EIGHTH EDITION

Racial and Ethnic Relations

Joe R. Feagin
Texas A&M University

Clairece Booher Feagin

Library of Congress Cataloging-in-Publication Data

Feagin, Joe R.
Racial and ethnic relations/Joe R. Feagin.—8th ed.
p. cm.
Includes bibliographical references and index.
ISBN–13: 978–0–13–224404–6
ISBN–10: 0–13–224404–7
1. Minorities—United States. 2. United States—Race relations. 3. United States—Ethnic relations. I. Title.
E184.A1F38 2007
305.800973—dc22
2007027161

Editorial Director: Leah Jewell
Publisher: Nancy Roberts
Editorial Assistant: Lee Peterson
Senior Operations Specialist: Sherry Lewis
Operations Specialist: Christina Amato
Production Liaison: Joanne Hakim
Production Editor: Shelley Creager/Aptara, Inc.
Director of Marketing: Brandy Dawson
Marketing Manager: Lindsey Prudhomme
Marketing Assistant: Jessica Muraviov
Senior Art Director: Nancy Wells
Art Director (Interior and Cover Design): Ilze Lemesis
Director, Image Resource Center: Melinda Patelli
Manager, Rights and Permissions: Zina Arabia
Manager, Visual Research: Beth Brenzel
Manager, Cover Visual Research & Permissions: Karen Sanatar
Photo Researcher: Rachel Lucas
Image Permission Coordinator: Ang'john Ferreri
Composition: Aptara, Inc.
Printer/Binder: Edwards Brothers, Inc.
Cover Printer: Lehigh Lithographers
Cover Photos: Students using laptop—*Gary Conner/PhotoEdit Inc.;* African American family—*Arthur Tilley/Taxi/Getty Images Inc.;* Preparing for Nisqually Ceremony—*Natalie Fobes/Corbis Bettmann;* Smiling Asian-American girl with basket—*Rita Ariyoshi/Pacific Stock;* Asian-American kids with grandparents—*National Geographic Image Collection;* Black man wearing traditional African clothing—*Cleo Photography/PhotoEdit Inc.;* Hispanic grandmother and granddaughter cooking—*David Young-Wolff/PhotoEdit Inc.;* Three generations of Latina women—*Patrik Giardino/Corbis Bettmann;* Muslim women on Brooklyn sidewalk—*Ricki Rosen/Corbis/SABA Press Photos Inc.;* Two senior citizen brothers—*Norbert Schaefer/Corbis Bettmann.*

Credits and acknowledgments borrowed from other sources and reproduced, with permission, in this textbook appear on page 475.

Pearson Education LTD., London
Pearson Education Singapore, Pte. Ltd
Pearson Education, Canada, Ltd
Pearson Education–Japan
Pearson Education Australia PTY, Limited
Pearson Education North Asia Ltd
Pearson Educación de Mexico, S.A. de C.V.
Pearson Education Malaysia, Pte. Ltd
Pearson Education, Upper Saddle River, New Jersey

10 9 8 7 6 5 4 3 2 1
ISBN-13: 978-0-13-224404-6
ISBN-10: 0-13-224404-7

Contents

Preface

Over the past few decades, numerous scholars, journalists, and politicians have argued that there is a "declining significance of race" or an "end to racism" in the United States. They have written or spoken optimistically about a decrease in discrimination and about an improving character of racial and ethnic relationships in the United States. Over the same period of time, however, the scholarly journals and mass media have been filled with accounts of crimes targeting people of color, accounts of the violent views and actions of white supremacist groups, college students and comedians doing openly racist skits or parties, talk show hosts openly stereotyping people of color, public discussions of many lawsuits over racial discrimination in employment and public accommodations, studies showing widespread housing discrimination, descriptions of community rebellions against local police brutality incidents, and controversies over affirmative action and other anti-discrimination programs. In recent years, we have also seen intense debates about the character and impact of recent immigrants to the United States, many of whom are immigrants of color from Latin American or Asian countries.

As we move well into the 21st century, much scholarly and public discussion and argument focus on continuing racial and ethnic discrimination, oppression, and conflict. Contrary to what some scholars and journalists assert, this debate reflects fundamental and foundational social, economic, and political realities in the United States. Today, many Americans are well aware, or are becoming aware, of the continuing significance of "race," racism, and ethnicity, not only in this country but also in other countries—from the Republic of South Africa to Northern Ireland, the former Yugoslavia, the former Soviet Union, France, Brazil, and the Middle East. Racial and ethnic oppression and conflict are extraordinarily important in the modern world and have the potential to tear apart any country, including highly industrialized countries that are said to be "advanced."

One result of the reinvigorated interest in racial and ethnic issues in many areas of the United States is the creation of college and university courses that focus on racial and ethnic divisions, cultural diversity, immigration, and multicultural or multiracial issues. We have revised this eighth edition of *Racial and Ethnic Relations* with this growing interest in U.S. racial and ethnic heritages, developments, conflicts, and coalitions in mind. This textbook is designed for sociology courses, other social science courses, and education courses variously titled "Racial and Ethnic Relations", "Race Relations", "Minority Groups", and "Minority Relations", and also for various other courses on cultural diversity, multiculturalism, and racial and ethnic groups offered in college, business, and governmental settings.

One purpose of this book is to provide readers with access to the important literature on racial and ethnic groups in the United States and, to a lesser extent, in certain other countries around the globe. We have drawn heavily on a broad array of sources, including articles, books, and other data analyses by sociologists, political scientists, social psychologists, anthropologists, historians, economists, investigative journalists, and legal scholars.

We have limited space, so we have not been able to deal with all the important racial and ethnic groups in the United States. Instead, we have focused on a modest number of major racial and ethnic groups, generally preferring to accent depth rather than breadth in the analyses. In recent decades, social science analyses have begun to dig deeper into the "what," "why," and "how" of racial and ethnic oppression and conflict. We draw heavily on this ever-growing research.

The introduction to Part I looks briefly at the origins of the racial and ethnic mosaic that is the United States. It serves as an introduction to Chapters 1 and 2, which discuss major concepts and theories in the study of racial and ethnic relations. The introduction to Part II sketches the political and economic history of the United States in order to provide some context for understanding the adaptation and oppression of the various immigrant groups that have come, voluntarily or involuntarily, to U.S. shores. Only one major group, Native Americans, cannot be viewed as such immigrants; indeed, as the original inhabitants of North America , they were often the victims of actions by the early immigrants (colonists) from outside the continent. The situations and experiences of indigenous societies and the various groups that have immigrated to North America are considered in Chapters 3–13. In Part III, Chapter 14 moves away from the United States to look at patterns of racial and ethnic adaptation, oppression, and conflict in several other countries around the world, mainly France, South Africa, and Brazil. In the latter two cases, we examine how global patterns of racial oppression and conflict have often been developed or fostered by the outside European colonizers and their descendants during the colonial and decolonization periods in the histories of such countries.

In this eighth edition of *Racial and Ethnic Relations* we have made many changes that should make the text more accessible to readers. We have added opening vignettes for numerous chapters, real-life vignettes that capture for the reader some poignant aspects of the issues raised later in the chapters. We have enhanced the organization of each chapter with the addition of big picture questions at the beginning of each and with the positioning of important questions for discussion throughout the various chapter sections. In order to accent for readers many of the important racial and ethnic terms, we have set these off as clearly marked key terms in each chapter. To sharpen the conceptual analysis, we have incorporated new (and accented older) social science concepts dealing with racial and ethnic matters, such as *systemic racism* and the *white racial frame*, and made more cross-references to various important social science concepts from one chapter to another.

We have also carefully revised and updated each chapter with much new material and research on racial and ethnic issues, including 2000 census analyses published by the U.S. census Bureau since our last edition and analyses of our own and others drawing on more recent Census Bureau surveys. We have also added much new racial and ethnic data from recent social science research and analysis in both scholarly journals and books. And we have incorporated significant material from media sources on current racial and ethnic events of consequence in the United States and, especially in the last chapter, in other countries.

Throughout, and especially in Chapter 13, we examine the implications for the United States of the forecasts by demographers that by the middle of the twenty-first century the United States will become a country whose population majority is composed of Latino, African, Asian, Middle Eastern, and Native Americans. The United States has long been a mosaic of many groups, and that mix is getting ever more complex, interesting, and significant as the decades pass.

Supplements

Instructor's Resource Manual with Tests (0-13-224405-5)

For each chapter in the text, this valuable resource provides a detailed outline and a list of objectives. In addition, test questions in multiple-choice, true/false, and essay formats are available for each chapter; the answers to all questions are page-referenced to the text.

TestGEN-EQ (0-13-224406-3)

This computerized software allows instructors to create their own personalized exams, to edit any or all of the existing test questions, and to add new questions. Other special features of this program include random generation of test questions, creation of alternate versions of the same test, scrambling question sequence, and test preview before printing.

ABCNEWS

ABC News/Prentice Hall Video Library for Sociology, Race and Ethnic Relations, Series 1 DVD (0-13-179107-9)

Prentice Hall and ABC News are working together to bring to you the best and most comprehensive video material available in the college market. Through its wide variety of award-winning programs—*Nightline*, *This Week*, *World News Tonight*, and *20/20*—ABC offers a resource for feature and documentary-style videos related to the chapters in *Racial and Ethnic Relations, Eighth Edition.* The programs have high production quality, present substantial content, and are hosted by well-versed, well-known anchors.

Companion Website™

Designed by sociology instructors, this online study guide provides unique support to help readers in their studies. Featuring a variety of learning tools, including online quizzes with immediate feedback, this site is a comprehensive resource organized according to the chapters in *Racial and Ethnic Relations, Eighth Edition.* It can be found at www.prenhall.com/feagin.

Research Navigator™

Research Navigator™ can help students to complete research assignments efficiently and with confidence by providing three exclusive databases of high-quality scholarly and popular articles accessed by easy-to-use search engines.

- **EBSCO's ContentSelect™ Academic Journal Database,** organized by subject, contains 50–100 of the leading academic journals for sociology. Instructors and students can search the online journals by keyword, topic, or multiple topics. Articles include abstract and citation information and can be cut, pasted, e-mailed, or saved for later use.
- ***The New York Times* Search-by-Subject™ Archive** provides articles specific to sociology and is searchable by keyword or multiple keywords. Instructors and students can view full-text articles from the world's leading journalists writing for *The New York Times*.
- **Link Library** offers editorially selected "best of the Web" sites for sociology. Link Libraries are continually scanned and kept up to date, providing the most relevant and accurate links for research assignments.

Gain access to Research Navigator™ by using the access code found in the front of the brief guide called *The Prentice Hall Guide to Research Navigator™*. The access code for Research Navigator™ is included with every guide and can be packaged for no extra charge with *Racial and Ethnic Relations, Eighth Edition*. Please contact your Prentice Hall representative for more information.

10 Ways to Fight Hate Brochure

Produced by the Southern Poverty Law Center, the leading crime-watch organization and authority on hate crime in the United States, this brochure walks students through ten steps that they can take on their own campus or in their own neighborhood to fight hate every day.

Acknowledgments

In writing this and previous editions of this textbook, we have received useful comments and suggestions from numerous colleagues, students, teachers, correspondents, editors, and reviewers. We are indebted to those whose advice, suggestions, and insights have made this a better book.

Among these are Edward Múrgía, Jóse Cobas, Elizabeth Aranda, Susan Eichenberger, Louwanda Evans, Ruth Thompson-Miller, Leland Saito, Gary David, Amir Marvasti, Nijole Benokraitis, Nestor Rodríguez, Melvin Sikes, Hernán Vera, Jim Fenelon, Kristin Lavelle, Jennifer Mueller, Glenn Bracey, Ruth Thompson-Miller, Chris Chambers, Rosalind Chou, Joane Nagel, Howard Winant, Edna Bonacich, Karyn McKinney, Eileen O'Brien, Leslie Inniss, Richard Alba, Debra Van Ausdale, Robert Parker, Daniel Duarte, Teun Van Dijk, Harriett Romo, Alice Littlefield, Wendy Ng, John R. Sosa, Jaime Martinez, Bud Khleif, Howard Leslie, Larry Horn, Doris Wilkinson, Anthony Orum, James Button, Ward Churchill, S. Dale McLemore, Gideon Sjoberg, Gilberto Cardenas, Nikitah Imani, David Roth, Joseph Lopreato, John Butler, Eric Woodrum, Andrew Greeley, Graham Kinloch, Lester Hill, Chad Oliver, Marcia A. Herndon, Rogelio Nuñez, Tom Walls, Samuel Heilman, Phylis Cancilla Martinelli, José Limon, Devon Peña, Diana Kendall, Robena Jackson, Mark Chesler, David O'Brien, Bradley Stewart, John Arthur, Barbara Mori, Robert Parker, William Smith, Leslie Houts Picca, Peter Chua, Lenard Wynn, Kenneth Stewart, Timothy Fong, Diane Wolf, and Yanick St. Jean. We are also indebted to many other colleagues and undergraduate and graduate students for their helpful comments on previous editions. We are especially indebted to Pinar Batur for revising Chapter 14.

Publishers' reviewers for this revision were:

Peter Chua, San Jose State University
Roberta Rosenberg Farber, Stern College/Yeshiva University
Celestino Fernández, University of Arizona
Timothy P. Fong, California State University, Sacramento
Tomás R. Jiménez, University of California, San Diego
Akil Kokayi Khalfani, Essex County College
Deirdre A. Royster, College of William and Mary
Kenneth L. Stewart, Angelo State University
Carol Ward, Brigham Young University
Lenard C. Wynn, Moraine Valley Community College
Diane L. Wolf, University of California, Davis

We also thank them for their timely and useful comments on this edition of the text book.

We hope that you find this eighth edition informative and intellectually stimulating. We welcome your comments. Please write to us at the Department of Sociology, Mailstop 4351, Texas A&M University, College Station, Texas 77843-4351.

Joe R. Feagin
Clairece Booher Feagin

PART I

The Racial and Ethnic Mosaic

BIG PICTURE QUESTION

- ***Why did the United States begin as a country that was substantially democratic*** **and** ***rooted in racial oppression?***

More than two hundred years ago, the new United States severed its colonial ties with Europe. Born in revolution, this new nation was portrayed as centrally dedicated to freedom and equality. Over the next two centuries, a vigorous society would emerge, with great racial and ethnic diversity.

However, the new society had its seamy side. Racial and ethnic oppression and conflict were imbedded in the founding period and in the subsequent history of the new republic. The European immigrants often took the lands of indigenous societies by force. By the end of the seventeenth century, the enslavement of Africans and African Americans was fundamental to the economy of the North American colonies, and resistance and revolt by these enslaved Americans were recurring problems for white slaveholders. In succeeding centuries other non-European peoples, such as Mexican and Chinese Americans, would suffer serious yokes of racial oppression. However, non-Europeans were not the only ones to face oppressive conditions. Discrimination against European immigrant groups was also part of the sometimes forgotten history of both the pre- and post-revolutionary periods.

In the earliest period, the colonial population on the prospering Atlantic coast was predominantly English in its origins and basic social institutions. Because of England's huge appetite for raw materials and new markets, English authorities encouraged non-English immigration to the colonies. However, there was popular opposition, verbal and violent, to the long line of new white immigrants. "Foreigners" soon became a negative category for many colonists. "Despite the need for new settlers, English colonials had mixed feelings about foreign arrivals. Anglo-Saxon mobs attacked Huguenots in Frenchtown, Rhode Island, and destroyed a Scotch-Irish frontier settlement in Worcester, Massachusetts."[1] In the 1700s, colonies such as Virginia, Pennsylvania, and Rhode Island attempted to restrict non-British immigrants.[2]

The basic documents of the new republic reflected its patterns of racial relations and racial subordination, and some of the republic's first laws were aimed at hampering groups of non-English origin. A relatively radical Declaration of Independence, prepared mostly by the young Thomas Jefferson, originally contained language accusing King George III of pursuing slavery, of waging "cruel war against human nature itself, violating its most sacred rights of life and liberty in the persons of a distant people who never offended him, captivating them and carrying them into slavery in another hemisphere, or to incur miserable death in the transportation thither."[3] Jefferson further noted that the English king had not attempted to prohibit the slave trade and had encouraged enslaved Africans to "rise in arms" against white colonists. But because of pressure from white slaveholding interests in the South and slave-trading interests in New England, this critique of the slave trade was omitted from the final version of the Declaration.

Even in this revolutionary period, the grand new doctrines of freedom and equality could not be extended to the black population, for criticism of King George III on the issue of slavery was in fact criticism of much of the North American social and economic system. Jefferson himself was a major slaveholder, whose prosperity and wealth were closely tied to an oppressive, slaveholding agricultural system.

The U.S. Constitution (1787) explicitly recognized racial subordination in several places. First, as a result of a famous compromise between northern and southern representatives to the Constitutional Convention, Article I originally stipulated that three-fifths of a given state's enslaved population was to be counted in the total for apportioning the state's legislative representation—that is, each enslaved American was officially viewed as three-fifths of a person. Significantly, at the Constitutional Convention, white southern slaveowners, seeking to enhance their representation in the new U.S. Congress, pressed for full inclusion of the enslaved African Americans in the population count, while northern interests were opposed.

In addition, a section was added to Article I permitting the slave trade to continue until 1808. The Constitution also incorporated a fugitive slave provision that required the return of runaways to their owners, a provision opposed by few whites at the time.[4] Neither the statement in the Declaration of Independence that "all men are created equal" nor the Constitution's soon-to-be-added Bill of Rights was seen as applying to Americans of African descent. Slavery, ironically, would last much longer in the new "democratic" republic than in the older aristocratic Britain.[5]

African Americans and Native Americans were not the only groups to suffer from the new government's action. Numerous other non-English groups continued to find themselves less than equal under the law. Anti-immigrant legislation in the late 1700s and early 1800s included the Alien, Sedition, and Naturalization Acts.[6] Irish, German, and French immigrants were growing in number by the late eighteenth century, and concern about the democratic political sentiments of the new immigrants was great. The Naturalization Act stiffened residency requirements for citizenship from five to fourteen years; the Alien Act gave the president the power to expel foreigners. President John Adams was pressed to issue orders deporting immigrants under the Alien Act and did so. Shiploads of immigrants left the country because of fear of exclusion.

Inequality in life chances and wealth along racial and ethnic lines was a fundamental fact of the new country's institutions. At first, liberty and justice were for men of British descent only. This situation did not go unchallenged. By the late eighteenth century, many Irish and German immigrants had come to the colonies. Indeed, a significant proportion of the 4 million persons enumerated in the first U.S. census in 1790 were of non-English origins.

Over the next two centuries, English domination was modified by the ascendance of other northern Europeans, such as the Irish. These groups in turn were later challenged by southern and eastern European and non-European groups trying to move up in the social, economic, and political systems. Gradually, the new society became an unprecedented mixing of diverse peoples.

Most in the non-British immigrant groups gradually came to adopt the English language and adjust to English-shaped economic, political, and legal institutions. All newly entering groups adapted, to some degree, to the dominant Anglo-Saxon culture and ways. European immigrant groups soon became viewed as "whites" and eventually gained substantial power and status in the process.

In contrast to white immigrants, the voluntary and involuntary immigrants from Africa, Asia, and Latin America, as well as Native Americans, have generally remained subordinate to white Americans in political, cultural, and economic terms. Racial and ethnic inequality and oppression were and continue to be part of the foundation of U.S. society. Nonetheless, racially oppressed Americans have long challenged their subordinate status, and they continue to do so. If current demographic trends continue, Americans of color will become the majority of the U.S. population by the middle of the twenty-first century. They already are the majority in several large states and in many larger cities.

Today, as in the past, issues of immigration, adaptation, inequality, and oppression are at the heart of the sociological study of racial and ethnic relations in the United States. They will continue to be central issues for the foreseeable future. In the two chapters of Part I, we will define basic terms used by social scientists and examine these concepts from a critical perspective. Chapter 1 examines terms such as *race*, *racism*, *ethnic group*, and *prejudice*. Chapter 2 reviews major conceptual frameworks, including a variety of assimilation theories and power-conflict theories, for interpreting the complex structure and long-term development of racial and ethnic relations in the United States.

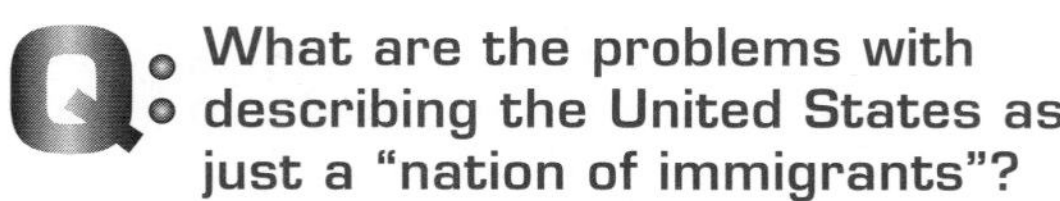

What are the problems with describing the United States as just a "nation of immigrants"?

CHAPTER 1

Basic Concepts in the Study of Racial and Ethnic Relations

BIG PICTURE QUESTIONS

- ***Why and how have human beings developed the powerful ideas of "race" and ethnicity?***
- ***How does racial or ethnic discrimination become institutionalized?***
- ***How do people respond to racial and ethnic oppression in the United States?***

In the 1980s, Susie Guillory Phipps, the wife of a white businessman in Louisiana, went to court to try to get the racial designation on her birth certificate at the Louisiana Bureau of Vital Records changed from "colored" to "white." A 1970 Louisiana "blood" law required that persons with one thirty-second or more "Negro blood" (ancestry) were to be designated as "colored" on birth records; before 1970, "any traceable amount" of African ancestry had been used to define a person as colored. The light-skinned Phipps was the descendant of an eighteenth-century white plantation owner and an enslaved black American, and her small amount of African ancestry was enough to get her classified as "colored" on her official Louisiana birth certificate. Because other records supported the designation, Phipps lost her case against the state of Louisiana.[1]

This significant controversy raises the basic question of how a person comes to be defined as *white* or *not white* in U.S. society. Only under racist assumptions does having one black ancestor make one black while having one white ancestor does not make one white. If the latter were the law in Louisiana, of course, many *black* residents there—those who have at least one white ancestor (often a white slaveholder)—would be classified as *white*! This revealing case illustrates that racial categories are constructed and defined socially and politically, not scientifically.

A logical place to start in making sense out of this U.S. system of racial and ethnic categorization is with basic terms and concepts. People have often used such terms as *racial groups* and *prejudice* without specifying their meaning. Because these are basic concepts in the study of intergroup relations, we will analyze them in detail.

Issues of Race and Racism

Racial Groups and Racialized Hierarchies

Both *racial group* and the more common term *race* have been used in a number of senses in social science and popular writings. *Human race, Jewish race, White race*—such terms in the literature suggest a range of meanings. In sixteenth- and early seventeenth-century Europe, the concept or word *race* was typically used for descendants of a common ancestor, emphasizing kinship linkages rather than physical characteristics such as skin color, hair type, or facial features. Only in the late eighteenth century did **race** come to mean a *category of human beings with distinctive physical characteristics transmitted by descent, and set in a racialized hierarchy*.[2]

Soon **racial hierarchy**, *a stratification of, and substantial inequality among physically distinct groups*, came to be widely accepted, with white Europeans at the top. Darker-skinned people from African societies were relegated by European observers to the bottom, in part because of these Africans' skin color and allegedly "primitive" culture, but also because such Africans were enslaved by Europeans. Economic and political oppression resulted in a low position in the white classification system, or what can be termed *racial subordination*.[3]

Immanuel Kant's use of the German phrase for "races of mankind" in the 1770s was one of the first explicit uses of the term *race* in the modern sense of biologically distinct, hierarchical categories of human beings. In 1795 Johann Blumenbach, a prominent German anatomist, established a racial classification system that became an influential typology. At the top of his racial hierarchy were the Caucasians (Europeans), followed in order by the Mongolians (Asians), the Ethiopians (Africans), the Americans (Native Americans), and the Malays (Polynesians). Blumenbach was the first to use the term *Caucasian*; he felt that the Europeans in the Caucasus mountains of Russia were "the most beautiful race of men." Ever since, people of European descent have been called by a racist term that originally applied only to a small area of Europe. Blumenbach also chose the term because he believed the earliest human beings came from the Caucasus area.[4]

The concept of race as a biologically distinctive, hierarchical category was developed by certain northern Europeans who, for much of their histories, had been largely isolated from contact with people who differed from them physically or culturally. Before the development of large sailing ships in the late 1400s, the Europeans had little contact with people from Asia, Africa, or the Americas. Soon, however, it was the colonizing Europeans who established slave systems in the Americas. The slave colonies were legitimated and rationalized by the colonizing Europeans, including the English, who classified enslaved Africans as a "lesser race." The idea of race was not developed from scientific observations of all human beings. Rather, "race was, from its inception, a folk classification, a product of popular beliefs about human differences that evolved from the sixteenth through the nineteenth centuries."[5]

From the eighteenth century to well into the twentieth century, most biologists, physical anthropologists, and other scientists accented this socially determined classification of what were seen as biologically distinctive groups. These scientists reflected their own racial prejudices and those of the white public. "The scientists themselves undertook efforts to document the existence of the differences that the European cultural worldview demanded and had already created."[6] Basic to this increasingly prevalent view was the theory of a fixed number of biologically distinct "races" with differing physical characteristics and the belief that these characteristics were hereditary and thus created a "natural" hierarchy of groups. By the late nineteenth century, numerous European and U.S. scientists and popular writers were systematically downgrading all peoples not of northern European origin, including southern and eastern Europeans (such as Polish and Jewish Europeans), as inferior "races."[7]

Thus, over four centuries of North American development, **racialization** has been *the process by which those in the dominant white group, especially its elites, have defined and constructed certain groups as being racially inferior or superior for the purposes of societal placement and of group enrichment, segregation, or oppression*. Racialization has operated in somewhat different ways for particular groups, but the process has generally been under the control of the dominant group, which from the late 1600s forward defined itself as "white." Since the seventeenth century, the dominant racial group has put into place a pervasive racial hierarchy, with a racial-status continuum that places white Americans at the top and African Americans and other Americans of color at or near the bottom. Over time, as we will see in later chapters, the white elite, assisted by rank-and-file whites, has determined where new immigrant groups, such as Irish or Chinese immigrants, are placed and racialized within that established racial hierarchy.

The singling out of people within the human species in terms of a biologized "race" hierarchy seems to have been a distinctively European and Euro-American idea, which has over recent centuries spread across all continents. In contrast, many "indigenous peoples ... have observed and appreciated cultural diversity as variations on cosmological themes. As a rule, the indigenous worldview encompasses all humanity."[8] In the view of M. Annette Jaimes, many indigenous peoples across much of the globe have been more likely than Europeans to emphasize building alliances across variety of a distinctive human groups. U.S. examples include the assistance in agricultural techniques given by Native Americans to early European colonists and later to Japanese Americans who were imprisoned during World War II (see Chapter 10) in the U.S. concentration camps located near indigenous communities in the western United States.[9]

How has the concept of "race" as a biologically distinctive category changed, or not changed, over several centuries?

Ideological Racism

The development of ideological racism is rooted in the European global expansion that began in earnest in the late 1400s. We can define **ideological racism** specifically as *an ideology that considers a group's unchangeable physical characteristics to be linked in a direct, causal way to psychological or intellectual characteristics and that, on this basis, distinguishes between superior and inferior racial groups*.[10] The "scientific racism" of such European writers as Count Joseph Arthur de Gobineau, a French diplomat in the mid-nineteenth century, was used to justify the spread of European colonialism in Asia, Africa, and the Americas. A long line of racist theorists followed in De Gobineau's footsteps, including the German Nazi leader Adolf Hitler. Sometimes they even applied the ideology of racial inferiority to culturally distinct white European groups, such as Jewish Europeans. In a racist ideology, real or alleged physical characteristics are linked to *cultural* traits that the dominant group considers undesirable or inferior.

Significantly, the word *racism*, first coined in the 1930s by German scholar Magnus Hirschfeld, is relatively new. Hirschfeld coined it for the ideology of biologically determined "races" of the German Nazis and other Europeans, who used that ideology to buttress their well-institutionalized system of racially oppressive practices. In its blatant and more subtle forms, ideological racism has long been common in the United States. For example, in 1935 an influential white University of Virginia professor wrote this blatantly racist analysis:

> The size of the brain in the Black Race is below the medium both of the Whites and the Yellow-Browns, frequently with relatively more simple convolutions. The frontal lobes are often low and narrow. The parietal lobes voluminous, the occipital protruding. The psychic activities of the Black Race are a careless, jolly vivacity, emotions and passions of short duration, and a strong and somewhat irrational egoism. Idealism, ambition, and the co-operative faculties are weak. They love amusement and sport but have little initiative and adventurous spirit.[11]

This example of crude ideological racism links physical and personality characteristics. Although this extreme, biologized, racist portrait passed for science before World War II—and in today's white supremacist organizations, it still does—it is *pseudoscience*. Modern biologists and anthropologists have demonstrated the wild-eyed irrationality of this racist mythology.

Found in many versions today, including some much more subdued, ideological racism accepts as true various stereotyped characteristics traditionally applied by whites to "outsider" groups of color. The assumption of this commonplace racist thinking is that physical differences such as skin color are intrinsically, even unalterably, tied to meaningful differentials in intelligence, culture, or "civilization." Yet, despite assertions of such a linkage by many, including pseudoscientists, no real scientific support for this assumed intrinsic linkage exists.

Indeed, there is *no* distinctive and enduring biological reality called "race" that can be determined by objective scientific procedures. Since at least the 1940s, the social, medical, and physical sciences have demonstrated this in numerous research studies. Since the 1990s, a renewed insistence on the genetic reality of "races" has been triggered by a few dissenting geneticists and social scientists, yet the older evidence and more recent research and analysis still strongly refute the notion of "races" being good categories for describing human genetic or biological diversity.[12] Given the constant blending and interbreeding of human groups over many centuries and into the present, it is impossible to sort human beings into unambiguously distinctive "races" on genetic grounds. There is too much overlapping of genetic characteristics across the variety of human populations. Two randomly selected individuals from the world's population would have in common, on average, about 99.8 percent of their genetic material. Most of the genetic variation in regard to human populations "occurs *within* populations, not *between* them."[13] Wherever they reside, human beings are remarkably similar genetically. There are genetic differences between geographically scattered human populations, but these differences are slight and exist because of different histories and geographical locations. The racial importance of the modest dissimilarities such as skin color variations is *socially*, not scientifically, determined.

Human populations singled out as "races" are simply groups with visible differences that certain people collectively decided to emphasize as important in social, economic, and political relationships. Such racial categorizing is neither objective nor scientific, but highly subjective. There are *many* different ways of classifying human populations in terms of genetic characteristics: "One such procedure would group Italians and Greeks with most African blacks. It would classify Xhosa—the South African 'black' group to which [South African] President Nelson Mandela belongs—with Swedes rather than Nigerians."[14] Antimalarial genes are not found among the light-skinned Swedes or dark-skinned southern African groups such as the Xhosas, but they are commonly found in northern African groups and among Europeans such as Italians and Greeks. These antimalarial genes are likely much more important for human beings than those that determine skin color variations, yet they are *not* used by biological-race thinkers, including pseudoscientists, for their racial classifications.[15]

There is only one human race *(Homo sapiens)*, to which we all belong. Every human being is in fact distantly related to every other human being on earth. The indigenous peoples' view of human beings, previously noted, is now accepted by most scientists.[16] Nonetheless, the lack of scientific support has not lessened the popularity of racist ideologies of various types. Ashley Montagu noted the extreme danger of ideological racism, a view shaped in part by the consequences of the German Nazi ideology, according to which there were physically distinct Aryan and Jewish "races."[17] That ideology lay behind Nazi-generated killings of millions of European Jews (and other Europeans) during the 1930s and 1940s.

In the case of North America, over several centuries now, variations on an old racist ideology have long been incorporated as part of a *white racial framing* of an ever more diverse society, a concept to which we will return later.

Racial Groups

Today, social scientists view "race" not as a given biological reality but as a socially constructed reality. Sociologist Oliver Cox, one of the first to underscore this social construction perspective, defined a "race" as "any people who are distinguished, or consider themselves distinguished, in social relations with other peoples, by their physical characteristics."[18] Similarly, a *racial group* has been defined by Pierre van den Berghe as a "human group that defines itself and or is defined by other groups as different from other groups by virtue of innate and immutable physical characteristics."[19]

Thus, a racial group is *not* something generated naturally as part of the self-evident order of the universe. A person's "race" is typically determined by, and important to, certain outsiders, although a group's own self-definition can be important. In this book we define a **racial group** as a *social group that persons inside or outside the group have decided is important to single out as inferior or superior, typically on the basis of real or alleged physical characteristics selected subjectively*. Racial group distinctions are rooted in some type of ideological racism, which, as noted previously, links physical characteristics to "inferior" or "superior" cultural and intellectual characteristics.

In the United States, numerous groups fit this definition. Asian Americans, African Americans, Native Americans, and Mexican Americans have had their physical characteristics, such as skin color, facial features, and eye shape, singled out by the dominant white group as badges of social, cultural, and racial inferiority. Some groups once defined as racial groups—and as physically and mentally inferior groups—are no longer defined that way. In later chapters we will see that Irish and Italian immigrants were for a time defined as inferior "races" by native-born Anglo-Protestant Americans. Later, the social definition of these European immigrants as distinctively inferior racial groups was replaced by a social construction of these groups as white and as *ethnic groups*, a term we examine later.

The examples of Irish and Italian Americans make clear that racial definitions are not necessarily fixed essences that last forever, but instead can be temporary social constructions shaped in sociopolitical struggles in particular times and places. Definitions of racial inferiority or superiority can and do change over time.

Why are some physical characteristics, such as skin color, selected as a basis for distinguishing racial groups, whereas certain other characteristics, such as eye color, seldom are? These questions cannot be answered in biological terms. They require historical and sociological analysis. Some have argued that such characteristics as skin color are "easily observed and ordered in the mind."[20] More important than ease of observation, however, is the way economic or political subordination creates a need to identify the powerless group in a certain way. In justifying economic or other exploitation, the dominant group often defines the real (or alleged) physical characteristics that are singled out to typify the exploited group as inferior racial characteristics. For example, technological differences in weaponry and firepower between European and African peoples facilitated the enslavement of Africans in the American colonies. In turn, the generally darker skin of the Africans and their descendants came to be used by white groups as an indicator of subordinate racial and cultural status. Skin-color characteristics have no inherent meaning; in group interaction they become important because they can be used to classify members of the dominant and subordinate groups.

In addition, knowledge of one's relatives often affects one's assignment to a racial group, particularly for those who lack the emphasized physical characteristics. At various times in many societies, people have been distinguished not only on the basis of their own physical characteristics but also on the basis of a socially determined "rule of descent."[21] For example, in Nazi Germany, Adolf Hitler's officials often identified Jewish Germans on the basis of their having one or more Jewish relatives.

How is the concept of "race" understood presently by almost all social scientists?

Ancestry and Multiracial Realities

The socially applied rules of descent have varied greatly from society to society. For example, in some countries there are special categories or designations for mixed-ancestry groups, such as the "Coloureds" term once used for people with African and European ancestry in South Africa. Many Latin American countries recognize several mixed-ancestry categories. Mixed-ancestry distinctions have been rare in the United States. In the case of African Americans, interracial blending has, over time, caused dark skin color to become a less reliable characteristic for those determined to make racial distinctions, and the rule of descent has gained more importance as a mechanism of racial identification to perpetuate discrimination. Today, black Americans "evidence an unusually wide range of physical traits. Their skin color extends from ebony to a shade paler than many 'whites.'"[22] Indeed, relatively few black Americans are literally "black." Most have a skin color that is some shade of brown.

In many U.S. communities, the social aspect of the defining process becomes obvious when a light-skinned person, say, of one-eighth African ancestry but with none of the physical traits most whites associate with African Americans, is regarded as "black" because one of his or her ancestors is known to be of African ancestry. Sometimes termed the "one drop of blood" rule, this odd rule of descent is unique to the United States. Indeed, in Caribbean nations such as Jamaica or in many parts of Africa, a person who is one-eighth African in ancestry and seven-eighths European would ordinarily be considered "white."

Golf star Tiger Woods hits his tee shot at a 1996 tournament.

Mixed racial ancestry does not fit neatly into traditional U.S. categorizing. Today, there are millions of children in interracial families, and growing numbers of interracial marriages take place annually. The existence and experiences of these Americans underscore the social construction of racial identities. Consider the case of Tiger Woods, a talented golfer. In 1997, Woods became the center of media attention when he won a number of major golf tournaments, including the Master's tourney, where he posted a record score.[23] Woods's ancestry is complex. He has described his ancestry as one-eighth white, one-eighth Native American, one-fourth African American, one-fourth Thai, and one-fourth Chinese. However, the mass media have usually portrayed Woods as African American. Following his major victories, his father also spoke of him as a black sports star, and Woods presented himself in some early commercials as black. Later Woods accented his mixed ancestry and seemed to some observers to play down his black ancestry or identity. After some criticism by African Americans who were proud of his achievements and his African ancestry, Woods issued a statement that he was proud of his African American *and* other ancestry.[24]

Nonetheless, many people in the media and elsewhere have continued to view Woods as a black sports star, and it seems likely that far more Americans see him as African American than as multiracial. After Woods won the Master's tourney, a white golfer, Fuzzy Zoeller, spoke about "that little boy" and joked that he hoped Woods would not pick collard greens and fried chicken for the Master's championship dinner.[25] This white golfer clearly saw Woods as an African American. (He later met with Woods and apologized for his comments.)[26]

In the late 1990s, Congress debated the addition of a "multiracial" category in the U.S. census for the year 2000, a change supported by many Americans of mixed racial and ethnic ancestry. However, some critics suggested that the presence of such a multiracial box for people to check on the census form might reduce the count in other categories, such as "black," which would hurt civil rights enforcement in some areas. Congress decided against the creation of a specific multiracial category for the 2000 census. Instead, individuals were allowed to mark multiple ancestry groups. This political and census debate clearly indicates that racial designations are socially constructed and maintained. Interestingly, in the 2000 census only 6.8 million Americans—out of a total of 281 million—indicated by checking multiple categories that they had multiracial ancestry.[27]

Of course, these 2000 census data represent only the tip of the iceberg; additional millions of Americans have multiracial backgrounds. Many Americans' ancestry is some mixture of European, African, Native American, Asian, Middle Eastern, or Latin American backgrounds, and today increasing numbers of people are willing to acknowledge this reality and assert their multiracial (and multiethnic) identities. Attention to issues of multiracial ancestry, intermarriage, and interracial families will likely escalate as the United States becomes ever more diverse.

Ethnic Groups

What Is an Ethnic Group?

The term *ethnic group* has been used by social scientists in two different senses, one narrow and one broad. Some definitions of the term are broad enough to include socially defined racial groups. For example, in Milton Gordon's broad definition, an ethnic group is a social group distinguished "by race, religion, or national origin."[28] Like the definition of racial group, this definition contains the notion of social set-apartness. However, here the distinctive characteristics can be physical or cultural, and language and religion are seen as critical markers or signs of ethnicity even when there is no physical distinctiveness. Today, a number of contemporary scholars, such as Werner Sollors, still view religious, national-origin, and racial groups as falling under the umbrella term *ethnic group*.[29]

Other scholars prefer a narrower definition of ethnic group, one that omits groups defined substantially in terms of physical characteristics (those called racial groups) and is limited to groups distinguished primarily on the basis of cultural or national-origin characteristics. *Cultural characteristics* include language; *national origin* refers to the country (and national culture) from which the person or her or his ancestors came.

The English word *ethnic* comes from the Greek word *ethnos*, originally meaning "nation." In its earliest English usage, in the fifteenth century, the word referred to culturally different "heathen" countries, that is, those not Christian or Jewish. The first usage of *ethnic group* to denote national origin developed in the period of heavy immigration from southern and eastern European countries to the United States in the early twentieth century. Since the 1930s, a number of prominent social scientists have suggested that the narrower definition of ethnic group, more in line with the original Greek meaning of nationality, makes the term more useful.[30]

Social scientist W. Lloyd Warner, who was perhaps the first to use the term *ethnicity*, distinguished between ethnic groups—which he saw as characterized by cultural differences—and racial groups, characterized substantially by physical differences.[31] More recent scholars have also preferred the narrower usage. In van den Berghe's view, for example, ethnic groups are "socially defined but on the basis of cultural criteria."[32]

In this book, the usual meaning of **ethnic group** will be the narrower one—*a group socially distinguished or set apart, by others or by itself, primarily on the basis of cultural or national-origin characteristics.* Such set-apart groups, such as Irish Americans or German Americans, usually develop a sense of a common cultural heritage and ancestry. Some broad social categories, such as the religious category of "Baptists," have been considered by some to be ethnic groups, but in the sense we use the term here they are not. Religious groups that are open to relatively easy conversion are not, strictly speaking, ethnic, because ethnicity says something about socially accepted lines of common descent or national origin as well as current cultural characteristics.

Many social analysts who use the broader defiinition that includes racial groups argue that the historical experiences of people defined as "nonwhite" are essentially similar to experiences of white groups. Some social scientists have argued that in the United States the situations and experiences of non-European groups such as African or Asian Americans are in broad ways similar to those of immigrants from Europe, especially with regard to the process of gradual integration into the

Anglo-Protestant core society. Some further assume that the experiences of both European and non-European groups are adequately explained by the same theoretical framework—typically an assimilation framework (see Chapter 2).[33]

In contrast, many analysts who prefer the narrower definition of *ethnic group* as a socially constructed category that differs in important ways from the term *racial group* view the experiences of subordinated racial groups as distinctively different from those of white European ethnic groups.[34] Moreover, the public and scholarly use of the umbrella term *ethnic group* for all groups, including racial groups, in the past two decades has often had political and racial overtones: "Indeed, the substitution of 'ethnicity' for 'race' as a basis of categorization is accompanied by increasing unwillingness among the dominant group to accept responsibility for the problems of racism."[35] Although this criticism is accurate for much popular and scholarly writing that views such groups as African Americans and Mexican Americans as just ethnic groups that are no different in their experiences from groups such as Italian Americans and Irish Americans, it does not apply to those scholars who prefer the term *ethnic group* because they feel its use indicates that all groups have genuine and significant cultural histories.[36]

In addition, many scholars emphasize the point that all socially constructed racial groups include subgroups that can be seen as ethnic groups because they have distinctive cultural identities. Examples of this include Italian Americans within the white racial group and Jamaican Americans within the black racial group.

Definitions of *racial group* and *ethnic group* that emphasize their social meaning and construction directly reject the biological determinism that views such groups as self-evident, with unchanging physical or intellectual characteristics. People themselves, both outside and inside racial and ethnic groups, determine when certain physical or cultural characteristics are important enough to single out a group for social purposes, whether for good or for ill.

A given group may be viewed by different outsiders or at different times as a racial or an ethnic group. Indeed, some groups have been defined by the same outsiders on the basis of both physical and cultural criteria. During the 1930s, for example, Jewish Germans were identified as a "race" in Nazi Germany, in part because of physical characteristics that were alleged to be different from those of other Germans. However, the actual identification of Jewish Germans for persecution and killing by Nazi bureaucrats and soldiers was based more on ethnic characteristics—cultural characteristics such as religion or language—and genealogical ties to known Jewish ancestors than on physical characteristics.

In their first contacts with European societies, darker-skinned Africans were viewed in ethnic rather than racial terms. St. Clair Drake's research on early African contacts with Europeans has shown that in the first centuries of contact—during the Egyptian, Greek, and Roman periods—European outsiders generally attached far greater significance to Africans' culture and nationality than to their physical characteristics. Before the sixteenth century, "neither White Racism nor *racial slavery* existed."[37] Similarly, Frank Snowden has demonstrated that the early encounters between African "blacks" and Mediterranean "whites" led to a generally favorable image of the Africans among Europeans and to friendships and intermarriage—much different from the black–white relations in modern race-conscious societies. Although some Europeans in these periods did express negative views of Africans' color, these views never developed into an acute color consciousness linked to an ideological view of Africans as an inferior species with intellectual deficits. Virulent color prejudice in the form of ideological racism emerged only in the modern world, primarily in the imperial expansion into Africa and the Americas by European nations seeking colonies between the 1400s and the 1800s.[38] Historical conditions have shaped whether and how skin color becomes a marker—usually in the social processes of exploitation and oppression.

Ancestry is important to the concept of ethnic group whether it is defined in a narrow or a broad sense. Perception of a common ancestry, real or mythical, has been part of outsiders' definitions and of ethnic groups' self-definitions. Sociologist Max Weber saw ethnic groups broadly as "human groups that entertain a subjective belief in their common descent."[39] In addition to a sense of common ancestry, a consciousness of shared experiences and of shared cultural patterns is important in shaping a group's identity.

A number of social scientists have focused on the ways in which people's constructions and conceptions of their own and others' ethnic identities change over time and from one situation to another. These social constructionists emphasize the importance of studying

The United States is a racially and ethnically diverse society.

the "ways in which ethnic boundaries, identities, and cultures are negotiated, defined, and produced through social interaction inside and outside ethnic communities."[40] Drawing on her field research, Mary Waters has shown the options white Americans have with regard to their ethnic identity. A white person of both English and Irish ancestry may choose either ethnic identity, both, or none, preferring in the latter case to identify only as "American."[41] Waters has also documented how Afro-Caribbean immigrants sometimes view themselves as African Americans and sometimes as an ethnic group distinct from native-born people within the African American racial group.[42] Nonetheless, Afro-Caribbean Americans generally have no choice in how they are viewed—as black Americans—by most people in the dominant white group.

Other terms for socially distinguished groups are used in racial-ethnic research. Among these are *majority group* and *minority group*.[43] Louis Wirth defined a **minority group** thus: *"A group of people who, because of their physical or cultural characteristics, are singled out from others in the society in which they live for differential and unequal treatment and who therefore regard themselves as objects of collective discrimination."*[44] However, many scholars today consider it more accurate to use the term **dominant group** instead of *majority group for the racial or ethnic group with the greatest power and resources in a society,* and the term **subordinate group** instead of *minority group for a group that is singled out because of physical and/or cultural characteristics for differential and unequal treatment and whose members become objects of substantial discrimination.* This usage is appropriate because a majority group can be numerically a minority, as was the case with white Europeans in numerous colonial societies. Indeed, if demographic trends continue, the white majority, in population terms, will likely become a statistical minority in the United States by the 2050s.

A Note on Cultures

Real cultural differences between groups are often at the heart of racial and ethnic conflict. Sociologists and anthropologists often define *culture* as the shared values, understandings, symbols, and practices of a group of people. The shared symbols are the means by which people "communicate, perpetuate, and develop their knowledge about and attitudes toward life."[45] There are cultural objects (the symbols and practices) as well as cultural creators and cultural receivers (the people who create and use the cultural objects).[46]

In Chapter 2 we will observe the importance of culture in the process by which one group adapts to another. We will examine the concept of *dominant culture,* the understandings and symbols created and controlled by a powerful group, as well as the concept of an *immigrant culture,* the understandings and symbols of an immigrant group entering the sphere of the dominant culture. Milton Gordon, an assimilation theorist, has argued that immigrant groups coming into North America after the English have given up much of their own cultural heritage to conform to a dominant core culture: "If there is anything in American life which can be described as an overall American culture which serves as a reference point for immigrants and their children, it can best be described, it seems to us, as the middle-class cultural patterns of, largely, white Protestant, Anglo-Saxon origins, leaving aside for the moment the question of minor reciprocal influences on this culture exercised by the cultures of later entry into the United States."[47]

In subsequent chapters we will also see how some subordinated racial and ethnic groups have drawn on their well-developed cultures to resist discrimination and slavish adaptation to a dominant Anglo-Protestant culture. Some analysts describe these as *cultures of resistance.*[48]

The cultural heritage and present cultural understandings of subordinated groups, such as African Americans or American Indians, often have positive significance. They not only foster a positive sense of identity and pride but also facilitate the group's survival and enhance its ability to resist oppression. Strong family and kinship values of Native American societies enabled them to survive the Euro-American invasions of their lands. Contrary to certain prevailing stereotypes, moreover, the strong family ties of African Americans have generally fostered a sense of pride and identity and have provided crucial support for coping with widespread discrimination.

A Racial Framing of Society

Central to the persistence of racial hierarchies in countries such as the United States is the development of a comprehensive racial frame, primarily by the dominant racial group. This broad racial framing typically includes more than the racist ideology discussed previously. We can define a **racial frame** as an *organized set of racial ideas, stereotypes, images, emotions, and inclinations to discriminate.* Today, as in the past, a racial frame provides an all-encompassing interpretive scheme that shapes evaluations of everyday events and encounters with people from various racialized groups. A racial frame is important because it interprets everyday worlds and generates discriminatory action in line with the frame. A strong racial frame captures territory in our minds and thus shapes how we act.[49]

In the case of North America, white colonists early developed a white racial framing of the new society to interpret and defend the increasingly institutionalized reality of white-on-black oppression and white-on-Indian oppression. This broad racial frame has been maintained, with some variation and periodic reworking, to the present day. Central to this frame is an interrelated set of cognitive notions and emotionally charged understandings that whites (and others) have used to rationalize and legitimate oppression. Early political leaders, such as Thomas Jefferson, James Madison, and George Washington, participated actively, and often emotionally, in the development of this racial framing, including its ideological racism, in order to defend white power and privilege as natural for this society. Historically, variations on the old racial frame have generated recurring discriminatory actions. Such racial framing of society has generated or rationalized anti-Indian genocide, African American slavery, legal segregation, and contemporary incarnations of racial discrimination.

Historically and in the present, whites have combined racial stereotypes (the cognitive aspect), ideas and concepts (the deeper cognitive aspect), images (the visual aspect), emotions (feelings like fear), and inclinations (to take discriminatory action) within a racial frame that is oriented to assessing other Americans of color in everyday situations. Learning racial (and ethnic) framing typically begins at a young age. The language and framing of "race" that is picked up in social settings often becomes what psychologist Lev Vygotsky has called "inner speech"; that is, it is deeply internalized.[50] Racial words and terms learned as children carry complex understandings going well beyond their apparent denotative meanings. Particular racial words learned in childhood embed and trigger an array of psychological linkages, emotions, and understandings. Our racialized language and broad racial framing often shape and limit our thinking about society.

Interestingly, there has been little research on the dominant white-generated framing, especially viewed as a whole. What evidence we do have suggests that there have been numerous variations on this white framing since the seventeenth century. Members of the dominant racial group in various regions of the country sometimes have accented different elements of the broad racial framing, although much of this old framing is shared across all subgroups and regions. From time to time new immigrant groups, such as Asian and Latino Americans, have been racialized and incorporated within the dominant framing. By constantly using the many elements of this old racial frame to rationalize and interpret this racialized society, by integrating new items into the frame periodically, and by applying learned stereotypes, images, and prejudicial interpretations in discriminatory actions, whites and others embed a racialized framing of the world deeply in their minds and, as well, many institutions of this society. Such deep embeddedness makes it difficult to alter or replace this centuries-old frame.

How has the racial framing of this society been maintained and reworked from the seventeenth century to the present day?

Prejudices and Stereotypes

Typically, a racial or ethnic framing of society in the minds of members of dominant groups, and of others influenced by them, includes negative stereotypes and prejudices concerning those in subordinate groups, as well as assertively positive views of the dominant group and its major institutions. These elements are centrally about the ways various racial and ethnic groups are represented, named, and discussed in the dominant framing of them. Let us now examine some of these important elements.

One often discussed element is *prejudice*, which in popular discourse is associated mostly with negative attitudes about members of racial and ethnic groups, especially subordinate groups. Some understanding of how and why these negative attitudes develop can be achieved by considering the concept of *ethnocentrism*, which was long ago described by William G. Sumner as the "view of things in which one's own group is the center of everything, and all others are scaled and rated with reference to it."[51] Individuals who develop *positive ethnocentrism* are characterized by a loyalty to the values, beliefs, and members of their own group. Ethnocentrism often prompts negative views of outgroups through a constant evaluation of outgroups in terms of ingroup values and ways. Such negative views are manifested in prejudices and stereotypes that influence the social, economic, and political interaction among groups.[52]

Prejudice has been defined by influential social psychologist Gordon Allport as "thinking ill of others without sufficient warrant."[53] The term *prejudice* comes from the Latin word *praejudicium*, or a judgment made prior to knowledge or experience. In English the word evolved from meaning "hasty judgment" to the present connotation of unfavorable bias based on an unsupported judgment. Although prejudice can theoretically apply to favorable prejudgments, its current usage in both popular speech and social science analysis is usually negative. Thus, **prejudice** is, to closely paraphrase Allport, *an antipathy based on a faulty generalization. It may be felt or expressed. It may be directed toward a group as a whole, or toward an individual because she or he is a member of that group.*[54]

As used in this text, *prejudice* has both an emotional and a cognitive aspect; it involves a negative feeling or attitude toward the outgroup as well as an inaccurate belief or image. An example might be "I as a white person hate black and Latino people because black and Latino people always smell worse than whites." The first part of the sentence expresses the negative emotion (the hatred); the last part, an inaccurate generalization. This latter cognitive aspect has been termed a **stereotype**—that is, *an overgeneralization associated with a racial or ethnic category that goes beyond existing evidence.*

Why do many people stereotype other people? Why have Irish Americans been stereotyped as lazy drunkards, African Americans and Latinos as indolent, Italian Americans as criminals with "Mafia" ties, Asian Americans as "treacherous Orientals"? Such questions encourage us to examine the role that prejudices and stereotypes play in the history and daily lives of individuals and groups and in the society in which they live.

Stereotypes involve social representations of various groups and take different forms. For example, anthropologist Jane Hill has researched the widespread use of "mock Spanish" as part of the negative representations and images of U.S. Latinos. Many non-Latinos sprinkle their language with mock-Spanish terms such as "no problemo," "el cheapo," and "hasty banana," and phrases such as "hasta la vista, baby." Mock-Spanish terms appear on billboards, in movies, in cartoons, on items in gift shops, and in elite board rooms—often in association with racial caricatures of

Mexican Americans or other Latino groups. This widespread mocking of the Spanish language and of Latinos typically signals racialized stereotyping.[55] Ridicule of Mexican American language or speech is racist because it has meaning mainly in relation to underlying racial stereotypes. Hill suggests that this mocking enables its (usually Anglo-white) perpetrators to support traditional hierarchies of racial privilege without seeming to be blatantly racist.

Recurring white attacks on certain distinctive language accents or on variants of English spoken by many Latinos and African Americans are not just concerned with language, for they reveal a "general unwillingness to accept the speakers of that language and social choices they have made as viable and functional. . . . We are ashamed of them, and because they are part of us, we are ashamed of ourselves."[56] Language mocking and language subordination are not about standards for speaking as much as they are about determining that some people (usually people of color) are not worth listening to and treating as equals. Thus, people who speak French-accented English rarely report discrimination, whereas those who speak Spanish-accented English often do. Stereotyped language or accent mocking often becomes part of "hundreds of taken-for-granted commonplace utterances that function to 'racialize' their targets, constructing them as members of a human group represented as essentially inferior."[57]

Stereotyping operates at both the conscious and the unconscious levels. For example, social psychologists have discovered that nearly 90 percent of whites who have taken a test of unconscious stereotyping associate black Americans with negative words and traits, such as "evil character." In these studies, whites have had more difficulty linking black faces than white faces to pleasant words and positive traits. In addition, when shown photos of black faces, even for only 30 milliseconds, key areas of white subjects' brains that are designed to respond to perceived threats light up automatically when scanned. Such data suggest how deeply embedded in the brain traditional racial stereotypes can be. As a result, a great many whites do not approach new encounters with black Americans and other people of color with minds that are truly open to new information or interpretations.[58] In addition, social psychologists such as Patricia Devine have found that virtually all whites are aware of major racial stereotypes no matter what their personal inclinations to act on them may be. The reason: Automatic mental processing brings up such racial stereotypes for whites whenever an appropriate stimulus appears, such as a member of a racial outgroup. Moreover, the research shows that very prejudiced people are more inclined to act on the activated racial stereotypes, whereas less prejudiced people often engage in a type of mental processing that ignores or rejects the activated stereotype.[59]

Explanations of Stereotyping and Prejudice

Sociological analysts of stereotyping and prejudice tend to emphasize group pressures on individuals for conformity or rationalization, whereas psychological analysts tend to stress individual irrationality or personality defects. Much research has highlighted the expressive function of prejudice for the individual. Frustration–aggression theories, psychoanalytic theories, and authoritarian personality perspectives generally focus on the **externalization function of prejudice**—*the transfer of an individual's internal psychological problem onto an external object, such as a particular racial group, as a solution to that internal psychological problem.* Psychologically oriented interpretations sometimes attribute racial or ethnic prejudice to special emotional problems of "sick" or "abnormal" individuals, such as a deep hatred of their own parents.[60]

In a classic study of prejudice and personality, *The Authoritarian Personality*, T. W. Adorno and his colleagues argued that people who hate such groups as Jewish Americans typically differ from tolerant people in regard to central personality traits—specifically, that they tend to exhibit "authoritarian personalities."[61] Those with **authoritarian personalities** *are characterized by a high degree of submission to authority, a strong tendency to stereotype, great concern for social status, a view of the world as threatening, and an intolerance of outgroups that occupy socially subordinate positions.*

Some scholars have raised questions about a too heavy stress on the expressive function of prejudice. They have suggested that social *conformity* may be a much more important factor for most prejudiced people. Most people accept their own social situations as given and hold the prejudices taught at home and school and by the mass media. The **conformity function of prejudice**—*holding prejudiced attitudes in order to conform to expectations of* *important social reference groups* such as relatives and friends—explains much individual prejudice. Many negative prejudices and stereotypes are formed from the informal lessons that people learn as children at home and school and as adults as they absorb messages from the media and socialize with relatives, co-workers, and friends.[62] In this conformity view, most racial and ethnic prejudices are not the result of deep psychological pathologies, but rather reflect shared social definitions of outgroups. In such cases, prejudice functions as a means of social adjustment. Most of us can think of situations in which we or our acquaintances have adjusted to new racial beliefs in moving from one region or setting to another. As Schermerhorn notes, "prejudice is a product of *situations*," not "a little demon that emerges in people simply because they are depraved."[63]

An additional function of prejudice is to help rationalize a subordinate group's powerless position. Herbert Blumer suggested that prejudice is more than a matter of negative feelings possessed by members of one group for another; it is also "rooted in a sense of group position."[64] The dominant group comes to defend and rationalize its privileged position. Modern prejudice, Oliver Cox argues, "is a divisive attitude seeking to alienate dominant group sympathy from an 'inferior' race, a whole people, for the purpose of facilitating its exploitation."[65] When peoples are racially subordinated, as in the cases of white enslavement of Africans in the North American colonies or restrictive quotas for Jewish Americans in U.S. colleges in the 1920s, those in power—in both cases, Anglo-Protestant whites—develop prejudices and stereotypes that help to rationalize the oppression of others.

Some analysts have suggested that certain members of dominant racial groups who today discriminate against subordinate groups are motivated just by a desire for economic or political gain. Such people strive to maintain their undeserved privileges, whether or not they rationalize that striving in terms of racial prejudices and stereotypes.[66] Such striving takes place within a societal system of inequality in which the dominant racial group benefits economically, politically, and psychologically—and acts to maintain its ill-gotten benefits. In the everyday world of racial discrimination, however, it is likely that the desire to protect racialized privileges will be accompanied by negatively stereotyped views of the subordinate group targeted for discrimination.

Are Racial Attitudes and Performances Changing?

Stereotyped images and other stereotypes of people of color held by whites today have many similarities with stereotypes of the past. Still, some changes have occurred, especially since the 1960s. Public opinion surveys of white attitudes toward Americans of color have shown a significant decline in the public expression of certain old-fashioned racist attitudes since the 1940s.

Researchers David Sears and John McConahay have identified what they term **symbolic** or **modern racism**, that is, *white beliefs that serious racial discrimination does not exist today and that black Americans in particular are making illegitimate demands for social changes.* Using survey-type measures, these social psychologists have suggested that, among whites, "old-fashioned racism" favoring rigid segregation and extreme stereotypes has largely been replaced by a modern racism whose proponents accept modest racial desegregation but resist the large-scale changes necessary for full integration of U.S. society. Sociologist Lawrence Bobo has suggested that whites have an "ideology of bounded racial change." That is, whites' support for changes in discrimination ends when such changes seriously endanger their standard of living.[67] In addition, social psychologist Thomas Pettigrew has noted certain white reactions to black achievements in recent decades and suggested that an "ultimate attribution error" on the part of whites includes not only blaming black victims for their failures, but also discounting black successes by attributing the latter to luck or unfair advantages rather than intelligence and hard work.[68] Research on modern versions of attitudinal racism has mostly examined white attitudes toward black Americans, but these new concepts can likely be used to interpret white prejudices and stereotypes directed at other people of color.

Much recent research shows that many people today vary their presentations and performances of negative racial attitudes depending on the social setting. For example, in a survey of white students on major college campuses, sociologists Eduardo Bonilla-Silva and Tyrone Forman discovered that racial attitudes expressed on short-answer survey items were frequently different from those expressed to questions requiring extended commentary. On a brief survey item, 80 percent of 451 white students indicated that they *approved* of marriages between white and black Americans. However, when a smaller but similar group of white college students was interviewed in depth, this figure dropped to only 30 percent. Given more time to answer and explain their views in in-depth interviews, the majority expressed significant reservations about marriage across the color line. Other attitudinal views showed a similar pattern of racial expression varying by setting. Moreover, in her research social psychologist Maria Krysan increased the privacy of the settings in which her respondents could express their racial views. As the privacy of settings increased, white respondents expressed more negative attitudes toward black Americans. Other psychological research has found that whites who reject some stereotypes, such as in settings where their expression is easy to control, nonetheless reveal these deeply held stereotypes in other situations where they are less able, or less concerned, to control them. Social conformity and desirability concerns constantly are factors.[69]

Several social scientists have used various qualitative research methods to explore the spatial and temporal variations in racist commentaries and performances. They too have demonstrated how whites vary their commentaries and performances depending on whether they are in public or private social arenas. In pioneering research on interactions in an all-white country-and-western group, sociologist Nina Eliasoph found that overtly racist commentaries were critical for socially integrating whites when they were interacting with each other. Racist talk, or complacency about it, facilitated interaction. Whites were aware of when and where to engage in overtly racist discussions; they understood the social setting was as important as the racist content. Researcher Karyn McKinney got college students to provide autobiographical journals about their private and public lives. One student pointed out that private settings were comfortable places for expressing racial attitudes: "I think that for people, other white people being around are a comfort zone to express any racist views. It is funny how some people assume that no white person will care about what they say or that they will even support their beliefs." Similarly, in an important and probing ethnographic study of "race talk," Kristen Myers and her associates recorded substantial comments made by ordinary people, whites and people of color, in private places. Myers and her ethnographers found that many whites used blatantly racist slurs and categorizations—an often ritualistic degregation of people of color—in their everyday interactions.[70]

Particularly significant is the finding of contemporary social scientists that many whites still make blatantly racist commentaries and do racist performances, such as racist joking or frequent use of racist epithets, when they are in settings with white friends and relatives. This behavior is termed *backstage racism* by Leslie Houts Picca and Joe Feagin, who draw on the ideas of Erving Goffman. Making use of thousands of journal accounts from hundreds of college students across the country, Picca and Feagin found that whites often seem to behave differently depending on whether they are in a backstage setting with white friends and relatives or in a frontstage setting that includes people of color. They report this recent journal account from a white female college student about a night out with several other white students:

> Three of my friends (a white girl and two white boys) and I went back to my house to drink a little more before we ended the night. My one friend, Dylan started telling jokes.... Dylan said: "What's the most confusing day of the year in Harlem?" "Father's Day...Who's your Daddy?" Dylan also referred to black people as "Porch Monkeys." Everyone laughed a little, but it was obvious that we all felt a little less comfortable when he was telling jokes like that. My friend Dylan is not a racist person. He has more black friends than I do, that's why I was surprised he so freely said something like that. Dylan would never have said something like that around anyone who was a minority.[71]

Here a white student told racist jokes, and others laughed along with him. Though they reportedly felt uncomfortable, the other whites did not openly object. The journal writer has rationalized her friend's racist actions, noting that he would not make such racist "jokes" in a frontstage setting with people of color around.

Although there have been some important shifts in whites' racist attitudes in recent decades, many of the old racial stereotypes and prejudices, as well as much of the old racist framing of society, remain firmly embedded in many white minds and evident in many whites' everyday commentaries and performances.

What are common methods of developing and rationalizing stereotypes and prejudices?

Discrimination

Distinguishing Dimensions

Public discussions of racial and ethnic discrimination and of government programs to eradicate it (for example, affirmative action) are often confusing because important dimensions of that discrimination are not fully distinguished. As a first step in sorting out the confusion, we suggest Figure 1.1. Key dimensions of discrimination include (a) motivation, (b) discriminatory actions, (c) effects, (d) the relation between motivation and actions, (e) the relation between actions and effects, (f) the immediate institutional context, and (g) the larger societal context.[72]

A given set of discriminatory acts—such as the exclusion of Jewish American applicants from Ivy League colleges in the 1920s or the exclusion of many children of color from numerous all-white public schools until the mid-1960s—can be looked at in terms of these dimensions. One can ask what the motivation was for this discrimination. Was it prejudice, stereotyping, or another motive? One can also ask what form the exclusionary practices actually took. For example, in the case of segregated public schools in the South or West during earlier decades, white school administrators often refused, on overtly racist grounds, black, Latino, or Asian American children entrance into their buildings. Also of importance are the many long-term effects and costs of these discriminatory practices. For example, one effect was the much poorer school facilities that many black, Latino, and Asian American children encountered.

These historicial practices were usually not just the actions of isolated white administrators. Rather, they were part of an institutionalized pattern of legally or customarily segregated education, the effects of which are still very evident in U.S. society. Such patterns of official school segregation were part of a larger social context of the general subordination of black, Latino, and Asian Americans across various institutional areas. Indeed, today, as in the past, racial discrimination remains a multidimensional problem involving most institutional areas of U.S. society.

How do stereotypes and prejudices maintain racial or ethnic discrimination?

Research on Prejudice and Discrimination

Much social science research on discrimination has focused on one type of motivation—prejudice [(a) in Figure 1.1]. Many social scientists emphasize the relation between prejudice and discrimination [(d) in

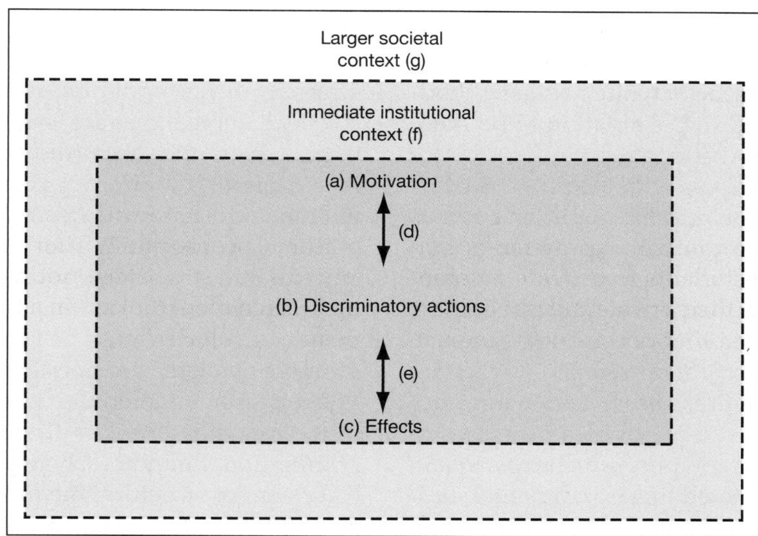

FIGURE 1.1 The Dimensions of Discrimination

Source: Adapted from Joe R. Feagin, "Affirmative Action in an Era of Reaction," *Consultations on the Affirmative Action Statement of the U.S. Commission on Civil Rights* (Washington, DC: U.S. Government Printing Office, 1982), pp. 44–48.

Figure 1.1], viewing racial and ethnic prejudice as the critical cause of discriminatory treatment of a singled-out group. Gordon Allport suggested that few prejudiced people keep their prejudices to themselves; they act out their feelings in discriminatory ways.[73] In his classic study, *An American Dilemma* (1944), Gunnar Myrdal saw racial prejudice as "the whole complex of valuations and beliefs which are behind discriminatory behavior on the part of white Americans." Later, sociologist Robert K. Merton suggested that for some people, discrimination is motivated not by their own prejudices, but by fear of the prejudices of others in their social group.[74]

Experimental studies by psychologists have focused on the relationship between prejudice and expressed discrimination. Numerous researchers have examined whether prejudiced people do, in fact, discriminate, and, if so, how that prejudice links to discrimination. Such studies have generally found a weak positive correlation between expressed prejudice (for example, on questionnaires) and certain discriminatory behavior. Thus, knowing how prejudiced a subject is does not necessarily help predict the character of his or her actions.

Some experimenters have tried to develop nonobvious measures of discrimination. One such measure involved setting up an experimental situation in which whites encountered a person (an assistant of the researcher) who needed help making a phone call at a public telephone. In this case the researcher found that the racial identity of the person needing help often affected the type of white response. Studies like this have found discrimination to be more likely in anonymous situations than in face-to-face encounters that whites have with black people they know. As noted previously, public opinion surveys have shown a decline in public expression of blatantly racist attitudes among whites in recent decades. Thus, several experimental researchers have also asked whether whites responding to such surveys with relatively liberal racial answers are concealing many racial prejudices. Reviewing laboratory studies that used less obvious measures of discrimination, such as the phone call experiment, these researchers have noted that experimental studies have found *much more* antiblack discrimination than they should have uncovered if the unprejudiced views that many whites express in surveys were their real views.[75] As the backstage racism research cited previously suggests, many whites do indeed hide their traditionally racist views in more public settings—including in surveys conducted by pollsters and social science researchers.

Defining Institutional and Individual Discrimination

The emphasis on individual prejudice and bigoted individuals in traditional assessments of racial and ethnic discrimination has led some analysts to accent the institutionalization of discrimination. Stokely Carmichael (Kwame Ture) and Charles Hamilton distinguished between the concepts of **individual racism**, *the racially hostile acts of an individual directed at members of another racial group* and exemplified by the actions of a Klan-type terrorist bombing a black church, and of **institutional racism**, *the institutionalized practices that differentially and negatively affect members of a subordinate racial group,* such as the accumulating institutional practices that lead to large numbers of children of color suffering because of seriously inadequate health care facilities in many cities.[76] Carmichael and Hamilton thus moved beyond individual bigots. In their view institutional racism often involves harmful actions in which many dominant group members have "no intention of subordinating others because of color, or are totally unaware of doing so."[77]

In his analysis of discrimination and mental health, Thomas Pettigrew has distinguished between *direct* and *indirect* racial discrimination, applying the latter term to restrictions in one institutional area (such as screening out job applicants because they do not have a college degree) that are shaped by racial discrimination in another area (the historical exclusion of Americans of color from important educational facilities, including many colleges, prior to the 1960s).[78]

Some conceptual work on discrimination emphasizes the close relationship between its individual ("micro") and institutional ("macro") dimensions, which should be viewed as two aspects of the same phenomenon. Social psychologist Philomena Essed has underscored the "mutual interdependence of the macro and micro dimensions" of racial discrimination. From the macro perspective, racism is "a system of structural inequalities and a historical process." From a micro perspective, racism involves individual discriminators whose specific actions are racist "only when they activate existing structural racial inequalities in the system."[79] In the U.S. case the routine actions of discriminators typically reinforce, and are shaped by, an old hierarchical system of racial dominance and inequality.

The group context of discriminatory actions is very important. The working definition of the serious **discrimination** we emphasize in this book is as follows: *actions carried out by members of dominant groups, or their representatives, that have a differential and harmful effect on members of subordinate groups*. The dominant and subordinate groups we focus on here are socially constructed racial and ethnic groups. From this perspective, the most serious discrimination involves harmful practices taken by members of *powerful* racial and ethnic groups against those with much less power and fewer resources. (Those on the middle rungs of a racial-ethnic hierarchy can and do discriminate against those below them in power.) Discrimination involves *actions* as well as one or more *discriminators* and one or more *victims*. A further distinction between *intentional* (motivated by prejudice or intent to harm) and *unintentional* (not motivated by prejudice or intent to harm) is useful for identifying different types of discrimination.[80]

Drawing on the two dimensions of scale and intention, we suggest four major types of discrimination. Type A, **isolate discrimination**, is *harmful action taken intentionally by a member of a dominant racial or ethnic group against members of a subordinate group, without the support of other members of the dominant group in the immediate social or community context*. An example is a white Anglo police officer who implements anti-Latino hostility by beating up Mexican American prisoners at every opportunity, even though the majority of Anglo officers and department regulations specifically oppose such actions. (If the majority of Anglo officers in that department behaved in this fashion, the beatings would fall under the heading of type C discrimination.) The term *isolate* should not be taken to mean that type A discrimination is rare, for it is indeed common.

Type B, **small-group discrimination**, is *harmful action taken intentionally by a small number of dominant-group individuals acting in concert against members of subordinate racial and ethnic groups, without the direct support of the norms and of most other dominant group members in the immediate social or community context*. The bombing of Irish Catholic churches in the 1800s by small groups of British Americans and the burning of crosses at the homes of people of color in several cities in the last decade by members of white supremacist groups are likely examples.

The Ku Klux Klan, created in the nineteenth century as a major terrorist group, marches at a recent rally in Houston.

Type C, **direct institutionalized discrimination**, is *organizationally prescribed or community-prescribed action that by intention has a differential and negative effect on members of subordinate racial and ethnic groups*. Typically, these actions are not sporadic but are carried out routinely by a large number of dominant-group individuals guided by the legal or informal norms of the immediate organizational or community context. Historical examples include the intentional exclusion, by law, of African and Jewish Americans from traditionally white neighborhoods and jobs. Type C discrimination can be seen today in the actions of those white real estate agents and owners who regularly create barriers for people of color seeking homes in traditionally white residential areas. These discriminating whites are acting in accord with informal norms widely shared by many whites in their communities.[81]

Type D, **indirect institutionalized discrimination**, consists of *dominant-group practices that have a* *harmful effect on members of subordinate racial and ethnic groups even though the organizational or community-prescribed norms or regulations guiding those actions have been established with no intent to harm.* For example, intentional discrimination institutionalized in the inadequate school facilities provided for subordinate-group members such as black, Latino, and Native Americans—resulting in inadequate educations for many—has often handicapped their attempts to compete with dominant-group members in the employment sphere, where hiring and promotion standards usually include certain educational credentials.

In addition, the effects of *past* discrimination linger on strongly in the *present*: Current generations of racial groups that were once severely and openly subordinated usually have less inherited wealth and fewer sociocultural (for example, educational or social networking) resources than current generations of the dominant racial group.

What is the relevance of the four types of discrimination discussed to present-day racial relations in the United States?

The Sites and Range of Discrimination

Discrimination usually includes a spatial dimension. For instance, in a white-dominated society, a racially subordinated person's vulnerability to discrimination can vary significantly. If the latter is in a relatively protected site, such as with close friends at home, the probability of experiencing racial hostility or discrimination from dominant-group members is low. In contrast, if that same person—for example, a college professor—is in a moderately protected site, such as in a departmental setting within a once predominantly white university that has undergone some desegregation, the probability of experiencing racial hostility and discrimination often increases, although the professional status of that professor may offer some protection there. The probability of overt racial hostility and discrimination often increases further as this person of color moves into historically white hotels, restaurants, and stores, or into city streets patrolled by white police officers. As we will see in later chapters, those members of subordinate groups who have ventured the most into settings once reserved for members of dominant groups, either in the past or in the present, have often been the most likely to face substantial discrimination and hostility.[82]

In his classic book, *The Nature of Prejudice*, Gordon Allport notes that discrimination by members of a dominant group against those in a subordinate group ranges from antilocution (speaking against), to avoidance, to exclusion, to physical attack, and finally, to extermination.[83] For example, a dominant-group member, such as an English Protestant American, may try to exclude a Jewish American from his or her university or club. Or a white American may hurl a racist epithet at a Chinese or Korean American walking nearby.

One can also distinguish subtle and covert categories of discrimination from the more blatant forms. **Subtle discrimination** can be defined as *unequal and harmful treatment of members of subordinate racial and ethnic groups that is obvious to the victim but not as overt as traditional, "door-slamming" varieties of discrimination.* In modern bureaucratic settings such as corporate workplaces, many white employers and managerial employees have internalized inclinations to subtle discriminatory behavior that they consider normal and acceptable. This type of discrimination often goes unnoticed by nondiscriminating members of the dominant group.[84]

For instance, in research on African American managers who have secured entry-level positions in corporations, Ed Jones found a predisposition among whites, both co-workers and senior managers, to assume the best about persons of their own color and the worst about people different from themselves in evaluating job performance. Like Pettigrew's "ultimate attribution error," this critical predisposition, which can be conscious or subconscious, can result in discrimination in promotions and other areas that is more subtle than the blatant discrimination of exclusion. The black managers interviewed by Jones and other researchers report that their achievements are often given less attention than their failures, while the failures of comparable white managers are more likely to be excused in terms of situational factors or just overlooked. This negative feedback on a black worker's performance makes it more difficult for her or him to perform successfully in the future.[85]

Covert discrimination, in contrast, is *harmful treatment of members of subordinate racial and ethnic groups that is hidden and difficult to document.* Covert discrimination includes acts of sabotage and tokenism. For example, in one research study, a black female mail carrier reported that white male co-workers were hiding some of her mail, so that when she returned from her route, there was still mail waiting to be delivered. Because of this sabotage, her white manager blamed her and gave her a less desirable route.[86] Asian, African, and Latino Americans are sometimes hired as "tokens" or "window dressing": They are placed in certain conspicuous positions just to make an organization look good instead of being evaluated honestly in terms of their abilities for higher-level employment. Some employers hire a few for "front" positions to reduce pressures to expand the number of employees from racially or ethnically subordinated groups to more representative proportions. Tokenism can thereby become a serious barrier to individual and group advancement.

Cumulative and Systemic Discrimination

Various combinations of blatant, covert, and subtle forms of discrimination usually coexist in a given organization or community. *Well-institutionalized patterns of discrimination that cut across major political, economic, and social organizations in a society* can be termed **systemic discrimination**. One National Council of Churches group portrayed systemic racial discrimination this way: "Both consciously and unconsciously, racism is enforced and maintained by the legal, cultural, religious, educational, economic, political, environmental and military institutions of societies. Racism is more than just a personal attitude; it is the institutionalized form of that attitude."[87]

Central to this systemic discrimination is the *cumulative* effect of much discrimination on its targets. Particular instances of racial or ethnic discrimination may seem minor to outside observers if considered in isolation. But when blatant actions, such as verbal harassment or physical attack, combine with subtle and covert slights, such as veiled sabotage, the cumulative effect of all this discrimination over months, years, and lifetimes is usually *far* greater than the sum of the individual instances. Racial and ethnic oppression is typically both systemic and cumulative, and its targets usually pay a heavy price.

Responding to Discrimination

The responses of subordinate-group members to discrimination can range from deference or withdrawal to verbal and physical confrontation to legal action. Even when dominant-group members expect acquiescence in discrimination, some subordinate-group members may not oblige. The targets of discrimination often organize and fight back. Thus, **civil rights movement** is a *collective movement to establish or improve the legal and political rights of a subordinate racial or ethnic group*. Such organized movements are exemplified by the black and Latino civil rights movements of the 1950s and 1960s. Sometimes however, the response is by individuals in everyday settings, especially if they are among those subordinate-group members with some monetary or legal resources. Discrimination that begins as one-way action may become two-way negotiation, often to the surprise of the discriminators.

Consider this example of a black woman manager in a U.S. corporation describes a meeting with her white boss about her job performance:

> We had a five scale rating, starting with outstanding, then very good, then good, then fair, and then less than satisfactory. I had gone into my evaluation interview anticipating that he would give me a "VG" (very good), feeling that I deserved an "outstanding" and prepared to fight for my outstanding rating. Knowing, you know, my past experience with him, and more his way toward females. But even beyond female, I happened to be the only black in my position within my branch. So the racial issue would also come into play. And he and I had some very frank discussions about race specifically. About females, but more about race when he and I talked. So I certainly knew that he had a lot of prejudices in terms of blacks. And [he] had some very strong feelings based on his upbringing about the abilities of blacks. He said to me on numerous occasions that he considered me to be an exception, that I certainly was not what he felt the abilities of an average black person [were]. While I was of course appalled and made it perfectly clear to him . . . . But, when I went into the evaluation interview, he gave me glowing comments that cited numerous achievements and accomplishments for me during the year, and then concluded it with, "so I've given you a G." You know, which of course just floored me . . . . [I] maintained my emotions and basically just said, as unemotionally as I possibly could, that I found that unacceptable, I thought it was inconsistent with his remarks in terms of my performance, and I would not accept it. I think I kind of shocked him, because he sort of said, "well I don't know what that means," you know, when I said I wouldn't accept it. I said,

> I'm not signing the evaluation. And at that point, here again knowing that the best way to deal with most issues is with facts and specifics, I had already come in prepared .... I had my list of objectives for the year where I was able to show him that I had achieved every objective and I exceeded all of them. I also had . . . my sales performance: the dollar amount, the products . . . both in total dollar sales and also a product mix. I sold every product in the line that we offered to our customers. I had exceeded all of my sales objectives. You know, as far as I was concerned, it was an outstanding performance.

Then she noted the final result:

> So he basically said, "Well, we don't have to agree to agree," and that was the end of the session. I got up and left. Fifteen minutes later he called me back in and said, "I've thought about what you said, and you're right, you do have an O." So it's interesting how in fifteen minutes I went from a G to an O. But the interesting point is had I not fought it, had I just accepted it, I would have gotten a G rating for that year, which has many implications.[88]

This example of employment discrimination is a common one and illustrates a number of points made in this chapter. Because of certain physical characteristics, this woman was viewed by her white supervisor as a member of a racial group he stereotypes as generally incapable. He discriminated against her by downplaying her accomplishments with a low evaluation. In this case she did not accept his rating. Because of prior experience with his negative attitudes, this woman came to the interaction with some expectation of having to counter his actions. The one-way action that was probably expected by the boss soon became two-way negotiation. This savvy woman made tactical use of her resources to win a concession and a changed evaluation.

Over the past two decades, there has been an increase in the number of middle-class people of color who have the resources to contest blatant discrimination more directly and, sometimes, successfully. Microlevel discrimination may only be the first stage in a two-way encounter. The initial discrimination, the counter, and the discriminator's response, as well as the resources and perceptions of those involved, are important aspects of everyday racism.

Moreover, thinking broadly, we should recognize how important the individual and collective struggles against discrimination and for civil rights have been to the development of U.S. democracy. The United States has been an officially free country *only since the late 1960s*. Prior to the 1960s' civil rights acts (the last in 1968), this country had been substantially grounded either in slavery or in legal segregation since the 1600s. For more than three centuries this country had a major portion of its population under such extreme oppression that describing the country as "free" was highly inaccurate. Over this period, moreover, the freedom struggles of African Americans and other Americans of color were central to creating the more democratic country we live in today.

Conservative Reactions to Antidiscrimination Programs

Many conservative scholars and commentators have written about "reverse discrimination" and "reverse racism" in recent decades. They have intentionally tried to change the public discussions of traditional racial discrimination. Most argue that whites suffer seriously from the implementation of affirmative action and other remedial programs that attempt to redress the extensive discrimination historically faced by subordinate racial groups. (**Affirmative action programs** are *private and governmental programs that seek to improve the economic or educational opportunities for formerly excluded racial, ethnic, and gender groups.*) Conservatives and others often use the phrase *reverse discrimination* to deflect attention from the large-scale patterns of institutionalized discrimination still directed by whites against racially oppressed people. Discrimination, as conceptualized by most social science scholars of racial and ethnic relations, emphasizes the dominant group–subordinate group context of discrimination. Racial discrimination usually refers to actions of members of dominant groups—for example, white Americans—that are taken to harm members of subordinate groups, such as African, Latino, Asian, Middle Eastern, or Native Americans. Historically and today, systemic white discrimination is not just a matter of occasional white bigotry but involves the dominant white group's power to enforce white prejudices in discriminatory practices in most major U.S. institutions.

On occasion, individual members of subordinated racial groups can be motivated by their prejudices to take action to harm those in the dominant white group. Yet, with scattered exceptions, members of racially subordinate groups usually do not have the power or institutional position to express the prejudices they may hold about whites in the form of substantial everyday discrimination.

Think carefully about the historical and contemporary patterns of racial discrimination directed by large numbers of whites against just one major group, African Americans. That mistreatment has meant, and still means, widespread blatant and subtle discrimination by whites against African Americans in most organizations in all major institutions in U.S. society—in housing, employment, business, education, health services, and the legal system (see Chapter 7). Over four centuries, many millions of whites have participated directly in discrimination against many millions of African Americans. Judging from opinion polls, a majority of whites currently hold some negative stereotypes of African Americans, and millions of these whites will discriminate under some circumstances. In addition, most whites still observe the antiblack discrimination that often takes place around them without working actively to stop it. This widespread and systemic discrimination has brought extraordinarily heavy social and economic losses (the latter estimated by some scholars to be in the trillions of dollars over nearly 400 years) for African Americans in many institutional sectors of this society.[89]

What would the *reverse* of this centuries-old antiblack discrimination really look like? The reverse of the institutionalized discrimination by whites against African Americans would mean reversing the power and resource inequalities for several hundred years. In the past and today, most organizations in major institutional areas such as housing, education, and employment would be run at the top and middle levels by a disproportionate number of powerful black managers and officials. These powerful black officials would have aimed much racial discrimination at whites, including many years of slavery and legal segregation. As a result, millions of whites would have suffered—and would still suffer—trillions of dollars in economic losses such as lower wages, as well as high rates of unemployment and political disenfranchisement for long periods, widespread housing segregation, inferior school facilities, and violent lynchings. That societal condition would be something one could reasonably call a condition that "reversed the discrimination" against African Americans. It does not now exist, nor has it ever existed.

What is usually termed *reverse discrimination* is something much different from this fictional antiwhite scenario. One usual reference is to affirmative action programs that, for a limited time or in certain places, have used racial screening criteria to overcome a small part of the past and present discrimination that has targeted racially oppressed people. Whatever modest costs a few years of antidiscrimination programs have meant for whites those costs do not add up to anything close to the total cost that inverting the historical and contemporary patterns of discrimination against people of color would involve. Affirmative action plans as currently set up—and there are now far fewer effective plans than most critics suggest—do not make concrete and devastating a widespread antiwhite prejudice on the part of people of color.[90] As established and implemented, affirmative action plans have mostly involved modest remedial efforts (typically designed some years ago by white men) to bring token-to-modest numbers of people of color and white women into certain areas of our economic, social, and political institutions from which these groups have historically been excluded.

A modest number of white men have occasionally paid some price for certain remedial programs. If affirmative action is successful, it will entail some cost to be paid by those who have benefited most from centuries of racial and gender discrimination. Yet, a white man who suffers as an individual from remedial programs such as affirmative action in employment or education suffers in but one area of life (and often only once) and because he is an *exception* to his privileged racial group. A person of color who suffers from racial discrimination usually suffers *in all areas* of his or her life and primarily because the whole group has been and still is subordinated, not because he or she is an exception.[91] Moreover, in spite of continuing high levels of discrimination targeting Americans of color, many private organizations and public agencies have in recent decades cut back even on their modest affirmative action programs because of white protests and judicial backtracking.

Summary

In this chapter we have examined an extensive array of basic concepts that are essential for making sense out of racial and ethnic contacts and conflicts. These concepts loom large in contemporary discussions of racial and ethnic issues. More than a century of discussion of these concepts lies behind the voyage we have set out on here. We must carefully think through the meaning of such terms as *race* and *racial group*, because such concepts have historically been used in the shaping of racial contacts and racial oppression, as they still are today.

Ideas about "race" and racial groups have been particularly dangerous because they have played an active role in the triggering, or the convenient rationalizing, of societal processes that have cost many millions of lives. Ideas do have an impact. The sharp cutting edge of "race," in the context of theorizing about "racial inferiority," can be seen in the enslavement by white Europeans of millions of Africans between the seventeenth and nineteenth centuries and in genocidal German Nazi actions taken against European Jews and others in the 1930s and 1940s. Sometimes it is easy to consider concepts as harmless abstractions. However, some reflection on both recent and distant Western history exposes the error in this view. The concept may not be "mightier than the sword," to adapt an old cliché, but it is indeed mighty.

Key Terms

race 4
racial hierarchy 4
racialization 5
ideological racism 5
racial group 7
ethnic group 9
minority group 11
dominant group 11
racial frame 12
prejudice 13
stereotype 13
externalization function of prejudice 14
authoritarian personalities 14
conformity function of prejudice 14
symbolic or modern racism 15
individual racism 18
institutional racism 18
discrimination 19
isolate discrimination 19
small-group discrimination 19
direct institutionalized discrimination 19
indirect institutionalized discrimination 19
subtle discrimination 20
covert discrimination 20
systemic discrimination 21
civil rights movement 21
affirmative action programs 22

CHAPTER 2

Adaptation and Conflict: Racial and Ethnic Relations in Theoretical Perspective

BIG PICTURE QUESTIONS

- ***How do initial contacts contribute to the creation of dominant and subordinate racial and ethnic groups?***
- ***Have long centuries of immigration made the United States a real melting pot?***
- ***What is the role of systemic racism in the United States today?***

In 1790 the first U.S. Congress limited naturalized U.S. citizenship to "white persons" only. This discriminatory law remained in effect until 1952. Because of the law, numerous immigrants coming into the United States in this long era petitioned U.S. courts to be viewed as "white" so that they could officially become citizens. The first challenge to the law came from Ah Yup, a man who had immigrated from China and petitioned a California court to be admitted as a citizen of the United States. However, after some research on racial hierarchy, and citing Johann Blumenbach's racial typology, the white judge decreed that Ah Yup was not a "white person" under the law, but rather a person of the "Mongolian race."[1]

How do groups that are termed racial groups or ethnic groups develop? How do groups come into contact with one another in the first place? How do they adjust to one another beyond the initial contact? A number of social science theories analyze how intergroup contact leads to initial patterns of racial and ethnic interaction and stratification. Various other theories explore the persistence of racial and ethnic patterns. Group domination and stratification, as well as intergroup conflict, are critical issues in these racial and ethnic theories.

Racial and Ethnic Hierarchies

Like many other societies, U.S. society is made up of a diversity of racial and ethnic groups. As in the 1790s, so in the present the number of racial and ethnic groups in North America remains impressive, although the mix of groups has varied over time. Racial and ethnic diversity is basic in the history of this society.

Yet, diversity, as the previously discussed terms *dominant group* and *subordinate group* suggest, has often been linked to a racial and ethnic *hierarchy*—to stratification, domination, and substantial inequality among groups. Human beings organize themselves for a number of different reasons—for example, for earning a living, for conducting religious rituals, and for governing. Among the important features of societal organization are social ranking systems. Such systems rank categories of people, not just individuals.

In most societies, several social ranking systems coexist. Some classify people by their racial or ethnic group, whereas others rank people by their gender, age, disability, sexuality, or class position. Each ranking system has distinct social categories; rewards, privileges, and power vary with a group's position within the system. Some categories, such as English Americans in the racial and ethnic system, have generally had much greater power and resources than other categories, such as Native Americans, African Americans, or Latinos. Such power and resource inequality tends to persist from one generation to the next. In racial and ethnic ranking systems, certain ascribed (that is, attributed, not achieved) characteristics—such as one group's racial characteristics as perceived by another group—become the criteria for very unequal social positions, privileges, and rewards.[2]

The image of a ladder makes the concept of racial and ethnic stratification clearer. In Figure 2.1 the positions of five selected racial and ethnic groups at a specific time in U.S. history are diagrammed on a hierarchical ladder. Some groups are higher than others, indicating that they have greater privileges—social, economic, and political—than the lower groups. A group substantially higher than another on an important dimension is viewed as a dominant

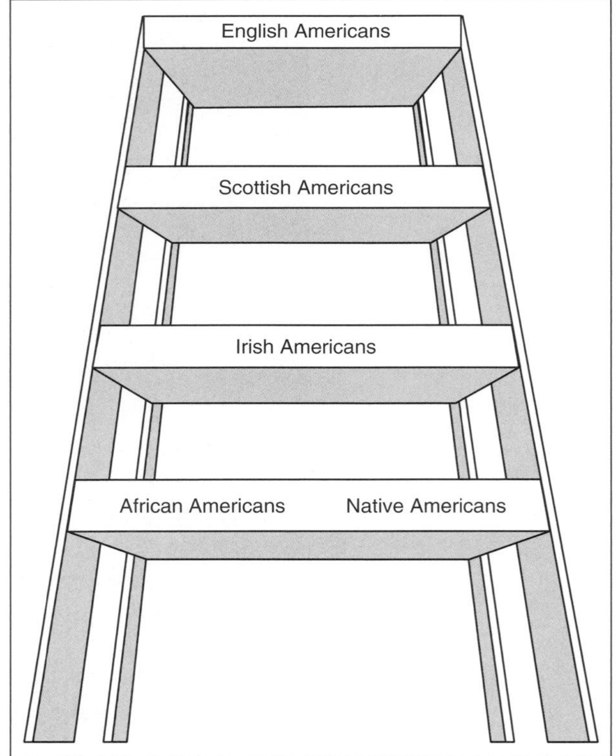

FIGURE 2.1 A Ladder of Dominance: The United States as of 1790

group; one substantially lower than another is seen as a subordinate group. The more groups there are in a society, the more complex is the image, with middle groups possibly standing in a relation of dominance to some groups and in a relation of subordination to others.

Consider the United States in 1790, about the time of its founding. For that era one might roughly diagram the five groups in Figure 2.1 in terms of such factors as overall economic or political power, so that the top group would be English Americans, with Scottish Americans a little down the ladder. Farther down would be the early (usually Protestant) Irish immigrants, a group composed at the time mostly of poor farmers and indentured servants. At the bottom in terms of power and resources would be African Americans, most of whom were in slavery in the South. Those Native American (Indian) groups and individuals within the boundaries of the new nation—most were still outside it—were also at the bottom of the racial and ethnic hierarchy in terms of economic and political power and resources. The new nation firmly embedded a racial and ethnic hierarchy from its beginning.[3]

Some Basic Questions

A number of social science theories have been developed to explain this societal diversity, domination, and stratification, as well as the related intergroup adaptation. In some contexts, *theory* means vague speculation; in the social sciences, however, **theory** refers to *a conceptual framework used to interpret or explain some aspect of everyday existence*. Theorists Ernest Barth and Donald Noel have summarized major questions raised in the analysis of racial and ethnic relations:

1. How does one explain the origin and emergence of racial and ethnic diversity and stratification?
2. How does one explain the continuation of racial and ethnic diversity and stratification?
3. How does one interpret internal adaptive changes within systems of racial and ethnic diversity and stratification?
4. How does one explain major changes in systems of racial and ethnic diversity and stratification?[4]

What methods have been used to create the racial hierarchy in the United States?

Migration and Group Contact

Racial and ethnic relations and stratification systems originate with intergroup contact as different groups, often with no common ancestry, come into each other's spheres of influence. Contact can be between an established or indigenous people and a migrating people (group A→land of group B) or between migrating groups moving into a previously uninhabited area (group A→new land←group B). The movement of the English colonists into the lands of Native Americans in the 1600s is an example of the first type of contact.

Migration has been viewed by Charles Tilly in terms of the following:

1. The actual migrating units (for example, individuals or families)
2. The situation at the point of origin (for example, the home country)
3. The situation at the destination (for example, a U.S. city)
4. The socioeconomic and political framework within which the migration occurs (for example, modern capitalism)[5]

Certain precontact factors shape both the migration and the outcome of the contact that results from migration. *Push* factors include what is happening in the immigrants' home country—high unemployment or intergroup hostilities, for example. Depressed economies or painful religious or political conflicts in sending countries have generated major migrations to the United States. *Pull* factors also generate migration. Immigrants may be attracted by the portrayal, accurate or inaccurate, of better conditions—such as abundant jobs—at the destination. The outcome of the initial contact is influenced by the resources and characteristics of the migrating group (such as its wealth or language) and of the receiving group (such as its receptiveness to newcomers). Technological assets, such as industrial skills or armaments (firepower), have proven an advantage to certain groups. Some argue, for example, that early European colonists were able to conquer (and often destroy) numerous Native American societies largely because of the latter's less developed weaponry.[6]

Types of Migration

In his book, *Comparative Ethnic Relations*, R. A. Schermerhorn suggested four major types of migration that generate racial and ethnic relations. These constitute a continuum running from involuntary migration to completely voluntary migration:

1. Movements of forced labor
2. Contract-labor movement
3. Movement of displaced persons and refugees
4. Voluntary migration[7]

Movements of forced labor include *involuntary immigration, such as the forcible removal of Africans to North America;* **contract-labor movement** includes the *migration of indentured Irish servants to the English colonies and of Chinese laborers to western North America.* **Political refugees** include the *streams of refugees produced by war,* such as Jewish immigrants from Europe in the 1930s and Vietnamese and Cuban refugees since the 1950s. **Voluntary migration** is *migration primarily by choice,* and includes the great migrations of southern and eastern European groups to the United States in the early twentieth century and of numerous Asian and Latin American groups since the 1960s.

The *voluntary migration of powerful colonizers,* sometimes termed **colonization migration**, often precedes the types just listed. Colonization migration can be seen in the English trading companies whose employees founded the first North American colonies, a development that led to the dispersal or brutal destruction of indigenous societies already inhabiting the continent.[8]

Patterns of Racial and Ethnic Adaptation

The Initial Contact

What happens when different human groups come into contact as the result of migration? Outcomes vary. In the initial stage, outcomes include the following:

1. Exclusion or genocidal destruction
2. Egalitarian symbiosis
3. An exploitive hierarchy and stratification system

Genocide is *the deliberate and systematic extermination of one group by another*—one outcome of contacts between European colonists and several Native American societies on the Atlantic coast of North America. **Egalitarian symbiosis** refers to *peaceful coexistence and a rough economic and political equality between two groups.* Occasional examples of this outcome can be found in the history of world migrations, but they are rare, especially in North America. Some authors argue that by the early nineteenth century, Scottish Americans were approaching equality with English Americans in many areas. A more common result of migration and contact is **hierarchy,** *a significant socioeconomic stratification.* Stanley Lieberson noted that **migrant superordination** occurs *when the migrating group imposes its will on indigenous groups, usually through more advanced weaponry and political or military organization.* The indigenous populations of the United States and Canada were subordinated in this fashion. **Indigenous superordination** occurs *when groups immigrating into a new society become subordinate to groups already there,* as was the case for Africans forcibly brought to North and South America by the established European colonists.[9]

Later Adaptation Patterns

Beyond the initial period of contact between two groups, the range of possible outcomes of intergroup contact includes the following:

1. Continuing genocide
2. Continuing egalitarian symbiosis
3. Replacement or modification of stratification by substantial inclusion along conformity lines
4. Replacement or modification of stratification by inclusion along cultural pluralism lines
5. Continuing subordination, ranging from moderate to extreme, of a racial or ethnic group

One type of outcome can be a continuing thrust by the dominant group to exterminate the subordinate group. Attempts by European Americans to kill off indigenous peoples continued until the early twentieth century. Alternatively, an egalitarian symbiosis can continue beyond initial peaceful interaction. Another outcome is for an initial hierarchy, characterized by a sharp inequality of power and resources, to be modified by extensive incorporation of the incoming group into the dominant culture and society. This can take two forms. In the first, inclusion of the new group occurs by means of substantial conformity to the dominant group's culture. By surrendering much of its cultural heritage and conforming to the dominant group, the incoming group gains increased acceptance and resource equality. Some have argued that many non-English European immigrant groups, such as Scots and Scandinavians, eventually gained rough equality with the English Americans in this way.

Another possibility is *cultural pluralism*—substantial economic and political assimilation and greater equality along with a significant persistence of subcultural (for example, religious) distinctiveness. In this outcome, the substantial adaptation of the immigrant group to the host group is primarily economic and political, with cultural distinctiveness continuing in certain major respects (such as religion). The interaction of certain white immigrant groups, such as Irish Catholic Americans, with the host-group English Americans offers a possible example of this outcome.

A fifth outcome of continuing intergroup contact is persisting and substantial racial or ethnic subordination and stratification. The extent and inequality of the stratification can vary, but for many non-European groups, such as Native Americans and Mexican Americans, political and economic inequality has remained so great as to constitute what some term a condition of *internal colonialism*. Even in this case, however, partial acculturation usually occurs in terms of significant adaptation to the dominant group's culture (for instance, to the English language).

Types of Theories

In the United States, explanatory theories of racial and ethnic relations have been concerned with migration, adaptation, exploitation, oppression, stratification, and conflict. Most such theories can be roughly classified as either order theories or power-conflict theories, depending on their principal concerns. **Order theories** are *racial and ethnic theories that accent patterns of inclusion—the orderly integration and assimilation of particular racial and ethnic groups to a dominant culture and society*, as in the third and fourth outcomes just described. The central focus is on progressive adaptation to the dominant culture and on stability in intergroup relations. **Power-conflict theories** are *racial and ethnic theories that accent the persisting and great inequalities in the power and resource distributions associated with racial or ethnic subordination in a society*, as in the first and fifth outcomes just described. Most assimilation theories are social-order theories. In contrast, internal colonialism theories and class-oriented neo-Marxist viewpoints are examples of power-conflict theories. Moreover, some theorists accent elements from both of these theoretical traditions.

Assimilation and Other Order Perspectives

In the United States, much social theorizing has heavily emphasized **assimilation**, *the more or less orderly adaptation of a migrating group to the ways and institutions of an established host group*. Charles Hirschman has noted that "the assimilation perspective, broadly defined, continues to be the primary theoretical framework for sociological research on racial and ethnic inequality." The reason for this dominance, he suggests, is the "lack of convincing alternatives."[10] The English word *assimilate* comes from the Latin word *assimulare*, meaning to make similar.

Robert E. Park

Robert E. Park, a major sociological analyst, argued that European out-migration was a major catalyst for societal reorganization around the globe. In his view, intergroup contacts regularly go through stages of a **race relations cycle**, in which *fundamental social forces, such as out-migration, lead to recurring cycles of contact and assimilation in intergroup history:* "The race relations cycle which takes the form, to state it abstractly, of *contacts, competition, accommodation* and *eventual assimilation*, is apparently progressive and irreversible."[11] In the contact stage, migration and exploration bring peoples together, which in turn leads to economic competition and thus to new social organization. Competition and conflict flow from the contacts between host peoples and the migrating groups. Accommodation, a critical condition in the race relations cycle, often takes place rapidly. It involves a migrating group's forced adjustment to a new social situation.

Park seems to view accommodation as involving a stabilization of relations, including the possibility of permanent caste systems. Sometimes he speaks of the race relations cycle as leading inevitably from contact to assimilation. At other times, however, he recognizes that the assimilation of a migrant group might involve major barriers and take a substantial period of time to complete.

Nonetheless, Park and most scholars working in this tradition have argued that there is a long-term trend toward large-scale assimilation even of subordinated racial and ethnic groups in modern societies. "Assimilation is a process of interpenetration and fusion in which persons and groups acquire the memories, sentiments, and attitudes of other persons or groups, and, by sharing their experience and history, are incorporated with them in a common cultural life."[12] Racially subordinate groups are expected eventually to assimilate into the "common culture" and institutions of the society.[13]

Stages of Assimilation: Milton Gordon

Since Park's pioneering analysis in the 1920s, many U.S. racial and ethnic relations theorists and other analysts have adopted some version of the assimilationist perspective, although most have departed from Park's framework in important ways. Milton Gordon, author of the influential *Assimilation in American Life*, offers a multidimensional perspective. There is a variety of initial encounters between racial and ethnic groups and an array of assimilation outcomes. Gordon presents three competing images of assimilation—the melting pot, cultural pluralism, and Anglo-conformity—but he focuses on Anglo-conformity as having been the usual historical reality for the United States. In Gordon's view, immigrant groups entering the United States have over time given up much of their cultural heritage and conformed substantially to an Anglo-Protestant core culture.[14] Cultural assimilation (also called acculturation)—the change of one group's cultural patterns to those of the host or dominant group—is a very important dimension of intergroup adaptation. Gordon's view emphasizes the way in which new groups must conform to the preexisting Anglo-Protestant culture that they face as they enter U.S. society.

Gordon notes that Anglo-conformity has been substantially achieved for numerous immigrant groups to North America, especially with regard to cultural assimilation. Most groups following the early English migration have adapted to the Anglo core culture. Gordon distinguishes seven dimensions of adaptation:

1. **Cultural assimilation:** *the change of one group's important cultural patterns to those of the core society*
2. **Structural assimilation:** *penetration of cliques and associations of the core society at the primary-group level*
3. **Marital assimilation:** *significant intermarriage*

A long line of European immigrants at Ellis Island (about 1900).

4. **Identification assimilation:** *development of a sense of identity linked to the core society*
5. **Attitude-receptional assimilation:** *absence of prejudice and stereotyping*
6. **Behavior-receptional assimilation:** *absence of intentional discrimination*
7. **Civic assimilation:** *absence of value and power conflict*

Whereas Park believed that structural assimilation, including new primary-group ties such as intergroup friendships, flowed from cultural assimilation, Gordon stresses that these are separate stages of assimilation and may take place at different rates.

For Gordon, structural assimilation generally relates to families and other primary-group relations. (*Primary groups* are small groups characterized by personal closeness, such as family groups and groups of close friends; *secondary groups* are specialized and impersonal groups such as corporations.) In his view, the movement of a new immigrant group into the secondary groups of the host society—that is, into the employing organizations, such as corporations or government bureaucracies, and educational and political institutions—is not a distinctive type of structural assimilation that should be incorporated in an assimilation typology.

The omission of a thorough discussion of this secondary-structural assimilation is a flaw in Gordon's typology. Looking at U.S. history, one sees that some admission into the society's important secondary groups, such as its economic institutions (workplaces), does not necessarily mean that one gets to enter the dominant group's friendship cliques or families. Also missing in Gordon's analysis is attention to residential integration and Anglo-conformity—to the movement of an incoming group away from segregated immigrant communities into the residential areas of the dominant group, a pattern that has received much attention in some demographic analyses. Moreover, the dimension Gordon calls *civic assimilation* is somewhat confusing, because he includes in it "values," which are really part of cultural assimilation, and "power," which is a central aspect of structural assimilation at the secondary-group level.[15]

Still, this assimilation theory is useful and continues to influence researchers. For example, Silvia Pedraza has made significant use of Gordon's conceptual framework in her research on Cuban and Mexican immigration, and Richard Alba has contrasted his view of the loss of strong ethnic identities among white ethnic Americans with Gordon's idea of identificational assimilation. Alba and Victor Lee have also pointed out that Gordon's concept of the core culture needs to be modified to take account of the fact that the cultures of new immigrants have sometimes had an effect on that core, particularly in areas such as religion and music. The cultural influence is not just one way. Moreover, in an assessment of Gordon's seven dimensions, J. Allen Williams and Suzanne Ortega examined interviews with a Midwestern sample and found that cultural assimilation was not necessarily the first type of adaptation to occur. Thus, Mexican Americans were less culturally assimilated than African Americans, yet more assimilated structurally. Those of Swiss and Swedish backgrounds ranked about the same on the study's measure of cultural assimilation, but the Swedish Americans were less assimilated structurally. Williams and Ortega concluded that assimilation varies considerably from one group to another and that Gordon's seven types can be grouped into just three general categories of structural, cultural, and receptional assimilation.[16]

In a later book, *Human Nature, Class, and Ethnicity*, Gordon noted that his assimilation theory neglects power issues and that there are different resources available to competing racial groups, but he gave little attention to the effects of economic power, material resource inequalities, or a capitalistic economic history on U.S. racial and ethnic relations.[17]

Focused on the millions of European immigrants and their adjustments, Gordon's model emphasizes *generational* changes within immigrant groups over time. For most European immigrant groups, substantial acculturation to the Anglo-Protestant culture has often been completed by the second or third generation. The partially acculturated first generation formed protective communities and associations, but the children of those immigrants were considerably more exposed to Anglo-conformity pressures from the media and in schools.[18] Gordon suggests that substantial assimilation along civic, behavior-receptional, and attitude-receptional dimensions has occurred for numerous European immigrant groups. Most have also made considerable progress toward equality at the secondary-structural levels of employment and politics, although the dimensions of this assimilation are not discussed in any detail by Gordon.

For many white, particularly non-Protestant, groups, substantial structural assimilation at the primary-group level is now accomplished yet still incomplete. Gordon suggests that substantially complete cultural assimilation (for example, adoption of the English language) along with some structural (primary-group) separateness form a characteristic pattern of adaptation for many white ethnic groups. Even these relatively acculturated white ethnic groups tend to concentrate informal friendships and marriage ties in their immediate ethnic groups or in their general socioreligious community. Following Will Herberg, who argued that there are three great community "melting pots" in the United States—Jews, Protestants, and Catholics—Gordon suggests that primary-group ties beyond one's own group are generally developed within one's broad socioreligious community.[19] According to the traditional **melting pot** view, *immigrants to the United States lose their racial and ethnic identities as they mix together in one new American blend.*

Gordon recognizes that racial prejudice and discrimination have retarded structural assimilation, but he seems to suggest that non-European Americans, including African Americans, particularly those in the middle class, will eventually be *fully* absorbed into the dominant culture and institutions. With regard to black Americans, he argues, optimistically, that the United States has "moved decisively down the road toward implementing the implications of the American creed [of equality and justice] for race relations"—such as in employment and housing. The tremendous progress that he perceives black Americans have made has, in his view, created a policy dilemma for the government: Should it adopt a traditional political liberalism that ignores racial groups or a "corporate liberalism" that recognizes group rights along racial lines? Gordon includes under corporate liberalism government antidiscrimination programs such as affirmative action, which he generally rejects.[20] The optimism of many assimilation analysts about the eventual implementation of the U.S. creed of equality for African Americans and many other non-European Americans is very problematical, as we will see in later chapters.

Some assimilation analysts have argued that certain once-prominent ethnic identities, especially of European Americans, are fading. An advocate of the continuing usefulness of the concept of assimilation is sociologist Richard Alba. He has argued persuasively that, while ethnic identity is still of some consequence for many whites, a new ethnic group is now being formed—"one based on a vague *ancestry* from anywhere on the European continent." In other words, such distinct ethnic identities as English American and Irish American are gradually giving way to identification as "European American." Similarly, Herbert Gans has suggested that increasingly, especially for white Americans, ethnicity is only "symbolic" and weakening greatly in social significance. Symbolic ethnicity involves little more than a desire to maintain some feeling for ethnic background without strong commitments to traditional ethnic behavior or networks and social ties.[21]

Interestingly, research on intermarriages linking white ethnic groups reveals that large proportions of the children of such marriages see themselves as having multiple ethnic identities, whereas others choose one of their heritages, or simply "American," as their identity. In addition, some scholars, such as Alba and Lee, have argued that in the near future skin color may not be the barrier to structural assimilation that it once was. In their view, perceptions of racial difference can change over time, and in the future some immigrant groups of color may, like earlier white ethnic groups, be allowed by the dominant white group to integrate fully into the core institutions of this society. They see signs of this in the favorable situation of many dark-skinned Asian-Indian Americans today (see Chapter 11). However, other social scientists, such as Mia Tuan, have examined the situations of third- and later-generation Chinese and Japanese Americans and found that, although they are substantially acculturated to the core culture, most have a strong sense of their racial and ethnic identity because whites regularly discriminate against them and *impose* the identity of "Asian foreigner" on them. Many whites (and others) view them in racialized Asian terms—as somehow not "real Americans." Thus, it seems unlikely that most Asian Americans will soon be accepted and absorbed fully into white middle-class society.[22]

Given the various assimilation theories, which one best describes the adaptation of present-day immigrants in the United States?

Ethnogenesis and Ethnic Pluralism

Some theorists working in the assimilation tradition reject the argument that most European American groups have become substantially assimilated to a generic Anglo-Protestant or Euro-American iden-tity and way of life. A few have explored models of adjustment that depart from Anglo-conformity in the direction of ethnic or cultural pluralism. It was a Jewish American of Polish and Latvian origin who early formulated a perspective called *cultural pluralism*. Horace Kallen (1882–1974) argued that membership in ethnic-cultural groups was not a membership one could readily abandon. Writing in *The Nation* in 1915, he argued that ethnic groups had a right to exist on their own terms; that is, democracy applied to ethnic groups. He argued against the ruthless Americanization advocated by many white Anglo-Protestant nativists at the time. By the 1920s he had given the name **cultural pluralism** to *the view that each ethnic group has the democratic right to retain its own cultural heritage without being forced to assimilate to the dominant culture.*[23] Kallen's pioneering analysis set early precedents for the perspective now called *multiculturalism* (see Chapter 13).

Social scientists adopting a cultural pluralism perspective accept some Anglo-conformity adjustment as inevitable. In *Beyond the Melting Pot*, Nathan Glazer and Daniel Moynihan agree that the original customs and home-country ways of European immigrants were mostly lost by the third generation. This did not, however, mean the decline of their ethnicity. The European immigrant groups usually remained distinct in terms of name, identity, and, for many, primary-group ties.[24]

Andrew Greeley developed the concept of *ethnogenesis* and applied it to white immigrant groups set off by nationality and religion. **Ethnogenesis** entails *the sociological theory that, over time, immigrant groups not only come to share cultural traits with the host group, but also retain many of their own nationality characteristics.* The traditional assimilation perspective assumes "that the strain toward homogenization in a modern industrial society is so great as to be virtually irresistible."[25] The direction of this assimilation is assumed to be toward the dominant Anglo-Protestant culture. However, from this ethnogenesis perspective, adaptation has meant much more than one-way conformity. The traditional assimilation model does not explain the persistence of ethnicity—the emphasis among immigrants on ethnicity as a way of becoming American and, in recent decades, also self-conscious attempts to create ethnic identity and to manipulate various ethnic symbols.

The complex ethnogenesis model of intergroup adaptation is shown in Figure 2.2. Greeley suggests, as shown in the left-hand box (host/common/immigrant), that in many cases host and immigrant groups had a somewhat similar *cultural* inheritance. For example, some later European immigrant groups

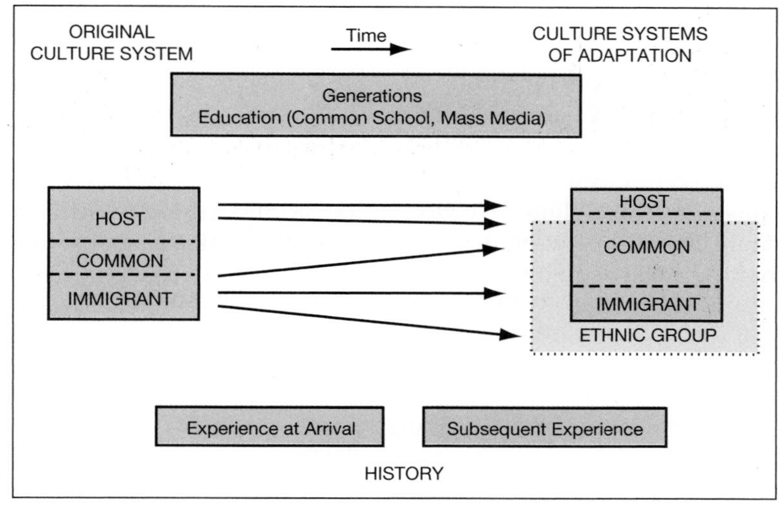

FIGURE 2.2 The Ethnogenesis Perspective

Source: Andrew M. Greeley, *Ethnicity in the United States* (New York: John Wiley, 1974), p. 309. Reprinted with permission.

had a cultural background initially similar to that of earlier English colonists. As a result of the interaction of subsequent generations with each other and with descendants of earlier immigrants, in public schools and through the influence of the media (symbolized by long arrows in the figure), the number of cultural traits common to the host and immigrant groups often increased. Yet, as is illustrated in the right-hand boxes, late in the adaptive process certain aspects of the heritage of the home country have remained important to the character of the immigrant ethnic group. Ethnic groups share traits with the host group but also retain major characteristics of their nationalities. A modern ethnic group is one part home-country heritage and one part common culture, mixed together in a unique way because of a distinctive history of development within the North American crucible.[26]

As we noted in discussing Milton Gordon's ideas about assimilation, some researchers argue that white ethnic cultures are blending and white ethnic identities are fading. Thus they do not see a persistence of strong ethnic identities as Greeley does. Nonetheless, a number of research studies have documented the presence today of still-distinctive white ethnic groups, such as Italian Americans and Jewish Americans, in numerous cities, from New York to Chicago to San Francisco, New Orleans, and Tucson. Several researchers have shown that ethnicity is an *emergent phenomenon*—that its importance varies in cities and its character and strength depend on specific historical conditions in which it grows.[27]

Some Problems with Assimilation Theories

Assimilation theorists often take as their primary examples of adaptation the European groups that migrated more or less voluntarily to countries such as the United States. But what of the adaptation and incorporation of non-European groups beyond the stage of initial contact? Numerous assimilation analysts include non-Europeans in their theories, despite the problems that sometimes arise from such inclusion. They have argued that traditional assimilation, cultural and structural, is the necessary, if long-term, answer to the "racial problem" of the United States. One prominent analyst, Gunnar Myrdal, argued some years ago that as a practical matter it is "to the advantage of American Negroes as individuals and as a group to become assimilated into American culture, to acquire the traits held in esteem by the dominant white Americans."[28] In Myrdal's view there was an ethical contradiction between the democratic principles announced in the Declaration of Independence and the still-institutionalized discrimination against black Americans. For Myrdal this represented a "lag of public morals," a problem solved in principle but still being worked out in an ongoing, one-way assimilation process that may or may not be completed.

Optimistic assimilation analysts have emphasized *progressive inclusion*, which they view will eventually provide racially subordinated groups with full citizenship in fact as well as in principle. For that reason, they expect ethnic and racial conflict to disappear as various groups become fully assimilated into the dominant culture and society. Scholars such as Nathan Glazer, Milton Gordon, and Talcott Parsons have stressed what they see as the essential egalitarianism of U.S. institutions and what they view as the ongoing emancipation of non-European groups. They have underscored the gradual assimilation of (middle-class) black Americans over several decades. Full membership for black Americans seems inevitable, notes Parsons, for "the only tolerable solution to the enormous [racial] tensions lies in constituting a single societal community with full membership for all."[29] The importance of racial, as well as ethnic, hierarchy and stratification is expected to decline as powerful, universalistic societal forces wipe out the vestiges of earlier ethnocentric value systems. As these analysts see it, white immigrants have desired substantial assimilation and have been absorbed. The same is expected to happen *eventually* for non-European groups.

Historically, some assimilation arguments and theories have been criticized for having a serious nativist or "establishment" bias. For example, a number of Asian American scholars and leaders have reacted vigorously to the application of the concept of assimilability (and, thus, unassimilability) to Asian Americans, arguing that the modern version of this concept originated in a period (about 1870–1925) of intense attacks by white Americans on the then numerous Chinese and Japanese immigrants. The term *assimilation* was thus tainted from the beginning by its association with the notion that the only "good groups" were those that could assimilate rapidly and in Anglo-conformity fashion.

Since the 1990s, several researchers have explored another assumption of traditional assimilationist thinking: the idea that new immigrants both should and do adapt to the core culture in a linear, one-directional manner. One old and common view is that new immigrants must gradually "become American" in order to overcome the "inferiority" of their old languages, cultures, and societies. However, this ethnocentric view ignores the fact that the assimilation process can have significant negative effects. Some research indicates that in certain ways the physical or mental health of immigrant groups *declines* as they become better off economically and more assimilated into the core culture. For example, over time, most immigrants gradually adopt the relatively unhealthy diet of many native-born Americans (and many become overweight) and experience family and social stresses (for example, teenagers become depressed) associated with adapting to mainstream U.S. customs. The shift from the culture of origin to the core culture is not necessarily a shift from an inferior to a superior culture, as many native-born Americans might assume.[30]

Assimilation theorists often do not analyze sufficiently the historical development of a particular racial or ethnic group within the larger international context of modern capitalism. Numerous social scientists have developed a perspective called *transnationalism*, which assesses how migration across national boundaries takes place within a highly developed global capitalistic context in which the imperialistic actions of major industrial ("core") countries often have (intended or unintended) effects on international migration flows from countries in the "periphery." Like traditional assimilation analyses, transnationalism emphasizes the fact that individual migrants tend to migrate along family and friendship networks; however, as an analysis of Israeli immigrants to the United States puts it, transnationalism also involves "large scale economic, political, and legal structures within which immigrants develop their communities and lives." Transnationalism views immigration as an "ongoing process through which ideas, resources, and people change locations and develop meanings in multiple settings."[31] Certain immigrants maintain a strong tie to the home country, with attachments to two "homes" at the same time. They seek opportunities in a new country but maintain strong ties to the old country. Some immigrants, such as many Puerto Ricans, come to the U.S. mainland to escape pervasive poverty in the home areas, yet return home periodically because of racial discrimination and other factors that make their lives difficult. (*Return* or *circular migration* is a term for this process.) For many Israeli, Puerto Rican, and undocumented Mexican immigrants—even some in the second generation—orientation and self-identity are very strongly linked to place of origin.

Biosocial Perspectives

Some social theorists, including some assimilationists, offer a biosocial perspective on racial and ethnic relations. The old European and American notion that racial and ethnic groups are deeply rooted in human beings' biological makeup has received renewed attention from a few social scientists and biologists in the United States since the 1970s. In *Human Nature, Class, and Ethnicity*, for example, Milton Gordon suggests that ethnic ties are rooted in the "biological organism of man." Ethnicity is a fundamental part of the physiological as well as the psychological self. Ethnicity "cannot be shed by social mobility, as for instance social class background can, since society insists on its inalienable ascription from cradle to grave." Gordon seems to have in mind the rootedness of intergroup relations in the everyday realities of kinship and socially constructed group boundaries, not the old racist notion of the unchanging biological character and separateness of racial groups. He goes further, however, emphasizing that human beings tend to be "selfish, narcissistic and perpetually poised on the edge of aggression." And it is these selfish tendencies that lie behind racial and ethnic tensions.[32] Gordon is here adopting a Hobbesian ("dog-eat-dog") view of human nature.

Critics of this biosocial view have suggested that it attributes to fundamental "human nature" what are in reality only modern capitalism's highly individualistic values. That is, under modern capitalism, much selfishness and narcissism are *learned* rather than inherent in the human biological makeup. Although decidedly different from earlier biological theories, the modern biosocial analysis remains problematical. The exact linkages between the deep genetic underpinnings of human nature and concrete racial or ethnic behavior are not spelled out beyond some vague analysis of kin selection and selfish behavior.

A major difficulty with any such biosocial approach is that in the everyday world, racial and ethnic relations are *immediately social* rather than biological. As numerous scholars have pointed out, many racial and ethnic groups have mixed biological ancestry. Jewish Americans, for example, have a very mixed ancestry—as a group, they share no distinctive biological characteristics. Biologically diverse Italian immigrants from different regions of Italy gained a sense of being Italian American (even Italian) in the United States. The bonds holding Jewish Americans and Italian Americans together were not genetically based or biologically primordial, but rather the result of real *historical* experiences as these social groups became firmly established in community settings in countries such as the United States. If ethnicity is primordial in a biological sense, it should always be a prominent force in human affairs. Sometimes ethnicity leads to recurring conflict, as in the case of Jews and Gentiles in the United States; in other cases, as with Scottish and English Americans, it mostly disappears in the mutual adaptation process. Sentiments based on common ancestry are important, but they are activated primarily in the concrete experiences and histories of specific migrating and host groups.[33]

Protests against legal and undocumented immigration have increased in recent years.

Emphasizing Migration: Competition Theory

Competition theory is a contemporary example of the exploration of migration issues more or less in the tradition of Robert Park. **Competition theory** is *a view of ethnicity that emphasizes the relative stability of ethnic population boundaries over time and the intergroup competition over resources that results from shifts in these boundaries because of migration.* Park emphasized that ethnic and racial relations stem from the migration of peoples, which in turn leads to competition for often scarce resources. Competition theorists have explored the contact and competition parts of the race relations cycle. Unlike some order-oriented theorists, they usually do address questions of protest and conflict, although they do not give much attention to racialized exploitation or wealth-inequality issues.[34]

Competition theorists view "ethnicity" in the broad sense as a social phenomenon distinguished by boundaries of language, skin color, and culture. They emphasize the general stability of many ethnic population boundaries, as well as the effects of shifts in boundaries; ethnic-group membership often coincides with the creation of a distinctive group niche in the labor force. Competition occurs when two or more ethnic groups attempt to secure the same resources, such as jobs or housing.[35]

According to competition theorists, intergroup tensions and conflict are fostered by immigration across geographical borders and by the expansion of once-segregated ethnic groups into the same labor and housing markets to which other groups have access. Attacks on immigrant workers or native-born workers of color, for example, increase at the city level when a group moves out of traditionally segregated jobs and thus challenges other groups and not, as one might expect, in cities where ethnic groups are locked into segregation and poverty.

Susan Olzak uses empirical data on ethnic and racial violence in the nineteenth century to show that collective action, such as Anglo-Protestant crowds attacking the newer European immigrants entering the United States, increased when immigration expanded and economic recessions occurred. The ethnic boundary of the native-born white Americans was mobilized against European immigrant (and black) workers "when ethnic competition was activated by a rising supply of low-wage labor and tight labor markets. In this case the ethnic groups that mobilized were not fully assimilated, but had retained aspects of their traditional identity and drew on that for mobilization against other groups."[36] Olzak suggests a distinction between (1) societal situations of economic decline, which can increase interethnic competition for jobs and other economic goals, and (2) situations of new ethnic mixing and integration, in which the breakup of once-segregated societies brings ethnic groups into new job competition and other economic competition.[37]

Competition theorists have emphasized that economic struggles often accompany political competition, which includes competition among ethnic groups for government positions and tax dollars. Joane Nagel has shown how contenders for political power often organize along ethnic lines and argues that "ethnicity is a convenient basis for political organizers due to the commonality of language and culture and the availability of ethnic organizations with ready-made leadership and membership."[38]

A power-conflict theorist might criticize the competition theorists for studying markets and interethnic competition in cities since the late nineteenth century without a clear sense of the substantial racial discrimination and deeply imbedded resource inequality that has undergirded urban job and housing markets in this country now for nearly four centuries. Missing from competition theory is a systematic concern with the issues of (especially racial) inequality, power, exploitation, and institutional discrimination that are accented by numerous power-conflict theories.

Power-Conflict Theories

The past few decades have witnessed an increased development of major *power-conflict* frameworks explaining racial and ethnic relations in this and other countries, perspectives that place much greater emphasis on economic stratification and power issues than one finds in most assimilation and competition theories. Within this broad category of power-conflict theories are a number of subcategories, including the caste perspective, the internal colonialism viewpoint, and a variety of class-based and neo-Marxist theories.

The Caste School

One early exception to the assimilation perspective was the *caste school of racial relations*, which developed in the 1940s mostly under W. Lloyd Warner and Allison Davis and their associates.[39] Focusing on white-on-black oppression in the South, these researchers viewed the position of black Americans as distinctively different from that of other racial and ethnic groups. After the Civil War, a new societal system, a "caste" system, replaced the slavery system of the South. The white and black castes were separated by a total prohibition of intermarriage as well as by great economic and social inequality. These social scientists were critical of the emphasis in most social science analysis on prejudiced attitudes and feelings. Instead, these proponents of the **caste school of racial relations** emphasized *well-institutionalized racial discrimination as the foundation of a castelike system of U.S. apartheid.*[40]

Early Class Theories of Racial Relations

W. E. B. Du Bois, one of the first sociological analysts in the United States, was a black scholar and civil rights activist who had experienced the brutality of white racism firsthand. Drawing on Marxist class analysis in his later writings, Du Bois was perhaps the first major social science theorist to emphasize that racial oppression and class oppression are inextricably linked. In his view, the interplay of racial oppression and modern capitalism explained why there has never been true democracy and freedom for all people in the United States. In a 1948 article titled "Is Man Free?" he argued that both black workers and white workers were prevented from exercising full democratic rights because of the control of a very small capitalist class (for example, the owners of major workplaces) over the U.S. economy and politics. He argued with evidence that a truly democratic society must include not only equality for Americans of color but also decision-making control of workplaces by workers. Du Bois's sociological ideas are still fresh and provocative, but to this point in time only a modest number of scholars have used them to analyze U.S. society.[41]

An early power-conflict analyst who drew on Du Bois and class analysis was Oliver C. Cox, a scholar whose work has been neglected, in part because of its Marxist approach. Cox also emphasized the role of the capitalist class in racial exploitation. He analyzed the economic dimensions of the forced slave migration from Africa and the oppressiveness of later conditions for enslaved African Americans. The slave trade was "a way of recruiting labor for the purpose of exploiting the great natural resources of America." The color of Africans was not important; they were chosen "simply because they were the best workers to be found for the heavy labor in the mines and plantations across the Atlantic."[42] A search for cheap labor by a profit-oriented capitalist class of whites led to a system of racial subordination. Racial prejudice developed only later, as part of a white-generated ideology rationalizing this economic subordination.

Internal Colonialism and "Coloniality"

An emphasis on power and resource inequalities across racial lines is at the heart of the internal colonialism theory and its recent descendant, "coloniality" theory.

Internal Colonialism The conceptual framework of internal colonialism is built in part on the work of analysts of *external colonialism*—the worldwide imperialism of certain capitalist nations, including the United States and European nations.[43] Balandier has noted that Europe's capitalistic expansion has affected non-European peoples across the globe since the fifteenth century: "Until very recently the greater part of the world's population, not belonging to the white race (if we exclude China and Japan), knew only a status of dependency on one or another of the European colonial powers."[44] **External colonialism** involves *the running of a country's economy and politics by an outside colonial power*. Many European colonies eventually became independent of their colonizers, such as Great Britain or France, but continued to have their economies directed by the capitalists and corporations from the former colonial powers. In contrast, European colonies that experienced a large in-migration of whites show a different pattern. In such cases external colonialism becomes **internal colonialism**, in which *the control and exploitation of non-European groups in the colonized country passes from whites in the home country to white immigrant groups within the newly independent country.*[45]

Non-European groups in the United States have been viewed in terms of internal colonialism. The origin and initial stabilization of internal colonialism predate the Revolutionary War. The systematic subordination of non-Europeans began with "genocidal attempts by colonizing settlers to uproot native populations and force them into other regions."[46] A great many indigenous Americans were killed or driven off desirable lands. Enslaved Africans were a cheap source of labor for white farmers before and after the Revolution. Later, Asian and Pacific peoples were imported as contract workers or annexed in the expansionist period of U.S. development. Robert Blauner, an internal colonialism theorist, notes that agriculture in the South often depended on black labor; in the Southwest, Mexican agricultural development was forcibly taken over by European Americans after the Mexican American War in the 1840s.[47]

In exploiting the labor of non-European peoples, who were enslaved or paid low wages, white agricultural and industrial capitalists often reaped enormous profits. From the internal colonialism perspective, contemporary racial and ethnic inequality is grounded in the long-term economic interests of whites in low-wage labor—the underpinning of capitalistic economic exploitation.

"Coloniality": Racial Colonialism Today In the past few years, colonialism theory has been reinvigorated by research showing how the global colonialism of the past created social structures of oppression that persist into the present. Drawing on the work of Aníbal Quijano, scholars Ramón Grosfoguel and Chloe Georas have shown that the current situation for key racial and ethnic groups in the United States is still one of "coloniality"—a situation of cultural, political, and economic oppression for subordinated racial and ethnic groups without the existence of an overt colonial administration and its trappings of legal segregation. Official decolonization does not mean an end to coloniality, for the colonial hierarchies of racial and ethnic oppression often remain. Indeed, seen from this perspective, most mainstream analyses of racial relations underestimate the major continuities between the overtly colonial past and the racial and ethnic hierarchies of the present.[48]

Grosfoguel and Georas cite the examples of Puerto Ricans and African Americans in the United States. Both were early colonial-racial subjects of a global U.S. empire, and their situations today show many aspects of that overt colonialism. Today, European Americans remain at the top of, and in control of, the racial hierarchy, and African Americans and Puerto Ricans remain racially subordinated groups at the bottom.

Cultural Resistance and Oppositional Cultures

Internal colonialism theorists accent the role of the cultural stereotyping and racist ideologies of dominant groups seeking to subordinate people of color. A racist ideology, itself part of a racist framing, dominates an internal colonialist society, intellectually dehumanizing the colonized. Stereotyping and prejudice, seen in many traditional theories as more or less temporary problems, are viewed by colonialism analysts as a way of rationalizing exploitation over a very long period. Attempts are made by the dominant group to envelop subordinate groups in dominant cultural values, traditions, and language—in the case of people of color, to "whiten" their cultures. In a system of internal colonialism, cultural as well as racial markers are used to set off subordinate groups such as Native Americans, Latinos, Asian Americans, and African Americans from the white European American group.[49]

A number of power-conflict scholars have honed the idea of **oppositional culture**—*the culture of resistance often found among subordinate groups*—as a basis for understanding the resistance of non-European groups to the dominant Euro-American culture. Bonnie Mitchell and Joe Feagin argue that the oppositional cultures of Americans of color are "distinct from the dominant Euro-American culture, while also reflecting or reacting to elements of the larger society. . . . In the colonies and later the United States the pressures on non-Europeans for conformity to the Euro-American culture forced minority Americans to become bicultural, to know both the dominant Euro-American culture and their own oppositional culture as well."[50]

The nation of the United States, created in the late 1700s, encompassed African enslavement and genocidal attacks on the indigenous (Indian) societies. Faced with oppression, these and other targets of white colonialism have long drawn on their own cultural resources, as well as their distinctive knowledge of Euro-American culture and society, to resist oppression in every way possible. The cultures of those oppressed by European Americans have not only provided a source of individual, family, and community resistance to racial oppression and colonialism but have also infused some significant elements into the evolving cultural mix that now constitutes the U.S. core culture. The cultures of racially colonized groups such as African, Latino, and Native Americans have also helped preserve key aspects of certain U.S. ideals, including the important tradition of civil rights, freedom, and social justice.[51]

Looking back over U.S. history, several social scientists have researched cultural strategies developed by subordinate racial and ethnic groups to resist oppression. For example, James Scott has shown that intentional deception is central to much interaction between the powerless and the powerful.[52] Most groups of color, including Asian, African, Latino, and Native Americans, have used a variety to techniques to hide their critical views of systems of oppression. The concealed discourse of oppressed groups includes ideological critiques that cannot be discussed publicly. For example, early Afro-Christianity was an example of how enslaved black Americans resisted the "ideological hegemony" (attempts to brainwash) of white slavemasters. In public religious services, enslaved African Americans often pretended to accept Christian teachings about obedience. However, when and where no whites were present, Afro-Christianity frequently emphasized "themes of deliverance and redemption, Moses and the Promised Land, the Egyptian captivity, and emancipation."[53] For many of these Americans, the "Promised Land" meant the North and freedom, and the afterlife was often viewed as a place where their white oppressors would be punished.[54] Surviving elements of African culture and religion were also major sources of the inclination to resistance and rebellion.

What are the major strengths and weaknesses of the order and power-conflict theories we have explained in this chapter?

Anticolonial Nationalism

Ideological resistance takes different forms. For example, anticolonial *nationalism* has developed as part of the cultural resistance to European colonialism and its racist ideology. Pan-Africanism and cultural nationalism are two examples of this resistance to both internal colonialism and liberal solutions for that colonialism.

From the early 1900s to the 1960s, for example, W. E. B. Du Bois was a major advocate of cultural nationalism. He saw pan-African nationalism as a partial solution for the colonized conditions in which people of African descent around the world found themselves; he argued that the pan-African movement "means to us what the Zionist movement must mean to the Jews."[55] Over objections from the U.S. State Department, Du Bois succeeded in putting together the first Pan-African Congress in 1919, which was attended by delegates from fifteen countries. The Congress did not ask for immediate decolonization of Africans and their descendants around the globe, but for more democratic treatment. The Congress called for abolition of slavery and for curtailment of colonial exploitation. The Pan-African Congress was an important step toward uniting people of African descent and was perceived as *radical* by most white European and American leaders.[56]

Many racially oppressed people have historically drawn on cultural nationalism as a means of resisting Euro-American cultural pressures and various forms of discrimination. For example, in Chapter 6 we will examine the cultural and other resistance of numerous Native American societies to the threat of both white violence and white cultural imposition. In Chapter 8 we will examine protests by Mexican Americans in New Mexico. The Alianza Federal de Mercedes, founded in the 1960s, sought to recover lands in New Mexico that had been taken by the Anglo-American invaders and to establish a stronger Mexican American identity with links to the Mexican heritage. A militant *Chicano* movement, which emphasized Mexican culture and national pride, also emerged among Mexican Americans in a dramatic way in the 1960s and 1970s.

In recent decades, African American scholars and activists have developed a comprehensive Afrocentric perspective that includes a strong critique of the cultural imperialism of European Americans. Sociologist Molefi Kete Asante, among others, has spurred the development of this perspective, arguing for the term *Afrocentricity*. Asante and his colleagues analyze the Eurocentric bias in the dominant culture, particularly the elements of that culture that have been absorbed by African Americans. Indeed, they are critical of the language of much "ethnic"

An African American family in African garb celebrates Kwanzaa.

analysis: "The use of the terms *ethnicity, disadvantaged, minority*, and *ghetto* are antithetical to our political consciousness which is indivisible from the international political struggle against racism."[57]

Similarly, anthropologist Marimba Ani writes: "European cultural imperialism is the attempt to proselytize, encourage, and project European ideology. . . . European nationalism implies European expansion, that, in turn, mandates European imperialism."[58] Beginning in the 1400s, European imperialism was supported by a well-developed theory of European supremacy, a worldview that attempted to destroy the cultures of African and African American peoples. From this perspective, the Euro-American worldview includes the myth of European cultural and national superiority, a celebration of materialism over cooperative and spiritual values, and a belief in the superiority of the Judeo-Christian religious tradition over other religious traditions. Because of the profound effect this Euro-American framing of the world has had on the subordinated peoples, Afrocentric theorists argue that African Americans must direct their "energies toward the recreation of cultural alternatives informed by ancestral visions of a future that celebrates . . . Africaness."[59] Numerous other Americans of color have engaged in similar struggles against a strongly Eurocentric dominant culture.

A Neo-Marxist Emphasis on Class

Analysts of racial oppression have sometimes combined an internal colonialism perspective with an emphasis on class stratification, drawing on the Marxist research pioneered by such analysts as Du Bois and Cox. For example, Mario Barrera suggests that the heart of internal colonialism is an interactive structure of class and racial stratification that divides U.S. society. Class, in the economic-exploitation sense of that term, is central in this perspective. Basic to current internal colonialism are four classes that have developed in U.S. capitalism:

1. *Capitalists*: that small group of people who control capital investments and the means of production and who buy the labor of many others
2. *Managers*: that modest-sized group of people who work as administrators for the capitalists and have been granted control over the work of others
3. *Petit bourgeoisie*: that group of small-scale merchants who control their own businesses and do most of their work themselves, buying little labor power from others
4. *Working class*: that very large group of blue-collar and white-collar workers who sell their labor to employers in return for wages and salaries

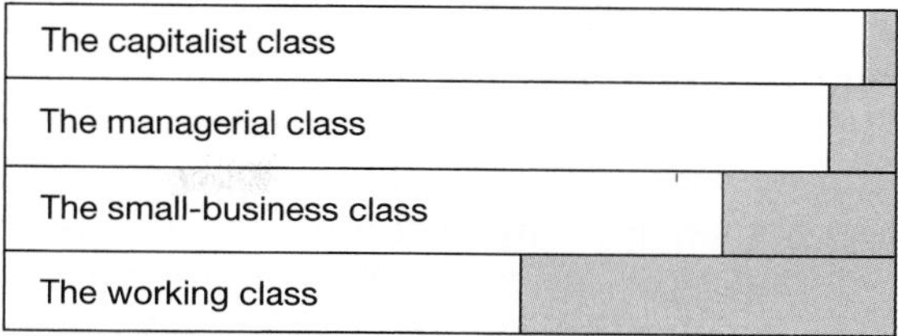

FIGURE 2.3 The Class and Racial Structure of Internal Colonialism

The dominant class in the U.S. political-economic system is the small capitalist class, which in the workplace subordinates workers from all racial and ethnic groups to its profit and investment needs. It is the capitalists who decide whether and where to create jobs.

As shown in Figure 2.3, each class is crosscut by a line of racial segmentation that separates those who suffer from institutionalized discrimination—such as African, Latino, Asian, and Native American workers—from those whites who do not. Take the example of the working class. Although these workers of color may share the same class position with white workers in that they are struggling against capitalists for better wages and working conditions, they are also in a subordinate position because of structural discrimination along racial lines within that working class. The dimensions of this racial discrimination often include lower wages for many subordinate-group workers, as well as their concentration in lower-status jobs.[60]

The Split Labor-Market View

Racial and ethnic analysts who emphasize class are sometimes unclear about whether all classes of whites benefit substantially from the colonization of people of color or just the dominant class of capitalist employers. A power-conflict perspective that helps in assessing this question is the **split labor-market view**, which *treats class in the sense of people's position in the economic "means of production" and argues that the white employer class and whites in the working class both discriminate against those in the working class who are not white*. For example, sociologist Edna

Bonacich argues that in U.S. society, dominant-group (white) workers do not share the economic interests of the top class, the capitalists, yet both the white employer class and the white part of the working class play key roles in discriminating against the racially subordinated part of the working class.[61]

Developing a neo-Marxist class analysis of racial subordination, Oliver Cox argued that the capitalist class, motivated by a desire for profit and cheap labor, sought African labor for the slave system in the United States. Ever since, this employer class has played the major role in keeping African Americans in a subordinate economic position in U.S. society. Similarly, Al Szymanski argued that because employers have not created enough jobs for all those who wish to work, black and white workers are pitted against each other for too few jobs, often to the broad advantage of capitalists as a class.[62]

However, Bonacich emphasizes that aggressive discrimination against black workers by white workers seeking to protect their own racial privileges is very important. Capitalists bring in black and other racially subordinated workers to decrease labor costs, but white workers resist because they fear job displacement or lower wages. For example, over the past century, white workers' unions have restricted the access of workers of color to many job ladders, thus splitting the labor market and significantly reducing those workers' and their families' incomes. Research on unions provides much historical evidence for this argument. For example, from the 1880s to the 1960s, in states such as Alabama, the industrial unions controlled by white workers "helped forge a labor framework" that created and perpetuated rigidly segregated white and black jobs.[63] Informal job restriction, if not actual segregation, of workers of color is still maintained by white workers in numerous U.S. workplaces to the present day. White workers both gain and lose from this racial discrimination. They gain because there is less competition for better-paying job categories from workers of color who are restricted or excluded. However, white workers have often lost in the long run because employers can use a cordoned-off sector of lower-wage workers of color to undercut them if they try to protest or strike for better working conditions.[64]

In the 1930s, W. E. B. Du Bois explained how both of these class perspectives might be brought together. Du Bois examined the "public and psychological wage" that white workers have received in the U.S. system of racial oppression.[65] Most working-class whites—those with far fewer resources than whites in the higher classes—have come to accept less in the way of economic and political resources and power because of their access to the racial privileges of whiteness. And it is the white elite that has historically convinced and pressured white workers to accept an ideology that celebrates "whiteness." When white working people, viewing themselves as racially superior, have refused to organize effectively with workers of color against stubborn white employers in order to secure better wages, they have often received fewer economic resources than might have been the case had they organized with workers of color. White workers often accept this lesser economic situation because they have come to prize the racial privileges of whiteness.

Ordinary whites suffer in the class-stratified society that is the United States, and the dominant racial ideology—with its racist stereotypes of Americans of color—makes it harder for most of these whites to understand not only the situation of the racialized "others" but also their own oppressed economic situation. Most whites do not feel powerful or privileged, especially relative to the white elite, but they are generally unable to see clearly the real sources of class and racial inequality in this society. Indeed, many whites target Americans of color as bearing primary responsibility for their, or the country's, serious economic difficulties. Some even join white supremacist groups (such as the Ku Klux Klan), which engage in threats of overt violence and acts of terrorism against Americans of color.

Middleman Minorities, Ethnic Enclaves, and Segmented Assimilation

Social scientists have often explored the in-between position, in terms of power and resources, that certain racial and ethnic groups have occupied in highly stratified societies such as the United States. These groups periodically find an economic niche as small-business people positioned between more powerful producers and less powerful consumers (often consumers of color). Some ethnic and racial groups become small-scale traders and merchants doing jobs that dominant groups are not eager to do. For example, many first-generation Jewish and Japanese Americans, excluded from mainstream employment by white Protestant Americans, became small-scale merchants, tailors, and restaurant operators. Such groups have held "a distinctive class position that is of special use to the ruling class." That is, they often "act as a go-between to this society's more subordinate groups."[66]

Edna Bonacich and John Modell found that Japanese Americans fit what has been termed the *middleman minority model*. A **middleman minority** is *a racial or ethnic group that occupies an in-between position in terms of societal power and resources*. Before World War II, for example, Japanese Americans resided in highly organized, mostly west coast, communities. Their local economies were based on self-employment, including gardening and truck farming, and on other nonindustrial family businesses. The social solidarity of the first generation of Japanese Americans helped them establish successful small businesses. However, they faced hostility from whites, and in fact were driven into the businesses they developed because they were denied many other employment opportunities by white discrimination.[67]

Some middleman groups, such as Korean or Cuban American merchants in certain central cities today, have become targets of hostility from groups that are less well off, such as low-income Mexican or African Americans. Strong ingroup bonds can make the middleman group an effective competitor, and even white capitalists may become hostile toward an immigrant group of color that competes too effectively in the economy. Historically and in the present day, in U.S. cities Korean or Jewish business people have been viewed negatively by better-off, white Protestant merchants who have the power to discriminate against them, as well as by the poor renters and customers of color with whom they deal as landlords and merchants. Some scholars have criticized the application of "middleman minority" theory to certain Asian American groups, arguing that groups such as Chinese or Japanese Americans, though substantially involved in trade, have rarely been a *middle* group of modest entrepreneurs situated between a poor racial-ethnic group and a richer racial-ethnic group. More generally, this middleman perspective also does not deal adequately with the movement, over time, of large numbers of a particular middleman group into a more powerful business group, as has happened for many Jewish Americans over the last century.

A somewhat similar perspective, *enclave theory*, examines secondary-structural incorporation into the economy, especially the ways in which certain non-European immigrant groups have created **ethnic enclaves**—*distinctive social and economic niches in numerous U.S. cities*. Both the middleman and the enclave perspectives give more emphasis to economic inequality and racial or ethnic discrimination than do the traditional assimilation perspectives such as Milton Gordon's. Thus, enclave theorists stress the incorporation of certain groups, such as the Chinese, Koreans, and Cubans, into the United States through the means of small businesses and specialized "ethnic economies." The major differences between the two viewpoints seem to stem from the examples emphasized. Groups studied by enclave theorists, such as Cuban Americans, have generally created enclaves that are more than merchant or trading economies; they often include manufacturing enterprises, for example. These economic enclaves may compete directly with established white-Anglo business elites. In contrast, the previously mentioned "middleman" groups have developed trading economies and have filled an economic niche that has complemented that of established white businesses.

Alejandro Portes and Robert Manning examined the communities of Cubans in Miami and Koreans in Los Angeles, groups that have developed many small businesses that cater to customers inside and outside their own racial-ethnic communities. Enclave economies require an immigrant group with entrepreneurial talents, business experience, some capital, and a pool of low-wage labor. These characteristics enabled Cuban Americans in Miami to build a strong enclave economy. These enclaves, unlike the "colonies" of internal colonialism, typically do not relegate newcomers to a more or less permanent position of inferiority. Enclave scholars sometimes criticize the internal colonialism and split labor-market viewpoints for trying to encompass all subordinated groups, although they agree that the situations of African Americans, Mexican Americans, and Native Americans can perhaps be better explained as variations on internal colonialism. Enclave analysts have so far paid insufficient attention to the exploitation that takes place in numerous enclave economies, such as the exploitation of low-wage immigrant workers by immigrant (for example, Cuban American) employers. They also tend to neglect the effects of the surrounding political and economic system—in the Cuban and Korean cases, multinational capitalism—which shapes the initial migration as well as the character of the specific enclave economies. In some ways, then, these enclave theorists straddle the fence between the order and power-conflict theories.[68]

Some researchers who are concerned with the structural barriers that prevent immigrants of color from assimilating as might be predicted from a traditional assimilation perspective have suggested the concept of *segmented* assimilation. Ruben Rumbaut has underscored the diversity of the adaptation experiences of various immigrant groups, calling on immigration researchers to spell out what is "being 'assimilated,' by whom, under what circumstances, and in reference to what sector of American society." Alejandro Portes and Min Zhou have argued that over time the outcomes of adaptation by immigrants to U.S. society vary greatly, with some confined to the lower economic rungs of the societal ladder and others experiencing rapid economic development while maintaining much of their traditional culture. An example of segmented assimilation is the situation of many second-generation Mexican Americans today. Unlike the children of earlier white immigrants from Europe, who soon moved into better economic circumstances and living conditions, many second-generation Mexican Americans continue to face very difficult economic circumstances, with low-paying jobs and inadequate housing (see Chapter 8). Over the generations, thus, the experiences of immigrants can involve upward or downward mobility, and thus reflect a variable and segmented assimilation in key areas such as the economy. The arguments about segmented assimilation parallel to some degree the ideas of the ethnogenesis theory. The main difference lies in the greater attention given by segmentation theorists to major structural barriers such as the discrimination and entrenched segregation that have faced many people of color.[69]

A Note on Market-Dominant Minorities

We should consider briefly who it is that has gained the top economic position in market-driven economies around the globe. In a provocative analysis of contemporary capitalism, legal scholar Amy Chua has developed the concept of *market-dominant minorities*. She shows that in many areas certain racial or ethnic minorities have come, by means of capitalistic markets, to economically dominate the population majorities in their countries. These market-dominant groups include, in her analysis, white South Africans in contemporary South Africa, people mainly of European descent (considered "whites") in many Latin American countries, Jewish Russians in contemporary Russia, Chinese Indonesians in contemporary Indonesia, Croatians in the former Yugoslavia, and Lebanese in several West African countries.

Historically, the European colonizers were market-dominant minorities in the areas on every continent where they came to dominate—almost always at the expense of impoverished indigenous peoples of color. Huge wealth increases came out of this process of greatly exploiting the labor, land, and natural resources of other peoples. In addition to these white Europeans becoming market-dominant minorities, the divide-and-conquer process of colonialism over time also favored certain other groups, "exacerbating ethnic wealth imbalances and fomenting group tensions. . . . most starkly in southern Africa but also in Latin America."[70]

Central to Chua's argument, as well as that of other recent U.S. analysts, is a concern that in many countries today the operation of capitalistic markets comes into serious conflict with the operation of political democracies. Markets tend to favor small groups of people, often people who have accented their own racial or ethnic superiority (and who are thus viewed as distinctive). Yet, the opening up of democratic political institutions means that impoverished, often racially denigrated and oppressed majorities, can gain political power and begin to counter and attack in various ways the smaller, economically privileged racial or ethnic groups.

Women and Gendered Racism

Most theories of racial and ethnic relations have neglected gender stratification. In recent years numerous social scientists have researched the situations of women within various U.S. racial and ethnic groups. Their analyses often assess the ways in which male supremacy, or a **patriarchal system**—*a social hierarchy in which men as a group dominate women as a group, especially in terms of socioeconomic power and resources*—interacts with and operates within a system of racial and ethnic stratification. For example, discussing racial and ethnic cultures around the globe, Adrienne Rich has explained a patriarchal system in more detail as "a familial-social, ideological, political system in which men—by force, direct pressure, or through ritual, tradition, law and language, customs, etiquette, education, and the division of labor—determine what part women shall or shall not play, and in which the female is everywhere subsumed under the male."[71]

Asking whether racism or patriarchy has been the primary source of oppression, social psychologist Philomena Essed examined the situations of black women in the Netherlands and the United States. She found racism and sexism interacting regularly. Thus, *societal oppression of women of color* is often a **gendered racism**.[72] For example, under slavery, African American women were exploited not only for labor but also often as sex objects for many white men, including powerful slaveholders. After slavery ended, these women were excluded from most job categories available to white men and white women; major employment changes came only with the civil rights movement of the 1960s (see Chapter 7). Today, racism has many gendered forms. In the mass media, the white woman is usually the standard for female beauty. Women of color are often stereotyped as exotic sex objects, matriarchs in female-headed families, or "welfare queens." In the economy they are found disproportionately in lower-paid "female jobs," such as nurse's aides and backroom or fast-food restaurant workers. Some women of color, such as Mexican American and African American women in the South and Southwest, are closely bound in their social relations with those who oppress them in such areas as domestic employment ("maids").

Sociologist Patricia Hill Collins has argued that a solid black feminist theoretical framework highlights and analyzes critically negative stereotypes of black women in this society—the white-generated, historical and contemporary stereotypes of the docile mammy, the domineering matriarch, the promiscuous prostitute, and the irresponsible welfare mother. These severely negative images, which are also sometimes applied to Mexican American and Puerto Rican women, are central to the old white racial frame and persist in the society because they are fostered by the mass media and because they undergird white discrimination against women of color.[73]

Scholars assessing the situations of women of color—including Native, Asian, Latino, and African Americans—have long emphasized the cumulative and interactive character of racial and gender oppression and the necessity of liberating these women from white stereotypes and discrimination. For example, Denise Segura has examined labor force data on Mexican American women and developed the concept of *triple oppression*—the mutually reinforcing and interactive set of racial, class, *and* gender forces the cumulative effects of which "place women of color in a subordinate social and economic position relative to men of color and the white population."[74] Indeed, numerous social scientists have called for much more research to explore the character, interaction, and consequences of the triple oppressions of "race," class, and gender.

Men in some racial or ethnic groups also face a type of gendered racism. For example, gender-specific stereotypes are often directed at men of color. Whereas black women are often stereotyped by whites and others as "welfare queens," black men are often stereotyped as oversexed criminals. In addition, Asian American and Mexican American women are sometimes stereotyped as exotic sex objects, and Asian American men are sometimes stereotyped as impotent or unmasculine.

How does gendered racism shape an individual's position in U.S. racial and gender hierarchies?

The State and Racial Formations

Looking at the important role of governments in creating racial and ethnic designations and institutionalizing discrimination, creative social theorists Michael Omi and Howard Winant have developed an innovative theory of *racial formation*. Racial tensions and oppression, in their view, cannot be explained solely in terms of class or nationalism. In **racial formation theory**, *racial relations are substantially defined by government actions that range from the passing of racist legislation, such as restrictive immigration laws, to the racially motivated imprisonment of groups defined as a threat* (for example, the Japanese American imprisonment during World War II discussed in Chapter 10).

The U.S. government has greatly shaped the contours and stereotypes of racial and ethnic relations in this country: The U.S. Constitution and a lengthy series of laws long defined racial groups and interracial relationships (for example, slavery) in openly racist terms. The U.S. Constitution, for example, counted each enslaved African American as only three-fifths of a person (for the purpose of white political representation), and the Naturalization Law of 1790 explicitly declared that only "white" immigrants could qualify to become naturalized U.S. citizens. Many non-Europeans, including Africans and Asians, were prevented from becoming citizens. Japanese and other Asian immigrants, for example, were banned by racist laws from becoming U.S. citizens *until the 1950s*. In 1854 the California Supreme Court even ruled that Chinese immigrants should be classified as "Indians," thereby denying them the political rights then available to white Americans.[75]

For centuries, as we will see in later chapters, the U.S. government officially favored northern European immigrant groups over southern Europeans, such as Italians, and over people of color from other continents. For example, the Immigration Act of 1924 was used to exclude Asian immigrants and most immigrants from southern and eastern Europe, those whom the Anglo-Protestant political leaders in Congress and the White House saw as racially inferior and a threat to their control of this society. Northern European Americans working through the government thereby greatly shaped the subsequent racial and religious mix of the United States. For example, today there are far fewer Catholic, Jewish, and Buddhist Americans than there would have been if the U.S. government had not enforced discriminatory immigration laws for decades.

Toward a Theory of Systemic Racism

All the social scientists and other scholars reviewed in the power-conflict theory section are grappling with important dimensions of racial oppression as it has developed in countries like the United States. Drawing on the research and ideas of these authors—particularly Du Bois, Cox, Blauner, and Ture and Hamilton—and using much recent research work by Joe Feagin and his colleagues, we can trace out briefly the contours of a more comprehensive power-conflict theory, one we can call a *theory of systemic racism*. **Systenic racism** encompasses *the white prejudices, stereotypes, emotions, discriminatory practices, and institutions that are integral to the long-term domination of Americans of color*. We suggest here key themes in the development and continuing maintenance of systemic racism in the United States:

1. *Initiation of oppression*: At an early point in time, European colonists established hierarchical group relations with the people of color they oppressed and exploited for their land (Native Americans) and labor (African Americans). Later, descendants of these self-named "white" colonists would add many other Americans of color to the system of racial exploitation and oppression. Typically, subordinated groups were viewed as culturally inferior and, by the 1700s, as biologically inferior "races."
2. *Mechanisms of oppression*: In the past and in the present, racial hierarchies are supported by a range of dominant-group ideas, feelings, and attitudes, including hostility, contempt, and fear. Racial stereotypes and prejudices are very important, and racial hierarchies are perpetuated centrally by the exploitative and other oppressive (discriminatory) practices carried out by members of the dominant racial group (in this case, white Americans) against those in subordinate racial groups.
3. *Privileges of oppression*: Great material and symbolic privileges come to those in the dominant racial group. Much misery and serious social and economic burdens come to those in subordinate racial groups. Critical to the maintenance of hierarchical group relations is the ongoing societal reproduction of this unjust enrichment for white Americans and unjust impoverishment for Americans of color, now over many generations.
4. *Elite maintenance of oppression*: Many actions of the white economic and political elites have created and maintained the institutions, interpretive frames, and ideologies that reflect the elites' interests in racial (and class and gender) hierarchies. Most nonelite whites have more or less accepted the society's racial hierarchy, along with fewer socioeconomic resources than the elites, because of their access to certain privileges and advantages associated historically with "whiteness."
5. *Rationalization of oppression*: Once the system of racial oppression and privilege was firmly put into place in the late 1600s and the 1700s, it was increasingly defended and rationalized by a racial framing and ideology. Since the 1700s a broad racist frame and ideology accenting

superior and inferior racial groups have been created and circulated by whites in power. That framing and ideology have been accepted and further circulated by rank-and-file whites.

6. *Resistance to oppression*: Opposition to systemic racism is a constant in North American history. Native Americans, African Americans, and other Americans of color have a long history of individual and group protest against the reality and burdens of racial oppression by white Americans. Some antiracist whites have periodically joined in this centuries-old struggle against systemic racism.

To varying degrees, these dimensions of racial oppression are relevant to understanding the oppressed situations of most non-European Americans, including Native Americans, African Americans, Latino Americans, Asian Americans, and Middle Eastern Americans. We will examine these dimensions in detail in later chapters, but let us illustrate them briefly here, with particular reference to white oppression of African Americans over nearly four centuries.

A previous history of oppression often explains many contemporary societal realities. For example, the pioneering W. E. B. Du Bois, in his book, *The World and Africa* (1946), showed how the great misery and poverty evident in Europe's many African colonies were linked directly to the "wealth and luxury in Europe. The results of this poverty were disease, ignorance, and crime. Yet these had to be represented as natural characteristics of backward peoples."[76] Du Bois argued that the history of African colonization has been omitted from most mainstream histories of European development, wealth, and affluence. He further demonstrated that a serious understanding of European wealth and prominence must *center* on the history of African colonialism, for the material and labor resources of Africans were exploited and taken to create much of that European wealth and prominence.

Similarly, a first step in developing a comprehensive theory of systemic racism in the United States is to put the four-centuries-long white exploitation and domination of people of color at the center of the analysis. From the beginning, European colonialism in North America involved racialized exploitation and oppression: European colonists built up much wealth by unjustly taking for themselves the material and labor resources of Native Americans and Africans. Today, a major educational task is to analyze critically the mythologized and falsified past history often taught in U.S. school books and to learn more about our actual racial and ethnic history.

Together with Du Bois, Oliver Cox was one of the first to examine the colonial origins of systemic racism in North America. He showed how capitalism, which was involved in the movement of Europeans overseas, created a situation that was "favorable for the development of white race prejudice."[77] Modern racial prejudice and racial ideology developed as these colonizers moved from viewing the early colonized populations of indigenous Americans and African Americans (and soon, Mexican and Chinese Americans) as "uncivilized savages" or "heathens" to seeing them as racially inferior and well below whites on the hierarchy of "races." Colonialism, with its theft of land and labor, created modern racial relations. The racial oppression of recent centuries did not arise out of some "abstract, natural, immemo-rial feeling of mutual antipathy between groups" but rather grew out of "a practical exploitative relationship" that was soon combined with a justifying social framing and ideology.[78]

Examining the origins of *racial hierarchies* in the colonialism and exploitation of particular historical periods, rather than in innate intergroup hostilities, is a second major theme for a comprehensive theory of systemic racism. "Race" is not an inborn human trait but rather a *way of relating* between individuals and groups. A comprehensive theory should begin with the real world of everyday exploitative and oppressive experiences and thus the historical relationships between large groups of human beings.

This conceptual framework recognizes the centrality of the history of material and economic exploitation in North America, which began with the seizure by whites of Native American lands (see Chapter 6) and the enslavement of Africans (see Chapter 7) by violent means. Land and labor obtained unjustly, by theft and chicanery, formed the economic and social foundation of what became the United States. Most Native Americans were killed or driven out of major white-controlled areas, while enslaved Africans were forced to become a central part of the economies of the new white communities. This genocidal action against many indigenous societies and the importation, subordination, and exploitation of enslaved Africans set in place the foundation for nearly four hundred years of group oppression in North America.

By the mid-1600s, the liberty and lives of Americans of African heritage were controlled by a system of racial oppression put into place by European Americans. For most, this meant legalized slavery. Transplanted and enslaved Africans became a major point of reference for whites in their construction of the colonial economy, polity, legal system, and values, and even "white" selves. African American subjugation became the common model for the treatment of other Americans of color in later periods. The white male elite among the colonizers reinforced this economy of oppression by legalizing it in the founding laws and political institutions of the new republic. The enslavement of African Americans was upheld in numerous provisions of the U.S. Constitution. Wealthy slaveholders—including George Washington, Thomas Jefferson, and James Madison—led in the creation of the legal and political arrangements of the new nation; Americans of color of that day, mainly Indian and African Americans, had *no* representation whatsoever in this nation-creating process. From the beginning, white-controlled local, state, and federal governments were used to create and enforce an extensive system of racial exploitation and oppression that would soon expand to encompass other groups, such as Mexican and Chinese Americans.

A third theme in this comprehensive overview is the importance of the power and privilege of whites and the related burdens of the racial "others." Oppression operates from a socially organized set of ideas and practices that deny Americans of color the privileges, power, opportunities, and rewards that this society offers whites as a group. The racial hierarchy offers generally different resources and life chances for the racially dominant and racially subordinate groups.[79] Thus, white Americans and Americans of color have different group interests because they have generally had unequal access to "life, liberty, and the pursuit of happiness" and to the material and other resources that shape everyday life.

For systemic racism to persist across generations, it must reproduce the necessary socioeconomic conditions. These conditions include a greatly disproportionate control by whites of major economic resources and of the political, police, and ideological power to control subordinate racial groups. This *social reproduction process* is often hard to see because it is so much a part of everyday existence. Every new generation of whites has inherited an array of social, economic, and political privileges that are associated with being white. For more than three centuries of this country's existence, racial oppression was firmly enforced and reinforced by legal and political institutions. Once legal slavery and official segregation were finally eliminated—the latter only in the late 1960s—this action did not eliminate the *racial hierarchy* that put privileged whites generally toward the top and disadvantaged people of color generally toward the bottom. Over centuries now, the majority of whites have inherited some economic resources—often in the form of a farm, some house equity, or family savings—or other valuable social resources, such as job training or the ability to get a good education, from their white ancestors. These ancestors usually benefitted significantly from legal slavery, legal segregation, or other legalized discrimination.

For example, under just one major federal program (set up by a Homestead Act), from the 1860s to the 1930s the federal government provided, for little or no money, some 246 million acres of land for some 1.5 million homesteads. Because of official discrimination and Klan-type violence, almost all of these homesteading families were white. Research by social scientist Trina Williams estimates that perhaps some 46 million (mostly white) people *today* are the descendants and heirs of those who received just this one major "affirmative action" benefit from the U.S. government.[80] The ancestors of contemporary African Americans were mostly excluded from this farm land and from many other economic resources by blatant, often violent discrimination. (We should note too that the land provided had often been stolen by violence from Native American societies.)

In addition, as we will document extensively in later chapters, many whites still discriminate today against Americans of color in order to protect their group interests and privileges. For example, frequent discriminatory actions by whites still restrict the access of many Americans of color to better-paying jobs, higher political positions, and some residential areas. This persisting discrimination outweighs the expressed commitments of many whites to the values of racial fairness and equality.[81] Note the continuing hierarchical structure of employment. Today, the majority of low-wage service and unskilled menial jobs in numerous employment sectors are held by workers of color; employees in these jobs often service better-off whites, such as employers, managers, and skilled workers. As a result, "these jobs entail a transfer of energies whereby the servers enhance the status of those served."[82]

The other side of white privilege is the set of material and psychological burdens that bear down on African Americans and other Americans of color. In its everyday operation, systemic racism dehumanizes those in a racially subordinated group. The most precious asset a person can have, substantial control over personal life and liberty, is often that which is most taken away. Institutionalized discrimination and inequality constitute the social structure of systemic racism, and part of its psychological dynamic is individual dehumanization. Our conceptual framework recognizes some degree of variation in these discriminatory burdens depending on the social position and gender of the oppressed individual. For example, women of color often face gendered racism—the double burden of suffering discrimination because they are not white and because they are female. Historically and in the present, institutionalized racial oppression has prevented most Americans of color from developing to their full human potential.

A fourth aspect of this theory of systemic racism recognizes the differential role of different class and gender groups among white Americans. The actions of the white elite—originally centrally composed of slaveholding planters, other farmers, merchants, and bankers, but later of industrialists and other major entrepreneurs—are critical in the creation and maintenance of the racist system at the foundation of U.S. society. As Du Bois and Cox made clear, in the process of protecting its top position, the overwhelmingly white (and mostly male) elite has worked to create organizations, institutions, and ideologies that substantially incorporate its interests. This elite holds disproportionate power and wealth. When its interests conflict with those of other societal groups, the white-dominated elite has worked hard to deflect challenges to its continuing dominance. The exploitative and discriminatory treatment of racially subordinated groups has varied, but in every case it is the dominant white group—and within it the ruling elite—that has set the basic terms for this treatment and, thus, for group development and mobility.[83]

In the economic arena, the white elite has been substantially interested in the exploitation of the land and labor of Americans of color, while the white working and middle classes have been more concerned about job and housing competition with Americans of color. Ordinary whites are important in enforcing discrimination in everyday life, because they constitute the majority of whites. Middle-class and working-class whites are responsible for much of the everyday discrimination against people of color, as recent studies of employment and housing discrimination show (see Chapters 6–12).

A fifth theme in our theory is that once racial oppression is in place, it is usually vigorously defended and rationalized. The taking of the land and labor of Americans of color is rooted not only in the laws and founding documents of U.S. society but also in a strong racial framing and ideology accenting the alleged cultural, intellectual, or biological inferiority of those at the bottom of the racial ladder. This ideology is structured by certain intellectuals and other elite leaders and communicated to the public in both overt and subtle forms, often through schools, churches, and the media.

Since the seventeenth century, white intellectuals and other leaders have frequently tried to hide the actual sources of racial and class inequalities. The dominant group has regularly generated images of itself as racially superior and explained inequality in racist terms. A comprehensive theory of oppression must include this rationalization process. From the seventeenth century onward, the religious, economic, political, intellectual, and media elites have perpetuated negative images of racialized outgroups in order to legitimate oppression. The often unseen power of the white elite still works through the racist frame's strong beliefs and images (for example, the woman of color as a lazy "welfare queen") perpetuated in the media, schools, workplaces, and churches of the country.

A sixth aspect of a complete theory of systemic racism emphasizes the many countering and resistance strategies developed by members of racially oppressed groups, both individually and collectively. Protest against racial oppression includes not only overt confrontation with members of the dominant group but also the development of an alternative perspective on the everyday world one must live in, a counter framing of society generated over a long period of time by those fighting discrimination and other domination. Americans of color are theorists of their own experience, as they have frequently made clear in the long history of antidiscrimination protest and civil rights movements. Out of their everyday experiences with the white-generated system of racism, Americans of color have created counter frames and countercultures of resistance that are the basis for individual and group strategies to challenge or destroy oppression.

Evidence of a counterculture of resistance, for example, can be seen in the black and Mexican American protest movements that were so powerful in the 1950s and 1960s. Organized protest against discrimination during this period included economic and bus boycotts, sit-ins, and demonstrations. African American resistance to segregation spurred the creation of civil rights organizations such as the Southern Christian Leadership Conference (SCLC). Many demonstrations included large-scale participation by Americans from all class and racial backgrounds. This organized activism was often rooted in a strong local base of churches, clubs, and other organizations. These groups provided money and mobilized people to enable civil rights organizations to achieve success in fighting the entrenched patterns of the then-legal racial segregation.[84]

In summary, then, a racially oppressive society can best be comprehended in its totality. These several dimensions are important to a fully developed framework for understanding systemic racism in the United States.

How has the U.S. racial hierarchy changed from the 1790s to the present?

A Note on the "Black–White Paradigm"

In recent decades, some academic researchers and other commentators have criticized what they see as a "binary black-white paradigm," which is said to dominate too much analysis of U.S. racial and ethnic relations.[85] These analysts feel that government, social science, and the media give (1) too much attention to white–black issues and (2) too little attention to the situations of certain other groups such as Asian, Latino, and Middle Eastern Americans. As we will see in later chapters, the view that these latter non-European groups have not received adequate public attention and social science research is generally quite accurate.

However, the critical power-conflict analysts we just discussed have shown that a thorough understanding of the current and historical oppression of all non-European groups requires a recognition that the economic and social *foundation* of the North American colonies, and later of the United States, was created and concretized with the enslavement of Africans and the destruction of Native American societies. As we have seen, once indigenous peoples were killed off or driven away and white-on-black oppression became an institutionalized foundation of the new European-American society, that system was enshrined in legal institutions and rationalized in a racist ideology that has endured to the present day.[86]

From this power-conflict perspective, U.S. society is not an array of disconnected racisms affecting peoples of color; rather, this society has a central racialized core that asserts and maintains substantial white (European American) superiority over all groups of color—a comprehensive system of racial domination that whites first developed for African Americans, and to some extent Native Americans, *within* the new society and then extended later to other non-European groups. Since the mid-nineteenth century, other groups of non-European workers—for example, Japanese, Chinese, Filipino, Puerto Rican, and Mexican Americans—have been brought into the racialized system to be exploited as low-wage labor. The more powerful white group generally exploited, evaluated, and imaged later non-European immigrants and their descendants from within the already well-institutionalized structural and ideological framework of white-on-black oppression.

The dominant white group has typically placed new non-European groups somewhere on a white-to-black continuum of status and privilege—with white Americans at the highly privileged end, black Americans at the bottom, and various other racial and ethnic groups placed in between, generally at the discretion of powerful whites. For nearly four centuries in North America, white minds and practices have constructed and maintained this hierarchical continuum of racial status, power, and privilege. As we will demonstrate in later chapters, at certain points in U.S. history white Americans have come to view certain groups among Americans of color as more socially acceptable than black Americans or than the darker-skinned, or less acculturated, members of those particular groups of color. For example, whites have periodically granted some non-European groups, such as Japanese and Cuban Americans, an intermediate-group status between the white and black ends of the white-generated racial ladder and continuum. The "model minority" stereotype that white commentators have applied to Japanese, Chinese, and other Asian American groups (see Chapters 10 and 11) provides evidence of this strategy. These latter groups did not create this "model minority" perspective; elite white commentators did.

Indeed, at earlier points in U.S. history, Chinese and Japanese immigrants' character, values, and societal position were very negatively stereotyped by whites—even as "black" or "near-black" on the socioracial continuum. In recent years, powerful whites have constructed certain groups, such as Japanese or other Asian Americans, as "model minorities" and as "nearer to white" on the socioracial continuum. They then criticize groups such as African or Mexican Americans for not possessing the work ethic, and for not achieving the economic successes, of such "model minorities." As Gary Okihiro has expressed it, whites have historically "upheld Asians as 'near-whites' or 'whiter than whites' in the model minority stereotype, and yet Asians have experienced and continue to face white racism 'like blacks' in educational and occupational barriers and ceilings and in anti-Asian abuse and physical violence . . . . This marginalization of Asians, in fact, within a black and white racial formation, 'disciplines' both Africans and Asians and constitutes the essential site of Asian American oppression."[87] By placing certain groups of color in an intermediate status on the socioracial ladder and continuum, white Americans as a group can effectively maintain and perpetuate the age-old racial hierarchy that began in this country with white oppression of Native Americans and African Americans.

When new immigrants arrive in the United States, what criteria are used to place them in the persisting racial hierarchy?

Summary

In this chapter we have reviewed major theories of migration and subsequent patterns of intergroup adaptation. Migration—varying from the movement of conquerors to slave importation to voluntary immigration—creates intergroup contact and thus racial and ethnic relations and conflicts. Adaptation can have different outcomes in the period of initial contact, ranging from genocide to peaceful symbiosis to some type of societal hierarchy and large-scale inequality. Further adaptation may lead to further genocide, to egalitarian symbiosis, to full adaptation to the dominant culture and institutions, to some type of cultural pluralism, or to continuing large-scale inequality and a persisting socioracial hierarchy.

Most theories discussed in this chapter fall more or less under the two broad categories of order theories and power-conflict theories. Both types of theories offer insights into the character and development of racial and ethnic relations. Assimilation theories tend to focus on voluntary immigrant groups and emphasize inclusion along conformity lines or pluralism outcomes. Assimilation analysts have pointed out the different dimensions of intergroup adaptation, such as acculturation and marital assimilation, and have often accented the role of value consensus in holding a racial and ethnic system together.

In contrast, power-conflict theories typically focus on involuntary immigration or colonial-type oppression and thus examine the substantial inequality and hierarchy in society. Power-conflict theories have certain recurring themes:

1. A central concern for major racial and ethnic inequalities in economic position, power, and resources
2. An emphasis on the interrelationship of racial oppression, the economic institutions of capitalism, and the subordination of women under patriarchal systems
3. An emphasis on the role of the government in legalizing and maintaining exploitation and segregation and in defining racial and ethnic relations
4. An emphasis on resistance to racial or ethnic domination by those who are oppressed

In analyzing U.S. history, power-conflict analysts have emphasized the forced character of much cultural and economic adaptation, particularly for non-European groups, and the role of coercion, segregation, exploitation, colonization, and institutionalized discrimination in keeping groups such as African, Latino, Asian, and Native Americans on or near the bottom rungs of the societal racial and ethnic ladder. Power-conflict perspectives have examined the role of governments in racial oppression and have stressed the importance of oppositional cultures in providing the foundations for subordinate-group resistance to that oppression.

Power-conflict theorists have often emphasized the importance of examining racial and ethnic relations in the context of the historical and global development of capitalism and patriarchy. In the introduction to Part II we will explore the utility of such an approach in evaluating the broad contours of racial and ethnic relations over nearly four centuries of North American and world history.

Key Terms

theory 27
movements of forced labor 28
contract-labor movement 28
political refugees 28
voluntary migration 28
colonization migration 28
genocide 28
egalitarian symbiosis 28
hierarchy 28
migrant superordination 28
indigenous superordination 28
order theories 29
power-conflict theories 29
assimilation 29
race relations cycle 29
cultural assimilation 30
structural assimilation 30
marital assimilation 30
identification assimilation 31
attitude-receptional assimilation 31
behavior-receptional assimilation 31
civic assimilation 31
melting pot 32
cultural pluralism 33
ethnogenesis 33
competition theory 36
caste school of racial relations 37
external colonialism 38
internal colonialism 38
oppositional culture 39
split labor-market view 41
middleman minority 43
ethnic enclaves 43
patriarchal system 44
gendered racism 45
racial formation theory 45
systemic racism 46

PART II

A Nation of Immigrants: An Overview of the Economic and Political Conditions of Selected Racial and Ethnic Groups

BIG PICTURE QUESTIONS

- ***How did the changing capitalistic economy influence major racial and ethnic groups immigrating to the United States?***
- ***Why have so many people come to the United States?***
- ***What push and pull factors have shaped large-scale migrations?***

In the chapters that follow, we examine a number of important racial and ethnic groups in U.S. society. For each we look at its history and analyze its current situation in terms of theories of racial and ethnic relations reviewed in Chapter 2. Before examining groups in detail, we will here set some major groups in the historical context of four centuries of North American economic and political development. We accent two important dimensions in our overview: the changing capitalistic economy and the expanding political institutions. Within these frameworks, each racial or ethnic group has worked out its own cultural and social patterns in an increasingly complex United States.

Immigration, the Economy, and Government

North American economic development has seen several stages: mercantilism and early commercial capitalism coupled to a plantation/slave economy, competitive industrial capitalism, and advanced multinational capitalism. Economic institutions and developments and related government actions have shaped the character of all periods of immigration and immigrant incorporation and adjustment.

Significantly, indigenous peoples were the original inhabitants of the lands to which the English and subsequent immigrants migrated; many in the indigenous societies lost their lives and lands as a result of the often brutal European invasion and conquests.

The table on the following pages briefly lists many of the immigrant groups discussed in this book. Each group entered North America under particular historical circumstances. Many started in slavery, low-wage jobs, small-scale farming, or small businesses. Political and economic conditions at the time of entry were very important. Some groups entered when low-wage jobs were plentiful on farms or in cities; others entered when fewer jobs were available. The extent of racial and ethnic discrimination and oppression has varied considerably. Also important were the economic and other resources brought by or available to particular immigrant groups. Those immigrants who came voluntarily

Selected Immigrant Groups: An Overview

Immigrant Group	Time of Entry	Economic Conditions in North America	Government Conditions and Actions
		Phase One: Commercial Capitalism and the Slave Society: Early 1600s–1860s	
1. English	1600s–1800s	Mercantilism; land taken from Native Americans; English entrepreneurs and yeoman farmers; commercial capitalism emerges.	English state creates land companies; colonial governments define individualized property and protect property.
2. Africans	1600s–1800s	Enslaved as property; became major source of labor for plantation capitalism.	Colonial governments establish slave codes; U.S. Constitution legitimates slave trade; U.S. government substantially controlled by slaveholding oligarchy.
3. Irish Catholics	1830s–1860s	Driven out of Ireland by English oppression and by famine; labor recruited for low-wage jobs in transport, construction.	U.S. government opens up western lands; Irish take over urban political machines from English Americans.
		Phase Two: Industrial Capitalism: 1860s–1910s	
4. Chinese	1850s–1870s	Contract labor and low-wage work in mining, railroads, construction; menial service work for whites.	Local governments recruit Chinese labor; anti-Chinese laws passed in California; 1882 Exclusion Act.
5. Italians	1880s–1910s	Moved as European peasants into U.S. industrial capitalism; overseas recruitment for low-wage industrial and construction jobs in the cities.	Government backing for labor recruitment; U.S. treaties with Europe; intervention in European affairs (World War I); incoming numbers reduced by 1924 Immigration Act.
6. Eastern European Jews	1880s–1910s	Industrial capitalism utilized their skilled and unskilled labor; small entrepreneurs established themselves; much anti-Semitism.	Government backing for labor recruitment; U.S. treaties with Europe; incoming numbers reduced by 1924 Immigration Act.
7. Japanese	1880s–1900s	Recruited as agricultural laborers for Hawaii; later migrated to west coast as laborers; served in domestic work; created small farms and businesses.	Government backing for labor recruiting; U.S. imperialism in Asia; conquest of Philippines and Hawaii; government actions soon exclude the Chinese and Japanese.
		Phase Three: Advanced Industrial (Multinational) Capitalism: 1910s–2000s	
8. Mexicans	1910s–2000s	With Asian/European labor cut off, Mexicans recruited for low-wage jobs on farms and in industry; substantial immigration, especially during war periods.	U.S. government provides labor recruitment programs, fosters U.S. agribusiness in Mexico, stimulating out-migration; growing U.S. Border Patrol monitors immigration; new laws restrict immigration.

Selected Immigrant Groups: An Overview *(Continued)*

Immigrant Group	Time of Entry	Economic Conditions in North America	Government Conditions and Actions
9. Puerto Ricans	1940s–2000s	Early farm labor migration; U.S. corporations recruit labor; blue-collar work in service economy; recurring and circular migration.	Conquest of Puerto Rico in 1898; U.S. government-supported agribusiness takes over economy, creates surplus labor, stimulates migration to mainland.
10. Recent Asian, Caribbean, Latin American, and Middle Eastern Groups	1960s–2000s	Many political and economic refugees; create economic niches, small businesses; important workers in the expanding service economy; face nativist racism.	U.S. involvement; in South Korea, Vietnam, Taiwan, Philippines stimulates out-migration; Cubans, Haitians, Middle Easterners flee political repression or wars.

and with a little economic capital, some education, or entrepreneurial experience frequently had access to better jobs or developed small businesses—opportunities not available to immigrants with less in the way of economic or cultural resources.

Commercial Capitalism and the Slave Society: 1600s–1860s

Colonial Society and Slave Labor

The colonial society that grew up on the east coast of North America during the 1600s was tied closely to England and the expansionist policies of the English political and economic elites. The early economic system in these colonies was a combination of state enterprises under the English king and enterprises developed by independent entrepreneurs, including, by the eighteenth century, the slave/plantation owners in the South and the merchants in the North. As was the case with other European colonial powers, the objective of English colonization was to secure raw materials and markets for English goods. The first joint-stock companies were formed by merchants under the auspices of King James I of England. Employees of the Southern Company settled Jamestown; this was the English colony that secured the first enslaved Africans from a ship flying a Dutch flag in 1619.

English merchants and entrepreneurs, early capitalists, invested capital in the extraction of raw materials for home industries. The colonies served the empire as a source of raw materials and agricultural products and as a dumping ground for surplus workers and peasants displaced by the expansion of aggressive capitalism and other economic changes in Europe. Capitalistic production for profit was not the only important economic dimension, for the colonies also became home to many English and other northern European immigrants—people displaced from the land in Europe and typically seeking to become small farmers or traders. In the colonies there were two major modes of production, the subsistence household (small-farm) mode and the profit-oriented capitalist (slave/plantation and merchant) mode.[1] The North American colonies had so much available land that it was difficult for English and English American entrepreneurs to secure enough cheap European labor, particularly for large-scale agriculture. They tried using white indentured servants, but these immigrants generally worked off their terms of servitude and then often went into farming for themselves.

From the late 1600s to the mid-1800s, people of African descent were a major source of (slave) labor for the white merchant and agricultural capitalists in the North American colonies. In the late eighteenth century, the emergence of cotton and sugar as international commodities created an even stronger demand for workers on slave plantations. The number of enslaved African Americans increased from 59,000 in 1714 to 3.9 million in 1860. This forced labor generated great wealth for many whites; it built up profits (capital) not only for further investments in expanding plantations and related business enterprises, but also for depositing in banks, where it could be used or borrowed by the white merchants, shippers, and industrialists of the North and South.

Civil War: The Southern Plantation Oligarchy Versus Northern Entrepreneurs

The South was generally the most prosperous and powerful region in the country from the late 1700s to about the 1850s. White southerners owned much of the productive land, much of the agricultural produce for export, many processing mills and other valuable equipment, and millions of enslaved African American laborers. These black laborers generated much wealth for white farms and trading businesses, including capital later invested in manufacturing enterprises. White southerners dominated U.S. politics, as most presidents between George Washington and Abraham Lincoln were slaveholders or sympathetic to slavery; until the 1860s few major decisions made by the federal legislative and judicial branches went against the critical interests of the slaveholding oligarchy and associated merchants. The Civil War was to a substantial degree a struggle for economic and political power between northern industrialists and small farmers, on the one hand, and the southern plantation oligarchy, on the other. The victory of the North in that bloody war marked the arrival of northern industrialists as a dominant force in the U.S. economy and national government.[2]

Immigrant Laborers in the North

During the 1800s in the northern states, the growing industrial working class and the class of small farmers were increasingly peopled by immigrants from Ireland, Germany, and Scandinavia. Immigrant labor often became the labor for the growing number of industrial enterprises—the textile mills, railroad shops, and foundries. The pull factors motivating millions of Irish Catholic immigrants to cross the Atlantic after 1820 were the same as those that have attracted immigrants for centuries to a country portrayed by industrial labor recruiters and others as the land of opportunity. There were major push factors as well. In Ireland a potato disease created severe food shortages; this crisis, plus the continuing political and economic oppression of Ireland by England, generated the migration of 1.6 million Irish to the United States over several decades. Many small farmers and artisans from Ireland sold their labor to U.S. employers; they became domestic servants, railroad laborers, miners, and industrial workers in cities.

The arrival of large numbers of white immigrants from northern Europe laid the foundation for new patterns of racial conflict. African Americans became a smaller percentage of urbanites in the North. Free black workers were used by industrial entrepreneurs in the North mostly as low-wage labor, sometimes as strikebreakers. Using them against white strikers increased the hostility of these workers toward black Americans. By the 1840s free black workers in the North were being forcibly displaced from jobs by white immigrants, including Irish American workers. Although the Irish immigrants arrived from a country where the English oppressed and stereotyped them as an "inferior race," within a generation in the United States the majority of the Irish had come to see themselves as part of a "superior white race."

Western and Global Expansion

In the early decades of the nineteenth century, the new nation of the United States began to expand its own empire well beyond that envisioned by its former British overlords. Since that time, the U.S. empire has gradually and continually expanded—first into Mexican and other lands to its west, later into Latin America, and eventually to Asia and around the globe.

Fostered by U.S. governmental decrees and military protection, the great westward expansion across North America in the nineteenth century brought not only Native Americans but also a new group—Mexicans—into the orbit of exploitation and oppression by white entrepreneurs, soldiers, and farmers. The racist frame and ideology accenting the "white man's civilizing responsibility" for non-European groups guided white expansionists and justified for them the taking of Mexican and Native American lands in the West. Expansionists believed the "Mexican race" and the "Indian race" should become subordinate to the "Anglo-Saxon race." The first Mexican citizens, who had long been residents of the Southwest, did not migrate; they and their land were brought into the United States by force as the result of the imperialistic Mexican-American War in the 1840s.

In 1822, President James Monroe announced, in what came to be called the Monroe Doctrine, that the Americas were now the U.S. sphere of influence and that no more European colonization would be tolerated. Soon, the United States replaced the European colonial powers as the dominant colonial power in the Americas. Since the middle of the nineteenth century, the U.S. government and businesses have expanded their involvement to western North America, Latin America, and all other continents. Since that time, U.S. economic and political ties have gradually become more extensive and complex than those of any other modern empire. They have included a myriad of business linkages and economic exploitations, as well as numerous military adventures, government aid of many kinds, and far-reaching media and other cultural linkages.

Over the past century and a half, U.S. involvement in most other countries has had far-reaching consequences, not only for these countries but also for the United States itself. As we will see, the character and history of immigration to the United States often parallels the development of economic exploitation and political or military adventures in other countries. Some have called this large-scale and continuing immigration "the harvest of the U.S. empire."

Industrial Capitalism: 1860s–1910s

Industrial Capitalism and Government Expansion Overseas

The Civil War was followed not only by westward expansion but also by an industrial boom. **Competitive capitalism**, *an economy dominated by small and medium-sized for-profit businesses*, gradually became one that was dominated by large enterprises. The growth of these enterprises was dramatic, and the United States soon surpassed Great Britain in numerous industrial production categories. The proportion of workers engaged in agriculture declined between the 1860s and the 1920s, while the proportion in manufacturing doubled. By the last two decades of the nineteenth century, many corporations were growing dramatically through mergers and acquisitions.

Leading U.S. industrialists expanded corporate investments and activities in numerous countries overseas, often backed by a U.S. government that was growing in military power. The movement of U.S. Navy ships, as well as merchants and missionaries, into countries such as China, Japan, and the Philippines often disrupted the economies and other social institutions in these countries, thereby increasing the surplus of farm workers and shaping out-migration. U.S. military and economic power pressured Asian countries to submit to U.S. influence. Given the often difficult economic conditions in these countries, U.S. labor recruiters enticed many Asian workers to Hawaii and the west coast of the United States. More than 200,000 Chinese laborers came to the United States between 1848 and 1882 to do the hard work in west coast mining, railroad, and service businesses. After the Chinese were excluded by a racist immigration law, Japanese immigrants were recruited for low-wage jobs. Japan sent many thousands of emigrants to Hawaii and the United States, a migration triggered by U.S. political influence and labor recruiting by U.S. employers.[3]

The U.S. victory in the Spanish-American War of the 1890s resulted in the annexation of Puerto Rico and the Philippines by the expansionist U.S. government and the effective domination of Cuba. When the United States took over Puerto Rico, much of that island was owned by small local farmers, but soon large U.S. companies were controlling much of the production. Puerto Rico, the Philippines, and Cuba would later send large numbers of emigrants to the U.S. mainland.[4]

African Americans: Exclusion from Western Lands

The second half of the nineteenth century was a period of major governmental growth and bureaucratization in the United States. Government action had a major influence on racial and ethnic relations. One of the first actions of president Abraham Lincoln and the new Republican legislators in the early 1860s was to pass a major Homestead Act, a wealth-building program for many white immigrant families seeking land, including Germans, Scandinavians, and Irish families. European American families who wished to farm were often provided 160 to 320 acres of land if they would develop it. After the Civil War, the U.S. Land Office ruled that most black Americans were ineligible for these land grants because they were not citizens when the act was passed. For the most part, black families did not have the opportunity that many white families had to build up landed wealth through farming, wealth passed down to millions of their descendants.[5]

In the late 1800s and early 1900s, southern black workers were one possible source of labor for northern industries, but the white oligarchy in the South, after a brief postwar Reconstruction period, took back control of the South's economy and state governments—to a substantial degree using terroristic Klan-type violence–and made certain that most newly freed black Americans remained in the South as low-wage laborers, tenant farmers, or sharecroppers. There was little distribution of plantation land to the black men and women who had made that land so fruitful for whites. They did not receive the "forty acres and a mule" that some government leaders had promised them.

Southern and Eastern European Immigrants

Unable to use southern black labor, or preferring not to use it, northern industrialists turned to Europe. The majority of the 20.7 million immigrants to the United States between 1881 and 1920 were from southern and eastern Europe. Labor shortages and increasing wages for native-born white workers encouraged U.S. industrialists to seek immigrant labor. A 1910 survey of twenty major manufacturing and mining industries found that six of every ten workers were foreign-born. Without this immigrant labor, the great industrial expansion of the United States probably would not have been possible.[6] In some cases these new workers displaced native-born white workers. Anti-immigrant hostility (nativism) among the workers in older European American groups increased as a result.[7]

European Immigrants and Black Americans

Writer Irving Kristol once argued that "The Negro Today Is Like the Immigrant of Yesterday." In this view the experience of black Americans moving to U.S. industrial cities has not been significantly different from that of white immigrant groups: African Americans should eventually move up economically and socially just as those immigrants did.[8] However, this argument overlooks important differences between the experiences of white and black immigrants to the industrial cities. Group mobility was possible for European immigrants because of the following.

1. Most arrived at a time when urban jobs were generally available, U.S. industrial capitalism was expanding, and opportunities were relatively abundant.
2. Many had some technical or other skills or a little capital—resources available to few African Americans at the time.
3. Most faced far less severe employment and housing discrimination than black workers in the cities.
4. Most found housing, however inadequate, reasonably near their workplaces.
5. In key cities, the political system was changing from Anglo-Protestant business dominance to shared power between these business elites and political machines oriented to new white immigrant voters.[9]

In the critical periods of large-scale European immigration, cities such as New York, Philadelphia, Boston, and Chicago were expanding centers of manufacturing. Blue-collar jobs were frequently available, if not plentiful. In the mid-nineteenth century, Irish and German immigrants were attracted to rural areas and to cities, where most found industrial, service, or government jobs. From 1890 to 1930, southern and eastern Europeans came in large numbers to the cities. One study notes that "the Italian concentration in construction and the Polish in steel were related to the expansion of these industries as the groups arrived."[10] Many migrated as a result of labor recruiting by U.S. employers in Europe.

Among the European immigrants who arrived in the period between 1880 and 1920 were large numbers of Jewish immigrants fleeing oppression in Europe. Although they were often poverty-stricken, many Jewish immigrants were part of an urban industrial proletariat and came with some experience in skilled trades. One study found that two-thirds of the Jewish immigrants were skilled workers, whereas other southern and eastern European immigrants were primarily peasant farmers or farm workers. When Jewish immigrants entered in large numbers around 1900, the clothing industry was moving to mass production and offered jobs for tailors and seamstresses, as well as unskilled jobs, and there were also chances for small-scale entrepreneurs in a number of cities.

The situation for the African Americans who began to move to the northern cities from the South after 1910 was quite different. Black workers who migrated from the South had little access to good government jobs and were regularly displaced by the white immigrant groups who forced them out of job after job, such as construction and transport jobs, and into marginal, low-paying jobs or unemployment. Stanley Lieberson has explored why southern and eastern European immigrants have done well in northern cities, compared with black Americans. Among his conclusions are that (1) black migrants were the victims of more severe discrimination over a longer period than were white immigrant groups and (2) economic competition between whites and the growing group of black workers in the urban North led to extensive hostility and institutionalized discrimination by whites.[11]

What factors contributed to the growing racial conflicts of the late 1800s and early 1900s?

Advanced Industrial (Multinational) Capitalism: 1910s–2000s

Mexican Immigrants

With the increased industrialization accompanying World War I came a sharp decline in the number of laborers available for agricultural work. The need was filled in part by Mexican labor, recruited with substantial help from the federal government. Mexican laborer and family migrations increased significantly in the 1920s. Agencies in cities such as Los Angeles and San Antonio recruited Mexican workers for agriculture and for low-skilled jobs in the steel, auto, and other urban industries. Internal colonialism theorist Robert Blauner has captured the contrast between the non-European and the European immigrants of this period and later: "America has used African, Asian, Mexican, and, to a lesser degree, Indian workers for the cheapest labor, concentrating people of color in the most unskilled jobs, the least advanced sectors of the economy, and the most industrially backward regions of the nation."[12]

Large Corporations and the U.S. Business Cycle

Since 1900, large corporations, many with an international orientation, have come to dominate the U.S. economy and politics. *The economic system that is dominated by large-scale, for-profit corporations that operate in many different countries, thereby creating an international market system,* is called **multinational capitalism**. By the 1920s, a large number of Americans, including immigrant workers, were working in the auto industry or in related industries such as steel. Aggressive competition among auto firms in the 1920s resulted in the production of more cars than were needed. This overproduction, a chronic problem in a capitalist economy, resulted in major cutbacks in employment in auto-related industries, thus helping to trigger the 1930s' Great Depression, which hit especially hard among African American and Mexican American migrants to industrial cities. Unemployed whites, including recent immigrants, took over many of the lower-paying jobs previously held by workers of color. The latter had very high unemployment rates. The federal government grew as U.S. political leaders tried to develop ("New Deal") government programs to save the foundering capitalist system. Nonetheless, racial discrimination was perpetuated in these New Deal social welfare programs of the 1930s. Typically, workers of color received lower wages than whites, were employed mainly as unskilled laborers, and were often employed only after whites.[13]

The Postwar Era: The United States and the World

For three decades after World War II, the U.S. government, the U.S. military, and U.S. multinational corporations substantially dominated the world economy, in large part because major industrial societies elsewhere, such as Germany and Japan, had been destroyed by the war. Since World War II, it has become easier for U.S. multinational corporations to move capital investments from the central city to the suburbs, from northern to southern cities, and from U.S. cities to cities overseas. Capital flight and job exports have resulted in many economically abandoned central cities. The federal government has facilitated this outward expansion of investment and jobs by funding home mortgage programs and highway systems often built in accord with the needs of large firms developing plants and of middle-class (disproportionately white) workers seeking to live outside central cities. As a result, after World War II many white Americans—often the children and grandchildren of European immigrants—followed the new manufacturing plants and allied workplaces to the outlying suburbs.

Into the central cities came yet other groups of workers and their families—African Americans, Puerto Ricans, Mexicans and Mexican Americans, Native Americans, Asian Americans, and Middle Eastern Americans. After World War II these immigrants to northern and western cities inhabited residential areas increasingly abandoned by industry and the children or grandchildren of earlier European immigrants. For example, among these immigrants were Puerto Ricans, many of whom were recruited for low-wage city jobs in the 1950s and 1960s. U.S. industrial and agribusiness development in Puerto Rico helped to stimulate a large out-migration. Many older cities have thus seen an increase in the political influence of Americans of color in recent years.

Government Involvement Overseas and Asian Immigration

Until the mid-1960s, U.S. immigration legislation was so restrictive that most people from Asian countries desiring to emigrate could not enter the United States. By the late 1960s, these discriminatory quotas had been lifted, and since then there has been a significant increase in immigrants, including Chinese, Korean, Filipino, Asian Indian, and Vietnamese immigrants. U.S. support for South Korea during and after its war with North Korea built strong ties between the United States and South Korea. A succession of dictators in South Korea drove out some dissenters, who migrated to the United States; other Koreans came for economic or educational reasons. The immigration of the Chinese, the Filipinos, and the Vietnamese is also generally related to the involvement of the U.S. government and corporations overseas. The U.S. arming and political support of the Philippine government and of the Nationalist Chinese government on Taiwan, and U.S. participation in the wars in Korea and South Vietnam, have played an important role in creating large groups of Filipinos, Koreans, Chinese, and Vietnamese oriented to the United States. More recently, increasing corporate and political ties between the United States and mainland China have encouraged the immigration of mainland Chinese here. As with earlier immigrants, Asian immigrants have generally migrated to the United States seeking better economic opportunities and/or greater political freedom.

Latin American Immigration

Caribbean immigrants to the United States since the 1960s have included Cubans and Haitians, who have often moved to Florida. The U.S. government long supported a right-wing dictatorship in Cuba, which was overthrown by a guerrilla movement led by Fidel Castro. Many Cuban businesspeople and professionals fled in the first period of emigration after Castro took power. These Cubans, many of whom had some economic or educational resources, established a major economic enclave and gained political influence in Florida. After 1980, a significant number of working-class Cubans also migrated to the United States, some of them having been expelled as alleged "undesirables" by the authoritarian Castro government. Most Cuban immigrants have been welcomed by the U.S. government as political refugees from a Communist government, and many millions of dollars in federal subsidies have been provided to facilitate their adjustment. In contrast, Haitians, who also fled politically repressive governments, were for the most part not welcomed by the U.S. government. Many were forced to return, and most of those allowed to stay were not provided the type of government support provided to Cuban immigrants. A major reason for this is that the Communist government in Cuba is seen as a political opponent, whereas repressive governments in Haiti have mostly been viewed as political allies of the U.S. government.

In recent decades much investment capital and federal government aid for development have shifted from northern to Sunbelt cities. The growing economy of the U.S. Sunbelt has created a demand for low-wage workers in sectors such as construction, manufacturing, and agriculture. Many people have migrated there from Mexico and Central America for economic reasons. Others, like earlier European groups, have come fleeing political oppression in Central America. Mexican immigrants still make up a significant portion of undocumented immigrants. They are constantly attracted by the possibility of jobs, and many are pushed by poor economic condition in their home country. Large U.S. corporations operating in Mexico have played a continuing role in generating Mexican outmigration. U.S. agribusiness firms have greatly stimulated the development of export-oriented agriculture in Mexico, in the process taking over large amounts of land for that purpose and driving off many small Mexican farmers who had farmed the land to feed their families. Many of these small farmers and their families have thus become migrants to Mexican cities and to the United States. Nativistic attacks on these undocumented immigrants by U.S. citizens typically ignore the U.S.-generated, economic push factors that drive many poor Mexicans to migrate to the United States.

Middle Eastern Immigration

Immigrants from the Middle East have been coming to the United States for more than a century. Arab immigrants from more than twenty countries comprise the largest group among these. Immigration from Arab areas has occurred in two major segments—the first from about 1880 to 1945, and the second, much larger immigration from 1946 to the present day. Between 1880 and World War II, Arab immigrants came in modest numbers. They were working-class and middle-class people who came mostly seeking economic opportunity. They were usually from what was then Greater Syria, an area that included what would later be known as Lebanon, Syria, and Palestine/Israel. By the mid-1920s, Arab Americans numbered an estimated 200,000; most were Christians. These early immigrants and their descendants make up a substantial proportion of Arab Americans today. The discriminatory 1924 Immigration Act sharply reduced immigration from the Middle East.

With the abolition of this blatantly discriminatory immigration law in the 1960s, immigration to the United States was opened to people of all countries, and the number of Arab immigrants increased. The 1970s' Lebanese civil war and the 1980s' Israeli military invasion of Lebanon generated numerous immigrants; others have fled other Middle East wars. Large numbers have come from Lebanon, Syria, Egypt, and Palestine. Whether Muslim or Christian, most have a strong sense of their Arab origins. Most have settled in large metropolitan areas.

Although those who came during the earliest period of immigration were generally poor, many who have immigrated since the 1960s have been educated professionals or businesspeople. Today, Arab Americans as a group are disproportionately self-employed in their own businesses.

Early Arab immigrants were frequently cataloged with southern and eastern European immigrants as "inferior races" by whites in the United States. In recent decades many people from the Middle East and Mediterranean areas, both Arab and non-Arab peoples, have continued to face widespread stereotyping. The U.S. media (including movies) have often portrayed Arabs, Arab Americans, and other Middle Eastern Americans (for example, Iranian Americans) in negative and racially stereotyped terms.

Immigration Restrictions

European immigrants made up more than half of all those coming to the United States during the decade of the 1950s. Their proportion dropped to one-third by the 1960s and to less than one-fifth in recent years. The change is substantially the result of the abolition of the discriminatory national-origin quotas in the 1965 Immigration Act. Since the 1960s many Asian, Latino, and Middle Eastern immigrants have been viewed as a "problem" by native-born Americans. Congress has passed additional immigration legislation with provisions to shape and restrict the recent, mostly non-European, immigration to the United States. Many native-born workers and leading politicians are concerned that the United States cannot absorb so many new immigrants, even though the ratio of immigrants to the native-born population was *higher* in the early twentieth century than it is now. The percentage of foreign-born in the U.S. population today is also smaller than that of other countries, including several in Europe. Implicit in many European American discussions of the new immigrants is a concern that most are from Asia and Latin America—that is, they are not white and not European.[14]

Significantly, the new immigrants from Asia and Latin America, and their children and grandchildren, are part of a growing population of Americans of color. In many areas of the United States, including half the country's hundred largest cities and the states of Hawaii, New Mexico, Texas, and California, Americans of color are now a majority of the population. They soon will be the majority in several other states. As their numbers increase, Americans of color will likely press even harder for more equitable treatment in U.S. social, economic, and political institutions. They will likely achieve increased representation in this society's major decision-making positions, including those in the economy and the federal government.

When and how did changing immigration laws bar certain racial or ethnic groups from entry into the United States?

Summary

In this overview we have briefly surveyed the economic and governmental contexts within which particular groups have immigrated and adjusted to life in the United States. The time of entry for particular groups and the resources they have brought have affected their relative economic and political success. A complete understanding of the character of U.S. immigration requires an analysis of the economic and political contexts of immigrants' entry and adaptation. Capitalist development and expansion, as well as U.S. political involvement overseas and domestic governmental action, not only have shaped the context and character of U.S. immigration and the patterns of racial and ethnic relations in North America for centuries but also have provided crucibles within which the family patterns, distinctive cultures, and political resistance to discrimination of specific immigrant groups have constantly developed.

Key Terms

competitive capitalism 57

multinational capitalism 59

CHAPTER 3

English Americans and the Anglo-Protestant Culture

BIG PICTURE QUESTIONS

- ***Who were the English colonists who began the North American experiment?***
- ***What influence did the English Americans have on major U.S. institutions?***
- ***How was the dominant Eurocentric culture established, and how has it been maintained?***

Cleveland Amory tells a story about prominent English American families in Massachusetts. A Chicago banking firm wrote a Boston investment company for a letter of recommendation for a young Bostonian. Eloquently praising the young man's virtues, the company's letter pointed out that his mother was a member of the Lowell family, his father a member of the Cabot family, and his other relatives were members of other prominent New England families. The bank wrote back, thanking the company but noting that this was not the type of letter of recommendation they had in mind: "We were not contemplating using Mr. _______ for breeding purposes."[1] Apocryphal or not, this story illustrates the elite status of certain Boston families and suggests their prominence in New England's history.

The story indicates too the importance of inbreeding, descent, and interlocking family ties over the generations. Ethnicity involves cultural or nationality characteristics that are distinguished by the group itself or by important outgroups, but lines of descent are major channels for passing along these ethnic characteristics to later generations.

English Americans—that is, *Americans of English ancestry*—are the third largest white ethnic group in the United States, after German and Irish Americans. Approximately 24.5 million Americans are estimated to have significant English ancestry according to a 2000 census report.[2] The term *English Americans* itself may sound a bit strange. Other terms are often used. Most common are the rather inaccurate terms *Anglo-Saxon* and *white Anglo-Saxon Protestant*. **Anglo-Saxon** *originally referred to Germanic tribes, the Angles and the Saxons, who came to the area now called England in the fifth and sixth centuries C.E. It was later applied to the inhabitants of England and to those English who came to North America.* **Anglo-Protestants** is *a more accurate term for those often referred to as Anglo-Saxons* or as **white Anglo-Saxon Protestant Americans**. Although in-depth analyses of this ethnic group are rare, numerous authors have commented on its central importance: "Our American culture, our speech, our laws are basically Anglo-Saxon in origin."[3]

Milton Gordon's view of the shaping effect this first large group of European immigrants had on the dominant culture of the United States was noted in a previous chapter: "If there is anything in American life which can be described as an overall American culture which serves as a reference point for immigrants and their children, it can best be described . . . as the middle-class cultural patterns of, largely, white Protestant, Anglo-Saxon origins."[4] This comment suggests the importance of this dominant culture in the adaptation process faced by later immigrant groups.

Note that the term *Anglo-Saxon* is an inadequate designation for the immigrants from England and their descendants. The term derives from the names for two Germanic tribes, the Angles and the Saxons, that came to the area now called England in the fifth and sixth centuries C.E. However, other people were there already—the Celts—and these Germanic tribes were followed by Normans from France. Thus, the English colonists in the North American colonies already embodied several centuries of the blending and fusion of several nationality types and cultures.[5]

Some authors have used *Anglo-Saxon* and related terms such as the ethnocentric "old-stock Americans" in a loose way to also include British groups other than the English, such as the Scots and the Welsh. Certain other northern European groups that have substantially adapted to the Anglo core culture—particularly Scandinavian and German Protestants—are also sometimes included by scholars in the terms *Anglo-Saxon* and *Anglo-Protestant*. In any event, when the terms *Anglo-Saxon*, *Anglo-Protestant*, and *British American* are used by scholars, English Americans and the dominant culture they generated are usually at the heart of the discussion.

Early on, Americans of British descent often expressed a sense of their superiority and prominence in the new nation. In the late 1780s, John Jay, the first chief justice of the U.S. Supreme Court, wrote in *The Federalist*, "Providence has been pleased to give this one connected country to one united people—a people descended from the same ancestors, speaking the same language, professing the same religion, attached to the same principles of government, very similar in their manners and customs."[6] This ethnocentric perspective—certainly inaccurate at the time—has been a central problem for non-English groups ever since.

The English Migrations

Some Basic Data

Although the English were not the first Europeans to come to North America (the Spanish came earlier, for example), they were the first Europeans to colonize it in large numbers. By the early eighteenth century there were approximately 350,000 English and Welsh colonists in North America. At the time of the American Revolution, this number was approaching 2 million.[7]

Migration to the North American colonies was heavily English until 1700. Then the English migration generally receded to modest levels, until well into the nineteenth century.[8] Nearly 3 million English migrated to the United States between 1820 and 1950; the majority came between 1880 and 1900. The English migration to the colonies, and later to the United States in the nineteenth century, was one of the largest population flows in this period. The English were the first sizable European group in what was to become the United States and continued to be an important segment of the European migration until World War I.[9]

The First Colonial Settlements

The English colonists' seventeenth-century migration, together with their pattern of settlement, was distinctive. This movement can be viewed as *colonization migration*, a concept explored in Chapter 2. Unlike other types of migration, colonization migration involves the subordination of indigenous societies. As we show in Chapter 6, the first victims of English and other European colonialism on this continent were many indigenous societies. English colonists participated actively in killing Native Americans and otherwise driving them off their lands.[10]

Why did the English Crown become interested in establishing these North American colonies? English advocates in the colonial period put forth various explanations for colonial development. The need for trading posts and for new sources of raw materials, as well as for new markets for English goods, received much attention.[11] Other colonial advocates emphasized Protestant missionary objectives, the search for a passage to Asia, the need to stop Spanish and French expansion, and the need for a place for England's surplus population. "What England primarily looked for in colonies was neither expansion of territory *per se* nor overseas aggregations of Englishmen, but goods and markets."[12]

The English colonization was a case of Lieberson's migrant superordination (see Chapter 2). It had dire consequences for the preexisting Native American

Pilgrims aboard the Mayflower sign the Mayflower Compact.

societies. Geographical expansion proceeded rapidly. At first, some Native American groups were treated in a friendly fashion, if mainly because the colonists depended on Native American food and advice for survival. As the colonists gained numerical superiority over the indigenous population, they forced the latter back into frontier areas or slaughtered them.[13] Few European colonists seemed concerned over the genocidal consequences of their aggressive colonialism. Most European invaders viewed the Native Americans as "savages" who should be driven off the valuable land.

The English established large settlements in North America, often using royal companies of various kinds. Recall from the introduction to Part I that some of these were early manifestations of European capitalism, an economic system that accents capital and profit. The first joint-stock companies were formed by merchants under the auspices of James I of England in the early 1600s. Employees of the Southern Company settled Jamestown, a colony where the primary goal was economic. Initially planning to develop the colony with poor white labor, the leaders at Jamestown soon perceived a labor shortage and secured enslaved Africans from a Dutch-flagged ship in 1619, laying the foundation for the institution of human slavery in North America. The northern colony of Plymouth was settled in 1620 under the auspices of another royal company. Many of these New England colonists—later called "Pilgrims"—were Puritans who had broken with the Anglican church.[14] Both settlements nearly expired in their early years because of disease and starvation. The Plymouth colony managed to survive only with the aid of supportive Indian communities.[15]

According to historian David Fischer, four distinctive English-speaking groups were among the first to immigrate to North America. First came the Puritans from England's eastern counties, who entered the Massachusetts area primarily between 1629 and 1640. They brought to New England "nucleated settlements, congregational churches, town meetings, and a tradition of ordered liberty."[16] A second group of immigrants came to the Virginia area between 1642 and 1675. This group consisted of a small number of Royalists from southern England and numerous indentured servants. Their culture was characterized by "extreme hierarchies of rank, strong oligarchies, Anglican churches, a highly developed sense of honor, and an idea of hegemonic liberty."[17] A third group—Quakers from the North Midlands of England and Wales, who came to the Delaware Valley between 1675 and 1725—established a "pluralistic system of reciprocal liberty" based on spiritual and social equality, austerity, and an intense work ethic.[18]

A fourth group of immigrants came to the Appalachian backcountry from the borderlands of northern Great Britain and northern Ireland between 1718 and 1775. This group represented a variety of ethnic ancestries (English, Scottish, and "Scotch-Irish") and had extreme socioeconomic inequalities, but its members shared the ideal of natural liberty.[19] Each of these four groups had a distinctive type of culture—distinctive speech patterns, architecture, family ways and child-rearing customs, dress and food ways, religious orientations, and conceptions of liberty and the organization of public life. Over time, their cultural patterns interacted with each other and eventually fused together to create the dominant Anglo-Protestant culture of the colonies and, later, the United States.

The American Historical Association has developed rough estimates of the "national stocks" of the white population in 1790 based on a surname analysis (see Table 3.1).[20] These estimates give the English the primary position among whites, with other British groups accounting for significant proportions. In addition, note that black Americans, then mostly enslaved, made up about *one-fifth* of the total population in 1790.[21]

TABLE 3.1 "National Stocks" as Percentage of the White Population (1790)

Surnames	White Population (%)
English	60.1
Scottish, "Scotch-Irish"	14.0
German	8.6
Irish (Free State)	3.6
Dutch	3.1
French, Swedish	3.0
Other	7.6
Total	100.0

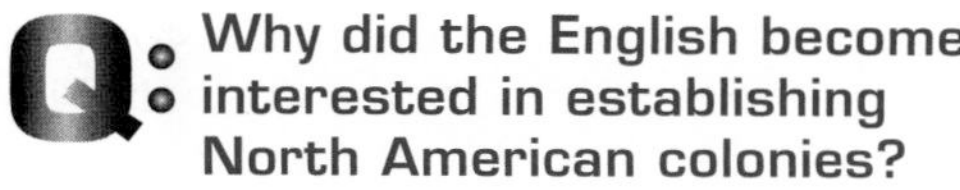

Later Migration

A modest number of British and other European immigrants entered the United States between the Revolution and 1820, but the century following 1820 saw the greatest Atlantic migration in history. English immigrants moved in large numbers from manufacturing and mining industries in England to comparable positions in U.S. industry; their skills helped spur the dramatic industrialization of the nineteenth century.[22] When English American workers were eventually displaced by machines or later immigrant groups, they or their children often moved up into managerial, professional, and technical positions. With their help, and also substantial investments by English capitalists, U.S. industrial productivity soon surpassed that of the home country.[23]

The ease with which many English immigrants moved into industrial workplaces suggests the swiftness of their assimilation at the level of secondary organizations. Their skills kept most from the poverty that many other immigrants faced. Larger numbers moved into clerical and professional jobs than was the case with many later white immigrant groups. Acculturation was easy. They were more readily hired where the ability to speak English was important. These immigrants avoided most of the anti-immigrant agitation that others faced. Indeed, new English immigrants often shared the ethnocentric or racist views held by previous English colonists, including the stereotyping of Jews, hostility toward black Americans, and dislike of southern Europeans. Structural assimilation in the *primary-relations sphere,* to use the concept of assimilation theorist Milton Gordon, was usually rapid for them. English immigrants never faced enforced residential segregation, and marriage with other English Americans was commonplace.[24]

Smaller numbers of English immigrants have come to the United States since 1910, generally fewer than a few thousand each year. In the 1930s, more people returned to England than came in as immigrants. The modest English migration since 1910, coupled with dramatic increases in immigration from other areas, has had a significant demographic effect. Since 1910, British Americans as a group have declined as a proportion of the total U.S. population.[25]

Other Protestant Immigrants

The terms *Anglo-Saxon* and *Anglo-Protestant* have sometimes been used by researchers to include not only the English but also the Scots, the Welsh, and even Scandinavians and Germans. The Welsh entered the colonies in relatively small numbers, beginning in the early 1600s. The total number who came has been estimated at just over 100,000. Many found employment in industrial jobs or farming. The first generations retained their customs, language, and distinctive communities, but most were soon substantially assimilated to the white Anglo-Protestant mainstream.[26]

In terms of political and economic power, the Scots were perhaps the closest to the dominant English group from the 1700s onward, although they too were subject to Anglo-conformity pressures. By the late eighteenth century there were perhaps 250,000 Scots in the United States, a number that was supplemented over the next century by three-fourths of a million migrants. In the colonial period, some Scots were prosperous merchants, clerks, soldiers, and middle-income farmers, although the majority probably were servants, laborers, and poor farmers. Many settled in rural and frontier areas. Scots experienced hostility from some English Americans in the early period. Assimilation to the English core culture gradually accompanied inclusion in the economic system; by the early 1800s many if not most Scots had achieved parity with their English American neighbors. They, too, were becoming an important segment of the white Anglo-Protestant mainstream.

German immigrants made up the largest non-British group during the eighteenth century. Germans constituted nearly one-tenth of the colonists, and in the century after 1820 several million more came to the United States. Some were Catholics and Jews, but the largest proportion was Protestant. Many became farmers, merchants, and, later, industrial workers. Over several generations much, but by no means all, of the German culture was reshaped or displaced by the well-established Anglo-American patterns. Cultural assimilation, together with substantial mobility in the economic and political spheres, came in a few generations for German Protestants. For years, however, some distinctiveness persisted in the form of certain German customs, festivals, and residential concentrations. Jewish Germans (see Chapter 5), who immigrated in the middle decades of the nineteenth century, remained somewhat distinctive, in part because of the often vicious anti-Semitism directed against them (and later Jewish immigrants) by many other Americans.

Scandinavian immigrants, such as Swedes and Norwegians, did not enter in large numbers until the 1870s and 1880s. In all, perhaps 2 million came. Many immigrants entered as farmers and laborers, but the second and third generations moved into skilled blue-collar and white-collar positions. Here, too, substantial assimilation to the British American core culture came in just a few generations. Still, some distinctiveness in family customs and residential location, especially in midwestern areas, persists today.

These white Protestant groups from northern Europe assimilated relatively rapidly in the cultural, economic, and political spheres, although this process was not always peaceful. In the period of early contact, some of these white northern European groups suffered physical attacks and extreme cultural conformity pressures from English Americans. However, this did not last long. Within a generation or so, English Americans were intermarrying with Scottish, Welsh, and "Scotch-Irish" Americans, and sometimes with Scandinavians and Germans. By the early twentieth century, the designations *white Anglo-Saxon Protestant* and *white Anglo-Protestant* increasingly came to blur the distinction between the English and the later northern European immigrant groups.

The Invention of the "White Race"

The eighteenth and nineteenth centuries saw the emergence of the "white race" as a deliberately constructed social group for the first time in North American or, for that matter, world history. From the beginning, English colonists and their descendants saw themselves as quite different from the indigenous Americans and black Americans, whom they initially stereotyped as "uncivilized," "idolaters," and "savages." English Americans saw themselves as "republicans" of great virtue; they were concerned with protecting the new nation and reserving it, as some explicitly stated in the 1790s, for the "worthy part of mankind."[27] By the early 1800s, the growing importance of southern plantations for the U.S. economy as a whole (northern entrepreneurs and bankers were often linked to the southern economy) increased the demand for Native American land and for enslaved African American workers. At the same time, slavery was being abolished, sometimes rather slowly, in most northern states.

As a result of these developments, a white Anglo-Protestant elite circulated the idea of an advantaged "white race" and of inferior Indian and African "races." Famous U.S. founders, men of English or Welsh descent, played a central role in making this racial framing of society central to the thinking of most white Americans. These included three early presidents, Thomas Jefferson, James Madison, and George Washington. For example, Jefferson, the main writer of the Declaration of Independence, wrote extensively in the first major book by a U.S. intellectual that African Americans were greatly inferior to white Americans with regard to not only skin color and physical form but also reason, familial love, forethought, and even the ability to feel pain and grief.[28] In an 1814 letter to a neighbor, Edward Coles, the aging Jefferson explained why he still thought that black Americans should not be freed; as he saw it, black Americans are "brought from their infancy without necessity for thought or forecast, are by their habits rendered as incapable as children of taking care of themselves, and are extinguished promptly wherever industry is necessary for raising young."[29] Jefferson reiterated the explicitly racist notions in his earlier writings as to the lack of forethought among black Americans and his view of their childlike dependency. In this letter to Coles, Jefferson also described the freed blacks in these terms: "In the mean time they are pests in society by their idleness, and the depredations to which this leads them." Many slaveholders like Jefferson, Madison, and Washington viewed those enslaved as a childlike and thus inferior "race."

Yet, these views were not just confined to powerful whites. The white elites of the founding era and later decades sought to provide some racial privileges for the propertyless British and other European immigrants and their children, and thus to prevent the latter from bonding with black Americans and other Americans of color. As sociologist W. E. B. Du Bois suggested, these white workers often accepted a lesser economic position and lower wages in return for the "public and psychological wage" that went with being members of a "white race." In return for acceptance of their subordinate class position, white workers, including new immigrant workers from Britain, were allowed or encouraged by the white elite to be part of a racial hierarchy in which all whites enforced deference from black Americans and other Americans of color.[30]

Historical research shows that many nineteenth-century European immigrants, who did *not* define themselves initially as "white" but rather as Irish, German, or Italian, gradually came to construct themselves as "white" as they moved up economically and politically in U.S. society. The development of a racist frame and white-supremacist ideology was accelerated during Andrew Jackson's presidency (1829–1837). (Jackson, of Protestant Irish descent, was infamous as a slaveholder and for his involvement in destroying Native American societies.) By the late nineteenth century or early twentieth century, not only the later English immigrants but also immigrants from Scotland, Scandinavia, Ireland, and Germany had come to accept a place in the "white race." Their racial privileges generally included the right to substantial personal liberty, the right to travel and immigrate, and (for men initially) the right to vote. Similarly, the white elite's response to eighteenth- and nineteenth-century farmer protests and union organization among white immigrants often included efforts to convince white farmers and workers to embrace racial solidarity within the socially invented "white race."[31]

What structural and cultural factors led to the social construction of the "white race"?

Nativist Reactions to Later European Immigrants

Nonetheless, in the 1700s and 1800s, some native-born white Americans, themselves descendants of earlier immigrants, expressed their hostility toward the new European immigrants. **Nativism**, *an anti-immigrant ideology that advocates the protection of the native-born inhabitants of a country from immigrants who are seen as threatening or dangerous,* goes far back in North American history, but the term appears to have been first used in the 1840s. Nativists were nationalists who saw themselves as the *only* true Americans.[32]

Before the American Revolution, nativists focused on the religious and moral undesirability of new immigrants. Certain religious groups (especially Catholics), "paupers," and convicts were discouraged by English Americans from entering the colonies. Antiforeign sentiment was directed primarily at some non-English immigrant groups, of whom French Huguenot refugees were one example. At least one Huguenot community was violently attacked by these nativists. "In the early years Englishmen treated the increasingly numerous immigrants from other European countries, especially Scottish and Irish servants, with much condescension and frequently with exploitative brutality." In Virginia and Maryland, discriminatory duties were placed on non-English servants coming into the colonies. Catholics among the Irish were "doubly damned as foreign and Papist."[33]

Established colonists felt ambivalence about the new immigrants. On the one hand, immigrants provided needed labor for employers, ship captains profited from immigration, and new immigrants were encouraged to settle in frontier areas to increase colonial security. On the other hand, immigrants were sometimes seen as a threat, and English American mobs occasionally tried to prevent their landing.[34]

More Fear of Immigrants

Antiforeign sentiment took legal form in the late 1700s after the Federalist party became concerned about political radicalism among certain new immigrants and about non-English immigrants' growing support for Jeffersonian Republicans. The 1798 Alien Act empowered the English American president (John Adams) to deport immigrants considered a threat to the new nation. The period of residence required to be eligible for citizenship was raised from two to five years in 1795 and to fourteen years in 1798. Attempts were also made to set an exorbitant fee for naturalization. These strategies were designed to limit the political power of the new non-English immigrants. Numerous attempts were made to reduce the influence of new immigrants by vigorously pressuring them to assimilate to English-dominated institutions.[35]

A nativistic concern about the many non-English immigrants who did not know the English language and customs led Benjamin Franklin to establish a school in Pennsylvania in the 1740s.[36] Even the "liberty-loving" Franklin held strong ethnic prejudices and stereotypes about German immigrants in his region; he feared they would "shortly be so numerous as to Germanize us instead of us Anglifying them."[37]

Anti-Catholic sentiment fueled much nativist agitation. Irish and German immigrants entering during the 1840s and 1850s were periodically targeted by bursts of nativist agitation; a variety of secret societies, sometimes termed the "Know-Nothing" movement, fought immigration and Catholicism. (When questioned, members of these societies are reported to have said, "I don't know nothing.") During the 1850s, ethnocentric Know-Nothings were elected to state legislatures, Congress, and state executive offices. They precipitated numerous violent attacks against both new immigrants and native-born Roman Catholics.[38]

Nativism was coupled with racist ideologies in the nineteenth century; other northern Europeans joined English Americans in this perspective. U.S. socioeconomic development was celebrated aggressively as the perfect example of what could be accomplished by the "Anglo-Saxon race." This racialized Anglo-Saxonism was picked up by white expansionists who lusted after Mexican lands in California and Texas. European Americans legitimated their vigorous military thrust into those areas by a perceived mandate to colonize the "inferior races" there. One European American expansionist commented that "the Mexican race now see in the fate of the aborigines of the North, their own inevitable destiny. They must amalgamate or be lost in the superior vigor of the Anglo-Saxon race, or they must utterly perish."[39] This Anglo-Saxonism was to play an important role in racist thought for decades. It provided the rationalization for U.S. imperialist military and business expansion overseas, in places such as the Philippines, in the late nineteenth and early twentieth centuries.

After the Civil War, some U.S. intellectuals came under the influence of **social Darwinism**, *a perspective that extended Charles Darwin's evolutionary thinking into the societal realm and thus argued for a culture that embraces the "survival of the fittest."* This perspective developed in England and the United States (continuing cross-fertilization across the Atlantic) and contained notions of Anglo-Saxon racial superiority linked to a theory of the social "survival of the fittest." One advocate, John Fiske, celebrated the superiority of English civilization and claimed it was the destiny of the English people to populate *all the world's* empty spaces.[40] Even more influential were popular U.S. writers such as Josiah Strong, a Congregationalist minister whose book, *Our Country* (1885), sold thousands of copies. Strong was a vigorous advocate of Anglo-Saxon superiority myths, which he and others combined with the view that native-born Catholics and non-British immigrants were both highly undesirable. The English peoples were multiplying, he argued, and the United States was destined to be the seat of an "Anglo-Saxon race" whose numbers would approach (by the 1980s, he inaccurately predicted) a billion strong![41]

Nativism and Racism Since 1890

Increased immigration from southern and eastern Europe and from Asia around the turn of the twentieth century focused anti-immigration sentiment on these groups. For example, Henry Cabot Lodge, an English American aristocrat from New England and a powerful political figure, was fiercely determined to defend the United States against immigrant "threats" in the 1890s and early 1900s. English Americans formed the Immigration League to halt southern and eastern European immigration. The League worked diligently for a literacy test, which passed Congress, and associated itself with the eugenics movement started by Sir Francis Galton, a prominent English Darwinist. The early U.S. eugenicists feared that allowing so-called "unfit" southern and eastern European (especially Catholic and Jewish) immigrants to enter would destroy the "superior race" of north Europeans. In their view, the unfit should be sterilized, excluded, or even eliminated.[42]

Perhaps the most prominent American to contribute to the development of racial nativism was Madison Grant, an American of English extraction who fused various racist ideas in his influential book, *The Passing of the Great Race* (1916). Worried about the influence of newer groups from southern and eastern Europe, Grant claimed that interbreeding with the inferior European "races" would lead to mongrelization. Northern Europeans—the "Nordic race"—were the superior "race."[43] By the 1920s this racist perspective (sometimes called "scientific" racism) helped fuel pressures for immigration legislation that discriminated against non-British white groups. Various national-origin quotas were set to restrict the then-substantial immigration from southern and eastern Europe.

The 1920s and 1930s saw an outpouring of racial nativism on many fronts. Nativist organizations such as the revived Ku Klux Klan, an old U.S. terrorist group, provided a social outlet for those who wished to subordinate African, Catholic, and Jewish Americans and preserve the "Anglo-Saxon race." Opposition to foreign immigration resurfaced again after World War II, when various members of Congress and (northern) European American organizations opposed legislation that would permit large numbers of political refugees, such as European Jews and Catholics, to migrate to the United States.

In recent decades some anti-immigrant and anti-Catholic nativism has continued to take the form of ethnic stereotyping and harassment of Americans not of northern European ancestry. For example, Democratic Party presidential and vice-presidential candidates have sometimes been targeted because of their Catholic or southern European ancestry. In the 1984 national election, attacks were leveled at the Italian immigrant ancestry of Democratic vice-presidential candidate Geraldine Ferraro. Among other things, some Republicans (often of northern European ancestry) alleged that she and her Italian American husband had connections to organized crime. Since the 1990s a number of Americans of Italian ancestry who are involved in politics, such as former Governor Mario Cuomo of New York, have suffered similar "mafia" stereotypes.[44]

Another recent form of nativism can be seen in the various anti-immigration organizations that have flourished in the past decade or two. Like their predecessors in the early twentieth century, these organizations have opposed and stereotyped recent immigrants, particularly those coming from Asia and Latin America since the late 1960s. Immigrants' languages and cultures have often been the focus of this nativist opposition. White-supremacy groups, including the Klan, have held rallies across the United States, published racist literature, and established websites that attack non-European immigrant groups (sometimes viciously called, together with black Americans, the "mud people") as a threat to "American jobs" and to the Anglo-Protestant culture. These contemporary nativist groups include not only significant representations of northern European Americans but also, ironically, many whites with southern and eastern European ancestries, those whose parents or grandparents were targets of earlier nativist organizations.

At a demonstration in Denver, right-wing skinheads give the Nazi salute.

The Dominant Culture and Major U.S. Institutions

Most analysts of the U.S. racial and ethnic scene have assumed that the dominant culture and institutions of the United States are substantially Anglo-Protestant in character. During the first century and a half of colonial settlement, an English heritage integrated most east coast colonies. As historian Sheldon Hanft has put it: "Since all but two of the original colonies were founded by Englishmen, were administered by English officials, were protected by England's army and navy, and were led by English-trained clergy, lawyers, and educators, they adapted English models in their laws, constitutions, educational system, social structure, and cultural pursuits." He adds that many wealthier colonists also sent their sons to English universities and "English styles in literature, poetry, music, architecture, industry, and clothing were the models to emulate until the twentieth century."[45]

The dominant U.S. political, legal, and economic institutions have generally been based on English models, but they have not been identical to those in England. For example, the early dominance of the Anglican church in several colonies soon gave way to significant religious diversity, and the availability of (Indian) land for (white) immigrants—the basis of much North American wealth—often fostered more democratic institutions. Traditional English ways were often modified under North American conditions.[46]

Language

Although contemporary nativists have tried to bring it about, the United States as yet has no official language. Nonetheless, the *de facto* dominance of the English language signals the huge impact of early English colonists and their descendants. When the English came, perhaps a thousand indigenous languages were spoken. Today, only a few hundred are still spoken, and the number of Americans speaking these indigenous languages is far smaller than those speaking the languages of the European conquerors.

The principal U.S. language over the past two centuries has not been a thorough blend of Native American and early immigrant languages, but an English language that has incorporated words from both European and U.S. sources. Some scholars have argued that "our customary way of life is most like the English, and our language is but one of the several English dialects." Historically, assimilation pressures on non–English-speaking immigrants have first taken the form of language pressure. As early as the 1740s, native-born Americans of British background attacked new immigrants (such as Germans) for their alleged threats to the persistence of the English language and Anglo-American culture. From then to the present, the dominance of the English language has been a major concern of each new generation of nativists.[47]

Today, millions of Americans live in homes in which a language other than English is often spoken. In recent decades this group of non–English speakers has been attacked as un-American by organized nativists, who worry that many newcomers, especially Latin American and Asian immigrants, will not accept English as their primary language. They are especially concerned that Spanish, spoken by an estimated 7 to 8 percent of Americans at home, is challenging the dominance of English. One result of lobbying by nativist organizations has been the introduction of legislation to make English the official language of the United States. In 1986, for example, California passed a ballot proposition that declared English to be the official language of this most populous state in the Union. In recent years numerous other states have passed this type of nativist legislation. In 1981 an English Language Amendment to the U.S. Constitution was introduced in Congress; it has been reintroduced in subsequent sessions of Congress but has not yet been passed.[48]

In the 1990s a group called National English Campaign announced that its goals were to (1) replace ethnic group identification and "hyphenated ethnicity" with an "American identity" based on individual citizenship and (2) establish English as the official language of government, schools, and elections.[49] Such goals suggest fear of a pluralism of racial and ethnic groups and cultures and an emphasis on an English-oriented U.S. identity.

Contemporary organizations with nativist undertones, such as the California English Campaign and the National English Campaign, have fought bilingual programs across the country. In 1997 they pressed for a California ballot initiative to limit instruction of immigrant children to one year in their native language before they moved into classes taught in English.[50] Such groups often argue that they are not trying to discriminate against immigrants but wish immigrants to quickly become part of the mainstream by adopting English as their primary language. However, one such group, called U.S. English, was a project of a nonprofit organization that supports significant immigration restrictions. A member of the U.S. Commission on Civil Rights resigned as president of U.S. English when she learned that its founder held anti-Latino views; among other things, the organization's founder had apparently forecast a political takeover of the United States by Hispanic Americans.[51]

Civil rights leaders have pointed out the discriminatory nature of several actions advocated by pro-English groups, in particular the prohibition of Spanish usage by government agencies, the elimination of bilingual programs in public schools, and the elimination of bilingual ballots in states with numerous Latino voters. A number of research studies have shown that children who are "denied the right to view the world through their language and culture are made to feel inferior" and sometimes react in such negative ways as dropping out of school or engaging in drug use or crime—outcomes that cost not only themselves but the greater society dearly.[52] The implementation of English-only laws can have other negative effects, including the banning of testimony by non–English speakers in court and the removal of language interpreters in government agencies.

Nativist campaigns that promote use of the English language underscore the traditional dominance of that language—and the uneasiness that, ironically, some descendants of *earlier immigrants* still feel in the presence of languages and cultures brought by relative newcomers to this "nation of immigrants."[53] As one legal scholar notes, their "first myth is that our national unity somehow depends solely on the English language, ergo we must protect the language through constitutional amendment or legislation. A corollary is that the only language of true American identity is the English language."[54]

What is ironic about the aggressive English-only movements is that most of the immigrants being attacked not only recognize that English is the language of much political, social, and economic discourse, but also strive hard to learn the language. In recent years, for example, tens of thousands of immigrants have been turned away or placed on waiting lists for adult English classes in cities such as Los Angeles. Significantly, three-fourths of Latino immigrants speak English *every day*.[55] In addition, English-only nativism serves to further segregate English-only supporters from the rest of the world. Lack of knowledge of languages other than English cripples many Americans who conduct business abroad or deal politically with people in other countries across the globe. A person who knows more than one language well typically has greater knowledge and ability, and is thus more intelligent in this regard, than a person who knows but one.

Religion and Basic Values

English religious influence on the United States has been of great importance since colonial days. The various English denominations represented a variety of beliefs and practices. Anglicans in Virginia were characterized by a hierarchy of priests and a liturgical form of worship. This group favored a state church supported by compulsory church taxes. Presbyterian churches in the Appalachian backcountry favored a national church governed by strong ministers. Congregationalists and Separatists in New England favored moderate separation of church and state and more democratic church governance. Baptists (Rhode Island) and Quakers (New Jersey and Pennsylvania) both advocated strict separation between church and state. The communally organized Baptists favored a fellowship-centered form of worship. The spirit-centered worship of Quakers followed from a belief in an Inner Light that dwells in all people.[56] It was these latter groups who established the principle of separation of church and state at the heart of the U.S. political system.

For the first two hundred years, English religious denominations, or variations thereof, dominated the North American scene. The Anglican church received some early government support but lost its privileged position during the era of the American Revolution. Anglican and Congregational churches were in the majority at the time of the Revolution, although Baptist and Presbyterian churches and Quaker groups were becoming numerous. In the century after 1776, English dominance of the country's religious institutions decreased as Catholic, Jewish, and other religious groups grew with each new era of immigration.[57]

The Catholic and Jewish faiths, as well as non-British Protestantism, have been greatly shaped by the "American way of life," a phrase the scholar Will Herberg applied to the dominant Anglo-Protestant culture.[58] One important study of Judaism has shown the substantial impact of Protestant institutions on eastern European Judaism. Immigrant synagogues made major changes over time in response to the dominant Anglo-Protestant culture. For example, Jewish religious schools adapted to Protestant American scheduling and Sunday school formats. Reform Jews adopted English as the language of worship and introduced Friday night services.[59] Yet, the Anglo-Protestant culture's effects on the non-Protestant religions of later immigrants have been uneven and incomplete. Although new immigrants have been expected to adapt in many areas, some religious heritages from the home countries have been preserved. Contemporary U.S. religious patterns can be accurately described as a type of cultural pluralism.

Certain Anglo-Protestant values have had significant effects on non-Anglo immigrants. The importance of the ascetic (austere and self-denying) Protestantism that early English immigrants brought to the colonies should not be underestimated. "American condemnation of British sexual and political impurities focused on the King. Idleness, wealth, and power had corrupted him."[60] Puritanism helped to establish the **Protestant work ethic**—*the idea of hard work as a duty of every individual, originally of an individual who seeks to please God*—at the center of the U.S. value system. This work ethic was linked by many to the persistent pursuit of personal profit. The expanding U.S. capitalistic system in the late 1700s and the 1800s was pervaded by the "pursuit of profit, and forever *renewed* profit, by means of continuous, rational, capitalistic enterprise."[61]

The influence of English religious traditions on music and the arts in the first two centuries is further evidence of the extensive effects of the English on early American culture. The first book published in New England was the *Bay Psalm Book* (1640), which drew heavily on the English music tradition. "Yankee Doodle" was probably an English tune whose original lyrics satirized ragtag colonial soldiers. Only when the Revolution began did American soldiers take it over from the British. Before, during, and after the Revolution, various English melodies were the basis of most popular and political songs.[62] Even the new national anthem, "The Star-Spangled Banner," took its melody from an English drinking song!

Interestingly, however, over the next two centuries English influence on U.S. popular music receded dramatically before the pervasive influence of African American music (jazz and rock and roll, for example), "Scotch-Irish" country music, and the Mexican American music of the Southwest. Today, popular music is one major area of U.S. culture from which the direct English influence has mostly disappeared.

Education

English and other British Americans took advantage of what few educational opportunities were available in the colonial period; more affluent parents sent their children to private schools established before 1800. With the public school movement, which began in earnest in the first decades of the nineteenth century, British American dominance of public schools became a fact of life. British Americans often saw urban public schools as a means of socializing non-British immigrants into Anglo-Protestant values. In the nineteenth century, most public school systems were established by British American industrialists and educators who shaped curricula and instruction and supervised schools. Although some—for example, John Dewey—believed that education should bring greater mobility opportunities for poor immigrants, many elite educators emphasized the social-control aspects of schools. The Americanization pressures on immigrant children were often intense. Whether children were Irish, Jewish, or Italian, Anglicization was designed to ferret out non-Anglo-Protestant ways and assimilate the children to Anglo-Protestant manners, work habits, and values.[63]

Public schools' social-control function and the Anglo-American influence on their operation remain evident today. More recent immigrants, such as Asians and Latinos, have faced Anglo-conformity pressures similar to those experienced by earlier Irish and Italian immigrants. Indeed, the public schools are still a major battleground for those concerned with making English the official language of the United States.

Political and Legal Institutions

The political and legal institutions that affect all Americans have been shaped fundamentally, and are still being shaped greatly, by the English heritage in at least two ways: the laws and traditions more or less inherited from the English, and their concrete application today by English immigrants' descendants. Given the early majority of English immigrants in colonial society, English legal institutions became dominant. Concern for the rule of law and insistence on the "rights of Englishmen" were central. The Mayflower Compact (1620), a political framework that theoretically provided for equality under the law, was part of this English political tradition. New England, with its Puritan institutions, often provided the model for later U.S. political and legal developments.[64]

The North American colonies developed distinctive political institutions—in some ways those characteristic of sixteenth- and seventeenth-century England. The basic political ideas in England and the soon-to-be United States included unity of government and society, subordination of government to law, a balance of power between the legislature (Parliament in England) and the executive (the king in England), and heavy reliance on local governments.[65] U.S. political and legal institutions, growing out of the U.S. Constitution, have generally reflected these ideas ever since. Nonetheless, some contrasts can be seen. Governmental authority and power were being centralized in England in the late 1700s, but in the new United States of 1789 governmental power was separated into three national branches—the executive, the judicial, and the legislative. The position of the U.S. president is thus unusual: The United States, unlike most modern political systems, does not distinguish between the head of the government and the chief of state. Indeed, numerous recent presidents have demonstrated how powerful the U.S. executive branch is relative to the Congress, whereas in most European countries the parliaments are very powerful versus the heads of governments. The United States is a relatively new society, but it is an "old" political state.

Representative government in the colonies and, later, the United States is another example of English influence. Using Parliament as its model, the British Crown established representative colonial assemblies almost from the start.[66] Gradually these assemblies grew in power vis-à-vis the London government. Indeed, Crown infringements on them helped to generate the Revolution.

The U.S. legal framework reflects great English influence. Before the Revolution, English common law was asserted to be "the measure of rights of Americans."[67] Tension between the new nation and England generated U.S. objections to the continuation of English-based laws. Some Americans wanted a new U.S. legal code, but for the most part U.S. officials and lawyers only "sought to reshape or add to the existing stock of authoritative legal materials."[68] Although there was variation in how English statutes were brought into the U.S. legal system, their implementation was thoroughgoing: "The use of English statutes was provided for at an early stage in twenty-six of the twenty-eight jurisdictions organized between 1776 and 1836."[69] Although the U.S. legal system has been patched many times, the basic cloth today is still English common law.[70]

Officeholding

In addition to their fundamental impact on the establishment and structure of U.S. political institutions, English Americans have had a major impact on their operation. The first U.S. president, George Washington, was of English ancestry, as was the forty-third president, George W. Bush, more than two centuries later. English Americans have filled a disproportionate number of major offices at various political levels throughout U.S. history.

The colonial assemblies were "almost exclusively English in makeup."[71] The Declaration of Independence was signed by fifty-six European American men, thirty-eight of whom were English by background or birth; nine were Scottish or "Scotch-Irish," three Irish, five Welsh, and one Swedish.[72] A majority of the fifty-five members of the U.S. Constitutional Convention were also English; the Constitution was framed around their concerns not only for (partially) democratic institutions reminiscent of English institutions but also for the protection of their own property and wealth. Most people of wealth in the new nation—merchants, slaveholders, financiers, shippers, wealthy farmers, and their allies—supported the Constitution, substantially out of economic self-interest. Enslaved Americans, indentured servants, poor farmers, laborers, and women had no say in the making of the U.S. Constitution. Those who crafted the new Constitution perpetuated class lines similar to those prevailing in England.[73]

Studies of U.S. presidents, Supreme Court justices, and members of Congress have revealed a distinctive pattern persisting to the present. Presidents and presidential candidates have been informally "required" to possess ancestry qualifications, preferably British American or other northern European ancestry. Of the U.S. presidents from Washington to Bush, about two-thirds had English ancestry and *all* the rest had other northern European backgrounds.[74] No southern Europeans, Jewish Americans, Latino Americans, Asian Americans, Middle Eastern Americans, or African Americans have been president. A study of the origins of Supreme Court justices from 1789 to 1957 found that more than half were of English or Welsh extraction. Northern Europeans have generally dominated the country's highest court.[75] Moreover, an analysis of 162 prominent political leaders (including presidents, representatives, senators, and Supreme Court justices) of the period between 1901 and 1910 found that more than half were of English or Welsh origin. These data show just how powerful elite members of the English or British American groups remain in U.S. society, even as their group's percentage of the population has long been less than 10 percent.[76]

Even when new immigrant groups have periodically managed to break into U.S. politics, as in the case of Irish and Italian Americans, they have often been subservient to Anglo-Protestant leaders who have continued to hold the highest political offices. Newer immigrants and their children did gain significant electoral and political power in the first decades of the twentieth century in some cities, but not as top elected officials at the national level. Indeed, as of 2007, only one Catholic American had *ever* been president, Irish American John F. Kennedy (1961–1963). His brief presidency marked only a temporary shift from a more or less homogeneous political establishment at the very top, for Kennedy was followed by more men of northern European Protestant stock.[77]

Although the domination of northern European Americans at the very top of national politics persists today, some challenges to this dominance can be seen at political levels below the top. For example, in the early 2000s the cabinet of President George W. Bush included a number of Americans whose ancestral background was not northern European. Bush's cabinet included people of Asian, Latino, and African American backgrounds, perhaps signaling some slowly growing racial and ethnic diversity in national politics.

What about the English American impact on local governments? A study of New Haven, Connecticut, up to 1960 illustrates English political dominance in New England. For many decades an Anglo patrician elite there "completely dominated the political system. They were of one common stock and one religion, cohesive in their uniformly conservative outlook on all matters, substantially unchallenged in their authority, successful in pushing through their own policies, and in full control of such critical institutions as the established religion, the educational system (including not only all the schools but Yale as well), and even business enterprise."[78] A study of the mayors of Cleveland, Ohio, in the period between 1836 and 1901 found that most were part of an Anglo-Protestant elite with strong ties to New England. Their political framework was guided by what was termed the "New England creed," one proposition of which was "The good society is white and Protestant."[79]

In recent decades Americans of British ancestry have had to compete with non-British immigrants and their descendants for power in local and state politics, and today the racial and ethnic mix in local and state political institutions varies considerably across the country. Irish, Italian, and, most recently, African, Asian, and Latino Americans have risen to political power in large cities of the Midwest, East, South, and West. Still, English and other British Americans continue to exercise disproportionate influence in many areas, especially in suburban politics, although they and their ethnicity receive little media attention.

Economic Institutions

Recall from previous sections that the English heritage is substantially reflected in U.S. economic institutions—in the norms and values that shape these capitalistic institutions and in the actual dominance of English American individuals. Just as the U.S. legal system incorporated portions of the English system, the forms of capitalism that dominated much of northern Europe during colonial times shaped the colonies' economic system. The British Crown wished to increase the raw materials and the markets available to the home country. To this end, the first English colonies were often capitalistic, especially those established by state-chartered trading companies or wealthy English investors.

Mercantile capitalism, which still existed in the colonies at the time of the Revolution, was a state-directed capitalism linked to English nationalism. The

American Revolution was in part a clash between English and British American commercial interests, a clash that unified the colonies and brought a political break between two rather similar economic systems.[80]

Industrial capitalism developed in the United States after 1830, again with intimate connections to the English system. Much investment and many technologies used for U.S. industrial development came from England; English capitalists and skilled workers provided much of the know-how for U.S. economic development. After the Revolution, as before, Britain and the United States formed a single north Atlantic economy.[81]

Direct Participation in the Economy

English and other British Americans have regularly influenced the operation of the U.S. economy through direct control of critical business and political positions. In the beginning they established most of the colonies and controlled much of land and wealth. Control of the colonies lay primarily in the hands of English and other British American landowners and merchants.[82] In the late prerevolutionary period, small and medium-sized farmers with their own land came to have more influence.[83] Whatever their background, English Americans with land and wealth often needed labor. Because they had no surplus population, the colonies imported labor from Europe and Africa. By the 1730s a substantial Irish migration had begun, and a large proportion of these immigrants were indentured servants. A brutal African slave trade eventually supplanted the trade in white indentured servants.[84]

As we move toward the Civil War period and then into the twentieth century, we find few studies on the English or British American dominance of the economy. A study of the wealth of men in 1860 concluded only that the wealth of "native-born males," doubtless mostly British Americans, was about twice that of "foreign-born males."[85] U.S. industrialization in the nineteenth century was fueled by English and Dutch capital. U.S. business elites have long been dominated by Americans of British or other northern European descent. In the nineteenth century, the most famous of these were industrialists and financiers, many of whom have been regarded as "robber barons." They included John D. Rockefeller, Leland Stanford, and J. P. Morgan, all men of great wealth and power. Their heritages were typically English, with a few other northern European heritages mixed in. Many of their associates or family members became U.S. senators, representatives, and governors.[86]

A study of top executives and entrepreneurs in the late-nineteenth-century iron and steel industry found that few came from recent immigrant families; most were native-born and had fathers with capitalist or professional backgrounds. Most did not fit the image of a poor immigrant "making good," as did the steel magnate Andrew Carnegie, who came to America as a poor boy. More than half were of English or Welsh ancestry; most of the rest were either Scottish or Irish.[87] A survey of two hundred major executives serving the largest companies from 1901 to 1910 found that 53 percent were of English or Welsh origin, 7 percent were Scottish, 14 percent were Irish, and 8 percent were Canadian or British (unspecified).[88]

A few studies have made clear the extent of British American dominance in local economies. For instance, in the 1930s Burlington, Vermont, was dominated by "Old Americans"—those who had been in the United States for four generations, probably heavily English and English Canadian. They controlled banking and manufacturing, and they constituted a disproportionate number of professionals and political officials.[89] A few studies of the economically influential have been done since the 1930s. The "proper Philadelphians" about whom Baltzell has written typically had English or British backgrounds. This is suggested by the dominance of Episcopalians and Presbyterians in the Philadelphia *Social Register* for the year 1940.[90] In an analysis of the 1950s and 1960s, Baltzell also underscored the continuing dominance of British Americans at the national level.[91]

What factors ensure the centrality of the Eurocentric culture and institutions?

Contemporary Elites

Thomas Dye's famous 1970s study of major U.S. decision makers identified four thousand people in top positions in corporations, government, and the public sector: "Great power in America is concentrated in a tiny handful of men. A few thousand individuals out of 200 million Americans decide about war and peace, wages and prices, consumption and investment, employment and production, law and justice, taxes and benefits, education and learning, health and welfare, advertising and communication, life and leisure."[92] Decisions of importance are reached at the middle and lower levels of the society, but it is the few thousand people in the top positions who make many of the most critical decisions—those affecting the lives of many millions in all racial and ethnic groups. Dye's research revealed that the social origins of the top four thousand were not representative of the population as a whole. Most were affluent, white, Anglo-Protestant men. There were very few African Americans and virtually no Mexican Americans, Native Americans, or Asian Americans. These elites were "at least 90 percent Anglo-Protestant," and Dye noted that "there were very few recognizable Irish, Italian, or Jewish names" in the group.[93]

In recent decades, popular U.S. magazines have proclaimed that those in the media, politics, and the universities who most influence American life are now a much more representative group. Elites "today represent a real break with their predecessors."[94] However, this view is inaccurate. One must be careful to distinguish social and economic realities from rags-to-riches myths. By the early 2000s the upper reaches of U.S. economic (and other) institutions had broadened to include not only British Americans but also those with other northern European ancestry, particularly German, Irish, and Scandinavian Americans, and a handful of Catholic and Jewish Americans were beginning to penetrate elite bastions of economic power. Yet, as we more well into the twenty-first century, Catholic and Jewish Americans are still *not* proportionately represented at the top of the U.S. economic pyramid. And few non-Europeans can be found at or near the very top of the largest U.S. corporations.

Research since the 1980s has indeed found a continuing pattern of disproportionately white, northern European Protestant dominance at the top levels of industrial, public-interest, and governmental organizations. One study found that 57 percent of business leaders were Anglo-Protestants, much higher than their proportion in the population. When other white Protestants were added in, the proportion rose to 79 percent.[95]

English Americans as a Group: Economic and Other Demographic Data

Demographic analysts using the 2000 census estimate that 24. 5 million Americans now claim English as their ancestry, about 8.7 percent of the population in 2000. As we can see in Table 3.2, a very small percentage of these Americans were born abroad.[96] The proportions of women and men in the English American population are similar to those of the total population, but the English American population is rather older than the population as a whole.

In the 2000 census data (Table 3.2) we also see that the educational attainment of English Americans as a

TABLE 3.2 People with English Ancestry: Selected Population Characteristics (2000 Census)

	People with English Ancestry	Total U.S. Population
Number	24,514,199	281,421,906
Median age (years)	44	35
High school degree or greater (25 years and over)	91%	80%
College degree or greater (25 years and over)	35%	24%
Foreign born	1.8%	11%
Female	52%	51%
Median family income in 1999	$60,615	$50,046
Percent below poverty line	5%	12%

group was higher than that of the total population, for the category of high school diploma or greater (91 percent versus 80 percent) and the category of at least a college degree (35 percent versus 24 percent). Taken as a group, English American families were economically better off than those in the total population—with substantially higher median family income of $60,615. The poverty rate for individuals of English ancestry was also less than half that of all Americans. Still, it is important to note that not all those with English ancestry are well off in terms of education and income.

English Americans Today

Although they constitute the group whose culture and institutions have usually been the standard against which other groups' degree of assimilation is measured, English Americans are rarely researched. A recent analysis by the first author using the Google search engine—and using many phrases with "English American" or "Anglo—Saxon American" in them—revealed *no* research articles or books dealing centrally with this group today. In the billions of websites that Google indexes there is no indication of a single recent research study of contemporary English Americans. This extensive neglect of such a powerful ethnic group suggests just how much the English Americans have blended into the sociocultural background of U.S. society.

Some 24.5 million Americans today claim partial or total English ancestry. Those of English descent appear to have some tendency to marry others with similar backgrounds. One older (1988) analysis found that just over half the women with English ancestry had mates who were at least of partial English ancestry.[97]

Residential dispersal has been characteristic of English Americans and other northern European Americans. One study of the New York region found that, by the 1980s, respondents with English ancestry had dispersed throughout the region. Their ancestors had immigrated to the area in the seventeenth and eighteenth centuries, and later descendants had much time to move around. In this study, 95 percent of those with English or Dutch ancestry reported mixed ethnic backgrounds; many had ancestors from several countries. Some 40 to 50 percent of those with British backgrounds said that their ethnic identity had *no importance* to them. Sociologist Richard Alba cautions that this latter response may mean that many have come to see their English or British American identity as synonymous with a "truly American" identity. They may have so completely integrated their English or British identity with their definition of what is American that they see no need to identify assertively with their country of origin. In contrast, more recent immigrant groups (for example, southern European Catholics) were much more likely to identify strongly with their national heritage.[98]

Although English Americans can be viewed for many purposes as a cohesive ethnic group, regional variations in English American culture are still evident. Concepts of liberty brought by the four groups of English immigrants in the 1600s and 1700s evolved in different ways in the colonies. In New England, the Puritans' concept of ordered freedom, which was codified into written laws, "became an instrument of savage persecution." Ordered freedom involved the liberty to impose individual restraints on the Puritans themselves without interference by outsiders, to grant certain exemptions from these restraints to particular individuals, and to practice the "true" religion and persecute dissenters. In Virginia, the idea of hegemonic freedom—the belief that liberty was the birthright of the free-born English and gave those with high status the right to rule people of lower ranks—"permitted and even required the growth of race slavery for its support." In the Delaware Valley, the Quakers' belief in reciprocal freedom, which recognized each individual's right to dissent, caused them to withdraw from the world. In contrast, "the [Appalachian] backcountry belief in natural freedom, which favored minimal government and the supremacy of private interests, sometimes dissolved into cultural anarchy."[99] All those of English descent, however, emphasized the importance of individual freedom as they saw it. All these interpretations can still be found today as different regional variations on the theme of freedom.

David Fischer has analyzed the relationship between regional diversity *today* in the United States and the distinctive colonial cultures of these four groups of English immigrants. Regional differences in homicide rates provide an interesting example. Homicide rates today are low in the areas of New England in which the early Puritans established a tradition of order and nonviolence, and high in the southern areas that were first settled by immigrants from Great Britain's northern borderlands, whose culture was somewhat violence-prone before emigration. Other social indicators examined by Fischer include education, attitudes toward gender equality, and patterns of local government and public life. Those areas with high rates of high school and college graduation today are generally the ones whose colonial culture valued education highly. Those states that failed to ratify the Woman's Suffrage Amendment (1918–1921) and the Equal Rights Amendment (1972–1978) were those in whose colonial culture women had a comparatively low status. Many New England communities today continue the colonial practice of democratic governance by town meetings. Current regional differences in the levels of taxation and public spending are broadly similar to what they were in the colonial period. Significantly, "each of the four cultural regions of British America . . . [has] kept its own customs of enculturation for many generations."[100]

One distinctive region is the South, which was settled substantially by English from the borderlands. The largest white ethnic group in the South today is still Americans of English descent. Sociologist Lewis Killian noted that another important part of the southern white population has descended from early Irish immigrants, those often called the "Scotch-Irish" Protestants (see Chapter 4). There are also large proportions of French, Spanish, or German descent in the South. Killian has argued that English and other British Americans have become mostly submerged in a larger, ethnically diverse white population that has emphasized whiteness above all else: "For a southerner, the salient fact was and is whether he was white or black; all else was secondary."[101]

The theoretical frameworks of assimilation analysts generally take the English (or British) Americans and their culture and institutions as the starting point for the analysis of assimilation in the United States. Gordon's important seven-stage framework (Chapter 2) generally assumes Anglo-conformity as the general trend of adaptation by subsequent immigrant groups in the North American colonies and, later, in the United States.

Looking at the history of English Americans, however, power-conflict theorists would emphasize the ways in which the English colonization process initiated racial and ethnic stratification in the United States. The initial violent subordination or extermination of Native Americans by English colonists is a clear example of *migrant superordination*, which takes place when a migrating group imposes its will on an indigenous group. The entry of later groups of immigrants and their relegation to a subordinate position in the stratification system by that time fully dominated by English Americans, as was the case for enslaved Africans, is an example of *indigenous superordination*. Such concepts acknowledge the social hierarchy, with its unequal power and resources, that developed over the course of U.S. racial and ethnic history.

What are the major consequences of maintaining a Eurocentric culture and institutions?

Summary

This chapter examines one of the most neglected of U.S. ethnic groups, English Americans. The degree to which they now blend into the background of U.S. culture and society often makes it difficult to assess the power, location, and achievements of these early immigrants and their many millions of descendants. Americans of English ancestry still make up a substantial proportion of the U.S. population, and they still tend to share certain values and customs and to marry others of northern European ancestry.

The English were the first to establish major colonies in the area that became the eastern United States. Dominance is the appropriate term for English influence on U.S. religious, economic, and political institutions. The colonization migration of the English created a dominant culture and hierarchical social structure to which subsequent immigrant groups were required to adapt. The study of group assimilation in the United States begins with the English. For centuries, English migrants and their millions of descendants have been disproportionately represented in key social, economic, and political positions in this society.

Between the mid-1800s and the present, English Americans have been joined in their dominant position by certain other European American groups. The result is a more diverse Anglo-Protestant group, but one that still holds disproportionately great power.

The tremendous impact of Anglo-Protestant Americans on U.S. culture and institutions does not mean that substantial segments have not remained working-class or poor. In addition, there have long been very significant regional and denominational differences within English and British American groups. Indeed, Episcopalians still differ from Congregationalists, and southerners differ from New Englanders.

Since World War II, the English and British Protestant dominance has been challenged by Catholic Americans and Jewish Americans with European ancestry as well as by non-European groups. Some analysts have argued that Anglo-Protestant influence is on the wane. Schrag, for instance, argued some time back that "Anglo-Saxon Protestants" were on the road to cultural decline and offered as evidence the increasing non–Anglo-Saxon dominance of music, literature, and art. However, even Schrag presented a different conclusion for the economic sphere: The Anglo-Protestant "elite still controls its own corporate offices, its board rooms, its banks and foundations."[102] Analyses declaring the significant decline of whites of English and British ancestry as a powerful force in many institutions of this society are, as the data above suggest, premature.

Key Terms

English Americans 64
Anglo-Saxon 64
Anglo-Protestants 64
white Anglo-Saxon Protestant Americans 64
nativism 69
social Darwinism 70
Protestant work ethic 74

CHAPTER 4

Irish Americans and Italian Americans

BIG PICTURE QUESTIONS

- ***Why are the neglected experiences of white ethnic immigrants in the United States important?***
- ***What factors have contributed to the incorporation of European immigrant groups into mainstream institutions?***
- ***How have discrimination and related barriers been faced by Irish and Italian Americans?***

The Menace, a Missouri newspaper that reached 1 million in circulation by 1914, was created by editor Wilbur Franklin Phelps. Phelps used the weekly to circulate extreme anti-Catholic ideas, including the contention that the Vatican was pushing politically radical Italian Catholics to immigrate to the United States instead of the allegedly more docile, Americanizing Irish Catholics. Phelps's publication accused the Knights of Columbus of seeking the extermination and mutilation of religious heretics. Fierce anti-Catholicism characterized much popular writing in the mass media of the late nineteenth and early twentieth centuries. These nativists sought to stem the flow of Catholic immigrants to the United States, with Irish and Italian Americans often being the center of their attention.[1]

Numerous discussions of ethnicity have focused on "white ethnics," a term sometimes used for white Catholic and Jewish Americans. White Anglo-Protestant Americans have, on occasion, blamed these groups for societal problems such as urban political machines or urban antiblack racism. They have spoken of white ethnic "hardhats" as though they were uneducated people with a corrupt and authoritarian bent. Not surprisingly, white ethnics have resisted, arguing that hypocritical Anglo-Protestants have little awareness of the historical experiences of Catholic and Jewish Americans with poverty and Anglo-generated discrimination.

IRISH AMERICANS

The purpose of this chapter on Irish and Italian Americans, and the next on Jewish Americans, is to analyze the neglected experiences of some non-English white Americans who have helped to build the United States. Irish Americans are one major group, especially in cities, that comes to mind when white ethnic groups are mentioned.

Irish Immigration: An Overview

Placed on the migration continuum from slave importation to voluntary immigration, the Irish migration to North America falls toward the voluntary end. Even so, this movement was less voluntary than the migrations of other European groups, for economic and political pressures to leave Ireland were often great. More than 200,000 Irish left for the American colonies before 1787; between 1787 and the 1820s, approximately 100,000 migrated.[2] The period of heaviest immigration was between 1841 and 1860, when 1.6 million Irish entered the United States. Migration peaked again in the 1880s and 1890s, then dropped sharply in subsequent decades.[3] For example, in the period 1961–1992, only about 107,000 Irish immigrants entered the United States.[4]

In the 2000 census, more than 30.5 million Americans listed "Irish" as their ancestry. Almost all were born in the United States. They now make up about 11 percent of the U.S. population.[5]

The Eighteenth-Century Migration

The first Irish came in the 1650s, when Captain John Vernon supplied 550 persons from southern Ireland as workers for the English colonists in New England. However, large numbers of Irish did not begin to arrive on North American shores until the 1700s. Both push and pull factors influenced Irish immigration. The image of North America as a land of opportunity was a major pull factor, but domestic pressures were also important. Traditional scholars have held that virtually all Irish immigrants before 1800 were "Scotch-Irish" Protestants from northern Ireland.[6] **"Scotch-Irish"** is a term for certain *immigrants from northern Ireland, some of whose ancestors are said to have immigrated to Ireland from Scotland.* However, Michael O'Brien has cited "unquestionable proof that every part of Ireland contributed to the enormous emigration of its people, and while there are no official statistics now available—for none were kept—to indicate the numerical strength of those Irish immigrants, abundant proof of this assertion is found in authentic records."[7] Many southern Irish immigrants gave up their traditional Catholicism because of the scarcity of Catholic churches in the North American colonies and because of the hostile Protestant environment in many areas of Ireland and the colonies that made open practice of Catholicism difficult.

Because the northern Irish in the first streams of immigration regarded themselves as Irish rather than "Scotch-Irish," the term *Scotch-Irish* was seldom used in the first two centuries of Irish presence in North America. New migrants gave Irish names to their settlements and joined organizations such as the Friendly Sons of Saint Patrick, not Scottish societies. The term *Scotch-Irish* came into heavy use only after 1850, when older Irish Protestant immigrants (and English Americans) sought to distinguish themselves from more recent Irish Catholic immigrants, who were the focus of hostile English American stereotyping and discrimination.[8] By the late nineteenth century, prominent Anglo-American politicians engaged in overt stereotyping when they often praised the members of the "Scotch-Irish race" as exemplary pioneers and democrats while damning the "Catholic Irish race as inferior and lazy."[9]

Early Life

In North America, perhaps half of the early immigrants became indentured servants; others became subsistence farmers or farm workers, often in frontier areas. English Americans treated their Irish Protestant and Catholic servants and other workers as lowly subordinates, to the point of brutality. Faced with anti-Catholic hostility, significant numbers of Irish immigrants gave up Catholicism. Not all converted to Protestantism, however. Pressing for religious tolerance, prominent Irish Catholics wrote President George Washington in the late 1700s asking that the full religious rights of Catholics be protected.[10]

The pull factors motivating millions of Irish Catholics to cross the Atlantic after 1830 were the same as those that have attracted European immigrants for centuries to North America, which was portrayed, in exaggerated terms, as the land of golden opportunity. Push factors loomed larger. The Irish famine of the 1840s spurred emigration. Irish peasants relied heavily on potatoes for food. A potato blight caused a massive failure of that crop, and many people starved and/or died from hunger-related diseases. Ireland produced more than twice enough food to feed its population, but English landlords saw to it that most foodstuffs were exported or consumed by those in Ireland who had money. English leaders advocated emigration to the United States and elsewhere as the solution for the poor Irish.[11]

The Atlantic crossing was often dangerous. Few ships arrived that had not lost a number of their poorly accommodated passengers to starvation or disease. Survivors usually chose urban destinations. New York became a major center, eventually housing more Irish than the Irish city of Dublin. Like most migrants, they went where relatives or fellow villagers settled. Early immigrants often clustered in small, dispersed settlements within cities, unlike the huge segregated communities that were often characteristic of later groups. These Irish settlements were reinforced by a second large group of immigrants from Ireland between 1870 and 1900 and by significant but declining numbers of immigrants from 1900 to 1925.[12]

From the beginning, Irish American women have been crucial to their communities. One distinctive aspect of Irish immigration was the presence of large numbers of young single women. Because they had no hope of inheritance and little hope of marriage in poverty-stricken Ireland, they saw the United States as a land of opportunity. Once here, they usually did not subscribe to the cult of womanhood that emphasized that the woman's place was only in the home. Most did not live lives of sheltered domesticity but rather became self-sufficient individuals with strong work histories outside the home. They made important socioeconomic contributions to the upward mobility of the Irish into the middle class.

For decades, young unmarried women came to the United States to avoid the terrible life that usually awaited them in Ireland. In contrast to male Irish immigrants and female immigrants from many other countries, these women were willing to postpone or forego marriage and to work as domestic servants. Many supported their families in the "old country." Their daughters often became schoolteachers or other white-collar workers. The decisions they made were an expression of life-choice values that persist among Irish Americans today.[13]

Stereotypes

Protestant and Catholic Irish Americans suffered from nativistic English American concerns over their presence and political persuasions. Yet, it was the nineteenth-century Irish, poor Catholics from the famine-ridden Emerald Isle, who were attacked the most frequently.

From the 1820s onward, the Anglo-American stereotype of the Catholic Irish emphasized alleged character faults, such as wickedness and ignorance. With the increase in Irish migration in the late 1840s, words such as *temperamental*, *dangerous*, *quarrelsome*, *idle*, and *reckless*—characteristics emphasizing conduct as much as character—came into use to stereotype the Irish. Anglo-American images of the Irish hardened and became less tolerant as the number of immigrants grew.[14]

Caricatures of Roman Catholic bishops as crocodiles supposedly threaten Protestant children on American shores.

The Ape Image

Irish Catholics were stereotyped in cartoons that used outrageous and hostile symbols—an apelike face, a fighting stance, a jug of whisky, a shillelagh (a wooden club or cudgel). The influential caricaturist Thomas Nast published cartoons of this type in *Harper's Weekly* and other magazines. One of his caricatures showed a stereotyped southern black man and an apelike Irishman, both portrayed as ignorant voters and a threat to orderly politics. The apelike image of the Irish was imported from England to the United States. With the rise of debates over human evolution in England, the Irish poor had been viewed by many in England and the United States as the "missing link" between the gorilla and the human race. With the constant threat of Irish rebellions on the one hand and the press of evolutionary Darwinism on the other, "it was comforting for some Englishmen to believe—on the basis of the best scientific authority in the Anthropological Society of London—that their own facial angles and orthognathous features were as far removed from those of apes, Irishmen, and Negroes as was humanly possible."[15] In rationalizing the exploitation of both the Irish and the Africans, white racist theorists and commentators on both sides of the Atlantic developed dehumanizing animal-like stereotypes.

Sociologist Andrew Greeley underscored the parallels in prejudice and stereotyping for early Irish Americans and for African Americans:

> Practically every accusation that has been made against the American blacks was also made against the Irish: Their family life was inferior, they had no ambition, they did not keep up their homes, they drank too much, they were not responsible, they had no morals, it was not safe to walk through their neighborhoods at night, they voted the way crooked politicians told them to vote, they were not willing to pull themselves up by their bootstraps, they were not capable of education, they could not think for themselves, and they would always remain social problems for the rest of the country.[16]

Changing Attitudes

In the early twentieth century, harsh attitudes toward Irish Americans gradually gave way to acceptance, as nativist hostilities were transferred to newer groups. However, not all negative attitudes disappeared.

As late as 1932, white students at Princeton University were given a list of character traits and asked to identify those they associated with certain groups, including Irish Americans. Five of the ten traits most frequently assigned to Irish Americans—"pugnacious," "quick-tempered," "quarrelsome," "aggressive," and "stubborn"—comprise the traditional stereotype of Irish aggressiveness. Significantly, fifty years later, a similar questionnaire given to a predominantly white sample of Arizona State University students found a significant decrease in negative imagery. Only "quick-tempered" and "stubborn" remained among the top ten traits assigned to the Irish.[17]

In a 1980s nationwide opinion poll that asked respondents whether various immigrant groups had, on balance, been good or bad for this country, Irish Americans received the second-highest percentage of *positive* answers, a little less than English Americans. The reduction in the stereotyping of Irish Americans that appears to have taken place since the 1930s indicates substantial *attitude-receptional assimilation*, to use Gordon's conceptual term. Yet, even today, stereotypes of Irish Americans exist. In a study of white ethnic groups in metropolitan New York, about one-fifth of those with Irish ancestry reported encountering stereotypes of Irish Americans as politicians and police officers, heavy drinkers, or poets. They also encountered the traditional image of Irish women as "long-suffering."[18]

Protest and Conflict

From their first decades, Irish Americans suffered not only verbal abuse and stereotyping but also intentional discrimination and violence from Anglo-Protestants. On occasion, Irish Americans retaliated, sometimes to the point of counterviolence. Irish Americans have also been responsible for starting racial or ethnic conflict. As noted in Chapter 2, intergroup conflict often involves a struggle over resources and can be generated by substantial racial or ethnic group inequality.

Traditional assimilation theorists tend to neglect the substantial conflict characterizing interethnic and interracial relations. Some social science and popular views of U.S. history embody a myth of peaceful progress. According to this assimilationist view, the members of each white ethnic group have ascended the socioeconomic ladder mainly by pulling themselves up by their bootstraps—by hard work, not by active protest and collective violence. This image is incorrect. To secure their "place in the sun," Irish Americans have had to struggle vigorously against many groups, from established Anglo-Protestants (over political-economic issues) to Native Americans (over land). They have been involved in conflict with groups above and below them in the U.S. hierarchy of power and position.

Early Conflict

Irish immigrants' first major conflict was with the established groups that controlled the major institutions in the North American colonies at the time of the initial Irish immigration. A few eighteenth-century Irish settlements were damaged or destroyed by Anglo-Protestant attacks. For example, British Americans attacked and destroyed an Irish community in Worcester, Massachusetts, in the eighteenth century. Catholic and Protestant Irish migrants faced widespread opposition from already-established white groups.[19]

In the colonial period, English Americans considered backcountry Irish Americans to be crude frontier people. Settling in frontier areas, the Irish sometimes defied laws made by English American officials and engaged in aggressive protest against them, as in the Whisky Rebellion and the Regulation movement, to relieve domination and expand their own political power. The Irish were encouraged to settle in frontier areas to protect and shield the dominant Anglo-Protestant interests from indigenous Americans living to the west. The bloody practice of scalping was institutionalized by English and Irish settlers determined to exterminate indigenous Americans. Placing bounties on the scalps of Native Americans became common in numerous colonies.[20]

By 1850 most large cities had seen anti-Catholic demonstrations and riots carried out by Protestants. Philadelphia became a center for anti-Irish violence. There, in 1844, major riots "resulted in the burning of two Catholic churches....the destruction of dozens of Catholic homes; and sixteen deaths."[21] In the 1850s, Anglo-Protestant nativist groups such as the Know-Nothings played a major role in open attacks on Irish Americans.

Conflict with Other Groups

Conflict in mining areas was a major feature of the Irish experience in the nineteenth century. For example, a major coal strike in 1875, the Long Strike, forced many Irish American miners to the brink of starvation. British American owners broke the strike and crushed attempts at unionizing. In response, secret Irish organizations linked to the Ancient Order of the Hibernians (AOH) sometimes resorted to assassination or sabotage. Owners reacted with violence against AOH groups. The Anglo-Protestant establishment engineered the shooting deaths of numerous Irish workers, and the miners replied with armed defense and guerrilla warfare.[22]

In addition to conflict with British Americans, Irish Americans found themselves contending with other groups for land and other economic resources. Irish American Protestant farmers seized Native American lands on the frontier. By the 1840s, Irish competition with and discrimination against black workers in northern cities engendered substantial hostility between the two groups. Between the 1840s and the 1860s, Irish workers attacked black workers in several cities. During the Civil War, Irish hostility toward African Americans increased; the two groups competed for many low-wage jobs in northern cities. Irish opposition to free black workers was partially economic—the fear of job competition from black Americans moving north. Excluded from discriminatory all-white unions, black workers sometimes were used by employers as strikebreakers. The use of black strikebreakers on the waterfront, combined with Irish opposition to the Civil War military draft, helped spur the 1863 Irish riot, usually termed the "Draft Riot"—the most serious riot in U.S. history. An estimated four hundred white rioters were killed in the streets, together with some black residents and some white police officers and soldiers. Irish American rioters attacked "Yankees," the police, and black men, women, and children.[23]

Within a generation or two, Irish Americans—once attacked by Europeans and English Americans as an "inferior race"—had come to see themselves (and be seen) as members of the "white race." As we discussed in Chapter 3, one response of the English American ruling class (political and business leaders) to unrest among these white immigrant farmers and laborers in the nineteenth century was to emphasize racial solidarity with them in what was termed the "superior white race."[24]

Between 1850 and 1890, most Irish Americans came to see themselves as "white" and, as a rule, began to develop the antiblack prejudices and stereotyping shared by other whites. Historical analyses have shown that, among Irish Americans, the movement from sympathy for the oppression of African Americans to their own version of the white-racist framing of society was intentionally fostered by the Anglo-American press, by some Anglo-Protestant and many Roman Catholic religious and community leaders, and especially by Democratic Party organizations.[25]

English Americans grudgingly accepted this change in the racial status of Irish Americans, in part because the Irish had growing political power in cities. David Roediger has underscored this point: "The emphasis on a common whiteness smoothed over divisions in the Democratic ranks within mainly northern cities by emphasizing that immigrants from Europe, and particularly from Ireland, were white and thus unequivocally entitled to equal rights."[26] Some Irish Americans aggressively opposed the racist thinking directed at black Americans, but they were not able to stem the tide.

Irish–black conflict has now persisted for more than a century and a half, especially in large cities. In recent decades, Irish American and other white ethnic groups' concern over modest black gains from government antidiscrimination programs has been a recurring issue. Many white ethnic Americans have felt that African Americans have received a disproportionate share of government attention and benefits, compared with what urban white ethnics have received. However, the evidence in this and later chapters shows that this notion is inaccurate.

What were some important factors that contributed to conflicts between new immigrant groups and existing racial-ethnic groups?

Politics and Political Institutions

When the Irish began arriving in the seventeenth century, much of the political framework of the colonies had already been fashioned by the English. However, the Irish immigrants who came in the eighteenth century did play a role in shaping the new nation's institutions. Eight of the fifty-six signers of the Declaration of Independence were Irish immigrants.

Seven Irish Americans were members of the Constitutional Convention, and at least four were members of the first U.S. Congress.[27]

Political Organization in the Cities

Most Irish who immigrated after the Revolutionary War settled in eastern cities, where they frequently became involved in urban politics. Discussions of urban politics have often focused on Irish Catholics and their "political bosses and machines." Indeed, the theme of corrupt urban machines has been tied to hostile views of Catholic immigrants. Many such analyses have characterized Irish Americans as being more corrupt in their political activities than other groups. In fact, Irish immigrants entered an urban political system that already included serious corruption. Anglo-Protestant political machines—by which those in power secured for their poor constituents jobs, housing, and food—already ruled in numerous cities before there were sizable Irish communities.

Urban politics was one means to upward socioeconomic mobility for Irish Americans, a way to achieve economic and political power in the face of Anglo-Protestant opposition. In the nineteenth and early twentieth centuries, the dominant perspective on government tended toward a conservative hands-off view. Against this do-nothing background, desperate urban Irish residents, plagued by unemployment, low incomes, and poor housing, joined large political organizations. Taking control of local party organizations, immigrant leaders shaped government programs to benefit their poor. Providing jobs was one of the political machines' critical functions.[28]

One of the first political machines was New York City's Tammany Society. In 1817, a group of Irish Americans, incensed at discrimination at the hands of this Anglo-Protestant machine, broke into one of its meetings and demanded the nomination of an Irish American for Congress. Although they were driven away that time, a few decades later Irish Americans were able to take over two New York political organizations, including Tammany Hall.

One Tammany Hall figure, William M. ("Boss") Tweed, has long been singled out by critics who have claimed that he was uniquely greedy and politically corrupt. In reality, Tweed was an urban leader who represented the underdog, including Irish and Jewish Americans, in nineteenth-century New York. He was tolerant of various religious beliefs, family-oriented, and ambitious. He identified with New York's poor immigrants and worked to build schools and hospitals. He was attacked by the Anglo-Protestant elite because of his identification with the poor.[29]

With the election of New York City's first Irish Catholic mayor in the 1880s, William Grace, Irish Americans began to play a major role in city politics. They held many elective posts and gained heavy representation in appointed positions. In vigorous competition with English and other British Americans, the Irish gradually won a place in the political sun in numerous east coast cities. By the 1960s these Irish political organizations were mostly gone, except in Chicago, where the paramount Irish "boss," Mayor Richard J. Daley, maintained enormous power into the 1970s. By the 1980s, Daley was dead, and Chicago's Irish-dominated political machine was weakening. However, in 1989 Richard M. Daley, son of the former mayor, was elected mayor and was still in office as of 2007. Today, Irish Catholic Americans hold many local and state political offices.[30]

Pragmatism in Politics

For most Irish Americans, politics is an honorable profession. In local politics, Irish Americans have often developed a pragmatic political style based on concern for individuals and loyalty to leaders. Indeed, pragmatic politics, with its themes of coalition and compromise, is a major Irish contribution to U.S. politics. In this framework, the political machine functions as a broker to balance the interests of the city's mosaic of racial and ethnic groups so that a coalition can hang together. Irish political leaders have pressed periodically for racially and ethnically balanced tickets, which have contributed to urban coalition building. Irish American political organizations have made major contributions to the bricks-and-mortar development of cities. Irish contractors associated with city political machines helped to meet the then-pressing needs for public buildings, streets, and subways in many cities.[31]

With suburbanization and intermarriage this Irish political style has begun to fade, but it has by no means disappeared. One study of fifty-one cities found that those with large Irish populations were more likely than other cities to have a government (often Irish-dominated) that provided a high level of public services for residents. These Irish-populated cities were more responsive to poor residents than other cities. Some analysts have attempted to link the upward mobility of Irish Americans to a growing "conservatism," noting that in the 1960s and 1970s Irish American electorates in areas such as New York and Connecticut preferred more conservative political candidates in mayoral, gubernatorial, and senatorial races. In many areas, however, Irish Americans have continued to vote for liberal and moderate Democrats in local and state races.[32]

National and International Politics

One study of the period between 1901 and 1910 found that 13 percent of 162 prominent political leaders, including presidents, senators, representatives, and Supreme Court justices, were Irish American (generally Protestants), compared with 56 percent who were of English or Welsh descent.[33] Irish Catholic influence at the national level was weak. Andrew Jackson, a slaveholder from Tennessee who served as president from 1829 to 1837, was the country's first Irish American president and the only one both of whose parents were immigrants. Woodrow Wilson, a "Scotch-Irish" Protestant from New Jersey, was president from 1913 to 1921. However, Wilson was not sympathetic to Irish Catholic causes and did not support the Irish struggle against English domination. More recently, at a precedent-setting 1994 Saint Patrick's Day White House dinner, which was attended by prominent Irish American industrialists, academics, and politicians, Ireland's prime minister presented President Bill Clinton with a genealogy of Clinton's Irish ancestors. Clinton had shown much concern with political conflict in Northern Ireland.[34]

In recent decades the issue of an independent, united Ireland has generated substantial financial and political support among Irish Americans. In the 1980s, Irish Republican Army (IRA) member Joe Doherty became a rallying point for Irish American opposition to British rule of Northern Ireland. From an Irish prison, Doherty wrote a popular column in the New York newspaper *Irish People* supporting the IRA's cause, and he received visits from more than one hundred members of the U.S. Congress, as well as from New York's Cardinal, in support of his request for political asylum. In 1992, following the Supreme Court's decision to deny Doherty refugee status, his supporters protested on a Manhattan street corner named in his honor.[35]

Irish American support for the Catholic Irish cause in Northern Ireland has created political tensions in the United States. Some non-Irish politicians have criticized Irish American support of the Catholic struggle in Northern Ireland and U.S. efforts to broker peace between the British government and Sinn Féin, the political arm of the IRA. Several times in the 1990s, Gerry Adams, the head of Sinn Féin, was granted a visa to visit the United States—first to participate in a conference on Northern Ireland, then to meet with U.S. government officials following his announcement of an IRA cease-fire in Northern Ireland, and again later to meet with President Bill Clinton.[36]

Many observers feel that Irish American political leaders' peace negotiation efforts and President Clinton's decision to lift a twenty-year ban on official U.S. contacts with Sinn Féin played a significant and positive role in encouraging the recent peace agreements in Northern Ireland. By the early 2000s republican and nationalist Sinn Féin had elected two dozen members to the Northern Ireland Assembly. As of spring 2007, Sinn Féin had agreed with the Democratic Unionist Party to share political power in Northern Ireland. Irish Americans have continued to be oriented to the politics of Northern Ireland. The controversy over Northern Ireland's future and possible independence from Britain not only illustrates an intergroup struggle (between Catholics and Protestants in Ireland) that continues to the present but also demonstrates how events in the country of origin of one U.S. population group can long affect ethnic relations in the United States. This theme will reappear regularly in this book—as, for example, in the effects of events in Italy on Italian Americans and in Japan on Japanese Americans. World politics remains an important larger context influencing interethnic and interracial relations in the United States.

The Only Irish Catholic President

Alfred E. Smith, the Democratic candidate for president in 1928, was the first Irish Catholic to carve out an important role in presidential politics. Yet, his Catholic religion counted against him in this first

The only Catholic (Irish) President in U.S. history, John F. Kennedy, takes the oath of office.

Irish Catholic presidential campaign.[37] Not until 1960, more than three hundred years after the first few Irish Catholics had come to the United States and more than a century after sizable Irish Catholic communities had been established, was the first and only Irish Catholic (also only Catholic) president elected. Six of the thirty-six presidents, from Washington to Nixon, had Irish American backgrounds, but except for John Kennedy all of these were Protestant Irish, as were the more recent presidents, Ronald Reagan and Bill Clinton.

In the 1960 presidential election, Irish Catholic votes in New England, New York, and Pennsylvania helped to create John Kennedy's narrow victory. As president, Kennedy acted not only on behalf of Irish Americans but also, to some extent, on behalf of America's other emergent urban political groups. Thus, Kennedy appointed the first Italian American and the first Polish American to a presidential cabinet and the first African American to head an independent government agency.[38]

The Irish in the Economy

One type of structural assimilation involves large-scale movement by members of an immigrant group into the secondary organizational levels of a society, such as into positions in government agencies and private economic organizations, including farms and factories. The majority of Irish immigrants started out at the bottom of the economic pyramid, filling the hard, often dirty, low-wage jobs in rural areas and cities. As with other immigrant groups, Irish immigrants found jobs through preexisting ethnic networks. "The process was cloaked in favoritism and operated quite independently of qualifications. The result can be called 'ethnic mobility, collective style.'"[39]

Irish labor was critical to industrial and commercial development in the United States. Irish immigrants after 1830 typically became urban workers, miners, or transportation workers. They migrated looking for work. Irish men found it in unskilled jobs, on the docks and in the factories of large cities; Irish women found it as servants, usually in Anglo-Protestant homes. Many Irish immigrants were single females unattached to family groups. Impoverished, these women frequently moved into live-in domestic work. In contrast, Jewish and Italian women immigrants generally came with families. Irish women who came alone did so not by choice but because of adverse economic conditions in Ireland.[40]

Male immigrants became farm laborers, railroad laborers, miners, and textile workers. Many died helping to build transportation systems, as the old saying, "There's an Irishman buried under every railroad tie," indicates. Irish Catholics encountered direct institutionalized discrimination in employment. Stereotyped as dumb, unskilled, or rowdy, Irish American men and women were often denied well-paid jobs by employers. Few would hire them except for unskilled positions. By the 1840s, Boston newspapers were carrying anti-Irish advertisements with the phrase, "None need apply but Americans."[41]

Upward Mobility

Significant numbers of Irish Catholics became upwardly mobile by the turn of the twentieth century. They entered the urban economy when expanding industries needed large numbers of low-wage workers. Major cities developed as Anglo-American capitalists centered new types of manufacturing in the industrial heartland, from Pittsburgh to Chicago to Detroit. Urban political machines facilitated mobility by providing jobs and other resources for the upward trek. Urban machines channeled money into building projects, facilitating the emergence of a business class. Irish Americans were important in labor organizations in Massachusetts and New York by the 1850s. By the early 1900s unions had become important for Irish dockworkers, construction workers, and miners. To the present day, Irish Americans have been prominent in labor organizations, including the AFL-CIO.[42]

Mobility among Irish Americans after 1900 suggests increasing economic security for a growing segment. The mostly Protestant descendants of pre-1830 immigrants were still disproportionately concentrated in farming areas, towns, and southern and border states. In the late nineteenth and early twentieth centuries, and probably in later decades, a significant proportion became relatively prosperous farmers, owners of small businesses, and skilled blue-collar workers, as well as part of many white-collar categories. Over time, many more or less blended into the Anglo-Protestant mainstream. By the 1930s, however, Irish Catholics had not yet blended fully into the Anglo-Protestant mainstream. A study of Newburyport found Irish Americans moving closer to native-born Yankee residents in socioeconomic status, yet no Irish could be found at the top. In addition, the Depression of the 1930s postponed for a decade a major economic breakthrough.[43]

Recent Successes

In recent decades many Irish Catholics have been employed in government jobs, such as in police, fire, and public works departments; in the courts; and in schools and colleges. In seeking government jobs, like other groups after them (for example, African Americans), they often faced less discrimination in government than in the business sector. By the 1970s, two-thirds of younger Irish Catholic men held white-collar positions, compared with 38 percent of their fathers. Both generations were more likely to be found in better-paid, white-collar jobs than their counterparts in most other ethnic Catholic groups. The occupational distribution for Irish Americans now roughly parallels that of the total white population. Moreover, as Table 4.1 shows, the median income of Irish American families ($58,594) is now well above that of the total population and is only a little lower than that of English Americans (see Chapter 3). The percent poor in the Irish American population is higher than for English Americans, at 6.7 percent, but substantially lower than that for the U.S. population. (Note that these data include people who report sole or partial Irish ancestry.)[44]

Today, Irish Americans hold positions of leadership in all areas of U.S. life. Mass media symbols of Irish American success have typically been athletes, entertainers, politicians, or, less often, entrepreneurs such as Joseph Kennedy, John Kennedy's influential father. Another group of Irish American heroes has received little notice—the growing group of Ph.D.s and academics. Catholics make up a significant percentage of faculty members in top state colleges and universities, and perhaps half of these are Irish. In addition, many graduate-trained Irish Catholics continue to move into local, state, and federal government as lawyers, administrators, researchers, and elected officials.[45]

Education

Organized education on a significant scale for Irish Protestants began after the Civil War. In the South, public schools spread during the often progressive Reconstruction period, and by the early twentieth

TABLE 4.1 People with Irish Ancestry: Selected Population Characteristics (2000 Census)

	People with Irish Ancestry	Total U.S. Population
Number	30,528, 470	281,421,906
Median age (years)	37	35
Foreign born	0.9%	11%
Percent female	52.5%	51%
High school degree or greater (25 years old and over)	90%	80%
Having at least a college degree (25 years old and over)	30%	24%
Median family Income in 1999	$58,594	$50,046
Percent below poverty line	6.7%	12%

century many of the Protestant Irish had taken advantage of them. The Catholic Irish, in contrast, relied on parochial and public schools in urban areas of the North for organized education. In part, because of the often severe anti-Catholicism, parochial schools did not become numerous until the period between 1820 and 1840. By the late 1800s and early 1900s a parish and parochial school system had become the center of the Irish Catholic community in numerous cities.[46]

By the 1960s the nearly 13,000 elementary and secondary Catholic schools had an enrollment of 5 million children. Irish Catholic Americans were at the center of this immense network. Gradually too, these parochial schools have come to receive significant government aid—aid that, like that for other religious groups, has periodically raised the issue of the separation of church and state. By 1910, Irish Catholics were enrolled in college in large numbers, above the national average for all whites. Educational achievements of Irish Catholics were increasingly impressive. Significant numbers of Catholic colleges were established, and college attendance continued to increase.[47]

Today, Irish Americans continue to place emphasis on education. As the 2000 census data in Table 4.1 show, educational attainment for of Irish Americans as a group is well above that of the U.S. population as a whole. Some 90 percent of those 25 years old or older have at least a high school diploma, and about 30 percent have at least a college degree. Older data indicate that the educational attainments of both Irish American Catholics and Protestants are increasing relative to the general white population.[48]

In the past decade a number of Irish American leaders have pressed for more coverage of Irish and Irish American history in U.S. schools and colleges. One California state senator of Irish heritage proposed a bill that would reshape the educational curriculum so that children in the diverse state of California could learn about the horrendous potato famines we discussed earlier. Similar efforts to change the educational curriculum to include more Irish history have been made in other states.[49]

Religion

In the political and economic spheres, Irish Americans were pressured early to assimilate to the established Anglo-Protestant culture. In the religious sphere, the earliest Irish immigrants, whether Catholic or Presbyterian, mostly blended into various Protestant denominations. However, later groups of Irish Catholic immigrants played a major role in establishing what may be the most influential non-Protestant institution in the United States—the Roman Catholic church. Although the Catholic church has had to adapt to some extent to the preexisting Protestant religious system, its growing strength has served to reinforce the right of all Americans to choose any faith. Indeed, the large migrations of Irish, other European, and Latin American Catholics to the United States have helped to make this country probably the most religiously diverse on earth.

Initially, Irish Catholics had to fight intense anti-Catholic prejudice and sometimes violent discrimination designed to prevent the Catholic church from taking root in Anglo-Protestant soil. Still, new churches sprang up wherever Catholic workers lived. The U.S. Catholic church's hierarchy has long been disproportionately composed of Irish Americans. One analysis of Catholic bishops from 1789 to 1935 revealed that 58 percent were of Irish extraction. In the early 2000s Irish Americans still account for a disproportionate number of Catholic priests but no longer generate a disproportionate number of Catholic bishops.[50]

In northern cities, many Irish neighborhoods were built around a parish church, and local politics was often blended with church and school. However, over recent decades, many central city churches have been closed or merged, as Irish Americans have moved to suburbs. Today, the Irish Catholic parish survives in the suburbs of many cities. Loyalty to the church remains strong; one 1990s survey found that more than half of Irish Catholics go to services every week, a higher proportion than for other whites.[51]

Irish American priests have shaped the U.S. Catholic church in a number of distinctive ways. Irish American archbishops and cardinals have often been politically and socially conservative, while many local Catholic priests have helped to lead progressive struggles, such as the struggle for expanded civil rights. For example, the former president of Notre Dame University and Congressional Gold Medal winner, Father Theodore M. Hesburgh, symbolizes the liberalism in Irish Catholicism. For many years, including those spent on the U.S. Commission on Civil Rights, Hesburgh was outspoken in his support for civil rights laws, antisegregation action, and affirmative action to benefit African Americans and other Americans of color.[52]

Assimilation Theories and the Irish

As we saw in Table 4.1, there are now about 30.5 million Americans with Irish ancestry, more than one-tenth of that U.S. population. Irish Americans are one of the largest U.S. racial-ethnic groups. As can also be seen in Table 4.1, they are roughly similar as a group in median age and percent female to the U.S. population as a whole, but they are much less likely to be foreign-born.

Let us now examine how the theories and concepts in Chapter 2 help to illuminate the experiences of Irish Americans. Some power-conflict analysts specifically omit immigrant groups such as "white ethnics" like the Irish Americans from their analyses, preferring to focus on racially subordinated groups because these have generally endured much greater violence and repression and for much longer. The assimilation theories of Milton Gordon and Andrew Greeley seem most relevant for analysis of groups such as Irish and Italian Americans. However, we should keep in mind something many assimilationists tend to forget—the substantial conflict and discrimination that has characterized the experiences of these ethnic Americans.

Each generation of Irish Americans has become ever more incorporated into the core institutions than previous generations. The eighteenth-century Irish, typically Protestants, moved up the socioeconomic ladders slowly. Substantial assimilation came by the late nineteenth century for many of their descendants. By the early 1900s the successful assimilation of these mostly Protestant Irish was considered a standard for subsequent immigrant groups to emulate.[53]

Cultural assimilation (acculturation) came relatively rapidly for early Irish immigrants and their descendants. And assimilation came slowly but surely at the level of structural integration into the economy and the polity and gradually at the level of primary social ties with the Anglo-American group. Sometime in the past century, many Protestant Irish became a difficult-to-distinguish part of the white Protestant mainstream.

Assimilation came more slowly for Irish Catholics who immigrated after 1830. Some adaptation to the dominant Anglo-Protestant culture, particularly learning the English language and the core culture's basic views and values, is necessary to successful achievements within mainstream institutions. Significantly, Ireland's customs and U.S. customs had similarities. The English language was familiar to many immigrants. Although assimilation at other levels took several generations, significant cultural assimilation usually took place in the first decade or so.[54]

Religion was an exception. Most Irish Catholic immigrants did not become Protestants. Conflict with the Anglo-Protestant nativists intensified Irish commitment to the Catholic church. Still, Catholic churches made adjustments to the English-dominated milieu in such areas as language and restructured their church organizations. Such adaptations made the U.S. Catholic church and school system an important medium within which new Catholic immigrants began their acculturation and some structural assimilation (for example, priests helped immigrants secure jobs).[55]

Has commitment to the Catholic religion declined in later generations of Irish American Catholics? Some analysts have claimed this, arguing that cultural assimilation will thus soon be complete. One Catholic scholar recently did a modest survey of Irish Americans and found that a substantial majority felt that their Irish heritage was more significant to them than their Catholic religion. (Indeed, certain persisting Irish religious customs, such as large wakes and funerals in commemoration of those who have died, are probably rooted in Celtic Irish roots as much as in the Catholicism that came to Ireland later in its history.) Still, some social science studies over the last few decades have not found a decline in Catholic religious commitment. As a group, Irish Americans have been among the most likely to attend mass of all Catholic groups.[56]

Since the mid-nineteenth century the Catholic Irish have experienced substantial changes in the dimensions of assimilation that Gordon calls behavior-receptional assimilation and attitude-receptional assimilation—in effect, discrimination and prejudice. Stereotyping has declined substantially since the days when the apelike image was commonplace, although negative feelings directed against Irish Catholicism have persisted among some Protestant Americans. Anti-Catholic discrimination has also declined significantly, although it still can sometimes be seen at the very highest levels of the U.S. economy and government.

Patterns of Structural Assimilation

At the structural-assimilation (secondary-group) level, Irish Americans made slow but significant movement, over several generations, into Anglo-Protestant organizations and institutions. We have seen the steady movement of the Irish from unskilled work into white-collar occupations—and the relatively high occupational levels of Irish American Catholics in recent decades. Residential dispersal, often to suburban areas, has paralleled these developments, although some residential self-segregation persists in some cities in the East and Midwest. After a century of struggle in the political sphere, Irish Catholics are now substantially integrated at the local and state government levels; in the past few decades, they have moved significantly into the judicial, legislative, and executive branches of the federal government, although they are not yet present in significant numbers at the very top of the political system.

Some have argued that the higher status that accompanies economic assimilation is causing many Irish Americans to move away from the Democratic Party. Urban politicians, particularly Democrats, have long given much attention to the Irish American community, and numerous Democratic Party leaders are still Irish. One research analysis found that 61 percent of Irish Catholics and 54 percent of Irish Protestants identified themselves as Democrats. These percentages question the accuracy of one assimilation theory of ethnic politics—that economic mobility destroys traditional ethnic voting patterns. As of the early 2000s, absorption into a Republican Party dominated by white Protestants has not happened for the majority of Irish American Catholics.[57]

As for structural incorporation at the level of primary-group ties, data on informal groups and voluntary associations point to some interesting trends. Since World War II, ethnic clubs and organizations have declined in importance for Irish Catholics. This probably indicates increasing integration into the voluntary associations of the larger white society. Irish American attendance at Catholic parochial schools has also declined.[58]

Intermarriage—*marriage between members of different racial or ethnic groups*—can be a major indicator of substantial assimilation at the primary-group level. One national survey in the 1960s reported substantial **endogamy**—*marriage within one's racial or ethnic group*—for Irish Catholics; 65 percent of respondents who had Irish fathers also had Irish mothers, and 43 percent of Irish married men had a wife with an Irish father. However, more than half the respondents to that national survey had a non-Irish spouse. One more recent survey of a large metropolitan area in New York found that 82 percent of Irish Americans were of mixed ethnic ancestry.

And in the late 1990s, one commentator estimated that at least two-thirds of Irish Americans were then marrying outside the group.[59]

Is There an Irish American Identity Today?

The intermarriage rate poses challenges to continuing Irish American identity. Among the final stages of assimilation is what Milton Gordon and Andrew Greeley have seen as "identificational" adaptation. Ultimately, this type of assimilation would mean a loss of a sense of "Irishness" and the development of a sense of "peoplehood" that is solely American or Anglo-Protestant American. One's sense of identity would no longer be Irish. This may have happened for many Irish Protestants, but the majority of Irish Catholics still have some sense of Irishness, however vague.

Some analysts argue that Irish Americans are losing their ethnic identity because of the decline in immigration from Ireland. For example, Marjorie Fallows has argued that the American Irish are fully acculturated to the Anglo-Protestant culture. In her view, distinctive ethnic traits that are culturally significant are rare among American Irish today. Even though there are still a few ethnically distinct Irish Catholic communities in northern cities, most Irish Catholics do not live in these communities. From this viewpoint, cultural and structural (primary-group) assimilation are all but complete for those Irish Catholics who live outside ethnic neighborhoods.[60]

Richard Alba interviewed respondents in eight white ethnic groups in a metropolitan area in upper New York State. He found a decline in the significance of ethnic identity among Irish Americans, especially in the fourth and later generations. However, those with pure Irish ancestry had a stronger sense of their ethnic identity than most of the other groups examined. Those with mixed Irish ancestry were also loyal to their Irish heritage. They were three times as likely to identify solely as Irish as they were to choose another ethnicity from their mixed background.[61]

Certainly, the Irish Catholic group has changed over generations of contact with the public school system and the mass media, but it has retained enough distinctiveness to persist as an ethnic group into the first decade of the twenty-first century. The theory of ethnogenesis discussed in Chapter 2 seems appropriate to Irish Catholic Americans. Over several generations, the large numbers of Irish who came after 1830 and their descendants forged a distinctive U.S. ethnic group. Ethnicity was an important way for the Irish Catholics to assert their own identity in a buzzing confusion of diverse nationality groups. Because of nativistic attacks and discrimination, ethnic identity was less voluntary for Irish Catholics in the first few decades than it was to become later. The Irish immigrants' cultural heritage was distinctly different from that of the British American host culture. Over several generations of sometimes hostile interaction with Anglo-Protestants, the Irish immigrants and their descendants adapted substantially to the host society. This process created a distinctive Irish American ethnic group that reflects elements of its nationality background and also much of the host culture.

In an analysis of opinion-poll data, Greeley examined survey questions that tap what he views as traditional Irish Catholic sociocultural traits: gregariousness, gathering in a public house, religious intensity, and activity in religious organizations. Greeley concluded that Irish Catholic distinctiveness persists, particularly in certain northern cities. He even found some evidence of a return to higher levels of self-conscious identification among young Irish Americans.[62] Other reports have also indicated a resurgence of interest in things Irish. One late-1990s survey reported a growing interest in studying the Irish language (Gaelic), Irish dance, and Irish music among Irish Americans. And we should note the pressures being placed on public schools to include more Irish and Irish American history. At least twenty-nine colleges and universities have developed some type of research and teaching program in Irish studies, usually as part of humanities departments; at least seven important universities have major Irish research programs. Today, the impact of the Irish background on Irish American thought and behavior remains strong.[63]

How would you apply assimilation theory to the experiences of Irish Americans?

Italian Americans

For many decades Italian Americans have been targets of hostility from other racial and ethnic groups, especially Anglo-Protestants. This mostly Catholic group has been attacked for being unsophisticated, superpatriotic "hardhats" with connections to the "Mafia." Many prominent writers, including Henry James and Arthur Miller, have written of the alleged criminality of Italians or Italian Americans as groups. By the 1960s, a counterattack had developed. Many white ethnic leaders, including Italian Americans, came to view Anglo-Protestant intellectuals and officials very critically and spoke out openly against such ethnic stereotyping.

The strong defense of things Italian and the achievements of Italian Americans had, by the 2000s, brought this group greater acceptance among other Americans. The rising prominence of Italian Americans in the United States can be seen in the selection of Geraldine Ferraro, an Italian American member of Congress, as the Democratic Party's first female vice-presidential candidate (in 1984) and in the substantial national support for New York Governor Mario Cuomo as a possible Democratic presidential nominee during the 1990s.

Italian Immigration

Italian explorers, including Cristoforo Colombo (Christopher Columbus), played a major role in opening the Americas to European colonization and exploitation. An Italian navigator, Amerigo Vespucci, made a number of voyages to the Americas shortly after Colombo's voyages. Because of his early maps, the continents came to be named after him.[64]

Many Immigrants

Since 1820, more than 5 million Italians have migrated to the United States. Very small numbers migrated to the North American colonies and the United States before the mid-1880s. Between 1880 and 1920, Italian immigration was heavy, with more than 4 million recorded immigrants. Before 1880, the relatively modest numbers of immigrants were from northern Italy. After 1880, very large numbers, mostly poor farmers and laborers, came from southern Italy. Most Italian Americans today are descendants of this southern migration.[65]

As we saw in Chapter 2, certain factors are relevant to the study of migration: the point of origin, the destination, the migrating units, and the larger context. As with the Irish, land and agricultural problems triggered much of the Italian outmigration. National unification under a government controlled by northern Italians had brought heavy taxes to southern Italy. Low income, poor soil, a feudal land system, unreasonable taxes, and government corruption were important push factors at the point of origin. The often exaggerated image of the United States as a place of expanding opportunity was a major pull factor. Some came to stay, but the majority of the early immigrants saw the United States as a temporary workplace.[66]

Migration along kinship networks, typical for poor and working-class migrants from European countries, lessened the pain of resettlement. Italians often came in groups from the same villages. Industrialized east coast cities were popular destinations. In the larger cities, many immigrants settled in **ethnic enclaves**—*residential, social, and economic niches*—that were frequently called "Little Italies," where fellow villagers already resided. Remigration for Italians was well above that of other groups. In some years in the early 1900s, returnees to Italy equaled 60 to 70 percent of new immigrants.[67]

Nativist agitation by Anglo-Protestant groups resulted in legislative attempts to restrict this southern European immigration. Between 1924 and 1965, nativist-motivated immigration quotas sharply curtailed Italian immigration. The Immigration Act of 1924 established a small discriminatory quota for Italians. By 1929 the annual quota for Italians was only 5802, compared with 65,721 for British immigrants. The quota system was based on nativists' belief that those countries that had furnished the most "good American citizens"—that is, Protestant immigrants prior to 1890—should receive the largest quotas. The British, Germans, Irish, and Scandinavians were given three-fourths of the total, although the demand from those countries had slackened considerably by that time.[68]

Pressure on Italy's small quota produced a backlog of 250,000 applicants by the time the 1965 Immigration Act replaced the discriminatory national-origin quota system. Gradually, by the late 1970s, that backlog was exhausted, and since that time the annual number of Italian immigrants has dropped sharply. More than 11 million Americans listed Italian as their first ancestry in the 1990 census; most of these were U.S.-born. Counting both the first and second ancestries listed by respondents in the 2000 census supplementary survey, the Census Bureau estimated that there were 15.7 million Italian

Americans in 2000, making them one of the largest European ancestry groups in the United States.[69]

Life for the Immigrants

What was life like for the large numbers of Italians who immigrated in the peak period between 1880 and 1920? Most worked as unskilled laborers, often on transportation systems such as canals and railroads and on water and sewer systems. Pay was low, and individuals as well as families were usually poor. They were often segregated in "Little Italy" areas within cities. Italian Americans often replaced earlier immigrant groups in inner-city areas of large cities, as part of a residential invasion-succession process. Yet other immigrant groups would follow on their heels.[70]

Some analysts have viewed working-class communities in cities as disorganized "slum" areas with little positive social life. This was not true for Italian American communities. As with the Irish before them, Italians developed their own extensive friendship and kinship circles, numerous political clubs, important avenues for upward mobility, and commonplace community celebrations. Festivals and indigenous organizations, including mutual-benefit societies whose members made monthly payments to ensure a proper funeral upon their demise, were central to Italian American communities.[71]

Stereotypes

By the end of the nineteenth century, nativist stereotypes of the "apelike" Irish were giving way to negative stereotypes of southern and eastern European immigrants, especially those who were Catholics or Jews. The Italian stereotypes were especially harsh and often racialized. Italian immigrants were regularly seen as an "inferior race" and scorned by white nativists as "dangerous, contemptible, inferior, and disloyal"—the "off-scourings of the world."[72]

Popular writers, scholars, and members of Congress warned of the peril of allowing these "inferior" racial-ethnic stocks from Europe into the United States. For example, Kenneth Roberts, a prominent journalist, expressed a common fear that the newer immigrants would make Americans a *mongrel* race: "The American nation was founded and developed by the Nordic race, but if a few more million members of the Alpine, Mediterranean and Semitic races are poured among us, the result must inevitably be a hybrid race of people as worthless and futile as the good-for-nothing mongrels of Central America and southeastern Europe."[73] Nativist writers of northern European origin included Italians and European Jews when they spoke of "Alpine, Mediterranean, and Semitic races."

Yet, in spite of these vicious attacks, Italian Americans were usually treated by various governments as "white." Unlike African Americans, they could vote, serve on juries, and intermarry with other European Americans. They had a paradoxical status and were pressured to become ever more acculturated to the white northern European core culture.[74]

Stereotypes of Inferiority in Intelligence

In the first three decades of the twentieth century, Anglo-Protestant stereotypes of southern and eastern European immigrants' intellectual inferiority were based in part on misreadings of the results of the new psychological tests that were often inaccurately labeled intelligence quotient or **IQ tests**. The term *intelligence quotient (IQ) test* is inaccurate because the tests measure only selected, learned verbal and quantitative skills, not a broad or basic intelligence. In 1912 the U.S. analyst Henry Goddard gave the European researcher Alfred Binet's diagnostic test and related tests to a large number of immigrants from southern and eastern Europe. His data supposedly showed that 83 percent of Jewish and 79 percent of Italian immigrants were "feeble-minded," a category naively defined in terms of low scores on the new English-language tests. During World War I prominent U.S. psychologists developed verbal and performance tests for large-scale testing of wartime draftees. Detailed analyses, published in the 1920s, gained public attention because of the racial-inferiority interpretation many British American psychologists placed on the test scores of the southern and eastern European immigrants among the draftees.[75]

In 1923 Carl Brigham, a Princeton psychologist who later played a major role in developing college entrance tests, argued for the intellectual inferiority of these (white) immigrant groups, including Italian Americans, drawing on data from the Army tests. The average scores for foreign-born draftees ranged from highs of 14.87 for English and 14.34 for Scottish draftees, to an average of 13.77 for all white draftees, to lows of 10.74 for Polish and 11.01 for Italian draftees. The relatively low test scores for groups such as Italian Americans were boldly explained in aggressively *racial* terms; those low-scoring groups were considered not only unintelligent but also "inferior racial stocks." Psychologists such as Brigham used these results to support the ideology of "Nordic" superiority that was being espoused by overtly racist theorists. Brigham and others argued that the sharp increase in southern and eastern European immigration had lowered the general level of American intelligence.[76]

The political implications of these tests were soon proclaimed: Immigration limits were necessary, and political means (immigration barriers and even government-ordered, forced sterilization) should be developed to prevent the continued propagation of these "defective strains" in the population.[77] Here was *pseudoscientific* support for such government action as the passage of the racist 1924 Immigration Act, which would soon severely restrict southern European immigration.

The U.S. government itself played an important role in the stereotyping of Italian immigrants, a point that Omi and Winant underscore in their racial formation theory (see Chapter 2). Psychologists working with government agencies helped to generate the official view of these European immigrants as undesirable racial-ethnic groups, and Congress used their research to support racist arguments against southern and eastern European immigration.

The "intelligence" differences measured by the usually brief psychological tests were assumed to reflect the inferior or superior genetic background of the European "racial" stocks. In the early decades of the twentieth century, few analysts and political leaders seriously considered the possibility that the linguistic (English), cultural (northern European American), and educational bias in the tests and in the psychologists' interpretive procedures could account for the "racial" differences.[78]

Immigrant leaders developed aggressive strategies for dealing with concern over "racial" lineage. One prominent Italian American leader, Fiorello La Guardia, suffered personal attacks that incorporated stereotypes. For his criticism of officials such as President Herbert Hoover he received letters such as the following: "You should go back where you belong and advise Mussolini how to make good honest citizens in Italy. The Italians are preponderantly our murderers and boot-leggers."[79] It is striking that even today, as one scholar has put it, "In TV shows, advertisements, children's cartoons, and even some university programs emphasizing cultural diversity, that bias [stereotypes of ignorance or criminality] persists despite the Italian-American intellectual foundation on the grandeur of Dante, the stateliness of Virgil, the experimentation of Pirandello, and the metaphysical complexity of Petrarch and the Troubadours," not to mention the art of Michelangelo and Da Vinci.[80]

Ethnic slurs and epithets, including *dago*, *wop*, and *guinea*, that have often been hurled at Italian Americans reveal the intensity of anti-Italian hostility. *Dago*, a corruption of the Spanish name Diego, was originally used for Spaniards or Mexicans. After 1880, however, it was applied by northern European Americans to Italian immigrants. Similarly, the term *guinea* was an early term for African Americans, whose ancestors had come from the Guinea coast of Africa. After 1880, northern European Americans used *guinea* to classify Italians as "no better than blacks."[81] The ease with which these racist epithets were transferred to later racial and ethnic groups reveals not only the fear that established groups often have of newcomers but also the way in which certain European newcomers have come to be classified, as in the case of the Italian immigrants for a time, as somehow *not* white.

The Mafia Myth

The most persistent Italian American stereotype has been the **"Mafia" myth**—*the stereotyped image of Italian Americans as being substantially involved in organized crime*. As early as the 1870s, Italians were depicted as lawless, knife-wielding thugs looking for a fight. Even a report of the influential U.S. Immigration Commission, issued in the early 1900s, argued that certain types of criminality were "inherent in the Italian race." However, the validity of the criminality stereotype is contradicted by government data. For example, in 1910 the imprisonment rate for Italian immigrants was *much lower* than public stereotypes would suggest: 527 prisoners per 100,000 for the Italian-born, compared with 727 for the English and Welsh foreign-born.[82]

Small-scale crime, fostered by poverty and discrimination, was a problem in most central city communities, but it usually did not involve a criminal conspiracy. Prohibition catapulted some Italian Americans into organized crime, which at the time was controlled mostly by Irish and Jewish Americans. By 1940 two dozen Italian American "crime families" were operating in major cities. For many immigrant groups, including Italian Americans, such crime has been one of the only avenues for economic mobility. Unfortunately, the Sicilian word *Mafia* has been used to describe organized crime, although many of these gangsters have been neither Sicilian nor Italian. Significantly, Italian Americans had *low* crime rates in the 1920s and 1930s.[83]

The image of Italian criminality has taken on a widespread mythological character; the stereotype of the Italian American male as a Mafia hoodlum committed to crime and violence persists. Into the 2000s now, Italian names for criminals in various TV programs and movies have often implied ties to a "Mafia." Without exception, every non-Italian respondent in Waters's study of white ethnics in California and Pennsylvania used the Mafia and gangsters to characterize Italian Americans; most said their ideas were based on mass media images. A mid-1990s national survey found that most of those surveyed still believed that the majority of Italian Americans are linked somehow to organized crime. In addition, a 2003 survey of teenagers reported in *Parade* magazine revealed that most still associated Italian Americans "with blue collar jobs or the mob."[84]

Moreover, in 1997 CBS aired a miniseries, *Bella Mafia*, about Italian American wives linked to organized crime. Some Italian Americans, including the National Italian American News Bureau, protested the gangster stereotypes of Italian Americans and encouraged viewers to protest by not watching the program. However, this program was soon followed by a more popular television program, *The Sopranos*, and by stereotypical movies such as *Analyze This*, which present Italian Americans as disturbed gangsters. *The Sopranos* show was highly praised by prominent media commentators as one of the great television shows. Not only is there the problem with the obvious stereotyping but, as Alba and Abdel-Hady have noted, "On a deeper level, contemporary stereotypes present Italian Americans as individuals who have advanced materially in American society but have not absorbed the values and mores of its middle class; in their outlooks and their lack of appreciation for intellectual matters, they are depicted as little different from their immigrant peasant forebears."[85]

Over the last few decades, Italian Americans have fought against stereotypes on labels and trademarks. One lawyer working with the Commission for Social Justice of the Order of the Sons of Italy in America—a group with half a million members—has successfully stopped the federal government from issuing label trademarks that are insulting to Italian Americans, including product labels with terms such as "Mafia Mob" or "Cosa Nostra." In November 2003, school children and their parents in New York protested the movie *Shark Tale* because its animated shark characters were depicted with the names, accents, and images of stereotypical "Mafia" types.[86]

Significantly, by the 1990s FBI statistics showed that only a very small percentage of the 500,000 Americans involved in organized crime were part of Italian American crime networks. In addition, except in a few New York City and Chicago neighborhoods, the power of famous Italian American "crime families" had declined significantly. As has often been the case in U.S. history, recent immigrant groups, including some now from Asia and Latin America, have taken over much of organized crime in cities from previous immigrant groups. For more than a century, organized crime has been a major avenue of socioeconomic mobility for U.S. immigrant groups.[87]

Stereotypes and Discrimination

One study of the portrayal of Italian Americans on prime-time television that examined a sample of 263 programs for one 1980s season found that negative images of Italian Americans outnumbered positive images by two to one. Most of the ninety-six Italian characters in the shows studied were men with low-status jobs.[88]

One Italian American in California described his experience with ethnic slurs: "When I joined the office in the new location I became a member of the Rotary Club, and of course there were very few Italian members. So the minute I came on board, they started referring to me as the Godfather of the country." He went on to say that he found this humor degrading; he had to explain that he had no ties to a so-called Mafia. Numerous Italian Americans have reported similar experiences, including barbed Mafia jokes and discrimination in corporate workplaces.[89]

The Mafia myth has caused serious problems for Italian Americans, especially those in the public sphere. It was used by some Republicans in the 1984 presidential election, when a smear campaign aimed at Democratic vice-presidential candidate Geraldine Ferraro, an Italian American, insinuated that *she* had important "mob connections" because her husband inherited a business founded by his father and the brother of a New York crime figure. Recalling the first time her son had been called a "wop," when he was young, Ferraro indicated that her family's encounters with anti-Italian attitudes were common. One 1990s national survey by the Joint Civic Committee found that three-fourths of Americans still viewed Italians as somehow linked to crime. Not surprisingly, thus, research has shown that this very common Mafia stereotype has hurt Italian American political candidates in numerous elections in recent decades.[90]

Among all European ancestry groups in Richard Alba's study of white ethnics in a metropolitan area in New York, Italian American respondents reported encountering the most ethnic stereotypes. Stereotyped images referred to physical appearance (big noses), mannerisms (talking with hands), family life (extremely family-oriented), as well as alleged Mafia connections. Waters's non-Italian white respondents in a California and Pennsylvania study held both negative and positive stereotypes of Italian Americans. Some described Italians as dirty, loud, temperamental, selfish, unambitious, combative, and not bright; others listed characteristics such as having excellent food, doing well in business, being affectionate, and being family-oriented.[91]

How have the stereotypes used in portrayals of Irish Americans, Italian Americans, and African Americans been similar and different?

Conflict

The old U.S. myth of peaceful progress is dispelled by the history of Italian Americans' struggles with Anglo-Protestant nativists, Irish Catholics, and African Americans. Irish and Italian Americans fought on the streets of Boston by the 1860s, and Italian parents sometimes accompanied their children to school for protection. By the 1880s Anglo-Protestant nativist attempts to control immigrants from southern Italy took the form of vigilante action. In the 1880s in Buffalo, New York, more than three hundred Italians—most of the local Italian population—were detained by police after an incident in which one Italian killed another; only two were found to be holding weapons. Replying to the governor of New York, the police chief explained, stereotypically, that he thought Italian Americans as a rule carried concealed weapons and threatened social order.[92]

Legalized Killings

In the South during this early period, dozens of Italian immigrants were killed by mobs motivated by economic competition and a desire to maintain racial-ethnic lines. Italian immigrants were viewed as a threat to white solidarity because they were more likely than other whites at that time to support civil rights for African Americans. They often worked as laborers alongside black Americans or sold to them as shopkeepers. In one town, five Italian American shopkeepers were lynched for this reason. One well-publicized attack occurred in New Orleans after the 1891 murder of a police superintendent who was investigating crime among Italian immigrants. Numerous immigrants were jailed for the murder; the police refused to intervene when a large group led by prominent citizens stormed the jail and lynched eleven of them. Anglo-American newspapers and major political figures praised the deed, using the incident to advance the stereotype of Italian criminality.[93]

One of the most famous U.S. murder trials was that of Nicola Sacco and Bartolomeo Vanzetti, Italian-born workers tried for robbery and murder in Massachusetts. Numerous witnesses testified that the defendants were elsewhere at the time of the crime, but the judge ignored the testimony of Italian-born witnesses. Anti-Italian prejudice was very evident at the trial. Although their guilt or innocence is still debated, the two men did not receive a fair trial. As suspected "radicals," they were executed in 1927 in the midst of public hysteria over left-wing, "un-American" activities.[94]

Conflict with African Americans

Since the 1930s, conflict has arisen between Italian Americans and groups lower on the socioeconomic ladder. "Law and order," school desegregation, and busing have been major issues in various metropolitan areas. During the 1960s and 1970s, some Italian American leaders complained that black Americans were the "darlings" of certain white liberals and received disproportionate federal aid. Italian Americans in some areas of such cities as Newark and Philadelphia found themselves surrounded by large numbers of black immigrants from other regions, who were often poor. Realistic fears about urban crime were coupled with exaggerated views of the black role in crime, much as Anglo-Protestant fears earlier had exaggerated the Italian role in urban crime.[95]

In 1990, a group of Italian American youths killed a black youth, Yusuf Hawkins, in predominantly Italian Bensonhurst in New York City. The attackers believed the victim was dating an Italian American woman. Actually, Hawkins had gone there to inquire about buying a car. Members of the Federation of Italian American Organizations actively sought to calm racial tensions, calling Italian residents' attention to their own history of being discriminated against.[96]

Opinion surveys of Italian Americans in the 1960s and 1970s showed significant antiblack prejudice and strong opposition to neighborhood desegregation. By the 1990s, Italian American attitudes expressed in opinion surveys, like those of many other whites, had liberalized on some racial matters. Sixty percent of Italian Americans, compared with 55 percent of all whites, said they would work for improved racial relations, and 85 percent of Italian Americans, compared with 79 percent of all whites, said they would vote for a black presidential candidate.[97]

Yet, among Italian Americans a sizable proportion remain openly racist in their attitudes toward black Americans, a situation that has on occasion fueled antiblack discrimination and violence, such as the Bensonhurst attack. Like many Irish Americans, many Italian Americans have abandoned much of the left-wing politics of their first generation and of relatives in Italy for conservative politics, including on racial issues. In research on Italian acculturation, scholar David Richards has shown the process by which Italian Americans came to "buy into" the U.S. racist system, thereby accepting a place in the "white race" and an orientation that weakened their earlier strong commitments to multiracial democracy. A recent book, titled *Are Italians White?*, summarizes social science research, including some on New York communities, that shows how central-city location and struggles against northern European discrimination eventually led many Italian Americans "to assert a white identity in order to effectively distance themselves from their Brown and Black neighbors, and receive the ample rewards that come with being white."[98]

Politics

The first major Italian influence on U.S. politics was that of Filippo Mazzei, a friend of Thomas Jefferson who came to the colonies to help with agricultural development. Mazzei helped Jefferson bring legal reforms to Virginia. Mazzei's writings speak vigorously of freedom and include phrases similar to those Jefferson later used in the Declaration of Independence—such as Mazzei's phrase, "All men are by nature created free and independent."[99]

City Politics

During and after the great migration of 1880–1920, Irish political leaders recruited Italian Americans into the Democratic Party. In Chicago, Italian Americans benefited from political patronage, and many were employed by the city. By 1892, they elected a Chicago alderman, and soon had a few representatives in the Illinois legislature. Italians had won significant elective offices in New York City by the 1920s.[100] By the 1930s, Italian Americans were mayors of large cities such as New York, San Francisco, and New Orleans, and of a few smaller cities. Prominent Italian American mayors in recent decades have included Anthony Celebrezze (Cleveland), Joseph Alioto (San Francisco), George Moscone (San Francisco), and Frank Rizzo (Philadelphia).

State and National Politics

Few Italians served in state and national legislatures before 1900. Prior to 1950, New York had sent only six Italian American representatives to Congress. The most famous was Fiorello La Guardia. In Congress he vigorously supported Italian immigration and attacked the anti-Italian immigrant quota system. He was the first Italian American to rise through ethnic politics in New York City, where he was elected mayor in 1934. In his political efforts, La

Italian Americans march in a Philadelphia parade.

Guardia demonstrated that Italian Americans often supported movements to reform urban machines and promote honest government.[101]

International politics has affected Italian American political activities. During the economically oppressive Great Depression of the 1930s, Italian fascist and dictator Benito Mussolini became a hero for many Italian (as well as non-Italian) Americans, although antifascist activity was also a significant force in Italian American communities.

During World War II, Italian Americans suffered political discrimination. Italian American subversion was widely alleged, but not proven, and the use of the Italian *language* on the radio was actually prohibited in New York and Boston. Several hundred Italian Americans, legal residents, were imprisoned at a Montana concentration camp where Japanese Americans were interned. More than half a million Italian Americans were officially seen as "enemy aliens," and some had their rights curtailed. The property of some was confiscated; restrictions were placed on travel; nighttime curfews were imposed; and some in coastal areas were forced to move. The justification for ignoring the civil rights of many Italian Americans was similar to the rationalizations for the internment of Japanese Americans (see Chapter 10). They were *alleged* without evidence to represent a security threat. Indeed, in the late 1990s legislation was introduced in Congress to require the government to acknowledge these civil rights violations. Nonetheless, during World War II federal action against Italian Americans was far less severe than that against Japanese Americans—perhaps because Italian Americans were by that time considered to be "white" by most government officials.[102]

World War II contributed to Italian American mobility and assimilation. The solidarity with other (especially white) Americans that was generated by the war effort against Germany and Japan helped Italian immigrants and their children assimilate rapidly to the Anglo-Protestant culture and institutions. Italian Americans enlisted in the armed forces in significant numbers and served in ethnically integrated units. (In contrast, African and Japanese Americans served in *segregated* units.) The war helped create a vision of the U.S. that encompassed these ethnic Americans as fully white in terms of citizenship and privilege. In addition, numerous white ethnics, including Italian and Irish Americans, benefitted greatly from a huge array of "welfare state" programs after World War II, such as federal home loan and veterans' programs, college aid programs, and Social Security programs. These and other whites had privileged access to these "affirmative action" programs, because white officials usually discriminated against Americans of color. In the postwar era, indeed, these ethnic Americans aggressively insisted on white privileges, to the point of violently resisting school and neighborhood racial desegregation and/or engaging in white flight to the suburbs. Over the last few decades, in contrast, small but significant numbers have joined groups—such as Italian Americans for a Multicultural United States—attacking racism and supporting democratic diversity, even as the majority of these ethnic Americans have continued to accent their white privilege.[103]

Between the 1970s and the 2000s, the number of Italian American cabinet members, governors, and state legislators has grown. This signals substantial political advances. Mario Cuomo was a contender for the Democratic Party's presidential nomination in the 1990s, whereas Geraldine Ferraro was the first woman nominated for vice-president. In the late 1990s, New York City's mayor and one of the state's U.S. senators were of Italian ancestry. Since the 1990s New York's mayor, Rudolph Giuliani, a Republican, has been heralded as a likely presidential candidate, and since the early 2000s he has been celebrated for his role in providing support for families of victims of the 9/11 World Trade Center attacks. Moreover, by the late 1990s, thirty-two Italian Americans were members of the U.S. House of Representatives.

In the 1960s Republican political strategists began efforts to win the white ethnic vote, including the Italian American vote, away from the Democratic Party. White ethnic fears of the civil rights demands of Americans of color were manipulated for this purpose. By 1990, poll data indicated that 49 percent of Italian Americans called themselves Republicans, compared with 39 percent who called themselves Democrats. Analysis of national opinion data also indicated that over recent decades Italian Americans as a group have moved to the right on major issues such as capital punishment and immigration restrictions. Still, the data indicate continuing political liberalism on such matters as increased government spending to help the poor and central cities.[104]

Italian Americans, like other U.S. ethnic groups, have lobbied politically on behalf of their home country. In the late 1990s the United Nations was considering a U.S. proposal to add Germany and Japan, but not Italy, as permanent members of the Security Council. Italian American groups organized protests against this "blatant insult" and argued that Italy should be on the Security Council because of its great historical importance in UN activities.[105]

The Economy

Structural adaptation by immigrant groups includes their movement into secondary-organization levels of the host society—into economic as well as political and educational organizations. Economic mobility means attaining higher levels of employment and the attendant economic benefits. Italian Americans started near the bottom of the ladder. The small number of immigrants before 1880 were mostly artisans, street merchants, and political exiles, primarily from northern Italy. The southern Italian immigrants, who came after 1880, were often economically exploited. They responded to the tremendous U.S. demand for unskilled labor in the late nineteenth century.[106]

Early Poverty and Discrimination

Urban poverty coupled with often low-wage and/or dangerous working conditions was the lot of most immigrants: "The Italian immigrant may be maimed and killed in his industrial occupation without a cry and without indemnity. He may die from the 'bends' working in the caissons under the river, without protest; he can be slowly asphyxiated in crowded tenements, smothered in dangerous trades and occupations (which only the ignorant immigrant pursues, not the native American); he can contract tuberculosis in unsanitary factories and sweatshops."[107] Some among the first generation of the post-1880 Italian immigrants were skilled workers, but most were unskilled. Women were often employed in trade occupations.

Isolate, small-group, and institutionalized discrimination (see Chapter 1) held Italian Americans back. From the first years of migration, new Italian residents were "abused in public and isolated in private, cuffed in the works and pelted on the streets, fined and imprisoned on the smallest pretext, cheated of their wages, and crowded by the score into converted barns and tumble-down shanties that served

Immigrant workers in a U.S. factory at the turn of the 20th century.

as boarding houses."[108] Discrimination in wages was blatant. An early ad for laborers to build a New York City reservoir listed daily wages as $1.30 to $1.50 for "whites" and $1.15 to $1.25 for "Italians."[109] Then, as now, informal social networks were a major means of circulating job information. In most job networks, Anglo-Protestant and Irish American sponsors functioned to protect their own kind and discriminated against Italian workers. Italian Americans thus constantly faced institutionalized discrimination.

Upward Mobility

Economic progress came slowly but steadily. The proportion of Italian American workers who were laborers dropped from 50 percent in 1916 to 31 percent fifteen years later. Small-business and skilled blue-collar positions were more common by 1931. Socioeconomic mobility was evident, but so was the persisting economic differential between Italian Americans and other whites. The Great Depression slowed advancement but did not stop it. By 1939 Italian Americans had begun to supplant Jewish Americans as the major group in a number of important unions of skilled workers. Indeed, first- and second-generation Italian Americans were very important in the development of industrial unions, participating in numerous major strikes from the 1910s to the 1920s, as well as important leftist (for example, socialist) movements of the period. Radical political movements in Italian communities were mostly ended by the execution of Sacco and Vanzetti and by the repressive Red Scare by the federal government in the 1920s, as well as by repressive McCarthyism during the 1950s. (In both eras, numerous Italian Americans, among others, were illegally arrested and targeted by federal and local governments for their progressive political activity.) One result of this political repression was to pressure Italian Americans to become more conservative. Today, Italian Americans are more politically conservative as a group than are Italians in Italy, as well as than their own immigrant ancestors.[110]

By the 1920s, organized crime was providing some better-paying jobs for Italian Americans in cities. Indeed, the "good citizens" of the cities, often non-Italian residents, were the ones who supported

TABLE 4.2 People with Italian Ancestry: Selected Population Characteristics (2000 Census)

	People with Italian Ancestry	Total U.S. Population
Number	15,723,406	281,421,906
Median age (years)	34	35
Foreign born	3.8%	11%
Percent female	50.4%	51%
High school degree or greater (25 years old and over)	87%	80%
Having at least a college degree (25 years old and over)	29%	24%
Median family income in 1999	$61,297	$50,046
Percent below poverty line	6.6%	12%

the bootlegging, prostitution, and gambling operations of these Italian Americans by their active patronage. Later, money from organized crime would flow to legitimate enterprises, as it had for earlier groups. Children of those who were successful in organized crime often moved out of illegitimate enterprises. This trend, according to Ianni, supports "the thesis that for Italian Americans, as for other ethnic groups, organized crime has been a way station on the road to ultimately respectable roles in American society."[111] Of course, only a few Italian Americans achieved upward mobility in this way. Most did it by means of legitimate work efforts.

Some Italian Americans have become nationally prominent as entrepreneurs and scientists. Amadeo Giannini, founder of the Bank of America, made his fortune in California financing businesses and ranches. Italian Americans such as Joseph Di Giorgio and the Gallo brothers began to play major roles in restaurant, agricultural, wine, and contracting businesses. Scientists Enrico Fermi and Salvador Luria won Nobel Prizes. As with groups before and after them, Italian Americans have found upward mobility in sports. Notable examples include boxer Rocky Marciano and baseball Hall-of-Famers Joe DiMaggio, Ernie Lombardi, Phil Rizzuto, Yogi Berra, Tony Lazzeri, and Tommy Lasorda.[112]

What key factors have contributed to the socioeconomic mobility of Irish Americans and Italian Americans?

Recent Decades

By the 1950s Italian Americans had advanced economically, yet at least one study suggested that second-generation Italian Catholics had still to equal white Protestants in the proportion holding higher-level white-collar jobs. Decades later, the 1990 census showed significant mobility. Compared with the total white population, Italian Americans now had a greater proportion in professional, managerial, technical, and other white-collar jobs—and a smaller proportion in blue-collar jobs.[113]

Socioeconomic progress continues. As can be seen in Table 4.2, the 2000 census revealed that median family income for Italian Americans ($61,297) was substantially higher than that of the general population, while the poverty rate for Italian Americans was substantially below that of the general population, though substantially higher than that for English Americans (see Chapter 3).[114]

Some Persisting Problems

Over the past few decades, ethnic discrimination targeting Italian Americans has sometimes been a problem at the highest occupational levels. For example, the failure to hire Italian Americans at the City University of New York (CUNY) was documented in a 1970s study: "In decision-making positions of Dean, Director and Chairman of the system's 18 colleges, there are only 20 Italian Americans out of a total of 504 positions."[115] In addition, only a small percentage of the faculty members were Italian. In

1975 an affirmative action program for Italian American faculty was put into place, but fifteen years later the percentage of Italian American faculty still had not increased. Little change occurred between the 1970s and the 1990s. At the beginning of the 1990s, Italian Americans still constituted less than 6 percent of CUNY's faculty, while the student body was 17 percent Italian American.[116]

In the 1990s, thus, CUNY professors protested discrimination in the hiring of Italian Americans in a class-action suit against the university. Eventually, CUNY settled a lawsuit brought by the director of the university's Italian-American Institute; CUNY's administration agreed to make the Institute a permanent part of Queens College and to hire a distinguished senior professor in Italian American studies. In the early 2000s, however, Italian American organizations were still reporting not only significant underrepresentation on the CUNY faculty (still about 6 percent) but also a decline in the number of full-time Italian American faculty members.[117]

In addition, one recent study of the American Academy of Arts and Sciences found a significant underrepresentation of Italian Americans among its 3700 distinguished U.S. members, drawn from numerous scientific and artistic fields. Although the percentage of that group that is Italian American has been growing, it still shows underrepresentation (1.3 percent of all members) when the percentage of Italian Americans on college and university faculties (4.6 percent) is used as a rough standard. By various mechanisms, probably including some anti-Italian stereotyping, Italian Americans are still excluded by the elite that chooses members of this prestigious organization.[118]

Over the past decade, some private clubs have continued to bar Italian Americans, and Italian Americans are still underrepresented in the top management of major corporations. Still, the overall picture of recent occupational and income mobility for Italian Americans, a white ethnic group discriminated against on a large scale only a few decades ago, is impressive. Some, like Giuliani and Lee Iacocca, have been touted as presidential candidates. Two, Antonin Scalia and Joseph Alito, are members of the U.S. Supreme Court. Italian American men are prominent among movie directors. Women of Italian American ancestry have moved into important positions in politics, notably the first woman Speaker of the U.S. House (2007), Nancy Pelosi, and in the mass media, major commentators such as Anna Quindlen. The majority of Italian Americans have made strides up the socioeconomic ladder, and on numerous socioeconomic indexes they have surpassed Anglo-Protestants.

Education

Many immigrants came from areas in Italy where the poor received little schooling. Like other immigrants, they often adopted a pragmatic approach to education, valuing it but asking, "What is the practical value of this for jobs, for later life?" Many families made sacrifices to put their first child through elementary school and then expected this child to get a job to put later children through school.

As with the Irish, Anglo-Protestant educators were concerned over the alleged corruption and inferiority of Italian Americans. Schools became "pressure cookers" of Americanization in which these educators sought aggressively to teach Italian immigrants and their children Anglo-Protestant norms about dress, work, and language. Ethnic discrimination was often a fact of school life. Public schools were Procrustean beds shaped in Anglo-centric form.[119]

Despite such obstacles, Italian Americans made dramatic progress in educational attainment. By 1970 Italian Americans' median level of educational attainment was higher than that of the total U.S. population and only slightly lower than that of the total white population. Table 4.2 shows that by 2000, Italian Americans 25 years old and older had achieved educational attainments—87 percent with at least a high school diploma and 29 percent with at least a college degree—well above those for the U.S. population as a whole.[120]

Religion

The Roman Catholic church has been very important in the lives of Italian Americans. Preexisting Irish Catholic churches were often overwhelmed by the numbers of Italian immigrants. For many Italians, Irish Catholicism was too orthodox. Religion was not an intimate part of political identity for the Italian immigrant, as it often was for the Irish immigrant, whose religious expression was tied to a nationalist heritage of anti-English agitation. Saints were important to Italian Catholics, as were religious festivals that played an important role in cementing Italian communities.[121]

Irish American priests often held negative views of the new Italian parishioners. Tensions sometimes escalated. When some ethnic parishes for Italian Americans were developed, the latter were warned away, on occasion forcefully, from Irish parishes. Many first-generation Italian Americans preferred to send their children to public schools rather than to Irish-dominated parochial schools. Gradually, Italian Catholicism, with its festivals and ceremonies, took its place alongside Irish Catholicism.[122]

A 1960s study of Italian and Irish Catholics in New York City suggested the controversial conclusion that third-generation Italians were becoming more "Irishized" in their religious practices. In national surveys between 1988 and 1991, only 70 percent of Italian Americans classified themselves as Catholics, and many of those were nonpracticing. Today, Catholicism genrally seems less central for Italian Americans than for Irish Americans. Still, in the early 2000s some Italian American communities, such as that on New York's Long Island, have important parades, feasts, and church bazaars honoring traditional saints or the Virgin Mary.[123]

Assimilation or Ethnogenesis?

Today Italian Americans make up more than 5 percent of the U.S. population, at about 15.7 million Americans. As Table 4.2 shows, their median age is slightly lower than that of the U.S. median, as is their percentage female. The percentage of the group that is foreign born, at 3.8 percent, is lower than that for the U.S. population as a whole, though higher than for English and Irish Americans.

Significantly, the pressures for acculturation to a British American culture came early for southern and eastern European immigrants. They spoke no English, nor were they familiar with the customs of the Anglo-Protestant society. Often concentrated in "Little Italies," Italian immigrants learned Italian dialects other than their own, although most picked up some English. In addition to language and community factors, cultural adaptation was slowed by poverty, the intention of some to return home, and anti-immigrant discrimination in the new environment.[124] The first-generation family was in transition, cross-pressured between the old Italian and new U.S. ways. Families often became less patriarchal, and kin solidarity often weakened somewhat, as did ties to conservative Catholic religion. Children were more on their own. Speaking Italian at home was a point of intergenerational conflict, because younger members felt school pressures to speak only English.[125]

Marriage was a second point of intergenerational conflict. First-generation parents saw it as a family matter, whereas children tended to see it as an individual matter. Given this tension, second-generation families adapted in different ways. One type substantially abandoned old ways, changing the Italian name and moving out of an Italian area. This was rare. A second type rejected the old ways in part, perhaps by moving out of a concentrated Italian community but maintaining close ties to the first generation. This was the largest group. A third type stayed in the old community and retained many of the old ways.[126] Today, though they have spread to states such as Florida and Illinois in significant numbers, Italian Americans are still concentrated in the North, and especially the northeastern states. They are no longer a predominantly central-city group but are about as likely to reside in suburbs as the average white American.

Structural Assimilation

Structural assimilation involves the movement of a group into the secondary organizations—the businesses and bureaucracies—of the larger society, as well as into its primary social networks: social clubs, neighborhoods, and friendship circles. Structural movement into workplaces and other areas by Italian Americans over the first several decades came with considerable resistance from earlier European groups. Positioning at the lower economic levels was a fact of life for a time. However, in recent decades Italian Americans have made impressive gains in employment, income, and education and significant advances in politics. This upward educational and occupational mobility has contributed to assimilation in other areas. Increasing equal-status contact with members of other white groups in the workplace, the suburbs, and colleges has in turn created cross-ethnic friendship networks and marriages.[127]

The economic success of Italian Americans and other white ethnic groups is sometimes compared with the relative lack of success of other groups, such as African Americans. Why were Italian Americans so successful in assimilating over time to Anglo-Protestant institutions and organizations? The answer to this question lies not only in the hard work and sacrifice of several generations of Italian Americans, for those factors are also characteristic of African Americans. It lies also in the timing of Italian immigrants' entry into the United States. Jobs and housing near jobs were available to the many Italians who arrived in the late nineteenth century and the early twentieth century. Second and third generations emerged with enough economic support from parents to obtain the education needed for better-paying jobs which opened up for white ethnics during and after World War II.[128] Expansion of jobs on the middle rungs of the occupational ladder made upward mobility possible for ethnic Americans. Of even greater importance is the fact that the poverty and discrimination that Italian immigrants faced, though serious, were never as thoroughgoing as the extreme poverty and the severe racial discrimination faced by African Americans and other non-European Americans.

During the World War II period, the earlier view of Italian Americans as an "inferior race" held by Anglo-Protestant officials was replaced by a conception of Italian Americans as part of the "white race." This change signalled the reality of reduced anti-Italian discrimination. Wartime solidarity hastened the assimilation of white ethnics, including Italian Americans, into Anglo-Protestant institutions, including the regular units of the armed forces. In contrast, African and Japanese Americans were kept in segregated units. After the war, many Italian Americans took advantage of new federal housing and veterans' programs, oriented primarily to whites, in order to buy homes and get a college education.

Residential patterns have contributed to a continuing ethnic identity. One 1980s study in a large New York metropolitan area found that Italian Americans there were still one of the most residentially concentrated white ethnic groups. They were more likely than other groups to name a relative as a close friend, and they had one of the highest rates of *intraethnic* friendships.[129] Although kinship and primary-group ties often remain strong, suburbanization has shrunk formerly large ethnic enclaves. In both 1980 and 1990, most of the nearly 3 million Italian Americans in the Greater New York area lived outside of concentrated Italian American neighborhoods. In the early 2000s, New York's Italian Americans are much less concentrated in primarily Italian neighborhoods than in previous decades.[130]

Studies of marriages in New Haven (1870) and Chicago (1920) found high rates of in-marriage for early Italians: 94 to 98 percent of all marriages were endogamous. In-marriage decreased in subsequent decades. Although 84 percent of the respondents in a 1970s study reported that both of their parents were of Italian ancestry, only 44 percent were themselves married to Italian Americans. Still, the rate of *religious* endogamy was high: Most marriages with non-Italians were with Catholics. Exogamous marriages were more likely for those with higher-status educational and occupational achievements. More recently, one 1997 analysis estimated that 73 percent of Italian Americans in their 30s were marrying outside their ethnic group.[131]

Sociologist Richard Alba argues that, although ethnicity is still important for earlier generations, a transition is underway, with a strong sense of ethnicity receding for the later generations. Italian Americans are becoming ever more structurally integrated into the white mainstream: Just over half of Italian American respondents in Alba's New York State study reported ethnically unmixed ancestry. However, for those born after 1940, the proportion dropped to one-third. National survey data today suggest high levels of mixed ancestry for Italian Americans. A much more structurally assimilated Italian American group is likely emerging as younger generations replace earlier ones.[132]

Across-the-board assimilation of Italian Americans is progressing, although this major ethnic group still encounters significant "Mafia" stereotyping and some private, corporate, and political discrimination. With a few exceptions, Italian Americans remain underrepresented at the very highest economic and political levels of U.S. society.

An Italian Identity?

Identificational assimilation involves giving up one's ethnic identity for that of the dominant Anglo-Protestant culture. For many Italian Americans this seems to be happening, but slowly. Ethnic ties and accents are still found in older generations and among all generations in ethnic community enclaves.

In numerous substantially Italian American neighborhoods in northern cities, older Italian Americans and new Italian immigrants of recent decades seem to be helping to keep some Italian cultural characteristics alive. One 1980s study of Belmont, a community in the Bronx with a substantial Italian American flavor, found some persisting ethnic neighborhoods and traditions.[133] And a 1980s study of Italian Americans in Scottsdale, Arizona, found that, rather than losing their cultural identity, these respondents had preserved some Italian American subculture. In the New York State study cited earlier, Italian Americans were the most likely of the white ethnic groups to feel a sense of ethnic identity and to consider ethnic identity very important.[134]

Historian Marcus Lee Hansen once argued that there is often an increase in ethnic awareness in the third generation of an immigrant group; this substantially assimilated generation vigorously searches out its ethnic *roots*. Younger Italian Americans have faced less discrimination and stereotyping than older generations. This has enabled younger generations to express their ethnicity more openly. However, in her 1990s New Jersey study, Tardi found a strong pride in ethnic identity among Italian Americans of the first, second, *and* third generations. The structural factors associated with greater freedom to express ethnic pride, such as diminishing overt discrimination and increasing numbers of visible Italian Americans in public life, have apparently affected all generations.[135]

One study of Italian Americans in California found a relationship between the strength of ethnic networks and identity and the work an individual does. Most working-class Italian Americans no longer worked with large numbers of other Italian Americans and therefore expressed their ethnic identity differently from shopkeepers and independent professionals, who were better able to express their ethnicity in their work, such as by serving a partially ethnic clientele. Participation in the economy may or may not work to destroy ethnic identity, depending on the character of one's participation and on where one works.[136]

Andrew Greeley's *ethnogenesis* model seems to fit the Italian experience. Italians came to the United States with significant differences from the dominant British American group, but they shared some historical background (in Europe) and a Christian religious tradition with that dominant group. Over time interaction in schools and media influence served to narrow the gap. Italian Americans assimilated in major ways to the Anglo-Protestant host culture, but in other ways retained distinctiveness. Because of their strong national heritage, residential segregation, and strong community and kinship networks, a distinctive U.S. ethnic group developed over time. Today, Italian Americans are no longer dominated by their national heritage, but most have not yet become just like British Protestant Americans. For the most part, they remain Italian *and* American. As a group, Italian Americans have experienced very substantial adaptation and incorporation in the society, but without complete assimilation as yet, at least at the level of identity.

Some scholars see structural forces such as increasing intermarriage, increasing education, loss of the Italian language, and residential mixing in suburbs as further diminishing, if not soon eradicating, this sense of ethnic identity among most Italian Americans. Membership in Italian American organizations is declining. And the remaining sense of Italian American identity has not retarded the increasing rates of intermarriage.[137] However, the continuing presence of significant numbers of foreign-born Italian Americans fosters certain connections to the old ethnic identity. In addition, among Italian Americans, and in the larger society, there is increased interest in both things Italian and in the Italian language, which has experienced a major increase in people interested in learning it in recent years.

How would you compare and contrast the patterns of assimilation for Irish Americans and Italian Americans?

A Note on Ethnic Diversity Among White Americans

There are numerous white ethnic groups other than the Italian, Irish, and English American groups that we have considered at some length. For reasons of space, we cannot assess in detail the many other groups that make up the U.S. white population. We will pause briefly to note how diverse this population is. A November 1999–December 2000 Census

TABLE 4.3 Ancestry Groups

Ancestry Group	Estimate
Estimated to Be Larger Than 2,000,000	
Dutch	5,221,803
English	28,264,856
French	9,775,761
German	46,488,992
Irish and Scotch-Irish	38,293,533
Italian	15,942,683
Norwegian	4,541,254
Polish	9,053,660
Russian	2,980,776
Scottish	5,423,030
Swedish	4,339,357
Estimated to Be in the 300,000–2,000,000 Range	
Austrian	795,131
Belgian	377,451
Canadian	635,400
Croatian	392,121
Czech	1,396,279
Danish	1,502,600
Finnish	797,642
Greek	1,179,064
Hungarian	1,519,788
Lithuanian	714,097
Portuguese	1,321,155
Romanian	397,576
Slovak	821,325
Swiss	998,009
Ukrainian	862,762
Welsh	1,898,279

Bureau sample survey interviewed respondents at 58,000 residential addresses in all states.[138] Surveyers asked about ancestry of respondents and recorded the first and second ancestries given. The survey estimates the numbers for certain national-origin populations. Table 4.3 lists national-origin groups with more than 300,000 people giving first and second ancestry responses (combined).

Those Americans in the eleven largest ethnic groups mostly have ancestries linked to northern and central Europe. The largest groups list German, Irish, English, Italian, French, and Polish ancestries, in that order. Russia and the Netherlands, as well as Sweden and Norway, have many representatives in the U.S. population. The second list refers to sixteen countries or areas that have generally supplied fewer immigrants than the first list, but that still constitute major places of origin for many ancestors of these contemporary (mostly white) Americans. Distinctive in the second list of ancestral origins are numerous countries or areas in central, southern, and eastern Europe, with a few northern European countries or areas sprinkled in. Leading this list are those with Welsh, Hungarian, Danish, Czech, Portuguese, and Greek as their first or second ancestries. One county in the Americas, Canada, is represented, a country with large populations that also have English, Irish, Scottish, or French ancestries.

Although these data do not include vague choices and are estimates from one sample survey (estimates that are sometimes higher than 2000 census figures), they do provide insight into how diverse the white population is at the beginning of the twenty-first century. The data also suggest how early European immigrations were limited to a few countries, for the English, Irish, and German ancestries are by far the largest categories.

Summary

Irish immigration to North America began with the arrival of indentured servants and farmers in the 1700s. This early immigration included more southern, or Celtic, Irish than often exaggerated accounts of the "Scotch-Irish" have suggested. Most descendants of early migrants were, or became, Protestants. They settled disproportionately in the South and in frontier areas. Over several generations many descendants of these early colonists became part of the white Protestant mainstream. However, a significant proportion remained poor.

After the 1830s, large numbers of Irish Catholic immigrants settled in the cities of the North, where many suffered discrimination and violence at the hands of Catholic-hating nativists. Movement toward economic equality with older groups was slow for the poverty-stricken Irish Catholics. Conflict, sometimes violent, marked their climb. Frequently political innovators, Irish Catholics shaped urban political organizations to facilitate their integration into dominant political and economic institutions.

They diversified U.S. religious institutions by bringing in a strong Catholic church-and-school complex.

Economic mobility has been so dramatic that by the 1990s Irish Americans ranked at or above the national average for all whites on a number of important socioeconomic indicators, including educational level, occupational distribution, and income. Today, at the beginning of the twenty-first century, Irish Americans are a major segment of Middle America.

Today, some descendants of the Italian immigrants who entered the United States over the past century are still clustered in certain northern cities and states. However, large and increasing numbers are now scattered across suburban areas with other white groups. The majority of Italian Americans remain Catholic, although many are not active. Italian Americans have played and continue to play an important role in the culture, politics, and economy of the United States. Poverty and difficult working conditions greeted the hard-working Italian immigrants. They too were not prepared for the intense nativist attacks from Anglo-Protestants, who stereotyped Italian Americans as an inferior, immoral, and criminal people and sought to prove Italian American "racial inferiority." To this day, Italian Americans have been stigmatized by a widespread "Mafia" myth and have endured substantial discrimination from other white Americans.

Political avenues were closed for a time to Italian immigrants; the economy often consigned Italian Americans to low-paid jobs; and public schools sought to transform them into carbon-copy Anglo-Protestants. Despite these problems, however, immigrants and their descendants persevered. Particularly after World War II, they began to succeed ever more conspicuously in politics, the economy, and education. Economic and political mobility has made them another U.S. success story, although a considerable cultural-conformity price was often exacted for that success.

Today, Italian Americans are one of the major groups in the U.S. drama of blending and pluralism. As a group they have retained ethnic distinctiveness that seems likely to persist for a time. Some researchers predict that societal forces such as suburbanization and intermarriage may soon diminish the Italian ethnic identity and accelerate identification with a "European American" or "white American" identity. In any case, they too are now an important segment of Middle America.

Key Terms

"Scotch-Irish" 83
intermarriage 94
endogamy 94
ethnic enclave 96
IQ tests 97
"Mafia" myth 98

CHAPTER 5

Jewish Americans

BIG PICTURE QUESTIONS

- ***What factors have generated numerous Jewish migrations to the United States?***
- ***What political and economic changes have Jewish Americans brought to the United States?***
- ***What social factors have shaped Jewish Americans as a distinctive U.S. ethnic group?***

In 1913 Leo Frank, a Jewish American and hardworking president of the Atlanta B'nai B'rith, was accused of the murder of a non-Jewish teenager who worked in his pencil factory. Later examination of the contradictory evidence indicated that he could not have committed the crime, but at the time the police were under heavy pressure to find the murderer of the young woman. Early targeted by anti-Semitism, Frank was arrested, tried for the crime, convicted, and sentenced to hang. Efforts by northern Jews to get his case appealed to higher courts failed, and many non-Jewish Georgians cited that legal effort in accelerating their strongly anti-Semitic views. Rabid political demagogues such as Georgia's Tom Watson spoke of Jewish Americans as the "scum and dregs of the Parasite Race." Many people were angry when the governor finally commuted Frank's sentence to life imprisonment and began boycotts of Jewish merchants. Soon, a vigilante group of the "best citizens" took Frank from a prison farm in Marietta, Georgia, and hanged him from a tree. For decades afterward, many non-Jewish Georgians strongly insisted that both their anti-Semitism and the brutal lynching were justified.[1]

Jewish groups have been scapegoats for the hatreds of the dominant peoples in various countries for thousands of years. From the Egyptian and Roman persecutions in ancient times to massacres in Spain in the 1400s to brutal pogroms in Russia in the 1880s to the infamous German Nazi massacres, Jews might be regarded as the most widely oppressed racial or ethnic group in world history. One reason we devote a chapter to Jewish Americans is because of this long and violent history, one that makes clear just how oppressive societies can become in regard to modest cultural or physical differences between groups.

Remembering this past is important to keep it from being repeated. Yet, today, a majority of adult Americans know little or nothing about this violent past. A recent survey of adults in seven countries—the United States, Germany, Great Britain, Sweden, Austria, Poland, and France—found that the U.S. respondents were the *least* likely to know that Auschwitz, Dachau, and Treblinka were the names of major German Nazi concentration and death camps. Majorities of respondents in all countries except the United States had heard of these extermination camps. Some 56 percent of U.S. respondents admitted that they did not know what these names referred to. Ironically, most U.S. respondents did agree that it is important to teach about the **Holocaust**, *the German Nazi extermination of millions of European Jews.*[2]

In spite of this large-scale and long-term oppression, however, Jews have forged very strong cultural traditions. Indeed, some intellectual pillars of Western cultures—Karl Marx, Sigmund Freud, and Albert Einstein—were Jews. Jewish Americans have made enormous contributions to the United States—as pioneers in commerce, industrial workers, professionals, scholars, government officials, and entertainers. They have benefited from a political structure that separates church and state and that prohibits religious qualifications for public office. Jewish immigrants have often come from countries in which they were always outsiders struggling just to survive physically. Unlike the situation in other countries, for the most part U.S. law never became their enemy. Still, more than any other white ethnic group, Jews have often been treated as outsiders even in the United States.

By tradition, Jewish ethnicity has been based on matrilineal ancestry: A Jew is one whose mother is Jewish. In the contemporary United States, many Jewish writers define Jews simply as those who identify themselves as Jews.[3] Some Jewish Americans focus their identity primarily on their religion; others define their Jewishness primarily in terms of group membership.*

Migration

From 1500 to World War II

Most early Jewish immigrants came to Atlantic coast colonies in the 1600s seeking economic opportunities denied them in Europe. The first Jewish community dates from the arrival in 1654 of twenty-three Jews who fled the Catholic Inquisition in Brazil. Most were Sephardic Jews, whose background was the Jewish subculture of Spain.[4] Over the next hundred years, small numbers of the descendants of those called **Marranos** (originally a derogatory term)—

*In this chapter we will often use the term *Jewish American* as shorthand for Jewish Americans of European descent. However, the reader should keep in mind that there are relatively small (and rarely researched) Jewish communities with national origins in Iran, Syria, North Africa, and the non-European areas of Russia. There are also small groups of African Americans who adhere to Judaism, as well as small groups of Latino and Asian Jews.

Jews who were forced to convert publicly to Christianity during the Spanish Inquisition under threat of death, but who privately maintained allegiance to Judaism—came to North American colonies. The immigration of Ashkenazi Jews from England, Germany, and Poland began slowly in the 1700s, and this group soon outnumbered Sephardic Jews. Many were attracted by reports of North American prosperity.[5]

After 1820, central European Jews came to the new United States in dramatically increased numbers in response to declining economic conditions and increasing anti-Semitism in Europe, as well as to U.S. economic expansion. These have often been called "German Jews," although they came from Bohemia and Moravia as well as Germany. By 1860, Jewish American communities and synagogues had been established in many cities. Geographic mobility facilitated acculturation.[6]

Eastern European Jews, the largest group of Jewish immigrants, began to arrive in the 1870s. Most came from Russian-controlled areas where anti-Semitism and lack of economic opportunities were major push factors. In Russia during the late nineteenth and early twentieth centuries, a series of **pogroms**—*organized, often officially encouraged attacks on Jews*—contributed to significant out-migration.[7] Jewish immigration to the United States from 1881 to the 1920s totaled 2.5 million. By the mid-1920s, Jewish Americans composed 3.5 percent of the U.S. population. Eastern European Jews constituted a large proportion. Unlike some non-Jewish immigrants, few returned home. These immigrants brought with them a distinctive language and culture (Yiddish), a strong sense of Jewish identity, and Orthodox religious observances.[8]

After the 1924 Immigration Act, an overtly racist law aimed at limiting eastern and southern European immigration, the numbers of Jewish newcomers declined. Between 1921 and 1936, fewer than 400,000 immigrants entered. President Franklin Roosevelt's administration did permit some modest increase in Jewish refugees from Germany because of the Nazi persecution during World War II. Yet Roosevelt, and especially his State Department, soon adopted the policy of requiring affidavits of financial solvency and good character and used visa regulations to slow the flow of Jewish refugees. In 1940 the State Department put an end to most immigration. More than 400,000 slots within U.S. immigration quotas for refugees from countries under Nazi control were left unused between 1933 and 1943. Some of these unfilled slots likely represent lives lost to extermination by the Nazis because of the openly discriminatory U.S. immigration policy.[9]

From World War II to the Present

After the arrival of thousands of postwar refugees in the late 1940s, Jewish migration tapered off to an estimated 8000 annually. By the 1970s, however, a new group, Israeli Jewish immigrants, were coming in significant numbers. Many were undocumented immigrants. By the 2000s there were at least 200,000 in the United States.[10]

Between the late 1960s and the 2000s, a new group of eastern European Jews, this time from the Soviet Union (later, the former Soviet Union), came to the United States. By 2000, this immigration totaled nearly half a million. Most have proudly asserted their Jewish heritage. Many emigrated because of resurgent anti-Semitism and social chaos in Russia. Significantly, since the end of the Communist regimes, "old ethnic and religious hatreds have reentered political discourse, appearing now as a resurgent nationalism" in eastern European countries.[11]

Recent estimates based on the National Jewish Population Survey (NJPS) put the current Jewish American population at about 5.2 million. Others argue that if a broader definition of who is Jewish is used, the figure is a bit higher, probably more than 6 million. In either case, that represents a large proportion of the world's Jewish population. Most Jewish Americans were born in the United States; the majority live in large metropolitan areas—especially New York–northern New Jersey, Los Angeles–Riverside–Orange counties, and Miami–Ft. Lauderdale. Since the peak year of 1937, Jewish Americans have declined as a percentage of the U.S. population, to about 2 percent today.[12]

Prejudice and Stereotypes

Jewish Americans have been socially defined by non-Jewish outsiders on the basis of physical and cultural characteristics. From the 1800s onward, numerous non-Jews in many countries have considered Jews to be a biologically inferior "race."[13] No group in history has suffered a broader range of stereotypes for a longer period than have the Jews.

For centuries, they have been targets of hostility—that is, **anti-Semitism**, which includes *stereotyping or prejudice toward, or discrimination against, the Jews*. For many centuries, and especially since the Middle Ages, the theological writings of Christendom have often been rife with anti-Semitism. Jews have been cursed as the "Christ killers," as those mainly responsible for Jesus's death, a view many Christian immigrants brought with them to North America. This erroneous view is still articulated by some Christian writers and ministers, as well as in some movies. However, the earliest Christian account, the Gospel of Mark, shows clearly that the Roman authorities were responsible for the crucifixion of Jesus, who was likely seen as a political threat, and only they had such power. The Roman authorities crucified *thousands* of Jews and others they considered as dissidents. If the Jewish authorities had been primarily responsible—and some did collude with the Romans—Jesus would have been stoned to death.[14]

Unlike African, Native, and Latino Americans, who are often stereotyped as unintelligent, Jewish Americans have often been seen as too intelligent and too crafty. This "devious" stereotype likely developed in part to rationalize Jewish Americans' success as "middleman" merchants in this society.[15]

In the late 1800s, a stereotype of Jewish Americans as social climbers was circulated in the media, including then-popular vaudeville shows. Clumsy Jewish figures speaking oddly inflected English were depicted as being out of place in high-society positions. By the 1880s, newspaper and magazine cartoons were caricaturing Jewish Americans as long-nosed, garishly dressed merchants speaking broken English. During this period, Jewish Americans were excluded from many organizations and institutions. For example, in 1877 a prominent banker was denied accommodation in a major New York hotel. The following year a Jewish American was excluded from the New York City Bar Association, and New York's City College banned Jewish Americans from fraternities.[16]

One particularly vicious attack on Jews was the fictional book called *The Protocols of the Elders of Zion*. This highly stereotypical tract was created by the Russian secret police and attempted to show that Jews, as anti-Christian agents, were taking covert control of the world and destroying Western civilization. Automobile pioneer Henry Ford worked to spread vicious anti-Semitic stereotypes. In May 1920, a summary of *The Protocols* appeared in Ford's newspaper in Dearborn, Michigan, boosting the circulation. By the 1920s this book was widely circulated. Ford's newspaper and *The Protocols* played an important role in a burst of malicious anti-Semitic stereotypes and discriminatory agitation.[17] Numerous hate groups and websites still circulate the vicious *Protocols* today.

In subsequent decades, numerous media cartoons and reports stereotyped Jewish Americans as "Communist" sympathizers and alleged that "Jews were taking over the U.S. government." Right after World War II, a *Fortune* magazine poll found that three-fourths of those who felt some U.S. groups had more power than was good for the country cited Jewish Americans.[18]

Various forms of anti-Semitism persist today in the United States and Europe. The president of a major Baptist organization stated publicly that God does *not* hear the prayers of Jews; a leader of a conservative group asserted that Jews had a "supernatural" talent for moneymaking. Recently, numerous conservative Christian ministers have written about Jews "being spiritually blind" and in need of Christianizing. Actor Mel Gibson's film, *The Passion of the Christ*, was assailed by Christian–Jewish dialogue groups and Jewish organizations for portrayals of Jewish leaders (or Jews) as primarily and collectively responsible for the death of Jesus—a notion heard for centuries in some Christian rituals and numerous Passion Plays (the latter also a favorite of Adolph Hitler) around the globe.[19]

In a 2005 national survey of Jewish respondents, 27 percent said that that anti-Semitism is still a very serious problem; another 65 percent said that it is somewhat of a problem. Many Jewish Americans single out the "religious right" as the most anti-Semitic group.[20] Significantly, recent surveys have found that many non-Jewish Americans seriously overestimate the Jewish American presence, often placing that group at about 25 percent of the U.S. population (instead of the actual 2 percent). This estimate may indicate the negative view that Jews are too dominant. In addition, a 2005 national survey found that one-third of U.S. respondents believed Jews were *more* loyal to Israel than to the United States. Thirty percent believed Jews were mainly responsible for the death of Jesus (an increase since a 2002 survey), and 15 percent thought that Jews had too much power in the United States. Overall, some one-seventh of the total population was estimated to be very anti-Semitic in beliefs, including larger proportions of Latinos (29 percent) and African Americans (36 percent). Still, substantial *majorities* of the survey respondents felt that there should tougher sentences for hate crimes and that the history of the Holocaust should be taught to schoolchildren.[21]

Numerous researchers have examined stereotyped images. One noted that stereotypically Jewish characters in the media are only one problem: "The prevalence of interdating and intermarriage plots (to a point where they have become the paradigm for any romance involving a Jewish character); the virtual disappearance of Jewish families; the artificial limits on the number of Jewish characters on a single show, which might stigmatize it as 'too Jewish'; and finally, the often tasteless representation of religious themes and characters are related issues."[22]

Joyce Antler has documented the critical roles that Jewish women have played in their communities. Through contributions to literature, cinema, radio, and television, Jewish women have "helped to shape the main currents of modern and postmodern life." However, popular culture continues to perpetuate many inaccurate stereotypes of Jewish women—images of the "Yiddish Mama," the assertive "Jewish Mother," and the "Jewish American Princess" (JAP). Negative images of women are commonplace in jokes and on greeting cards. Numerous women scholars and media personalities have worked to reduce these negative images of Jewish women, as well as of Jews in general. In major films, Barbra Streisand, an influential Jewish American singer, has portrayed "feisty Jews and feisty women," creating positive images with staying power.[23]

Oppression and Conflict

During the 1880s, Jewish American merchants in the South suffered violent attacks from non-Jewish farmers who blamed them for economic crises; in the 1890s, farms and homes of Jewish merchants were burned in Mississippi. In the early 1900s, riots erupted against Jewish factory workers in New Jersey. Just before World War I, Leo Frank, a Jewish American in Georgia, was convicted of killing an employee and then lynched by an angry mob.[24]

About this time the Ku Klux Klan was also revived, and these white terrorists waged violence against black, Jewish, and Catholic Americans. During the 1920s and 1930s, crosses were burned on Jewish properties; synagogues were vandalized. On occasion, victims fought back. In the 1920s, Jewish and Catholic immigrants protested parades and gatherings of the Klan in Ohio and New Jersey.[25]

Organized Anti-Semitism and Hate Crimes

Between 1932 and 1941, openly anti-Semitic organizations grew to number more than one hundred. Two dozen were large-scale operations that held numerous anti-Semitic rallies, some of which drew thousands of people. Millions of anti-Semitic leaflets and newspapers were distributed. Father Charles Coughlin's organizations—the National Union and the Christian Front—were active in anti-Jewish agitation in the 1930s. In 1940 the FBI arrested more than a dozen members of a Christian Front terrorist group that reportedly intended to kill "Jews and Communists, 'to knock off about a dozen Congressmen,' and to seize post offices, the Customs House, and armories in New York. In the homes of the group were found 18 cans of cordite, 18 rifles, and 5,000 rounds of ammunition."[26]

Increased anti-Semitism in Germany was an important factor in the rising number of Nazi attacks against Jewish Americans. The Nazi Holocaust began with restrictions on Jewish communities, which were soon followed by deportation to forced-labor camps and extermination. An estimated 6 million European Jews (as well as millions of others, such as Gypsies and homosexuals) were killed by the Nazis. In the United States, the sense of oppression among Jewish Americans was reinforced not only by newspaper reports of European refugees but by the growing knowledge that the U.S. government was aiding Nazi actions in Germany—at first by continuing economic and diplomatic relations (until 1941) and later by turning its back on thousands of Jewish refugees.[27]

Violent attacks on Jewish Americans, their property, and their synagogues were common after World War II. In the last three decades their number has decreased, but they are still a significant problem. Generally, only blatant instances of anti-Semitism are reported to the Anti-Defamation League (ADL). The League's first survey (1979) counted 129 reported cases of anti-Semitic vandalism, including arson and the painting of swastikas (the Nazi

Anti-Semitic vandalism remains common in many areas of the United States.

"twisted cross") on synagogues. Between 1979 and 1984, some 3694 anti-Jewish incidents were reported, and today annual figures remain significant. Reported incidents include physical and verbal attacks on individuals, acts of vandalism against property, assaults, and harassment. For example, in 1996 a bomb was set off at a Jewish Center in New York. Members of one neo-Nazi group, The Order, which was formed to conduct war against the "Zionist Occupation Government," machine-gunned a Jewish talk-show host in Denver, committed robberies, counterfeited money, set fire to a synagogue, and killed police officers. The number of hate crimes by racist skinheads (white neo-Nazis who shave their heads) has grown in recent years.[28]

In 1990 Congress passed the Hate Crime Statistics Act, requiring the U.S. Justice Department to collect hate crime data from police departments. **Hate crimes** are defined as *crimes against people and property generated by prejudice against racial, ethnic, religious, disability, or sexual orientation groups*. The most recent (2003) FBI hate crimes report counted more than 7400 hate crimes, with about 9200 victims; about 12.5 percent (931) were anti-Semitic incidents. (Other groups suffered even more such incidents.) More recently, in its 2005 report, the ADL counted 1821 anti-Semitic incidents in forty-four reporting states and the District of Columbia, the highest figure in nine years. Most occurred in northern and midwestern states or in Florida. The reasons for the increase included "activity by organized neo-Nazi hate groups and a spike in reports of anti-Jewish harassment and intimidation in America's schools." Similar incidents are reported regularly in France, Germany, Italy, Russia, and Canada. The ADL has also noted increases in anti-Semitic groups participating in a global network, spreading racist propaganda via Internet sites. Note that most hate crimes are not reported to police agencies; according to the Southern Poverty Law Center, the actual figure is likely to be at least 50,000 annually.[29]

In recent years more than forty state legislatures have passed hate crimes laws, and most make religious desecration a special crime. Numerous state legislatures have increased penalties for crimes involving racial and ethnic hatred. A more comprehensive federal approach to dealing with anti-Jewish and other hate crimes, such as the Hate Crimes Prevention Act (introduced in Congress in 1999), has been supported by Jewish and other civil rights organizations, but has so far been stalled by conservative members of Congress.[30]

Religious Discrimination and Conflict

Federal court cases have periodically dealt with religious discrimination. During the 1950s and 1960s, Jewish business owners contested local "blue laws" that required businesses to close on Sunday, the Christian holy day; they argued that such laws violated their First Amendment right not to be penalized for religious practices. The Supreme Court, however, upheld the blue laws. Christian religious observances, such as reciting the Lord's Prayer, were once standard in public schools. The imposition of these and other Christian religious practices on Jewish children was contested in state courts, and in the 1960s the Supreme Court ruled against officially sanctioned religious practices in public schools. Although since the 1980s a conservative Supreme

Court has upheld the practice of prayers in legislatures and the government practice of putting Christian nativity scenes on public property, the Court has also reaffirmed the principle of the separation of church and state.[31]

In 1986 the Supreme Court ruled that the U.S. Air Force could require an Orthodox rabbi serving as a chaplain to remove his religious head covering—called a yarmulke—when working indoors. For Orthodox Jews, religious law requires adult men to wear head coverings at all times. The impact of such cases has been to give court sanction to government decisions that decide which religious expressions are permissible in the government sphere and which are not.[32]

What has been the basis for much of the prejudice and discrimination targeting Jewish Americans?

Jewish Americans Fight Back

Fear of crime and anti-Semitism led to the formation of self-protective associations. In 1968, Rabbi Meir Kahane, an ultraconservative Jewish nationalist, organized the Jewish Defense League (JDL) in New York, in part to deal with threats against Jewish communities. The JDL's goals included reinvigoration of ethnic pride and use of armed citizen patrols to protect communities from crime. During the 1980s, some JDL members protesting the treatment of Jews in the Soviet Union disrupted Soviet diplomatic activities and tried to assassinate high-level diplomats.[33] Kahane was assassinated in 1990, but the organization has continued aggressive efforts to defend Jewish issues and communities, especially against neo-Nazi groups. The Anti-Defamation League has condemned the JDL's "reckless violence against Jews [who do not agree with the group] and non-Jews" and for their "cult of violence and racism who speak only for themselves."[34] Most Jewish Americans condemn such extremist groups.

Jewish–Black Relations

African Americans and Jewish Americans share a long history of mutual assistance. This history has been very important for both groups, as more than a dozen recent books on black–Jewish relations have made clear. For example, Cheryl Greenberg's 2006 book, *Troubling the Waters,* shows how, from the 1930s to the 1960s, the black–Jewish alliance helped build a strong civil rights movement in spite of major ongoing conflicts. Actually, the relationship goes back more than a century. In the 1850s, three Jewish immigrants participated in abolitionist John Brown's well-known armed struggle against slavery. And in 1917 a Jewish newspaper condemned antiblack violence in the white-led East St. Louis riot. Joel Spingarn, a Jewish American, was chairperson of the then new black civil rights organization, the National Association for the Advancement of Colored People (NAACP), between 1914 and 1939. Moreover, at the end of World War II, an all-black unit in the racially segregated U.S. armed forces was photographed and shown to be among the first units to liberate the Jews in the Nazi concentration camps. Although they were denied equality at home, black troops risked their lives for the U.S. cause and helped free Jewish victims of Nazism. Later, during the 1960s civil rights movement, Jewish Americans comprised more than half of the white students who went to the South to register black voters and of the white lawyers who defended imprisoned civil rights protesters. Some were murdered by white southerners for this effort.[35]

Conflict has, however, erupted periodically between Jewish Americans and African Americans. In the 1960s black urban rebellions—and in similar 1980s–1990s rebellions—black rioters have sometimes attacked local Jewish (and other white as well as Asian) businesses they considered to be exploiting their communities. These developments generated a backlash among Jewish Americans. Controversies between Jewish and African Americans in New York City have often gained media attention. In the 1970s there was conflict between black New Yorkers (especially parents) and Jewish New Yorkers (especially teachers) over the experimental decentralizing of the control of public schools, mainly in predominantly black districts. Later, in the 1990s, tension escalated between Hasidic Jewish residents and black residents in Brooklyn after crime patrols, set up by the Hasidic community, harassed and beat black and Latino residents from nearby areas who ventured into the community. In nearby Crown Heights, a Hasidic driver accidentally ran over a black child, setting off anti-Jewish rioting by angry black residents in which a rabbinical student was killed. The traffic death, rioting, and other violence greatly increased tensions between black and Jewish residents.[36]

Since the 1960s, some black anti-Semitism and black leaders' criticism of Israeli treatment of Palestinians have alienated numerous Jewish Americans from participation in intergroup coalitions. In recent decades a few black leaders have aimed anti-Semitic remarks at Jewish merchants and landlords whom they believed were exploiting black communities economically.[37] Some black leaders have been unwilling to disavow the comments of Louis Farrakhan, a leader of the Nation of Islam, whose anti-Semitic utterances included a reference to Judaism as a "gutter religion."[38] Into the 2000s, negative statements about Jews and Judaism by some Nation of Islam ministers, and a few other black leaders, have helped to perpetuate major tensions between Jewish and black communities. Antiblack sentiments have also been found among some Jewish Americans.

Perceptively, Letty Pogrebin has given important reasons for continuing tensions: "The differences between blacks and Jews are rarely more obvious than when each group speaks about its own 'survival,' a word that both use frequently but with quite dissimilar meanings .... Blacks worry about their actual conditions and fear for the present; Jews worry about their history and fear for the future." Members of each group fear the other, but for different reasons: Some Jewish Americans fear the urban black Americans and leaders who make anti-Semitic remarks. Some African Americans, in contrast, fear Jewish Americans primarily because they are part of the dominant white group. Indeed, as recent analyses such as those of Karen Brodkin and Ira Katznelson have made clear, in the decades since World War II American Jews have clearly become "white." As a result, the many postwar educational, veterans', and housing programs benefitted them greatly, even as the same programs often routinely excluded or marginalized African Americans.[39]

Still, these tensions between Jewish and African Americans have not substantially affected Jewish commitments to civil rights. Among white groups, Jewish Americans remain the most liberal on racial issues. In recent decades, opinion polls have found that Jewish views on racial matters are closer to those of African American respondents than to those of white Protestants and Catholics. A major nationwide survey found that Jewish Americans were more likely than other whites to believe that black Americans do not receive equal treatment in the economic, educational, or judicial arenas. Their views on racial matters were also much closer to those of black Americans than to those of other whites.[40]

Today, many Jewish individuals and organizations strongly support black civil rights causes and communities. For example, although some Jewish businesses were burned by rioters during a 1990s Los Angeles riot, thirty synagogues and Hillel centers (campus organizations) provided substantial clothing and food for relief of black families in riot areas.[41] The pattern of mutual support has been evident in the national political arena for decades. One study by the American Jewish Congress of the votes of the thirty-nine black and thirty-two Jewish members of the U.S. Congress found that much of the time the two groups voted *alike* on matters of interest to both communities, including issues of separation of church and state and important government social services.[42]

Indeed, there is even a little overlap in the membership of the groups called African American and Jewish American. A few small groups of African Americans adhere to Judaism, and some of these religious adherents have created the Alliance of Black Jews.

Since the 1990s, black and Jewish citizens in numerous dialogue groups have sought ways to ease tensions between these two traditional allies in the struggle for civil rights. For example, in several cities, black and Jewish teenagers join in celebrating Martin Luther King, Jr.'s birthday, such as by volunteering in local soup kitchens. Operation Understanding, a cooperative group created by a black member of Congress and a Jewish executive, is sponsored by the Urban League and the American Jewish Committee. Each year the group has brought together significant groups of Jewish and black students in several major cities to build interracial bridges, such as by visiting sites of cultural importance to each group—Ellis Island, New York, where large numbers of eastern European Jews entered the United States, or the Mississippi location of the murder of black and Jewish civil rights workers.[43]

Considering the decades since World War II, what has been the relationship between Jewish Americans and African Americans?

Politics

From their first arrival in the colonies, Jewish immigrants were treated as outsiders. Members of the first Jewish community, in Dutch New Amsterdam, were barred from holding public office; and, in general, voting and officeholding in the English and Dutch colonies were limited to Christians. Nonetheless, later on, Jewish Americans made very substantial contributions to the American Revolution, and the government to which the Revolution gave birth brought benefits to Jewish citizens by establishing the (unique for the time) separation of church and state. The U.S. Constitution's prohibition of religious qualifications for public office and the Bill of Rights' protection of speech and religious choice granted political freedom at the federal level. Political enfranchisement was slower to come at the state level. Indeed, by 1790 only five states had removed voting and officeholding restrictions; six others carried Christians-only provisions for political participation *as late as 1876*. Still, fierce "anti-Semitism never became rooted in the political tradition of American society," as it had in Europe.[44]

In the first years of the U.S. republic, anti-Jewish practices by Federalist party officials, combined with their support for the new anti-immigrant Alien and Sedition Laws, guaranteed that most Jewish Americans would support the more liberal Jeffersonian political party, later to become the Democratic Party. Although Jewish Americans supported Democrats for decades, some gravitated to the antislavery Republican Party in the 1850s.[45]

The voting power of Jewish Americans increased as they became concentrated in northern cities at the beginning of the twentieth century. Socialist Party candidates received strong support, but many Jewish Americans remained Republicans or supported the Irish-dominated Democratic machines, which provided jobs and shelter to needy urban immigrants. Whereas Irish Americans used ethnic politics to advance immediate economic and family interests—for example, to create jobs—Jewish Americans, although concerned with bread-and-butter matters, were more political-issue–oriented, particularly with regard to expanding civil rights.[46]

Jewish Americans and Political Parties

By 1910, few Jewish Americans had won electoral office. An occasional city council member, one or two state legislators, a judge—this was the extent of political success. Political representation at the national level was modest. The appearance of an internationalist Democratic candidate, Woodrow Wilson, brought a majority of Jewish voters to the Democrats for the first time in decades. Wilson appointed a few Jewish Americans to important positions, including the legal genius Louis Brandeis to the Supreme Court.[47]

Franklin Roosevelt brought Jewish Americans firmly into the Democratic fold in 1932. Roosevelt's anti-Nazi rhetoric, support of social programs such as Social Security, and support of labor unions won over many Jewish voters. For the first time, Roosevelt brought numerous Jewish Americans into the federal government. Benjamin Cohen, Felix Frankfurter, and Louis Brandeis served as advisers to Roosevelt, and Roosevelt appointed Henry Morgenthau, Jr., Secretary of the Treasury.[48]

Yet, Roosevelt did *not* take dynamic action on behalf of refugees from Nazi-dominated Europe. One reason was his fear of the intense anti-Semitism prevailing in the United States during the 1930s and 1940s, especially among the gentile (non-Jewish) members of Congress. Anti-Jewish discrimination was then common in politics, social affairs, education, employment, jury selection in certain states, and real estate decisions.[49]

Since Roosevelt, decade after decade, a substantial proportion of the Jewish vote has usually gone to Democratic presidential candidates. Recently, in the 2005 Annual Survey of American Jewish Opinion (ASAJO), 54 percent of Jewish respondents identified with the Democratic Party, and only 16 percent with the Republican Party, probably the lowest for any white ethnic group. In addition, 44 percent spoke of themselves as liberal, 29 percent as middle-of-the-road, and only 26 percent as conservative. In the survey, we also see a strong commitment to liberal political issues, especially social justice, a view likely honed by centuries of anti-Semitic oppression.[50]

Historically, Jewish Americans have been underrepresented among elected and appointed officials. It was not until 1974 that a Jewish American (Abraham Beame) became mayor of New York City. Also in the 1970s, Dianne Feinstein became the first Jewish woman to be elected mayor of a major city, San Francisco. Only somewhat more than one hundred Jewish Americans have ever held the office of state governor, U.S. senator, or member of the U.S. House

Senator Joseph Lieberman (D–CT.), here campaigning in 2000 with his wife Haddassah, was the first Jewish American to be nominated for vice-president by a major political party.

of Representatives. The only Jewish American ever nominated for president by a major party was Barry Goldwater (a convert to the Episcopal religion), who was defeated in 1964. So far, only a half-dozen Jewish Americans have ever served on the U.S. Supreme Court, although perhaps one-fifth of the country's lawyers in recent decades have been Jewish. In 1993 President Bill Clinton appointed the first Jewish American woman (the second woman ever) to the Supreme Court—Ruth Bader Ginsburg. By the early 2000s there were two Jews on the U.S. Supreme Court. As of 2006 Jewish Americans held numerous important positions in the U.S. House (twenty-six members) and Senate (eleven members), a proportion (nearly 7 percent) substantially higher than the Jewish percentage of the population—though likely in line with the Jewish percentage among Americans who are most active in politics. In 2000 the Democratic Party, for the first time in major party history, chose a Jewish American, Senator Joseph Lieberman of Connecticut, as its vice-presidential candidate.[51]

Discrimination still plays a role in limiting the number of Jewish Americans who occupy political offices in numerous states and cities. In these areas the proportion of Jewish Americans in elected office is low given their relatively high proportion among political activists and contributors. Moreover, although there are somewhat more Jews than Presbyterians and Episcopalians together in the United States, in recent years Jewish Americans have not held even half as many congressional offices as have members of these powerful Protestant groups (most recently, ninety-one members).[52]

In the political arena, what have been primary concerns for many Jewish American voters?

Unions and Community Organizations

Eastern European immigrants protested oppressive working conditions in the 1890s, organizing to fight long hours, low pay, and unsafe conditions. New York City data for the 1930s show large numbers of Jewish Americans in food, entertainment, clothing, and jewelry unions. Jewish union leaders often went beyond the problems of wages and working conditions to grapple with broader issues, such as developing health, pension, and educational programs that would be imitated by other unions. Jewish Americans also played an important role in the growth of the American Socialist Party and subsequent labor–liberal parties.[53]

By the 1930s, several important civic and civil rights organizations had been established: the Anti-Defamation League, the American Jewish Congress, the American Jewish Committee, and the United Jewish Appeal. Since 1906 the American Jewish Committee has vigorously fought anti-Semitic discrimination. The American Jewish Congress has long fought for civil rights. The Anti-Defamation League has carried out a long campaign to root out anti-Semitism. The United Jewish Appeal, established in 1939, has been a successful fund-raising organization that has aided numerous causes, including those of political refugees and the state of Israel. The United Jewish Communities, a merger of earlier humanitarian and philanthropic federations and organizations, is currently made up of 155 Jewish federations and 400 independent organizations serving Jewish Americans. An important agent of civic Judaism, this humanitarian movement has long stressed social services, social justice activism, and progressive political issues.[54]

The survival of Israel has been a major concern of Jewish organizations in recent decades. During the 1950s, political pressure for U.S. government support for Israel was largely unheeded, but by the 1960s such support had sharply increased. Since the 1960s, Jewish American political pressure has been mobilized for numerous other causes, such as opposition to political candidates who support Middle Eastern policies viewed as hostile to Israel. More recently, new liberal organizations have developed, and these reveal the diversity of views on the Middle East, Israel, and Palestinians among Jewish Americans. The New Israel Fund, a partnership involving Americans, Canadians, Israelis, and Europeans, provides funding for social justice efforts designed to benefit both Arab and Jewish residents of Israel. The Jewish Peace Lobby and the Jewish Voice for Peace attempt to provide constructive criticism of U.S. and Israeli policies and to take a more progressive approach to issues involving Israeli Jews and Palestinian Arabs than some older organizations.[55]

In addition to combating anti-Semitism, some organizations have worked to eliminate all racial prejudice and discrimination and to ensure separation of church and state. For example, early in his first term as president (2001), George W. Bush proposed a "faith-based initiative" to involve private religious organizations in providing social services with federal aid. At a meeting between a Bush representative and the Jewish Council for Public Affairs, a coalition of 123 Jewish organizations working on public policy and social service issues, concerns about separation of church and state were articulated. Jewish American leaders feared that government support might go to specifically religious activities, which would violate the principle of government neutrality.[56]

In recent years, some Jewish Americans have accused the well-off board members of the American Jewish Committee, the American Jewish Congress, the United Jewish Appeal, and the Anti-Defamation League of being more sympathetic to the needs of employers than to traditional concerns for workers, the poor, and discrimination. This criticism may be unfair to some degree, but it highlights a dilemma faced by Jewish Americans. As perhaps the most affluent of white ethnic groups, Jewish Americans might be expected to develop the generally conservative orientation of other high-income white groups.[57] Some have indeed become politically conservative. Yet, given their past experiences with racial-ethnic discrimination and continuing anti-Semitism, Jewish Americans generally remain more liberal, both politically and economically, than non-Jewish whites.

The Economy

Jewish immigrants have contributed to the prosperity of North America from colonial times. One immigrant from Poland, Haym Salomon, played a critical role in financing the American Revolution with a loan to the struggling revolutionary government. The opening of commerce in the Americas presented opportunities for many European Jews, especially those with centuries of experience as a "middleman" trading minority in Europe, where they were excluded from land ownership. However, their success in certain commercial pursuits in Europe had made them a scapegoat for the non-Jewish poor, who often saw them as exploiters, and for the non-Jewish rich, who viewed them as an economic threat. In North America the often marginal nature of their businesses, as well as discrimination, fostered the growth of an ethnic economy in which Jews relied on economic aid from one another to maintain their businesses and communities.[58]

Establishing an Economic Niche: A "Middleman Minority"?

The rate of penetration of a new immigrant group into the core economy depends on its economic background as well as conditions at the point of destination. Most German and other central European Jews were poor when they came to the United States. However, they arrived when frontier development and industrial growth were expanding, and they often found that their experience as merchants was in demand. As street vendors, they roamed city streets and the countryside. Many eventually became prosperous shopkeepers.[59] By the 1890s, a majority of the German and other central European Jews were moving up the economic ladder.

The next large group of immigrants, from eastern Europe, also entered the expanding industrial economy at an opportune time. Most were poor and poorly educated, but their experience in coping with oppression in Europe provided them a heritage replete with strategies for finding economic niches in which to survive. Men, women, and children often engaged in low-wage manufacturing work. The long hours and poor working conditions of industrial capitalism's factories, often miserable sweatshops, led to participation in union movements on the part of these immigrants. In the early 1900s, more than one-third of eastern European Jewish immigrants were employed in the garment industry, one-fourth were in building trades, and one-fifth were in retail trade. Members of the second generation were encouraged by their parents to seek white-collar jobs, and many went into law, medicine, and other white-collar professions.[60]

Jewish women contributed significantly to family incomes. A Philadelphia study in this period found that one in three Jewish households had a woman working outside the home, including most unmarried women. Because of the low wages of male and female workers, families needed the wages that women earned working outside the home or by taking in sewing or laundry to do at home. Wives often joined their husbands in small retail shops that supplied many neighborhoods. Many working-class women were left to raise their children alone when their husbands died or deserted the family.[61]

From the Depression to 1950

The solidarity of the Jewish American community and its heavy involvement in small and medium-sized businesses were sources of survival during the Great Depression of the 1930s. Whenever possible, Jewish American businesses dealt with one another and hired unemployed relatives. Organized crime provided a way out of poverty for a small proportion in early decades, but participation in organized crime declined significantly as large numbers moved out of the working class and into the middle class, and suburban areas, following World War II.[62]

The Jewish ethnic economy provided a fallback position for those who faced discrimination from gentiles. One goal of anti-Semitic organizations was to reduce the number of Jewish Americans in private and public employment. Non-Jewish whites in the teaching, banking, medical, legal, and engineering professions often sought to prohibit Jewish Americans from employment in these fields. In many cities Jewish workers found it very difficult to secure skilled blue-collar jobs and clerical jobs. The Great Depression increased this problem. Signs proclaiming "No Jews need apply" were commonplace. Jews faced discrimination in the teaching profession, particularly in smaller cities and at colleges. From 1900 to the 1950s, discrimination was rife in housing, from Philadelphia to Boston and Chicago, as well as in smaller cities. Even for the significant numbers who managed to move to suburbs, Protestant-oriented organizations and recreational facilities were often off-limits.[63]

One obsession of anti-Semites, even to the present day, has been the alleged Jewish "dominance of banking." This fear increased in the 1930s. However, a 1936 *Fortune* magazine survey found very few Jewish Americans in banking and finance. Another survey found that *only six hundred* (far less than 1 percent) of 93,000 banking officials were Jewish. Jewish Americans were also *rare* in heavy industries, public utilities, the press, and radio. The only sectors in which Jewish Americans were overrepresented were clothing, textiles, and the movies. Even in law and medicine, Jews held few powerful positions. The author of the 1936 *Fortune* article seemed puzzled by the clusters of Jews found in certain industrial and business areas and explained the situation in the stereotypical terms of Jewish clannishness. Such clustering patterns were not mysterious, for they reflected the extent to which Jewish workers and entrepreneurs were forced to work outside mainstream industries and businesses because of blatant and well-institutionalized anti-Semitism. They were channeled by gentile discrimination into higher-risk economic spheres that were often marginal to the mainstream economy.[64]

After World War II, extensive employment discrimination continued. Job advertisements included anti-Jewish restrictions, and employment agencies discriminated against Jews. Even so, many Jewish Americans were able to share in postwar prosperity, particularly in new industries such as television and plastics. Jewish workers still were concentrated primarily in trade, clothing, and jewelry manufacturing; commerce; merchandising; certain light industries; mass communications; and certain white-collar professions. In 1957 the Census Bureau found that three-fourths of Jewish men were employed in white-collar jobs, compared with 38 percent of white Protestants. Yet, in 1950 no more than 3 percent of corporate executives, presidents, and board chairpersons were Jews. Given the preponderance of Jewish Americans in commercial and business employment, this proportion was much lower than it would have been absent discrimination. A large proportion of Jewish executives made it to the top only in Jewish-owned businesses.[65]

Individual and Family Success

The most recent National Jewish Population Survey (NJPS) estimated median annual income for Jewish American households (including both families and single individuals) to be $54,000. The median income for all U.S. households was significantly less.[66] (Household income figures are usually less than family income figures.) The median Jewish household is thus substantially better off in terms of income than the median U.S. household—another sign of economic mobility over recent generations. Still, about 5 percent of Jewish households report incomes that fall below the federal poverty line.

Continuing occupational mobility has characterized Jewish Americans over the last few decades. In the 1960s, occupational data for major east coast cities showed that 20 to 32 percent of Jewish American males were in professional positions, with another 28 to 54 percent in managerial positions. More than half of Jewish workers in all the cities fell into these two major categories, while most of the rest held either clerical or sales positions. In comparison, the majority of the total employed population in each of these cities held blue-collar positions. More recent data confirm this trend toward white-collar employment. One 1990s survey revealed that most Jewish American workers held salaried white-collar positions or were self-employed.[67]

In recent decades, as earlier, Jewish executives have not controlled U.S. banking. Excluding one New York bank (31 percent of whose top managers were Jewish), in 1976 only 2.5 percent of the executives of commercial banks nationwide were Jewish. A decade later, another analysis found that 3.4 percent of the executives at ten of the largest banks were Jewish.[68] A 1980s study of Jewish Americans in the corporate elite found that most were in Jewish-founded corporations or occupied lower managerial positions in other corporations. Those who have cracked the top of the corporate establishment, such as Irving Shapiro, formerly head of DuPont, have usually been brought in from outside. They have rarely been given the chance to start at the bottom and work their way to the top.[69]

Abraham Korman's 1988 study of the distribution of Jewish American executives in corporate America found that they constituted less than 5 percent of senior executives in many of the largest corporations in terms of annual sales and number of employees. Korman's interviews with consultants and managers documented the "outsider" status of Jewish managers. These interviewees agreed that, to succeed in the corporate hierarchy, Jewish Americans must divest themselves of *all visible Jewish identity*. As we will document throughout this book, this more or less forced one-way assimilation to the dominant Anglo-Protestant norms and arrangements is still an oppressive aspect of this society. Some Jewish respondents cited specific anti-Jewish actions that blocked career advancement; some were even denied job titles appropriate to their duties. Like many Asian Americans, many found that they could hold professional or staff positions but would never be considered for higher executive positions.[70]

Until the past two decades, higher-level government positions have rarely been open to Jews. One Jewish American noted that when he began his career in the 1960s, "the State Department (and the CIA and FBI) was virtually closed to Jews."[71] Interestingly, in the late 1990s the media made much of the fact that a dozen top people in the State Department were Jewish, including then Secretary of State Madeleine Albright, who had converted to Episcopalianism. This did mark a significant change, yet such intense media attention was problematical, because similar attention was not given to the prevalence of Presbyterian or Catholic government officials.

Perhaps because the academic sphere may offer greater freedom than other employment spheres, many of the country's college professors have been Jewish, though only in recent decades. Jewish Americans have been well represented among distinguished scholars at major universities and among top literary figures. They have included Nobel laureate Saul Bellow and prominent intellectuals such as Noam Chomsky, Stephen Jay Gould, Irving Howe, and Seymour Martin Lipset.

How did Jewish Americans come to play a role as a "middleman minority"?

Persisting Discrimination

In the 2005 ASAJO, most Jewish respondents thought anti-Semitism was still a problem in the United States. *Only 10 percent* believed it would decrease in the future.[72] There is still significant anti-Jewish discrimination in both public and private organizations. Thus, an employee at a major rental car company reported that he was told by supervisors that Hasidic Jews were "the worst people to rent to." Two employees reported that supervisors rejected business accounts from Jewish applicants. Although the company denied the allegations, the complaints suggested the likelihood of continuing economic discrimination against Jewish Americans.[73]

The effects of anti-Semitism keep many Jewish Americans from the full social recognition and political power that economic success brings to others. Only in 1985, for example, did New York City finally pass a law banning anti-Jewish and other discrimination in private clubs. In 1992, a bill banning racial and gender discrimination in private country clubs made its way through the New York State senate after being blocked for years by white Protestant opponents. In March of the same year, a similar bill banning discrimination in private clubs finally passed the Florida legislature. The American Jewish Congress headed a coalition of civil rights groups that worked together to get the bill passed. As of today, Florida is one of relatively few states with strong laws prohibiting racial or gender discrimination in private clubs. Recently, the governor of Maryland was criticized for attending a fundraising gathering at an all-white country club. Like numerous states, Maryland laws generally allow private clubs to exclude Jews, blacks, and women.[74] Some experts estimate that the majority of private country clubs have no black members, and many have no female or Jewish members. Others have very small numbers. Much discrimination has been hidden by secrecy at this high socioeconomic level of society. Often this discrimination is defended as private, yet many such "private" organizations benefit greatly from public laws and actions, such as tax exemptions and liquor licenses. Given such government benefits, Jewish and other civil rights groups have argued, they are in effect public facilities that should be subject to antidiscrimination laws.

Education

Education was not as high a priority for the earliest groups of Jewish immigrants as it was for later groups; earlier arrivals focused on (small) business success rather than on entering a profession or preserving the European tradition of religious scholarship. Significant participation in public schools came in the nineteenth century with the surge of eastern European immigrants, for whom secular education was a means of becoming "American." Parents pushed their children to succeed in school so that they could prosper economically and be accepted socially. College was valued as a door to a career for the young. Eastern European immigrants established numerous schools that taught Jewish religious practices to ensure that U.S.-born children would retain their ethnic and religious identity. Educational mobility for second- and third-generation Jewish Americans often came swiftly. Large numbers graduated from high school; many pursued college educations. By the late 1930s, about 9 percent of the country's 1.1 million college students were Jewish.[75]

Discriminatory Quotas for Jewish Students

Jewish progress in higher education was countered in part by discrimination on the part of Anglo-Protestant whites. Restrictive quotas for Jewish students were imposed at numerous colleges and universities from the 1920s to the 1950s. In 1918, Dean Frederick Jones of Yale University called for a ban on Jewish students because they were winning too many scholarships; in 1922, Harvard president A. L. Lowell called for discriminatory quotas. Covert methods to limit Jewish admissions, such as "character" tests and requirements for "geographic balance," were employed by many colleges. Various states restricted Jewish admissions to law schools and to the bar.[76]

Jewish Americans were often excluded from teaching positions. Between the 1920s and the 1940s, Jewish Ph.D.s found it difficult to secure appointments at Anglo-Protestant–dominated universities. However, the sudden increase in college enrollments following World War II created a demand for college teachers; by 1970 the proportion of Jewish faculty members on faculties in institutions of higher education had risen significantly, to 9 percent.[77]

Affirmative Action Programs

Affirmative action programs, which seek to improve educational opportunities and job chances for black and other non-European groups, have become a political issue for some Jewish Americans. Jewish Americans have long been among the vigorous supporters of the principle of individual merit, because of quota restrictions that once denied them access to higher education and to jobs. Some have thus opposed contemporary affirmative action programs, such as in college admissions, because of Jewish Americans' heavy commitment to higher education—a commitment that reflects past exclusion from many sectors of the academic world. College admissions preferences for non-Jewish groups, it has been argued, disproportionately affect Jewish access to college degrees and perpetuate the effects of past anti-Semitic discrimination.[78]

However, voicing support for affirmative action, Alan Dershowitz, a prominent Jewish American law professor, notes that the "real difference between the institutional impact and intensity of the hurt suffered as part of an invidious pattern of racial *subordination* and as part of a benevolent pattern of racial *equalization*." He points out the bias of college admission programs, such as those in Ivy League colleges, that hold fairly constant the number of students admitted from certain white Anglo-Protestant pools (descendants and relatives of alumni and those admitted to achieve "geographic balance"), yet at the same time make room for certain affirmative action applicants (Latinos and blacks) by reducing the numbers of other groups (Jewish and Asian Americans) who are admitted. He argues that it would be *much more* equitable for those white Anglo-Protestant groups that have long benefited from the exclusion of some racial and ethnic groups to bear a *heavier share* of the costs of equalization through affirmative action.[79] This perspective takes history and societal background into serious consideration, suggesting how past white privileges should be taken into account in considering contemporary remedies for continuing racial and ethnic inequalities.

Continuing Achievements in Education

Severe anti-Jewish discrimination declined after World War II, and since that time the educational attainment of Jewish Americans has reached ever higher levels. One 2000 survey of 1010 Jewish adults found that an amazing 86 percent had secured some college education, with 60 percent reporting at least a college degree. These figures are much higher than for the U.S. population as a whole.[80]

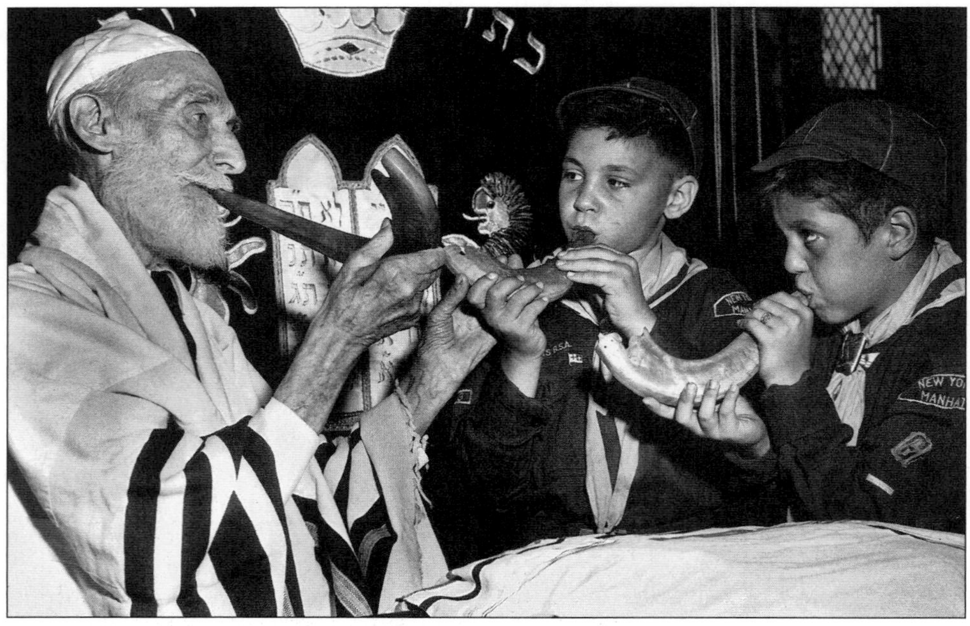

A Jewish elder shows youngsters how to blow a shofar, the ram's horn used in religious observances.

Schooling in Jewish religion and culture also persists. Surveys of Jewish Americans in recent decades have found strong support among parents for some Jewish education for their children, and large percentages of adults and children have reported receiving such education. The 2000–2001 NJPS report for "more engaged" Jewish Americans (about 93 percent of the Jewish population surveyed) estimated that much more than half of these adults and children had received some Jewish education. The emphasis on formal learning of one's heritage and religion in lower grades has carried over to colleges, for some 41 percent of current Jewish college and graduate students (the "more engaged" in the survey) reported having taken a Jewish studies class.[81]

Religion and Zionism

The degree of freedom allowed for people of various religious organizations varied across the American colonies, but most restricted Jewish participation in colonial life. Such anti-Jewish bias generated and sustained a vigorous oppositional culture among Jewish Americans that has formed the base for protest of religious and other oppression to the present day. Although the new country remained substantially Christian after 1790, religious freedom gradually became law in each new state.

As the numbers of German and other central European Jews increased, they founded their own synagogues. Jewish communities often had multiple synagogues representing different religious traditions. During the 1850s and 1860s, most Jewish congregations Americanized their religious practices, in part to achieve greater respectability from non-Jews. The American Reform movement became organized in the Union of American Hebrew Congregations in the 1870s. Reform temples had shorter services, organ music, and English prayers.[82]

The role of *Judaism* (the Jewish religion) in Jewish identity was a point of conflict between established German Jews and later eastern European immigrants. German Jews saw themselves as Americans whose religion happened to be Judaism. They generally endeavored to be inconspicuous. In contrast, new immigrants from eastern Europe generally had a strong desire to maintain their old ethnic identity. Most were Orthodox, observing the Sabbath and kosher dietary laws if they could. Theirs was a grass-roots adaptation of Orthodoxy that focused on family and group feeling and stressed charitable acts and observance of rituals.[83]

Conservative Judaism, which began in the 1880s as a modified traditionalism in reaction to Reform groups, appealed to later generations. Conservative synagogues observed many Orthodox traditions but discontinued strict dress codes and the separation of men and women at services. By 1935, Orthodox synagogues had about 1 million members, Conservative synagogues about 300,000, and Reform temples about 200,000. The authority of the rabbi, as well as traditional ritual, became less important as one moved from Orthodox to Conservative to Reform congregations. Many synagogues built in new middle-class neighborhoods after the 1920s were designed as community centers as well as religious centers. The Jewish atmosphere in concentrated neighborhoods provided a strong sense of group solidarity. Secularism, socialism, labor radicalism, and Zionism became the new "religions" of many younger Jewish Americans during and after the 1930s Depression.[84]

Trends in Religious Practice and Identity

Expanding suburbanization for Jewish families after World War II brought an increase in suburban congregations. As a small minority in suburbs, Jewish families sought a way to ensure the Jewishness of their children. Synagogue membership and ritual observances saw marked increases.[85]

Jewish American religion currently reflects a substantial interest in the traditional heritage, maintenance of the synagogue as a community center, and home religious practices. In the 2005 ASAJO, some 57 percent of the Jewish respondents reported belonging to a synagogue or temple. Moreover, there was substantial diversity: 10 percent identified as Orthodox, 32 percent as Conservative, 29 percent as Reform, and 28 percent stated that they were "just Jewish" or listed other commitments. Many Jewish Americans now do not see themselves as religious.[86]

Judaism has become one of the major U.S. religious traditions. Modern Judaism is a voluntary faith. Some call much of contemporary Judaism a "cardiac" religion, emphasizing the "heart" (ethics) rather than traditional ritual and doctrine. There are different denominations within U.S. Judaism, as within U.S. Protestantism. Orthodox Judaism, which bases Jewish identity on descent from a Jewish mother, still involves ritual observance with fewer adaptations to the secular world. In contrast, Reform Judaism accepts Jewish heredity through either a Jewish father or mother and emphasizes humanitarian Jewish principles rather than traditional ritual. Conservative Judaism represents a middle path between Orthodoxy's traditionalism and Reform's strong humanitarianism.[87]

Israel and Zionism

Concern for the survival and prosperity of Israel occupies a place near the center of modern Jewish consciousness. Whether religiously active or not, many Jewish Americans share a commitment to **Zionism**—*a worldwide movement for the establishment in Palestine of a national homeland (Israel) for the world's Jewish communities*. This commitment to the nation of Israel has affected Jewish voting patterns and Jewish–black relations (because of pro-Arab sentiments among some black leaders), as well as Jewish philanthropy. In the 2005 ASAJO, three-fourths of the respondents felt close to Israel; 42 percent reported having gone to Israel.[88] However, many Jewish Americans have periodically raised questions about the direction of Israeli or U.S. Middle East politics. One-fourth of the respondents and numerous leaders in an earlier American Jewish Committee survey agreed that Israel's continued occupation of Arab territories captured by force would "erode Israel's democratic and humanitarian character." Most have periodically favored "territorial compromise for credible guarantees of peace" and peace negotiations between Israel and the Palestine Liberation Organization (PLO) if the latter organization recognized the state of Israel and renounced terrorism.[89]

Since 1990 there have been ongoing negotiations between the Israeli government and the PLO over the future of the Palestinian population. An agreement was reached giving the PLO some political authority over the Palestinian population in certain occupied areas. A majority of Jewish Americans have backed peace negotiations between the PLO and the Israeli government, although many remain skeptical about a lasting peace. One late 1990s U.S. survey found that 82 percent supported the creation of a Palestinian state if Israel's security could be guaranteed (a "two-state solution").[90] However, in the 2005 ASAJO, 60 percent were opposed to Israel compromising on the status of Jerusalem as a united city under Israeli jurisdiction in order to secure peace. In that survey, 78 percent of the respondents also agreed with the pessimistic view that the "goal of the Arabs is not the return of occupied territories but rather the destruction of Israel."[91]

Assimilation or Pluralism?

At least two different theoretical perspectives have been used to explain the experiences of Jewish Americans—Anglo-conformity perspectives and cultural pluralism approaches. Most scholarly analyses have reflected an assimilation viewpoint. The dominant perspective among Jewish Americans themselves has been at least partially assimilationist: the view that substantial adaptation to the surrounding Anglo-Protestant culture is critical to achieving economic success and avoiding anti-Semitic prejudice and discrimination.[92]

Since the early 1800s, certain Jewish leaders have favored cultural pluralism as an alternative to Anglo-conformity assimilation. Horace Kallen, a Jewish American scholar, best formulated this perspective (see Chapter 2). He argued that for most people, ethnic-cultural group membership is not easily abandoned and that ethnic groups have a right to exist on their own terms—that is, democracy should be fully applied to U.S. ethnic groups. He argued against the ruthless Americanization long advocated for European immigrants by Anglo-Protestant Americans. Kallen gave the name *cultural pluralism* to this view. However, some scholars have argued that Kallen's cultural pluralism is not a useful perspective for understanding the adaptive history of Jewish Americans, because massive acculturation and substantial assimilation in other areas have been facts of life for most.[93]

Patterns of Assimilation

Partial cultural assimilation came relatively quickly for each of the three major groups of Jewish immigrants and their children. Most Sephardic and German Jews rapidly adapted, picking up English and certain North American folkways but maintaining a strong commitment to Judaism. Then came large numbers of eastern Europeans. German Jews pressed these immigrants to Americanize, yet most of the new arrivals were committed to retaining their distinctiveness and sense of Jewish peoplehood. Their European Yiddish culture, which in the United States became in part an oppositional culture, played a crucial role in perpetuating their Jewish heritage. These immigrants had no illusions that they would cease to be outsiders in a predominantly non-Jewish society, yet they aggressively embraced opportunities for jobs, citizenship, and education.[94]

Second-generation (and later) eastern Europeans were more affected by assimilation pressures and rapidly picked up the language and Anglo-Protestant values pressed on them in the media and the schools. Like the young Italian Americans (Chapter 4), they were caught between the culture of their parents and the Anglo-Protestant culture, a situation guaranteed to create family tensions. Their Judaism was usually Americanized. Many of the third generation moved out of predominantly Jewish neighborhoods. Still, they too were often eager to accent their Jewishness in their religious and secular practices.[95]

Riv-Ellen Prell has researched dilemmas faced by young Jewish women in the second and third generations. Many second-generation women were pressured to reject their mothers' strong-woman reality and adopt instead more servile "lady-like" virtues of the Anglo-Protestant culture, which included devotion solely to home and family. "My mother's task growing up was to become simultaneously an American and a woman, and her mother could be of little help in either pursuit.... Power was the last thing she needed: Propriety and normality were her paths."[96] In their turn, later-generation women often struggled against their more conservative mothers for a liberated woman's life less constrained by gender expectations and limitations.

Central and eastern Europeans advanced relatively quickly in the sphere of structural assimilation at the secondary level of the economy and, sometimes, politics. A large portion achieved substantial economic success in the first generation. As a group, eastern Europeans moved from a blue-collar concentration to a white-collar concentration in three generations. The ethnic niche economy was critical for many. Hard work and mastery of the educational system generally facilitated upward socioeconomic mobility.

However, even today, Jewish Americans' occupational distribution underscores the point that many of the prosperous among them are not yet fully integrated into upper reaches of the economy and society. The underrepresentation or absence of Jewish Americans at the very top in many spheres of the economy and politics is indicative of continuing, if often covert or subtle, anti-Jewish discrimination.

Why were Jewish Americans generally able to move up the economic ladder so successfully? Some have explained this in terms of values and religious traditions. Nathan Glazer has argued that "Judaism emphasizes the traits that businessmen and intellectuals require, and has done so at least 1,500 years before Calvinism.... The strong emphasis on learning and study can be traced that far back, too. The Jewish habits of foresight, care, moderation probably arose early."[97]

Others have argued that this relative success has had less to do with religion than with historical and structural conditions. Although eastern Europeans were among the poorest, least-educated European Jews, most were not illiterate. Those who came between 1880 and 1920 were generally from urban areas of Europe, where they had worked in urban occupations such as manufacturing, craftwork, and small-scale commerce. Their literacy was relatively high compared with that of most other immigrants. European Jews migrated at a time of expanding manufacturing and trade in the United States. Contrary to what Glazer has argued, Jewish immigrants did not need to rely only on their religious values; they came in with "occupational skills that gave them a decisive advantage over other immigrants."[98] The fit between Jewish skills and economic circumstances at this critical time was better than it would be for later migrants (such as African Americans and Puerto Ricans) to the big northern cities.

In addition, Hertzberg attributes these immigrants' success to their "'Jewish head'... the heritage of siege mentality, of centuries of being an embattled bastion in a hostile 'exile,' and of having only one tool for survival, the use of one's wits." This interpretation suggests a type of oppositional culture that facilitates survival under often extreme anti-Semitic oppression.[99]

In recent decades the decreasing residential concentration of Jewish Americans has not eliminated their informal social cohesion and strong voluntary organizations. Geographic mobility is based on the same factors as that of other Americans: housing markets, life-cycle, and economic constraints. However, informal social ties remain relatively strong among Jewish Americans in many towns and cities. For example, the large Jewish community in Los Angeles has an active online journal and is substantially interconnected in terms of Jewish organizations and family ties despite a dispersed housing pattern. Nationally, too, the pattern of having Jewish friends and related community connections seems strong. In the most recent NJPS, over half of the more engaged Jewish respondents reported that at least half their close friends were Jewish.[100]

Despite the affluence of current generations, some economic and social discrimination against Jewish Americans persists. Some time ago, the leading assimilation theorist, Milton Gordon, argued that while Jewish Americans have experienced partial assimilation at the behavior-receptional level (that is, discrimination has declined), less assimilation has occurred at the attitude-receptional level because of the aggressive persistence of anti-Semitic views.[101] Today, anti-Semitic prejudice can still be found in communities across the United States. Indeed, the development of white supremacist websites on the Internet in recent years has kept many anti-Jewish images—and thus, organizations—very much alive.

Intermarriage

Opposed by some on the grounds that it threatens the survival of the Jewish community, intermarriage has generally increased with each successive generation, probably reflecting the decline of negative images of Jews and a greater acceptance of ethnic diversity. One 2000s study found intermarriage to be more common among young adults, those in the West, those with little Jewish religious education, those with less education generally, and children of those who had intermarried. Since the 1960s, the proportion of interfaith marriages has risen steadily, to 47 percent of those who married between 1996 and the early 2000s. In another 2000 national survey, 85 percent of the Jewish respondents (of all ages) who were married had a Jewish spouse, but 64 percent reported that one or more children had a non-Jewish spouse.[102] The American Jewish Committee has recently concluded that the traditional "taboo on mixed marriage has clearly collapsed." According to a national survey, more than half (56 percent) of the respondents disagreed with the assertion that "It would pain me if my child married a gentile." Some 40 percent said they were "neutral," while 16 percent viewed such marriages as a "positive good."[103]

Some analysts have speculated on whether Jewish Americans as a group will eventually disappear, given this intermarriage rate. Yet, some intermarried couples, along with their children, have embraced Judaism and identify themselves as Jewish. One 2000–2001 survey indicated that perhaps one-third of intermarried couples had taken this step.[104] Thus, Goldscheider has argued against the view that intermarriage can be regarded as an unambiguous measure of assimilation because "strong communal bonds and networks link the intermarried to the community.... There is evidence as well that an increasing proportion of American Jews are accepting the intermarried within the community."[105]

Is the Jewish American community concerned that intermarriage is destroying Jewish identity and solidarity? The 2005 ASAJO suggests that a majority may not be. Asked whether anti-Semitism or intermarriage was the greater threat to the continuing Jewish presence in the United States, 62 percent of those respondents picked anti-Semitism, 33 percent cited intermarriage, and 3 percent cited both equally. This survey found much more concern over external threats than over internal threats of intermarriage, and concern over the latter seems to be declining compared to previous surveys.[106]

The declining birth rate and related aging of the population may be most significant. The Jewish population is rapidly aging. Jewish women in all age groups have had fewer children than for all women in those groups. The Jewish population's median age today (42) is about seven years higher than for the U.S. population as a whole. This likely means a declining Jewish population in the future.[107]

How well have Jewish Americans been assimilated into the dominant Anglo-Protestant culture and society?

Recent Immigrants: Strong Jewish Identity

The social and economic adjustment of recent Jewish immigrants raises interesting issues concerning assimilation and U.S. culture. Close ties between

Israel and the United States make this trek westward easy for Israeli immigrants, who generally are more economically successful than most other immigrants. Many come with professional or managerial experience. Still, Israeli immigrants often maintain some distance from native-born Jews in language and values.[108]

In her important book, *The Soviet Jewish Americans* (1999), Annelise Orleck has shown a significant diversity in adaptive patterns for Jewish immigrants from the former Soviet Union. Immigrants from Eastern regions of the Soviet Union were less assimilated to western European ways (and thus were more patriarchal and religious) than the immigrants from European-influenced areas of the Soviet Union (such as Moscow). Those who immigrated before the 1991 collapse of the Soviet Union were more likely to be anticommunist and more inclined to support the U.S. Republican Party, whereas those who immigrated after the collapse were more positive about the old Soviet Union, especially its social services. Many immigrants have reported difficulty assimilating to U.S. culture. Many left their homeland because of anti-Semitism. Although most émigrés in one survey rated their lives as Jews, as well as housing, income, and standard of living, as better in the United States than in the former Soviet Union, most reported having trouble with English and finding a job. Most considered their cultural environment worse in the United States, and large percentages felt their friendships, social status, and workplace atmospheres were worse here. They liked the freedom, but disliked the "low" cultural tastes here. This mostly well-educated group appears to be assimilating satisfactorily to the U.S. economy but is having trouble with certain social and cultural adjustments. Orleck notes that "depression, anxiety, high blood pressure, and psychosomatic illnesses are common among this and other recent immigrant groups."[109]

Steven Gold has examined adaptation among a diverse group of refugees from the former Soviet Union in Los Angeles and San Francisco. There the Jewish population has been geographically concentrated; residents of the full-faceted Los Angeles community can lead an active life without any knowledge of English. Some, particularly younger, well-educated émigrés, found desirable jobs and moved into the middle class. Many middle-aged émigrés who had no transferable job skills or who were unwilling to take a lower-prestige job than they had held before had more difficulty adapting and often remained isolated from fellow émigrés. Few voluntary support organizations had been formed in either California city. The strong sense of Jewish identity (often nonreligious) of these immigrants is another factor reinforcing Jewish American identity.[110]

Although many immigrants from former Communist countries have aligned themselves with the Republican Party, most have been concerned over Republican attempts to limit immigration and government services. In the past decade many immigrants have allied themselves with Latino, Asian, and Caribbean American groups to fight attempts to restrict legal immigration and to support programs for immigrants. Interestingly, in one 2000 survey of all Jewish American groups, one-fifth of the respondents supported increased immigration to the United States from countries overseas, and another 46 percent were satisfied with the current (substantial) level of immigration.[111]

Contemporary Jewish Identity and the Future of the Community

What does it mean to be Jewish American today? Many scholars stress that in U.S. society all Jews are "Jews by choice."[112] Although this view is exaggerated, it does indicate the degree of change that has occurred since the intense, highly racialized anti-Semitism of the early to mid-twentieth century. In that era, many gentiles targeted Jews for persecution. Today, most people of Jewish ancestry can make their identity choices in an atmosphere of less discrimination.

Asked to specify the basis of Jewish identity, 90 percent of the respondents to one survey cited cultural or ethnic group membership. Fewer than 5 percent defined Jewishness only as religious. Still, the 2000–2001 NJPS found that most children of Jewish parents had some Jewish schooling, and that there had been an increase in the number of children attending Jewish schools. Such schooling sustains Jewish identity. Significantly, Israel has been a major focus of Jewish American consciousness—which also reduces the possibility of Jewish identificational assimilation shifting to "just American."[113]

The *ethnogenesis* perspective (Chapter 2) recognizes the reality of cultural differences among contemporary ethnic groups and helps in interpreting the Jewish experience. Jewish Americans are a composite group made up mostly of Sephardic, central European, eastern European, and Israeli origin. In the United States, Jewish immigrants and their descendants have forged a *distinctive ethnic group*, shaped partially by their Jewish and (mostly) European cultural heritage and partially by the long history of adaptation to the Anglo-Protestant culture. Despite substantial adaptation, ethnic distinctiveness remains. Persisting anti-Semitism (if much less than in the past), respect for an ancient heritage, commitment to Israel, and parents' desire to socialize children in the Jewish heritage continue to shape the behavior and beliefs of most Americans of Jewish ancestry.

Sociologist Sylvia Barack Fishman has described Jewish Americans' pattern of adaptation to the core culture as *coalescence*. The liberal American social and political values held by most American Jews have come to be seen simply as "Jewish" values. Through adaptive coalescence, Jewish Americans have merged their ideas with certain American ideas, incorporating "American liberal values such as free choice, universalism, individualism, and pluralism into their understanding of Jewish identity."[114]

How strong is Jewish identity today? Is it, as Herbert Gans argues, only a "symbolic ethnicity" without lasting significance? In this view, ethnicity for many white ethnic Americans is today little more than a desire to maintain some feeling for ethnic background without a strong commitment to ethnic behavior or to traditional social ties. Thus, some scholars have argued that the weakening of religious ties among Jewish Americans indicates that Jewish ethnicity is "well on its way to becoming memory."[115]

A Jewish history professor has pointed out the identity dangers of Anglo-conformity assimilation, which he argues is not just "assimilation to American culture" but "actually assimilation to Christian culture." In his view, "There is no such thing in the United States as a strictly secular organization. You cannot treat Sunday as a day of rest or hold a Christmas party and claim to be strictly secular ... the choice is not between Jewishness and secularism. It is between a Jewish model of secularism and a Christian model. And given the inherent anti-Semitic bias of the Christian religion, it is suicidal ... to choose the Christian model. It means placing yourself in a situation where you are always at a disadvantage, where you always have to prove yourself."[116] From this perspective, Jewish Americans have already become *too* conforming and Christianized as they have adapted to the Anglo-Protestant core culture and society; and, if they are to survive as a specifically *Jewish* people, they must work hard to overcome the effects of that substantial Anglo-Protestant assimilation.

In addition, some Jewish American leaders have expressed concern over changes at the voluntary organization level. Numerous Jewish philanthropic and service agencies have recently faced a decline in private and governmental support. Jewish organization leaders are worried that assimilated Jewish Americans with a weak sense of identity may not support such organizations to the extent that their parents and grandparents did. However, the emergence of newer Jewish organizations, such as the Jewish Voice for Peace and the New Israel Fund, has involved many American Jews, especially younger generations. Diverse cultural organizations and media have arisen as well, such as those for younger Jews and for gay-lesbian groups. Such organizations, as well as increases in Jewish day schools and festivals and the continuing importance of Jewish community centers, suggest that such worries are at least premature.[117]

One study of Jewish youth indicates that parents today face enormous problems: The "all-pervasive consumer society that surrounds us increasingly affects the environment of American children. The sophisticated marketing of fashion in clothing, toys, foods, films, etc., uses peer pressure to help produce a highly materialistic, present-oriented youth culture which is at odds with Jewish values of spirituality, learning, tzedakah [charity], and self-discipline as exemplified by Sabbath observance."[118] This study concludes with a call for an expanded role for Jewish community organizations in helping families socialize new generations of children in the Jewish religion and traditional values.

Still, recent surveys of Jewish Americans have found that most still have substantial connections to Jewish subculture and communities. One report concludes that "Most Jews participate in selected holidays and forms of cultural involvement, maintain strong social connections to other Jews, and regard being Jewish as very important." But the report further noted that "Smaller proportions of Jews—ranging from a quarter to a half—are variously engaged in other aspects of Jewish life as well, such as synagogue affiliation, charitable giving, volunteering, and many ritual observances." In effect, the majority are still connected to Jewish culture and community, and a substantial minority are very active in more organized Jewish American life.[119] Certain distinguishing features of Jewish culture and history—in particular, their extensive social networks, especially those rooted in religious congregations and schools, and their long tradition of survival as a minority in non-Jewish societies—support the long-term survival of their ethnic identity.[120]

Interestingly, the greater acceptance of Jewish Americans in a largely non-Jewish society today, compared with decades back, seems to make Jewish Americans less likely to abandon their Jewishness, for their identity has ceased to be the focal point of massive discrimination and has instead become a badge of pride linked to a worldwide Jewish struggle such as that of Israel. From this perspective, a sense of Jewishness is likely to remain strong for the majority of Jewish Americans for the foreseeable future. In the 2005 ASAJO, 55 percent ranked "being Jewish" as "very important" in their life; another third ranked it as "fairly important."[121]

There is also the related issue of the impact of Jewish characteristics and views on the larger society. In a 2006 review of research that assessed the ways in which Jewish characteristics, such as family styles and food habits, have penetrated popular culture (for example, television sitcoms), researcher Caroline Litwack suggests that "Jewishness" may have in some sense become the "marker of all ethnicity in 21st century America ... the history and connection of Jews with humor may serve as a model for the masses, easing people's anxiety in the face of adversity. Immediately recognizable to the audience because they rely on ingrained stereotypes, 'crypto-Jews' appear often on sitcoms adding humor and drama with their paranoia, kvetching, or guilt."[122]

Accepting and Challenging White Privilege

Jewish Americans remain significantly differentiated in identity, history, and experience from other white Americans, yet for the most part they are now accepted as "white." As recently as World War I, most white Anglo-Protestants regarded Jewish Americans as an "inferior race" that was not fully part of the "white race." After World War II, in part because of Nazism and its anti-Semitic Holocaust, the dominant white gentile group granted Jewish Americans, albeit slowly, access to institutionalized white privileges, especially greater occupational and residential mobility.

In addition, as Jewish social scientist Karen Brodkin has shown, many American Jews worked hard to become accepted as "white." Many moved to suburban areas, changed their names, or underwent cosmetic surgery in order to assimilate better to the image of successful Euro-American whiteness. After World War II prominent Jewish Americans, such as writers and entertainers, publicly and successfully embraced white gentile values and institutions and perpetuated images of Jewish Americans as a "high-achieving minority." Brodkin documents how many ordinary Jewish Americans came to accept a range of Anglo-Protestant values and views as part of becoming white. Similarly, in a 2006 book, *The Price of Whiteness*, Eric Goldstein shows how Jewish Americans sought acceptance and privileges as whites by conforming strongly to preexisting Anglo-Protestant values, even as this meant giving up some of their distinctive Jewish group heritage or identity.[123]

Both Brodkin and Goldstein have also shown that many American Jews have been uncomfortable with the group move to embracing white privilege, given their long history of fighting racial and ethnic oppression. Looking to the future, Brodkin suggests that "the challenge for American Jews today is to confront that whiteness as part of developing an American Jewishness that helps build an explicitly multiracial democracy in the United States."[124]

In what ways have many Jewish Americans challenged the "white" privilege that they have gained?

Summary

Jewish Americans, most of whom are descendants of central and eastern Europeans, have become substantially assimilated in the cultural arena. A prosperous ethnic group that has made dramatic progress up the socioeconomic mobility ladder, Jewish Americans have constantly struggled against widespread prejudice and discrimination. Theirs is substantially a success story, but they have paid a significant price. Anti-Semitism still persists today and often limits movement to the very top in the economy and in presidential politics. Coupled with substantial vertical progress over the decades has been horizontal mobility in the form of suburbanization.

Central to an adequate understanding of Jewish Americans today is an understanding of their ties to Israel. The creation of Israel and periodic Arab–Israeli conflicts have generated a strong commitment to Israel, both philosophically and financially. Jewish Americans continue to see Israel as an essential place of refuge for a people that has survived the Roman persecution, the Spanish Inquisition, Russian pogroms, and the Nazi Holocaust. This commitment has motivated thousands of Jewish Americans to visit or to immigrate to the work camps, towns, and cities of Israel. Yet, in recent decades a significant number of Israeli immigrants have come to the United States seeking to escape the violence of the Middle East. And many Russian Jews have come seeking better economic and political opportunities. These immigrants provide a contemporary reminder of the sojourner nature of much of historical Jewish experience.

In this chapter we have demonstrated how diverse the United States still is—a diversity that fosters vitality and creativity. Jewish participation in U.S. institutions means that this country is *not* by official definition a Christian country; it is a country of many religious groups, including a diverse array of Protestants, Catholics, Jews, Muslims, and others. One contribution of Jewish Americans has been their stand for the Jewish religious and cultural heritage—and thereby for the expansion of liberty for all U.S. residents.

Jewish Americans have contributed substantially to the national emphasis on education, to high achievement in arts and sciences, and to values of social justice and tolerance. Jewish Americans have not been passive victims of anti-Semitic discrimination; they and their organizations have often occupied the forefront of the fight against racial and ethnic prejudice and discrimination that continue to plague U.S. society.

Key Terms

Holocaust 113
Marranos 113
pogroms 114
anti-Semitism 115
hate crimes 117
Zionism 128

C H A P T E R 6

Native Americans

BIG PICTURE QUESTIONS

- ***What have been the consequences of colonization migration for indigenous American societies?***
- ***What impact have Native Americans had on the dominant U.S. culture and society?***
- ***How do conceptions of assimilation and resistance relate to the experiences of Native Americans?***

Recently, an Italian American leader in Denver, Colorado, tried to bring back the Columbus Day Parade, which he and others viewed as a celebration of the heritage of Italian Americans. This proposal was opposed by local Native Americans on the grounds that Columbus was a brutal conqueror who with his men slaughtered and enslaved indigenous peoples. The U.S. Justice Department worked out a modification whereby the march would be renamed The March for Italian Pride. Still, Native American, African American, and Latino protesters objected to the celebration of Columbus under any name and sat down in the street to block the parade. This event is but one in a long series of protests by Native Americans against the genocidal conquests of indigenous peoples by European colonizers in the Americas.[1]

In the 1990s, Native American groups across the nation held protests against the celebration of the five-hundreth anniversary of Columbus's 1492 voyage to the Americas. In Washington, D.C., protesters spray-painted "500 years of genocide" on a statue of Columbus and read a list of human rights violations.[2] Suzan Shown Harjo has explained the prevalent Native American position regarding the Columbus Quincentenary: "As Native American peoples... we have no reason to celebrate an invasion that caused the demise of so many of our people and is still causing destruction today. The Europeans stole our land and killed our people."[3]

With this chapter we begin to consider non-European groups that were racially subordinated during European colonial expansion. The term *white* as a self-designation for Europeans developed in the context of contact with the usually darker-skinned peoples of Africa and the Americas, whom Europeans generally came to call *black* and *red*, respectively.[4] Many groups were subordinated economically, politically, and culturally. In this and subsequent chapters, we observe major differences in the past and present experiences of European and non-European Americans. We also examine the relevance of assimilation and power-conflict theories for interpreting the experiences of subordinated racial groups.

The first victims of European colonization on this continent were indigenous peoples—hundreds of Native American groups that were present at the time. Called collectively (and erroneously) "Indians" by their conquerors, indigenous peoples have long suffered at the hands of white intruders. Reflect for a moment on the notion of Europeans "discovering" America. In fact, the fifteenth-century European explorers were *latecomers*, for the continent they happened upon was already peopled by millions. Ancestors of contemporary Native Americans had discovered the continent at least 20,000 years earlier—when, most scholars believe, they migrated across the land bridge from Asia to Alaska.

Conquest by Europeans and European Americans

Human migration varies from voluntary movement to forced slave importation. Migration often involves the incorporation of a new immigrant group into a societal framework by a dominant racial or ethnic group already established within certain geographical boundaries. In the case of Native Americans, however, the dominant group itself migrated: Europeans moved into the territories of indigenous groups. This process can be termed *colonization migration*. Unlike other migration, **colonization migration** involves the *conquest and domination of a preexisting geographical group by outsiders*. Such migration illustrates *external colonialism*.

How many Native Americans were there when Europeans came to North America? Early on, some analysts estimated the indigenous population in the year 1500 at about 1 million. Recently, this estimate has been revised upward. One considered estimate puts the number at 15 million at the time of conquest, with tens of millions in Central and South America as well. Other careful assessments support a much larger figure. Low figures have been used to legitimate the European conquest of an allegedly unoccupied land.[5]

By 1890, the combined effects of European diseases and violence had sharply reduced the number of indigenous people to approximately 250,000. This population remained below 400,000 until the 1950s, when it began to grow. Thus, in the 2000 census, 2,475,956 people identified themselves as American Indians (including indigenous Alaskans). Another 1,082,683 people identified themselves as white *and* Indian, while 182,494 identified themselves as black and Indian. (The 2000 census was the first to allow people to indicate a multiracial identity.) The total of these three groups and other (Indian—other) groups is more than 4.1 million, which marked a substantial increase in the self-designated Indian population since 1990. States with the largest percentages (14.2 to 4.7 percent) of Native Americans in their populations are, in order, Alaska, New Mexico, South Dakota, Oklahoma, Montana, North Dakota, and Arizona. Other states have proportions of less than 2 percent. States with the largest number of Native Americans are California, Oklahoma, Arizona, and Texas.[6]

Today most of the more than 550 federally recognized Indian tribes have fewer than 10,000 members. According to the 2000 census, only five have populations of more than 100,000—in order of numbers, Cherokee, Navajo, Choctaw, Sioux, and Chippewa. Only 36 percent of Native Americans (including indigenous Alaskans) live on reservations, on trust lands, or in other Indian areas, most of which are rural. Most live in towns and cities.[7]

In recent decades, the number of Americans claiming Indian ancestry has increased. For example, the enrollment officer of the Cherokee Nation receives hundreds of applications a month from people who wish to claim Cherokee ancestry.[8] Drawing on interview data, Joane Nagel suggests that one reason for the increase is identity switching—the change in self-identification from non-Indian to Indian in response to Native American activism promoting pride in being Native American. The tendency for Americans with partial Indian ancestry to openly assert this is increasing. One reason is that the stigma of being part-Indian has declined. Some have also suggested that government or tribal benefits available to members of some Indian groups may have accelerated the willingness of non-Indians to claim Indian ancestry.[9]

The term *Indian* and most government names for major Native American groups were given by whites. In most history books, not one major Native American group is recorded under its own original name. For example, the "Navajo" call themselves *Diné*, meaning "The People."[10] The renaming by outsiders is a result of their racial subordination and suggests one major difference between colonized groups and European immigrants: Colonized peoples often have had little or no control over the group naming process.

Although many non-Indians today think of Indians as a single category, the latter have for centuries been a diverse array of nations, with major differences in population, economies, polities, language, and customs. Native American groups have ranged from small bands to complex, hierarchically organized nations with large territories. The diversity is important to keep in mind, as the image of the typical Indian in the non-Indian mind is of a Plains Indian living in a tipi, hunting bison, and wearing a feathered headdress.

Most Native Americans have never fit this image. As one researcher has noted, "Lumping Indians together into one group presumed to have the same cultural and physiological characteristics is the same as assuming that all Europeans are alike, that they speak the same language, have the same heritage, and share the same values. Historic tribes differed substantially in regard to religious beliefs and practices, language, dress, hairstyles, physiology, political organization, social structures, gender roles, world view and living conditions in response to the environment, which varied from forests, deserts, mountains, plains and coasts to subarctic and arctic areas."[11]

Early Cultural Borrowing

The cultures of the Native American societies encountered by European colonizers in the Western Hemisphere were often more highly developed than those of European societies. Some indigenous nations built great cities and roads, developed advanced agricultural systems, and created calendars and numerical systems superior to those of Europeans. In what came to be called "the Americas," most indigenous societies had complex and "sophisticated systems of government, community organizations, economy, means of communication, gender roles, arts, and elaborate clothing and hairstyles. Indians were and are extremely religious."[12] European invaders borrowed heavily. Thus, an estimated *60 percent* of foods (for example, potatoes, corn, peanuts, and many grains) eaten by people around the globe today were *first* developed by indigenous peoples in the Western Hemisphere. Many medicinal plants and their derivatives (for example, quinine) were borrowed from Native Americans—without which cultural borrowing some readers of this book, and many others, would likely not be alive.[13]

In the first decade of English settlement, numerous colonists deserted to Indian communities in search of better living conditions. In the winter of 1609–1610, one in seven of Jamestown (Virginia) colonists deserted to Algonquian communities. Better nourished than whites, the Algonquians hunted, fished, gathered food, and cultivated beans and maize. Their matrilineal society had no social classes, no state, and little economic specialization. The chiefs, who were not called by their titles, worked alongside other members. English workers were leaving a colony where the authorities had established severe punishments to prevent desertion. Not surprisingly, the reality of societies without property holding, kings, classes, and states provoked much worry among European American elites.[14]

Geographical Location and Relocation

Hundreds of indigenous societies were thriving at the time of European invasions. (In this chapter we will sometimes speak of these many groups as though they were one Native American group; at other times we will speak of one specific group within the larger category.) Initially, many were forced to move westward as whites advanced. Most Native American groups have at some time faced substantial pressure to migrate. *Forced migration* at gunpoint was the lot of some indigenous groups after their defeat by whites. Groups in the West, such as the Navajo, were rounded up after military engagements and forced to migrate to barren reservations. Perhaps the most famous forced march was the "Trail of Tears," in which thousands of Cherokees, Creeks, Chickasaws, Choctaws, and Seminoles were relocated from their eastern lands to the so-called "Indian Territory" in present-day Oklahoma.

Internal migration over the past century has involved relocation from reservations and other rural areas to the cities. During the 1950s and 1960s, an urban relocation program was expanded by the federal government to cover many Indian groups and numerous cities; a Bureau of Indian Affairs (BIA) branch was set up to oversee relocation services.[15] The scale of internal migration can be seen in the more than 200,000 Native Americans who moved to the cities between the 1950s and 1980s. By the year 2000, more than half resided in cities.[16]

The Colonial Period

White historians and others have asserted that white "settlers" encountered roving bands of Indians with whom they often came into conflict. In reality, it was the indigenous Americans who were *settlers*—they were the ones who had long settled the land, used it, and developed it. European colonists developed various strategies for dealing with those whose land they coveted. These ranged from honest treaty making with equals to deceptive treaty making, to attempts at extermination, to enslavement like that of Africans, to confinement in often barren, prison-like areas called reservations.[17]

European colonists slowly gained dominance over Indian groups, usually forcing them into frontier areas or killing them. Few whites seemed concerned about the genocidal consequences of this expansion. Some colonists relied on friendly Native Americans to survive the first devastating years, yet the colonists soon turned on their neighbors. In New England, a war with the Pequots in 1637 ended when whites massacred several hundred inhabitants of a Pequot village and sent survivors into slavery. The English defeat of the French resulted in the French withdrawal from the continent in the mid-1700s. This brought more indigenous societies into contact with the often less sophisticated and generally more brutal Indian policies of the English.[18]

Treaties, Reservations, and Genocide

With the founding of the United States in 1787, indigenous peoples found themselves in a strange position. They were viciously stereotyped and attacked in the Declaration of Independence, where Jefferson accused the British king of working "to bring on the [white] inhabitants of our frontiers, the merciless Indian Savages, whose known rule of warfare is an undistinguished destruction of all ages, sexes and conditions." Later, the U.S. Constitution only briefly mentioned Indians, giving Congress the power to regulate commerce with them.

By action or inaction, federal officials supported the recurring theft of Indian lands. A French observer of the 1830s noted the hypocrisy of official treaties: "This virtuous and high-minded policy [of treaty making] has not been followed. The rapacity of the settlers is usually backed by the tyranny of the government."[19] The procedure was often not one of immediate expropriation of land but rather of constant encroachment by whites, a gradual land-taking process sanctioned after the fact by the government treaties.

The subordination of Native Americans was encouraged by Andrew Jackson, a slaveholding president who was critical of much treaty making. Jackson encouraged states to defy Supreme Court rulings that favored Indians. Gradual displacement gave way to brutally oppressive marches over hundreds of miles at gunpoint, a near-genocidal policy designed to rid regions of those stereotyped by whites as "savages." Congress passed the Indian Removal Act in 1830, and within a decade many groups in the East had migrated "voluntarily" or at gunpoint to lands west of the Mississippi—often under the auspices of "negotiated" treaties. Atlantic and Gulf Coast tribes, as well as midwestern tribes, were forcibly removed to the Indian Territory along the infamous "Trail of Tears." Large numbers died, and the relocated peoples faced serious survival problems in the new lands.[20]

Westward-moving whites precipitated struggles with the Plains societies, many of which had by that time abandoned farming for a nomadic lifestyle. The often genocidal actions of federal troops and white farmers were a new experience. The nomadic, horse-oriented Plains peoples came to symbolize "the Indian" in white imaginations. Media presentations have severely distorted the reality of the Plains wars, which, unlike Hollywood's version, usually did *not* involve warriors in war bonnets on stallions facing a brave collection of U.S. Army officers backed by heroic soldiers on a sun-swept plain.[21]

What are the consequences of being made a colonized people?

Myths About Conflict

Movies and television have portrayed the years between 1840 and 1880 as an era of large-scale and constant conflict between white overlanders and Indians. Movies and television have created unforgettable, often racist images of the West—wagon trains moving across the West, wagons in a circle, whooping Indians on ponies, thousands of dead whites and Indians, and treacherous "red savages." However, research studies by John Unruh and others have made clear that these prevailing images are often mythical. Between 1840 and 1860, approximately 250,000 whites made the journey across the plains to the West Coast; fewer than two in every thousand died at the hands of the resident Native Americans. Between 1840 and 1860, a total of *only*

An etching of a meeting between U.S. Army generals and Sioux and other Native American leaders at North Platte, Nebraska.

362 whites and 426 Native Americans died in *all* the recorded battles between the two groups along wagon train routes. There is only *one* documented attack by Indians on a wagon train in which there were as many as two dozen casualties for the white settler-invaders. Most white accounts of massacres by Indians are either fictions or great exaggerations of minor encounters.[22] Indeed, Native Americans often provided food, horses, or guidance for weary white travelers.

A recurring pattern emerged in the conflict between whites and indigenous inhabitants. White farmers would move onto Indian lands. The U.S. government, by means of a treaty resulting from threat or coercion, would provide land for resettlement of the Indians affected. More white farmers, prospectors, or hunters moving from the East would intrude on these new Native American lands. This new land theft would later be legitimated by another government treaty, and the process would begin again. Or, sometimes, a U.S. government treaty promise of supplies to those Indians living in a restricted area would be broken, and some would leave the area seeking food or revenge. The U.S. Army would take repressive action, sometimes intentionally punishing an innocent group and precipitating more uprisings.

Many treaties, still part of U.S. law, were masterpieces of fraud; consent was gained by deception or threat. More than three hundred treaties with Indian groups were made between 1790 and the Civil War. Most have *not* been honored in full by the U.S. government. As time passed, treaties established regulations governing Indian behavior and provided for restricted areas whites called "reservations." This treaty process was abandoned by the U.S. government by 1871. Still, hundreds of ratified treaties between the United States and many Native American groups remain in effect.[23]

White Massacres of Native Americans

Serious treaty violations by whites often led to conflict. In an 1862 uprising in Minnesota, the eastern Sioux killed some white farmers after losing much of their land to invading whites and suffering at the hands of government agents. Delays in supplies promised by the government resulted in the Sioux burning and killing throughout the Minnesota Valley, and massive white retaliation followed. About the same time, conflict occurred in Colorado between indigenous groups and a state militia left in charge when the U.S. Army was withdrawn. Indian guerrilla warfare was often met with savage retaliation. In 1864, Colonel John Chivington, a Christian minister, and his Colorado volunteers massacred nearly two hundred Cheyennes in a peace-seeking band at Sand Creek. The massacre was one of the most savage in history: "Children carrying white flags were slaughtered and pregnant women were cut open. The slaughter and mutilation continued into the late afternoon over many miles of the bleak prairie."[24]

After the Civil War, with government support, large railroad corporations gobbled up millions of acres in the West. Buffalo were slaughtered by the millions, and the hunting economy of the Plains was destroyed. White farmers, miners, and soldiers repeatedly violated treaties. One example was the Dakota Territory of the Sioux. Conflict over illegal white invasion escalated; troops were sent in to force Sioux bands onto a smaller reservation, even though the Sioux were already on what the government regarded as "unceded Indian territory." Among this force was Colonel George A. Custer. The most widely known battle of the Plains struggle occurred at the Little Big Horn in 1876, when a miscalculating Custer and his soldiers were wiped out by a Sioux group and its allies that had refused to settle on the reservation.

One of the last engagements took place at Wounded Knee Creek fourteen years later. Attempting to round up the last Sioux bands, the Army intercepted one and forced the Sioux to camp. A white colonel ordered a disarming, which was carried out ruthlessly. One Sioux shot into a line of soldiers; the troops replied by shooting at close range with rifles and machine guns. Approximately three hundred unarmed Indians, many of them old men, women, and children, were killed on the spot or while running from the camp.[25]

In the Southwest, Indian resistance was, on occasion, substantial. Military expeditions against the scattered Navajo and Apache communities in the Southwest attempted to destroy them or hem them in. Colonel Kit Carson convinced the Mescalero Apaches to agree to reside on a reservation. Establishing headquarters in Navajo territory, Carson began a scorched-earth program, destroying Navajo fields and herds. He then herded his captives three hundred miles to a reservation—the infamous "Long Walk" that is central to the Navajo collective memory of oppression. By 1890 most of the remnants of the Native American groups had been forced onto reservations.[26] Still, even on the reservations, most groups attempted to maintain their historic cultures, including language and religion, and drew on their cultures to resist pressures of acculturation to white folkways.

What are some long-term effects of the forced migrations of indigenous peoples?

Racist Images and Stereotypes

Soon after the arrival of European colonizers in the Americas, stereotypes of Native Americans as lazy and wild and of Europeans as hardworking and steady, along with group classification by physical characteristics, served to distinguish colonizers from colonized. One early European myth, that of the "child of nature" or "noble savage," was a mixture of appreciation and anti-Indian prejudice. By the late 1600s, an array of anti-Indian stereotypes and ideologies became an early part of a comprehensive white racial framing of the new colonial society that was developing, a framing that included views of African Americans enslaved to work land that had been taken from Indians. To the present day, this racist framing of Native Americans has been maintained by many in the dominant white group.[27]

European colonists were initially shocked at the strength of Indian societies and their unwillingness to submit to the "civilizing" pressures of white missionaries and farmers. Violent resistance reinforced the white stereotype of the "Indian savage." This image became common after battles in which Indians resisted seizure of lands. By the mid-1600s, Europeans were writing that the Indians were "wild beasts" who should be hunted.[28]

The era of westward expansion imprinted on the white mind, in popular novels and later in films and TV programs, the image of "cruel" Indian "warriors" attacking "helpless" white families. The media have seldom focused on the more significant savagery of attacks on Indian families, farms, and communities by white soldiers, hunters, and farmers. Ironically, a staggering number of fictional Indians have been killed in the media, especially in pulp fiction: "The Indian, who had been all but eliminated with real bullets, now had to be resurrected to be killed off again with printer's ink."[29] Cowboy-and-Indian movies added to false images of Indian "savagery." Distorted images of Indians can still be found in many books used in U.S. schools.

One erroneous image is that of the "primitive hunter" who made little use of the land. Most indigenous groups that were killed off or forced off their lands were composed *not* of nomadic hunters but of part-time or full-time farmers. Groups such as the Cherokee had, by the time of their forced removal in the 1830s, developed significant agricultural enterprises.[30]

Paradoxical stereotypes have long been applied to Indian women, based mostly on the women's relationship with white men: a "Princess" who may save a white man from her own people, and a "Squaw" (another derogatory epithet) who becomes the white man's sexual partner. The image of the esteemed Princess, portrayed as only slightly darker-skinned than Europeans and often with distinctly European features in books and movies (such as in Disney movies), became a symbol of the New World in Europe, a many-faceted "Mother figure—exotic, powerful, dangerous, and beautiful."[31] In contrast, the "Squaw" was portrayed negatively by racist thinkers as darker, fatter, and cruder than the "Princess." She often shared the stereotyped traits of drunkenness, stupidity, and thievery attributed by whites to Indian men.

Research on elementary, high school, and college textbooks have found numerous stereotypes. Most history textbooks deal at least briefly with indigenous peoples, but often only in the past. Some children's books today portray Indians as Pocahontas-type "princesses," "squaws," or "warriors." In an analysis of a social science textbook series for kindergarten through eighth grade, Communities United, a group that seeks to remove old racial stereotypes from textbooks, found "justifications and trivializations of some of the most vicious social practices in our history."[32] James Loewen's study of high school textbooks found significant improvements in recent years, with more attention to the diversity of early Indian societies and some recognition of their important cultures. Still, the textbooks are riddled with erroneous assumptions about Indians and whites.[33]

Studies of the media, including popular films, have revealed various stereotypes, including the continuing use of "Indian warrior" and "Indian princess" images. Scholars have criticized the tendency of white observers to define Native Americans and their ancient traditions in terms of nineteenth-century white images. This old imagery has influenced North American art, literature, the media, and the mainstream view in general and has contributed to the invisibility of contemporary Indians.[34] The Academy Award–winning film *Dances with Wolves* (1990) is an example of the focus on the past. Although that now-classic film presents a more sensitive treatment of white–Indian history than its predecessors, it views the historical Indian experience as proceeding to an inevitable and negative conclusion. The film diverts attention from the present reality of Native Americans.[35]

Note, too, that *Dances with Wolves*, *Last of the Mohicans* (1993), and more recent Hollywood films often feature *white* actors playing Indians to attract white audiences. Even the much-viewed Disney film *Pocahontas* (1995) continues to perpetuate backward stereotypes. What appears to be a fun movie about a real-life character is pseudo-history that distorts the real history. One researcher notes that the Disney producer said he sought to dramatize the "essence" of the real Pocahontas story. However, "the logic of that reasoning may be difficult to follow, but evidently to depict her 'essence' they needed to change her age and her body, and give her a motive for her actions that boils down to falling desperately in love with the first white man she sees."[36] The historical Pocahontas was actually a 10- to 12-year-old child when she was involved with John Smith, not the much older Barbie look-alike of the Disney movie. As a child, she was an Indian living at a time when European colonizers were invading Indian lands—and soon would decimate her society and others by violence and disease. Her actual life included kidnapping and rape by whites, a trip to England, a marriage to a white planter, and an early death from disease. This is not the story that non-Indians like to hear, and not usually the one told in the media. The mainstream film industry has yet to make a fully honest film about the oppression of indigenous American societies, one told substantially from the perspective of Native Americans and filled with Native American actors.

There are only a few studies of white attitudes toward Native Americans. In a 1920s research study, white college students were asked how close to themselves, on a scale from 1 ("would marry") to 7 ("would not allow them in nation"), they would allow a given racial or ethnic group. White students rejected all close contact (such as friendships) with Native Americans. Using the same social-distance scale, a later (1970s) study found that white respondents still rejected Indians in primary-group relations, such as marriage and club membership. White views of Native Americans still mixed romantic stereotypes with traditional negative stereotypes.[37]

Today, stereotypes are commonplace and have serious consequences. Stereotyped views in the minds of white officials lead to discrimination in policing, arrests, and sentencing. Reports on prisons and juvenile facilities have shown that Indians are overrepresented and tend to receive harsher sentences compared with comparable white arrestees. One review of Montana prisons suggests that "Socially sanctioned racism can and does seep into every level of the criminal justice system from the numbers of police arrests, severity of charges, sentencing, treatment by correction officers, and parole board decisions."[38] One reason is that many whites, including police, view Indians as outsiders and hold images of them as lazy, drunken troublemakers. The "drunken Indian" stereotype is one of the most extreme. Although indigenous societies have had problems with some members' alcohol abuse, relatively few Native Americans today have such problems. In one recent survey, only 5.8 percent of Native Americans, as compared to 5.1 percent of whites, had seriously abused alcohol over a recent year. Contrary to popular images, the *majority* had *not*—even though few groups in society have faced the cultural destruction and intensive racial oppression, past and present, that Native Americans have encountered. In addition, numerous communities facing alcoholism problems have taken aggressive actions, including the use of both traditional healing approaches and Western medical treatment programs.[39]

Members of white hate groups have carried out crimes against Indians and have developed websites circulating negative, often vicious stereotypes. Suzane Shown Harjo, founding trustee of the National Museum of the American Indian, has noted that "There is no such thing as a good stereotype. . . . It reduces people or a person to a consumable, easily digestible, prejudged image or word. It sets up a system or prejudice either for or against a person or a people and, in that way, denies the humanity of that person or people . . . or it wrongly characterizes people."[40] In the 1990s, the Cable News Network (CNN) aired "Native Americans: The Invisible People," a rare series that presented the historical circumstances surrounding contemporary Indian issues, including land-use treaty violations, federal recognition of Native American nations, and protection of sacred sites.[41] It is interesting that CNN should be the first major television network to detail such historical and contemporary realities; CNN's founder, Ted Turner, also owned the Atlanta Braves baseball team, whose supporters have helped perpetuate negative Indian stereotypes through their continuing use of the team's name on sports gear and their insistence on the famous "tomahawk chop." The team's name and fans' behavior have generated protests by Native American organizations.

The CNN program and some changes in the accuracy of school textbooks may signal a slow trend toward more honesty in dealing with U.S. history. Interestingly, 57 percent of the respondents in a recent nationwide poll of registered voters reported that they believed public schools do not teach enough about Native American history, and three-fourths thought that colleges should provide more courses on Native Americans.[42]

In recent decades, numerous Native American writers, novelists, and moviemakers have fought traditional racist images and portrayed more realistic and nuanced images of Native Americans. For example, in his writings, such as the novel *Reservation Blues* (1995) and the movie *Smoke Signals* (1998), Sherman Alexie generally portrays Native Americans in their own terms, constantly questioning racial stereotypes and accenting his studied representations of how Native Americans act and think. James Cox notes that Alexie's fictional characters constantly "struggle for self-definition and self-representation against the oppressive technological narratives that define Native Americans as a conquered people, as decontextualized, romanticized, subservient Tontos, and Native America as a conquered landscape." Similarly, Laguna poet and novelist Leslie Marmon Silko has dealt deeply with real Indian life, sense of place, spirituality, and struggle with the white world in her poetry and novels, such as *Ceremony* (1977) and *Almanac of the Dead* (1991). Native American writers have contributed much important and critical analysis to the public discussion of the images and ideas of indigenous peoples and cultures.[43]

How has a white racial frame persisted in the maintaining and reworking of stereotypes targeting Native Americans?

Politics

Native American Cultures and Societies: Before European Influence

European Americans have often viewed Native Americans as not having had "civilization" until it was brought to them by European colonizers. Yet, at initial contact most indigenous societies were at least as old as European societies and had civilizations that were at least as developed. Many indigenous societies were more egalitarian than European societies. Generally, in these societies both men and women had societal respect and significant social status. Women often played as important a social or political role as men. Some groups, such as the Cherokees and the Iroquois, were matrilineal; "the husband-father role was to sire children, who belonged to their mother's clan, lived in their mother's family's home and inherited her property. Chiefs were from the women's side of the family."[44] Among the Iroquois, women elders chose the tribal leadership. Women had significant political input in other societies as well. Democratic political institutions were commonplace in Indian societies. Benjamin Franklin, Thomas Jefferson, and other colonial leaders admired the democratic institutions of indigenous nations such as the Iroquois. The symbol of the United States, an eagle clutching a bundle of arrows, was copied from Iroquois eagle and arrow symbols.[45]

The fact that much written Native American history has been compiled by whites is perhaps one reason why the important roles of Indian women have been ignored or downplayed. Contact with Europeans frequently forced Indian groups to alter these gender roles; white leaders usually refused to deal with Indian women as leaders. Efforts of white political officials and missionaries to convince Indian groups about the inferiority of women and the superiority of men resulted in some decline in social power for women in numerous Indian communities.[46]

The Politics of the European Invasion

At first, European colonizers dealt with Native Americans as independent *nations*. As European communities gained strength, they began to treat these nations as groups to be exterminated or as dependent wards. Many eastern groups were destroyed or decimated. Those remaining in the East were militarily weak enough by the 1830s for the government to force them westward. During the 1830s Supreme Court decisions made it clear that indigenous societies were "domestic dependent nations" to be supervised, like children, by the U.S. government. The powerful bureaucratic agency, the Bureau of Indian Affairs (BIA), was established to coordinate federal relations with Indians; its work ranged from authoritarian supervision of reservations to provision of some supplies. Until the 1880s, the BIA's role of attempting to protect Native Americans put it in conflict with a U.S. military policy that often promoted genocidal extermination.

Under BIA domination, traditional Indian leaders were often replaced by white-controlled leaders. Indigenous religions were suppressed, and large numbers of Christian missionaries were imported. With the end of treaty making between the U.S. government and Indian nations in 1871 and the removal of many nations to white-determined reservations by the 1890s, Indians entered into a unique "trust relationship" with white America: They are the only subordinated racial or ethnic group whose life has been routinely administered directly by a bureaucratic arm of the U.S. government. The action of the BIA is a clear example of *government* defining and controlling U.S. racial and ethnic groups, a point underscored by the theory of racial formation (see Chapter 2). Later, we will see how the federal government has mismanaged Native American lands and trust funds that were supposedly protected under the "trust relationship."[47]

From the Dawes Act to the New Deal

A major federal policy shift regarding land took place in the late nineteenth century. Indians, whites often argued, should be taught new rules of land ownership. Congress's 1887 Dawes Act provided that reservation lands now be divided among individual families—even though the European tradition of private ownership and development of land was an alien value system for most indigenous peoples. White advocates hoped that individual land allotments would convert Indian societies into collections of individualistic owners. Unallotted lands would be sold to white outsiders. This new policy soon resulted in large-scale land sales to whites. Through fair means and foul, the remaining 140 million acres of Indian lands were further reduced to 50 million acres by the mid-1930s.[48]

In 1884 an Indian named John Elk had moved to Omaha, Nebraska, where he had adopted white ways and attempted to vote. Denied this citizenship right, Elk took his case to court, where he argued that the Fourteenth Amendment made him a citizen and that the Fifteenth Amendment guaranteed his right to vote.[49] The white court ruled that he was *not* a U.S. citizen—that he was a citizen of a *foreign* nation and not entitled to vote. However, under the 1887 Dawes Act, the Indian "wards" of the government could become citizens if they showed themselves competent in managing their individual land allotments. Belatedly, in 1924, Congress passed the Indian Citizenship Act, granting citizenship to all Native Americans.

More change came a few decades later. The 1934 Indian Reorganization Act (IRA) established yet another federal policy for indigenous peoples. Designed by Commissioner of Indian Affairs John Collier, the law was intended to establish Indian civil and cultural rights, allow for semiautonomous tribal governments, and foster better economic development on reservations. The IRA would end land allotment, require BIA supervision of the land sales, and provide for preferential hiring of Indians at the BIA. Indian groups were supposed to vote on whether they wanted to come under this act.[50]

However, this supposedly progressive law ignored fundamental economic problems and maintained the subordinate relationship of Native Americans to the federal government. The law gave the Secretary of the Interior what many Indians saw as excessive power. The Secretary, called the "dictator of the Indians," made rules for elections, could veto constitutions, supervised expenditures, and made regulations for land management on reservations.[51] One analyst noted that "the expressed purpose of this law was finally and completely to usurp the traditional mechanisms of American Indian governance (e.g., the traditional chiefs, council of elders, etc.), replacing them with a system of federally approved and regulated 'tribal councils' ... structured more along the lines of corporate boards than of government entities."[52]

Many Native Americans saw the IRA as a violation of the sovereignty guaranteed them by treaties, and the law was ratified locally often by manipulation of the voting process. After four years, 189 Native American nations were reorganized, many with central councils and constitutions reflecting the values of the surrounding white culture. The seventy-seven groups that voted down participation operated under their traditional cultures. In this era numerous groups began some self-government, managing their own property and governing their own affairs under federal supervision.[53]

The Termination Policy

In 1946, after World War II, with a growing number of claims being made with regard to U.S. government violations of older treaties made with various Native American communities, the federal government set up an Indian Claims Commission. This Commission received numerous claims for compensation for lands taken, though in the first decade most of the Indian claims were denied.

In the 1950s, federal Indian policy again changed dramatically. House Concurrent Resolution 108 called for the *termination* of federal supervision of Indian groups. The intent was to reject the Indian Reorganization Act and return to the policy of forced conformity to white values with regard to land ownership. Termination was supported by land-hungry whites and their political supporters seeking to cut government costs, as well as by some acculturated Indians living off reservations. Thus, between 1954 and 1960, federal guardianship of several dozen Indian groups was "terminated." Because of its negative effects, including problems with unfriendly white officials and land entrepreneurs, this termination policy soon came to be viewed as a major failure. Termination was costly for many Indian groups that were still unprepared to deal with the land greed of the outside world.[54]

In the 1960s, federal policy toward Indians shifted once again. President Richard Nixon called on Congress to maintain Indians' close ties to the federal government and to prohibit any termination without consent. Congress passed legislation that made credit available for business purposes and established a self-determination procedure whereby Indian nations would assume self-administration of certain federal programs. Thus, since the 1970s, some groups have been able to run their own schools and social service programs.[55]

The Controversial Role of the BIA

The powers of the Bureau of Indian Affairs have long been far-reaching. That agency defines who is an "Indian" by determining which tribal groups are officially acknowledged by the government. It keeps records of fractions of "blood" lines to identify who is eligible for tribal membership. Official status usually brings a number of benefits to a group, including development, health, education, and housing benefits. To obtain federal recognition, a tribal group must document a continuous history and prove that its members are Indians. Several groups have been denied recognition, an action that amounts to administrative death.[56] The government-controlled process of defining who is an Indian and what is a tribe is one that is often emphasized by racial formation theorists. Governments intrude importantly into processes by which racial or ethnic groups are defined.

Today, the BIA continues to supervise Indian governments, banking, utilities, and highways, as well as millions in Indian trust funds. The BIA supervises the sale of land, and, until recently, all control of social services was in the hands of federal agencies. Some Native Americans regard the BIA as the lesser of two evils, noting that in recent decades it has to some extent protected them against predatory exploitation by white outsiders and has periodically expanded tribal self-determination. From this perspective, to terminate the BIA would be to end what protection the federal government does provide.[57]

Growing numbers of Indians have called for an end to BIA control and have worked for recognition of their groups as sovereign nations. The Indian Self-Determination and Education Assistance Act was amended to enable several nations to plan for autonomous governance. Federal support for self-government was furthered when a U.S. Senate investigation revealed extreme BIA mismanagement.

One Indian leader pointed out that federal actions "still retain the legally groundless presumption that Indian nations are somehow inherently subordinate to the United States."[58]

In 1996 several Indian leaders filed a lawsuit on behalf of the half-million Indians who sought a financial accounting and reform of the government's trust account system, which had been mismanaged for a century. To this point in time, the U.S. government has fought the lawsuit. Soon after the lawsuit was filed, a federal judge ordered the departments of Interior and Treasury to produce records for the trust accounts for the named plaintiffs. These trust accounts stem from land allotments made to individual Indians in the nineteenth century. Profits from the land—such as leasing fees and royalties for oil, logging, and other land uses—should have been held in trust by the government. However, the government has not yet produced the records, in part because it has not kept records or has lost those that it had. The federal judge referred to this as "fiscal and government irresponsibility." Most recently (2006), members of Congress have proposed an Indian Trust Reform Act. If it is passed, this legislation would provide $8 billion as a settlement to individual trust account holders and also give some Indian groups control over trust assets on reservations. As of 2007, some federal officials were still blocking the settlement.[59]

What are the strengths and weaknesses of government policies designed to assist Native Americans?

Growing Pressures for Political Participation

For Native Americans on reservations, political participation has often been directed at reservation elections and service in tribal governments. Indian governments have often combined legislative and executive functions into one elected council, and voter turnout for elections has often been substantial. Political conflict has occurred periodically between leaders who prefer to work closely with the BIA and those who support tribal sovereignty.[60]

Native Americans did not have the right to vote in all states (outside reservations) until the 1924 Indian Citizenship Act. Even then, states such as Utah, Arizona, and New Mexico barred reservation Indians from voting until the 1940s; as late as 1970, some states made voting and jury participation difficult. State literacy tests and gerrymandered voting district lines have reduced Indian voting power in several western states. The number of potential voters has risen to substantial proportions in nonreservation areas; in some urban areas, Indian voting strength is great enough to function as a **swing vote** (*a bloc that can affect close elections*).

The number of Indians running for political office has gradually increased over the last few decades. Until recently, only a handful had ever served in state and federal legislatures. For example, the New Mexico legislature had its first Indian representatives only in 1964. By 2007, however, the number had grown significantly in the western states, Alaska, and Hawaii—to about seventy-three members of state legislatures. Few have ever served in Congress—perhaps a half-dozen representatives and two senators. The most famous, Charles Curtis, was born on the Kaw reservation in 1860. Said to be one-fourth Indian, Curtis was a representative for fourteen years, a senator for twenty, and vice-president under Herbert Hoover.[61]

Since 1935 only a handful of Native Americans have served in the U.S. Congress; there has rarely been more than one at any time. Ben Reifel, a Sioux, was a representative (R–S.D.) from 1961 to 1971. In 1992, Congress's only Native American member at the time, Representative Ben Nighthorse Campbell (R–Colo.) was elected senator from that state. In 2000 Campbell was joined by Brad Carson, who was elected in Oklahoma with the help of an organized campaign to get out Indian voters. Carson was elected in the congressional district with the largest Indian population and was at the time the only Native American (Cherokee) in the House. In 2007, only one Native American, Thomas Cole (Chickasaw), a House member (R–Okla.) elected in 2002, serves in either branch of Congress. The number of Indian voters has grown significantly over the past few decades, substantially as a result of voter registration campaigns. As a result, Indian voters have been very important in some state races in the West, such as in helping the Democratic candidate for the U.S. Senate, Jon Tester, win in Montana in 2006.[62]

The modest-to-slight Indian representation in state legislatures and Congress is paralleled in town and city governments. Even in metropolitan areas with substantial Indian populations, few have been elected to city councils, school boards, or county governments. Police harassment of Indians in towns near reservations is sometimes a problem, which often reveals discrimination by local authorities. Periodically, complaints by Indian leaders have focused on the lack of efforts in various towns and cities with significant Native American populations to recruit Native Americans as police, parole officers, and government attorneys.[63]

The recent economic gains that have come from industrial and gaming operations, which we will examine later, have enabled a few Indian groups to contribute significant amounts of money to political campaigns and to fund lobbying in Washington, D.C., thereby expanding their political influence. This political influence has already helped to stop the passage of legislation detrimental to Indian interests. In recent years, a few of the (white) lobbyists working for Indian interests, as well as for non-Indian interests, have been accused or convicted of corruption and illegal practices. In addition, we should note that the large *majority* of Native American groups have not yet been able to prosper economically and politically in the United States.[64]

Over the last decade or so a conservative U.S. Supreme Court has handed down a series of major decisions that limit the political and judicial power of reservation governments. During the same era that tribal governments have asserted their rights and powers under treaties (including over whites on reservations), the U.S. Supreme Court has, as a recent National Congress of American Indians (NCAI) report puts it, "significantly limited the civil and criminal jurisdiction of tribal governments over events that occur within their territorial boundaries. The most recent Supreme Court cases make it clear that tribal governments are in an increasingly defensive posture in the federal courts.... In the long term, this erosion of jurisdiction threatens to make tribal governments ineffective in protecting the cultural identities of their communities."[65]

Protest and Conflict

Organized Native American protest against subordination has perhaps been the most sustained of any group in the history of North America. Armed resistance to European and European American oppression between the 1500s and the 1890s produced great protest leaders and movements; the end of armed conflict after the 1890s did not end the protests. By the late nineteenth century, new protest organizations had sprung up. One was the Indian Rights Association, founded by whites concerned with protecting and "civilizing" Native Americans. By exposing the corruption and discrimination on reservations, such progressive groups did lay the basis for reforms in federal policies. The Society of American Indians was one of the first formed by Native Americans. The goals of this self-help-oriented organization included developing a national Indian leadership and improving educational and job opportunities.[66]

In the 1920s, John Collier organized the American Indian Defense Association to fight attempts by government officials to establish "executive order reservations" not covered by treaty and thus more accessible to exploitation by whites who wished to extract minerals. The NCAI, the largest advocacy group, was formed in the 1940s and has pressed for education, legal aid, and progressive legislation. The NCAI vigorously opposed the termination policy of the 1950s and campaigned for tribal self-determination. It has campaigned against anti-Indian stereotyping, including sports teams' use of caricatured Indian symbols. The National Indian Youth Council, created in 1961, has fought vigorously for civil rights, sometimes organizing civil disobedience protests. The Youth Council has been active in education and in protection of Native American lands.[67]

Significantly, over the last few decades many Native American groups have organized and pressed hard to relieve continuing discrimination and other modern effects of historical anti-Indian oppression. Many have reasserted their sovereignty over lands and reservations that have long been controlled by federal and local governments.

Confrontation with the Federal Government

The term *Red Power* appeared during a period of expanded Native American activism in the 1960s. Protest actions during the 1960s continued a long tradition of pressuring white-controlled institutions into fair concessions. Civil disobedience involved such activities as delaying dam construction, occupying government facilities, and picketing.[68] Numerous protest actions have brought significant changes benefiting Native Americans.

In 1968 the American Indian Movement (AIM) was organized to address problems ranging from police brutality to discrimination in housing and employment. In 1973 the AIM organized a large-scale occupation of Wounded Knee, South Dakota, a hamlet on the Pine Ridge Reservation. Several hundred AIM members participated in armed protest directed against the U.S. Justice Department's decision to send federal agents to Pine Ridge to support a Sioux leader who was being challenged by activists who wanted to replace him with a traditional council of elders.[69]

In its attempts to convict AIM protesters, the government behaved like a police state and used illegal wiretaps, altered evidence, and paid witnesses—which led a federal judge to dismiss the case. Afterward, U.S. government agents participated in a campaign to destroy the AIM and were thought by knowledgeable observers to have been involved in suspicious accidents and murders involving AIM members. Two hundred AIM members were harassed and arrested; few were ever convicted. This political struggle was a major example of an open confrontation between militant Native Americans and a Native American establishment supported by the BIA and other white officials.[70]

Leonard Peltier: A U.S. Political Prisoner

In recent years numerous Native American protest efforts have sought to free Leonard Peltier, a Lakota Sioux Indian. Seen by many, including the international civil rights group Amnesty International, as a political prisoner, Peltier has been in a federal penal institution for decades. He is accused of shooting two FBI agents in the confrontation between Indians and government agents at the Pine Ridge Reservation in 1975. Initially, several men were accused, but only Peltier was tried. Federal officials admit that it is unclear who shot the agents, and numerous members of Congress have supported a new trial for Peltier. Revelations that the FBI withheld documents (including a critical ballistics test) from Peltier's defense attorneys have added support to international calls to free him. Millions around the globe have signed petitions or joined groups protesting Peltier's confinement as a U.S. political prisoner, and legal efforts to free him have continued to the present day.[71]

Anti-Indian Racism and Sports Mascots

In recent decades the AIM and other Indian organizations have protested the use of Indian names, sacred symbols, and "tomahawk chop" gestures by white-oriented sports teams. Before one 1990s Super Bowl, the AIM sponsored a conference on racism in sports. Nationally televised sports events have brought degrading caricatures into the homes of Indians who otherwise have little contact with such racist imagery and behavior. "We couldn't ignore it anymore," one protester stated. "People started coming up to me at work and going, 'chop-chop' and 'woo-woo.'" Prominent team names such as *Redskins* are racially derogatory and vicious, yet many people still refuse to acknowledge this fact. Most names such as *Redskins*, *Chiefs*, and *Braves*, together with the associated caricatures used by many teams, involve offensive anti-Indian images and stereotypes. White parodies of sacred chants, face paint, headdresses, and drums for entertainment purposes are taken by many Indians as assaults on their cultures, in part because most of these have spiritual significance.[72]

For years now, people associated with the National Coalition on Racism in Sports and the Media have joined protesters challenging the Cleveland baseball team's use of the highly caricatured "Chief Wahoo" symbol. Called the *Indians*, Cleveland's team has come under intensive criticism for an image that is seen by many Native Americans and other Americans as extremely negative and racist. Images and mascots like Chief Wahoo are "invented Indians," as the book *Team Spirits* (2001) puts it. They are not real but "perpetuate inappropriate, inaccurate, and harmful understandings of living people, their cultures, and their histories.... Through fragments thought to be Indian—a headdress, tomahawk, war paint, or buckskin—Native American mascots reduce them to a series of well-worn clichés, sideshow props, and racist stereotypes."[73]

Today, many colleges and universities still use such Indian logos, often in connection with sports. Debates similar to those in Cleveland have taken place around Chief Illiniwek, the dancing Indian present at sports events, who has long been a symbol for the University of Illinois. In 2001 most of that university's trustees expressed support for this racist symbol for the university. Finally, in March 2007, facing much protest, the University of Illinois board of trustees decided to retire the Chief Illinewek image, name, and regalia. Researcher David Prochaska argues that these Indian mascots catch on because of "imperialist nostalgia," a mutated celebrating by whites of those whom their ancestors killed or forced onto reservations. The fictional Chief Illiniwek was *not* dressed like the Woodlands Illiniwek after whom he was named. Instead, whites "playing Indian" at sports events dressed up in a pseudo-Sioux costume with a war bonnet like a Plains Indian. Such actions were *not* attempts to celebrate authentically the country's indigenous inhabitants.[74]

Such mascots and related fan actions are often based on stereotypes of Native Americans as wild "savages" or blood-thirsty warriors and ignore the historical reality of the savage European takeovers of Native American lands and the often genocidal policies directed at indigenous peoples.[75] The symbolism chosen by college and other sports teams also stereotypes Indians as historical peoples rather than as contemporary peoples. Indians are portrayed as a generic "Indian" group rather than as diverse nations and are thus robbed of control even over their public images. Use of these stereotyped symbols often mocks the religious significance of Indian sacred symbols. Vigorous opposition among some non-Indian men to the elimination of Indian sports symbolism may even suggest that the protest movement threatens a particular version of male identity that is rooted in the mythology of the American West. Note the following statement made by a prominent professional football player: "The reason there's so much violence in football is we can't kill Indians anymore."[76]

Significantly, the U.S. Census Bureau decided not to include pictures of sports teams that still use these stereotyped Indian symbols in the Bureau's promotional materials. In 2001 the U.S. Commission on Civil Rights issued a statement condemning the use of stereotyped Indian images as sports symbols and noting that such images are especially insensitive in view of the history of oppression of Native Americans. In 2005 the National Collegiate Athletic Association (NCAA) decided that college sports teams that use Indian names and logos will not be allowed to use that imagery in NCAA-related postseason games.[77]

Recent Gains and Continuing Protests

The Indian civil rights movement has achieved some gains in raising public consciousness. Films portraying Native Americans as savages and white people as heroes have become less common. Films such as *Powwow Highway* and *Dances with Wolves* have portrayed Native Americans in a more sympathetic, if often paternalistic, light. Since the 1970s some colleges and universities, such as Dartmouth and Stanford, have dropped the name *Indians* for their teams. In 1992, in response to AIM protests, the *Oregonian* became the first newspaper to discontinue using names that stereotype Indians.[78]

In the 1990s a coalition of petitioners sued to force the Washington Redskins football team to change its name. In 1999 a federal agency voided the trademark rights of the team because its logo was racially derogatory and violated the law. Over the last two decades several colleges and universities, including Stanford University and the University of Illinois, have given up their Indian logos, while numerous local governments, especially school boards, have had to face the issue. Numerous high schools have changed team names and dropped offensive mascots. The Minnesota Board of Education and the Los Angeles and Dallas school districts have forced local schools to give up Indian mascots.[79]

Other recent protests have focused on a variety of issues. Protests in Oklahoma led the legislature to pass a resolution that requires local governments to delete the derogatory word "squaw" from names of geographic places. In 2001, in Austin, Texas, several hundred Native Americans and supporters rallied at the Capitol to press for a repatriation and grave-protection law. This legislation would protect unmarked Indian graves and their contents on both public and private lands in Texas. However, the Texas state government continued its anti-Indian reputation by opposing this reasonable law. At the rally, organized by an Indian student group at Texas A & M, an Indian leader spoke effectively of her tribe's long history of oppression in Texas.[80]

Honoring Treaties: Fishing Rights and Land Claims

Fishing rights and land claims have provoked conflict between Indians and whites in several states. For more than a century, indigenous nations have struggled with whites over fishing rights in the

Pacific Northwest and Great Lakes regions. Shootings and court battles have occurred in Washington state over Indian rights to catch fish, particularly salmon and trout—rights guaranteed by official treaties between the Indian nations and the U.S. government. White anglers and commercial companies object because fishing opportunities are reduced when Native Americans exercise old treaty rights. A court decision, *U.S.* v. *State of Washington* (1974), ruled that indigenous rights reserved by the treaties are different from those allowed whites. The court ordered the state to protect Indian anglers.[81]

White anglers defied the decision, and the state appealed. Indian fishers were harassed and assaulted, and white protests were directed at the judge. The federal government spent millions to increase fish available and compensate whites. In 1979 the Supreme Court upheld the lower-court ruling, and government enforcement gradually reduced illegal fishing by whites. This decision helped to revitalize reservation economies in Washington state. In the words of one Indian leader, "the opportunities created directly or indirectly from the legally secured right to fish are the difference between staying and leaving" for many families in numerous communities.[82]

Historically, Native American lands were taken by force or secured by fraud and/or without adequate compensation. The underlying cause of an east coast land-claims conflict was stated by the U.S. Commission on Civil Rights:

> The basic Eastern Indian land claim is that Indian land in the East was invalidly transferred from Indians to non-Indians in the 18th and 19th centuries because the Federal Government, *although required to do so,* did not supervise or approve the transactions.[83]

In recent decades many groups, such as the Oneida and Mohawks in New York and the Passamaquoddy in Maine, have pressed land claims in court. The Mohawks successfully pressed a claim for the return of many acres of land in New York. In 1980, after a lengthy court battle, the U.S. Supreme Court awarded the Lakota Sioux $122.5 million for more than 7 million acres taken illegally in the 1870s. Although the land had been guaranteed to the Sioux by an 1868 treaty made by the U.S. government, it was stolen by whites later when gold was discovered on the reservation. Following a war between the Sioux and the U.S. Army, the Lakota and others lost control of a large area. In 1987, a U.S. senator introduced a bill to return substantial land and to offer money damages for some stolen land. The bill gained considerable support from the Lakotas before it was withdrawn. From 1981 to 1987, Native Americans staged an occupation of Camp Yellow Thunder in the Black Hills to protest the government's failure to live up to its treaty.[84]

Recently, Alex White Plume, president of the Oglala Lakota Nation, wrote a letter to President George W. Bush, asking on behalf of the Nation that the "United States fulfill its obligation to respect and protect the human rights of Indian peoples in this country." He then discussed sacred Indian sites that are endangered by white development and other projects, calling on government to honor its legal obligation to protect these sites. He added: "We are also calling on the United States to fulfill its legal and moral obligations to Indian peoples by voting to approve the Declaration on the Rights of Indigenous Peoples at the upcoming September session of the U.N. General Assembly. The United States cannot meet its existing legal and moral obligations under international law, nor its fiduciary obligations under federal Indian law, by voting against (or abstaining from voting on) the declaration."[85] Sioux leaders were part of the U.N. committee that wrote this Declaration on the Rights of Indigenous Peoples, which provides for the "restitution of the lands, territories and resources" and the "enforcement of treaties." Indigenous organizations representing more than 300 million indigenous people around the world have pressed the UN General Assembly to pass this Declaration, which has already been approved by the UN Human Rights Council. That action has been resisted by several powerful countries, including Canada and the United States.[86]

White backlash against Native American land claims, fishing claims, and other militant protests led to the creation of a national organization called the Interstate Congress for Equal Rights and Responsibilities and a variety of other antitreaty organizations. Senator Mark Hatfield of Oregon noted publicly that this "very significant backlash. . . by any other name comes out as racism in all its ugly manifestations." White members of Congress introduced bills to break treaties, overturn court decisions, and extinguish native land claims, arguing that the demands by Indians had soured "friendly relations." Native American groups responded that they were seeking what was *legally* theirs under official agreements with the U.S. government. Whites had become hostile because of the expense of living up to U.S. law and, as one Indian leader noted, "because of the lack of educational systems to teach anything about Indians, about treaties."[87] White ignorance of official treaties has played an important role in white opposition to Indian struggles for justice.

The Native American Rights Fund (NARF), a nonprofit national legal defense firm, has represented various tribes in lawsuits and negotiations for treaty-guaranteed land and natural resource rights and for restoration of the status of tribes as sovereign nations. The NARF has won hundreds of victories. The organization has secured the return of land to the Passamaquoddy and Penobscot nations in Maine; Native American control over taxation, local courts, and educational programs; and new economic enterprises on reservations.[88]

Human rights groups have documented continuing harassment and violence perpetrated by whites against Native Americans in recent decades. Native Americans have been victims of property crimes as well as beatings and murder, especially in southwestern states. Many hate crimes have occurred in rural white communities that border reservations. Indians in urban areas have also been targeted. Hate crime incidents seldom receive media coverage. One prominent author, Rodney Barker, has reported that numerous Native Americans have told him of hate crimes that they or their families experienced, but the local "newspaper was refusing to carry those reports... Everyone tries to dissociate themselves from the historical pattern and say, 'Well, this is an aberration, it's not representative of what's going on here.' And yet, how many of those (crimes) does it take before you see the pattern is still in evidence?"[89]

How have Native Americans resisted white-generated government policies and persisting discrimination?

Fighting for Fairness: Suing the Department of Agriculture

Native Americans are the oldest farmers in North America, yet most have had to struggle to maintain a living at this occupation. The U.S. government has an uneven record regarding fairness to farmers who are not white. In early 2000 more than 890 Native American families joined a class-action suit against the U.S. Department of Agriculture (USDA) charging that government agency with discrimination.[90]

The lawsuit, which as of 2007 was still pending, cites several types of discrimination. First, Indian farmers are often discouraged from applying for USDA disaster assistance or farm support loans, while this is not the case for comparable white applicants. Second, Indian applicants are often asked to fill out more complicated forms or to fill out the forms with less assistance from USDA employees than is offered to comparable whites. Third, USDA guidelines are interpreted more advantageously for white than for Indian farmers. The latter also tend to receive smaller amounts when they do manage to secure loans. In addition, the USDA's locations favor white farmers and make it difficult for many Indian farmers to get to the offices. The USDA has denied the lawsuit's charges of systemic discrimination. However, the history of U.S. government treatment of Native American and African American farmers suggests that a deeper investigation of USDA policies is in order.[91]

Activism and Self-Determination

Since the 1970s many Indian groups have renewed pressure on the U.S. government to accept the terms of long-neglected treaties with Indian nations. Protests of various kinds, including lawsuits, have led to restoration of lands and other resources and have been important to the passage of congressional laws that increase Indian self-determination. Tribal control of lands and resources has increased because of such laws as the 1975 Indian Self-Determination and Education Assistance Act, the 1979 Archaeological Resources Protection Act, the 1983 Land Consolidation Act, and the 1988 Indian Gaming Regulatory Act. Numerous other legislative acts are linked to this trend, including the 1978 American Indian Religious Freedom Act and the 1990 Native American Languages Act. This legislation indicates that earlier termination of tribal groups has ended. Coupled with these legislative changes are changes on reservations, where "communities are developing tribal court systems, establishing tribal education systems including tribal colleges, extending tribal sovereignty and control over resources and taxation, enforcing tribal hunting, fishing, and water rights, and building economic development programs."[92]

The resurgence of Indian self-determination has been accompanied by a renewed emphasis on Indian cultures and spirituality. The 1989 National Museum of the American Indian Act authorized construction of a museum on the mall in Washington, D.C., to bring together in one place the Smithsonian's dispersed collection of Indian sacred objects. This museum is now mostly under Native American control. The Act requires that extensive government holdings of Indian funerary objects and burial remains be returned. This Act provides recognition of the long struggle of Native Americans for respect for burial sites and sacred objects. The Native American Graves Protection and Repatriation Act (1990) requires museums to notify Indian groups of government holdings of Indian objects and to facilitate their return.[93]

The greatly increased Native American activism since the 1960s is now bearing fruit in a strong resurgence of Native American cultures and societies and a strong insistence on indigenous and civil rights across the United States. For example, in communities near reservations, protests against discrimination have periodically been organized. In fall 2006 in Farmington, New Mexico, a substantial number of Indians participated in a march down a major highway to protest recent instances of hate crimes, police brutality, and other local discrimination that had taken place in urban areas bordering the Navajo nation.[94] Still, while protests may be on the increase, as is the case for other racial and ethnic groups, most Native Americans have not participated in the public protests engaged in by an activist minority. The majority of Native Americans likely agree with numerous goals of the active protestors, although they are more likely to seek change by more conventional political and social means.

The Economy

Before being forced onto reservations, most indigenous groups, which ranged from the Pueblo agriculturalists of the Southwest to hunting societies on the Plains to mixed agricultural-hunting societies elsewhere across the continent, had self-sufficient, land-based economies.

The loss of land to whites destroyed traditional economies. Melissa Fawcett Sayet, a Mohegan elder, has explained how she cried in anguish when her high school teacher taught the concept of **manifest destiny**, which stated that *the United States had a right to expand from the Atlantic Ocean to the Pacific and would inevitably do so*. By the 1880s, Native American nations had lost millions of acres as whites proceeded westward; millions more acres were lost with the breakup of the remaining lands under the 1887 Dawes Act. Native American lands were usually reduced to areas considered at the time to be the least valuable to white farmers and entrepreneurs. Today Native Americans control only 3 percent of the land in the continental United States, although indigenous peoples have legal claims to ten times that amount.[95]

Economic exploitation accompanied the growth of industrial capitalism and urbanization in the nineteenth century. Encroachment on Indian lands by white lumbering, ranching, and railroad interests redirected resources from rural Indian lands to fuel growth in cities. Bison and other game were killed for skins to be sold in eastern cities, and whites took lands for cattle raising and agriculture, hastening the impoverishment of Native Americans. Rural poverty increased as corporations reached out from metropolitan areas to develop more and more land; this in turn pressured many Native Americans to migrate to the cities. Joseph Jorgensen has shown that the poverty of rural Native Americans is "not due to rural isolation [or] a tenacious hold on aboriginal ways, but results from the way in which U.S. urban centers of finance, political influence, and power have grown at the expense of rural areas."[96] Over centuries, much Indian wealth and many resources have been unjustly transferred to the white population.

Poverty and Land Theft

The poverty of many reservations is rooted in destruction of local economies and mismanagement by BIA officials. Testifying before a congressional committee on the food situation in 1883, a member of the Assiniboine nation pointed out that its members were healthy until the buffalo were destroyed, and that substitute BIA rations were very inadequate:

> They gave us rations once a week, just enough to last one day, and the Indians they started to eat their

> pet dogs. After they ate all their dogs up they started to eat their ponies. All this time the Indian Bureau had a warehouse full of grub.... Early [the next] spring, in 1884, I saw the dead bodies of the Indians wrapped in blankets and piled up like cordwood in the village of Wolf Point, and the other Indians were so weak they could not bury their dead; what were left were nothing but skeletons.[97]

Government agents were responsible for supplies, instruction in farming, and supervision of lands. Unfortunately, many agents were corrupt or incompetent.

The 1930s reorganization policy, which provided for some self-government, put a partial brake on corruption and land theft, but federal policy later fluctuated between tribal self-determination and the forced individualism of the "termination" policy. Some Indian lands were sold to pay taxes, and many Indian groups fell deeper into severe economic deprivation as land resources were depleted. For many years, Indian lands have been taken for dams, national parks, and highways. Sale of lands to white lumbering and mineral interests continues. In addition, much of the substantial money made from agriculture or ranching operations on Indian reservations has actually flowed to whites. Facing local and USDA discrimination and often having limited schooling, technical assistance, and capital to buy seeds, livestock, or machinery, many Indian farmers have faced a low agricultural yield or having to lease to white outsiders.[98]

Land, Minerals, and Industrial Development

Reservations have about one-third of all low-sulfur coal, 6 percent of oil and gas reserves, and half of known uranium reserves. Yet, historically, whites have benefited the most from these resources. White corporate executives have eagerly eyed these resources, and some have called for abolition of reservations and the Bureau of Indian Affairs so that these resources can be better exploited. Historically, when desirable mineral resources have been found on Indian land, the land has often been taken over by white corporations. An example is the 1952 mineral extraction agreement between the Navajo Tribal Council and Kerr-McGee Corporation. Over eighteen years, Kerr-McGee profited greatly, employing 150 Navajo men to mine uranium on Navajo land and paying them two-thirds of the prevailing off-reservation wage. Once the easy-to-reach deposits were mined, the company closed the facility, leaving radioactive debris that threatened water supplies. Many Indian miners contracted terminal cancers related to their mining of uranium.[99]

Three dozen tribes made national headlines in the 1970s when they announced the creation of the Council of Energy Resources Tribes (CERT) and hired a former Iranian oil minister to help them get better contracts with white-owned companies. Many whites worried that CERT would seek to be completely independent in making contracts with energy corporations. Today, CERT's membership has expanded to fifty-seven U.S. and Canadian tribal groups. By providing technical and financial assistance to help member groups control their energy resources, the organization has brought new jobs and increased income to numerous Indian communities. It has also provided a forum for discussions of the effects of new economic development on traditional cutlures.[100]

Persisting Economic Problems

Before 1940 most Indian men were poor farmers or unskilled workers. With urban migration, the proportion in farm occupations has dropped dramatically—from 68 percent in 1940 to less than 2 percent today. Urban workers have usually been concentrated in the **secondary labor market**—*that sector characterized by job instability, low wages, and little mobility*, and disproportionately composed of workers who are not white. The **primary labor market**—*the sector characterized by skilled jobs, higher wages, and greater mobility*—is composed predominantly of white workers.

Recent census survey figures for workers aged 16 years and older (Table 6.1) compare the recent occupational distribution of workers who reported (only) Indian ancestry with that of all U.S. workers.[101] Today, Native Americans are less likely than U.S. workers as a group to hold managerial or professional positions (26.1 percent versus 34.1 percent). Native American men tend to be concentrated in blue-collar and service-sector jobs, while most Native American women hold clerical, sales, or service-sector jobs. (The pattern is very similar when those who listed Indian and other ancestry are added in.)

TABLE 6.1 Occupational Distributions: Native American Workers (Including Native Alaskans) and All Workers (2005)

	Native American Workers*	All Workers
Managerial and professional	26.1%	34.1%
Sales and office	23.0	25.9
Service	21.3	16.3
Farming, forestry, and fishing	1.2	0.7
Construction, Extraction, and Maintenance	13.5	10.0
Production, Transportation, and Material Moving	15.0	13.0
Total	100.1%	100.0%

**These census data are for those who reported only Indian ancestry.*

Moreover, Native American civilian employees in the executive branch of the federal government (Table 6.2) are most heavily represented in clerical, technical, and blue-collar job categories. Their percentage is lowest for professional positions. The percentage of Native American workers is highest at the lower pay levels and lowest at the highest pay levels.[102].

Through the years, unemployment rates for Indians have been far higher than for most other groups. In 1940, one-third of all Indian men were unemployed, compared with fewer than one-tenth of white men. By 1960 the rate had risen to 38 percent, compared with 5 percent for all men. This increase reflected in part the move from agriculture to the less certain work opportunities in urban areas. By 1990 the unemployment rate had dropped but was still high. For Native American men, the 15 percent rate was also three times that of white men, and the 13.1 percent rate for Native American women was almost three times that of white women. In that year the unemployment rate for Native Americans

TABLE 6.2 Civilian Employees in Executive Branch Agencies, 2004 (Percentage of Employees by Category and Racial Group)

	Native American	White
All white-collar workers	2.0%	69.0%
Professional workers	1.4	76.5
Clerical workers	3.1	55.9
Blue-collar workers	3.0	65.7
Pay plans		
General schedule	2.0	68.7
GS1	1.1	53.7
GS2	3.3	55.1
GS3	3.9	55.8
GS4	4.5	57.3
GS15	0.8	82.6
Senior pay levels	0.8	86.0

living on reservations was much higher, at 26 percent. In recent estimates from the Bureau of Labor Statistics (2005), the Native American unemployment rate was estimated at 9.3 percent, still more than twice the estimated white rate of 4.4 percent.[103] Note that these rates do *not* include the large proportion of Indian workers who have given up looking for work or who can find only part-time work.

Prevailing notions about poor Native Americans are full of old myths that help keep our often oppressive racial system in place. One elite-sponsored, stereotypical view of poor people of color is that they are unemployed because they are lazy or do not have necessary skills because of their "culture of poverty." However, research has made it clear that the *main* reason for their unemployment is the unwillingness or inability of local employers in rural and urban areas to provide enough decent-paying jobs. Recent research by scholars such as Kathleen Pickering has shown that poverty-stricken Native American communities, such as the Lakota Pine Ridge Reservation (South Dakota), involve local residents in much work activity. Many Native Americans there not only hold regular jobs in urban areas, off and on, but also engage in much other work activity in their home reservation areas—making traditional Lakota goods (such as star quilts), making clothes, catering, repairing cars, and doing other personal services. Native Americans do a great deal of sharing goods and income across their extended families. Like Native Americans in other communities, Lakota lives frequently involve movement back and forth between a reservation, where conventional paid work is scarce, and towns or cities where they work until (usually white) employers lay them off. In this way, the local community economy involves both subsistence work on the reservation and work beyond its borders—with supporting family networks being the central motivation for this extended economic effort across space and time.[104]

For decades Native Americans have had the lowest median family income and per-capita income of any major racial or ethnic umbrella group. The income of Native Americans on reservations has been lower than that of those living in nonreservation areas. In 1939 the median income of men on reservations was less than one-fourth of the median income for all U.S. men. Some improvement has occurred in the decades leading up to the present, but in 2005 (the most recent data) median family income for Native American (including Alaskan) families ($38,588) was still much less than the median income of non-Hispanic white families ($62,300). The median income of households on rural reservations was even lower. Today, some 21.2 percent of Native Americans (including Alaskans) live below the poverty line, more than three times the non-Hispanic white figure of 6.3 percent.[105]

Part of Native Americans' economic improvement in recent decades may be an effect of the large increase of people who now identify themselves as Native American. That is, people of mixed ancestry now reclaiming their heritage are frequently more affluent than others.[106] Still, in this twenty-first century, many Native Americans remain among the poorest of all Americans.

Poverty and unemployment are accompanied by inadequate living conditions. Generally speaking, Native Americans face the worst housing conditions of any U.S. group. Today, Native Americans are much more likely than whites to have inadequate nutrition, to die of tuberculosis or diabetes, to live in small apartments or houses, and to have inadequate water or other facilities. Thus, some 12 percent of Indian homes do not have safe water, as compared to 1 percent for the rest of the U.S. population. Recent data on mortality rates show that they are much higher than for the population as a whole. For example, the tuberculosis death rate is 533 percent higher for Indians than for the population as a whole. Native Americans also have the highest prevalence of type 2 (adult-onset) diabetes of any group across the globe. Although life expectancy for Native Americans has increased in recent years, it is still well below the national average. Current federal officials tend to blame Native Americans for these problems, citing their "lifestyles" and diets. However, inadequate jobs, incomes, and medical facilities constitute a major part of the problem. Cutbacks in federal health programs by conservative U.S. administrations since the 1980s have also reduced Indian access to medical care.[107]

Recent Economic Developments

With the growing self-determination movement and the recognition of tribal sovereignty in the courts, dozens of Indian nations have developed gambling and other enterprises in attempts to improve local economies. According to a 2006 report, there were

420 Indian gaming operations operated by 227 tribal groups in thirty states. Annual revenues totaled about $22.7 billion in the most recent year. While this economic development is significant, Indian gaming still constitutes a small percentage of the total U.S. gaming industry.[108] Media reports have greatly exaggerated the economic return from these operations, to the point that many non-Indian Americans hold to the myth that Indians are now mostly well off because of casinos (or oil wells). However, most Native Americans have *not* benefited at all from casino gaming, nor do most get significant payments from community or federal government programs. Most Indian societies are still struggling to overcome serious poverty and unemployment. The majority of the 500-plus federally recognized Indian groups have *no* such gaming operations. Indeed, a few dozen of the Indian operations receive most gaming revenues.[109]

Profits from gaming enterprises have constituted the first regular income for some Indian groups. Federal law requires that gaming profits be used for such things as education, economic development, courts and policing, and physical infrastructure. Where gaming revenues are significant, they have paid for educational and health care facilities, water treatment plants, job training, roads, and housing, and have reduced unemployment for Indians. Gaming revenues have also helped to create new businesses. For example, profits from the Choctaw Nation's bingo hall in Durant, Oklahoma, helped create truck stops, a motel, and a restaurant. These enterprises employ numerous Choctaws. Tourist dollars generated by Indian operations also provide substantial benefits to nearby white businesses.[110]

Over recent decades, the Mississippi Band of the Choctaw Nation has been successful in developing industrial parks and other areas that have attracted *Fortune* 500 companies, thereby increasing local employment. They have also developed a forestry management company, a major nursing home facility, and some golfing resort developments (see www.choctaw.org). Similarly, in recent years Oregon's Confederated Tribes of Warm Springs have developed substantial recreation and tourism facilities, a casino, a hydroelectric power enterprise, and a joint enterprise to develop diatomaceous earth products (see www.warmsprings.com). In Oklahoma the Cherokee Nation Industries has used gaming profits to build a plant that manufactures cable boxes and another that manufactures cables, some of which have been used on the International Space Station. Numerous Indian groups are investing gaming profits in more diversified businesses.[111]

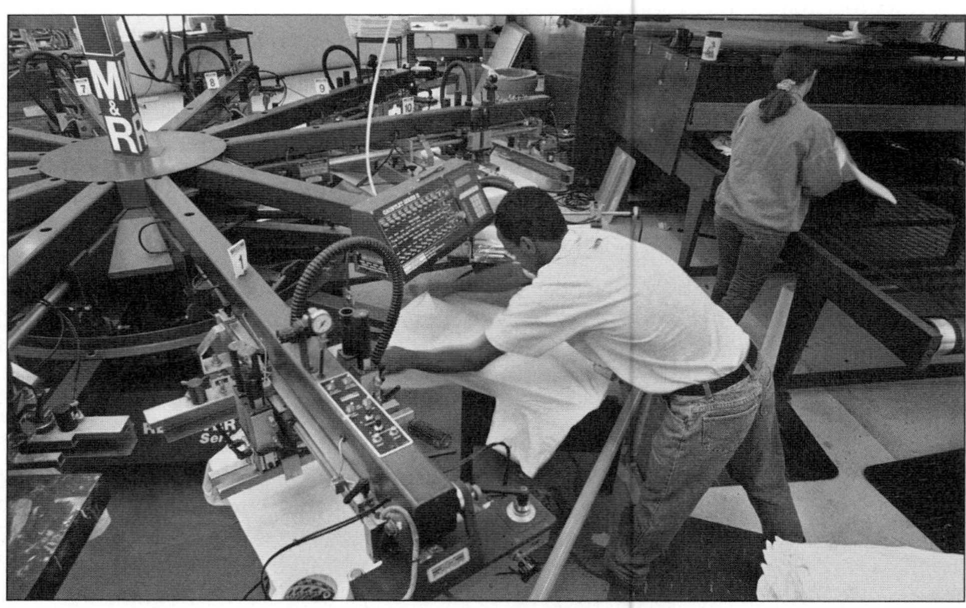

Workers print designs on T-shirts at a factory owned by the Oneida Nation.

Interestingly, a poll of registered voters nationwide found that three-fourths felt Indian nations should be permitted to use reservation lands to develop such enterprises as casinos, gas stations, and golf courses. Nonetheless, white investors, lenders, and management firms have claimed a large share of revenues from many of the Indian gambling operations. One federal investigation found that many tribes had been victims of economic exploitation and embezzlement by white firms.[112]

In addition, certain economic opportunities have been rejected. For example, in recent years numerous reservation leaders have been approached to provide landfill space for outside garbage or nuclear waste. Reservations are attractive to waste management companies because of their low population density and because they are not generally subject to state environmental regulations or taxes. Enforcement of federal pollution regulations has often been lax on reservations. Most tribes have rejected the offers, though some have become badly divided between tribal members seeking economic development and those trying to protect their lands. One Sioux leader stated, "we're still fighting the invaders, only now they're trying to make us take their trash."[113] The widespread problem of *government and private dumping in communities populated by Americans of color* is documented by a growing body of research. Such dumping is often a type of **environmental racism**.

Education

The first extended experiences of subordinated Native Americans with white-dominated education came early in the reservation period. Influential whites supported education as the channel of forced acculturation to white culture. In white-controlled schools, "wild Indians"—as whites often stereotyped them—could be "civilized." By 1887, some 14,300 Indian children were enrolled in 227 schools, most operated by the BIA or white religious groups.[114]

Still, by 1900 only a modest percentage of children were receiving schooling in white-oriented schools. In the Southwest, perhaps one-fourth of school-age children in the four decades after 1890 had experience with BIA and other boarding schools; a small percentage of the rest attended public schools. BIA and mission schools were usually run with an Anglo-conformity assimilationist approach. Intensive efforts were made to destroy Indian ways; students were punished for speaking their home languages. By the 1930s, some boarding schools were being replaced by day schools closer to home, and a bilingual policy was being discussed by white officials. Yet, even by 1945, large proportions of Native American children were still not enrolled in schools of any type.[115]

Enforced acculturation has been a recurring issue in BIA and local public schools, where white administrators and teachers have blamed educational problems on cultural differences and thus emphasized the contrast between the often collective values of Indians and the intense individualism of most white Americans. Many white teachers have attempted to make their pupils "less Indian." To this day, many public and private school textbooks provide little to help Native American children identify with their own ancient and distinguished cultures.[116]

Partly because of organized protest since the 1960s, government aid for primary, adult, and vocational education has expanded substantially. Government attention has been refocused on local public and BIA schools, and many federal schools have developed Native American advisory boards, added Native Americans to their staffs, and added classes in Indian art, dance, and language. However, in the words of one AIM member, the central "curriculum taught in Indian schools [has] remained exactly the same . . . indoctrinating children with exactly the same values as when the schools were staffed entirely by white people."[117]

The movement of many Native Americans to the cities has resulted in a decline in the proportion of children in BIA schools. Most now attend local public schools. One U.S. Department of Education task force concluded that local and federal educational systems have failed to meet the needs of Indian students. Their report cited the absence of an Indian perspective in the curricula, the loss of Indian languages, the shift away from Indian values, and the racist views of many white teachers. The report called for implementation of multicultural curricula that embody respect for Indian history and culture. In addition, a 2006 report found that a large national sample of Native American fourth- and eighth-grade students had lower average reading and math test scores than did non-Indian students.[118]

Today Native American educational attainment levels remain below those of the general population. Educational gains have been made since the 1960s, and by 2005 nearly 77 percent of Native Americans over the age of 24 were high-school graduates, but that figure was still a little lower than for all Americans.[119] Some groups, such as the Navajos (in the 2000 census, 62.7 percent), have significantly lower high school attainment. Indian students in predominantly white public school systems have often been disproportionately placed in "special education" classes and been disproportionately disciplined, often for overtly racial reasons. In several midwestern schools with a significant number of Indian students, organizations such as the American Civil Liberties Union (ACLU) have recently documented discriminatory treatment of Indian students by white personnel, as well as recurring harassment by white students who throw rocks or hurl epithets such as "dirty Indian" or "greasy Indian" at the Indian students. Not surprisingly, U.S. Department of Education reports and other sources put the proportion of Indian students who drop out of high school at a figure of at least 60 percent, the highest for any racial or ethnic group and much higher than that for whites.[120]

Over the last few decades, nonetheless, Indian youth have attended and graduated from two- and four-year colleges in ever larger numbers, doubling the number of college degrees received annually in the last two decades or so. Today, more than 176,000 Native American (including Alaskan) students are enrolled as undergraduate or graduate students in various types of colleges nationwide. While most of these attend predominantly white colleges, many attend the thirty-three Indian-controlled colleges, where efforts are made to integrate Indian history into courses and attention is given to tribal cultures. In addition, since the 1960s more than one hundred colleges and universities have provided facilities for study of Indian issues, such as by establishing American Indian Studies centers.[121]

Religion

Native American groups have periodically pressured museums and other facilities to return religious and art objects, many of which were acquired illegally. Native Americans have protested the display of Indian skeletal remains in museums and have called for their return for proper burial ceremonies.

Students register at a Navajo college in the Southwest.

Following enactment of the Indian Arts and Crafts Act (1988) and the Native American Graves Protection and Repatriation Act (1990), the U.S. government has required white-controlled museums to consult with Indian groups about returning these holdings.

For example, in 1989 the Omaha tribe in Nebraska celebrated the return of their four-hundred-year-old sacred pole, which had been in the possession of a Boston museum. The tribe has raised funds for a new Indian museum to house the sacred pole, which they regard as a living person, as *Umon'hon'ti*.[122] Problems of storage and protection are becoming common as more historical documents and sacred objects are returned to Native American groups that often lack the economic resources to house and preserve adequately the sacred objects.

Pressures on Native Americans to adapt to European American culture have been clear in the case of religion. Early white conquerors often attempted to convert those stereotyped as "heathen Indians" to Christianity. With the reservation period came a jockeying among various Christian denominations for control; reservations were often divided up among these denominations. For a number of reasons, including fear of whites, many Indians became loosely affiliated with a Christian denomination.[123] Today, however, only a minority of Native Americans identity exclusively with a Christian denomination.

Revitalization Movements as Protest

Colonized peoples have sometimes reacted to European oppressors by joining **millenarian movements** *oriented to a "golden age" in which supernatural events will change their oppressive conditions.* Among Native American millenarian movements were the Ghost Dance groups that emerged on the Great Plains. In the 1870s a prophet called Wodziwob told of a vision in which ancestors of indigenous peoples would come on a train to Earth with explosive force, after which the Earth would swallow up the oppressive whites. Several Indian groups joined in the movement in hope of salvation from oppression. The movement declined when the cataclysm failed to occur, but it experienced a resurgence in the 1880s when a new prophet, Wovoka, told of a vision that ordered him to found another Ghost Dance religion. Religious fervor spread through the Plains tribes. The cooperation among indigenous peoples increased solidarity, but the movement was suppressed by white officials disturbed by the millenarianism.[124]

Long used by individual Indian practitioners to treat sickness, peyote rituals became part of a new religion that spread through the Plains between 1880 and 1900. This new religion reflected an ambivalence toward Christianity. Rituals involved singing and praying but were distinctive in the visionary experiences induced by eating peyote (a hallucinogenic plant). Attacks on the religious movement by Christian missionaries and government officials welded believers together, and in 1918 the Native American Church was formally incorporated as an association of distinctive Christian groups using the traditional sacrament of Peyote. White legislators in seven states passed antipeyote laws, yet in the 1930s the commissioner of Indian affairs finally came to the defense of indigenous religions and allowed their resurgence. By the 1960s, 40 percent of Native Americans on some reservations were Native American Church members.[125] Today, the Native American Church has at least 103,000 members in numerous states, and many other adherents in Mexico and Canada. The legality of the peyote sacrament was not assured, however, until the Religious Freedom Restoration Act was passed in the 1990s.

In contrast to Christianity, most traditional religious beliefs and practices of Native Americans are not exclusive; a person can be both a Christian and a traditional believer. Because of this, a great variety of traditional and Christian religious practices have coexisted among Indian groups. Historically, numerous Native Americans have criticized Christianity as a crude religion stressing blood, crucifixion, and bureaucratized charity rather than practicing true sharing and love for others. In addition, Native American religious and political leaders often stress that Europeans are newcomers who sharply accelerated conflict in North America and mostly betrayed the Indians who aided them in becoming established. Europeans and their cultural ways are also viewed as having greatly polluted the surrounding physical environment, which is frequently viewed as sacred.[126]

Indigenous Americans Overseas

Although most residents of the continental United States are unaware of it, the United States has significant colonies overseas. Because of imperial conquests in the 1800s and 1900s, numerous indigenous groups on Caribbean and Pacific islands were brought under U.S. political-economic control. Now supervised and controlled by the U.S. Department of Interior, these areas still officially belong to the U.S. empire, and they do not have voting representation in Congress. These colonies include Puerto Rico (a commonwealth) and the Virgin Islands (an unincorporated U.S. Territory) in the Caribbean, and six colonial jurisdictions in the pacific: the Northern Mariana Islands (a commonwealth); Guam and American Samoa (unincorporated U.S. Territories); and the Federated States of Micronesia, Republic of the Marshall Islands, and Republic of Palau (euphemistically called "sovereign nations"). The total indigenous population of these Pacific islands is now nearly half a million. In addition, the official government census designation, "U.S. Pacific Isanders," includes the indigenous peoples of Hawaii—the largest single group. The latter have political rights in the state of Hawaii, which lies far from the continental United States. In addition to the indigenous residents, some islands (especially Hawaii and Guam) contain large populations of more recent immigrants of various backgrounds and their descendants. Pacific Islanders who live within the fifty states of the United States are resident mostly in Hawaii and California.[127]

As a group, colonized Americans of Hawaiian, Polynesian, Micronesian, and Melanesian ancestry have a high poverty level and median family incomes much lower than for the continental United States. They have worse disease and mortality rates than the U.S. population as a whole. Like other indigenous peoples, those in island communities have periodically organized to deal with the reality of unjust impoverishment. They have aggressively raised the issue of European Americans taking their lands and destroying their environments. Indigenous Hawaiians often argue that the natural environment has frequently been seriously polluted by the testing of weapons by the Department of Defense, as well as by large-scale tourism. Sacred sites have been desecrated by large developments for retirees and other mainland U.S. immigrants. Leaders of the indigenous Hawaiian Nation have pressed for sovereignty, the return of stolen lands, and a land trust for indigenous Hawaiians. Several U.S.-controlled Pacific islands have been sites of nuclear bomb and other military tests that polluted the land and water sources with dangerous chemicals. Food grown on the islands is often polluted with these toxins.[128]

Our search of social science databases has turned up only two rather sketchy articles on political-economic conditions faced by these colonized Americans. Virtually all specific articles on these Pacific Islanders are concerned with individualized health issues or substance abuse. No research seems to examine the economic and political exploitation of these colonized peoples by Americans from the mainland.

Assimilation and Colonialism

The classical *external* colonialism model applies to Native American encounters with Europeans, making this group distinct among North American racial and ethnic groups. In the earliest period, indigenous societies on the Atlantic coast had their lands seized and members driven off or killed by European outsiders. The primary colonial strategy was to remove indigenous peoples. This process prevailed as whites moved westward from the Atlantic over several centuries. A policy of genocide often preceded, or coexisted with, a segregation ("reservation") policy.

Assimilation Perspectives

Some observers have argued that the opportunity to assimilate to the core culture is more open for Native Americans than for other people of color. Since the 1920s, even a few Indian professionals have argued that Indians should voluntarily follow the lead of European immigrants and blend quietly into the dominant European American culture.[129]

Applying an assimilation model to Indians, social science and other analysts tend to focus on the extent to which traditional Indian cultures have undergone Europeanization. White-run schools and missions did bring changes in religion, language, and dress styles to many indigenous groups. Other changes, such as in land-ownership orientation, have also been substantial. Assimilationists cite the cultural adaptations to the dominant culture as evidence of Indians' movement toward gradual inclusion in the white-dominated society, yet often argue that Indian cultural traditions remain barriers to further incorporation.[130]

Living patterns and the sense of Native American identity today vary widely. For example, people in the

Sioux and Navajo societies generally have a strong group identity, whereas other groups have lost their old ways and strong identities. Some reservation groups, such as the western Pueblos, the Navajo, and the Sioux, often confine substantial social contacts to their group. Yet others, such as a significant segment of the Blackfeet, have intermarried with whites and substantially acculturated to European American ways.[131]

The intensive, often forced in the past, acculturation has failed to destroy many of the indigenous cultures. Cultural survival despite extremely unfavorable conditions is evident in the persistence of traditional Indian languages. Something like 130 Native American languages are still spoken in the United States today, although most are dying because they are spoken only by a few older people. In 1990 the U.S. Congress finally passed the Native American Languages Act, which commits the federal government to working with Native Americans to "ensure the survival of these unique cultures and languages." Some Indian communities (for example, the Ojibwe and Blackfeet) have developed intense immersion language programs so that younger members can learn their indigenous languages.[132]

Structural integration at other than low-paid job levels in the economy has come slowly for Native Americans. Movement into the economic mainstream did not begin until the urban migration of the past few decades. Today, urban integration has often involved less-well-paid blue-collar positions and inadequate housing conditions, though great effort on the part of many Native Americans has gradually led to better educations and jobs. Some political integration has also taken place in towns and cities, though much political discrimination and underrepresentation remains.

Social integration (at Milton Gordon's primary-group level) with white families has come slowly, especially for those on reservations. One 1960s Spokane, Washington, study found little social integration of Native Americans into white voluntary associations. In recent decades, intermarriage with other groups has been on the rise. Estimates suggest that half of Indian marriages now involve non-Indian spouses, with many of these being white. Intermarriages between members of different Native American groups have also become common, especially in cities.[133]

Assimilation-oriented analysts suggest that adaptation has occurred on Milton Gordon's other

A Native American dancer at a recent Pow Wow.

dimensions of assimilation (attitude-receptional, behavior-receptional, and identificational assimilation). Some movement can be glimpsed in the area of white attitudes; overt stereotyping of Native Americans by whites appears to have declined somewhat, at least in areas such as government publications. However, the stereotypical use of Indian mascots by sports teams persists, often with extremely racist defenses of such practices being made. Blatant discrimination against Native Americans may have decreased in certain societal sectors, but data on the economy, education, and politics indicate that many types of direct and indirect discrimination continue to restrict Native Americans today.

Attachment to ancestral identity is often strong among those who have predominantly Native American ancestry. Some have emphasized an umbrella or panethnic identity. Thus, a number of organizations, including the National Congress of American Indians and the National Indian Education Association, have tried to build a "pan-Indian identity" and promote unity across many Indian groups. Since the 1980s, regular pan-Indian conferences and Pow Wows have been held in all regions of the United States. Still, local group membership remains very important for many Native Americans, and most on reservation lands identify themselves in local terms, such as Navajo or Sioux, rather than in pan-Indian terms.[134]

Recent research using the 2000 census shows that over the last few decades Native Americans in major metropolitan areas have experienced a degree of spatial assimilation, at least as measured by residential dispersion within predominantly white neighborhoods. On standard measures of residential segregation from the (non-Latino) white population, metropolitan Native Americans are the least segregated non-European group. That is, they are most more likely than black, Asian, or Latino Americans to live among whites. Still, many urban Native Americans remain scattered among low-income neighborhoods populated by poor whites and other people of color. And a large proportion of Native Americans remain residentially separate in rural (often reservation) areas.[135]

Historically, when Indians have moved from reservations to cities, their ties to traditional tribal cultures have weakened in the urbanization process. However, in the last few decades increased self-determination on numerous reservations has sparked some "retraditionalization." Many city dwellers have regularly returned to home reservations to participate in traditional ceremonies, thereby countering urban pressures for assimilation to the dominant culture. Countervailing trends can be seen, one decreasing ties to traditional cultures and another increasing them. These trends are accentuated by the growing numbers of Indian Americans who aggressively assert their Indian ancestry, such as those who are creating educational settings to teach disappearing languages.[136]

How do assimilation concepts pertain to the experiences of Native Americans?

Power-Conflict Perspectives

Because of the colonialism history of Native Americans, some social science theorists have persuasively argued that power-conflict models are particularly relevant to their experience. They often discuss Native Americans as an "externally colonized minority."[137]

Power-conflict analysis accents the deception, genocide, and land theft that were part of the subordination process. Much assimilation rhetoric—"civilizing the Indians"—has been a cover for the aggressive exploitation of indigenous peoples by often land-hungry whites. Later on, treaties and laws allowed individual Native Americans to become U.S. "citizens," usually only after meeting such criteria as accepting individualized land allotments. Thus, becoming a citizen generally involved great pressure, even coercion, to adapt in a one-way fashion to white customs and laws. Unlike most assimilation analysts, power-conflict analysts stress the reality of acculturation and incorporation processes often having *force* behind them. This government force is evident, for example, in the statement by the commissioner of Indian affairs in 1879:

> Indians are essentially conservative, and cling tenaciously to old customs and hate all changes: Therefore the government should force them to scatter out on farms, break up their tribal organizations, dances, ceremonies, and tomfoolery; take from them their hundreds of useless ponies, which afford the means of indulging in their wandering, nomadic habits, and give them cattle in exchange, and compel them to labor or to *accept the alternative of starvation*.[138]

On reservations, forced acculturation to the English language and white folkways was often the rule in Christian missions and public and private boarding schools, where children were usually isolated from their families.

Since the 1970s some Indian children have been removed from their homes to white foster homes or institutions. White social workers have sometimes argued that the homes of poor Native Americans are not "fit" places for these children. Anthropologist Shirley Hill Witt has written of one child-placement program that aggressively sought the removal of Native American children. A former president of the Mormon church stated:

> When you go down on the reservations and see these hundreds of thousands of Indians living in the dirt and without culture or refinement of any kind, you can hardly believe it. Then you see these boys and girls [placed in Mormon homes] playing the flute, the piano. All these things bring about a normal culture.[139]

It is odd and ironic that white culture should be held up as the "normal culture" against which poor Native Americans are judged, because the poverty in their lives is substantially the result of whites' destruction of indigenous peoples' resources, theft of land, and continuing discrimination. In recent years, implementation of the Indian Child Welfare Act (1978) has gradually achieved a reduction in the number of children removed from parents and placed in non–Indian homes.

Power-conflict analysts frequently accent the one-way character of social adaptation pressures. One study of Indian students at the University of Oklahoma found that those students with a strong Native American identity were more likely than more "assimilated" Native Americans to drop out, regardless of academic ability. The conventional white-oriented college context is problematic for many students of color. The social changes that are expected by (usually white) educators are typically unidirectional: The Native American student is expected to conform to a typically Eurocentric college environment. As a rule, historically white institutions do not change significantly to reflect the cultures, values, and needs of Native American students or other students of color who are integrated physically into them.[140]

At all educational levels, Native American children typically face great and one-way acculturation pressures; most capitulate to some degree, with some even adopting white stereotypes of Indians and many thinking and behaving constantly in white-preferred ways. This adaptive behavior can damage the inner self and create great stress and, thus, health problems. Caught between their commitment to indigenous cultures and white pressures to conform, some children, as well as adults, have committed suicide or turned to drugs or alchol.[141]

A colonialism analyst would stress that many Native Americans remain isolated politically and geographically—on the reservations, in rural areas, or in segregated urban areas. Many remain, in effect, colonized on their own lands. This is reminiscent of the external colonialism of imperialistic countries. Today, whites, including policymakers, are often ignorant of Indian conditions. For example, in states such as Oklahoma, many whites hold the misconception that reservation groups such as Cherokees are dying out. Yet the Cherokee nation is one of the largest, and is for the most part holding strongly to many of its traditional values.[142] By denying the existence of enduring communities, whites can ignore Native American neighbors and persisting problems of discrimination and inequality rooted in earlier centuries of violent land theft and colonialism.

The continuing relevance of some type of colonialism model can be found in data on Native American income, employment, housing, education, and political participation. Although there have been some important gains, many Native Americans remain on the lower rungs of the U.S. economic ladder. Many in rural areas and central cities live in or near poverty; reservations have long had high unemployment rates. To a disproportionate degree, Native Americans in urban areas have had to face a lack of economic resources, low-wage jobs, absentee landlords, and racial discrimination.

Still, many Native Americans are fighting back against European American oppression, such as organizing to protest the racist symbols used by many sports teams and the waste dumping on their lands by outsiders (environmental racism). A renaissance of Indian cultures can be seen in numerous protest movements and Pow Wows of recent decades. We see a resurgence in the strong self-determination efforts of many Indian nations and in numerous economic development projects on reservations. We observe growing numbers of Americans reclaiming their Native American identities publicly and returning to reservations for group action, including community celebrations.

Power-conflict analysts are likely to emphasize the importance of the struggle against white pressures and continuing racial oppression. Resistance and resurgence are generally rooted in the historical cultures of Native Americans, the ancient cultures that frequently emphasize harmony with the natural world and the dangers of self-indulgent individualism. Traditional cultures, thus, seem to provide a valuable source of the humanitarian, earth-centered values that many see as too weak today in U.S. society.

Richard Williams, director of the American Indian College Fund, has noted that in recent decades North American Indians have "made their return from near annihilation to revival and renaissance in one of the greatest survival stories in all of human history." Since the 1960s, organized efforts by Native Americans have forced the federal government to uphold treaties and respect Indian rights, and thus have brought a dramatic revival of Native Americans as a powerful national group. "For the first time," Williams notes, the government is "being held accountable to its own laws and treaties with Indian nations under its own legal system."[143] Federal laws passed since 1970 have facilitated self-determination for Indian communities and have improved education, health, and other social programs on and off reservations. Growing numbers of Native Americans have reasserted their rights and identities as part of the evolving mix in this increasingly multiracial and multiethnic nation.

How might a power-conflict perspective be used to explain Native American experiences?

Summary

Native Americans today remain highly diverse, with many different rural and urban groups. Today, many are still discriminated against by whites who have greater economic, political, and bureaucratic (BIA) power. Native Americans are descendants of the only groups that did *not* immigrate to North America within the past five hundred years. They were brought into the European American sphere over a long period, during which many fought battles against the violent invaders. Genocide, the destruction of all Native Americans in an area, was often the goal of these invaders. The era of battles with whites was followed by the present reservation era, with its long line of white bureaucrats and private actors, such as missionaries and entrepreneurs, seeking to dominate Native Americans.

Often stereotyped by whites as culturally or intellectually inferior, Indian Americans have long suffered and still face individual and institutionalized discrimination in the economic, political, religious, and educational spheres. In the economic sphere, they have had their lands taken, they have been forced by job circumstances to relocate to racially inhospitable cities, and their mobility has been limited by continuing discrimination. While significant economic gains have occurred, for many on and off reservations this progress has been slow and has yet to be matched by substantial political influence. The BIA remains an intrusive bureaucracy, although it has gradually become more progressive and now employs many more Native American officials than in earlier years. Recently, the U.S. government has been investigated for serious mismanagement of large Indian trust accounts, an issue that has yet to be resolved.

For centuries, assertive protest movements have underscored the strengths and discontent of Native Americans. In recent years, activists have emphasized the cultural uniqueness of Indian respect for the larger human community and for the natural environment. Many groups have organized to regain fishing rights and lands long ago stolen by whites. Calls for maintaining cultural distinctiveness and recognizing the virtues of Native American cultures have been heard. Opposing celebrations of Columbus's "discovery of America," Native Americans have called attention to the reality of past and continuing oppression. Native Americans inhabited North America prior to European settlement or government and thus have a unique position with regard to citizenship. Indeed, some argue that they are *not* citizens of the United States; because they *predate* the European invasions, they are citizens of their own long-established nations, which should regain their original sovereignty.

The desire for full recognition of their sovereignty is strong for many nations. Although the U.S. government has made moderate progress in returning land and control of various aspects of everyday life to many groups, most still have a neocolonial relationship to the government. In recent years many Native American nations have pressed for a direct government-to-government relationship that would replace this current neocolonial relationship with the government of the United States.[144]

Key Terms

colonization migration 136
swing vote 146
manifest destiny 152
secondary labor market 153
primary labor market 153
environmental racism 157
millenarian movements 159

CHAPTER 7

African Americans

BIG PICTURE QUESTIONS

- ***What role have African Americans played in building up this country's wealth and institutions?***
- ***What are the long-term consequences of interracial contacts between European Americans and African Americans?***
- ***What methods have African Americans used to resist systemic racism?***

A few years ago one of the country's most talented journalists, Leanita McClain, committed suicide. Just thirty-two years old, she had won major awards and was the first black person to serve on the Chicago Tribune's editorial board. Why did such a talented person commit suicide? The answer is complex, but one factor looms large: the problem of coping with a discriminatory white world. Reviewing her life, one friend noted the conformity to white ways that is faced by black women in historically white workplaces: "Black women consciously choose their speech, their laughter, their walk, their mode of dress and car. They trim and straighten their hair.... They learn to wear a mask."[1] Black Americans in the corporate workplace not only face subtle and blatant discrimination but also suffer from intense pressures to adapt to values and ways of that typically white world.

Interestingly, many African Americans have family trees in this country that date back to the 1600s or 1700s, well before the American Revolution. They were among the very first immigrants, and as a group they have been here far longer than many white immigrant groups. That a people who have been here almost as long as the first European settlers should still find themselves so discriminated against, so unwelcome in many traditionally white institutions, is a problematical dilemma for them and for the future of this country.

Forced Migration and Slavery

The black experience in North America is an example of the slave-importation end of the migration continuum discussed in Chapter 2. Formally, **slavery** involves *the legal ownership and exploitation of one human being by another*. Unlike white immigrants, who mostly came voluntarily, most Africans had no choice until recently; for centuries they came enslaved and in chains. Their destinations were determined by European or European American slave traders and slaveholders. Many whites saw such enslavement as a solution to the demand for cheap agricultural labor on farms throughout the Americas.

The European Trade in Human Beings

Dutch and French companies early dominated the forcible importation of Africans; England entered the trade in the 1600s. Some Africans were enslaved directly by Europeans, who raided local African societies and took people away by force. In other cases, African coastal rulers, motivated by greed or by fear of European firepower, succumbed to European slave-trade pressures and became go-betweens serving European slave traders. Nonetheless, this bloody Atlantic slave trade was invented and dominated by Europeans and, later, participated in by European Americans.[2]

Once they were captured, enslaved Africans were often chained in corrals called barracoons, where they were branded and held for transportation. The Atlantic voyage was usually a living hell. Enslaved Africans were chained together with little room. The horror was summed up by one African:

> I was soon put down under the decks, and there I received such a salutation in my nostrils as I had never experienced in my life: so that with the loathsomeness of the stench, and crying together, I became so sick and low that I was not able to eat, nor had I the least desire to taste any thing.... On my refusing to eat, one of them held me fast by the hands, and laid me across, I think the windlass, and tied my feet, while the other flogged me severely.[3]

Suicides were common among enslaved Africans, and uprisings brought death to Africans and white sailors alike. The white myth that Africans passively endured their fate is contradicted by the 155 recorded shipboard uprisings by Africans between 1699 and 1845; many other violent attacks on slavers doubtless went unrecorded.[4]

In 1619, twenty Africans were brought to the new European colony at Jamestown (Virginia) by a Dutch-flagged ship, and by the mid-1600s the slave status of Africans had been fully institutionalized in colonial laws. From the mid-1600s to the 1860s, virtually all Africans were imported for the purpose of involuntary servitude. Estimates of the number brought alive to the Western Hemisphere range from 10 to 15 million. Most were brought to the West Indies and South America; only 5 percent were brought directly to North America. From the 1600s to the Civil War, an estimated half-million Africans were brought into the colonies and, later, the United States.[5] In addition to those who arrived alive, millions more died in the brutal process of transportation across the Atlantic.

Many European Americans in the early period were wealthy because they *owned* other human beings.

These included George Washington, James Madison, and Thomas Jefferson. In an early draft of the Declaration of Independence, the slaveholder Jefferson actually attacked slavery, but he was careful to blame it on England's King George III. Yet, because of other slave owners' opposition, this antislavery language was not included in the final version of the Declaration. One of the great democratic manifestos in world history was severely compromised by the unwillingness of slaveholding whites to include African Americans within its powerful framework.[6]

Slaveholding interests forced the recognition and support of slavery in several major sections of the U.S. Constitution. These included a provision that each slave be counted as three-fifths of a person for the calculation of congressional representation (for whites); a fugitive-slave provision; and the postponement of prohibition of slave importation to 1808. Moreover, although the slave trade was finally and officially abolished as of 1808, that ban was not seriously enforced. Thousands of Africans were still forcibly imported into a "democratic" United States.[7]

Most white families did not own enslaved African Americans. In 1860, only one-fourth of the 1.6 million white families in the South owned 3.8 million African Americans. A majority of those enslaved were held on larger farms and plantations, where they performed most of the labor and produced agricultural products to be marketed for the profit of slaveholders and their descendants. Most plantation owners were agricultural capitalists attuned to trade for profit. The wealth and power of the slaveholding gentry rose dramatically as a result of this slave-based agriculture. This plantation gentry dominated the economy and federal government from the late 1700s to the 1850s.[8] Power-conflict theorists emphasize the government's role in creation of such oppressive racial arrangements (Chapter 2). For centuries the U.S. government and southern and border (and some northern) state governments passed laws to benefit the powerful slaveholding gentry and thus to reinforce the racialized definition of and extreme oppression of black Americans.

The Lives of Africans Under Slavery

There has long been a magnolias-and-mint-julep mystique about the slave system, which lingers on, particularly in highly racist Hollywood movies such as the still-popular *Gone with the Wind*. According to this fictional white imagery, residing in a big plantation house with multiple columns surrounded by magnolia trees, a paternalistic white master "cared kindly" for the "contented, happy slaves."

However, slave autobiographies describe the extreme brutality and oppressiveness of actual living conditions. Most rose before dawn, then worked in the house or fields until dark or later. Food, clothing, and housing were typically crude and inadequate. The whip and chains, and other forms of torture, were common mechanisms of control. White masters were frequently brutal and violent, such as the owner of one African American who told about moving from Georgia: "Then he chains all the slaves round the necks and fastens the chains to the hosses and makes them walk all the way to Texas. My mother and my sister had to walk. Emma was my sister. Somewhere on the road it went to snowing, and Massa wouldn't let us wrap anything round our feet. We had to sleep on the ground, too, in all that snow."[9] African Americans could not legally protest such extreme brutality, for slaveholders controlled the state militias and the courts.

Although many analyses of slavery provide little discussion of enslaved women, one should recognize that the slave system included black women and children. Most women, as one put it, "worked in the fields every day from 'fore daylight to almost plumb dark."[10] The brutality of many slaveholders was not tempered when it came to the women: "Beat women! Why sure he [master] beat women. Beat women just like men. Beat women naked and wash them down in brine."[11] African American women were victims of much coercion and violence, including frequent rape by white overseers and slaveholders, a major source over the centuries of "racial mixing."

Whites, including many social scientists, have long been preoccupied with black families; contemporary problems of poverty and so-called broken families have often been traced back to the conditions of slavery. Until recently, supportive family life was viewed as nonexistent for the majority of enslaved African Americans. However, there is historical evidence that paternalistic slave owners fostered enslaved families—if often in their own self-interest—and, most significantly, that enslaved African Americans worked hard to preserve their families to the extent possible under extreme slavery conditions. Typical families were protective, supportive environments that helped enslaved African Americans to survive. These enslaved people frequently ran away as family units; the desire to find lost loved ones was a common reason for fleeing a plantation. In his analysis of enslaved families, Herbert Gutman found that enslaved women were expected to have children by one man; that the names of fathers were given to sons; that adoption was used to ease disruption caused by death or breakup of families; and that many families managed to persist over generations. Of course, the threat to these families was typically great. Marriages were likely to be disrupted at some point, by death or sale of a spouse by the slaveholder. An accurate picture of the slave family must include the strong African American attempts to maintain family stability *and* the frequent disruption of families by callous slaveholders.[12]

Faced with physical torture and white attempts to eradicate their cultures, many peoples of Africa among those enslaved—the Yorubas, Akans, Ibos, Angolans, and dozens of other groups—became a single African American people and forged a distinctive African American culture.[13] Drawing on African spiritual roots, these new Americans shaped their religion, their art and music, and their philosophical and political thinking about oppression, liberation, and social justice. In the colonies and, later, the United States, pressures on African Americans to conform to the dominant Eurocentric culture forced them to become *bicultural*, to know the dominant culture as well as their own. Since the first two centuries of slavery, African Americans have struggled to maintain what Mitchell and Feagin, among others, have termed an *oppositional culture*, a culture that is part African and part an African American adaptation to the history of white oppression.[14] This culture has provided the foundation for active black resistance to white oppression for centuries.

Active Resistance

Enslaved African Americans often had to be submissive, but this was only one response to domination. A more assertive reaction, often grounded in African American culture, was common. Many observed the servile etiquette when necessary, but rebelled in dozens of small and large ways when they could.

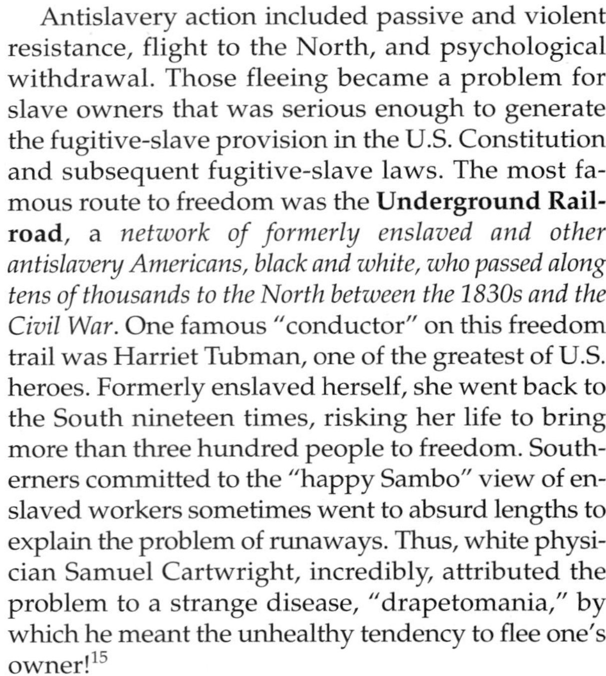

Antislavery action included passive and violent resistance, flight to the North, and psychological withdrawal. Those fleeing became a problem for slave owners that was serious enough to generate the fugitive-slave provision in the U.S. Constitution and subsequent fugitive-slave laws. The most famous route to freedom was the **Underground Railroad**, a *network of formerly enslaved and other antislavery Americans, black and white, who passed along tens of thousands to the North between the 1830s and the Civil War*. One famous "conductor" on this freedom trail was Harriet Tubman, one of the greatest of U.S. heroes. Formerly enslaved herself, she went back to the South nineteen times, risking her life to bring more than three hundred people to freedom. Southerners committed to the "happy Sambo" view of enslaved workers sometimes went to absurd lengths to explain the problem of runaways. Thus, white physician Samuel Cartwright, incredibly, attributed the problem to a strange disease, "drapetomania," by which he meant the unhealthy tendency to flee one's owner![15]

Nonviolent resistance often took the form of a slow working pace, feigned illness, or strikes. Violent resistance was directed at property and at slave owners or overseers. Tools, livestock, fields, and farmhouses were periodically destroyed; slavemasters and overseers were killed. In addition to mutinies aboard slave ships, there is evidence of at least 250 slave revolts or conspiracies to revolt during the long years of legal slavery. Newspapers of the day provide considerable evidence that whites feared uprisings by those enslaved.[16]

In 1800 a group of enslaved black Americans led by Gabriel Prosser gathered weapons and planned to march on Richmond. The governor of Virginia took action to protect the state capital from the rebels. One thousand armed African Americans rendezvoused, but a heavy rain cut them off from the city and they disbanded. Betrayed, the leaders were arrested; at least thirty-five were put to death.[17]

In 1831, Nat Turner, a very religious man, led a rebellion in Southampton County, Virginia. Seventy enslaved people recruited by Turner attacked, and dozens of whites were killed. The freedom fighters were eventually defeated by hundreds of white soldiers. Turner escaped but was captured and executed. Leaders of slave revolts took seriously the U.S. principle of "liberty and justice for all" and could be included among U.S. revolutionary heroes.

African culture and religion were one important source of the black revolutionaries' resistance-oriented philosophy and inclination to rebellion.[18]

These revolts contradicted the white apologists' notion of "happy slaves"; given the opportunity, those enslaved did resist. Slavery destroyed lives and wasted energies of millions of African Americans and denied most any opportunity to create wealth for their descendants. Slavery also brought major, though generally less recognized, costs for whites and their descendants. Especially In the southern and border states, whites involved with slavery lost much of their own humanity, as well as much of their own freedom of speech and press, because of the repressive legal controls and requirements of a more or less totalitarian slave system. The country as a whole lost as well from its failure to live up to its own egalitarian ideals.

Many free African Americans joined abolitionist organizations to work for the liberation of their brothers and sisters. Frederick Douglass, formerly enslaved himself, was an important leader among the abolitionists. In a July 4, 1852, speech in Rochester, New York, Douglass spoke eloquently: "What, to the American slave, is your Fourth of July? I answer: A day that reveals to him, more than all other days of the year, the gross injustices and cruelty to which he is the constant victim. To him your celebration is a sham."[19] Another influential black abolitionist was Isabella Van Wagener, better known as Sojourner Truth, who had been enslaved in New York; in the mid-1800s she became an influential antislavery lecturer and an early advocate of women's rights. Clearly, black women played a key role in antislavery movements.

Outside the Rural South

Between the 1600s and the early 1800s, many *northern* whites either owned African Americans or considered the U.S. slavery system to be legitimate. Significant numbers of people were enslaved in northern states. The wealth of many northern whites was built up with forced black labor, as well as the labor of European immigrants. Benjamin Ringer notes that "despite the early emancipation of slaves in the North, [racialized colonialism] remained there, not merely as fossilized remains but as a deeply ingrained coding for the future."[20] Consider Massachusetts, where slavery was legalized in 1641, right after Africans were brought in. Massachusetts merchants played a central role in the slave trade. Not until the 1780s did public opinion and court cases come together to abolish slavery in New England. Even then, it was not white recognition of the rights of African Americans that ended slavery, but pressure from white working people who objected to competition from enslaved labor. In New York, those enslaved made up 7 percent of the population by 1786. A statute of emancipation was not passed there until 1799, and even then the law only provided for gradual emancipation. A realization that slavery was long entrenched in the North's economic and legal system is essential for an understanding of the various forms of racial discrimination that black Americans still face today in the North.[21]

Before the Civil War, **"Jim Crow" laws** in the North enforced *the racial segregation of ostensibly "free" African Americans in public transportation, hospitals, schools, churches, and cemeteries.* Racially segregated railroad cars were established first in Massachusetts. In northern cities, whites enforced severe housing discrimination and segregated housing areas. Residents in numerous northern areas tried to drive out any black immigrants who tried to settle there.

Q: What early methods of resistance were used by African Americans, and what were the consequences?

Racist Ideologies and Associated Stereotypes

Over time, the dominant group in a racial hierarchy, such as whites in the United States, develops strong beliefs to rationalize an unjustly gained economic, social, and political position. For nearly four centuries—in pamphlets, books, and articles—white intellectuals, theologians, and politicians have devised racist stereotypes and theories of the biological, mental, and moral inferiority of black Americans to rationalize the latter's exploitation. These racist stereotypes, theories, and ideologies are part of a comprehensive, deep racial framing of society, one created and maintained by the dominant group yet often accepted to some degree by members of other groups.

Negative views of African peoples existed in Europe before 1600, but until the 1700s these did not develop into a systematic racist ideology and racist framing of society. Recall from Chapter 1 eighteenth-century notions of a racist hierarchy that included a social construction of an "African race" as inferior to "Caucasians." Thomas Jefferson took up these European notions and developed a racist ideology that personified the moral dilemmas of American whites in the eighteenth century: He wrote an indictment of slavery in the original draft of the Declaration of Independence yet was the owner of two hundred human beings. Jefferson wrote of his strong opposition to interracial sex yet enslaved a black teenager, Sally Hemings, who, according to DNA evidence, probably bore him at least one child, whom he also enslaved.[22] (Until the DNA evidence revealed this likely relationship, most white scholars and other commentators denied that he could have had children with Hemings.) Jefferson wrote of the inferiority of African Americans and held many in slavery, yet even he occasionally foresaw that they would ultimately have to be freed from slavery if the country was to make progress. Still, he freed few of those he himself had enslaved, even at his death. And he, as an advocate of black colonization overseas, thought that those who were eventually freed should be pressed to leave the United States. A slaveholder with a very racist mindset, Jefferson could not envisage the United States as a multiracial democracy.[23]

Seeing African Americans as Inferior: White Stereotypes

The white racial framing of society has long included an array of antiblack stereotypes. For example, by the 1600s and 1700s whites considered the dark color of enslaved African Americans to be problematical or ugly. By the mid-1800s white defenders of slavery were even portraying African Americans as "apelike" creatures who were somehow not fully human. Significantly, this was the same vicious and stereotyped image that Anglo-Protestants had applied a little earlier to new Irish immigrants.[24] Many antiblack stereotypes have become widespread since the first century of North American slavery. As Thomas Jefferson, among many other whites, asserted, black men and women were alleged to have an offensive odor. Black women have been stereotyped as immoral or exotic; black men, as oversexed and potential rapists. Extreme white images of black sexuality may reflect deep white psychological problems with the idea and reality of "racial mixing." Indeed, much white guilt and anger over "racial mixing" may ultimately be linked to the historical fact that much intimate interracial contact before and after 1865 involved the rape of black women by white men, particularly by white overseers and slave owners.

Patricia Williams, a distinguished law professor, has illustrated this point by relating the story of Austin Miller, her great-great-grandfather. Miller, a thirty-five-year-old white lawyer, bought Williams's eleven-year-old black great-great-grandmother Sophie and her parents. Soon Miller forced the youngster Sophie to become the mother of Williams's great-grandmother Mary. Like many African Americans, Williams must deal with the reality that her white ancestor was not only a prominent lawyer but also a rapist and a child molester.[25]

The Pseudoscience of "Intelligence" Testing

The theme of intellectual inferiority along racial lines has received much public attention since World War II. Earlier in the twentieth century, this theme was applied to white immigrants from southern and eastern Europe, who were considered to be inferior in intelligence to native-born Americans of northern European descent. However, in the past few decades the focus has been on black Americans and other Americans of color. For example, Arthur Jensen and Richard Herrnstein, along with a small handful of other white social scientists, have alleged that differences in "intelligence test" (IQ) scores are not determined primarily by environmental factors such as education, socialization, racial discrimination, and socioeconomic circumstances, but reflect genetic differences between black and white groups. They argue that differences in intelligence can be reliably measured by relatively brief paper-and-pencil and object (or symbol) manipulation tests that are inaccurately labeled "IQ tests." Groups with low social status or income are argued to be, on the average, intellectually and genetically inferior to groups with greater status and income levels simply because the former average lower scores on these brief tests. These academics and associated conservative writers often argue that poor and rich Americans, or black and white Americans, have such different types of intelligence that they require different educational techniques. They also express concern about high black birthrates, which they believe lower the national intelligence. Richard Herrnstein and Charles Murray's best-selling book, *The Bell Curve*, published in 1994, argued for the discredited theory that there are significant genetically determined differences in intelligence between black Americans and white Americans.[26]

Although the reactionary views of Jensen, Herrnstein, and Murray have been successfully refuted by many social scientists—especially their denial of environmental effects on test results—their notions about intelligence have spread to analysts and politicians around the globe. For example, a philosophy professor at a New York college has cited Jensen's research on white and black intelligence to support his arguments against affirmative action programs.[27] In 1971, Patrick Buchanan, an adviser to President Richard Nixon who later became a Republican presidential candidate, picked up on Herrnstein's arguments. In a memo to Nixon, Buchanan alleged that "every study" showed black groups had lower IQs than white groups and that Herrnstein's views about race and IQ provided "an intellectual basis" for considering cuts in certain government programs.[28]

In the 1930s a number of social psychologists began seriously questioning whether IQ test results could be used as evidence of genetically determined differentials. They showed how white–black differences in IQ test scores reflected major differences in education, income, and other living conditions. Numerous studies showed that test scores of black children improved with better economic and educational environments. Results from large-scale IQ testing revealed that black children and adults in some northern states scored *higher* than whites in some southern states.[29] Using the logic of Jensen, Herrnstein, and Murray, one would be forced to conclude that white southerners were mentally and "racially" inferior to black northerners. Most such white analysts would doubtless avoid this interpretation; obviously they, as defenders of a theory of black IQ inferiority, do not wish to argue that data on IQ might actually show black intellectual superiority. Rather, they would accept an *environmental* explanation for uncomplimentary regional IQ-score differentials for whites. Not surprisingly, thus, testing differentials favoring whites are also most reasonably interpreted as reflecting environmental conditions such as family income and quality of schooling, not genetic factors.

Some analysts have focused on the cultural bias—specifically, the white middle-class bias—inherent in traditional achievement and other psychometric tests (including IQ, SAT, and GRE tests), which measure only certain types of learned skills and certain acquired knowledge—skills and knowledge that are not equally available to all racial and ethnic groups because of centuries of discrimination and, thus, of low family incomes and lesser-quality educational facilities. Social scientists have also found that advanced skills in achievement-test taking itself are skills that white middle-class children are more likely to possess because they and their parents have access to more substantial learning resources (including access to expensive tutoring programs) and are typically more familiar and experienced with such paper-and-pencil testing.[30]

The most fundamental problem for those who insist on racial differences is the equation of these relatively brief tests' results with general intelligence. From the beginning, the so-called intelligence (IQ) tests have been intentionally misnamed. These tests measure only selected verbal, mathematical, or manipulative *skills*. Clearly, they do not measure well many aspects of human abilities, such as much human creativity and imagination. They do not measure musical, artistic, farming, fishing, and many other skills that reflect human intelligence. They penalize those who do not spend their lives enmeshed in the culture of the test makers. Intelligence is much broader than what relatively short paper-and-pencil or symbol-manipulation tests can measure. Intelligence is more accurately defined as a complex ability to deal creatively with one's environment, whatever that environment may be. At best, only a very small portion of human intellectual ability can be revealed on any short test. Given this problem of what social scientists call the *validity* of a measure, the modest and brief "intelligence" tests by no means reveal what the defenders of racial inequality claim that they do.[31]

Why was it important for whites to establish a racist ideology with negative stereotypes?

Contemporary Antiblack Prejudices and Related Views

To what extent does the white public still accept negative stereotypes of African Americans? Surveys of whites since 2000 continue to show that a majority still think in stereotypical terms about African Americans. An early 2000s survey of whites by Harvard researchers found that a majority (58 percent) of whites stereotyped African Americans. A majority agreed that one or more of these traits characterized African Americans: lazy, aggressive or violent, prefer to live on welfare, or complaining. One-third of whites agreed with two or more of these negative traits. Similarly, a 2004 survey of white college students in Pennsylvania asked them to rate how other whites viewed African Americans; views of African Americans as hostile, lazy, impolite, doing drugs, criminal, and unintelligent got the greatest emphasis.[32]

Negative images of black Americans seem to be deeply embedded in many whites' consciousness. Psychological studies have demonstrated that, when given a test of unconscious stereotyping, nearly 90 percent of whites quickly associate black faces with negative traits such as evil character or failure. In these studies whites have more difficulty in linking black faces to positive traits than they do white faces. Moreover, in research in which whites are showed photos of black faces for a few milliseconds, key brain areas designed to respond to perceived threats light up automatically. The more unconscious stereotyping they show on paper-and-pencil tests, the greater their brains' threat responses. Whites' underlying emotional states, such as fear of the racial "other," can apparently trigger brain reactions and, thus, discriminatory actions.[33]

Negative white stereotypes are harmful for African Americans across the spectrum of life experiences. For example, negative stereotypes can affect health care. In an older survey of practicing psychiatrists, Doris Wilkinson found that "cultural conditioning to racial beliefs and attitudes...pervades therapeutic contexts in which minority women are clients."[34] One recent study used actors to portray black and white patients with symptoms of coronary disease. Several hundred physicians were asked to view recorded interviews and patient data to assess the probability of coronary artery disease and suggest treatment. Black patients were less likely to be recommended for cardiac catheterization than white patients with similar dress, occupations, and medical histories. A study of lung cancer patients found that black patients were less likely than white patients to receive the best surgical treatment. White doctors' stereotyped images of black patients—such as the view that they are not intelligent patients—may affect their medical treatment. Recent studies have also found racial discrimination or inequality in the cancer drugs carried by pharmacies (fewer in neighborhoods of color), in nursing home care, in avoidable hospitalizations, and in the provision of medical care to communities of color (for example, fewer physicians). In addition, black medical students have also reported significant racial harassment during their medical educations. Building black trust in the U.S. medical care system is difficult in the face of widespread racial discrimination.[35]

Examining white views, John McConahay and colleagues have described what they call **modern racism**: *the white view that black Americans have illegitimately challenged cherished white values and are making illegitimate demands for changes in U.S. racial relations*. This white hostility is reflected in negative views of certain black actions and achievements. Citing survey data, McConahay and his associates have argued that the most extreme antiblack stereotypes and white opposition to all racial desegregation have to some extent been replaced by new racial prejudices and stereotypes.[36] Unlike the white segregationists of the 1950s, most whites today publicly state their support for equality of opportunity. A great many believe that serious racism is no longer widespread and that African Americans today have equal opportunities with whites. For example, a *Washington Post* poll of 779 whites found that on a general question about opportunities in life, 71 percent of the respondents thought African Americans had opportunities in life that were equal to or better than those of whites. On specific issues, a majority viewed the average black person as having health care access equal to or better than that of the average white person. About half felt that blacks had a level of education similar to or better than that of whites. Half felt that, on average, blacks were about as well off as whites in jobs they hold, and 42 percent thought that the average black worker earned at least as much as the average white worker. However, the demographic and other data on these issues show that in no case is there real racial equality. Considering these four areas together, a large majority (70 percent) of these whites were holding one or more erroneous beliefs about white and black inequalities.[37]

Today, racial discrimination remains a very serious problem for black Americans, yet again black and white Americans hold dramatically different views about particular types of discrimination. In an early 2000s *New York Times* nationwide poll, large proportions of the black respondents said that in their local communities blacks were less likely to be fairly treated than whites in such areas as the workplace (40 percent, versus 11 percent of white respondents agreeing), local malls (46 percent versus 10 percent), local restaurants and theaters (45 percent versus 10 percent), and local policing (66 percent versus 25 percent). Two-thirds of the black respondents indicated that they had been victims of discrimination because of their racial characteristics.[38]

Do racial prejudices and stereotypes generate discrimination? One review of numerous research studies found that whites who express prejudice tend to be more likely to discriminate than those who do not and that whites "systematically alter their expressed racial attitudes and behaviors to appear in a more socially desirable—unprejudiced and egalitarian—light." Experimental research suggests that the apparently significant decrease in negative white racial attitudes since the 1960s has represented conformity to a more liberal social climate rather than a basic change in racist attitudes.[39] Today, many whites continue to conceal their antiblack views in order to appear socially acceptable.

Thus, research on white university students has found that attitudes expressed on short-answer survey items are often different from those expressed in reply to questions requiring detailed commentary. Recall that in one study cited in Chapter 1, 80 percent of 451 white students said that they approved of marriages between blacks and whites when the issue was presented as a brief survey item. However, when a similar but smaller group was interviewed in depth, the proportion that unequivocally approved of intermarriage dropped to 30 percent. Given time to explain, the majority expressed reservations about marriages across the color line.[40]

One recent research project had 626 white students at more than two dozen colleges keep journals about racial events for part of a semester. In their brief journals these students recorded about *nine thousand* racial events, most of them involving negative and racist performances by well-educated whites, often college students. A great many accounts of racist performances, such as the commonplace telling of "N-word" jokes at a party, described what are termed "backstage" settings–that is, social settings composed only of white friends and relatives. After recounting racist joking or other racist performances by whites (more often men than women) in these private spaces, the journal writers would often go on to say something like, "but these guys are really nice, and they would not say or do racist stuff in public." From the perspective of these recent research studies, the apparent decrease in antiblack prejudices and stereotyping among whites seen in public opinion surveys over recent decades may reflect, for many whites, increased concern for social acceptability rather than abandonment of the white racial framing and its old racist stereotypes.[41]

How is the negative white racial framing of African Americans harmful across the spectrum of their life experiences?

Interracial Conflict

Antiblack Violence

Lynching is one of the most brutal forms of **ethnoviolence**—*violence directed at an individual or group because of that individual's or group's ethnic or racial identity*—in which human beings engage. **Lynching** is *a group killing carried out by vigilantes seeking revenge for an actual or imagined crime by the victim.* Before the Civil War, most lynchings in the United States were carried out by white mobs against whites. After the Civil War, lynching became primarily a means of keeping African Americans subordinated—"in their place," as white southerners often said. Table 7.1 shows the racialized pattern of recorded lynchings from the 1880s to the 1950s.[42]

Whites have also engaged in lynchings more recently. In 1981, in Mobile, Alabama, Ku Klux Klan

TABLE 7.1 Recorded Lynchings, 1882–1956

Years	White Victims	Black Victims
1882–1891	751	732
1892–1901	381	1,124
1902–1911	76	707
1912–1921	53	533
1922–1931	23	201
1932–1941	10	95
1942–1951	2	25
1952–1956	0	3

members hanged a black man, and in 1998, white supremacists dragged James Byrd, Jr., to death near Jasper, Texas. Experts estimate that, from the end of the Civil War to the present, at least half of all lynchings have gone unrecorded. Some experts estimate the actual number to be at least *six thousand* for the decades since the Civil War. African Americans have faced this extreme white violence for more than a century; in many periods there was an "inclination to abandon such relatively mild and decent ways of dispatching the [lynch] mob's victim as hanging and shooting in favor of burning, often roasting over slow fires, after preliminary mutilations and tortures... a disposition to revel in the infliction of the most devilish and prolonged agonies."[43]

White lynchers usually expected that brutal lynchings would discourage black challenges of practices such as legal segregation. Until recently, white lynchers have seldom been punished; many lynchings have taken place with the acquiescence or participation of white police officers. Some have been public; others have been carried out in secret. Many black civil rights advocates—and some white civil rights workers—were killed by whites, often in secret attacks, between the 1940s and the 1960s.[44]

Beginning in the World War I period, many black southerners moved to northern cities to escape oppressive conditions, but in the North they often met more violence. In a riot of whites in 1900 in New York City, for example, a substantially Irish American police force encouraged working-class whites to attack black residents. One of the most serious white-dominated race riots occurred in 1917 in East St. Louis. White workers, who saw new black workers as a job threat, attacked a black community. Thirty-nine black residents and nine of the white attackers were killed. This riot was followed in 1919 by a string of white-generated riots against black citizens from Chicago to Charleston.[45]

Opposition to black workers seeking better jobs has long been a cause of white violence. African Americans, as well as Asian, Latino, and Jewish Americans, have often been inaccurately blamed for economic troubles by white workers who have little understanding of how a capitalistic system works. For example, many do not recognize that job cutbacks and job displacement are frequently the result of decisions by white employers and investors to export jobs to low-wage labor areas outside the United States in pursuit of higher profits.

White supremacy groups have long been in the forefront of those who blame black, Latino, Asian, and Jewish Americans for problems rooted elsewhere. The Ku Klux Klan, a leading white supremacy group for most of the past century and more, started as a violent terrorist group right after the Civil War, then went into decline after its victories in restoring the old white oligarchy's rule in the South. It regained strength in the 1920s, and once again during the civil rights era of the 1960s. Other supremacist groups, such as the White Aryan Resistance (WAR), have emerged in recent decades. One recent count by the Southern Poverty Law Center found that more than 697 Klan, neo-Nazi, racist-skinhead, Christian Identity, neo-Confederate, and other white hate groups, involving thousands of white Americans, were active in most states. Some hate groups make extensive use of the hundreds of white supremacist websites, thereby increasing the readers of their literature. They often augment their supremacist ideologies with white-power music. White supremacy groups have been involved in numerous attacks on and murders of blacks and other people of color; until 1987, no supremacist group had been found guilty of such attacks.[46]

In recent years there have been numerous hate-motivated murders and hate-inspired assaults, including many against African Americans. Fewer than half of all hate crimes are reported to police, and many hate crimes that are reported are not classified as such. In 1998, a black man, James Byrd, Jr., was killed near Jasper, Texas, by white men whose racial views strongly suggested ties to white-supremacist ideas. They dragged him along a road until his body was dismembered. After this lynching-type killing, a Klan group held a rally nearby for the supremacist cause. This murder triggered copycat crimes in at least two other cities.[47]

In the Brooklyn's Flatlands area in the summer of 2005, a group of ten white teenagers attacked a small group of black men, one of whom was unable to escape. He was chased by the white group, in cars and on foot, some of whom yelled racist slurs. Once caught, he was beaten and ended up in the hospital. Plea bargains got several white teenagers off with just probation and community service. This incident was not isolated, for a few weeks before in the Queens area of New York City some white men had similarly attacked three black men and beaten one of them with a bat.[48]

Some conservative political groups, such as Focus on the Family and the Traditional Values Coalition, have worked against tougher hate crimes legislation. In contrast, given the increase in hate groups and, periodically, in hate crimes against Jewish Americans, Americans of color, and gay/lesbian Americans, many civil rights groups have called for increased penalties for perpetrators. Some state legislatures have passed such legislation.[49]

Black Protest Against Oppression

As with other groups we have examined, it is important to distinguish violence used to oppress black Americans from violence used by black victims to *resist* oppression. Since the 1930s, black urbanites have, on occasion, rebelled violently against oppressive racial and socioeconomic conditions in their cities. Historically, large-scale white violence to enforce racial oppression preceded most black attacks on that continuing oppression.

A few urban revolts involving pitched battles between black residents and white police officers, often sparked by police brutality or other police malpractice, occurred during the 1930s and 1940s, especially in New York City. The underlying causes involved extensive job discrimination and discriminatory restrictions on political participation by whites, issues that have periodically prompted black Americans to lash out in nonviolent resistance movements as well as in violent revolts. During the 1960s and 1970s, many cities experienced black uprisings against local symbols of racial oppression, especially discriminatory white police officers, businesses, and landlords. Large-scale black rebellions occurred in Los Angeles in 1965, in Detroit and Newark in 1967, and in Washington, D.C., in 1968. An angry generation of black Americans showed their willingness to engage in aggressive protests against racial discrimination and related economic problems.[50]

Rebellions against oppressive conditions have continued in recent decades. In the spring of 1980, black anger over local discrimination erupted in Miami. Black residents lashed out at white and Cuban American police officers and discrimination by the larger white society. Rioting there cost sixteen lives, caused four hundred injuries, and resulted in $100 million in property damage. Afterward, 27 percent of a national sample of African Americans said they felt the rioting was justified, and another 25 percent were unsure.[51] More uprisings occurred in Miami between 1982 and 1991, all triggered by incidents involving white or Latino officers shooting an African American or being acquitted for such actions. In Los Angeles in the spring of 1992, the acquittal of officers videotaped beating an unarmed black man named Rodney King triggered the most costly uprising in U.S. history. During days of rioting in central Los Angeles, more than 10,000 blacks and Latinos were arrested, and more than fifty people were killed. Property damage exceeded $1 billion. At one point, 20,000 police officers and soldiers patrolled the area.[52] Protests also broke out in other cities. As in the 1960s riots, the underlying conditions fuelling the uprisings included present-day discrimination and the poverty, unemployment, and poor housing that have resulted from centuries of racial discrimination and inequality.

In 2001, the killing of a black man by white officers in Cincinnati sparked a large-scale rebellion by residents there. Local and national civil rights organizations had warned that police practices, as well as underlying employment and housing problems, could trigger rioting in major cities, including Cincinnati, 43 percent of whose population is African American. Numerous suspicious killings of black citizens by police officers had occurred in Cincinnati, and no officer had ever been convicted for such a killing. Days of rioting resulted in eight hundred arrests, dozens of injuries, and extensive property damage. In March 2001 the American Civil Liberties Union (ACLU) and local citizens filed a lawsuit against the city for **racial profiling**, *a practice used by some police departments that unfairly singles out citizens of color as potential criminals and often results in extensive harassment of innocent people.*[53]

In Cincinnati in June 2001, African Americans engage in a nonviolent protest against the killing of a young unarmed black man by the police.

The role of white officials and police in generating or accelerating nonviolent protests and urban revolts by black Americans, while overlooked by many whites, has been significant. Police malpractice targeting Americans of color remains a major problem in many cities. One national survey asked black respondents if they had faced police discrimination. Strikingly, 15 percent of all the respondents, and 34 percent of young men, reported that they had been treated unfairly by police in just the past month.[54] In a search of major newspaper articles from a several-year period in the 1990s, one researcher found reports of 130 incidents of serious police brutality. White officers were involved in more than nine of every ten of these cases; black or Latino citizens were the victims in 97 percent of the incidents. Yet, an officer was actually punished in *only 13 percent* of the incidents, and the punishment was typically slight. Police brutality is often a racialized crime in the United States.[55]

Racial profiling has recently become more visible as a national issue. In a summer 2006 agreement, the Arizona Department of Public Safety (DPS), which a lawsuit had charged with racial profiling of black and Latino motorists, agreed to make its data on traffic stops by state police officers public and to take other actions to reduce the likelihood of officers engaging in racial profiling or other malpractice. An *Arizona Daily Star* review of the DPS records had revealed that black and Latino motorists were searched much more often than white motorists on suspicion of possessing drugs and other contraband, yet were less likely than whites to have been found with that contraband.[56] Such discriminatory racial profiling (termed by some "driving while black") has been reported in numerous towns and cities across the United States.

The Economy

According to traditional assimilation perspectives, most members of an immigrant group coming into the society will gradually experience secondary-structural assimilation into the economy (Chapter 2). Over several generations, most members of a particular racial or ethnic group are expected to move into ever higher levels of employment and living conditions. However, this assimilation view of economic mobility does not apply very well to African Americans. Thus, although they have been in North America since 1619, they have still not been incorporated, in representative numbers, in many of the country's better-paying job categories and they still face much discrimination in areas such as housing.

White Enrichment, Black Losses

Over the course of North American history, whites at most class levels have benefitted greatly from the racial oppression that has targeted African Americans for nearly four centuries. This white privilege typically includes an array of material benefits and socioeconomic advantages inherited by most in each generation of whites. Such white privilege began in early white gains from the economic exploitation of slavery, persisted as a result of socioeconomic discrimination under legal segregation, and continues as a result of contemporary discrimination and the societal failure to redress the current effects of past discrimination.

For centuries, African Americans have been critical to the growth of this country's wealth and prosperity.

From the 1600s to the present, they have provided much of the hard labor necessary for economic growth and societal affluence. From the 1600s until the 1860s, the labor of most African Americans was stolen as they toiled for white slaveholders on farms and in cities. Much of the economic capital (wealth) and success of the country's white families and communities came directly, or by means of economic multiplier effects on the larger society, from the African slave trade and the slave plantations. The slave trade and plantations generated many jobs for whites (such as overseers and local officials), much commercial trade, numerous banking enterprises, and many other enterprises throughout both the southern and northern regions of the country. Much British, French, and North American industry, shipping, and banking depended on enslaved labor or the capital-generating effects of that labor. From the 1600s to the 1800s, most major agricultural exports in the Atlantic trade were produced by enslaved Africans. Without this enslaved labor, it seems unlikely that the successful British and U.S. textile industries would have developed when they did. Without that first major industry (textiles), it is unclear how or when Britain and the United States would have become major industrial powers. Indeed, even James Watt's improved steam engine, which greatly accelerated Western industrialization, was financed by British investors with capital accumulated in the Atlantic trade in enslaved human beings and slave-produced products.[57]

Since the 1600s, over the course of nearly four centuries, the exploitation of black Americans has redistributed material rewards and wealth earned by black labor to many generations of whites, leaving the former relatively impoverished as a group and the latter relatively privileged as a group. Consider the value of the African American labor that was stolen. One researcher has calculated that the value (in 1983 dollars) of the slave labor expropriated by whites from 1620 to 1865 was somewhere between $1 and $97 trillion, depending on the rate of (lost) interest chosen. Even more labor was stolen under legal segregation in the form of the commonplace discriminatory wages. Another research study estimated the cost of this labor discrimination for just 1929–1969 (in 1983 dollars) at $1.6 trillion.[58] Calculating the cost of antiblack discrimination from the end of slavery (1865) to the end of legal segregation (1969), and putting that calculation into current dollars would likely increase the wage-loss estimate under segregation to several trillion dollars. Since the end of official racial segregation, which took place only about 1968, black Americans have suffered additional economic losses from continuing racial discrimination in employment and other areas. The sum total for the current value of all the black labor stolen by whites through slavery, segregation, and contemporary discrimination is staggering—trillions of dollars.

Whites have benefited from numerous federal programs that gave away critical resources that could be used to accumulate individual and family wealth over generations. Thus, in the late 1800s and the 1900s, the federal government distributed land, mineral rights, airline routes, radio/television frequencies, and other important resources. Throughout this period, black Americans, even though they were present in large numbers, were generally excluded from such benefits because of racial segregation and other white discrimination. Under the 1860s Homestead Act, from that time to the 1930s, the federal government provided about 246 million acres at minimal cost to 1.5 million homesteads. Research by Trina Williams estimates that roughly 46 million Americans *today* are the likely beneficiaries, to varying degrees, of this huge wealth-generating land-providing program.[59] Almost all these beneficiaries are white, for black families were largely excluded from this huge land giveaway. (One might also note that much of this land had been stolen from Native Americans.) Stephen DeCanio's research suggests that much of the long-term racial gap in income and wealth is a direct result of this racial gap in access to arable homestead land.[60]

After the Civil War, some Republican Party proposals sought to give those who had formerly been enslaved some arable land taken from those slaveholders who had rebelled against the union—the famous "40 acres and a mule." Yet, this did not happen. With no major land distribution to accompany their emancipation from slavery, most formerly enslaved workers were forced to sell their labor to former slave masters and other whites because whites continued to control the agricultural system in southern and border states. Exploitative, semislave farm labor became the lot of many. Black sharecroppers and tenant farmers were often tied to one rural area by mounting debts owed to the often exploitative and discriminatory, white-controlled lending and provisions system. With less money and much less legal protection than whites and faced with discrimination in land and consumer-product transactions, most freed blacks who remained in the South were unable to become independent, land-owning farmers who could build up wealth to pass along to later generations. Those who migrated to cities fared little better. Most black men in cities were confined to service-sector jobs; unemployment was common. Few manufacturing jobs were open to black women or men.[61] The effect of racism-generated poverty was severe. Reflecting on the high rate of stillbirths among black mothers in this period, a physician commented, "Why should we be surprised at the great number of still-births among our women?... They do heavy washing, make beds, turn heavy mattresses, and climb the stairs several times during the day, while their more favored white sister is seated in her big armchair, and not allowed to move, even if she wanted to."[62]

What are some political and economic consequences of established white power and privilege?

The Migration North

In 1900, most black citizens lived in southern states. Soon, however, the bustling economy in northern and border cities, the declining significance of "King Cotton" in the South, and the violent cruelty of southern segregation stimulated increasing numbers to move north. After the anti-immigrant legislation of the 1920s and the subsequent decline in overseas immigration, demand for black laborers in northern industries increased. The major push factors were violence-enforced racial segregation and the declining viability of cotton farming; the major pull factor was service and industrial employment.[63]

By the mid-twentieth century, millions had migrated to what many saw as an economic "promised land." They went to the cities in the Northeast, Midwest, and West. Generally, they were forced to settle in low-income areas already occupied by black families, swelling their size. Some traditional assimilation theorists argue that this northern migration brought great opportunities for economic mobility to black Americans, whom they see as just another in a line of urban immigrant groups (such as the Irish and the Italians) successfully seeking to improve their lives in cities. However, if we accept this view, we would expect that black economic gains between 1900 and the 2000s would have gradually closed the white–black economic gap. The reality, however, has been quite different.[64]

The racial division of labor in cities was enforced by discriminatory laws, violence, or informal discrimination at the hands of whites. The urban economy can be viewed as having primary and secondary employment sectors—the split labor market described in Chapter 2. The primary labor market, composed disproportionately of privileged white workers, is characterized by skilled jobs, high wages, and job ladders that offer significant upward mobility. The secondary labor market, composed disproportionately of workers of color, is characterized by more instability, lower wages, and less upward mobility.[65] The dramatic rise of corporate capitalism after 1900 that created employment for large numbers of workers resulted in union organizing to expand workers' wages and rights. However, to counter the white workers' increasing demands, white employers often offered noneconomic concessions, including separating the white workers from less privileged workers of color in the workplace. In this way, white workers got what W. E. B. Du Bois called a **psychological wage** (that is, *the white workers' sense of white superiority and privilege*) in return for accepting lower monetary wages than they would have gotten by organizing more aggressively in unions with black workers.[66]

Increasing numbers of black men and women moving out of farm occupations found themselves channeled into relatively unskilled jobs in urban industrial and service sectors. The principal occupations of black men became truck driver, porter, janitor, and cook. Black women served as maids, restaurant workers, and dressmakers as white women began to move into clerical and professional jobs.[67] Census figures for 1930 revealed the continuing dominance of agricultural and domestic service jobs. Of every 1000 black workers, 648 were in agricultural or domestic service jobs, compared with 280 of every 1000 whites. Most of the remainder held other unskilled blue-collar positions. Most of the few black professionals were teachers, ministers, and physicians serving the black community; likewise, black businesspeople usually served a black clientele. As a result of extensive racial discrimination, black incomes and savings were sharply lower than those of whites, a situation that again resulted in little in the way of resources to pass along to future generations.[68]

Most labor unions were racially segregated. By the late 1930s, black pressure and federal legislation had forced many American Federation of Labor (AFL) unions to begin to reduce discrimination in recruiting black workers. The new Congress of Industrial Organizations (CIO) began with an official nondiscriminatory policy in order to attract black workers in the automobile, steel, and packing industries. However, in 1930 at least twenty-six major unions *officially* barred black workers from membership; by 1943 the number had dropped to fourteen. Nonetheless, official discrimination was usually replaced by informal exclusion or restriction of black workers on a large scale in the historically white unions, practices that have persisted in more subtle forms in some unions to the present day.[69]

Economic Changes Since the 1940s

During World War II, industries with severe labor needs were forced to make concessions to black demands for antidiscrimination laws and better job opportunities. Under pressure from civil rights leaders, President Franklin Roosevelt issued executive orders that reduced job discrimination somewhat in war-related industries. At the end of the war this progress came to an abrupt end: Layoffs hit black workers much harder than whites, and discrimination increased again in most areas.[70]

During the civil rights era and the economic expansion between 1955 and 1972, the proportion of black workers in professional, managerial, sales, clerical, crafts, and operatives jobs increased. By the 1980s growth in the proportion of black employees in better-paid job categories slowed. In the 2000s black workers are still significantly less likely than white workers to be in better-paid managerial, professional, technical, sales, and crafts job categories. In 2005, BLS data (annual averages) showed that 26 percent of black workers held managerial and professional jobs, compared with 36 percent of whites. Black workers were more likely than white workers to hold blue-collar jobs in service, production, and transportation categories (41 percent compared with 28 percent).[71] Moreover, in 2004 black civilian employees in the executive branch of the federal government were most heavily represented in clerical positions. Their percentage of blue-collar workers was more than twice that of professional workers. The percentage of black workers is highest at low pay levels and lowest at the highest pay levels (Table 7.2). Even within white-collar categories, black workers tend to be in subcategories with lower pay and lesser job status. For example, within the professional-technical category, black employees today are most commonly found in social work, kindergarten teaching, vocational counseling, dietetics, and health care. They are less often found among lawyers and judges,

TABLE 7.2 Civilian Employees in Executive Branch Agencies, September 2004 (Percentage of Employees by Category and Racial Group)

	Black	White
All white-collar workers	16.7%	69.0%
Professional	9.0	76.5
Clerical	27.7	55.9
Blue-collar workers	18.4	65.7
Pay plans		
General schedule	17.3	68.7
GS1–4	24.2	56.7
GS14–15	8.9	80.7
Senior pay levels	6.5	86.0

dentists, artists, engineers, and professors at historically white universities. In addition, white urbanites are much more likely to be self-employed than black urbanites.[72]

Persisting Discrimination: A Business Example

Recall that 71 percent of white respondents in a recent survey thought black Americans had at least the same opportunities as whites. Surveys such as this indicate that many whites refuse to accept the experienced testimony of the majority of African Americans to the effect that they still face serious discrimination in the workplace and many other areas. Numerous research studies confirm that racial discrimination today continues to confront black employees working for wages and also those trying to succeed in businesses of their own. In several research studies, the first author has conducted or supervised interviews with hundreds of working-class and middle-class African Americans in numerous cities. Many have related concrete stories of discrimination in employment or business settings that document the types of discrimination discussed in Chapter 1. The reader will recall that isolate discrimination involves the actions of an individual acting alone, such as a white manager expressing antiblack views by discriminating against black employees without the support of fellow workers or a discriminatory company policy. Following is a description of the actual experience of the successful owner of a consulting firm:

> I have a contract right now with a southwestern city government; and I practically gave my services away. I had to become very creative, you know. I wanted the contract because I know I could do the work, and I have the background and the track record to do it. However, in negotiating the contract, they wanted to give it to all these other people who never had any experience... simply because they're a big eight accounting firm, or they're some big-time institution. So, I had to compete against those people. But it was good because it proved that I could be competitive.

She then explained that a professional panel evaluating the bids gave her the highest rating because of her track record. But a barrier was thrown up, because:

> ... the director of their department made a very racial statement, that "they were very sick and tired of these niggers and these other minorities because what they think is that they can come in here and run a business. None of them are qualified to run a business, especially the niggers." (Now, a white person, female, heard this statement, and because they had some confrontational problems—I think the only reason she really told me was because of that.) He was going to use that, not overtly, but in his mind that was going to be his reason for rejection .... Even though they [the panel] all recommended me (I got all five consensus votes), he was going to throw it out.... I had to really, really do some internalizing to keep myself from being very bitter.[73]

This incident involved one white man's attempt to restrict a talented black person's advancement, apparently without overt support of other whites. Although this event happened more than a decade ago, current research indicates that such discrimination strongly persists. Self-employment outside black communities remains difficult for black entrepreneurs, especially with the decline of antidiscrimination programs. A 2006 National Bureau of Economic Research study looked at receipt of public contracts in the construction industry and found a major decrease for black contractors and other contractors of color. The causes of this decline include racial discrimination in the construction industry, as well as lawsuits by white contractors that have forced a reduction of government antidiscrimination programs. As the director of the Lawyers' Committee for Civil Rights recently put it, "Self-employment rates of minorities, black contractors in particular, collapse when these programs are replaced or weakened through court challenges."[74]

Clearly, examples of isolate discrimination motivated by prejudice are still common in the lives of African Americans today. Small-group discrimination is also common. Small-group discrimination, such as that shaped by prejudiced supervisors or union officials wishing to subvert company or union regulations that require the hiring or promotion of skilled black employees, continues to be omnipresent in U.S. workplaces.

Discrimination in Corporations, Sports, and the Military

In addition, direct institutional discrimination remains a serious problem for black workers. This discrimination consists of organizationally prescribed actions carried out routinely by whites in business and government workplaces. Today, this often takes an informal or covert form. Examples include outright exclusion, the relegation of black employees to special jobs or sections, or restricting the mobility of black employees beyond entry level. Several audit studies conducted in the mid-2000s of employer responses to in-person applications and mail applications have shown that white applicants are much more likely to get callbacks about jobs than black applicants with similar resumes.[75] In addition, in 2005 some 417 lawsuits were filed by the federal Equal Employment Opportunity Commission (EEOC), and tens of millions in damages were won for employees. In 2005 the federal Office of Federal Contract Compliance won $45.2 million for nearly 15,000 workers who were targets of discrimination. This has been true for other recent years as well. Numerous lawsuits and other agency actions demonstrate the reality of well-institutionalized discrimination in the United States. These cases show continuing discrimination in hiring, working conditions, and pay raises in a great array of workplaces.[76]

Having abandoned the traditional, overt, and exclusionary barriers of earlier decades, many white employers and managers have retreated to a second line of discrimination: hiring black workers for nontraditional jobs and putting them in powerless or marginalized positions. Research on the corporate world documents that African Americans moving into professional and management jobs frequently find themselves tracked into special "job ghettos," such as members or heads of departments of affirmative action, "community affairs," or "special markets."[77] In a 2004–2005 survey, more than half of the 132 black and Latino professionals working in public relations (40 percent in middle management) reported facing subtle and/or overt discrimination by current or past employers. Most felt that they had to be better qualified than a white person for the job they held. Some 60 percent felt that they were placed into slow-moving job career tracks, and more than half felt that they were often given menial jobs. The respondents underscored the failure of top management in the industry to seek out more employees of color.[78] A recent survey of partners involved in hiring in eighty-three large law firms found that racial biases color the "way minority law students' achievements and aspirations are evaluated, that minority candidates are penalized for the high attrition rate of minority practitioners from law firms, and that there are still a significant number of inappropriate comments being made about minority candidates in the evaluation process." In the survey, one partner noted that senior lawyers in firms often set the stage for well-qualified lawyers of color to fail: They greatly exaggerate youthful mistakes and put them under the microscope, increasing their likelihood of failure.[79]

An example of racial problems in major corporations came to public attention in the late 1990s when the *New York Times* quoted from the taped transcript of a meeting of top executives at Texaco, then the country's fourteenth largest corporation, to discuss a lawsuit filed by black employees. According to the transcript, these top corporate officials discussed destroying documents requested by the plaintiffs. Black employees were called "black jelly beans" who "seem to be glued to the bottom of the bag." The EEOC found that Texaco had discriminated against black employees with regard to promotions. In an affidavit, a white manager in a midwestern office reported a black employee's discrimination complaint to a senior executive. That executive reportedly replied that he would "fire her black ass." When the manager pointed out that Texaco's policy protected those who complained from dismissal, the senior executive reportedly said, "I guess we treat niggers differently down here." At the time only six of Texaco's 873 highest-paid executives were black.[80]

In 2006 there were only four black executives heading *Fortune* 500 companies, less than 1 percent of the CEOs. Today, there are about seventy-five black executives in all the senior executive ranks of the country's top 1000 publicly traded companies. Indeed, about 95 percent of top corporate officials (vice presidents and above) are white men, yet they make up about 38 percent of the adult population. Even finding data on progress, or lack thereof, is difficult. Thus, 46 percent of the Standard and Poor's 100 top publicly traded companies have ignored the request of the federal Glass Ceiling Commission to regularly and openly report full data on the racial, ethnic, and gender characteristics of their employees. Without such public reporting, those concerned with truly desegregating the U.S. workforce cannot tell if a company is making progress in eradicating racial or gender discrimination in hiring and promotion processes.[81]

In numerous sports programs, one finds racial discrimination at the coaching and front office levels. For example, even though a very large percentage of Division 1A college football players have been black for decades, data on the 414 head coach openings at Division 1A colleges and universities between 1982 and the 2005–2006 season indicate that black coaches had been picked for such positions just twenty-one times, only 5 percent of the total. Among the many 2005–2006 Division 1A football programs, only Mississippi State, UCLA, Kansas State, Washington, and the University of Buffalo had black head coaches.[82]

Considering more ordinary jobs in cities, the racial mismatch of jobs in many cities is the result of corporate executives' intentional movement away from black populations in those cities. One recent report on workers of color in Atlanta, Boston, Detroit, and Los Angeles found that, in general, the movement of jobs away from central cities to suburban areas by employers has severely limited employment opportunities for many urban black workers. Apparently, some employers intentionally selected workplace locations that would be inaccessible to black workers. In Boston and Los Angeles, surveys found that employers were more likely to express a desire to move away from neighborhoods with increasing numbers of black families than from other city neighborhoods. In this large-scale study, numerous employers admitted that their hiring decisions involved a white racial framing, with its racist stereotypes about the personality traits, attitudes, and behaviors of workers of color. White employers held stereotyped images that white workers work better than black workers and rejected skilled black workers even before checking on their abilities. In addition, a 2003 research study of California temporary employment agencies found white job applicants were significantly preferred over black applicants for jobs that often become a gateway to better jobs. Using paired and similar white and black testers in sixty-four undercover tests, the researchers found that "temporary agencies preferred white applicants 4–1 over African Americans in Los Angeles and more than 2–1 in San Francisco." The study results were the same as those of an earlier 1990s study.[83]

A major survey of 40,000 U.S. military personnel, enlisted and officers, found that one-fifth of the black personnel had faced career-related racial discrimination in the previous year. Three-fourths had faced negative racial encounters; 52 percent had been told offensive racist stories; 49 percent had suffered unwelcome attempts to draw them into offensive discussions of race; 46 percent had endured acts of racial condescension; 37 percent had encountered hostile racial stares; and 28 percent had endured racist comments or epithets. Six percent had been physically threatened or intimidated because of their racial characteristics. A large percentage also reported racial harassment from the civilian community.[84]

Government Action and Inaction on Discrimination

Freedom from long centuries of widespread, overt discrimination in the form of slavery and legal segregation did not come for black Americans until the 1960s—that is, only in the last 10 percent of our history. The 1960s brought the first major civil rights laws in a century. The 1964 Civil Rights Act and its amendments prohibit racial discrimination in employment. The Equal Employment Opportunity Commission (EEOC) was created to enforce the act, primarily by investigating complaints, seeking conciliation, and filing suit to end discrimination by labor unions, private employers, state governments, and educational institutions. Until the 1980s, the federal courts and the EEOC made significant progress in reducing racial barriers in traditionally white employment arenas.

However, under the Ronald Reagan and George H. W. Bush administrations in the 1980s and early 1990s, aggressive EEOC efforts to halt racial discrimination in workplaces declined substantially. The EEOC reduced field investigations of class-action complaints of discrimination as well as other broad, institutionally focused investigations of discrimination. The Reagan administration eliminated or weakened numerous civil rights enforcement agencies, and, for the most part, President George H. W. Bush continued this negative approach. In addition, Presidents Reagan and Bush appointed justices to the U.S. Supreme Court, who subsequently handed down a number of backtracking decisions on civil rights enforcement and antidiscrimination issues.

During the 1990s the Bill Clinton administration enforced the civil rights laws more vigorously, but this enforcement progress was mostly discontinued under the administration of George W. Bush, beginning in 2001. Indeed, in late 2006 the EEOC was dealing with major budget cuts and the loss of many important staff members. The agency continues to have a large backlog of at least 30,000 discrimination complaints, and thus has had a slow resolution process for complaints made to it.[85]

In addition, the existing civil rights laws do not guarantee real equality of opportunity in everyday settings for Americans of color. Relatively few of the millions of cases of discrimination perpetrated by white Americans each year against African Americans and other Americans of color are countered by effective private or government antidiscrimination remedies. Generally, federal and state government agencies have neither the resources nor staff to vigorously enforce antidiscrimination laws. Over the past few decades, many victims of discrimination have given up on the government's ability or willingness to deal with discrimination. In a 1989 decision, one of the few progressive justices on the Supreme Court, Harry Blackmun, asked whether the conservative majority on the court, and by implication in the country, "still believes that race discrimination—or, more accurately, race discrimination against nonwhites—is a problem in our society, or even remembers that it ever was."[86]

Unemployment, Income, and Poverty

For decades the black unemployment rate has been more than twice the white rate (Table 7.3).[87] In 1989 the black–white unemployment ratio reached a record high of 2.53. Since then it has fluctuated, but it has remained high, at 2.3 times the white rate into the twenty-first century. During economic recessions black workers tend to lose their jobs at a higher rate than white workers and to be recalled at a slower rate. The movement of investment capital and jobs to mostly white suburbs is a contributing factor to unemployment.

Even higher than the unemployment rate is the **underemployment rate**, which includes *those with no jobs, those working part-time, and those making poverty-level wages*. Nationwide surveys have found that large numbers of black workers have part-time work even though they want full-time work, receive very low wages, or are discouraged workers (those who have given up looking). Recent state reports indicate that one-quarter or more of black workers typically fall into subemployment categories, while the proportion for whites is usually much lower.[88]

For key years since 1950, black family income has not risen above 62 percent of white family income (Table 7.4).[89] Moreover, in 2005 black median family income and per-capita income were less than 60 percent of the respective white figures.[90] Families headed by single, separated, or divorced mothers tend to be poorer than those in which two parents are present. The proportion of black families headed by women increased from 18 percent in 1950 to just over 44 percent in 1999.[91] From 1970 until the mid-1990s, the poverty rate for black female–headed families with children under eighteen years old remained well over 50 percent, peaking at almost 64 percent in 1982. By 2005 this poverty rate was still high, but lower, at just over 39 percent. In contrast, only 22 percent of non-Hispanic white families in this female-headed category were below the poverty level in that year.[92] One leading scholar has noted: "Families headed by black women are primarily

TABLE 7.3 Unemployment Rates

Year	Black (or Nonwhite)	White	Ratio
1949	8.9%	5.6%	1.6
1959	10.7	4.8	2.2
1969	6.4	3.1	2.1
1979	12.3	5.1	2.4
1989	11.4	4.5	2.5
1999	8.0	3.7	2.2
2005	10.0	4.4	2.3

TABLE 7.4 Black (or Nonwhite) Median Family Income as a Percentage of White and Non-Hispanic White Family Income (U.S. Census Categories)

Year	Percent of White Family Income	Percent of Non-Hispanic White Family Income
1950	54%	
1960	55	
1970	61	
1980	58	57%
1990	58	56
2004	62	58

poor, not because they do not have husbands, but *because they do not have jobs.*"[93] Like black men, black women face major employment problems in part because of intentional discrimination by white employers in the present and in part because of the continuing effects of past discrimination in workplaces and schooling.

Whatever the type of family, black Americans have on average significantly fewer dollars than whites. In 2005, black families were four times as likely as white families to live in poverty (24 percent versus 6 percent). One-fourth of all black Americans, and one-third of black children, fell below the poverty line. In 2005, about 9.2 million black Americans lived in poverty in "the world's richest country." Note too that a much smaller proportion of black families than non-Hispanic white families owned their home (48 percent compared with 76 percent), and a substantial majority of black families nationwide cannot afford a modestly priced house in their local community.

Over centuries, most African Americans have had little opportunity to build up multigenerational wealth. Today, black households as a group have a much lower net worth than white households. The median net worth of white households is *many* times that of black households. Table 7.5 reveals that in 2005 more than 29 percent of black households had zero or negative net worth, and the net worth of an additional 16 percent was less than $5,000, altogether about 45 percent. The high percentage of black households at this low wealth level has changed little since a 1995 survey. Nearly half of white households had a net worth of $100,000 or more, four times the percentage of black households at that level.[94]

Most of the economic wealth held by more affluent black families is in cars and houses. White families are far more likely than black families to have interest-bearing bank accounts and to hold stocks. One striking thing about the wealth data is that they show the long-term effect of centuries of

TABLE 7.5 Percent Distribution of Household Net Worth by Racial Group and Amount of Net Worth, 2000

	White	Black
Negative or $0	11.3%	29.1%
$1–$4,999	7.2	16.0
$5,000–$24,999	12.4	18.9
$25,000–$99,999	24.6	25.3
$100,000–$249,000	22.2	8.0
$250,000 or over	22.2	2.7

racial oppression. Some data even indicate that white families with modest incomes have *greater* net worth than black families with much higher incomes. The likely reason for this is the fact that these modest-income white families are more likely than the higher-income black families to have built up some significant equity in a house—which has often been made possible because the white families have inherited a house or some money from their parents, or because they have not faced discrimination in holding a good job or finding decent housing in the past. Many middle-class African Americans are first-generation middle-class, and while their incomes may be good for the present, they have not inherited the wealth that enables them to build up much future wealth. In addition, many middle-class African Americans are likely to be assisting parents or relatives who are poor or working-class. One should also note that mid-2000s research indicates that the proportion of African Americans in the middle class, as measured by income, has stayed roughly the same (about a quarter) since the early 1980s.[95]

How do racial framing and discrimination relate to the unemployment and income inequality of African Americans?

Is There a Distinctive African American "Culture of Poverty"?

For decades, numerous commentators have contended that the black community is divided or polarized between an affluent middle class and the poor. Sometimes they argue that discrimination has mostly been eradicated for middle-class black Americans, thus lessening the need for antidiscrimination programs. Often the plight of the black poor is discussed as though economic conditions were not the main problem; their values and behavior are said to be the main source of problems. From this perspective, poor black Americans (sometimes called "the underclass") are locked into a lower-class "culture" or "culture of poverty," with its alleged immorality, "broken" families, delinquency, and lack of work emphasis. These stereotyped arguments about poor Americans are recent versions of the largely discredited culture-of-poverty views that have been made since at least the 1960s.[96]

Perhaps the greatest weakness of arguments that focus on the alleged cultural inferiority of poor African Americans (and other poor Americans) is the serious neglect of several centuries of structural discrimination and related socioeconomic factors. For example, many economic problems faced by poor Americans are actually created by corporate executives who move jobs overseas or from central cities to suburbs. In addition, overt, subtle, and covert discrimination remains commonplace in workplaces and in the housing sector. If the common notion that discrimination is irrelevant were true, poor black Americans should face roughly the same economic, political, and housing conditions as comparably poor white Americans. This is not generally the case. Because of continuing discrimination, overt and covert, poor black families do *not* live in integrated neighborhoods with comparable white families. African Americans, including low-income workers, are *more* likely to be laid off in recessions than white Americans. Poor blacks are *less* likely than comparably poor whites to get unemployment compensation when they are laid off. They tend to hold lower-paying and less secure jobs than poor whites, and they face far more discrimination at the hands of white police officers and other whites than do poor whites. The "class" situation of poor black Americans does not account for the differences in treatment between them and poor white Americans. The cumulative effects of past and present racial discrimination on socioeconomic problems faced by poor black Americans must be recognized. As many research studies show, past official segregation and centuries of exploitative discrimination, coupled with blatant, subtle, and covert discrimination today, are likely reasons for much black poverty, unemployment, and underemployment.[97]

Discrimination in Housing

The 1968 Civil Rights Act, together with later amendments, officially banned most housing discrimination in the United States. However, antidiscrimination laws have often been weakly enforced, and discriminatory practices in housing persist widely. One 2000 study across several cities, using numerous white and black testers, found that the white testers were favored over black testers 20 to 30 percent of the time with regard to such issues as housing availability, inspections, and cost. Local audit studies in New Orleans, Montgomery, Fresno, and San Antonio have shown even higher rates of discrimination, especially for black testers seeking rental housing.[98] This widespread discrimination is often covert, as in the case of a landlord falsely telling a black renter that an apartment has been rented or a real estate salesperson steering home buyers or providing housing information with substantial attention to their racial characteristics.

Insurance companies create discriminatory barriers. One investigation had black, Latino, and white testers pose as homeowners seeking insurance. They contacted major insurance companies in nine cities. Overall, 53 percent of the black and Latino testers—ranging from 32 percent in Memphis to 83 percent in Chicago—experienced racial discrimination in offers of insurance coverage and price. Whites were often offered more insurance options and lower rates.[99]

Residential apartheid is still the reality in cities. The white population of central cities has decreased, and most suburbs are predominantly white. Today most whites live in suburbs or nonmetropolitan areas, while the majority of people of color live in cities. Ironically, many whites now have some racial fears stemming from the residential segregation that they or their ancestors have created by centuries of racially exclusionary practices. Residential segregation has serious societal consequences, including little or no interracial contacts for many white Americans. Thus, one study by several journalists examined adjacent but largely segregated working-class residential areas of Chicago, one white and one black. According to field interviews, the whites live in an insulated world in which they "live out entire lives without ever getting to know a black person." The study found racial fear and suspicion of the other group in both residential areas. However, the black residents were "fearful because much of their contact with white people was negative," whereas "whites were fearful because they had little or no contact."[100]

Politics and Protest

Before 1865, African Americans, whether enslaved in the South or theoretically free in the North, were not allowed to participate as equals with whites in the political system. Some petitioned white legislatures and officials for redress of their grievances, but most petitions were ignored. The Civil War brought an end to slavery and increased black participation in electoral politics. The Thirteenth Amendment to the Constitution abolished slavery, the Fourteenth Amendment asserted that civil rights of black Americans could not be denied by the states, and the Fifteenth Amendment guaranteed black men (but not women) the right to vote.

From Reconstruction to the 1920s

Following the Civil War, the Reconstruction period came to the South as a breath of fresh air. **Reconstruction** was *the period in U.S. history following the Civil War during which an attempt was made by the federal government to disenfranchise the former slaveholding oligarchy and to improve the economic, educational, political, and human rights conditions of poor whites and blacks in the South.* Federally enforced Reconstruction policies were precipitated by southern elites' unwillingness to make major changes in the discriminatory treatment of freed blacks or to prevent unrepentant leaders of the rebelling Confederacy from resuming political power. A brief period of limited federal military occupation resulted. Reconstruction brought much political progress to black southerners. Black men gained the right to vote. New state constitutional conventions included black delegates, although in most states the majority of delegates were white. Between 1869 and 1901, twenty black men served in the U.S. House and two in the U.S. Senate. Hiram R. Revels and Blanche K. Bruce, from Mississippi, were the first ever to serve in the Senate.[101] Indeed, the fact that *only three* African Americans—Edward Brooke (R–Mass.), Carol Moseley Braun (D–Ill.), and Barack Obama (D–Ill.)—have served in the Senate since Revels and Bruce testifies to the continued pervasiveness of discrimination in U.S. politics.

During Reconstruction the new southern state governments were mostly controlled by whites who had not been wealthy and powerful supporters of the Confederacy, including farmers of modest means. But reactionary forces in the South brought an end to Reconstruction by the late 1870s. Few Americans today know that a major reason for the end of this progressive Reconstruction era was *white terrorism*. Many in the South's white elite, helped by the neglect or collusion of U.S. presidents and many other whites in the North, conducted an extensive terrorist campaign against Reconstruction governments and newly freed black southerners. A leading Confederate general, Nathan Bedford Forrest, was the first Grand Dragon of the newly created Ku Klux Klan, and no less a figure than General Robert E. Lee pledged his "invisible" support to the Klan. The terrorist actions of Klan-type white supremacist groups gradually destroyed the often progressive southern governments, and thousands of men, women, and children were severely beaten, raped, or killed by members of these violent groups. The Confederacy had lost the four-year war, but fought on for "twelve more years—using every weapon at its disposal, including the ultimate one of mass terrorism—until the nation finally acceded to most of the Confederacy's modified war aims."[102] After a few years of this open white terrorism, northern interest in the South waned. Most northern whites were not interested in punishing those white Southerners who had led the southern rebellion; indeed, few Confederate leaders were imprisoned for war-making activities or for participation in the subsequent white terrorism.

Although considerable racial segregation existed during the brief Reconstruction era, that segregation was not nearly as all-encompassing as it would later become. By the early 1900s, enforced racial segregation became the rule in southern and border states. It was legitimated by a U.S. Supreme Court decision. *Plessy* v. *Ferguson* (1896) upheld racial segregation in Louisiana railroad cars and asserted the legality of "separate but equal" facilities for black Americans. The all-white Court reasoned openly that white racist attitudes were natural and that "legislation is powerless to eradicate racial instincts or to abolish distinctions based upon physical differences, and the attempt to do so can only result in accentuating the difficulties of the present situation."[103]

In 1915 the Supreme Court began a slow swing back to the protection of some black civil rights by declaring unconstitutional southern laws' "grandfather clauses" (stipulating that a person could vote only if eligible in a previous year when black southerners could not vote). Black voter registration increased very slowly. By the 1920s, black migration to the cities had brought a few black leaders to the political forefront in the North. Independent political organizations were established in a few cities, but the only major success was that of Adam Clayton Powell, Jr., in New York City. In 1945, Powell, a black Democrat, became a member of Congress. In the North, most black voters supported the Republican Party, but by the 1930s they had begun to shift to the Democratic Party.[104]

The Limits of Black Progress: Political Discrimination

Southern voter registration increased between the 1940s and the 1970s, raising the number of black voters from 250,000 to 4 million. A big jump in registration occurred after the belated passage of the federal Voting Rights Act of 1965. Since their reenfranchisement, black southerners have developed numerous effective political organizations and campaigns. In 1965 there were approximately seventy black elected officials in the South. Three years later, the figure had climbed to 248. More than three decades later, in 2001, the number was 9101 for all states. About one-third were women. Still, black officials remained less than 2 percent of all U.S. elected officials. In 2007 there were only thirty-seven black voting members of the U.S. House, and there was only one in the U.S. Senate. The increase in elected officials that began in the late 1960s was linked to the 1965 Voting Rights Act, "perhaps the single most successful civil rights bill ever passed."[105]

Over the past few decades, black voters have continued to face attempts to reduce the efficacy of their political participation. Researchers such as Chandler Davidson and a recent report by the National Commission on the Voting Rights Act have demonstrated that *serious* electoral discrimination persists in the twenty-first century in such forms as vote dilution, gerrymandering, changing elective offices into appointive ones, majority runoff requirements, annexing of white residential areas, and unnecessary revisions in qualifications for office. A major example of vote dilution is the at-large electoral system, whereby candidates are elected citywide rather than from smaller districts. In numerous cities this system has sharply reduced the participation of candidates and voters of color in local political campaigns. As long as black voters constitute well under half of the voters in a city, black candidates are unlikely to win elected office in an at-large system because many whites will rarely or never vote for a black candidate. Responding to conservative white supporters in the 1980s, the Reagan administration tried to weaken the Voting Rights Act. In 1982, after a long battle, civil rights forces persuaded Congress to pass a twenty-five-year extension of key provisions. Between 1982 and 2006 the number of Department of Justice objections to local or state electoral changes, the frequent withdrawal of requests for changes, and the imposition of thousands of federal observers of local elections all indicated the continuing reality of racial discrimination in U.S. voting practices. In 2006 the nonpermanent features of the Voting Rights Act were again extended for twenty-five years, actions strongly supported by black and Latino civil rights organizations.[106]

African American voters also face discrimination in the form of purges of voter registration rolls, unannounced changes in polling places, intentionally difficult registration procedures, and threats of retaliation. These practices have been documented from Florida to Texas.[107] Indeed, the 2000 and 2004 elections in which George W. Bush was elected president were marked by continuing local and state discrimination against black voters, more than 90 percent of whom voted for the Democratic candidate. Protests from civil rights groups focused national attention on this discrimination in states such as Florida, Ohio, and Illinois. Black voters had sometimes been harassed by the police and turned away by poll officials, who claimed, erroneously, that they were not on the voter registration lists. Some black polling places were moved suddenly.[108] The persistence of these and other discriminatory practices has renewed debates over governmental remedies. Since the early 1980s, voting rights issues have been at the center of debates about democracy in the United States. A number of legal scholars have pointed out that, while the enforcement of the Voting Rights Act has helped to increase the number of black-majority voting districts and elected officials, it has not reshaped local and state legislative bodies to give black officials a proportionate influence on their everyday operations.

Legal scholar Lani Guinier has suggested remedies that might increase black influence on government bodies, one of which is *cumulative voting*, a procedure in which each voter is given a number of votes equal to the number of positions to be filled in a legislative body. If ten members of a commission are to be elected, each voter has ten votes and may use them to vote for one candidate for each of the positions or may cast all ten votes for one candidate. Cumulative voting is currently used in selecting corporate boards of directors. Guinier argues that this strategy would increase the probability that a black candidate would be elected in an area in which the majority of voters are white. Some cities, such as Alamogordo, New Mexico, and Peoria, Illinois, have already experimented with this procedure. Other mechanisms, such as the requirement of legislative "supermajorities" to pass most laws, might be considered if cumulative voting and traditional strategies do not generate significant black political power.[109]

Some analysts argue that increased black votes and more black elected officials accomplish much for black voters, while others feel that black citizens are unlikely to gain much through an electoral process that is still mostly controlled by whites. Thus, in most jurisdictions, black elected officials have been unable to dramatically reorder local priorities in employment, housing, and education. However, they have sometimes been able to bring some expansion of capital-based services to local black residential areas. In Florida, though, James Button found that black elected officials were often more effective in changing employment opportunities for their constituents than in improving these capital-based services. Many black officials have had a positive influence on voter turnout. They have become a "direct and effective conduit for political input from black citizens," and the legitimacy of holding elected office has given them "influence and power in the public realm that other black leaders and organizations [have] rarely had."[110]

African Americans have won mayoral elections in a number of major cities with large black populations—including Philadelphia, Detroit, New York City, and Los Angeles—and also in a few predominantly white cities, such as Seattle and Kansas City. In 1990 the state of Virginia elected L. Douglas Wilder, the grandson of a slave, as the first black governor of any state.[111]

The Federal Government

The New Deal era (1933–1940) was the first period since Reconstruction in which the federal government gave serious attention to the needs of its black citizens. President Franklin Roosevelt appointed more than one hundred African Americans to important government positions. New Deal programs helped black Americans survive the Great Depression, even though most economic recovery agencies discriminated substantially in favor of white citizens.[112]

Between 1901 and 1929, Congress had *no* black members, and from 1929 until 1945, only one. In 1945, Adam Clayton Powell, Jr. (New York) joined William Dawson (Illinois) in the House, and ten years later Charles Diggs was elected from Michigan. By 1992, in part thanks to the registration of new black voters after the 1960s civil rights revolution, there were twenty-six black members, including four women, in the U.S. House. The redrawing of election districts following the 1990 census to bring states into compliance with the 1982 amendments to the Voting Rights Act increased the number of black-majority congressional voting districts. By the late 1990s, there were thirty-nine black representatives, including eleven women, in the U.S. House and one black woman (the first ever), Carol Moseley Braun of Illinois, in the Senate. However, Moseley was defeated in her bid for a second term.[113]

The first black person ever to serve in a presidential cabinet was Robert Weaver, appointed Secretary of Housing and Urban Development by President Lyndon Johnson in 1967. Johnson also appointed Thurgood Marshall as the first black Supreme Court justice.[114] From the 1970s to the present, the pattern of a few token black appointments in presidential cabinet positions and of one Supreme Court appointment has persisted under both Republican and Democratic presidents. African Americans continue to be significantly underrepresented in federal legislative, executive, and judicial positions.

The black vote has sometimes been very important in federal elections. Black voters played a role in Franklin Roosevelt's fourth election in 1944, and they were important to Harry S Truman's election in 1948.[115] The black vote in a few key states reportedly decided the 1960 presidential election in favor of the Irish Catholic John Kennedy. Black voters also played a role in electing Lyndon Johnson in 1964 and Jimmy Carter in 1976. They voted overwhelmingly for Al Gore in 2000 and helped provide him with a popular vote (but not electoral college) majority. During recent elections, African American voters have continued to help elect white and black (usually Democratic) members of Congress who support civil rights issues, to some extent offsetting the effect of conservative white voters. African American voters have long been centrally important in pressing the nation in the direction of its stated political ideal of "liberty and justice for all."

What are the societal implications of political segregation along racial lines?

The Republican Appeal to White Voters: A Shift from the Past

Black voters have often voted for losing presidential candidates since the late 1960s, largely because of the barely disguised pro-white strategy of many leaders in the Republican Party. This political strategy, used by Richard Nixon in winning the 1968 presidential election, was celebrated in Kevin Phillips's book, *The Emerging Republican Majority*. Phillips suggested that Republicans did not need "urban Negroes" and other "vested interests" to win elections. In recent decades, the Republican Party has moved from the party of Abraham Lincoln, one that advocated expanded civil rights for black Americans, to a party opposed to most aggressive government or private action (including affirmative action) to eliminate discrimination against African Americans and other Americans of color in employment and other institutional areas.[116]

Since 1990, speeches or advertisements by some Republican candidates for election or reelection (for example, Senator Jesse Helms in North Carolina) have included racially charged code words, such as "racial quotas" and "unqualified minorities," in attempts to win white votes. Partially as a result of these racialized appeals to whites, the overwhelming majority of black voters have supported Democratic candidates at local, state, and national levels. Between 1992 and 2006 the Republican Party got only 8 to 12 percent of the black vote in national elections. In recent decades southern states have increasingly been divided between a Republican Party that is overwhelmingly white and a Democratic Party that is multiracial and diverse. Recent Republican conventions have had a relatively small percentage of black delegates, and the Republican National Committee has had tiny numbers of black members. In 2004, for example, there was only one black representative from the fifty U.S. states among the 165 members of the Republican National

Committee. (This compared to the ninety-seven black members on the Democratic National Committee, a substantial proportion of its membership.) Most black Americans in positions in state Republican organizations work in minority outreach, in contrast to the far more numerous black members of state Democratic Party organizations, who are active mostly outside outreach programs. In 2004 *all* black Congress members, and almost all black officeholders at all government levels, were members of the Democratic Party. This highly segregated pattern of political party interests and participation has characterized U.S. politics since the 1960s.[117]

Still, even with this inclination to the Democratic Party, however, black allegiance has not always been enthusiastic—in part because some white Democratic candidates have also used barely disguised antiblack tactics to court white voters.

African American Organization and Protest

Certain fundamental values held by most African Americans have long provided a source of strength to cope with and resist discrimination. Black commitment to civil rights and human liberty is one of the major sources of support for civil liberties today. Over the centuries, black resistance to white-generated discrimination and oppression has ranged from legal strategies and the ballot, to nonviolent civil disobedience, to violent attacks on the racist system.

The goals of protest movements over the past century and more have included desegregation of public accommodations and schools and the opening up of housing and employment reserved for whites. In 1905, in reaction to the pro-white accommodationist position of black leaders such as Booker T. Washington, the path-breaking black sociologist W. E. B. Du Bois together with other black and white leaders formed the Niagara movement to press for legal and voting rights as well for economic changes. Soon, some of these leaders helped to create the still-influential National Association for the Advancement of Colored People (NAACP).

From the 1900s to the 1950s, Du Bois played an important role in the development of pan-African nationalism as a partial solution for oppression faced by people of African descent across the globe. In 1919, working with other black leaders, Du Bois put together the first Pan-African Congress, to which delegates from fifteen countries came. About the same time, cultural nationalism was also strong in the 1920s Harlem Renaissance, a dramatic flowering of literature and the arts that celebrated black perspectives, traditions, and history.

Black organizations directed at self-help and philanthropic activity, such as the Urban League, were created in the early twentieth century. These provided aid for the poor and worked to end legal segregation. Lawsuits were a major strategy. One early NAACP victory was a 1917 Supreme Court decision, *Buchanan* v. *Warley*, that knocked down a Louisville, Kentucky, law requiring residential segregation—one of the first steps in reversing the segregationist position the Court had taken since the late 1800s. Nonetheless, most Supreme Court decisions before the 1930s only reinforced racial segregation in schools, transportation, and the jury system.[118]

Against fierce white resistance, the NAACP began a large-scale attack on legal segregation in schools, voting, transportation, and jury selection. Beginning in the 1930s, NAACP and other civil rights lawyers won a series of cases that over the next several decades expanded legal rights of defendants, eliminated all-white political primaries, protected black voting rights, reduced union discrimination, voided discriminatory housing covenants, and desegregated schools and public accommodations. The Supreme Court's separate-but-equal doctrine in *Plessy* v. *Ferguson* increasingly came under attack. Dramatically reversing its 1896 position, the Supreme Court in *Brown* v. *Board of Education* (1954) finally ruled that "in the field of public education the doctrine of 'separate but equal' has no place."[119]

By the 1940s and 1950s, black communities were generating more antidiscrimination protests. During World War II, a threatened march by black Americans on Washington, D.C., helped pressure President Roosevelt to issue an order officially desegregating wartime employment. After World War II, black leaders organized against the peacetime draft on the basis that black citizens should not have to serve in a racially segregated army. President Truman eventually set up an agency to rid federal employment of official discrimination and a committee to oversee desegregation of the armed forces. The U.S. military became, and probably still is, the most racially desegregated of major U.S. institutions.[120]

The 1950s and 1960s brought another increase in protests. One strategy was the *boycott*, such as that of racially segregated buses in Montgomery, Alabama, in the 1950s, that began when NAACP member Rosa Parks refused a white driver's order to give up her seat on a racially segregated bus to a white person. Her arrest triggered a successful boycott by the black community that brought the young leader, Dr. Martin Luther King, Jr., into national prominence. King became the head of the new Southern Christian Leadership Conference (SCLC). In 1960, a sit-in by students at a whites-only lunch counter in Greensboro, North Carolina, touched off a long series of sit-ins by thousands of black southerners and white allies. "Freedom Rides" on interstate buses came in 1961; blacks and whites tested federal court orders desegregating public transportation.

In 1963, Dr. King, other black leaders, and many black citizens launched demonstrations against discrimination in Birmingham, Alabama. Fire hoses and police dogs used aggressively against peaceful demonstrators, many of whom were children, gained national publicity for the movement. An agreement desegregating businesses and employment ended these protests, but another round of demonstrations was touched off when a black home and motel were bombed. Then came the massive 1963 March on Washington, in which Dr. King dramatized rising aspirations for freedom in his famous "I Have a Dream" speech before thousands of black and nonblack supporters.[121]

Direct action against informal racial segregation in the North began in earnest in the 1960s with boycotts in Harlem, sit-ins in Chicago, school sit-ins in New Jersey, and demonstrations in Cairo, Illinois. The Congress of Racial Equality (CORE) accelerated protests against discrimination in housing and employment. Led by Stokely Carmichael (Kwame Ture), the Student Nonviolent Coordinating Committee (SNCC) helped to germinate a national movement for desegregation and real "black power" and for representative participation in all societal institutions. The growing number of organizations oriented toward black nationalism and self-help included the Black Panthers, a group of young men and women who started breakfast programs for children and engaged in surveillance of white police officers to try to reduce police brutality against black urbanites. The Nation of Islam was expanding in membership and established black-controlled social programs and businesses. Outspoken commitment

Dr. Martin Luther King, Jr., gives his "I Have a Dream" speech at a large civil rights demonstration in Washington, D.C., in 1963.

to protest and to reducing racial segregation was growing in most black communities in the North.[122]

Some white commentators on the nonviolent civil rights era have suggested that Dr. King's strong image was largely a media creation and that the civil rights movement was primarily middle-class. Neither is true. Many local demonstrations included large-scale participation by African Americans from *all* economic backgrounds. Research on black movements has demonstrated that most were grounded in organized activism, which was rooted in what Aldon Morris has called "a well-developed indigenous base."[123] This broad base included community churches, clubs, and other voluntary organizations that provided money and mobilized people, thus enabling more visible activists in organizations such as the SCLC and SNCC to successfully fight discrimination and segregation across the country.

Progress and Retreat

The 1960s civil rights movement played an important role in pressuring Congress to pass major legislation prohibiting discrimination in employment, voting, and housing—the Voting Rights Act of 1965 and the Civil Rights Acts of 1964 and 1968. However, as noted previously, many of these advances have been undercut since the 1980s by conservative presidential administrations. From 1981 to 1993, for example, government civil rights agencies reduced important enforcement activities, such as compliance reviews of government contractors and class-action suits against discriminatory employers. The 1980s Reagan administration even tried to cut back the Voting Rights Act.[124] The George H. W. Bush administration (1989–1993) continued the negative approach to African Americans, who responded by pressing their fight to improve civil rights enforcement. The arrival of Bill Clinton in the White House in 1993 brought some hope for better civil rights enforcement. Clinton did appoint more black Americans to important government positions, including judgeships, than his predecessors, and his administration put greater emphasis on civil rights enforcement. For example, class-action suits brought on behalf of black individuals who reported discrimination at Denny's restaurants were resolved by a consent decree in which the company agreed to pay $46 million in damages. This more aggressive Department of Justice involvement in antidiscrimination lawsuits was a clear break from the policies of previous administrations.[125]

The national elections in 2000 and 2004 brought another conservative president, George W. Bush, to power. His conservative political appointments brought further backtracking on civil rights enforcement in many areas. A draft report by the experienced staff of the U.S. Commission on Civil Rights summarized Bush's first years in office as a "retreat" from the antidiscrimination legacy of the past:

> President Bush seldom speaks about civil rights, and when he does, it is to carry out official duties, not to promote initiatives or plans for improving opportunity... the administration's words and deeds often conflict.... In his first three years in office, the net increase in President Bush's requests for civil rights enforcement agencies was less than those of the previous two administrations. After accounting for inflation, the President's requests for the six major civil rights programs...amount to a loss of spending power for 2004 and 2005.... While judicial and legislative achievements of the 1960s and 1970s largely broke down the system of segregation and legal bases for discrimination, the effects persist and hamper equal opportunity in education, employment, housing, public accommodations, and the ability to vote. President Bush has implemented policies that have retreated from long-established civil rights promises in each of these areas."[126]

Later reports by civil rights groups concluded that the Bush administration's antidiscrimination efforts continued to be weak or backtracking. This could be seen in the administration's appointment of several very conservative members to the Commission in 2004. The new Commission deleted staff reports, such as *Redefining Civil Rights*, which were critical of the Bush administration, from its official website.

The periodic dominance of conservative political officials unconcerned with civil rights since the 1980s has generated bursts of new organizational activity in support of civil rights enforcement and expansion of equal opportunity. Numerous civil rights groups have continued to protest on behalf of expanded opportunities for African Americans and other Americans of color. Washington, D.C., and other cities have seen important demonstrations against discrimination and the weakening of civil rights enforcement. Since the late 1980s black leaders have held a State of the Black America overview conference annually. In 2006 a document, "The Covenant with Black America," was presented to nearly eight thousand attendees at the seventh conference in Houston, a book-length statement of strong recommendations to policy-makers that would improve the lives of African Americans. In addition to suggesting action options for African Americans with regard to issues such as renewal of voting rights legislation and boycotting discriminatory companies, these conferences have generated renewed interest in an array of political campaigns accenting issues of concern to black communities. From time to time, the NAACP Legal Defense Fund, the Leadership Conference on Civil Rights, and other civil rights organizations have mounted enough pressure to stop top white government officials from achieving racialized political goals, such as appointing whites who are not supportive of civil rights advances to federal judgeships.[127]

Even with its ups and downs, the black-led civil rights movement has contributed greatly to the expansion of civil rights for all Americans, especially since the 1960s. Black men and black women have always been central to this centuries-old movement for liberty and justice for all. Researchers such as Patricia Hill Collins have demonstrated that black women were an integral part of the civil rights movement of the 1960s, even though leadership roles were generally reserved for men. In recent decades black women have moved into important positions in civil rights and political groups and have pressed for increased attention to the joint effect of sexism and racism on women of color.[128]

Education

During the Reconstruction period after the Civil War, black southerners gained their first access to schools, both those sponsored by the federal government and by private organizations. However, by 1900, public schools in southern and border states were legally segregated under "separate but equal" laws, and educational facilities for black students were grossly inferior. In 1900 some southern counties spent *ten times* as much per capita for the education of white children as for black children.[129]

African American author and teacher Toni Morrison is a Nobel Prize winner.

Despite relentless discrimination and segregation by whites, blacks pressed on toward their dream of good educations for all. By the early 1900s, a million-and-a-half black children were enrolled in schools. The South had thirty-four predominantly black colleges. Influenced by Booker T. Washington, who advocated vocational education, black college curricula typically focused on skills suitable for an agricultural economy, which at that time was declining. Other leaders, such as W. E. B. Du Bois, felt that Washington was too deferential to white views, and advocated instead a full range of educational opportunities for black youth.[130]

African Americans have long taken advantage of educational opportunities wherever these become available. In 1940 more than half of black adults over the age of twenty-four had less than a sixth-grade education. Fewer than 8 percent were high school graduates (versus 26 percent of whites). Forty years later, the proportion of black adults (aged twenty-five and older) with high school diplomas had risen above 50 percent; and by the early 2000s nearly three-quarters were high school graduates and 14 percent had completed four years of college or more (compared with 80 percent and 24 percent, respectively, of the total population). Although educational opportunities and attainments for blacks today are still not equal, the educational attainment gap has narrowed much more than the large economic gap between white and black Americans.[131]

The Struggle for Desegregation

Movement toward school desegregation began in earnest in the 1930s with a savvy, long-term NAACP legal strategy. Lawsuits attacking discrimination in graduate schools were the first to expose the "separate-but-equal" doctrine for a sham. In the 1930s and 1940s federal court decisions thus forced the racial desegregation of law schools and other graduate programs at major universities. Then, in 1954, brave black parents won the famous school decision, *Brown* v. *Board of Education of Topeka*. This decision forced the desegregation of schools in Topeka, Kansas, and a few other school systems and set in motion government action to officially desegregate all school systems. This government action met massive resistance. White judges, often fearing violent reactions by whites, generally allowed school desegregation to proceed at a snail's pace during the decade after *Brown*. Most white-dominated school systems circumvented *Brown* as long as they could, and most black children remained overt targets of racial discrimination. Increasingly, whites set up private schools and/or resorted to open defiance and violence. In 1956, President Dwight Eisenhower was forced to federalize the Arkansas National Guard to protect black children braving violent white mobs to desegregate a high school in Little Rock.[132]

The 1960s and early 1970s finally brought widespread desegregation throughout the South and some court orders to desegregate certain northern school systems. In *Swann* v. *Charlotte-Mecklenburg Board of Education* (1971), one of a series of court cases following *Brown* that expanded the attack on racially segregated schooling, the Supreme Court upheld the use of busing as a means of disestablishing a dual school system. However, by 1974 a more conservative Court began to back off from comprehensive desegregation in a ruling that rejected inclusion of suburban districts in central-city desegregation plans. In *Milliken* v. *Bradley* (1974) the Court overturned a lower-court order requiring the integration of the substantially black Detroit school system with surrounding predominantly white suburban school systems. In one incremental step after another, between *Milliken* and the present, the Supreme Court and numerous other federal courts have retreated. In the major 1990s' cases of *Board of Education of Oklahoma* v. *Dowell* (1991) and *Freeman* v. *Pitts* (1992), the Court permitted informal resegregation of schools where there was no longer official segregation. Since the 1980s, majority white perspectives and interests have taken precedence over a national interest in a fully desegregated society.[133]

The Current Situation in Public Schools

Since the 1960s, the racial desegregation of public schools, when done reasonably well, has had positive effects on the academic achievement of African American children and other children of color who attend majority-white schools, when that is compared with achievement in schools that have a majority of children of color. A Charlotte, North Carolina, area study of 1800 children found that black and white children did better in terms of test scores and track placements in substantially desegregated schools than in more segregated schools. The reasons are mainly the better resources available, which children and parents of color eagerly seek out when school desegregation makes them available. Not surprisingly in this still discriminatory society, predominantly white schools generally get much more economic and human resources, such as good media and internet centers, newer and more computers, newer buildings, and more classes for advanced students. When schools are racially desegregated, white officials tend to spend more money on them. When public schools resegregate, as they now are doing, the opposite usually happens. In addition, children of color from desegregated schools usually have much better access to good job and information networks. Research shows too that they are also more likely than similar students from segregated schools to attend desegregated colleges, work in desegregated settings, and acquire friends from other racial groups.[134]

However, most black children, who remain in schools composed predominantly of children of color, have not gotten access to first-rate educational opportunities and resources. They never have gotten the level of socioeconomic resources invested in their educations that typical white children have received. In spite of *Brown*, the promise of integration has never been delivered. There has not been one year in this country's history when *even half* of black children were in integrated schools where a majority of children were white. Judge Robert Carter, an NAACP lawyer in *Brown*, has condemned the country's "dismal progress" toward educational equality: "Thus far, for most black children the constitutional guarantee of equal education opportunity which *Brown* held was secured to them has been an arid abstraction, having no effect whatsoever on the bleak offerings black children are given in the deteriorating schools they attend."[135]

Although polls show that the overwhelming majority of Americans support equal educational opportunities, since the 1990s resegregation has taken place in many school systems. Recent research drawing on government data indicates that segregation of black from white children in city schools remains very high. This segregation has increased even as urban residential segregation has decreased a little in recent years. Indeed, in larger cities there are relatively few white children left in most public schools.[136] According to Harvard's Civil Rights Project, the proportion of black students in majority-white schools *decreased* from 1988 to the present. In the 2003–2004 school year, most *(73 percent)* black students attended predominantly segregated (more than 50 percent children of color) schools, and some 38 percent attended intensely segregated (90 percent or more children of color) schools. This represents significant resegregation compared with the low point of school segregation, in 1980, when 63 percent were in predominantly segregated schools and 33 percent were in intensely segregated schools. In addition, predominantly black schools have a much higher concentration of poverty than do predominantly white schools.[137]

School resegregation is in part the result of the policies of Republican presidential administrations that have opposed mandatory desegregation and supported voluntary desegregation or segregated neighborhood schools. Recent administrations have cut back efforts to desegregate schools and instead supported charter schools or tax deductions for private-school tuition. Local authorities have mostly supported these policies. In some districts, school-choice policies have had an overwhelming effect on racial diversity. Thus, a middle school in Winston-Salem, North Carolina, went from two-thirds white to 97 percent black over one summer after school choice was offered to parents. Indeed, today our U.S. educational system offers considerable choice for parents in the form of magnet schools, charter schools, home schooling, and private schools, yet such "choice" has not reduced racial segregation and inequality in the United States.[138]

School desegregation often increases housing desegregation. Cities with metropolitan-area school desegregation plans have experienced more rapid housing desegregation than cities without such plans. The extent of housing desegregation in cities of similar size and racial mix is related directly to the scope of their school desegregation programs. Cities with school desegregation plans that cover only the central cities have had less housing desegregation than cities that desegregated schools in both central cities and suburbs.[139]

Racial tracking and other forms of institutionalized, internal discrimination also persist in public school systems. A report by the community organization ACORN on New York City schools found widespread discrimination in the treatment of parents and children. Trained testers, posing as parents, were sent to twenty-eight elementary schools in half the city's community school districts. White parent-testers were able to speak with an educator, such as the principal, much more often than black and Latino parent-testers. Whites were two-and-one-half times more likely to get a school tour and, on average, whites were given much more information. The report describes these actions as "institutional racism" that is likely rooted in conscious prejudices, malign neglect by officials, and the "dysfunction that results when a vital public responsibility is managed by people whose racial, class, and cultural reality is totally different from that of the people whom they are supposed to serve."[140]

Black students are often placed in school tracks lower than their measured abilities indicate. Students in higher tracks typically get more attention and better resources. Those put in privileged tracks in early grades tend to perform better in later schooling, and thus over time "racially stratified tracks create a discriminatory cycle of restricted educational opportunities." Eliminating or reducing ability tracking has had beneficial effects, as sociologist Roslyn Michelson has recently summarized: "When schools consistently employ practices to enhance equality of opportunity (including the elimination of tracking and ability grouping), desegregation brings clear, though modest academic benefits to black students and does no harm to whites."[141]

In her Charlotte-Mecklenburg study, Mickelson found that breaking down tracking often benefits white students, for such heterogeneous schooling helps to counter traditional racial stereotyping.

In the 2000s, St. Louis is one of the few major cities with a long-standing school desegregation plan bringing together inner-city children of color with children in mostly white suburbs. By the desegregation plan's eleventh year, black students made up at least 15 percent of the student population in most suburban school districts. Drawing on interviews with three hundred educators, parents, students, and lawyers, an evaluation study of the impact of desegregation reported that many black students had achieved academic, and sometimes social, success in integrated suburban schools. Most black children struggled "endlessly to maintain their self-esteem and to carry their cultural heritage with them to the other side of the color line so that whites might partake of it and eventually learn to value it."[142] Each year about one in ten of the black students who transferred to white schools found the social demands of white suburbia too great or the hostile attitudes of white teachers too intolerable and returned to their central-city schools.

However, the majority of children of color have not yet benefitted from this program. Today, the St. Louis (central city) school system—composed of 81 percent black students, 15 percent white students, and 4 percent other students of color—is facing recurring financial crises and includes a very large percentage of children from economically disadvantaged families. That central-city school system, like many others, is struggling to meet the needs of these poor children and continues to have a high dropout rate and low high school graduation rate. Recent government remedial programs, such as those generated by the George W. Bush administration's No Child Left Behind Act, have mostly documented the continuing racial inequality in resources between predominantly white schools and those with mostly children of color (and often punished weakly performing schools), yet have yet to provide the large-scale funding necessary to bring weakly performing schools up to the level of providing equal opportunities.[143]

As in the past, black parents today often face a major dilemma. What significantly desegregated school settings still exist, while holding out promise of better educational resources, often remain hostile or unsupportive places for black children. White hostility in desegregated schools can have significant negative effects on black children. Thus, since 1980 many local black leaders have shifted their emphasis away from comprehensive school desegregation plans to other educational objectives. Many educators have become more concerned with the survival of black children, especially black males, than with desegregation, which is in any case declining. Thus, educators in some cities with substantially black school enrollments, such as Atlanta and Washington, have developed a curriculum with more emphasis on the cultural heritage of African American children. In numerous cities, black educators have also created special schools, or programs within public schools, for poor black males. This survival strategy attempts to support black children and black community institutions in the face of continuing antiblack discrimination and little government action against that discrimination. However, this understandable strategy has significant limits, especially with regard to the majority of black children who still must attend regular public schools. Separate-but-equal policies for schools do not generally work because, for the most part, those children and parents with poor school opportunities are in communities with little political clout over the mostly white politicians who control the government money necessary to creating truly equal school opportunities. Without that clout, getting white government officials to provide government resources that facilitate concentrated-poverty schools becoming equal to middle-class schools is highly unlikely. Black American children do not need white children in order to thrive educationally, but in this still-racist society they will ordinarily get the full array of educational resources they need only if they are in school with children whose parents have this substantial economic and political clout.[144]

Growing research indicates that whites also pay a significant price for continuing school and housing segregation. Gary Orfield, a leading school researcher, notes that most whites who grow up in relatively segregated suburban enclaves have "no skills in relating to or communicating with minorities."[145] As the country becomes more diverse, this lack of skills will become even more of a disadvantage in social and political interaction, and in getting jobs with globally focused companies and government agencies. Such white isolation will be a major handicap as the country becomes more involved in international trade and diplomacy in a world in which non-European nations are ever more powerful.

College Attendance and College Experiences

In one opinion survey, 96 percent of black youths aged eleven to seventeen stated that their biggest hope for their future was to go to college. Yet, in 2000, only 56 percent of black students entered college immediately after high school graduation, compared with 66 percent of their white counterparts.[146] In 2005 the proportion of African Americans between the ages of twenty-five and twenty-nine who were college graduates (17.1 percent) was a little less than half that of whites in this age group (35 percent).[147]

Until the 1960s, black college students in southern and border states were generally restricted by law to all-black colleges. The 1960s desegregation movements and laws opened many historically white colleges and universities for black students, including many in the North that had been informally segregated. By the 1970s, three-fourths of black college students nationwide were in predominantly white schools. Still, many black students today attend historically black colleges, where the campus culture is more hospitable to black students than that of traditionally white schools and where they are more likely to graduate and go on to graduate schools.[148]

Today, black students face serious problems of discrimination at predominantly white colleges and universities. "Frequently black students find white universities to be hostile places where they are seen as 'special admits' and beneficiaries of affirmative action. Moreover, adjustment requires adherence to white cultural norms, thereby necessitating the abandonment of black cultural roots."[149] African American students often establish their own networks, in part because of exclusion from white networks. Research conducted by the first author at a major historically white university found many racial barriers. A questionnaire given to three dozen black juniors and seniors asked them to assess this statement: "Today the [State University] is a college campus where black students are generally welcomed and nurtured." Most (89 percent) disagreed with this statement. One female student stated the following:

> This university does cater to white students. The commercial strip near the university is for white people. You know, bars everywhere—all white boys in it, no black people. The frat row's white. No black Greeks, nothing. So they're coming from where they're coming from.... Sometimes I'm like, "God, if I was white, I'd have the best time."... They get to have parties at frat houses; they don't have to pay for it. You know, they just have the best time. Everything is geared toward them. Their [campus] paper is geared toward them.[150]

A tragic aspect of the barriers at predominantly white colleges is that African American students often identify these colleges not primarily with educational experiences to be savored but rather with an "agonizing struggle" with campus racism just to get a college degree.

Religion and Culture

One of the first major stereotypes of Africans and indigenous people in the Americas involved what Europeans saw as "savagery." The irony of slave-trading, warring Europeans seeing Africans as "savage" was lost on Europeans at the time and has been lost on most of their descendants. The enslaved Africans brought sophisticated African religions and music. At first, slave owners feared that "Christianizing" African Americans would give them ideas of freedom—as though they did not already have those ideas. Protestant missionaries were specifically instructed to tell their converts that conversion to Christianity did not bring freedom. Later, white slave owners actively encouraged missionaries, such as Baptists and Methodists, to convert those enslaved so that they could be better controlled.[151]

Over time, African American religion mixed various African and European elements, and African perspectives often prevailed. Afro-Christianity often developed a strong element of protest. The view of God that many held—for example, the emphasis on God's having led the Israelites out of slavery—was not what slaveholders had hoped for. Hidden in Christian symbolism, the text of slave spirituals sometimes embodied a strong yearning to be free. Regular religious meetings sometimes provided opportunities to plan open revolts. Those enslaved were permitted to preach, and some preachers became important resistance leaders. The freedom discourse that African Americans developed in private was different from the discourse used in the presence of oppressive slavemasters.[152]

Because African Americans, enslaved or free, were excluded from full participation in white churches, they developed their own churches. In Philadelphia, Absalom Jones and Richard Allen, after being mistreated at a white Methodist church, established the Free African Society in 1787. Later, Jones established the first Negro Episcopal church, and Allen played a role in the emergence of the influential African Methodist Episcopal church.[153]

Black churches became very important after the Civil War as mutual-aid societies, which ministered to those facing sickness and death. They functioned as centers for pooling economic and other resources. Many new schools established after the Civil War were under religious auspices. Later, with migration to cities after World War I, many African Americans shifted to a less otherworldly style in numerous religious organizations. Urban social programs and civil rights activity increasingly became part of church life. Urban churches became both religious and political forces. One important urban group is the Nation of Islam, a group that broke with the black Christian heritage. Nation of Islam leaders have pressed for a religious approach suffused with black pride and a strong self-help philosophy. Afrocentric leaders have arisen from this movement, including Malcolm X.[154]

Today, African Americans mostly attend Protestant churches. They belong to a great diversity of groups, from older Methodist and Baptist denominations to newer evangelical groups. Whatever its form, however, the black church is often, as one minister has explained, "the hub of existence in the black community," a "holistic ministry," and a "social center."[155]

Organizations protesting oppressive conditions have long been rooted in African American religion. Religious gatherings and leaders have played a significant role in spreading protests against racial oppression for centuries. Since the 1800s, black ministers have often been political and protest leaders. The nonviolent civil disobedience movement that took place from the 1950s to the 1970s had religious underpinnings. The prominent minister Dr. Martin Luther King, Jr., raised in a religious family known for its support of civil rights, came naturally to his religious view of the legitimacy of nonviolent protest as a way to win concessions while at the same time healing the wounds of oppressed and oppressor. King led black and white citizens in effective civil rights protests, for which he earned a Nobel Peace Prize, and he died a hero whose example today inspires Americans of all backgrounds.[156]

The effectiveness of churches in providing leadership, and in mobilizing millions of formerly disenfranchised people in the civil rights movement, is rooted in African American culture. The call-and-response format of many religious services, which allows the congregation to give the minister feedback on the sermon, has provided a supportive context for response to calls to register to vote and participate in other political activities by black religious and political leaders. Political and protest leaders have harnessed the religious sentiments of an oppressed people to mobilize action against racial discrimination. In addition, African American music and singing have frequently reflected a strong element of protest against prejudice and discrimination–from the days of the spirituals to more recent blues, jazz, gospel, and hip-hop traditions.[157]

Recent Immigrants from Africa and the Caribbean

In the mid-1990s and again in the 2000s, Colin Powell, a retired U.S. Army general and son of Jamaican immigrants, has been mentioned as a possible Republican vice presidential or presidential candidate. For a time, General Powell, formerly head of the Joint Chiefs of Staff, was called by some, "the most respected figure in American political life."[158] In 2001 he became the first African American to serve as U.S. secretary of state. Powell is a representative of one of several ethnic groups that today make up the broad group called African Americans.

Among the 28.4 million foreign-born Americans in 2000, just 2.2 million were black. Approximately 6 percent of the black population today is made up of immigrants, mostly from Africa and the Caribbean, and mostly having arrived since 1970.[159] The most recent (2000) census data reveal about 613,000 African-born individuals among black Americans, with most having arrived since 1980 and many fleeing political problems in home countries or seeking greater economic opportunities. Large concentrations live in Washington, D.C., and New York. This is a highly educated population, with a higher median family income, lower unemployment rate, and lower poverty rate than native-born African

Sen. Barack Obama, D-Ill., answers a question during a Democratic presidential primary debate before the 2008 election.

Americans. Nonetheless, despite substantial achievements, they are still less well off economically than whites.[160]

The 2000 census data indicate about 1.5 million black Americans of Caribbean ancestry. Many have immigrated since 1980, and a majority live in New York or Florida. Taken as a whole, these Caribbean Americans also have an educational level somewhat higher and a median family income substantially higher than that for multigeneration, native-born African Americans, with significantly lower unemployment and poverty rates as well.[161] Like recent African immigrants, these Caribbean immigrants have often immigrated to the United States with substantial educational or economic capital; they generally represent the better-off residents of their sending countries. Caribbean Americans include numerous national-origin groups, including Martinicans, Guadeloupeans, Dominicans, Haitians, Trinidadians, and Jamaicans. The members of each usually do not identify as "Caribbean Americans," but rather expect their national-origin identities to be respected. They sometimes view themselves as African Americans and sometimes as an ethnic group distinctive from others in the general black group. Nonetheless, Afro-Caribbean Americans have no choice about the "black" designation assigned to them by the dominant white group, most of whom see only their "blackness."[162]

In recent decades, Haitian immigrants have received more public attention than other Caribbean newcomers. Since the 1970s, thousands of Haitians have sought political refuge in the United States. Those fleeing a brutal dictatorship were permitted to enter the United States until 1981. In contrast to Cuban refugees who fled political persecution, and who have generally qualified for permanent residence and been provided with much support from the U.S. government, Haitians have received no significant financial support from the U.S. government and have generally been left to cope on their own. Between 1981 and mid-1994, most Haitians were refused entry; the U.S. Coast Guard intercepted immigrants and returned them to Haiti, where they often faced persecution. This U.S. policy drew criticism from human rights organizations. Amnesty International described Haitian prisons as death traps. Beginning in 1981, those reaching the United States were held at U.S. detention centers.[163]

The ouster in 1991 of Haiti's democratically elected president by military leaders created another flight of Haitians. To stop attempts to immigrate, the U.S. government repatriated five hundred immigrants in 1991. In 1994, President Bill Clinton announced that the U.S. government would no longer send Haitian refugees home without a hearing.[164] Following the UN- and U.S.-supported overthrow of Haiti's military government in 1994, large numbers of the Haitian refugees opted to return home. Soon, however, the new government itself was overthrown and Haitians again tried to immigrate to other countries, including the United States, where they still faced detention and deportation in the mid-2000s. One of the ironic aspects of the troubled situation of Haiti today is that Haiti is the only country in the modern era whose enslaved African-origin population rose up and overthrew their colonial (French) slavemasters; in the late eighteenth century Haitians set up a new country led by their talented military leader, Toussaint L'Ouverture, an independent country that frightened slaveholders such as the new U.S. President Thomas Jefferson.[165]

Economics and Education

Caribbean Americans are generally better off economically than other African Americans, although their situation is closer to that of other African Americans than to that of white Americans. Immigrants are often willing to take lower-wage jobs than native-born Americans. A study of native-born and immigrant black workers at a New York City worksite found that white managers preferred immigrants over native-born black workers for food-service jobs because the former were thought to be "more flexible" and "loyal." In areas such as New York, whites have often singled out West Indian immigrants as a type of "model minority," as "better" than native-born African Americans who are negatively stereotyped as lazy and criminal. This sometimes results in West Indian immigrants getting somewhat less discriminatory treatment from whites. Still, West Indians, particularly second and later generations, do indeed face substantial racial discrimination.[166]

Racial History and Racial Discrimination

The relatively recent Caribbean and African immigrants have had a different racial history than African Americans whose ancestors came to North America generations back and in chains. In most cases neither they nor their recent ancestors have experienced legal segregation in the United States. Most come from countries in which black people are the majority and have a significant role in major institutions, including politics, education, and the economy. In numerous Caribbean nations, many if not most police officers, government officials, and white-collar workers are of African ancestry. Most immigrants have not grown up under recent white domination but only experience it when they immigrate to the United States.

Because they have lived in a society that is not controlled by whites, Caribbean Americans often question the U.S. system of racial categorization. Thus, a common Haitian perspective is illustrated by a humorous story about one Haitian official's reply to a journalist who asked him what percentage of the Haitian population was white:

> "Ninety-eight percent." The startled American journalist was sure he had either misheard or been misunderstood, and put his question again. Duvalier assured him that he had heard and understood the question perfectly well, and had given the correct answer. Struggling to make sense of this incredible piece of information, the American finally asked Duvalier: "How do you define white?" Duvalier answered the question with a question: "How do you define black in your country?" Receiving the explanation that in the United States anyone with any black blood was considered black, Duvalier nodded and said, "Well, that's the way we define white in my country."[167]

African Americans who have grown up in the United States are constantly dealing with discrimination at the hands of whites and are routinely reminded of the significance of their African origin. In contrast, in the Caribbean immigrants' home countries, racial identity typically has much less significance. When most of the population is black, it is common for a person not to be constantly conscious of racial identity.[168]

Haitian American sociologist Yanick St. Jean has noted that many Caribbean immigrants continue to see themselves as culturally different, as "foreigners" in the United States regardless of their length of residence. For that reason they feel, usually erroneously, that white Americans are more likely to accept them than they are to accept other African Americans and that racial discrimination is directed mainly at other blacks and only indirectly at them. Indeed, Waters' interviews with Caribbean American workers revealed that many shared some white stereotypes of African Americans (that is, some of the white racial frame).[169]

Although they have a strong black or African identity, Caribbean and African immigrants sometimes distance their identity from that of other African Americans. One reason is that there has been friction between these immigrants and native-born African Americans, many of whom expect immigrants to reject their island identities and heroes and to speak without a foreign accent. St. Jean has noted that for many Caribbean and African immigrants, "the level of resistance to assimilation into African American groups is extremely high. As one social scientist correctly said: 'They want to be black; they are proud of being black; they just don't want to be black in the United States.'... The notion of blackness in this country is so different from their own. In the Caribbean, blackness is strength. In the United States it is not. Assimilating means moving from a positive image to a less than positive one."[170]

Initially, many Caribbean immigrants think that native-born African Americans exaggerate the discrimination they face. After they have lived for a substantial time in the United States, however, they usually change this view because they too experience exclusion and other forms of antiblack discrimination. When asked in an interview by the first author, "How do you personally feel being black in a mostly white society?" one Caribbean American professional, Mark R. (a pseudonym) stated the following:

> I usually interact with American whites from a distance. Most are acquaintances, not friends. Co-workers do not know who I am, what I really want. I am not invited to their informal gatherings. Occasional exchanges in hallways are only superficial. I feel I am expected to live in an intellectual ghetto, a very special and preset place which I call "colonization of thinking." From all appearances, I am expected to fail. I am denied even the basic respect due to me as a human being.... Some things I would never admit to. They are just too demeaning.
>
> I feel my differences are neither acknowledged nor respected. I am a Haitian American. I cannot and will not discard my Haitian origins. But in this society everyone must move in the same direction. It simplifies. It unifies. And to the extent that it also inferiorizes, the denial is a perfect tool to keep "others," and blacks in particular, within the boundaries of American cultural definitions. If and when my differences are acknowledged, AIDS, poverty, and religion are quick to surface as if these were synonymous with Haitian.

Why do many U.S. whites associate AIDS and so-called "voodoo" religion with Haitian immigrants? Many Americans have erroneously believed that AIDS originated in Haiti or that Haitians have extremely high rates of AIDS. In 1990, acceptance of this stereotype led officials in the U.S. Food and Drug Administration to ban blood donations by Haitians, an action that provoked civil rights protests. The evidence contradicted the notion that Haitians then had a uniquely high AIDS rate. San Francisco's rate of new AIDS cases was then about *ten times* that of Haiti, and other U.S. cities also had rates significantly higher than Haiti's. Yet, people in these cities were not generally banned from donating blood. Stereotypes of and discrimination against Haitian Americans are often rooted in racial images of "savage and exotic" African peoples.[171] Many whites also devalue the cultures of other Caribbean Americans and hold racial stereotypes against people with any African background. Note, for example, common white (and thus media) images of African-origin "voodoo" religion. Even this term is a white creation. The accurate term is "vodou" or "vodun." White images of this and other traditional African religions are replete with racist stereotypes.

What historical and societal pressures have led to the recent migration of people from Africa and the Caribbean?

Assimilation for African Americans?

Assimilation Theories

Assimilation theorists such as Milton Gordon and Nathan Glazer have argued that the mainstream theory of assimilation is applicable to all ethnic and racial groups. Gordon has applied his scheme to black Americans, whom he viewed as substantially assimilated at the cultural level (for example, to English and Protestant religion), with some cultural differences remaining because of a so-called lower-class subculture. Beyond acculturation, however, Gordon (writing in the mid-1960s) noted little integration of black Americans into what he viewed as the "core" (white Anglo-Protestant) society at the structural level—that is, little intermarriage, modest erosion of discrimination, and no demise of racial group identity.[172]

Nonetheless, Gordon wrote optimistically about what he saw as the eventual full assimilation of African Americans in a white-dominated society, a trend he and others have asserted can be seen in a now substantial black middle class. Similarly, prominent Harvard sociologist Talcott Parsons argued that racial and ethnic inclusion is basic to U.S. society and that this process would eventually encompass black Americans.[173]

In recent decades, numerous social scientists and popular analysts have argued that there has been a major collapse of antiblack discrimination and that the full integration of black Americans into the core economy and society is well underway. These assimilationist scholars cite what they view as dramatic progress for the black middle class as proof of ongoing assimilation. They often suggest that the major remaining problem is a troubled black "underclass," whose difficulties are in their view not related to current discrimination. While recognizing that some discrimination remains, many assimilationist scholars have in effect blamed black Americans for their slower economic and social mobility. In a famous 1960s report, Daniel P. Moynihan viewed black families headed by women as a serious retardant to progress. These family-blaming arguments have been regularly resurrected from the 1970s to the present. Some analysts have pointed to a so-called poverty subculture among low-income black Americans as a continuing barrier to their progress. The theme of certain white analysts boils down to "Why can't black people be like us?" This notion is an old part of white racist framing and suggests that black individuals, like those in white immigrant groups, should be able to move up through the various levels of the Anglo-dominated economy, society, and polity if they would only work harder and address their internal family and cultural problems.[174]

Power-Conflict Perspectives: The Continuing Significance of Racism

Power-conflict analysts reject the optimistic assimilationist view of African American mobility and incorporation into society. From this perspective, the traditional assimilationist is viewed as denying the persistence of racial discrimination and its large effects on society. The contemporary situation of African Americans is much more resistant to change than that of white immigrant groups. Once racial oppression became systemic in the 1600s, those whites initially in the superior racial-hierarchy position, and their descendants, continued to monopolize the lion's share of the economic, political, and educational resources and capital. Only since the late 1960s, when the last major civil rights law went into effect, has the United States even been an officially "free" country. Even then, legal segregation in employment, education, and housing—which lasted nearly a century—has been replaced by informal, but still extensive, racial discrimination targeting Americans of color.

Articulating a theory of internal colonialism, Robert Blauner has argued that major differences exist in the levels of social and economic oppression that black Americans and white immigrant (ethnic) groups have faced over long periods of time.[175] Africans were enslaved and brought in chains. Incorporated into the economy against their will, they and their descendants provided hard labor to build up the wealth of many whites in this society—first as enslaved laborers, later as exploited tenant farmers, then as exploited urban workers. Even with the great northward migration after World War I, their lesser economic position relative to whites was little altered. They faced extensive discrimination even as the U.S. economic system was industrializing. Historically, the initial incorporation of white immigrants into U.S. society occurred voluntarily, most often at the lower economic levels, but those offering some chances of upward mobility. This was not the case for most Africans and their descendants. Enslaved Africans suffered white attempts to destroy their African cultures and were forced to give up many traditional ways as part of their incorporation into slavery. Protestant religion and English were forced on them. They were generally forced to give up control of their own bodies, which became the property of whites. Over time, many thousands of biracial children resulted from the coercion and rape of African American women by white slaveholders or overseers—and, later on, by some white male segregationists. In contrast with the assimilation view, power-conflict theorists emphasize the *forced* acculturation and *forced* secondary-structural incorporation of African Americans into a white-controlled society.

Power-conflict perspectives take a different view of the lack of full assimilation of black Americans into the society in recent decades. They view the so-called subculture of poverty as actually a description of a structural condition and point of view historically created by whites' racial hostility, stereotyping, and discrimination, both individual and institutionalized. When European immigrants such as the Irish began arriving in cities, they did not gain socioeconomic mobility solely by hard work and fair competition. Coming to see themselves as "white" in the U.S. hierarchy, they often displaced and discriminated against free black urbanites, who were thus relegated to the lowest-paid jobs or unemployment. By the mid-nineteenth century, white immigrants were crowding free black workers out of numerous urban occupations.[176]

After the Civil War, most black families in the South had to remain there, becoming poor tenant farmers or sharecroppers again exploited by white landowners. The new industrial economies of growing cities mostly drew workers from Europe, not from the South. Widespread racial discrimination prevented black structural incorporation into the burgeoning industrial economy on an equal-status basis with European immigrants. After World War I, with the trek northward, black southerners moved into low-paid jobs in northern industries; not until World War II did a significant proportion of black workers find some better-paid jobs in industry. Then, increased racial discrimination against skilled black workers after World War II generated, once again, a major black unemployment problem, which persists today. Southern migrants found that the economic opportunities in northern cities were much paler than the promised-land image that had drawn them. For many decades now, racial discrimination in all regions has seriously limited black opportunities in jobs, education, and housing.[177]

In Chapter 2 we also noted the resurgence of an Afrocentric perspective emphasizing the long-term role of European imperialism and colonialism in enslaving and dispersing Africans around the globe and in seriously damaging once-advanced societies in Africa. This approach examines the continuing Eurocentric bias in the dominant U.S. culture: Euro-American worldviews often include a myth of white cultural superiority over many other cultures. From this point of view, because of the Euro-American views' negative effects on African Americans, the latter should direct their efforts to re-create cultural alternatives more fully informed by their African heritage; they should develop a reinvigorated African diaspora culture.[178]

Power-conflict analysts often underscore the reality of racial oppression today: White racist framing and discrimination significantly handicap black Americans today in major institutional arenas, from public accommodations to employment, business, education, and housing. Power-conflict theorists are usually pessimistic about full incorporation of African Americans into these critical institutional arenas without substantial changes in the racist framing and discriminatory actions of the white majority.

Summary

Social, economic, and political progress by African Americans in this society has been severely restricted by the lasting effects of centuries of slavery and legal segregation, which existed for nearly 90 percent of our history. Even during the last great migrations of European immigrants in the early 1900s, African Americans—many of whom were already multi-generation Americans—were still extremely segregated and violently oppressed. This was in great contrast to the upward mobility open to most European immigrants. Long decades of Jim Crow segregation greatly hampered the lives, including the economic mobility, of black Americans freed from slavery and several generations of their descendants. Later, the northward trek of black Americans reflected protest against southern oppression, protest in this case "by the feet." Other types of protest against racial subordination, nonviolent and violent, have regularly punctuated the long course of U.S. racism. The legal segregation period was followed by a long epoch, still in process today, of widespread and informal racial discrimination.

Today, most African Americans live in cities, North and South. In recent years, the migration pattern of African Americans has changed; more are now moving to the South than are leaving. Wherever they live, African Americans continue to face much racial discrimination and much educational, economic, and housing inequality. The Civil Rights Acts of 1964, 1965, and 1968 (and later amendments) have made many acts of racial discrimination illegal, but have not ended the millions of cases of blatant, subtle, and covert discrimination in business, jobs, housing, education, and public accommodations each year. Government antidiscrimination programs have been too modest to remedy this widespread anti-black discrimination.

The twenty-first century specter of "slavery still unwilling to die" can be seen today everywhere: Major barriers to black voting continue in various states; most black children still attend racially segregated schools; the majority of black families still live in mostly segregated residential areas; most black Americans at all income levels face informal discrimination by banks, real estate agents, and landlords; many black defendants are tried by juries in which black citizens are underrepresented or absent; and most black workers face recurring blatant or subtle discrimination in the workplace.

The effects of this racial discrimination remain painful, stifling, and cumulative. Reflecting on the costs of racism, a successful black entrepreneur has commented on what it is like to be black today in a predominantly white society:

> *One step from suicide!* What I'm saying is—the psychological warfare games that we have to play everyday just to survive. We have to be one way in our communities and one way in the [white] workplace or in the business sector. We can never be ourselves all around.[179]

Key Terms

slavery 166
Underground Railroad 168
"Jim Crow" laws 169
modern racism 172
ethnoviolence 173
lynching 173
racial profiling 175
psychological wage 178
underemployment rate 183
Reconstruction 186

Mexican Americans

BIG PICTURE QUESTIONS

- ***How does capitalistic globalization contribute to Latin American immigration to the United States?***
- ***What role have Mexican Americans played in building up this country's wealth and institutions?***
- ***What are the societal consequences of discrimination by European Americans against Mexican Americans?***

Not long ago, three men were drinking beer in suburban San Diego. After a while, these Anglo whites* decided to "shoot some aliens" at the U.S.–Mexico border. Using a rifle, one man killed a Mexican youngster who was crossing the border. The killer was sentenced to only two years in jail. The life of the immigrant was not considered valuable by his killer or, indeed, by the judge. In recent years, hostility toward Latin American immigrants has reached intense levels—with new white-dominated citizen groups, such as the Minutemen, patrolling the Mexican border. One group demonstrated and burned a Mexican flag in front of a Mexican Consulate in Arizona. In addition, the U.S. Congress passed billion-dollar legislation to create a 700-mile security fence between the United States and Mexico. Anti-immigrant hostility has been fed by highly stereotyped assertions about Mexican immigrants by poorly informed politicians and media. These assertions have helped to spur white supremacists and nativists, who have even made death threats against Latino leaders, such as Los Angeles Mayor Antonio Villaraigosa, because of their speaking out on behalf of undocumented immigrants.[1]

Many Americans have historically held stereotypical views of the people in Mexico as sleepy farmers with big sombreros, "wetbacks," mustachioed banditos, or ignorant people involved with magical religious views. Popular images are supplemented by negative treatments of Mexicans and Mexican Americans in schoolbooks that distort the history of the Southwest, as in the historical myths that glorify heroic white Texans in the 1830s confronting a backward Mexican government and army. In addition, popular and scholarly accounts of U.S. history by European Americans frequently omit significant references to Mexican American contributions to the past and present development of the United States.

The last (2000) census counted just over 35 million **Latinos (Hispanics)**, *persons whose national origins (or whose ancestors' national origins) are in the countries of Latin America*—that is, much of the Caribbean, Central, and South America. This figure was estimated to have grown by the mid-2000s to 42 million, about 27 million of whom were Mexican Americans.[2] U.S. Latinos are now one of the two largest groups of Americans of color, along with African Americans. The umbrella term *Hispanic*, which was coined by the U.S. government relatively recently, is widely used to designate persons of Mexican, Puerto Rican, Cuban, Dominican, and Central or South American heritage. Yet *Hispanic* is an English word derived from *Hispania*, the Roman name for Spain. This term emphasizes Spanish heritage while ignoring other (for example, Indian and African) backgrounds. *Latino*, an alternative collective designation, recognizes the complex Latin American origins of these groups. It is a Spanish-language word preferred by many Spanish-speaking scholars and others.[3] Though each term has its critics, both are widely used not only by members of this group but by outsiders. The use of these terms also reflects a new collective consciousness among these groups that did not exist until recently. The relatively new idea of a Latino group is an example of the "emergent" character of ethnic and racial identities that William Yancey and his associates suggested in their analysis of adaptation patterns of earlier European immigrants (see Chapter 2).

Note too that combining the various national-origin groups into one Latino or Hispanic category masks their significant diversity. Most people are likely to name their own group first and foremost in terms of its national origin, such as Mexican, Cuban, or Puerto Rican. Latino groups differ economically, politically, in their histories, and in certain cultural forms—for example, food, religious practices, music, and political inclinations. Although the Latino population is increasingly dispersed, geographic distinctiveness remains. Eight in ten live in the southwestern states or in Florida, Illinois, New York, and New Jersey. Mexican Americans are disproportionately concentrated in the Southwest; Puerto Ricans and other Caribbean Latinos, in the Northeast; and Cuban Americans, in the Southeast.

In this and the following chapter, we examine three large Latino groups: Mexican Americans, mainland Puerto Ricans, and Cuban Americans—all of whom have diverse histories and heritages as well

*The terms *whites* and *Anglos* are generally used in this and other chapters as shorthand for "European Americans," or what the U.S. Census Bureau calls "non-Hispanic whites." A recent survey of 2900 Latinos indicates that a significant majority, and more than 80 percent of Mexican Americans, do not prefer the term white for their group when given a wide range of choices. The largest percentage prefer Hispanic/Latino. Cases where they opt for a "white" identity will be discussed later.

as different experiences in U.S. society. Today, about 63 percent of U.S. Latinos are Mexican Americans; 15 percent are of Central, South American, or Dominican origin; 10 percent are mainland Puerto Ricans; 4 percent are Cuban Americans; and 8 percent fall into an "other" category.[4] This chapter focuses principally on Mexican Americans.

The Conquest Period, 1500–1853

Beginning in the 1500s, Spaniards conquered and sought to Catholicize the indigenous population in what is now Mexico and the southwestern United States and to concentrate this population in agricultural and mining communities for economic exploitation. Because only very modest numbers of Spanish women migrated to the Americas, sexual liaisons, often forced, between Spanish men and indigenous women were common. The offspring, sometimes called *mestizos* ("mixed peoples"), soon outnumbered Spanish colonizers, and they usually occupied a middle social position in colonial society, below the Spanish immigrants but above Indians, persons of mixed Indian and African heritage, and enslaved Africans. It is also important to remember that many of the Spanish colonizers had some African ancestry *before* they arrived, because of Spain's long centuries of contact with, and invasion by, peoples from Africa.[5]

After centuries of exploitation, Mexico won independence from Spain in 1821. Before the invasion of Anglo-American immigrants in the 1830s, Mexicans had established numerous communities in what is now the southwestern United States. Several thousand, with a Mexican way of life and a self-sufficient economy, lived on Mexican land grants in what would become the U.S. state of Texas. Thousands of European Americans from the United States moved into the area, and in a few years the new migrants outnumbered the Mexican population.[6]

The Texas Revolt: Myths and Reality

Mexican government actions, including freeing enslaved people and placing restrictions on U.S. immigration, angered U.S. immigrants. The causes of the 1836 Texas revolt included the growing number of immigrants coming illegally from what was then the United States, racist attitudes of these immigrants toward native-born Mexicans, and the resentment of immigrant slaveholders toward Mexican antislavery laws. Until recently, relatively few U.S. analysts have been inclined to see the Texas revolt as territorial aggression by U.S. citizens against another sovereign nation, which it was, but have excused the behavior of the Texans and blamed the Mexican government.[7]

Myths about the revolt that praise white Texans' heroism persist. The most widely known is the legend of the Alamo, which portrays 180 principled native-born white Texans courageously fighting thousands of Mexican troops. Actually, most of the men at the Alamo mission, located in what is now San Antonio, were newcomers, not native Texans. Many, such as James Bowie and Davy Crockett, were adventurers, not men of principle defending their homes. The Alamo was one of the best fortified sites in the West; its defenders had twice as many cannons, much better rifles, and better training in riflery than the poorly equipped Mexican recruits.[8]

The Texas rebellion was a case of U.S. colonizers going beyond an existing U.S. boundary and intentionally trying to incorporate new territory. The 1845 annexation of Texas precipitated a war. Provocative U.S. troop actions in a disputed boundary area generated a Mexican attack, which was followed by a U.S. declaration of war and victory. Mexico fell victim to what was in effect a U.S. conspiracy to seize its territory by force. In 1848 the Mexican government was forced to cede a huge area (now the U.S. Southwest and West) for $15 million. Mexican residents had the choice of remaining or moving to Mexico; most stayed, assured on paper of legal rights by the Treaty of Guadalupe Hidalgo.[9] However, white immigrants used both legal and illegal means to take much of the land still owned by the existing Mexican occupants.

California and New Mexico

In the early 1800s the 7500 non-Indian residents of California lived mostly on Mexican-run ranches. After gold was discovered in 1849, U.S. whites poured into California, once again taking lands from Mexicans.[10] At the time of U.S. acquisition, the 50,000 Mexicans in what became New Mexico had long maintained their cultural traditions. Established villages—Santa Fe dates from 1598—provided the organization to withstand some effects of the U.S. invasion. Initially, Mexican American landholders in these western areas continued to play an important role in commerce and politics.[11]

Soon, though, many lost their lands to invading whites. By the mid-nineteenth century, the U.S. system of private land ownership was replacing a Mexican system that included significant communal lands. Despite U.S. treaty promises, old land grants were ignored; communal land was treated as U.S. government land. Everywhere Mexican landholders lost much land. The invasion of the Southwest was not a heroic period in which U.S. "settlers" appropriated unused land, but rather a period of imperialistic expansion and colonization of Mexicans who had long been resident in the area.[12]

Past and Present Immigration

Estimates of Mexicans within the expanding United States range up to 118,000 for the 1850s. In the decades that followed, millions entered the United States, pushed by political upheavals and economic conditions in Mexico and pulled by expanding economic opportunities in U.S. fields and factories. Peak immigration periods have been 1910–1930, 1942–1954, and 1965 to the present. Immigrants have included (1) those with official visas ("legals"); (2) **undocumented immigrants** or **"illegals"** *(immigrants without legal immigration papers)*; (3) **braceros** *(seasonal farm workers on contract)*; (4) commuters (those with official visas who live in Mexico but work in the United States); and (5) "border crossers" (those with short-term permits, many of whom become domestic workers).[13] Exclusion of Asian immigrants by federal action (see Chapter 11) and the pull of World War I–era industrialization sharply decreased the number of U.S.-born laborers available for agricultural work in the Southwest, and Mexican workers were thus drawn there. Under pressure from U.S. employers, federal authorities waived immigration restrictions, allowing many thousands of Mexican workers to enter legally during World War I.[14]

This was an indication of the globalizing character of capitalism. U.S. employers went beyond the U.S. labor pool to secure low-wage workers from outside. Recruitment of overseas labor by U.S. employers has for a century been a major source of racial and ethnic diversity.

Several hundred thousand Mexican workers and their family members entered the United States in the 1920s. Improved canning and shipping technologies opened markets for agricultural produce. U.S. business interests opposed restrictions on immigration. The 1924 Immigration Act, which barred most southern and eastern European immigrants, did *not* exclude Mexicans, for Mexico had become a major source of low-wage labor for U.S. employers. Still, white nativists then objected strongly to this growing Mexican population, which they feared would create a "problem" that was greater than, as they put it in their racist framing, "the negro [sic] problem of the South" and thus would threaten white racial "purity" here.[15]

The Border Patrol of the Immigration and Naturalization Service (INS), created in the 1920s, has played a major role in the lives of immigrants. In 1929, legislation made illegal entry a felony. Although it was given authority to keep out undocumented workers, the Border Patrol has historically tried mostly to regulate the number, allowing enough to come in to meet the labor needs of U.S. employers. In times of economic recession, however, the Border Patrol has sometimes conducted exclusion or deportation campaigns. Then, in better times, more immigrant workers have often been allowed in, and enforcement of immigration restrictions has been less rigorous.[16]

During the Great Depression of the 1930s, federal enforcement of literacy tests and local white hostility greatly reduced the number of immigrants. Considerable pressure was put on Mexicans already here, whether citizens or not, to leave. Many were forcibly deported in massive campaigns; thousands, *including U.S. citizens,* were expelled in organized caravans by agencies eager to reduce government expenditures for relief during the Depression.[17]

Braceros *and Undocumented Workers: Encouraging Immigration*

In the World War II era, a 1942 Emergency Farm Labor *(Bracero)* agreement between the United States and Mexico again provided Mexican workers for U.S. agriculture. Over two decades, nearly 5 million *braceros* were brought in at the request of U.S. employers, who were once again going beyond U.S. borders for low-wage labor. This government program stimulated the migration of yet more undocumented workers. Mexico, with the largest Spanish-speaking population of any country, has been the major supplier of immigrant workers for U.S. employers for decades.[18]

Today, most such workers are not rural migrants but come from urban areas in Mexico. Mexican workers' entry has periodically met intense opposition. Union officials have called for restrictions to protect the jobs of native-born Americans. Growing concern among nativist groups led finally to the inclusion of restrictions on legal Mexican immigration in the 1965 Immigration Act, which got rid of earlier immigration quotas but then set an annual limit of only 20,000 per year for Mexican immigrants, thereby making it more difficult for Mexican immigrants to join relatives in the United States legally. Subsequent U.S. legislation has attempted to limit undocumented immigration.[19]

The U.S. economy, however, depends heavily on immigrants from Latin America. Undocumented workers are the "backbone of Dole, Green Giant, McDonald's, Stouffers, Burger King, the Octopus car wash chain, Del Monte, Chicken of the Sea, Heinz, Hunt's, Rosarito, Campbell's *m-m-m good*, Wendy's, Taco Bell, Lean Cuisine, Dinty Moore, Hormel, midnight shifts, front lawn raking, pool scrubbing, gas station back rooms, blue-jean stitching, TV assembly, [and] athletic-shoe sole gluing."[20] Mexican workers and U.S. employers are closely linked.

Migration and U.S. Involvement in Latin America

U.S. involvement in Latin America has long involved the U.S. government and major corporations, and the goals often have been political and economic colonization—the expansion of the U.S. empire to the south. The U.S. military has intervened many times in Latin America to protect U.S. interests. In addition, the growing U.S. economy has created much demand for low-wage workers in sectors such as construction, agriculture, and food services.[21]

On the one hand, most immigrants are attracted by U.S. jobs. On the other, many are pushed by serious economic problems in their home countries, and the U.S. government or corporations are sometimes implicated in these economic problems. For decades, U.S. corporations operating in Mexico have helped to generate out-migration. Some U.S. firms have built large farming operations in Mexico to grow food for export, thereby taking over large amounts of land and driving off small farmers who traditionally farmed the land to feed their families. U.S. corporations' expropriation of agricultural land and other resources in Mexico has forced many Mexicans to move from rural areas to large cities in Mexico, where jobs are scarce. These urban workers often seek work in the United States in order to support their families at home. Indeed, a large proportion of Mexico's total revenues comes from money sent home to Mexico by immigrant workers in the United States.[22]

Since the 1960s, U.S. manufacturing and industrial corporations have built many factories in Mexico. Many companies have built **maquiladoras**, *manufacturing operations in northern Mexico near the U.S. border*, where they can take advantage of low-wage labor and weak environmental standards while avoiding certain tariffs and duties. International trade agreements such as NAFTA (the North American Free Trade Agreement) have accelerated U.S. investment and manufacturing in Mexico. One consequence of the border plants is that workers who migrate from southern Mexico to border areas learn that wages are far higher across the border, and some leave for the United States. The increased number of low-wage jobs in border plants has not benefitted most Mexican workers. The era of "free trade," which was supposed to bring economic benefits to most Mexican workers, has mainly benefited a modest number of affluent Mexicans and U.S. capitalists.[23] The Mexican government has made little effort to stop cross-border migration, which relieves poverty pressures in Mexico. This Mexican perspective and increased U.S. hostility toward undocumented immigrants have created major political tensions between the U.S. and Mexican governments.

The number of Mexican workers entering illegally for permanent residence is less than many U.S. media accounts and anti-immigrant groups suggest. One major study found that most of the Mexican border crossers apprehended annually "are temporary labor migrants who are caught more than once by the INS and who do not intend to live in the U.S. in any case. . . . A large reverse flow into Mexico goes virtually unnoticed and unreported."[24]

The best estimate for the number of undocumented immigrants in the United States by the mid-2000s was about 12 million, with a bit more than half of these coming from Mexico. We should note that a large proportion come from elsewhere—from Europe, Asia, and other Latin American countries. In the decade of the 2000s, an estimated 500,000 to 600,000 undocumented immigrants have entered annually. A substantial majority are male workers—which contrasts with legal immigrants, who are majority female. One study of undocumented workers found that most had friends or relatives in the United States through whom they found employment. The low-paid, often impermanent jobs available to most undocumented immigrants offer limited economic opportunities. They work hard and rely mostly on their personal resources.[25]

Most pay considerably more in income and other taxes than they receive in government benefits such as Social Security, food stamps, or schooling for their children. Research studies indicate that undocumented immigrant workers work mainly in low-wage jobs that most U.S. workers consider undesirable, and thus they have little effect on, or in some cases even increase, the employment rate of native-born workers as a whole. The major exception is in urban areas, where there are many unemployed workers of color. Native-born workers in the lowest-wage job categories in these areas are sometimes displaced by undocumented Latin American workers.[26]

How has U.S. capitalism shaped Mexican migration and employment patterns?

The 1986 Immigration Act, the 2006 Secure Fence Act, and Undocumented Immigrants

Growing concern over the presence of undocumented immigrants led to passage of the 1986 Immigration Reform and Control Act (IRCA). It authorized (1) the legalization of undocumented immigrants resident continuously in the United States since 1982; (2) sanctions for employers who hire undocumented aliens; (3) reimbursement of governments for added costs of legalization; (4) screening of welfare applicants for migration status; and (5) programs to bring in agricultural laborers.[27] Just over 3 million undocumented immigrants applied for legalization by the deadline; 1.7 million applications were accepted for adjustment to legal residence. Mexican immigrants made up three-fourths of those legalized.[28]

Many analysts feared that the IRCA would encourage employers to discriminate against anyone who looked like an immigrant, especially an immigrant of color. One federal study found that numerous firms were discriminating against U.S. citizens in hiring to ensure that they were not hiring undocumented workers. Other researchers have found a similar response by many employers and "an IRCA-induced decline in job opportunities" for "unauthorized-looking natives."[29] A 1990 Immigration Act was passed to correct some of these problems, but employer discrimination against "immigrant-looking" native-born workers continues to be reported.

Debates over regulatory legislation have periodically revived anti-immigration arguments. Many native-born whites have long been concerned that the country could not absorb so many immigrants, even though the ratio of immigrants to the native-born population was higher in the early twentieth century, when southern and eastern Europeans were immigrating to the United States. In 1910 the foreign-born represented 14.6 percent of the population; today that figure is only about 12 percent, giving the United States a smaller percentage of foreign-born than some other nations.[30] Given its long history of successful absorption of immigrants, it is unlikely that the United States will soon be overwhelmed by these immigrants. Implicit in many discussions of these new immigrants is a racialized concern that most are from Latin America and Asia—that is, that they are not whites of European origin.

Anti-immigrant stereotypes and political actions have been commonplace in recent decades. One white legislator in California distributed a racist poem titled "Ode to the New California" to state legislators that mocked Mexican immigrants with lines such as "I come for visit, get treated regal. So I stay, who care illegal.... We think America damn good place. Too damn good for white man's race."[31] Many newspaper and web commentators have claimed that these immigrants cause employment problems for many Americans, significantly increase crime, and seriously overburden government services. Some white politicians and citizen groups forced the anti-immigrant Proposition 187 onto the California ballot, and it passed with a substantial majority in 1994. Proposition 187 sought to restrict undocumented immigrants' access to public services and required public employees to report undocumented

Farmworkers harvest grapes in California.

immigrants. After legal challenges, it was overturned in 1999. In 2004 Arizona voters passed a similar measure, which has also faced major legal challenges. The Arizona effort created a national group that is working to get anti-immigrant propositions on other state ballots.

In 1996 the U.S. Congress passed yet another act, the Illegal Immigration Reform and Immigrant Responsibility Act (IIRIRA). This law established regulations restricting legal immigration as well as undocumented immigration. The IIRIRA increased the number of border control agents and imposed a substantial income requirement for families that wish to sponsor immigrant relatives. These requirements discriminate against prospective Latino sponsors because their family incomes are, on average, significantly lower than those of white families.[32]

In fall 2006, after more months of immigration debates, Congress passed another piece of punitive immigration legislation, the Secure Fence Act, which was estimated to cost taxpayers $35 billion. The law again increased the number of border enforcement personnel, as well as surveillance technology on the border. It required construction of physical barriers to Latin American immigrants, including a long, double-layered border fence to be completed by 2008. (Other immigration reforms, such as amnesty for hard-working undocumented immigrants long resident in the United States, were postponed.) From 1994 to the mid-2000s punitive actions in border states had already cost an estimated four thousand lives of undocumented men, women, and children trying to cross the U.S. border, yet political pressures from conservative elements and a looming 2006 congressional election resulted in a rush to pass this restrictive legislation especially targeting Mexican immigrants.[33]

The punitive immigrant legislation of recent decades has been motivated in part by a concern that immigrants become dependent on public welfare programs. Yet much research on Mexican and other Latino immigrants contradicts these often stereotyped notions. Generally, Latino immigrants are employed at higher rates, and use social welfare programs less often, than other major racial and ethnic groups. Thus, the notion that Mexican immigrants come to the United States just to get on welfare is contradicted by the high proportion (69 percent) of Latinos in the labor force. This is higher than for the non-Latino population (66 percent). Indeed, today Latinos rank second only to white Americans in total number of workers in the workforce.[34]

In the twenty-first century Latin American immigration has become, as in the 1930s, a major political issue that is hotly debated in the media and by politicians. Undocumented Mexican immigrants have been constructed as a major threat, as numerous U.S. politicians and media commentators accent new arguments about "homeland security" and an "unprotected southern border." Yet, the often harsh language about immigrants and security is rarely extended to the even longer border that the United States has with Canada—a sign that racialized thinking about the skin color and culture of those immigrating may be central to much renewed opposition to these immigrants. In addition, the increasing barricading of the U.S.–Mexican border since the 1980s has led to some unintended consequences—such as actually increasing the number of undocumented workers living in the United States because the large number who are interested in working in the United States for only part of the year cannot easily go home to Mexico.

Have recent immigration laws contributed to discrimination against Mexican Americans?

Population and Location

Today the umbrella group termed Latinos is currently the fastest-growing major racial-ethnic segment of the U.S. population, numbering more than 42 million, about one-seventh of the population. The majority are Mexican Americans. Although immigrants make up a substantial portion of this population, the majority of Mexican Americans today have been born and raised in the United States. The Latino, mostly Mexican American, population of just one metropolitan area, Los Angeles, is now larger than the total population of numerous states. Latinos (mostly Mexican Americans) are more than one-third of the residents of California, the largest state, and growth in Latino communities has been substantial in other states in recent decades. Primarily because of recent growth in Latino and Asian populations, California and Texas now have population *majorities* that are not European American. In addition, U.S. Census Bureau and other data for the last decade reveal that the Mexican American population is increasingly becoming dispersed, for large numbers are now neighbors of other Americans in every region. Indeed, southern states from Arkansas to Georgia and South Carolina have seen particularly rapid growth in Latino populations, especially of foreign-born male workers filling low-wage jobs in these areas.

Stereotypes and Related Images

Early Images

In the 1830s and 1840s, U.S. whites migrating to the Southwest generally did not react favorably to the people already living there. Most whites coming from eastern and southern states applied the white racial framing and its stereotypes, which they had developed previously for African Americans, to the resident peoples of the Southwest, including Mexicans and Indians. For example, they attributed laziness and backwardness to what they saw as a distinctive "Mexican race." Most Mexicans in what would become the U.S. Southwest were of mixed ancestry, the descendants of Spaniards, Indians, and mestizos from farther south, and many had some African ancestry. (Some scholars estimate that a majority of Mexicans then had some African ancestry because of the African ancestry of some of the original Spanish invaders and because of centuries of African slavery in Mexico.) European American immigrants brought with them a well-developed racist framing already rationalizing the subordination of African Americans and making it easy for them to stigmatize the generally darker-skinned Mexican Americans also as racially inferior.

Apparently, few white colonizers saw Mexicans as "white," but compared them to black or Indian groups. They placed Mexicans at the bottom of the old white-racist continuum. In the words of one land agent, Mexicans were "swarthy looking people resembling our mulattos, some of them nearly black." Sam Houston, a leader of white immigrants coming to Texas, called them inferior "half-Indians." The widespread white view that Mexicans had a "filthy, greasy appearance," as one traveler wrote, probably led to the derogatory epithet "greaser" for Mexicans.[35]

In the 1850s, John Monroe reported to Washington that the people in the New Mexico area "are thoroughly debased and totally incapable of self-government, and there is no latent quality about them that can ever make them respectable."[36]

Ironically, these Mexicans' knowledge of ranching and mining laid the foundation for successful economic development by later white immigrants.

Later on, increased Mexican immigration after 1900 triggered more attacks. White-supremacist groups raided labor camps and beat workers. A "brown scare" hysteria developed in California between 1913 and 1918 amid fears that the Mexican Revolution would spread to the United States. Whites characterized Mexican immigrants as a menace to communities' health, and pressure for deportation mounted.[37] In the 1920s a white member of Congress stereotyped Mexicans as a mongrelized mixture of Spanish and "low-grade Indians" plus some African slave "blood." In 1928 an "expert" witness testified to the House Immigration Committee and branded the "Mexican race" a threat to the "white race."[38] Nativist writers expressed fear of "race mongrelization." A Princeton professor spoke fearfully of the future elimination of Anglo-Saxons through interbreeding in "favor of the progeny of Mexican peons who will continue to afflict us with an embarrassing race problem."[39] Interestingly, an explicit category of "Mexican race" was used in the 1930 census, the only census ever to include such.

Much public commentary since the 1920s has stereotyped the Mexican American male as crime-oriented. For example, a report by a white lieutenant in the Los Angeles Sheriff's Department after the 1943 "zoot suit" riots (discussed later) alleged that the Mexicans' desire to spill blood was an "inborn characteristic," a view endorsed by his superior. Then as now, stereotypes linked assumed social or cultural traits to alleged biological inferiority: "The Mexican was 'lawless' and 'violent' because he had Indian blood; he was 'shiftless' and 'improvident' because that was his nature."[40]

Since the 1920s, the results of so-called IQ testing have often been used to argue for the intellectual and group inferiority of Mexican Americans and other Latinos, as well as of black Americans. A version of this highly stereotyped view of Latinos was expressed in a best-selling 1990s book called *The Bell Curve* (see Chapter 7).[41]

Contemporary Stereotypes and Prejudices

Negative stereotypes and prejudices can be found at all class levels, including economic and political leaders. George Murphy, former senator from California, argued that Mexicans were "ideal for 'stoop' labor—after all, they are built close to the ground."[42] In 1965 a leading historian, Walter Prescott Webb, wrote that "there is a cruel streak in the Mexican nature.... It may and doubtless should be attributed partly to the Indian blood."[43]

In recent decades, overtly racist stereotyping by whites, especially those in elites (see below), has often changed for the better, but there are still many who assert and act on negative anti-Mexican images. For example, speaking at a meeting on border issues and Mexican immigration in the 1990s, a California state senator argued that public education should not be provided to the children of undocumented immigrants: "It seems rather strange that we go out of our way to take care of the rights of these individuals who are perhaps on the lower scale of our humanity." Latinos who criticized the senator's comments were themselves attacked in the media.[44]

For many decades, numerous public commentators and scholars have stereotyped Mexicans or Mexican Americans as passive or fatalistic. Some social science studies have reinforced the view that Mexican culture is one of fatalism, "machismo," and a too-extreme family orientation. Oscar Lewis and William Madsen, thus, portrayed what they thought was a folk culture of fatalism and familism in Mexican villages, a view later extended to Mexican American communities.[45] Numerous social scientists have pointed out the errors in such stereotyped assumptions. Many analysts have overlooked the substantial diversity in Mexican American culture and communities from Texas to California—and, more recently, in midwestern and southern states. A characteristic such as the assumed male domination in Mexican families varies significantly with the class and educational background of Mexican Americans, just as it does among other racial and ethnic groups.[46]

Drawing still-negative images from the media, political speeches, and other sources, many people often stereotype Mexican Americans and other Latinos.[47] Thus, in one 1990s survey, white college students expressed the belief that Hispanics were more likely than whites to be physically violent, dirty or smelly, uneducated, poor, and criminally inclined. These respondents felt that, compared with whites, Hispanics placed less value on learning, mature love, physical fitness, and economic prosperity.[48] A majority of white respondents in a National Conference survey regarding interethnic attitudes believed that Latinos "tend to have bigger families than they are able to support." One-fifth of whites felt that Latinos lacked "ambition and the drive to succeed."[49] In contrast, an examination of data from twenty-one surveys of Mexican Americans and European Americans found that Mexican American workers were *not* less work-oriented than European Americans; the former had a strong work ethic and were productive in their workplaces.[50]

What are important commonalities in stereotypes targeting Native Americans, African Americans, and Mexican Americans?

Views of Immigration and Immigrants

In spite of increasing anti-immigrant discussions across the country, recent surveys have found that a *majority* of Americans still prefer to see legal immigration kept at the current level or increased. Yet, there is substantial concern about Mexican and other immigration among a substantial number of Americans. In one recent national survey, 52 percent agreed with a statement that immigrants today are a "burden because they take jobs, housing," while 41 percent preferred instead the statement that immigrants "strengthen the U.S. with their... talents." Nonetheless, only 21 percent of these respondents also said that immigration was a "very big" community problem. Even with politicians making immigration a major issue, only 4 percent volunteered immigration as the most important problem facing the country. Numerous other issues, such as dissatisfaction with government and concern with terrorism, were listed ahead of immigration, There is also a lot of variation in how Americans see ending illegal immigration. In this same survey, just 27 percent of the respondents said that all illegal immigrants should be required to go home, with no temporary worker program being provided by government as a substitute. Another 25 percent said that these undocumented immigrants should be required to return home but that such a temporary program should be provided, while yet another 40 percent said that illegal immigrants should be allowed to stay under some government program. In addition, when asked how to stop illegal immigration, the largest proportion of respondents (49 percent) thought that penalizing employers was best, while 33 percent preferred increased border patrolling and just 9 percent thought a border fence was a good idea. We should note too that surveys of Latinos have found that they are much more supportive of the current level of immigration than the general population.[51]

In numerous local areas, especially in Arizona, Nevada, Indiana, and North Carolina cities that have experienced substantial Mexican immigration, anti-immigrant sentiment is often stronger. Two-thirds of the respondents in a survey in North Carolina, where the Latino population has increased significantly in recent years, felt their neighbors would not accept Hispanics into the neighborhood. Just over half said that they themselves were not comfortable around Spanish speakers. Fear of job competition appeared to fuel these negative attitudes.[52]

Moreover, in the mid- to late 2000s numerous demonstrations against Latin American immigrants were held by white-supremacist groups, including Ku Klux Klan, neo-Nazi, and neo-Confederate groups, Today, on numerous websites as well as in videos and books, these and other white-supremacist groups describe Mexican and other Latino immigrants as a "cultural cancer," a "wildfire," or a "gang of illegals" making the country "less beautiful." (They also portray African Americans with similar viciousness.) Since the early 2000s some whites have created violent video games with which one can play at killing undocumented immigrants coming across the U.S.–Mexico border.[53]

Using less flamboyant language, Harvard Professor Samuel Huntington argues that Latin American immigrants are a serious danger to Anglo-American culture. In his generally ethnocentric view, certain immigrant groups are dividing the country because they and their allies "deny the existence of a common culture in the United States... and promote the primacy of racial, ethnic, and other subnational cultural identities and groupings." He is explicitly concerned that today the problematical immigrants are people of color, "overwhelmingly from Latin America and Asia." Yet, as we will show below, most of these immigrants either desire to return home after working for a while in the United States or aggressively seek to adapt to the dominant U.S. "common culture."[54]

Negative Images in the Mass Media

As a result of protests from Mexican American communities, the use of some extreme stereotypical depictions of Mexican Americans in advertising and the media has decreased in recent years. Organized protests and the recognition of the increasing importance of Latino viewers has led U.S. media elites to present more positive images in the movies and on television, in part by featuring more Latino actors, such as Jennifer López, Eva Longoria, Edward James Olmos, and Javier Barem.

However, serious problems remain in the mass media. One mid-1990s' study of the portrayal of Mexican Americans and other Latinos in television programming found that most shows ignore Latinos or present them disproportionately as criminals. Though the percentage of Latinos as actors on television shows has increased, an early 2000s study found that they are still only 2 percent of regular television characters and are still often portrayed as criminals or, more recently, in law enforcement occupations. Another study of local television news shows also found a bias, with Latinos being much less likely to be shown as defenders of the law than whites.[55]

Numerous Hollywood films remain problematical as well. One media scholar has commented: "The way we are treated in movies represents a way that we are marginalized in the larger society. In that way it is a very accurate portrayal."[56] For decades, Hollywood films, such as *Dirty Harry* (1971) and *Falling Down* (1993), as well as numerous theater and television crime movies in more recent years, have portrayed Latinos disproportionately as criminals, drug users, or welfare mothers. In addition, the absence of Latinos in Hollywood films has been serious. A study of G-rated family films produced between 1990 and the mid-2000s, many of which are still widely viewed on DVDs in homes, found that only 1.9 percent of the speaking characters were Latino, far less than the Latino proportion in the U.S. population over this period. Whites were substantially overrepresented.[57]

Media stereotyping, prejudice, and discrimination are often subtle, as in the absence or infrequency of positive pictures and images of Latinos in many U.S. magazines and newspapers, especially those outside the entertainment industry. Marco Portales, a Mexican American scholar, has noted: "Since the 1950s, when I grew up, I have periodically observed that pictures of Hispanic people are not selected for the covers and inside pages of national and regional mainstream magazines, advertisements, and promotional brochures in the United States."[58] By such omissions, members of this subordinate group are made less visible by members of the dominant group.

Newspapers and magazines communicate negative images in the routine language and metaphors they choose. Analyzing everyday language used in a major newspaper, linguistics scholar Otto Santa Ana has shown that editors and reporters often write racialized reports on Latino immigrants. His examination of articles written around the time of Proposition 187 (see above) documents frequent use of negative language, especially metaphors, that portrayed Mexican and other Latino immigrants as animals, invaders, or disreputable persons. Numerous articles characterized public programs as "a lure to immigrants" and have spoken of the electorate's appetite for "the red meat of deportation," INS agents catching "a third of their quarry," Proposition 187 supporters who "devour the weak and helpless," and the need to "ferret out illegal immigrants." The articles' use of strong metaphorical language—words such as *burden, dirt, disease, invasion,* or *waves flooding the country*—conveyed an image of Latino immigration as threateing or dangerous.[59]

As with the mock Spanish we discuss next, such metaphorical language, which non-Latinos often use without thinking, bolsters a negative view of immigrants and plays down the humanity of immigrants, who are human beings mostly seeking to make better lives for themselves and their families.

Mocking Spanish

Anthropologist Jane Hill has examined the widespread use of a mocking type of Spanish by otherwise monolingual (in English) whites across the country. Mock Spanish includes made-up terms such as "no problemo," "el cheapo," "watcho your backo," and "hasty banana," as well as the use of phrases such as "numero uno" and "no way, José." On the surface these terms often seem light-hearted, but they subtly incorporate "a highly negative image of the Spanish language, its speakers, and the culture and institutions associated with them." Mock Spanish, which is common in gift shops, in board rooms, at country club gatherings, and in the media, especially in the Southwest, is mostly created by college-educated whites. These whites also create greeting card texts, coffee cup slogans, video games, children's cartoons, and other cartoons that mock Spanish speakers. Movies such as *Terminator 2* use "adiós," "hasta la vista, baby," and similar Spanish terms in an insulting way not common among native Spanish speakers. In a society in which openly racist talk is often frowned upon, mock Spanish is used to perpetuate negative images of Mexicans and Mexican Americans: "Through this process, such people are endowed with gross sexual appetites, political corruption, laziness, disorders of language, and mental incapacity."[60]

Such language mocking, like that mocking African American vernacular English, is much more serious than occasional light-hearted joking about numerous other languages and accents because it is linked intimately to racialization and institutionalized discrimination. Social science and linguistics researchers have demonstrated how certain accents in English are used as markers for this racialization. While native speakers of languages such as French or Gaelic-Irish do not generally face job or other serious discrimination because of their accents when they speak English, many speakers of Spanish-accented English do face such discrimination, especially at the hands of white native-English speakers. As one scholar has noted, "It is crucial to remember that it is not all foreign accents, but only accent linked to skin that isn't white, or which signals a third-world homeland, that evokes such negative reactions."[61] Certain accents are closely linked to the stigmatization of groups such as Mexican Americans, Puerto Ricans, and Cuban Americans.

A Racialized Identity: The Contemporary Situation

Historically, Mexicans and Mexican Americans have been socially constructed by most Anglo whites as a distinctive, inferior racial group. Regardless of how they saw, or see, themselves, they have typically been racialized by the dominant group as inferior and not white. As David López and Ricardo Stanton-Salazar explain, "However ambiguous on the individual level for Mexican Americans, on the group level Mexicans have a history of stigmatization, economic exploitation and racial exclusion in California and the Southwest."[62] In recent decades, Mexican Americans, including recent immigrants from Mexico, have inherited this historical burden of being racialized in negative terms by a majority of whites.

Today the terms *Mexican* and *Mexican American*, as used by those outside the group so designated (especially by those in the dominant white group), usually involve a view of Mexican Americans as being distinctive in racial and ethnic terms. Recall that a racial group is one that is socially constructed centrally on the basis of physical characteristics considered important by the dominant group, and an ethnic group is one that is socially constructed mainly on the basis of cultural or national-origin characteristics. Today, research evidence indicates that a substantial majority of whites view Latino groups as racially distinctive and as *not white*. We recently gave a questionnaire to 151 white college students asking for them to place a long list of racial and ethnic groups into "white," "not white," and "other" categories. Overwhelming majorities classified each Latino group listed—including Mexican Americans, Cuban Americans, and Puerto Ricans—as not white. The majority of these well-educated whites are operating with a white framing and racial-status continuum in mind when they place various U.S. groups into racial categories. For most, all groups of color are viewed as closer to the black (or nonwhite) end of the old racial-status continuum than to the white end; no group among the many groups of color is, as yet, significantly "whitened." In addition, late 2000s television and radio news discussions of Latino immigrants reveal clearly that leading white news commentators think of Latinos in racialized terms, such as by periodically alluding to them as a "race."[63]

Today, non-Latinos may use language, accent, or surname as well as physical characteristics to identify a person as Mexican American or Hispanic/Latino. This typically means that most of the latter who are lighter-skinned will usually be identified by Anglo whites as Hispanic/Latino—and therefore as *not* European American or white.

A subordinate group's reactions to the experience of being socially constructed by the dominant group adds yet more layers to the social reality. Typically, a subordinate group comes to see itself in certain racial or ethnic terms, yet this view is often not the same as that constructed for them by the dominant white group. Subordinated racial groups, including Mexican Americans and other Latinos, often resist the racialization imposed by whites in various ways. Some may insist that they are "white" just like European Americans. This strategy is often painful and may involve alienation from relatives and other members of the group, but it does make some psychological and social sense, for "white" status carries with it privileges, power, and no racial subordination. A small percentage of Mexican Americans recognize the significant African ancestry of many people born in Mexico and assert their kinship with African Americans, while many others assert a distinctive Mexican American identity of their own that does not recognize this African ancestry. The latter often view themselves as part of a proud *la Raza Unida* and/or identify with a broader Hispanic/Latino community. Indeed, the Chicano movement since the 1960s (see below) has accented *la Raza* and thus accelerated the willingness of many to identify themselves as part of a mestizo group, which is not white and has some Indian ancestry. Today, surveys suggest the diversity of Mexican American (and other Latino) responses to their societal situation. One 1990s Houston-area survey found that the majority of Hispanic respondents, including nearly two-thirds of the U.S.-born, did not consider Hispanics to be part of the "white race." Similarly, an early-2000s national survey of 2900 Latinos by the Pew Hispanic Center found that a substantial majority of Latinos, and of Mexican Americans, preferred to classify themselves as something other than "white" or "black," with only 17 percent of Mexican Americans consistently preferring "white."[64]

However, when forced by the 2000 census to categorize themselves only in terms of a very limited racial-group listing—white, black, Indian, Asian, or other race—about half of those who self-identified as Hispanic or Latino chose a racial category other than white. However, the fact that 48 percent of self-identified Hispanics/Latinos did designate themselves on this limited census continuum as "white" (few chose "black") may indicate the strength of social pressures to appear white, as well as the complexity of chosen racial-ethnic identities today. The centuries-old, white-imposed system of racial categorization, running from white to black, is generally viewed as problematical by Americans of Latin American descent.[65]

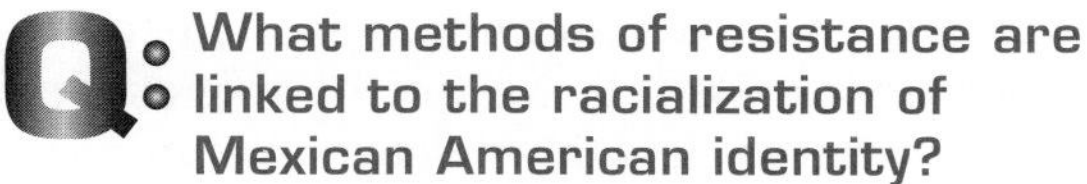

Conflict and Protest

Oppression and Resistance

Coercion was a fundamental factor in white domination in the Southwest in the nineteenth century. Mexican land and agricultural development were taken over by theft and force. Many Mexicans and Mexican Americans resisted. Folk ballads along the border have long praised the Mexican "bandits," who were often rebel Mexican leaders unwilling to bear quietly the burdens imposed on their people. Their resistance actions are regarded as "crimes" by those in the dominant group, but often *not* by those subordinated. Mexican rebels (for example, Pancho Villa) were protected and praised by Mexican people on both sides of the U.S.–Mexico border. Moreover, much land theft and other oppression of Mexicans in the Southwest had an official or semiofficial status. Law enforcement officers such as the Texas Rangers terrorized Mexicans and Mexican Americans. The commonplace myth of heroic Texas Rangers covers up the oppressiveness of a police force that was long used to repress the Mexican American population.[66]

Over the next century Latinos suffered violence by whites throughout the Southwest. For example, in Los Angeles in the summer of 1943, violent attacks by white sailors on Mexican American youths, particularly those dressed in baggy attire whites called "zoot suits," marked the beginning of white-generated "zoot suit" riots. Groups of whites roamed Los Angeles beating up Mexican Americans, and the latter sometimes organized retaliatory attacks. The local media exaggerated Mexican American crime, and police harassment of Mexican Americans was common. The years leading up to the riots had seen a sharp increase in the *Los Angeles Times*'s use of "zoot suit" to refer to Mexican Americans. Such derogatory labeling fostered white hostility toward local Mexican American residents.[67]

Over more recent decades, to the present, some whites have continued to use violence against Mexican Americans and other Latinos. We cite elsewhere the recent attacks by whites on undocumented immigrants crossing the U.S.–Mexico border, as well as the numerous websites with violent anti-immigrant video games or intensely racist commentaries on immigrants and Spanish speakers. Hate crimes against Mexican Americans and immigrants seem to be on the increase. Recently, in the San Diego area, a restaurant owned by a Mexican family was firebombed, and racist grafitti was sprayed on its wall. In Houston, a Latino teenager was attacked and raped by two white youths, who reportedly were shouting racist comments.[68]

Protests Since the 1960s

During the 1960s and 1970s, dozens of Mexican American protests against discrimination took place in southwestern cities. Young Mexican Americans, including groups such as the Brown Berets, took to the streets to fight back against police harassment and other discrimination. East Los Angeles protests were among the most important. In August 1970, police attacked demonstrators at the end of a National Chicano Moratorium on the Vietnam War march, in which 20,000 Mexican Americans took part. (Activists in the 1960s and 1970s preferred the term *Chicano* to *Mexican American*. Today the term *Chicano* is still used occasionally, mainly by activists and academics.) Hundreds were arrested. Other Mexican American protests during a Mexican Independence Day parade resulted in one hundred injuries and sixty-eight arrests.[69]

Local governments have sometimes used their police forces, which historically have included few if any Mexican Americans, to counter legal strikes and protests by Mexican Americans. From the 1960s to the present, the common practice of preventive police patrolling in Mexican American communities, with its "stop and frisk" and "arrest on suspicion" tactics, has led periodically to unfavorable police contacts for Mexican Americans. Two-thirds of Latinos in one early-1990s Los Angeles poll reported that incidents of police brutality were common. At public hearings, an independent citizens' commission investigating the Los Angeles Police Department heard testimony from Mexican Americans that the department "acted like an army of occupation," treating them as the "enemy."[70] This pattern has persisted to the present. In a more recent *Los Angeles Times* poll, 31 percent of Latinos were strongly critical of the local police department and disagreed that "most Los Angeles police officers are hard-working and honest." Many supported active oversight of the Los Angeles Police Department by federal monitors.[71]

Incidents of police brutality trigger protests and riots. In the major 1992 South Central Los Angeles riot—many called it a rebellion—large numbers of Latinos joined black residents in aggressive and violent protest against general racism, police brutality, and oppressive living conditions (see Chapter 7). And in 1996, Riverside County (California) sheriff's deputies were videotaped, and condemned for, clubbing a Mexican woman and man, both undocumented immigrants, with batons in the process of arresting them.[72]

Widespread anti-immigrant sentiment and the introduction of anti-immigrant ballot measures have stimulated Mexican Americans to organize and take action. In some communities Mexican Americans have responded to anti-immigrant nativism with school walkouts and protests. A large Los Angeles demonstration against one proposition (Proposition 187) illustrated broad-based community support for Mexican American political concerns. In the fall of 1996, about 30,000 Mexican American and other Latino demonstrators in Washington, D.C., denounced restrictions on immigrants and called for an increased minimum wage, better educational programs, and an end to discrimination.[73]

Over the first decade of the twenty-first century, anti-immigrant attitudes and legislation have generated numerous large-scale marches, demonstrations, and strikes by hundreds of thousands of Mexican Americans and their allies in other racial and ethnic groups in cities from Washington and New York to Miami, to Chicago and Denver, to San Francisco and Los Angeles. Thus, in the spring of 2006, hundreds of thousands of (some estimated a million) demonstrators from numerous Latino and other groups participated in the largest public demonstrations in Chicago and Los Angeles history. Participants demanded social justice, fair treatment, and legalization for undocumented immigrant workers and their families. Speaking at the demonstration, the mayor of Los Angeles and the son of Mexican immigrants, Antonio Villaraigosa, asserted that "We cannot criminalize people who are working, people who are contributing to our economy and contributing to the nation." On May 1, 2006, International

Worker's Day, many millions of workers and activists in some two hundred cities boycotted routine school, work, and shopping activities as part of a national protest against the treatment of immigrants. Not surprisingly, recent surveys of Latinos have found that more than 60 percent think the pro-immigrant protests signal a social movement "that will go on for a long time" and that over half say that they would participate in future protests. Numerous analysts have viewed these very large-scale movements as a sign of something new in U.S. protest history—protests that are clearly linked to transnationalism, border crossings, and the globalization of modern capitalism.[74]

The Economy

Recall that Mexicans were initially incorporated into the U.S. economy by often violent conquest and takeovers of Mexican lands. Some 2 million acres of private lands and 1.7 million acres of communal lands were lost to Anglos between 1854 and 1930 just in what is now New Mexico. Across the Southwest, those who lost land often became landless laborers. In the 1850s, one-third of Mexican Americans in the rural south Texas labor force were ranchers and farm owners, one-third were skilled laborers or professionals, and one-third were manual laborers. By 1900 the proportion of ranchers and farm owners had dropped sharply, to 16 percent, while the proportion of laborers—many working on white-owned ranches and farms—had climbed to two-thirds.[75]

Note that Mexican Americans were the original *vaqueros* (Spanish for cowboys) on ranches across the Southwest, and large numbers became agricultural workers there. From the late 1800s to the early 1900s working conditions in agriculture were often so severe and the pay so low that few whites competed with Mexicans for these jobs. Women were concentrated in agriculture, domestic service, and manufacturing, particularly in the garment industry and canneries. Mexican American workers generally earned less than whites and were usually assigned the more physically demanding tasks.[76]

Stratification and Discrimination in the Workplace

Thus, Mexican Americans have long faced individual and institutional discrimination. Beginning in the early 1900s, many white-run agricultural firms, mining companies, and other firms openly paid differential rates for "whites" and "nonwhites"; the latter category included Mexican Americans. The constant availability of undocumented workers allowed white employers to keep wages low. Many white-controlled unions also discriminated against Mexican American workers. Attempts to create farm labor unions for Mexican American and other low-income workers date back several many decades, but they were not successful until the 1960s.[77]

By the 1940s there was some improvement, but discriminatory barriers kept most Mexican Americans in low-wage positions. In 1943, President Franklin Roosevelt's antidiscrimination order and the tight labor supply temporarily opened some jobs at decent wages to Mexican Americans, but virtually none moved up into skilled positions. Poorly paid jobs and housing discrimination restricted most to segregated urban areas sometimes called *barrios*. Restrictive housing covenants were used by whites to exclude Mexican Americans from better housing areas. Since World War II, many Mexican American workers have occupied secondary-labor-market positions as farm workers, laborers, domestic-service workers, or other service workers and earned wages far below those of whites.[78]

Beginning in the 1960s, U.S. firms began building labor-intensive manufacturing plants *(maquiladoras)* in the northern border region of Mexico to take advantage of low-wage Mexican labor. By the 1990s, approximately 1800 U.S.-owned maquiladoras employed half a million people in furniture, electronics, food processing, and other industries. Wages in maquiladoras have been far lower than in similar U.S. plants. Large numbers of Mexican workers in border cities today live in shacks without water, electricity, or sanitation facilities.[79] Many migrate to border areas to work in the maquiladoras just long enough to earn money to migrate to the United States.

Many employers in the southwestern, southern, and midwestern states have long sought out undocumented Mexican workers because they will work, today as in the past, for low wages and can often be exploited more easily than U.S.-born workers. For example, if undocumented workers protest oppressive working conditions, an employer can report them to immigration authorities. Agricultural and service-sector employers frequently rely heavily on undocumented workers and circumvent laws that prohibit hiring them.[80]

In recent years, investigative reporters have discovered numerous immigrants working under slavery-like conditions. In New York, deaf immigrants were forced to sell trinkets for very low wages and live in extremely crowded conditions. Yet, the few exploited workers who come to public attention represent a small portion of those forced to work under extreme conditions. Many restaurant employees work long (for example, fourteen-hour) shifts for less than the minimum wage. Large numbers of domestic workers, housekeepers, and nannies from Mexico, Central America, and the Caribbean work in affluent U.S. households. The "maids and servants" category of workers in the United States has long been racialized. In recent years this occupational racialization has developed a global dimension as affluent U.S. families purchase household and other services from workers from poor countries, especially Latin American countries. These workers tend to work long hours for less than minimum wage. Interviewing 153 Latina domestic workers, Pierrette Hondagneu-Sotelo found that these women pay a high price for their employment: "the loss of dignity, respect, and self-esteem; the inability to even live with their [own] children; and the daily hardships of raising families on poverty-level wages." These immigrant workers are among the most economically and politically oppressed members of this society.[81]

Over the last decade or so, Mexican American and other Latino workers in several New York communities have cited numerous incidents of employment and housing discrimination at the hands of local whites. For example, a "quality of life" group in Farmingville, New York, has been described as a "hate group" concerned mainly with keeping immigrants out. Indeed, in 2001, Farmingville's county executive and legislative body vetoed a proposal to fund a new and safer immigrant laborer hiring site and community center. The beating of two immigrant laborers, apparently by local white supremacists, was not enough to secure action for improved hiring conditions for workers desired by local employers.[82]

Mid-2000s employment testing has documented continuing discrimination against Mexican Americans and other Latinos, as well as for black Americans. Indeed, white job applicants with felony drug convictions are about as likely to be called back or given job offers as Latino applicants *without a criminal record*.[83] Many urban employers in Atlanta, Los Angeles, Detroit, and Boston have admitted that stereotypes about the personality traits and behavior of Latino and black workers influence their hiring decisions. Many employers believe that workers of color are suitable primarily for lower-paying jobs regardless of their skills, and they seldom consider such workers for skilled positions. Even before they have specific knowledge, many employers stereotype Latino and black applicants as less likely than whites to possess skills of interpersonal communication; thus, these applicants are less likely to be hired.[84]

Recent research by Millard and Chapa in several midwestern areas found significantly less job, housing, and school integration of Latinos and Anglos than they expected. "The two groups are quite separate in all sectors of the workplace, including factories, commerce, and services.... Anglos generally pay little attention to the newcomers, who are often left to the practices and prejudices of an Anglo minority that exploits them and another, larger group of Anglos that rebuffs them." Discrimination by a minority of Anglos took place regularly in the context of majority Anglo indifference.[85]

In a San Diego survey, two-thirds of Mexican American youths reported that they had personally faced discrimination. One young woman reported that as a high school senior, despite a good job interview over the phone, she failed to get the job. She noted that "I guess they heard me over the phone, and I guess I sounded kind of white. Once I got to the store, I saw there were only white girls working there. Well, they never called me back."[86] Additional forms of discrimination often await those workers who are hired. A survey of Mexican American and other Latino workers in Los Angeles found that 31 percent had faced racial discrimination in the workplace recently. Discrimination included racial slurs at work and being denied a job or promotion because of their racial background. Recent national surveys of Mexican Americans and other Latinos have found that 38 percent view discrimination as a major problem in the workplace, with an additional 37 percent saying it is a minor but still present problem. More generally, 58 percent think discrimination is a major problem in securing success in U.S. society, with another 24 percent thinking it is a minor problem. Majorities also report that Latinos face discrimination in schools and housing and that debates over immigration have increased anti-Latino discrimination.[87]

In what ways are Mexican American workers exploited economically?

Continuing Language Discrimination

Language discrimination in the workplace involves treating people unfairly because they speak a language that is not English, or because they speak a dialect of English that is not in favor. The Equal Employment Opportunity Commission (EEOC) has reported increases in complaints against employers who bar Spanish-speaking employees from speaking Spanish in job-related or private conversations at work. English-only rules are common in job settings. Many legal scholars feel that such practices constitute national-origin discrimination and thus violate Title VII of the 1964 Civil Rights Act. EEOC regulations state that an English-only rule is discriminatory unless the employer can show a strong business necessity for it.[88]

Court decisions have varied. In *García* v. *Gloor* (1981) the U.S. Supreme Court upheld an employer's right to fire an employee for speaking Spanish. A Mexican American employee of a lumber company was fired for answering a fellow employee's question in Spanish. The Court reasoned that Title VII of the 1964 Civil Rights Act did not equate national origin with primary language and that language discrimination was in this case permissible.[89] In a 1988 case, the Court of Appeals for the Ninth Circuit came to the opposite conclusion after evaluating an English-only rule: "The cultural identity of certain minority groups is tied to the use of their primary tongue." Referring to EEOC regulations, the court stated that "English-only rules... can 'create an atmosphere of inferiority, isolation, and intimidation' [and] can readily mask an intent to discriminate on the basis of national origin." This case was appealed to the U.S. Supreme Court, but the parties reached a settlement before the Court considered it.[90] In 1991 a federal district judge in California ruled that an English-only requirement for employees in a meat-packing plant was discriminatory. Fluency in English had not been a requirement when the employees were hired.[91]

Lawsuits over language discrimination against Mexican Americans and other Latinos have become more common in recent years. A few federal courts have knocked down English-only laws aimed at

TABLE 8.1 Civilian Employees in Executive Branch Agencies, September 2004 (Percentage by Job Category and Group)

Latino civilian employees in the executive branch of the federal government are most heavily represented in the "Other White-Collar" category, in which Latinos make up significant percentages of Border Patrol agents, nuclear materials couriers, and correctional officers. Relatively few hold professional positions. The percentage of Latino workers is highest at low pay levels and lowest at the highest pay levels.

	Latino	White
All white-collar workers	7.3%	69.0%
Professional	4.8	76.5
Clerical	8.3	55.9
Other	17.0	61.3
Blue-collar workers	7.8	65.7
Pay plans		
General schedule	7.2	68.7
GS 1–4	9.3	56.7
GS 14–15	3.9	80.7
Senior pay levels	3.5	86.0

restricting Spanish speech in government settings, on First Amendment grounds. In 2000 the Court of Appeals for the Eleventh Circuit decided *Sandoval* v. *Hagan* and knocked down Alabama's English-only driver's license examinations as a violation of the 1964 Civil Rights Act. However, in the summer of 2001 the U.S. Supreme Court overturned the decision on the grounds that the applicable law did not allow a "private right of action," but the Court did not rule on the argument that language discrimination was national-origin discrimination. Moreover, in the spring of 2001 a Catholic university in Texas reached a $2.4 million settlement in an EEOC lawsuit brought by cleaning personnel. Latino housekeepers charged that they were called "dumb Mexicans" and told by their supervisor to speak only English, even at lunch and on their breaks.[92] The federal law on language discrimination is still developing, but bars to Spanish speaking are viewed as discrimination under EEOC guidelines and a few federal court decisions.

Language discrimination has periodically drawn organized protest from Mexican Americans. In a demonstration of intragroup solidarity in La Puente, a Los Angeles suburb, local Mexican American women organized with Mexican immigrants to stop school board attempts to replace their district's bilingual program with an English-only policy.[93]

Unemployment, Poverty, and Income

Unemployment rates for Mexican Americans have been relatively high for decades. Mexican Americans' unemployment rate for early 2006 (6.2 percent) was significantly higher than that of non-Latino whites (4.1 percent). In Table 8.2, Mexican American workers are more highly concentrated in low-wage job categories than are white workers. Census data treat some Hispanics as white and present both a "white" category and a "non-Hispanic white" category. Data here labeled "European American" represent the latter category. Although there is a significant proportion of Mexican American workers in the white-collar (sales) category, Mexican American workers are heavily concentrated in the production, transportation, construction, natural resources, and service-worker categories, whereas European Americans are more heavily concentrated in white-collar positions. Indeed, Mexican American workers make up a significant percentage of the workers in numerous blue-collar and service categories. (For government employment, see Table 18.1).[94]

Mexican American incomes have been consistently low compared with those of white Americans. Table 8.3 compares family income levels and poverty rates as determined by the Census Bureau in its American Communty survey for Latinos of Mexican, Puerto Rican, and Cuban ancestry with figures for the European ancestry population. On family income measures, Mexican Americans as a group ranked as the poorest, followed by (mainland) Puerto Ricans. The median income for Mexican-origin families was less than 60 percent of that of European-origin families. Mexican American families were nearly three times as likely as European-American families to be poor. In addition, the fact that many Mexican American workers hold relatively low-wage or temporary jobs has meant that economic slowdowns bring an actual decline in wages for workers in these families. Many of the poorest families include workers who immigrated from Mexico in recent decades with

TABLE 8.2 Employment Distribution (2005)

	European American	Mexican American
Managerial and professional specialty	37.7%	14.2%
Sales and office occupations	26.8	19.7
Natural resources, construction, maintenance	10.2	21.9
Production, transportation, materials moving	11.6	20.6
Service occupations	13.7	23.6
Total	100.0%	100.0%

TABLE 8.3 Family Income Levels and Poverty Rates (2005)

	Puerto Rican American	Mexican American	Cuban American	European American
Median family income	$37,534	$35,838	46,717	$62,300
Percentage of:				
Families below poverty level	23.1	22.0	12.8	6.3
Children less than 18 years old below poverty line	32.8	30.5	17.2	10.8

little in the way of educational or economic capital.[95] To make matters worse for these and other Mexican American families, there are dramatic differences in the reported wealth of Latinos (Mexican Americans and other groups) and European Americans (see Table 8.4). According to 2002 data analyzed by the Pew Hispanic Center, the median net worth of Latino households, at $7932, was less than 10 percent of that of the median net worth for white households.[96]

Are covert methods used by some whites in discriminating against Mexican Americans?

Problems of Economic Adaptation

Some analysts have suggested that the processes of adaptation for later immigrant groups, such as Mexican immigrants, are, or should be, similar to those for early-twentieth-century groups, such as Italian immigrants. However, the first large groups of Mexican immigrants and their children—those who came between World War I and the 1950s—did not achieve the same socioeconomic mobility as southern and eastern European immigrants because of discrimination, economic exploitation, and segregation. Later groups of Mexican immigrants, those who have come since the 1960s, have also faced different circumstances. The white southern and

TABLE 8.4 Percentage Distribution of Household Net Worth by Group and Amount of Net Worth, 2000

In the most census recent data (2000), more than one-quarter of Hispanic households had zero or negative net worth, and the net worth of an additional 15.9 percent was less than $5000. Four in ten white households had a net worth of $100,000 or more, compared with one in six Hispanic households. Just 5.1 percent of Hispanic households had a net worth of $250,000 or more, compared with a fifth of white households.

	White	Hispanic
Negative or $0	11.3%	27.6%
$1–$4,999	7.2	15.9
$5,000–$24,999	12.4	17.2
$25,000–$99,999	24.6	22.8
$100,000–$249,000	22.2	11.4
$250,000 or over	22.2	5.1

eastern European immigrants did not experience the high levels of job, residential, and school segregation and the racist stereotyping that have long been experienced by Mexican and other Latino immigrants. Most Europeans came during a period of rapid industrialization and had access to blue-collar jobs that required little education. These conditions usually enabled white immigrant workers and their children to advance economically.

In contrast, today the United States has a predominantly service-work-dominated economy with increasingly few industrial jobs. Most well-paid jobs today require more than a high school education. Unlike European immigrants in the early 1900s, many recent Mexican and other Latino immigrants, especially those with relatively little formal education, have been able to find only low-paid jobs with little chance of mobility. Thus, segmented assimilation describes the experience of many Mexican American workers and their children. The children of these immigrants, second-generation Mexican Americans, today often do not move up the socioeconomic ladder as the second generation of earlier white immigrant groups did. This is substantially the result of the U.S. economy no longer providing enough decent-paying blue-collar jobs, as it did for much of the twentieth century for white immigrants and their children.

Recent research shows two divergent patterns of economic mobility over the first few generations of Mexican American adaptation. Researcher Zulema Valdéz has shown from census data that "earnings of low-skilled, foreign-born Mexicans *decrease* as immigrants reside in the United States longer.... In contrast, the earnings of high-skilled, foreign-born Mexicans *increase* as immigrants reside in the United States longer. . ." Immigrant status, level of education, and continuing discrimination all make a difference. Elsewhere Valdéz suggests that data indicating a large economic gap between Mexican Americans and whites and a persisting "intergenerational, low-wage, low-skilled Mexican laboring class" are not surprising for a country that has "a racialized and gendered labor market, growing wage inequality, tougher immigration policy, and an upsurge in anti-Mexican-immigrant sentiment."[97]

Moreover, as we saw in Chapter 7, the concept of a troubled "underclass"—one characterized by multigenerational poverty, high violent-crime rates, a school dropout problem, teenage pregnancy, and long-term drug use—has been accepted by some social scientists and media analysts as a way of explaining the impoverished conditions of certain racial and ethnic groups, including African Americans and Mexican Americans. Assessing Mexican American and other Latino communities in cities from Los Angeles to New York, several social scientists have examined these communities' cultures and strengths, as well as their problems.[98] Even in the face of substantial poverty and political and economic discrimination, these communities generally maintain strong family and community support structures, community organizations, and enclave economies. For example, an analysis of social and economic conditions in Laredo, Texas, found that the city's border location facilitates illegal drug trafficking, yet the area's strong Latino extended families and residential stability have created "a strong sense of community structure and identification."[99] In several cities, small local businesses and off-the-books enterprises such as street vending have promoted the economic vitality of numerous Latino communities.

The movement of large numbers of immigrants into many Latino communities has also buttressed local economies and maintained a demand for businesses that provide Latino goods and services. The concentration of the poor that underclass theorists emphasize as negative can be positive. Thus, residential concentration of immigrants in cities like Houston has stimulated development of an enclave economy, reinforced job and housing networks, and provided a supportive cultural setting. Recent research continues to confirm the strengths of families, religion, and organization in Mexican American communities, with their still large populations of working poor.[100]

Contrary to conventional underclass notions, researchers do not find just one pattern of responses to poverty conditions. The character of poverty varies from community to community, but each has used its oppositional culture and social, economic, and religious resources for survival. Although many of the characteristics associated with the conventional underclass portrait can be found, such conditions do not fundamentally *define* the character of these communities. Extended family and other networks, as well as strong cultural frameworks, remain at the core of these communities;

these are reinforced by religious organizations and, frequently, additional community organizations.

Immigrant Workers: Targeted for Discrimination

Mexicans and Mexican Americans are now the neighbors of other Americans in all U.S. regions. For the most part, Mexican and other Latin American immigrants work hard under difficult conditions and often for little pay. They perform much hard labor shunned by others: harvesting crops, building and cleaning houses, cutting lawns, and washing dishes in restaurants.

However, when it comes to having these workers as neighbors, many other Americans treat them as unwanted outsiders. Growing numbers report housing and related discrimination by their white neighbors. Local officials periodically enforce local housing codes so as to discriminate against Latino workers. A lawsuit by landlords in the Babylon area on Long Island accused town officials of using rental permits and apartment regulations to drive out Latino immigrant workers. An organization representing Mexican American and other Latino farmworkers in Riverside County, California, reached a settlement with county officials resolving complaints of discrimination in code enforcement there. A U.S. Department of Housing and Urban Development (HUD) investigation confirmed that county officials had used discriminatory code enforcement to exclude Latino residents from mobile home parks.[101] HUD also cited officials in Elgin, Illinois, for violating an agreement to end discrimination in local code enforcement. In 1999 the city had settled complaints filed by Latino families, but officials failed to honor their promises to change code enforcement and accept HUD monitoring. These represent only a few of many such cases. One recent report shows that at least thirty towns have considered, and six have passed, some type of local legislation aimed at discriminating against immigrant workers. In addition to housing discrimination, various new or proposed laws attempt to deny business permits to employers who hire undocumented workers or to require the language of business or government to be only in English.[102]

In many cities, housing discrimination by landlords plagues Latino families, both immigrant families and those whose members have been citizens for generations. Audit studies using Latino and white testers in San Antonio and Fresno have found substantial rates of housing discrimination. Moreover, in the summer of 2000, a large apartment management firm in Orange County, California, paid $226,000 in damages and penalties to settle a case brought by the county's Fair Housing Council that charged the company with discrimination against Latino and black renters in eight apartment complexes.[103]

Not surprisingly, given these patterns of intentional discrimination in housing, coupled with the desire to live with fellow Latinos who have similar experiences and backgrounds (including knowledge of how to cope with discrimination), more than 40 percent of Latinos now live in Latino-majority neighborhoods. This U.S. proportion is high, though somewhat less than that for African Americans, and increased between 1990 and the mid-2000s.[104]

Politics and Protest

Before 1910 only a few Mexican Americans, usually hand-picked by whites, held office in territorial and state legislatures in the Southwest. White ranchers and those who controlled railroads, mining interests, land companies, and other large enterprises dominated local and state politics.[105] By means of a poll tax, an all-white primary, and threats of violence, these interests kept Mexican American voting strength low. Similarly, between 1910 and the 1940s, few Mexican Americans voted in the Southwest. Over subsequent decades, voting strength was expanded by legal victories in the form of the Twenty-Fourth Amendment, which banned poll taxes, and a California court case that knocked down an English-only literacy requirement for voting.

In some areas the gerrymandering of voting districts has continued to dilute Mexican American voting strength and prevent the election of Mexican American political candidates. Lawsuits, for example, *Garza* v. *County of Los Angeles* (1990) and *Williams* v. *City of Dallas* (1990), have challenged intentional discrimination against the Latino voting population, such as the discriminatory use of at-large city council elections.[106] These lawsuits have forced some white-controlled governments to create single-member districts that allow for the possibility of elected Latino political officials.

Voter registration and voter turnout among Mexican Americans and other Latinos have risen substantially over the past three decades. In this period the number registered to vote "increased from 2.5 million to more than 10.5 million. In fact, the number of new Latino registered voters increased by over 3 million between the presidential election of 2000 and the presidential election of 2004."[107] However, as of late 2006, only about 39 percent of Latinos were U.S. citizens over the age of eighteen and thus eligible to vote—which was much less than the 77 percent of whites who were eligible. Latino voters then made up only 8.6 percent of all U.S. voters, albeit a figure growing significantly each year.[108] Large numbers of potential Latino voters are, as yet, too young or have not yet become citizens.

Growing Political Representation

Recent surveys indicate that Latinos are very committed to working together to increase Latino political participation and political power. Numerous examples of slowly expanding, sometimes regressing, political participation can be seen in the counties and cities of the Southwest and other regions, from the late 1940s to the present. Los Angeles, with the largest Mexican American population of any U.S. city, elected its first Mexican American city council member in 1949. However, the city had no Mexican Americans on its council between the early 1960s and the early 1970s. In 1991, Gloria Molina, the daughter of a Mexican immigrant laborer, became the first Mexican American, and first woman, elected to the Los Angeles County Board of Supervisors.[109]

The National Association of Latino Elected and Appointed Officials Educational Fund has become one of the important organizations seeking to empower Latinos. The organization's thousands of members come from all government levels; the organization has played a major role in increasing Latino voter registration and turnout. A study of 435 congressional districts found that one-fourth have a Latino population percentage of at least 12 percent, enough to be politically significant. In recent years, many of these districts have had Republican members of Congress. Given that a majority of Latino voters—with the exception of Cuban Americans—still vote Democratic, the future translation of now-young Latino Americans into voters may bode well for Democratic Party candidates.[110]

Since World War II, the total number of Mexican Americans serving at all political levels has increased gradually but significantly, to about 5160 in 2006. Gradually, the growing numbers of registered Latino voters have brought the group greater political power. Mexican Americans and other Latinos currently constitute the largest voting bloc in Miami, San Antonio, Los Angeles, and New York.[111] Several cities, small and large, have had Mexican American mayors. In 1981, Henry Cisneros, who later served as secretary of housing and urban development in the Bill Clinton administration, was elected mayor of San Antonio, the first Mexican American mayor of a large city. His victory was the culmination of ten years of organization. Cisneros was elected by means of a political alignment between a white business elite and the city's new Latino middle class. In 2001, a young city councilmember, Ed Garza, was elected as San Antonio's mayor with a similar coalition. Such coalitions of Anglo business elites and the Latino middle class have been successful in several cities, including those along the U.S.–Mexico border. The most successful Latino politicians since the 1980s have tended to be business- or professional-oriented rather than community activists or labor leaders. In the early 2000s, five major cities had Mexican American mayors (San José and Santa Ana, California; El Paso and San Antonio, Texas; and Albuquerque, New Mexico); four of these had a business or professional background. In 2005, Antonio Villaraigosa, the son of Mexican immigrants, was elected mayor of Los Angeles, the country's second largest city.[112]

Between the 1960s and the mid-2000s, the number of Latinos in state legislatures increased significantly, with the largest numbers in Texas, California, and New Mexico. As of 2005, Texas had about 2000 Latino elected officials, the largest number of any state; these included about 19 percent of Texas House members and about 23 percent of the Texas Senate members, most of whom were Democrats. California had nearly one-fifth of all Latino elected officials (1080), including about one-quarter of all state legislators, most of whom were also Democrats. New Mexico had the third largest number of Latino elected officials (668).[113]

Still, the number of Mexican American and other Latino elected and appointed officials at the state and national levels remains low relative to the Latino population percentage. Only a handful have ever

In a 2001 election, former California Assembly speaker Antonio Villaraigosa came close to being elected the first Latino mayor of Los Angeles. In a 2005 election he was elected mayor.

served in top state executive positions, such as governors. In 1988, President Ronald Reagan appointed Lauro Cavazos as secretary of education, the first Mexican American (and Latino) ever appointed to a presidential cabinet. President Bill Clinton appointed two Mexican Americans to cabinet posts, and in 2001 President George W. Bush appointed one Latino, a Cuban American, to his cabinet. In addition, as of late 2006 there were twenty-three Latino members of the U.S. House of Representatives (nineteen of them Democrats). This representation marked a significant increase over recent decades, but the Latino percentage (5.3 percent) of House members was well below the Latino percentage (14 percent) of the population. By late 2006 there were also three Latinos in the U.S. Senate (from New Jersey, Florida, Colorado) and one Latino governor (New Mexico).[114]

These growing numbers are politically significant in many ways. For example, the international concerns of many Mexican Americans have helped to expand the political involvement of Mexican American and other U.S. leaders in the international arena, including the U.S. government placing a greater emphasis on relations between the United States and Mexico. Moreover, where Mexican Americans and other Latinos have been elected to office and increased their numbers in state and local bureaucracies, including as officials and teachers in school systems, significant educational and other socioeconomic advancements (such as high school graduation) have been demonstrated.[115]

Support for the Democratic Party

In national elections since 1990, a majority of Latino voters nationwide have supported Democratic Party candidates. In the 1996 election, Latino voters, the majority of whom were Mexican American, for the first time voted at a rate greater than the national rate. This Latino turnout had an important impact not only on the presidential election but also on local and state elections from New York to California. Most voted for Democratic candidates, although one survey revealed that the percentage voting for the Democratic presidential candidate (Bill Clinton) declined from 93 percent of the first-generation (immigrant) respondents to 75 percent of the fourth generation.[116]

In the 2000 presidential election, an estimated 63 percent of Latinos voted for the Democratic candidate. Significantly, both the Democratic candidate, Al Gore, and the Republican victor, George W. Bush, spoke Spanish during the campaign and actively sought Latino voters, a first for presidential elections. In his first year in office, Bush became the *first* president to give a White House address in Spanish. Moreover, in the 2004 presidential election, exit polls suggested that 44 percent of Latino voters had given their votes to President Bush for reelection, an increase since 2000. However, in the 2006 elections for the U.S. Congress, the Latino vote increased for Democratic candidates across the country, as Latino voters apparently showed their negative reaction to the moves of the Republican-majority Congress to support anti-immigrant legislation. Surveys of registered Latino voters revealed that just 19 percent were planning to vote for Republican candidates in those congressional elections. In recent decades a majority of Latinos have voted for Democratic Party candidates in most state, Local, and federal elections. Clearly, Latino voters are now having a significant influence on U.S. politics.[117]

The Courts and the Police

Mexican Americans have long been underrepresented in the U.S. judicial system, as jurors, judges, and prosecutors. In *Hernández* v. *Texas* (1954), the U.S. Supreme Court upheld an appeal of an all-white jury's conviction of a Mexican American defendant on the grounds that Mexican Americans were excluded. The judge noted that the lack of Mexican American representation on any jury over a period of twenty-five years in a county that was 14 percent Mexican American was evidence of discrimination.[118]

Not until the 1960s was the first Mexican American federal judge appointed. Since the 1970s the number has slowly increased, but it is still relatively low today. Mexican Americans are underrepresented in most historically white police departments. Over recent decades, numerous Mexican American applicants have been denied police positions by the indirect discrimination of height requirements and by English-language requirements, as well as by too-low scores on conventional English-language examinations. Today all Latinos taken together make up about 11 percent of police officers, but only 6 percent of first-line supervisors in police agencies. They make up only 3.5 percent of lawyers and 6 percent of various judicial workers. Very few Latinos have ever served at the higher levels of federal law-enforcement agencies, although in 2007 the U.S. attorney general, Alberto Gonzáles, was a Mexican American.[119]

Arizona, California, and Colorado have required jurors to be able to speak English, screening out many citizens. In these and other states, the pool of jurors has until recently been selected by whatever method has suited (usually white) jury commissioners. Recent research in major Texas cities has shown that Latinos make up less than 10 to 13 percent of those called for jury duty in cities whose populations are at least 30 percent Latino. Many juries have included no Latino jurors. Thus, Mexican Americans charged with crimes have frequently been judged by juries containing few if any of their peers. Courtrooms in which no one understands Spanish present a problem for some defendants. Besides facing an absence of Spanish interpreters, defendants have been subjected to excessive bail, poor legal counsel, and stereotyped views of white judges. In some cases, white prosecutors have successfully excluded Latinos from juries on the basis of language. One 1990s Supreme Court decision upheld a prosecutor's exclusion of bilingual Latino jurors who had hesitated before agreeing to accept the official English translation of the Spanish-language testimony in a trial. In contrast, a judge in San Diego County, California, dismissed indictments by a grand jury because the pool from which jurors were selected did not represent a fair cross section of the county.[120]

Moreover, a recent survey of Latinos found that only 35 percent felt that Latinos usually or always "receive fair outcomes when they deal with the courts" in their communities, which compared to 57 percent and 21 percent, respectively, of white and black respondents. Latino and black respondents also had substantially *less* favorable views of the police in their communities than did whites. Early 2000s data for San Diego police officers stopping motorists showed that Latino and black motorists were overrepresented in comparison to the driving-age population and were more likely to be searched when stopped. The same pattern of racial profiling characterizes other major cities. In 2006 a national survey of local residents' views of police behavior found that a significant percentage (45 percent) of Latino respondents felt that their local police officers were stopping people without good reason and were engaging in racial profiling.[121]

The Chicano Political Movement

Disenchantment with the accomodationist perspectives of some middle-class Mexican American leaders led to the emergence of the 1960s' **Chicano**

political movement, *a social movement that sought greater political power and less discrimination for Mexican Americans*. Lacking influence in mainstream political parties, many Mexican Americans joined the La Raza Unida Party (LRUP). The LRUP's goals included significant representation in local governments and pressing the latter to better serve the Latino community. LRUP's major electoral and political successes occurred in Crystal City, a Texas city populated mostly by Mexican Americans. During the 1960s the LRUP became a leading political force, and by 1970 Mexican Americans had won control of the school board and city council. However, white officials cut off state and federal funding, almost bankrupting the city, and then blamed the Mexican American leadership for the difficulties. By the 1980s, Mexican Americans were no longer identified with the LRUP but rather with the state Democratic party. Yet, the LRUP had brought democratization to some southwestern communities and a substantial increase in political participation.[122]

Mexican American women held a range of important leadership roles within the LRUP. Most of those elected to office in the Crystal City area were women. This feminism came "easily for Chicanas because of the woman's traditional role and strength as center or heart of the family.... The tradition of activism inherited from women's participation in armed rebellions in Mexico and in the political life of Mexico has also strengthened the Chicanas' position."[123] Mexican American feminists have faced major barriers. For decades, many issues of great concern to them, including poverty and discrimination, have not been central to the mainstream (white) women's movement.

What is the long-term significance of growing political participation among Mexican Americans?

Other Organizations and Protest

Union organization has a long history among Mexican Americans. The first permanent organization was the Confederación de Uniones Obreras Mexicanas (CUOM), organized in California in 1927 with 3000 members. One CUOM strike was stopped by deportation to Mexico and numerous arrests. Mexican American women participated in early strikes as members of the International Ladies Garment Workers Union. In addition, mutual-benefit associations developed early. These included worker alliances that pooled resources and provided individual and group support. The League of United Latin American Citizens (LULAC) was organized in southern Texas in the 1920s. Oriented toward civic activities, LULAC also pressed for an end to discrimination.[124]

After a Texas cemetery refused to allow the burial of a Mexican American (World War II) veteran, the American GI Forum was established to organize Mexican American veterans and work for expanded civil rights. In Los Angeles the Community Service Organization worked to organize voters. Two groups that formed about 1960—the Mexican American Political Association in California and the Political Association of Spanish-Speaking Organizations in Texas—focused mostly on political goals. Protests intensified in the 1960s. Youth organizations including the Mexican American Youth Organization and the Brown Berets worked for better education, employment, and housing. A new ideology of *Chicanismo* that espoused a philosophy of self-esteem and antiracism developed in many circles. The Alianza Federal de Mercedes was founded in 1963 by Reies Lopez Tijerina after he had researched old Mexican land grants. In July 1966 a group of Alianza members marched to Santa Fe, New Mexico, and presented a statement of grievances about Anglo theft of Mexican land grants in the state.[125]

Since the 1980s, the Southwest Voter Registration Education Project and similar groups have participated in many voter-registration campaigns and joined in filing lawsuits to dismantle discriminatory election systems. The Mexican American Legal Defense and Education Fund (MALDEF), founded in 1968 to address problems of jury discrimination, police brutality, and school segregation, is another active force for change. MALDEF has filed numerous class-action lawsuits targeting discrimination and has worked to increase political representation.[126] With the recent growth in Mexican American and other Latino populations in states outside the Southwest, MALDEF has expanded its civil rights efforts to the east coast, opening an Atlanta office in 2002, where another Latino organization, the National Council of La Raza, has also recently set up a regional office. Discrimination targeting Mexican Americans and other Latinos in the southeast has influenced the expansion of antidiscrimination efforts by these important civil rights groups.[127]

Today, Mexican American women remain active in grass-roots organizing. For example, Mothers of East Los Angeles is an effective grass-roots organization that works to defend its community's quality of life against environmental racism and corporate pollution. At a neighborhood meeting, MELA members confronted an oil company representative seeking to build a pipeline through a Latino community in Los Angeles:

> "Is it going through Cielito Lindo [former President Ronald Reagan's ranch]?" The oil representative answered, "No." Another woman stood up and asked, "Why not place it along the coastline?" Without thinking of the implications, the representative responded, "Oh, no! If it burst, it would endanger the marine life." The woman retorted, "You value the marine life more than human beings?"[128]

César Chávez marches at the head of United Farm Workers during a 1979 protest.

Unions for Low-Wage Workers

In the 1960s, Jessie López, Dolores Huerta, and César Chávez created the Agricultural Workers Organizing Committee (AWOC) and the National Farm Workers Association (NFWA). In 1965, AWOC workers struck the Delano, California, growers; the NFWA met in Delano and voted to join the strike, demanding better wages. White growers refused to talk; picket lines went up; and guns were fired at workers. The NFWA remained nonviolent in the face of provocation by growers and police. A grape boycott was organized and spread. Picket lines formed wherever grapes were sold, and a massive march on Sacramento was organized. In 1966, AWOC and NFWA merged into the United Farm Workers Organizing Committee.[129]

In 1973, the largest California winery, Gallo Brothers, chose not to renew its contract with the United Farm Workers (UFW). As other wineries followed suit, many observers argued that the union was dying. But the struggle continued. Governor Jerry Brown of California worked for legislation to protect workers, and in 1975 signed the Agricultural Labor Relations Act, which provided for protection of union activities.[130] The UFW has been the most successful farm workers' union in history and has altered the structure of power in rural California by using the power of organized numbers to pressure for economic and political change. Among other issues, the UFW has addressed the issue of pesticide spraying of farm products in a nationwide campaign to force farmers to "stop poisoning workers and consumers."[131]

In the spring of 1994, one year after the death of César Chávez, more than eighty current and former farm workers, some of whom had made the first such pilgrimage twenty-eight years earlier, walked the 340 miles from Delano to Sacramento, California, signing up thousands of new UFW members along the way. From then to the present day the UFW has continued to organize and strike on behalf of farmworkers. A recent report from the UFW website summarizes the results of organizing drives, including a long campaign that led to a new contract with the Gallo winery. The union also "mounted a major organizing drive among Central Valley table grape workers resulting in a summer election at Giumarra vineyards, America's largest table grape producer.

Labor observers say it is one of the largest private sector union election campaigns in the nation in 2005."[132]

Today, many Mexican American and other farmworkers across the country still get low wages and few benefits. They often live in very crowded conditions, and many who favor unions are harassed by employers. In the early 2000s, at least 60 percent of farm-worker families remained below the federal poverty line. The UFW, once at 80,000 members, is now down to about 27,000. In 2006 the UFW left the AFL-CIO and joined a more aggressive union coalition that included the Service Employees International Union, the Teamsters, and the United Food and Commercial Workers. Today, more farm workers are undocumented than in the early days of the UFW. These workers are often afraid to organize. Still, union membership has again been growing slowly. Explaining the decline and recent increase, union leaders note that the 1975 Agricultural Labor Relations Act was weakly enforced under sixteen years of rule in the 1980s and 1990s by Republican governors of California. In the early 2000s, however, there was a Democratic governor more sympathetic to workers and labor unions and to enforcement of the act. Soon, however, in 2003 he was replaced by a moderate Republican governor (Arnold Schwarzenegger), whose support for unions was weaker.[133]

Today, an increasing number of Mexican Americans are members of mainstream unions that represent auto workers, miners, teamsters, dockworkers, and railroad, cannery, garment, steel, and construction workers. Unionizing efforts have periodically been successful among undocumented urban workers.[134] In Los Angeles in the late 1990s, the local of the Hotel Employees and Restaurant Employees International Union called for an international boycott of the New Otani Hotel because of its poor treatment of Latino and Asian workers. Workers began large-scale picketing and made it clear that the diverse composition of the workforce did not deter union organization. Latinas, in particular, were critical to the union and its protests. Women activists proved wrong traditional notions that women would be "unorganizable because of their family responsibilities, marginal commitment to the labor market, and submission to patriarchy." In August 2000, as the boycott and strike continued, a protest against working conditions at the hotel by four hundred union workers was met by two hundred police officers in riot gear. Forty workers were arrested for blocking the intersection with clothes symbolizing the "dirty laundry" the hotel was unwilling to face.[135]

In the mid- to late 2000s, a few other unions, including the Service Employees International Union (SEIU), have aggressively organized Latino workers. Recently, an SEIU branch in Houston, called Justice for Janitors, has organized hundreds of janitors, who clean much Houston office space. Most are Mexican American women and other Latinas. The union has drawn on a significant multiracial coalition of Houston community organizations, religious groups, and other labor unions. As Glenn Bracey describes it, "Catholic churches and majority Latino organizations, such as CRECEN and LULAC, united with majority African American organizations, such as ACORN and NAACP, to push for improved living conditions for Houston's working poor. In many ways, Justice for Janitors' Houston campaign provides a model for interracial coalitions and exemplifies the power multiracial coalitions can have, even in traditionally hostile political environments."[136] In Houston most such janitors have typically gotten a minimum wage and have been limited to just four hours a day of work, with no health insurance benefits. In late 2006 the Houston union went on a successful strike against cleaning companies that refused to sign a reasonable contract adding some health benefits for these hard-working janitors. Many of the 225,000 janitors organized by SEIU in numerous cities are Latino. Today, union efforts to improve Latinos' working conditions continue across the United States.

Other Recent Challenges: Latinos and African Americans

The growing Mexican American and other Latino populations in urban areas have brought Latinos into situations of political conflict and cooperation with long-time African American residents. Together, the two groups now make up a majority of the population in numerous U.S. cities. Capitalistic globalization is drawing Mexican and other immigrant workers to the United States, and the shift from an industrial to a service economy is reducing the number of higher-wage, unionized, blue-collar jobs available for both groups. Modern capitalism sometimes pits new immigrants against established citizens who rely substantially on lower-wage blue-collar and service jobs.

Debates in the policy and scholarly literatures sometimes focus on whether recent Latin American and Asian immigration has affected the economic situations of native-born Americans. According to available data, employment problems have increased for many African Americans since the 1970s. National Research Council (NRC) and similar recent reports indicate that immigration has had a generally positive effect on the U.S. economy as a whole, with same negative effects on employment opportunities for other recent immigrants and some native-born Americans. Most undocumented workers labor in just two dozen or so low-wage occupations and earn wages near the minimum wage, if not below, and thus most native-born workers are not affected in a negative way. Recent undocumented immigration has brought significant benefits to employers and better-off native-born workers, because they are the most likely to use the low-cost labor or services (for example, household work) of immigrants. The negative impact is greatest for high school dropouts and less skilled workers, including those Latinos and African Americans working in low-paid jobs. One analysis of immigration's effects concluded that "studies provide compelling documentation that the overall positive economic effects of immigration emphasized by the NRC in the country as a whole do not extend to African Americans.... In general, the economic implications of immigration appear less than benign."[137]

Capitalism-generated competition between immigrants and less skilled native-born workers has the potential to generate recurring conflict, but so does general political competition between larger groups of Latinos and African Americans. In Dallas, for example, a struggle between the two groups over who should become school superintendent was resolved by the appointment of a black Puerto Rican candidate. Substantial conflicts between Latino and black groups related to elections in Miami, public housing in Chicago, and school and hospital hiring in Los Angeles have occurred. Typically, the issues involve a growing Latino population that has not achieved full representation in public jobs and elected positions, which are often held by black urbanites.[138]

White-controlled mass media tend to focus on conflict and neglect cooperation, which is more common than conflict. For example, the head of the Los Angeles Human Rights Commission has reported that at the neighborhood level Latinos and blacks there are generally finding ways to coexist and cooperate. Some black elected officials are working hard to better serve their new Latino constituents, many of whom have recently moved into formerly black areas.[139] Over recent decades, black and Latino communities in Texas have often shown respect for one another. One 1970s study of Mexican American attitudes in Texas found more positive feelings toward African Americans, more sensitivity to discriminatory barriers, and more support for civil rights protest than were found among whites. More recently, black leaders and union members marched with Latinos in San Antonio to demonstrate against California's Proposition 187. And in a late-1990s Houston election, Latino voters helped elect a black mayor against white opposition. In surveys, a majority of Houston's black and Latino leaders report that they interact frequently with leaders of other groups. In the late 2000s black leaders and organizations there worked closely with Latinos to create a strong service-workers union, the Justice for Janitors group mentioned previously.[140]

Education

In the early twentieth century, little official attention was given to the public education of Mexican Americans. Whites who controlled the economy of the Southwest pressed for low-wage labor without the expense of public education. Schooling was typically minimal. Before World War II, Mexican American schoolchildren from Texas to California were often racially segregated. However, as a rule, Mexican Americans were segregated by local laws or by informally gerrymandered school district lines rather than by state law. Extensive white-generated discrimination in housing reinforced school segregation.[141]

Recurring Education Problems

After World War II, many communities began to demand changes. A major conference in 1946 called for an end to segregation, the adoption of a Mexican-oriented curriculum, better teacher training, and improved school facilities. In *Méndez* v. *Westminster* (1946), a federal judge ruled that segregation of children in "Mexican schools" in California violated the Fourteenth Amendment because these children were separated on the basis of their surnames. The educational theory expressed in the *Méndez* case anticipated the Supreme Court's ruling in *Brown* v. *Board of Education* almost a decade later. After *Méndez*, California laws allowing segregation were repealed.[142]

For decades, some schools with high percentages of Mexican American students prohibited all manifestations of Mexican American subculture. Teachers' classroom behavior, which has a strong relationship to student achievement, often downgraded the children's heritage. Teachers often anglicized children's names (for instance, Roberto became Bobby). One 1960s study found that the average teacher praised white children more often than Mexican American children, questioned them more often, and used their ideas more often. Mexican American children were overrepresented in classes for the mentally retarded. Most in these classes were only "six-hour retarded" children—capable of functioning well in the outside world yet mislabeled largely as a result of in-school discrimination and poor testing. Tests of children were (and often still are) usually conducted in English.[143]

Current Education Issues: Segregation and Bilingualism

Although certain discriminatory practices, such as disproportionate placement in classes for the "mentally retarded," had been eliminated from most schools by the 1980s, some discrimination has remained. In the 2000s, public schools still place too many Mexican American children in learning-disabled classes, school textbooks still neglect Mexican American history, and *de facto* racial segregation persists. Recent research by the Civil Rights Project of Harvard University found that intense segregation for Latino students is greater today than at the beginning of the civil rights revolution more than thirty years ago. In 1968 some 23 percent of Latino students attended intensely segregated schools (minority enrollment of 90 percent or more); recent data indicate that at least 39 percent of Latino students (including those in the Southwest) attend such highly segregated schools. In addition, the study reports that most of the segregated schools have high concentrations of children from low-income families.[144] A spokesperson for the National Council of La Raza has explained, "... Latinos are highly concentrated in schools that don't have the requirements that research has shown are necessary for a quality education—small schools, small classes, qualified teachers, decent facilities, quality curriculum, high expectations."[145]

Significantly, from its colonial beginning, the United States has been a land of many languages. In the eighteenth century the Articles of Confederation were officially published in English, German, and French. California's first constitution (1849), published in Spanish and English, provided that "all laws, decrees, regulations, and provisions" be printed in both languages. New Mexico's laws were published in Spanish and English from the time this area became a U.S. territory through the first forty years of statehood, until—under nativist pressure—languages other than English were labeled "foreign."[146]

When placed in English-only classrooms, children with limited English proficiency frequently become discouraged, develop low self-confidence, and fail to keep pace with their native-English-speaking peers. Many Latino students today face such a situation. For this reason, effective bilingual programs remain important. Although the Elementary and Secondary Education Act (1968) established a way for the federal government to fund bilingual programs in schools to meet the needs of language-minority children, by 1973 no southwestern state had taken more than a few token steps. The Supreme Court decision in *Lau* v. *Nichols* (1974), which established a child's ability to understand classroom instruction as a civil right, made it illegal for school systems to ignore English-language problems of language-minority groups. For a time, federal programs provided substantial funding for local school district programs to increase the English proficiency of children whose primary language is not English. Yet, apart from some stellar programs in schools with sensitive principals in scattered school systems, the overall picture is now one of decline, backtracking, and organized opposition. A majority of voters in California, Massachusetts, and Arizona voted in recent years to eliminate bilingual education, while one state's voters (Colorado) voted against ending programs. Forced immersion into English, regardless of the effect on immigrant children, is the view of a non-Latino majority in many areas.[147]

One researcher has summed up the bleak trends this way:

> Bilingual educators find themselves increasingly isolated and hard-pressed to resist attacks. [Limited-English-proficient] students have fewer options, as many school districts limit access to native-language instruction and others convert to English-only models altogether. The nation's 30-year experiment with bilingual education, despite its success in many schools and its benefits to many children, is branded a failure in the public mind.[148]

One stubborn myth about bilingual instruction, often propagated by nativist organizations, is that there is no research evidence that bilingual programs are effective. Yet, numerous research studies show that well-crafted and adequately funded bilingual programs are successful. Effective bilingual programs do not create or foster ethnic enclaves. Today, Latino immigrants and their children, including those in bilingual programs, are generally learning English *much faster* than earlier European immigrants.[149]

Educational Achievement and Continuing Problems

In 1950 more than half of Mexican American adults had less than a sixth-grade education, and fewer than 8 percent were high school graduates. By 2004 about half were high-school graduates and almost 8 percent had at least a college degree. However, Mexican Americans currently have the lowest levels of education of any major U.S. group. Table 8.5 compares the educational attainment in 2005 of Mexican-American, mainland Puerto Rican, Cuban-American, and European-American adults over twenty-four years of age.[150]

Mexican Americans' educational attainment is the lowest of the three Latino groups and lower than that of European Americans. This is in part because of the recent large-scale infusion of poorly educated immigrants. Today a majority of foreign-born Mexican American adults are not high school graduates. In addition, economic and other pressures generate a high dropout rate. Recent research by the UCLA Chicano Studies Research Center has found that for every one hundred Mexican American students beginning first grade, less than half (forty-six) become high school graduates, only eight graduate from college, and only two secure a graduate or professional degree. For whites the figures are much higher, with eighty-four of one hundred graduating from high school, twenty-six from college, and ten getting a graduate or professional degree. The educational levels of the Mexican-origin population today not only show evidence of decades of limited economic and educational opportunities, often because of overt discrimination, but also indicate the recent large-scale immigration of many less educated immigrants.[151] Limited education contributes to the wide income gap between Mexican American and white workers. "It's a vicious circle. This wage differential makes it so everyone in the family has to work, which is one of the biggest reasons for the [school] dropout rate."[152]

The dropout rate—some call it the pushout rate—for Mexican American students in public schools remains high. Variations in reporting methods for dropout rates and the fact that students drop in and out of school make it impossible to arrive at an exact figure, but estimates for all Latino groups combined range from two times to three times that of non-Latinos, and Mexican Americans rank at the high end among Latino groups. Poverty and the need to earn money to help support their families are obstacles. Nonetheless, a few schools have increased graduation rates significantly by providing programs to address such student concerns as jobs, substance abuse, and teen parenthood.[153]

TABLE 8.5 Educational Attainment, 2005 (Percentages at Selected Levels by Racial or Ethnic Group)

	Mexican American	Puerto Rican American	Cuban American	European American
Less than high school	47.2%	28.8%	27.0%	11.0%
High school graduate or more	52.8	71.2	73.0	89.0
Bachelor's degree or more	8.4	14.8	24.3	30.0

In the late 1980s, researchers Harriet Romo and Toni Falbo began tracking a group of one hundred Mexican American high school sophomores at high risk of dropping out. Within two years, 40 percent had dropped out. Many who graduated did so with the help of special programs, and their skills were often scarcely better than those of the students who dropped out. Interviews with the students revealed that their school experience had been demeaning and demoralizing. Some expressed the feeling that someone was "always on my back." Many students felt they were better off after they left school.[154]

Nonetheless, education was *highly* valued by both the students and their families; the anguish of school failure was keenly felt. "School failure involves threats to the self-esteem of the students as well as the status of the family and results in complex intra-family tensions and conflicts.... After a student dropped out, parents felt devastated and angry."[155] In most families, mothers were primarily responsible for children's education. The mothers derived much of their own sense of self from the successes of children and tended to blame themselves, or felt that school personnel blamed them, for their children's failures. These mothers' strategies for helping their children stay in school involved giving encouragement and pointing to individual models of success. They reported experiencing frustration over the school's unwillingness or inability to provide help and sometimes encountered hostility from teachers, counselors, or administrators.

Mexican American parents and children value education highly. One 2004 survey of Latinos, a majority of whom are Mexican American, found that nine out of ten thought it was very important for Latino children to get a college education. Three-quarters of these thought that the government was spending too little on education and that an equal amount of money should be spent on schoolchildren no matter how affluent or poor their school districts are.[156] Ethnographic research has also shown that immigrant families are very interested in education for children, although they frequently have little knowledge about how to become involved in U.S. schools. This research also shows that public school administrators in the United States typically make little effort to involve immigrant parents with their children's education in a meaningful way.[157]

In a critique of the major explanations offered for the poor school performance by many students of color, Catherine Walsh argues that attributing school problems to alleged individual or cultural inadequacies is blaming the victim. Blaming the incompatibilities arising from the cultural differences between Latino students and the white-dominated educational system on the victims is to overlook the historical and ongoing sociological significance of these differences. That all culturally different students do not perform equally poorly in school points to the relevance of additional factors. The problem is one of unequal power. To locate the root of school problems, one must look to the character of the Eurocentric school system, not to the student. For example, the mainstream curriculum is built on the dominant northern European culture and the centrality of English, and usually equates individual and group success with the adoption of that dominant culture and language. Mexican American history, culture, language, and life experiences are typically ignored. The dominant white group generally controls the structure of public schools and tends to view Latino cultures as negative environments from which students need to escape. Walsh suggests that poor school performance is often a response to alienating and oppressive conditions that have robbed students of identity, dignity, and voice. Learning or not learning can thus be a political statement. Lack of school funding and resources are also major factors. Other recent research has shown that Mexican American and other Latino high school students are *far more likely* than white students to attend very large public high schools, to be in classrooms with a high student–teacher ratio, and to be in schools with large numbers of students from low-income families. These very large public schools in cities tend to have much less in the way of teaching and learning resources than those attended by whites in suburban areas.[158]

Including the Spanish language and Mexican American culture in the classroom, involving the students' parents in the learning process, and increasing meaningful interaction between students and teachers are important steps toward improving public education. In addition, from the Walsh perspective, the severe imbalance of power and authority in public school systems must be corrected in order for Mexican American students to be accorded respect and the possibility of establishing a positive identity in schools.

Once in college settings, moreover, Mexican Americans and other Latinos still face much discrimination and a threat to self-esteem and positive identity. Thus, recent research involving interviews with middle-class Mexican Americans reveals this subtle and blatant discrimination. In one account from a recent study by Cobas and Feagin, a professional woman reports that a white professor

> in college refused to believe that I had written an essay... because she assumed that Mexicans don't write very well and so therefore I couldn't have written this paper.... And so she asked that I write it over again.... I rewrote the assignment and she still didn't believe that it was my own.... She still refused to believe that it was my handwriting or my writing because she still felt that Mexicans could not express themselves well in English.[159]

Here a well-educated white instructor, apparently with a head filled with Mexican stereotypes, used her power to discriminate twice against a talented Mexican American college student. Such occurrences are often reported by Latino and black students in colleges across the country, and have a negative effect on self-esteem and thus on learning for success in society.

Religion

Historically, most Mexican Americans have been Roman Catholics, yet many of the formal doctrines of the Catholic church are not now major factors in the lives of Mexican Americans. What has been termed "popular Catholicism," a blend of formal Catholicism and popular beliefs and rituals, has played a more important role. Indeed, a current concern among numerous Latino theologians and their allies is that the U.S. Catholic Church does not take seriously enough these popular religious practices and does not "endorse their inclusion into the official and often traditional teachings of the Church." A key feature of the popular religion has been an emphasis on miracles and on the maternal and family aspects of Christianity, including an accent on the Virgin Mary and Our Lady of Guadalupe.[160]

Many Mexican immigrants and their children have not been prepared for a U.S. Catholic church that is generally dominated by European American priests and officials. Indeed, before 1940 the European-oriented Church often provided little sustenance to a Mexican American population troubled by significant poverty and racial discrimination, sometimes including discrimination within the church. However, by the 1950s some non-Mexican priests began to take an active role in community protests and union activities to benefit Mexican Americans. In the 1960s, War on Poverty programs were operated in connection with church projects, and a number of groups were formed to protest urban poverty. Initially, Catholic officials prohibited priests from participating in these programs and protests, though later a few high Catholic officials supported Mexican American protests and unionization. In addition, the U.S. Catholic hierarchy has sometimes actively discriminated against Mexican Americans. Very few Mexican Americans achieved positions of responsibility before the 1960s. The first Mexican American bishop was designated, in San Antonio, only in 1970. By the mid-1990s, twenty-two of several hundred bishops in the United States were Mexican American.[161]

In recent decades, the church's influence on secular issues appears to be waning in many Mexican American communities; rejection of the church position on issues such as abortion and birth control has been widespread. Morever, other changes are evident. Many dioceses require priests to study Spanish, and there is a growing Mexican American and other Latino lay leadership in many areas. Celebrations of the feast day of Our Lady of Guadalupe are still popular in Mexican American communities. In many areas the Catholic church still creates a central place for Sunday mass and Latino holiday celebrations and community gatherings. In response to rapidly growing numbers of Spanish-speaking parishioners, many older Catholic parishes in major cities have reoriented at least some of their services and programs to the needs of Mexican American and other Latino members. Numerous new churches have been established in areas where Mexican immigration has been substantial, including the suburbs. In cities such as Chicago, where a substantial proportion of the metropolitan area is now Latino, there has been a large-scale movement of Latinos (Mexican American, Puerto Rican, and other groups) out from central city areas to inner suburbs, a process that has resulted in a significant expansion of Catholic services, and construction of buildings, in these suburban areas. In these suburban areas, Mexican Americans continue to practice an often distinctive version of Catholicism.[162]

Recent research on large Mexican American populations across the country demonstrates a significant decline in identification with the Catholic Church. Whereas 81 percent of first-generation Mexican American respondents in San Antonio and Los Angeles identified themselves as Catholic, only 57 percent of the fourth-generation Mexican American respondents did likewise.[163] One reason for this decline is that many Mexican Americans and other Latinos have converted to Protestant, particularly evangelical, denominations that increasingly welcome Mexican Americans and make them feel, as one put it, like "part of a family." Some scholars also argue that the evangelical churches help Mexican Americans to move away from a more hierarchical Catholic church and way of thinking to a religious perspective that better fits in with the intensely competitive individualism of U.S. society.[164]

Assimilation or Internal Colonialism?

An assimilation perspective is implicit or explicit in much research on Mexican Americans. In addition, some media and political commentators have argued that, except for the recent immigrants, Mexican Americans are gradually becoming assimilated to the U.S. core culture and society. Assimilationists argue optimistically that Mexican Americans are moving up the mobility ladder like earlier European ethnic groups, and thus are proceeding slowly but surely into the U.S. mainstream at all assimilation levels described by Milton Gordon. Reviewing the situation of Mexican Americans and other Latinos today, one recent article in *The Economist* concluded that "most of the evidence suggests that the latest immigrants are bedding in at least as quickly as their predecessors" and cites Latino rates of home ownership, intermarriage, and gaining citizenship as evidence.[165]

An assimilation theorist might emphasize that only 100,000 Mexicans were initially brought in by U.S. military conquest. Most have arrived later as voluntary immigrants and have generally been able to improve their economic circumstances relative to people in Mexico. Aspects of traditional culture have begun to disappear as acculturation, a key stage in assimilation, has proceeded. Cultural assimilation for the first generation, the Mexican immigrants, primarily involves adjustment to English and to conventional U.S. norms in public settings. Religious and other home-country values are less affected; respect for Mexico remains strong. Later generations, however, have experienced increased cultural adaptation as well as significant structural assimilation into the U.S. economy. Urbanization and increased incomes have made possible separate residences for nuclear families, and the number of traditional large and extended families in urban areas has declined. Seen from this assimilation perspective, Mexican American fertility and family values, as well as their sociopolitical views, are now often, though not always, similar to those professed by a majority of whites.[166]

However, a substantial degree of Mexican cultural heritage persists. Most Mexican Americans and other Latinos see no problem in adopting many aspects of the dominant culture, yet seek to preserve key elements of their own cultural background as

Mexican Americans celebrate Mexican Independence Day.

well. Spanish remains part of a pattern of **bilingualism**, *the ability to speak two languages*, for many families into at least the second generation. Surveys in Los Angeles and San Antonio have found that most Mexican Americans wish their children to retain some ties to Mexican culture, particularly to language, customs, and religion.[167] Still, most immigrant parents and their children recognize the clear social and economic advantages of learning English. Recent research reports indicate that *97 percent* of Latinos surveyed think the ability to speak English is essential to success in the United States, and 84 percent think government programs to teach English to immigrants should be expanded. Majorities indicate that immigrants must learn English to consider themselves a serious "part of American society." Recent research indicates that most Mexican Americans use English every day after they have lived in the United States for a decade or so, and that by the third generation English is the dominant or only language used by most Mexican Americans (and most people in other Latino groups). By the fourth generation Spanish is *not* spoken by 95 percent of Mexican Americans to their children.[168]

One U.S. problem is structural, for private and public organizations do not now provide enough language training. Research by the National Association of Latino Elected and Appointed Officials (NALEO) examined 184 organizations that provide English-language training in sixteen states. More than half had waiting lists, some involving many years of waiting. Numerous programs had a "decreased quality of instruction, from overwhelmed teachers, inadequate facilities and materials, to the inability to publicize services." In addition, most classes were for beginning students, making it difficult for immigrants to move beyond elemenatry English.[169]

Widespread use of English among immigrants and their children underscores how wrong-headed xenophobic calls for English-only laws and school policies are. In general, Latino immigrants are learning English *somewhat faster* than their European immigrant predecessors. (In addition, we might note that it would be advantageous for most Americans to be bilingual.) A mid-2000s review of the literature on several generations of Mexican Americans concluded that the fears of nativist commentators such as Samuel Huntington about the unassimilability of Mexican immigrants is much too pessimistic: "Based on information about what happens to individual immigrants after entry and about what happens to their children, we find in the data examined here that many are undergoing changes that knit them more closely into the political and economic fabric of the country." They make active efforts to become acculturated and to move toward citizenship. Even undocumented immigrants are often incorporating themselves by trying to secure legal permanent-resident status and pressing hard for educational advances for their children. However, half the Latino foreign-born population is now undocumented; their ability to move up the socioeconomic ladder is limited unless they can convert to legal status, which is difficult to secure under U.S. law. Given that reality, Mexican American mobility will not likely be the same as for earlier white ethnic immigrants.[170]

Structural assimilation, especially upward mobility, at the economic level has come slowly even for many in the second and third generations of Mexican Americans. Discrimination and the concentration of many workers at lower wage levels persist. Mexican Americans' limited participation in political institutions has also been problematical, although recent progress can be seen. Registration efforts such as that of the Southwest Voter Registration Project and the success of court cases stipulating the more democratic single-member districts have increased Mexican American voter strength in some areas.

Behavior-receptional assimilation and attitude-receptional assimilation have varied considerably within the Mexican American group and over time. Widespread prejudice and severe discrimination faced the Mexicans who were conquered during nineteenth-century U.S. expansion, as well as later Mexican immigrants. Over time, however, many lighter-skinned Mexican Americans, especially in larger cities, often faced somewhat less prejudice and discrimination. In contrast, darker-skinned Mexican Americans, like African Americans, have often been treated in discriminatory ways by whites. Today, considerable prejudice and discrimination are still directed against Mexican Americans in many parts of the United States. Many Anglos still view Mexican Americans as an "inferior race" based primarily on certain physical features seen as typical of the group.[171] Thus, two-thirds of the Mexican American youth in one 1990s California survey reported that they had personally faced discrimination. More than 80 percent said there was racial discrimination against U.S. Latinos. More recently, mid-2000s interviews with middle-class Mexican Americans similarly found an array of types of discrimination still confronting them in daily contacts with white Americans.[172]

The Limits and Pacing of Assimilation

Neither structural assimilation at the primary-group level nor marital assimilation, to use Gordon's terms, have over recent decades yet reached a high level for Mexican Americans, though assimilation in other areas is proceeding rapidly.

Studies in the 1970s reported some increases in intergroup friendship contacts, particularly for Mexican American children in desegregated environments, although most still had predominantly Mexican American friends. Later on, in a 1990s survey, the vast majority of Latinos in predominantly Mexican American areas of the country reported that their close friends (as well as their neighborhoods) were Latino. The majority of marriages are still within the Mexican American group. In the early 1900s, fewer than 10 percent of Spanish-surname individuals married outside the group. By the mid-1990s about 10 percent of first-generation Latinos were intermarried, compared with second- and third-generation percentages being at least double that percentage.[173] The current rate of out-marriage appears to be growing and is higher for younger generations. One recent large-scale study of Mexican Americans in Los Angeles and San Antonio found that 9 percent of the first generation had out-married, but that percentage increased gradually to 29 percent for the fourth generation, a figure well below that for white ethnic groups such as Italian and Irish Americans. Note too that those increasing numbers who are intermarrying with whites, or who are the children of parents who intermarried, often find themselves in a dilemma. Some opt to pass as "white," if they can, yet this often means that they have to break ties to family members who are not light-skinned and that they must also live in fear of being discovered in a European American world.[174]

Significant numbers of Mexican Americans demonstrate movement toward identificational assimilation. Today, the diversity of self-identification labels used by persons with ties to Mexico—designations such as *Latino*, *Hispanic*, *Chicano*, and *Mexican American*—indicates a diversity of opinion about such naming and/or identity within an ever more multicultural and multiracial United States. A study of second-generation Mexican Americans found that those who were Mexican-born preferred "Mexican"; the U.S.-born preferred "Mexican American," "Latino," or "Hispanic."[175] In a recent survey, moreover, some 69 percent of Hispanic adult respondents reported that they were more Hispanic than American, while 26 percent said they were equally Hispanic and American, and 5 percent said they were more American than Hispanic. Interestingly, when asked what of Hispanic culture and tradition was most important to preserve, 56 percent stressed strong family values. The importance of the Spanish language was stressed by 54 percent, while respect for parents and elders was emphasized by 47 percent. Two of these three top preservation concerns fit well with traditional family values emphasized in the dominant Anglo culture.[176]

Racial and ethnic identification varies with class, age, and experience, and with whether it is self-defined or imposed. Research at the University of California has found that numerous Mexican American undergraduates there had been sheltered by parents who encouraged them to view themselves as more or less "white" and/or to assimilate fully to Anglo-American ways. As a result, these students often experienced shock upon arrival at a campus where they were considered by others to be "Mexican" or "Mexican American," and/or as part of a distinctive racial group.[177] The campus experience brought them out of sheltered families and into a highly racialized society in which whites still mostly determine how racial or ethnic identities are *imposed*.

Structural socioeconomic incorporation has its limits as well. Ease of movement and incorporation into white-controlled institutions often varies with perceived class and skin color. Middle-class professionals often face fewer overt racial barriers from whites than members of the working class, although they still do face much subtle and covert discrimination. Sociologist Edward Murguía and others have argued that today Anglos often allow lighter-skinned, middle-class Mexican Americans to fit in to some degree in historically white institutions. Murguía and colleagues have also argued that the "presentation" of a person that gets them defined for negative or positive treatment, as a member of a distinctive social group, often includes more than skin color, such as other physical characteristics (facial features, hair, height), as well as often associated sociocultural characteristics such as clothing, language accent, or name.[178]

Today, as long as there are major immigration streams from Mexico into Mexican American communities, traditional assimilation will probably be slowed, on some but not all major dimensions. The movement of significant numbers of immigrants into established communities perpetuates significant aspects of traditional Mexican culture, supports much in-group marriage, and encourages respect for, and maintenance of, the Spanish language. Immigrants also create a constant stream of new customers and workers for Mexican American businesses, thereby stimulating the growth of an enclave economy. Immigrants from Mexico, as well as those from Central and South America, have furnished both the means and the reason for the growth of various enterprises, such as authentic Mexican-cuisine restaurants, spiritualist healing centers, and Spanish-language media.

Many Mexican Americans and other Latinos are interested in developing or viewing their own mass media, including magazines, radio, and television. Latinos are the country's fastest-growing television audience in the 2000s, and much of this audience is watching Spanish-language networks—Univision Television Network and Telemundo Network Group—both of which have been acquired in recent years by Anglo-controlled firms. In some cities, television stations affiliated with these networks have more viewers than major English-language stations. Spanish-language networks show programs from numerous Latin American countries and provide much more coverage of Latin America and U.S. Latinos than English-language stations. Today, Spanish-language networks are under some pressure to hire more darker-skinned Latinos and to focus even more on issues of particular interest to U.S. Latinos.[179]

Is the core culture itself responding to the growing Latino population? Some of the larger society's adaptations to the growing Latino population are relatively modest or superficial, such as the proliferating Mexican food outlets and listening to Latino music. Other societal adaptations, such as bilingual education and Spanish-language ballots and Internal Revenue Service forms, represent a recognition of the reality of a different culture. In the twenty-first century the mainstream media are also paying much more attention to Latino consumers, by selective advertising to Latinos and by featuring more Latino actors in movies and on television. Recognition of the changing character of the consumer market has also prompted major corporations to recruit bilingual employees. Some observers have even spoken, usually in exaggerated ways, of these modest changes as the "Hispanicizing of America."[180]

Applying a Power-Conflict Perspective

Power-conflict analysts focus on the extent to which many Mexican Americans have *not* moved toward speedy incorporation into the dominant society and its institutions because of external discrimination and other persisting oppression. For example, significant economic assimilation and political assimilation into the higher levels of this society are not yet part of the societal reality for most Mexican Americans.

Internal colonialism analysts note that Mexican American history began with whites' ruthless conquest of northern Mexico between 1836 and 1853. This conquest created a colonial situation for early Mexicans, whose land and labor were brought into the United States by force. Parallels can be seen between their experience and that of externally colonized populations: Land is taken by military force, the indigenous population is subjugated, the indigenous culture is suppressed, and the colonizing power favors a small elite to help maintain its economic and political domination.[181]

One problem in applying a traditional colonialism perspective to Mexican Americans is that most have entered as voluntary immigrants after the initial conquest. Thus, internal colonialism analysts have focused on important differences between these Mexican immigrants and their European predecessors. Mexican migrants have not come into a new environment; people of their background have long been in what is now the southwestern United States. Socially and culturally, they have moved within one geographical area, all of which was originally Mexico. Relatively little time is usually required to move back and forth across the border (though this is becoming more difficult)—in sharp contrast with the travel time historically required of most European immigrants.[182]

The most significant difference between the Mexican and European immigrant experience lies in the intensive discrimination and great cultural subordination that later Mexican immigrants encountered in the United States. "The colonial pattern of Euro-American domination over the Mexican people was set by 1848 and carried over to those Mexicans who came later to the Southwest."[183] From the beginning to the present, the Mexican American experience has been different from that of European immigrant groups, whose level of residential and school segregation has generally declined sharply with length of residence in the United States. Mexican Americans have been racially subordinated and intentionally segregated to a far greater extent and over a longer period of time than European immigrant groups.

Mexican immigrants have entered an environment in which their progress and mobility have generally been limited by low wages, inferior schools, and various types of racialized discrimination. Intense societal pressure and even coercion have historically been used to acculturate Mexican American schoolchildren and adults to the Anglo core culture. John Ogbu has suggested that the rejection of public education by some Mexican American youth is a reaction to their enforced and colonized status.[184] Racial stereotyping, especially of darker-skinned Mexican Americans, has helped preserve the U.S. racial hierarchy and its white racial framing. Land theft and the exploitation of Mexican American labor have long been justified by theories of biological and cultural inferiority. Mexican immigrants have been forcefully subordinated by means of rigorous Border Patrol searches and the deportation of those immigrants (and sometimes citizens) whom authorities deemed unworthy. Residential segregation has often reflected racial discrimination. Indeed, much informal discrimination against Mexican Americans in employment and housing persists today. Whites have gained substantial psychological as well as economic benefits from long decades of discrimination against Mexican Americans.

As we discussed in Chapter 2, Mario Barrera analyzes the Mexican American experience using an internal colonialism model emphasizing institutionalized racism and exploitative capitalism in the shaping of past and present racial inequalities. Each of the major classes of capitalism, the capitalist class and the working class, contains segments defined by racial characteristics. Each class is divided by a racial line that separates those who suffer institutionalized discrimination, such as Mexican Americans, from those Anglo whites who do not. While Mexican American workers generally share a similar class position with ordinary white workers, in that both are struggling against employers for better wages and working conditions, the former are in a subordinate economic position within the working class because of structural discrimination along racial lines. The dimensions of this discrimination include lower wages for similar work and concentration in lower-wage occupations.[185]

Internal colonialism analysts argue that white employers have intentionally created a split labor market from which they have received enormous profits; they have fostered distrust within the working class by focusing the attention of many white workers on Latinos and other racially oppressed workers as a threat to white jobs. Given the dual-market segmentation of the labor force by employers, many white workers have periodically tried to solidify their positions and work in various ways, including through unions, to restrict or bar workers of color from better jobs.

Power-conflict analysts emphasize the continuing reality that the majority of white Americans still see Mexican Americans as *not* white and as an inferior racial group distinguishable by both physical characteristics and culture. Given this racialized reality, Mexican Americans could not be fully assimilated into the institutions of U.S. society even if they were to abandon entirely their cultural heritage and Spanish surnames. Even most of those who are light enough to pass visually as white are not likely to abandon their families and relatives or give up their cultural heritage, whereas the latter heritage often enables whites to distinguish them for continuing individual discrimination.[186]

Assimilation analysts have questioned the extent of Mexican American identification with assertive social movements. Sociologist Nathan Glazer once characterized the assertive Chicano movement of the 1960s as having only "extreme views espoused by a minority for a short period."[187] However, at the time a majority of younger Mexican Americans supported much of the assertive Chicano perspective, and many in older generations were quietly supportive of goals to accent the Mexican heritage and end discrimination. Indeed, since the 1960s the perspectives and actions of political and union activists, such as those involved in recent Justice for Janitors organizing in several cities, have reflected themes rooted deeply in the Mexican historical heritage and garnered the support of a great many Mexican Americans.

Still, as historian Rodolfo Acuña has noted, Mexican Americans and other Latinos feel great pressure to see whiteness, and things white, as best. In the past, Mexican American organizations, such as the League of Latin American Citizens (LULAC) pressing lawsuits against segregation in the 1930s, argued that the U.S. census takers should classify Mexican Americans as "white." By insisting they were "white," some Mexican Americans have tried to overcome extensive racial segregation by whites (who have generally seen them as an "inferior race") that they faced in the Southwest, especially from the 1930s to the 1960s. Today, some Mexican Americans still insist they are partly or wholly "white" (or "Spanish"). Many adults will comment unfavorably on the dark skin of a newborn child or play down their Indian and African backgrounds. In an effort to position their group closer to whites, they may also articulate anti-immigrant or antiblack attitudes. As Acuña notes, "the acceptance and internalization of the dominant society's racism by Mexicans and Latinos is irrational and produces a false consciousness. For instance, it is not uncommon for first-year Chicano university students to talk about reverse racism toward whites or express anti-immigrant sentiments."[188]

Indeed, many Latino immigrants come to the United States with some aspects of the white racial frame already in their heads, such as racially stereotyped attitudes directed against African Americans, even though they have met no (or few) African Americans. Based on interviews with Latino immigrants, one Mexican American scholar has explained that negative views of black Americans are created by the U.S. media south of the border: "I have traveled to Guatemala and have seen theaters showing the same violent, racist movies we show here. When I asked one migrant in Houston why some migrants have antiblack attitudes, he responded that they first learn about blacks from U.S. movies."[189] Similarly, a research study of foreign-born and U.S.-born Latinos in Houston found that the former had *more* negative attitudes toward black Americans than did the latter.[190] New immigrants from all parts of the globe often arrive with negative views of African Americans and other Americans of color gleaned from white-controlled U.S. mass media productions, which now have a global circulation. Such views make coalitions with African Americans more difficult. Most immigrants to the United States feel enormous pressure to conform to the dominant white views on racial issues.

To make matters even more complicated, some native-born Mexican Americans feel that recent Mexican immigrants jeopardize the status of established Mexican Americans in U.S. society because whites constantly link them to the immigrants. As one recent study of tensions between the native-born and recent immigrants in California put it, "Realizing that members of the dominant society may not differentiate among the heterogeneous Mexican-origin community... [some] distance themselves spatially, socially, and culturally from immigrants."[191]

A Pan-Latino Identity

Continuing anti-Latino discrimination across the society has led many Mexican Americans and others to adopt a broader Hispanic or Latino identity in efforts to be "real authentic Americans with dignity. They are beginning to embrace the new and less precise categories of Hispanic or Latino so that they can be part of a larger and more influential group..."[192] Power-conflict analysts see the possibility of decreasing oppression and of an improved economic, political, and cultural situation in pan-Latino organizations and their periodic protests against discrimination.

The collective Latino/Hispanic consciousness has developed since the 1960s and unites people with such diverse national-origin identities as Mexican American, Cuban American, Puerto Rican, Salvadoran, Nicaraguan, and Dominican. Since that era, for example, many Mexican Americans and Puerto Ricans have to a significant degree transcended old identities and adopted the collective identity of Latino/Hispanic, while in some important ways still asserting their national-origin identities. In numerous U.S. towns and cities, this pan-Latino process has emerged as a political strategy to accomplish political goals shared by the component groups. The discrimination, imposed inequalities, and political opposition that Latinos have faced at the hands of whites have contributed to the formation of this collective consciousness. As Félix Padilla has stated, "at the heart of Latino or Hispanic ethnic identity are the circumstantial conditions of structural or institutional inequality."[193]

This pan-Latino consciousness is facilitated by a shared language and similar home country cultures. On a national level, and in numerous cities where Hispanic/Latino populations contain more than one national-origin group, the Hispanic/Latino consciousness contributes to a broader sense of community and political solidarity and helps subgroups achieve the collective strength to address local problems of education, bilingualism, jobs, and discrimination. A "dual identity" based on both national origin and a collective identity forged in the context of broader Hispanic/Latino concerns is clearly emerging.[194]

What are some factors generating the significant differences in poverty and family income between European Americans and Mexican Americans?

Summary

Mexican Americans have an ancient and proud ancestry, substantially Indian with significant Spanish and African infusions. Their vital cultural background is partly Native American but heavily Spanish in language and Catholic in religion. After the European American conquest of what is now the U.S. Southwest, Mexican Americans became part of the complex U.S. mosaic of racial and ethnic groups. They have suffered racialized stereotyping similar to that of other groups of non-European ancestry, and discrimination in the economy, education, and politics has been part of their lot from the beginning.

The literature on racial and ethnic relations has often compared the situations of Mexican Americans and African Americans, now the largest subordinated groups in the United States. Both groups face substantial prejudice and discrimination at the hands of whites even as we move well into the twenty-first century, especially with regard to jobs, business, and housing. Today, across the country, we find both competition and cooperation between these two groups of Americans as they try to make a better place for themselves in a historically racist society.

A distinctive aspect of Mexican American communities today is the constant infusion of documented and undocumented workers. This immigration often renews ties to Mexico, thereby undergirding Mexican American communities and identity. The Spanish language has a much longer history in the United States than the languages of most white ethnic immigrants, and bilingualism is a facet of numerous U.S. communities. A significant aspect of continuing Latino immigration is that many who come to the United States regularly return, if they are not prevented by increased border barriers, to their home countries. Demographers estimate that a substantial majority of undocumented Mexican immigrants will, if not prevented, return to Mexico after a few years working in the United States, and indeed that most Mexicans who have ever immigrated to the United States are *now* living in Mexico.[195] Historically, thus, the Mexican migration to the United States has been both significant and circular.

Close ties to the culture of the home country Mexico—probably the closest for any immigrant group in U.S. history—slow certain aspects of the incorporation process by providing an external and supportive foundation for the home culture and social networks. Today, the dominant Eurocentric culture of the United States is under increasing pressure to change significantly as ever larger numbers of non-Europeans insist on the importance and validity of their own cultures and experiences.

Mexican Americans have helped to generate the pan-Latino consciousness that ties them to other Latinos and contributes to a stronger sense of social solidarity. This consciousness is reflected in political efforts to address common problems of education, jobs, and discrimination. A "dual identity" based on national origin and on a collective identity forged in the context of broader Latino issues has indeed emerged across the United States.

Key Terms

Latinos 206
braceros 208
undocumented immgrants or "illegals" 208
maquiladoras 209
Chicano political movement 228
bilingualism 238

CHAPTER 9

Puerto Rican and Cuban Americans

BIG PICTURE QUESTIONS

- ***What roles have Puerto Rican and Cuban Americans played in building this country's wealth and institutions?***
- ***What are the persisting barriers to social and economic mobility for Puerto Rican and Cuban Americans?***
- ***How would assimilation and power-conflict theorists explain current Puerto Rican and Cuban American socioeconomic realities?***

Puerto Rico and Cuba, Spanish-speaking islands in the Antilles, are points of origin for large numbers of the 42 million U.S. Latinos. For a century, Puerto Rico has been a subordinated part of the U.S. empire. San Juan, Puerto Rico, is the oldest city under the U.S. flag. All Puerto Ricans are U.S. citizens, yet Puerto Rico is not a state. Puerto Ricans send nonvoting delegates to Congress but cannot vote in federal elections. Today, the island's future is debated by groups that support independence, statehood, or a continuation of the commonwealth status. Unlike the Cuban case, these on-island political debates have been less important to migration, which is greatly influenced by the pull of the mainland U.S. economy, government-encouraged migration (to reduce island population pressures), and the ease of migration for these U.S. citizens. Island Puerto Ricans are only "quasi-citizens of the United States. They can give their lives fighting for the country in U.S. forces, but they cannot vote in national elections. They have only observer status in the U.S. Congress, but they can migrate to the mainland freely."[1] In the mid-2000s, just about 3.8 million Puerto Ricans resided on the mainland, while the population on the island was just over 3.9 million. Including both, Puerto Ricans make up about 2.5 percent of the U.S. population.[2]

The island of Cuba has "oscillated between a corrupt democracy and dictatorships of both right and left, accompanied by a humiliating dependence on a superpower."[3] This oscillation has generated large out-migrations that have increased the populations of the U.S. Latino communities, particularly in the southeast. Many Cubans came as refugees fleeing the Communist government on their island, during several different periods of migration. Most settled in east coast cities, particularly in Florida, and today they and their descendants number nearly 1.5 million. Cuba has a long history of struggle for independence, replete with heroes such as Jose Martí, a nineteenth-century leader whose maxim was "a nation... but no master." The struggle for independence continues to be an important theme in the present history and politics of Cuban Americans.[4]

Cuban Americans and mainland Puerto Ricans have been important to the expansion of the U.S. Latino population and culture in an increasingly multicultural United States. (*Mainland* refers to the U.S. mainland, as distinct from the territory of Puerto Rico.) Most in both groups express a strong identification with their homelands and traditions, and both groups are committed to carving out a permanent place in the United States.

Puerto Ricans

Borinquén, the original name for Puerto Rico, had an indigenous population of 50,000 in 1493 when Spanish imperialism reached the island. Spain used indigenous residents as forced labor in mines and fields. Forced labor, disease, brutal killings, and violent suppression of rebellions caused a genocidal decline in the population, and enslaved Africans were imported. Later, during the nineteenth century, immigrants from numerous countries, both European and Latin American, made their way to Puerto Rico. A census in 1827 found that the proportions of whites and people of color in Puerto Rico were almost equal. By 1900 the island's population comprised thirty-four nationalities. The inhabitants of Puerto Rico today are the product of several racial and ethnic heritages.[5]

From Spanish to U.S. Rule

In 1897, Puerto Ricans pressured the Spanish into granting them autonomy. The following year, during the Spanish-American War, U.S. troops occupied the island. In the 1899 treaty ending that war, Spain gave Puerto Rico to the United States, whose leaders made it into a naval station and a profitable agricultural enclave. After centuries of Spanish rule, Puerto Rico came under U.S. control with no input from its inhabitants.[6]

As a U.S. possession, Puerto Rico had a governor from the mainland appointed by the U.S. president. Manuel Maldonado-Denis describes early governors:

> The criterion used by the President of the United States to choose the colonial governor and his cabinet was, with very few exceptions, one of compensation for political favors received. Many of these men came to Puerto Rico without knowing the language or, at times, even the location of the island.[7]

Acts of the local legislature were subject to veto by the U.S. Congress, the president, or the appointed governor. English became mandatory in schools. In 1917 the Jones Act awarded U.S. citizenship to all Puerto Ricans.[8]

In 1948 Puerto Ricans were finally permitted to elect their governor, and in 1952 the Commonwealth of Puerto Rico was created with a constitution approved by the U.S. Congress. Considerable home rule was granted, including the right to elect officials, make legal codes, and run schools. These changes came only with the permission of the U.S. government, the colonizing power that still oversees Puerto Rico. Those living in Puerto Rico still have no vote in national U.S. elections and no voting members of the U.S. Congress.

When the U.S. government took over Puerto Rico, much land was owned by small farmers who raised coffee, sugar, and other foodstuffs. Puerto Ricans owned most farms. Under U.S. control, heavy taxes and restrictions on credit forced many to sell their land to U.S. companies. Independent farmers were also driven out by U.S.-forced devaluation of the Puerto Rican peso and by the closing of European markets under U.S. occupation. By 1930, absentee-owned companies controlled most sugar production and monopolized tobacco production and shipping lines. The island had moved from a locally controlled, diversified economy to one dominated by external U.S. companies. Many small farmers and their families were thus forced to seek jobs with the absentee-owned companies or leave for the U.S. mainland.[9]

In the 1940s, Operation Bootstrap, a program designed by the Puerto Rican governor to bring economic development by attracting U.S. corporations, was implemented. Lured by low wages and exemption from taxation, 1700 factories located there by 1975. Per-capita income increased. However, tax exemptions for new industries left the burden of financing public infrastructure on the local population, resulting in a high income tax. Operation Bootstrap's emphasis on industry and neglect of agriculture tilted the economy farther away from its heritage of locally owned farms. Today, little of the island's economy is agricultural.

Since the 1970s, high unemployment rates have hurt many island workers, encouraging migration to the mainland. Recurring recessions have brought cutbacks in industrial plants, increasing unemployment. By the late 1990s the real unemployment rate (including part-time workers who want full-time work) was estimated at 40 percent or higher.[10] In the 1990s the Puerto Rican government privatized communications, shipping, and other public services and undertook major infrastructure projects in an attempt to attract outside investors again. But jobs did not increase rapidly, and the government has faced debt, employee layoffs, and financial crises. Moreover, in 1996 the U.S. Congress passed legislation to gradually end by 2006 the tax incentive that encouraged U.S. firms to locate in Puerto Rico. Local tax incentives, including low business income taxes, have not been adequate replacements. As a result, from the mid-1990s to the late 2000s, even as some new investments have been made, many factories have been moved to cheaper labor and taxation areas around the globe, continuing the economic crisis and stimulating yet more outmigration.[11]

Migration to the Mainland

Migration Patterns

By 1900 some 2000 Puerto Ricans lived on the mainland, mostly in New York. Significant immigration to the mainland began in the 1920s; by 1940, mainland Puerto Ricans numbered almost 70,000. Over the next two decades, the number increased more than tenfold, to 887,000, largely because of Operation Bootstrap, which resulted in a net loss of local jobs and encouraged emigration. Between 1945 and 1970, about one person in three left the island. Puerto Rican communities were established in New Jersey, Connecticut, and Chicago, although the majority settled in New York.[12]

Puerto Rican writer Jack Agüeros has described the impact of the new immigration on established mainland communities:

> Into an ancient neighborhood came pouring four to five times more people than it had been designed to hold. Men who came running at the promise of jobs were jobless as [World War II] ended. . . . The sudden surge in numbers caused new resentments, and prejudice was intensified. Some were forced to live in cellars. . . .[13]

Puerto Rican workers brought to New Jersey farms in the 1940s were "flown up here to a strange land, in the dark of the night, and by morning some are in the farmers' fields ready to work. There is no time for any sort of adjustment."[14] Workers also came to textile sweatshops in New York; steel mills in Pennsylvania, Ohio, and Indiana; foundries in Wisconsin and Illinois; and electronics industries in Illinois.[15]

The decades since 1970 have often involved the return or circular migration that we discussed in Chapter 2. Under conditions of globalizing capitalism and transnationalism, many Puerto Ricans fleeing the island's poverty and economic crises have come to U.S. cities, which also have problems of unemployment and poverty, as well as the added problem of racial discrimination. Economic recessions along with deteriorating neighborhoods and discriminatory conditions on the mainland, combined with family ties and a desire to nurture children in island culture, have prompted some number to return to Puerto Rico. Yet, as Gina Pérez has argued, one must be careful not to overemphasize the return or circular migration, for it involves only a modest minority of Puerto Ricans in most cities, with the rest settling well into mainland communities. In addition, the circular migration has long been government-encouraged and involves attempts to overcome built-in structural poverty in *both* places. It is not just the result of idiosyncratic personal factors, as some analysts have argued, thus "blaming the victims." Often, those who return to Puerto Rico come back to the mainland after a time because of poor economic conditions on the island. Manufacturing wages on the island have been less than those on the mainland, and Puerto Rico's per-capita income has been less than that of the poorest U.S. state. In recent years the number of well-educated Puerto Rican workers coming to the mainland has increased, in part because of an absence of appropriate jobs in Puerto Rico. One recent study of these middle-class workers found that they too face economic difficulties on the island, and some make several cycles of mainland migration and return to the island. They develop, as Elizabeth Aranda puts it, "emotional bridges that connect island and mainland social spaces," a key reality that is an aspect of contemporary transnationalism. Facing discrimination on the mainland, and isolation from their extended families, they periodically go back to the island to recharge their personal energies. They are caught between two emotional and social worlds.[16]

In the mid-2000s, nearly half of all Puerto Ricans resided in mainland communities, where they make up nearly one-tenth of all Latinos. Increasingly, many have settled in areas other than New York state, where in the mid-2000s about 30 percent of Puerto Ricans resided. In recent years, secondary migrations from the Northeast to other parts of the United States have increased, especially to southeastern metropolitan areas such as Miami, Tampa, and Orlando, where there are more Latino residents and there is generally less overt discrimination.[17]

What are the strengths and weaknesses of the reciprocal social and economic relationship between the United States and Puerto Rico?

Joined by Other Latinos: Diversity in the New York Area

U.S. census data show that New York City's population is about 8 million. During the decade of the 1990s, the city's Anglo white population decreased to less than half the city's population. Most new growth came from Latino and Asian immigrants. In the mid-2000s, Puerto Ricans (some 787,000) accounted for a little more than one-third of the city's Latinos. Like immigrant groups before them, many Puerto Ricans have gradually moved to suburban areas near New York City. In addition, in recent decades increasing numbers of Mexicans, Dominicans, Salvadorans, and other Latin Americans have moved to the bustling metropolitan area, including Long Island.[18]

By the early 2000s Long Island's Latino population had increased to 282,693, more than 10 percent of the total population. This Latino population is approximately 27 percent Puerto Rican and 8 percent Mexican or Cuban American. The rest are of other Caribbean, Central, or South American origin. Since the 1980s, large numbers of people from the Caribbean and Central and South America have joined Long Island's substantial Puerto Rican community. Unlike earlier migrations, many Latino immigrants today are not moving to the large central cities but rather directly to suburban areas near large cities such as Long Island.[19]

Increasingly, those who work in Long Island's restaurants and homes and on construction sites are Salvadorans, Colombians, and Dominicans. Many of the estimated 2 million Salvadorans in the United States today are refugees from repressive civil wars in El Salvador. (One-third of people born in that country now live outside it, mostly in the United States). Long Island is one of the major areas of Salvadoran settlement, the others being Los Angeles,

San Francisco, Washington, D.C., and Houston. Latino diversity in areas such as Long Island has encouraged a pan-Latino (pan-Hispanic) consciousness. Thus, the town of Brentwood there renamed its Puerto Rican Day Parade the Hispanic Day Parade.[20]

Prejudice and Stereotypes

Puerto Ricans have long suffered racial stereotypes similar to those targeting Mexican Americans and African Americans. The first important stereotypes were mostly developed by white military officers and colonial administrators. (The terms *white* and *Anglo* in this chapter again refer to those identified by the U.S. census as non-Hispanic whites.) In the 1890s one Anglo officer noted that "the people seem willing to work, even at starvation wages, and they seem to be docile and grateful for anything done for them. They are emotional."[21] Other U.S. officials saw the colonized Puerto Ricans as "lazy natives."

Images of lazy, submissive, emotional Puerto Ricans persist today, including among white professionals with Puerto Rican clients. For example, some white teachers have held images of Puerto Ricans as lazy and immoral. Alfredo López has reported attending a college meeting in New York at which an experienced teacher from a poor school spoke about instilling "middle-class values" of thrift, morality, and motivation in the children. López confronted the white teacher about her image of Puerto Rican children:

> It was when I asked what morality was and where it was practiced among middle-class people or what motivation was lacking in our people and how she discovered this, or finally, how the hell a person could be thrifty on eighty-four dollars a week that she began to do some thinking.[22]

Though this is a report from the 1970s, this stereotyped framing of Puerto Ricans is still common today.

Criminalizing Puerto Ricans

Often referred to by the derogatory term *spic*, Puerto Ricans have been viewed by many whites, like Italian, African, and Mexican Americans before them, as a criminal lot. An Aspen Institute conference report noted that the English-language news media often exaggerate certain aspects of Puerto Rican and Mexican American life—poverty, gang violence, and illegal immigration. Crimes by Puerto Ricans have also been sensationalized in New York City newspapers and other media. J. Edgar Hoover, one-time director of the FBI, promulgated the following racist stereotype:

> We cooperate with the Secret Service on presidential trips abroad. You *never* have to bother about a President being shot by Puerto Ricans or Mexicans. They don't shoot very straight. But if they come at you with a knife, beware.[23]

Stereotypes of Puerto Ricans as criminals and drug users influence police actions in Puerto Rican communities, which are often more closely patrolled than affluent white areas. In the words of one Puerto Rican rights activist, "There is this idea that young Hispanics are all drug abusers who come here to terrorize people." Yet, a 2005 anonymous survey found that only small percentages (ranging from 1 to 15 percent) of Latino high school students had *ever* used hard drugs such as cocaine or heroin, percentages only a little higher than for white students.[24] However, such empirical data have not yet corrected the racial bias in drug-use stereotypes circulated by government agencies and in the mass media.

In Chapter 8 we cited data indicating that Latino characters are rare in G-rated movies and that Latino actors are significantly underrepresented on television programs, especially as primary recurring characters. When Latino actors are used, they are often lighter-skinned (such as Jennifer López) or are more likely than whites to be portrayed as criminals. In the early 2000s, Puerto Rican actor Esaí Morales was given a major part as the police lieutenant on the then-popular television program *NYPD Blue*. This marked some modest change, though Puerto Rican actors still were mostly getting roles as law enforcement officers, drug dealers, other criminals, drug or alcohol abusers, or, in the case of women, stereotyped sex objects. Morales has been an activist for civil rights and a co-founder of Washington's National Hispanic Foundation for the Arts. This organization has been very critical of the stereotyped roles that are often offered to Latino actors.[25]

Other Negative Images

In the 1970s, *New York Magazine* ran an article including the following negative metaphorical description of Puerto Ricans: "They came in swarms like ants turning the sidewalks brown, and they settled in, multiplied, whole sections of the city fallen to their shiny black raincoats and chewing-gum speech."[26] Such negative metaphors of swarming or flooding have often been used by anti-immigrant groups. In addition, negative imaging of Puerto Ricans has also been circulated by some social scientists. *In Beyond the Melting Pot,* prominent social scientists Nathan Glazer and Daniel Moynihan argued that Puerto Rican society was "sadly defective" in its culture and family system. They characterized Puerto Rican families as disorganized and suggested that was the reason they usually did not move into better-paying jobs.[27] Anthropologist Oscar Lewis accented the concept of a **culture of poverty**—*the stereotyped idea that poor people usually develop a defective and deviant subculture.* He applied the concept to the poor on the island of Puerto Rico and in the United States, arguing that the culture of the poor is "a way of life which is passed down from generation to generation along family lines."[28] Popular and scholarly views of poor communities have been significantly influenced by Lewis's culture-of-poverty generalizations. However, culture-of-poverty and similar analyses do not recognize clearly the role that widespread structural unemployment and underemployment play in the creation of poverty and related problems for many Americans.

A late-1990s report on the local economy in New Britain, Connecticut, revealed some stereotypes similar to the traditional culture-of-poverty notion. The report, issued by whites in the business elite, alleged that Puerto Ricans' "poor" language skills, family values, and work ethic contributed to the city's economic problems and suggested that Puerto Ricans should be encouraged to leave the city. Puerto Rican residents organized the Puerto Rican Organization for Unity and Dignity to counter this overt anti-Latino stereotyping and related discrimination and to increase their political clout. Frequently, in such reports one finds whites emphasizing the accents or Spanish language spoken by Puerto Ricans and other Latinos as problematical, when they do not do the same for those who speak English with other types of accents (such as French-accented English). Recall that social science research has shown that only a few accents in English, such as those of native Spanish speakers, are regularly used as markers for negative stigmatization and discrimination.[29]

In an early-2000s radio interview, Republican Jim Hansen, then a member of House Armed Services Committee, expressed concern about protests by Puerto Ricans against Navy bombing near the island: "I don't see where Puerto Rico should get any favorite treatment over the rest of these people. Now what have they done to get it? They sit down there on welfare and very few of them are paying taxes, got a sweetheart deal." This image of lazy Puerto Ricans on welfare is still found at high levels of government. Some whites couple negative images of Puerto Ricans and other Latinos with fearful views of immigrants. Recall from Chapter 8 white supremacist groups' hostile verbal and physical attacks on Latinos. Other whites, in various areas, including those who are not members of such supremacist groups, sometimes articulate hostile views. Homeowners in a mostly white New York town received letters warning of a threat to their area by Latino immigrants, who were described as "forces of evil" and "low-income trash" seeking to convert the area to a Latino outpost.[30]

Color Coding and White Prejudices

Prejudices and stereotyping motivate much discrimination against Puerto Ricans and thereby have a negative effect on their lives. To better understand the Puerto Rican experience on the mainland, we should note the somewhat different racial situation in Puerto Rico. Puerto Rico, like other Latin American societies, recognizes a spectrum of racial-ethnic categories based on multiple physical and cultural characteristics and not just skin color. One family's members may represent a variety of socially distinguished skin colors. Today, Puerto Rican society is more racially integrated than mainland society. An individual's treatment in the areas of housing, political rights, government policy, and education is less likely to be as racially differentiated, at least overtly, as on the mainland. Still, dark-skinned individuals sometimes face significant discrimination, particularly in socializing and marital arrangements, and there is often an attempt to disguise a particular family's significant African ancestry, which is usually not seen positively. In Puerto Rico, in other Latin American countries, and among Latinos on the U.S. mainland, there is a strong tendency to play down the African ancestry of Latinos. As Marta Cruz-Janzen has commented:

> Africa is alive in all Latinos; the African [influence]...clamors in the Spanish flamenco, resonates in the Mexican corrida, palpitates in Mexico's *La Bamba,* and laments in the Argentinian tango. It is alive in Diego Rivera's painting. It calls to us in today's popular salsa sounds from the Caribbean. Just as earth is mother to us all, Africa is Latinos' other mother....Awareness is the first step in personal change....[31]

European Americans have generally viewed Puerto Ricans as "not white," frequently grouping them with African Americans or Mexican Americans. One reason for this **color coding**—*social stratification or discrimination based on skin color*—is the long colonial relationship that Puerto Ricans have had with the U.S. government.[32] Whatever their actual skin color, Puerto Ricans have been associated in the white mind with colonized people. Until they come to the mainland, most Puerto Ricans, especially those whose complexion is medium brown in tone, have seldom dealt with blatant racial discrimination, especially on a large scale. Recalling an experience in high school when a girl whom he had asked to dance turned him down, Piri Thomas, a Puerto Rican who grew up in New York City and became well known as the author of the autobiographical *Down These Mean Streets*, wrote about his anger at whites' denial of his Puerto Rican identity:

> "Who?" someone asked.
>
> "That new colored boy."
>
> I couldn't see them, but I had that for-sure feeling that it was me they had in their mouths....
>
> "Christ, first that Jerry bastard and now him. We're getting invaded by niggers."[33]

The use of racist epithets in connection with an imposition of the white framing of Puerto Ricans as more or less black, when the home culture sees racial and ethnic diversity as a more complex matter, has often created confusion and anger. Statements such as "You don't look Puerto Rican," or "Are you 100 percent Puerto Rican?" commonly confront Puerto Ricans on the mainland. Indeed, faced with the task of categorizing Puerto Rican school children as either "Negro" or "Caucasian" in 1954, New York officials proposed abandoning the white/black terminology and listing them just as "Puerto Rican," even though this would imply that they were a separate racial category.[34]

Research has revealed a substantial difference in the self-perception of Puerto Ricans and how they think others perceive them. In one survey, most Puerto Rican respondents indicated that they felt other Americans saw them as white (58 percent) or black (42 percent). However, this is not an accurate perception, at least in the twenty-first century. In a recent survey of a large number of white college students in the southeastern United States, only 6.9 percent said unambiguously that they considered Puerto Rican Americans to be a white group. Most saw Puerto Ricans as definitely not white.[35]

How do Puerto Ricans view their own racial-ethnic identity? The 1980 census was the first to ask individuals if they were "Hispanic," with a separate question asking about "race." Fewer than 4 percent of Puerto Ricans in New York City stated that their "race" was black; 44 percent classified themselves as white. Just under half wrote something like "Spanish" in the space of "Other-Specify." More recently, however, a 2002 survey found that most Puerto Rican respondents said that they did *not* prefer "white" as their racial group; some 52 percent preferred "Hispanic" or "Latino." This complex reaction indicates, among other things, the conflict between the U.S. racial structure and the island's own racial categorizing with which most Puerto Ricans are familiar.[36]

Why might some Latinos play down their African ancestry?

Economic and Related Conditions: The Mainland

Writing as an early immigrant, Jesús Colon explained that Puerto Ricans did hard labor for the mainland society and that poverty was often their lot. He and his brother worked different hours and shared clothes: "We only had one pair of working pants between the two of us."[37] Discrimination was common for Puerto Rican immigrants; those with darker skin suffered the most. In *Down These Mean Streets*, Thomas recounted a 1945 interview for a job as a door-to-door salesperson. He was not hired; a lighter-skinned friend was. Dark-skinned Puerto Ricans, he discovered by asking other applicants, were discriminated against by white employers.[38]

Occupation and Unemployment

For decades Puerto Rican immigrants have brought with them many talents and skills. Some are artists and musicians; others are skilled in crafts. Some operated a business on the island; others held positions of responsibility in the educational, medical, legal, or political systems. On the mainland, however, immigrants' skills have often gone unused. Regardless of background, many have faced a limited range of jobs. They have often done the "dirty work" for European Americans, such as low-paying factory or restaurant jobs. They have cleaned up as busboys and janitors and worked in garment-industry sweatshops. Many have faced recurring unemployment.[39]

Table 9.1 shows the occupational distribution for employed Puerto Ricans on the mainland in the mid-2000s.[40] Although some progress has been made in recent decades, male workers are disproportionately in lower-paid blue-collar and service jobs. Once mostly less skilled blue-collar workers, Puerto Rican women are now concentrated in service, sales, and clerical jobs. Today, Puerto Rican men are significantly less likely to hold managerial or professional positions than European American men and are twice as likely to be employed in service jobs. Note too that those in white-collar jobs tend to occupy lower-paid positions, such as teacher or librarian, rather than doctor or lawyer. In recent decades, Puerto Rican laborers on the east coast have done much low-paid field work that puts vegetables on U.S. tables.[41]

Unemployment at all points has been much higher for mainland Puerto Ricans than for white workers. Unemployment and subemployment rates for Puerto Ricans have been among the highest of any racial or ethnic group in eastern cities. In the mid-2000s, some 7.8 percent of Puerto Ricans were officially unemployed, compared with 4.4 percent of whites.[42] Such official rates underestimate the employment problem. To ascertain the total number of unemployed and underemployed Puerto Ricans, we must add large numbers who are discouraged from looking for work as a result of long-term unemployment, those who are working part-time but who desire full-time work, and those who receive very low wages.

For several decades, mainland Puerto Rican communities have had distinctive social classes, including a relatively small group of professionals and managers at the top of the community's social structure, many of them employed in government agencies, and a large group of workers doing blue-collar, service, and clerical work. Much smaller are the groups of business entrepreneurs, small and large, and of "skilled technical workers who provide stability" for mainland communities.[43]

Employment Discrimination

Institutionalized discrimination against Puerto Ricans has long been rooted in color coding and linguistic

TABLE 9.1 Occupational Distribution (2005)

	Men		Women	
	European American	Puerto Rican American	European American	Puerto Rican American
Managerial and professional specialties	35.3	21.1	40.4	30.6
Sales and office occupations	18.6	19.8	36.3	39.2
Production, transportation, and material moving occupations	17.2	22.0	5.2	6.8
Construction, extraction, and maintenance occupations	17.5	16.2	0.8	0.7
Service occupations	10.7	20.6	17.1	22.5
Farming, forestry, and fishing	0.7	0.3	0.2	0.1
Total	100.0%	100.0%	100.0%	99.9%

prejudice. This discrimination restricts access to many jobs, contributing to the disproportionate concentration of Puerto Ricans in lower-level employment and to a relatively high unemployment rate.

In recent decades, in places such as New York City, Puerto Ricans have been underrepresented, relative to their population percentage, in government jobs. Thus, one recent study of nonprofit hospitals by the Institute for Puerto Rican Policy found relatively few Puerto Ricans and other Latinos "in policy-making positions at New York's private non-profit hospitals... [and] concludes that Latinos face barriers in receiving care in these hospitals, including a lack of interpreters."[44] This absence of Latinos occurs in part because they are not well integrated into the important (white-dominated) job information networks. In addition, job tests that are often, and unnecessarily, given only in English screen out Puerto Ricans from good jobs. This procedure is discriminatory when Puerto Rican applicants are capable of doing the jobs and screening tests are not job-related. Even trash collection jobs have sometimes required screening tests on which those who speak English score better. As with other Latinos, Puerto Ricans have found themselves unfairly stigmatized as being of "low intelligence" because of a limited command of English.

Institutionalized discrimination can be seen in height and weight requirements that use white men as the standard. Such requirements have sometimes disqualified Puerto Rican applicants, who are often smaller than Anglo white applicants, for police and fire department jobs. Even Puerto Ricans' status as U.S. citizens has been a source of discrimination. In some cases, mainland officials have asked Puerto Ricans to prove their U.S. citizenship. For other jobs, their citizenship status has proved to be a handicap. In a Civil Rights Commission interview, a Puerto Rican woman in California reported that employers there often prefer "Mexicans (particularly illegals) because they know that unions don't represent them, so they can be exploited easier. At least Puerto Ricans have citizenship and can get into unions."[45]

Employment opportunities are heavily shaped by discrimination. Many white employers classify Puerto Ricans as "black" or "nonwhite" and discriminate against them. Historically, many unions, especially those representing skilled workers, have excluded or restricted Puerto Ricans. Government officials have sometimes winked at these discriminatory practices. Recall the mid-2000s employment testing we noted in Chapter 8. In one recent study, white job applicants with felony drug convictions were about as likely to be called back or given job offers as Puerto Rican applicants without criminal records. (As a group, Puerto Rican applicants got somewhat better treatment than African American applicants.) Research also shows that middle-class professional and managerial workers still face racial discrimination. One 2007 study of such workers found that many go back to Puerto Rico periodically, to rest from the stress of discrimination as well as for family reasons. In spite of significant educational and other human capital, they had significant encounters with "prejudice, ethnocentrism, and xenophobia, all revealing the persistence of racism in the United States."[46]

Industrial Restructuring

A variety of changing structural factors in the economy have contributed to high unemployment. Early Puerto Rican immigrants came to mainland cities to fill manufacturing jobs. By the time of the later migration of 1946–1964, however, the large central cities had mostly entered a period of gradual manufacturing decline. As New York City moved from an industrial to a service-oriented economy, production jobs once open to Puerto Ricans began to disappear. Between 1960 and 1980, New York City lost many manufacturing jobs, and this decline has generally continued to the present. Then and in subsequent decades, the availability of low-paying service jobs has not kept pace with the decline in production jobs. Technological innovations—automation and computerization—have eroded the number of less-skilled production jobs. Many city plants have moved to the suburbs, the South, or overseas, taking jobs out of the geographical reach of city workers who do not qualify for white-collar jobs being newly created in cities.[47]

The presence of employed workers is crucial for any community's survival. Thus, in one area of Brooklyn, New York, numerous unemployed Puerto Ricans have lived in dire straights, yet have resided next to regularly employed blue-collar workers who help them and also maintain the community's social institutions. A community can usually handle unemployment as long as this does not become the dominant economic reality.[48]

Income and Poverty

Mainland Puerto Ricans are relatively poor compared to other U.S. groups. As we saw in Table 8.3, in the mid-2000s, median family income for mainland Puerto Ricans ($37,534) was only 60 percent of that of Anglo whites ($62,300). Moreover, about 37 percent of Puerto Rican full-time, year-round workers earned less than $25,000 in 2003, compared with 23 percent of their Anglo counterparts.[49] In areas such as New York City, where many Puerto Ricans reside and which has recently seen significant increases in its Latino population, their per-capita income is one-third that of the Anglo population. In the mid-2000s, the Census Bureau reported that nearly a quarter (and a larger proportion of children) of mainland Puerto Rican families fell below the federal poverty line, compared with just 6.3 percent of non-Latino whites.[50]

Table 8.4 suggests the significant inequality in wealth that faces Latinos, including Puerto Ricans. The desperate nature of some Puerto Ricans' economic situations is evident in their substantial use of public assistance, which is especially significant given the reluctance most have in taking such aid. "I'd rather starve than go on welfare" is an often-stated sentiment among Puerto Ricans.[51]

What is the relationship of systemic racism to the unemployment, underemployment, and poverty facing Puerto Ricans?

Housing Problems

For decades, housing discrimination has been a significant problem for Americans of Puerto Rican descent. At one 1980s U.S. Civil Rights Commission hearing, a Rutgers University professor testified that Puerto Ricans have been excluded from most good housing markets and get "housing scraps" that no one else wants. Compared with other major groups, Puerto Ricans use a larger percentage of their income for housing and are more likely to live in dilapidated housing. In the mid-1990s, fewer than one-fourth of Puerto Rican households owned a home, compared to more than 70 percent of white households. As low-income renters, many Puerto Ricans are vulnerable to the effects of both urban decay and gentrification. Overcrowding and deteriorating housing are characteristic of numerous city neighborhoods. The South Bronx, home to a large Puerto Rican community, is a grim example. Once composed of stable communities, this area has been gutted by highway construction, redlined by bankers, and abandoned by employers. Since the 1970s, the area has lost much population. In addition to psychic stress and severed community ties, neighborhood decay has had negative effects on school quality and increased distances to shopping and workplaces.[52]

In recent years Puerto Rican neighborhoods in New York City, such as those in East Harlem ("*El Barrio*") have experienced gentrification because of affluent whites seeking central city housing and entrepreneurial opportunities. In the process of whites returning to the central city and generating housing gentrification, which is also occurring in Chicago, those with more money drive out those with less. Recent research by Arlene Dávila shows how East Harlem neighborhoods have faced increasing gentrification to the benefit of new white middle-class residents and businesses, as well as a modest number of middle-class Puerto Ricans. One irony of this gentrification is how some officials use the language of "Latin culture" and "Latinidad" to get Puerto Rican and other Latinos to acquiesce in neoliberal development projects that result in white and other middle-class people eventually displacing working-class Puerto Ricans.[53]

Puerto Rican and other Latino leaders have pressed New York's attorney general for action against housing discrimination experienced by Latino workers in Long Island communities. For example, numerous Puerto Rican, Dominican, and other Latino residents in Freeport have reported home invasions, illegal searches, and harassment by building inspectors. Many local whites seem to prefer a community that segregates whites and "browns" in separate residential areas. In other New York communities, Puerto Ricans, Dominicans, Salvadorans, and others have also reported that their homes are inspected for housing-code violations far more frequently than those of white residents. They also report racial profiling and police harassment.[54]

Discrimination by local officials persists despite federal measures to stop such actions. Under a consent decree with the federal government, officials in Mount Kisco, in New York's Westchester County, agreed to stop using building codes and park regulations to discriminate against laborers, many of whom were from Central America. This consent decree had to be extended because of continuing complaints that a housing ordinance was being used to unfairly target Latino residents. Similarly, in 2005 a Puerto Rican legal defense organization won an injunction against the Town of Brookhaven (Long Island) for evicting Latino renters, most of whom were laborers doing hard labor for white employers, without notice and due process. Some had to live in nearby woods as a result.[55]

Data on housing discrimination suggest that Latinos with darker skin are more likely than those with lighter skin to suffer discrimination from whites. (Those with lighter skin and a certain accent may also suffer more discrimination.) A few studies show that certain Latino groups are *more* segregated from African Americans than they are from whites, but research also shows that Puerto Ricans and Dominican Americans are *less* segregated from African Americans than from whites. One likely reason is the substantial African ancestry of many Puerto Ricans and Dominican Americans. Dominican immigrants, yet another group under the Latino umbrella category, are more recent and somewhat more skilled and educated on average than Puerto Rican immigrants, and they have often settled in Puerto Rican communities. Grosfoguel and Georas have noted that despite their "higher-class background," Dominican Americans are usually placed by whites in the same racially subordinate category in the "coloniality of power" that they place Puerto Ricans.[56]

Recent surveys indicate that more than 80 percent of Puerto Ricans view racial discrimination to be a problem in general. More specifically, they cite discrimination against Latinos in workplaces (72 percent) and in schools (83 percent). Some 36 percent report that they or people close to them have been discriminated against in recent years. For Latinos this proportion reporting significant discrimination increases with level of education, with 42 percent of the college educated reporting such. For Puerto Ricans, as for other Latinos, racial discrimination remains a serious problem.[57]

Education

In the 2005 census survey, just over 71 percent of Puerto Ricans more than twenty-four years old had completed high school, compared with about 89 percent of whites. Some 14.8 percent had completed college, just half the figure for whites.[58]

High dropout rates, which are often *pushout* rates, remain a nationwide problem. Nationally, nearly half of all Latino high school students do not graduate. These rates tend to be highest in central-city school districts, such as those of Chicago and New York City. Despite its high position among the states in per-pupil expenditures, New York ranks near the bottom in student retention. New York City has a dismal record in educating Puerto Rican students, whose retention rates there have been very low. The overall graduation figure for New York City schools has been below 50 percent. Some have characterized the poor educational opportunities of Puerto Rican youth as "premarket discrimination"—that is, discrimination that inhibits future success in the labor market.[59]

The low college graduation rate for mainland Puerto Ricans restricts socioeconomic mobility. As for African and Mexican Americans, historically white college settings are usually alien environments for Puerto Rican students. Morales-Nadal has noted the determination and struggles of Puerto Rican women to get educations in order to secure good jobs: "It is not uncommon for some mothers to take their children with them to class in some public colleges." Within the context of higher education, curricula and intergroup exchanges that respect the culture and identity of Puerto Ricans seem vital to the empowerment of more Puerto Rican youth.[60]

For decades, Puerto Rican parents have struggled against an educational system that has typically failed their children. Numerous community organizations have been formed to examine educational problems and work for change. When school boards have ignored the findings of critical evaluation reports, Puerto Rican leaders and organizations have sometimes turned to the courts. Yet, deficient urban school systems have proved highly resistant even to court-mandated change; white school administrators' attention to the rights and needs of culturally different students has often been resistive or halfhearted.[61]

Barriers to Social and Economic Mobility

Few Puerto Ricans have moved into influential positions in education, and Puerto Rican communities usually have little control over educational policies and curriculum decisions affecting children. White authorities frequently are insensitive to Puerto Rican history and concerns; the standard curriculum is often based on the assumption that Puerto Ricans are culturally or linguistically deficient. Neglect of Puerto Rican history and culture undoubtedly contributes to a lack of self-esteem among students. The public schools attended by most students are *de facto* segregated, with a high concentration of students of color. A 2003–2004 Harvard study of northeastern public schools found that 78 percent of Latino (substantially Puerto Rican) children were in schools in which more than half the students were students of color. More than four in ten were in schools that were 90 to 100 percent children of color. Yet, the number of Puerto Rican teachers and administrators, especially compared to the number of Puerto Rican students, is quite low.[62] As we have seen in the case of African Americans and Mexican Americans, racially segregated schooling has negative implications: low retention rates, many students who read below grade level, high student–teacher ratios, less qualified teachers, and low teacher expectations. A strong correlation has been established In educational research between teachers' expectations and students' academic achievement. Students, in any group, whose teachers respect them and expect them to achieve are more likely to succeed in life.

Language

Few schools today are structured appropriately to deal with non–English-speaking students. Prior to the American Revolution, bilingual education (in German, for example) was commonplace and continued to be available to many European immigrants and their children in private, and sometimes publicly funded, schools in the eighteenth, nineteenth, and early twentieth centuries. Only in recent decades has bilingual education become "un-American" and the target of anti-immigrant organizations.

In the current atmosphere of hostility to bilingual education, limited English proficiency creates barriers for Puerto Rican and other Latino students. Without well-crafted bilingual programs, children who are unable to understand English instruction fall behind native–English-speaking classmates. Puerto Rican students are often inaccurately assigned to low-ability groups, "language-disabled" classes, or lower grades. On average, Puerto Rican students do less well than white students on conventional achievement tests, most of which are given in English. One psychologist has underscored the inaccuracy of test scores: "In my clinic, the average underestimation of IQ for a Puerto Rican kid is 20 points.... When we test in Spanish, there is a 20 point leap immediately—20 higher than when he's tested in English."[63] In addition, some Spanish-language achievement tests are more or less translations of English-language tests and maintain the cultural biases of the original version.

Puerto Rican educator Hermán La Fontaine once noted that a viable "definition of cultural pluralism must include the concept that our language and our culture will be given equal status to that of the majority population."[64] Many Puerto Rican educators have argued that children should be taught to read well in Spanish first, taught subjects in that language, and then taught English as a second language. Civil rights groups have pressed for substantial and well-designed bilingual education programs for Latino children. Thus, in struggles against the New York City and Chicago school systems, Puerto Rican parents and organizations have regularly sought comprehensive educational programs that recognize the significance of Puerto Rican history and culture and of the Spanish language. Interestingly, some researchers report that students in bilingual programs have higher attendance and completion rates and that such programs contribute to more positive self-concepts for students. Nonetheless, as we noted in Chapter 8, well-crafted, well-funded bilingual programs have not become part of the public school curriculum for most Latino children.[65]

Official English Policies and Spanish Speakers

Support for English as the *official* U.S. language has grown dramatically in recent years. Much of this movement is nativist; leaders have mainly targeted Spanish and Spanish speakers, from Florida to California. An amendment to the Arizona Constitution went so far as to make English the language "of all government functions and actions," but a federal judge ruled that it violated the U.S. Constitution. (Florida voters rejected an English-only constitutional amendment.)[66]

Xenophobic Americans praise English-only government policies as a means to unify diverse groups within U.S. society and promote certain "traditional" (that is, European American) cultural values. Educator Catherine Walsh reports that instead "such efforts toward linguistic cohesion resonate with a kind of colonial domination, a hegemony that threatens to silence the less powerful [and attempts] to render invisible the complex, abstract, psych-ideological nature of language."[67] Far more than just neutral symbols, language reflects and imbeds a group's history and culture and thus is inseparable from group and personal identity. Walsh documented the daily struggle faced by language-minority students over whose language and therefore whose knowledge, perspectives, and experiences are recognized and whose are omitted. She quotes one young bilingual student: "Sometimes I two-times think," she said. "I think like in my family and in my house. And then I think like in school and other places. Then I talk. They aren't the same, you know." Realizing that the language context of her home was not only different but less acceptable than that of the school, this child often told her teacher, "It makes me feel funny, all alone... different."[68]

Politics

In Puerto Rico, a substantial majority of the island's registered voters usually cast votes on election days. Among mainland Puerto Ricans, however, voting rates have often been much lower. Similar to the experiences of other subordinated racial communities, weak electoral support of Puerto Rican candidates by white voters, a lack of campaign funds, a lack of representation in political party leadership, and a feeling of hopelessness regarding political change contribute to this relatively low political participation. In one older survey of mainland Puerto Ricans who were not registered to vote, the most frequently cited reasons were "not interested in politics" and "voting makes no difference."[69] However, voter registration and turnout have generally increased for mainland Puerto Ricans since 1990, especially in areas where governments are responsive to community needs. As a result, in several recent elections Puerto Rican voters have played an important role in deciding the results. Gradually, researchers have begun to examine the political views of Puerto Ricans. Thus, in a 2002 national survey, half the Puerto Rican respondents indicated that they would be willing to pay higher taxes if government provided more services, a figure significantly higher than that for whites in similar surveys. Some 38 percent felt that you could trust government officials most or all the time, while 49 percent felt you could trust them only some of the time. This pattern was about like the response of whites, but more trusting than that of African Americans in similar surveys.[70]

Election to major political office has come slowly for mainland Puerto Ricans. Since the 1930s, Puerto Ricans have participated in Democratic Party politics in New York and New Jersey, but until recent years that participation has usually been token. The first Puerto Rican American was elected to the New York state assembly in 1937; it would be fifteen years before another was elected. In 1965, Hermán Badillo became the first Puerto Rican elected president of a New York City borough; six years later he became the first voting member of Puerto Rican background in the U.S. House. His seat was later filled by José Serrano. Puerto Rican representation in the U.S. House tripled in 1992 with the election of Nydia Velázquez (D–N.Y.) and Luis Gutiérrez (D–Ill.). However, by the mid-2000s there were still just three Puerto Ricans in the U.S. House and none in the Senate.[71]

Local and State Government

In recent decades Puerto Ricans have served on numerous city councils and as mayors of small towns and a few cities. For example, Miami had a Puerto Rican mayor from 1973 until 1985. By the late 1990s, Puerto Ricans had won twenty-one elected positions in New York City. In 1989 the National Hispanic Caucus of State Legislators was founded; as of the mid-2000s, its members include more than three hundred elected Latino state legislators (including numerous Puerto Rican legislators) in the United States, Puerto Rico, and the Virgin Islands. (By 2006 there were about 58 Latinos serving in state senates and 180 serving in state lower houses.) The organization's first legislative summit was held in 2001, and in summits since then its stated goals have included improving socioeconomic conditions and government services for Latinos across the United States and its territories.[72]

The long-term effects of institutional discrimination can be seen in state and city government employment, in which Puerto Ricans are still significantly underrepresented. Partly as a result of this modest representation, many Puerto Ricans report poor treatment by government and private agencies. Government officials who serve them seldom speak Spanish. Government services have historically been less accessible to Puerto Ricans, and job training and employment services have often been slow in coming to Puerto Rican communities.[73]

In the 1980s, the governor of Puerto Rico announced a campaign to register mainland Puerto Rican voters and thus expand their political power. Local leaders welcomed this intervention, which demonstrated the close alliances between mainland and island communities. The project registered many new voters in areas such as New York City, and Puerto Rican voter turnout increased, resulting in more Puerto Ricans in government. In the 2000s the Puerto Rico Federal Affairs Administration, an organization working for the Commonwealth of Puerto Rico in the United States, has continued to work aggressively to register hundreds of thousands of Puerto Rican and other Latino voters.[74]

Politics and Recent Intergroup Conflict

We have previously noted the success of political coalitions between black and Latino communities in some cities. In New York City, where Latino and African Americans now make up half the population, there has been a long history of successful coalitions, as well as periodic tensions. Latino voters were critical to the elections of the city's first black mayor, David Dinkins, in 1989. Later, in 2001, a key New York black leader, Rev. Al Sharpton, went to jail with Puerto Ricans protesting the U.S. Navy's test bombing of a Puerto Rican island. A Puerto Rican mayoral candidate, Fernando Ferrer, was also supported that year by black officials. However, other cities have been characterized mostly by political competition. For example, consider the case of Providence, Rhode Island. The population is one-fourth Latino, half of whom are from the Dominican Republic and the rest from Puerto Rico, Mexico, and South America. African Americans make up about 15 percent of the population; whites are a bare majority. In recent years Latino political organizations have grown in strength. In 2000, two Latino candidates tried to unseat progressive black elected officials. The primary and general elections saw a large turnout of Latino voters, and one Latino successfully displaced a black official; a second came close to ousting another. Local observers suggested that the white elite had backed the Latino attempt to unseat black officials; others argued that the conflict was primarily the result of growing numbers of Latino voters. Local activists expressed much concern about the lack of a strong progressive coalition of voters of color.[75]

Protest

In Puerto Rico, protests against colonial status have periodically punctuated U.S. rule. Contrary to the stereotype of docility, Puerto Ricans have fought hard to retain their language and culture and end the island's status as the "last major U.S. colony." In the 1930s, large numbers of Puerto Ricans attacked colonial government buildings in periodic protests. The Nationalist Party began pushing for expanded freedom and independence.[76] In 1950, police raided Nationalist Party meetings, precipitating armed revolt. Hundreds were killed, and two thousand were arrested for advocating island independence. On the mainland, Puerto Rican nationalists seeking independence conducted an armed attack on the residence of President Harry Truman and on members of the U.S. House while it was in session.

Recent platforms of the Republican and Democratic parties have supported statehood for Puerto Rico. Although pro-statehood sentiment on the island has increased over the decades, in a 1993 nonbinding plebiscite, island voters narrowly favored continuing the island's commonwealth status. In the late 1990s the U.S. House passed a bill permitting a Puerto Rican plebiscite on the island's future, but the bill did not pass the Senate. Significantly, the bill admitted that the U.S. government had never permitted Puerto Ricans to have self-determination and recognized that commonwealth status was a temporary status on the way to statehood or "separate sovereignty." Today, island Puerto Ricans are divided between the options of commonwealth status and statehood.[77] Supporters of statehood argue that commonwealth status is a second-class status. Opponents fear the economic changes and loss of Puerto Rican culture that statehood might bring. Rubén Berríos Martínez, president of the Puerto Rican Independence Party, has noted that "As a state, Puerto Rico is bound to pay the heaviest of prices: cultural assimilation. In the American system the only way out of an ethnic ghetto is through cultural assimilation into the Anglo-American mainstream, which would subordinate the island's Spanish language and distinct culture. . . . In any case, assimilation is unacceptable to Puerto Ricans, including statehooders."[78] One sign of this threat of assimilation is the view of many mainland whites that Puerto Rico should not become a state unless it adopts English as its official language. In a significant show of support for independence, more than two hundred delegates from nearly two dozen countries met in Panama in 2006 as part of the Latin American and Caribbean Congress for Puerto Rico's Independence. Numerous Latin American leaders, including the president of Panama, noted that Puerto Rico was the only Latin American country remaining under colonial control and that it should be free to become an independent country.[79]

Tensions between island leaders and U.S. politicians increased significantly in the early 2000s. Numerous protest demonstrations targeted the U.S. Navy's bombing range on the island of Vieques just off Puerto Rico. Puerto Rican demonstrators regularly protested the negative impact of Navy bombing on island inhabitants. Some New Yorkers went to Puerto Rico to protest. Bronx Democratic Party chair Roberto Ramírez, assembly member José Rivera, and borough presidential candidate Adolfo Carrión, Jr., as well as black civil rights leader Al Sharpton, were arrested in protests on the island. The Navy bombing was abandoned finally in 2003.[80]

In Washington, D.C., demonstrators protest the U.S. Navy's use of the Puerto Rican island of Vieques for bombing and other military operations.

On the Mainland

Arriving for the most part poor and stigmatized as inferior, Puerto Ricans have developed significant organizations to cope with discrimination and other barriers. Some of the major organizations are the Puerto Rican Legal Defense and Education Fund and the National Puerto Rican Coalition. Puerto Rican teachers associations have worked to increase representation of Puerto Ricans among teachers and principals and expand bilingual programs. Puerto Ricans have been active in union organizations on the mainland since the late 1800s.[81]

Protest activity increased in the 1960s and 1970s. In the spring of 1969 the Young Lords, a militant youth group, occupied the administration building of Chicago's McCormick Theological Seminary to publicize poverty there. They opened a community day-care center and school, protested the use of urban-renewal land for a tennis club, and set up a people's park on urban-renewal land.[82]

In New York City, another Young Lords group occupied the First Spanish Methodist Church and organized a day-care center, a breakfast program, and a clothing program. They created a newspaper, *Palante* ("Forward"), and led a demonstration to protest squalid conditions at a hospital.[83] The Young Lords articulated a thirteen-point program for a democratic-socialist society. Asserting their Puerto Rican identity, they called for "liberation and power in the hands of the people, not Puerto Rican exploiters." At the peak of their influence, Young Lords had chapters in twenty cities. The Young Lords, like other militant groups, were subject to police repression, including infiltration by government agents. Leaders were prosecuted, sometimes in rigged trials, or co-opted into government antipoverty programs.

By the 1970s, the Young Lords had disbanded. Still, many former members later became influential Puerto Rican professionals and leaders in community organizations.[84]

In recent decades, numerous Puerto Rican organizations have worked for a better quality of life and increased participation in the political process. In cities with a significant number of Puerto Ricans, social and cultural clubs seek to preserve elements of Puerto Rican culture. Grass-roots activists have created a number of organizations in the New York and New Jersey areas, seeking to improve day-care, bilingual education, and social services. The Puerto Rican Legal Defense and Education Fund has since 1972 engaged in litigation in support of civil rights; the organization Aspira has worked hard to improve education for Latino youth; and the National Puerto Rican Forum has focused on employment and job training. The National Puerto Rican Coalition, representing many local organizations, has served as a liaison between Puerto Rican communities and government officials and lobbied for educational, health, economic, voting rights, and other civil rights programs. Under the pressure of organizations such as these, as well as activism by Puerto Rican students and professors, several New York and New Jersey universities have developed Puerto Rican studies programs. This effort has encouraged new research on Puerto Ricans and the creation of the Puerto Rican Studies Association, as well as a new generation of Puerto Rican researchers, artists, and writers. Puerto Ricans have also led in struggles to keep open admissions at New York City universities.[85]

More Community Protest

Puerto Rican communities have long protested discrimination by local whites. The previously cited research on East Harlem neighborhoods describes how Puerto Rican organizations in that area have fought against various types of discrimination by getting involved in politics, including lobbying school boards and planning boards. Puerto Rican groups there have made use of the idea of *Latinidad*, of Latino cultural unity, in struggles against gentrifying urban development projects. Chicago community organizations have similarly protested gentrification by affluent whites moving back into the city, as well as housing discrimination and police brutality directed at Puerto Ricans and other Latinos. Reports of police injustice, including unwarranted arrests and searches and the use of excessive force, are common in cities with significant Latino populations. In 1990 a major riot that involved hundreds of Puerto Ricans occurred in Miami after six police officers were acquitted in the fatal police beating of a Puerto Rican drug dealer. Residents of the impoverished Puerto Rican neighborhood reported that the violent uprisings were related directly to the sense of powerlessness that many there felt.[86]

Problems with police persist. In 2001, after a National Puerto Rican Day parade in New York, a milling crowd rioted and protested when police, according to community observers, began arguing with, and then beating and pepper-spraying, people in the crowd. Some community residents were injured. Police authorities defended their violent actions as appropriate, but some in the community questioned what they saw as a pattern of continuing police malpractice in the area. Mid-2000s research in Chicago has found similar community reports of police discrimination against working-class Puerto Ricans and other Latinos on the streets, as well as poor police responses to citizen reports of crimes.[87]

Some protest movements have brought significant changes. Pressures from community activists led to the founding of a community college in the South Bronx and helped create supportive programs for Latino students at the City University of New York. City and state governments have provided more funds for community projects and hired more Puerto Ricans. Public schools have added more Puerto Rican studies and bilingual programs and hired more Puerto Rican teachers, and colleges have set up Puerto Rican studies programs.[88]

Coalitions of grass-roots organizations and older established groups, including the National Congress for Puerto Rican Rights, have been created to improve the economic conditions of Puerto Ricans. Since the 1990s, leaders and members of state branches of the National Congress have pressed state and local governments for fair treatment in the courts and for better schools for Latino children; they have participated in protest demonstrations, sometimes with black organizations, against government indifference to poverty, discrimination, and police brutality. The National Congress and other

Puerto Rican organizations have pressed the mass media for better reporting on Latino communities and more Puerto Rican and Latino journalists and editors.

In the last decade or two, numerous mass media outlets have belatedly responded to community pressures for better coverage and representation. By the late 1990s some Puerto Ricans, such as David González, the *first* Latino to write the *New York Times* column "About New York," had begun to articulate a Latino perspective in mainstream media. Also the *Times*'s Caribbean and Central America bureau chief, González noted that he "took the column's title at face value. I wanted to make sure the groups I knew, my people, were reflected not just in terms of the usual issues—the social issues, which are important—but also the cultural issues in these neighborhoods whose residents exist in New York."[89] Integrating local media outlets not only voices historically excluded communities but also increases the knowledge available to all citizens and policymakers in an increasingly diverse U.S. society. The deepest understandings of this society's distinctive racial and ethnic communities often come from those who are native to those areas' cultures and languages.

Annual Puerto Rican Day parades have been held since the 1950s in several U.S. cities, especially in New York and New Jersey. One late-1990s parade in New York City that drew 200,000 people, including elected officials, celebrated the strong sense of Puerto Rican identity and asserted concern over discrimination. Significantly, a few days before this parade, a white businessperson urged businesses to close their doors and protect their premises during the event, and a former New York columnist writing in a prominent magazine called Puerto Ricans "fat," "dusky," and "semi-savages." These comments, which triggered protests, reveal continuing stereotypes of Puerto Ricans in certain white business and media elites. Significantly, the mid-2000s parades were generally friendly and family-oriented and had as many as 80,000 participants.[90]

Religion

Catholicism has long been the main religion among Puerto Ricans on the mainland, as in Puerto Rico. Interestingly, Puerto Rican and Cuban Americans have also developed some distinctive branching religions. For example, some Puerto Ricans have adopted aspects of the syncretic Santería religion that blends traditional practices of once enslaved Africans (mainly Yoruba) with those of Catholicism (see below, on Cuban Americans).

On the mainland, Puerto Rican Catholics have generally been led by non–Puerto Rican clergy. One exception to the dependence on non–Puerto Rican clergy is the bishop of Puerto Rico, who periodically visits mainland parishes. Sociologist Joseph Fitzpatrick has argued that Puerto Rican Catholicism is more a religion of the community than of the parish. Community celebrations and processions are important, as is reverence for the Virgin Mary and certain saints. Formal church worship has often been less important than communal celebrations and home ceremonies. Still, many remain devoutly religious whether or not they attend mass regularly. On the mainland, Puerto Ricans have often shared parishes with black and other Latino parishioners. Research by Susan Eichenberger suggests that the pan-Latino diversity of some parishes can leave some Puerto Rican parishioners feeling alienated because of the diverse approaches to religion among the Latino groups. Increasingly, Latino caucuses have developed within the Catholic church to press for Spanish-language services and for more priests of Latino background. In Fitzpatrick's words, "the principal demand of the Puerto Ricans and other Latinos is for a policy of cultural pluralism in the church that will provide for the continuation of their language and culture in their spiritual life and the appointment of Puerto Ricans and other Latinos to positions of responsibility."[91] Gradually, if too slowly, the U.S. Catholic church has moved to integrate Puerto Ricans and other Latinos into parishes and leadership positions.

As is the case for other Latinos, many Puerto Ricans have left the Catholic church for evangelical Protestant churches, which they feel offer a warmer reception and a community feeling. Protestant evangelical groups have made significant inroads into Puerto Rican communities, and many communities now have numerous storefront evangelical churches. Research by Andrew Greeley has shown that moving out of Catholicism is seen by some Puerto Ricans as assisting their social mobility in a predominantly Protestant society.[92]

Assimilation or Colonialism?

Assimilation Perspectives

In an influential 1971 book, Joseph Fitzpatrick uses an assimilation model to interpret Puerto Rican experiences. At that time he reported a significant degree of overall assimilation, including substantial cultural assimilation, particularly for the mainland-born Puerto Ricans who identified with U.S. society and adopted English as their second language.[93] Yet, other scholars, then and now, such as Catherine Walsh, have argued that this cultural adaptation is more variable and limited and generally gives a "false hope" of full sociocultural inclusion. Thus, some Puerto Rican schoolchildren deny knowing Spanish when speaking with non-Latinos, even if they use Spanish at home. Earlier, in *Up from Puerto Rico* (1958), Elena Padilla had argued that second-generation Puerto Ricans generally have a different reference group than the first-generation immigrants—that is, the mainland society rather than island society—and as a result many hide their Spanish-language facility in an attempt to assimilate culturally in a Eurocentric environment.[94]

Manuel Maldonado-Denis suggests that the "American ethic is a messianic one, and all ethnic groups are required to assimilate culturally as a condition for achieving a share in the material and spiritual goods of American society."[95] Cultural assimilation pressures begin in Puerto Rico, where for decades the colonial government pressured islanders to assimilate to a Eurocentric U.S. culture, such as by requiring English in schools. More recently, in a 1990s survey, Strategy Research Corporation ranked the cultural assimilation level of Latinos. The majority (59 percent) of mainland Puerto Rican heads of household were then classified as partially assimilated, with only 10 percent fully assimilated. English language use was one measure of cultural assimilation. Many were bilingual or only Spanish speakers. Since the 1990s, however, an ever-growing percentage of mainland Puerto Ricans have come to speak mainly or only English. Indeed, recent research shows that the ability to speak any significant Spanish dies out in *three* generations or less for Puerto Ricans and other Latinos. The United States is a burial ground for non-English languages.[96]

Over the decades, many Puerto Ricans have resisted complete acculturation. The quest for a Puerto Rican identity in the United States has sometimes taken the "form of a strong assertion of the significance of Puerto Rican culture, including language, and also the definition of Puerto Rican interests around militant types of political and community action."[97] Puerto Rican studies programs in some public schools and a few colleges have periodically buttressed the sense of a distinctive Puerto Rican identity. However, some Puerto Rican leaders argue that they must assimilate more thoroughly to key aspects the Eurocentric culture to secure better jobs and socioeconomic positions. Some argue that this can be done with a minimum of selling out—that is, with a strong persistence of Puerto Rican culture. Others worry about the heavy cost of thoroughgoing cultural assimilation to Puerto Rican identity; they fear that assimilation pressures will lead to rootlessness. In addition, one should distinguish those Puerto Ricans who have made a permanent home on the mainland and have cut many ties with the island and those who still maintain very strong ties to their families and communities on the island—and often return there periodically. One recent study of middle-class Puerto Ricans who return periodically to the island suggests that they engage in selective acculturation–that is, they "embrace U.S. patterns of living" and certain U.S. measures of success, but also maintain strong cultural and family ties to the island of Puerto Rico. They are part of an increasing global migration and are also caught between two sociocultural worlds. With this large group among mainland Puerto Ricans, including people of all class backgrounds, it is unlikely that Puerto Ricans will ever fully assimilate to the dominant culture and society as earlier European immigrants did.[98]

There is also the continuing racialization of Puerto Ricans by influential whites. For example, some research shows that many white school teachers are engaged in an ongoing cultural struggle with their Puerto Rican and other Latino students. The outcome varies; students may become culturally assimilated, fully or partially, or they may drop out. Researchers have found that favorable treatment of Latino students in school increases as their "difference" from whites, as perceived by non-Latino teachers, decreases. For earlier white immigrants,

Puerto Ricans wave the flag of Puerto Rico in a New York City parade.

acculturation frequently led to significant denial of their ethnicity, and cultural differences became a source of shame. For Americans of color, however, full cultural assimilation and loss of racial identity are impossible; the differences usually are too visible and important in whites' racial judgments. Rather than becoming de-racialized or de-ethnicized "Americans," Puerto Ricans and others of color typically remain distinctive and substantially subordinated.[99]

Today, overt job discrimination against Puerto Ricans appears to be declining, although substantial covert and subtle discrimination remains. Blatant, covert, and subtle forms of mistreatment continue in other areas such as housing rentals and sales. For the most part, the level of behavior-receptional assimilation, to use Gordon's term, is relatively low. Secondary-structural incorporation at the level of higher-paying white-collar jobs has been slow; Puerto Ricans are still disproportionately concentrated in blue-collar, service, and lower-wage white-collar jobs, as well as among the unemployed. The level of Puerto Rican participation in mainland political institutions also remains relatively low, although it has grown significantly in the last decade.

Structural assimilation of Puerto Ricans at the primary-group level and marital assimilation have not reached levels comparable to those of past European immigrants. Several studies have found regular interaction between immigrant parents and their U.S.-born married children. Despite the wrenching experiences of migration and several decades on the mainland, the older immigrant generation remains substantially linked to children and grandchildren. The better jobs and educations of many in the second and later generations have not ended this family integration for most. However, out-marriage appears more significant for second and later generations and may be slowly breaking down intergenerational ties. One 1990s study of New York City marriage records showed that some 87 percent of first-generation Puerto Rican brides married within their group or married other Latinos. The percentage was still high, about three-quarters, for second-generation brides. These exogamy percentages were similar to those for Dominican Americans, but substantially higher than for Mexican and Cuban Americans in New York City. However, 2000 census data showed that, taking the country as a whole, Puerto Ricans were more likely to be married to non-Latinos (at 21 percent) than Cuban

Americans and other Latinos. The proportion had increased from about 10 percent in 1970.[100]

As in other immigrant communities, generational conflict has been a problem. Children who grow up in the mainland U.S. culture pick up values that sometimes conflict with traditional Puerto Rican values. For example, the traditional chaperoning of girls has given way to less restrictive mainland dating patterns. Still, identificational assimilation, in Gordon's terms, has come slowly for young and old. Most, whether island-born or mainland-born, still see themselves as Puerto Rican. Even those born on the mainland have retained strong symbolic ties to the island of Puerto Rico.[101]

Power-Conflict Perspectives

Power-conflict analysts agree that Anglo-conformity pressure on Puerto Ricans has been heavy, but they stress how colonized Puerto Rican Americans as a group remain. Assimilation into the economic and political mainstream has been relatively slow, which suggests that many non-European migrants such as Puerto Ricans are not being progressively incorporated into U.S. society, contrary to the views of some assimilation analysts, just like the European immigrants earlier in the twentieth century.

Issues of a multiracial Puerto Rican identity and history surfaced in a late-1990s debate among some Puerto Ricans about a new Puerto Rican "Barbie" doll issued by Mattel Corporation in its "Dolls of the World" series. Puerto Rican critics argued that the doll's appearance (skin and hair) was too white European and did not reflect Puerto Ricans' strong Indian and African ancestries. Some also noted that the description of the island on the doll's box neglected this Indian and African ancestry, as well as the long U.S. colonial oppression of the island. As we move well into the twenty-first century, some scholars and other analysts are paying much more attention to the substantial African ancestry and African cultural background, as well as colonial history, of Puerto Ricans.[102]

Power-conflict analysts of the U.S. treatment of Puerto Ricans are generally concerned more than most assimilation analysts about the negative effects of racialization, racial discrimination, unemployment, and deteriorating housing areas on the socioeconomic futures of Puerto Ricans, especially the youth.[103] Indeed, Puerto Ricans are one social group that has had the distinctive experience of *external* colonialism. Unemployment in the U.S. "possession" of Puerto Rico is often cited as a reason for outmigration; the prosperity of the mainland economy is cited as a pull factor. However, unemployment and mainland prosperity would not have created the great migrations without the long colonial relationship. The economic history of Puerto Ricans is grounded in the history of the colonial relationship between the United States and the island of Puerto Rico. After the war with Spain, the United States took the island by force as an external colony. Since that time the inhabitants have been subject to constant U.S. economic and political intervention. Indeed, it was the creation of a one-crop agricultural society dominated by absentee sugar companies that originally displaced a large group of agricultural workers from the land.

With the later industrialization of Puerto Rico under the auspices of large U.S. corporations, many Puerto Rican workers became part of a growing surplus labor population that frequently made its way to mainland cities. These immigrants from an external colony often became part of the *internal* colonialism of U.S. central cities, where Puerto Ricans are usually racialized by whites as "not white" and live mostly in significantly segregated communities. Colonialism theorists also argue that today a coopted Puerto Rican middle- and upper-class elite frequently exerts political and social control over Puerto Rican communities to keep the populations there from rebelling strongly against oppressive socioeconomic conditions.[104]

Internal colonialism can be seen in numerous "urban enterprise zones" created in older cities since the 1980s. (New Jersey alone currently has thirty-two such zones.) Typically these are urban poverty areas that offer significantly reduced taxes and regulations to corporations that open plants there. Some power-conflict analysts view this program as economic exploitation of Latino and black communities because participating corporations have often paid low wages yet received major government benefits. Frank Bonilla and Ricardo Campos have compared this "puertoricanization" of central-city communities to the economic colonialism of Operation Bootstrap on the island of Puerto Rico.[105]

How have Puerto Ricans resisted institutional discrimination?

Cuban Americans

Cuban Americans are one of the largest U.S. Latino groups, at nearly 1.5 million. (A few more recent immigrant groups such as Salvadoran Americans may now be somewhat larger in number.) Like Puerto Ricans, this group has its roots in an important Caribbean island, Cuba, one with more than a century of close ties to the United States. Indeed, even through the recent decades of dramatic political conflict between the U.S. and Cuban governments, the U.S. government has maintained a major symbol of past colonialism on the island—the military base at Guantánamo Bay, Cuba.

Patterns of Immigration

Early Immigration: 1868–1959

Most migrations from Cuba to the United States have stemmed from political upheaval or economic distress on the island. Nineteenth-century wars of independence brought the first immigrants, mostly from Cuba's middle and working classes. Some went to New York, Philadelphia, and Boston, but most settled in Florida because of its proximity to Cuba. By 1873, Cubans were the majority of the population in Key West. After 1885, Ybor City and Tampa in south Florida became home to many Cubans when cigar factories located there. These Cuban Americans were committed to independence of their homeland from Spain and contributed soldiers and financial assistance to the war with Spain. When Cuba won its independence, many returned. Yet, tens of thousands stayed in the United States where they had homes and jobs. These early Cuban Americans made major contributions to their adopted homeland; they organized Florida's first labor union and established Key West's first fire department and bilingual school.[106]

These early Cuban exiles lobbied for official U.S. support of Cuba's liberation from Spain. Initially, the U.S. government supported Spanish rule of Cuba. Later, after attempting to purchase the island, the United States sent troops to Cuba. Spain was driven out in 1898, and the United States occupied the island. In 1902, Cuba became a U.S. protectorate. The Platt Amendment to a 1900–1901 U.S. military appropriations bill gave the United States the right to military intervention in Cuba to preserve the island's "independence." During the early twentieth century, the United States intervened militarily to settle political disputes. After the 1920s, diplomatic interference replaced military intervention. So great was U.S. power that no elected president of the island who was opposed by the United States could remain in office. Cuba was in effect a U.S. colony from 1898 until the Cuban revolution in the 1950s. During this long period, U.S. financial domination was no less extensive than its political domination. Within fifteen years after Cuba gained independence from Spain, U.S. investments grew from about $50 million to $220 million. By the late 1950s, U.S. businesses controlled 90 percent of Cuba's mines, 80 percent of its utilities, half of its railways, 40 percent of its sugar production, and one-fourth of its bank deposits. Cuba was indeed an economic and political colony.[107]

The political turbulence accompanying a succession of repressive dictators in Cuba during the first half of the twentieth century brought political exiles to the United States. Many stayed only briefly before returning to Cuba. They were often replaced in the United States by those Cubans from whose power they had earlier fled. During the corrupt dictatorship of Fulgencio Batista in the 1950s, between 10,000 and 15,000 refugees per year entered the United States.[108]

Recent Immigration: 1959 to the Present

Large numbers of Cubans migrated to the United States after Cuba's 1959 revolution, when Fidel Castro, a U.S.-educated leader of the grass-roots insurrection that overthrew Batista, came to power. To the majority of Cubans, Castro's victory brought hope for economic and political reforms. Land grants to tenant farmers, guaranteed compensation for small growers, and nationalization of utility companies were among Castro's stated goals. However, these reforms were not welcomed by Cuba's business, industrial, and political elites, or by U.S. investors. Exaggerated views of the Cuban revolution's threat to U.S. business and political interests, suspicions that Castro was a Communist, and Castro's declarations that he would not tolerate outside manipulation of Cuba led to open U.S. government and business hostility, a break in diplomatic relations, and a U.S. government policy that welcomed refugees from Cuba's "Communist oppression."[109] This U.S. opposition helped tilt Cuba to supportive Communist regimes in Europe.

The first major immigration after the revolution began with Cuba's monied elite—former government officials, bankers, and industrialists who had done well under the Batista dictatorship and feared Castro's revolutionary orientation. During a second wave of immigration, which began in 1961, large numbers of middle-income and upper-income Cubans chose exile from their native island rather than life under Fidel Castro's increasingly authoritarian government. This group was predominantly composed of professionals, managers, merchants, and landlords and included more than half of Cuba's teachers and doctors. Many cited loss of jobs, possessions, or sources of income as reasons for departure. Others reported political persecution or fear that they would be imprisoned. More than 14,000 children were sent alone by parents who feared having their children educated by a Communist state. Early groups of immigrants were composed primarily of lighter-skinned Cubans. (In 1953 the island's population was at least 27 percent Afro-Cuban.) By 1962, almost 200,000 Cubans had entered the United States. Smaller numbers continued to arrive by boat or by way of other countries after air travel between Cuba and the United States was suspended in 1962.[110]

As with earlier Cuban immigrants, Florida, only 90 miles from Cuba, was the usual destination. Because they were fleeing a Communist government, they found the U.S. government a willing host. Both the immigrants and the U.S. government initially viewed Cubans as refugees forced into temporary exile, but who intended to return home when Castro was overthrown. To provide for the needs of refugees, the U.S. government created the Cuban Refugee Emergency Center in Miami and allocated federal funds. Soon the John Kennedy administration expanded aid by establishing a Cuban Refugee Program that assisted refugees with resettlement, helped locate employment, and provided for health services, education and training programs, and food distribution. Unlike many other Latino and Caribbean immigrants, Cubans were well treated and welcomed as allies in the struggle against Communism.[111]

A third group of immigrants, totaling more than 250,000, arrived between 1965 and the 1970s. In 1965, almost five thousand relatives of refugees in the United States were allowed to leave Cuba aboard hundreds of boats. This exodus was followed by an airlift. Hope for a better standard of living in the United States as well as disagreement with Cuba's regime were major push factors for this largely lighter-skinned, working-class and small-business group. These refugees also settled primarily in Florida, although by the 1970s some were spread among Cuban communities in other states. A nationwide study of immigrant families found that relocation patterns reflected family associations: More than three-fourths of new immigrant families had relatives already in the United States. Occupational orientation was also found to be an important criterion in selecting a relocation city. For example, some with a background in government chose Washington, D.C.[112]

By the late 1960s, increasing numbers had begun to think of themselves as permanent residents of the United States, more interested in improving their lives and less involved in efforts to bring about the demise of Castro's government. Many were developing businesses, had bought homes, and had become integrated into the social, economic, and political institutions of their communities. Many became naturalized citizens.

The Mariel Immigrants

A fourth infusion of immigrants, *the entry of 125,000 Cubans who came from Cuba to the United States in 1980* often called the **Mariel boatlift** (after the port from which they sailed), gave rise to popular stereotypes that characterized these refugees as "undesirables"—poorer and less educated than earlier immigrants and containing a large percentage of criminals and the mentally ill. Some in this group left Cuba voluntarily and some, considered undesirable by the Cuban government, were forced to leave. However, of the entire group, only a few hundred were mentally ill and required institutionalization, and fewer than one in five had been in prison in Cuba. Among this latter group, almost one-fourth had been political prisoners, and the offenses of an additional 70 percent consisted of acts that were not crimes in the United States. Fewer than 2 percent were subsequently imprisoned in a U.S. penitentiary. The education level of this Mariel group was actually similar to that of the 1970s' immigrants. More than 11 percent were professionals; 71 percent were blue-collar workers. Unlike earlier immigrants, most of whom were lighter-skinned, approximately 40 percent of the Mariel group were darker-skinned Cubans with more substantial African ancestry. More than half came to waiting families or sponsors, and two-thirds of the rest were easily placed in communities across the country.[113]

Because their reasons for immigration were substantially economic, most Mariel immigrants were working class and came with often different political experiences from earlier immigrants. They had lived under a Communist government for long periods. Yet, they were ineligible for the financial support available to earlier political refugees. They were allowed to stay by the creation of a special category, "Cuban-Haitian entrant," which included eligibility for emergency assistance, medical services, and supplemental income. Upon arrival the immigrants were housed in tent cities in the Miami area and flown to military bases elsewhere. Some were held in processing centers for an extended time while the government attempted to identify refugees who were "dangerous." However, the vast majority were not criminal. Many became angry at the contrast between their actual socioeconomic conditions in the United States and exaggerated reports they had heard in Cuba about life in the United States. Disillusionment and crowded conditions in detention centers led to scattered confrontations between refugees and the police or National Guard troops. Most were eventually integrated into Cuban American communities, but as a group these later immigrants have not done nearly as well economically or politically as earlier immigrants.[114]

In 1994 the Cuban government again lifted its ban on emigration, and 35,000 Cubans left for Florida, mostly on rafts and small boats. Reversing earlier policy, the U.S. government stopped admitting immigrants, sending them instead to camps at the Guantánamo Bay naval base on Cuba. The U.S. and Cuban governments negotiated an agreement whereby the United States would increase visas for Cubans to at least 20,000 annually, and Cuba would halt the exodus. The U.S. government agreed to send back Cubans who had not departed legally and were intercepted by the Coast Guard. Since the mid-1990s, the number of immigrants has often not reached the allowed quota because of fees and other barriers imposed by the Cuban government. The sometimes heated discussions over immigration and travel issues have continued between the two governments to the present. Attempts to reach the United States

Some of the Cuban refugees not allowed into the United States were held at the Guantánomo naval base in Cuba.

illegally have persisted. Under U.S. law, migrants who reach the U.S. shoreline are permitted to stay (at least temporarily). In addition, the Nicaraguan Adjustment and Central American Relief Act, in effect since the late 1990s, has given legal resident status to many Cubans and Central Americans who came illegally.[115]

Nearly 1.5 million Cuban Americans live in the United States, mostly in urban areas. In a 2005 Census Bureau survey, the median age for Cuban Americans was just over forty years, higher than for the U.S. population as a whole and for other Latino groups.[116] Nearly two-thirds were born in Cuba. One scholar notes that "Dissatisfaction with socialist revolutionary change was likely to be highest among the elderly. In issuing permits, the Cuban government has given preference to the dependent elderly while restricting the emigration, for example, of males of military age."[117]

What pressures and attractions have led to Cuban migrations?

Intergroup Conflict

One major result of the Cuban migrations is the significant change in the population mix of Florida. By the 1980s, Latinos had become a majority in Miami. The 1980 migration swelled public-assistance rolls, increased school overcrowding, and created major expenses for local governments hurting from federal cutbacks. The millions paid to care for new Cuban immigrants angered many non-Latinos, and many of the latter unfairly blamed the Cuban immigrants for local social problems.

Tensions Between Cuban Americans and African Americans

Tensions accelerated between Cuban immigrants and Miami's black residents, many of whom felt that Cuban Americans were getting too much government assistance and were taking jobs away from African Americans. Today, the larger and generally more affluent Cuban American community in south Florida controls many businesses, many of which prefer to hire Cuban Americans. This creates friction with the black population, which often faces high unemployment. In one 1980s mayoral election, most black voters voted against the Cuban American candidate. Since 1980, several racial riots have occurred in the Miami area. Miami's 1980 Liberty City riot and 1982 Overtown riot by working-class African Americans were precipitated in part by police involvement in killing black men. The Overtown uprising began after a Cuban American police officer shot and killed a black man playing a video game. More rioting took place in 1984 when the officer was acquitted in connection with the killing. After the riots some Anglo landlords and businesses that had been damaged were replaced by Latino landlords and businesses. One black school official complained that "after a generation of being Southern slaves, blacks now face a future as Latin slaves." The 1989 shooting of an unarmed black motorist by a Latino officer precipitated another uprising in black areas of Miami. After the incident the U.S. attorney began an inquiry into complaints of police brutality by Anglo and Latino officers. Latino officers asked not to be assigned to black areas of the city where anti-police hostility remained high after the riot.[118]

More recently, Cuban American leaders angered the black community when they ignored visiting black officials, including South African President Nelson Mandela, who had maintained relations with the Cuban government. In addition, black groups have sued Cuban American–controlled local governments for what they see as the obstruction of fair political representation. In the late 1990s, the head of a civil rights group, People United to Lead the Struggle for Equality, commented, "We are very much on edge here, and it's getting worse because of the constant elimination of African Americans from jobs and political offices. They [Cuban Americans] are becoming the oppressor."[119]

Political tensions between African Americans and Cuban Americans surfaced again in the 2000 and 2004 presidential elections. Black voters in Florida overwhelmingly supported the two Democratic candidates, while Cuban Americans voted in large numbers for the Republican candidate. Black leaders charged that local election officials, some of whom were Cuban Americans, had played a role in creating discriminatory barriers for black voters. Today, intergroup rivalry and competition remain strong in Florida, where a very old immigrant group (African Americans) often loses in a political power struggle with a new immigrant group (Cuban Americans).

Inconsistent U.S. government treatment of the often lighter-skinned Cuban refugees and the darker-skinned Haitian refugees, discussed in Chapter 7, has been another source of intergroup tension. Thousands of Haitians, as well as hundreds of thousands of Salvadorans and Guatemalans, have been refused refugee status in the United States since the 1970s; many have been deported to face persecution at the hands of dictatorial governments. In a clearly biased maneuver, Cuban immigrants were for some years defined as "political refugees" eligible for U.S. citizenship by friendly U.S. officials, while most Haitian and Central American immigrants were classified as "economic refugees" ineligible even for entry into the United States. (Beginning in 1994 the federal government finally placed more restrictions on Cuban immigrants.) This differential treatment of immigrants has fueled significant tensions between Miami's Cuban and Haitian communities.[120]

Racial Division Among Cuban Americans

The Cuban American population is diverse in terms of the racial gradient that is central to U.S. society. In Cuba, before the revolution, the society was substantially segregated; lighter-skinned Cubans generally had more residential and economic privileges than darker-skinned Cubans with more African ancestry. After the revolution, Castro's government decreed that darker-skinned Cubans should be treated equally with lighter-skinned Cubans, and the former generally gained greater access to better jobs and housing. Racial status became less important, though it did not disappear. In the United States, Cuban immigrants faced a world in which dominant European Americans classify people on a continuum running from preferred "white" to denigrated "black" and in which societal privileges are linked to racial classification. A *New York Times* report described the experiences of two men who had been close friends in Cuba, but who had grown apart when they moved to the Miami area.[121] The light-skinned one integrated easily into the predominantly light-skinned Cuban population, while the other, darker-skinned, was viewed as black by European Americans and forced to reside in a black community. Although they lived a few miles apart, the friends inhabited separate racialized worlds. The reporter who interviewed them recounted the experiences of the darker-skinned man (Mr. Ruiz):

> He had seen barrios in Havana with more blacks than others, but he had never lived in a place where everybody was black. Far from feeling comfortable, he yearned for the mixing he had known in Cuba.... [H]e had been taught to see skin color... as not much more important than, say, the color of his eyes. But this was not Cuba. This was Miami, and in Miami, skin color easily trumps nationality.[122]

In the United States, Ruiz felt constantly under surveillance from Anglo whites. Many of the latter, as well as many lighter-skinned Cubans, stereotype black Americans as dangerous, lazy, or criminal. Soon after arrival, Ruiz faced police harassment from a light-skinned Cuban American officer, just because he was black. The rigid U.S. racial division forces Latin American immigrants into a new world that is often hard to navigate.

What has been the relationship between Cuban Americans and African Americans?

Stereotypes and Discrimination

Cuban Americans are sometimes stereotyped as mostly being anti-Castro militants or extremists and have been described in some media reports, including newspaper editorials, as "crazies" for their aggressive protests over such incidents as that involving the young Cuban boy, Elián González (see below). Certainly, some media accounts of this latter case suggested stereotypes of Cubans as overly emotional. Myriam Márquez, a Cuban American journalist, has argued that many other Americans hold a stereotyped view: "We are circling our wagons, hunkering down for battle and waving a foreign flag on American soil. You are sure we will riot because there's no question in your mind that Miami long ago turned into a Banana Republic with a Wild West flair."[123] However, although some Cuban Americans have joined far-right groups, most reject political extremism and support participation in U.S. politics using traditional electoral approaches.

Some analysts have stereotyped Cuban Americans as a predominantly successful or affluent group that does not face racial discrimination. However, as Susan Eckstein has noted, "Cuban separateness resulted partly from Anglo rebuff. The Anglo upper class and the Anglo professional and business community excluded Cuban immigrants from their informal social circles and from their economic interest groups."[124] Cuban Americans as a group are generally more prosperous than other Latino groups, but this relative affluence should not be exaggerated, for a large proportion live in modest circumstances or poverty. Indeed, a recent census report found 14.4 percent to be below the poverty line, compared with 8.2 percent of the Anglo population.[125]

As we saw in the last chapter, many non-Latinos, and especially in Florida, express distaste for Spanish or other aspects of Latino cultures. In the 1980s, Florida voters overwhelmingly approved an "official English" ballot initiative that many Latinos understandably considered hostile. This initiative mandated that government business be conducted in English. One Cuban American leader noted that such legislation "opens the way for bigotry and discrimination."[126] The desire of some private clubs in Florida to provide a place in which European American members do not have to hear Spanish spoken has led them to establish policies that exclude Latinos and other Americans of color. Federal judge Kenneth Ryskamp's connection to a Miami country club with such a policy was one of several actions that apparently led the Senate Judiciary Committee to reject his nomination to a Court of Appeals seat in the 1990s. (In most U.S. regions, the Spanish heard by middle- and upper-income Anglos is spoken primarily by working-class Latinos. However, Spanish speakers make up a majority of the Miami population and are to be found in every social class.) Judge Ryskamp echoed the sentiments of many Florida Anglos when he explained that his wife was annoyed because many store clerks spoke mostly Spanish and it was difficult for her to shop because stores stocked merchandise preferred by Spanish-speaking customers. Many Anglos have appeared unwilling to make even small adjustments to changing racial and ethnic conditions in their communities.[127]

Like other Latinos, Cuban Americans have experienced discrimination at the hands of Anglo whites. In the 1960s, signs outside some apartment buildings proclaimed, "No Dogs, No Kids, No Cubans." Immigrants have also faced employment barriers. One Cuban American FBI agent, Fernando Mata, helped bring a successful class-action lawsuit against the FBI. The court ordered the agency to eradicate discrimination against its Latino employees. After the lawsuit, Mata, a decorated counterintelligence specialist, lost his security clearance and was suspended because of allegations that he was spying for Cuba. However, civil rights activists outside the agency saw no proof of spying activity and argued that Mata was being harassed because of the lawsuit. Mata's attempt to sue the FBI for retaliation was rejected by federal courts for "national security" reasons.[128]

Other Cuban Americans have reported discrimination in government agencies. In the early 2000s, a Drug Enforcement Administration (DEA) senior agent, Sandalio González, sent materials to Congress indicating that he was being transferred out of the Miami office for what appeared to be discriminatory reasons. The highest-placed Cuban American in the agency, González had protested anti-Latino discrimination in the office. He filed a lawsuit seeking to stop the transfer. Significantly, one 2006 national survey found that 45 percent of Cuban American respondents thought that anti-Latino discrimination was still a major problem, albeit a figure somewhat lower than that for Puerto Ricans (59 percent) and Mexican Americans (58 percent).[129]

The Economic Situation

Many Cuban immigrants experienced a dramatic decline in occupational status when they entered the U.S. economy. A 1966 survey of Cubans in the Miami metropolitan area found that the percentage of immigrants who were employed as professionals, proprietors, technicians, and managers dropped from about 48 percent to about 13 percent, while the percentage of those employed as unskilled laborers doubled (32 percent in the United States compared with 16 percent in Cuba). Even though many were willing to take jobs far below their previous occupational level, unemployment was widespread.[130]

The increased Cuban presence in Florida has elevated Miami's importance as a center for Latin American and other international commerce. The area's growth has expanded the volume of international trade as well as the number of international corporations that have located their headquarters for Latin America there. In the eyes of many, Miami has become the "capital of Latin America" because of its dominant position in Latin American trade and banking as well as in the underground economy of the drug trade.[131]

Compared with other Latino groups, Cuban Americans have generally enjoyed a greater degree of economic success. There are several interrelated reasons for this. The relatively high-level educational and occupational characteristics of many immigrants, especially earlier arrivals, have helped many attain significant economic success. In addition, large numbers of immigrants in one metropolitan area (Miami) make possible the development of what some term an "ethnic enclave" (a concentrated community) with strong support networks greatly facilitating social and economic adjustment. Examining Miami's Cuban enclave, some researchers have suggested that Cubans have done relatively well economically because they migrated not as poor individuals in isolated circumstances over long periods of time but rather as a group that had substantial resources, access to important social networks, and major support from government programs. Researcher Silvia Pedraza has underscored this government role. Motivated greatly by government concern to "fight Communism," large-scale federal programs played a major role in advancing the structural assimilation of immigrants by reinforcing their initial social-class advantage and creating a cumulative advantage for them in the economy.[132]

U.S. government assistance provided to Cuban immigrants was unprecedented. The first federally funded bilingual programs were started for Cubans in the 1960s, and the Cuban Refugee Program lasted until 1974. Over time the government provided $1.2 billion in aid to Cuban refugees, an average of about $63,000 per family (in 2000 dollars). About three-fourths received some government assistance. Specific government programs to support new businesses, such as loans from the Small Business Administration, were targeted to Cuban Americans. As Grosfoguel and Georas found in their data analysis, "In Miami, as well as in Union City, New Jersey, and in New York City, metropolitan areas where large numbers of Cubans settled, the Small Business Administration (SBA) practiced institutionally racist policies against Puerto Ricans and African-Americans while favoring disproportionately the Cubans in the provision of loan programs."[133] Numerous local government programs were also established to benefit Cuban refugees. More than half the "minority contracts" for Miami-Dade County's new transit system went to Latino contractors. Cuban immigrants are the only large group of Latin American immigrants who have ever been granted such extensive federal aid. This assistance has been critical in helping Cuban refugees and their descendants to adapt to the mainstream economy and culture.

In addition, the wide range of occupations among the Cuban immigrants has facilitated the development of a large and interdependent local economy capable of providing jobs and incomes for many in Florida's Latino communities, including immigrants from Central and South America. The enclave economy has given Cuban American entrepreneurs access to less skilled workers arriving later from Cuba. Appeals to group solidarity have helped some businesspeople exploit their compatriots as low-wage workers.[134]

Although these individual and group factors are important in Cuban Americans' economic adjustment, they do not fully account for this group's mobility. Another factor is the economic organization of the Cuban American family. The Cuban American family has generally been "organized around realizing aspirations of economic achievement." Although relatively few women participated in the paid labor force prior to the revolution, gainful employment became an economic necessity for upward mobility in the United States; after immigration, women viewed work outside the home as an opportunity to help the family. Cuban American women, including those who are married with husband present and those with children, have over the decades been more likely than other Latinas to do paid labor; Cuban American women have been more likely to work full-time and year-round than other Latinos. In addition, three-generation families under one roof are more common among Cuban Americans. Such families provide a major source of child care and additional wage earners.[135]

Among Latino groups, Cuban Americans have relatively high levels of economic status. In a 2005 Census Bureau survey, 32 percent reported managerial and professional occupations, with 28 percent in sales and office positions. The rest were in blue-collar and service positions, about the same distribution as for the U.S. population as a whole. Our comparison of income, poverty rates, educational attainment for Mexican Americans, Puerto Ricans, and Cuban Americans in Chapter 8 shows that

Cuban Americans are nearer the non-Latino white population on several socioeconomic measures than are Mexican Americans and Puerto Ricans. As we saw in Table 8.5, the proportion of Cuban Americans with at least a high school diploma is the highest of the three largest Latino groups (at 73 percent), but significantly less than the 89 percent for Anglo whites. The rate of college completion for Cuban Americans is substantially higher than for Puerto Ricans and Mexican Americans. As we saw in Table 8.3, the median family income ($46,717) for Cuban Americans is about 75 percent of that ($62,300) of Anglo whites. In contrast, median family income for mainland Puerto Ricans and Mexican Americans was substantially less. Cuban Americans also have a high rate of home ownership (61 percent versus 47 percent for other Latinos.) The relatively higher economic status of Cuban Americans compared with other Latino groups does not mean that they face no discrimination. Given this group's relatively high level of education, their median income figure is lower than it is for comparably educated Anglos. Employment discrimination by Anglos has long been a problem for Cuban Americans.[136]

As we have already noted, the prosperity of Cuban Americans compared with other Latino groups does not mean that all Cuban Americans are affluent. In the mid-2000s, as we saw in Table 8.3, the poverty rate for Cuban American families was double that of Anglo whites; about 17 percent of Cuban Americans under age eighteen lived below the official poverty line.[137]

Politics

The expectation that the Fidel Castro regime would be short-lived led most post-1959 Cuban immigrants to remain politically inactive in the United States for a number of years, although they sought to influence U.S. policy toward Cuba. The 1970s saw an increase in naturalized citizens, followed by an increase in voter registration and participation in politics. Political views were often shaped by concern with Cuba. In the 1980s, the Cuban American marketing director of the *Miami News* stated, Cuban Americans are "definitely super-conservative. Communism for us is the enemy. On domestic issues, we will be more toward the center... but the Cuban business community is still more in favor of Reaganomics than Mexicans or Puerto Ricans."[138] However, although many identify with the Republican Party, which they consider to be more anti-Castro, they left a legacy of progressive programs in Cuba, where social reforms, such as an eight-hour work day, free school lunches, and a minimum wage, instituted in the 1930s, have remained in effect through a succession of Cuban dictators. Cuban Americans still are more likely to support such social programs than Anglos.[139]

Since the 1980s, Cuban Americans have become more politically active. Two-thirds of adults are citizens, and they register and vote in large numbers. They hold many elective and appointive offices in Florida, including powerful positions in the Florida legislature. In recent years, the mayor of Miami, the mayor of Miami-Dade county, the superintendent of the Miami-Dade County public schools, the county police chief, the presidents of major local colleges, and numerous state legislators from the area have been Cuban American. Cuban Americans have also made political advances in urban areas in other states, particularly New Jersey. In 1993, Ileana Ros-Lehtinen, a Cuban American from Miami, became the first Latina ever to serve in the U.S. House of Representatives. (She continued there as of the 2006 election.) In the 1990s two more Cuban Americans joined Ros-Lehtinen in the House. In the early 2000s, President George W. Bush appointed the first Cuban American, Mel Martínez, to a cabinet position, as Secretary of Housing and Urban Development. Martinez was later elected to the U.S. Senate (Florida). In 2006 he also became chair of the national Republican Party. In the mid-2000s Robert Menendez, a Democrat, became the first Cuban American to serve in the U.S. Senate from New Jersey. Cuban Americans in south Florida remain strongly committed to the Republican Party. One 2006 survey found that 72 percent of adults surveyed were registered Republicans, with those immigrating before 1980 being the most likely to be Republicans.[140]

Many Cuban Americans remain involved in the politics of Cuba. One major example was the 2000 case of Elián González, a Cuban boy whose mother drowned while trying to bring him on a boat to the United States. Elián's U.S. relatives waged a custody battle with his father, who sought to have Elián returned to Cuba. In April 2000 (during the Bill Clinton administration), U.S. agents seized the boy from U.S. relatives and let him return. Both actions

U.S. Senator Robert Menendez (D-NJ) speaks during a campaign rally in October 2006.

upset many in the Cuban American community and cost the Democratic presidential candidate in 2000 many Cuban American votes, and perhaps the election.[141] This is another example of how many U.S. racial and ethnic groups remain actively concerned about the politics of home countries. Some U.S. political analysts, such as Samuel Huntington, worry that U.S. foreign policy is no longer unified but instead has become a "balkanized" collection of the overseas interests of diverse U.S. nationality groups. Huntington also sees Cuban Americans and other Latinos as intentionally creating a separate America and a threat to cultural unity (by which he means, a threat to the Anglocentric culture he prefers).[142]

One influential group has been the Cuban American National Foundation (CANF), established in 1981 and eventually involving thousands of members and offices in Miami, Washington, and other cities. It has been active in lobbying Congress on legislation dealing with Cuba. In a 2001 speech, the chair of CANF indicated that his organization still supported the U.S. embargo on trade with Cuba, which was under increasing attack from humanitarian groups. However, by the early 2000s a majority of Cuban Americans indicated in surveys that they thought the embargo had not worked, and in early 2006 a group of moderate Cuban American leaders created a new group, called ENCASA, to press for an end to trade and travel embargos. By late 2006, with the serious illness of Fidel Castro and the rise of his brother Raúl Castro to prominence, the CANF and other Cuban American organizations were shifting their hard-line approach to working for more contacts and interaction with the Cuban people and government. Thus, in late 2006, after months of discussion, a dozen Miami exile groups, including CANF, put together a petition to the U.S. government to end regulations banning family travel to Cuba. The reasoning accented the "ethical obligation" of Cuban Americans to "loved ones" left behind in Cuba. Still, a 2006 survey of Cuban Americans in south Florida found that 49 percent supported (with 45 percent opposed) tough new George W. Bush administration restrictions on family travel and remittance transfers to Cuba, restrictions added because of the lobbying efforts of a new far-right Cuban organization called the Cuba Liberty Council. Significantly, in the 2006 survey over half of those who immigrated since 1980 opposed these new restrictions. Clearly, the Cuban American community is currently divided over the proper U.S. government response to the Cuban government.[143]

In a recent sociological analysis, Susan Eckstein has shown that this political division is substantially a result of the different views and experiences of immigrants who came in the 1959–1965 era and those who have come since the 1980s. Those who came in the early period have tended to be more economically mobile and more politically conservative, and have had much more political influence (especially with Republican officials) in Florida and in the country, than those who have come since the 1980s, who have mostly been working-class and have not moved up economically as rapidly. The latter are more likely to reject trade and travel restrictions to Cuba, especially because they have left families there relatively recently.[144]

In the past, some Cuban exiles have engaged in paramilitary training and terrorist acts directed against the Fidel Castro government. Exiles recruited by the CIA were involved in the unsuccessful Bay of Pigs invasion in 1961. Members of at least one anti-Castro group practiced mock invasions well into the 1990s. In 1991, three Miami Cubans entered Cuba by boat with small arms and explosives, but they were captured and tried for sabotage. Mid-2000s opinion surveys have found that 60 percent of Cuban Americans still support military actions by exile groups against the Cuban government. In addition, Cuban Americans have been active in the operation of Radio Martí, a federally funded station, and its affiliate, TV Martí, which transmit news and public affairs programming from Washington to Cuba via Florida. Some critical analyses, however, suggest that the programming is often of low or propagandistic quality and that few Cubans have even heard of these expensive efforts ($27 million annually).[145]

The collapse of the Soviet Union in 1991 brought severe economic hardships to Cuba's people; the two countries had been linked by billions of dollars in trade for decades. In 2001 a group of prominent Cuban Americans, including Miami-area Cuban American mayors, met to hear a presentation from Ramón Saul Sánchez regarding nonviolent actions to help the Cuban people with humanitarian supplies and undermine the Cuban government. Sanchez has headed the Democracy Movement, a major Cuban-exile group that has demonstrated on behalf of Cubans trying to sail from Cuba. Over the 1990s and 2000s the group has brought a flotilla of boats to Cuba numerous times on anti-Castro and pro-democracy missions, and the U.S. Coast Guard has tried to stop the efforts. In addition, in 2006 the U.S. Secretary of Commerce, Cuban American Carlos Gutiérrez, headed up a George W. Bush Administration planning group to aid the island to move toward a government more in line with U.S. interests when the Castro government ended.[146]

The recurring involvement of Cuban Americans in the politics of Cuba is yet another example of the way in which the development and situations of U.S. racial and ethnic groups interact with and are dependent on the world context. U.S. racial and ethnic relations are intrinsically international.

How did migration to the United States change the economic situation of many Cuban Americans?

Religion

Like many Puerto Ricans, many Cuban immigrants to the United States brought with them *a type of syncretic religion that included aspects of both Catholicism and older African religions*, religious practices referred to as Cuban **Santería**. Over centuries, Cuban Santería practitioners have dressed up African nature deities (orishas) in the religious symbolism of Catholic saints, thus combining aspects of Catholic ideas and ritual with folk religious practices rooted in the religions of Africans who were once enslaved in Cuba. Today, Santería practices and ideas are important for many Cubans. They not only provide therapeutic support for many people, but also shape the ways in which these people practice Catholicism in the United States and Cuba. Interestingly, mid-2000s surveys have found that Cuban Americans are less likely than those in other major Latino groups to say that religion is the most important thing in their lives. Just 28 percent reported being regular (at least weekly) attenders of church services, a figure lower than that for other Latino groups. (In addition, Cuban Americans report that they are less opposed to abortion than are Puerto Ricans or Mexican Americans.) Those who are actively involved in Catholic parishes, especially in Florida, may find an increasingly diverse Latino Church. Numerous formerly white Catholic parishes have become mostly Latino, with a significant number ministering to a diversity of Latino populations—Cuban Americans, Puerto

Ricans, Mexican Americans, Dominican Americans, and South and Central Americans. As with Puerto Ricans, this pan-Latino diversity leaves some Cuban parishioners feeling alienated because of the different approaches to Catholic religion even among Latinos.[147]

Assimilation or Colonialism?

Assimilation Issues

Cuban Americans are a relatively recent addition to the bubbling cauldron that is the United States. Like other Latinos, they have faced prejudice and discrimination, including language discrimination and restriction or exclusion in Anglo-dominated organizations and institutions.

Efforts to maintain the Cuban culture and social order, as well as to bypass country club discrimination by European Americans, led to the creation in the 1960s of the Big Five Club, an elite, mostly Latino Miami social club. In recent years the club's membership has included many of the Cuban American community's most distinguished families. (Affluent Anglos have their own, mostly Anglo clubs.) Over the last decade or two, however, the younger, U.S.-born generation has seemed less interested in joining elite Cuban social clubs. As one Big Five president put it, "The ones born in this country feel they are more American than Cuban." Nonetheless, many Cuban Americans in various generations have joined an array of mostly or entirely Latino business and professional associations and are sending their children to predominantly Latino parochial schools. (Significantly, private-school segregation can be seen in south Florida. Affluent Anglos, thus, often place their children in elite private schools with few Latino children.)[148]

Identificational assimilation has come slowly for Cuban Americans. Some, especially those who are older and Cuban-born, still consider themselves exiles rather than immigrants and speak of a "fractured identity." Others—especially those who left Cuba as children and the U.S.-born generations (the latter now more than one-third of the population)—say they have a "double" identity. However, a recent survey of Cuban Americans found only 13 percent expressing any inclination to return to Cuba permanently if the current government were to be replaced. In addition, over half have indicated in surveys that the U.S. government should be in overt dialogue with the Cuban government. More than 70 percent of Cuban Americans surveyed in 2006 favored negotiations between the U.S. government and a new Cuban government that showed a willingness to improve relations with the U.S. and the Cuban exile community. Recently, a majority has also shown a willingness to have cultural exchanges with Cuba, such as by allowing Cuban musical groups to perform in the United States.[149]

One 2000s study compared the identifications of Cuban American and African American women. The African American women felt they were indeed "American," but that they were not seen as such by Anglo whites, and they felt they still were economically and socially excluded by whites. In contrast, Cuban American women did not feel they were American and did not think Anglo whites saw them as American. However, their reported feelings of societal inclusion increased with length of residence. The longer they had been in the United States, the more economically and socially included they felt.[150]

The preservation of Cuban culture and identity in the enclave communities in Florida provides a crucial foundation for Cuban Americans' economic and political integration into U.S. society. The community solidarity originally created by the first groups of immigrants was rooted in kinship and friendship ties and formed the socioeconomic context into which later immigrants entered. In the mid-1970s, researchers interviewed 590 male immigrant heads of household at the time of their arrival in Miami and again several years later. In the initial interview, 99 percent expressed an intention to remain in the Miami area; at the time of the final interview, 97 percent still resided there. The Miami area's strong enclave community has provided a context in which immigrants and their children adapt to the dominant Anglo culture yet continue to carry out routine activities within a Cuban American setting. Six years after these respondents entered the United States, more than one in five were self-employed in the Cuban American community, and almost half worked for a Cuban American business. At the economic level, most of these immigrants did not assimilate directly to the dominant economic institutions but rather to the enclave economy.[151]

Over time, Cuban Americans have made significant economic achievements, which increasingly link them into the mainstream economy and politics.

Scholars David Hayes-Bautista and Robert Stein have argued that "Latino entrepreneurship has turned Miami into a bustling center of international trade, self-declared gateway to the economies of Latin America and self-appointed music center of Latino USA. Latino politicians run the city and county; Latinos are involved in the fine arts, academia, journalism and broadcasting."[152] Although this summary neglects continuing problems with racial discrimination and stereotyping that Cuban Americans face at the hands of Anglo whites, it underscores the important point that, of all major Latino groups, Cuban Americans are probably the most integrated into Anglo-dominated U.S. economic and political institutions.

Cuban Americans are similar to a few other immigrant groups that achieved a significant degree of economic prosperity and integration during the first generation. Like some Jewish immigrants in the first half of the twentieth century, Cuban immigrants did not have to wait their turn in the urban economic queue, as did Italian, Polish, and certain other immigrant groups. Instead, many in the first three Cuban immigrant groups advanced into an economic niche as small-business owners or professionals, often laying a basis for their children's educational mobility and movement into better business and professional jobs. As a result, many of their children and grandchildren are now relatively advantaged. Media reports from Florida underscore the growing affluence of many. For example, children's first communions (receiving the Roman Catholic sacrament) for many families have become costly celebrations. As Daniel Álvarez has noted, "We are a very tight community, and we want to do whatever we can to hold on and keep our kids in touch with their Cuban Catholic heritage."[153] The presence of a large and cohesive group of immigrants in an enclave community provides a context of support for later generations. However, the enclave community has brought significantly less socioeconomic mobility for the most recent group of Cuban (Mariel and later) immigrants.[154]

Cultural assimilation pressures on Cuban immigrants have created cross-generational problems similar to those of earlier European immigrants. Language assimilation is significant for the younger generation. One 1980s survey of Miami's Cubans revealed that the young already preferred English-language programs on radio and TV, whereas their parents switched between English and Spanish programs. Like immigrant grandparents before them, the grandparents preferred to hear and speak Spanish. Parents and grandparents worried about the excessive freedom and lack of parental respect of U.S. teenagers. Parents and grandparents tended to emphasize Cuban traditions and food; grandchildren preferred things American. The older generations were strongly committed to overthrowing Cuba's Communist government and to returning home. The less politically active youth saw the United States as their permanent home. Family and community ties were strong, and the young were proud of their Cuban identities.[155]

In the 1990s, Strategy Research Corporation (SRC) ranked the Cuban Americans as the least *culturally* assimilated of major Latino groups, based on language use and behavioral and attitudinal measures. The high density of Cuban Americans in Florida and the group's older average age were likely factors. Fewer than one-third reported then that they spoke or wrote English well. However, the SRC survey presented a different picture for younger Latinos in the Southeast. Fewer than half of the youth classified themselves as "very Hispanic," and only 40 percent felt they would be "very Hispanic" ten years in the future. Three-fourths spoke English at school and felt more comfortable speaking English than Spanish. More recently, a 2004 Miami survey found that nearly half of Cuban Americans speak English outside their homes and that most work with non-Cubans. And a 2004 national survey by the U.S. Census Bureau found that the overwhelming majority of Cuban Americans under eighteen spoke English well, although most reported that some Spanish was spoken at home, doubtless to older relatives. As with other Latinos, however, the Spanish language is slowing dying out as the generations pass.[156]

Cuban Americans, especially in south Florida, have adapted selectively to their new country. They have developed a vigorous enclave economy and substantial group resources, with increasing links to the outside, Anglo-dominated economic and political institutions. Many have also tried to preserve the Spanish language and traditions. Recent surveys have shown that 70 percent view fluency in Spanish as useful in securing jobs, especially as multinational corporations expand their operations in Latin America and locate facilities in Florida.

Nonetheless, the younger generations are assimilating more rapidly than the Cuban-born to the dominant culture. Interestingly, one major recent survey found that Cuban Americans were the *only* major Latino group in which a majority said that they *preferred* to identify as "white" over other common identifications such as Latino, Hispanic, and black. The survey also found that for Latinos as a group, and probably for Cuban Americans, the tendency to identify as "white" was much higher for those over age fifty-five than for those who were younger.[157]

The dominant Euro-American culture does regularly make some modest adjustments to new groups entering the society. For example, as the U.S. Latino population has grown, Cuban, Mexican, and other Latino music and foods have become popular. Many restaurants now feature Cuban and Mexican foods, and major store chains, especially in areas with substantial Latino populations, carry foods of interest to Latinos. In south Florida cities, major chain grocery stores carry such things as plantains, guava paste, and corn husks. Although smaller Latino-operated stores *(bodegas)* have more goods for Latinos, chain retailers have discovered this group's buying power (at least $400 billion) and are striving to discover what products they seek. In this process, non-Latino customers are also exposed to Latino tastes in food and other products.[158]

A Power-Conflict Perspective?

To our knowledge, no one has applied a sustained power-conflict perspective to the case of Cuban Americans. Some might argue that the internal colonialism and other power-conflict perspectives are not useful to interpreting the development of the predominantly light-skinned Cuban American group, which has not been so strongly racialized and victimized as much by long-term economic and political discrimination as other Latino groups. Many of the relatively well-off Cubans who migrated to the United States before 1980 had been, to some degree, the beneficiaries of U.S. economic and political control over Cuba prior to the 1959 revolution. Instead of becoming low-wage laborers for non-Latino agribusiness and industrialists, as was (and often still is) the case for many Mexican Americans and Puerto Ricans, many Cuban Americans have become part of a south Florida niche economy and enclave society that have helped speed their economic and social mobility.

The opportunities and accomplishments of the U.S.-born generations of Cuban Americans (at least of the lighter-skinned majority), which include growing numbers of businesspeople, professionals, and managerial workers, seem in some ways more similar to those of older white ethnic groups (for example, Italian or Polish Americans) at a comparable point in time than to those of other Latinos. Indeed, the adaptive development of lighter-skinned Cuban Americans may best be interpreted as a variation on the ethnogenesis model. This group has experienced substantial cultural adaptation as well as some economic and political integration into certain Anglo-controlled institutions. Still, the process of ethnogenesis means that *major* aspects of home-country heritage remain very important to the immigrant-ethnic group identity for a long period of time. Relatively new groups like (lighter-skinned) Cuban Americans are, to a substantial degree, increasingly being integrated politically and economically with the dominant European American group, yet retain major characteristics of their home cultures and nationalities as well. From the ethnogenesis perspective, a new ethnic group is one part home-country heritage and one part common culture mixed together in a distinctive way because of a unique history of social and political development within the U.S. crucible.

Substantially greater political and civic integration with the dominant group can occur only if later generations of Cuban Americans disperse residentially from what is now a relatively concentrated and cohesive community in south Florida. Residential dispersion will likely accelerate this societal incorporation process. Language is a major obstacle to full cultural assimilation of Cuban Americans to the dominant Anglo culture and institutions. Powerful English-speaking Anglos have periodically organized to impose English as the dominant language. Such nativist movements mark a type of cultural colonialism that rejects cultural pluralism if it threatens the core culture. Most Anglo whites still seem to classify Cuban Americans, even those who are light-skinned, as not white. In addition, as a group they will not be fully accepted by the dominant Anglo group until they reject Spanish and other important aspects of their Cuban heritage and culture, probably including Spanish surnames. An even more dramatic Cuban sacrifice on the altar of nativism will be required for the Anglo majority to welcome Cuban Americans fully into the dominant culture and society. Even then, the many Cuban Americans whose ancestry is substantially and perceptibly African (especially from an Anglo point of view) will likely not be admitted into European American social groups and institutions on the same terms as Anglos. Indeed, given persisting problems of anti-Latino discrimination and English language and other Anglo cultural domination, one could well construct a developed power-conflict perspective in regard to understanding the societal reality for a majority of Cuban Americans.

How do you explain the economic and educational differences among Cuban Americans, Puerto Ricans, and Mexican Americans?

Summary

The United States now has the fourth largest Spanish-speaking population among all countries, and in the near future the Latino population will reach 45 million people. In Chapter 8 we examined Mexican Americans, the largest Latino group in the United States. In this chapter we have examined two other large Latino groups.

Puerto Ricans on the mainland are second in population size to Mexican Americans. Puerto Ricans are an important and distinctive American group with an ancient heritage. Like Mexican Americans, they represent a fusion of Native American, Spanish, and African heritages. Today, Puerto Ricans are a divided people with one foot on the mainland and one foot on a Caribbean island. The more or less external-colony situation of the island population greatly complicates its future political-economic development.

The island of Puerto Rico is self-contained, with a variety of classes, including a local capitalist class and a local working class, as well as a small elite of U.S.-based multinational capitalists. Some argue that social-class problems on the island are different from those on the mainland, where most Puerto Ricans are working-class; there are few mainland Puerto Rican capitalists. Other commentators downplay class and stress that there is only one Puerto Rican people. As one Puerto Rican social scientist has stated, "No matter how we see ourselves internally, the Yanqui always sees us and deals with us as one class and one people with the same problems. Therefore we should band together and not divide ourselves to fight for our nation against the colonizer."[159]

Concentrated in the Northeast, mainland Puerto Ricans have been important to the social health and economic vitality of the New York City area, especially as whites are leaving the region. Many Puerto Rican workers face hard lives doing difficult, low-wage jobs. Levels of poverty and unemployment remain relatively high.

Like Puerto Ricans, Cuban Americans are rooted in a Caribbean island. One of the largest Latino groups, they are relatively better off than other groups, with higher levels of education and income. Today they are an urban population mostly concentrated in the southeastern United States. Cuban Americans' relative prosperity stems substantially from the fact that a majority of early immigrants migrated with some important personal and group resources, including access to major federal assistance. Smaller families and a relatively high level of participation of women in the paid labor force have contributed to upward mobility. Cuban Americans' achievements affirm the advantages of migrating under the auspices of strong family networks and of receiving government support.

Cuban Americans have developed a powerful community centered in Miami. This population's size and resources have allowed Cuban Americans to develop a strong economic and political niche and to maintain their Spanish language as well as many Cuban cultural practices. As is the case with other immigrant groups, members of the younger generation have moved rapidly toward the dominant culture in many areas, including language, often to the disappointment of the older generation.

The pride that most Latinos feel in their heritages can be seen in their desire to maintain the Spanish language as well as other cultural patterns. The growing numbers of U.S. Latinos provide support for Spanish-language media, Latino organizations, and the marketing of Latino-oriented products. Puerto Ricans and Cuban Americans have helped generate a new pan-Latino consciousness. They share with Mexican Americans a common language, a common religion, and similar home cultures. The pan-Latino consciousness contributes to a sense of solidarity that is reflected in efforts to address common problems of education, jobs, and racial discrimination.

In recent years, the now substantial Latino population has had an increasing impact on the larger society. Latin American immigration is a major source of the country's population and economic growth, and U.S. Latinos are the most likely Americans to see immigration in a positive light. (However, Mexican Americans are more favorable than Cuban Americans and Puerto Ricans.)[160] Increasingly in some areas, major businesses are actively recruiting Puerto Rican, Cuban American, and other Latino workers—especially the better educated. Major U.S. corporations, as varied as Chevron, PepsiCo, and Pricewaterhouse Coopers, have operated recruitment programs at high schools and colleges with large Latino populations, hired Spanish interpreters, and provided mentoring for Spanish-speaking employees. Executives in these companies seem aware of the increase in Spanish-speaking consumers as well as growing international trade with Spanish-speaking countries.[161] Growing numbers of Latinos are citizens and voters, and thus are having an increasing impact on U.S. politics.

Key Terms

culture of poverty 249
color coding 250
Mariel boatlift 265
Santería 273

CHAPTER 10

Japanese Americans

BIG PICTURE QUESTIONS

- ***What role have Japanese Americans played in building up this country's wealth and institutions?***
- ***How has a white racial framing shaped negative perceptions of Japanese Americans?***
- ***Does the "middleman minority" theoretical perspective fit the experiences of Japanese Americans?***

Mitsuye Yamada, a Japanese American professor of English, has described white students in an Ethnic American Literature class who had read a book in which outspoken Asian American writers wrote critically of discrimination they faced. One white student "blurted out that she was offended by its militant tone and that as a white person she was tired of always being blamed for the oppression of all the minorities." Professor Yamada noted that she saw numerous other students nodding in agreement. She pointed out to the students that they had read other critics of society who were black, Native American, and Latino, but that the students had not been as offended by these analyses. Significantly, white students indicated that they had expected the frustration and anger of these other writers, but not the frustration and anger about discrimination of the Asian American writers. One white student summarized the feelings of numerous students: "It made me angry. *Their* anger made *me* angry, because I didn't even know the Asian Americans felt oppressed. I didn't expect their anger." At that very time, Professor Yamada herself had filed a grievance against her academic employer for violation of her rights as a long-time community college teacher, yet some white administrators seemed to view her stereotypically as just a quiet Asian American and were thus shocked at her speaking out.[1]

Introduction: Asian Americans

Changes in U.S. immigration laws since 1965, especially the elimination of openly discriminatory immigration quotas, have allowed a substantial increase in immigration from Asia and the Pacific Islands. Asian-Pacific Islander Americans constitute the fastest-growing racial group in the United States. More than a dozen groups of Americans have roots in Asia or the Pacific Islands. Since their earliest days of immigration, Asian-Pacific groups have sought to maintain their distinctive cultures and identities.

Diverse groups are included under the relatively new terms **Asian American** and **Asian-Pacific American**, *umbrella terms for Americans with ancestral roots in Asia or the Pacific Islands*. In 1940, these Americans were less than one-half of one percent of the U.S. population. By the 2000 census, they numbered more than 10 million. In the mid-2000s their numbers are still growing, now at about 14 million (about one-third living in California), and they constitute nearly 5 percent of the population. Table 10.1 shows the numbers for various groups at three points in time (1980, 1990, and 2005). In the 2005 census count, the largest of the Asian-Pacific groups was Chinese American. Including those of partial Chinese ancestry (the census tabulates certain groups for sole reported ancestry as well as those with partial ancestry), they totaled more than 3.3 million. In numbers, Filipino Americans were not far behind, at 2.8 million. Japanese, Korean, Asian-Indian, and Vietnamese Americans constitute the other large Asian American groups. Note too that in the mid-2000s Asian Americans as a group had the highest educational attainment and median household income among all U.S. racial groups, although there is great variation within and among the Asian American groups.[2] In this chapter we examine the critical case of Japanese Americans; then we turn to other groups in Chapter 11.

Japanese Americans

Japanese Americans, now more than 1.2 million in number, are one of the two oldest Asian American groups. They hold a distinctive place in U.S. history because of their experiences during World War II. They are the *only* group of Americans to have been forcibly placed in concentration camps on a large scale in the past eighty years. Japanese Americans, as well as Americans collectively, are still paying a significant price for that extreme violation by the U.S. and California governments of their human rights. Today, Japanese Americans are considered by many to be the most successful and assimilated of Asian Americans, and since the 1960s they have been central to the **model minority stereotype**—*which characterizes certain Asian American groups as exemplary in socioeconomic and moral characteristics, often as compared to other people of color.* For these reasons, we devote an extended discussion to their experiences.

Although large proportions of major Asian American groups live in western states, Japanese Americans are among the most heavily concentrated there. Among Asian Americans, Japanese Americans have the highest percentage who are U.S.-born, an indication of the group's early entry and small

TABLE 10.1 Asian-Pacific American Groups (1980 to 2005)

	1980 Census	1990 Census	2005 Census Survey (Group Alone)*	2005 Census Survey (Group Alone Plus Combinations)**
Japanese	716,331	866,160	833,761	1,204,205
Chinese	812,178	1,648,696	2,889,280	3,336,966
Filipino	781,894	1,419,711	2,282,872	2,807,731
Korean	357,393	797,304	1,246,240	1,406,687
Vietnamese	245,025	593,213	1,418,334	1,521,353
Asian Indian	387,223	786,694	2,319,222	2,479,424
Hawaiian	172,346	205,501	151,878	436,404
Cambodian	16,044	149,047	217,438	241,025
Laotian	47,683	147,375	193,247	209,627
Hmong	5,204	94,439	183,265	188,900
Thai	45,279	91,360	143,169	188,043
Samoan	39,520	57,679	56,736	98,681
Guamanian or Chamorro	30,695	47,754	76,062	109,985

**This category includes census estimate from a survey for people who reported only one specific Asian group.*

***This category includes census estimate from a survey for people who reported one detailed Asian group plus people reporting two or more Asian groups and people who reported some Asian and some non-Asian ancestry.*

number of recent immigrants.[3] For many non-Asian Americans, Japanese Americans still conjure up racial stereotypes of "crafty Orientals," images of militaristic Japanese expansionism in the 1930s, or resentment of "unfair" Japanese economic competition today. Even in recent years, movies, political speeches, and vandals' graffiti have included such phrases as "fat Japs" and "little Nips," and Japanese and other Asian Americans have been targets of vandalism and violence. Periodically, Japanese American community facilities are vandalized, and Japanese firms are considered dangerous if they purchase U.S. companies. Indeed, individuals are sometimes attacked; thus, a "Japanese businessman in California is killed, apparently after receiving an anti-Japanese threat."[4] Such verbal and physical attacks seem to be motivated by fear of Japanese product imports and corporations or resentment of Japanese competition in world trade. Anti-Asian hostility has increased during periodic U.S. economic recessions as non-Asians have sought scapegoats for problems rooted in faulty economic decisions of non-Asian executives, investors, or workers.

Migration: An Overview

Serial and Chain Migration

Asian and Pacific Americans include many immigrant groups: the Chinese, Japanese, Koreans, Filipinos, Vietnamese, and Asian Indians, as well as smaller groups such as Cambodians, Laotians, the Hmong, the Thai, Samoans, and Guamanians. Historians have often neglected Asian immigrants in the epic story of U.S. migration. Nonetheless, Americans have "come from many different shores—Europe, the Americas, Africa, and also Asia."[5]

Historically, immigration of early Asian groups proceeded serially. This was largely the result of actions of white employers seeking new laborers and of white workers motivated by racist prejudices to stop immigration by a particular Asian worker group. As we discuss in Chapter 11, the first substantial group of Asian immigrants was composed of Chinese workers. From the 1860s to the 1880s, Chinese workers migrated in large numbers to the west coast to do low-wage work in construction and other industries. After racist agitation and exclusionary legislation stopped most Chinese immigration in the 1880s, Japanese workers were aggressively recruited to fill the demand for labor on farms and in construction and mining projects. Similarly, the termination of Japanese immigration in 1908 in its turn spurred employers to recruit Filipinos to fill their labor needs on the mainland and in Hawaii.[6]

Early Immigration

Japan's initial contact with the United States involved **gunboat imperialism** *(imperialism backed by the use or threat of military force)*. In 1853, U.S. Commodore Matthew Perry sailed warships into Tokyo Bay and coerced a treaty granting the United States trading rights with Japan. Later, the U.S. colony of Hawaii became the first destination for Japanese immigrants entering the U.S. sphere. At least 231,000 migrated there between 1868 and 1929. After 1884, thousands of Japanese laborers were brought to Hawaiian plantations, usually under contract labor agreements. There were relatively few white laborers in the islands, and Japanese immigrants became part of a racial hierarchy headed by white planters. When labor agreements expired, most Japanese workers stayed, laying the basis for Hawaii's present-day Japanese American population. In 1898 Hawaii came under U.S. government control.[7]

Japanese workers were numerous on the islands. Dependent on the plantations owned by a few big corporations, they learned that they could not "advance themselves through individualism and small business," as on the mainland. Rather, as laborers, they adopted a strategy of "unionization, politics, and collective action."[8]

Mainland Migration

Between the 1880s and the so-called Gentlemen's Agreement in 1908 (see below), more than 150,000 Japanese entered; between 1909 and the 1920s, another 100,000 came. The immigrants to the mainland moved into a greater diversity of economic positions, from farm labor and mining to shopkeeping and truck farming, than did immigrants to Hawaii. Some came under contract to employers, some under the auspices of relatives, and others on their own. The pre-1908 Issei (literally, "first generation") had a harder time than those who came afterward, since later immigrants were able to move directly into Japanese American communities.[9] (*Issei*, *Nisei*, *Sansei*, and *Yonsei* are Japanese terms for the first four generations of Japanese Americans. Issei were born in Japan.)

White employers favored labor immigration; white workers and unions opposed it. About 1900 one San Francisco mayor campaigned against the Japanese, arguing that they were "unassimilable" and a competitive threat. In 1905, white-run California newspapers began a racist campaign against what they called the "yellow peril," that is, Asian immigrants seen as a threat. The all-white California legislature passed a resolution calling for exclusion of the Japanese because, given their racial differences, they would not assimilate. Racist agitation and related factors led President Theodore Roosevelt to negotiate a prohibition of immigrants. In 1907–1908, Roosevelt persuaded the Japanese government to agree to an infamous Gentlemen's Agreement whereby no passports would be given by Japan to Japanese workers except those already in the United States and their close relatives.[10]

Unlike earlier Chinese immigrants, Japanese immigrants were able for a time to bring in families. Before 1920, thousands of "picture brides" entered, after proxy wedding ceremonies conducted in Japan to husbands they had never met. The large proportion of women and children among Japanese immigrants between 1910 and 1920 led white supremacy groups to allege that a "disloyal alien race" would soon overpopulate California.[11]

More Racist Agitation and Restrictions

White writers and politicians who proclaimed the threat posed by southern and eastern Europeans to "Anglo-Saxon superiority" also expressed fear of Asian immigrants. The American Legion and the California Farm Bureau Association pressed for exclusion. By the 1920s, the U.S. Congress succumbed to agitation by passing the 1924 Immigration Act, which established racist quotas that gave preference to "Nordic" countries and excluded Japanese by prohibiting all "aliens ineligible for citizenship" from entry into the United States. (In *Ozawa* v. *United States* [1922], the U.S. Supreme Court had previously ruled that only immigrants of white or African origin could become U.S. citizens.) One striking feature of the new immigration restrictions was that Japanese and other Asian immigrants already in the United States, unlike their European counterparts, were now prohibited from bringing in wives they had left behind. The extreme Cable Act (1922) also stipulated that *any* U.S. woman, whether white or Asian American, who married an alien ineligible for citizenship (that is, an Asian) would lose *her own* citizenship. These restrictions served to block many avenues of incorporation into the larger society for Asian immigrants.[12]

Government action against Asians, often spurred by white-controlled labor unions and hate groups, persisted. Much of the labor movement supported exclusion of Japanese immigrants. Not until 1952 did the federal government provide even a small quota for the Japanese and permit first-generation Japanese Americans to become naturalized citizens, and anti-Asian restrictions were not fully removed from U.S. immigration law *until 1965*.[13]

As late as 1965, Asian Americans numbered only about 1 million, and Japanese Americans were the largest group. The reform-oriented 1965 Immigration Act finally permitted significant numbers of new immigrants from Asia, and, since the 1970s, Asian and Pacific peoples have been a major component of U.S. immigration.[14] Since the end of openly racist immigration quotas in 1965, Japanese immigrants have been allowed to enter, but relatively few have taken the opportunity. Japanese numbers have been lower than those of numerous other Asian groups, in part because of the advanced character of the Japanese economy in recent decades. However, the immigration of a modest number of college students and of professionals and executives of U.S. branches of Japanese corporations and their families has contributed to the revitalization of some Japanese American communities.

How did U.S. government action shape Japanese migration to the United States?

Stereotypes

White and other non-Asian Americans have long held strong stereotypes about Asian Americans, which take a variety of forms. For example, in recent decades Japanese and other Asian Americans have often been called "model minorities"—that is, viewed as especially successful in moving up the socioeconomic ladder because of distinctive cultural values. In contrast, movies about World War II and the Vietnam War have often portrayed Asians as devious, corrupt, or evil "gooks." In recent years anti-Asian graffiti such as "Look out for the Asian invasion" and "Stop the Yellow Hordes" have been scrawled on college dorm walls and highway overpasses.[15]

Robert Lee has listed the racist images applied to those whom non-Asians view as "Orientals" (an offensive term): "Six images—the pollutant, the coolie, the deviant, the yellow peril, the model minority, and the gook—portray the Oriental as an alien body and a threat to the American national family."[16] White Americans, in particular, have often applied the stereotypes they developed for early Chinese and Japanese immigrants to later Asian immigrants. All Asian groups have suffered from similar stereotypes, such as the "dangerous or wily Oriental" image. In the nineteenth century and later on, Chinese immigrants were stereotyped as "docile," "crafty," or "dirty." Initially, whites tended to consider new Japanese immigrants around 1900 less threatening and more family-oriented than the Chinese and evaluated them less negatively. Soon, however, white images came to include the negative notions that the Japanese were docile, servile, and devious. Immigrants heard cries of "Jap go home."[17] Since those early decades, the word "Jap" has become a shorthand term used routinely by some non-Asian Americans for Japanese Americans or Japan, sometimes by those with clearly hostile intent and sometimes by those who do not clearly understand its derogatory origins.

Within a short period, many early laborers managed to gain land to farm by contract or lease. However, hostile white farmers and workers often exaggerated this Japanese American land use, which never involved more than a small percentage of western farmland. Another widespread myth was that Japanese Americans were incapable of assimilation because of their distinctive culture. Like other whites, V. S. McClatchy, a Sacramento editor, argued that the Japanese were "for various reasons unassimilable, and a dangerous element."[18] The irony in this was clear to anyone who understood that by state or federal law Japanese immigrants were *not allowed* to become citizens, own land directly, or marry whites. They were legally prohibited from even trying to assimilate along these social dimensions.

From U.S. presidents and senators to ordinary whites, many exaggerated the differences between themselves and Japanese immigrants, often in racist terms. James Phelan, U.S. senator from California, argued openly that Japanese Americans were a threat to the "future of the white race, American institutions, and Western civilization."[19] Again we see how an influential framing of whiteness is based on biased views of the meaning of "civilization," as well as on negative views of disliked outgroups.

The U.S. movie industry has played an important role in circulation of stereotypes of Asian Americans—as it has for other oppressed Americans. Historically, movie images have reinforced stereotypes of Japanese Americans as treacherous and immoral. In the formative period of the movie industry in the early twentieth century, Chinese and Japanese characters were pictured as outsiders and villains. Asians and Asian Americans were crudely stereotyped as "inscrutable," poor at speaking English, and dangerous.[20] Between 1900 and 1930, vicious images of forward, buck-toothed "Japs" exploded across the media. In his widely circulated "Letters of a Japanese Schoolboy," journalist Wallace Irwin articulated and stimulated various stereotypes, including a mode of speech mocked and parodied with phrases such as "so sorry, please." White legislators and other leaders spoke of the alleged immorality of Japanese Americans, sometimes using the apelike image applied earlier to Irish and African Americans.[21]

War Propaganda

From the 1890s to the 1930s, anti-Japan sentiment grew. The Japanese were considered an "inferior race" with the brashness to challenge European and American interests in the Pacific. Well before the attack on Pearl Harbor, white politicians and labor leaders were portraying Japanese Americans as disloyal. This image expanded after the bombing of Pearl Harbor, and many white-generated rumors of spying circulated, including such unsubstantiated stories as Japanese American farmers planting flowers in a pattern to guide attacking airplanes![22]

California's attorney general (later U.S. chief justice), Earl Warren, depicted Japanese Americans as dangerous. In 1943, west coast military commander General John DeWitt argued that "A Jap's a Jap. . . . The Japanese race is an enemy race, and while many second- and third-generation Japanese born on U.S. soil, possessed of U.S. citizenship, have become 'Americanized,' the racial strains are undiluted."[23] With no evidence whatsoever, the national press argued that there were many enemy agents in this "large alien population." The main reason for the existence of this "alien" population was the racist law that had intentionally prohibited Japanese immigrants from becoming U.S. citizens. Significantly, and contrary to recent books again trying to justify the World War II discrimination, *no* Japanese American was *ever* proven to have collaborated with the enemy during World War II—a reality that contrasts with that of German Americans, who included a few supporters of Hitler's regime but who (as whites) were never put into concentration camps on a large scale (see below).

After the war, the stereotypes slowly began to change. By the 1960s, new stereotypes had developed. Magazines and newspapers periodically praised Japanese Americans for being acculturated and successful. However, as Dennis Ogawa has noted, the "highly Americanized" and "successful citizens" stereotypes are not really positive, for they usually suggest that one must act or think "very white" in order to be a good citizen. The model minority stereotyping was and continues to be used to defend the overall U.S. racial record. It implies that because Japanese Americans have been English-speaking, work-ethic models of virtue, they can now be accepted by whites as better than certain other non-European groups. Whites who hold this view often allege that groups such as African Americans and Latinos can succeed if they too work harder and assimilate aggressively as Japanese and other Asian Americans are said to do.[24]

Recent Distortions, Stereotypes, and Omissions

One study of Japanese American images in 1970s school history textbooks found numerous distortions of Japanese American history along with the model minority stereotype. Most omitted the fact that U.S. employers in Hawaii and California brutally exploited Japanese laborers. One prominent textbook tiptoed around the oppressive circumstances of this history by speaking of the Japanese as being "added" to the U.S. population. Indeed, few school textbooks dealt with the Japanese American experience in U.S. concentration camps (see below) until the U.S. government apologized in the late 1980s. Today, analyses of textbooks have shown that many textbooks have finally included a mention of the wartime camps but still do not assess critically this illegal internment. Like recent best-selling popular books, many school textbooks—termed "whitewashed" by one *AsianWeek* commentator—view wartime oppression of Japanese Americans as part of the "hysteria of war" and do not discuss the long history of anti-Japanese discrimination leading up to the imprisonment. One reason for the weak history involves educational "reforms," which have led to watered-down textbooks frequently oriented to a "teaching to the tests" approach to public education. One result of such inferior education is that many people are so uninformed about the concentration camp events that they vigorously defend them, as did leading Republican House member Howard Coble in 2003. On a talk show, the ill-informed Coble argued that the U.S. government did the right thing to protect national security and the imprisoned people themselves, assertions that provoked protests from civil rights groups.[25]

Stereotypes and other misperceptions remain commonplace. In the 1980s, Senator Spark Matsunaga of Hawaii, a Japanese American assisting the White House at a reception for visiting Japanese officials, was mistaken for the latter by U.S. Secretary of State Alexander Haig, who shook Matsunaga's hand and wished him a nice visit! In addition, Senator Daniel Inouye, a Japanese American who lost an arm fighting for the United States in World War II, has periodically received hate mail telling him things like he should "go home to Japan where he belongs." Japanese American and other Asian American officials have reported that whites frequently congratulate them on how well they speak English, as though they were foreign-born. Many non–Asian Americans seem unaware that the United States has numerous Japanese American elected officials, that their birthplace is the United States, and that their native language is English.[26]

Racist imaging sometimes takes the form of mocking the language and cultures of Americans of color. On a radio show, U.S. Senator Alfonse D'Amato (R–N.Y.) once spoke in a mock foreign-Asian accent as he criticized the Japanese American judge, Lance Ito, who was presiding over the O. J. Simpson murder trial. (Other commentators since then have done similar accent mocking.) Yet Judge Ito has *no* such accent, and he, like D'Amato, is a third-generation American![27]

Previously we noted that several sports teams have discontinued use of stereotyped racial symbols of groups such as Native Americans. Similarly, Seattle's Shoreline Community College abandoned its Japanese Samurai Warrior mascot, a Japanese caricature. Racist caricatures of Japanese people periodically surface in the media, in novels, and on Internet sites. For example, Michael Crichton's novel, *Rising Sun*, and the movie made from it, develop negative racialized caricatures. Japanese characters in this Los Angeles–based mystery are portrayed, to quote a reviewer, as "inscrutable, technologically proficient, predatory aliens who . . . subsist through unpalatable foods, manipulate *everything* and *everyone*, and enjoy kinky, violent sex with white women."[28] The novel's characters embody age-old stereotypes. The Media Action Network (MANAA), an Asian American organization formed to combat anti-Asian stereotyping, initiated talks about the film's racial content with Twentieth Century-Fox, the studio that made the film, and organized demonstrations against the use of racially stereotyped images of the Japanese in the film.[29]

Debates about negative Asian images in the media emerged again in the early 2000s with the release of the Disney movie *Pearl Harbor*. The film's use of the derogatory epithet, "Japs," as well as its one-sided portrayal of Japanese military aggression in the World War II period, resulted in an increase in anti-Japanese sentiment. Japanese Americans reported derogatory comments from non-Asians because of the movie, responses that indicate that old prejudices are still alive. One California news report quoted a number of Japanese American students who stated that others blamed them for starting World War II and called them derogatory epithets such as "'Nips" or "Chino." One student noted, "People are still against Japan. They treat us like we [Japanese Americans] did something wrong."[30]

In the mid-1990s a white disk jockey for a San Francisco radio station was suspended for anti-Asian comments and for allowing callers to make anti-Asian remarks. He reportedly spoke of "stinking Japanese," told a Japanese American caller he would hate the Japanese forever, and even predicted another war with Japan. The station received vigorous complaints from Asian American groups, including the Japanese American Citizens League (JACL). In 2006 a disc jockey at a Toledo, Ohio, radio station called Japanese and other Asian restaurants numerous times making offensive mock-Asian commentaries, such as "ching, chong chung" and "me speakee no English," to those who answered. Protests by a local Asian American civil rights group led to his dismissal. That year a talk show host on the CBS radio network also mocked an Asian Excellence Awards ceremony by playing a fake excerpt with "Asian men" saying things such as "ching chong, ching chong, ching chong." Protests by civil rights groups were initially ignored. Also in 2006, comedian Rosie O'Donnell was criticized for using a repeated "ching chong" to mock Chinese speech on an ABC talk show. In mid-2000s the Adidas company was also criticized by civil rights groups for making shoes that had a negative caricature of a buck-toothed, slant-eyed Asian as a logo, an image like that used in earlier decades against Japanese and Chinese groups. Such aggressive stereotypes are intergral parts of the old white racial framing of society and are thus long-lasting.[31]

Repression and Violent Attacks

Japanese Americans have suffered not only hostile stereotyping and prejudices but also economic discrimination and physical attacks. The first acts of violence against immigrants came within a decade of their arrival. After the 1906 San Francisco earthquake, mob violence directed at Japanese Americans increased. Scientists sent by Japan to help with earthquake relief were attacked by white men, and newspapers condoned such actions. Japanese businesses were boycotted, and shopkeepers were attacked.[32]

Anti-Japanese exclusion movements sometimes turned to violence, as in California in 1921, when large numbers of Japanese farm workers were driven out of some farm areas. In the 1930s, white farmers in Arizona attempted to throw out Japanese American farmers by force. Violent attacks escalated at the beginning of World War II. In 1942 whites carried out dozens of violent attacks on Japanese Americans and their property, from Seattle to San Diego.[33]

The Ugly Specter of U.S. Concentration Camps

Japanese military victories in the Pacific in the 1930s and 1940s, including the attack on Pearl Harbor, increased fear of a Japanese invasion of the mainland. Members of Congress and the media parroted anti-Japanese stereotypes and escalated fear of Japanese Americans across the country. By 1942, the "evacuation" and "relocation," to use the government's euphemistic bureaucratic terms, of Americans of Japanese ancestry was being suggested by many whites. Some were motivated by economic self-interest; the Western Growers Protective Association and similar groups seemed committed to destroying Japanese American business competition.[34]

In the first major phase of federal action against Americans whose ancestry was linked to countries at war with the United States, a small number of Japanese, German, and Italian aliens were moved from sensitive areas and their travel was restricted. The second stage began with Executive Order 9066, issued on February 19, 1942, by President Franklin Roosevelt and validated by Congress, which instructed the secretary of war to establish areas from which any person could be excluded. The west coast military commander established western California, Washington, and Oregon, and southern Arizona, as areas where no Japanese, Italian, or German aliens could reside. However, *only* those of Japanese ancestry—U.S. citizens and noncitizens alike—were detained in large numbers in assembly centers and transported under guard to barbed-wire concentration camps in the West.[35]

Japanese American businesses usually had to be sold at a loss. By fall 1942, inland areas in the West housed about 120,000 Japanese Americans, more than two-thirds of them *native-born U.S. citizens* whose only crime was to be perceived by whites as racially different.[36] Racist oppression took many forms. The administration at California's Tule Lake Camp arranged for inmates to be hired out as domestics at the very low wage of $30 per month. The camp administration spent some of these earnings on facilities for white personnel. Barracks were typically bare-board with few furnishings. Families were forced to live in small rooms or partitioned-off

Japanese Americans forced out of their homes in San Francisco await transportation to U.S. concentration camps.

areas. Men, women, and children faced severe discrimination and the consequent psychological and physical stress.[37]

Japanese Americans protested their discriminatory treatment in numerous demonstrations; six thousand renounced their citizenship. Gradually, several thousand college students and workers on agricultural assignments were released, and others were allowed to join the Army, where, ironically, many served in Europe with extraordinary valor in racially segregated units.[38] In 1944, the order to evacuate was rescinded. Most returned to the west coast region and found their farms and businesses in white hands or in ruin, household goods destroyed, and whites hostile if not violent. The U.S. government spent about $250 million on the process of imprisonment; Japanese American losses are estimated to have been at least $400 million. The psychological costs and other human losses were incalculable.[39]

Why the Camps Were Created

The U.S. Supreme Court upheld the military decision—even though two-thirds of those imprisoned were U.S. citizens. This imprisonment was a clear violation of civil rights guaranteed by the Constitution.[40] President Franklin Roosevelt and other high officials held racist attitudes toward Japanese and other Asian Americans. Roosevelt believed that people of Japanese descent were racially inferior, and he and other leaders saw the emerging struggle in the Pacific as a *racial* war. Racist attitudes made it easier for top officials to intern U.S. citizens of Asian descent (but not large numbers of citizens of German descent) in barbed-wire concentration camps.[41]

Japanese Americans fought unsuccessfully in courts and with demonstrations. When evacuees confronted authorities at a California assembly center, some destroyed camp property and rioted. The freedom-oriented revolt was suppressed by armed police. In fall 1942, internees called a strike at the Poston camp to protest imprisonment.[42] In December 1942, at the Manzanar camp in California, an assault on a Japanese American who collaborated with whites and the imprisonment of the attacker led to a meeting attended by 4000 and demands for an investigation of camp conditions. The director, escorted by police armed with machine guns, met the crowd. A crowd again formed at night and was fired upon; two Japanese Americans were killed.[43] Ironically, this authoritarian and highly racialized oppression of U.S. citizens occurred at a time when the U.S. government was proclaiming the values of "freedom" and "democracy" to a war-torn world.

Later Impact

After World War II, most Japanese Americans moved back to the west coast, where they continued to face economic discrimination and violent attacks. The epithet "Jap" became commonplace in white comments and anti-Japanese graffiti. Hate crimes—including murders, assaults, threats, and harassment—targeting Japanese and other Asian Americans in their homes, businesses, and places of employment have persisted now well into the twenty-first century; indeed, the fastest-growing category of hate crimes in recent decades has been that involving Asian Americans as targets.

One can also see the effects of the concentration camp experience in many areas of the lives of Japanese Americans today, as we will see in later sections. One individual example is the court martial of Lieutenant Ehren Watada, an American officer of Japanese and Chinese descent. A fine student and an Eagle Scout in Hawaii, he joined the Army in the early 2000s as a patriotic response. When he was ordered to go to Iraq, and after careful study of the Iraq invasion and rationale, he decided that the war violated U.S. and international law and became the first commissioned officer to refuse to be sent to the Iraq war zone (including an Army offer of a safe desk job). The U.S. Army decided to court-martial him, rejecting his argument that the invasion violated the law. The charges against him included his public comments critical of the war. While his parents, veterans for peace groups, and some civil liberties groups supported his decision, often strongly, the Japanese American community was divided, with Representative Michael Honda speaking out on behalf of his conscientious stand and several Japanese American veterans groups condemning his actions. In an interview, Watada directly *connected* his conscientious stand with that of Japanese Americans during the World War II concentration camp era who actively stood up to that political oppression.[44]

What have been some long-term socioeconomic consequences of Japanese American internment in U.S. concentration camps?

The Political Arena

Because of racist U.S. naturalization laws, the Issei and other first-generation Asian Americans were not allowed to become citizens until the 1950s. Thus, they could not be active politically. Political and civic organizations were created in the 1930s, when older Nisei (second-generation) formed political clubs in west coast cities. The Japanese American Citizens League (JACL), under Nisei leadership, advocated accommodation strategies of self-help and individual enterprise and pressed moderately for civil rights and voter registration.[45]

Compensation Pressures and Political Progress

Since World War II, the JACL, with other Japanese American organizations, has won important political and legal victories. By 1946 the JACL and some newer organizations were pressing for compensation for the imprisonment losses, citizenship for the first generation, and changes in discriminatory laws. Meager compensation for business and property losses came with the 1948 Japanese American Evacuation Act, and the Japanese American recipients were paid less than 10 percent of their actual losses.[46]

Japanese American organizations continued to press the government for adequate repayment for losses. As advocates for the country's "liberty and justice for all" tradition, these organizations helped secure public admission of racial discrimination. In 1987, after years of foot-dragging by congressional leaders and initial opposition from the Ronald Reagan White House, Congress passed a bill, which President Reagan signed into law, that provided $1.2 billion in reparations to Japanese Americans. The law contained an admission that the "basic civil liberties" of Japanese Americans were violated because of "racial prejudice" and included a formal apology.[47] Finally, by 1994, all reparations checks were mailed. Each internee, or his or her heirs, received a modest $20,000. President George H. W. Bush wrote each a letter of apology. Some, such as U.S. Representative Robert Matsui of California, refused the check but accepted the apology, saying, "All of us feel like we are home again."[48] Not all Americans were willing to see Japanese Americans receive justice, however. In Oxnard, California, for example, non-Asians unable to distinguish between

Japanese Americans, who are U.S. citizens, and the Japanese government, circulated anti-Japanese leaflets that claimed that no apology to Japanese Americans for unconstitutional imprisonment was necessary because the Japanese government had detained U.S. soldiers in World War II.[49]

In 2001, a well-designed memorial to Japanese Americans who were incarcerated and to Japanese American soldiers who served in the U.S. military was dedicated in Washington, D.C., near the Capitol.[50] In addition, in the 1970s, pressure from Japanese American organizations helped win the repeal of the infamous Title II of the 1950 Internal Security Act, which permitted government imprisonment of citizens deemed potential collaborators with an enemy in time of crisis, and the rescinding of Executive Order 9066, which ordered wartime imprisonment of Japanese Americans.[51] These were victories of significance for the civil rights of all U.S. citizens.

Norman Mineta, a leading Japanese American official, has served in the cabinets of Democratic and Republican presidents.

Government Officials

In 1930, the first Japanese Americans were elected to the territorial legislature of Hawaii. Later on, World War II veterans, intent on expanding participation, became active in Democratic attempts to overthrow the Republican domination of the islands, and several were elected to the legislature. Their efforts facilitated Congress's conferral of statehood on Hawaii in the 1950s. Statehood had been opposed by white politicians with openly racist views, such as rabidly segregationist Senator Strom Thurmond (R–S.C.).[52]

War hero Daniel Inouye was elected the first U.S. representative from the new state and the first Japanese American to serve in Congress. In 1962, Spark Matsunaga became the second to serve in the House, when Inouye was elected to the U.S. Senate. In 1964, a second House seat was won by Patsy Takemoto Mink, the first Japanese American woman, and the first woman of color, ever to serve in Congress.[53] In 2007, Inouye and Daniel Akaka, of native Hawaiian and Chinese American, ancestry were Hawaii's U.S. senators.

Political victories on the mainland have been difficult because of the dilution of Japanese American votes in predominantly non-Asian populations. Few have been elected until recent decades. In the 1960s, a few were elected to city offices in Los Angeles County, Oakland, and San Jose, California. In 1972, Carl Ooka was elected county commissioner in Washington state, the first Japanese American elected to office in that state.[54] Since the 1970s, only a handful of mainland Japanese Americans have held elected positions at higher government levels. In the 1970s Samuel I. Hayakawa was elected U.S. senator from California, the first on the mainland, and Norman Mineta of California became the first mainland representative of Japanese descent to the U.S. House. Robert Matsui was elected in 1978 and remained in the U.S. House in 2001 when he was joined by fellow Californian Michael Honda, also Japanese American. In 2006 Mazie Hirono was elected to the U.S. House from Hawaii, the first Japan-born person to serve there. As of 2007 Hirono, Honda, and Matsui's wife Doris (who was elected in 2005 to replace Matsui after his death and was reelected in November 2006), together with Inouye, were the Japanese American members of Congress. Only one Japanese American has ever held a presidential cabinet post. Norman Mineta was appointed Secretary of Commerce by Bill Clinton in 2000. In 2001 he became Secretary of Transportation in the George W. Bush administration.

Historically, many Asian Americans, including Japanese Americans, have been reluctant to participate actively in politics out of fear of intensifying discrimination against their group. Even in the past decade, Japanese and other American Americans have been less likely than whites to register to vote or to actually vote. Some researchers have speculated that Asian Americans tend to view politics and politicians as corrupt or disreputable or to vote for white politicians rather than run their own candidates because they feel that whites have "more political clout."[55]

Japanese and other Asian Americans who venture into the political arena sometimes encounter overtly racist reactions. For example, in 1992, a Democratic Party leader at a Spokane, Washington, party meeting referred to owners of a local hotel as "chinks." Later, at a meeting to examine the incident, the party's white vice-chair bowed and clasped her hands in front of her in response to a Japanese American participant who would not shake her hand. This mocking gesture combined with the other leader's racial slur led the JACL to sue the state party for overt discrimination.[56]

Politics, Stereotyping, and Competition with Japan

Acts of vandalism and violence by whites against Japanese Americans have often been motivated by fear of economic competition from Japan, which might be seen as a variation of the classic racist view of "Oriental hordes" threatening white America. For example, an exhibit at a 1980s Flint, Michigan, auto show portrayed a car with a Japanese face falling like a bomb on Detroit.[57] In recent decades, Japan's economic development has surpassed that of the United States in a number of areas. In response, "buy-American" cartoons featuring caricatures of "wily Japs" and "crafty Orientals" have appeared in U.S. print media. Old stereotypes have reappeared on the Internet, in public conversations among whites, and in newspaper articles. Increasing unemployment in local and national recessions of the 1980s, 1990s, and 2000s have periodically fueled a tendency among some non-Asians to blame the Japanese and other Asians for U.S. economic troubles. This scapegoating is sometimes reflected in political action. Anti-Japanese protectionist bills have periodically been introduced in Congress. Yet, congressional and other critics have often ignored Japanese investments in the United States that create thousands of jobs. U.S. recessions are not the result of Japan's investments or its competitive economy; the real causes lie elsewhere—often in poor U.S. corporate management and capital flight.[58]

In 1992, a Japanese businessperson was killed in the Los Angeles area. Not long before, he had been threatened by a man who blamed him for a U.S. economic recession.[59] In Baton Rouge, Louisiana, a white butcher shot and killed a sixteen-year-old Japanese exchange student, mistaking the youth for a robber. A Louisiana jury found the man not guilty, and white spectators applauded. In Beaumont, Texas, a Japanese American resident who tried to get a road sign reading "Jap Road" changed received hate mail and death threats. Clearly, anti-Japanese hostility among non-Asians can still turn to threats or violence today.[60]

Protest Organizations and Group Pride

Voluntary associations were formed in the early 1900s to combat anti-Japanese discrimination. Japanese workers in Hawaii participated in work stoppages to protest poor conditions, and substantial labor organizing took place on the mainland, with strikes for better wages and conditions from the 1890s onward. Japanese American workers were involved in agricultural and mining strikes in California, Utah, Colorado, and Washington. However, white labor leaders often blocked admission of Japanese Americans into unions with the racist argument that the latter were racially unassimilable.[61]

Japanese Americans protested incarceration in World War II concentration camps; thousands renounced their citizenship and returned to Japan after the war. During the 1960s, new pan-Asian organizations and publications appeared, often established by the younger generations. *Amerasia Journal* and similar journals urged collective action and attention to problems of Japanese and other Asian Americans. Sugar-coated images of Asian American success were increasingly challenged.[62]

Helping to stimulate new scholarship on Asian Americans that questions traditional white views and provides a more honest appraisal of U.S. history, numerous colleges and universities have developed Asian American studies programs, including campuses of the University of California and the

California State University, the University of Washington, and the University of Hawaii. Most programs have become institutionalized.[63]

In recent years, hate crimes directed against Japanese and other Asian Americans have persisted on campuses. Hundreds of Asian American students at Indiana University received hate (e-mail) messages in three incidents. In the late 1990s, a naturalized U.S. citizen from El Salvador, writing under the alias, "Asian hater," and upset by successful Asian American students at the University of California (Irvine), was sentenced to a year in prison for e-mailing death threats to Asian students.[64] He was the first to serve time for violating civil rights laws in cyberspace.[65] Because of such hostility, which often increases as the number of Asian American students on historically white campuses grows, many Japanese American and other Asian American students have become more interested in development of strong Asian American organizations and academic programs on these campuses.

The Economy

Most Japanese immigrants started out at the bottom of the U.S. economic pyramid, filling hard farming, mining, and construction jobs. One California study in 1909 found 65 percent of Japanese American workers in agriculture, 15 percent in domestic service, 15 percent in small businesses, and 5 percent in other work. In many areas Japanese workers did much of the "dirty work" and generally were paid less than whites.[66]

Finding an Economic Niche

Gradually, many first-generation immigrants (Issei) found land to farm on their own. Although the amount of land owned was not large, their economic role was important. In some areas they grew most of certain food crops. Some also created small businesses in urban areas in which institutionalized discrimination barred them from manufacturing and white-collar employment. The Issei came to play what has been called a "middleman minority" role in western states (see Chapter 2). Operated on a small scale, some enterprises catered primarily to a Japanese American clientele, but many eventually served non-Asians as well. Issei solidarity helped create a niche economy, and this small-business economy in turn reinforced group solidarity. Bonacich and Modell conclude that "the Japanese minority filled a particular and specialized niche in the western economy and was important to it, providing key products and services."[67]

Most early immigrants came from just eleven Japanese prefectures, and each was represented by an association in the United States. These prefectural clubs became mutual-aid associations for immigrants caught in an often hostile environment. They aided immigrants' movement into the economy by providing training for workers and directing clients to small businesses. Businesses succeeded because they could usually draw on prefectural networks for workers and loans. Informal money-pooling organizations called *tanomoshi* provided capital for entrepreneurs who could not secure funds from white-owned banks.[68]

Opposition to these immigrant workers and entrepreneurs came swiftly. In urban areas, white-controlled labor movements often led the opposition, using boycotts and anti-Japanese advertising. One such action by the Anti-Jap Laundry League attempted to drive Japanese Americans out of the laundry business.[69] A 1913 California Alien Land Law, passed under pressure from white farmers, stipulated that "aliens" could not buy land or lease it for more than three years. (Recall that all Issei were forced to remain "aliens" because of discriminatory naturalization laws.)[70] This California land law interfered with agricultural activity, but some found ways to circumvent it, such as by registering land ownership under children's names. Discriminatory land laws significantly reduced the number of Japanese American farms. These laws were passed in other states and remained on the books of Florida, New Mexico, Kansas, and Wyoming into the twenty-first century.[71]

Those forced out of farming or otherwise attracted to cities often became gardeners or nursery operators. The 1930 California census showed that half of male Japanese workers were in agriculture or gardening, one-fourth were in trade or business, 2 percent were in the professions, and most of the rest were in other urban occupations.[72] By the beginning of World War II, some were moving into white-collar positions. Half the Japanese American men in Los Angeles County in 1940 held white-collar positions, and most of the rest had blue-collar jobs.[73] Then the economy collapsed. Median economic losses per family in Los Angeles from the forced wartime imprisonment were estimated at about $10,000 (in 1940 dollars) in goods, property, income, and expenses. Losses were similar elsewhere.

In research on the labor of women before World War II, Evelyn Nakano Glenn found that "from the moment they arrived, Japanese American women labored alongside the men to secure their own and their families' livelihood."[74] Much hard work done by Issei women was unpaid family labor, but some women and their daughters worked as domestic servants to whites. Before World War II, discrimination kept Japanese American women out of white-collar work that had been available to European immigrant women. Domestic workers often resisted oppression in covert ways, such as by evading work pressed on them by exploitative employers. This resistance gave them a sense of self-reliance that was critical for their personal and political development and for that of their children. They sometimes struggled against husbands as well; subordination to white women in domestic employment was often reinforced by subordination to husbands at home. Yet, they struggled to maintain dignity, and "despite the menial nature of employment, the Issei achieved a sense of their own strength, and in some cases, superiority to employer and husband within their own area of competence."[75]

What methods have been used by Japanese Americans to resist racial discrimination?

The Postwar Economy

As the need for labor grew in the booming postwar economy, white employers finally began to hire Japanese Americans. However, racial discrimination continued, keeping the second generation out of certain occupations. University of California education departments discouraged Japanese American students from considering the teaching profession because of the difficulty of placement in schools.[76] Self-employment continued to be important. By 1960 there were 7000 Japanese-owned businesses, mostly small, in Los Angeles. The middleman minority model seems to fit the Issei generation well, but second and later generations have gradually moved away from the small business niche economy to professional and other white-collar jobs. In 1960 about half the Nisei were involved in niche businesses, but many used education funded by parents to move into white-collar jobs.[77]

Occupational Mobility, Income, and Persisting Employment Barriers

Numerous popular and scholarly books and articles have related the postwar Japanese American experience as a story of achievement. The usual socioeconomic indicators in census data show that Japanese American progress since the 1950s has indeed been dramatic. For example, for those reporting only Japanese ancestry, in 2005 both men and women were more likely to hold managerial or professional jobs than were their white counterparts (51.9 percent versus 35.3 percent for men; 47.6 percent versus 40.4 percent for women). The occupational percentages are only slightly lower when those with partial Japanese ancestry are added in. Japanese Americans' unemployment rate was less than that of whites (2.1 percent versus 3.2 percent) and less than that for all Asian Americans as a group. If those with partial Japanese ancestry are added in, the unemployment rate climbs to just 2.7 percent.[78]

Income data reveal economic success. According to a 2005 census survey of those reporting only Japanese ancestry, mid-2000s median income for their families was substantially more than that for white families ($74,301 versus $62,300). In addition, only a small percentage of Japanese American families (5 percent) fell below the federal poverty line, a figure lower than for whites (6.3 percent) and for Asian Americans as a group (8.9 percent). Note, however, that Japanese American workers are significantly concentrated in western states, especially Hawaii and California, which have both high wages and a high cost of living. The difference in median incomes between Japanese American families and white families in California is reversed ($77,243 versus $78,842), thus favoring whites, in contrast to family incomes nationally. Per-capita income for Japanese Americans is also a little lower than that for whites ($35,558 versus $38,083).[79] With one exception, per-capita income in California (reduced to $30,941), the income figures above change little when people with partial Japanese ancestry are included. Note that the pattern of lower per-capita incomes holds true for certain other Asian American groups and should be kept in mind in assessing the relative socioeconomic achievements of Asian American groups considered in the next chapter as well.

Although Japanese Americans have achieved significant success, they still face exclusion from certain positions in many business, entertainment, political, and civil service areas, regardless of abilities. Examinations of television and Hollywood filmmaking in recent decades have found relatively few Japanese and other Asian American actors, except in stereotypical positions such as gardener, geisha, and tourist. One 2006 examination of television programs on four major networks found continuing underrepresentation of Asian Americans—with only slight improvements recently in number of Asian American actors in key roles and a *decline* in the number of Asian American writers and producers.[80] In addition, indirect discrimination in the form of white-normed height and weight requirements has played a restrictive role for Asian American entry into occupations such as firefighters and police officers. Because of anti-Asian stereotypes, positions at the highest administrative, managerial, and professional levels are often off-limits to Japanese and other Asian Americans, and whites with lesser credentials or ability are sometimes promoted at a faster rate.[81]

Asian Americans now make up about 5 percent of the population, yet one early 2000s estimate put the percentage of Japanese and other Asian Americans on the boards of the 500 top firms at far less that 1 percent and noted that *only one* Asian American served as the top executive of any *Fortune* 500 firm not founded by an Asian American.[82] One *Wall Street Journal* story noted that Asian Americans have a hard time climbing corporate ladders because "ironically, the same companies that pursue them for technical jobs often shun them when filling managerial and executive positions."[83] Top corporate executives have been quoted as saying that Asian Americans, including Japanese Americans, are best as technical workers and not as corporate executives. Because of this stereotype, Asian Americans may be hired as engineers, computer experts, and technicians but are often not considered for upper management positions. Knowing that discrimination awaits them if they depart from the stereotype, many younger Asian Americans have pursued scientific and technical educations and rejected the humanities and social sciences. The promotion ceiling also exists in higher education; one mid-2000s study estimated that the ratio of Asian American college administrators to Asian American college faculty and professionals is a little more than one-third that for other major racial groups and far below the national average.[84]

Blatant discrimination still occurs in various settings. Thus, a third-generation Japanese American, Bruce Yamashita, entered a Marine Corps' Officer Candidate School. A talented man with a law degree, Yamashita faced overt discrimination from the first day, when a sergeant told him to "go back to your own country." Other sergeants called him by names of Japanese-made motor vehicles. A fellow candidate asked why he had not joined the Japanese army. No Marine Corps officers intervened to stop the harassment, and Yamashita was terminated for "leadership failure." In 1994, after a legal battle during which Yamashita, with the assistance of the JACL, uncovered a *pattern* of discrimination against non-European American officer candidates, the Secretary of the Navy commissioned Yamashita a captain in the Marine Corps.[85]

Overall trends in the U.S. economy have affected employment opportunities. Many student career choices are influenced by the past discrimination that channeled Japanese Americans into certain occupations such as school teaching. Business opportunities are still sometimes limited by anti-Japanese sentiment. Japanese and other Asian Americans periodically report a "glass ceiling" in corporations or exclusion from business networks. (A **glass ceiling** is *an unwritten and unofficial policy in some organizations that limits the advancement of certain persons, usually based on their racial group or gender.*) Response to this discrimination has often come in the form of organization. For example, in 1992 several businesspeople created the Japanese American Chamber of Commerce to foster business development. That Japanese Americans have achieved remarkable economic success against enormous odds is indicated in the socioeconomic statistics. What they could have achieved without persisting racial discrimination can only be imagined.

Education

Racism and Early Segregation

The Issei had a strong commitment to education; most viewed education as a way to escape arduous farm and nursery jobs and secure better-paying positions. Parents enrolled children in school more often than most other immigrant group parents, and many pursued formal education for themselves.[86]

In 1906, the white mayor of San Francisco, in a move supported by newspapers, secured a resolution from the board of education establishing a segregated public school for Asian American children. Reflecting white fears of "racial mixing," one member of the legislature spoke of the danger to "pure maids of California" posed by older Japanese students in primary grades. The Japanese government protested, and the U.S. government took action to force the San Francisco board to give Japanese American children the equal rights promised by a U.S.–Japan treaty. Whites were so angered by this rare federal show of support for Japanese Americans that they talked of *state secession*. President Theodore Roosevelt and San Francisco officials worked out a compromise that allowed most Japanese American children to return to integrated schools. In exchange, Roosevelt executed the infamous Gentlemen's Agreement, which soon terminated most Japanese immigration.[87]

Japanese Americans developed their own schools to educate children in the Japanese language and culture. By 1928 there were more than 4000 pupils in 118 schools. White supremacists vigorously attacked language schools as centers of emperor worship and Buddhism that they alleged made children "disloyal" to the United States. The California legislature passed a bill, which was vetoed by the governor, abolishing these schools.[88]

Educational Progress

By the 1930s, Japanese Americans were making great strides, from primary grades to college, despite widespread discrimination. At University of California branches, the ratio of Japanese American college students to the Japanese American population was a little higher than the figure for the total population. A 1930 survey showed that Japanese Americans' educational attainments were already at least equal to those of whites in California.[89]

Wartime imprisonment interrupted these pursuits. Second- and third-generation Japanese Americans received part of their schooling behind barbed wire. After the war, major gains resumed. In recent decades the median educational level for adult Japanese Americans has been substantially higher than that for all adult Americans. Recent data for those reporting only Japanese ancestry, who were twenty-five and older, showed that most (93 percent) had a high school education or higher, and 44 percent had a bachelor's degree or higher, compared with 89 percent and 30 percent of whites, respectively, in this age group. (These figures change only slightly when those with partical Japanese ancestry are added in.) Today, Japanese Americans are among the most educated Americans.[90]

However, racial discrimination persists. As we noted above, Japanese Americans remain underrepresented in higher administrative positions in education. Japanese and other Asian Americans continue to be underrepresented, relative to their abilities and personal goals, or differentially treated in certain graduate programs at U.S. universities, often because of continuing stereotypes about their personalities or technical abilities. Moreover, although the education levels of Japanese Americans are significantly higher than those of the white population, some research indicates that their income levels are lower than one would predict on the basis of their high levels of education.[91]

Religion

Japanese immigrants brought Buddhism and Shintoism with them. These religious traditions are now significant in the United States. Once the Japanese arrived, Protestant missionaries tried to convert many to Christian beliefs. Protestant missions were often crucibles of acculturation in which many young Japanese Americans began to absorb the language and values of the dominant culture.[92]

By the 1920s there were many Buddhist temples, which often adapted to the U.S. environment with Christian-style Sunday schools and church organizations. Some white exclusionists, ignorant of the fact that Buddhism does *not* involve emperor worship, claimed that the temples were hotbeds of emperor worship and antipatriotic teaching.[93] Jingoistic agitation branded Buddhism (and Shintoism) as un-American, and some temples were vandalized. After

A Buddhist temple in Los Angeles.

the war, the number of temples increased as Buddhism regained its important position in local communities. Japanese Americans founded the Buddhist Churches of America, the oldest U.S. Buddhist group and one that involves Jodo Shinshu Buddhism. Today there are many Buddhist temples across the country, including those of other types of Buddhist groups brought by immigrants from various Asian countries.[94]

Today many Japanese Americans are members of Protestant churches. A San Francisco study found that churches of various kinds were second in importance only to family in cementing the community; a majority of respondents were at least occasional participants in church activities. One trend that has emerged in the last decade is an emphasis on panethnic Protestant churches, which include members from different Asian groups, such as Japanese and Chinese Americans. Moreover, the percentage of Buddhists among Japanese Americans has declined in recent years. Buddhist groups tend to attract older members; younger Japanese Americans have preferred Protestant churches or no religion at all.[95]

Yet, there has been a resurgence of interest in Buddhism in recent decades among many Americans, Asian and non-Asian. Buddhist festivals have been celebrated in Japanese and other Asian American communities. Colonel Ellison Onizuka, the first Asian American in space and one of those who died in the 1986 space shuttle explosion, was a member of the Buddhist Churches of America. His Buddhist funeral made many Americans aware of the significant presence of Buddhists in the United States.[96]

Assimilation Perspectives

Japanese Americans have received much attention in social science and popular theorizing about group adaptation in the United States. Early on, as we have seen, many white leaders and other citizens considered Japanese Americans to be very "unassimilable." In recent decades, however, many social scientists and popular analysts have adopted an assimilation perspective and heralded Japanese Americans as probably the most assimilated to the Euro-American core culture of all Asian American groups, or of all Americans of color. Assimilation analysts often emphasize that younger generations have intermarried at relatively high rates and have little facility in the Japanese language.

Today, most Japanese Americans are not immigrants. Because relatively few Japanese immigrants have come to the United States in recent decades, Japanese Americans' ties to the home country are not generally as strong as for other Asian American groups. All but a few were born in the United States and have grown up under the pressures of the dominant culture and white-controlled institutions.

An assimilation theorist might argue that some cultural assimilation came at an early point for most Issei, although some acculturated to the dominant culture more rapidly than others. Numerous Issei sought to survive discrimination by socially isolating and immersing themselves in things Japanese; others sought to acculturate rapidly, at least in those areas where acculturation was permitted, while maintaining strong social ties to relatives and friends. Historically, Issei influence in the Japanese community was wide-ranging, but their ability to cope with the dominant culture was restricted by the massive discrimination they faced. Cultural assimilation, especially with regard to language, religion, and orientation to white-collar employment, has come rapidly for later generations. Second-generation Nisei became bicultural and operated successfully in their communities and in Euro-American institutions. Studies of third-generation Sansei underscore the apparent closing of the gap with some aspects of the dominant culture. In one study, Nisei and Sansei respondents showed substantial acculturation in that they spoke mostly English and seldom read Japanese literature. By the late 1980s about half of Japanese Americans in Los Angeles spoke English only, the highest proportion for any Asian American group.[97]

A 1990s study of Japanese and Chinese Americans in California found that those who were third or fourth generation were highly oriented to the norms and styles of white middle-class culture and retained few Japanese and Chinese traditions. They chose to keep only the parts of ancestral cultures that fit their current way of life. "What they have retained of cultural traditions is largely symbolic and a novelty."[98] However, a deeper assessment of their values and worldview would likely have shown strong continuity with some basic values of parents and grandparents, particularly with regard to family, community, and education.

By the 1990s and 2000s, some key community institutions were in decline. Several important civic organizations have disappeared, and Japanese American newspapers have ceased publication in recent years. In the mid-2000s, *Rafu Shimpo*, a Japanese American newspaper in publication since 1903, was changing, such as by adding a website on the Internet, and today reports about 45,000 daily readers. This is the largest remaining Japanese American paper and now covers issues of interest to all Asian Americans. Current readers are mostly younger-generation Japanese Americans, as well as more recent Asian immigrants and their children. It is also the largest bilingual newspaper now published in the United States.[99]

Structural assimilation at secondary-group levels has been significant for Japanese Americans, particularly in the economy. Typically, second- and later-generation families have achieved relatively high levels of education, income, and occupational position. Explanations for this success tend to focus on work, family values, and community or economic organization. Ivan Light, for example, has opted for a traditional-culture explanation for the development of Japanese Americans' small-business economy, a niche economy that in his view sets them apart from African and Mexican Americans. Light emphasizes the role of a "culturally preferred style of economic organization," by which he means rotating-credit associations and similar organizations established by Japanese immigrants.[100]

What Milton Gordon refers to as behavior-receptional assimilation and attitude-receptional assimilation showed little change for Japanese Americans until after World War II. Blatant discrimination and prejudice marred the lives of Issei and Nisei for the first sixty years. Since World War II, discrimination and prejudice have decreased. In the early 1900s, Japanese Americans were seen by whites as the "lowest of the low" and were often negatively grouped with black Americans, but, according to Paul Spickard, by the 1980s whites did "not see them as very different from themselves, and that fact is remarkable."[101] Spickard judges white attitudes indirectly from relatively high rates of Japanese American intermarriage with whites, which suggest to him that whites generally do not feel hostile about Japanese–white marriages.

However, analysts like Spickard are probably too optimistic in equating intermarriage rates with strongly positive white views. In recent decades, as we have demonstrated, white hostility and discrimination are periodically directed toward Japanese and other Asian Americans. Thus, in one 1980s survey, one-fifth of those surveyed reported experiencing considerable discrimination as adults;

another 65 percent reported a little discrimination. Three-fourths felt that Japanese Americans as a group did experience discrimination. Given the reluctance of many to speak about personal matters or to speak ill of their country, these responses likely underestimated the amount of discrimination. Indeed, mid- to late 2000s field interviews with Japanese and other Asian Americans by Rosalind Chou show that they still experience substantial levels of subtle, blatant, and covert discrimination, even though much of that discrimination does not get researched by social scientists or dealt with in the mass media.[102]

Assimilation analysts often accent assimilation at the level of primary social ties and voluntary associations. Integration in these areas did not occur to any significant degree until after World War II. Researchers have found that primary-group integration with outsiders has been limited for the Nisei but has been more extensive for younger generations. One study of 148 Japanese American men found that two-thirds had mostly Japanese Americans as close friends; Sansei were somewhat more socially integrated with whites than Nisei. However, majorities in both groups lived in neighborhoods in which at least half their neighbors were white.[103] Other data suggest a trend toward primary-group assimilation since the 1960s, especially for those who have moved away from areas with a "critical mass" of Japanese Americans.[104]

Until the late 1940s, laws in western states made Asian–white marriages officially *illegal*. Los Angeles data show an outmarriage rate of just 2 percent in the years between 1924 and 1933 and a rate of 11 to 20 percent for the 1950s. A 1967 national survey of young Sansei, however, discovered that one-third had out-married or were planning to out-marry.[105]

The 1990 census data on intermarriage indicated that, for Japanese Americans in California, outmarriage rates to whites was relatively high—13 percent for men and 28 percent for women as a group. These were then the highest figures for any large Asian American group. A recent examination of 2000 census data for Japanese Americans found that 69 percent of husbands and 51 percent of wives had Japanese spouses, while 9 percent of husbands and 5 percent of wives were married to other Asian Americans. About 18 percent of Japanese American husbands had white wives, with 37 percent of Japanese American wives having white husbands. (The others who were intermarried had black or "other" spouses.) Both are increases since 1990. Still, a majority are married within the Japanese American group. Significant here too is the fact that numerous Japanese and other Asian Americans marry outside their own group yet marry interethnically—that is, to other Asian Americans. A substantial majority of marriages are still within the Asian American umbrella group.[106]

Viewed from Gordon's concept of identificational assimilation, few Japanese Americans have rejected their Japanese cultural heritage or identity. They hold this identity for positive reasons, and it is also imposed on them by non-Asians who still often view them as "foreigners." Japanese identity is strong in all generations. Most are bicultural, with a foot in two cultural worlds. Substantial differences in value orientations between Japanese and white Americans have been found in recent decades. The authors of one study asked Japanese Americans whether they saw differences in Japanese American and white orientations toward social affairs, church life, and family relations. Large percentages saw significant differences, from 42 percent for social life to 65 percent for family life and 75 percent for church life. Most did *not* consider that they were assimilating rapidly to the dominant culture in regard to certain important areas such as family and religion.[107]

Younger Japanese Americans are retaining at least some of their distinctive organizations and traditions. Japanese American athletic leagues established by the Nisei have survived through subsequent generations, and where possible many younger Japanese and other Asian American college students have joined Asian American fraternities and sororities rather than white-dominated organizations. The Sansei and Yonsei have also maintained numerous Japanese American rituals, parades, and festivals, especially in west coast areas. Although geographical concentrations ("Japantowns") are declining in population, significant family and community connections remain, even for many who have intermarried with whites or other Asian Americans. Recently, one Japanese American entrepreneur noted: "The community's alive and well and thriving. What's declining are these historical and geographic icons like Japantowns."[108]

Surveys of Japanese American college students also reveal that, while the students show signs of significant acculturation to the core culture and support interracial dating and marriage, most hold values close to those of their parents. Most place great value on family, community, hard work, and education. They also report being most comfortable with people of Asian descent and often are members of Asian American organizations.[109]

Developing a broad view of assimilation, Kitano and Daniels suggest that Japanese and other Asian Americans can be grouped into major categories based on (1) degree of overall assimilation to the dominant Eurocentric culture and institutions and (2) the strength of what they term "ethnic identity." Among Japanese and other Asian Americans, many in third and later generations, especially those isolated from large communities, are in a "high assimilation, low ethnic identity" category; that is, they have made many adaptations to the dominant Anglo-American culture in terms of language and lifestyle and retain only weak ties to the old language and culture. Japanese Americans in this category have strong social ties to whites or have married whites. In contrast, another large group of Japanese Americans belongs to a "high assimilation, high ethnic identity" category. They move easily in both Japanese American culture and community and in the dominant culture. In contrast with the first group, they are more knowledgeable about Japanese American history and culture and have a stronger racial-ethnic identity. A third and much smaller group includes those who have immigrated in recent decades and those who have spent most of their lives within Japanese American communities; they belong to a "low assimilation, high ethnic identity" category. Marriages are only within the Japanese American group, and Japanese identity is very strong. Kitano and Daniels note that assimilation is incomplete even for the first two subgroups because many whites in the larger society still regard Japanese Americans as racially and ethnically distinct, and this visibility forces "the retention of ethnic identity, no matter how slight."[110]

One might also view Japanese Americans as an example of Greeley's concept of ethnogenesis—partly in but partly outside the dominant European American culture and society. To our knowledge, no analyst has yet developed this perspective for Japanese Americans, although Petersen argued that this group has become a "subnation" in the United States, achieving integration in the economy and making some cultural adaptation, but often maintaining cohesive, family-centered communities.[111]

Younger generations of Japanese Americans are among the most integrated of all non-European groups into European American culture and communities. How this adaptation and integration will develop in the future is unclear. We have already noted the significant level of intermarriage to other Asian Americans, which has increased in recent years as Asian American populations have grown. For many Asian Americans today, integration with whites may no longer be as important, at least in the primary-social sphere, as integration with other Asian Americans. In addition, some Japanese Americans view the children of mixed marriages as Japanese American and are working to integrate them well into Japanese American traditions. Those of *mixed ancestry* called ***Hapa*** (from a Hawaiian word meaning "half") are seen by some as the leading edge of change among Japanese Americans. Greg Mayeda has explained that eventually the typical Japanese American will be a Hapa:

> Community leaders must recognize this and encourage Hapas and their multicultural families to participate in Japanese-American organizations and customs. If given the opportunity, Hapas can unify and reinvigorate the Japanese-American community.[112]

A Power-Conflict View

Only a few analysts have interpreted the Japanese American experience systematically from a power-conflict perspective. Robert Blauner has suggested that Japanese Americans might be viewed as a partially colonized racial group, especially in the first half-century of their experience in the United States. Many early immigrants worked in a position of debt servitude or migrated to the United States under economic or political pressure.

Over the centuries an important economic relationship has existed between the labor needs of U.S. capitalism and the many infusions of immigrant workers. Asian labor has often filled the needs of U.S. capitalism, such as on the west coast frontier in the nineteenth century. Chinese and Japanese laborers were seen as "colored" labor, with far fewer rights than whites. Because the United States was an imperial power in the Pacific, U.S. labor agents had easy entry into Asian countries and could often dictate labor agreements benefiting U.S. employers. The latter recruited Asian laborers because they could be made to work for very low wages. U.S. employers had the backing of the U.S. government in securing low-wage labor from Japan and China. Neither country then possessed the power that European nations had to protect their immigrant workers. Because Japanese immigrants could not become citizens under U.S. law, they could be excluded if employers later found them unsuitable.[113]

In the beginning, Japanese Americans, much like Mexican Americans, were forced by white-generated discrimination to mostly become low-wage laborers. Alien-labor laws that barred land ownership, the race-based exclusion of Japanese immigrants in 1924, and the massive imprisonment in World War II constituted semicolonial treatment. Japanese Americans' experiences were quite different from the experiences of most European immigrants on which the conventional assimilation models are typically based.

Acculturation might be viewed differently from a systematic power-conflict perspective. Pressures to acculturate were largely coercive for the first two generations. Early commitment to cultural assimilation in Japanese communities was substantially a reaction to severe racial discrimination. In public schools, acculturation pressures took the form of attacks on the Japanese heritage. By 1910, Japanese American leaders were exhorting their constituents to be exemplary in their hard work and deference to whites in order to gain some acceptance. In early decades, Japanese Americans' experiences with systemic racism were quite similar to those of African, Mexican, and Native Americans.

Note too the implicit bias in the traditional assimilation model. The assimilation theory of early social scientists emerged in a period of intense white agitation *against* Japanese immigration and reflected those white scholars' often racist views of the Japanese. Indeed, applying the assimilationist perspective to Japanese and other Asian Americans prior to the 1950s is inappropriate in one fundamental respect. Asians were generally *prevented* from even trying to assimilate politically and in other important ways. Unlike European immigrants, Japanese and other Asian immigrants were denied the right to become naturalized citizens.

U.S. government agencies have long played a central role in defining racial groups, a point underscored in racial formation theory (see Chapter 2). For example, in the important 1922 *Ozawa* case, the U.S. Supreme Court ruled that Asian immigrants were *not white* and could not become citizens. In a similar case the following year, *U.S.* v. *Bhagat Singh Thind*, the same racist reasoning was applied to an Asian Indian who sought to become naturalized. The Court declared that, in contrast to children of Asian parentage, "the children of English, French, German, Italian, Scandinavian, and other European parentage quickly merge in to the mass of our population and lose the distinctive hallmarks of their European origin."[114] This racist reasoning by an arm of the U.S. government misses the point that at the time—and indeed into the 1950s—Asian immigrants were legally barred by U.S. law from political and civic assimilation.

Returning to the present situation, intermarriage data might be viewed from a power-conflict perspective. Increasingly, many Asian Americans marry within the Asian American umbrella group rather than with whites, especially on the west coast. Even among later generations of Asian Americans, the proportions of marriages to other Asian Americans is substantial. The interethnic marriage rate has been growing because of the growing size of the Asian American population, the consequent expansion of social networks, the similarity in economic achievements for many in Asian American groups, and a shared Asian American identity. Another important factor is "a growing racial consciousness in American society, which is perceived by many Asian Americans as increasingly racially polarized and stratified.... Race, more so than ethnicity, shapes the experiences and the development of identity among Asian Americans."[115]

How is the "model minority" stereotype harmful to Japanese and other Asian Americans?

Criticizing the "Model Minority" Stereotype

Paramount among the weaknesses in many assimilation analyses is reliance on a "model minority" stereotype. In recent decades, as we have noted, newsmagazines and television commentators have carried glowing reports on the achievements of

Asian Americans in various occupations and in education.[116] The success of Japanese and other Asian Americans, frequently viewed as rooted in distinctive cultural values and family styles, is cited not only in the white-dominated media but also by other whites as a reflection of the great opportunities in the United States and as a model for what other people of color, particularly African Americans and Latinos, could achieve if they would only follow the Asian American example.[117] However, stereotypes of Japanese Americans as paragons of hard work and docility often carry a negative undercurrent. The model imagery was created not by Asian American groups but rather by white outsiders, including scholars and media analysts, for their own ideological reasons.[118] During the period when African Americans protested during the 1960s, these whites *intentionally* created the model minority image and term in order to suggest that African Americans could achieve the American dream by working harder rather than by protesting institutional discrimination.

However, one must recognize the historical realities. Pre–World War II educational opportunities (greater than those available to legally segregated African Americans) in states such as California helped prepare many Japanese Americans for white-collar jobs that opened up after that war. It was not Asian values alone that brought success, but better access to education and certain white-collar jobs. Critics of the model minority notion have noted other factors in the economic success of Japanese Americans: the Japanese government's early support of immigrants and the availability of an important small-business niche in west coast areas. At an early point, Japanese Americans created many successful businesses through which they served one another and the needs of the frontier economy of the West. Out of economic necessity, Japanese American employers and employees, many with kinship ties, worked together against hostile white competitors.

Success often came at the price of being marginalized in the small-business economy and, later, in certain professions. As with Jewish Americans, Japanese Americans have, to a substantial degree, succeeded economically by carving a distinctive niche for themselves—a process of adaptation that is not in line with the more idealistic assimilation models. The long-term effects of racial discrimination are still reflected in the disproportionate concentration of Japanese and other Asian Americans in certain professional and technical occupations. The movement of Japanese Americans into white-collar jobs has not indicated full emancipation from white discrimination. A 1980s study of Japanese American workers in the San Francisco metropolitan area found that those in white-collar jobs were clustered in such occupations as computer programming, clerical work, architecture, engineering, dentistry, and pharmacy. The highest-level white-collar personnel, such as managers, financial officers, and management analysts, still tended to be white men. Indeed, the model minority stereotype operates in white minds to "delegitimize Asian Americans' concerns and protests against racial inequalities. Asian Americans still face serious discrimination in society, yet their complaints about discrimination are often not taken seriously." As we have noted previously, some of these problems remain as we move well into the twenty-first century, especially at higher managerial and business levels.[119] In addition, Japanese Americans often receive smaller economic benefits from their high levels of education than do comparably educated whites.[120]

Paul Takagi has pointed to another bias in the traditional cultural-background explanation of Japanese American success—the idea that the racial and ethnic groups whose values are closest to those of the dominant white group are the ones who will be, and should be, successful. Success is evaluated in terms of values prized by the dominant white group. Although Japanese Americans have acculturated in numerous ways, the price they have often paid in terms of conformity, lost creativity, and lost contributions to this society has been great.[121]

In her important documentary work, Japanese American media analyst Janice Tanaka has examined the negative impact of the great pressures for assimilation on third-generation Sansei. Tanaka's interviews with Sansei found that most of their parents were interned as youths in the wartime camps. These Nisei were greatly affected by that incarceration, and during and after World War II they placed great pressure on themselves and their children to *conform* to white perspectives and customs. Fearful of a reoccurrence of extreme oppression, they responded to this brutal racism with the orientation that would later get them labeled, in an ironic twist of stereotyping, as model minorities. Many Nisei and Sansei conformed rigidly to white ways in an effort to prevent such a racist outrage as the concentration camps from targeting Japanese Americans again. However, the Nisei and their children have paid a heavy price. The effects of this aggressive conformity often have been negative: Many Sansei have encountered, and continue to endure, great personal distress, painful self-blame, mental and physical illnesses, or alcoholism and drug abuse. Some have committed suicide because of the intense pressure to conform. Not surprisingly, the negative reactions of the Sansei have in turn affected their own children, the Yonsei. The costs of white-imposed racism persist over generations. The internment experience continues to exert a terrible price, and the tepid U.S. government response in terms of modest reparations has not been enough to lift this heavy burden from Japanese Americans.[122]

Over recent decades, Japanese Americans have reported that no amount of cultural assimilation protects them from whites who insist on stereotyping Japanese and other Asian Americans as outsiders. Ronald Takaki, a University of California professor, visited an east coast city where a taxicab driver congratulated him on his good English and inquired how long he had been in the country. Takaki told the driver his family had been here for *three* generations—since 1886.[123] Despite the fact that many Japanese Americans have grown up in mostly white neighborhoods and gone to mostly white schools, they often report discrimination and do not feel that they are fully accepted by large numbers of white Americans.[124]

From the beginning, Japanese immigration and Japanese American integration into the dominant culture and society have been shaped by U.S. corporations' intervention in the world economy. The action of the U.S. government in forcing Japan into the world economy in the nineteenth century was eventually followed by the recruitment of Japanese laborers for U.S. business enterprises. Today, as the Japanese economy vies successfully with the U.S. economy for Pacific and world dominance, the world economy still forms the backdrop. New economic alliances on the Pacific Rim, such as the Association of Southeast Asian Nations, are bypassing the United States. Japan is a powerful economy in these alliances, and that economic success is one reason there has been relatively little recent migration from Japan to the United States.

Some non-Asian Americans, angry over domestic economic troubles, confuse Japanese Americans and other Asian Americans with the Japanese and blame them unfairly for economic troubles caused by U.S. employers investing overseas or by the federal government. As a Japanese American Citizens' League commentary has put it, "When the U.S. economy declines, attention often shifts to the role that other countries play in providing 'unfair' competition. Asian Pacific Americans are often perceived to be 'foreigners' who take jobs away from 'real' Americans. . . . [For a time] Japan was perceived as 'taking over' the U.S. by buying companies and real estate. Little attention was given to the fact that Great Britain was then the largest foreign investor in the U.S., while Canada held the largest percentage of foreign-owned real estate."[125] Such periodic negative imaging and attacks are yet another constant indication to Japanese Americans that somehow they have not been accepted as "true Americans" by many non-Asian Americans.

How would you use assimilation or power-conflict perspectives to explain key aspects of the Japanese American experience?

Summary

Japanese Americans are a very important group in U.S. history. In the beginning they were severely exploited and treated as a greatly "inferior race." Many entered as laborers, facing violence and intense discrimination. They later endured complete exclusion as a result of overtly racist immigration legislation. During World War II, they suffered the only large-scale imprisonment of U.S. citizens in U.S. concentration camps. Against terrible odds they prospered. Yet, in spite of substantial cultural and other assimilation, Japanese Americans are still not fully integrated into the dominant European American institutions.

Students of racial and ethnic matters should realize that the success story of Japanese and other Asian Americans is partially a myth. Japanese Americans have suffered in the past and still suffer from discrimination. Fewer Japanese Americans than whites fully realize earnings levels that parallel their high educational levels. Few rise to top management in *Fortune* 500 corporations, major law firms, or government agencies. Although significant numbers of Asian Americans have lived in the United States for more than 150 years, not one has ever served on the U.S. Supreme Court, as Speaker of the U.S. House, or as president or vice-president of the United States. Few have ever served in the U.S. Congress.

Japanese Americans have often been stereotyped by non-Asian Americans, including many government officials. Across the United States white employers and government officials have spoken of Japanese Americans and other Asian Americans as though they were "foreigners," not "true Americans." Japanese Americans are considered by many other Americans to be a "model minority" with no need of government protection against discrimination. However, as we have seen, there is still anti-Japanese sentiment among other Americans that results in discrimination and violence. White Americans will have to change their attitudes and practices if Japanese Americans are to enjoy full equality. David Mura, author of *Turning Japanese: Memoirs of a Sansei*, has argued that whites must see that the "problem of race is one of giving up power." In his view, whites must begin to take part in "dismantling racism and redistributing power."[126]

Working harmoniously together, the seven-person crew of the ill-fated space shuttle *Challenger* included an African American born to sharecroppers (Ronald McNair), a Jewish American of the Orthodox faith (Judith Resnik), and a Japanese American of the Buddhist faith (Ellison Onizuka). Onizuka, the grandson of Japanese laborers who immigrated to Hawaii to work in the 1890s, was born on a farm. He became an aerospace engineer and participated in two space missions. As the first Asian American astronaut, Onizuka has come to symbolize for many the heroic character of the Asian American struggle for success.

Hawaii was the first U.S. state in which no racial or ethnic group constituted a majority of the population. Today Japanese Americans are the single largest group in Hawaii, but they are not a majority. Compared with other areas of the United States, racial and ethnic relations in Hawaii have generally been more cooperative and less conflict-ridden. Although Hawaii has seen serious interracial tensions, and native Hawaiians have suffered much poverty and discrimination, some observers have suggested that multiracial, multiethnic Hawaii can provide a few lessons on how diverse racial and ethnic groups on the U.S. mainland can work together to build a viable multiracial society and democracy.[127]

Key Terms

Asian American 280
Asian-Pacific American 280
model minority stereotype 280
gunboat imperialism 282
glass ceiling 293
Hapa 298

Chinese, Filipino, Korean, Vietnamese, and Asian-Indian Americans

Source: Copyright Lia Chang Gallery

BIG PICTURE QUESTIONS

- ***What role have Asian American groups played in building up this country's wealth and institutions?***
- ***How has systemic racism affected the Asian American experience?***
- ***Why have numerous Asian groups recently migrated to the United States?***

Elaine H. Kim, a Korean American professor at the University of California, has written insightfully about the major Los Angeles riot that took place in the 1990s. She has noted how the media played up visual images of conflict between black and Latino rioters and Korean merchants, while ignoring the important histories of these racialized groups. Korean Americans, African Americans, and Latinos have all been victims of a long tradition of violence and other discrimination by white Americans. Recalling her experience, Kim noted that:

> Korean-Americans have been and continue to be used for someone else's agenda and benefit, whether we are hated as foreigners who refuse to become "good Americans," stereotyped as diligent work machines or simply treated as if we do not exist. Throughout my childhood, the people who continually asked, "What are you?" knew nothing of Korea or Koreans.[1]

Korean Americans are one of five major Asian American groups—each with a strong identity and a rich history and culture—discussed in this chapter. The others are Chinese, Filipino, Vietnamese, and Asian-Indian Americans. Although these groups have contributed much to U.S. development, they still suffer greatly from racial stereotyping and discrimination by non-Asian Americans.

Members of these and other Asian American groups often find themselves pressured by the dominant Eurocentric culture to conform in a one-way direction to certain norms of that culture. Thus, in recent edited books titled *YELL-Oh Girls!* and *Asian American X,* several hundred young Asian Americans, many from groups discussed here, write about their lives, experiences, and understandings. Although they were not asked specifically to write about the racism they face, a great many recount frequent experiences dealing with intense, often coercive pressures to assimilate to the white end of the dominant racial-status continuum—to white-dominated ways of dress, speech, goal-attainment, thinking, and physical being. Most are torn between the culture of parents and home country, which provides respect for their "Asian-ness," and the pressures of the white-dominated society. As one young Korean American male who grew up in a white community and Southern Baptist church puts it, the historical dominance of whiteness in the United States helps to explain the "thoughtless ways white Americans often inhabit a sense of entitlement and egocentric normality. But when that entitlement becomes married to an acute perception of moral authority and clarity borne of a patriarchal and Anglocentric notion of rectitude and religion, the outcome . . . is acidic and threatening to nuanced or complex thought."[2]

Migration: An Overview

Since the 1980s, Filipinos, Chinese, Koreans, Vietnamese, and Asian Indians have been among the fastest-growing U.S. immigrant groups. For key periods from 1820 to the present, Table 11.1 lists those immigrants gaining permanent legal resident status (tourists and temporary visitors are not included) in each group.[3] Relatively few Filipinos, Koreans, Vietnamese, or Asian Indians immigrated to the U.S.

TABLE 11.1 People with Legal Permanent Resident Status, by Country of Last Residence, 1820–2005

	1820–1899	1900–1919	1920–1939	1940–1959	1960–1979	1980–1999	2000–2005
Chinese*	304,208	40,800	36,522	39,410	314,896	993,679	399,483
Filipino	**	**	391	21,344	408,386	1,036,394	295,042
Korean	**	**	**	4,928	268,240	502,478	112,271
Vietnamese	**	**	**	290	124,665	476,011	174,201
Asian-Indian	687	6,504	2,630	3,542	166,635	584,177	362,934

**Figures include Hong Kong and Taiwan.*

***Figures not available for this period.*

mainland before the 1960s. Thereafter, immigration increased dramatically. The number of Filipino, Korean, and Vietnamese immigrants rose from so few that records of their arrival were not kept to more than 2.5 million since 1980. Most Asian Indians have come since the 1960s. Chinese immigration has followed a different pattern, with two major periods. The first began about 1850 and lasted until the passage of the 1882 Chinese Exclusion Act, which prohibited direct immigration from China. Although some Chinese immigration occurred in the years following the 1882 act, large-scale immigration did not resume until the immigration reforms in 1965. A substantial majority of all Chinese immigrants have come relatively recently.

The 1924 Immigration Act excluded people in Asian countries from immigrating to the United States. The 1952 Immigration and Nationality Act began to eliminate some of the anti-Asian discrimination in the 1924 act. That 1952 act established principles for immigration policy: (1) reunification of families; (2) protection of the domestic labor force; and (3) immigration of persons with needed skills. It permitted small-scale Asian immigration and for the first time made immigrants from Asia eligible for U.S. citizenship. In 1965, Congress took a major step toward providing Asians the opportunity to immigrate on a scale similar to earlier European groups. The 1965 Immigration Act abolished the overtly racist national-origins quotas and established a significant annual quota for individual Asian countries. The proportion of Chinese, Filipinos, Koreans, Vietnamese, and Asian Indians among the total number of immigrants rose from a tiny 0.2 percent for 1901–1920 to 27 percent in the 1970s, and has remained above one-fifth in the 1990s and 2000s.

Because the 1965 act and its amendments give preference to family members of people already in the United States, many recent legal permanent residents are relatives of previous immigrants or are sponsored by the latter. The majority of immigrants have gone to areas where earlier immigrants settled, particularly the west coast. Today, the largest Asian-Pacific American populations are in large cities; Los Angeles, New York, Honolulu, and San Francisco lead the list. Because of past U.S. immigration barriers for Asians, most today are either foreign-born immigrants or the children of foreign-born parents. Chinese and Japanese American populations have the largest third- and later-generation components.

Chinese Americans

Over time, the Chinese have been one of the two largest groups of Asian immigrants. Migration began in substantial numbers in the decade before the U.S. Civil War, with a quarter-million coming during three decades after 1860. Most were men and entered as low-wage workers, brought in to do the "dirty work" for white employers in the West. Many were recruited to remedy labor shortages in railroad work or fill menial positions in such personal-service areas as laundry and restaurant work.

The few women who immigrated usually came alone, often brought by force to work as prostitutes. In 1875, Congress passed a law prohibiting the importation of women for prostitution—the first direct regulation of immigration in U.S. history. Significant numbers of women were not permitted to enter until the 1940s. Between 1946 and 1952, almost 90 percent of Chinese immigrants were women, typically wives of men who had immigrated earlier.[4]

As the 1870s began, the U.S. economy entered a depression; at the time, white labor leaders, newspaper editors, politicians, and the general public accused Chinese Americans of driving wages to a substandard level or taking jobs from whites. They blamed the Chinese for the country's economic difficulties.[5] The 1882 Chinese Exclusion Act officially prohibited direct immigration. Over the next decades, the act reduced the flow of immigrants, which had reached a high of 123,201 in the 1871–1880 era. Because most immigrants were male, exclusion of new immigrants resulted in a 40 percent decline in the Chinese American population by 1920.[6] In 1905 President Theodore Roosevelt strongly affirmed his support for this racist law, stating that Chinese laborers must be kept out of this country "absolutely."[7] Significantly, this openly racist Exclusion Act was not repealed *until 1943*, when China became a wartime ally against Japan. At that time, a tiny quota of 105 was set for new Chinese immigrants.[8]

The second major period of immigration took place after the 1965 immigration reform. Between 1960 and 1979, more than 300,000 Chinese, mainly from Hong Kong and Taiwan, came to the United States. Large numbers, nearly 1.4 million, have entered since 1980 (Table 11.1). During this most recent period the proportion from Hong Kong and Taiwan has fallen as the proportion from the mainland of China has grown. Between 1980 and 2005, the Chinese American population, the largest among Asian Americans, increased substantially—from 812,178 to about 3.3 million, including those with partial Chinese ancestry. According to a 2005 census survey, Chinese Americans constituted about one-fourth of all Asian Americans, and more than four in ten lived in western states.[9]

Filipino Americans

When the islands that make up the Philippines were taken over by the U.S. government after the Spanish–American War, an imperialistic relationship was established. The U.S. government ignored Filipino desires for independence, and U.S. military forces killed many who fought for independence. Between 1901 and 1913, a U.S. form of government was established, and a system of education was introduced in which U.S. teachers taught Filipino children U.S. cultural norms and values.

Because the Philippines was a U.S. colony, Filipinos were exempt from anti-Asian exclusionary provisions of the 1917 and 1924 Immigration Acts. This allowed them to immigrate freely, and U.S. employers actively recruited them to work on sugar plantations in Hawaii and in fields on the west coast. However, few came to the mainland.[10] After passage of the 1924 Immigration Act, employers increased recruitment of Filipinos as laborers to replace Asian and other workers excluded by the act. Between 1924 and 1929, approximately 24,000 Filipinos came to California to do low-wage work. As numbers increased, so did anti-Filipino sentiment among white workers. In 1934, Congress responded to this sentiment by passing an act granting independence to the Philippines and imposed an immigration quota of only fifty persons per year.[11]

Although Filipinos could enter without restriction until 1934, advantages ended there. Filipino Americans held an ambiguous legal position, which was only resolved in 1946 when they were finally declared eligible for U.S. citizenship. Most states did not allow Filipinos to practice law, medicine, or other professions. Congress began moving toward citizenship for Filipinos during World War II, since it was hard to defend the idea of freedom for the Philippines from Japanese rule while denying citizenship to Filipino Americans.

During World War II, 30,000 Filipinos were recruited to fight with U.S. forces battling the Japanese in the Philippines. President Franklin Roosevelt promised these fighters that they could come to the United States and become U.S. citizens. The government soon backed out of the promise and left thousands of veterans stranded. These veterans were not granted the right to U.S. citizenship until passage of the Immigration Act of 1990.[12] Even then, most of the thousands who have resided in the United States in recent decades have not been eligible for many veterans' benefits. As of mid-2007, the "Filipino Veterans Equity Act," first introduced in Congress in 1993, still had not been passed. A study of Filipino American veterans in California found that most have lived on low incomes, and often with serious medical problems. In recent years the Filipino American Veterans Campaign and the Filipino-American Service Group have fought hard to secure belated justice for these veterans.[13]

Between the 1950s and the 1970s, the number of Filipinos residing in the United States almost doubled. Since the 1960s and 1970s, Filipino immigration has increased dramatically (Table 11.1). In 2005, the Census Bureau estimated from a national survey that more than about 2.8 million Americans had at least some Filipino ancestry, making this group the second largest. Today, a large majority are foreign-born. Many Filipino Americans live in the Los Angeles area, and they are numerous in larger midwestern cities.[14]

Korean Americans

Immigration of a few Koreans began in the early 1900s, and by 1905 some 1000 Korean Americans lived in California. They too confronted low wages and other racial discrimination. They were segregated, refused housing in many areas, and denied service in public facilities. After learning of these conditions, Japan, which occupied Korea beginning in 1910, pressured the Korean government to impose a ban on emigration that restricted entry of Koreans into the United States for decades.[15] Nonetheless, a few—primarily "picture brides" and students—managed to come. Because most who arrived before the 1910 restrictions were single men, and because interracial marriage was banned by U.S. anti-intermarriage laws, Korean men sent their pictures to prospective brides in their homeland. Thus, *marriages were arranged on the basis of photographs, without the bride and groom having met*, leading to use of the term **picture brides**. From 1910 to 1924, more than 1000 Korean brides came to the United States.[16]

During the U.S. intervention in the 1950s Korean War, many in South Korea came to admire Americans and the United States. U.S. military support for the South Korean government, then authoritarian and undemocratic, built strong ties between the countries. Most Koreans who immigrated from 1950 to 1965 were brides of U.S. soldiers and as such came in outside the regular immigration system. Children and grandchildren stemming from these marriages are today part of a substantial U.S. multiracial population making its voice heard for greater respect for intermarriage and multiracial ancestry.

Changes in immigration laws in 1965 opened up new possibilities. Lack of economic or educational opportunities in Korea has prompted many to emigrate. Some have been political dissidents who opposed the dictatorial regimes that dominated South Korea for decades. Others have been students who completed their education and stayed. Once established, immigrants have used the immigration law's family reunification clause to bring in more family. Between 1960 and 1965, only a few thousand entered each year, but after 1965 numbers increased; within a decade the annual number exceeded 30,000. Immigration peaked at 35,849 in 1987 and dropped to less than 14,000 annually by the late 1990s, then increased over the early 2000s, reaching 26,002 in 2005.[17] Improvements in South Korea's economy over recent decades have contributed to this relatively low rate of immigration compared to other Asian countries.

In 2005, the Census Bureau estimated there were about 1.4 million Americans with Korean ancestry, around 10 percent of the Asian American population. About one-third presently reside on the west coast, down from 40 percent in 2002. By the mid-2000s, many Korean Americans had moved away from the west coast, often settling in larger midwestern or eastern cities.[18]

Vietnamese Americans

Most Vietnamese immigrants to the United States have come since 1975, when U.S. involvement in the Vietnam War ended abruptly. When French military forces withdrew in 1954, and Vietnam was divided in two, the United States became a military ally of the South Vietnamese government, which was a political dictatorship. U.S. troops and dollars flowed to what slowly became an unpopular war. In the face of advancing enemy forces at the war's end, U.S. plans to evacuate some South Vietnamese included those (and their families) employed by the U.S. government or U.S. businesses. In just one week, thousands fled their country.[19]

The large numbers of Vietnamese refugees who began to enter the United States in 1975 were admitted outside the usual immigration process as political refugees.[20] As Table 11.1 shows, very few immigrated before 1960, in part because of anti-Asian immigration laws. Following changes in immigration laws and the end of the U.S. military intervention in Vietnam, many Vietnamese entered the United States just between 1975 and 1980.

In the 1980–1990 period, the number of Americans with Vietnamese ancestry grew 142 percent—the largest percentage increase for the larger Asian groups. Between 1990 and 2000, this population again increased dramatically. The population continues to increase, numbering more than 1.5 million in the mid-2000s. A large percentage are foreign-born, and many live in western states.[21]

Asian-Indian Americans

Of all the major Asian–Pacific groups in the United States, perhaps the least well known is the group the Census Bureau calls "Asian Indians"—those from India. The first Indian immigrants were Sikhs who worked on the railroads or in agriculture on the West Coast in the 1800s, but their number remained very small until the 1960s. Asian Indians have immigrated in significant numbers only since the 1965 Immigration Act. The 1990 census reported almost 787,000 Asian-Indian Americans, but by 2005 this population had increased sharply to nearly 2.5 million.[22]

Three periods are evident in the migrations. In the 1960s, many immigrants were male professionals and managers and easily found jobs. Wives were usually not well educated. Today, their children are a new adult generation. A second group came in the 1970s; it included a more diverse occupational mixture, with more well-educated professional women. A third and much larger group has come since the 1980s and includes many relatives sponsored by earlier immigrants. Compared with earlier immigrants, this latter group tends to be less well educated and more likely to move into service work or into family-owned businesses.[23]

The majority of Asian-Indian Americans do not live on the west coast, although the number there is growing. In 2005, over 449,000 Asian Indians resided in California. Still, the majority of Asian-Indian Americans live in the Northeast, and a large proportion live in the Midwest and the South. A half-million live in the greater New York City area and New Jersey.[24]

In metropolitan areas on the east and west coasts, many Asian-Indian Americans have had the economic resources to move directly into suburbs rather than settling first in central-city areas like most other U.S. immigrant groups, past and present. As a result, they are more scattered geographically than other Asian immigrants. There are no large central-city concentrations as there are for other Asian groups. Even so, wherever there is a substantial Asian-Indian population in a metropolitan area, there are usually numerous community organizations, such as Indian (for example, Hindu) houses of worship.

Asian Women as Immigrants

Many discussions of Asian immigrants, and Asian Americans in general, stereotype the women in these groups as being rather withdrawn and docile. However, Asian immigrant families do include many women who are strong figures in their own right. Min Zhou and James Gatewood write, "As immigrants, Asian American women are agents in their own destiny, often making painful decisions to come to America but, more often than not, having some control over their choices. They play an active role."[25] The immigration experience often reshapes traditional gender relationships so that these women immigrants take a much more active role in providing economic and other support for their families than they typically did in the home country. This in turn can reshape their relationships with the men in their families. As with women in earlier immigrant groups, such as the Irish and the Jews, Asian women are often important decision makers in the immigration process and in group adaptation to the host society.[26]

How have anti-Asian sentiments shaped U.S. immigration laws and decisions?

Stereotypes

Anti-Asian stereotyping and hostility have a long history in the United States. One common stereotype about Asian Americans is that they are basically the same, physically and culturally. Japanese Americans are commonly mistaken by non-Asians for Chinese Americans, who in turn may be mistaken for Vietnamese or Korean Americans. Asian Americans are frequently viewed by non-Asians as "foreigners" rather than as "Americans" because of their non-European appearance. Historically, U.S. films and television programs have portrayed Asians as criminal, dangerous, or fanatical. Stereotyped images, such as the "evil Jap" of World War II and the "Communist gook" in the cases of China and Vietnam, were created primarily by white Americans and have been recycled as U.S. foreign policy has changed over time. This *uninformed and stereotypical way of thinking of Asian peoples*, sometimes called **Orientalism**, is common among non-Asian Americans and shapes much anti-Asian discrimination and some government policies.[27]

One Chinese American leader has commented, "To the larger society, Asian Americans are either invisible, or forever foreigners, or honorary whites, or problems." Recent studies of Asian American students at various U.S. colleges and universities have found that they are regularly targets of racialized stereotyping as "foreigners" or as supposedly "typical Asian students."[28] Anti-Asian stereotypes have serious implications. For example, a white member of South Carolina's State Board of Education commented thus at a board meeting: "Screw the Buddhists and kill the Muslims." Even with this stereotyped outburst, he was able to keep his position on the board. Moreover, a study of relatively recent Chinese immigrants who settled in Monterey Park, California, found that many long-term residents—both powerful white residents and some older Japanese American and Latino residents—developed a stereotyped distinguishing between "good immigrants" for their own ancestors and "bad immigrants" for more recent Chinese immigrants. Good immigrants were said to have blended in and been quietly subservient, while bad immigrants were those like some Chinese who questioned the established social and economic order. Longer-term residents of numerous cities have used this fallacious distinction as they try to hold onto local power by accenting what Leland Saito calls the "mythical image of how 'good immigrants' [are] supposed to act."[29]

As we noted in Chapter 10, numerous Asian American groups have been stereotyped as "model minorities." According to this view, which many who use it think is positive, Asian Americans have moved ahead rapidly in society, generally unhindered by racial prejudice and discrimination, mainly by dint of hard work and thrift. There are indeed many exemplary individuals in Asian American communities, but the model minority stereotype overstates their economic situation and progress and underplays the racial barriers they still face.

Specific Images of Asian Americans

Coming to the west coast, the first Chinese workers became subjects of white workers' anger. They were called "coolies" and maligned as "heathen," "mice-eaters," or "Chinks." For decades white leaders, as well as the white public, viewed Chinese Americans not as Americans in any sense, but as an alien "race." Sociologist Claire Jean Kim has noted how Asian immigrants have been negatively evaluated by whites along the axes of superior/inferior and insider/foreigner.[30] The Chinese were thus inferior foreigners. In 1896, even as he defended some rights for black Americans as the dissenter in the famous *Plessy* v. *Ferguson* racial segregation decision, Supreme Court Justice John Marshall Harlan added this comment: "There is a race so different from our own that we do not permit those belonging to it to become citizens of the United States. Persons belonging to it are, with few exceptions, absolutely excluded from our country. I allude to the Chinese race."[31] Such "alien race" images have persisted to the present.

Modest changes in white attitudes came after the United States declared war on Japan in 1941. China and the United States became allies against Japan. The Chinese were suddenly friends. After the entry into World War II, *Time* magazine printed the following racist explanation of the differences between Chinese and Japanese:

> How to Tell Your Friends from the Japs: Virtually all Japanese are short. Japanese are likely to be stockier and broader-hipped than short Chinese. Japanese are seldom fat; they often dry up and grow lean as they age. Although both have the typical epicanthic fold on the upper eyelid, Japanese eyes are usually set closer together. The Chinese expression is likely to be more placid, kindly, open; the Japanese more positive, dogmatic, arrogant. Japanese are hesitant, nervous in conversation, laugh loudly at the wrong time. Japanese walk stiffly erect, hard heeled. Chinese, more relaxed, have an easy gait, sometimes shuffle.[32]

Ironically, those white editors who published this wildly stereotyped statement likely thought they were saying something positive about their "friends" the Chinese. Yet, this is an example of the crude stereotyping that has long been part of much white thinking.

Historically, stereotypes of Filipino immigrants have fluctuated according to their usefulness to employers recruiting them as low-wage labor, such as for agricultural plantations in Hawaii. When white employers were recruiting Filipinos, they often characterized them as "unintelligent" and "docile." When these workers were no longer needed, they were also stereotyped as "lazy, shiftless, and unmanageable." All of these are stereotypes that these whites had drawn out of the white racist framing of society developed for earlier Americans of color.[33]

The Vietnamese arrived in the United States when unemployment was relatively high, and many non-Asian Americans feared that these refugees would take jobs or drain sources of public assistance. During the 1970s this anti-Vietnamese sentiment was reflected in one Gallup poll in which 54 percent of the respondents felt that Vietnamese refugees should not be permitted to stay.[34] Many influential and rank-and-file whites apparently wanted to forget Vietnam and its people. Some non-Asian Americans still see the Vietnamese as alien or "the enemy" because of the U.S. intervention in Vietnam and thus use the racist epithet *gooks*. Senator John McCain, a periodic Republican presidential candidate, has used the racialized term "gook" for the Vietnamese who fought the U.S. intervention. And in 2006 a Dallas-area police chief retired early after making a comment that he would not have "gooks" on his force and after protests by Asian American residents. Many non-Asians still regard Vietnamese Americans as strange, clannish, or hard to approach. One survey of Vietnamese American residents of Orange County, California, found that six in ten felt anti-Vietnamese prejudice was still a problem. Today, non-Asian Americans harbor negative views of other groups as well. Thus, one recent national survey found that one-quarter of respondents admitted they held negative attitudes about Chinese Americans and would be uncomfortable voting for an Asian American for U.S. president. A similar proportion opposed the idea of intermarriage with an Asian American. One-third or more thought that Chinese Americans were more loyal to China than to the United States, had too much influence on U.S. technology, and might pass secrets to the Chinese government.[35]

The movie industry has long perpetuated a variety of negatively stereotyped images of Asian men and women. Asian men have often been portrayed as weak or sexless. As UCLA Professor Russell Leong has noted, "Racist myths and assumptions about smaller stature—smaller eyes—and less sexual and erotic drive—have stymied the development and acceptance of Asian American men as full erotic beings."[36]

One severe type of stereotyping is faced by Asian American women—that of the exotic sex object. Numerous Asian women have written of how some men, especially white men, seek them out with heads full of images of exotic sexual relationships and/or submissive wives in their heads. Numerous Internet websites are devoted to such themes, including sites devoted to finding Asian sexual partners and wives for white men. Other gendered stereotyping can be seen in another problem faced by Asian American women: the mainstream North American standard of ideal female beauty that is white, fair-haired, and relatively busty and tall. Faced with this constant imaging of ideal female beauty, and like some other women of color, many Asian Americans feel themselves to be inadequate or inferior—even to the point of having plastic surgery (which has become more acceptable) to "improve" facial or breast characteristics. One recent report showed a sharp increase in cosmetic surgery for Asian Americans, to whom much aggressive advertising is directed by plastic surgeons. The three most common surgeries for Asian American women are eyelid surgery, nose reshaping, and breast augmentation. Much surgery is directed at making Asian women look more like the white beauty ideal. Writing at age nineteen about her current reaction to years of pressures from female relatives to have plastic surgery on her face, one Chinese American has recently written thus: "Asian is beautiful. After all these years of wanting to open up my eyes with tape and glue and surgery, I have opened up my eyes to a different definition of beauty, one that embraces differences and includes every girl...because being *Asian is beautiful*."[37]

More Stereotyping in the Media and Popular Entertainment

The movie industry's productions have often been a double-edged sword. Some movies, such as the pioneering martial arts movies of Bruce Lee and those who have immitated him, have created some relatively positive images of strong, virtuous Asians. As a result of Lee's movies, martial arts movies have become generally popular not only among Asian American youth but among American youth generally. However, as sociologist C. N. Le has put it, "The success of these martial arts movies...also demonstrates the fine line that the Asian American community must walk. On the one hand, most of us are proud of the success of these martial arts movies and [their] Asian and Asian American stars. However, we must be wary of the possibility that these movies will only reinforce and perpetuate the cultural stereotype that all Asians know martial arts...In this case, it could be very easy to see all Asian Americans as martial arts experts and then associate that with being a 'foreign thing' and that therefore, all Asian Americans are again foreigners."[38]

Over many decades now, the mostly white-controlled media stereotyping has negatively targeted many Asian groups. Television series such as *The Simpsons* have derided Indian and other South Asian clerks, while the David Letterman show has made fun of Bangladeshi newsstand operators.[39] Since the 1990s the ever-popular musical *Miss Saigon*, produced in cities across the world, has been sharply and regularly criticized by Asian Americans, who have noted that the central character, a Vietnamese "bar girl" abandoned by a white GI, is a crude racial stereotype. Vietnamese and other Asian American leaders have periodically called on theatergoers and actors to boycott the play. Moreover, a study of images of people of color in news coverage found numerous portrayals of Asian Americans as manipulative, mysterious, and inscrutable. The study found widespread trivialization of Asian customs, ridicule of Asian American pronunciation, and use of derogatory clichés and inflammatory metaphorical phrases such as "Asian invasion," terminology that reinforces views of Asian Americans as undesirable foreigners.[40]

In recent decades several Asian Americans have been targets of widespread stereotyping in the investigation of alleged illegal contributions to political campaigns. For example, under pressure to raise money for the Democratic Party in the 1990s, John Huang, a Chinese American, and other Asian American fundraisers raised several million dollars in contributions, some of which were alleged to have been illegally contributed by overseas donors, including in Taiwan. Media discussions included considerable stereotyping of Asian Americans as mysterious, underhanded, or corrupt. Old racist images of "Orientals" were resurrected. Although investigation of illegal contributions is certainly legitimate, blatant stereotyping is another matter. Indeed, the media did *not* so vigorously target for investigation other foreign contributions, such as those from overseas corporations, to Democratic and Republican Party activities. And the white media also did not single out the racial or ethnic characteristics of other questionable contributors.[41]

Commenting on Huang's testimony before a Senate committee, a white U.S. senator made fun of what he thought to be Chinese American speech patterns: "No raise money, no get bonus." Amazingly, the senator contended that his mocking was not intended as a slight. A Georgia representative made a comment about illegal donations being the "tip of the egg roll." As Mia Tuan has suggested, "That both men felt free enough from recrimination to engage in such racist witticisms speaks volumes about the atmosphere during the hearings."[42] Such commentary suggests that powerful whites still harbor negative stereotypes of Asian Americans.

A graphic commentary on the fund-raising investigations that appeared on the cover of a 1997 issue of the magazine *National Review* showed caricatures of then President Bill Clinton and wife Hillary as slant-eyed, buck-toothed Chinese in Mao suits and Chinese hats. Daphne Kwok, of the Organization of Chinese Americans, described these images as racist because they resurrected stereotypes about Asian Americans' characteristics and dress. Since the nineteenth century, white cartoonists have portrayed Chinese and other Asian Americans in such stereotyped terms to express fear of the "yellow peril." Appearing on NBC's *Today* show with Daphne Kwok, the editor of *National Review* admitted that the caricatures were an attempt to portray Asian characteristics but refused to apologize. Several civil rights groups protested outside the magazine's New York offices and called for a boycott of the magazine.[43]

In a similar incident recently, an animation company made a cartoon called *Mr. Wong* with an extreme caricature of a Chinese "hunchbacked, yellow-skinned, squinty-eyed character who spoke with a thick accent and starred in an interactive music video titled 'Saturday Night Yellow Fever.'"[44] There was significant national protest, especially from Asian Americans, over the cartoon, while many whites and a few Asian Americans (including a few who helped make it) defended it as "only humor." When the Asian Pacific American Media Coalition heard that a company was considering making it into a movie, they conducted a letter-writing campaign to convince the company to back off and to get advertisers to pull ads from the company's website. In addition, the filmmakers of a 2004 puppet movie, *Team America: World Police*, had a Korean political leader speaking gibberish in a mock Asian accent. As one Asian American reviewer noted, "Team America was an hour and a half of racial mockery with an 'if you are offended, you obviously can't take a joke' tacked on at the end." Such episodes reveal how conventional racial stereotypes are passed off as harmless joking, when in fact such "joking" reinforces the white-generated racial framing lying behind ongoing discrimination against Americans of color.[45]

Clearly, media and elite stereotypes of Asian Americans still include notions of the latter as threatening, relatively unassimilated, and racialized foreigners. Such negative stereotypes have deep roots in the language of everyday discourse among whites, including children. In recent years numerous Asian Americans, including many young people, have noted that they periodically encounter hostile racist words from whites, including younger people, such as these: "Ching chong Chinaman sitting on a rail, along came a white man and snipped off his tail"; "Ah so. No tickee, No washee. So sorry, so sollee"; and "Chinkee, Chink, Jap, Nip, zero, Dothead...Flip, Hindoo."[46] Moreover, Asian immigrants interviewed by researchers have noted that they did not see themselves in racial terms until they arrived here. Asian-Indian scholar Sharmila Rudrappa has summarized this point from her field research: "Upon arrival in the United States we postcolonial immigrants suddenly become racialized....From being persons with no tangible race—we do not think of ourselves in racial terms in India—we become people of color in this society." As a result, conformity to white norms seems necessary, especially in public places, and one's home is often the only safe place to accent Asian culture and backgrounds.[47]

Discrimination and Conflict

Hate Crimes and Other Ethnoviolence

Violence, harassment, and vandalism directed against Americans of Asian descent have occurred since the earliest days of Asian immigration. Until relatively recently, few local or state governments have collected data on the scale of this ethnoviolence. Each year many anti-Asian hate crimes are reported to law enforcement. Since 1998, at least nine Asian Americans have died in hate crime attacks.[48] Hate crimes range from killings to verbal slurs and hate messages painted on homes and businesses.

Periodically, some anti-Asian discrimination is thoroughly reported in the media. In 1997 several Asian American students were denied service at a Syracuse, New York, restaurant. When they left, they were beaten by white patrons, and the restaurant's security personnel reportedly did not try to intervene. A lawsuit was filed against the restaurant, but the case was eventually dismissed by a judge. The media gave some attention to these events. Asian American leaders have attributed the significant number of hate crimes and other public discrimination in part to anti-immigrant sentiment and anti-Asian images in the media.[49]

The U.S. Commission on Civil Rights has noted that ethnoviolence is underreported, especially in the case of Asian Americans. Many of the latter are immigrants who distrust the police, have a limited understanding of their civil rights, and have a limited knowledge of English. Some have been mistreated or killed by police officers. One important county where many Asian Americans live, Orange County, California, has reported 150 to 170 hate crimes annually in recent years, with an increase in 2005. Los Angeles has also reported hundreds of hate crimes each year. Although African American residents are usually the most frequent targets of hate crimes in cities, Asian Americans have been singled out for a variety of hate crimes, which range from racist graffiti—painted on homes or businesses or circulated on the Internet—to violent threats and attacks.[50]

The U.S. Civil Rights Commission and its advisory boards have found that adequate police protection is often not provided for Asian Americans. Asian American community organizations in various cities have urged police and other officials to prosecute hate and other crimes more vigorously.[51] Some white-dominated police departments seem insensitive or hostile to Asian American communities. When Asian Americans do have contact with white officers, their rights are sometimes jeopardized by language barriers, and few police departments have adequate interpretive services for non–English-speaking Americans. When Asian Americans report a crime, they frequently do not receive an adequate police response. The Asian and Pacific Islander Advisory Committee of the California attorney general's office has reported that "one of the most commonly repeated experiences is one in which the perpetrator is allowed to go free and the victim [an Asian American] is arrested."[52]

One controversial police strategy is photographing youths because they fit a "gang profile." Asian Americans—like African Americans, Latinos, and Arab Americans—are sometimes the targets of extensive racial profiling by white authorities. Some communities have organized to challenge such police harassment. A spokesperson for one such community organization explained, "Culturally, the Asian community does not speak out against such things as police harassment. By nature, our people do not complain or report abuse, so by having some speak out, we hope to encourage others to do the same."[53] This is beginning to change, for a growing number of Asian Americans are organizing and speaking out for the full range of their civil rights.

Have hate crimes targeting Asian Americans been similar to or different from those involving other racial and ethnic groups?

Chinese Americans

During the nineteenth century, openly anti-Chinese sentiments were common in union policies and political platforms, as well as in the press. Chinese immigrants were attacked violently by whites in western states. In recent decades, Chinese Americans have continued to be the targets of racially motivated attacks, if on a smaller scale. For example, a Chinese American woman in New York was pushed in front of a subway train by a man with a "phobia about Asians."[54] And a teen-aged white supremacist in California was charged with numerous felony crimes, including the attempted murder of a Chinese American council member and the fire-bombing of NAACP and Japanese American Citizens League offices.[55]

In Detroit in 1982, the murder of Vincent Chin, a Chinese American, brought racially motivated actions against Asian Americans to public attention. Two white auto workers, apparently believing Chin was Japanese and blaming him for auto industry problems, started an argument with him, then beat him to death. A Michigan judge sentenced each to only three years' probation and a fine of $3780. Many Americans expressed outrage at the extraordinarily lenient punishment. The U.S. Commission on Civil Rights concluded that the leniency was "suggestive of very little value being placed on an Asian American life."[56] The U.S. Department of Justice later brought federal charges against the assailants for civil rights violations. A U.S. District Court jury found one of the defendants guilty of violating Chin's civil rights, thereby acknowledging the racial motivation of the attack. The other, apparently not involved directly in the beating, was acquitted. The guilty defendant was sentenced to twenty-five years in prison, but his conviction was overturned by an appellate court for technical reasons. In a retrial he was acquitted.[57]

A similar incident took place in Raleigh, North Carolina, in 1989. This time the Chinese American victim, Ming Hai Loo, was killed by two white brothers who thought he was Vietnamese and were angry about U.S. battle deaths in Vietnam. In 1990, the brother who struck the fatal blow was sentenced to thirty-seven years in prison for second-degree murder and simple assault, but with the possibility of parole after serving four-and-a-half years. The maximum penalty for such crimes under North Carolina's law is life in prison. The other assailant, who made hostile racist remarks, received a six-month misdemeanor sentence. The following year he was found guilty in federal court of violating the victim's civil rights and received a four-year sentence, which was shorter than the minimum sentence specified by federal guidelines. Significantly, this case was the *first* successful federal prosecution of a civil rights case in which the target was Asian American. Yet, this violence, like more recent violence against Asian Americans, has received little national media attention, a neglect that perpetuates non-Asian Americans' lack of awareness of anti-Asian violence. For example, in the summer of 2006 in Queens, New York, several Chinese American teenagers were attacked and beaten by whites whom a witness said were yelling racist slurs and saying, "Stay out of our neighborhood." This attack made the local news, but again there was no significant national discussion of such hate crimes.[58]

Anti-Asian attacks often illustrate not only racist violence but also the confusion of non-Asians about Asian Americans. Many non-Asians are not aware that Asian–Pacific Americans include many nationality groups, and many non-Asians periodically mistake a person from one Asian American group for someone from another. This confusion may have been reflected in several incidents since the 1990s in which Secret Service and other federal guards have treated with suspicion, as though they were foreigners, Asian Americans entering the White House or other government buildings.[59]

In the late 1990s, the federal Los Alamos National Laboratory was investigated for security compromises, and Dr. Wen Ho Lee, a naturalized U.S. citizen from Taiwan, was fired for allegedly being a spy for the Chinese government. He was indicted on fifty-nine counts of "mishandling classified information." In the fall of 2000, after months of media and political speculation about Chinese intrigues and Lee's involvement, and after Lee had served months in solitary confinement, he was freed on a plea bargain in which all but one relatively minor charge (downloading secret files to an unsecured computer) were dropped. Some news stories seemed to view Chinese Americans as mysterious or disloyal. President Bill Clinton was openly critical of the investigation and long incarceration, yet he asserted that no anti-Asian animosity lay behind what happened. However, many Asian Americans protested the stereotyping of Chinese Americans as disloyal, as well as the scapegoating and mistreatment of Dr. Lee. In 1997 the U.S. Commission on Civil Rights held a briefing on an American Civil Liberties Union (ACLU) petition that charged the

U.S. Congress, the Democratic National Committee, and the Republican National Committee with creating a hostile environment for Asian Americans in the United States.[60]

Filipino Americans

Among the earliest of Asian–Pacific immigrants, Filipino Americans have suffered many violent attacks from white Americans. In the 1910s–1930s period, for example, white farm laborers often clashed with Filipino workers in California. Revealing discrimination, Filipino wages were considerably lower than the wages of white workers, yet the latter still wanted to get rid of Filipino workers. In October 1929, whites rioted against Filipino workers in a San Joaquin Valley community. White workers were bitter about farmers' use of Filipinos. Attacks began at a carnival where whites were shooting Filipinos with rubber bands. After days of harassment, a Filipino laborer used a knife to defend himself when a white group attempted to attack him. He escaped, but a mob formed. Whites went to a nearby labor camp, ordered Filipinos out, then burned the camp. The police chief refused to take action against the mob despite the criminal acts.[61]

The most prolonged riot by whites occurred near Watsonville, California, in 1930, a riot reflecting a decade of increasing tensions and exacerbated by newspaper commentaries blaming Filipino Americans. Anti-Filipino demonstrations erupted; a vigilante mob of five hundred whites marched on a Filipino dance hall. On January 22, 1930, the anti-Filipino attacks reached a peak when hundreds of vigilantes attacked the Northern Monterey Filipino Club. One person was killed, and many Filipino Americans were severely beaten.[62]

In more recent decades, whites have directed hostility toward Filipino Americans. In the early 1990s, white guests at a party at Chicago mayor Richard Daley's estate called Filipino American youths racist names and threw them out.[63] In 1999, Joseph Ileto, a Filipino American mail carrier, was killed in Los Angeles by a white supremacist who killed him because of his skin color. (Supremacist groups often attack Americans of color as inferior "mud" people.) In response, Ileto's family has become active in protests against hate crimes, including pressing the U.S. Congress to pass significant new hate crimes legislation. Filipino American organizations rallied against this hate crime in several cities. Such hate crimes persist. Early in 2006 another white supremacist, a woman who had published a newsletter called *The Racist Press*, went on a rampage in Santa Barbara, California, and killed fellow postal workers. She targeted six people, including one Filipino, one Chinese, one Latino, and three black workers.[64]

Filipino Americans have also been targeted via racial profiling by the U.S. government. In one recent incident, U.S. government officials detained, treated roughly, and derided ten Filipino American airline mechanics on allegations that they were linked to terrorist cells. After being detained for nearly six months without bail for routine immigration charges, seven were released with simple misdemeanor violations and three others, who were tried, were acquitted. None was convicted of any terrorist act. Others who were picked up at the same time for similar offenses were quickly released, leading Filipino leaders to suspect aggressive racial profiling.[65]

Korean Americans

Koreans are relatively recent immigrants, yet they too have been hit by anti-Asian violence. Like white ethnic merchants, Korean American merchants in some communities of color have faced hostility, and their businesses have been targets of economic boycotts. Black city residents have sometimes charged that the merchants treat black customers rudely and refuse to hire black employees. The merchants, in turn, cite the high level of crime they often face at the hands of poor black criminals.

African American residents in New York and California have demonstrated against Korean American businesses. Each group has accused members of the other of racially motivated violence. In 1991 a Korean storekeeper in Los Angeles killed a fifteen-year-old black girl (Latasha Harlins), whom the storekeeper mistakenly thought was shoplifting. Black rage over this incident, which intensified after a judge imposed a lenient sentence, played a role in the major 1992 Los Angeles riot (see Chapter 7). Historian Mike Davis has described the looting of 2000 Korean-owned businesses during that riot as, in part, the product of "the black community's unassuaged grief over Harlins's murder."[66]

During the riot, Los Angeles's Korean Americans felt betrayed as they saw police officers protect large shopping centers owned by whites while smaller

Korean-owned stores were destroyed by black and Latino rioters. Note that this was a three-way racial conflict. Social scientist Elaine Kim has commented that "the so-called black–Korean problem masks a deeper racism in this country.... When the Los Angeles Police Department and the state government failed to respond to the initial outbreak of violence in South Central, I suspected that Korean Americans were being used as human shields to protect the real source of rage."[67]

One factor that contributes to continuing tensions is that many Asian immigrants already have strong negative stereotypes of black Americans when they arrive in the United States. They, like other recent immigrants, pick up negative stereotypes from U.S.-made movies and television programs that are seen by hundreds of millions in countries around the globe. In one study, Asian respondents in rural Taiwan were interviewed about their views of black Americans. Although they had never been to the United States, and although some respondents realized that U.S. television programs, movies, and newspapers engaged in racial stereotyping, most still accepted the negative stereotypes of African Americans that they had learned from the now-global U.S. mass media.[68]

The negative stereotypes Korean and other Asian immigrants bring with them can become a basis for negative interactions with African Americans. In their turn, African Americans sometimes develop negative views of the Asian immigrants who stereotype them. Negative stereotyping of Asian Americans that African Americans pick up from the same white-controlled media often affect how they see Asian American merchants in their communities. Negative attitudes of immigrants toward African Americans—and negative attitudes of African Americans toward Asian immigrants—are part of a much larger, indeed global, system of (disproportionately) white-generated and white-circulated racial framing of various racial-ethnic groups.[69]

Sociologist Claire Jean Kim has shown that Korean–black conflict should be understood in the context of this systemic racism. Such conflict is not just about stereotyping and scapegoating by African Americans or Korean Americans, but reflects the larger white-racist framework and its racial hierarchy. As we have noted previously, in this U.S. racial hierarchy, white Americans are at the top and black Americans are at the bottom, while other racially oppressed groups, such as those of Asian descent, are often caught or positioned in between (see Chapter 2). This white-created hierarchy stimulates conflict among the racial groups positioned differently in it. The hierarchy generates legitimate protests against a group's hierarchical placement and the racist barriers associated with that. "The differential positioning of Blacks and Asian Americans (including Korean immigrants) in the American racial order and their physical juxtaposition in the urban economy creates an immanent tendency for conflict between the two groups."[70] Collective black actions against Korean merchants in black communities are not only about black stereotyping of these merchants, but are also part of centuries of black resistance to outside economic control of their oppressed communities. Resistance arises no matter who (Irish, Jewish, or Korean) the outside merchants are.

Another source of bitterness on the part of some African Americans is the largely unfounded belief that the federal government helps Korean Americans start small businesses. In fact, Korean Americans usually pool family resources to purchase businesses in low-income black and Latino neighborhoods.[71] Many Korean immigrants have started businesses in black and Latino communities because such businesses require only modest capital and can be very profitable. The gamble the Korean American entrepreneurs take in poor communities is "necessitated by the constraints they face—the near impossibility of a professional career or white-collar work, and the daunting difficulties in opening a store in an affluent neighborhood."[72] Contrary to the "American dream," these Korean immigrants are usually not able to start businesses in heavily white areas because they face anti-Asian discrimination or do not have enough capital. Many have graduated from Korean colleges yet are unable to find employment in line with their educations, in part because of white discrimination and in part because they do not yet have the necessary language skills. Like white ethnic merchants before them, Korean Americans have sometimes become the latest "middleman minorities."[73]

In recent years, conflict has erupted between Korean Americans and Latinos in California. Some researchers and reporters have found strong antagonism between the two groups. For example, many of the rioters looting Korean American businesses during the 1992 Los Angeles riot were Latinos. In addition, Korean American garment industry subcontractors are often seen by their low-wage Latino employees as profit-seeking exploiters who are indifferent to workers' well-being. In their turn, these Korean American contractors report frequent verbal disputes in the workplace and acts of vandalism by Latino workers. The Korean American subcontractors are themselves exploited by white manufacturers, who make use of a subcontracting system designed for flexible and profitable production of garments.[74]

Vietnamese Americans

Many recent Vietnamese immigrants fished as a livelihood in their homeland, and some have moved to fishing communities on the U.S. Gulf Coast. In the 1970s, they were encouraged to move there because of its labor shortage. They generally took low-paying jobs, such as cleaning fish or working in restaurant kitchens, and in these positions they were mostly accepted by whites. But as they began to buy boats and offer competition to white fishers, white attitudes changed. Many whites have resented the Vietnamese Americans' success and have blamed them for economic recessions on the Gulf Coast.

Vietnamese Americans have faced hostility and violence by whites. A 1979 conflict between Vietnamese Americans and whites in Seadrift, Texas, culminated in the shooting death of a white fisher. Vietnamese refugees were arrested for the shooting, which followed an argument over placement of crab traps. Within hours of the death, Vietnamese boats were burned, one house was fire-bombed, and an attempt was made to bomb a packing plant where Vietnamese Americans worked. The attacks caused most Vietnamese Americans to flee to another town. Those arrested were eventually acquitted of the shooting. In response, some whites turned to the Ku Klux Klan for "protection of their industrial interest."[75]

Vietnamese Americans have faced racial violence in a number of other areas. Between 1983 and 1987, the Boston police department reported that nearly one-fourth of the racial violence in the city was directed at Vietnamese and other Asian Americans. And in 1989 one Vietnamese and four Cambodian children were gunned down in Stockton, California, by a white man with a semiautomatic weapon. He attacked the children at his old school, which now had mostly Asian American children. He had expressed hostility toward Asians. Significantly, major media reports on the killings generally ignored the issue of anti-Asian racism raised by the incident.[76]

Conflict similar to that between Korean American business owners and the black residents of the communities where they operate has also arisen between Vietnamese American owners and community residents. In the summer of 1996, open conflict arose in New Orleans, including a fight between the son of a Vietnamese American shopkeeper and a black resident. Black residents and their Committee for Justice boycotted the Vietnamese-owned grocery store, charging the owners with discrimination and other mistreatment. In their turn, the owners charged black residents with "untrustworthiness and years of tolerating obscene language and repeated taunts to 'go back to your own country.'"[77] The owners closed the store and filed a lawsuit against local black organizations. Both sides engaged in intensive stereotyping of the other. Eventually, several hundred Vietnamese and African American church members met to try to better understand each others' perspectives and cultures.

Asian-Indian Americans

Asian-Indian Americans have also faced racial hostility and discrimination. For example, anti-Indian leaflets have been circulated in New Jersey cities. In public schools, Asian-Indian children have been called derogatory names (e.g., "dot heads") and physically abused because of their Indian ancestry. Religion-based hazing targeting South Asians has become common in some schools. In recent years white politicians have made numerous hostile and stereotyped comments about South Asians, periodically alluding to them as "foreign" or not rooted in America. In a 2005 election for city council in Orange City, Florida, a white candidate spoke of his Asian-Indian opponent as being linked to 9/11 ("these kind of people") and asserted that "I don't want an Indian in my government." In his 2006 try for reelection, Senator George Allen (R–Va.) publicly called a South Asian campaign worker a racially derogatory term ("macaca").[78] Asian-Indian and other South Asian Americans (for example, Pakistanis and Bangladeshis) have also faced significant racial violence. In Queens, New York, Rishi Maharaj received multiple head injuries when he was beaten with bats by white men shouting racist epithets and threats. Two days later, a Pakistani American gas attendant was killed with a baseball bat on Long Island.[79]

Exaggerated stereotypes of the successfulness of Asian Indians have contributed to interracial struggles in several states, including California. For example, non-Asians in San Francisco have vigorously opposed attempts to include Indians as Asians in affirmative action programs designed to help small Asian American businesses. In addition, in recent years Asian-Indian Americans have faced significant harassment at the hands of police officers and other community members. For example, in Edison, New Jersey, a community rally was held in 2006 by Asian Indians to protest incidents seen as police brutality targeting people of Asian descent. When local authorities refused to redress the problem, several dozen members of South Asian communities held a demonstration, which was countered by whites with racist and anti-immigrant signs saying "You must've slid under the border to come here" and "You're all cockroaches! Go home!"[80]

How does the dominant white racial frame shape relations between Asian Americans and other Americans?

Organizing and Activism in the Political Arena

The number of Asian American voters is increasing dramatically in numerous areas, especially in California and New York. Some have called this vote a "sleeping giant" of U.S. politics. Asian Americans have already distinguished themselves politically, despite anti-Asian prejudices. However, except in the state of Hawaii, Asian Americans still have limited political representation. Even in the mid-2000s, federal appointed offices, including congressional staff positions, have largely been inaccessible. As noted in Chapter 10, Norman Mineta, a Japanese American, has held two presidential cabinet posts. In 2001, President George W. Bush appointed Elaine Chao as Secretary of Labor, making her the *first* Chinese American and the *first* Asian American woman to hold a Cabinet post. No other Asian Americans have been represented at this political level. As of 2007, there were also just eight voting members in both houses of Congress with Asian ancestry, three of whom were elected from Hawaii. Four were the Japanese Americans (Matsui, Honda, Hirono, and Inouye) mentioned in the last chapter. Two others were Chinese Americans. Of Chinese and native Hawaiian ancestry, Daniel K. Akaka (D–Hawaii) was elected U.S. senator in 1990. In 1999 David Wu

Taiwan-born U.S. Congressman David Wu of Oregon (left) is greeted by Taiwanese President Chen Shui-bian at the Presidential Palace in Taipei.

(D–Ore.) became the first Chinese American ever to serve in the U.S. House; he remained in that office in 2007. In 2003 Bobby Jindal (R–La.) became only the second Asian-Indian American ever elected to Congress; he remained there in 2007. In addition, one representative, Robert Scott (D–Va.), is of Filipino, black, and white ancestry; he has served since 1993. Very few other Asian Americans have ever served in the U.S. Congress.[81]

Advances at the state level have come slowly, although growing numbers of Asian Americans have run for office since the 1990s. In the mid-1990s the state of Washington elected a Chinese American governor, Gary Locke, the first Asian American elected governor outside Hawaii. However, in the mid-2000s, California, whose more than 4 million Asian Americans made up more than 12 percent of its population, had only two Asian American members of Congress (both Japanese American) and seven Asian American members in its state legislature. (In 2004 Van Tran, a Republican, became the first Vietnamese American elected to the California state legislature.) In the mid-2000s only about sixty-seven Asian Americans were serving among the country's approximately 7400 state legislators, less than 1 percent. A majority of Asian American elected officials at the state level serve in Hawaii's legislature or executive branch. A serious lack of representation in government also exists in most local areas with substantial Asian American populations. For example, until 2002, when Chinese American John C. Liu became a councilmember from the district of Queens, no Asian American had ever served on New York City's council. While Asian Americans have had little representation in big-city politics in the past, Asian American leaders forecast imminent changes. The number of candidates for office has grown. Christopher Kui, director of Asian Americans for Equality, has commented on New York City: "It's encouraging to see so many Asian Americans voting and running for City Council in this year's elections, but that's only part of what needs to happen."[82]

Nationally, a large proportion of Asian Americans have immigrated too recently to be eligible to vote, and the registration rate of eligible (native-born and naturalized) Asian Americans has been relatively low, although this is now changing. Some scholars suggest that many Asian Americans have not registered or voted because they come from (or fled) countries with undemocratic political systems, and they still do not trust politicians or political systems. Anti-Asian prejudice and discrimination on the part of white officials and the white public also play a role in the modest level of Asian American political involvement. Participants in Civil Rights Commission conferences have pointed to several barriers to political participation: (1) apportionment policies that dilute the voting strength of Asian American voting blocs; (2) the unavailability of Asian-language election materials; and (3) anti-Asian sentiments among non-Asian voters and in the mass media.[83]

In recent years numerous Asian American voters have faced discrimination at the polls, including faulty translations of candidates' names on ballots, being turned away at the polls because of inadequate voting facilities, racist remarks from poll workers, and a lack of assistance for voters with limited English proficiency. Large proportions of Chinese and Korean American voters in New York City reportedly have this limited proficiency and difficulty in voting. Asian American civil rights groups have recently filed a lawsuit contending discrimination in numerous local voting procedures.[84]

Pan-Asian Organizations and Coalitions

Nineteenth-century and early twentieth-century Asian immigrants, divided by language and cultural differences and historical tensions between their countries of origin, held fast to distinctive cultural identities, resisting the tendency of non-Asian Americans to lump all Asians together. This has remained true for most first-generation immigrants in recent decades. However, among the large number of second- and later-generation Asian Americans, language and cultural barriers are not as significant, and a pan-Asian identity and solidarity have developed in many cities. Beginning on college campuses in the 1960s and spreading to community activists and professional organizations by the 1970s, pan-Asian organizations and news media have helped to forge group consciousness among many students, artists, professionals, and other Asian Americans. This movement to **panethnicity**—*the generalization of solidarity among ethnic subgroups*—is fostered by shared cultural backgrounds, common experiences of racial and ethnic oppression in the United States, and a common interest in fighting that oppression. All Asian American groups have experienced being considered unwanted "foreigners" by other Americans, especially white Americans.[85]

The term *Asian American* has developed since the 1960s, in part because the collective term *Oriental*, with its roots in European colonialism and imperialism, is strongly rejected as erroneous. Asia is East (Oriental) only if the point of reference is Europe. The term *Oriental* has long been associated with white-generated stereotypes of Asian deviousness, passivity, and acquiescence. For many, *Asian American* means respect and empowerment.[86]

Note, too, that not all Asian Americans were empowered by the early pan-Asian movement. Women reported that they were too often restricted to subordinate roles in organizations, and those who challenged sexism in the movement were often ridiculed as "traitors" to Asian American unity. Feeling alienated from the mainstream (mostly white) women's movement, as have other racially oppressed women, Asian American women have formed their own groups within the context of the Asian American identity, often emphasizing their triple oppression based on gender, racial group, and class. Indeed, organizations of racially oppressed women have helped bring the issue of multiple forms of stratification—of race, gender, and class—into sharper focus in recent racial-ethnic scholarship.[87]

Asian American reactions to early pan-Asian movements ranged from support to apprehension and hostility. Not until the 1980s did a national pan-Asian *political* organization specifically address broad Asian American concerns. The first major political effort began in 1986 with the founding of the Asian-American Voters Coalition, which included organizations representing Japanese, Chinese, Asian-Indian, Filipino, Korean, Vietnamese, and Thai Americans. From then to the present day, the organization has sought to consolidate Asian Americans into an effective bloc of voters that can significantly influence elections in states from California to New York; protect Asian Americans' civil rights; and fight anti-Asian legislation, distorted media images, hate crimes, and employment discrimination.[88] Since the 1980s, the Asian Pacific American Legal Center of Southern California, the country's largest legal organization serving Asian–Pacific Americans, has often taken action to protect Asian immigrants' rights, such as the right to speak their own languages in workplaces, and has addressed other important civil rights and community issues.

In the mid-1990s, numerous Asian American (now twenty-one) organizations, including the Japanese American Citizens League and the Organization of Chinese Americans, joined to form the National Council of Asian Pacific Americans (NCAPA). The Council continues to be concerned with such problems as hate crimes, discrimination, immigration rights and restrictions, and the unfair singling out of Asian Americans during various official investigations.[89]

Coalitions with non-Asian groups have also been created. Latino, African, Vietnamese, Korean, Chinese, and other Asian American leaders in Los Angeles created the Multicultural Association for Voter Registration to encourage all people of color to register to vote and become more active politically. Numerous west coast coalitions reflect a growing awareness that cooperation generates greater political power. For example, Korean American community organizations' support for Latino hotel workers' unions involved in a dispute with a Los Angeles hotel owner was hailed by Latino union leaders as a major example of coalition building among people of color.[90]

Chinese Americans

Chinese Americans have had a long history of immigration and have been the most politically active of groups discussed in this chapter. After about 1920, Chinese Americans became increasingly involved in numerous political organizations. Labor-oriented organizations were created, such as in New York's Chinese American communities, where a large concentration of Chinese Americans then lived. Between 1900 and 1930, the Chinese-language newspaper *Chung Sai Yat Po* was an advocate of civil rights for Chinese Americans, including rights of women. The paper's emphasis on political events in China, where the role and status of women were progressing toward equality, contributed to the social awakening of Chinese American women.[91]

With the new immigration after the U.S. immigration reforms of 1965 came renewed political activity. Explaining barriers, Michael Woo, one of relatively few yet to hold a major city government position, has argued that one challenge in getting out the vote is that Chinese and other Asian Americans "traditionally view all political activity as suspect."[92] Earlier, Irving Chin, chair of the

Unionized Asian American health care workers picket for better wages and working conditions in Los Angeles.

Chinatown Advisory Committee to the Borough President of Manhattan, had told a U.S. Senate committee that Chinese American political activity was limited because of problems with English, fear of and lack of familiarity with government, and a traditional reluctance to engage in political action. Ling-chi Wang, chair of Asian American studies at the University of California (Berkeley), spoke to this committee in support of social programs. Wang, sometimes called the "Chinese Martin Luther King, Jr.," has been active in many civil rights causes.[93]

Influenced by Wang and others, immigrant parents pressed a lawsuit for bilingual education in public schools, an effort that resulted in a 1974 U.S. Supreme Court decision ordering such bilingual education. More recently, Wang has been active in efforts to get rid of discriminatory height requirements for police officers and fire fighters, to eliminate disproportionately tough admissions standards for Asian American students at elite universities, and to have SAT-type tests given in Asian languages.[94]

In the 2000s, concerned about a range of local and national issues, including attacks on immigrants, Chinese and other Asian Americans have become more politically active at national and local levels. For example, in mid-2006 Chinese and other Asian Americans organized a protest in New York City against a bill in the U.S. House that made undocumented immigrants into felons. Action on local issues is also increasing. One example is Monterey Park, California, a Los Angeles suburb whose population is predominantly Asian American and Latino. This is one of the largest Chinese American communities, with other Asian American groups well represented. When white council members passed a resolution saying that Monterey Park did not consider itself a sanctuary for "illegal aliens" and that English should be the official language, many Asian American residents were outraged. Some 4000 people signed petitions demanding that the council rescind the resolution, which it did. The controversy indicated a serious rift within the community between fearful whites, who contended that the Asians are not trying "to assimilate" and are "taking over," and Asian Americans who actually seek the traditional middle-class dream.[95]

Chinese Americans are growing in political influence, with a number of "firsts" in the last decade or so. In the 1990s Gary Locke, the son of immigrants, became the first Chinese American to serve as a mainland governor. In 1998 Oregon's David Wu was the first Taiwan-born American to serve in

Congress. In the 2006 election the first Asian American was elected to Connecticut's legislature, Chinese American William Tong. Several Chinese Americans have served on city councils in communities in the Los Angeles area and in San Francisco. In 2006 California elected Leland Yee, the first Asian and Chinese American to serve in its Senate. However, getting political representation remains an uphill battle against racial stereotyping and discrimination. Thus, in the spring of 2001, David Wu and his legislative director, both Chinese Americans, were detained and questioned at a Department of Energy security check-in about their citizenship status and about whether their identification cards were legitimate. Apparently, they did not fit what congressional officials were supposed to look like. Moreover, in 2002 David Chiu, mayor of San Marcos, Texas, lost a runoff election when a letter was circulated by a group called "Citizens for Traditional Values" that called on voters to reject him because he was an immigrant from "Communist China."[96]

Chinese Americans have become increasingly active in national politics and have pressed major political parties to select Chinese candidates. Yet, as we have noted, few Chinese Americans have so far served in the U.S. Congress. Note too that a majority of Chinese Americans usually vote for Democratic Party candidates.

Like other groups with a substantial number of immigrants, Chinese Americans are concerned about U.S. foreign policy. Since the 1980s many have pressed for changes in U.S. government policy toward China. The killing of protesting students in Beijing's Tiananmen Square in 1989 prompted the creation of an organization called the Committee of 100. Headed by influential Chinese Americans, including well-known architect I. M. Pei, the organization has sought to increase cultural exchanges, improve discussions on outsourcing, and change U.S. government policy on China. Many Chinese Americans have pressured the U.S. government to take stronger action to persuade China to improve its human rights policies. Even though there is continuing concern about the Chinese government's authoritarian record, in 2001, Chinese Americans throughout the United States were pleased when Beijing, China, was chosen to host the 2008 Olympic Games. Many Chinese Americans reportedly felt that bringing the world's media to Beijing, and focusing attention on China, would have a beneficial, liberalizing effect on that country.[97]

Filipino Americans

The most successful farm workers' union, the United Farm Workers (see Chapter 8), was created by a merger between a Mexican American organizing drive and a Filipino labor organization, the Agricultural Workers' Organizing Committee (AWOC). These groups conducted a major strike against poor working conditions on grape farms of California. Larry Itliong, head of the AWOC and a Filipino American activist, worked very hard to organize laborers from Alaska to California to South America. Numerous other Filipino labor and political organizations have been created in recent decades.[98]

New resistance tactics have emerged since the 1980s. The National Filipino American Council, an umbrella group of 3000 Filipino social, community, and civil rights groups across the country, has fought for fairer immigration laws. Since the 1990s, Filipino Americans have also held national conferences to generate political strategies to win elected and appointed offices in cities where they make up a significant percentage of the population. For example, at a conference organized by the Council and other Filipino organizations, one issue was getting the Filipino Veterans Equity Act passed, legislation that would finally give Filipino veterans of World War II the veterans' benefits long promised by the U.S. government.[99]

According to one study of 1969–1978 U.S. naturalization data, Filipinos already had one of the highest naturalization rates of any immigrant group. That rate has remained high to the present day. Despite the common stereotyped images of "foreigners," Filipinos and members of other Asian immigrant groups have long been eager to become naturalized U.S. citizens.[100]

In spite of this commitment to becoming citizens, Filipino Americans have rarely been elected or appointed to major political offices, even in areas where their numbers are large. As of mid-2006, the California legislature still had no Filipino members, though the state has a large Filipino population. In 1990 David Valderrama was the *first* Filipino American elected to a state legislature in a mainland state (Maryland). In 1994, Benjamin Cayetano became the *first* Filipino American ever elected to a top state office in the United States, as governor of Hawaii. In recent years a few Filipino Americans have been elected as state senators and representatives, mayors, city council members, and school board members. By 2000 there were about ten Filipino Americans serving in state legislatures in Hawaii, Washington, Ohio, Maryland, and West Virginia. Another dozen served as elected officials in towns and cities, mainly in California. By the mid-2000s numerous Filipino Americans were running for office, yet none had yet made it into mainland gubernatorial positions. As we noted previously, Robert Scott, a member of the House from Virginia, was of partial Filipino descent, the *only* person of Filipino ancestry ever to serve there.[101]

Numerous Filipino American organizations have responded to the Philippine government's call for investment in the islands to overcome economic crises. Again we see global influences on U.S. racial and ethnic groups. In addition, the overthrow of the Ferdinand Marcos dictatorship in the Philippines in the 1980s boosted Filipino American pride. Filipino identity was strengthened by the advent of political democracy there, and that democratic change reinforced the commitment of Filipino Americans to greater political participation in the United States. Significantly, in the late 1990s Filipino American leaders in San Francisco protested the installation of a granite column celebrating Commodore George Dewey's victory over the Spanish in Manila Bay in 1898.[102] Dewey is accurately criticized for bringing U.S. imperialism to the Philippines.

Korean Americans

Korean American political activity has also been inspired by events in the homeland. During the years 1905–1919, Korean Americans were active in the fight for Korean independence from Japan. Only in recent years, however, have Korean Americans gained significant political organization and power in the United States. In 1983 a Korean American Coalition was formed as an advocacy organization seeking to increase Korean American participation in political and civic affairs; recent efforts have accented voter registration, citizenship drives, and community service and educational programs. Although Korean Americans have been active in the Asian-American Voters Coalition, until the early 1990s not one had held major political office in a western state. In 1992 in California, Jay C. Kim became the first and only Korean American—and the first Asian immigrant—ever elected to the U.S. House.[103]

After the 1992 Los Angeles riot, the local Korean American Coalition became active. Jerry Yu, a member of the coalition, noted that during the riot, "Korean Americans really saw with their own eyes the lack of political strength that we as a community have."[104] In the last several presidential elections, Korean and other Asian Americans have become very active in registering voters and in mostly supporting Democratic Party candidates. During the Democratic Party's 1997 inaugural celebrations, 1000 Korean and other Asian Americans attended the first-ever Asian American inaugural ball, an indication of growing political influence.[105]

Periodically, Korean Americans have vigorously demonstrated against discrimination and other mistreatment. Not long after the 1992 Los Angeles riot, in which Korean American businesses were

Calling for rebuilding, Korean Americans protest the destruction of Korean businesses in a major Los Angeles riot.

destroyed, more than 30,000 Korean Americans marched to protest police brutality, lack of justice in the legal system, and media bias. Though it was the largest protest demonstration ever carried out by Asian Americans against injustice, it received little media attention. More recently, in 2006 Korean Americans organized to support a march in Los Angeles against growing anti-immigrant sentiment and legislation, while in other cities (for example, Philadelphia) some political activists organized forums on immigration issues.[106]

Many Korean Americans maintain close ties to Korea. After the 1992 riot, officials from Korea visited riot areas of Los Angeles, arriving even before U.S. presidential candidates in that election year. When North Korea faced serious food shortages in the 1990s, Korean Americans sent more than a million dollars for assistance. In 2001 many Korean Americans signed a petition to the U.S. Secretary of State supporting U.S. government negotiations with the North Korean government to unite Korean families that were divided by the Korean War. Many Korean Americans have relatives in North Korea. In the late 2000s many Korean Americans have become involved in U.S. policy debates over the securing of nuclear weapons by North Korea, fearing that their families might be among the first to suffer if such weapons were ever used.[107]

Vietnamese Americans

The home country also remains important for Vietnamese Americans. In recent years the once icy political relationship between Vietnam and the United States has thawed. By the late 1980s, surveys found half of Vietnamese Americans favoring the establishment of diplomatic ties with Vietnam. The issue of reestablishing ties to a Communist homeland has been a topic of heated debate within Vietnamese American communities, just as it has been in Cuban American communities. Indeed, in the late 1990s many Vietnamese Americans (and others) protested for weeks outside a store in Westminster, California, when the owner put up a Vietnamese flag and a picture of the Communist leader Ho Chi Minh. Others have been successful in getting some city and state governments to replace the current flag of Communist Vietnam with the old South Vietnamese flag when there is need for a Vietnamese flag to be used in the United States.[108]

Like other Asian Americans, Vietnamese Americans are still often stereotyped as "foreigners." In Orange County, California, a group of Vietnamese Americans seeking a permit for a parade to honor Vietnamese war dead was turned down by the council because whites did not consider that to be "American." Vietnamese stores and signs were defaced by white vandals. A white council member remarked, "If they want to be South Vietnamese, go back to South Vietnam." After protests from the community, however, the council member apologized. For a decade, southern California has had an active Vietnamese-American Political Action Committee working for expanded political participation and influence for Vietnamese Americans.[109] As concern over domestic political and economic issues in recent years has replaced the intense anti-Communist views that brought many Vietnamese immigrants to the United States, many Vietnamese Americans have moved their political allegiance from the Republican Party, which they once supported strongly, to the Democratic Party.

In recent decades Vietnamese Americans have created numerous important community organizations and institutions, including Buddhist temples and Vietnamese radio stations. In the 1990s, the Vietnamese Community of Southern California was created to unify some three hundred local Vietnamese American organizations and to develop employment, immigrant, and youth programs. Similar organizations have been created in other areas. Very slowly, Vietnamese Americans are moving into important government positions. For example, in 1997, Thang Nguyen Barrett became a Santa Clara County Municipal Court judge, the first Vietnamese American to serve as a judge in California. In 1992, Tony Lam, a restaurant owner, was elected to the Westminster city council in Orange County and became the *first* Vietnamese American elected to political office in the United States. In 2001 he was serving a third term. Lam came to the United States as a political refugee in the 1970s. Subsequently, Vietnamese Americans have been elected to the city councils of Garden Grove and San Jose in California. In the mid-2000s, Van Tran and Hubert Vo were the first to be elected to the California and Texas legislatures. By 2006, one source estimated that more than a dozen Vietnamese had run for office in California just that year. Still, as of the late 2000s, very few Vietnamese Americans have served as elected officials anywhere in the United States.[110]

Vietnamese Americans have developed important national organizations working for southeast Asian American concerns. One such group, the Southeast Asia Resource Action Center (SEARAC) in Washington, D.C., engages in political action and educational efforts for the Asian American community and has worked particularly on domestic social programs, foreign policy, and immigrant rights and other civil rights issues. SEARAC provides leadership training and technical assistance for numerous community organizations. One program helps local organizations fight mass media stereotyping faced by Asian Americans.[111]

Asian-Indian Americans

Because of their relatively recent arrival in large numbers, Asian Indians have relatively little political visibility. In the history of the U.S. Congress, only two Asian-Indian Americans have served, the first being Californian Dalip Singh Saund, elected in the 1950s. He was also the *first* Asian-American member of Congress. By the 1990s, Asian-Indian Americans were forming organizations designed to increase political influence. Resulting in part from this activity, Pitambar Somani was appointed Ohio's director of health in the mid-1990s, the first Asian Indian to serve in a governor's cabinet. Since then, the number of Asian-Indian Americans running for political office has slowly grown in New Jersey and other states with rapidly increasing Asian-Indian American populations. Recall that in 2003 Jindal (R–La.) became the second Asian Indian American ever in Congress. In 2006 two South Asians were elected to the state legislature of Maryland, and a few others were elected to other state legislatures. Slowly, their representation is increasing. Moreover, in recent decades Asian-Indian Americans have created organizations to fight discrimination. For example, a Hartford, Connecticut, group has pressed for changes in discriminatory licensing requirements for foreign-born physicians and lobbied for government aid for India. This is yet another example of the influence of international context on the political orientations of U.S. immigrant groups.[112]

In the 1990s the New York Taxi Workers Alliance organized a large group of South Asian taxi drivers to protest poor working conditions and poor treatment by city officials. Representing many taxi drivers, the group included Asian Indians as well as taxi drivers from Pakistan and Bangladesh. Faced with twelve-hour shifts, low incomes, and no fringe benefits, the drivers staged a successful strike against officials' attempts to impose unfair regulations on taxis. The strike helped organize drivers from a diverse array of South Asian groups to work together for working conditions. Broad South Asian coalitions such as the Alliance have increased in number. Especially since 9/11, groups have organized to counter the numerous hate crimes committed against South Asians, often because ignorant non-Asians think they are Middle Easterners.[113]

How have pan-Asian organizations and coalitions helped in resisting stereotypes and discrimination?

The Economy

In recent decades the U.S. Civil Rights Commission, among other agencies, has documented the exploitation of Asian and other immigrants, who are often unaware of their rights, by employers who violate laws regarding fair working conditions, wages, and hours. As with other Americans of color, civil rights laws and Supreme Court decisions have often failed to protect Asian American workers from serious discrimination.[114]

Even highly educated Asian immigrants with managerial or professional experience have faced significant barriers. Employers often discount immigrants' experience and credentials. Eventually, some are hired for research, engineering, and other technical positions, yet they remain underrepresented at management levels in most large companies. A 1990s Civil Rights Commission study found that U.S.-born Asian American men with good English proficiency were less likely to hold managerial positions than white men with comparable qualifications. Today, as then, Asian Americans are unlikely to hold top management and professional positions in U.S. corporations. Asian Americans seeking to be directors, top managers, and senior professionals report a significant "glass ceiling." One mid-2000s survey found that just 1 percent of the members of the boards of directors of *Fortune* 500 companies were Asian American—far less than their population percentage of about 5 percent. Only

10 percent of *Fortune* 1000 boards had even one Asian American director. Asian Americans qualified to be directors and top executives face "good old boy networks" and racial stereotyping about their alleged "lack of leadership abilities" and "nerdiness." One study of Asian American managers in California found that they were often seen as docile workers who could be hired and fired at will because they would not complain. Out of frustration, numerous Asian American professionals and lower-level managers have drawn on their own entrepreneurial skills, left major corporations, and started their own companies. Some analysts see this discriminatory situation changing slowly as more corporations expand their business operations into Asian countries.[115]

One 1990s Civil Rights Commission study found discrimination to be even more severe for Asian American women. These workers are vulnerable not only to racial discrimination but also to sexual harassment and other gender discrimination on the job, and many have little knowledge of their legal rights. They are frequently excluded from informal networks of white co-workers and enjoy fewer sources of support than white women when confronted with harassment. The Civil Rights Commission report noted that "because of the stereotypic expectation of compliance and docility, a formal complaint from an Asian American woman might have been considered as a personal affront or challenge." Recent studies in the 2000s have found continuing job problems. Women professionals and other workers often report being channeled into certain jobs seen as appropriate for women, being limited in the training they can do for promotion, and being excluded from critical "good old boy" networks that provide essential job information. Their experiences also include making significantly less than men—and only about 79 percent of the wages of white men.[116]

Discrimination based on physical appearance, language proficiency, or verbal accent is common for a variety of Asian American employees. In the mid-2000s, for example, nine Asian American and Latino plaintiffs sued Abercrombie & Fitch Co. for discrimination. According to a *Current Events* report, they charged that the company's policy of hiring "attractive" employees actually favored "a blond, blue-eyed staff" and discriminated "against people of color in hiring, job assignment, compensation, and termination."[117] Moreover, in a major decision, the Ninth Circuit Court of Appeals upheld an employer's right to consider an applicant's verbal skills when these were relevant to job performance, although the court cautioned employers not to misuse language proficiency to discriminate on the basis of national origin. Numerous Asian and Latin American immigrants are adversely affected by English-only rules in the workplace, many of which are inappropriate because no business necessity for them can be demonstrated.[118]

Chinese Americans

In the nineteenth century, Chinese immigrants were recruited to fill the lower rungs of the U.S. occupational ladder. The first large-scale use of Chinese labor—more than 12,000 workers—was in the construction of the transcontinental railroad, completed in 1869. Early immigrant workers converted swampland in California to farmland; their planting, cultivating, and harvesting skills were used extensively at white-owned vineyards, orchards, and ranches. Chinese factory workers were an important part of the California economy. Most labored long hours in poor working conditions for very low wages. Later on, the demand for large numbers of factory workers in World War II defense plants opened opportunities for Chinese Americans. Between 1940 and 1950, more than one-third of Chinese American men remained in service occupations, but the percentages in craft, technical, and professional occupations more than doubled. War industries also provided increasing numbers of Chinese American women with clerical and technical jobs.[119]

In recent decades, many Chinese immigrants' prospects have not been very good because they lack money, skills, and the ability to speak English well. Most have settled in preexisting urban Chinese American communities, where men typically find service jobs and women work in nonunion garment factories in or near Chinese American residential areas. Working conditions are often substandard or dangerous, and pay is often very low. The better educated among these postwar immigrants—such as engineers, doctors, mathematicians, and scientists trained in China, Taiwan, or the United States—have usually found better jobs in U.S. industries and universities and generally have had an easier time adjusting to their new country than the large number of poorer immigrants.[120]

Globalization of the U.S. economy since the 1970s can be seen in the major growth in high-tech industries, including those on the west coast. U.S. employers' desire for cheaper labor has led many high-tech employers to recruit skilled labor from overseas, especially from China, India, and the Philippines. Attracted by high-tech employment, many new U.S. engineers and medical personnel since 1980 have been immigrants from abroad, often from Asia. Many of these have been educated in overseas colleges and universities oriented to a Western curriculum or have been international students at Western universities.[121] Some have become entrepreneurs, creating high-tech U.S. firms.

By the early 2000s white executives at some major companies doing business in Asia had discovered that hiring Chinese and other Asian American executives for overseas management positions was smarter than sending white executives. One business report notes that "When Starbucks was looking to hire someone to lead its Asia Pacific operation in the late 1990s, it chose Pedro Man, a Canadian Chinese. In 2002, David Wang, a Chinese American, was appointed president of Boeing-China. Many of these newly appointed execs were born in Asia and educated in the West." The article notes that such executives are familiar with Asian and U.S. cultures and can act as human bridges operating "between the two parts of the world." Note, however, that Asian American managers or professionals are much less likely to be chosen to head up major corporate facilities *within* the United States.[122]

Table 11.2 presents the most recent data available on the occupational distribution of the groups considered in this chapter as well as that of whites. (The table includes data only for those who reported only one group for ancestry.)[123] Today, workers who listed only being of Chinese descent in the census survey are heavily concentrated in white-collar and small-business jobs; some 53.9 percent hold professional and managerial positions, a category that apparently includes some small entrepreneurs. (The occupational percentages change only a little when those with partial Chinese ancestry are added.) The proportion of Chinese Americans exceeds that of whites in this category, but whites are more likely to be in higher-paying jobs in this broad category. Chinese Americans are a little more likely to be in blue-collar

TABLE 11.2 Occupational Distribution by Group (2005 Census Survey)

	Chinese American	Filipino American	Korean American	Vietnamese American	Asian-Indian American	White American
Managerial and professional specialty	53.9%	41%	45%	29.8%	61.8%	37.7%
Sales and office occupations	21.2	25.9	28	18.1	21.2	26.8
Construction, extraction, maintenance, and repair occupations	3.0	4.3	3.9	5.9	1.9	9.7
Production, transportation, and material moving occupations	7.2	9.2	8.8	21	7.7	11.6
Service occupations	14.7	19.3	14.3	25	7.3	13.7
Farming, forestry, and fishing	0.0	0.3	0.0	0.3	0.1	0.5
Totals	100%	100%	100%	100.1%	100%	100%

service-sector jobs than whites. (The occupational distribution for people who listed both Chinese ancestry and non-Chinese ancestry is similar.) In the mid-2000s, Chinese Americans' unemployment rate was lower than that of the population as a whole (3.2 percent versus 4.5 percent).[124]

The Chinese American community is represented at both extremes of the economic spectrum. An Wang, former head of his own computer firm, became a billionaire. I. M. Pei is one of the country's leading architects. In recent decades Chinese American novelists have written insightfully about the experiences of their group. One of the first to become well known was Maxine Hong Kingston, whose 1970 novel, *The Woman Warrior*, won major book awards. Amy Tan is perhaps the best-known Chinese American author. Her novel, *The Joy Luck Club*, which became a movie, has helped to stimulate much novel writing on the part of Asian Americans in all the groups covered in this chapter. Kingston and Tan draw on important experiences in Chinese communities, especially on mother–daughter relationships. Maya Lin, the innovative Chinese American architect, designed the National Vietnam Veterans Memorial on the mall in Washington, D.C., while still in her twenties, as well as the major memorial to civil rights workers in Montgomery, Alabama.[125]

At the other end of the economic continuum, however, nearly 10 percent of Chinese American families live below the poverty line. Table 11.3 presents the most recent data available on income and poverty for the Asian American groups (those reporting one country for ancestry).[126] In the mid-2000s, median family income for Chinese Americans families ($71,416) was higher than that of white families. In evaluating these higher median incomes for Asian American groups, however, one should recognize that Asian American families generally have *more workers* per family than whites, as well as more family members. Per-capita incomes thus tend to be *lower* than for whites. The typical Asian American is also more likely to live in an expensive metropolitan area on the west coast (or in New York) than the average white person. In addition, in the mid-2000s the proportion of Chinese American families living in poverty was significantly greater than that of white families. (The data change little when those reporting both Chinese and non-Chinese ancestry are added in.) The economic range is related to length of residence. U.S.-born Chinese Americans tend to be better educated, to hold managerial or professional jobs outside the small-business economy, and to live outside the "Chinatowns" of the larger cities. Recent immigrants are more likely to have less education, be unemployed or hold low-wage jobs, and live in inner cities.[127]

One study of Manhattan's Chinese American community revealed that the area did not fit the common image, sometimes seen on television crime shows such as *NYPD Blue*, of an exotic urban zone with dangerous and mysterious "Orientals" and "red light districts." Instead, it is mostly peopled by hard-working Chinese Americans, many of them immigrants, who have created a booming local economy and a community "that is the center of economic and social life for the Chinese population throughout the New York City metropolitan area."[128] Yet, this community periodically faces urban redevelopment pressures, such as when white officials who view the area in "exotic" terms propose redevelopment projects to "clean up" the area. The

TABLE 11.3 Income Level by Group (2005 Census Survey)

	Chinese American	Filipino American	Korean American	Vietnamese American	Asian-Indian American	White American
Median family income	$71,416	$75,722	$60,498	$54,626	$82,610	$62,300
Below poverty level (families)	9.9%	4.5%	11.2%	12.3%	6.1%	6.3%

community is also shaped by the U.S. government's changing immigration policies.

Economic discrimination faced by Asian Americans takes many forms and affects consumers and businesses as well as workers. A study by Leland Saito examined the redevelopment of a shopping center in Monterey Park, California, which is now a majority Asian American community. The white minority forced an important redevelopment project to be done their way. "Rather than reflecting the city's current and future position as a major node for Asian-themed businesses, the shopping center was remodeled [with a Mediterranean design] to provide a place where whites could shop and 'feel at home.'"[129]

Filipino Americans

Filipinos were first recruited as farm workers for Hawaiian sugar plantations and west coast farms. Most were single men who endured grueling work and meager wages. In the 1930s, thousands, constituting 40 percent of California's Salinas Valley agricultural workforce, formed the Filipino Labor Union (FLU). An FLU-led strike of workers was met with violence from white growers supported by police. Strikers eventually won wages of $0.40 an hour and recognition of the union. "The FLU represented. . . the entrance of Filipinos into the labor movement in America. . . . The involvement of the Filipinos in the labor movement reflected a changing consciousness—a sober recognition of shattered dreams and a new sense of ethnic unity."[130]

Military-related Filipino communities were created on the west coast in the 1950s and 1960s, when U.S. armed forces began recruiting Filipinos into its civilian workforce. For decades U.S. hospitals have recruited Filipino nurses. Many Filipino engineers and other professionals have emigrated because of political and economic crises at home.[131]

Table 11.2 shows a concentration of Americans reporting only Filipino ancestry in white-collar jobs, and they are less heavily represented in professional and managerial positions (which includes some small businesses) and more heavily represented in technical, sales, and administrative support jobs than Chinese Americans. Filipino Americans are more likely to hold service-sector jobs and less likely to hold skilled blue-collar jobs than are whites. (These figures change only slightly when those with partial Filipino ancestry are added in.) Significantly, the mid-2000s unemployment rate for Filipino Americans was lower than that of the general population.[132]

In the mid-2000s Filipino Americans had a relatively high median family income, higher than that for whites ($75,772 versus $62,300). However, again these figures are misleading because on average more family members work among Filipino Americans than in non-Asian population, and most Filipino Americans live on the west coast, where wages and living costs are often higher. This is the case for most Asian American groups. Note too that Filipino Americans have the lowest family poverty rate of any group in Table 11.3. The income and poverty rate figures change only a little ($74,094 and 5.2 percent) when those with partial Filipino ancestry are added in.

For decades Filipino Americans have faced serious job discrimination, including language discrimination. A 1988 lawsuit filed with the Equal Employment Opportunity Commission charged that the San Francisco city government systematically discriminated against Filipino Americans. Statistical data indicated that Filipino Americans held only 1 percent of the city's administrative and supervisory positions although they made up 12 percent of the city's professional workers. Filipino American organizations charged that whites in government stereotyped Filipino American professionals as incapable of leadership and penalized them because of their accents.[133] In the 1990s, a federal judge upheld a Los Angeles hospital's ban on speaking Tagalog, the native language of many Filipinos. The hospital prohibited Filipino nurses from speaking Tagalog, even on breaks. In Hawaii, a Filipino American unsuccessfully sued officials who discriminated against him by turning him down for a white-collar job because of his Filipino accent. Over the 1990s and the 2000s so far, numerous court cases have continued to target English-only workplace rules and discrimination by employers against employees with non-English accents, especially those of native Spanish speakers.[134]

Korean Americans

Language barriers and racial discrimination kept early Korean immigrants from obtaining employment

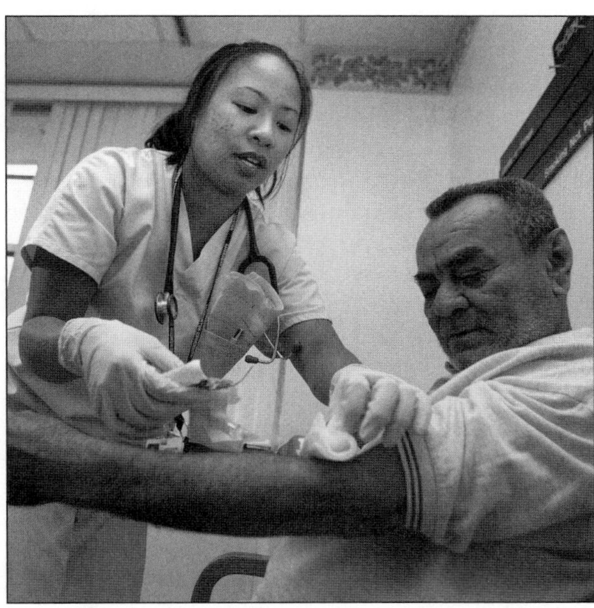

Filipino Americans constitute a large proportion of the nurses in New York area hospitals.
Source: The New York Times

in accordance with their abilities. The early-twentieth-century Korean immigrants engaged in hard labor for low wages. Many, including professionals, worked as agricultural laborers or as dishwashers, housekeepers, or janitors in urban areas.[135] Koreans arriving in recent decades have included scientists and other professionals. A significant percentage have become entrepreneurs, starting small stores, often in low-income areas. With the largest percentage of any Asian or white group being self-employed (24 percent in the 2000 census), Korean Americans have filled an important small-business niche in New York, Philadelphia, Los Angeles, and other large cities. Surveys of Korean American small-business owners have found that few had been small-business owners in Korea; most had held white-collar jobs in their homeland.[136]

Many immigrants have been forced into self-employment because of *exclusion* from professions for which they were trained. Limited English proficiency is one factor, but anti-Asian discrimination is also a reality. Korean Americans holding white-collar jobs are often passed over for promotions, especially to higher management ranks, regardless of language skills. Several news reports have indicated that some managers and professionals have actually moved back to Korea, where their skills allow them to move up the corporate ladders.[137]

Given discriminatory barriers, many prefer the freedom afforded by self-employment. Korean immigrants have arrived at a time when earlier immigrant groups are moving out of the inner-city small-business niche into white-collar jobs. Many immigrants, especially women, have little knowledge of English, and thus their main employment option is a family business. One of the dramatic changes brought by international immigration is the greatly increased participation of Korean women in the workforce, often in family businesses. This participation has had some effect on the strong patriarchal values that immigrants brought with them from Korea. These new roles for Korean American women have often "reduced their husbands' patriarchal authority, creating new sources of marital conflict and sometimes leading to separation and divorce." They have also influenced the preference among growing numbers of Korean women for white men as partners and husbands.[138]

Many Korean immigrants arrived with some capital, and often have the support of the larger Asian American community, including banks. One Los Angeles survey found that those Korean American merchants whose customers are primarily black or Latino earn more than those whose customers are primarily white. Many of these merchants take the money they earn in low-income communities and move out to middle-class areas. Black resentment over Korean merchants taking money out of the black community has contributed to the hostility that many black urbanites feel toward these entrepreneurs. Researchers have found a high degree of geographic mobility among Korean Americans in Los Angeles. Many live for only a short time in a heavily Korean inner-city area before moving out to a suburb. Later on, especially in the 2000s, some (or their adult children) have moved into central-city "Koreatowns" to enjoy the excitement of life there.[139]

Table 11.2 shows that today Americans who report only Korean ancestry are more likely to hold professional and managerial jobs and to hold sales and administrative support jobs than whites. Korean Americans are a little more likely to be in service occupations and less likely to hold skilled blue-collar jobs than whites. In the mid-2000s the unemployment rate for Korean Americans was well below that of the general population. The 2005 median family income for Korean Americans ($60,498) was also below the white median ($62,300). Korean Americans have a relatively high poverty rate among the groups considered in Table 11.3. (These economic figures change only slightly when those with partial Korean ancestry are added in.) In addition, one 2006 report on Korean immigrant workers, nearly 30 percent of whom were undocumented, found that many low-wage service workers—often working in restaurants, groceries, nail salons, construction, and dry cleaning businesses—are seriously exploited by their employers, some of whom are also Asian American. They are often made to work long hours and are not given work benefits to which they are entitled. In addition, because of the significant number of undocumented Korean workers in Korean American communities, there is significant support there for the increased protests in U.S. cities against anti-immigrant legislation.[140]

Vietnamese Americans

Vietnamese Americans have a relatively short history in the United States. Those who came immediately after the fall of Saigon were often more affluent and better educated than those who came later. Some had been in business in their country. After immigrating, however many suffered downward mobility. One survey found that more than six in ten immigrants with white-collar jobs in Vietnam held blue-collar jobs in the United States. The remainder held white-collar jobs, primarily clerical or sales work. Professionals also experienced downward mobility.[141]

Vietnamese Americans still face overt discrimination. In the 1990s, one large convenience store chain settled a class-action lawsuit charging that one of its managers had ordered discrimination against Vietnamese American employees. Two supervisors reported that they had been told to fire Vietnamese workers and hire whites. In the settlement, the company agreed to hire more Vietnamese American managers. Soon, however, the employees of the chain were back in court again, protesting continuing discrimination in some company stores. Vietnamese immigrants and their children have also faced discrimination when they have tried to run a small business. For example, in one recent account a white health inspector, who made openly racist comments like "You yellow people don't know how to run a business," forced a Vietnamese American family to close a business in a small town in Oregon.[142]

Many later Vietnamese immigrants have faced low-wage jobs and poverty. They have not been as economically successful as first arrivals. Table 11.2 shows that in 2005, Americans reporting only Vietnamese ancestry held professional-managerial positions or sales-occupational positions at lower rates than other Asian Americans or whites. Vietnamese Americans held the highest proportion of blue-collar jobs of any of the Asian groups. More than half held blue-collar or service jobs. This occupational situation was reflected in median family income ($54,626), which was substantially below that of European Americans ($62,300) and other large Asian groups (Table 11.3). Nearly one in eight Vietnamese families fell below the poverty line. (These economic data change only slightly when those with partial Vietnamese ancestry are added in.) In the mid-2000s the unemployment rate was slightly lower (at 4.2 percent) than the national population figure but the highest of any Asian group.[143] We should put the economic data into context too: As with other Asian Americans, many live in the relatively high-cost state of California. They also still face racial discrimination in the job market in California and other areas.

Asian-Indian Americans

Most of the country's more than 2.4 million Asian-Indian Americans have roots in relatively recent immigration. Most have not settled in preexisting communities on the west coast like other Asians, but rather have created new neighborhoods, mostly in east coast cities. Many have brought monetary capital and cultural capital in the form of college educations and professional training. Today, the majority are white-collar workers or businesspeople. The rate of creation of Asian-Indian American businesses has been twice that for the country as a whole. By the 1990s, Asian-Indian Americans owned 93,000 U.S. businesses, most in retail trade or services. By the mid-2000s they owned many more. They owned half of all economy lodging properties, including 35 percent of all hotels, as well as 60 percent of convenience stores, across the United States.[144]

Since the 1980s, many skilled Asian-Indian immigrants have gone to California, especially to the high-tech Silicon Valley. Many have prospered in the economic boom there, and one business journal estimates that 35 percent of start-up high-tech firms there are owned by Asian-Indians. However, those with limited work visas have had to return to India; others have scrounged for low-wage jobs in order to remain in the United States.[145]

Americans reporting only Asian-Indian ancestry have by far the largest proportion of college graduates and professional and managerial employees of all Asian–Pacific American groups (Table 11.2). The proportions are also much higher than for whites. According to one estimate, about 38 percent of U.S. doctors are now Asian-Indian, as well as 12 percent of all scientists, including 36 percent of NASA scientists. Reportedly, some 40 percent of New York diamond traders are Asian-Indian. Not surprisingly, thus, in the mid-2000s Asian-Indian Americans had the highest median family income among the Asian groups in Table 11.3. (Occupational and income figures change very little when those with partial Asian-Indian ancestry are included.)[146]

Still, all in this group have not achieved economic success; in the same year, 6.1 percent of families were below the poverty level. About 4 percent were unemployed, a little below the national percentage. Certainly, the large numbers of less well educated Asian-Indian immigrants in Silicon Valley or certain east coast cities, who tend to hold service jobs such as taxi drivers and restaurant workers, have had a much harder economic struggle in recent years than most of the Asian-Indian American professionals and managers who work in the same areas.[147]

What effects have anti-Asian stereotypes and discrimination had on Asian American economic and educational achievements?

Education

In earlier decades, Chinese, Japanese, and other Asian American children were often segregated in separate schools. A 1927 decision by the Supreme Court upheld Mississippi's segregation of children of the "Mongolian race." This segregation began to break down after World War II, but *de facto* school segregation persisted in many cities because discriminatory housing covenants kept Asian Americans out of white residential areas.[148] Still, this overt discrimination did not keep Asian Americans from pressing hard for better educational opportunities.

High Achievement Amid Persisting Problems

Most Asian American groups place heavy stress on educational success. Asian American students have often been overrepresented among students who do well in science competitions, such as the Westinghouse scholars program. However welcome these prizes are to the winners, they are a mixed blessing for Asian Americans as a group. Winning science competitions has reinforced stereotypes of Asian Americans as "naturally" gifted in science fields. Yet, Asian Americans have often criticized such "model minority" stereotypes, pointing out that many Asian Americans excel in areas other than the sciences. Being stereotyped as high achievers also puts a heavy burden on both the achievers and on Asian American students who are not at the top of their class. In addition, many Asian American children, especially poorer children, do not have well-funded educational environments, yet the "model" stereotype reduces the likelihood of government action to meet their needs.

Some Asian Americans, particularly youth growing up in predominantly white suburbs, come to accept these stereotypes themselves. Some have come to view themselves or their group in terms of the white-crafted model minority imagery because it appears only positive. However, these young people often do not understand the ideological purpose for which this stereotyped imagery was created by whites, and acceptance of it may limit their own opportunities and life choices, as well as their ability to work with people of color in coalitions against the continuing racial discrimination faced by all.[149]

Many immigrant children, along with some U.S.–born children of recent immigrants, face problems of limited English proficiency and the shock of an unfamiliar culture when they enter schools. Non-Asian teachers and administrators are often ignorant of Asian cultures and insensitive to the needs of these students. Some teachers have also been unwilling to protect Asian American students

In Austin, Texas, Vietnamese American children work on their geography lesson.

from mistreatment by non-Asian students. In addition, many students from Southeast Asia still have vivid memories of the horrors of war in their homeland; for many, a war-generated posttraumatic stress syndrome may also interfere with success in school.[150]

In one 1990s report the U.S. Civil Rights Commission reported that only a small proportion of limited-English-proficiency Asian American students had teachers who spoke their native languages, despite the legal obligation of public schools to help students develop English proficiency. Contrary to media stories, recent immigrants who are not proficient in English frequently have low grades and high dropout rates. A study of San Diego high school students found that Vietnamese, Cambodian, and Pacific Islander students had higher dropout rates than white students.[151] A late 1990s report of the organization Asian-American/Pacific Islanders in Philanthropy showed that only 1.2 percent of teachers in U.S. schools were Asian American, yet 3.2 percent of the children in these schools were Asian American. School authorities often have shown little concern for these children's language problems or for the hostility they receive from non-Asian children. Studies in the 2000s continue to show similar patterns of low Asian teacher–Asian student ratios, especially for Southeast Asians.[152]

Indeed, public schools in various cities have been settings for substantial hostility against Asian students. One recent survey of research on Korean, Vietnamese, and Hmong students in elementary and secondary schools found that they faced significant racial discrimination. In one study, more than 60 percent of Asian American students "reported that American students were 'mean' to them. Being insulted or laughed at by classmates were cited as reasons for not liking school and lacking friends."[153] They also reported physical atttacks by other students. Similarly, a mid-2000s report found that a New York City high school had "repeatedly denied Asian immigrant students an adequate education by discharging them early, and also had not addressed repeated incidents of hate violence against Chinese and Pakistani immigrant students on school grounds."[154]

Research studies indicate the problems faced by Asian American college students, who may be viewed positively only with regard to their educational achievements. One recent summary of research notes that most stereotypes of Asian American students by non-Asians "are negative, such as non-Asians' perceptions that Asians 'don't speak English well,' 'have accents,' and are 'submissive,' 'sneaky,' 'stingy,' 'greedy,' etc." Such stereotypes create hostile campus climates and, thus, much stress. In addition, anti-Asian hate crimes are also common on numerous college campuses. At the University of California (Davis), a group of whites, including students, beat up five Korean American students while spouting racist epithets. Asian American civil rights organizations, on and off campus, have worked hard to counter such discrimination.[155]

Educational Attainment

Many observers have noted the fact that Asian Americans have higher educational levels than the population as a whole. They are much more likely to have a college degree than the average American.[156] This figure is misleading, however, because of wide variations among the Asian American groups as well as within each group. Using the latest available data for persons over twenty-four years of age, Table 11.4 compares the educational attainment of five groups with that of whites and the total population.[157] Vietnamese Americans ranked the lowest in educational attainment. They were the only Asian group to fall below the national percentage for college completion. While Chinese Americans fell a little below the national percentage for high school graduation, the rate at which this group completed college was nearly double the national rate. Asian-Indian, Korean, Filipino, and Chinese Americans are much more likely to have graduated from college than the general population. (These educational distributions change little when those with partial group ancestries are added.)

Various explanations have been offered to explain much Asian American success in education. Some commentators argue that it is rooted in Asian cultures' traditional reverence for learning or in strong family support. Indeed, in one national Educational Testing Service poll of Asian-Indian high school seniors, every student said that parents had pressed them to secure a college degree. However, most U.S. groups also have high expectations for their youth. There is much more to these educational statistics than too-quick cultural interpretations suggest. When reviewing such statistics, one should keep in mind that the U.S. immigration system now *favors* immigrants with significant education. Many Asian immigrants have come with significant educational or other socioeconomic resources—resources that are important for their own mobility as well as that of their children. In addition, many Asian Americans aggressively pursue education as a weapon against anti-Asian prejudice and discrimination in this society; educational effort has become part of an oppositional culture in which education is viewed as a matter of group achievement and a counter to racial barriers. We should also keep in mind the significant variation in educational access and achievement within Asian American groups, as well as the fact that continuing discrimination in the job market has kept many Asian Americans from achieving the economic success they should have gained based on their abilities and educational achievements.[158]

TABLE 11.4 Educational Attainment by Group (2005 Census Survey)

	Chinese American	Filipino American	Korean American	Vietnamese American	Asian-Indian American	White American	Total Population
Less than high school diploma	17.3%	9.1%	9.3%	27.7%	9.6%	11%	15.8%
High school graduate or more	82.7	90.9	90.7	72.3	90.4	89	84.2
Bachelor's degree or more	52.4	46.8	53.4	25.5	68.2	30	27.2

Asian American educational achievement is often compared, especially by whites, with African American and Latino achievements. However, this comparison is problematical for the reasons just mentioned, as well as for certain geographical reasons. As a group, Asian American students have had greater access to educational institutions, such as those in California cities and suburbs, that have historically facilitated socioeconomic mobility better than many of the public schools attended by many black and Latino students in the states from the Carolinas to New Mexico. In addition, Asian American students in most U.S. metropolitan areas are not as likely as other students of color to be segregated residentially from the white middle-class students whose schools typically have first-rate facilities.

Controversy in Higher Education

In recent decades some elite colleges and universities have reportedly discriminated against Asian American applicants. For example, Ivy League universities began admitting a large percentage of Asian American applicants in the 1970s, but acceptance rates often dropped as the number of Asian American applications increased. Critics accused some universities of using such nonacademic pretexts as lack of alumni parents and the necessity for a regional distribution to exclude Asian American students.[159]

For example, the proportion of Asian Americans among the students admitted at Brown University rose from 2.6 percent for the class of 1979 to 14.8 percent for the class of 1993, although the proportion of Asian American applicants admitted fluctuated between 14 percent and 41 percent during this period. Studying the sharp drop in the proportion of Asian applicants admitted between 1982 and 1983, investigators found that the admissions staff had assigned comparatively low nonacademic ratings to Asian American applicants and had sought to hold steady the number of Asian American students admitted, even though their applicant pool had tripled.[160] Harvard and Yale have faced similar charges of covert discrimination against Asian American applicants.

How does the "model minority" stereotype relate, if at all, to Asian American socioeconomic attainments?

Full Assimilation for Asian Americans?

Assimilation Views

Milton Gordon argued that his assimilation theory applied to a wide range of ethnic and racial groups. While Gordon did not apply his scheme to Asian Americans, other assimilation-oriented analysts have argued that most Asian American groups are on their way to full integration into the Eurocentric core society—at least at the dominant-culture level and at the secondary-structural level in terms of job placement. Assimilation-oriented analysts tend to be optimistic about the eventual thoroughgoing assimilation of Asian American groups, including full incorporation into the U.S. middle class.

Assimilation-oriented analysts have underscored Asian American progress in economic integration. Sociologist Talcott Parsons argued that racial and ethnic inclusion is a powerful and ongoing process in U.S. society, and this includes Americans of color (see Chapter 2). Numerous scholarly analysts of Asian Americans argue that anti-Asian discrimination is collapsing and assimilation into dominant institutions is well underway. For example, some media analysts of Filipino Americans have argued thus. "With a command of English, light brown skin, and Spanish-sounding names, Filipinos have few problems assimilating into American society," asserted James Madore of the *Christian Science Monitor*.[161] Not surprisingly, many assimilation-oriented analysts view Filipino and other Asian Americans as indeed "model minorities." In their view, a non-European group has succeeded when its economic attainments, measured by quantitative socioeconomic indicators of occupation, education, and income, are at least comparable to those of the dominant white group.[162]

Interestingly, the National Asian Pacific American Bar Association (NAPABA) opposed U.S. Supreme Court nominee Clarence Thomas at his 1991 Senate confirmation hearings, in part by challenging Thomas's publicly asserted image of Asian Americans as "model minorities." Thomas argued that Asian Americans "transcended the ravages caused even by harsh legal and social discrimination" and should not be the beneficiaries of affirmative action because they are "overrepresented in key institutions." Then as now, the NAPABA has regularly pointed out the racial hostility and discrimination faced by Asian Americans. In the NAPABA's experienced view, affirmative action programs continue *today* to be critical for diversifying U.S. colleges and universities, as well as to Asian American workers' employment in historically white job categories.[163]

Recall Kitano and Daniels' assimilation model (Chapter 10) distinguishing types of group adaptation: (1) high assimilation, low ethnic identity; (2) high assimilation, high ethnic identity; and (3) low assimilation, high ethnic identity. In this view, Asian Americans who fall into the high assimilation/low ethnic identity category are more "core American" than Asian. Their language, lifestyle, and expectations are more like those of whites, and traditional culture is mostly forgotten. High rates of marriage to non-Asians occur in this group. While a significant (although still modest) proportion of Japanese Americans seem to fall into this Kitano-Daniels category of advanced assimilation, the proportions for the groups in this chapter appear to be smaller.

Those Asian Americans in the high assimilation/high ethnic identity category differ from those in the first because they retain a *strong* group identity. They move easily in and out of both cultures, and their friendship patterns and interests reflect a bicultural perspective. They are usually comfortable with their identity and resist persisting anti-Asian discrimination. A significant proportion of Filipino and Asian-Indian Americans appear to fall into this category. They remain substantially bicultural. One scholar has suggested that Asian-Indian children are constantly operating in two cultures. Most speak English well and are influenced by U.S. pop music and movies, yet also watch Indian movies and often "follow the ways of their elders when it comes to such traditions as marriage and child-rearing." Most Asian-Indian American young people still have a strong sense of their group identity.[164]

One study of Chinese and Japanese Americans found that those in the third and fourth generations were often highly oriented to white middle-class cultural styles. They were assimilated culturally and retained little traditional culture. However, most of these culturally assimilated Asian Americans still had a strong sense of group identity. One reason is that many whites expect them to accept and accent their Asian identity. Unlike white ethnics such as Italian or Polish Americans, Asian Americans do not have a choice, for their racial-ethnic position is constantly imposed on them by whites and other outsiders who ask repeatedly, "What are you?" or "Where are you from?" Answers such as "American" or "New York City" often anger these questioners.[165]

Asian Americans in Kitano and Daniels's third major category, low assimilation/high group identity, are usually recent immigrants or those who have spent their lives in traditional urban enclaves. Most have made some adaptations to the dominant culture but prefer their communities and form friendship and marriage bonds there. Many if not most recent Korean and Vietnamese immigrants fall into this category. A significant proportion of recent Filipino and Chinese immigrants seem modestly assimilated at the cultural level but firmly rooted culturally and socially in their communities.[166] Moreover, tensions between recent immigrants and the native-born are often seen in Asian American communities. Immigrants in Chinese American communities sometimes call the native-born "ABCs" (American-born Chinese). New immigrants criticize ABCs' lack of touch with traditional Chinese culture. In return, native-born Chinese and other Asian Americans sometimes call new immigrants "FOBs" (fresh off boats) and make fun of certain traditional ways that they accent.[167]

The 2000 census found that most adult Asian Americans who spoke a language other than English also reported being linguistically assimilated—that is, they spoke English reasonably well. At an early point, most Asian and Latino immigrants seek to learn and use English. Still, a 1989 survey of Vietnamese American adults in Orange County, California, found that the Vietnamese language was important in most households. Two-thirds also said that their families remained strongly Vietnamese in customs and tradition; three-fourths reported regular contact with relatives in Vietnam. Many were concerned about accelerating their acculturation. One-third said the greatest community need was more English classes.[168]

In Asian American communities generational conflicts are increasingly conspicuous. In recent years, Vietnamese American parents have complained that their children have given up the Vietnamese language, are not interested in entering the family business, and often move from old neighborhoods. For their part, young Vietnamese

Americans today refer to the conflict in the hyphenated term "Vietnamese-American" as "riding the hyphen." A group of Vietnamese American leaders in Garden Grove, California have met to establish an institute of Vietnamese studies to offer courses in Vietnamese language and history. One unstated purpose is to combat a too-rapid assimilation of the younger generation. California's Vietnamese-language radio and television programs also help to keep Vietnamese culture and language alive.[169]

Most first-generation Korean immigrants are also committed to their home-country language and culture and to maintaining close ties to relatives, and they have built strong institutions within their communities. In "Koreatown," in Los Angeles, Korean Americans have created many important institutions, including newspapers, schools, an orchestra, and churches. Religion has often facilitated the adjustment of many Koreans. South Korea has one of the largest Protestant populations of any Asian nation, and many Korean immigrants come as Christians. These immigrants have established many churches, which typically combine Western practices and Korean-language services.[170]

A study by Karen Pyke examined the views that seventy-three children of Korean and Vietnamese immigrants had of family life. Most accepted the dominant U.S. conception of the "normal" family as their framework. They often criticized their parents as too strict or emotionally distant and thought the latter should more closely resemble the "normal" family. These children had assimilated the dominant view of family. However, when they discussed plans for taking care of their parents in later life, they expressed strong traditional Korean and Vietnamese values, described parents' family practices positively, and retained important filial values drawn from their parents. Other studies of Korean American young people have also shown significant assimilation to the dominant culture, especially with regard to language and the popular culture. The adaptation pattern for the children (and probably grandchildren) of these Asian immigrants blends aspects of the culture of origin with aspects of the dominant U.S. culture, as is suggested by Greeley's ethnogenesis perspective. However, such adaptation can be stressful, and a minority of Asian American youth develop mental health problems. One mid-2000s study of Korean, Chinese, and Japanese American high school students found mental health problems for some students who had experienced substantial "cultural stress, such as being caught between two cultures, feeling alienated from both cultures, and having interpersonal conflicts with whites."[171]

Many Asian-Indian Americans are relatively well integrated into the dominant culture. Coming from a country that was once a colony of England, they often know English well, and many reside in predominantly white neighborhoods where children spend much time with white teachers and students. The majority of adults work in predominantly white settings. Most have adopted key aspects of the European American core culture. One study of 629 first-generation Asian-Indian Americans found that most came from urban areas in India and were already exposed to many aspects of U.S. culture through the mass media. The majority spoke English well. The group as a whole scored in the middle range on a cultural assimilation scale that included language use and music, food, and media preferences. Yet, most families maintain essential aspects of traditional culture. The majority still marry within the group. Asian-Indian Americans have built numerous Hindu temples. For example, the Hindu temple in Silicon Valley opened in a warehouse in 1994 with 380 families, but with immigration had grown to 4800 families by the early 2000s.[172] Asian-Indian Americans are generally very acculturated on some dimensions of adaptation and highly Indian on other dimensions. They are indeed straddling two cultures.

One sign of the somewhat slower overall assimilation of most Asian–Pacific groups in this chapter, compared with the assimilation rate for Japanese Americans, may be their lower out-marriage rates to non-Asians. Some 1990 census data showed relatively high out-marriage rates to whites for California's younger-generation Japanese Americans. The rates of out-marriage to whites were generally lower for the younger adults in four other Asian American groups discussed in this chapter.[173] Significantly, an analysis of these census data for California found that interethnic marriages (within the Asian American umbrella group) were increasing.

More recent 2000 census data for California plus all other states reveal an interesting pattern. A recent examination by C. N. Le of national data for Chinese, Korean, Filipino, Vietnamese, and Asian-Indian Americans found that 83 to 90 percent of husbands and 63 to 92 percent of wives had spouses from within their own Asian American group. Another 1 to 4 percent of husbands or wives were married to spouses from other Asian American groups. There was substantial variation in terms of intermarriages with whites, with one-quarter of Korean and Filipino wives having white husbands, but only 4 to 12 percent of Asian-Indian, Vietnamese, and Chinese wives having white husbands. (The percentages of white spouses for husbands were, with the exception of Asian-Indians, significantly lower than for wives, that is, in the 3–10 percent range. The others who were intermarried had black or "other" spouses.) In 2000 the overwhelming majority were married within their own Asian American group; and all groups examined in this chapter were outmarried to whites at lower rates than Japanese Americans (see Chapter 10).[174]

In some areas the rate of marriage within the Asian American umbrella group has grown in recent years, in part because of the now large and growing population of Asian Americans and because of the growing panethnic consciousness among Asian Americans, especially with regard to continuing discriminatory treatment at the hands of others because they are Asian.[175]

Significantly, one recent study of Asian–white interracial relationships in the Southwest found that "contrary to popular utopian celebration of mixed-race marriage as a sign of multiracialization, interracial intimacy is still regulated by racial, gender, class, and national hierarchies." That is, the Asian American women interviewed "saw white men as sources of power through which they might transform their [socioeconomic and gender] marginality" in their communities and the larger society.[176] Thus, Asian and Asian American women sometimes see white men as avenues of liberation and mobility from the patriarchal or modest-income realities of their own backgrounds, even as white men are often attracted to them because of old stereotypes of Asian female docility or exotic sexuality. Clearly, interracial partnering and marriage involving such motivations do not necessarily signal a trend to a more egalitarian and less racist society.

Researcher Nazli Kibria has used the ethnogenesis model to assess the adaptations of Asian groups to each other. Her research on second-generation middle-class Chinese and Korean Americans revealed what she terms a pan-Asian ethnogenesis. Members of each second-generation group are developing a sense of a shared Asian American identity in addition to their country-of-origin identities. The construction of this Asian American identity is a "process that involves recognition of the shared personal experiences and orientations of Asian-origin persons, including that of being racially labeled as Asian by the dominant society, of growing up in an Asian home, and of adhering to the Asian values of an emphasis on family, education, hard work, and respect for elders."[177] However, particular nationality ties, such as Chinese or Korean, are still strong and will likely continue to exist alongside an accent on a shared Asian American identity. In addition, a white-frame-imposed identity of "foreign Asian" cannot be escaped in U.S. society. Being defined as racially different plays a significant role in shaping Asian American identity. Racial consciousness is particularly strong where there has been a recent history of anti-immigrant political campaigns, hate crimes, and white flight.[178]

Some Questions from a Power-Conflict Perspective

Power-conflict analysts of Asian Americans reject numerous aspects of the more optimistic assimilationist perspectives, including much "model minorities" imagery. Among other things, the model minority view ignores the origins of many Asian immigrants who came as middle-class immigrants with good educations and some capital. It also exaggerates Asian American progress and downplays continuing problems with poverty and discrimination.[179]

The image of Asian immigrants is often one of poor immigrants working their way up to success by dint of hard work. However, while they were certainly hard-working, the majority of the Asian immigrants who came between the mid-1960s and the mid-1970s were middle-class people with white-collar backgrounds. Their monetary capital or educational backgrounds often enabled them to establish themselves as middle-class Americans and to provide advantages for their children. In contrast, the Asian immigrants who came after the mid-1970s included more working-class people, many of whom secured low-wage jobs in garment and assembly industries. Asian Americans, "particularly immigrant Asian workers, have a highly visible position in both ends" of the economy. "Despite the fact that a large number of Asian Americans are successful, a disproportionate number of Asian Americans are poor."[180]

Recall from Chapter 10 that, in response to black and Latino American protesting in the 1960s, some whites developed the model minority stereotype to suggest that all Americans of color could achieve the American dream not by protesting discrimination but simply by working as hard as Asian Americans. This negative assessment of African Americans is illustrated in a 1960s *U.S. News & World Report* article entitled "Success Story of One Minority Group in U.S." that compared Chinese Americans and African Americans. By praising the hard work and morality of Chinese Americans, the article implied that if black Americans possessed such virtues (which of course most do), it would not be necessary to spend "hundreds of billions to uplift" them. The article omitted any mention of the widespread racial discrimination.[181]

Power-conflict analysts have shown how, over centuries, powerful whites have positioned non-European groups in the established hierarchy of racial oppression. The earliest and most fundamental of the racial oppressions generated *within* the early colonies themselves, and later *within* the United States, targeted enslaved African Americans brought in to do labor to build up substantial white wealth. Later, white employers brought other non-European groups, including Mexican, Chinese, Japanese, and Filipino immigrants, into the economy as low-wage labor. Whites have evaluated later non-European immigrants and their descendants from within the earlier, well-established framework of white-on-black oppression, with its ideology of white superiority. New immigrant groups are placed, principally by dominant whites, somewhere in the long-established white-to-black hierarchy of exploitation and social status. In white practice and minds, the white rung of this hierarchy is the superior, privileged, and preferred rung, while the black rung is the most inferior, impoverished, and denigrated rung.[182]

At certain times in history, whites have elevated some Asian Americans, as individuals or as groups, from a lower rung to an intermediate rung in this white-to-black hierarchy of status. At least in their images of contemporary society, white leaders and the white public position certain non-European groups in an intermediate, sometimes even near-white, status. This helps maintain an intact but flexible hierarchical system. When white commentators and politicians write positive things about the success of Asian American groups, they usually single out those who are most white-oriented and acculturated. They point to achievements of groups such as middle-class Asian Americans to suggest that the latter are working harder and for that reason succeeding better than most black or Latino Americans.[183]

However, as some power-conflict analysts note, at earlier points in history most Asian Americans were placed on or near the bottom rung of the racial hierarchy for economic and other exploitation—and were thus typed negatively as "black" or "near-black" in status. Frank Wu has noted how historically various racially oppressed people, such as Asian Americans, have often been seen by whites as "constructive blacks," at or near the black end of the racist hierarchy.[184]

Today, in contrast, certain Asian American groups are publicly constructed as "nearer-to-white," but once again often to serve white purposes. Given this construction, whites can then move to criticize African or Latino Americans for not being like the stereotyped Asian American model in efforts and achievements. However, as Gary Okihiro has noted, whites have periodically "upheld Asians as 'near-whites' or 'whiter than whites' in the model minority stereotype, and yet Asians experienced and continue to face white racism 'like blacks' in educational and occupational barriers and ceilings and in anti-Asian abuse and physical violence.... This...'disciplines' both Africans and Asians and constitutes the essential site of Asian American oppression."[185]

The model minority perspective obscures the problems and needs of many Asian Americans who face continuing discrimination, stereotyping, and poverty. For example, many Southeast Asian immigrants, especially those from rural backgrounds with little education, have experienced severe economic strain from the 1980s to the present. Instead of dealing with these difficult socioeconomic realities, the media celebrate particular Asian American individuals who have been successful, even portraying them in "rags-to-riches" terms. For example. Chang-Lin Tien, the distinguished former chancellor of the University of California (Berkeley) is portrayed as a poor immigrant who came to the United States without knowing English. What is less often noted is that he was from a wealthy Chinese family with close ties to the pre-Communist ruler of China, Chiang Kai Shek. Numerous other leading Asian Americans have come from families with substantial economic or educational resources.[186]

Indeed, given the variation in assimilation among Asian groups and subgroups, the segmented assimilation view of analysts such as Min Zhou seems appropriate. Those Asian immigrants with greater family and group resources generally have had a different experience adapting to U.S. society than those with fewer resources, such as the many working-class Vietnamese and Hmong immigrants.[187]

The secondary-structural integration of many Asian Americans into the economy is also not as untroubled as assimilation analysts suggest. Many still suffer racialized discrimination in employment and educational institutions. We have noted the informal quotas sometimes used to reduce Asian American participation, such as those at some universities in the past two decades. Once in a historically white institution, moreover, many Asian Americans report an array of blatant and subtle barriers that are thrown in their paths. In employment settings, for example, many find that the jobs available are not as good as what their educational and experience credentials should have secured. Many Asian Americans excel in college, but they often receive a lower rate of return on their educational investments than whites do. In addition, although many are hired by major companies, many also find that promotions to higher management and upper professional levels are very unlikely.[188]

Optimistic assimilation analysts infrequently discuss in substantial ways the continuing problems of anti-Asian violence. Few pay sufficient attention to continuing racial violence and profiling that handicap Asian Americans and affect long-term assimilation probabilities. Many non-Asian Americans still view Asian Americans in hostile racial terms and as foreigners or even "mud people." We have seen recent violence on both coasts, such as the killing of Joseph Ileto in California and the 2006 killings in Santa Barbara, and the various attacks on Asian-Indian Americans in New Jersey cities. In numerous areas, anti-Asian violence has persisted since the 1990s.

Recall the study of third- and later-generation Chinese and Japanese Americans. Even though most are culturally assimilated, most also have a strong group identity. This is in part because many whites impose the identity of "foreigner" on them. Many view them in racialized terms—as not "real Americans." A power-conflict analyst would suggest that for this reason most Asian Americans will not soon be fully absorbed into the white middle-class mainstream. Analyzing experiences of second-generation Filipinos, Le Espiritu found that they "have to confront simultaneously the political pressure to assimilate and the racism that signals to them that they will never be accepted." They must adapt to the dominant culture, yet maintain some aspects of the home culture, in part because they have never been fully accepted because of their skin color. Research on younger Vietnamese Americans by Hung Cam Thai has found that they, like many younger Asian Americans, try hard to be "American by acting and being white to fit in." The pressure to conform to whiteness is intense, yet conforming does not bring acceptance because of the white racial mindset. Mia Tuan has noted that "Generations of highly acculturated Asian ethnics who speak without an accent have lived in this country, and yet most white Americans have not heard of or ever really seen them. They are America's invisible citizenry."[189]

Asian Americans have long struggled to protect their civil rights and growing political power. In 1992, for example, the Asian American Legal Defense Fund fought hard for an extension of the 1965 Voting Rights Act in order to protect the right of non–English speakers to bilingual election materials. White senators argued that Asian American voters needed no protection, even though the Senate itself, then as now, included not one Asian American from the forty-eight mainland states.[190]

Using assimilation or power-conflict perspectives, how would you explain differences in economic mobility and political achievements among Asian American groups?

Summary

Many Korean, Filipino, Asian-Indian, and Vietnamese Americans—and the newest Chinese Americans—are among the most recent of the immigrant additions to the bubbling U.S. cauldron. Like immigrants before them, they have been targets of much racial prejudice, hostility, and violence. In general, their socioeconomic success has been so significant that several groups have been stereotyped as model minorities. Those who portray Asian Americans thus often have the ulterior motive of criticizing non-Asian groups such as African and Latino Americans for alleged individual or community deficiencies. Assimilation-oriented social scientists are inclined to focus on Asian American socioeconomic progress but to downplay persisting problems of violence, discrimination, and poverty.

From a power-conflict perspective, an Asian American group has not achieved complete success until it can participate fully in the mainstream of the economy, politics, and society without paying higher social, material, and psychological costs than the dominant group.[191] No Asian American group has attained comfortable equality with the oldest white immigrant groups. Physically distinguishable, Asian Americans have remained disadvantaged and have experienced political or economic problems, racist framing, recurrent discrimination, and only modest recent gains in political power.

Immigration has taken "a central position on the American social agenda" and nativist talk and action have focused on regaining "control of U.S. borders."[192] Much white opposition to immigration seems to go beyond the question of immigrants taking jobs to the issue of their racial characteristics, because most recent immigrants have been Asian and Latin American. Asian immigrants continue to be the victims of extensive anti-Asian stereotyping.

However, Asian and Latino immigrants are at the heart of what makes U.S. society great. They are the ones who have supplied much of the energetic imagination and new labor necessary as the older immigrant groups and their descendants age. The hard work and abilities of these new immigrants have helped to make the United States a vigorous nation, yet one that is still very much in the making. The new-immigrant dimension of this process has helped the United States, time and again, to surge out of socioeconomic stagnation into new societal developments and enhanced creativity.

Key Terms

picture brides 307
Orientalism 308
panethnicity 318

CHAPTER 12

Arab and Other Middle Eastern Americans

BIG PICTURE QUESTIONS

- *What role have Arab Americans played in building up this country's wealth and institutions?*
- *What effect has the ideology of* Orientalism *had on U.S. society?*
- *How have Arab Americans challenged U.S. religious and racial stereotypes?*

An Arab American correctional officer at a federal prison in Virginia has described experiences there after the attacks of September 11, 2001 (9/11). An immigrant from Lebanon, he was one of a few Arab Americans working at the prison. Before 9/11 he had suffered some discrimination because of his appearance in this rural area of Virginia, but after the attacks he suffered much more. Fellow employees quit speaking to him, and some told him to "go back where you came from" or "go bomb something—your people are good at that." He was called "camel jockey" and "sand nigger" and endured hate e-mails and a note on his car that said "death to Muslims. In 2003 his office was ransacked and personal records and photos were taken." His superiors would not let him transfer from the facility. "It was degrading. Suddenly I became a second-class citizen. I became a criminal, a target, a person with no rights for something I had nothing to do with."[1]

Middle Eastern Americans

Many people in the United States seem confused about three important categories of Americans that overlap—Middle Eastern Americans, Arab Americans, and Muslim Americans. These are not the same. One of the fastest-growing umbrella groups in the United States, **Middle Eastern Americans**, (*a term for Americans whose ancestry lies in any of the Middle Eastern countries*) is a category now in the process of social formation and one much like other umbrella groups such as Latino Americans and Asian Americans. **Arab Americans** is an umbrella term as well, one that covers *people from numerous Arab countries*. Arab Americans are but one major group within the larger category of Middle Eastern Americans. Within the latter are also non-Arabs, especially Iranian, Turkish, and Pakistani Americans. Both the Middle Eastern and Arab American umbrella categories include Muslim Americans, a religious group, but this designation of Muslim encompasses many people who are not Middle Eastern. These Muslim Americans include many African Americans and South Asian Americans, who make up two-thirds of all U.S. Muslims.

Especially since the events of 9/11, this umbrella group, "Middle Eastern Americans," has become more important. Americans with Middle Eastern ancestry often face violence and other racialized discrimination no matter what country they are from or whether they are Christian or Muslim, Arab or non-Arab. Since 2001 the U.S. government, as well as private agencies, have frequently used "Arab," "Middle Eastern," and "Muslim" interchangeably to name a new political "enemy" and to target these people for an array of discriminatory actions, including unfounded interrogations, arrests, detentions, wiretapping, property seizures, and deportations of those here legitimately. These discriminators have had an effect: By targeting people from the Middle East, discriminators often force those targeted to see themselves as sharing significant experiences, backgrounds, and identities.[2] Indeed, 2000 census data and recent research reveal that a growing number prefer to identify themselves as "Arab American" or "Middle Eastern American" rather than by their specific country of origin, though the latter choice is still that of many.

Consider the three eras of immigration of Middle Eastern and Muslim immigrants. The first Muslim migration, largely unrecognized, came early and involved the involuntary immigration of enslaved people from Muslim societies in Africa. Brought here from the 1600s to the 1800s, they were the first Muslims in what later became the United States. The next period of immigration came much later, between the 1880s and World War II. These immigrants were mostly Arabs from the Middle East, including both Christians and Muslims. In recent decades a third era of immigration has encompassed more Arab immigrants and many non-Arab immigrants from countries such as Iran, Turkey, and Pakistan, many of whom have fled strife in the Middle East.

In this chapter we will not consider in detail non-Arab Middle Eastern groups, but they should be kept in mind as we explore the situations of Arab Americans. For example, Iranian Americans are a large portion of recent Middle Eastern immigrants and a growing U.S. group, one with a significantly different nationality and linguistic background from that of Arab Americans. Their increased presence has helped to create the umbrella designations of both Middle Eastern Americans and Arab Americans.[3]

Arab Americans

Most Americans are not aware that the development of European civilization was heavily influenced by advanced Arab cultures from the tenth to twelfth centuries. In that early period, for example, Arab scholars made critical breakthroughs in mathematics, such as the development of the place-value decimal system, well before European scholars did. They also made major contributions to the sciences, such as optics and medicine, and to seafaring technologies (for example, the compass). Much knowledge developed by Arab scientists and scholars was later imported into European civilizations.[4]

The widespread use of the Arabic language indicates just how far the Arab empire once spread. Today, Arabic is a language spoken by more than 300 million people, the seventh most commonly spoken language. It is spoken in the Middle East and North Africa, Malta, and Sicily, and was spoken in Spain for centuries prior to 1500. Modern Persian (Iran) and Urdu (Pakistan and India) are written in Arabic script, which is also used in parts of China, Russia, and the Philippines. From the eighth century to the fifteenth century, Arab Islamic (Moorish) culture was especially influential in Spain and the Spanish diaspora across the globe. From this Moorish period and other avenues of Arabic influence, some 2400 Arabic-origin words and place names have come into English—such as algebra, almanac, camel, chemistry, cipher, coffee, cotton, jar, mattress, nadir, orange, sofa, syrup, and zero. These reveal the substantial influence of Arab cultures, including Arab sciences and commerce.[5]

Today the Arab World ranges from Mauritania and Morocco in North Africa to Iraq and Saudi Arabia in what is now termed the *Middle East*. It includes countries in the League of Arab States, those with Arabic language and cultures. (Some countries in the Middle East, such as Turkey and Iran, are *not* Arab states but have large Muslim populations.) Although many Americans with origins in Arab countries consider themselves to be Arab Americans, others from these areas—some Lebanese Maronites, Coptic Americans, Armenians, and Chaldean Americans—often do not. They prefer to accent their ethnoreligious origins.[6]

Before the Arab–Israeli conflicts of the 1960s, most immigrants from Arab countries identified themselves by religion, country, or family. After these conflicts, a stronger pan-Arab identity developed in the Middle East. This pan-ethnic Arab identity is also a political reaction to the stereotyping of Arab peoples in the United States and to an anti-Arab tilt by the U.S. government in some Middle Eastern conflicts. Numerous pan-Arab organizations, including the National Association of Arab Americans, the Arab American Institute, and the Arab American University Graduates, have been created since the 1960s conflicts. These groups have spent much time and energy trying to influence U.S. foreign policy with regard to Middle Eastern political-economic issues.[7]

Pan-Arab sentiments are not unique to the United States, nor have they arisen only recently. The concept of pan-Arabism initially developed in the early twentieth century and grew during the 1950s, especially under the influence of President Gamal Abdel Nasser of Egypt. Even with the political, religious, and cultural differences in the Middle East and in the United States, a strong Arab pan-ethnic identity continues to exist in both areas.

TABLE 12.1 Population with Arab Ancestry by Detailed Group: 2000 Census

Detailed Group	Alone*	Alone or in Combination**
Lebanese	244,525	440,279
Egyptian	123,489	142,832
Syrian	75,517	142,897
Palestinian	61,691	72,112
Jordanian	36,104	39,734
Moroccan	30,352	38,923
Iraqi	29,429	37,714
"Arab" or "Arabic"	167,166	205,822
Other Arab	81,754	82,337
Totals	850,027	1,189,731

**Includes people who reported Arab ancestry only, regardless of whether one or more Arab ancestries were reported.*
***This category includes people who reported one or two Arab ancestries and people who reported both Arab and non-Arab ancestry. The total figure is less than the sum of rows because double-ancestry people are tabulated in two rows.*

This chapter focuses on Arab Americans. According to the 2000 census, there are about 1.2 million Americans with some Arab ancestry, with about 850,000 of those reporting only Arab ancestry (Table 12.1).[8] The largest group is Lebanese, while the next largest groups are Egyptian and Syrian. These three groups make up over half the Arab American population. Note, too, that Arab American leaders consider the official U.S. census figure, which only counts people identifying certain Arab country backgrounds, to be a serious undercount, because of methodological weaknesses in census enumeration techniques, Arab American distrust of government surveys, and significant out-marriage. A current estimate of the Arab American Institute Foundation is that there are about 3.5 million Arab Americans.[9]

How have Arab civilizations in the Middle East shaped the development of European and American societies?

Migration

The Early Period

Today, many Arab Americans are immigrants or the children of immigrants. There have been two major periods of immigration from Arab areas and countries to the United States—one from 1880 to 1945, and a second migration from 1946 to the present.

Between 1880 and World War II, immigrants entered in modest numbers. They were primarily Christians from rural villages who, like most immigrants, viewed the United States as a land of opportunity. *Many planned to make some money and return home*, a type of **sojourner immigration**. They were generally from Greater Syria, an area that included what would later be known as Lebanon, Syria, Jordan, and Palestine/Israel. By the 1920s, Arab Americans numbered about 200,000. Their descendants now make up a major proportion of Arab Americans.[10] Significantly, the discriminatory 1924 Immigration Act sharply reduced immigration from the Middle East, as well as from southern Europe and Asia.

Later Immigration

Most Arab immigrants—more than 750,000—have entered the United States since 1967. According to the 2000 census count of the foreign-born Arab American population, nearly half arrived between 1990 and 2000, which compares with 42 percent of the total foreign-born U.S. population. Moroccans, Iraqis, and the census category "other Arabs" are the groups with the largest proportions of recent arrivals, with about 60 percent of each arriving between 1990 and 2000. In addition, many immigrants have fled violent conflicts in the Middle East and Africa. Immigrants have come from at least twenty countries, ranging from Morocco in western Africa to the United Arab Emirates in the Middle East. The 1970s' Lebanese civil war and the 1980s' Israeli invasion of Lebanon generated numerous immigrants, including many Muslims. Yet other immigrants have fled wars between Iraq and Iran and between Iraq and Kuwait, as well as the civil war in Yemen. Many are Palestinians. Whether they are Muslim or Christian, they have often entered with a strong Arab nationalism and a greater inclination to criticize U.S. government policy in the Middle East than earlier immigrants. The largest numbers have been people from Lebanon, Syria, and Egypt, as well as Palestinians. Most have been Muslim. Most have settled in metropolitan areas, especially in Washington, D.C., New York, Chicago, Detroit, and Los Angeles. Indeed, the Arab American population is today more urban than the general U.S. population.[11]

However, since the events of 9/11, immigration authorities have created barriers to Arab immigration. Arab and Muslim immigrants have faced much racial profiling, and U.S. government officials have rejected more Arab visa applications, such as from tourists and businesspeople. Immigration regulations have been violated or applied disproportionately to Arab and Muslim immigrants. After the Homeland Security Act created the Department of Homeland Security, in 2003 the new agency gained control of immigrants and conducted a special registration program for men who had entered the United States legally from twenty-five countries, all but one predominantly Arab or Muslim. These men were required to be photographed and fingerprinted. Although much of this profiling program was soon ended for these Arab immigrants (but not for new entrants coming temporarily from several Arab countries), an array of other U.S. government actions since 2001 have resulted in significant mistreatment of Arab immigrants, mistreatment that groups such as the American-Arab Anti-Discrimination Committee

(ADC) have described as racial profiling and discriminatory.[12]

In recent decades, as we have suggested, most later immigrant groups have more or less coalesced into an Arab American umbrella group, at least for key social and political goals. Most third-generation descendants of earlier Greater Syrian immigrants have also come to see themselves as Arab Americans. One Detroit study surveyed leaders of Middle Eastern (including Arab) organizations to discern if there were cultural traits shared across diverse Middle Eastern groups. The research found that most stressed the importance of extended kinship networks. One respondent commented, "The most important [thing] in our tradition is respect for the family. And closeness of family."[13] Thus, Middle Eastern leaders, and presumably the immigrants they represent, have been concerned that U.S. culture tends to break up families through divorce and too-lenient supervision of children.

Many of these Detroit respondents mentioned religion, which has been central to Arab and other Middle Eastern cultures. Most Arab Americans come from backgrounds with a "common language, tradition, cultural traits, and values," even though they have diverse national identities.[14] Although there are differences (such as in marriage practices) within the Arab American community between Christians, Muslims, and Jews, the dominant society's anti-Arab stereotypes and hostility have provided pressures that tend to unite the Arab American community. In addition to family and religion, other cultural traits accented by this midwestern study's respondents included an emphasis on tracing ancestry to Arab or Middle Eastern lands, an orientation to Arabic and other Middle Eastern languages, and a strong commitment to entrepreneurship to build strong community economies.[15] Americans from Arab and other Middle Eastern areas may have different physical features and religious backgrounds but often share certain cultural traits and political concerns. Still, only in a loose way can one speak of an umbrella groups called "Arab Americans" or "Middle Eastern Americans."

What are the consequences of racial profiling for Arab Americans and the larger society?

Stereotyping and Prejudice

Classified as an "Inferior Race"

In the first period of Arab immigration, U.S. officials sometimes classified these immigrants as "Turks" and sometimes as "Syrians." Judges, too, were confused about how to classify them. Between 1909 and 1944 at least eight court decisions legally assessed whether certain Arab Americans were "white." Four ruled that they were white and four ruled that, by "common knowledge" or "legal precedent," they should *not* be considered white. Thus, in 1914 a South Carolina court ruled that while a Syrian immigrant "may be Caucasian," he or she was *not* what the 1790 Naturalization Act called a "free white person"—and thus could not become a U.S. citizen. In 1915 this decision was reversed on the grounds that the relevant laws were those of 1873 and 1875, which allowed Syrians to be considered enough like Europeans to be officially "white." Later decisions would sometimes disagree, asserting that Arab Americans were not white.[16]

The right of Arab immigrants to citizenship and to claim whiteness continued to be challenged in many institutional arenas, including courts, at least until the 1940s. Racist writers of the early twentieth century saw them as "parasites" and "Mongolian plasma" that would "contaminate the pure American stock."[17] Syrian immigrants were cataloged with southern and eastern Europeans as "inferior races" by leading European American intellectuals such as Madison Grant. Nativists termed Syrians the "most foreign" of immigrants. Many suffered extreme stereotypes and related notions that many whites drew from the entrenched white racist frame, including derogatory terms such as "blackie," "camel jockey," and "sheeny."[18]

Recent Stereotyping and U.S. Politics

Strong negative images of Arab Americans and other Middle Eastern Americans have been circulating among other Americans for decades now. For example, a 1975 undergraduate guide at Columbia University described one Arabic course by suggesting that every other word in Arabic was about violence and that this signaled the character of the Arab mind.[19] One survey of portraits of Arab peoples in U.S. textbooks reported that they portrayed Arabs as ignorant about other peoples and anti-Jewish sentiment as the link holding diverse Arab peoples together. A 1981 survey of Americans found that 44 percent of respondents considered Arabs to be "barbaric" or "cruel," while about half thought they were "treacherous" or "cunning." More than half thought they were "warlike" and that men "mistreat women."[20]

A 2006 national *USA Today*/Gallup survey found that many Americans still hold negative stereotypes and favor discrimination against Muslim Americans, many of whom are Arab Americans. Four in ten openly admitted they were prejudiced against Muslims. More than four in ten thought Muslims were extreme in their religious beliefs, and a majority felt they were not respectful of women. Some 31 percent admitted that they would be fearful if they saw a Muslim man on a plane with them. Given these negative and fearful views, it is not surprising that one-fifth said they would oppose a Muslim as a neighbor and that 40 percent favored discriminatory security measures—such as Muslims being required to carry special identification and being searched more thoroughly at airports.[21]

Since the 1960s, U.S. government policies regarding the Middle East have generated or accelerated the spread of negative stereotypes of Arabs and Arab Americans. For example, Terrel Bell, Ronald Reagan's Secretary of Education, reported that in the 1980s mid-level aides in the White House and other government agencies made racist comments about Arab peoples as "sand niggers," as well as similar derogatory comments about African Americans. These racist perspectives were at the time linked to an intentional government weakening of enforcement of U.S. civil rights laws.[22] The common labeling of Arab and other Middle Eastern peoples with old terms such as "camel jockeys" and "sand niggers" during the Gulf War of the early 1990s and more recent Middle Eastern conflicts has helped to rationalize U.S. interventions overseas in the minds of many non–Middle Eastern Americans.

Today, as in the past, political figures in the Middle East are sometimes characterized in biologically racist terms. Cartoons have long shown Arab leaders as evildoers with "sharply hooked noses" and a "mustachioed leer." The late Palestinian leader Yasser Arafat was portrayed by leading U.S. newspapers as having "pendulous lips," and other Arab leaders have been portrayed in the media and on the Internet as having "beak-like noses." These portrayals are similar to old anti-Jewish stereotypes.[23] The media have stereotyped Arab men as militaristic extremists and Arab women as distinctively servile. The stereotyping in such anti-Arab views is underscored in Evelyn Shakir's comments on her family: "Terrorist, oil sheik, master of the seraglio—it was impossible for me to connect these terms with my uncle who baked blueberry muffins for his wife's breakfast and washed out her underthings by hand, or with my other uncle who belonged to the Rotary Club, voted Republican, and was a deacon in the Baptist church."[24] Note, thus, the *omission* from much of the mass media of positive images of Arab and other Middle Eastern Americans. As the scholar Karyn McKinney Marvasti has put it recently, "So the only cultural resources 'average' Americans have to draw on in thinking about these groups are the negative, 'terrorist' images they've seen the most. This is particularly likely since relatively few non-Arab Americans have Arab American neighbors and friends."[25]

Television programs and the movies have often circulated harshly stereotyped images of "male terrorists" or "veiled, dominated women" and have largely ignored important differences among Middle Eastern peoples. The influential Arab scholar, Edward Said, famously described the negative and stereotyped views of Middle Eastern peoples as a western ideology of *Orientalism*. Orientalism targets Middle Eastern and Asian peoples with many hostile stereotypes and goes back centuries in Western thought, pervading much scholarly work as well as popular thinking. Viewing U.S. immigrants from the Middle East and Asia as "threatening foreigners" or "deviants" allows those who target them to view discrimination against them as actually "patriotic" and "pro-American."[26]

Challenging Stereotyping

Until recently, few U.S. leaders outside Middle Eastern American communities have been willing to challenge these racialized images. In a speech to the 1984 Democratic Party national convention, Jesse Jackson, an African American leader, was perhaps the first major U.S. political leader to speak publicly of Arab Americans in strongly positive terms and as a people facing the "pain and hurt of racial and religious rejection." Yet, Jackson paid a price for speaking out against this stereotyping. For a time, whenever he spoke positively about Arab Americans or questioned what he saw as one-sided U.S. government policy favoring Israel in Arab–Israeli conflicts, Jackson was attacked in the media or by other politicians.[27]

In one survey, Arab and other Middle Eastern American leaders expressed concern about the common stereotyping and discrimination directed at their communities. They cited the frequency of negative images of Muslims as well as the infrequency of positive commentaries in the media. These leaders noted that among Arab Americans, those of the Muslim faith are the most likely to be targets of overt hostility and discrimination. They also noted that those who possess the physical or cultural traits associated with Arab or Middle Eastern Americans in the minds of other Americans are more likely to be targeted for hostility than those who do not fit these images.[28]

Stereotypes and Arab American Women

Arab and Arab American women, as well as women from other Middle Eastern countries, have faced a range of stereotypes in the United States. They have frequently been portrayed as exotic, passive, or totally dominated by men, with the latter frequently being stereotyped as hot-tempered bullies. The religion of Islam and Arab culture are often viewed as extremely oppressive of women. For decades, numerous Western writers have circulated the notion that marital arrangements such as the "harem" are typical of some Arab societies, when in fact such arrangements of several wives have never involved more than a small elite in a few countries. The "harem" has been much more important in European fantasy than in the real world of contemporary Arab societies.[29]

The reality of life for Arab women in the many Arab countries and the United States is more varied and should be put in a comparative context. For example, several Arab and other Middle Eastern countries—such as Iraq, Pakistan, Afghanistan, and Tunisia—have a *greater percentage* of women in their governing bodies than the United States. Women in numerous Arab countries do face issues of an imposed *hijab* or *burka*—that is, covering clothing—though in many cases they themselves choose such covering out of respect for traditions or to be liberated from a "sex object" status in society. The issues here are often complex. As one scholar has noted, "many veiled women report feeling full of dignity and self-esteem and enjoy that their physical, personal self does not enter into social interactions." In addition, indigenous feminist movements in Middle Eastern societies are currently pressing to reduce barriers and improve the lives of women therein. We should note, too, that U.S. women are not "free" of gender domination. They face being objectified in an often extreme form that accents a certain image of (for example, bikini-clad, white, or thin) female beauty, which leads to pressure to diet in extreme ways or have cosmetic surgery to meet a socially constructed, usually male-oriented image. Historically, most women in Arab societies have lived under strong patriarchal conditions, yet this condition of strong patriarchal dominance has been characteristic of most non-Arab families in Western societies until recent decades. Many U.S. families are today strongly patriarchal, especially those most firmly situated in conservative religious (Christian or Jewish) traditions. In addition, today, as in the past, when it comes to everyday decisions, many wives and mothers in Arab families have substantial decision-making power.[30]

Generally speaking, traditional values in Arab countries have emphasized family honor and stipulated that women be modest and protected when around male strangers. For Arab American women, this gendered value system sometimes comes into conflict with prevailing U.S. values relating to such behaviors as dating or patriarchy. Some Arab American women "have engaged in outright rebellion against their parents' or husbands' authority. Others have been able to invoke traditional values to justify unconventional behavior; in the name of service to family and community, much has been permitted."[31] Over time, many Arab American women have gained greater autonomy, sometimes creating tensions in their families. Moreover, women are particularly important to the persistence of Arab culture in the United States; some studies have found them to be the "anchor of the group's sense of identity."[32]

The centrality of a certain body imagery in the U.S. media—such as that of the often thin, light-skinned, or blonde models in advertising—creates problems for Arab American women. As a result, "dark pigmentation and, especially, dark body hair, have been sources of shame to [Arab American] girls growing up in the United States." Some feminist groups have emerged among Arab American women, in part because of their concern with the common U.S. image of ideal female beauty.[33]

How have U.S. government policies regarding the Middle East shaped the spread of racial and ethnic stereotypes?

Oppression, Discrimination, and Conflict

Early Discrimination

The early Arab immigrants and their children sometimes faced a clearly racialized discrimination, especially in southern areas where whites often classified them with African Americans. Considered to be "not white," Arab Americans were sometimes turned away from voting places, restaurants, and rest rooms by racist whites in various southern and border states.[34] Across the country as a whole they faced less discrimination than did African Americans, but they were nonetheless often seen by others as not being white.

Current Patterns of Discrimination

Although the U.S. Census Bureau now defines Arab immigrants and their descendants as "white," many non-Arab Americans still view them as "not white." Indeed, one recent survey of college students found that *just 5 percent* felt that the group termed "Arab Americans" was unambiguously white, with only 7 percent indicating that the group termed "Middle Eastern Americans" was white. For a majority of these well-educated (self-identified) white Americans, Arab Americans are not considered as white. Classification as "white, non-European" by the U.S. Census Bureau has not prevented continuing racial imaging, prejudice, and discrimination.[35]

For decades, to the present day, discrimination has been a problem. The Council on American-Islamic Relations (CAIR) has dealt with many complaints of employment discrimination faced by millions of Arab and Muslim Americans. For example, CAIR reported a significant increase in job discrimination and other civil rights complaints in 2005, altogether 1972 as compared with 1522 in the previous year. (These are likely just the tip of the iceberg according to Arab American officials.) The largest number of these were in California. A mid-2000s research study by the Discrimination Research Center sent some 6000 fictitious job résumés from qualified applicants to a variety of California employers. An identifiably Middle Eastern name, Abdul-Aziz Mansour, got the lowest response rate.[36]

The array of contemporary discrimination is broad, from being forced to endure racist jokes, cartoons, and e-mails from fellow employees to not being hired or promoted because of Islamic religious observance or wearing traditional religious dress, to being taunted by people on the street on the way to work or school. Many cases of employer discrimination involve workplace prohibitions against religious practices, such as not allowing Muslim men to wear beards in the workplace, not permitting Muslim women to wear the *hijab*, or not permitting daily prayers. Protests against this discrimination by CAIR and other Middle Eastern American organizations has led to the rehiring of some employees who were mistreated or fired for such practices. Discrimination also affects Arab Americans in the U.S. legal system. Some lawyers have feared going to jury trials for Arab American clients because of negative depictions of Arab peoples in the media.[37] Unlike older white ethnic groups, most Arab Americans do not yet have the choice of escaping their racial and ethnic identities, even if they wished to do so.

International Politics and Discrimination

The commonplace "Orientalist" distortions of Arab and other Middle Eastern peoples have serious implications for U.S. government policies regarding overseas matters. This is especially true for U.S. policies in the Middle East, a region where the U.S. government has long been heavily invested, in part because of its continuing concern for oil supplies. For decades U.S. policymakers in Washington, D.C., and U.S. diplomats in the Middle East have often not been well informed about the region's history or cultures. Edward Said's earlier assessment is still accurate today: "The Middle East experts who advise policymakers are imbued with Orientalism almost to a person.... If in the meantime the Arabs, the Muslims, or the Third and Fourth Worlds go unexpected ways after all, we will not be surprised to have an Orientalist tell us that this testifies to the incorrigibility of Orientals and therefore proves that they are not to be trusted."[38] Such Orientalist views have become conspicuous recently in various U.S. interventions in the Middle East, such as in Iraq. That U.S. invasion and occupation of a sovereign country was conducted mostly by people with little accurate knowledge of that country (or region), little or no ability to speak local languages, and a propensity to stereotype those there as backward.

Much recent discrimination, including violent attacks on Arab Americans, is linked to international issues and conflicts and to stereotypes held by many non-Arab Americans. Since the 1960s, the United States has had a "negative atmosphere for Americans of Arab descent, due to the stereotyping, harassment, defamation, and exclusion of Arab Americans brought on by the widespread perception of Arabs as immigrants from hostile, enemy lands."[39] For example, influenced by this negative perception, President Richard Nixon responded to the 1972 killing of Israeli athletes in Germany by some Palestinians by establishing a secret government operation targeting people of "Arab ancestry." Although the attacks on Israelis had nothing to do with the United States, the CIA and the FBI collected information on Arab Americans and harassed thousands.[40]

The anti-Arab stereotyping has persisted since the 1970s, at the highest levels of the government. The 1990s Anti-Terrorism and Effective Death Penalty Act and the Illegal Immigration Reform and Immigrant Responsibility Act have given federal authorities powers to detain and interrogate immigrants suspected of being linked to terrorist organizations, without the usual civil rights protection such as the right to a speedy and fair hearing at which the evidence for detention is presented. These and more recent laws have often been used in discriminatory ways against U.S. immigrants and citizens with Arab or Muslim backgrounds, or those Americans who look like they might be Arab or Muslim (but are not).[41] As we have noted in the chapters on Japanese and Italian Americans, in the past some U.S. citizens have been viewed by their government as guilty until proven innocent, in contradiction to U.S. law, and only because of their racial or ethnic backgrounds.

Since the 1970s, Arab American community activists, especially those who critical views of U.S. government policies, have been targets of harassment and violence. Some have received threatening phone calls, had property vandalized, or found dead animals on their front steps. In 1985 a regional director for one Arab American organization was killed by a bomb at his office. Some police authorities attributed the bombing to the extremist Jewish Defense League, which did express satisfaction at the bombing. In addition, the U.S. government has periodically conducted overt investigations or secret surveillance operations targeting Arab Americans solely because of their ancestry, appearance, or political views.[42]

U.S. involvement in the Middle East, especially in ongoing conflicts and the invasions of Iraq, has periodically generated outbreaks of overt hostility and violence against Arab Americans in the United States. Hate crimes often seem linked to media reports of particular events. Since the late 1980s, and increasingly since 2001, some Islamic mosques have been bombed or set on fire, and others have been vandalized. Many physical attacks on Americans of Middle Eastern descent took place following the 1991 Gulf War. In the early 1990s more than 150 anti-Arab hate crimes were reported to police. Since that war, Arab Americans have been blamed for events such as the April 1995 Oklahoma City bombing plot targeting a federal building by white terrorist Timothy McVeigh and his white associates. In the days after that bombing, there were more than two hundred attacks on Arab and Muslim Americans. More recently, the attacks and other discrimination have continued. In 2005 CAIR alone received 141 reports of actual or threatened violence against Muslim Americans, adding to more than a thousand such incidents since 2001. In addition, one poll found that since 2001 nearly three-quarters of Muslim respondents had experienced anti-Muslim harassment or physical attack, or knew someone who had experienced that. And a poll of Arab Americans found that nearly 30 percent had endured some discrimination, and also that one-third had not traveled by air since 2001 for fear of such discrimination. Since 2001 many Arab and other Middle Eastern Americans have reacted to these hate crimes, and their own experiences with related types of hostility, by changing the way they dress, talk about social and political matters, and practice their religion.[43]

In addition, in the 1990s the FBI and the Immigration and Naturalization Service developed a plan to imprison Arab Americans in the event of a war between the United States and Arab countries.[44] Apparently, federal government agencies have not yet learned the lessons that became clear during the 1940s imprisonment of Japanese American citizens solely because of their racial characteristics. Persisting into the present, government actions based on racial stereotyping are not only unconstitutional, but a violation of international human rights treaties. Historically, they have also not enhanced national security (see Chapter 10).

The Effects of the Attacks on the World Trade Center and the Pentagon: 2001 and After

The September 11, 2001, attacks by Middle Eastern terrorists—who were apparently angry about U.S. policies in the Middle East—on the World Trade Center and the Pentagon generated many hate crimes against Arab Americans or those who were thought to look like Arabs. Such crimes were principally about stereotyping and ignorance, for they were committed in spite of the fact that no Arab American citizen was implicated in the attacks and that seventeen of the nineteen men involved were from Saudi Arabia and the United Arab Emirates, countries of origin for few Arab Americans (and, ironically, close allies of the U.S. government in the Middle East that have as yet suffered no serious repercussions for the attacks). In nine weeks after September 11, there were at least 520 violent attacks on people thought to be of Arab or Middle Eastern ancestry. These attacks included assaults, arson, and six murders. Some of those assaulted or killed were not Arab but were assumed to be so by ignorant attackers. In addition, hundreds of cases of employment discrimination were reported in this brief period, as well as increased discrimination in the form of racial profiling and other discrimination by law enforcement and airline personnel. Since this 2001 report, as we noted previously, many more cases of violent discrimination, employment discrimination, and racial profiling targeting Arab Americans have also been documented.[45]

In addition, the 2001 USA Patriot Act, passed quickly after the 9/11 attacks, gave the federal government broad authority to detain noncitizens with little or no due process and to carry out searches and surveillance with less judicial review. Many Americans concerned about civil liberties feared that laws said to be designed to reduce the possibility of terrorism would be used to target selected immigrants, particularly those who looked like Middle Eastern Americans. As the American-Arab Anti-Discrimination Committee put it, "These serious civil liberties concerns should be alarming to all Americans, but there can be little doubt that it is the Arab American and Muslim communities who are facing the gravest threats to their rights and that these communities will bear the brunt of any major diminution of civil liberties in the United States."[46]

This assessment has been accurate, to the present day. Many Arab and other Middle Eastern Americans have been targeted by federal agents and private security personnel in recent years because of the way they look. They have been removed from airliners. In one recent case Muslim religious officials *(imams)* were taken off a plane just because they were praying. This surveillance problem has become so general that Arab Americans have a term for it—"FWA," for "flying while Arab." In addition, the FBI, among other police agencies, has targeted Islamic mosques since 9/11, but has apparently not done the same surveillance of conservative Christian churches, a few of whose members have been linked to various terrorist acts in the United States. Much surveillance of Muslim Americans assumes a fallacious connection between their everyday religion and certain terrorist actions. One should also recognize that the "actions of the September 11 terrorists are not condoned under Islamic law."[47]

Taking Action Against Discrimination

Arab Americans have taken action against some of this stereotyping and discrimination. Lawsuits by civil rights groups such as the American Arab Anti-Discrimination Committee have criticized the Homeland Security Department for using racial profiling to target Middle Eastern entrants into the United States. Civil rights protests have been aimed at the Chicago *Sun-Times* newspaper for stereotyping Arabs and for neglecting reporting on the Arab American community. Arab American groups organized a

People celebrate at the Arab American International Festival in Michigan.

boycott of the paper; protests called attention to editorials that claimed the late Palestinian Authority leader Yasser Arafat was primarily responsible for Middle Eastern violence. Antidiscrimination groups have protested several movies such as *The Siege* (1998), which shows Arabs as terrorists and a threat to the United States, further feeding stereotyped images. The film directly links Islam to terrorism, showing Muslim rituals being conducted before acts of violence. Hala Maksoud, head of an antidiscrimination organization, described this film as "insidious, dangerous, and incendiary" and as inciting "hate which leads to harassment, intimidation, discrimination, and even hate crimes."[48]

Many Arab Americans, and especially civil rights organizations such as CAIR, are taking action against anti-Arab and anti-Muslim discrimination. Various strategies are used. For example, CAIR often attempts mediation with employers to make them more sensitive to the religious needs of their Arab and other Muslim employees. If that fails, they may go to court.[49]

Local Conflict and Cooperation with Other Groups

In areas such as Detroit, where Arab Americans have established many small businesses, periodic conflicts with other racial and ethnic groups have occurred. Some black groups have reported that the relatively new Arab American merchants sometimes treat black customers with disrespect or discrimination. Arab American merchants have complained that black youngsters sometimes steal from their stores. This conflict is reminiscent of similar conflicts between Korean (or, earlier, Jewish) merchants and African American residents. Some local efforts—for example, at Detroit's Wayne State University and on Youth Day at Belle Isle in Detroit—have been directed at improving communication between the African American and Arab American communities.[50]

In recent years some local Jewish American and Arab American groups have made substantial efforts to increase contacts and dialogue. For example, in Chicago, members of the Arab-American Bar Association and the Decalogue Society of Jewish lawyers have committed themselves to more positive intergroup contacts, especially among young people. In addition, groups of New York Muslims, Jews, and Arab Christians, including religious leaders, have met to work for increasing understanding between these groups and to reduce local interpersonal and intergroup violence.[51]

What strategies of resistance have Arab Americans used to counter stereotyping and discrimination?

Politics and Political Emergence

Gradual Increase in Political Activity

By the 1930s a few Syrian Americans held elected public office, but it was not until 1958 that the first Arab American was elected to Congress. Greater political representation has come slowly. The first U.S. senator of Arab descent, South Dakota's James Abourezk, was not elected until 1980. By the late 1980s a few Arab Americans were named to major appointed positions in government, including White House chief of staff. Over the past decade or two, a modest number of Arab Americans have moved into positions of influence in the U.S. political system.

Recent Political Involvement

In the fall of 2000, a majority of New York City's council members passed a resolution on the Palestinian–Israeli conflict that condemned Palestinian violence and called the Palestinian leader a terrorist but did not criticize Israel's violent role in the continuing conflict. Several council members left that meeting in protest over its one-sided character.[52] Such protests show again how international tensions spill over into local and national politics.

Arab and Muslim Americans have increased their political activity significantly since 1990. Major voter registration drives by Arab American organizations have led to a substantial increase in Arab voter participation. Nearly 90 percent are now registered to vote, and surveys suggest that these U.S. citizens pay more attention to politics and donate to political campaigns more than people in numerous other groups. Numerous Arab and Muslim Americans have been elected at state and local levels across the country. So far, the political campaigns of the 2000s have seen many Muslim and Arab American political candidates, more than ever. In the 2006 election, from California to Michigan to West Virginia and Connecticut, thirty Arab Americans ran for local and state positions, such as those in state legislatures, and eighteen were elected to office. These included John Baldacci, as governor of Maine. In addition, some Arab Americans have been appointed as ambassadors and placed on national and local political commissions. The presence of Arab American officials has had an effect in both large and small ways. For example, there is now a Friday (Muslim) prayer service held by two dozen congressional aides in the Capitol building, and more attention is being given to the Arab American view of ongoing Middle Eastern conflicts.[53]

For the first time, in 2000 both Republican and Democratic national conventions had Muslim clergy giving prayers. In the November 2000 and 2004 elections there were many Arab American voters, mostly located in New Jersey, Ohio, Pennsylvania, and Michigan. In these presidential elections, states with significant numbers of Arab and Muslim American voters, such as Michigan, received substantial attention from presidential candidates. Candidate George W. Bush consulted with Islamic leaders in Michigan, where the Muslim community supported him in his 2000 presidential bid. (They shifted away from Bush significantly in his 2004 reelection campaign because of concerns over racial profiling and other discrimination by federal agencies.) As president, Bush appointed Arab Americans Spencer Abraham (Energy Secretary) and Mitchell Daniels (Director of the Office of Management and Budget) to his cabinet. (Donna Shalala was the first Arab American to serve in a presidential cabinet, for Bill Clinton in the 1990s.) In the mid-2000s five Arab Americans served in Congress: Nick Joe Rahall II (D–W. Va), Ray LaHood (R–Ill.), Charles Boustany (R–La.), and Darrell Issa (R–Calif.) in the U.S. House; and John E. Sununu (R–N.H.) in the U.S. Senate. About a dozen others have served in the U.S. House and Senate since George Kasem was the first Arab American to be elected to Congress in 1958. Numerous others have recently

Spencer Abraham, a Lebanese American, has served as U.S. Secretary of Energy.

served in state legislatures. Consumer advocate Ralph Nader, a Lebanese American, ran for president in the 1996, 2000, and 2004 elections. And in 2003 the first Arab American Muslim, Abdul Haidos, was elected mayor of a U.S. city (Wayne, Michigan).[54]

Negative images of Arab Americans have interfered with their ability to participate fully in politics. In recent decades political candidates have returned contributions of Arab or Muslim Americans, often with a public display, because the candidates were afraid to be seen as accepting contributions from them. For example, during the fall 2000 New York state senate campaign, the Democratic campaign returned a contribution by Muslim donors because of public reaction. Conventional stereotyping of Arab and Muslim Americans seems to be just below the surface of such discriminatory reactions to citizen contributions, which are usually actively sought by politicians.[55]

International Politics and Linkages

Social and political ties to countries of origin remain important to immigrants and their descendants generations after they have become fully established in the United States. Today, for many Arab Americans, such as Lebanese, Iraqi, or Palestinian Americans, ties to home countries or lands are still of much importance. They closely watch political events in the Middle East and the U.S. government's involvement there.

In recent years many Arab and Muslim Americans have been critical of U.S. foreign policy in the Middle East, faulting it for tilting too far in support of Israel (Israel is currently the largest recipient of U.S. foreign aid) and too much against the interests of the numerous Arab countries in the region. Arab Americans are often critical of Israel's treatment of Palestinians and their lands. Ibrahim Hooper, communications director of CAIR, has put it this way: "You're not going to find a Muslim who is not going to support the Palestinians' efforts to free themselves from occupation." Nonetheless, like most other Americans, most Arab and Muslim Americans do *not* support terrorism in any country. As Dr. Agha Saeed, chair of the American Muslim Alliance, an organization working for civic education and leadership training, has noted: "We are critical of Israel but not supporters of terrorism."[56] Not surprisingly, then, Arab Americans in cities from Atlanta to Detroit to Riverside, California, have peacefully protested Israeli treatment of Palestinians and called for increased efforts to bring peace there.

The influence of Arab American organizations' efforts to bring their perspective into U.S. discussions of the Middle East can be seen in recent opinion polls. The majority of U.S. respondents in one 2006 national poll expressed a desire for the U.S. government to take an even-handed approach to the Israeli–Palestinian conflict, one not favoring either side. In addition, most (79 percent) felt that Palestinians should have equal rights with Israelis, while nearly two-thirds also supported an independent Palestinian state. In addition, recent surveys also show that overwhelming *majorities* of Arab Americans and Jewish Americans favor both an independent Palestinian state and the right of Israel to be a secure and independent state.[57]

Arab American political activists and organizations have also actively focused on critical domestic issues such as immigration reform and health care. Arab Americans and other Middle Eastern Americans have created a large array of important voluntary associations and organizations to provide support for their communities. Cities with large Middle Eastern communities have many voluntary associations, including Islamic and Christian religious groups, media groups, village societies, professional groups, educational associations, human service groups, and political organizations such as the Arab American Political Action Committee.[58]

Many Middle Eastern community leaders are working to build greater community and political cooperation across various Arab American and other Middle Eastern organizations. One leader has noted that "The one thing I wish is for a united community with one organization and leaders... who are most qualified and can accomplish things whether they're Palestinian, Lebanese, Yemeni, Shi'a, Sunni, Muslims, non-Muslims."[59] To promote such cooperation, organizations such as the American Muslim Political Coordinating Committee have been formed to link Arab and other Middle Eastern Americans politically across the country. Today the American Muslim Alliance, another relatively new political organization, has thousands of members in many states.[60]

The Economy

Like other immigrants, some early Arab immigrants were attracted by the relatively high wages paid by Henry Ford in his automobile plant in Michigan. However, unlike many European immigrants, most early-twentieth-century Arab immigrants, those from Greater Syria, bypassed new industrial occupations expanding dramatically in the decades after 1890, and instead became peddlers or small merchants. As a result, they often had somewhat higher incomes than new industrial workers. Most settled in just a few cities, where many established grocery stores, fruit stands, and dry-goods stores. There they built residential and economic enclaves like other immigrant groups such as Italian and Cuban Americans.[61]

Early immigrants were often working-class, but many who immigrated more recently have been professionals and businesspeople. Indeed, Arab Americans today are disproportionately self-employed. Table 12.2 gives the current occupational distribution for those who gave their ancestry as only Arab in the 2000 census.[62] Compared to all U.S. workers, they are more likely to be white-collar and in managerial, professional, sales, and office occupations (which include entrepreneurs). They are less likely than U.S. workers as a whole to be in blue-collar, service, and farming occupations. (This pattern remains roughly the same if one adds those who told the Census Bureau they had both Arab and non-Arab ancestry.) Numerous Arab Americans have achieved prominence in professional and managerial occupations. Some we have already mentioned. Others include Dr. Michael DeBakey (inventor of the heart pump), Gibran Khalil Gibran (poet), John Abizaid (top U.S. general), and Helen Thomas (dean of the White House press corps in the 1990s and 2000s). An Arab American schoolteacher, Christa McAuliffe, was among the astronauts who died in the space shuttle *Challenger* explosion.

Arab Americans are more prosperous economically than numerous other racial and ethnic groups. In Table 12.3 we observe that those of (only) Arab ancestry had a median income ($52,318) just a bit higher than that of the total population. They had a poverty rate for families significantly greater (at 16.7 percent) than that for the total population. This is partially because numerous recent immigrants earn low wages. When one adds into the group those who listed both Arab and non-Arab ancestry, these figures change substantially. This larger group has a greater median income ($66,195) and a smaller percentage in poverty (7 percent) than the Arab-only group and the general population.[63]

Arab Americans are concentrated in a few major cities, with the largest number living in the Detroit area. Although the Detroit metropolis is often seen as a distinctively African American city, its population now includes hundreds of thousands of Middle Eastern Americans. It has the largest Arab American population of any U.S. city and the largest Arab-origin population outside the Middle East and north Africa. Areas of the city have significant Iraqi, Egyptian, Lebanese, Palestinian, and Syrian communities. Metropolitan Detroit is home to the national headquarters of the U.S. Chaldean church and an Islamic Institute. Middle Eastern immigrants and their children, like other recent immigrants, have helped greatly

TABLE 12.2 Occupational Distribution: 2000

Occupation	Arab Americans	All Workers
Managerial, professional, and related	42.0%	33.6%
Sales and office	30.2	26.7
Construction, extraction, and maintenance	5.3	9.4
Production, transportation, and material moving	10.7	14.6
Service	11.7	14.9
Farming, fishing, and forestry	0.1	0.7
Total	100%	99.9%

TABLE 12.3 Median Family Income and Poverty Rates: 1999

	Arab Americans	Total Population
Median family income	$52,318	$50,046
Poverty rate	16.7%	12.4%

to bring renewed prosperity to areas of Detroit and Michigan. Many Middle Eastern restaurants operate in the area, and Arabic-language signs advertise many Arab American shops and professional offices. Early 1900s' Arab immigrants went into the automobile industry in the area, and during the 1960s and 1970s Lebanese Muslims and Chaldeans (Catholics from Iraq) migrated there too. Many in this latter group became merchants with small stores. By the early 2000s more than 13,000 Arab American businesses were located in metropolitan Detroit.[64] Dearborn, part of metropolitan Detroit, is called the center of Arab America because of its large Arab population. Once known principally for being the home of the automobile industry, this area has become a city of mosques and Middle Eastern restaurants and shops and, recently, home of the country's only museum about Arab Americans.[65]

Education

The average Arab American is better educated than the average American. The 1980, 1990, and 2000 censuses all reported that Arab Americans had higher average educational levels than the U.S. population averages. Table 12.4 shows two examples from the 2000 census.[66] For those of only Arab ancestry, 84 percent had at least a high school diploma, while 41 percent had completed at least a bachelor's degree. Both figures are higher than those for the general population. When those who reported both Arab and non-Arab ancestry are added in, both figures increase, to 94 percent and 45 percent, respectively. One major survey of leaders of Middle Eastern organizations found a very strong emphasis on the importance of education, an emphasis serving to unite various Middle Eastern subcommunities. These leaders stressed education in part because education and knowledge have long been important within Islamic and other Middle Eastern cultures and in part because of its importance in facilitating advancement in society.[67]

Some parents send their children to private Muslim schools, but most send them to public schools. As with earlier immigrants and their children, tensions have sometimes arisen between schoolteachers and administrators, on the one hand, and students or parents, on the other. One Arab educator has noted that non-Arab teachers often fail to realize that not all Arab Americans share a cultural background. They or their ancestors have come from many countries. Conflicts arise when teachers are unaware that their Arab students come from diverse countries and cultures, when they make incorrect assumptions about the cultural backgrounds of students, or when they impose certain ill-considered school restrictions. For example, one teacher made the stereotyped and very inaccurate assumption that Lebanese women are not allowed to walk freely in the street. Other non-Arab teachers are unaware of the strong tradition of education and the extensive systems of schools in many Arab countries. Misunderstandings about appropriate roles and behaviors are another source of conflict. Muslim students have been suspended from schools, such as in Muskogee, Oklahoma, just for wearing the *hijab*. In addition, non-Arab teachers

TABLE 12.4 Educational Attainment: Percent of Population 25 Years and Older, 2000

	Arab Americans	Total Population
High school graduate or more	84.0%	80.4%
Bachelor's degree or more	41.2	24.4

An Arab American girl attends school in Dearborn, Michigan.

often see Arab American parents as too strict with children, while the Arab parents may view teachers as too lax with disruptive students.[68]

Educator Wendy Schwartz notes that public schools have a responsibility to deal with racial and ethnic stereotyping faced by children: "Because prejudice against Arab Americans increases when political events involve Arabs, or are even speculated to involve them, educators need to be prepared to respond to possible harassment of Arab American students resulting from negative news reporting, and to invoke school policies against hate crimes and discrimination as appropriate."[69] Most are not currently prepared. Schwartz calls on educators to become sensitive to major cultural practices of Arab Americans, such as by respecting major Islamic holidays, and to become better informed about Middle Eastern history and contemporary sociopolitical issues in the Middle East.

Religion

Religion has long been central to Middle Eastern countries and cultures, and many Arab Americans take religion very seriously. Some are Christian, a few are Jewish, and many are Muslim. Among Christians and Muslims there are distinctive subgroups.

Most early Arab immigrants were Christian. Generally, they immigrated from Maronite, Melkite, and Syrian Orthodox areas in Greater Syria. As late as the 1960s, most Arab Americans were Christian. Since the 1960s most immigrants have been Muslim. They and their descendants account for a significant proportion of the current U.S. Muslim population. Estimates vary as to the percentage Muslim among Arab Americans, with some estimating about half. Other analysts put the Muslim percentage at just 24 percent, with two-thirds estimated to be Christians today.[70]

Islam has been practiced in North America since the first century of European settlement (some enslaved Africans were Muslims) but did not become visible to most Americans until the 1940s or so. By the early 1950s, when the Federation of Islamic Associations of the United States and Canada was created, there were at least fifty-two mosques in the United States, not including African American mosques. Note that many U.S. Muslims are South Asian Americans and African Americans, with many of the latter being associated with distinctive Islamic subgroups such as the Nation of Islam. Indeed, the *first* Muslim elected to the U.S. Congress, in 2006, was Keith Ellison, an African American who had converted to Islam. By the late 2000s there were more than 2000 mosques in the United States, more than double the number of a decade before. According to some estimates, Muslims are now the second largest U.S. religious group.[71]

The arrival of Arab and other Middle Eastern Muslim immigrants since the 1970s has brought conflicts to some Islamic mosques and organizations. New arrivals have sometimes expressed surprise at deviations in U.S. mosques from what they regard as traditional Islamic teachings. Like Christian churches and Jewish synagogues, mosques have been significantly shaped by the U.S. environment. For example, Sunday schools have been set up, and Sunday prayer services have become more popular than traditional Friday services. Conservative Islamic

People gather outside a new mosque in Orange County, California.

revivalists have worked to bring U.S. mosques back to more traditional practices, seeking elimination of such events as raffles and teenage dances and segregation or reduction of participation of women in mosque affairs.[72]

Surveys of U.S. Muslims indicate that only 3 to 4 percent attend Friday prayers weekly. This is much lower than the 40 percent of Christians who attend church at least once a week. However, 47 percent of U.S. Muslims report that they fast for the month of Ramadan. Moreover, nationwide there are hundreds of Islamic day schools and even more Sunday and weekend schools. As of the mid-2000s, fewer than 5 percent of children with Muslim backgrounds are receiving direct schooling in Islam outside the home.[73] In the 1990s a training program for religious leaders was established in Herndon, Virginia, by the International Institute of Islamic Thought, which offers degrees in Imamate Studies and provides U.S. Islamic communities with religious imams educated in the United States. Until this was established, most leaders came from overseas, and the inability of some overseas leaders to understand U.S. society periodically created tensions with those served, especially with youth influenced by the dominant U.S. culture.[74]

Islamic scholar Yvonne Haddad has noted that while practicing Islam in the United States is becoming easier, problems remain: "The practice of religion is to pray five times a day, to perform ablutions before the prayers, to fast the month of Ramadan, to give alms, to go on the hajj once in a lifetime. Fasting is not as easy as fasting in a Muslim country, where the workday is shortened."[75] Finding places to do ablutions and pray in the workplace can be difficult, but the growing numbers of practicing Muslims are pressuring employers to become aware of the need to provide facilities.

However, unlike the various denominations of Christianity (Catholic, Orthodox, and Protestant groups), Islam is not yet fully accepted in the United States. Its practitioners still suffer widespread prejudice and stereotyping. In this regard the practitioners of Islam suffer much as Jewish Americans once did for practicing Judaism in the United States. (Indeed, Jewish synagogues are still sometimes targets for anti-Jewish hate crimes.) U.S. media periodically connect mainstream Islam to extremists and terrorism. The media often refer to numerous incidents as involving "Islamic terrorists"—as though the religion of Islam routinely generated this terrorism. Yet, the same reporters and editors would never refer routinely to the terrorists in places like Northern Ireland as "Christian terrorists," even though Christian sectarian ideologies (Catholic versus Protestant) have often been linked to recent terrorism on that island. Clearly, in neither case is the broader religion, Islam or Christianity, responsible for extremist terrorism. Today, as Suad Joseph has noted, the portrayal of Islam is too often "achieved by misrepresenting and then essentializing and homogenizing a highly complex and diverse religion that has many different sects, legal systems, beliefs, and practices."[76]

The recurring linkage of the religion of Islam to extremist terrorism creates serious dilemmas for many Muslim Americans. Much religious intolerance still confronts them in their everyday lives. Continuing anti-Arab and anti–Middle Eastern stereotyping and discrimination can create serious problems of identity and self-esteem for Arab and other Middle Eastern Americans. As a result, many have decided to deny or "de-emphasize their Arab or Islamic background." This reaction is the same as that of numerous other immigrants groups, past and present, for whom the U.S. sociocultural context has often been a painful Procrustean bed, one with great pressure for one-way conformity to the dominant culture.[77]

Adaptation and Assimilation Issues

Patterns of Assimilation

Partial cultural assimilation has come relatively quickly for most Arab immigrants and their children. Earlier Greater Syrian immigrants soon adapted to new cultural and social environments, picking up English and certain U.S. folkways, even as most maintained their distinctive religious traditions. Intentional discrimination by European Americans played a role in frustrating the rise of first-generation Arab Americans and their children. In response to discrimination, they often anglicized their names, gave up Arabic, and tried to appear as Anglo-American as they could, especially in public.[78]

In the sphere of structural assimilation at the secondary level of economy and politics, these early Arab Americans advanced and gradually achieved substantial success. In the early period whites saw their nationality as "Syrian," not "Arab." Indeed, most did not see themselves as Arabs at that point, although most had deep Arab cultural roots. While many had come to make money and return home, in the entrepreneurial process they came to be proud of their contributions to the United States. Their constant contacts with other Americans drew them into the individualistic culture and language habits of the dominant culture. As they became more attached to their new homeland, their attachment to Syria and Lebanon declined significantly.[79]

In contrast, Arab immigrants who have entered since the 1960s have assimilated more slowly at most levels, perhaps because their numbers have been much larger and because of more intense anti-Arab sentiment in the United States recently.

Contemporary Assimilation Issues and Patterns

One major survey of Middle Eastern Americans in Michigan found that the issues receiving the greatest emphasis were immigration, cultural preservation, citizenship, and assimilation. Preservation of Arab and other Middle Eastern cultures, especially language and religion, is of great concern in Arab and other Middle Eastern communities.[80]

Generally speaking, significant language and other cultural assimilation is taking place in Arab American communities today. While the 2000 census revealed that 69 percent of Arab Americans over the age of four, and either foreign-born or born of two Arab parents, speak a language besides English at home, therein two languages are the norm. In many homes Engligh is increasingly dominant. This is especially true for those who have intermarried with people from other racial and ethnic groups. Probably because of the growing Arab American population and continuing Middle East crises, interest in Arabic language and culture among native-born Arab Americans has increased in recent years. Those in the second and third generations usually have to take Arabic classes to become fluent, for most do not develop Arabic fluency at home.[81]

Although some Arab Americans oppose marriage outside the group because it threatens Arab American solidarity, intermarriage is increasing. Many second- and third-generation Arab Americans, as well as other Middle Eastern Americans, are moving out of enclave communities and intermarrying outside traditional nationality and religious groups. One recent study of Muslim Americans (mostly

Arab Americans) and converts in Houston found two major types of contemporary marriage patterns. Twelve of the twenty-seven respondents, mostly first or second generation, had traditional arranged marriages that were also endogamous. But fifteen of the twenty-seven had exogamous marriages outside their immediate nationality group, all of which were self-initiated. In addition, along with vertical economic progress for Arab Americans has come horizontal mobility, especially suburbanization. First-generation immigrants, like those in other immigrant groups, tend to live in older urban areas, while subsequent generations have been the most likely to move to suburbia. Indeed, many in all generations have moved to the suburbs.[82] This suburbanization, however, has often reduced attendance at mosques and weakened commitment to Islamic traditions.

Assimilation and Generational Conflicts

Today, Arab American and other Middle Eastern American groups are relatively young populations; a large proportion are under the age of twenty-five. This pattern is characteristic of populations containing large numbers of recent immigrants. As with earlier Arab immigrants, assimilation pressures have led more recent Arab immigrants and their children to adopt the English language and some mainstream values constantly articulated in the media and public schools. As they become better educated, Arab and other Middle Eastern Americans, especially the young, are being drawn away from cultures of origin to the dominant U.S. culture. Education is essential for advancement, but results in greater acculturation to the Eurocentric core culture. Some in U.S.-born generations even mock the first generation, especially newcomers, as "boaters" who speak English with a strong accent or are not in tune with the dominant culture. In its turn, the first generation sometimes views later generations as far too assimilated and losing touch with their heritage.[83]

Like children of other immigrants, Arab children are caught between parents' culture and the dominant U.S. culture; family conflicts often result. Parents and community leaders worry that young people are enticed away from traditional values and practices by negative aspects of U.S. culture—drugs, sexual promiscuity, and violence. As in other groups, many Arab American teenagers prefer the more permissive core culture. U.S.-born teenagers seek to fit in by adopting such practices as coloring their hair unusual colors, wearing jeans, or listening to rap music. Some young people arrange dates at shops or in malls away from parents.[84] While parents are disturbed at their children's lack of respect for the old ways, children frequently feel they are unfairly restricted. As one young Yemeni American put it, "I think it is not fair; I was born in a different society. I am in America." At the opposite extreme, one young Jordanian American was sent for counseling because he had beaten his younger sister, who was dating a boy at school without permission.[85]

Some Middle Eastern community leaders fear that anti-Arab prejudice and discrimination will cause the youth to desire to abandon their heritage or ancestry even more rapidly. Indeed, some youth do try to hide their identities. In one interview, an Arab American girl told of a friend who passed herself off as half-black and half-Puerto Rican to avoid anti-Arab racism. However, she herself said, "I could constantly find an excuse to deny my culture, but I'm not."[86] In addition, the targeting of Arab and Muslim Americans by racist outsiders and discriminators has often had the effect of encouraging youth to accent these identities. Thus, one recent research study of second-generation Arab Americans on the west coast found that many were accenting their Muslim identities (often in a Muslim first, Arab second pattern) in response to stereotyping and discrimination. This became one of the vehicles "for self-reinvention and public action, particularly among those who participated in Muslim student activism on college campuses."[87]

How might assimilation or power-conflict theories be used to explain generational conflicts among Arab Americans?

Creating a Hybrid Culture

Recall Andrew Greeley's *ethnogenesis* perspective (Chapter 2), one that recognizes the reality of cultural differences within contemporary racial and ethnic groups and seems to fit the Arab American experience in certain ways. Arab Americans constitute more than a single Middle Eastern group. Their origins lie in nearly two dozen different countries.

Today they are becoming a composite group of diverse cultural origins. Within the U.S. context, immigrants from various Arab countries and their descendants have increasingly forged a distinctive Arab American umbrella group shaped by their Arab heritages and by adaptation to the European American culture. Despite substantial adaptive changes, significant Arab cultural distinctiveness remains.

One study found that Michigan's Arab American organizations have helped young people to become assimilated to certain good features of U.S. culture and society while at the same time cautioning them about bad features and emphasizing traditional Arab family and religious values. As one leader has put it, "We even actually encourage our kids to assimilate in American society."[88]

Gary David and Kenneth Ayouby have defined **mediated assimilation** as *the process whereby Arab American organizations act as cultural filters to screen out some undesirable features of U.S. culture*. The pattern of using strong community organizations for both assimilation to and resistance to the dominant culture has been typical of many immigrants to the United States. This view of the effects and role of community organizations differs from the view that these organizations are interested only in promoting ancestral traditions and maintaining old cultural ways. In the mediated assimilation model, these organizations attempt to maintain some adherence to tradition, but also help create a new "Arab American" mixture. A hybrid Arab American culture appears to be developing, one that includes elements of ancestral and home-country practices but that also adapts these elements to the assimilation patterns within a specific community. The new hybrid Arab American culture is "specific to the community's experiences both in the new and old lands."[89] This hybrid particularly helps to blend together groups of people, young and old, whose ancestral roots are in different countries into an umbrella Arabic American culture.

Power-Conflict Issues: Identities in the Face of Hostility

A power-conflict perspective underscores certain distinctive aspects of the Arab American experience. The dominant European American majority has the major say in how Arab Americans are portrayed in the media and how they are viewed and treated in the many U.S. institutions. In public discussions and settings, the European American view of Arab Americans customarily decides whether the latter as a group are placed toward the darker, more socially undesirable end of the prevailing racial-ethnic continuum or toward the lighter, more socially desirable ("white") end. Recall the numerous European American judges who, between 1909 and 1944, vacillated on whether certain Arab American groups could be considered "white." Indeed, one important dimension of daily interaction with European Americans for Arab Americans is that they are treated as, at worst, "sand niggers" and "terrorists," or, perhaps with less overt hostility, as "not yet white," even as they are officially listed as "white" by the Census Bureau.

Continuing societal stereotyping and discrimination, usually at the hands of European Americans, have pressed some Arab Americans to deny or deemphasize their Islamic or Arab ties. Although the majority continue to openly claim their nationality and religious backgrounds, they often restrain their reactions to anti-Arab prejudice and discrimination even as they may work quietly to eliminate them. Moreover, some Arab Americans, such as those represented by the Arab American Institute, have sought to have Arab Americans officially classified as a distinctive non-European group, like the "Hispanic" category devised by the U.S. Census Bureau. Also, many Arab Americans publicly identify themselves as "people of color," and thus link themselves to the long struggle of movements against racial oppression in the United States.[90]

Clearly, the racial-ethnic identity of Arab Americans today is much more than a "symbolic identity" without lasting significance—the view some analysts hold of group identity in white ethnic groups such as Irish Americans. In this color-conscious society, Arab Americans' array of physical characteristics presents a continuing problem for their group and for European Americans who think in racist terms about them. Arab Americans vary from very dark-skinned to blue-eyed and blond, although most have brown eyes, dark hair, and olive or light brown skin.[91] Although some can and do pass as phenotypically white, many others who might do so in fact reject this option and emphasize certain differences from European Americans. They are usually proud of their national origins. Some intentionally assert that their identities are *not* white European.[92] Most European Americans, for their part, seem to view Arab Americans and other Middle Eastern Americans, taken as a group, as "not white." The persistence of anti-Arab stereotyping and hostility both encourages and discourages movement away from a strong Arab American identity.

Summary

Middle Eastern immigrants have been coming to the United States for more than a century. The largest group among these are Arab immigrants from more than twenty countries. By the 1920s there were about 200,000 Arab Americans, mostly Christians. They and their descendants make up a substantial proportion of today's Arab American population. The rest of this group encompasses many recent immigrants from Arab countries, most of whose religious background is Muslim. These immigrants and their descendants have helped to make Islam the second largest U.S. religion. As has been the case for other immigrant groups, economic and political conditions in countries of origin are major reasons for recent migration. Many immigrants have fled wars in the Middle East, including the civil war in Lebanon. Most have a strong sense of Arab origins and an inclination to be critical of traditional U.S. policies in the Middle East.

Today, Arab Americans have established strong communities in a number of large cities. The largest number live in metropolitan Detroit. Many have become successful professionals or businesspeople, and some are beginning to move into important political offices. Arab Americans still face widespread stereotyping and significant and sometimes violent discrimination. Hate crimes have frequently targeted Islamic mosques, as well as Middle Eastern individuals and their families and homes. Negative images of Arabs and Arab Americans are common in some media; men are often portrayed as extremist or domineering and women as servile or repressed. Only a few U.S. leaders outside Arab American communities have yet been willing to challenge these stereotyped images in a regular and sustained way.

Arab Americans are today in the forefront of those fighting racial and ethnic stereotyping and religious discrimination. Like other groups facing serious discrimination, they have created important community and civil rights organizations that have pressed for expanded civil rights not only for Arab and other Middle Eastern Americans but also for all Americans.

Key Terms

Middle Eastern Americans 342
Arab Americans 342
sojourner immigration 344
mediated assimilation 360

CHAPTER 13

Ongoing Racial and Ethnic Issues in the United States: Some Final Considerations

BIG PICTURE QUESTIONS

- *How is the commonplace rhetoric about current immigrants similar to that for past immigrants?*
- *How does the changing U.S. demographic situation challenge white Americans' traditional power and privilege?*
- *Is the United States truly a democracy?*

In the 1990s, David Spritzler, a twelve-year-old student at the distinguished Boston Latin School, refused to say the Pledge of Allegiance with other students. He explained that, because "liberty and justice for all" does not exist in the United States, he did not want to do something that violated his principles. Facing disciplinary action, the boy went to the Massachusetts Civil Liberties Union, which sent the headmaster a letter noting that federal court decisions supported the boy's understanding of free speech. Inside and outside the school, reaction to the boy's courageous assertion of his rights was positive and negative. One hostile letter that he received was accompanied by a copy of his newspaper photograph marked with a bullet-riddled Star of David and a swastika.[1]

The United States began as a land of great promise for colonists who came from Europe. Early poets such as Philip Freneau, in his 1788 poem, "The Pictures of Columbus," spoke of the new land as "paradise anew" and "another Canaan" excelling the old. Thomas Jefferson and other founders used strong language about liberty, freedom, and democracy for the new nation created in the late 1700s.[2] Yet, as Latino scholar Ilan Stavans has noted, this celebrated image is not the reality of the past four centuries. Instead, North America has always been "the crossroads of hope and violence, democracy and intolerance. America the beautiful and America the ugly."[3] Today, the United States is still a country of hope with grand ideals of equality, freedom, and democracy, but it is also "America the ugly," where a great many "others" are still second-class citizens who face racial or ethnic discrimination or other oppression that is substantially under the control of still-dominant European Americans.

Currently, U.S. society is undergoing important changes in its racial and ethnic composition. Challenges and conflicts brought by these demographic changes will likely continue for the next century. Among these are challenges to white domination of U.S. society, both in terms of the white population majority and of white power and privilege. The proportion of whites in the population is now decreasing. Significant challenges to white social, political, and educational domination are already arising from large-scale population changes and new organizational developments those changes bring. People of European descent are today less than a fifth of the world's population and still decreasing in proportion. They are also a decreasing proportion of the U.S. population. White Americans are today a statistical minority in the central-city areas of the major metropolises of New York City and Chicago and of the entire metropolitan areas of Los Angeles and Houston. They are a minority in many of the country's one hundred largest cities. Whites are also a minority of the population in California, Texas, New Mexico, and Hawaii. If future birth and immigration rates are at least roughly similar to those of the present, more than half the population will be Americans of color no later than the 2050s.[4]

This ongoing demographic shift is significant, for European Americans have not been a statistical minority of the North American population since the 1700s. Today, much discussion of these demographic changes, especially among European Americans, has a fearful tone. Many have a deep concern about non-European challenges to the dominant Euro-American culture. For example, Patrick Buchanan, former contender twice for the Republican presidential nomination and presidential candidate for the Reform Party, has expressed the concerns of many whites about a country that is no longer predominantly white. Buchanan has asserted that "Our Judeo-Christian values are going to be preserved and our Western heritage is going to be handed down to future generations and not dumped on some landfill called multiculturalism." In a best-selling 2006 book that got him on many television network programs, called *State of Emergency,* Buchanan draws in part on white-nationalist and other extremist authors to argue that the United States is being submerged by "third world" immigrants who will take over the country socially in coming decades—that is, that current young people will live to see the "end" of the United States if something is not done to stop the migration.[5] Writing in the influential policy journal *Foreign Affairs,* Harvard professor Samuel Huntington asserted a similar point: "If multiculturalism prevails and if the consensus on liberal democracy disintegrates, the United States could join the Soviet Union on the ash heap of history."[6] He, too, fears that domestic forces pushing toward heterogeneity, diversity, and multiculturalism are disintegrating the country.

Even otherwise liberal analysts have expressed variations on this strongly negative view of cultural pluralism and multiculturalism. Historian Arthur Schlesinger, Jr., has written about multiculturalism as dominating all levels of education. In his view, this involves "an astonishing repudiation" of "a unifying American identity" and an "assault on the Western tradition" by multicultural "tribalism."[7] Many such analysts, thus, see efforts to create a multiracial democracy whose core culture is no longer predominantly European as a disturbing challenge to European American values and interests and to "European civilization."

A Nation of Immigrants

Yet the United States has *always* been a *nation of immigrants*. Recurring immigration is its uniqueness and one of its strengths. In numbers and diversity, the many millions who have come from all corners of the globe are unparalleled in the rest of the world. These millions have brought dozens of languages and cultures, a great diversity of resources, and an array of physical and cultural characteristics. This diversity can be seen in something as simple as the array of Asian, Mexican, African, European, Middle Eastern, Asian-Indian, and South American restaurants in cities, or in something as complex as recent voting patterns in California or New York and ongoing debates over multicultural education in the schools.

European countries have supplied nearly 60 percent of the 70 million immigrants who have legally entered the United States over this 185-year period.[8] Numerous European countries have supplied at least 700,000 immigrants to the growth of the United States; Austria/Hungary, Germany, Ireland, Italy, Norway/Sweden, Russia, and the United Kingdom have each contributed more than 2 million immigrants. Canada, populated mostly by European immigrants and their descendants until relatively recently, has supplied more than 2 million. Significantly, only five countries from the populous areas of Asia and the Middle East have contributed 700,000 immigrants or more to the U.S. mix, and not one of these has yet contributed 2 million. Only two countries from the Caribbean have reached the level of 700,000 immigrants, and *no* country in Central America, South America, Africa, or Oceania has sent as many as 700,000 legal immigrants. Indeed, Mexico is the *only* country outside of Europe and Canada that has contributed more than 2 million immigrants to the mix. These patterns reflect the highly discriminatory effects of U.S. immigration laws before 1965. Some groups of immigrants do not appear in official statistics for various reasons. One group is

IMMIGRANTS TO THE UNITED STATES, 1820–2005

*Persons Obtaining Legal Permanent Resident Status by Region and Country of Last Residence: 1820–2005***

Official government records show that between 1820 and 2005, just over 70 million immigrants entered the United States. Only a small number of countries have sent more than 700,000 people. Listed below are the countries from which at least 700,000 immigrants have arrived during this long period. Asterisked countries are those from which at least 2 million immigrants have come during this period.

Europe (total = 39,216,290)
- Austria and Hungary*
- France
- Germany*
- Greece
- Ireland*
- Italy*
- Norway and Sweden*
- Poland
- Russia*
- United Kingdom*

North America (11,593,899)
- Canada and Newfoundland*
- Mexico*

Asia and Middle East (10,113,486)
- China
- India
- Korea
- Philippines
- Vietnam

The Caribbean (4,052,575)
- Cuba
- Dominican Republic

Central America, South America, Africa, Oceania (5,032,797)

***Data for years prior to 1906 refer to country of origin; data from 1906 to 2005 refer to country of last residence.*

Puerto Ricans, who are not counted because they are officially U.S. citizens. And from the 1600s to the 1850s many Africans were forced to immigrate. For most, their point of origin on the African continent is unknown because of the brutal conditions of forced emigration. These involuntary immigrants numbered at least a half-million, but they are uncounted in government records.

Why do people migrate? What affects migration? We have examined these issues throughout this book. Distinctive economic and political conditions in the United States and sending countries for particular historical periods have shaped which countries supply immigrants and how many come. For many decades between the late nineteenth century and the mid-1960s, the United States imposed major barriers to immigrants from many areas. For those who were able to come more or less voluntarily, economic and political conditions in homelands that were distressing to personal and family development pressed people to leave. During boom times, when many jobs are available, the U.S. economy has particularly attracted immigrants from many lands.

Many indigenous peoples were already present in North America when strangers from distant shores arrived. Ancestors of contemporary Native Americans had migrated to these shores, probably from Asia, thousands of years before Europeans and Africans stepped off boats. Immigration from Europe brought genocide, forced migration to reservations, and many material and other losses to these indigenous peoples.

Political actions by colonial and U.S. governments have long helped to determine the character of immigration patterns. For centuries now, the U.S. empire has expanded as the government and corporations have expanded activities globally. U.S. ties overseas, more extensive than those of previous empires, include corporate and military linkages, often generated by U.S. military interventions overseas; extensive government aid to countries; and far-reaching mass media linkages, including television and movies. Large-scale immigration often parallels the development of U.S. political and economic linkages internationally. We saw this in the first great migrations of needed workers to North America, the migration of English and Irish laborers in the eighteenth and nineteenth centuries. We have also seen it in later migrations, such as the Chinese laborers who built infrastructure projects in western states, the Mexican laborers who have done much hard labor in agriculture since 1900, and Korean immigrants who have established thousands of small businesses in cities.

An elderly Chinese American woman recites the Pledge of Allegiance with a diverse group of 1700 other new U.S. citizens in San Jose, California.

In the United States, leading officials have often used restrictive laws to control migration according to their racial and ethnic prejudices and preferences. As an article in a 1914 magazine noted, "Immigrants who came earlier and their descendants have always tried to keep this country for those who were already here and for their kinfolk."[9] The discriminatory Chinese Exclusion Act (1882) and discriminatory national-origin quotas in the 1924 Immigration Act guaranteed that by the 2000s the U.S. population mix would include fewer Americans from Asia and from southern and eastern Europe than would otherwise have been the case. The 1924 law sharply reduced the number of Catholic immigrants from countries such as Italy and Poland and of Jewish immigrants from eastern Europe. As a result, the country is today majority Protestant; a minority of the population is Catholic, Jewish, or Muslim. Asian Americans today constitute only about 5 percent of the population.[10]

Beginning in 1965, openly exclusionary and racist quotas in U.S. immigration laws were replaced with general limits on the number of immigrants allowed to enter from any one country. Still, both the 1986 Immigration Reform and Control Act and later immigration acts have again reflected dominant-group concerns about who was immigrating. For example, the 1986 act was intended to limit immigrants from south of the U.S. border, particularly from Mexico. Not surprisingly, the act's restrictive provisions have led to some racial profiling of Latinos who are U.S. citizens.

The 1990 Immigration Act set an official annual limit of all legal immigrants at 675,000. This limit most affects immigrants from countries, such as Asian countries, from which many people seek to emigrate and contrasts with the generally unlimited immigration allowed before 1910, when most potential immigrants were European. The 1990 act established several visa categories, the largest of which is for family members of legal U.S. residents in order to facilitate family reunification. In addition, 140,000 employment-based visas are reserved primarily for highly skilled workers, and visas for unskilled workers are virtually unavailable. The act also designated a special category of visas to provide legalization for certain illegal immigrants from some (mostly European) countries and to set aside visas for wealthy immigrants willing to invest at least $1 million to create U.S. jobs. A 1996 immigration act significantly increased federal surveillance over illegal immigrants, and other federal legislation excluded most undocumented immigrants from federal welfare benefits. Statistical calculations including allowances for regular legal immigrants, refugees, and undocumented immigrants (and excluding temporary visitors, workers, and students)—and subtracting out-migrants—indicate that a net figure of approximately 1.2 to 1.3 million people have been added to the United States annually over the 2000s.[11]

In recent years, immigration and proposed immigration restrictions (including such things as a fence on the Mexican border) have been debated by Congress, by the public, and by media commentators. Many native-born business leaders and politicians question the character and values of the Latin Americans and Asians who constitute the majority of recent newcomers. These arguments are similar to those made by opponents of immigration in the nineteenth century against many immigrants *from Europe*.

Most respondents in recent opinion surveys indicate that they feel the diverse cultural composition of the United States is an important asset. However, when commenting on immigration, the public shows mixed feelings. For example, a 2006 Pew Research Center national survey asked respondents to indicate the most important problem facing their communities. Crime, education, unemployment, drugs, traffic, taxes, and roads all ranked higher in the list than did immigration issues. Still, when asked specifically, 52 percent agreed that immigrants were a burden in terms of jobs, housing, and health care. About 42 percent, however, accented an alternative view—that immigrants strengthen the country with hard work and talents. A majority felt that the level of legal immigration should stay the same or be increased, and about half (49 percent) thought today's immigrants were at least as willing to assimilate as European immigrants in the early 1900s (44 percent did not agree). In addition, most negative opinion about immigrants was directed at the undocumented. A majority felt that they should not have access to social services; about half thought that employers should be penalized for hiring them. Nonetheless, a third felt that undocumented immigrants already here should be allowed to stay permanently, while another third thought they should be allowed to stay in a temporary work program, with only 27 percent agreeing that they should be forced to leave.[12]

Although many respondents in this and other polls *believe* that immigrants are taking away many U.S. jobs, most research studies have shown that immigrants do not generally take away more jobs than they create. Immigrants' presence creates new demands for housing and other commodities. Drawing on several studies showing that immigrants actually create more jobs than they take, one report of the Council of Economic Advisors concluded that the low-wage jobs "taken by immigrants in years past have . . . increased employment and income for the population as a whole." An overview study by the National Academy of Sciences concluded that "the evidence points to the conclusion that there is only a small adverse impact of immigration on the wage and employment opportunities of competing native groups. This effect does not appear to be concentrated in the local areas where immigrants live, but instead is dispersed across the United States."[13]

Over the past decade, growing misinformation about and hostility toward immigrants, those who are legal and those who are not, have too seldom been countered by educators and public officials willing to speak on the truth about immigration. For example, government data indicate that immigration from Asia and Latin America since the 1960s is not fueling a uniquely large population expansion. The 1980s saw a population increase of only 10 percent, the second-lowest rate of increase for any decade in U.S. immigration history. The 1990s saw a somewhat faster increase (13 percent), but this, too, was smaller than increases for most decades over the past century and a half. For example, in the decades from the 1850s to the 1920s, the percentage increases in population ranged from a low of 15 percent over the 1910s to a high of 36 percent over the 1850s.[14]

Between 1901 and 1910, some 8.8 million immigrants entered the United States, mostly from Europe. This was the largest number of immigrants to the United States for any decade prior to the 1990s. (This was an era with little restriction on immigration from Europe.) Immigration and Naturalization Service (INS) data for 1991–2000 show that total legal immigration was the largest yet, nearly 10 million. However, during that early-twentieth-century decade, the U.S. population was much smaller than today—92 million, as compared with 281 million in 2000.[15] The ratio of legal immigrants to the native-born population is thus *lower* today than the immigrant/population ratio was in the late nineteenth and early twentieth centuries. (Adding in current undocumented immigrants is difficult because numbers are rough and variable; many also return home.) Today, even adding in estimates for undocumented immigrants who stay permanently, the United States has not only a smaller percentage of foreign-born than it had in earlier decades but also a smaller percentage of foreign-born than some other countries. Given its long history of successful absorption of immigrants and the size of its native-born population and geographical area, the United States is unlikely to be overwhelmed by the current rate of immigration.

Some social analysts argue that immigrants make mostly positive contributions to this country: As a group, immigrants are "upwardly mobile, ambitious, saving; they have traditional values, care about their children, all that sort of stuff. They've done something very dramatic to upgrade themselves."[16] Immigrants are generally hard-working and seek to make a good life for themselves and their families. If it were not for the many immigrants in recent decades, numerous cities would now have declining populations. The 2000 census showed that several major cities—including Chicago, Boston, and New York City—whose populations have declined over the past half-century, are growing again. (Several of the states with the largest percentages of the foreign-born have seen economic booms.) Other major cities, including Pittsburgh and Philadelphia, without as great an immigrant influx, have continued to decline. Some city officials have sought to support their economies by encouraging immigration. In the late 1990s, the city of Boston established an Office of New Bostonians to assist immigrant settlement. Other cities have reportedly looked to similar strategies to stem some urban decline.[17]

Interestingly, over the next half-century, the United States will likely face a shortage of young workers as large numbers of baby boomers retire. The aged population will gradually grow to more than one-fifth of the population, and additional numbers will near retirement age. The current workforce is insufficient to meet heavy demands for health care and other public and private services this aging population will likely require. Numerous analysts have asked whether the United States can survive without the constant infusion of immigrants from abroad.[18]

The Melting Pot: Early Images of Immigrant Incorporation

There has never been a consensus on how new immigrants are to be incorporated into this society. Pressures for cultural assimilation are often matched by immigrants' desire to maintain their own cultures. For a century, one prominent idealized image for immigrant incorporation has been the "melting pot." In the early 1900s, immigrant playwright Israel Zangwill made an influential statement of this idea in his play, *The Melting Pot,* in which a Russian immigrant argues:

> America is God's Crucible, the great Melting-Pot where all races of Europe are melting and re-forming! Here you stand, good folks, think I, when I see them at Ellis Island, here you stand in your fifty groups, with your fifty languages and histories, and your fifty blood hatreds and rivalries. But you won't be long like that, brothers, for these are the fires of God. . . . A fig for your feuds and vendettas! Germans and Frenchmen, Irishmen and Englishmen, Jews and Russians—into the Crucible with you all! God is making the American.[19]

Zangwill's optimistic image of a crucible that melts many different groups to form an "American blend" symbolizes a mutual adaptation process in which old and new groups blend together on a more or less equal basis. However, actual intergroup adaptation has usually involved much more one-way assimilation and group conflict. Also, Americans of color—including African, Asian, Latino, and Native Americans—seem to be absent from this melting-pot imagery. Middle Eastern Americans are also missing.

Assimilation theorists such as Milton Gordon argue that in practice the melting pot has diverged greatly from Zangwill's ideal. Immigrant adaptation has typically been in the direction of Anglo-conformity as those in each new group of immigrants have given up much of their cultural heritage for the dominant culture: "If there is anything in American life which can be described as an overall American culture which serves as a reference point for immigrants and their children, it can best be described, it seems to us, as the middle-class cultural patterns of, largely, white Protestant, Anglo-Saxon origins."[20]

How have U.S. government immigration policies shaped past and present demographic trends?

Multicultural and Multiracial Democracy Issues

In recent years melting-pot and pluralistic imagery have become common. As we have seen, some modern-day assimilationists have expressed great concern over integration of groups from Asia and Latin America into the U.S. mix. Popular and scholarly debates over the meaning of the melting-pot idea occur in colleges, corporate boardrooms, Congress, and the White House. Indeed, in 1997 President Bill Clinton set up a White House advisory panel to hold hearings across the country on how to deal with growing diversity and preserve "One America." Contemporary discussions are filled with terms such as **multiculturalism**—*the idea that modern societies should include and accept diverse racial and ethnic groups with equal social and political status*—and **cultural diversity**—*acceptance of a variety of cultures*—that stress the importance of respecting the many groups and subcultures contributing to U.S. development, especially the contributions of non-European groups. A variation of the cultural pluralism perspective (Chapter 2), multiculturalism, emerged out of the racial and ethnic protest movements of the 1960s and has spread. Some multiculturalists seek modest changes in existing institutions, while others, often called "strong" multiculturalists, seek fundamental structural and cultural changes, especially in institutionalized racial and ethnic discrimination.

Numerous colleges and universities, as well as elementary and secondary schools, have developed a few multicultural courses or programs to give voice to the racially oppressed people (and sometimes white women) who have done much hard work that has built this society. Since the 1980s, universities as different as Stanford University, the University of Michigan, the University of California at Irvine, Texas A&M University, and Tufts University

Many U.S. colleges and universities, such as the University of California (Berkeley), have become more racially and ethnically diverse over the past few decades.

have added courses on aspects of U.S. (and global) cultural and/or racial-ethnic diversity to B.A. requirements. As of the late 2000s, well over half of major U.S. colleges and universities report having some type of diversity requirement. Studies show these courses are often effective in reducing some cognitive stereotypes. Multicultural programs, usually modest in scope, have been implemented at many public schools. Teachers at one high school in Brooklyn's predominantly white Bensonhurst section, where a black man shopping for a used car was killed by a white mob, pioneered a successful multicultural class that was imitated in other high schools. Their goal was to shatter racial and ethnic stereotypes and provide students with an opportunity to discuss the causes of intergroup stereotyping and strife.[21]

Some publishers and voluntary organizations have made multicultural teaching materials more readily available to colleges and public schools. For example, the Southern Poverty Law Center in Montgomery, Alabama, has developed a program for public schools that includes the high-quality magazine, *Teaching Tolerance*, and other curriculum materials for multicultural school programs.

A "strong" version of multiculturalism has been enthusiastically embraced by numerous scholars and other Americans with roots in Africa, Asia, Latin America, and the Middle East who seek a sharp reduction in ideological racism and racial and ethnic discrimination, as well as a greater respect for their home countries and their cultures. Some white analysts view this stronger variant of multicultural thought as an attack on the dominant Euro-American culture. The late historian Arthur Schlesinger put it this way: "The contemporary ideal is not assimilation but ethnicity. We used to say *e pluribus unum*. Now we glorify *pluribus* and belittle *unum*. The melting pot yields to the Tower of Babel."[22]

Social scientists and popular writers who make such arguments reflect the "order theory" framework we have discussed. Critics of an assertive multiculturalism, fearful of losing the centripetal forces of Euro-American culture, argue that Anglo-conformity is still the best assimilation model for non-European groups. Their "melting pot" is not so much a mutual blending as a melting of newcomers (and some older groups) into the dominant Euro-American culture. Although they may recognize contributions of non-Europeans to the core culture, critics of multiculturalism emphasize Anglo-conformity assimilation when they assert that the United States is founded on European individualism, not on a philosophy of ethnic and racial pluralism. Schlesinger argued, "It is not that the Western cultures are superior to other cultures as much as it is, for better or worse—our culture."[23] From this perspective, the Eurocentric bias generally found in the U.S. educational system, as well as other societal sectors, is not problematic, but essential to the integration of diverse groups into one societal whole.

The strong version of multicultural thought suggests that the United States should be viewed, not as a melting pot, but as a grand mosaic, a country that celebrates its diversity with "rainbow" language and framing. Traditional images of the melting pot and assimilation assume that European culture and institutions should form the foundation of U.S. society. No early melting-pot analysts paid serious attention to Americans of color, and even many pluralists have "presupposed a set of criteria for successful participation in American plural society: middle-class values, English-language dominance, and acceptance of Western political and cultural ideas."[24] In contrast, mosaic theorists do not see the dominant culture as necessarily central to the American identity, but rather see an evolving and increasingly rainbow nation. "Ironically, it is in minority communities that the idea of the 'gorgeous mosaic' has been embraced most enthusiastically: the least powerful are advancing the most encompassing and egalitarian notion of social relations."[25] As Amitai Etzioni has noted, "The mosaic is enriched by continuous elements of different colors and shapes, but it is held together by a frame and glue. The mosaic depicts a society in which various communities maintain their religious, culinary, and cultural particularities, proud and knowledgeable about their specific traditions—while recognizing that they are integral parts of a more encompassing whole."[26]

Strong multicultural analysts believe that vigorous multiculturalism and diversity programs provide a necessary corrective to the dominance of Euro-American culture. One reason is that relatively few Americans, of any age, know much detail about the country's variegated history. One survey, using multiple-choice questions, found that most respondents could *not* choose 1775 as the year the Revolutionary War started, nor could they pick Virginia as the area where that war ended. A government survey of high school seniors found that most lacked knowledge even of simple historical facts.[27] Even those who think they know U.S. history often accept many misconceptions and myths taught in school. Research shows that high school textbooks communicate much inaccurate, distorted, or elliptical information about U.S. history, particularly with regard to racial and ethnic matters. Typical high school and college textbooks put a pleasant face on an often bloody U.S. racial and ethnic history. Most textbooks leave out inconvenient historical information—such as the fact that New York's Wall Street was a large colonial market where whites sold enslaved Africans, a savage business that lasted there until 1862, *after* the Civil War started.[28]

Many multicultural studies "have encouraged us to look at traditionally excluded cultures and study them on their own terms rather than seeing them through the eyes of the dominant class." Multiculturalism is not separatist but encourages "people to see in plural ways, so that they are not seeing through the lens of any single culture, but understanding the relationships of cultures to each other."[29] Analyses such as that of Schlesinger miss the fact that strong multicultural education is very much in tune with the changing U.S. demographic reality.

Debates over multiculturalism and cultural diversity programs often become heated when they encompass issues of racial and ethnic inequality and white privilege and power. Some social science and other analysts view the function of multicultural courses as simply to expose students to racial and ethnic groups and their cultures, but other analysts, such as "critical race" theorists, want such courses to analyze deeply the oppressive stratification that underlies U.S. racial and ethnic relations. Some have called this strongest version a "revolutionary multiculturalism." Its focus is power and resource inequality, and its goal is to eventually effect major change through large-scale democratic restructuring of this still-ineqalitarian society.

Power-conflict analysts argue that multiculturalism in college curricula should acquaint all students well with the perspectives of nondominant racial and ethnic groups, and that college administrators and faculty should carefully scrutinize and change the curricula in all disciplines so that they "fairly represent the variegated nature of American culture."[30] From this perspective, a strong multiculturalism should also bring a real change in college hierarchies so that people of color (and white women) are well and fairly represented at all levels of the faculty and administration and are thus an empowered presence in policy making on admission of students, hiring of administrators and faculty, drafting of curricula, and college investments.[31] These analysts believe that a strong commitment to multiculturalism and real multiracial democracy should lead to a major alteration of the hierarchies of all private and public organizations, including corporations and government agencies, so that people of color (and white women) are substantially and meaningfully represented at all levels of decision making.

Equality and a Pluralistic Democracy

An Egalitarian Society?

The equality and social justice sought by all subordinated racial and ethnic groups has an ancient heritage. Indeed, the view that "all men are created equal" was articulated for and by the white male "founders" in the Declaration of Independence. Many groups since that time have taken this ideal very seriously. However, these words were initially meant to apply only to white, European, Protestant male immigrants and their male descendants—and generally only those with property. This very limited equality of access to political institutions was certainly a dramatic step forward in an autocratic and feudalistic era, but it still excluded the American *majority,* which at the time included women, African Americans, and Native Americans. Even the few Jewish and Catholic Americans in the country at the time usually had limited citizenship.

Over the following centuries, the U.S. conception of who could claim this equality and justice has become more inclusive. The ideal of equality has been a major driving force in U.S. history as the social, economic, and political systems have gradually become more inclusive and egalitarian. The concept of equality has evolved to include equality of worth among individuals, equality of opportunity, equality before the law (civil rights), and, for many, equality of results in the socioeconomic system. Over time, most subordinated ethnic and racial groups have achieved some advancement in at least some of these categories.

Between the early 1800s and the early 1900s, dramatic economic development brought opportunity and advance to millions of European immigrants. Although they suffered initial discrimination, substantial majorities of these groups eventually achieved much socioeconomic and political success. Many assimilation analysts argue that non-European groups are also moving, if more slowly, toward substantial social, economic, and political equality.

However, the rosy view of U.S. society as long committed to "liberty and justice for all" remains today, as always, very inaccurate. Substantial movement up the economic and political ladders did come for white immigrants from Europe. But an overly optimistic view ignores the great misery and discrimination that many white ethnics endured, for a generation at least, as poorly paid laborers, servants, or peddlers in an exploitative economic system. We have documented capitalistic exploitation of early Italian, Irish, and Jewish Americans. Immigration for the allegedly "inferior races" from southern and eastern Europe was severely restricted by the racist immigration law in effect until 1965. These white ethnic Americans faced stereotyping for several decades; for some, such as Jewish Americans, serious stereotyping persists, sometimes resulting in significant discrimination.

The optimistic picture of U.S. equality and freedom glosses over continuing discrimination faced by Americans with roots outside of Europe. Historically, Native, Asian, African, Latino, and Middle Eastern Americans have pressed hard for expanded equality and an end to discrimination and other oppression. Periodically, over the course of U.S. history, significant improvements have occurred in legal rights and socioeconomic opportunities, such as those that accompanied the civil rights movement of the 1960s. Nonetheless, major problems of continuing racial and ethnic discrimination remain imbedded in the informal operation of U.S. economic, educational, political, and other social institutions, in which whites frequently discriminate against people of color, often with impunity. Today, major U.S. civil rights laws are often only weakly enforced.

Family members, who are proud of their mixed racial and ethnic ancestries, explore the art of origami at their home in Arizona.

Racial Discrimination: The Present Day

The year 1992 marked the 500th anniversary of the landing of Christopher Columbus and his soldiers in the Americas. The Quincentenary celebrations generated protests from many Americans, especially Native Americans, who have worked hard to counter mythical images of beneficent European explorers "discovering" America. They have shown how arrogant and imperialistic it was for Europeans to claim to discover a land already occupied by millions of people for thousands of years. As we documented extensively in Chapter 6, "liberty and justice for all" has often bypassed the original Americans, who generally remain forgotten Americans.

As we saw in Chapters 10 and 11, the broad category of Asian Americans includes many groups, including Chinese, Korean, Filipino, Vietnamese, Asian-Indian, and Japanese Americans. Today they too struggle with much anti-Asian sentiment and discrimination from non-Asian Americans concerned about job competition and economic restructuring. Indeed, Asian countries have sometimes replaced the former Soviet Union as "enemies" somehow responsible for U.S. economic and other troubles. Anti-Asian sentiment continues to generate serious discrimination, including violence, against Asian–Pacific Americans across the country. As we documented in earlier chapters, hate violence remains relatively high in the United States.

Latinos, including Puerto Ricans, Mexican Americans, and Cuban Americans, also continue to face many problems in securing justice and equality. As we saw in Chapters 8 and 9, research studies provide much evidence of continuing anti-Latino discrimination. Studies document discrimination by white employers against Latinos, as well as by white landlords. As a group, Latinos, from California to Texas to New York, continue to find progress toward equality and justice limited by racial stereotyping and discrimination.

African Americans, as we have seen, face a great many obstacles in securing the equality and justice promised by the American creed. In the late 1860s and 1870s the Reconstruction era, one of progress in opportunities, was followed by a dramatic resurgence of extreme white-generated oppression, including legal segregation. In the late twentieth and early twenty-first centuries, only a few decades after public policy expanded opportunities for Americans of color (in the 1960s and 1970s), U.S. society and most federal, state, and local governments again moved backward. From 1981 to 1992, and again since 2001, powerful conservative political leaders, including Republican presidents, have cut back or kept ineffective various equal opportunity, affirmative action, and other programs designed to redress racial discrimination. In the 1990s the Democratic (Clinton) presidential administration placed somewhat greater emphasis on enforcing civil rights laws and expanding opportunity, but the election of more conservative Congresses in the 1990s brought renewed efforts to curtail affirmative action and other antidiscrimination programs. After the election of George W. Bush in 2000 (and 2004), the executive branch of the U.S. government moved even farther away from an aggressive commitment to end racial discrimination. Indeed, President Bush withdrew early a delegation to a major international conference on racism held in South Africa in the summer of 2001.

Decades after civil rights laws were passed, racial and ethnic discrimination remains very serious and widespread, and many federal and local government agencies and private institutions have backed away from effective programs to counter such persisting discrimination. No large-scale and lasting changes in racial composition and influence have yet occurred at or near the top levels in most major U.S. institutions. Whites (usually white men) still, overwhelmingly, dominate upper-level and (often) middle-level positions in most major organizations—from the executive branch of the U.S. government to *Fortune* 1000 corporations, major universities, most state legislatures, major banks, and large supermarket chains.

As we demonstrated in Chapter 7, many research studies show that discrimination against African Americans, mainly by white Americans, remains common in employment, housing, and education. Since the 1980s, most white Americans have shifted attention away from eradicating this pervasive racial discrimination. Indeed, in recent years a majority of whites seem to be in denial even about the severity of continuing racial discrimination. However, the deep reality and great pain of this discrimination can be seen by any person who sincerely wishes to see it. For example, when asked what it is like being black in America, a retired professor who has lived in several regions of the country replied as follows:

> I feel angry. I feel betrayed. Sometimes I feel very cynical. Most of the time I feel that I live in a country where I'm still not respected as a person. I lived at a time when I was told that if I got a good education, did all the right things, that I could be anything I wanted to be. I got a good education. I did all the right things, but even today I run into situations where my opportunity structure is limited because I am black. So I found that all along, no matter what I did, no matter how hard I tried, limitations were placed on me strictly because of the color of my skin. So I feel betrayed by the Constitution that guaranteed me certain rights. I feel betrayed by the Pledge of Allegiance to the flag, which says "liberty and justice for all."[32]

This statement was made in the late 1980s but, when we asked him recently if he still felt this way, he replied a firm "yes," adding that in some ways the situation was getting worse. In the aftermath of protests by African Americans, in the 1960s and recently, many whites have asked why they still rebel. Across the country African Americans and other Americans of color have protested because of continuing frustration and anger over pervasive individual and institutional discrimination. The equality-and-justice agenda of this country remains substantially rhetorical and unfinished. Contrary to the views of many, periodic group protests by Americans of color about flaws in U.S. society are usually realistic and at base about racism, economic equality, and civil rights.

How has the global expansion of the U.S. government and corporate operations shaped patterns of U.S. immigration?

Conclusion

We began this chapter with a brief discussion of demographic changes taking place in the United States. In some ways the country remains rather segregated geographically, along racial and ethnic lines. Many new immigrants, primarily Asian and Latin American, have settled on the coasts—in Los Angeles, New York City, San Francisco, Miami, Baltimore, Houston, San Diego, Boston—and in a certain midwestern cities such as Chicago. In contrast, significant numbers of whites have left numerous coastal cities in favor of outlying suburbs, rural areas, and smaller metropolitan areas, especially in the south Atlantic, Pacific, and Mountain regions. Still, to complicate the demographic picture, many Americans of color, including longer-resident Latino and Asian immigrants and their children, are now moving in larger numbers to many cities other than the entry cities on the coasts.

Even though the U.S. population has grown substantially in recent decades, without immigration many major cities (such as New York and Los Angeles) from which whites have departed would have experienced serious population declines. Numerous high-immigration (especially coastal) metropolitan areas are now heavily populated by Americans of color, while much of the center of the United States remains disproportionately white. Today, about half the white population lives in the Northeast or Midwest, but a much smaller proportion of all Americans of color live in those same areas. Americans of color are already a majority of the populations in California, New Mexico, Hawaii, and Texas. The populations of eight additional states, including New York, New Jersey, and Florida, are projected to be more than 40 percent Americans of color by the 2020s. In contrast, twelve states, including several in New England and in the Mountain and North Central areas, are projected to be overwhelmingly white.[33]

The ongoing population shift from a predominantly white country to one in which no racial or ethnic group has a population majority has significant economic, social, and political implications. In our view, much more thought needs to be given by all Americans, including social researchers and policy makers, to the likely effects of these changes and to ways to create a truly democratic multiracial country.

For example, consider the educational system. Twenty-seven of the eighty-eight metropolitan areas with populations over a half-million already have populations under fifteen years of age that are a majority of children of color. These include Los Angeles, San Francisco, Phoenix, Miami, Las Vegas, Tucson, and Washington, D.C. School systems in these and many other cities already have majority populations that are not white.[34] Indeed, about the late 2030s, the U.S. educational system as a whole will be composed predominantly of students of color. Such a population change will increasingly pose major challenges to the traditional white control of the structure, administration, and curriculum of public schools. Increasingly, parents, students, and teachers of color will likely press for much more input into how these schools are structured and run. Current discrimination against Americans of color is not likely to be tolerated when these groups have significant organizational and political power. School officials will likely become much more concerned with issues of expanded multiculturalism, enhanced diversity, varying group conflict, and imbedded institutional racism.

In addition, by the 2050s, if not before, demographic forecasts suggest that a majority of working Americans will no longer be white, while a majority of the older retired population will be white. One can wonder how, to take just one issue, workers of color will view paying various taxes to support elderly whites on Social Security and other support programs when many of those whites were the ones who created and maintained the patterns of racial discrimination that have oppressed these workers of color and their parents over decades.

Intergroup debates about and conflict over sociopolitical power, discrimination, diversity, and related public policy issues—such as serious affirmative action programs or laws to restrict immigrants—are likely to increase. Areas in which a majority of voters are people of color are not likely, depending on the area and groups involved, to elect whites who have a history of strong opposition to legal immigration, affirmative action, or other antidiscrimination programs. We already see this in states such as California and New York. A 2000 survey of voters leaving New York City polling places found that at least one-fifth of the voters were foreign-born (mostly voters of color). Some 13 percent of the foreign-born were Asian American voters, who are doubtless seeking expanded political representation in a city where up to now they have had little representation. Not surprisingly, Asian American leaders forecast major political changes for that city, including more attention to the needs of the city's Asian American communities. As voting constituencies change to reflect ongoing demographic changes, the composition of political bodies, juries and justice systems, educational systems, and other government institutions at all levels is likely to change significantly—unless, as some analysts fear, reactionary white political and business leaders take action to stop these likely changes in the direction of expanded democracy.[35]

Is it possible to move in the direction of much greater racial and ethnic equality and justice? These ideals have long been part of an authentic American dream and framing of a better society. The roots of that dream lie in many Americans' aspirations for liberty, human rights, and social justice over four centuries. These ideals were articulated in the Declaration of Independence, a path-breaking document that more than two centuries ago reflected this country's movement toward greater liberty and democracy. However, the Declaration and the U.S. Constitution were very seriously marred by a capitulation to white supporters of the slavery system. After the abolitionist movement and the Civil War, the Constitution was amended to abolish slavery and expand the liberties of African Americans, although Supreme Court and other government decisions soon severely limited the benefits stemming from the constitutional changes. Later, in the mid- and late twentieth century, under pressure from the numerous civil rights and women's movements, Supreme Court decisions and new civil rights laws brought formal equality and greater opportunities for Americans of color (and white women). Still, antidiscrimination laws and court decisions have often gone unenforced or have been weakly enforced. In addition, these civil rights laws do not protect against, and thus cannot eradicate, many informal types of racial and ethnic discrimination that persist now in the twenty-first century.

Whether equality and social justice for subordinated racial and ethnic groups can become the reality in the United States remains to be seen. In the recent and distant past, the expansion of human rights, equality, and justice has often resulted from the effective and large-scale organization of racially and ethnically oppressed people and their white allies against persisting racial and ethnic oppression. The likelihood of a further expansion seems to be conditional on renewed and successful political action and organization by Americans of all backgrounds and creeds who are committed to the eradication of such oppression and to the full implementation of the grand ideals of human rights, equality, and justice.

Key Terms

multiculturalism 368 **cultural diversity** 368

PART III

Global Realities

BIG PICTURE QUESTIONS

- ***How has European imperialism impacted racial and ethnic oppression and conflict in colonized societies?***
- ***How does neocolonialism continue the process of exploitation of former European colonies?***

Today, there is much racial and ethnic oppression and conflict in countries across the globe. In this third section we go beyond the United States to look at some major racial and ethnic issues as they have arisen on other continents—South America, Europe, and Africa. Until European imperialism began in earnest in the 1400s, most local intergroup oppressions and conflicts were shaped by local histories and contexts. In the long period of European imperialism, numerous European countries sent explorers and colonists to seize the labor, lands, and other material resources that would expand the wealth of the home countries. Eventually, most of the globe was under European domination. This colonialism involved the organized theft, the exploitation, of the labor and land of a great many indigenous societies overseas.

In his probing and brilliant book, *The World and Africa*, savvy sociologist W. E. B. Du Bois summarized the bloody effects of much European colonialism:

> There was no Nazi atrocity—concentration camps, wholesale maiming and murder, defilement of women and ghastly blasphemy of childhood—that the Christian civilization of Europe had not long been practicing against coloured folk in all parts of the world in the name of and for the defense of a Superior Race born to rule the world.[1]

Indigenous societies were destroyed or greatly reshaped by the impact of the European invaders and their military, political, economic, and religious organizations. This colonization was usually defended by an ideology of white European (usually Christian) superiority.

In addition, if there was already intergroup conflict in the colonized country, it was usually shaped or redirected by the European intervention. European imperialism also had a rebound effect, later or at the same time, on racial and ethnic oppression and conflicts within the colonizing societies themselves. We see this in the major example of France in the next chapter, as we have already seen evidence of this effect in the case of U.S. involvement overseas, such as in South Korea and Vietnam.

After centuries of direct European colonialism, colonizers and colonized have often remained linked. In *The World and Africa*, Du Bois examined how the poverty and disease of Europe's many African colonies have been closely linked to the great wealth and continuing prosperity that have persisted over centuries now in numerous European countries. A full understanding of that European prosperity must incorporate how extensive European colonialism took by force the labor and mineral resources of many colonized countries, especially those African countries (indeed, most of them) that were European colonies.

Today, economic neocolonialism typically continues the process of resource exploitation of former colonies. We see the effect of this colonialism and neocolonialism in the cases of South Africa and Brazil, which are examined in Chapter 14. In major ways the stolen economic resources of land and labor created the basis for much wealth in contemporary European countries while leaving the former colonies with a great range of major, and lasting, social and economic problems often not of their own making. Thus, the histories and current societal realities of the three countries examined in the next chapter are closely connected to the European colonization of Africa and Latin America. These important case studies show the major and continuing effects of Europe's overseas colonization on both the colonized and the colonizers.

Global Racism in Systemic Perspective

The global colonialism and imperialism examined earlier in this book and in the chapter that follows were typically rationalized in terms of a white racist framing of the social events. As we showed in previous chapters, especially Chapters 1 and 2, social theorists have often examined the origins of racial and ethnic formation and differentiation, as well as the reasons for the adaptation, perpetuation, and alteration of thereby-created racial and ethnic groups. Social theorists are interested in group interaction over long periods of time, which interaction has varied from peaceful coexistence and cooperation to substantial exploitation to genocidal destruction. Theorists examine differences in political, economic, and cultural foundations of racial and ethnic patterns of behavior that link to group enslavement, marginalization, and assimilation, among other possibilities of group interaction. In order to answer the question of how and why racial and ethnic patterns change over time, social theorists frequently explore key historical factors, such as the development of modern capitalism, that often generate social formations such as external colonialism and internal colonialism.

Considering this history, our concept of *systemic racism* provides a solid basis for understanding the origins, perpetuation, and maintenance of global racial oppression, as well as the large-scale resistance to that oppression. In previous chapters we have shown how this oppression has long been systemic and institutionalized, and how its modern forms have been generated and maintained, principally but not exclusively, by people of European descent—who by the 1400s were oppressing peoples around the globe and who saw themselves as civilizing and Christianizing supposedly "uncivilized" (by the 1600s, "not white") peoples. Understanding the systematizing and institutionalized reality of this oppression, this systemic racism, provides us with a comprehensive theory with which to examine the racial (and ethnic) relations shaped by four centuries of white exploitation and domination of people of color, not only in the United States but in most areas of the globe where Europeans intruded. As Chapter 2 explains, W. E. B. Du Bois and Oliver Cromwell Cox were probably the first to evaluate this racial oppression from a deep global and historical perspective, from which they examined not only the distinctive historical route of the North American experience but also how this experience paralleled the imposed changes of Eurocentric imperialism in many parts of the world. As a result of this European performance, similar racialized patterns have emerged in the experiences of people of color around the globe. Thus, we have the reality and pervasiveness of racism on a global level.

In this chapter we examine global racism further. We put the theory of systemic racism even more within a cross-cultural context in order to better understand some of its constituent elements. As previous chapters demonstrate, the study of racial and ethnic relations and oppressions, of racial-ethnic domination and resistance, generally requires a multifaceted inquiry. Studying the comparable societal cases of South Africa, Brazil, and France gives us an enhanced and nuanced perspective on global racism, including an increased understanding of our highly racialized United States.

Besides the crucial step of putting European and Euro-American domination of people of color at the center of historical and cross-cultural analysis, a theory of systemic racism encourages us to understand how the deeply imbedded racial hierarchies of these societies reflect centuries of institutionalized material and economic exploitation. For example, in North America, white colonizers seized Native American lands, just as white colonizers seized Bantu and Zulu lands in South Africa and the lands of many indigenous peoples in Brazil. Enslaved African laborers were often used to work the stolen lands. Once land and labor were stolen, through a centuries-old social reproduction process, systemic racism persisted and expanded, thereby destroying or limiting socioeconomic and other life possibilities for many racial and ethnic groups. Just in regard to economic conditions, the racial hierarchy means racially fractured and segmented job markets. The worldwide reality is that the majority of low-wage jobs are now held by workers of color, and unemployment rates are typically much higher for those on the lowest rungs of the racial hierarchy in the United States, South Africa, Brazil, and France. In addition, racialized social segregation has long been part of the experience of domination for various oppressed racial groups in all these countries. Moreover, in the United States, beginning in the slavery era, individual and group resistance to this racial oppression has involved an ongoing struggle. And this U.S. struggle against racial oppression is by no means unique. This battle for freedom has been fought, and is still being fought, in South Africa, Brazil, and France—in each case in terms demanding that allegedly democratic governments deliver on old promises of equality, justice, and progress for all.

Throughout this book we have seen how this system of racial oppression constantly overlaps and interrelates with other systems of social domination, especially gender and class domination. Thus, white *male* elites in the United States, South Africa, Brazil, and France generally maintain great privilege and power over both white women and women and men of color.

Not only reproducing the system, but also legitimizing it and creating institutions for such ends has become an important aspect of the perpetuating racial ideology and framing of systemic racism, so much so that not only the white oppressors, but also people of color, begin to believe that it is "normal" and this cannot be changed.

As we have seen and will see in Chapter 14, however, societal change is very possible. The struggle against oppression is an integral part of the racial and ethnic history of the United States, and the overthrow of apartheid in South Africa, the civil rights groups' efforts to force the Brazilian government to fulfill its commitments to "racial democracy," and the protests by African Muslims in France all demonstrate both the imperative and importance of confronting racial oppression, as well as the difficulties of overcoming deeply imbedded systems of racial oppression. By looking at some important global manifestations of systemic racism in the next chapter, we begin to understand how societal structures and complexities exhibit the significance, depth, and adaptability not only of racist ideology and oppression but also of antiracist resistance and confrontation, all at the global scale.

How does the concept of systemic racism help in understanding global racial oppression?

CHAPTER 14

Colonialism and Postcolonialism: The Global Expansion of Racism

BIG PICTURE QUESTIONS

- ***How has modern capitalism shaped global patterns of racial exploitation and inequality?***
- ***What are the legacies of European colonialism in African and Latin American countries?***
- ***Where can systemic racism be found outside the United States?***

This chapter was written by Pinar Batur of Vassar College.

In the spring of 1994, after the first elections in which black and white South Africans voted together, South Africa's new black president, Nelson Mandela, commented: "Today is a day like no other before it. Today marks the dawn of our freedom. . . . We are starting a new era of hope, reconciliation and nation-building."[1] That day, 30 million South Africans felt free of racial **apartheid**, *the rigidly institutionalized system of racial segregation and social, economic, and political inequality that had long invaded most aspects of daily life in South Africa.* The newly elected South African government outlawed apartheid and promised to move toward equality in rights and in black access to everything whites had in South Africa.

With this assurance, Nkosingthi Msesizwe, a black miner, believed he could now ride the same elevator with white miners in postapartheid South Africa. But Msesizwe was beaten by white miners, who shouted that "this hoist is for whites. It is not for you."[2] Even though South Africa's new government assured South Africans that equality would be achieved through constitutional changes, the transition has been difficult. More than a decade after the election that marked the end of apartheid, institutionalized racism, including overt discrimination, is still the everyday reality in contemporary South African society. Government statistics reveal that the proportion of households earning less than $90 a month rose from 20 percent of the population in 1995 to 28 percent in 2000. As a result, the poorest half of all South Africans, almost all black, earned just 9.7 percent of the national income in 2000, down from 11.4 percent in 1995.[3] The pattern seems to be similar to the persistent pattern of racial inequality in the United States. Other countries show similar patterns. Thus, when we examine Brazil, considered a "racial democracy" by some, we see that it too has one of the world's most unequal distributions of income, one of the indicators of persistent racial inequality between white and black Brazilians. The data indicate that white Brazilians earn at least 50 percent more than black Brazilians with the same level of education.[4] Why does examination of these countries, on different continents, with different histories and cultures, reveal similar patterns?

In this chapter we assess the cases of South Africa, Brazil, and France in order to examine how colonialism and the global reality of systemic racial discrimination and other elements of racism have been implemented and maintained by whites of European ancestry in countries other than the United States. The case of South Africa demonstrates the major life-determining and life-threatening consequences of European colonialism and the thoroughgoing institutionalization of overt antiblack racism, whereas Brazil exhibits how a racist culture overtly and covertly links to and maintains racist institutions. Turning to France, we explore the legacy and effects of racialized colonialism in one of the major European colonizing powers. In our view, students of contemporary racial and ethnic relations should know about more than intergroup relations and stratification in their own country. In order to understand the global realities of the twenty-first century, students must know about the history and development of colonialism, imperialism, and racialized societies around the globe.

Colonialism and Racism

In F. Scott Fitzgerald's classic 1920s novel, *The Great Gatsby,* one discussion among wealthy white characters focuses on a racist book that argued that, if not prevented, "the white race will be... utterly submerged. It's all scientific stuff; it's been proved.... It is up to us, who are the dominant race, to watch out or these other races will have control of things." One of the white characters then whispers, "We've got to beat them down."[5] As revealed in such novels as well as in government policy decisions, the white racial frame and its ideological racism have long validated for the white public imperialist expansion and colonialism around the world. Economic and political exploitation has long targeted people who are not of the dominant racial group, while the white-generated ideology of racism has rationalized this exploitation. This white-racist framing has long rationalized the subordination of people of color in many societies colonized by Europeans, including not only the United States but also South Africa and Brazil.

The expansion of Western capitalism around the globe since the 1400s has fostered the division of people according to racial group, including the assignment of superior and inferior characteristics to certain designated "races." As we noted in Chapter 2, the dynamics of this Western capitalistic expansion, which created numerous colonies of subordinated peoples, made racial inequality a permanent part of global existence through white racial framing and its racist ideologies, and associated discriminatory practices. Western capitalistic expansion integrated white racist framing and action into global and local economic and political arrangements and cultural production. The international development of Western capitalism also fostered the advancement of ideological and "scientific" racism, integrating them into a global system of oppression with its distinctive racialized culture. The examination of racism as a global reality is important to the study of racial relations because white racism's institutions superimpose themselves on local institutions in societies that it invades, and those institutions shape the construction of personal identities and everyday experiences of both colonizers and colonized.[6] By the eighteenth century global racism had become a process of defining and building communities and societies based on racialized privileges and a continuing hierarchy of power with whites of European background at the top and racially oppressed people at or near the bottom.

The global expansion of European capitalism through colonialism and imperialism gave white racist thinking and framing a global scope; indeed, by the early 1900s a majority of the earth's peoples were more or less under the control of European colonizers. In W. E. B. Du Bois's famous words, these dynamics lead to establishment of a global demarcation: "The problem of the twentieth century is the problem of the color line," because "force and fear have hitherto marked the white attitude" and permeated every major aspect of many societies. "Regardless of color, we carry the color abhorrence in our hearts."[7]

The History and Legacy of Colonialism

Western colonialism began with the major overseas expansion of Spain and Portugal, whose rulers sought to enhance their treasuries with gold, silver, and other goods taken from the world's peoples. The legal and ideological rationale for this colonialism was provided by Roman Catholic popes in several papal bulls, declarations echoing papal justifications for the Christian crusades against Muslims in earlier centuries.[8] On May 3, 1493, Pope Alexander VI issued a bull of demarcation, a document resolving Spanish and Portuguese disputes over colonization. As revised by the Treaty of Tordesillas in 1494, this bull put all the world's non-Christian ("pagan") peoples at the economic disposal of these growing colonial powers.[9] The Christian justification for expansion was for a time in tension with the profit-making desire of European entrepreneurs for land and slave labor. For a short period, some Catholic theologians and priests, most notably the Spanish priest Las Casas, opposed the ruthless enslavement of the indigenous populations. However, in a 1550 debate with Las Casas in Spain, theologian Gaines de Sepulveda carried the day with his argument that it was lawful to make war on and enslave the indigenous populations because of their heathen, sinful, and barbarous "natures," which obligated them to serve those (the Spanish) with the "superior" culture and virtues.[10]

After the 1500s, European expansion led by the Netherlands, England, and France (and later by Germany and Belgium) spurred the global expansion of capitalism, in the process fostering great economic and racial inequality between colonizers and colonized.[11] These countries generated scholars, theologians, and politicians who developed theories of the superiority of white Europeans and the animal-like inferiority of non-European peoples. Europeans distinguished themselves from so-called savages in many ways. Often, the colonized peoples were demonized and considered to have the vices that the English and other Europeans feared in themselves: wildness, brutishness, cruelty, laziness, sexual promiscuity, and heathenism. "Far from English civilization, they had to remind themselves constantly what it meant to be civilized—Christian, rational, sexually controlled, and white."[12] By the 1700s and 1800s, well-developed theories of the cultural and racial inferiority of the overseas "savages" were pronounced by English and other European leaders, as we noted in Chapter 1. As one of the major racist ideologues of the nineteenth century, Joseph de Gobineau, put it:

> [White people] are gifted with reflective energy, or rather with an energetic intelligence. . . . They have a remarkable, even extreme love of liberty, and are openly hostile to the formalism under which the Chinese are glad to vegetate, as well as the strict despotism which is the only way of governing the Negro.[13]

At an early point in time, colonialism became a system of control based on a colonial political administration, an exploitative commercial trade, and a missionary zeal to convert indigenous populations to Christianity and "civilization." In Asian, Oceanic, African, and American societies, this threefold domination fostered colonial administrations' oppressive rule, unequal trade practices, and the imposition of Christianity and Western culture. Desire for raw materials motivated European colonial expansion, such as the desire to obtain black pepper and lumber from Brazil or tea and spices from India. Securing these resources frequently required use of military violence—which violence, after the initial conquest, was carried out by a colonial administration. Everyday life in the colonies was reshaped by the European oppressors, who controlled colonized societies politically, economically, and culturally. Exploitation of colonized peoples and their many valuable natural resources was usually accompanied by systematic violence.[14]

Violence and exploitation were justified through an ideology of cultural and racial superiority that penetrated religious and political views and even everyday language. White racial framing and its racist ideology not only were an integral aspect of the dominant group's racial identity, but also often seeped into the subordinate group's racialized construction of its own self-conception. Pervasive material and ideological racism fostered the view of the colonized as subordinate and powerless.[15] Albert Memmi, a North African author educated in French colonial schools, wrote about the penetrating effect of such colonial rule:

> I am ill at ease in my own land and I know of no other. My culture is borrowed and I speak my mother tongue haltingly. I have neither religious beliefs nor tradition and am ashamed of whatever particle of them has survived deep within me.... I am Tunisian, but of French culture.[16]

European colonialism altered the lives of the colonized; it also had major effects on colonizers and their home countries. The flow of raw materials from the highly exploited colonies demanded a docile working class in both the colonized and the colonizing societies. Thus, the French Empire subjugated African areas such as Algeria, and the system of economic subjugation and racist rationalization reached well back into French society, thereby shaping negatively the conditions for the white working class in France. The white working class's acceptance of colonialism and the ideology of white racism, as well as of their own class oppression in France, was fostered by their own false sense of racial superiority and their uncritical acceptance of their own political and economic system. For example, French colonialism long oppressed Algerians in Africa, and in today's postcolonial France whites' racist views and actions greatly influence the political and economic positions of first- and second-generation Algerians now residing in France. In the United States, as we have documented, European colonial oppression included African slavery, the extermination of Native Americans, and the conquest of Puerto Rico and the Philippines. The scars of this colonial oppression likewise continue to influence contemporary social and political events in the United States.

Drawing on old racist ideologies and verbally or physically attacking racially oppressed people in their midst, white neo-Nazi groups and racist political parties have reemerged in most of the former colonizer societies of Europe and North America. The ongoing relationships between colonizing and colonized societies have firmly established the white framing and its ideology of racial superiority as a central mode in global thinking—a racial framing that shapes images of the (formerly or currently) colonized as well as the institutionalized practices of everyday oppression.[17] During the postcolonial era, the white racist framing and the practices of institutional racism are continuing global realities.

We now turn to an exploration of the effects and the legacy of colonialism in the colonized societies of South Africa and Brazil and in the colonizing society of France.

To Whom Does Southern Africa Belong?

In many areas, those who come to occupy the land often ask, "To whom does this land really belong?" According to racist constructions of colonial history, the land is usually "discovered" by "civilized" white people, who are the first to "use the land in a productive way." For white colonizers, the real history of a place begins with European or Euro-American colonization.

The Khoisan people resided in the area now called South Africa when the ancestors of the current Bantu-speaking black majority arrived there around 300 A.D.[18] The first European expedition to the area came *much later* in the form of Portuguese explorers in 1487. The first significant European settlement in southern Africa dates to 1652, when Jan van Riebeeck established a station for the Dutch East India Company. As Dutch colonial settlements spread, confrontations with the Bantu peoples led to a series confrontations, which Europeans called "kaffir wars."

In Arabic, *kaffir* originally meant "infidel." In South Africa, whites used it is as a hostile and degrading racist term (like "nigger" in the United States) for the black peoples in South Africa. Early European invaders and occupiers there saw their colonization as a religious and civilizing mission that justified the killing, subjugation, and enslavement of indigenous people. Drawing on the spreading and powerful white racist framing, Europeans rated themselves as racially and religiously superior to indigenous Africans, whom they considered to be animal-like, and they often stereotyped them as heathens, "idolatrous and licentious, thieving and lying, lazy and dirty."[19] Europeans often rationalized what they saw as the inferiority of Africans through "scientific" racism, arguing that the tropical environment was responsible for producing immature, childish, and "beastlike" creatures who could be "civilized" only by the European work ethic and Christian discipline. European colonists thus legitimated their invasion, occupation, and enslavement of black Africans as a vehicle to lift the latter from their "barbarism."[20]

While the white invaders agreed among themselves about the black "inferiority," they continued to fight each other for control. The Dutch colonial interest in southern Africa collided with British determination to control the sailing route to India around the tip of Africa. Britain's conquest of southern Africa's Cape Colony in 1806 and British colonial settlement beginning in 1820 fueled the out-migration of 15,000 **Boers**—*white South Africans of Dutch descent*—into the interior, a movement these whites called the "Great Trek." The British imperialists abolished slavery and changed the regulations on black labor. The Boers interpreted British actions as putting black people "on an equal footing with [white] Christians, contrary to the laws of God and the natural distinction of race."[21] These views were asserted by Dutch ministers and also reflected the goals of the Dutch East India Company, which had tried to create a racially divided society to maintain the slave trade and theft of raw materials.[22]

Dutch leaders began to promote Dutch settlers as the true "white tribe of Africa" and called themselves **Afrikaaners** (*white speakers of the Afrikaans language*).[23] According to the racist ideology, there were "no native blacks" prior to the arrival of Europeans. This erroneous view persists today: "Basically we came here more or less at the same time. We both belong to South Africa. There is no one black man who can say that this is his country more so than a white. We belong here as much as they do."[24] In addition, in defense of earlier slavery and current labor conditions, the Afrikaners have long argued that "we make the [black] people work for us in consideration of allowing them to live in our country."[25]

Are there similarities in contacts between Dutch colonists and Bantu peoples and those of European colonists and Native Americans?

Formation of the State and Apartheid

European interest in southern Africa was further stimulated by the discovery of diamonds and gold in the late nineteenth century. Under growing colonial control and violence, the oppressive working conditions in mines as well as on agricultural plantations shaped the brutality of everyday life for black Africans. In 1910 the Union of South Africa was created, which united British areas with Boer areas and redefined South Africa in terms of the common heritage of European Christianity and a "civilizing" mission. The new white-controlled state imposed extensive racial segregation on the politically defined population of "blacks" and "**coloureds**," the latter being *people of mixed white–black ancestry*. The 1913 Native Lands Act limited land ownership and settlement for black and coloured South Africans, but not for white South Africans, to restricted areas. Voting rights and political representation were reserved for whites. As gold and diamond mining and other industries expanded, the labor force was sharply divided between whites, who held skilled and supervisory positions with better wages and working conditions, and black workers, who were unskilled and worked under severe conditions with little pay.[26]

Black South Africans drew on their home cultures to resist the racialized oppression and inequality. Organized opposition to increasingly racist policies came from the African National Congress (ANC), founded in 1912 to demand voting rights, freedom of residence, and land ownership for black Africans. White voters elected the National Party in 1948 on a platform of apartheid that mandated separate development and complete racial segregation. The supporters of apartheid drew on a virulent form of white-racist and fascist ideologies. Afrikaner whites, like the Nazis in Germany, constructed South Africa as a "special nation with a special mission: The Afrikaner believes that it is the will of God that there should be a diversity of races and nations and that obedience to the will of God therefore requires the acknowledgment and maintenance of that diversity."[27] Afrikaner nationalists argued that "the preservation of the pure race tradition of the [Boers] must be preserved at all costs.... Any movement, school, or individual who sins against this must be dealt with as a racial criminal by the effective authorities." Church-sanctioned racist thinking was a great buttress for racial oppression; the Dutch Reform Church of South Africa became a citadel for the National Party.[28]

Apartheid had several interconnected aspects. One was the racially hierarchical structure in which whites, about 18 percent of the population, ruled over the 82 percent who were "not white." This racialized hierarchy was fostered by a white-controlled nation-state that denied full citizenship to Africans of color. A critical aspect of racial apartheid was widespread and well-institutionalized discrimination, which included extensive racial segregation in everyday life.[29]

Apartheid was reinforced by many racist laws. For example, the 1950 Population Registration Act established legal registration by racial group; the Group Areas Act prohibited black South Africans from residing outside of racially zoned areas. In the 1950s, the government sought to control opposition to apartheid by passing security legislation against so-called Communist activities, and until the 1980s this law enabled the government to silence any black or white South Africans opposed to government racial policies through the use of aggressive intimidation, imprisonment, and state violence. To control the transfer of knowledge, in 1953 the white government took control of public education, creating a separate and inferior educational system for black South Africans.[30] In addition, the Bantu Self-Government Act forced much of the black population into territorially fragmented areas, called *homelands*, with very limited material resources. Recognized by white South Africans, and only by them, as "independent countries," these homelands were yet another form of racial apartheid. Another example of the brutality of apartheid was the 1956 decision to order 100,000 non-Europeans to leave their homes in the city of Johannesburg within one year in order to make residential space available for whites. In 1964, new laws expanded apartheid by regulating black employment, giving the police power to hold suspects for months without trial, and prohibiting political organizations composed of racially diverse members.

Scholars have debated the role of South African capitalists in maintaining apartheid. Clearly, these white capitalists benefited from apartheid, yet some were opposed to its more extreme manifestations. A good example is Harry Oppenheimer, who in 1957 inherited the Anglo-American Corporation and DeBeers Consolidated Mines, which controls much of South Africa's and the world's gold, diamonds, and copper, as well as almost all coal production in South Africa. After 1959, Oppenheimer supported the Progressive Party, which advocated incorporation of black Africans into the political system. In 1976 he established the Urban Foundation for social support projects in black areas. However, Oppenheimer also took advantage of the racist labor structure by holding down the wages of his black workers. Even though some capitalists objected to apartheid because it was bad for the country's image, they mostly played a key role in supporting and prolonging apartheid because it kept labor costs down.[31]

Opposition to Apartheid

As apartheid intensified, so did efforts of the ANC and another resistance group called the Pan-African Congress (PAC), both of which were banned by the government in 1960.[32] In 1964, after the infamous Sharpeville massacre, in which the police killed sixty-nine black demonstrators in an urban area,

Black South Africans line up to use their new voting rights in democratic municipal elections in Cape Town.

Nelson Mandela and other ANC and PAC leaders were sentenced to life in prison. These imprisonments were followed by the torture and deaths of some leaders held in police custody. As the support for racial apartheid became more violent, the antiapartheid movement in South Africa became stronger in response. A growing number of demonstrations, including numerous student demonstrations, resulted in hundreds of deaths of black protesters at the hands of brutal police forces.[33]

By the late 1970s, open opposition to apartheid in black townships near the larger cities forced the government to search for new ways to legitimize its control. White leaders first tried co-optation. Beginning in 1978, the restrictions on black labor unions and multiracial political parties were lifted. Meanwhile, the ANC enlarged its political base and changed its emphasis from armed struggle to mass political mobilization.[34]

For a time, the white government attempted to continue control by exacerbating divisions in the black and coloured populations. Differences among black South Africans were used by white leaders to channel anger away from white oppression. Thus, the South African government funded the black Inkatha Zulu separatist movement and secretly provided it with military training in order to fuel Zulu (one black group) hostility toward the ANC and its primary supporters, especially the Xhosa people (a different black group).[35] Also, by providing for some limited political participation by Asian and coloured people in the 1984 constitution, the white-controlled government tried to divide the population further, provoking widespread opposition among black South Africans. Demonstrations in townships were again met with brutal suppression. Declaring a state of emergency, the government tried to prevent the press from reporting clashes and detained thousands; some 250,000 black mineworkers responded to these actions with a three-week strike.[36] For a few years, such divide-and-conquer strategies allowed the white government to continue to impose its rule; but, by accentuating racial and ethnic divisions, these actions produced lasting problems for the development of a democratic South Africa in the current era.

White resistance to the antiapartheid movement had its limits. Black protests, together with an international economic boycott, made life increasingly difficult for whites. The white elite, particularly the economic elite, was disturbed by the social chaos and loss of profits. In 1989, after becoming the head of the government, F. W. deKlerk began to dismantle the policies of racial apartheid under pressure from black and white opponents of the old racist regime. After 12,000 deaths in political clashes over four years, the South African government finally moved to hold the first free elections. In April 1994, two and one-half years after being freed from prison,

Nelson Mandela, the head of the ANC, was elected to the presidency of South Africa. This marked a dramatic shift in political power, from oppressors to oppressed, something rarely seen in human history without large-scale revolution.

The Future of South Africa

Today, however, the racist past is still having an effect on South African society. Racial oppression is well institutionalized in everyday life, from the city of Pretoria—which white Afrikaner separatists still see as their spiritual capital—to the rural Zulu homelands, where many Zulus still consider the ANC and its leaders to be the continuation of white oppression.[37] In the most recent period, critical issues for South Africa have included (1) "black on black" violence, which often reflects group differences among black South Africans; (2) the political and economic problems that plague the segregated homelands; and (3) the perpetuation of racial inequality in housing, education, employment, and health care.

In June 1999 a new South African president was elected, ANC leader Thabo Mbeki. The ANC has facilitated a peaceful transition from white to black political rule and provided significant economic relief for many poor black South Africans. To this point, however, it has proven mostly inadequate in its policies in reducing unemployment and stimulating regional development that will benefit the entire black population. According to government statistics, as the average black African household income fell 19 percent from 1995 to 2000, to about $3700 per year, white household income enjoyed a 15 percent increase, to about $22,600 per year.[38]

The government has also failed to acknowledge the seriousness of the AIDS epidemic in South Africa. As AIDS activists warn that up to 10 million South Africans might die of AIDS in the first decade of the twenty-first century, the Mbeki government plans to extend antiretroviral therapy from 235,000 to 650,000 by 2011.[39] The Treatment Action Campaign general secretary, Sipho Mthathi, has said that "Our task is to end 1000 new HIV infections daily and to reduce the AIDS death rate of more than 900 deaths every day," but critics of the government argue that these efforts are too late and too little.[40] As a result, South Africa faces the challenge of one of the world's highest infection rates, with AIDS likely claiming the lives of one in three adults, and creating 2.5 million orphans, by 2010 unless the government takes strong action.[41]

President Mbeki was elected in the past because a new political opposition, the Democratic Alliance, represents white power to many of the country's black citizens. In the presidential election, the ANC distributed pamphlets showing that the opposition included among its members white supremacists who use old Nazi salutes. However, many black South African voters now seem to be losing hope for real economic development and new prosperity. Many black and white South Africans are growing disinterested in politics. Indeed, turnout for regional elections dropped from 89 percent in 1999 to 50 percent in 2000.[42]

Frantz Fanon once asked, "What is South Africa?" He answered his own question: "A boiler into which thirteen million blacks are clubbed and penned in by two and a half million whites."[43] Today, South Africa is changing, but whites still have much economic control, and most black South Africans feel the country is not changing fast enough to provide them hope and real sustenance. The case of South Africa shows how European colonialism has historically operated through a trilogy of domination—administration, trade, and religion—to establish a system of white control and violence and to extract, vampire-like, an area's great resources for (mostly) white use and wealth. After three long centuries of intensive colonial exploitation for white profit, the lives of the black people of southern Africa have been changed fundamentally and irrevocably, mostly for the worse. These changes have made the struggle against systemic white racism integral to the past, present, and future of South Africa.

How have black South Africans resisted segregation and other racial oppression?

Brazil: The Legacy of Slavery and the Illusion of Equality

The country of Brazil in South America has the largest African-origin population outside of Africa—reported to be just under half, about 80 million, of the country's 170 million people. Slavery was abolished in Brazil more than one hundred years ago, but systemic racism still has major effects on black Brazilians today. For example, in many restaurants black customers are harassed or excluded by being told that all empty tables are reserved. A major television soap opera that showed a white man and black woman kissing generated numerous angry protests. Black women complain that in apartment buildings they are presumed to be maids and are shown the service elevator. Almost all of the many thousands of teenagers on whom the police reportedly have detailed files are not white. Many employers routinely choose white over black applicants for better-paying jobs.[44]

Even without the nine decades of legal segregation that the United States experienced, or a long era of racial apartheid as in South Africa, politically and economically, the differences between black and white Brazilians demonstrate the harsh realities of great racial inequality. For example, only 15 of the 513 members of the Brazilian Congress, and 3 of 81 senators, are black. The judicial system is dominated by the 98.5 percent of judges who are white.[45] About 40 percent of the black population works in minimum-wage jobs.[46] Though they comprise nearly half the population, black Brazilians constitute just 2 percent of students enrolled in the universities, and only 17 percent of university graduates admit to mixed racial ancestry.[47] At the very large University of São Paulo, for instance, only a few of the 5000 faculty members are black. Overall, black Brazilians have the highest rates of unemployment, underemployment, illiteracy, and substandard housing.[48] This reality of major social, economic, and political inequality along racial lines is the great legacy of the long era of European colonization and slavery.

Brazil was colonized during the early period of the imperialistic expansion of Spain and Portugal, when European knowledge of the world beyond Europe was sketchy. The Portuguese sought to establish a commercial empire, and explorer Pedro Alvarez Cabral claimed this land for the Portuguese crown. The Portuguese elite named the land after a dye extracted from native trees. The emerging European textile industry consumed so much of the dye that, by the end of the 1500s, one hundred ships traveled regularly between Brazil and Portugal. The Portuguese established sugar cane plantations in numerous colonial settlements. Some indigenous inhabitants were enslaved, although most were slaughtered during wars between indigenous groups and the European colonizers or in wars between the Portuguese and other European powers coming into Brazil. Or, like indigenous peoples in the United States, these indigenous peoples died from European diseases because they had no immunity to them.[49]

Human rights marchers march against racism in Brasilia, Brazil.

By the nineteenth century, Brazil resembled the U.S. South. Large numbers of enslaved Afro-Brazilians worked on large plantations to produce sugar, coffee, and rubber for the ever-expanding, Europe-dominated, capitalist world market.[50] Brazil's enslaved population, mostly of African origin, numbered about 5 million—more than half its population—just before the abolition of slavery in 1888. Brazil became independent of Portugal in 1822, and in 1889 the local military overthrew the monarch and declared a republic. Since that time, Brazilian history has been marked by recurring military intervention in national politics and by continuous debates about the establishment of real democracy in a multiracial society.

Ever a Racial Democracy?

When Brazil's slave system ended, one stated national goal was to establish racial equality, but this did not develop. Indeed, black citizens continued to live under slavery-like conditions. Nonetheless, an official myth emerged that Brazil had "benign patterns" of racial relations and that Brazil was, and currently is, a unique *racial democracy*. Many Brazilians, especially whites, have loudly proclaimed their society to be a true racial democracy. This notion usually does not recognize the existence of significant and widespread racial prejudice and discrimination, much less the need for major policies of racial remediation and reparation. Instead, it claims that black Brazilians are equal in this multicultural society. The mainstream white ideology in Brazil argues that because of "Brazilian exceptionalism"—the allegedly equal treatment of the formerly enslaved population and the allegedly equal opportunities available to all—multicultural Brazil is not so starkly divided along racial lines as the United States and South Africa.[51] However, this view ignores Brazil's continuing, large-scale patterns of institutional racism and the associated white racist framing and racist ideology, all of which foster economic and political inequalities and the cultural marginalization of black and indigenous Brazilians.

Since the late nineteenth century, one aspect of Brazil's racial framing has been an obsessive focus on racial mixing. Many whites, including intellectuals, have argued that people of mixed descent exhibit the worst characteristics of their parents' racial groups and that Brazilian society will degenerate with the increased "mixing of the races." This societal-degeneration view was imported from the racist framing of the United States and Europe. Based on nineteenth-century assumptions about the origins and hierarchy of "races" (see Chapter 1), this notion fits well with white stereotypes and fears about losing control to a growing Afro-Brazilian population. Opponents of racial mixing have often supported their argument with a "whitening thesis," which claims that the "stronger and better white genes" are essential to the "progressive" evolution of the Brazilian population. Even though these racist notions assume the racial superiority of whites, they are clearly contradictory. On the one hand, the fear of racial mixing seems to encourage racial segregation while, on the other, the whitening notion seems to favor interracial marriages that would supposedly improve society's "gene pool."[52]

Emerging together in the nineteenth century, these racist assumptions remain part of Brazil's culture and still influence many white (and some black) Brazilians' thinking about the state of their country. Today, this perspective can be seen in immigration policies that favor white Europeans, in negative white attitudes to interracial marriages, and even in many black Brazilians' adherence to a color hierarchy that shows a decided preference for lighter skin tones.

Many light-skinned Brazilians believe that differences between racial groups are less important in their country than such differences in South Africa or the United States. However, Brazilians use many words for racial identification. The word for "black" does not have the same meaning in Brazil as in the United States or South Africa. In Brazil, *preto* (black) describes a person with mostly or all African ancestry. Yet, a racially mixed person who would likely be called "black" in the United States is identified in Brazil as *pardo* (brown) or *moreno*. Morenos are further divided into light (*morenos claros*) and dark (*morenos escuros*). The term *mulatto* is used to refer specifically to a person of mixed African and European backgrounds. In addition, because the term *Negro* includes *pretos* and *morenos*, it has provided a political term for black-power movements, as in Brazil's *Movimento Negro*.[53] As displayed by this diverse terminology, the country's racial hierarchy is supported by strong white stereotypes that view black people as "bad-smelling, dirty, unhygienic, ugly" and view those termed mulattos as "pushy and envious of whites." According to one revealing Brazilian ditty, "The white man goes to heaven, the mulatto stays on earth, the caboclo (mestizo) goes to purgatory, the black goes to hell."[54]

Today, as in the past, whiteness is a symbol of superiority and the key to social and political power. Indeed, in national censuses the number of people who identify as "mulatto" has grown faster than is statistically possible. Many people who are not white seem to be choosing this term because they believe that "brownness" is an escape hatch that will allow them to achieve greater upward mobility by acquiring an intermediate, and whiter, racial status. Moreover, by downplaying real racial differences in much public discussion, Brazil's white elites and political leaders avoid addressing problems of racially based economic inequality as well as racial inequalities in education and in mortality rates. Brazil has had periodic economic booms, but the benefits have flowed heavily to the upper middle class and the upper class, which have long been almost exclusively white.[55]

Are the present consequences of European colonialization in Brazil similar to those for the United States?

A Century of Lies

The colonial histories of Brazil and the United States are different, but racial inequality is similar in both countries. The inequality between Brazil's racial groups has sharpened between the 1960s and today, during the country's movement to economic integration and modernization. Transnational corporations, many headquartered in the United States, have sought low wages and new markets and invested heavily in Brazil. As black Brazilians have confronted elites and demanded equal-opportunity legislation to secure greater access to education and employment, they have developed important political movements resembling U.S. civil rights and black-power movements. Moreover, since the 1980s, as U.S. politicians and administrations have reduced federal commitments to expanded civil rights and to affirmative action and curtailed government efforts to reduce inequality (see Chapter 7), Brazil's government has acted in a similar backtracking fashion. As in the United States, powerful whites have criticized affirmative action for Afro-Brazilians with the inaccurate and confused term "reverse racism."[56]

While affirmative action policies are relatively new in Brazil, the country has a history of significant racial policies, including some in its constitution and other major laws. In 1960 the government declared racism a punishable offense. The 1988 Constitution declared such racism a crime with no statute of limitations, included provisions to protect black cultural practices, and granted some economic reparations—such as the granting of land titles to surviving families of the "quilombos," the communities formed by runaway slaves prior to emancipation in 1888. The election of Fernando Henrique Cardoso, a progressive and a sociologist, in 1995 led to more comprehensive policy initiatives regarding the goal of racial equality. Later, substantial gains were also made with the 1996 Human Rights Program, which officially recognized racial groups and the need for targeted remedial policies. Following the 2001 World Conference on Racism—from which U.S. officials withdrew, in part to avoid discussing reparations for indigenous nations and black Americans—Brazil announced some multilayered affirmative action policies. For example, the Agrarian, Culture, Justice and Foreign Ministries announced affirmative action programs involving 30 percent quotas for black Brazilians. In 2001, Rio de Janeiro established a 40 percent quota for its two universities. President Cardoso argued the need for recognition and active confrontation of racial inequality and declared that Brazilians "lived wrapped in the illusion that this was a perfect racial democracy when it wasn't, when even today it isn't."[57]

These changes occurred as a result of pressures from black individuals and organizations. For example, on May 13, 1988, marking the centennial of slavery's abolition, the government organized a celebration, but Afro-Brazilian groups put together counterdemonstrations. Demonstrators protested persisting racial inequality and institutionalized discrimination. Labeling the celebration a "farce" and "100 years of lies," they called for a "march for the real liberation of the race." Afro-Brazilians demanded the elimination of inequality in jobs and political power; they addressed issues of racial categorization and the African influences on Brazilian culture. They advocated a strengthening of cultural and other ties between black Brazilians and others in the

African Diaspora in order to challenge white-imposed racial oppression everywhere.[58] Another protest movement demanded significant land reform. Because 5 percent of the Brazilian population, which is overwhelmingly white, controls 95 percent of the land, more than 50,000 rural poor marched in the late 1990s to protest the slow pace of change and to demand much-needed land reform.[59]

Yet another growing social movement is that of indigenous Brazilians. Even though the recent census indicates a rapid growth of the indigenous population—from 294,000 in 1991 to 386,000 in 2001—twelve of the 216 indigenous groups in Brazil are still facing extinction. These indigenous groups make up an important part of the population, yet their voices have been largely undermined or ignored for centuries.[60]

Under Cardoso's administration (1995–2003), visible gains occurred mainly in the government bureaucracy. Cardoso's advisory council on racial issues was chaired by the first black government minister ever in Brazil. Under this progressive administration, Brazil also gained its second black general and its first black police commander.[61] Not surprisingly, many black Brazilians have demanded much faster change. Interestingly, some rap groups, such as Racionais MC'S and Thaide & DJ Hum, are strengthening the black civil rights movement by using popular music to criticize racial prejudice and discrimination in Brazilian society.[62]

Helio Santos, a black university professor, has underscored the contradictions in his country today: "Brazilian society discriminates against blacks at every point, but it is hidden, disguised. . . . There is an illusion of social democracy in Brazil. . . . Blacks internalize discrimination so often they can't see it."[63] As in the United States, the illusion of equality serves elites' social and political purposes while racial discrimination remains integral to society. According to C. L. P. Oliveira, a researcher in Brazil, "People have an idea of the proper place for blacks in society. . . . They see blacks as soccer players, musicians, workers . . . but it's very hard for many people to recognize them as doctors or lawyers, and other highly qualified professionals."[64] These realities indicate the continuation of struggle for black Brazilians. Indeed, whites receive college degrees at a rate much greater than that of black and indigenous Brazilians of the same age.[65] Only 17 percent of university graduates are of mixed racial ancestry, and only 2 percent are black. While some government affirmative action policies are now targeting these problems through setting up such things as remedial quotas for college student admission, the retention rate in college has been influenced by black students' economic conditions, which often force them to leave school in favor of low-paying jobs to support themselves or their families. As a result, the large racial gap in advanced education has not changed significantly for over one hundred years in Brazil.[66]

The Brazilian case shows the effects of European colonialism not only on economic and political institutions but also on ideological racism's development and its perpetuation in the popular culture. Racial subordination of black Brazilians, although considered by whites to be a thing of the past, remains a central part of Brazil's present and promises to continue to influence the country's future through the dominance of the white racist framing and ideology in elite thinking, institutionalized practices, and the mass media.

Does the systemic racism concept help explain racial conflict in Brazil?

Colonialism and Colonizer in France: The Violence of Inclusion and Exclusion

European colonialism legitimated using violence on subordinated peoples through a dichotomous construction of the colonial world in terms of "good" and "evil."[67] This symbolism of "good" colonizing Europeans and "evil" and unworthy colonized subjects was an integral aspect of racial subordination and conflict during the long colonial period and during the subsequent postcolonial period. This symbolism of good Europeans and evil "colonials" has deep religious roots and has long been part of the white racial framing of non-Europeans. Attempts at assimilation and integration in colonial areas have long been fundamentally challenged by these racist assumptions, and postcolonial societies are still confronted by them. Although there are many examples of this, contemporary France is a very important case that we will examine here.

The Character of French Colonialism

French colonialism differed from British and Portuguese colonialism in that it claimed the newly colonized peoples as "citizens of France." To realize this social fiction, colonial administrators propagated French culture and language in a vigorous attempt to assimilate colonized peoples into the French culture and empire. However, at no point in its history has France itself been unified or monocultural. Subordinated racial and ethnic groups in France, such as French Jews, have long been targets of racial hostility and exclusion. In a famous case, Alfred Dreyfus, a Jewish captain in the French army, was falsely accused by his superiors and convicted in 1898 of selling military secrets to the Germans. The trial became a major political issue in the French elections of that year, and many candidates adopted anti-Semitic platforms. Yet French Jews made up a tiny 0.2 percent of the population at the time. In the first two months of 1898, French Jews were the targets of no fewer than sixty-nine anti-Semitic riots in which 4000 people participated; the rioters destroyed Jewish businesses and synagogues and attacked many individual Jews.[68]

France's anti-Semitic orientation emerged again during World War II in the southern pro-Nazi Vichy area of France. While the French-run Vichy government opposed the exportation of French Jews to German extermination camps, it did not resist deportation of foreign Jews in the region.[69] When former French President Francois Mitterand's association with the pro-Nazi Vichy government was later revealed in the press, he responded only that, at the time, "I did not think about the anti-Semitism of Vichy."[70] Official and popular obliviousness to racist framing and action, even among some "left" politicians, is integral to an enduring societal system of racism.

What role has anti-Semitism played in French patterns of racial thought and discrimination?

Muslim Immigrants and Racism

Since the period of overseas colonialism, debates surrounding immigration to France have often reflected overt and subtle racist thinking about government immigration policies. Today, it is estimated that one in every four French citizens has a non-French parent or grandparents.[71] The contemporary complexities surrounding the assimilation and integration of immigrants stem substantially from the French government's relations with about 5 million immigrant Muslims from Africa, most of whom settled in France after the Algerian War of 1954–1962. About two-thirds of this relatively new population have become French citizens.

Algeria, a country in northern Africa, became a French colony in the 1830s, although the Algerians vigorously resisted the French invasion. French colonists confiscated land and stripped Algerians of political and economic rights. In response, some Algerians advocated complete assimilation into French social and cultural ways; others demanded total independence from France through organized resistance. Interestingly, when France itself was controlled by the Germans during World War II, Algiers (in Algeria) became the capital of "Free France." During the war, Algerians even fought in the French army against Germans, largely in expectation of Algerian independence from France. However, this political liberation did not come as expected. Following the war, a growing Algerian nationalist movement led by the National Liberation Front (FLN) met with violent suppression from the French government. The Algerian war of independence did not end until 1962, when Algeria finally gained political independence from France.

Since the 1960s, the migration of Algerians to France has made Islam the country's second major religion, after Roman Catholicism. The large number of darker-skinned Muslims in France has not only kept alive memories of the brutal colonial war but also brought a hostile and racialized reaction from many whites who fear the loss of the "essence" of French culture.[72] Many French whites have argued that the cultural differences between them and the African immigrants are more important than the racial division. Intellectual and popular debates among whites tend to focus on immigrants' assimilation into, or conflict with, existing French culture, and try to play down the importance of racial perceptions held by whites, a strategy that is also common in the United States.[73] For example, when French whites view the omnipresent racial segregation in housing as a result of immigrants' "individual choices," they intentionally dismiss the dynamics of the racial discrimination routinely

Sitting in a courtyard, these undocumented African immigrants await a court decision on whether they can stay in France.

directed against Afro-French groups in housing markets in France.

Indeed, the term *immigrant* in French (as, increasingly, in English) is popularly used to define only those immigrants of non-European origin, and especially Muslim Africans. According to one social worker, *immigrant* and *foreigner* are pejorative: "I am a foreigner. You and I are foreigners. We are not victims of racism. An immigrant is someone who is forced to leave his country, the poor bloke—Arabs and so on."[74] Officially, people in France are classified in terms of nationality as "foreigners" or "nationals." There is little white recognition that those Muslim Africans who are naturalized are also *citizens of France*. The proportion of immigrants in the French population has not increased: Immigrants account for about the same proportion of the population today as in 1931. In addition, 80 percent of those popularly classified as "immigrants" have lived in France for more than ten years, and one-fourth were actually born in France.[75]

Especially since 1980, the issue of African immigration has come to the forefront of political debate, pressed in particular by the reactionary Jean-Marie Le Pen and the French far right, which has received as much as 15 percent of the vote in elections. Le Pen's support is greatest from white French voters in urban areas with sizable numbers of Muslim Africans. Far-right groups advocate ending African immigration, providing job priority only for native-born French whites, forcing Africans to return to Africa, and reimposing the death penalty for criminals.[76] The far-right particularly objects to the acquisition of French nationality by second-generation Africans, whose parents are often criticized for their attachment to certain African cultural values and for teaching these values to their French-born children.[77] Some rightist politicians have made arguments that the increasing numbers of Muslims in Europe are a threat to the "Christian core" of Western civilization, thereby sounding like some political extremists in the United States. Such arguments have roots dating back to the early Christian Crusades.

In an effort to attract voters who support the racist right, the French government has pursued some repressive policies against African immigrants and their supporters. For example, in the summer of 1996, when three hundred African immigrants, as well as non-African intellectuals, staged a mass protest in a church, the government sent 1000 police officers to break down the gates of the church "so that law and order be respected."[78]

Issues of racism have often divided France in recent decades. An antiracist association called SOS Racism, which includes native-born French and immigrants, has actively challenged xenophobia, anti-Semitism, and racism. SOS Racism advocates equality of rights and giving immigrants the right to vote. SOS Racism had 350 local committees and 50,000 followers at its inception and attracted media attention in the 1980s when it organized an antiracist demonstration attended by hundreds of thousands.[79]

Still, the attacks on African (especially Arab) immigrants continue. The most extreme form of discrimination is "Arabicide," a term some use for the more than two hundred unsolved murders of Muslim Arab residents of France in recent decades. French law includes no category for hate crimes, and the police do not classify such killings in a way that shows the pattern of violence against the French Arab community. These murders are often dismissed by whites as the "settling of accounts" between rival Arab factions. This official government attitude is similar to the French government's response to the 1961 Papon massacre during the Algerian War. In that case, a demonstration in Paris organized to protest the nightly curfew for Algerians in France was met with massive police violence. Protesters were clubbed, machine gunned, or driven into the Seine River by the police. At least 140 Algerians were killed, and 400 people were declared missing. According to the official government report, these were all "gangland killings" between the National Liberation Front and the Algerian National Movement. The police were thereby excused for their many killings.[80]

In addition to the anti–African-Muslim violence, racial discrimination in housing, workplaces, and education is commonplace. Muslim communities also face attacks on their culture and traditions. One issue is the right of Muslim girls to wear traditional head scarves in French schools. In the Muslim community, depending on the circumstances, the wearing of these head scarves has different meanings. Some Muslim feminists have argued that the traditional head scarves of women represent the oppression of patriarchy if forced on women by men. However, other Muslim feminists have argued that the head scarves represent an assertion of women's rights if they are worn by women of their own free will. They can thus represent a political statement. The controversy in France began in 1989, when three Arab students wearing head scarves were excluded from school classes. In 1994, the French government banned the wearing of head scarves in public schools, arguing that the practice violated the tradition of secular education. The Education Minister claimed, "We must respect the culture and faith of Muslims, but the history and will of our people was to build a united secular society specifically where schools were concerned."[81]

In this view, scarves divided Muslims from non-Muslims, therefore violating the separation of church and state. The French government has interpreted the increasing number of students wearing head scarves in schools as an indication of the increasing appeal of Muslim fundamentalism, including French Muslim support for Algeria's Islamic Salvation Front, which is fighting to establish an Islamic government in Algeria. In fact, the Education Ministry's ban on head scarves coincided with police raids in which the residents of Arab neighborhoods in French cities were arrested on suspicion of being Muslim militants.[82]

Since the 1990s, the French government has been deeply involved in the civil war between militant Islamic groups and the government in Algeria. The French government has supported the oppressive military government in Algeria. In addition, France's President Jacques Chirac aroused the racist sentiments of whites in France by accusing Algerian immigrants of being "welfare cheats," who produce many children in order to benefit from the welfare system.[83]

France's movement into the European Union (EU) has brought the complexities of the "New Europe" into its own society. The European Union stresses workers' rights, the standardization of policies with regard to communities of color, and a stable immigration policy. However, EU politics have also fostered a resurgence of rightist, protectionist, racist, anti-immigration, and anticommunity rights political platforms in several countries. Le Pen supporters in France would like to expel "foreigners" from the country. These pressures are fostering anti–European Union movements, sometimes known as "EuroNat."[84] Hate crimes against people of color have risen significantly in frequency. Indeed, racist music, such as the song "Beating Up Blacks," has had some popularity. A French television executive was fined for allowing this song to be performed on air, which includes lines such as "can't stand the foreigners, the darkies… flick on the lighters, we're going to set them on fire."[85]

In June 2005, a French newspaper asked, "Suburbs: A Colonial Problem?"[86] Unlike in the United States, where the poor are in inner cities mostly separated from those in suburbs, in France the poor are often concentrated in suburbs. As a response to this article, a group called Indigénes de la République published a manifesto accenting "liberté, egalité, fraternité!" (liberty, equality, brotherhood)—the cry of the peasants and workers during 1789 French Revolution. The manifesto announced: "We the daughters and sons of colonized peoples and immigrants, are engaged in a struggle against oppression and discrimination by the post-colonial-republic."[87] A few months later in many towns and cities, riots resulted in the burning of 10,000 cars and two hundred public buildings, and in three deaths. Most who participated in the rebellions were young men living in the poverty-stricken suburbs and suffering from a 40 percent unemployment rate. Most in these predominantly Muslim and African areas had lost hope that the French government would address their severe economic problems. Some expressed the desire to live under an Islamic government, but most said that they wanted a French government that would assist them economically, and without racial discrimination.[88]

Significantly, according to researchers, Muslim French voters' political patterns are similar to others in France who share their socioeconomic backgrounds. For example, according to opinion polls, Muslim French voters recently opposed the European Union Constitution in about the same proportion as the country as a whole.[89] In a way, assimi- lationist government policies seem to have succeeded on this political front. Even as a group of citizens who have been racially targeted and excluded, French Muslims do not act as a distinct voting bloc. Perhaps that is one reason why in 2007 President Chirac, serving his last term, did not make any attempts to address the economic needs of many Muslim Arab citizens.

Colonialism brings oppression and violence not only to the land of the colonized but also to the land of the colonizer, especially if the colonized migrate to the colonizing country. In the postcolonial era both the racial framing of non-Europeans and the well-institutionalized discrimination that accompanies it persist vigorously in countries such as France.

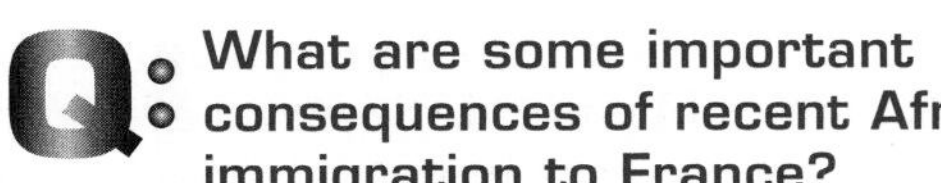

The Future of Colonialism and Postcolonialism

Some General Considerations

During the era of European colonialism and during the postcolonial era, Europeans and European Americans have often believed that the seeds of "Westernization" and "modernization" will eventually bring "civilization" to colonial or formerly colonial areas. Expecting a slow evolution, modernization theorists have argued that European colonialism spread Western culture and ideology to the lands of the "uncivilized" and "inferior." Following Westernization, conflict between the colonizers and the colonized was expected to disappear eventually as the colonized peoples gradually assimilated into the "superior" European culture. Thus, the Westernization process demands that colonized peoples acquiesce in the continuation of global patterns of racial and ethnic inequality by accepting external European and U.S. economic and political domination. This view is clearly racist in its assumptions, and is based on the oppressed willingly accepting their oppression.

Challenging such racist perspectives, power-conflict analysts generally reject the assimilationist Westernizing perspective. They argue that today, as in the past, white-generated racism is a global reality. From the power-conflict perspective, the awareness of global diversity should emphasize the creation of new terms of human coexistence and equality in order to establish real societal and international peace. Current world conditions often do not allow for the careful exploration of political and economic alternatives to external colonialism or its postindependence indirect colonialism, in part because warring factions in many postcolonial countries are rooted in divisions created by past colonialism and continue to practice group subordination backed by violence. In addition, in the United States, South Africa, Brazil, and France, systemic racism, with its many discriminatory mechanisms, continues to destroy the lives and communities of large numbers of oppressed people.

From a power-conflict perspective, colonialism is an exploitative system that has brought great racial and ethnic inequalities and misery to many countries. Racial subordination integrated segregation and racial inequality into the everyday lives of people in North America, South Africa, Brazil, and France, as well as people in many other countries. In the postcolonial era the painful realities of Euro-colonialism are evident in the continuing racial inequality in such areas as education, housing, business, employment, public accommodations, and health care. Around the globe, such inequalities influence the life chances of all people who were (and are) racially, ethnically, and religiously oppressed. Although the modes of inequality and segregation may be different, oppression and associated state violence have been perpetuated in the postcolonialist era in both colonizing and colonized societies.

The enslavement of human beings, whether of indigenous or imported populations, which was a common aspect of colonialism, had effects that have lasted to the present. As slavery destroyed human beings and their cultures, it and its ideology became integrated into social institutions that still dominate postcolonial societies. For example, South Africa is today confronting the lingering effects of slavery and its ideology under its slowly disintegrating apartheid system; African Americans and Afro-Brazilians are demanding abolition of the contemporary effects of slavery in their lives and communities. From a strong power-conflict perspective, a realistic assessment of the present and future of postcolonial societies requires a confrontation with entrenched racial inequality and segregation and a major struggle against the persisting practices and pernicious effects of systemic racism and its global realities. After World War II, the conditions of the Cold War era often defined the possibilities for colonial societies as they revolted against their colonial masters. The Cold War between the Soviet Union and the United States and its European allies shaped the economic dependency and cultural experiences of many postcolonial societies. **Neocolonialism**—*the continuation of the economic and cultural dominance of the former colonial states*—is an extension of the Cold War. When the Soviet Union and its empire broke up after the late 1980s and the Cold War ended, many people in the former Soviet Union and in its satellites pressed toward full independence, with the expectation that colonialism and neocolonialism, including that of the former Soviet Union, would end.

However, this has not been the case. In most of these countries, Communism has been replaced by a form of capitalism that constitutes a new type of economic and political colonialism with close ties to Western banks and corporations. And many former European colonies in Africa and Asia have faced a similar neocolonialism. As the capitalist system recreates itself in new neocolonial forms, it creates new modes of inequality and segregation that usually remain pervaded by the global system of racial and ethnic hostility and subordination.[90]

Colonialism, Capitalism, and Racism: A Note on Contemporary Genocide

The last century has often been marred by large-scale hate and massive killings, increasingly forcing the term *genocide* into widespread use. Genocide has come to be understood as "the coordinated plan of different actions aiming at the destruction of essential foundations of the life of national groups with the aim of annihilating the groups themselves."[91] As Israel Charny has warned:

> There needs to be a growing consensus on the part of human beings and organized society that penetrates the very basis of human culture that mass killing is unacceptable to civilized peoples, otherwise the prevailing momentum of historical experience will continue for generation after generation that genocide is a phenomenon of nature, like other disasters, and this view of the inevitability of genocide as an almost natural event will continue to justify it in the sense of convincing people that nothing can be done.[92]

Genocide is an old human problem, as we saw in Chapter 6 when we assessed Euro-American tactics attempting to exterminate indigenous Americans. In recent decades, the numerous examples of genocide have remained terrifying and inhuman in the extreme. In the late twentieth and early twenty-first centuries, a common response of the majority of white Europeans and Euro-Americans is to view genocide among peoples of color as natural and inevitable. Typically, they view such genocidal events through the old white racial frame, which inclines them to not notice, or to excuse, such genocidal events. The global system of racial oppression, gradually expanded by Europeans from the fifteenth century onward until it circled the globe, not only involved early European genocidal attacks on indigenous peoples but also developed the racist framing of "superior" peoples and "inferior" peoples that rationalized genocide and other forms of racial oppression.

Now that this racial framing of superior and inferior, of civilized and uncivilized, has been firmly in place for centuries—in some form in the minds of most people in the world's ruling elites—a great many people have acted on, and continue to act on, its racialized stereotypes, images, emotions, and interpretations. Thus, not surprisingly, recent genocides in Africa and the former Soviet Union implicate the white racial framing and its contextual system of racial-ethnic hierarchy and oppression. Those actually perpetrating genocidal action are often themselves acting out of some racial and ethnic categories generated, in part or in whole, by the white racial frame, and/or in relation to territorial boundaries created by Euro-colonialism's administering officials. At least as important is the fact that the old white racist framing legitimates great indifference and inaction on the part of the world's powerful European and Euro-American elites and associated international organizations. Wherever they have occurred in recent decades, as in earlier centuries, genocidal thinking and actions have often been linked in one way or another to the long history of European colonialism and neocolonialism.

One recent example is that of the Darfur region of Sudan in Africa, where at least 100,000 people have died and millions have been displaced, starving, and in desperate need of emergency aid for food, shelter, and medical treatment. The Darfur conflict has been escalated by two groups of allies. The Sudan Liberation Army and the Justice & Equality Movement, allies seeking federation or independence and representing the non-Arab majority, are fighting against what they view as intense political oppression of the Sudanese government's army and affiliated militia units, allies representing the country's Arab minority. (We use here the terms "Arab" and " non-Arab" although the groups in opposition sometimes overlap in their ancestry and religious commitments.)

Events in Darfur are rather complex. The minority-controlled government is northern and Arabized, while the rebels are southern and western and are fighting political and economic oppression and marginalization. The current Sudanese government is the *direct* descendant of the British colonial government, which handed over power to the Sudanese Arab elite. Some of the numerous groups resisting this minority and repressive government are Islamic in religion, as are the government leaders, yet others in the resistance in the south are Christian or animist. There is also a division today between non-Arab farmers and nomadic Arab herders over control of fertile lands.[93]

The current divisions and fighting in Sudan link closely to the long direct and indirect (through Egyptian officials that The British government controlled) colonization of the area by the British, who withdrew after long decades of colonial control only in 1956. During their many years of control, British colonial administrators used the method of "divide and conquer." To establish full colonial control and incorporation of the area into Euro-capitalism, which they legitimated in terms of a strong white-racist and colonialist framing, the British oppressors manipulated the existing group tensions between Arabized peoples mostly in northern Sudan and non-Arab (sometimes termed "black") Africans in southern and western areas. The British imposed their racialized thinking in ways that *inferiorized* the darker-skinned local population, a framing to some extent picked up, later on, by Sudan's Arab leaders and government officials who have sought the subordination and Arabization of Sudan's southern non-Arab areas.[94]

Much fighting has been linked to control of the oil extracted from southern Sudan and piped through a new pipeline to the Red Sea. One of the southern non-Arab groups, the Nubas, are among the major victims of the Arab government in this complex conflict. The Nuba Mountains, bordering Sudan's oil pipeline, are on the front line of conflict. Though they are non-Arab Africans, the Nuba speak Arabic, the official language of the country. About half are Muslim, and half are Christian and/or animist. When the Nuba joined the Sudan Liberation Army, government forces pushed them up into the mountains, where they could no longer grow food. When the government banned humanitarian airlifts, many Nuba died of hunger, especially children.[95]

In spite of their earlier colonial involvement and their significant shaping of political events there for many decades, Western (and other) leaders have so far delayed responding significantly to this ongoing violence, even debating whether the events in Darfur actually represent a case of "genocide." Westerners have debated how long killings on a large scale have been occurring, how to count nomadic peoples and villagers who have fallen victim, and how to calculate victims when some have fled to neighboring countries or perished from the side effects of violence such as related malnutrition and disease. Central to the debate on "genocide," which finally began in 2004, has been whether these horrific events are just internal, civil war skirmishes that do not warrant international intervention. Finally, in July 2004 the U.S. House of Representatives unanimously passed a resolution labeling the violent events as "genocide." The resolution called on the

George W. Bush administration to act according to the international Genocide Convention. Secretary of State Colin Powell then insisted that naming the Darfur events "genocide" would not change favorable U.S. policy toward Sudan's government even as he commissioned an in-depth study on whether the events merited the term. The U.S. government was not alone in being slow to call the events genocide, for Canadian, British and EU officials, along with the UN secretary general, continued to call Darfur "a massive violation of human rights," not genocide.[96] Groups such as Human Rights Watch called the Darfur situation "ethnic cleansing" and argued that it involved the "forced removal of an ethnic group," not its annihilation. Belatedly too, UN Secretary General Kofi Annan finally appointed a UN commission to determine whether genocide had occurred there. Debates came to a halt when Colin Powell finally did assert that genocide, not just civil war, was taking place in the Sudan.[97]

This belated declaration brought a new set of dilatory questions in the West: What kind of international intervention was justified to stop the violence, and when should it have taken (or take) place? As of 2007, waffling, delays, and lack of concern were still the order of the day, as leaders in the West seemed more concerned about the country's oil or ties to trade with China than the fact that thousands were buried in mass graves in the Darfur area and many others were near death. In the face of this genocide, the Western leadership silence of "none of our business," the inaction resulting from vacillating debates over "war" or "genocide," or the studied indifference to the lives of others thought to be engaged in local "ethnic cleansing" and "sectarian violence" revealed once again the old white framing that was honed so well during earlier European imperialism and colonialism. If these events were happening to Europeans in Europe, they would likely have received a quite different and more concerned response.

A peace accord was signed in May 2005 between the Arab-led government and the non-Arab opposition forces, but as of 2007 it has not ended the killings. The African Union sent 7000 peacekeepers to monitor the refugee camps, but this small force and the vastness of the county seriously hampered their effectiveness. The African Union ran out of money and time and withdrew in late 2006.[98] In summer 2007 the Sudanese government, under international political pressure, finally agreed to the deployment of a new peacekeeping force (United Nations and African Union soldiers). It impact is yet to be seen, and the genocide continues in Darfur.

The racial and ethnic differences among the people that were fostered and accentuated during British colonial rule have survived today under neocolonialism as Western leaders seem unconcerned with the violence there (as they were in the earlier case of Rwanda), yet seem very concerned about who gets the oil now flowing out of southern Sudan. The past actions of, and current collective indifference of, leaders in Western countries exhibits the ways in which white political-economic control, directly or indirectly, but always in terms of the pervasive racial framing, still dominates the globe.

Summary

White racism became a global reality substantially as a result of European and Euro-American colonialism, which operated through bureaucratic administrations, exploitative trade, and a missionary type of Euro-Christian culture. European and later U.S. colonizers rationalized colonial expansion and violence by defining themselves as superior peoples whose duty it was to Westernize and modernize the "uncivilized." The construction of colonized peoples as racially inferior, within the age-old white racist framing, was a fundamental aspect of the legitimizing of this colonial exploitation. Colonialism destroyed local economies and political arrangements, and it shaped colonized peoples' conceptions of themselves and their future possibilities. Racist framing, culture, and social institutions were integral to European colonialism, and white racial oppression has persisted into the postcolonial era. Around the globe, systemic racism can be still seen in pervasive racial prejudices, emotions, practices, and institutions.

The colonization of black South Africans by European states began in the seventeenth century. Over a four-hundred-year period, a powerful white racist framing, ideology, and society evolved that has shaped most aspects of the existence of black and other South Africans, from housing to education to employment. The racist system of apartheid created separate racial communities. Since the free election of 1994, white, black, and other South Africans have attempted to reconcile deep differences and inequalities within a postapartheid system. However, they still face major obstacles because of persisting racist thought and discriminatory action, as well as continuing neocolonialism in the form of white control of the country's powerful economy.

In contrast to systemic racism in South Africa, Brazilian racism is often more subtle and wrapped in the myth of "racial democracy." Brazil was colonized in the sixteenth century. Even today, however, Brazilian politics, economy, and society reveal the effects of that colonization and the slavery system imposed by whites. Even though slavery was abolished more than one hundred years ago, systemic racism is evident in widespread racial discrimination, in many media and intellectual discussions, and in elements of popular culture. A white racist framing penetrates the images Brazilians have of who they are and works to divide Brazilians, including those with African ancestry, according to shades of skin color. More than a century after the abolition of slavery, systemic racism persists in the discriminatory ways in which whites treat people of African ancestry and in the ways in which most Brazilians see themselves and their communities.

European colonialism left major scars on the colonized lands and also on the colonizing countries. The postcolonial lives of colonized and colonizers have been plagued by chronic racist framing, social disruption and oppression, and much group violence. For example, France, a colonizer, has experienced continuing racial violence in the postcolonial era. Racialized framing and practice still target French Muslims from Africa, who experience job discrimination, destruction of property, and attacks on their Muslim culture.

The European community, the United States, and even the United Nations have been hesitant to condemn many of the oppressive acts, including violence and genocide, that are shaped by global racism. They have often been reluctant to name and confront forms of institutionalized racism in societies around the world. Today, the world appears to be in the increasingly tight grip of a culture of racist thinking and hostility and a global structure of racial oppression long propagated by variations on European colonialism and neocolonialism. And this world of oppression is often accepted as an everyday reality.

Further confrontation of and resistance to white-generated racism will likely come from bridging various local understandings and especially from the everyday struggles of people with racial oppression in numerous societies. From this perspective, understanding white-generated racism better in France or Brazil can contribute significantly to confronting and resisting similar racial oppression in the Americas or South Africa. Similarly, understanding racism better in the latter areas can contribute substantially to resistance to racial oppression in the former areas. Undoing contemporary systems of racism remains a major and enduring challenge for all concerned peoples in the twenty-first century.

Key Terms

apartheid 381
Boers 384
Afrikaaners 384
coloureds 384
neocolonialism 396

Glossary

affirmative action programs Private and governmental programs that seek to improve the economic and educational opportunities for formerly excluded racial, ethnic, and gender groups.

Afrikaaners White South African speakers of the Afrikaans language.

Anglo-Protestant Americans A more accurate term for those often referred to as Anglo-Saxon Protestant Americans.

Anglo-Saxon A term that originally referred to Germanic tribes who came to the area now called England in the fifth and sixth centuries C.E.; it was later applied to white inhabitants of England and to those English who came to North America.

anti-Semitism Stereotyping of, prejudice toward, or discrimination against Jews.

apartheid The rigidly institutionalized system of racial segregation and social, economic, and political inequality that invaded virtually every aspect of daily life in South Africa from 1948 until the 1990s.

Arab Americans Umbrella term for Americans whose ancestral roots are in Arab countries.

Asian Americans Umbrella term for Americans whose ancestral roots are in Asia.

Asian-Pacific Americans Umbrella term for Americans whose ancestral roots are in Asia or the Pacific Islands.

assimilation An incoming group's adoption of the cultural traits (e.g., language) and identity of the host group and/or integration into the primary networks and secondary organizations of the host group.

attitude-receptional assimilation Milton Gordon's term for the absence of prejudice and stereotyping.

authoritarian personalities Personalities characterized by a high degree of submission to authority, a tendency to stereotype, great concern for status, a view of the world as threatening, and an intolerance of out-groups that occupy socially subordinate positions.

behavior-receptional assimilation Milton Gordon's term for the absence of intentional discrimination.

bilingualism The ability to speak two languages; relates to school programs for certain non-English-speaking children learning to speak English.

Boers White South Africans of Dutch descent.

braceros Farm workers on seasonal contracts (for example, some Mexican farm workers).

caste school of racial relations Power-conflict theory that emphasizes institutionalized discrimination as the foundation of a castelike system of U.S. apartheid.

Chicano political movement A militant movement that began during the 1960s and has sought increased power and respect for Mexican Americans.

civic assimilation Milton Gordon's term for the absence of value and power conflict between two racial or ethnic groups, mainly between a host group and a recent immigrant group.

civil rights movement A collective movement to establish or improve the legal and political rights of a subordinate racial or ethnic group.

colonization migration Conquest and domination of a preexisting geographical group by outsiders.

color coding Social discrimination or stratification based on skin color.

coloureds The South African term for people of mixed black–white ancestry.

competition theory A view of ethnicity that emphasizes the relative stability of ethnic population boundaries over time and the intergroup competition over resources that results from shifts in these boundaries because of migration.

competitive capitalism An economic system dominated by competition between small and medium-sized for-profit businesses.

conformity function of prejudice Prejudiced attitudes held in order to conform to the expectations of an important social reference group.

contract-labor movement Migration such as that of indentured Irish servants to the English colonies and of Chinese laborers to western North America.

covert discrimination Harmful treatment of members of subordinate racial and ethnic groups that is hidden and difficult to document.

cultural assimilation The change of one group's important cultural patterns to those of the host or dominant group.

cultural diversity The variety of cultures in a specific region, a nation, or the world; often relates to respect for diverse cultures.

cultural pluralism The view that each racial or ethnic group has the democratic right to preserve and practice important elements of its own cultural heritage without being forced to assimilate to a dominant culture.

culture of poverty The stereotyped idea that poor people typically develop a defective and deviant subculture.

direct institutionalized discrimination Organizationally prescribed or community-prescribed action that by intention has a differential and negative effect on members of subordinate racial and ethnic groups.

discrimination Most often, the actions carried out by members of dominant groups, or their representatives, that have a differential and harmful effect on members of subordinate racial or ethnic groups.

dominant group A racial or ethnic group with the greatest power and resources in a society; also called a majority group.

egalitarian symbiosis Peaceful coexistence and a rough economic and political equality between two racial or ethnic groups.

endogamy Marriage within one's own racial or ethnic group.

English Americans Americans of English ancestry.

environmental racism Government and private waste dumping in communities populated by Americans of color.

ethnic enclave The economic (often market), social, and often residential niche that certain racial and ethnic groups have developed as a way of surviving or prospering in U.S. cities.

ethnic group A group that is socially distinguished or set apart, by others or by itself, primarily on the basis of cultural or national-origin characteristics.

ethnogenesis The sociological theory that, over time, immigrant groups not only come to share cultural traits with the host group but also retain many of their own nationality characteristics.

ethnoviolence Violence directed at an individual or group because of the individual's or group's ethnic or racial identity.

external colonialism The economic or political exploitation of a society by a powerful group, such as (imperialistic) aristocrats or capitalists, from another, geographically separate society.

externalization function of prejudice The transfer of an individual's internal psychological problem to an external racial or ethnic group as a way of repressing or denying that problem.

gendered racism The interaction of racial discrimination and gender discrimination, which especially affects women of color.

genocide The deliberate and systematic extermination of a nationality or racial group.

glass ceiling An unwritten and unofficial policy in some organizations that limits the potential for advancement of certain persons, usually based on their gender or racial group.

gunboat imperialism Nineteenth-century imperialism backed by the use or threat of military force.

Hapa Persons of mixed Japanese-other ancestry (from a Hawaiian word meaning "half").

hate crimes Crimes against people and property generated by prejudice against racial, ethnic, religious, disability, or sexual orientation groups.

hierarchy A significant socioeconomic stratification.

Hispanics Persons of Mexican, Puerto Rican, Cuban, Dominican, and Central or South American heritage. (Also termed **Latinos**.)

Holocaust The planned extermination of the Jews by the government in Nazi Germany in the 1930s and 1940s, in which an estimated 6 million European Jews (and many others) were murdered.

identification assimilation Milton Gordon's term for an incoming group's development of a sense of identity linked to that of the host group.

ideological racism An ideology that considers a group's unchangeable physical characteristics to be linked in a direct, causal way to psychological or intellectual characteristics, and that on this basis distinguishes between superior and inferior racial groups.

illegals Undocumented immigrants.

indigenous superordination A societal condition in which immigrant groups are placed in a subordinate position to a host-dominant group.

indirect institutionalized discrimination Dominant-group practices that have a harmful effect on members of subordinate racial and ethnic groups even though the organizational or community-prescribed norms (informal or legal rules) guiding the actions were established with no intent to harm.

individual racism Racially hostile acts of an individual directed at one or more members of another racial group.

institutional racism Institutionalized practices that differentially and negatively affect members of a subordinate racial group.

intermarriage Marriage between members of different racial or ethnic groups.

internal colonialism The colony-like control and exploitation of subordinate groups by a dominant group *within* a given society.

IQ tests Paper-and-pencil or object/symbol manipulation tests that advocates claim can measure a global human intelligence.

isolate discrimination Harmful action taken intentionally by a member of a dominant racial or ethnic group against members of a subordinate group without direct and significant support from the immediate social or community context.

"Jim Crow" laws State and local laws, in the North before the Civil War as well as in the South afterwards, which enforced the racial segregation of ostensibly "free" African American in public transportation, hospitals, schools, churches, and cemeteries.

Latinos See **Hispanics**.

lynching The illegal killing of a person by a mob, such as by hanging.

"Mafia" myth A stereotype of Italian Americans as being substantially involved in organized crime.

majority group See **dominant group**.

manifest destiny A concept put forth in the nineteenth century that the United States had a *right* to expand from the Atlantic Ocean to the Pacific and would inevitably do so.

maquiladoras Manufacturing operations of U.S. firms that are located in northern Mexico near the U.S. border, where they can take advantage of low-wage labor and weak environmental standards while avoiding certain tariffs and duties.

Mariel boatlift The immigration of 125,000 Cubans who departed from Cuba's Mariel Harbor for the United States in 1980.

marital assimilation Significant intermarriage between one racial or ethnic group and another racial or ethnic group.

Marranos Jews who were forced to convert publicly to Christianity during the Spanish Inquisition under threat of death but who privately maintained allegiance to Judaism.

mediated assimilation David and Ayouby's term for the process whereby Arab American organizations act as cultural filters to screen out undesirable features of U.S. culture (applicable to other groups).

melting pot The view that immigrants to the United States lose their racial and ethnic identities as they mix together in one new American blend.

Middle Eastern Americans Umbrella term for Americans whose ancestral roots lie in any of the Middle Eastern countries.

middleman minority A racial or ethnic group that occupies an in-between position in terms of societal power and resources.

migrant superordination A societal condition in which immigrants assume a dominant position over an indigenous population.

millenarian movements Movements among indigenous groups, such as Native Americans, that have included the belief in a golden age in which supernatural events would change present oppressive conditions.

minority group A group that is singled out because of physical and/or cultural characteristics for differential and unequal treatment and whose members become objects of discrimination; it typically has less power and resources than the dominant group; also called a subordinate group.

model minority stereotype The stereotype that views certain Asian American (and sometimes other) groups as exemplary in socioeconomic and moral characteristics, often as compared to other people of color.

modern racism See **symbolic racism**.

movements of forced labor Involuntary immigration, such as the forcible removal of Africans to North America.

multiculturalism Cultural pluralism; the political or educational movement to respect the human rights of all Americans and to recognize the diverse cultural ways of the many U.S. racial and ethnic groups, particularly those that have suffered widespread racial or ethnic discrimination.

multinational capitalism An economic system dominated by large-scale, for-profit corporations that operate in many different countries, thereby creating an international market system.

nativism An anti-immigrant ideology that advocates the protection of the native-born inhabitants of a country from recent immigrants who are seen as threatening or dangerous.

neocolonialism The continuation of the economic and cultural dominance of the former colonial states.

oppositional culture The culture of resistance often found among subordinate groups; somewhat or greatly distinct from the dominant culture, it reflects in part the struggle with that dominant culture.

order theories Racial and ethnic theories that accent group adaptation patterns involving the orderly and progressive assimilation of particular racial and ethnic groups to a dominant culture and its related institutions.

Orientalism An uninformed and stereotypical way of thinking of Asian and Middle Eastern peoples.

panethnicity The generalization of solidarity among ethnic subgroups.

patriarchal system A social system in which men generally predominate in power and status over women and in which men work to maintain or reinforce subordinate social roles for women.

picture brides So-called because their marriages were arranged on the basis of photographs, without the bride and groom having met.

pogroms A Russian term, originally meaning "riot," that came to be applied to a series of organized, often officially encouraged attacks on Jews, especially during the late nineteenth and early twentieth centuries.

political refugees Streams of refugees produced by war or political oppression.

power-conflict theories Racial and ethnic theories that accent the persisting and great inequalities in the power and resource distributions associated with racial or ethnic subordination in a society.

prejudice An antipathy (negative feeling), felt or expressed, that is usually based on a faulty generalization and directed toward a group as a whole or toward individual members of a group.

primary labor market The sector characterized by skilled jobs, higher wages, and greater mobility.

Protestant work ethic A religiously based view of everyday life that promotes hard work and strong self-discipline.

psychological wage W. E. B. Du Bois's term for white workers' sense of white superiority and privilege.

race A term developed in the 1700s by European analysts to refer to what is also called a racial group (see **racial group**).

race relations cycle Robert E. Park's view of a progressive sequence of intergroup events that usually results from one group's migration into a host society: contact, competition, accommodation, and eventual assimilation.

racial formation theory The view that racial and ethnic relations and identities in a society are socially defined, especially by the historical actions of governments.

racial frame An organized set of racial ideas, stereotypes, images, emotions, and inclinations to discriminate.

racial group A social group that persons inside or outside the group have decided is important to single out as inferior or superior, typically on the basis of real or alleged physical characteristics that are selected subjectively.

racial hierarchy (racialized hierarchy) Stratification of, and substantial inequality among, a society's racial groups.

racial profiling A practice used by some police departments that unfairly singles out citizens of color as potential criminals and often results in extensive harassment of innocent people.

racialization The process by which those in the dominant white group, especially its elites, have defined and constructed certain groups as being racially inferior or superior for the purposes of societal placement and of group enrichment, segregation, or oppression.

Reconstruction The period in U.S. history following the Civil War during which an attempt was made by the federal government to disenfranchise the slaveholding oligarchy and to improve the economic, educational, political, and human rights conditions of poor whites and blacks in the South.

Santería A type of syncretic religion that includes aspects of both Catholic and older African religions.

"Scotch-Irish" immigrants Immigrants from northern Ireland, some of whose ancestors are said to have immigrated to Ireland from Scotland.

secondary labor market That sector characterized by job instability, low wages, and little mobility.

slavery The legal ownership and exploitation of one human being by another; the system that makes the trade in and ownership of human beings possible.

small-group discrimination Harmful action taken intentionally by a small number of dominant-group individuals acting in concert against members of subordinate racial and ethnic groups without the support of the immediate organizational or community context.

social Darwinism A perspective that extended Charles Darwin's evolutionary thinking into the social realm and that accents a perspective on society that embraces the notion of the "survival of the fittest."

sojourner immigration Nonpermanent immigration for the purpose of making money and then returning to the country of origin.

split labor-market view A power-conflict perspective that argues that the white employer class and the white part of the working class both discriminate, to a substantial degree independently, against the racially subordinated part of the working class.

stereotype An overgeneralized image, usually negative, of a racial or ethnic outgroup that is false or that greatly distorts the real characteristics of the targeted group.

structural assimilation Milton Gordon's term for an incoming group's penetration of the primary social networks of the host group; extended by other analysts to include penetration of secondary groups.

subordinate group A group that is singled out because of physical and/or cultural characteristics for differential and unequal treatment and whose members become objects of discrimination; it typically has less power and fewer resources than the dominant group.

subtle discrimination Unequal and harmful treatment of members of subordinate racial and ethnic groups that is obvious to the victim but not as overt as traditional "door-slamming" varieties of discrimination.

swing vote A bloc that can affect close elections.

symbolic racism Beliefs held by many whites that serious antiblack discrimination does not exist today and that African Americans or other people of color are making illegitimate demands for social and racial change.

systemic discrimination Institutionalized patterns of discrimination that cut across major political, economic, and social organizations in a society.

systemic racism The white prejudices, stereotypes, emotions, discriminatory practices, and institutions that are integral to the long-term domination of Americans of color.

theory In the social sciences, a conceptual framework used to interpret or explain some aspect of everyday existence.

underemployment rate Includes not only those with no jobs, but also those who are working part-time and those who are making poverty-level wages.

Underground Railroad A network of formerly enslaved and other antislavery Americans, black and white, who passed along tens of thousands of enslaved people from the South to the North between the 1830s and the Civil War.

undocumented immigrants Immigrants without legal immigration papers.

voluntary migration Migration primarily by choice.

white Anglo-Saxon Protestant Americans A label often applied to white Protestant Americans whose ancestry is English or British.

Zionism A worldwide movement for the establishment in Palestine of a national homeland for the world's Jewish communities.

Notes

Part I

1. Leonard Dinnerstein and Frederic C. Jaher, "Introduction," in *The Aliens*, ed. Leonard Dinnerstein and Frederic C. Jaher (New York: Appleton-Century-Crofts, 1970), p. 4.
2. Leonard Dinnerstein and Frederic C. Jaher, "The Colonial Era," in *The Aliens*, ed. Dinnerstein and Jaher, p. 17.
3. Quoted in Peter M. Bergman, *The Chronological History of the Negro in America* (New York: Harper & Row, 1969), p. 52.
4. John Hope Franklin, *From Slavery to Freedom*, 2nd ed. (New York: Knopf, 1963), pp. 141–143.
5. Ibid., p. 143.
6. Samuel E. Morison, *The Oxford History of the American People* (New York: Oxford University Press, 1965), p. 353.

Chapter 1

1. Frances F. Marcus, "Louisiana Repeals Black Blood Law," *The New York Times*, July 6, 1983, p. A10.
2. Wilton M. Krogman, "The Concept of Race," in *The Science of Man in the World Crisis*, ed. Ralph Linton (New York: Columbia University Press, 1945) p. 38.
3. Winthrop D. Jordan, *White over Black* (Baltimore, MD: Penguin, 1969), p. 217.
4. Stephen J. Gould, "The Geometer of Race," *Discover*, November 1994, pp. 65–66.
5. Audrey Smedley, *Race in North America* (Boulder, CO: Westview, 1993), pp. 303–305.
6. Ibid, p. 26.
7. Peter I. Rose, *The Subject Is Race* (New York: Oxford University Press, 1968), pp. 32–33; Thomas F. Gossett, *Race* (New York: Schocken Books, 1965), p. 3.
8. M. Annette Jaimes, "Liberating Race," in *The State of Asian America: Activism and Resistance in the 1990s*, ed. Karin Aguilar-San Juan (Boston: South End Press, 1994), p. 369.
9. Ibid., p. 370.
10. See Pierre L. van den Berghe, *Race and Racism* (New York: Wiley, 1967), p. 11.
11. Robert Bennett Bean, *The Races of Man* (New York: University Society, 1935), pp. 94–96, quoted in *In Their Place: White America Defines Her Minorities, 1850–1950*, ed. Lewis H. Carlson and George A. Colburn (New York: Wiley, 1972), p. 106. See also Magnus Hirschfeld, *Racism* (Port Washington, NY: Kennikat Press, 1973 [1938]), pp. 35–99, 266–318.
12. Eugenia Shanklin, *Anthropology and Race* (Belmont, CA: Wadsworth, 1994); Josephy L. Graves, "What We Know and What We Don't Know: Human Genetic Variation and the Social Construction of Race," Social Science Research Council, http://raceandgenomics.ssrc.org/Graves (retrieved June 12, 2006); Alan Goodman, "Two Questions About Race," Social Science Research Council, http://raceandgenomics.ssrc.org/Goodman (retrieved June 12, 2006).
13. James Shreeve, "Terms of Estrangement," *Discover*, November 1994, p. 60; see also Paul Hoffman, "The Science of Race," *Discover*, November 1994, p. 4.
14. Jared Diamond, "Race Without Color," *Discover*, November 1994, p. 84.
15. Michael Banton and Jonathan Harwood, *The Race Concept* (New York: Praeger, 1975), pp. 13–50.
16. See Nathan Rutstein, *Healing Racism in America* (Springfield, MA: Whitcomb, 1993), pp. 1–51, 121–129.
17. Ashley Montagu, *Race, Science and Humanity* (Princeton, NJ: D. Van Nostrand, 1963).

18. Oliver C. Cox, *Caste, Class, and Race* (Garden City, NY: Doubleday, 1948), p. 402.
19. Van den Berghe, *Race and Racism*, p. 9.
20. Michael Banton, *Race Relations* (New York: Basic Books, 1967), p. 57; see also p. 58.
21. Charles Wagley and Marvin Harris, *Minorities in the New World* (New York: Columbia University Press, 1958), p. 7.
22. Thomas F. Pettigrew, *A Profile of the Negro American* (Princeton, NJ: D. Van Nostrand, 1964), p. 69.
23. Bill Zimmerman and Bob Herzog, "Golf: From Sheep to Tiger," *Newsday*, August 13, 1997, p. A34.
24. Denene Millner, "In Creating a Word to Describe His Racial Makeup, Golfer Tiger Woods Has Also Stirred Up a Round of Controversy Among Blacks," *New York Daily News*, June 8, 1997, p. 2.
25. Wire reports, *Newsday*, May 20, 1997, p. A57.
26. Joe Drape, "Woods Meets Zoeller for Lunch," *The New York Times*, May 21, 1997, p. B13.
27. Barbara Vobejda, "Hill Reassured on Racial Check-off Plan for Census," *The Washington Post*, July 26, 1997, p. A4; Art Shriberg and Carol Lloyd, "Interracial Marriages Still Taboo," *Tampa Tribune*, June 5, 1997, p. 1.
28. Milton M. Gordon, *Assimilation in American Life* (New York: Oxford University Press, 1964), p. 27.
29. Werner Sollors, *The Invention of Ethnicity* (New York: Oxford University Press, 1989).
30. William M. Newman, *American Pluralism* (New York: Harper & Row, 1973), p. 19.
31. W. Lloyd Warner and Leo Srole, *The Social Systems of American Ethnic Groups* (New Haven, CT: Yale University Press, 1945), pp. 284–286.
32. Van den Berghe, *Race and Racism*, p. 10.
33. See Nathan Glazer, "Blacks and Ethnic Groups: The Difference, and the Political Difference It Makes," *Social Problems* 18 (Spring 1971): 447.
34. D. John Grove, *The Race vs. Ethnic Debate: A Cross-National Analysis of Two Theoretical Approaches* (Denver, CO: Center on International Race Relations, University of Denver, 1974); Robert Blauner, *Racial Oppression in America* (New York: Harper & Row, 1972).
35. Philomena Essed, *Understanding Everyday Racism* (Newbury Park, CA: Sage, 1991), p. 28.
36. Letter to authors from Edna Bonacich, October 1994.
37. St. Clair Drake, *Black Folk Here and There* (Los Angeles: UCLA Center for Afro-American Studies, 1987), 1: xxiii. See also vol. 2 of this work.
38. Frank Snowden, *Color Prejudice* (Cambridge, MA: Harvard University Press, 1983), pp. 3–4, 107–108.
39. Max Weber, "Ethnic Groups," in *Theories of Society*, ed. Talcott Parsons et al. (Glencoe, IL: The Free Press, 1961), vol. 1, p. 306.
40. Joane Nagel, "Constructing Ethnicity: Creating and Recreating Ethnic Identity and Culture," *Social Problems* 43 (February 1994): 152.
41. Mary Waters, *Ethnic Options: Choosing Identities in America* (Berkeley, CA: University of California Press, 1990).
42. Mary Waters, "The Intersection of Race and Ethnicity," paper presented at the Annual Meeting of the American Sociological Association, Cincinnati, OH, 1991.
43. This term was suggested by Donald M. Young in *American Minority Peoples* (New York: Harper, 1932), p. xviii.
44. Louis Wirth, "The Problem of Minority Groups," in *The Science of Man in the World Crisis*, ed. Linton, p. 347.
45. Clifford Goertz, *The Interpretation of Cultures* (New York: Basic Books, 1973), p. 89.
46. Wendy Griswold, *Cultures and Societies in a Changing World* (Thousand Oaks, CA: Pine Forge Press, 1994), p. xiv.
47. Milton M. Gordon, *Assimilation in American Life* (New York: Oxford University Press, 1964), pp. 72–73.
48. See Bonnie Mitchell and Joe Feagin, "America's Racial-Ethnic Cultures: Opposition Within a Mythical Melting Pot," In *Toward the Multicultural University*, ed. Benjamin Bowser, Gale Auletta, and Terry Jones (Westport, CT: Praeger, 1995), pp. 65–86; Patricia Hill Collins, *Black Feminist Thought: Knowledge, Consciousness, and the Politics of Empowerment* (Boston: Unwin Hyman, 1990).
49. I blend here framing ideas of George Lakoff, David Snow, and Rob Benford. See George Lakoff, *Don't Think of an Elephant: Know Your Values and Frame the Debate* (White River Junction, VT: Chelsea Green, 2004). Also, generally, in this section we draw heavily on Joe R. Feagin, *Systemic Racism: A Theory of Oppression* (New York: Routledge, 2006), especially pp. 25–27.
50. L. S. Vygotsky, *Mind in Society: The Development of Higher Psychological Processes*, eds. M. Cole, V. John-Steiner, S. Scribner, and E. Souberman (Cambridge, MA: Harvard University Press, 1978). We draw here on Debra Van Ausdale and Joe R. Feagin, *The First R: How Children Learn Race and Racism* (Lanham, MD: Rowman & Littlefield, 2001), chap. 1.
51. William G. Sumner, *Folkways* (New York: Mentor Books, 1960), pp. 27–28.
52. Robin M. Williams, Jr., *Strangers Next Door* (Englewood Cliffs, NJ: Prentice Hall, 1964), pp. 22–25.
53. Gordon Allport, *The Nature of Prejudice*, abridged ed. (New York: Doubleday Anchor Books, 1958), p. 7 (italics omitted); see also pp. 6–7.

54. Ibid., p. 10 (italics added).
55. Jane H. Hill, "Mock Spanish: A Site for the Indexical Reproduction of Racism in American English," unpublished research paper, University of Arizona, 1995; we draw here on Joe R. Feagin, *Racist America: Roots, Current Realities, and Future Reparations* (New York: Routledge, 2000), p. 119.
56. Rosina Lippi-Green, *English with an Accent* (New York: Routledge, 1997), p. 201.
57. Hill, "Mock Spanish"; Jane H. Hill, "Junk Spanish, Anglo Identity, and the Forces of Desire," paper presented at Symposium on "Hispanic Language and Social Identity," Albuquerque, NM, February 10–12, 1994.
58. See the summaries in Shankar Vedantam, "Many Americans Believe They Are Not Prejudiced. Now a New Test Provides Powerful Evidence That a Majority of Us Really Are," *The Washington Post*, January 23, 2005, p. W12; and Associated Press, "Racism Studies Find Rational Part of Brain Can Override Prejudice," www.beliefnet.com/story/156/story_15664_1.html (retrieved November 28, 2004).
59. Patricia G. Devine, "Stereotypes and Prejudice: Their Automatic and Controlled Components," *Journal of Personality and Social Psychology* 56 (1) (1989): 5–18; Patricia G. Devine and A. Elliot, "Are Racial Stereotypes Really Fading? The Princeton Trilogy Revisited," *Personality and Social Psychology Bulletin* 21 (1995): 1139–1150; R. H. Fazio, J. R. Jackson, B. C. Dunton, and C. J. Williams, "Variability in Automatic Activation as an Unobtrusive Measure of Racial Attitudes: A Bona Fide Pipeline?" *Journal of Personality and Social Psychology* 69 (1995): 1013–1027.
60. See Thomas F. Pettigrew, *Racially Separate or Together?* (New York: McGraw-Hill, 1971), pp. 134–135.
61. T. W. Adorno et al., *The Authoritarian Personality* (New York: Harper, 1950), pp. 248–279.
62. See Williams, *Strangers Next Door*, pp. 110–113; Pettigrew, *Racially Separate or Together?*, p. 131; Charles R. Lawrence, "The Id, the Ego, and Equal Protection," *Stanford Law Review* 39 (January 1987): 317–323; Gerald D. Jaynes and Robin Williams, Jr., eds., *A Common Destiny: Blacks and American Society* (Washington, DC: National Academy Press, 1989).
63. R. A. Schermerhorn, *Comparative Ethnic Relations* (New York: Random House, 1970), p. 6.
64. Herbert Blumer, "Race Prejudice as a Sense of Group Position," *The Pacific Sociological Review* 1 (Spring 1959): 3–7.
65. Cox, *Caste, Class, and Race*, p. 400.
66. David M. Wellman, *Portraits of White Racism* (Cambridge: Cambridge University Press, 1977).
67. David O. Sears, "Symbolic Racism," in *Eliminating Racism*, ed. Phyllis A. Katz and Dalmas A. Taylor (New York: Plenum Press, 1988), pp. 55–58; John B. McConahay, "Modern Racism," in *Prejudice, Discrimination and Racism*, ed. John F. Dovidio and Samuel L. Gaertner (Orlando, FL: Academic Press, 1986); and Lawrence Bobo, "Group Conflict, Prejudice, and the Paradox of Contemporary Racial Attitudes," in *Eliminating Racism*, ed. Katz and Taylor, pp. 99–101.
68. Marylee Taylor and Thomas Pettigrew, "Prejudice," in *Encyclopedia of Sociology*, ed. Edgar F. Borgatta and Marie L. Borgatta (New York: Macmillan, 1992), p. 1538.
69. Eduardo Bonilla-Silva and Tyrone A. Forman, "'I Am Not a Racist but. . .': Mapping White College Students' Racial Ideology in the U.S.A.," *Discourse and Society* 11(2000): 51–86; Maria Krysan, "Privacy and the Expression of White Racial Attitudes: A Comparison Across Three Contexts," *Public Opinion Quarterly* 62 (Winter 1998): 506–544.
70. Nina Eliasoph, "'Everyday Racism' in a Culture of Political Avoidance: Civil Society, Speech and Taboo," *Social Problems* 46 (November 1999): 479–495; Karyn McKinney, *Being White: Stories of Race and Racism* (New York: Routledge, 2005), p. 205; and Kristen Myers, *Racetalk: Racism Hiding in Plain Sight* (Lanham, MD: Rowman & Littlefield, 2005).
71. Leslie Houts Picca and Joe R. Feagin, *Two-Faced Racism: Whites in the Backstage and the Frontstage* (New York: Routledge, 2007), pp. 17–18.
72. Figure 1.1 is adapted from Joe R. Feagin, "Affirmative Action in an Era of Reaction," in *Consultations on the Affirmative Action Statement of the U.S. Commission on Civil Rights* (Washington, DC: U.S. Government Printing Office, 1982), pp. 46–48.
73. Allport, *The Nature of Prejudice*, p. 14.
74. Gunnar Myrdal, *An American Dilemma* (New York: McGraw-Hill, 1964; originally published 1944), vol. 1, p. 52; Robert K. Merton, "Discrimination and the American Creed," in *Discrimination and National Welfare*, ed. Robert MacIver (New York: Harper, 1949), p. 103.
75. Faye Crosby, Stephanie Bromley, and Leonard Saxe, "Recent Unobtrusive Studies of Black and White Discrimination and Prejudice," *Psychological Bulletin* 87 (1980): 546–563. See also Joe R. Feagin and Douglas L. Eckberg, "Discrimination: Motivation, Action, Effects, and Context," in *Annual Review of Sociology*, ed. Alex Inkeles, Neil J. Smelser, and Ralph H. Turner (Palo Alto, CA: Annual Reviews, 1980), pp. 3–4.
76. Charles Hamilton and Stokely Carmichael, *Black Power* (New York: Random House/Vintage Books, 1967), p. 4. See also *Institutional Racism in America*, ed. Louis L. Knowles and Kenneth Prewitt (Englewood Cliffs, NJ: Prentice Hall, 1969), p. 5.

77. Anthony Downs, *Racism in America and How to Combat It* (Washington, DC: U.S. Commission on Civil Rights, 1970), pp. 5, 7.
78. Thomas F. Pettigrew, "Racism and the Mental Health of White Americans: A Social Psychological View," in *Racism and Mental Health*, ed. Charles V. Willie, Bernard M. Kramer, and Bertram S. Brown (Pittsburgh: University of Pittsburgh Press, 1973), p. 271.
79. Essed, *Understanding Everyday Racism*, p. 39.
80. Joe R. Feagin, "Indirect Institutionalized Discrimination," *American Politics Quarterly* 5 (April 1977): 177–200.
81. Diana M. Pearce, "Black, White, and Many Shades of Gray: Real Estate Brokers and Their Racial Practices," Ph.D. dissertation, University of Michigan, Ann Arbor, MI, 1976); Diana Kendall, "Square Pegs in Round Holes: Nontraditional Students in Medical Schools," Ph.D. dissertation, University of Texas, Austin, TX, 1980).
82. Joe R. Feagin, "The Continuing Significance of Race: Antiblack Discrimination in Public Places, " *American Sociological Review* 56 (February 1991): 101–116.
83. Allport, *The Nature of Prejudice*, pp. 14–15.
84. Nijole V. Benokraitis and Joe R. Feagin, *Modern Sexism*, 2nd ed. (Englewood Cliffs, NJ: Prentice Hall, 1995), pp. 39–43.
85. Ed Jones, "What It's Like to Be a Black Manager," *Harvard Business Review* 64 (May/June 1986): 84–93; Thomas Pettigrew and Joanne Martin, "Shaping the Organizational Context for Black American Inclusion," *Journal of Social Issues* 43 (Spring 1987): 41–78; Joe R. Feagin and Melvin Sikes, *Living with Racism: The Black Middle Class Experience* (Boston: Beacon Press, 1994).
86. Benokraitis and Feagin, *Modern Sexism*, p. 135.
87. Quoted in Itabari Njeri, "Words to Live or Die by," *The Los Angeles Times Magazine*, May 31, 1992, p. 23.
88. Joe R. Feagin and Melvin P. Sikes, *Living with Racism*, pp. 145–147.
89. See Joe R. Feagin and Hernan Vera, *White Racism: The Basics* (New York: Routledge, 1995), chap. 8; Feagin and Sikes, *Living with Racism*.
90. See Joe R. Feagin and Aaron Porter, "Affirmative Action and African Americans: Rhetoric and Practice," *Humboldt Journal of Social Relations* 21 (1995): 81–104. Nijole Benokraitis and Joe R. Feagin, *Affirmative Action and Equal Opportunity: Action, Inaction, Reaction* (Boulder, CO: Westview Press, 1978).
91. We draw here on Feagin and Porter, "Affirmative Action and African Americans: Rhetoric and Practice."

Chapter 2

1. In re. Ah Yup, 1 F. Cas. 223 (C.C.D.Cal. 1878).
2. Tamotsu Shibutani and Kian M. Kwan, *Ethnic Stratification* (New York: Macmillan, 1965), pp. 28–33; and Donald L. Noel, "A Theory of the Origin of Ethnic Stratification," in *Majority and Minority*, ed. Norman R. Yetman and C. Hoy Steele (Boston: Allyn & Bacon, 1971), p. 32.
3. William M. Newman, *American Pluralism* (New York: Harper & Row, 1973), pp. 30–38.
4. Ernest A. T. Barth and Donald L. Noel, "Conceptual Frameworks for the Analysis of Race Relations: An Evaluation," *Social Forces* 50 (March 1972): 336.
5. Charles Tilly, *Migration to an American City* (Wilmington, DE: University of Delaware Agricultural Experiment Station, 1965).
6. Barth and Noel, "Conceptual Frameworks," pp. 337–339.
7. R. A. Schermerhorn, *Comparative Ethnic Relations* (New York: Random House, 1970), p. 98.
8. Ibid., p. 99.
9. Stanley Lieberson, "A Societal Theory of Racial and Ethnic Relations," *American Sociological Review* 29 (December 1961): 902–910.
10. Charles Hirschman, "America's Melting Pot Reconsidered," *Annual Review of Sociology* 9 (1983): 397–423.
11. Robert E. Park, *Race and Culture* (Glencoe, IL: The Free Press, 1950), p. 150 (italics added).
12. Robert E. Park and Ernest W. Burgess, *Introduction to the Science of Society* (Chicago: University of Chicago Press, 1924), p. 735.
13. Janice R. Hullum, "Robert E. Park's Theory of Race Relations." (Master's thesis, University of Texas, Austin, TX, 1973), pp. 81–88; see Park and Burgess, *Introduction to the Science of Society*, p. 760.
14. Milton M. Gordon, *Assimilation in American Life* (New York: Oxford University Press, 1964), pp. 72–73.
15. On the levels, see ibid., p. 71. On residential assimilation, see Doug Massey and Nancy Denton, "Suburbanization and Segregation in U.S. Metropolitan Areas," *American Journal of Sociology* 94 (1988): 592–626.
16. Silvia Pedraza, *Political and Economic Migrants in America: Cubans and Mexicans* (Austin: University of Texas Press, 1985), pp. 5–7; Richard Alba, *Ethnic Identity: The Transformation of White America* (New Haven, CT: Yale University Press, 1990), p. 311; Richard Alba and Victor Nee, "Rethinking Assimilation Theory for a New Era of Immigration," *International Migration Review* (1997): 829–837; J. Allen Williams and Suzanne T. Ortega, "Dimensions of Assimilation," *Social Science Quarterly* 71 (1990): 697–709.

17. Milton M. Gordon, *Human Nature, Class, and Ethnicity* (New York: Oxford University Press, 1978), pp. 67–89.
18. Gordon, *Assimilation in American Life*, pp. 78–108.
19. See Will Herberg, *Protestant–Catholic–Jew*, rev. ed. (Garden City, NY: Doubleday/Anchor Books, 1960).
20. Milton M. Gordon, "Models of Pluralism: The New American Dilemma," *Annals of the American Academy of Political and Social Science* 454 (1981): 178–188.
21. Alba, *Ethnic Identity*, p. 3; Herbert J. Gans, "Symbolic Ethnicity," *Ethnic and Racial Studies* 2 (1979): 1–20.
22. See Stanley Lieberson and Mary Waters, "Ethnic Mixtures in the United States," *Sociology and Social Research* 70 (1985): 43–53; Cookie White Stephan and Walter Stephan, "After Intermarriage," *Journal of Marriage and the Family* 51 (May 1989): 507–519; Alba and Lee, "Rethinking Assimilation Theory for a New Era of Immigration," p. 846; Mia Tuan, *Forever Foreigners or Honorary Whites?: The Asian American Experience Today* (New Brunswick, NJ: Rutgers University Press, 1998).
23. Milton R. Konvitz, "Horace Meyer Kallen (1882–1974)," in *American Jewish Yearbook, 1974–1975* (New York: American Jewish Committee, 1974), pp. 65–67; Milton Gordon, *Assimilation in American Life*, pp. 142–159.
24. Nathan Glazer and Daniel P. Moynihan, *Beyond the Melting Pot* (Cambridge, MA: M.I.T. Press and Harvard University Press, 1963).
25. Andrew M. Greeley, *Ethnicity in the United States* (New York: John Wiley, 1974), p. 293.
26. Ibid., pp. 295–309.
27. William L. Yancey, D. P. Ericksen, and R. N. Juliani, "Emergent Ethnicity: A Review and Reformulation," *American Sociological Review* 41 (June 1976): 391–393. See also Greeley, *Ethnicity in the United States*, pp. 290–317.
28. Gunnar Myrdal, *An American Dilemma* (New York: McGraw-Hill, 1964), vol. 2, p. 929.
29. Talcott Parsons, "Full Citizenship for the Negro American? A Sociological Problem," in *The Negro American*, ed. Talcott Parsons and Kenneth B. Clark (Boston: Houghton Mifflin, 1965–1966), p. 740.
30. Rubén G. Rumbaut, "Paradoxes (and Orthodoxies) of Assimilation," *Sociological Perspectives* 40 (1997): 483.
31. Steven J. Gold, "Transnationalism and Vocabularies of Motive in International Migration: The Case of Israelis in the United States," *Sociological Perspectives* 40 (1997): 410–411. We draw here too on Gina M. Pérez, *The Near Northwest Side Story: Migration, Displacement, and Puerto Rican Families* (Berkeley: University of California Press, 2004), pp. 12–14.
32. Gordon, *Human Nature, Class, and Ethnicity*, pp. 73–78; See also Clifford Geertz, "The Integrative Revolution," in *Old Societies and New States*, ed. Clifford Geertz (New York: The Free Press, 1963), p. 109.
33. Edna Bonacich, "Class Approaches to Ethnicity and Race," *Insurgent Sociologist* 10 (Fall 1980): 11.
34. Frederik Barth, "Introduction," in *Ethnic Groups and Boundaries: The Social Organization of Culture Difference* (Oslo: Universitets Forlaget, 1969), pp. 10–17.
35. Susan Olzak, "A Competition Model of Collective Action in American Cities," in *Competitive Ethnic Relations*, ed. Susan Olzak and Joane Nagel (Orlando, FL: Academic Press, 1986), pp. 17–46.
36. Susan Olzak, "Have the Causes of Ethnic Collective Action Changed over a Hundred Years?" (technical report, Department of Sociology, Cornell University, Ithaca, NY, 1987), p. 18.
37. Susan Olzak, *The Dynamics of Ethnic Competition and Conflict* (Stanford, CA: Stanford University Press, 1992).
38. Joane Nagel, "Resource Competition Theories," *American Behavioral Scientist* 38 (January 1995): 442.
39. W. Lloyd Warner, "Introduction," in Allison Davis et al., *Deep South* (Chicago: University of Chicago Press, 1941), pp. 4–6; W. Lloyd Warner and Leo Srole, *The Social Systems of American Ethnic Groups* (New Haven, CT: Yale University Press, 1945), pp. 295–296.
40. Compare Robert Blauner, *Racial Oppression in America* (New York: Harper & Row, 1972), p. 7.
41. William E. B. Du Bois, "Is Man Free?" *Scientific Monthly* 66 (May 1948): 432–434. See also Manning Marable, *How Capitalism Underdeveloped Black America* (Boston: South End Press, 1983), pp. 3–15.
42. Oliver C. Cox, *Caste, Class, and Race* (Garden City, NY: Doubleday, 1948), p. 332.
43. Ronald Bailey and Guillermo Flores, "Internal Colonialism and Racial Minorities in the U.S.: An Overview," in *Structures of Dependency*, ed. Frank Bonilla and Robert Girling (Stanford, CA: privately published by a Stanford faculty–student seminar, 1973), pp. 151–153.
44. G. Balandier, "The Colonial Situation: A Theoretical Approach," in *Social Change*, ed. Immanuel Wallerstein (New York: John Wiley, 1966), p. 35.
45. Pablo Gonzalez-Casanova, "Internal Colonialism and National Development," in *Latin American Radicalism*, ed. Irving L. Horowitz et al. (New York: Random House, 1969), p. 130; Bailey and Flores, "Internal Colonialism," p. 156.
46. Bailey and Flores, "Internal Colonialism," p. 156.
47. Blauner, *Racial Oppression in America*, p. 55. Our analysis draws here on Blauner's discussion.
48. Ramón Grosfoguel and Chloe S. Georas, "Coloniality of Power and Racial Dynamics: Notes Toward a Reinterpretation of Latino Caribbeans in New York

City," *Identities: Global Studies in Culture and Power* 7 (2000): 85–125.

49. Guillermo B. Flores, "Race and Culture in the Internal Colony: Keeping the Chicano in His Place," in *Structures of Dependency*, ed. Bonilla and Girling, p. 192.
50. Bonnie Mitchell and Joe Feagin, "America's Racial-Ethnic Cultures: Opposition Within a Mythical Melting Pot," in *Toward the Multicultural University*, ed. Benjamin Bowser, Gale Auletta, and Terry Jones (Westport, CT: Praeger, 1995), pp. 65–86. See also Michael Hechter, Debra Friedman, and Malka Appelbaum, "A Theory of Ethnic Collective Action," *International Migration Review* 16 (1982): 412–434.
51. Carol B. Stack, "Sex Roles and Survival Strategies in an Urban Black Community," in *Woman, Culture and Society*, ed. Michelle Zimbalist Rosaldo and Louise Lamphere (Stanford, CA: Stanford University Press, 1974), p. 128; Ronald Angel and Marta Tienda, "Determinants of Extended Household Structure: Cultural Pattern or Economic Need?" *American Journal of Sociology* 87 (1981–1982): 1360–1383.
52. James C. Scott, *Domination and the Arts of Resistance* (New Haven, CT: Yale University Press, 1990); John Gaventa, *Power and Powerlessness* (Urbana, IL: University of Illinois Press, 1980).
53. Scott, *Domination and the Arts of Resistance*, p. 116.
54. Sterling Stuckey, *Slave Culture* (New York: Oxford University Press, 1987), pp. 27, 42–46.
55. W. E. B. Du Bois, "The Future of Africa," *Advocate of Peace* 81 (January 1919): 12, as quoted in Manning Marable, *W. E. B. Du Bois: Black Radical Democrat* (Boston: Twayne, 1986), p. 100.
56. Marable, *W. E. B. Du Bois*, p. 101.
57. Molefi Kete Asante, *The Afrocentric Idea* (Philadelphia: Temple University Press, 1987); Molefi Kete Asante, *Afrocentricity* (Trenton, NJ: Africa World Press, 1988).
58. Marimba Ani, *Yurugu: An African-Centered Critique of European Cultural Thought and Behavior* (Trenton, NJ: Africa World Press, 1994), p. 567.
59. Ani, *Yurugu*, p. 570.
60. Mario Barrera, *Race and Class in the Southwest* (Notre Dame, IN: University of Notre Dame Press, 1979), pp. 214–217.
61. Bonacich, "Class Approaches to Ethnicity and Race," p. 14.
62. Cox, *Caste, Class, and Race*; Al Szymanski, *Class Structure* (New York: Praeger, 1983), pp. 420–440; Al Szymanski, "Racial Discrimination and White Gain," *American Sociological Review* 41 (1976): 403–414.
63. Stanley B. Greenberg, *Race and State in Capitalist Development* (New Haven, CT: Yale University Press, 1980), p. 349.
64. Barrera, *Race and Class in the Southwest*, pp. 201–203; Bonacich, "Class Approaches to Ethnicity and Race," p. 14.
65. W. E. B. Du Bois, *Black Reconstruction in America 1860–1880* (New York: Atheneum, 1992 [1935]), p. 700; Joe R. Feagin, *Racist America: Roots, Current Realities and Future Reparations* (New York: Routledge, 2000), pp. 30–31, 178.
66. Bonacich, "Class Approaches to Ethnicity and Race," pp. 14–15.
67. Edna Bonacich and John Modell, *The Economic Basis of Ethnic Solidarity* (Berkeley, CA: University of California Press, 1980), pp. 1–37.
68. Alejandro Portes and Robert D. Manning, "The Immigrant Enclave: Theory and Empirical Examples," in *Competitive Ethnic Relations*, ed. Olzak and Nagel, pp. 47–68.
69. Rumbaut, "Paradoxes (and Orthodoxies) of Assimilation," p. 483; Alejandro Portes, "Segmented Assimilation Among New Immigrant Youth: A Conceptual Framework," in *California's Immigrant Children*, ed. Rubén Rumbaut and Wayne Cornelius (La Jolla, CA: Center for Mexican American Studies, University of California, 1995), pp. 71–76; and Min Zhou, "Growing Up American: The Challenge Confronting Immigrant Children and Children of Immigrants," *Annual Review of Sociology* 23 (1997): 63–95.
70. Amy Chua, *World on Fire: How Exporting Free Market Democracy Breeds Ethnic Hatred and Global Instability* (New York: Doubleday, 2003), p. 121. See also pp. 22–30 and 120–123.
71. Quoted in Michael Albert et al., *Liberating Theory* (Boston: South End Press, 1986), p. 35.
72. Philomena Essed, *Understanding Everyday Racism* (Newbury Park, CA: Sage, 1991), pp. 30–32.
73. Patricia Hill Collins, *Black Feminist Thought: Knowledge, Consciousness, and the Politics of Empowerment* (Boston: Unwin Hyman, 1990), pp. 40–48.
74. Denise A. Segura, "Chicanas and Triple Oppression in the Labor Force," in *Chicana Voices: Intersections of Class, Race and Gender*, ed. Teresa Cordova et al. (Austin, TX: Center for Mexican American Studies, 1986), p. 48.
75. Omi and Winant, *Racial Formation in the United States*, pp. 75–76.
76. William E. B. Du Bois, *The World and Africa* (New York: International Publishers, 1965 [1946]), p. 37; for a more detailed development of these ideas, see Feagin, *Racist America*.
77. Cox, *Caste, Class, and Race: A Study in Social Dynamics*, p. 578.
78. Ibid., p. 332.
79. Andrew Hacker, *Two Nations: Black and White, Separate, Hostile, Unequal* (New York: Scribner's, 1992).

80. Trina Williams. "The Homestead Act—Our Earliest National Asset Policy," paper presented at the Center for Social Development's symposium, Inclusion in Asset Building, St. Louis, MO, September 21–23, 2000. See also, Feagin, *Racist America*, chap. 6.
81. Ian Craib, *Modern Social Theory: From Parsons to Habermas* (New York: St. Martin's Press, 1984), p. 53.
82. Iris Young, *Justice and the Politics of Difference* (Princeton, NJ: Princeton University Press, 1990), p. 52.
83. Tomas Almaguer, *Racial Fault Lines* (Berkeley, CA: University of California Press, 1994), p. 7.
84. Aldon Morris, *The Origins of the Civil Rights Movement* (New York: The Free Press, 1984).
85. See, for example, Juan F. Perea, "The Black/White Binary Paradigm of Race: The 'Normal Science' of American Racial Thought," *California Law Review* 85 (October 1997): 1219–1221.
86. See, for example, Lewis R. Gordon, *Her Majesty's Other Children: Sketches of Racism from a Neocolonial Age* (Lanham: Rowman & Littlefield, 1997), pp. 5, 53. This section draws on Feagin, *Racist America*, chap. 7.
87. Gary Y. Okihiro, "Is Yellow Black or White?" in *Asian Americans: Experiences and Perspectives*, ed. Timothy P. Fong and Larry H. Shinagawa (Upper Saddle River, NJ: Prentice Hall, 2000), p. 75.

Part II

1. Edna Bonacich, "United States Capitalist Development: A Background to Asian Immigration," in *Labor Immigration Under Capitalism*, ed. Lucie Cheng and Edna Bonacich (Berkeley, CA: University of California Press, 1984), p. 82.
2. Herbert Aptheker, lectures on American history, University of Minnesota, 1984.
3. Lucie Cheng and Edna Bonacich, "Imperialism, Distorted Development, and Asian Emigration to the United States," in *Labor Immigration Under Capitalism*, ed. Cheng and Bonacich, pp. 214–217.
4. Bonacich, "United States Capitalist Development," pp. 99–110.
5. Coretta Scott King, "It's a Bit Late to Protest Preferential Treatment," *Detroit Free Press*, December 13, 1985, p. 9A.
6. Stephen Steinberg, *The Ethnic Myth* (New York: Atheneum, 1981), p. 36.
7. Bonacich, "United States Capitalist Development," pp. 112–115.
8. Irving Kristol, "The Negro Today Is Like the Immigrant of Yesterday," *The New York Times Magazine*, September 11, 1966, pp. 50–51, 124–142.
9. Theodore Hershberg et al., "A Tale of Three Cities: Blacks, Immigrants, and Opportunity in Philadelphia: 1850–1880, 1930, 1970," in *Philadelphia*, ed. Theodore Hershberg (New York: Oxford University Press, 1981), pp. 462–464.
10. William Yancey, E. P. Ericksen, and R. N. Juliani, "Emergent Ethnicity," *American Sociological Review* 41 (June 1976): 393.
11. Stanley Lieberson, *A Piece of the Pie* (Berkeley, CA: University of California Press, 1980), pp. 377–383.
12. Robert Blauner, *Racial Oppression in America* (New York: Harper & Row, 1972), p. 62.
13. H. Sitkoff, *A New Deal for Blacks* (New York: Oxford University Press, 1978), pp. 37–38; C. G. Wye, "The New Deal and the Negro Community," *Journal of American History* 59 (December 1972): 634.
14. Charles B. Keeley, "Population and Immigration Policy: State and Federal Roles," in *Mexican American and Central American Population Issues and U.S. Policy*, ed. Frank D. Bean, Jurgen Schmandt, and Sidney Weintraub (Austin, TX: Center for Mexican American Studies, 1988).

Chapter 3

1. Cleveland Amory, *The Proper Bostonians* (New York: Dutton, 1947), p. 11.
2. U.S. Census Bureau, *Census 2000 Supplementary Survey*. Table PCT 024. Ancestry-First Reported, http://factfinder.census.gov/home; U.S. Census Bureau, *Census 2000 Supplementary Survey*. Table PCT 025. Ancestry-Second Reported, http://factfinder.census.gov/home (retrieved January 28, 2002); U.S. Bureau of the Census, *1990 Census of Population: Social and Economic Characteristics: United States*, CP-2-1 (Washington, DC: 1993), p. 166.
3. Carl Wittke, "Preface to the Revised Edition," in *We Who Built America*, rev. ed. (Cleveland, OH: Case Western Reserve University Press, 1967).
4. Milton M. Gordon, *Assimilation in American Life* (New York: Oxford University Press, 1964), p. 72.
5. Rowland T. Berthoff, *British Immigrants in Industrial America* (Chicago: University of Chicago Press, 1953), p. 1.
6. John Jay, Alexander Hamilton, and James Madison, *The Federalist* (London: Penguin Classics, 1987 [1788]), p. 91.
7. Wilbur S. Shepperson, *British Emigration to North America* (Oxford: Basil Blackwell, 1957), p. 3.
8. Conrad Taeuber and Irene B. Taeuber, "Immigration to the United States," in *Population and Society*, ed. Charles B. Nam (Boston: Houghton Mifflin, 1968), p. 316.

9. Immigration and Naturalization Service, *1975 Annual Report* (Washington, DC: 1975), pp. 62–64.
10. Alice Marriott and Carol K. Rachlin, *American Epic* (New York: Mentor, 1969), p. 105.
11. Samuel Eliot Morison, *The Oxford History of the American People* (New York: Oxford University Press, 1965), pp. 48–49.
12. Klaus E. Knorr, *British Colonial Theories, 1570–1850* (Toronto: University of Toronto Press, 1944), p. 126.
13. Marriott and Rachlin, *American Epic*, pp. 104–106; Winthrop D. Jordan, *White over Black* (Baltimore, MD: Penguin, 1969), p. 89.
14. This paragraph and the following paragraph draw on Morison, *Oxford History of the American People*, pp. 50–154; and Maldwyn A. Jones, *American Immigration* (Chicago: University of Chicago Press, 1960), pp. 10–38.
15. Morison, *Oxford History of the American People*, p. 74.
16. David Hackett Fischer, *Albion's Seed: Four British Folkways in America* (New York: Oxford University Press, 1989), pp. 6, 13–205, 785–786.
17. Ibid., pp. 207–418.
18. Ibid., pp. 419–603.
19. Ibid., pp. 605–782.
20. *Proceedings of the American Historical Association*, vol. 1 of *Annual Report of the American Historical Association* (Washington, DC: American Historical Association, 1932), p. 124.
21. Jones, *American Immigration*, pp. 34–35.
22. Berthoff, *British Immigrants in Industrial America*, pp. vii, 28–29; Charlotte Erickson, "English," in *Harvard Encyclopedia of American Ethnic Groups*, ed. Stephan Thernstrom (Cambridge, MA: Harvard University Press, 1980), pp. 324–332.
23. Shepperson, *British Emigration to North America*, pp. 27–32, 84; Berthoff, *British Immigrants in Industrial America*, pp. 46–87, 122; Charlotte Erickson, "Agrarian Myths of English Immigrants," in *In the Trek of the Immigrants*, ed. O. Fritiof Ander (Rock Island, IL: Augustana Library Publications, 1964), pp. 59–64.
24. Berthoff, *British Immigrants in Industrial America*, p. 125.
25. Stanley Lieberson and Mary C. Waters, *From Many Strands* (New York: Russell Sage, 1988), pp. 40–41.
26. Charles H. Anderson, *White Protestant Americans* (Englewood Cliffs, NJ: Prentice Hall, 1970), pp. 28–71, 79–87. See also Ian C. Graham, *Colonists from Scotland* (Ithaca, NY: Cornell University Press, 1956); and Albert B. Faust, *The German Element in the United States* (New York: Steuben Society, 1927).
27. Ronald Takaki, *Iron Cages* (New York: Oxford University Press, 1990), pp. 12–14.
28. Thomas Jefferson, *Notes on the State of Virginia*, ed. Frank Shuffelton (New York: Penguin, 1999 [1785]), pp. 144–166; I draw here on Joe Feagin, *Systemic Racism: A Theory of Oppression* (New York: Routledge, 2006), especially chap. 3.
29. "The Letters of Thomas Jefferson: 1743–1826; Emancipation and the Younger Generation," http://odur.let.rug.nl/~usa/P/tj3/writings/brf/jefl232.htm (retrieved May 10, 2004).
30. William E. B. Du Bois, *Black Reconstruction in America: An Essay Toward a History of the Part Which Black Folk Played in the Attempt to Reconstruct Democracy in America, 1860–1880* (New York: Atheneum, [1935] 1992). We draw here on Joe R. Feagin and Aaron Porter, "White Racism: Bibliographic Essay," *Choice* 33 (February 1996): 903–914.
31. Theodore W. Allen, *The Invention of the White Race* (New York: Verso, 1994), pp. 21, 184; David Roediger, *Towards the Abolition of Whiteness: Essays on Race, Politics, and Working Class History* (New York: Verso, 1994).
32. John Higham, *Strangers in the Land* (New York: Atheneum, 1963), p. 4.
33. Quotes are from Jordan, *White over Black*, pp. 44, 86. See also Henry P. Fairchild, *Immigration* (New York: Macmillan, 1920), p. 47; Jones, *American Immigration*, p. 44.
34. Jones, *American Immigration*, pp. 41–46.
35. Fairchild, *Immigration*, pp. 57–58.
36. Michael Kammen, *People of Paradox* (New York: Knopf, 1972), p. 66.
37. Quoted in Nancy F. Conklin and Margaret A. Lourie, *A Host of Tongues* (New York: The Free Press, 1983), p. 69.
38. Higham, *Strangers in the Land*, p. 6; Marcus L. Hansen, *The Immigrant in American History* (New York: Harper Torchbooks, 1964), pp. 111–136; Wittke, *We Who Built America*, p. 505.
39. Quoted in Richard Hofstadter, *Social Darwinism in American Thought*, rev. ed. (Boston: Beacon Press, 1955), pp. 171–172.
40. Higham, *Strangers in the Land*, p. 33.
41. Hofstadter, *Social Darwinism in American Thought*, pp. 178–179; Lewis H. Carlson and George A. Colburn, *In Their Place* (New York: John Wiley, 1972), pp. 305–308. Carlson and Colburn provide excerpts from the writings of Strong.
42. Higham, *Strangers in the Land*, pp. 96–152.
43. E. Digby Baltzell, *The Protestant Establishment* (New York: Random House/Vintage Books, 1966), pp. 96–98; Higham, *Strangers in the Land*, pp. 148–157.
44. Richard Alba, *Ethnic Identity: The Transformation of White America* (New Haven, CT: Yale University Press, 1990), p. 365.
45. Sheldon Hanft, "English Americans," www.everyculture. com/multi/Du-Ha/English-Americans.html (retrieved June 15, 2006).

46. Jones, *American Immigration*, pp. 36–38.
47. W. Lloyd Warner and Leo Srole, *The Social Systems of American Ethnic Groups* (New Haven, CT: Yale University Press, 1945), p. 287; Juan F. Perea, "Demography and Distrust: An Essay on American Languages, Cultural Pluralism and Official English," *Minnesota Law Review* 77 (1992): 269.
48. Susanna McBee, "A War over Words," *U.S. News & World Report*, October 6, 1986, p. 64.
49. "National English Campaign Supports English as the Official Language of the United States," *Business Wire*, February 11, 1997.
50. "English for the Children—California English Campaign Endorses Initiative," *Business Wire*, August 28, 1997.
51. Clarence Petersen, "Tribune Books," *Chicago Tribune*, October 31, 1993, p. C8.
52. Bill Piatt, *Only English? Law and Language Policy in the United States* (Albuquerque: University of New Mexico Press, 1990), p. 159.
53. Amado Padilla et al., "The English-Only Movement," *American Psychologist* 46 (February 1991): 120–130; National Education Association, *Official English/English Only* (Washington, DC: National Education Association, 1988), pp. 5–7.
54. Perea, "Demography and Distrust."
55. National Education Association, *Official English/English Only*, p. 7; Carl J. Veltman, *Language Shift in the United States* (Berlin: Mouton, 1983).
56. Fischer, *Albion's Seed*, pp. 795–797.
57. Edwin S. Gaustad, *Historical Atlas of Religion in America* (New York: Harper & Row, 1962), pp. 1–20.
58. Will Herberg, *Protestant–Catholic–Jew*, rev. ed. (Garden City, NY: Doubleday/Anchor, 1960), p. 82.
59. Marshall Sklare, *Conservative Judaism* (Glencoe, IL: The Free Press, 1955), pp. 31–117.
60. Takaki, *Iron Cages*, p. 7.
61. Max Weber, *The Protestant Ethic and the Spirit of Capitalism*, trans. Talcott Parsons (New York: Scribner's, 1958), p. 17; see also p. 50.
62. David Ewen, *History of Popular Music* (New York: Barnes & Noble, 1961), pp. 1–10.
63. See Samuel Bowles and Herbert Gintis, *Schooling in Capitalist America* (New York: Basic Books, 1976).
64. Morison, *Oxford History of the American People*, p. 55.
65. Samuel P. Huntington, "Political Modernization: America Versus Europe," *World Politics* 18 (April 1966): 147–148.
66. Jack P. Greene, *The Quest for Power* (Chapel Hill: University of North Carolina Press, 1963), pp. 1ff.
67. Roscoe Pound, *The Formative Era of American Law* (Boston: Little, Brown, 1938), pp. 7–8.
68. Ibid., p. 12.
69. Elizabeth G. Brown and William W. Blume, *British Statutes in American Law, 1776–1836* (Ann Arbor: University of Michigan Law School, 1964), p. 44. See also Lawrence M. Friedman, *A History of American Law* (New York: Simon & Schuster, 1973), pp. 96–100.
70. Pound, *The Formative Era of American Law*, p. 81.
71. Maurice R. Davie, *World Immigration* (New York: Macmillan, 1939), p. 36.
72. Henry J. Ford, *The Scotch-Irish in America* (Princeton, NJ: Princeton University Press, 1915), p. 491.
73. Charles A. Beard, *An Economic Interpretation of the Constitution of the United States* (New York: Macmillan, 1947), p. 17.
74. Joseph N. Kane, *Facts About the Presidents*, 3rd ed. (New York: Wilson, 1974).
75. John R. Schmidhauser, "The Justices of the Supreme Court: A Collective Portrait," *Midwest Journal of Political Science* 3 (February 1959): 1–57.
76. William Miller, "American Historians and the Business Elite," *Journal of Economic History* 9 (November 1949): 202–203.
77. On Protestant presidents before Kennedy, see ibid., p. 21.
78. Robert A. Dahl, *Who Governs?* (New Haven, CT: Yale University Press, 1961), pp. 15–16.
79. Matthew Holden, Jr., "Ethnic Accommodation in a Historical Case," *Comparative Studies in Society and History* 8 (January 1966): 172.
80. Rowland Berthoff, *An Unsettled People* (New York: Harper & Row, 1971), p. 13; Oliver C. Cox, *Caste, Class, and Race* (Garden City, NY: Doubleday, 1948), pp. 338–339; Barrington Moore, Jr., *Social Origins of Dictatorship and Democracy* (Boston: Beacon Press, 1966), pp. 112–113.
81. Frank Thistlewaite, *The Anglo-American Connection in the Early Nineteenth Century* (Philadelphia: University of Pennsylvania Press, 1959), pp. 5–11.
82. Jesse Lemisch, "The American Revolution Seen from the Bottom Up," in *Toward a New Past*, ed. Barton J. Bernstein (New York: Random House, 1968), p. 8; J. O. Lindsay, ed., *The Old Regime*, vol. 7 of *The New Cambridge Modern History* (Cambridge: Cambridge University Press, 1957), pp. 509–511.
83. Morison, *Oxford History of the American People*, p. 89.
84. Abbot E. Smith, *Colonists in Bondage* (Chapel Hill: University of North Carolina Press, 1947), pp. 25, 336; Jordan, *White over Black*, p. 47; Howard Zinn, *The Politics of History* (Boston: Beacon Press, 1970), p. 68.
85. Lee Soltow, *Men and Wealth in the United States, 1850–1870* (New Haven, CT: Yale University Press, 1975), p. 149.
86. Matthew Josephson, *The Robber Barons* (New York: Harcourt, Brace & World, 1934), pp. 32–35, 315–452.

87. John N. Ingham, *The Iron Barons* (Westport, CT: Greenwood Press, 1978), pp. 14–16.
88. Miller, "American Historians and the Business Elite," p. 202.
89. Elin L. Anderson, *We Americans* (Cambridge, MA: Harvard University Press, 1937), p. 137; see also pp. 21–247.
90. E. Digby Baltzell, *An American Business Aristocracy* (New York: Collier, 1962), p. 267.
91. Baltzell, *The Protestant Establishment*, p. 321.
92. Thomas R. Dye, *Who's Running America?* (Englewood Cliffs, NJ: Prentice Hall, 1976), pp. 3–8, 150–153. See also Thomas R. Dye, *Who's Running America? The Carter Years* (Englewood Cliffs, NJ: Prentice Hall, 1979), pp. 171–177.
93. Thomas R. Dye, letter to author, April 11, 1977.
94. Julia Reed, "The New American Establishment," *U.S. News & World Report*, February 8, 1988, p. 38.
95. Richard D. Alba and Gwen Moore, "Ethnicity in the American Elite," *American Sociological Review* 47 (June 1982); see also Dye, *Who's Running America?* pp. 170–173.
96. U.S. Census Bureau, Census 2000 Demographic Profile Highlights: Selected Population Group: English, http://factfinder.census.gov (retrieved June 16, 2006); see also U.S. Bureau of the Census, 1990 Census of Population: Ancestry of the Population of the United States, CP-3-2 (Washington, DC: 1993), p. 33.
97. Lieberson and Waters, *From Many Strands*, p. 173.
98. Alba, *Ethnic Identity*, pp. 49–82.
99. Fischer, *Albion's Seed*, pp. 199–205, 412, 597, 777–782, 897–898.
100. Ibid., pp. 887–897, quotation on p. 896.
101. Lewis M. Killian, *White Southerners* (New York: Random House, 1970), p. 16.
102. Peter Schrag, *The Decline of the WASP* (New York: Simon & Schuster, 1971), p. 164.

Chapter 4

1. John Higham, *Strangers in the Land: Patterns of American Nativism 1860–1925*, rev. ed. (New York: Atheneum, 1975), p. 180.
2. U.S. Department of Justice, Immigration and Naturalization Service, *Annual Report* (Washington, DC, 1973), pp. 53–55. The figures for the period between 1820 and 1867 represent "alien passengers arrived"; for later periods they represent immigrants arrived or admitted.
3. Cited in William Peterson, *Population*, 2nd ed. (New York: Macmillan, 1969), p. 260.
4. U.S. Bureau of the Census, *Statistical Abstract of the United States 1991* (Washington, DC, 1991), p. 10; U.S. Bureau of the Census, *Statistical Abstract of the United States 1994* (Washington, DC, 1994), p. 11.
5. U.S. Census Bureau, Census 2000 Demographic Profile Highlights: Selected Population Group: Irish, http://factfinder.census.gov (retrieved June 16, 2006); U.S. Bureau of the Census, *1990 Census of Population: Ancestry of the Population in the United States*, CP-3-2 (Washington, DC, 1993), pp. 50, 65; U.S. Bureau of the Census, *1990 Census of Population: Social and Economic Characteristics: United States*, CP-2-1 (Washington, DC, 1993), p. 166; U.S. Census Bureau, Census 2000 *Supplementary Survey*, Table PCT 024.
6. Philip H. Bagenal, *The American Irish* (London: Kegan Paul, Trench, 1882), pp. 4–5; Henry Jones Ford, *The Scotch-Irish in America* (Princeton, NJ: Princeton University Press, 1915), pp. 125–128, 183–186; James G. Leyburn, *The Scotch-Irish* (Chapel Hill: University of North Carolina Press, 1962), pp. 160ff.
7. Michael J. O'Brien, *A Hidden Phase of American History* (New York: Devin-Adair, 1919), p. 249; we also draw on pp. 267, 287–288.
8. Thomas D'Arcy McGee, *A History of Irish Settlers in North America* (Boston: Office of American Celt, 1851), pp. 25–34; Leyburn, *The Scotch-Irish*, pp. 331–332.
9. Quoted in Ford, *The Scotch-Irish in America*, pp. 520–521.
10. Winthrop D. Jordan, *White over Black* (Baltimore, MD: Penguin, 1969), pp. 86–88; McGee, *A History of Irish Settlers in North America*, p. 79.
11. Arnold Shrier, *Ireland and the American Emigration, 1850–1900* (Minneapolis: University of Minnesota Press, 1958), pp. 13–16; T. A. Jackson, *Ireland Her Own* (New York: International Publishers, 1970), pp. 243–245; Kerby A. Miller, *Emigrants and Exiles* (New York: Oxford University Press, 1985), p. 556.
12. Carl Wittke, *The Irish in America* (Baton Rouge: Louisiana State University Press, 1956), pp. 24–27; Theodore Hershberg et al., "A Tale of Three Cities," in *Majority and Minority*, 3rd ed., ed. Norman Y. Yetman and C. Hoy Steele (Boston: Allyn & Bacon, 1982), pp. 184–185; Bagenal, *The American Irish*, p. 72; Wittke, *The Irish in America*, p. 46.
13. Ronald Takaki, *A Different Mirror* (Boston: Little, Brown, 1993), pp. 154–160; Hasia R. Diner, *Erin's Daughters in America* (Baltimore, MD: Johns Hopkins University Press, 1983), pp. xiii–xv.
14. Dale T. Knobel, *Paddy and the Republic* (Middle-town, CT: Wesleyan University Press, 1986), pp. 24–27; Bill Bryson, *The Mother Tongue: English and How It Got That Way* (New York: William Morrow, 1990).
15. Lewis P. Curtis, Jr., *Apes and Angels: The Irish in Victorian Caricature* (Washington, DC: Smithsonian Institution Press, 1971), p. 103. See also p. 59.

16. Andrew M. Greeley, *That Most Distressful Nation* (Chicago: Quadrangle, 1972), pp. 119–120.
17. Leonard Gordon, "Racial and Ethnic Stereotypes of American College Students over a Half Century," paper presented at meetings of the Society for the Study of Social Problems, Washington, DC, August 1985, pp. 14–15.
18. American Institute of Public Opinion, *Roper Center*, 1982; Richard D. Alba, *Ethnic Identity: The Transformation of White America* (New Haven, CT: Yale University Press, 1990), p. 156.
19. Leonard Dinnerstein and Frederic C. Jaher, "Introduction," in *The Aliens*, ed. Leonard Dinnerstein and Frederic C. Jaher (New York: Appleton-Century-Crofts, 1970), p. 4.
20. Leyburn, *The Scotch-Irish*, pp. 234, 301–316; Ford, *The Scotch-Irish in America*, pp. 291–324; Leyburn, *The Scotch-Irish*, pp. 225–230.
21. Dennis Clark, *The Irish in Philadelphia* (Philadelphia: Temple University Press, 1973), p. 21; see also Wittke, *The Irish in America*, p. 120.
22. Wayne G. Broehl, Jr., *The Molly Maguires* (Cambridge, MA: Harvard University Press, 1964), pp. 198–199; Anthony Bimba, *The Molly Maguires* (New York: International Publishers, 1932), pp. 70–73.
23. Takaki, *A Different Mirror*, pp. 150–152; Oscar Handlin, *Boston's Immigrants, 1790–1865* (Cambridge, MA: Harvard University Press, 1941), p. 137; James McCague, *The Second Rebellion* (New York: Dial Press, 1968).
24. Theodore W. Allen, *The Invention of the White Race* (London: Verso, 1994), p. 21; David Roediger, *Towards the Abolition of Whiteness* (London: Verso, 1994), p. 12.
25. Allen, *The Invention of the White Race*, pp. 21–50; Joe R. Feagin and Hernan Vera, *White Racism: The Basics* (New York : Routledge, 1995), pp. 1–18.
26. Roediger, *Towards the Abolition of Whiteness*, p. 140.
27. Ford, *The Scotch-Irish in America*, pp. 246, 462, 491; McGee, *A History of Irish Settlers in North America*, p. 71; Shane Leslie, *The Irish Issue in Its American Aspect* (New York: Scribner's, 1919), p. 8.
28. Wittke, *The Irish in America*, p. 104; Edward M. Levine, *The Irish and Irish Politicians* (Notre Dame, IN: University of Notre Dame Press, 1966), pp. 6–9.
29. Leo Hershkowitz, *Tweed's New York* (New York: Doubleday/Anchor Books, 1987), pp. xiii–xx.
30. Nathan Glazer and Daniel P. Moynihan, *Beyond the Melting Pot* (Cambridge, MA: M.I.T. Press and Harvard University Press, 1963), pp. 218–262; Robert A. Dahl, *Who Governs?* (New Haven, CT: Yale University Press, 1963), p. 41; Mike Royko, *Boss: Richard J. Daley of Chicago* (New York: Dutton, 1971); Sam Roberts, "In Search of Irish, or the Greening of the Suburbs," *The New York Times*, March 17, 1988, p. B1; Alba, *Ethnic Identity*, p. 156.
31. Greeley, *That Most Distressful Nation*, pp. 206–209; Dennis J. Clark, "The Philadelphia Irish," in *The Peoples of Philadelphia*, ed. Allen F. Davis and Mark H. Haller (Philadelphia: Temple University Press, 1973), p. 145.
32. Terry N. Clark, "The Irish Ethnic and the Spirit of Patronage," *Ethnicity* 2 (1975): 305–359; Mark R. Levy and Michael S. Kramer, *The Ethnic Factor* (New York: Simon & Schuster, 1972), pp. 130–135; Andrew M. Greeley, *The Irish Americans* (New York: Harper & Row, 1981), pp. 168–169.
33. William Miller, "American Historians and the Business Elite," *Journal of Economic History* 9 (November 1949): 202–203.
34. John Aloysius Farrell, "Clinton Staff Alters Blair Brown's Status," *Boston Globe*, March 19, 1994, p. 3.
35. Linda Greenhouse, "Supreme Court Ruling Clears Way for Deportation of an I.R.A. Man," *The New York Times*, January 16, 1992, p. A1; "O'Connor Seeks Aid for I.R.A. Fugitive," *The New York Times*, February 1, 1992, sec. 1, p. 25; Cal McCrystal, "Notebook: A Tug-of-War for America's Irish Soul," *Independent*, February 2, 1992, p. 23.
36. Steve Fainaru, "Adams, in New York Limelight, Asks for U.S. Help on Peace," *Boston Globe*, February 2, 1994, p. 1; Gerald Renner, "Sinn Fein Leader Urges Peace Plan Support," *Hartford Courant*, September 26, 1994, p. A1; Kevin Cullen, "Loyalist Extremists Call Ulster Cease-Fire," *Boston Globe*, October 14, 1994, p. 1; "Northern Ireland Peace Talks," National Public Radio, "Weekend Edition," September 21, 1997.
37. William V. Shannon, *The American Irish* (New York: Macmillan, 1963), pp. 151–181.
38. Glazer and Moynihan, *Beyond the Melting Pot*, p. 287; Shannon, *The American Irish*, pp. 395–411; Levy and Kramer, *The Ethnic Factor*, pp. 126–127.
39. *Reporting for the Russell Sage Foundation*, no. 6 (May 1985): 6.
40. Stephen Steinberg, *The Ethnic Myth* (New York: Atheneum, 1981), pp. 160–164.
41. Handlin, *Boston's Immigrants*, p. 67.
42. Greeley, *That Most Distressful Nation*, p. 120; Clark, "The Philadelphia Irish," p. 143; Wittke, *The Irish in America*, pp. 217–227.
43. Lloyd Warner and Leo Srole, *The Social Systems of American Ethnic Groups* (New Haven, CT: Yale University Press, 1945), pp. 93–95.
44. Ronald P. Formisano, *Boston Against Busing: Race, Class, and Ethnicity in the 1960s and 1970s* (Chapel Hill: University of North Carolina Press, 1991), p. 15; Harold J. Abramson, *Ethnic Diversity in Catholic America* (New York: John Wiley, 1973), pp. 41–44; Levy and Kramer, *The Ethnic Factor*, p. 125; see also

U.S. Bureau of the Census, *1990 Census of Population: Ancestry of the Population in the United States*, pp. 353, 371, 455, 473; U.S. Bureau of the Census, *1990 Census of Population: Social and Economic Characteristics: United States*, pp. 45, 48, 49.

45. Roberts, "In Search of Irish," p. B1; Tim Unsworthy, "The Irish: Faith Persuasive as Metamucil in an Old Priest's Diet," *National Catholic Reporter*, March 15, 1996, p. 16.
46. John T. Ellis, *American Catholicism* (Garden City, NY: Doubleday/Image Books, 1965), p. 62; Clark, *The Irish in Philadelphia*, p. 123.
47. David O. Moberg, *The Church as a Social Institution* (Englewood Cliffs, NJ: Prentice Hall, 1962), p. 193; Andrew M. Greeley, *Ethnicity, Denomination and Inequality* (Beverly Hills, CA: Sage, 1976), pp. 45–53.
48. U.S. Census Bureau, *Census 2000 Demographic Profile Highlights: Selected Population Group: Irish*, http://factfinder.census.gov (retrieved June 16, 2006).
49. "Bill to Require Teaching of Irish Famine," United Press International, March 17, 1997.
50. Wittke, *The Irish in America*, pp. 52–61, 205; Owen B. Corrigan, "Chronology of the Catholic Hierarchy of the United States," *Catholic Historical Review* 1 (January 1916): 267–389; Edwin S. Gaustad, *Historical Atlas of Religion in America* (New York: Harper & Row, 1962), p. 103; Ellis, *American Catholicism*, p. 56; Wittke, *The Irish in America*, p. 91; Greeley, *That Most Distressful Nation*, p. 93.
51. National Opinion Research Center, 1990 General Social Survey. Tabulations by authors.
52. Greeley, *The Irish Americans*, pp. 130–132.
53. *Saturday Evening Post*, December 12, 1901; *Saturday Evening Post*, August 28, 1902.
54. Clark, *The Philadelphia Irish*, p. 178.
55. Stephan Thernstrom, *Poverty and Progress* (Cambridge, MA: Harvard University Press, 1964), p. 179.
56. Bede Jagoe, "Celtic Cult to Celtic Culture," paper presented at O.P. International Conference on Constructions of Irishness: The Irish in Ireland, Britain and Beyond, March 23, 2002; Abramson, *Ethnic Diversity in Catholic America*, p. 111; Greeley, *The Irish Americans*, pp. 149–151.
57. Andrew M. Greeley, "The Success and Assimilation of Irish Protestants and Irish Catholics in the United States," *Sociology and Social Research* 72, no. 4 (July 1988): 236; Raymond E. Wolfinger, "The Development and Persistence of Ethnic Voting," *American Political Science Review* 60 (1965): 907.
58. Joseph P. O'Grady, *How the Irish Became American* (New York: Twayne, 1973), p. 141; Marjorie R. Fallows, *Irish Americans: Identity and Assimilation* (Englewood Cliffs, NJ: Prentice Hall, 1979), p. 147.
59. Abramson, *Ethnic Diversity in Catholic America*, p. 53; Alba, *Ethnic Identity*, p. 47; Nona Claren, "The Trouble with the Melting Pot," *Baltimore Sun*, June 24, 1997, p. 9A.
60. Fallows, *Irish Americans*, pp. 148–149. See also Richard D. Alba, "Social Assimilation Among American Catholic National-Origin Groups," *American Sociological Review* 41 (December 1976): 1032.
61. Alba, *Ethnic Identity*, pp. 55, 61.
62. Greeley, *The Irish Americans*, p. 206; Andrew M. Greeley, *Ethnicity in the United States* (New York: John Wiley, 1974), p. 311.
63. S. L. Berry, "In Step with the Irish Heritage; Irish-Americans Struggle to Learn Ancestral Language," *Indianapolis Star*, March 17, 1997, p. E1; Jagoe, "Celtic Cult to Celtic Culture."
64. Giovanni Schiavo, *The Italians in America Before the Civil War* (New York: Vigo Press, 1934), pp. 55–180.
65. U.S. Department of Justice, Immigration and Naturalization Service, *Annual Report* (Washington, DC, 1973), pp. 52–54; Schiavo, *The Italians in America*, p. 204; Carl Wittke, *We Who Built America*, rev. ed. (Cleveland, OH: Case Western Reserve University Press, 1964), p. 441; Humbert S. Nelli, *The Italians in Chicago, 1880–1930* (New York: Oxford University Press, 1970), p. 5; Grazia Dore, "Some Social and Historical Aspects of Italian Emigration to America," in *The Italians*, ed. Francesco Cordasco and Eugene Bucchioni (Clifton, NJ: Augustus M. Kelley, 1974), p. 7.
66. We are indebted to Phyllis Cancilla Martinelli for her useful suggestions in sections that follow. Joseph Lopreato, *Italian Americans* (New York: Random House, 1970), pp. 23–27; John S. MacDonald, "Agricultural Organization, Migration, and Labor Militancy in Rural Italy," *Economic History Review*, 2d ser., 16 (1963–1964): 61–75; Luciano J. Iorizzo and Salvatore Mondello, *The Italian-Americans* (New York: Twayne, 1971), pp. 57–59; Michael La Sorte, *La Merica* (Philadelphia: Temple University Press, 1985), pp. 1–13, 189–202.
67. Antonia Stella, *Some Aspects of Italian Immigration to the United States*, reprint ed. (San Francisco: R & E Associates, 1970), p. 33; Rudolph J. Vecoli, "Contadini in Chicago," in *Divided Society*, ed. Colin Greer (New York: Basic Books, 1974), p. 220; William Petersen, *Population*, 2nd ed. (New York: Macmillan, 1969), p. 260; La Sorte, *La Merica*, pp. 189–202.
68. John Higham, *Strangers in the Land*, rev. ed. (New York: Atheneum, 1975), pp. 312–324.
69. U.S. Bureau of the Census, *Statistical Abstract of the United States 1994* (Washington, DC, 1994), p. 11; U.S. Bureau of the Census, 1990 *Census of Population: Ancestry of the Population in the United States*, CP-3-2 (Washington, DC, 1993), p. 50; U.S. Census Bureau,

Census 2000 Supplementary Survey, Table PCT 024, Ancestry-First Reported, http://factfinder. census.gov/home; U.S. Census Bureau, *Census 2000 Supplementary Survey,* Table PCT 025, Ancestry-Second Reported, http://factfinder.census.gov/home (retrieved January 28, 2002).

70. Stanley Lieberson, *Ethnic Patterns in American Cities* (Glencoe, IL: The Free Press, 1963), pp. 209–218; La Sorte, *La Merica,* pp. 61–158.
71. William F. Whyte, *Street Corner Society,* 2nd ed. (Chicago: University of Chicago Press, 1955), pp. 272–273; Walter Firey, *Land Use in Central Boston* (Cambridge, MA: Harvard University Press, 1947), pp. 187–188; Wittke, *We Who Built America,* p. 446.
72. Rita J. Simon and Susan H. Alexander, *The Ambivalent Welcome: Print Media, Public Opinion, and Immigration* (Westport, CT: Praeger, 1993), pp. 84, 131; see also Eliot Lord, John J. D. Trenor, and Samuel J. Barrows, *The Italian in America,* reprint ed. (San Francisco: R & E Associates, 1970), pp. 17–18.
73. Kenneth L. Roberts, *Why Europe Leaves Home,* excerpted in "Kenneth L. Roberts and the Threat of Mongrelization in America, 1922," in *In Their Place,* ed. Lewis H. Carlson and George A. Colburn (New York: John Wiley, 1972), p. 312.
74. Jennifer Guglielmo, "White Lies, Dark Truths," in *Are Italians White?: How Race Is Made In America,* eds. Jennifer Guglielmo and Salvatore Salerno (New York: Routledge, 2003), p. 11.
75. Leon J. Kamin, *The Science and Politics of I.Q.* (New York: John Wiley, 1974), pp. 15–19.
76. Carl C. Brigham, *A Study of American Intelligence* (Princeton, NJ: Princeton University Press, 1923), especially pp. 124–125 and 177–210. Brigham later recanted.
77. See Roberts, *Why Europe Leaves Home,* for earlier views.
78. See Kamin, *The Science and Politics of I.Q.,* p. 30.
79. Quoted in E. Digby Baltzell, *The Protestant Establishment* (New York: Random House/Vintage Books, 1966), p. 30.
80. Fred Misurella, "Truth Behind the Fiction of Italian-Americans," *The Christian Science Monitor,* April 15, 2002, p. 9.
81. Irving L. Allen, *Unkind Words* (New York: Bergin and Garvey, 1990), pp. 32, 60.
82. Iorizzo and Mondello, *The Italian-Americans,* pp. 35–36; quotation in Nelli, *The Italians in Chicago,* p. 126; Stella, *Some Aspects of Italian Immigration,* pp. 60–61, 73.
83. Philip di Franco, *The Italian American Experience* (New York: Tom Doherty Associates, 1988), pp. 84–86; Richard Gambino, *Blood of My Blood* (Garden City, NY: Doubleday/Anchor Books, 1975), pp. 293–298; Lopreato, *Italian Americans,* p. 126; Nelli, *The Italians in Chicago,* pp. 154–155.
84. Mary C. Waters, Ethnic Options: Choosing Identities in America (Berkeley: University of California Press, 1990), pp. 142–143; the earlier survey is cited in Richard Alba and Dalia Abdel-Hady, "Galileo's Children: Italian Americans' Difficult Entry into the Intellectual Elite," *The Sociological Quarterly* 46 (2005): 7; the *Parade* survey is cited in Italic Institute, "Shark Tale—Overview, Argument, & Position Summary," http://italic.org/shark.htm (retrieved July 6, 2006).
85. Alba and Abdel-Hady, "Galileo's Children," p. 6.
86. "Italian American Group Rips CBS for 'Mafia' Stereotypes," (New York) *Daily News,* November 18, 1997, p. 96; William F. Miller, "Lawyer Fights Italian American Stereotypes," (Cleveland) *Plain Dealer,* June 15, 1996, p. 7B; Italic Institute, "Shark Tale—Overview, Argument, & Position Summary."
87. Gambino, *Blood of My Blood,* pp. 300–301; Selwyn Raab, "The Mob in Decline," *The New York Times,* October 22, 1990, p. A1.
88. Robert Lichter and Linda Lichter, "Italian-American Characters in Television Entertainment," report prepared for the Commission for Social Justice, Order of Sons of Italy, May 1982.
89. Quotation cited in Micaela di Leonardo, *The Varieties of Ethnic Experience* (Ithaca, NY: Cornell University Press, 1984), pp. 160–161; Susanna Tardi, *Family and Society: The Case of the Italians in New Jersey* (Ann Arbor, MI: UMI Dissertation Service, 1991), p. 189.
90. S. Luconi, "Mafia-Related Prejudice and the Rise of Italian Americans in the United States," *Patterns of Prejudice* 33 (1999): 43—57; Donna Haupt, Jan Mason, and Penny W. Moser, "The Embattled Queen of Queens," *Time,* October 1, 1984, p. 34; Vivienne Walt, "Cuomo: Hurt by Prejudice Toward Italians," *Newsday,* July 23, 1991, p. 19.
91. Alba, *Ethnic Identity,* pp. 141–142; Waters, *Ethnic Options,* pp. 142–43; see also Ross Harano and Jeryl Levin, "Capone Image Hurts Italian-Americans," *Chicago Tribune,* August 3, 1993, p. N16.
92. William F. Whyte, "Race Conflicts in the North End of Boston," *New England Quarterly* 12 (December 1939): 626; Iorizzo and Mondello, *The Italian-Americans,* pp. 35, 66.
93. Luciano J. Iorizzo, "The Padrone and Immigrant Distribution," in *The Italian Experience in the United States,* ed. Silvano Tomasi and M. H. Engel (New York: Center for Migration Studies, 1970), pp. 49–51; Gambino, *Blood of My Blood,* p. 119; Higham, *Strangers in the Land,* p. 169; di Franco, *The Italian American Experience,* p. 85; Gambino, *Blood of My Blood,* pp. 118, 280–281.

94. William Young and David E. Kaiser, *Postmortem* (Amherst: University of Massachusetts Press, 1985); Gambino, *Blood of My Blood*, pp. 120–21.
95. Iorizzo and Mondello, *The Italian-Americans*, p. 207; Gerald D. Suttles, *The Social Order of the Slum* (Chicago: University of Chicago Press, 1968), pp. 102–103; Richard Krickus, *Pursuing the American Dream* (Garden City, NY: Doubleday/Anchor Books, 1976), p. 280.
96. Curtis Rist, "Prosecutor: Race Riot in Bensonhurst," *Newsday*, April 17, 1990, p. 4.
97. Levy and Kramer, *The Ethnic Factor*, p. 174; National Opinion Research Center, General Social Surveys, 1989 and 1990.
98. Guglielmo, "White Lies, Dark Truths," p. 4; see also David A. J. Richards, *Italian American: The Racializing of an Ethnic Identity* (New York: New York University Press), 1999.
99. Schiavo, *The Italians in America Before the Civil War*, pp. 163–166.
100. Nelli, *The Italians in Chicago*, pp. 75–76; Wittke, *We Who Built America*, p. 447; Lopreato, *Italian Americans*, pp. 113–117; Giovanni Schiavo, *Italian American History* (New York: Vigo Press, 1947), 1: 499–504.
101. di Franco, *The Italian American Experience*, pp. 146–147. Salvatore J. LaGumina, "Case Studies of Ethnicity and Italo-American Politicians," in *The Italian Experience in the United States*, ed. Tomasi and Engel, p. 147; Krickus, *Pursuing the American Dream*, pp. 174–181.
102. "World War II Italian American Internment," Bill Ritter, Charles Gibson, ABC *Good Morning America*, October 30, 1997; Wittke, *We Who Built America*, p. 450; Iorizzo and Mondello, *The Italian-Americans*, pp. 200–205, 208; Gambino, *Blood of My Blood*, p. 316.
103. Richard Alba, *Italian Americans* (Englewood Cliffs, NJ: Prentice Hall, 1985), pp. 78–81; Guglielmo, "White Lies, Dark Truths," pp. 11-12.
104. Alba, *Italian Americans*, p. 143; General Social Surveys, 1989 and 1990. See also Andrew M. Greeley, *Ethnicity in the United States* (New York: John Wiley, 1974), pp. 94–101; "Italian Americans: Big Swing?" *Campaigns & Elections*, August 1996, p. 63.
105. John M. Goshko, "Italian Americans Lobbying UN for Their Motherland," *International Herald Tribune*, September 18, 1997, p. 10.
106. Iorizzo, "The Padrone and Immigrant Distribution," p. 43.
107. Stella, *Some Aspects of Italian Immigration*, p. 94; Gambino, *Blood of My Blood*, p. 85; Leonard Covello, "The Influence of Southern Italian Family Mores upon the School Situation in America," in *The Italians*, ed. Cordasco and Bucchioni, p. 513; Lord, Trenor, and Barrows, *The Italian in America*, pp. 16–19;E.P. Hutchinson, *Immigrants and Their Children, 1850–1950* (New York: John Wiley, 1956), pp. 137–138.
108. Higham, *Strangers in the Land*, p. 48.
109. Gambino, *Blood of My Blood*, p. 77; see also Stephan Thernstrom, *The Other Bostonians* (Cambridge, MA: Harvard University Press, 1973), p. 161.
110. John J. d'Alesandre, "Occupational Trends of Italians in New York City," *Italy-America Monthly* 2 (February 1935): 11–21; Marcella Bencivenni, "Lost and Found: The Italian-American Radical Experience," *Monthly Review* 57 (January 2006): 60; W. Lloyd Warner and Leo Srole, *The Social Systems of American Ethnic Groups* (New Haven, CT: Yale University Press, 1945), pp. 96–97; Gambino, *Blood of My Blood*, p. 101; Wittke, *We Who Built America*, p. 443.
111. Nelli, *The Italians in Chicago*, pp. 211–214; Smith, *The Mafia Mystique*, p. 322; Ianni, *A Family Business*, p. 193.
112. Andrew F. Rolle, *The American Italian* (Belmont, CA: Wadsworth, 1972), pp. 89–93.
113. Thernstrom, *The Other Bostonians*, p. 171; U.S. Bureau of the Census, *1990 Census of Population: Ancestry of the Population in the United States*, p. 356; U.S. Bureau of the Census, *1990 Census of Population: Social and Economic Characteristics: United States*, p. 45.
114. See U.S. Bureau of the Census, *1990 Census of Population: Ancestry of the Population in the United States*, pp. 307, 356, 458.
115. National Center for Urban Ethnic Affairs Newsletter 1, no. 5 (1976): 8.
116. Robert Viscusi, "Giving the Boot to Italians," *Newsday*, May 30, 1991, p. 74
117. "CUNY Settles Suit by Italian Institute," *The New York Times*, January 9, 1994, sec. 1, p. 22; Felipe Pimentel, "The Decline of the Puerto Rican Fulltime Faculty at the City University of New York (CUNY) from 1981–2002," Hunter College, www.centropr.org/downloads/FacultyBrief(R).pdf (retrieved July 6, 2006).
118. Alba and Abdel-Hady, "Galileo's Children," pp. 3–18.
119. Lawrence A. Cremin, *The Transformation of the School* (New York: Alfred A. Knopf, 1961),pp. 67–68; Colin Greer, *The Great School Legend* (New York: Basic Books, 1972), pp. 3–6.
120. U.S. Bureau of the Census, *U.S. Census of Population, 1970: Subject Reports—National Origin and Language*, PC(2)-1A (Washington, DC, 1973), p. 165; U.S. Census Bureau, Census 2000 Demographic Profile Highlights: Selected Population Group: Italian, http://factfinder.census.gov(retrieved June 16, 2006).
121. Rudolph J. Vecoli, "Contadini in Chicago: A Critique of the Uprooted," in *The Aliens*, ed. Leonard Dinnerstein and Frederic C. Jaher (New York: Appleton-Century-Crofts, 1970), p. 226; Harold J. Abramson,

Ethnic Diversity in Catholic America (New York: John Wiley, 1973), pp. 136–139.

122. Silvano M. Tomasi, "The Ethnic Church and the Integration of Italian Immigrants in the United States," in *The Italian Experience in the United States*, ed. Tomasi and Engel, pp. 167–188; Nelli, *The Italians in Chicago*, p. 195; di Franco, *The Italian American Experience*, pp. 269–270.
123. National Opinion Research Center, *A Profile of Italian Americans: 1972–1991*, March 1992; Stuart Vincent, "Devotion to Saints a Part of Life; Festivals Have an Italian Flavor," *Newsday*, May 1, 1996, p. A6.
124. Covello, "The Influence of Southern Italian Family Mores," p. 515.
125. Paul J. Campisi, "Ethnic Family Patterns: The Italian Family in the United States," *American Journal of Sociology* 53 (May 1948): 443–449; Covello, "The Influence of Southern Italian Family Mores," pp. 525–530.
126. Irvin L. Child, *Italian or American?* (New Haven, CT: Yale University Press, 1943) (an important excerpt from this book can be found in *The Italians*, ed. Cordasco and Bucchioni, pp. 321–336); Alba, *Italian Americans*, p. 114.
127. Alba, *Italian Americans*, p. 166.
128. See ibid.
129. Alba, *Ethnic Identity*, pp. 47–48, 59–61, 70–71, 224–226.
130. Commentary from Richard Alba given to authors, May 1994 and June 1997; Anthony L. LaRuffa, *Monte Carmelo: An Italian-American Community in the Bronx* (New York: Gordon & Breach, 1988), pp. 135–139.
131. Francis X. Femminella and Jill S. Quadagno, "The Italian American Family," in *Ethnic Families in America*, ed. Charles H. Mindel and Robert W. Habenstein (New York: Elsevier, 1976), pp. 74–75; Ruby Jo Reeves Kennedy, "Single or Triple Melting Pot? Intermarriage in New Haven, 1870–1950," *American Journal of Sociology* 58 (July 1952): 56–59; Nelli, *The Italians in Chicago*, p. 196; James A. Crispino, *The Assimilation of Ethnic Groups: The Italian Case* (New York: Center for Migration Studies, 1980), p. 105; Alba, *Italian Americans*, pp. 146–147; Waters, *Ethnic Options*, p. 104; Nona Claren, "The Trouble with the Melting Pot," *Baltimore Sun*, June 24, 1997, p. 9a.
132. Alba, *Italian Americans*, pp. 159–162; Alba, *Ethnic Identity*, p. 47.
133. LaRuffa, *Monte Carmelo*, pp. 17–28.
134. Phyllis Cancilla Martinelli, *Ethnicity in the Sunbelt* (New York: AMS Press, 1989), pp. 234–258; Alba, *Ethnic Identity*, pp. 59–60, 70.
135. Marcus Lee Hansen, "The Third Generation," in *Children of the Uprooted*, ed. Oscar Handlin (New York: Harper & Row, 1966), pp. 255–271; P. J. Gallo, *Ethnic Alienation* (Rutherford, NJ: Fairleigh Dickinson University Press, 1974), p. 194; John M. Goering, "The Emergence of Ethnic Interests," *Social Forces* 49 (March 1971): 381–382; Tardi, *Family and Society*, pp. 179–192.
136. di Leonardo, *The Varieties of Ethnic Experience*, p. 156.
137. Richard D. Alba, "Identity and Ethnicity Among Italians and Other Americans of European Ancestry," in *The Columbus People: Perspectives in Italian Immigration to the Americas and Australia*, ed. Lydio Tomasi, Piero Gautaldo, and Thomas Row (Staten Island, NY: Center for Migration Studies, 1994), pp. 21–41.
138. U.S. Census Bureau, *Census 2000 Supplementary Survey*, Table PCT 024, Ancestry-First Reported; Table PCT 025, Ancestry-Second Reported.

Chapter 5

1. Leonard Dinnerstein, *Anti-Semitism in America* (New York: Oxford University Press, 1994), pp. 181–184; John Higham, *Strangers in the Land: Patterns of American Nativism 1860–1925*, rev. ed. (New York: Atheneum, 1975), p. 186.
2. American Jewish Committee, "Thinking About the Holocaust 60 Years Later: A Multinational Public-Opinion Survey," March–April 2005, www.ajc.org/site/apps/nl/content3.asp?c=ijITI2PHKoG&b=846741&ct=1025513 (retrieved July 12, 2006).
3. Arthur Hertzberg, *The Jews in America* (New York: Simon & Schuster, 1989), pp. 377–388; Bernard J. Wolfson, "African American Jews: Dispelling Myths, Bridging the Divide," in *Black Zion: African American Religious Encounters with Judaism*, ed. Yvonne Chireau and Nathaniel Deutsch (New York: Oxford University Press), pp. 34–38.
4. Hertzberg, *The Jews in America*, pp. 13–28.
5. Charles E. Silberman, *A Certain People* (New York: Summit Books, 1985), pp. 42–45; Chaim I. Waxman, *America's Jews in Transition* (Philadelphia: Temple University Press, 1983), pp. 6–8.
6. Silberman, *A Certain People*, pp. 42–49; Hertzberg, *The Jews in America*, pp. 102–104.
7. Hertzberg, The Jews in America, pp. 152–154, 185; Silberman, *A Certain People*, p. 49; Waxman, *America's Jews in Transition*, p. 43; Frank K. Flinn, "Who Killed Jesus? A Guide to Viewing Mel Gibson's Movie," Washington University, http://newsinfo.wustl.edu/news/page/normal/711.html (retrieved January 25, 2007).
8. Hertzberg, *The Jews in America*, pp. 160–176, 224; Silberman, *A Certain People*, pp. 49–51.
9. Milton Meltzer, *Never to Forget: The Jews of the Holocaust* (New York: Harper & Row, 1976), p. 45.
10. Douglass Stanglin, Kenneth Walsh, Edward Pound, Charles Fenyvesi, and Josh Chetwynd, "Quale's

Newest Place in the Sun," *U.S. News & World Report*, August 26, 1996, pp. 16, 19.

11. Maurice J. Karpf, *Jewish Community Organization in the United States* (New York: Arno, 1971), p. 33; Sidney Goldstein, "American Jewry: A Demographic Analysis," in *The Future of the Jewish Community in America*, ed. David Sidorsky (New York: Basic Books, 1973), p. 71; Alvin Chenkin, "Jewish Population in the United States," in *American Jewish Yearbook, 1973* (New York: American Jewish Committee, 1973), pp. 307–309; Arthur A. Goren, "Jews," in *Harvard Encyclopedia of American Ethnic Groups* (Cambridge, MA: Harvard University Press, 1980), pp. 591–592; Rita J. Simon and Julian L. Simon, "Social and Economic Adjustment," in *New Lives*, ed. Rita J. Simon (Lexington, MA: Heath/Lexington Books, 1985), pp. 26–41; Stanglin et al., "Quale's Newest Place in the Sun," pp. 16, 19; Annelise Orleck, *The Soviet Jewish Americans* (Westport, CT: Greenwood Press, 1999), p. 7.
12. United Jewish Communities, "The National Jewish Population Survey 2000-01: Strength, Challenge and Diversity in the American Jewish Population," 2003–2004, www.ujc.org/content_display.html?ArticleID=60346 (retrieved July 7, 2006); "Religion in Brief," *Atlanta Journal and Constitution*, September 6, 1997,p. 6E; Jerome A. Chanes, "A Primer on the American Jewish Community," www.ajc.org/pre/primer.asp (retrieved March 13, 2001).
13. See David Sidorsky, "Introduction," in *The Future of the Jewish Community in America*, ed. Sidorsky, pp. xix–xxv; and Stephen D. Isaacs, *Jews and American Politics* (Garden City, NY: Doubleday, 1974), pp. ix–x.
14. Charles Y. Glock and Rodney Stark, *Christian Beliefs and Anti-Semitism* (New York: Harper & Row, 1966), p. 64 et passim.
15. Carey McWilliams, *A Mask for Privilege* (Boston: Little, Brown, 1948), pp. 164–165, 170–173; John Higham, "Social Discrimination Against Jews in America, 1830–1930," *Publication of the American Jewish Historical Society* 47 (September 1957): 5.
16. Silberman, *A Certain People*, p. 48; Hertzberg, *The Jews in America*, pp. 86–87, 188–189; Higham, "Social Discrimination Against Jews in America," p. 47.
17. Leonard Dinnerstein, *Antisemitism in America* (New York: Oxford University Press, 1994), pp. 80–82.
18. Gustavus Meyers, *History of Bigotry in the United States*, rev. ed. (New York: Capricorn Books, 1960), pp. 277–313; Isaacs, *Jews and American Politics*, pp. 51, 98.
19. Gary A. Tobin, *Jewish Perceptions of Anti-Semitism* (New York: Plenum Press, 1988), pp. 106–112; "Anti-Jewish Elements Intact in Gibson's 'Passion Recut,'" www.adl.org/PresRele/ASUS_12/4665_12.htm (July 10, 2006); "Resources on the Mel Gibson movie, The Passion of the Christ," Boston College Center for Christian-Jewish Learning, www.bc.edu/research/cjl/meta-elements/texts/cjrelations/resources/education/PASSION_resources.htm (July 10, 2006).
20. American Jewish Committee, "2005 Annual Survey of American Jewish Opinion," www.ajc.org/site/apps/nl/content3.asp?c=ijITI2PHKoG&b=846741&ct=1740283 (retrieved July 11, 2006); www.ajc.org/pre/Survey2000.asp (retrieved March 13, 2001).
21. "Anti-Semitism Concerns Surveyed," *San Diego Union-Tribune*, June 6, 1997, p. E5; Anti-Defamation League, "ADL Survey: Anti-Semitism Declines Slightly in America; 14 Percent of Americans Hold 'Strong' Anti-Semitic Beliefs," www.adl.org/PresRele/ASUS_12/4680_12.htm (retrieved July 11, 2006).
22. American Jewish Committee, "Introduction," *Television's Changing Image of American Jews*, www.ajc.org/pre/journal12-index.asp (retrieved March 13, 2001).
23. Joyce Antler, "Introduction," in *Talking Back: Images of Jewish Women in American Popular Culture*, ed. Joyce Antler (Hanover, NH: Brandeis University Press, 1998), pp. 1, 10.
24. Henry L. Feingold, *Zion in America* (New York: Twayne, 1974), pp. 143–144; C. Vann Woodward, *Tom Watson* (New York: Oxford University Press, 1963), pp. 435–445.
25. Rufus Learski, *The Jews in America* (New York: KTAV Publishing House, 1972), pp. 290–291; John Higham, *Strangers in the Land* (New York: Atheneum, 1975), pp. 298–299.
26. Milton R. Konvitz, "Inter-Group Relations," in *The American Jew*, ed. O. I. Janowsky (Philadelphia: Jewish Publication Society of America, 1964), pp. 78–79; Donald S. Strong, *Organized Anti-Semitism in America* (Washington, DC: American Council on Public Affairs, 1941), pp. 14–20; Strong, *Organized Anti-Semitism in America*, p. 67.
27. Lucy S. Dawidowicz, *The War Against the Jews: 1933–1945* (New York: Holt, Rinehart & Winston), p. 148; see also pp. 164, 403.
28. Lewis H. Carlson and George A. Colburn, "The Jewish Refugee Problem," in *In Their Place*, ed. Lewis H. Carlson and George A. Colburn (New York: John Wiley, 1972), pp. 290–291; Stephanie Chavez, "Anti-Semitic Incidents Reported Rising," *Los Angeles Times*, February 7, 1992, p. A3; Lenni Brenner, *Jews in America Today* (Secaucus, NJ: Lyle Stuart, 1986), pp. 205–206, 209; Chavez, "Anti-Semitic Incidents Reported Rising," p. A3.

29. Anti-Defamation League, "Anti-Semitism—U.S.," www.adl.org/main_Anti_Semitism_Domestic/default.htm (retrieved July 10, 2006); Kevin Johnson, "Hate-Motivated Murders Reach 5-Year High," *USA Today*, February 14, 2001, p. 3A.
30. Greg Wilson, "Hate Crimes Law to Make Debut in Attack on Bronx Synagogue," (New York) *Daily News*, October 20, 2000, p. 30.
31. Konvitz, "Inter-Group Relations," pp. 85–95; Alan Dershowitz, *Chutzpah* (Boston: Little, Brown, 1991), p. 326; Linda Greenhouse, "Justices Affirm Ban on Prayers in Public School," *The New York Times*, June 25, 1992, p. A1.
32. Robert F. Drinan, "The Supreme Court, Religious Freedom and the Yarmulke," *America*, June 12, 1986, pp. 9–11.
33. Gerald S. Strober, *American Jews* (Garden City, NY: Doubleday, 1974), pp. 149–176.
34. Anti-Defamation League, *Extremism in the Name of Religion: The Violent Legacy of Meir Kahane* (Washington, DC: ADL, 1995).
35. Cheryl Lynn Greenberg , *Troubling the Waters: Black-Jewish Relations in the American Century* (Princeton, NJ: Princeton University Press, 2006); Ronald Takaki, *A Different Mirror: A History of Multicultural America* (Boston: Little, Brown, 1993), p. 406.
36. "Two Deaths Ignite Racial Clash in Tense Brooklyn Neighborhood," *The New York Times*, August 21, 1991, p. A1; Scott Minerbrook and Miriam Horn, "Side by Side, Apart," *U.S. News & World Report*, November 4, 1991, p. 44.
37. Silberman, *A Certain People*, pp. 41, 340.
38. Ibid., pp. 333, 339–343; Dershowitz, *Chutzpah*, pp. 241, 301–302.
39. Letty Cottin Pogrebin, *Deborah, Golda, and Me: Being Female and Jewish in America* (New York: Crown, 1991); Karen Brodkin, *How The Jews Became White Folks: And What That Says About Race in America* (New Brunswick, NJ: Rutgers University Press, 1998); Ira Katznelson, *When Affirmative Action Was White: An Untold History of Racial Inequality in Twentieth-Century America* (New York: W. W. Norton, 2005).
40. Joe R. Feagin and Leslie Inniss, "Racial Attitudes in Four Socio-religious Groups," research paper, University of Florida, spring 1992; Anti-Defamation League, *Highlights from an Anti-Defamation League Survey on Racial Attitudes in America* (New York: ADL, 1993), pp. 51, 55, 61, 80–86.
41. Tom Tugend, "L.A. Jews Step Up Aid to Riot-Hit Areas," *Jerusalem Post*, May 12, 1992, n.p.
42. Buddy Nevins, "Idea of Saving Bucks Doesn't Compute with School Officials," *Ft. Lauderdale Sun-Sentinel*, December 18, 1994, p. B4.
43. Gene Warner, "Black, Jewish Teens Team Up to Honor King Legacy," *Buffalo News, January* 21, 1997, p. 1B; and Judith Reitman, "Black, Jewish Teens Look to Past to Find New Understanding," (New Orleans) *Times-Picayune*, March 9, 1997, p. A3; Jenna Portnoy, "Going Far to Get Close," Citypaper.net, http://citypaper.net/articles/2006-06-29/naked.shtml.
44. Waxman, *America's Jews in Transition*, pp. 5–10, quotation from p. 10; Hertzberg, *The Jews in America*, pp. 62–69; Lawrence H. Fuchs, *The Political Behavior of American Jews* (Glencoe, IL: The Free Press, 1956), pp. 23–25; Silberman, *A Certain People*, p. 44.
45. Hertzberg, *The Jews in America*, pp. 108–109; Mark R. Levy and Michael S. Kramer, *The Ethnic Factor* (New York: Simon & Schuster, 1972), p. 101; William R. Heitzmann, *American Jewish Voting Behavior* (San Francisco: R & E Research Associates, 1975), pp. 27–28.
46. Irving Howe, *World of Our Fathers* (New York: Simon & Schuster, 1976), pp. 362–364; Emanuel Hertz, "Politics: New York," in *The Russian Jew in the United States*, ed. Charles S. Bernheimer (Philadelphia: John Winston, 1905), pp. 256–265; Edward M. Levine, *The Irish and Irish Politicians* (Notre Dame, IN: University of Notre Dame Press, 1966); Isaacs, *Jews and American Politics*, pp. 23–24; Feingold, *Zion in America*, p. 321.
47. Hertz, "Politics," pp. 265–267; Heitzmann, *American Jewish Voting Behavior*, p. 37; Fuchs, *The Political Behavior of American Jews*, pp. 57–58.
48. Hertzberg, *The Jews in America*, pp. 282–283.
49. Heitzmann, *American Jewish Voting Behavior*, p. 49; Fuchs, *The Political Behavior of American Jews*, pp. 99–100.
50. American Jewish Committee, "2005 Annual Survey of American Jewish Opinion."
51. Chanes, "A Primer on the American Jewish Community"; Isaacs, *Jews and American Politics*, pp. 23, 201; Levy and Kramer, *The Ethnic Factor*, pp. 102–103; Howe, *World of Our Fathers*, p. 118; Milton Plesur, *Jewish Life in Twentieth Century America* (Chicago: Nelson Hall, 1982), pp. 143–145; Andrew Herrmann, "Buddhists See Cup as Half Full," *Chicago Sun-Times*, January 21, 1995, p. 13.
52. Isaacs, *Jews and American Politics*, pp. 12, 118–119.
53. Nathan Reich, "Economic Status," in *The American Jew*, ed. Janowsky, pp. 70–71; Karpf, *Jewish Community Organization in the United States*, pp. 11–12; Howe, *World of Our Fathers*, pp. 391–393; Feingold, *Zion in America*, pp. 235–236.
54. Karpf, *Jewish Community Organization in the United States*, pp. 62–65; Naomi Cohen, *Not Free to Desist* (Philadelphia: Jewish Publication Society of America, 1972), pp. 3–18, 37–80, 433–452; Jonathan S.

Woocher, *Sacred Survival* (Bloomington: Indiana University Press, 1986), pp. vii–viii.

55. Arnold Foster and Benjamin R. Epstein, *The New Anti-Semitism* (New York: McGraw-Hill, 1974), pp. 155–284; Strober, *American Jews*, pp. 7–42.
56. Leonard, Mary, "Many Jews Hit Faith Plan Funding," *Boston Globe*, February 28, 2001, p. A2.
57. Brenner, *Jews in America Today*, p. 10.
58. Hertzberg, *The Jews in America*, pp. 17–28, 63; Feingold, *Zion in America*, p. 12; McWilliams, *Brothers Under the Skin*, pp. 305–306.
59. Wittke, *We Who Built America*, p. 325; George Cohen, *The Jews in the Making of America* (Boston: Stratford, 1924), pp. 120–122; Silberman, *A Certain People*, pp. 44–45; Waxman, *America's Jews in Transition*, pp. 22–24.
60. Nathan Goldberg, *Occupational Patterns of American Jewry* (New York: Jewish Teachers Seminary Press, 1947), pp. 15–17; Marshall Sklare, *America's Jews* (New York: Random House, 1971), p. 61; Isaac M. Rubinow, "Economic and Industrial Conditions: New York," in *The Russian Jew in the United States*, ed. Bernheimer, pp. 110–111; Jacob Lestschinsky, "Economic and Social Development of American Jewry," in *The Jewish People* (New York: Jewish Encyclopedic Handbooks, 1955), 4:74–77; Rubinow, "Economic and Industrial Conditions," pp. 103–107; Waxman, *America's Jews in Transition*, p. 58; Hertzberg, *The Jews in America*, p. 198.
61. Charlotte Baum, Paula Hyman, and Sonya Michel, *The Jewish Woman in America* (New York: Dial Press, 1976), p. 98; Hertzberg, *The Jews in America*, pp. 198–201.
62. Karpf, *Jewish Community Organization in the United States*, pp. 9–14; Lestschinsky, "Economic and Social Development of American Jewry," pp. 91–92; W. Lloyd Warner and Leo Srole, *The Social Systems of American Ethnic Groups* (New Haven, CT: Yale University Press, 1945), p. 112; Silberman, *A Certain People*, pp. 127–130.
63. McWilliams, *A Mask for Privilege*, pp. 38, 40–41; Karpf, *Jewish Community Organization in the United States*, pp. 20–21; Higham, "Social Discrimination Against Jews in America," pp. 18–19.
64. For the February 1936 *Fortune* survey, see Karpf, *Jewish Community Organization in the United States*, pp. 9–11; McWilliams, *A Mask for Privilege*, pp. 143–150.
65. Lestschinsky, "Economic and Social Development of American Jewry," pp. 71, 87; McWilliams, *A Mask for Privilege*, p. 159; Reich, "Economic Status," pp. 63–65; Dershowitz, *Chutzpah*, p. 74; Barry R. Chiswick, "The Labor Market Status of American Jews," in *American Jewish Handbook*, ed. M. Himmelfarb and D. Singer (New York: American Jewish Committee, 1984), p. 137; Mabel Newcomer, *The Big Business Executive* (New York: Columbia University Press, 1955), pp. 46–48.
66. United Jewish Communities, "The National Jewish Population Survey 2000-01," p. 6. Median household income is usually lower than median family income in census data.
67. Goren, "Jews," p. 593; Sklare, *America's Jews*, pp. 61–62; Goldscheider and Goldstein, *The Jewish Community of Rhode Island*, pp. 11–12; Barry A. Kosmin et al., *Highlights of the CJF 1990 National Jewish Population Survey* (New York: Council of Jewish Federations, 1991), p. 12.
68. Abraham K. Korman, *The Outsiders: Jews and Corporate America* (Lexington, MA: Heath/Lexington Books, 1988), pp. 79–82.
69. Richard L. Zweigenhaft and G. William Domhoff, *Jews in the Protestant Establishment* (New York: Praeger, 1982), p. 46.
70. Korman, *The Outsiders*, pp. 35–41, 66–88.
71. Dov B. Levy, "Top Jobs," *Jerusalem Post*, March 30, 1997, p. 6.
72. American Jewish Committee, "2005 Annual Survey of American Jewish Opinion."
73. Allen Myerson, "At Rental Counters, Are All Drives Created Equal? Avis Finds Itself at the Center of Discrimination Complaints," *The New York Times*, March 18, 1997, p. D1; Ellen Neuborne, "Car Renters Outline Charges at State Hearing," *USA Today*, April 1, 1997, p. 1B.
74. "Florida Legislature Passes Bill," PR Newswire, March 13, 1992; Sklare, *America's Jews*, p. 65; McWilliams, *Brothers Under the Skin*, pp. 310–311.
75. Hertzberg, *The Jews in America*, pp. 50, 273; Silberman, *A Certain People*, p. 51; Waxman, *America's Jews in Transition*, p. 53; J. K. Paulding, "Educational Influences: New York," in *The Russian Jew in the United States*, ed. Bernheimer, pp. 186–197; Cohen, *The Jews in the Making of America*, pp. 140–141; Karpf, *Jewish Community Organization in the United States*, p. 57; Waxman, *America's Jews in Transition*, p. 137.
76. Silberman, *A Certain People*, pp. 52–55; Hertzberg, *The Jews in America*, pp. 246–247; Higham, "Social Discrimination Against Jews in America," p. 22; Karpf, *Jewish Community Organization in the United States*, p. 19; McWilliams, *A Mask for Privilege*, pp. 128–129.
77. Silberman, *A Certain People*, pp. 98–100; Hertzberg, *The Jews in America*, p. 309; Dershowitz, *Chutzpah*, pp. 73–74.
78. Strober, *American Jews*, pp. 120–130; Maurice R. Berube and Marilyn Gittell, "The Struggle for Community Control," in *Confrontation at Ocean Hill–Brownsville*, ed. Maurice R. Berube and Marilyn Gittell (New York: Praeger, 1969), pp. 3–12 et passim; Joe R. Feagin and Harlan Hahn, *Ghetto Revolts* (New York: Macmillan, 1973), pp. 327–328; Nathan Glazer, *Affirmative*

Discrimination (New York: Basic Books, 1975), pp. 33–76, 196–221.

79. Dershowitz, *Chutzpah*, pp. 75–79, quotation from pp. 78–79.
80. Hertzberg, *The Jews in America*, p. 309; Kosmin et al., *Highlights of the CJF 1990 National Jewish Population Survey*, pp. 10–11; Holly J. Lebowitz, "High Holy Days Can Be Lonely for Students," (Cleveland) *Plain Dealer*, September 7, 1996, p. 6E; American Jewish Committee, "Responding to Intermarriage Survey, Analysis, Policy"; American Jewish Committee, "2000 Annual Survey of American Jewish Opinion."
81. United Jewish Communities, "The National Jewish Population Survey 2000-01," p. 15. Silberman, *A Certain People*, pp. 171–172; Robert Alter, "What Jewish Studies Can Do," *Commentary* 58 (October 1974): 71–74.
82. Waxman, *America's Jews in Transition*, p. 10; Hertzberg, *The Jews in America*, pp. 117–123, 146–147, 254–262, quotation from p. 120. See also Silberman, *A Certain People*, p. 46.
83. Hertzberg, *The Jews in America*, pp. 159–161, 167–168, 195, 214–236.
84. Ibid., pp. 277–279; Waxman, *America's Jews in Transition*, p. 17; Wolfe Kelman, "The Synagogue in America," in *The Future of the Jewish Community in America*, ed. Sidorsky, pp. 157–158; Louis Lipsky, "Religious Activity: New York," in *The Russian Jew in the United States*, ed. Bernheimer, pp. 152–154; Silberman, *A Certain People*, pp. 170–177; Hertzberg, *The Jews in America*, pp. 277–279.
85. Silberman, *A Certain People*, pp. 176–181.
86. American Jewish Committee, "2005 Annual Survey of American Jewish Opinion."
87. J. L. Blau, *Judaism in America* (Chicago: University of Chicago Press, 1976), as summarized in Samuel C. Heilman, "The Sociology of American Jewry," in *Annual Review of Sociology*, ed. Ralph Turner, vol. 8 (Palo Alto, CA: Annual Reviews, 1982), p. 147; Michael Greenstein, *The American Jew: A Contradiction in Terms* (New York: Gefen, 1990), pp. 1–5.
88. American Jewish Committee, "2005 Annual Survey of American Jewish Opinion."
89. Monty Noam Penkower, *At the Crossroads: American Jewry and the State of Israel* (Haifa, Israel: University of Haifa, 1990), p. 27.
90. "U.S. Jews Favor Palestinian State: Poll," Agence France Presse, September 29, 1997; Stanley Reed, "Will Palestine's Peace Dividend Buy Peace?" *Business Week*, May 16, 1994, p. 53
91. American Jewish Committee, "2005 Annual Survey of American Jewish Opinion."
92. Howe, *World of Our Fathers*, p. 645; Karpf, *Jewish Community Organization in the United States*, pp. 37–39, 49–50; Tobin, *Jewish Perceptions of Anti-Semitism*, p. 84.
93. Milton R. Konvitz, "Horace Meyer Kallen (1882–1974)," in *American Jewish Yearbook, 1974–1975* (New York: American Jewish Committee, 1974), pp. 65–67; Milton Gordon, *Assimilation in American Life* (New York: Oxford University Press, 1964), pp. 142–159.
94. Hertzberg, *The Jews in America*, pp. 102–130, 167–176, 195.
95. Sidney Goldstein and Calvin Goldscheider, *Jewish Americans* (Englewood Cliffs, NJ: Prentice Hall, 1968), p. 226; Silberman, *A Certain People*, pp. 173–181.
96. Riv-Ellen Prell, *Fighting to Become Americans: Jews, Gender, and the Anxiety of Assimilation* (Boston: Beacon Press, 1999), p. 8. See also pp. 6–10.
97. Nathan Glazer, "The American Jew and the Attainment of Middle-Class Rank: Some Trends and Explanations," in *The Jews*, ed. M. Sklare (Glencoe, IL: The Free Press, 1958), p. 143, as quoted in Stephen Steinberg, *The Ethnic Myth* (New York: Atheneum, 1981), p. 93.
98. Steinberg, *The Ethnic Myth*, pp. 94–102.
99. Hertzberg, *The Jews in America*, pp. 167–171, 195, 254–255, quotation from p. 171; Waxman, *America's Jews in Transition*, pp. 55–58.
100. Calvin Goldscheider, *Jewish Continuity and Change* (Atlanta, GA: Scholars Press, 1986), pp. 17–18; Sidney Goldstein, "Jews in the United States: Perspectives from Demography," in *American Jewish Yearbook, 1981* (New York: American Jewish Committee, 1980–1981), p. 28; Kosmin, et al., *Highlights of the CJF 1990 National Jewish Population Survey*, p. 35; United Jewish Communities, "The National Jewish Population Survey 2000-01," p. 7.
101. Gordon, *Assimilation in American Life*, pp. 76–77.
102. United Jewish Communities, "The National Jewish Population Survey 2000-01," p. ix; American Jewish Committee, "2000 Annual Survey of American Jewish Opinion."
103. American Jewish Committee, "Responding to Intermarriage Survey, Analysis, Policy."
104. United Jewish Communities, "The National Jewish Population Survey 2000-01," p. 130; see Alan Dershowitz, *The Vanishing American Jew: In Search of Jewish Identity for the Next Century* (New York: Little, Brown, 1997).
105. Goldscheider, *Jewish Continuity and Change*, pp. 15–19, quotation from p. 16.
106. American Jewish Committee, "2005 Annual Survey of American Jewish Opinion."
107. United Jewish Communities, "The National Jewish Population Survey 2000-01," p. 3.

108. Marilyn Henry, "Israeli Immigrants to the United States Moving Up the Ladder," *Jerusalem Post*, August 13, 1996, p. 12; Henry summarizes a report in the 1996 *American Jewish Yearbook* by Steven Gold and Bruce Phillips.
109. Orleck, *The Soviet Jewish Americans*, p. 3, see also pp. 4–100; Steven J. Gold, "Review of *The Soviet Jewish Americans*," *Journal of American Ethnic History* 20 (Fall 2000): 107; Simon and Simon, "Social and Economic Adjustment," pp. 27–38.
110. Steven J. Gold, *Refugee Communities* (Newbury Park, CA: Sage, 1992), pp. 39–44, 67–89.
111. Orleck, *The Soviet Jewish Americans*, pp. 190–193; American Jewish Committee, "2000 Annual Survey of American Jewish Opinion."
112. David Biale, "The Melting Pot and Beyond," in *Insider/Outsider: American Jews and Multiculturalism*, ed. David Biale, Michael Galchinsky, and Susan Heschel (Berkeley: University of California Press, 1998), p. 31.
113. Kosmin et al., *Highlights of the CJF 1990 National Jewish Population Survey*, pp. 3–6, 14–17, 28; United Jewish Communities, "The National Jewish Population Survey 2000-01," p. 15.
114. Sylvia Barack Fishman, *Jewish Life and American Culture* (Albany, NY: SUNY Press, 2000), pp. 1–16.
115. Hertzberg, *The Jews in America*, p. 386; see also Herbert J. Gans, "Symbolic Ethnicity," *Ethnic and Racial Studies* 2 (1979): 1–20; Richard Alba, *Ethnic Identity: The Transformation of White America* (New Haven, CT: Yale University Press, 1990), p. 306.
116. Robert Wolfe, "Reviving the Jewish Left," http://pnews.org/art/5art/JEWISHleft.shtml (retrieved July 13, 2006).
117. The report is cited in Ira Rifkin, "Jewish Social Agency Finds Support Eroding," *Sacramento Bee*, December 2, 1995, p. G5. We are indebted to Diane L. Wolf for suggestions here.
118. Ariela Keysar, Barry A. Kosmin, and Jeffrey Scheckner, *The Next Generation: Jewish Children and Adolescents* (Albany, NY: SUNY Press, 2000), pp. 103–104.
119. United Jewish Communities, "The National Jewish Population Survey 2000-01," p. viii.
120. Alba, *Ethnic Identity*, p. 310.
121. American Jewish Committee, "2005 Annual Survey of American Jewish Opinion"; Silberman, *A Certain People*, pp. 25, 159–324.
122. Caroline Forman Litwack, "'You Don't Have to Be Jewish'": The Representation of Jews on Television Sitcom," M.A. thesis, Georgetown University, Washington, DC, 2006, p. 89.
123. Brodkin, *How the Jews Became White Folks*, pp. 139–178; Eric Goldstein, *The Price of Whiteness: Jews, Race, and American Identity* (Princeton, NJ: Princeton University Press, 2006).
124. Brodkin, *How the Jews Became White Folks*, p. 187.

Chapter 6

1. Peggy Lowe, "Columbus Day Case Dropped; Charges to Be Dismissed Against 139 Protesters Arrested at October March," *Rocky Mountain News*, March 7, 2001, p. 5A.
2. "Counter-Quincentenary Protesters Encounter Celebrators at Kickoff of Quincentenary Year," *Indigenous Thought* 1, nos. 4 and 5 (October 1991): 1–3.
3. "We Have No Reason to Celebrate an Invasion," *Rethinking Columbus* (Milwaukee, WI: Rethinking Schools, 1991), p. 4.
4. For a discussion of the development of the designations *white* and *red*, see David R. Roediger, *The Wages of Whiteness* (New York: Verso, 1991), pp. 21–23.
5. Henry F. Dobyns, "Estimating Aboriginal American Population," *Current Anthropology* 7 (October 1960): 395–416; Kirkpatrick Sale, *The Conquest of Paradise* (New York: Knopf, 1990); Lenore A. Stiffarm and Phil Lane, Jr., "The Demography of Native North America," in *The State of Native America*, ed. M. Annette Jaimes (Boston: South End Press, 1992), pp. 23–28; see also Russell Thornton, *American Indian Holocaust and Survival* (Norman: University of Oklahoma Press, 1987); C. Matthew Snipp, *American Indians: The First of This Land* (New York: Russell Sage Foundation, 1989).
6. U.S. Census Bureau, "Overview of Race and Hispanic Origin, Census 2000 Brief," March 2001, pp. 2–5; U.S. Census Bureau, "2005 American Community Survey," *American Factfinder,* http://factfinder.census.gov (September 14, 2006).
7. U.S. Bureau of the Census, *1990 Census of Population: Social and Economic Characteristics: United States*, CP-2-1 (Washington, DC, 1993), p. 105; U.S. Bureau of the Census, *We the First Americans* (Washington, DC, 1993), pp. 2–3, 7–8; Public Information Office, U.S. Census Bureau, "Census Bureau Facts for Features," November 2000, CB00-FF.13, www.census.gov (retrieved June 7, 2001); U.S. Census Bureau, *The American Indian and Alaska Native Population: 2000* (Washington, DC, 2002), pp. 1–11.
8. Carol Morello, "Native American Roots, Once Hidden, Now Embraced," *The Washington Post*, April 7, 2001, p. A01.
9. Joane Nagel, *American Indian Ethnic Renewal: Red Power and the Resurgence of Indian Identity and Culture* (New York: Oxford University Press, 1996); Morello, "Native American Roots, Once Hidden, Now Embraced."

10. Edward H. Spicer, *Cycles of Conquest* (Tucson: University of Arizona Press, 1962), pp. 20–23; Clyde Kluckhohn and Dorothy Leighton, *The Navajo*, rev. ed. (Garden City, NY: Doubleday/Anchor Books, 1962), pp. 23–27 et passim.
11. Devon A. Mihesuah, *American Indians: Stereotypes and Realities* (Atlanta, GA: Clarity Press, 1996), p. 20.
12. Ibid., p. 43.
13. Jack Weatherford, *Indian Givers: How the Indians of the Americas Transformed the World* (New York: Ballantine, 1988), pp. 39–133.
14. Peter Linebaugh and Marcus Rediker, *The Many-Headed Hydra: Sailors, Slaves, Commoners, and the Hidden History of the Revolutionary Atlantic* (Boston: Beacon Press, 2000), pp. 32–34.
15. Howard M. Bahr, "An End to Invisibility," in *Native Americans Today*, ed. Howard M. Bahr, Bruce A. Chadwick, and Robert C. Day (New York: Harper & Row, 1972), pp. 407–409; James E. Officer, "The American Indian and Federal Policy," in *The American Indian in Urban Society*, ed. Jack O. Waddell and O. Michael Watson (Boston: Little, Brown, 1971), pp. 45–60.
16. U.S. Bureau of the Census, *1990 Census of Population: General Population Characteristics: Urbanized Areas*, CP-1-1C (Washington, DC, 1992), p. 48.
17. Spicer, *Cycles of Conquest*, pp. 5, 306–307; Murray L. Wax, *Indian Americans* (Englewood Cliffs, NJ: Prentice Hall, 1971), pp. 6–7; Lynn R. Bailey, *Indian Slave Trade in the Southwest* (Los Angeles: Westernlore Press, 1966), pp. 73–140.
18. D'Arcy McNickle, *The Indian Tribes of the United States* (London: Oxford University Press, 1962), pp. 13–28; Alice Marriott and Carol K. Rachlin, *American Epic* (New York: Mentor Books, 1969), pp. 104–108; John Collier, *Indians of the Americas* (New York: Mentor Books, 1947), p. 115; William T. Hagan, *American Indians* (Chicago: University of Chicago Press, 1961), p. 14; Ruth M. Underhill, *Red Man's America* (Chicago: University of Chicago Press, 1953), pp. 321–322; Wax, *Indian Americans*, p. 13.
19. Alexis de Tocqueville, *Democracy in America* (New York: Random House/Vintage Books, 1945), 1:364.
20. Virgil J. Vogel, "The Indian in American History, 1968," in *This Country Was Ours*, ed. Virgil J. Vogel (New York: Harper & Row, 1972), pp. 284–287; McNickle, *The Indian Tribes of the United States*, pp. 40–41.
21. Ralph K. Andrist, *The Long Death* (London: Collier-Macmillan, 1964), p. 3.
22. John D. Unruh, *The Plains Across* (Urbana: University of Illinois Press, 1979), p. 185 et passim.
23. Vogel, "The Indian in American History, 1968," p. 285; Wendell H. Oswalt, *This Land Was Theirs* (New York: John Wiley, 1966), pp. 501–502.
24. William Meyer, *Native Americans* (New York: International, 1971), p. 32; Andrist, *The Long Death*, pp. 31–68, 78–91; Thornton, *American Indian Holocaust and Survival*.
25. Andrist, *The Long Death*, pp. 240–250, 350–353; Alvin M. Josephy, *The Indian Heritage of America* (New York: Bantam, 1968), pp. 284–342; Theodora Kroeber and Robert F. Heizer, *Almost Ancestors* (San Francisco: Sierra Club, 1968), pp. 14–20.
26. Spicer, *Cycles of Conquest*, pp. 216–221, 247–270.
27. Robert F. Spencer, Jesse D. Jennings, et al., *The Native Americans* (New York: Harper & Row, 1965), pp. 495–496; David Miller, "The Fur Men and Explorers View the Indians," in *Red Men and Hat Wearers*, ed. Daniel Tyler (Fort Collins, CO: Pruett, 1976), pp. 26–28; Roediger, *The Wages of Whiteness*, pp. 21–23.
28. Peter Farb, *Man's Rise to Civilization as Shown by the Indians of North America from Primeval Times to the Coming of the Industrial State* (New York: Dutton, 1968), pp. 246–249; Tyler, ed., *Red Men and Hat Wearers*, passim.
29. Lewis H. Carlson and George A. Colburn, "Introduction," in *In Their Place*, ed. Lewis H. Carlson and George A. Colburn (New York: John Wiley, 1972), p. 44.
30. Vogel, "The Indian in American History, 1968," pp. 288–289; de Tocqueville, *Democracy in America*, 1:355–357.
31. Rayna Green, "The Pocahontas Perplex: The Image of Indian Women in American Culture," in *Unequal Sisters*, ed. Ellen Carol DuBois and Vicki L. Ruiz (New York: Routledge, 1990), pp. 15–21, quotation from p. 17.
32. "Children's Secret Lessons," *Indigenous Thought* 1, nos. 4 and 5 (October 1991): 24.
33. James W. Loewen, *Lies My Teacher Told Me: Everything Your American History Textbook Got Wrong* (New York: The New Press, 1995), p. 91.
34. See Jacquelyn Kilpatrick, *Celluloid Indians: Native Americans and Film* (Lincoln: University of Nebraska Press, 1999; Snipp, *American Indians*, pp. 23–25; Jimmie Durham, "Cowboys and... ," in *The State of Native America*, ed. Jaimes, pp. 423–425.
35. Ward Churchill, *Fantasies of the Master Race* (Monroe, ME: Common Courage Press, 1992), pp. 243–247, quotation from p. 246.
36. Jacquelyn Kilpatrick, *Celluloid Indians: Native Americans and Film*, p. 152; see also pp. 151–153.
37. Howard M. Bahr, Bruce A. Chadwick, and Robert C. Day, "Introduction: Patterns of Prejudice and Discrimination," in *Native Americans Today*, ed. Bahr, Chadwick, and Day, pp. 44–45; Emory S. Bogardus, *Immigration and Race Attitudes* (Boston: Heath, 1928); Beverly Brandon Sweeney, "Native American: Stereotypes and Ideologies of an Adult

Anglo Population in Texas," M.A. thesis, University of Texas at Austin, 1976, pp. 125–133.

38. Alexandra Witkin-New Holy, "American Indian Religious Rights: Inside Montana Prisons," Center for Native American Studies, Montana State University (Bozeman), http://tlc.wtp.net/american_indian_religious_rights.htm (retrieved June 7, 2001).
39. Bridget F. Grant, Deborah A. Dawson, Frederick S. Stinson, Patricia Chou. Mary C. Dufour, and Roger P. Pickering, "The 12-Month Prevalence and Trends in DSM–IV Alcohol Abuse and Dependence: United States, 1991–1992 and 2001–2002," *Alcohol Research & Health* 29 (2006): 84,
40. Gayle Pollard Terry, "Los Angeles Times Interview with Suzan Shown Harjo: Fighting to Preserve the Legacy and Future of Native Americans," *The Los Angeles Times*, November 27, 1994, p. M3.
41. Jeff Cohen and Norman Solomon, "Using History, CNN Delivers Improved Coverage of Indians," *Star Tribune*, November 30, 1994, p. A17.
42. "Nationwide Poll Shows Support for Native Issues; Saginaw-Chippewa Commissions Zogby Research Firm to Reach Average Americans," *Oklahoma Indian Times Online*, www.okit.com/gaming/2001/feb/poll.htm (retrieved June 6, 2001).
43. James Cox , "Muting White Noise: The Subversion of Popular Culture Narratives of Conquest in Sherman Alexie's Fiction," *Studies in American Indian Literatures*, 9 (Winter 1997): 57; Robert M. Nelson, "A Laguna Woman," in *Leslie Marmon Silko: A Collection of Critical Essays*, eds. Louise Barnett and James Thorson (Albuquerque: University of New Mexico Press, 1999), pp. 15–22.
44. Mihesuah, *American Indians: Stereotypes and Realities*, pp. 61–63.
45. Loewen, *Lies My Teacher Told Me*, p. 104.
46. Mihesuah, *American Indians: Stereotypes and Realities*, pp. 63–65.
47. U.S. Bureau of Indian Affairs, *Federal Indian Policies* (Washington, DC, 1975), p. 6.
48. Ibid., p. 7; Spicer, *Cycles of Conquest*, p. 348.
49. *Elk* v. *Wilkins*, 112 U.S. 94 (1884); see also Vine Deloria, Jr., *Of Utmost Good Faith* (New York: Bantam, 1972), pp. 130–132.
50. Spicer, *Cycles of Conquest*, pp. 351–353; McNickle, *The Indian Tribes of the United States*, p. 59; Alison R. Bernstein, *American Indians and World War II* (Norman: University of Oklahoma Press, 1991), pp. 4–10.
51. Virgil J. Vogel, "Introduction," in *This Country Was Ours*, ed. Vogel, pp. 196–197.
52. M. Annette Jaimes, "Federal Indian Identification Policy: A Usurpation of Indigenous Sovereignty in North America," in *The State of Native America*, ed. Jaimes, p. 124.
53. Ibid., pp. 95–98.
54. W. A. Brophy and S. D. Aberle, *The Indian* (Norman: University of Oklahoma Press, 1966), pp. 179–193; Rebecca L. Robbins, "Self-Determination and Subordination: The Past, Present, and Future of American Indian Governance," in *The State of Native America*, ed. Jaimes, pp. 98–100.
55. U.S. Bureau of Indian Affairs, *Federal Indian Policy*, p. 12.
56. Jaimes, "Federal Indian Identification Policy," pp. 123–137; Susan Campbell, "A Mohegan Family," *Hartford Courant*, March 1, 1992, p. 10; Anne Fullam, "Tribe Seeks U.S. Recognition," *Newsday*, February 11, 1992, p. 20.
57. Jack Forbes, *Native Americans of California and Nevada* (Berkeley, CA: Far West Laboratory for Educational Research and Development, 1968), pp. 80–82; Alan L. Sorkin, *American Indians and Federal Aid* (Washington, DC: Brookings Institution, 1971), pp. 48–65; Vogel, "Introduction," p. 205; James S. Olson and Raymond Wilson, *Native Americans in the Twentieth Century* (Provo, UT: Brigham Young University Press, 1984), p. 209; E. S. Cahn, *Our Brother's Keeper* (New York: World, 1969), pp. 157–158.
58. Robbins, "Self-Determination and Subordination," pp. 98–112, quotation from p. 109.
59. Elouise Cobell, "After five years of delay, will the Bush Administration treat the Trust Accounts lawsuit any differently?" *Oklahoma Indian Times Online*, www.okit.com/opinion/2001/janfeb/trust.htm (retrieved June 7, 2001); NCAI, "Senate Committee Schedule to Meet with Tribes to Discuss Indian Trust Reform Act of 2006 and Fractionation Problem," www.ncai.org/Home.9.0.html?&no_cache=1 (retrieved September 7, 2006).
60. Brophy and Aberle, *The Indian*, pp. 33–44; Olson and Wilson, *Native Americans in the Twentieth Century*, pp. 189, 191.
61. Virgil J. Vogel, "Famous Americans of Indian Descent," in *This Country Was Ours*, ed. Vogel, pp. 310–351.
62. U.S. Census Bureau, "Census Bureau Facts for Features," October 26, 2004, www.census.gov/Press-Release/www/releases/archives/facts_for_features_special_editions/002957.html (retrieved September 5, 2006).
63. Olson and Wilson, *Native Americans in the Twentieth Century*, p. 186.
64. "Indians Flashing Casino Profits in D.C.: The Mashantucket Pequot Tribe, for Example, Employs a Full-Time Lobbyist in Washington," *Providence Journal-Bulletin*, July 13, 1997, p. 5A.
65. NCAI, "Tribal Sovereignty Protection Initiative," www.ncai.org/Sovereignty_Protection.91.0.html (September 7, 2006).

66. Hazel W. Hertzberg, *The Search for an American Indian Identity* (Syracuse, NY: Syracuse University Press, 1971), pp. 20–21, 42–76, 180–200.
67. Ibid., pp. 200–208, 291–293; Isabel Wilkerson, "Indignant Indians Seeking Changes," *The New York Times*, January 26, 1992, p. 14.
68. Robert C. Day, "The Emergence of Activism as a Social Movement," in *Native Americans Today*, ed. Bahr, Chadwick, and Day, pp. 516–517.
69. Robbins, "Self-Determination and Subordination," p. 103.
70. Meyer, *Native Americans*, p. 88; "Pine Ridge After Wounded Knee: The Terror Goes on," *Akwesasne Notes* 7 (Summer 1975): 8–10.
71. Greg Toppo, "Group Wants a Peltier Pardon," *Santa Fe New Mexican*, December 8, 1996, p. B1.
72. Richard Meryhew, "Be It Redskins, Chiefs, or Lions, Indians to Protest," *St. Paul Star Tribune*, January 3, 1992, p. 1B; Wilkerson, "Indignant Indians Seeking Changes," p. 14.
73. C. Richard King and Charles Fruehling Springwood, "Introduction," in *Team Spirits: The Native American Mascots Controversy*, ed. C. Richard King and Charles Fruehling Springwood (Lincoln: University of Nebraska Press, 2001), p. 7; "Doby's Best Pitch Comes at Playground," *Austin American-Statesman*, July 9, 1997, p. C4.
74. Susan Dodge, "Illiniwek Not Going Anywhere," *Chicago Sun-Times*, March 08, 2001, p. 1; David Prochaska, "At Home in Illinois: Presence of Chief Illiniwek, Absence of Native Americans," in *Team Spirits*, ed. King and Springwood, pp. 165–169.
75. Laurel R. Davis, "Protest Against the Use of Native American Mascots: A Challenge to Traditional American Identity," *Journal of Sport and Social Issues* 17 (April 1993): 9–22; quotation on p. 13.
76. Ibid., p. 19.
77. Randi Hicks Rowe, "NCAA Decides; New Policy Prohibits Usage of Racially Abusive Names by College Teams," *American Indian Report* 21 (2005): 8–9.
78. Quoted in "Newspaper Defends Dropping Native American Names from Teams," *Reuters News Service*, February 19, 1992.
79. Terry, "Los Angeles Times Interview with Suzane Shown Harjo"; "Indian Mascots Are Out, Says Vote in L.A.," *The Los Angeles Times*, September 10, 1997, p. A6; C. Richard King and Charles Fruehling Springwood, "Introduction," in *Team Spirits*, ed. King and Springwood, p. 5.
80. Zach Maxwell, "Rally for Repatriation," *Oklahoma Indian Times Online*, www.okit.com/news/2001/feb/rally.htm (retrieved June 7, 2001).
81. U.S. Commission on Civil Rights, *Indian Tribes: A Continuing Quest for Survival* (Washington, DC, 1981), pp. 61–99; Institute for Natural Progress, "In Usual and Accustomed Places," in *The State of Native America*, ed. Jaimes, pp. 223–226.
82. Institute for Natural Progress, "In Usual and Accustomed Places," pp. 224–226.
83. U.S. Commission on Civil Rights, *Indian Tribes*, p. 103. Italics added.
84. Olson and Wilson, *Native Americans in the Twentieth Century*, p. 195; Ward Churchill, "The Earth Is Our Mother," in *The State of Native America*, ed. Jaimes, pp. 151–169.
85. Alex White Plume, "An Open Letter to President George W. Bush, *Indian Country Today*, August 31, 2006, www.indiancountry.com/content.cfm?id=1096413572 (September 12, 2006).
86. Haider Rizvi, "Indigenous Rights: Native Peoples Demand Self-Determination," Inter Press Service, August 9, 2006, n.p.
87. U.S. Commission on Civil Rights, *Indian Tribes*, pp. 1–2 (Hatfield quotation from p. 1; quotation from tribal leader from p. 2); Institute for Natural Progress, "In Usual and Accustomed Places," pp. 223, 231, 233–234.
88. "Shattering the Myth of the Vanishing American," *Ford Foundation Letter* 22, no. 3 (Winter 1991): 1–5.
89. "The Hidden Victims: Hate Crimes Against American Indians Under-Reported, *Southern Poverty Law Center Intelligence Report*, October 1994, pp. 1–4; quotation on p. 4.
90. Jeff Shaw, "Bitter Harvest; Indian Farmers Allege Years of Discrimination at the USDA," *In These Times*, October 2, 2000, p. 20.
91. Ibid.
92. Alvin M. Josephy, Jr., Joane Nagel, and Troy Johnson "Introduction: 'You Are on Indian Land!'" in *Red Power: The American Indians' Fight for Freedom*, 2nd ed., Alvin M. Josephy, Jr., Joane Nagel, and Troy Johnson (Lincoln: University of Nebraska Press, 1999), p. 5. We draw here on pp. 3–6.
93. Alvin M. Josephy, Jr., Joane Nagel, and Troy Johnson, "The National Museum of the American Indian Act," in *Red Power*, ed. Josephy, Nagel, and Johnson, p. 228; Alvin M. Josephy, Jr., Joane Nagel, and Troy Johnson, "The Native Americans Graves Protection and Repatriation Act," in *Red Power*, ed. Josephy, Nagel, and Johnson, p. 233.
94. Associated Press, "Navajos March Against Discrimination, Violence," www.lakotaarchives.com/ictnews.html (retrieved September 8, 2006).
95. Ward Churchill and Winona LaDuke, "Native North America: The Political Economy of Radioactive Colonialism," in *The State of Native America*, ed. Jaimes, pp. 241–262; Campbell, "A Mohegan Family," p. 10. See also Sar A. Levitan, Garth L. Mangum, and Ray

Marshall, *Human Resources and Labor Markets*, 2nd ed. (New York: Harper & Row, 1976), p. 441.

96. Joseph G. Jorgensen, "Indians and the Metropolis," in *The American Indian in Urban Society*, ed. Waddell and Watson, p. 85.
97. Quoted in Deloria, *Of Utmost Good Faith*, pp. 380–381; see also Hagan, *American Indians*, pp. 126–127; Spicer, *Cycles of Conquest*, pp. 349–356.
98. Cahn, *Our Brother's Keeper*, pp. 69–110; Rupert Costo, "Speaking Freely," *Wassaja* 4 (November–December 1976): 2; Sorkin, *American Indians and Federal Aid*, pp. 70–71; Jorgensen, "Indians and the Metropolis," pp. 96–99.
99. Olson and Wilson, *Native Americans in the Twentieth Century*, p. 181; Robert Bryce, "Indians Seek Control of Tribal-Land Resources," *The Christian Science Monitor*, September 14, 1994, p. 4.; Churchill and LaDuke, "Native North America," pp. 247–248.
100. Michael Parfit, "Keeping the Big Sky Pure," Perspectives 13 (Spring 1981): 44; Bryce, "Indians Seek Control of Tribal-Land Resources"; Michelle Dearmond, "Tribes, Officials Talking Energy," *Riverside Press Enterprise*, June 21, 2005, p. B01.
101. U.S. Bureau of the Census, *Population, 1940: Characteristics of the Nonwhite Population by Race* (Washington, DC, 1943), pp. 83–84; U.S. Bureau of the Census, *1990 Census of Population: Social and Economic Characteristics: United States*, p. 45; U.S. Bureau of the Census: "American Fact Finder: Selected Population Profiles in the United States," http://factfinder.census.gov/servlet/IPTable?_bm=y&-geo_id=01000US&-qr_name=ACS_2005_EST_G00_S0201&-qr_name=ACS_2005_EST_G00_S0201 PR&-qr_name=ACS_2005_EST_G00_S0201T&-qr_name=ACS_2005_EST_G00_S0201TPR&-reg=ACS_2005_ EST_G00_S0201:009;ACS_2005_EST_G00_S0201PR:009;ACS_2005_EST_G00_S0201T:009;ACS_2005_EST_G00_S0201TPR:009&ds_name=ACS_2005_EST_G00_&-_lang=en&- redoLog=false&-format= (retrieved January 25, 2007). In chapters 6–12 we use data from the American Community Survey (ACS), a large national survey done to supplement the decennial census. It provides excellent survey estimates for key population statistics, but not full population counts.
102. Daniel Gonzalez, "TV Reporter Keeps Ties to Heritage," *Arizona Republic*, February 25, 2001, p. B3; the data in Table 6.2 are from Office of Personnel Management, www.opm.gov, September 30, 2004.
103. U.S. Bureau of the Census, *Sixteenth Census of the United States: The Labor Force, Part I: U.S. Summary* (Washington, DC, 1943), p. 39; U.S. Department of Health, Education and Welfare, *A Study of Selected Socio-Economic Characteristics of Ethnic Minorities Based on the 1970 Census*, vol. 3, *American Indians* (Washington, DC, 1974), p. 49; U.S. Bureau of the Census, *1990 Census of Population: Social and Economic Characteristics: United States*, p. 44; U.S. Bureau of the Census, *1990 Census of Population: Social and Economic Characteristics: American Indian and Alaska Native Areas*, CP-2-1A (Washington, DC, 1993), p. 56; the 2005 data were supplied by Randy Ilg, Bureau of Labor Statistics, personal communication, September 11, 2006.
104. Kathleen Pickering, "Alternative Economic Strategies in Low-Income Rural Communities," *Rural Sociology* 65 (2000): 148-167.
105. U.S. Bureau of the Census: "American Fact Finder: Selected Population Profiles in the United States," http://factfinder.census.gov/servlet/IPTable?_bm=y&-geo_id=01000US&-qr_name=ACS_2005_EST_G00_S0201&-qr_name=ACS_2005_EST_G00_S0201 PR&-qr_name=ACS_ 2005_EST_G00_S0201T&-qr_name=ACS_ 2005_EST_G00_S0201TPR&-reg=ACS_2005_EST_G00_S0201:009;ACS_2005_EST_G00_S0201PR:009;ACS_2005_EST_G00_S0201T:009;ACS_2005_EST_G00_S0201TPR:009&-ds_name=ACS_2005_EST_G00_&-_lang=en&-redoLog=false&-format= (retrieved January 25, 2007); see also U.S. Census Bureau, "Income Climbs, Poverty Stabilizes, Uninsured Rate Increases," *U.S. Census Bureau News*, August 29, 2006, pp. 1–2.
106. See Nagel, American Indian Ethnic Renewal.
107. U.S. Department of Health and Human Services, Regional Differences in Indian Health (Washington, DC, 1994), pp. 33, 45, 56–61, 90; Charles W. Grim, "Statement Before the Senate Committee on Indian Affairs on the Status of Indian Health," Department of Health And Human Services, April 13, 2005, www.senate.gov/~scia/2005hrgs/041305hrg/grim.pdf (September 11, 2006).
108. Kavan Peterson, "Indian Casinos Boon to Tribes and States," Stateline.org, June 21, 2006, www.stateline.org/live/ViewPage.action?siteNodeId=136&languageId=1&contentId=121398 (September 11, 2006).
109. National Indian Gaming Commission, "Helping Indian Nations Recover from Centuries of Economic and Social Neglect," *Oklahoma Indian Times Online*, www.okit.com/gaming/2001/feb/helping.htm (retrieved June 7, 2001).
110. Bob Doucette, "Tribes Compete and Contribute," *The Oklahoman*, June 6, 2001, www.oklahoman.com/cgi-bin/show_article?ID=696797&TP (retrieved June 7, 2001); and National Indian Gaming Commission, "Helping Indian Nations Recover from Centuries of Economic and Social Neglect."
111. Bob Doucette and Mark A. Hutchison, "Tribes Build Businesses from Gaming," *The Oklahoman*, June 4, 2001, www.oklahoman.com/cgi-bin/show_article?ID=

696799&pic=none&TP=getarticle (retrieved June 7, 2001).

112. "Nationwide Poll Shows Support for Native Issues; Saginaw-Chippewa Commissions Zogby Research Firm to Reach Average Americans," *Oklahoma Indian Times Online*; Bill Lueders, "Casino Cowboys Take Indians for a Ride," *Progressive*, August 1994, pp. 30–33.
113. Associated Press, "Goshute Reservation in Skull Valley, Utah—2006 Update, Nuclear Dump Glance," June 24, 2006; the quote is in Bob von Sternberg, "Tribe Fights Storage of Reactor's Spent Fuel," *St. Paul Star Tribune*, November 27, 1991, p. 2B.
114. U.S. Bureau of Indian Affairs, *Federal Indian Policies*, p. 5; Jorge Noriega, "American Indian Education in the United States," in *The State of Native America*, ed. Jaimes, pp. 371–383.
115. U.S. Bureau of Indian Affairs, *Federal Indian Policies*, pp. 5–6; Spicer, *Cycles of Conquest*, p. 349; Noriega, "American Indian Education in the United States," pp. 381–383; U.S. Bureau of Indian Affairs, *Federal Indian Policies*, p. 9.
116. Noriega, "American Indian Education in the United States," pp. 384–385.
117. Interview with Phyllis Young, quoted in ibid., p. 387.
118. *Indian Nations at Risk: An Educational Strategy for Change*, report of U.S. Department of Education Task Force (Washington, DC, 1991), cited in Kenneth Cooper, "Multicultural Focus Recommended for Education of Native Americans," *The Washington Post*, December 27, 1991, p. A19; National Center for Education Statistics, *National Indian Education Study, Part 1: The Performance of American Indian and Alaska Native Fourth- and Eighth-Grade Students on NAEP Reading and Mathematics Assessments* (Washington, DC, 2006), executive summary (np).
119. U.S. Bureau of the Census: "American Fact Finder: Selected Population Profiles in the United States," http://factfinder.census.gov/servlet/IPTable?_bm=y&-geo_id=01000US&-qr_name=ACS_2005_EST_G00_S0201&-qr_name=ACS_2005_EST_G00_S0201PR&-qr_name=ACS_2005_EST_G00_S0201T&-qr_name=ACS_2005_EST_G00_S0201TPR&-reg=ACS_2005_EST_G00_S0201:009;ACS_2005_EST_G00_S0201PR:009;ACS_2005_EST_G00_S0201T:009;ACS_2005_EST_G00_S0201TPR:009&-ds_name=ACS_2005_EST_G00_&-_lang=en&-redoLog=false&-format= (retrieved January 25, 2007); see also U.S. Bureau of the Census, *We the People: American Indians and Alaska Natives in the United States* (Washington, DC, 2006), p. 8.
120. David Melmer, "ACLU Intervenes at High School," *Indian Country Today*, July 4, 2005, www.indiancountry.com/content.cfm?id=1096411180 (September 12, 2006); Valerie J. Shirley, "On the Right Path," *Black Issues in Higher Education* 21 (2004): 88.
121. National Center for Educational Statistics, "Digest of Education Statistics," 2005, http://nces.ed.gov/programs/digest/d05/tables/dt05_205.asp (September 14, 2006); Noriega, "American Indian Education in the United States," pp. 391–392; Office of Indian Education Programs, *Fingertip Facts: 1994* (Washington, DC: U.S. Bureau of Indian Affairs, 1994), p. 16.
122. Paul Hammel, "Tribes Offered Help In Preserving Relics, Treasured Artifact," *Omaha World-Herald*, February 26, 2001, p.1
123. Vine Deloria, Jr., *Custer Died for Your Sins* (London: Collier-Macmillan, 1969), pp. 108–116.
124. Vittorio Lanternari, *The Religions of the Oppressed* (New York: Mentor Books, 1963), pp. 110–132; Spencer et al., *The Native Americans*, pp. 498–499; Wax, *Indian Americans*, p. 141.
125. Lanternari, *The Religions of the Oppressed*, pp. 99–100; Hertzberg, *The Search for an American Indian Identity*, pp. 239–240, 251, 280; Hertzberg, *The Search for an American Indian Identity*, pp. 246, 257, 271–274, 280–284; Elaine G. Eastman, "Does Uncle Sam Foster Paganism?" in *In Their Place*, ed. Carlson and Colburn, pp. 29; Deloria, *Of Utmost Good Faith*, pp. 177–180; Deloria, *Custer Died for Your Sins*, pp. 110–115.
126. Olson and Wilson, *Native Americans in the Twentieth Century*, p. 219; Deloria, *Custer Died for Your Sins*, pp. 122–124.
127. National Asian Pacific American Families Against Substance Abuse, "Pacific Islander Substance Abuse Fact Sheet," Los Angeles, April 26, 2005.
128. Intercultural Cancer Council, "Native Hawaiians/Pacific Islanders & Cancer," http://iccnetwork.org/cancerfacts/cfs5.htm (July 20, 2006); Anonymous, "Pacific Islanders Threatened," *Environmental Action* 25 (Winter 1994): 32.
129. For example, Lurie, as quoted in John A. Price, "Migration and Adaptation of American Indians to Los Angeles," *Human Organization* 27 (Summer 1968): 168–175.
130. See Snipp, *American Indians*, pp. 23–25
131. Olson and Wilson, *Native Americans in the Twentieth Century*, p. 212; see also pp. 210–211.
132. Alvin M. Josephy, Jr., Joane Nagel, and Troy Johnson, "Native American Languages Act," in *Red Power*, ed. Josephy, Nagel, and Johnson, p. 199; Michelle Nijhuis, "Tribal Immersion Schools Rescue Language and Culture," *The Christian Science Monitor*, June 11, 2002, www.csmonitor.com/2002/ 0611/p11s01-legn.html.

133. Prodipto Roy, "The Measurement of Assimilation: The Spokane Indians," *American Journal of Sociology* 67 (March 1962): 541–551;C. Matthew Snipp, *American Indian and Alaska Native Children in the 2000 Census* (New York: The Annie E. Casey Foundation and The Population Reference Bureau, April 2002).
134. Lynn C. White and Bruce A. Chadwick, "Urban Residence, Assimilation, and Identity of the Spokane Indian," in *Native Americans Today*, ed. Bahr, Chadwick, and Day, p. 243; Brophy and Aberle, *The Indian*, p. 10; Spicer, *Cycles of Conquest*, p. 577.
135. Joan Weibel-Orlando, *Indian Country, L.A.* (Urbana: University of Illinois Press, 1991), pp. 22–43; John Iceland, Daniel H. Weinberg, and Erika Steinmetz, "Racial and Ethnic Residential Segregation in the United States: 1980-2000," paper presented at the annual meeting, Population Association of America, Atlanta, GA, May 9–11, 2002.
136. Josephy, Nagel, and Johnson, "Introduction," in *Red Power*, pp. 7–8; Nijhuis, "Tribal Immersion Schools Rescue Language and Culture."
137. Robert Blauner, *Racial Oppression in America* (New York: Harper & Row, 1972), p. 54; Spicer, *Cycles of Conquest*, pp. 573–574.
138. Quoted in Francis McKinley, Stephen Bayne, and Glen Nimnicht, *Who Should Control Indian Education?* (Berkeley, CA: Far West Laboratory for Educational Research and Development, 1969), p. 13 (italics added).
139. Quoted in Shirley Hill Witt, "Pressure Points in Growing Up Indian," *Perspectives* 12 (Spring 1980): 31.
140. Wilbur J. Scott, "Attachment to Indian Culture," *Youth and Society* 17 (June 1986): 392–394.
141. Witt, "Pressure Points in Growing Up Indian," pp. 28–31; Robert W. Blum et al., "American Indian–Alaska Native Youth Health," *Journal of the American Medical Association* 267 (March 25, 1992): 1637–1644; U.S. Department of Health and Human Services, *Regional Differences in Indian Health* (Washington, DC, 1994), p. 56; Donald Warne, "Research and Educational Approaches to Reducing Health Disparities Among American Indians and Alaska Natives," *Journal of Transcultural Nursing* 17 (July 2006): 266–271.
142. Albert L. Wahrhaftig and Robert K. Thomas, "Renaissance and Repression: The Oklahoma Cherokee," in *Native Americans Today*, ed. Bahr, Chadwick, and Day, p. 81.
143. Richard B. Williams, "The Indian Renaissance in America," *Denver Post*, June 6, 2001, p.B7.
144. Institute for Natural Progress, "In Usual and Accustomed Places," pp. 228–236.

Chapter 7

1. Bebe Moore Campbell, "To Be Black, Gifted, and Alone," *Savvy* 5 (December 1984): 69.
2. James H. Dorman and Robert R. Jones, *The Afro-American Experience* (New York: John Wiley, 1974), pp. 72–74; Thomas R. Frazier, pre-face to chapt. 1, in *Afro-American History: Primary Sources*, ed. Thomas R. Frazier (New York: Harcourt, Brace & World, 1970), pp. 3–5.
3. Olaudah Equiano, "The Interesting Narative of the Life of Olaudah Equiano," in *Afro-American History*, ed. Frazier, pp. 18, 20.
4. Dorman and Jones, *The Afro-American Experience*, pp. 80–82.
5. Philip D. Curtin, *The Atlantic Slave Trade* (Madison: University of Wisconsin Press, 1969), pp. 87–93; U.S. Bureau of the Census, *Historical Statistics of the United States* (Washington, DC, 1960), p. 770.
6. Carl N. Degler, *Out of Our Past* (New York: Harper, 1959), pp. 161–163; John Hope Franklin, *From Slavery to Freedom*, 4th ed. (New York: Knopf, 1984), p. 88.
7. Franklin, *From Slavery to Freedom*, pp. 132–133.
8. U.S. Bureau of the Census, *Historical Statistics of the United States*, p. 11; Degler, *Out of Our Past*, pp. 163–164; Ulrich B. Phillips, *Life and Labor in the Old South* (Boston: Little, Brown, 1929), pp. 339ff; Kenneth M. Stampp, *The Peculiar Institution* (New York: Random House/Vintage Books, 1956), pp. 383–418.
9. Ben Simpson, "Ben Simpson: Georgia and Texas," in *Lay My Burden Down*, ed. B. A. Botkin (Chicago: University of Chicago Press, 1945), p. 75; see also John W. Blassingame, *The Slave Community* (New York: Oxford University Press, 1972), pp. 155–160.
10. Quoted in Jacqueline Jones, *Labor of Love, Labor of Sorrow: Black Women, Work, and the Family, from Slavery to the Present* (New York: Random House/Vintage Books, 1985), p. 16. We have amended the quotation slightly for clarity.
11. Quoted in ibid., p.19.
12. Herbert Gutman, *The Black Family in Slavery and Freedom, 1750–1925* (New York: Pantheon, 1976); Stanley Elkins, "The Slavery Debate," *Commentary* 46 (December 1975): 46–47.
13. Patricia Williams, "Alchemical Notes: Reconstructing Ideals from Deconstructed Rights," *Harvard Civil Rights and Civil Liberties Review* 22 (1987): 415.
14. Bonnie Mitchell and Joe Feagin, "America's Racial-Ethnic Cultures: Opposition Within a Mythical Melting Pot," in *Toward the Multicultural University*, ed. Benjamin Bowser, Gale Auletta, and Terry Jones (Westport, CT: Praeger, 1995), pp. 65–86; see also

Patricia Hill Collins, *Black Feminist Thought: Knowledge, Consciousness, and the Politics of Empowerment* (Boston: Unwin Hyman, 1990), pp. 40–48.

15. Eugene G. Genovese, *Roll, Jordan, Roll* (New York: Random House, 1974), p. 650.
16. Herbert Aptheker, *American Negro Slave Revolts* (New York: International, 1943), pp. 12–18, 162.
17. Ibid., pp. 165, 220–225, 249–250, 267–273.
18. Herbert Aptheker, *Essays in the History of the American Negro* (New York: International, 1945), pp. 39, 49–51; Sterling Stuckey, *Slave Culture* (New York: Oxford University Press, 1987), pp. 42–46.
19. Quoted in *Bartlett's Familiar Quotations*, 15th ed., ed. Emily M. Beck (Boston: Little, Brown, 1980), p. 556.
20. Benjamin B. Ringer, *"We the People" and Others* (New York: Tavistock, 1983), p. 533.
21. A. L. Higginbotham, *In the Matter of Color* (New York: Oxford University Press, 1978), pp. 144–149.
22. Jerry Fresia, *Toward an American Revolution: Exposing the Constitution and Other Illusions* (Boston: South End Press, 1988), pp. 1–2; Dinitia Smith and Nicholas Wade, "DNA Evidence Links Thomas Jefferson to Slave's Offspring," *Gainesville (Fla.) Sun*, November 1, 1998, p. 4A.
23. Thomas F. Gossett, *Race* (New York: Schocken Books, 1965), pp. 42–43; see Thomas Jefferson, *Notes on the State of Virginia*, ed. Frank Shuffelton (New York: Penguin Books, 1999 [1785]).
24. See, for example, Samuel Cartwright's infamous 1850s article, "The Prognathous Species of Mankind," in *Slavery Defended*, ed. Eric L. McKitrick (Englewood Cliffs, NJ: Prentice Hall, 1963).
25. Williams, "Alchemical Notes," pp. 401–434. See also Duncan J. MacLeod, *Slavery, Race, and the American Revolution* (London: Cambridge University Press, 1974), p. 158.
26. Richard J. Herrnstein, *IQ in the Meritocracy* (Boston: Little, Brown, 1973); Arthur R. Jensen, "How Much Can We Boost IQ and Scholastic Achievement?" *Harvard Education Review* 39 (1969): 1–123; Tom Wilkie, "The American Association for the Advancement of Science: Research Revives Dispute over IQ," *Independent*, February 19, 1991, p. 7; Richard J. Herrnstein and Charles Murray, *The Bell Curve: Intelligence and Class Structure in American Life* (New York: The Free Press, 1994), p. 311; see also pp. 295–316.
27. Cited in Richard Brookhiser, "Fear and Loathing at City College," *National Review*, June 11, 1990, p. 20.
28. "Buchanan Campaign Rhetoric," *Boston Globe*, January 12, 1992, p. 68. Samuel Francis, "Out of the Mouths of Japanese," *The Washington Times*, February 11, 1992, p. F1.
29. See data gathered by Otto Klineberg as cited in I. A. Newby, *Challenge to the Court* (Baton Rouge: Louisiana State University Press, 1967), p. 74. See also Thomas F. Pettigrew, *A Profile of the Negro American* (Princeton, NJ: D. Van Nostrand, 1964), pp. 123–126.
30. Leon J. Kamin, *The Science and Politics of IQ* (New York: John Wiley, 1974), pp. 175–178.
31. N. J. Block and Gerald Dworkin, "IQ, Heritability, and Inequality," in *The IQ Controversy*, ed. N. J. Block and Gerald Dworkin (New York: Random House, 1976), pp. 410–540.
32. Lawrence Bobo, "Inequalities That Endure?: Racial Ideology, American Politics, and the Peculiar Role of the Social Sciences," paper presented at conference on "The Changing Terrain of Race and Ethnicity," University of Illinois, Chicago, October 26, 2001; Srividya Ramasubramanian, "Effects of Media Literacy Training on Explicit and Implicit Racial Stereotypes," Ph.D. dissertation, Penn State University, State College, PA, 2004, p. 16.
33. Shankar Vedantam, "Many Americans Believe They Are Not Prejudiced. Now a New Test Provides Powerful Evidence That a Majority of Us Really Are," *The Washington Post*, January 23, 2005, p. W12; and Associated Press, "Racism Studies Find Rational Part of Brain Can Override Prejudice," www.beliefnet.com/story/156/story_15664_1.html (accessed November 28, 2004). I draw here on Leslie Houts Picca and Joe R. Feagin, *Two-Faced Racism: Whites in the Backstage and Frontstage* (New York: Routledge, 2007), pp. 2–12.
34. Doris Wilkinson, "Minority Women: Social-Cultural Issues," in *Women and Psychotherapy*, ed. Annette M. Brodsky and Rachel T. Hare-Mustin (New York: Guilford, 1980), pp. 295–297. See also A. Thomas and S. Sillen, *Racism and Psychiatry* (New York: Bruner-Mazel, 1972), pp. 57–58.
35. Kevin A. Schulman et al., "The Effect of Race and Sex on Physicians' Recommendations for Cardiac Catherization," *New England Journal of Medicine* (February 25, 1999): 618–626; Peter B. Bach et al., "Racial Differences in the Treatment of Early-Stage Lung Cancer," *New England Journal of Medicine* (October 14, 1999): 1198–1205; Robert W. Putsch and Linda Pololi, "Distributive Justice in American Healthcare," *American Journal of Managed Care* 10 (September 2004): SP48–SP49.
36. John B. McConahay and Joseph C. Hough, "Symbolic Racism," *Journal of Social Issues* 32 (1976): 38.
37. Richard Morin, "Misperceptions Cloud Whites' View of Blacks," *The Washington Post*, July 11, 2001, p. A01; for data on these areas, see Joe R. Feagin and Karyn McKinney, *The Many Costs of Racism* (Lanham,

MD: Rowman & Littlefield, 2003), pp. 10–17. We draw on this discussion here.

38. "New York Times Poll: Race Relations in America," June, 2000, www.ropercenter.uconn.edu (retrieved September 18, 2006).
39. John F. Dovidio, John C. Brigham, Blair T. Johnson, and Samuel L. Gaertner, "Stereotyping, Prejudice, and Discrimination: Another Look," in *Stereotypes and Stereotyping*, ed. C. Neil Macrae, Miles Hewstone, and Charles Stangor (New York: Guilford, 1995), pp. 276–319.
40. Eduardo Bonilla-Silva and Tyrone A. Forman, "'I Am Not a Racist but...': Mapping White College Students' Racial Ideology in the U.S.A.," *Discourse and Society* 11 (2000): 51–86; I draw here on Joe R. Feagin, *Racist America: Roots, Current Realities, and Future Reparations* (New York: Routledge, 2000).
41. Picca and Feagin, *Two-Faced Racism*.
42. U.S. Bureau of the Census, *Historical Statistics of the United States*, p. 218.
43. W. J. Cash, *The Mind of the South* (New York: Random House/Vintage Books, 1960), p. 125.
44. See Gunnar Myrdal, *An America Dilemma* (New York: McGraw-Hill, 1964), 2: 1–198.
45. Gilbert Osofsky, *Harlem: The Making of a Ghetto* (New York: Harper & Row, 1963), pp. 45–51; Arthur I. Waskow, *From Race Riot to Sit-In, 1919 and the 1960s* (Garden City, NY: Doubleday, 1966), pp. 209–210 et passim; Elliot M. Rudwick, *Race Riot at East St. Louis* (Carbondale: Southern Illinois University Press, 1964), pp. 3–30.
46. "Active U.S. Hate Supremacist Groups in 2005," Intelligence Report, www.splcenter.org/intel/map/hate (retrieved September 18, 2006); "Going After the Klan," Newsweek, February 23, 1987, p. 29.
47. See "Violent Hate Crime Remains at Record Levels Nationwide," *Intelligence Report*, March 1994, pp. 1, 4–5; Thomas Fields-Meyer, Bob Stewart, Michelle McCalope, and Michael Haederle, "One Deadly Night: Deep in the Woods of East Texas, James Byrd Died a Terrible Death, Leaving a Town and a Nation in Shock," *People*, June 29, 1998, p. 46; Howard Chua-Eoan and Hilary Hylton-Austin "Beneath the Surface; A 'New South' Town is Haunted by 'Deep South' Ghosts—And a Fresh, Ugly Murder," *Time*, June 22, 1998, p. 34.
48. Andy Newman, "Plea Agreements Worked out in Brooklyn Hate-Crime Beating," *The New York Times*, March 9, 2006, http://gothamgazette.com/community/45/news//184 (retrieved September 18, 2006); Robert D. McFadden, "Black Man Is Attacked by Whites in Brooklyn, Police Say," *The New York Times*, www.nytimes.com/2005/08/08/nyregion/08bias.html?ex=1281153600&en=8f7ecc53eb288e6a&ei=5090&partner=rssuserland&emc=rss (retrieved September 19, 2006).
49. People for the American Way, "Right Wing Organizations," www.pfaw.org/pfaw/general/default.aspx?oid=7069&print=yes&units=all (retrieved September 19, 2006); "U.S. Supreme Court Upholds Stiffer Sentences for Hate Crimes," *Intelligence Report*, September 1993, pp. 4–5.
50. Joe R. Feagin and Harlan Hahn, *Ghetto Revolts* (New York: Macmillan, 1973), p. 134.
51. "The Mood of Ghetto America," *Newsweek*, June 2, 1980, pp. 32–34.
52. Lara Parker, "Violence After Police Shooting Exposes Miami Racial Tensions," *The Washington Post*, June 29, 1991, p. A2.
53. Associated Press, "Cincinnati City Manager Resigns," *The New York Times*, May 2, 2001, www.nytimes.com (retrieved May 3, 2001).
54. Gallup, *Black/White Relations in the United States* (Princeton, NJ: The Gallup Organization, 1997), pp. 29–30, 108–110.
55. Kim Lersch, "Current Trends in Police Brutality: An Analysis of Recent Newspaper Accounts." master's thesis, University of Florida, Gainesville, 1993.)
56. Howard Fischer, "DPS to Track Stops for Profiling," *Arizona Daily Star*, July 29, 2006, www.azstarnet.com/allheadlines/139930.php (retrieved September 19, 2006).
57. William M. Wiecek, "The Origins of the Law of Slavery in British North America," *Cardozo Law Review* 17 (1996): 1711–1792; Robert S. Browne, "Achieving Parity Through Reparations," in *The Wealth of Races: The Present Value of Benefits from Past Injustices*, ed. R. F. America (New York: Greenwood Press, 1990), pp. 199–206.
58. Cited in David H. Swinton, "Racial Inequality and Reparations," in *The Wealth of Races*, pp. 153–162.
59. Trina Williams, "The Homestead Act—Our Earliest National Asset Policy," paper presented at the Center for Social Development's symposium, Inclusion in Asset Building, St. Louis, MO, September 21–23, 2000.
60. Stephen J. DeCanio, "Accumulation and Discrimination in the Postbellum South," in *Market Institutions and Economic Progress in the New South 1865–1900*, ed. G. Walton and J. Shepherd (New York: Academic Press, 1981), pp. 103–125.
61. Doris Y. Wilkinson, "The Segmented Labor Market and African American Women from 1890 to 1960," in *Research in Race and Ethnic Relations*, vol. 6, ed. Rutledge M. Dennis (Greenwich, CT: JAI Press, 1991), p. 89. See also Ray Marshall, *The Negro Worker* (New York: Random House, 1967), pp. 7–12; MacLeod, *Slavery, Race, and the American Revolution*, pp. 151–153;

Pete Daniel, *The Shadow of Slavery: Peonage in the South* (London: Oxford University Press, 1972); and Myrdal, *An American Dilemma*, 1:228.

62. Quoted in Jones, *Labor of Love, Labor of Sorrow*, p. 123.
63. Karl E. Taeuber and Alma F. Taeuber, *Negroes in Cities* (Chicago: Aldine, 1965), pp. 12–13.
64. Charles Tilly, "Race and Migration to the American City," in *The Urban Scene*, ed. Joe R. Feagin (New York: Random House, 1973), p. 35; Taeuber and Taeuber, *Negroes in Cities*, pp. 144–147.
65. Edna Bonacich, "Class Approaches to Ethnicity and Race," *Insurgent Sociologist* 10 (Fall 1980): 11. See also Bennett Harrison, *Education, Training, and the Urban Ghetto* (Baltimore: Johns Hopkins, 1972).
66. W. E. B. Du Bois, *Black Reconstruction in America: An Essay Toward a History of the Part Which Black Folk Played in the Attempt to Reconstruct Democracy in America, 1860–1880* (New York: Atheneum, 1992 [1935]).
67. Wilkinson, "The Segmented Labor Market and African American Women from 1890 to 1960," pp. 90–94.
68. U.S. Bureau of the Census, *Negroes in the United States, 1920–1932* (Washington, DC, 1935), p. 289; Jones, *Labor of Love, Labor of Sorrow*, p. 179; Myrdal, *An American Dilemma*, 1:304–306.
69. Marshall, *The Negro Worker*, pp. 23–24, 56–57.
70. U.S. Bureau of the Census, *Population*, vol. 3, *The Labor Force* (Washington, DC, 1943); see also Sidney M. Wilhelm, *Who Needs the Negro?* (Cambridge, MA: Schenkman, 1970), p. 57.
71. U.S. Bureau of Labor Statistics, "Annual Average Tables from the January 2005 Issue of Employment and Earnings, Table 10: 'Employed Persons by Occupation, Race, Hispanic or Latino Ethnicity, and Sex,'" January 2005, www.bls.gov/cps/home.htm#annual (retrieved September 19, 2006). Note that BLS data are *annual averages*. Economic and educational data for black Americans who listed only black ancestry are similar to those who listed only and partial black ancestry.
72. Ibid., "Table 11: Employed Persons by Detailed Occupation, Sex, Race, and Hispanic Origin"; the data in Table 7.2 are from Office of Personnel Management, www.opm.gov, September 30, 2004.
73. Joe R. Feagin and Melvin P. Sikes, *Living with Racism: The Black Middle Class Experience* (Boston: Beacon Press, 1994), pp. 191–194;
74. "Statement of Barbara R. Arnwine Executive Director Lawyers' Committee for Civil Rights Under Law," U.S. Equal Employment Opportunity Commission, www.eeoc.gov/abouteeoc/meetings/4-19-06/foreman.html (retrieved September 19, 2006).
75. Lincoln Quillian, "New Approaches to Understanding Racial Prejudice and Discrimination," *Annual Review of Sociology* 32 (2006): 308; Devah Pager and Bruce Western "Discrimination in Low-Wage Labor Markets: Evidence from an Experimental Audit Study in New York City," research paper, Princeton University, http://72.14.209.104/search?q=cache:hltEuw40fgkJ:paa2005.princeton.edu/download.aspx%3FsubmissionId%3D50874+discrimination+job+Hispanic+testers+matched+cities+research&hl=en&gl=us&ct=clnk&cd=1H (retrieved October 24, 2006).
76. LRA Ontline, "Backtracking at the EEOC," June 13, 2006, www.laborresearch.org/story2.php/418 (retrieved September 19, 2006).
77. Sharon M. Collins, "The Making of the Black Middle Class," *Social Problems* 30 (April 1983): 369–381; Sharon Collins, "Blacks on the Bubble: The Vulnerability of Black Executives in White Corporations," *Sociological Quarterly* 34 (August 1993): 429–447.
78. Public Relations Society of America, New York Chapter, "National Survey of Multicultural Public Relations Practitioners Reveals Barriers to Diversity," Press Release, New York, June 9, 2005.
79. Arin N. Reeves, "Colored by Race: Bias in the Evaluation of Candidates of Color by Law Firm Hiring Committees," Minority Corporate Counsel Association, www.mcca.com/site/data/magazine/2006-09/colored_by_race.shtml (retrieved September 25, 2006).
80. Kurt Eichenwald, "Texaco Executives, on Tape, Discussed Impeding a Bias Suit," *The New York Times*, November 4, 1996, p. A1; Kurt Eichenwald, "The Two Faces of Texaco," *The New York Times*, November 10, 1996, sec. 3, p. 1.
81. Glass Ceiling Commission, *Good for Business: Making Full Use of the Nation's Human Capital* (Washington, DC, 1995); Walden Asset Management, "Report: Nearly Half of America's Largest Companies Responding to Survey Do Not Voluntarily Disclose Equal Employment Opportunity Data on Women, Minorities," Washington, DC: Walden Asset Management, December 7, 2005, p. 1.
82. Black Coaches Association, *"Scoring the Hire:" Division 1A and 1AA Football Head Coaching Positions in American Higher Education* (Ann Arbor, MI: Paul Robeson Research Center, 2006), pp. vi–vii.
83. "The Multi-City Study of Urban Inequality," *Russell Sage Foundation Newsletter*, Fall 1999, pp. 1–3, and on an attached supplement to that newsletter; and Philip Moss and Chris Tilly, *Stories Employers Tell: Race, Skill, and Hiring in America* (New York: Russell Sage, 2001); the quote is from Jenny Bussey and John Trasviña, "The Treatment of White and African American Job Applicants by Temporary Employment Agencies in California," research report, Discrimination Research Center, December 2003, http://72.14.209.104/search?q=cache:9B6I8O0NUi0J:

www.impactfund.org/DRC%2520December% 2520 2003%2520Report.pdf+%22employment+testing% 22+testers+matched+cities+research&hl=en&gl=us &ct=clnk&cd=2 (retrieved October 24, 2006).

84. Jacquelyn Scarville et al., *Armed Forces Equal Opportunity Survey* (Arlington, VA: Defense Manpower Data Center, 1999), pp. 46–85; Office of the Under Secretary of Defense Personnel and Readiness, *Career Progression of Minority and Women Officers* (Washington, DC: U.S. Department of Defense, 1999), pp. 83–85.
85. LRA Ontline, "Backtracking at the EEOC."
86. *Wards Cove Packing Co.* v. *Atonio*, 109 S. Ct. 2115 (1989).
87. U.S. Bureau of the Census, *The Social and Economic Status of the Black Population in the United States, 1971* (Washington, DC, 1972), p. 52; U.S. Department of Labor, Bureau of Labor Statistics, "Annual Average Data, Table 24: Unemployed Persons by Marital Status, Race, Hispanic or Latino Ethnicity, Age, and Sex," ftp://ftp.bls.gov/pub/special.requests/lf/aat24.txt (retrieved September 24, 2005).
88. See, for example, the figures for Laura Dresser and Joel Rogers, *The State of Working Wisconsin: Update* 2003 (Madison: Center on Wisconsin Strategy), August 31, 2003, www.cows.org/pdf/jobs/soww/rp-soww-03.pdf (retrieved September 22, 2006).
89. U.S. Census Bureau, "Historical Income Tables—Families, Table F-5: Race and Hispanic Origin of Householder—Families by Median and Mean Income: 1947 to 2004," published December 20, 2005, www.census.gov/hhes/income/histinc/incfamdet.html. "Nonwhite" here consists mostly of black Americans.
90. U.S. Bureau of the Census, "Income, Poverty, and Health Insurance Coverage in the United States: 2005, Table 1: Income and Earnings Summary Measures by Selected Characteristics: 2004–2005," published August 2006, www.census.gov/prod/2006 pubs/p60-231.pdf.
91. U.S. Census Bureau, "Historical Income Tables—Families, Table F-7B: Type of Family—Black Families by Median and Mean Income: 1967 to 1999," published October 30, 2000, www.census.gov/hhes/income/histinc/incfamdet.html.
92. Joseph Dalaker and Bernadette D. Proctor, U.S. Census Bureau, Current Population Reports, Series P60-210, *Poverty in the United States*, 1999 (Washington, DC: U.S. Government Printing Office, 2000), pp. B-15, B-17; U.S. Bureau of the Census, *Income, Poverty, and Health Insurance Coverage in the United States: 2005*, published August 29, 2006, www.census.gov/prod/ 2006pubs/p60-231.pdf.
93. Robert B. Hill, "The Economic Status of Black Americans," in *The State of Black America, 1981*, ed. J. D. Williams (New York: Urban League, 1981), pp. 5–6, 33. Italics added.
94. U.S. Bureau of the Census, *Asset Ownership of Households* (Washington, DC, 2005), Table 4, www.census.gov/hhes/www/wealth/1998_2000/wlth00-4.html. See also note 90.
95. U.S. Census Bureau, "Asset Ownership of Households: 1995, Table 1: Median Value of Assets for Households, by Type of Asset Owned and Selected Characteristics: 1995," published April 9, 2001, www.census.gov/hhes/www/wealth/1995/wealth 95.html; U.S. Census Bureau, "Asset Ownership of Households: 1995, Table 2: Asset Ownership Rates for Households, by Selected Characteristics: 1995," published April 9, 2001, www.census.gov/hhes/www/wealth/1995/wealth95.html; U.S. Commission on Civil Rights, *The Economic Stagnation of the Black Middle Class* (Washington, DC, 2005), pp. 7–9.
96. See William J. Wilson, *The Declining Significance of Race* (Chicago: University of Chicago Press, 1978); Ken Auletta, *The Underclass* (New York: Random House, 1982); William J. Wilson, *The Truly Disadvantaged* (Chicago: University of Chicago Press, 1987); and Joe R. Feagin, *Subordinating the Poor* (Englewood Cliffs, NJ: Prentice Hall, 1975), p. 22.
97. Joe R. Feagin, *Racist America* (New York: Routledge, 2000); Joe R. Feagin, *Systemic Racism: A Theory of Oppression* (New York: Routledge, 2006).
98. Quillian, "New Approaches to Understanding Racial Prejudice and Discrimination," p. 306; see also Fair Housing Council of Fresno County, "Audit Uncovers Blatant Discrimination Against Hispanics, African Americans and Families with Children in Fresno County," press release, Fresno, CA, October 6, 1997.
99. Shanna L. Smith and Cathy Clous, "Documenting Discrimination by Homeowners Insurance Companies Through Testing," in *Insurance Redlining: Disinvestment, Reinvestment, and the Evolving Role of Financial Institutions*, ed. Gregory D. Squires (Washington, DC: Urban Institute, 1997), pp. 106–117; "Housing Segregation Background Report: Brooklyn, New York," National Fair Housing Alliance, New York, New York, October 2006, pp. 2–3.
100. Isabel Wilkerson, "The Tallest Fence: Feelings on Race in a White Neighborhood," *The New York Times*, June 21, 1992, sec. 1, p. 18.
101. Franklin, *From Slavery to Freedom*, pp. 252–253; Chuck Stone, *Black Political Power in America*, rev. ed. (New York: Dell, 1970), pp. 30–31.
102. Stetson Kennedy, *After Appomattox: How the South Won the War* (Gainesville: University Press of Florida, 1995), p. 3; see also Cedric J. Robinson, *Black Movements*

in America (New York: Routledge, 1997), pp. 86–88. We draw in this section on Feagin, *Racist America*, pp. 57–58.

103. *Plessy* v. *Ferguson*, 163 U.S. 551–552.
104. Hanes Walton, Jr., *Black Politics* (Philadelphia: Lippincott, 1972), pp. 100, 119.
105. Chandler Davidson and Bernard Grofman, "The Voting Rights Act and the Second Reconstruction," in *The Quiet Revolution in the South* (Princeton, NJ: Princeton University Press, 1994), p. 386; the data here are from the Joint Center for Political and Economic Studies, http://nuance.dhs.org/ibotalk/0012/0083.html (retrieved May 3, 2001).
106. Chandler Davidson, *Minority Vote Dilution: An Overview*, Reprint 85-1 (Houston, TX: Institute for Policy Analysis, Rice University, 1985), pp. 17–18; Frank R. Parker, *Black Votes Count* (Chapel Hill: University of North Carolina Press, 1990); Davidson, *Minority Vote Dilution*, pp. 17–18.
107. Davidson, *Minority Vote Dilution*, pp. 17–18.
108. Earl Ofari Hutchinson, "Bamboozled at the Voting Booth," *Mother Jones,* November 16, 2000, www.motherjones.com/reality_check/bamboozled.html (retrieved May 3, 2001).
109. William E. Forbath, "Civil Rights, Economic Justice, and the Meaning of the Guinier Affair," *Legal Times*, June 28, 1993, p. 21; Michael Isikoff, "Readings in Controversy: Guinier's Pivotal Articles," *The Washington Post*, June 4, 1993, p. A10; Lani Guinier, *The Tyranny of the Majority: Fundamental Fairness and Representation Democracy* (New York: The Free Press, 1994).
110. Quotes are from James W. Button, *Blacks and Social Change* (Princeton, NJ: Princeton University Press, 1989), pp. 226–227.
111. Data are from the Joint Center for Political and Economic Studies, personal communication, 1995.
112. Myrdal, *An American Dilemma*, 1:503; Raymond Wolters, *Negroes and the Great Depression* (Westport, CT: Greenwood Press, 1970), p. xi and elsewhere.
113. Congressional Black Caucus, *Directory of the 104th Congress* (Washington, DC, 1995).
114. Stone, *Black Political Power in America*, pp. 68–72.
115. Ibid., p. 47. Cf. Henry L. Moon, *Balance of Power* (Garden City, NY: Doubleday, 1948).
116. Kevin Phillips, *The Emerging Republican Majority* (New Rochelle, NY: Arlington House, 1969); Joe R. Feagin, "White Elephant: Race and Electoral Politics in Texas," *Texas Observer*, August 23, 1991, pp. 15–16.
117. We draw here on Feagin, *Systemic Racism*, p. 257, and on David A. Bositis, "Blacks and the 2004 Republican National Convention," Joint Center for Political and Economic Studies, Washington, DC, 2004, pp. 1—10.
118. Feagin and Hahn, *Ghetto Revolts*, pp. 81–85; Loren Miller, *The Petitioners* (New York: Random House, 1966), pp. 250–256; see also Mitchell and Feagin, "America's Racial–Ethnic Cultures," pp. 65–86
119. Miller, *The Petitioners*, pp. 260–347.
120. Lerone Bennett, Jr., *Confrontation: Black and White* (Baltimore, MD: Penguin, 1966), pp. 164–169.
121. Ibid., pp. 223–234; Bryan T. Downes and Stephen W. Burks, "The Historical Development of the Black Protest Movement," in *Blacks in the United States*, ed. Norval D. Glenn and Charles Bonjean (San Francisco: Chandler, 1969), pp. 322–344.
122. Feagin and Hahn, *Ghetto Revolts*, pp. 92–94; Bennett, *Confrontation*, pp. 234–237; Inge P. Bell, *CORE and the Strategy of Nonviolence* (New York: Random House, 1968), pp. 13–16.
123. Aldon Morris, *The Origins of the Civil Rights Movement* (New York: The Free Press, 1984).
124. U.S. Commission on Civil Rights, *The Federal Civil Rights Enforcement Effort: Fiscal Year 1983* (Washington, DC, 1982), pp. 5–7; Andrew Rosenthal, "Reagan Hints Rights Leaders Exaggerate Racism to Preserve Cause," *The New York Times*, January 14, 1989, p. 8.
125. Joe R. Feagin and Hernan Vera, *White Racism: The Basics* (New York: Routledge, 1995), pp. 52–57.
126. Office of Civil Rights Evaluation, U.S. Commission on Civil Rights, *Redefining Rights in America; The Civil Rights Record of the George W. Bush Administration, 2001–2004*, www.thememoryhole.org/pol/usccr_redefining_rights.pdf (April 12, 2005); see Law Librarian Blog, "One Step Closer to Book Burning," http://lawprofessors.typepad.com/law_librarian_blog/2005/02/one_step_closer.html (retrieved September 25, 2006).
127. Michael H. Cottman, "7th State of the Black Union Gathers but HUD's Alphonso Jackson Misses It," February 27, 2006, www.blackamericaweb.com/site.aspx/bawnews/stateofblackunion227; and Sheila D. Collins, *The Rainbow Challenge* (New York: Monthly Review Press, 1986), pp. 128–143.
128. Collins, *Black Feminist Thought*.
129. Franklin, *From Slavery to Freedom*, pp. 280–281; Myrdal, *An American Dilemma*, 1:337–344; Henry A. Bullock, *A History of Negro Education in the South* (New York: Praeger, 1967), pp. 1–99.
130. Bullock, *A History of Negro Education in the South*, pp. 170–186; Franklin, *From Slavery to Freedom*, pp. 284–286.
131. See U.S. Bureau of the Census, *We the People: Blacks in the United States* (Washington, DC, 2006), p. 10; U.S. Bureau of the Census, *Statistical Abstract of the United States 1993*, p. 152; and discussion of education below.
132. Bullock, *A History of Negro Education in the South*, pp. 211–212, 225–230; Miller, *The Petitioners*, pp. 347–358.
133. *Milliken* v. *Bradley*, 418 U.S. 717 (1974); *Swann* v. *Charlotte-Mecklenberg Board of Education* 402 U.S. 43

(1971); U.S. Commission on Civil Rights, *Twenty Years After Brown* (Washington, DC, 1975), pp. 11–41.

134. We draw here on Joe R. Feagin, "Heeding Black Voices: The Court, *Brown*, and Challenges in Building a Multiracial Democracy," *University of Pittsburgh Law Review* 66 (Fall 2004): 57–81; see R. A. Mickelson, "The Academic Consequences of Desegregation and Segregation," *North Carolina Law Review* 81 (2003): 1513–1546; see also Joe R. Feagin and Bernice M. Barnett, "Success and Failure: How Systemic Racism Trumped the *Brown v. Board of Education* Decision," *University of Illinois Law Review* 2004 (2004): 1099–1130; Gary Orfield and Susan Eaton, *Dismantling Desegregation: The Quiet Reversal of Brown v. Board of Education* (New York: The Free Press, 1996); Rethinking Schools Project, *The Return to Separate and Unequal* (Milwaukee: Rethinking Schools Project, 2001); J. H. Braddock and T. M. Eitle, "The Effects of School Desegregation," unpublished manuscript, University of Miami, n.d.

135. Quoted in William H. Freivogel, "Black, White, and Brown: Desegregation Ruling Established a Legal Landmark, Unkept Promises," *St. Louis Post-Dispatch*, May 15, 1994, p. 1B.

136. John R. Logan, Choosing Segregation: Racial Imbalance in American Public Schools, 1990–2000, unpublished research report, Lewis Mumford Center, University at Albany, Albany, NY, March 29, 2002, n.p.

137. Gary Orfield and Chugmei Lee, *Racial Transformation and the Changing Nature of Segregation* (Cambridge, MA: Harvard Civil Rights Project, 2006), pp. 6–12.

138. Gail Russell Chaddock, "U.S. Schools Slip Back Toward Segregation," *The Christian Science Monitor*, July 18, 2001, www.csmonitor.com; Brett Lane, "Choice Matters: Policy Alternatives and Implications for Charter Schools," Northwest Regional Educational Laboratory, www.nwrel.org/charter/policy.html (retrieved October 3, 2006).

139. Orfield and Lee, *Racial Transformation and the Changing Nature of Segregation*, p. 32.

140. New York ACORN Schools Office, *Secret Apartheid: A Report on Racial Discrimination Against Black and Latino Parents and Children in the New York City Public Schools* (New York: ACORN, 1996), p. 2.

141. Roslyn A. Mickelson, "The Academic Consequences of Desegregation and Segregation: Evidence from the Charlotte-Mecklenberg Schools," *North Carolina Law Review* 81 (2003): 1513–1529.

142. Amy Stuart Wells, Robert L. Crain, and Susan Uchitelle, *Stepping over the Color Line: African American Students in White Suburban Schools* (New Haven, CT: Yale University Press, 1997).

143. St. Louis City School District, "2004-05 School Accountability Report Card," http://dese.missouri.gov/planning/profile/arsd115115.html (retrieved October 3, 2006); Orfield and Lee, *Racial Transformation and the Changing Nature of Segregation*, p. 38.

144. We draw here on Feagin, "Heeding Black Voices," pp. 76–80; see also Juan Williams, "The Seduction of Segregation, and Why King's Dream Still Matters," *The Washington Post*, January 16, 1994, p. C1.

145. Gary Orfield, as quoted in George J. Church, "The Boom Towns," *Time*, June 15, 1987, p. 17.

146. "Black Students and Educational Aspirations," *Race Relations Reporter*, August 15, 1994, p. 1; U.S. Census Bureau, "School Enrollment, October 2000, Social and Economic Characteristics of Students, Table 13: Enrollment and Employment Status of Recent High School Graduates 16 to 24 Years Old, by Type of School, Attainment Level for People Not Enrolled, Sex, Race, and Hispanic Origin," published June 1, 2001, www.census.gov/population/www/socdemo/school.html.

147. U.S. Department of Education, "Action Plan for Higher Education: Improving Accessibility, Affordability and Accountability," published September 2006, www.ed.gov/about/bdscomm/list/hiedfuture/actionplan-factsheet.html.

148. Mary Jordan, "Black College Enrollment Up," *The Washington Post*, January 20, 1992, p. A14; "Is the Dream Over?" *Newsweek on Campus*, February 1987, pp. 10–14.

149. Komanduri S. Murty and Julian B. Roebuck, "The Case for Historically Black Colleges and Universities," *Journal of Social and Behavioral Sciences* 36 (1992): 177–178.

150. Joe R. Feagin, Hernan Vera, and Nikitah Imani, *The Agony of Education* (New York: Routledge, 1996), p. 55.

151. Stampp, *The Peculiar Institution*, pp. 156–162; Aptheker, *American Negro Slave Revolts*, pp. 56–60.

152. Stuckey, *Slave Culture*, p. 27; James Scott, *Domination and the Arts of Resistance* (New Haven, CT: Yale University Press, 1990).

153. Richard C. Wade, *Slavery in the Cities* (New York: Oxford University Press, 1964), pp. 161–163; Winthrop Jordan, *White over Black* (Baltimore: Penguin, 1969), pp. 422–425.

154. E. Franklin Frazier, *The Negro Church in America* (New York: Schocken Books, 1964), pp. 35–39; Myrdal, *An American Dilemma*, 2:938–939; E. U. Essien-Udom, *Black Nationalism* (New York: Dell, 1964).

155. Quoted in Michael Hirsley, "Churches Are Sources of Power," *Chicago Tribune*, February 5, 1992, p. C6.

156. Frazier, *The Negro Church in America*, p. 44; Joseph R. Washington, Jr., *Black Religion* (Boston: Beacon Press, 1964), pp. 2–29; David L. Lewis, *King* (Baltimore: Penguin, 1970), p. 390.

157. We draw here on research by Bonnie Mitchell for Mitchell and Feagin, "America's Non-European Cultures."
158. Joe Klein, "Can Colin Powell Save America?" *Newsweek*, October 10, 1994, p. 26.
159. U.S. Bureau of the Census, *We the People: Blacks in the United States*, p. 7.
160. John R. Logan and Glenn Deane, *Black Diversity in Metropolitan America* (Albany, NY: Lewis Mumford Center, 2003), pp. 4-6.
161. Ibid., pp. 3-6.
162. Personal communication between authors and Professor Yanick St. Jean, September 1994.
163. Felix Robert Masud-Piloto, *With Open Arms: Cuban Migration to the U.S.* (Totowa, NJ: Rowman & Littlefield, 1988), pp. 111–125; see also Paul Farmer, *The Uses of Haiti* (Monroe, ME: Common Courage Press, 1994); Amy Wilentz, *The Rainy Season: Haiti Since Duvalier* (New York: Simon & Schuster/Touchstone, 1989).
164. Gwen Ifill, "President Names Black Democrat Advisor on Haiti," *The New York Times*, May 9, 1994, p. A1; Eric Schmitt, "Tents for Haitians Rise Again at Guantánamo," *The New York Times*, July 2, 1994, p. 1.
165. Testimony of Steven David Forester, Esq., Senate Foreign Relations Committee Hearing on the "Success and Challenges of United States Policy to Haiti," July 15, 2003, http://foreign.senate.gov/testimony/2003/ForesterTestimony030715.pdf (retrieved October 3, 2006).
166. U.S. Bureau of the Census, *1990 Census of Population: Social and Economic Characteristics: United States*, p. 45; U.S. Bureau of the Census, *1990 Census of Population: Ancestry of the Population in the United States*, p. 393; U.S. Bureau of the Census, *1990 Census of Population: Ancestry of the Population in the United States*, p. 394; Mary C. Waters, "Ethnic and Racial Identities of Second Generation Black Immigrants in New York City," *International Migration Review* 28 (Winter 1994): 795–820; Ramón Grosfoguel and Chloe S. Georas, "'Coloniality of Power and Racial Dynamics: Notes Toward a Reinterpretation of Latino Caribbeans in New York City," *Identities: Global Studies in Culture and Power* 7 (2000): 85–125.
167. Barbara J. Fields, "Ideology and Race in American History," in *Region, Race, and Reconstruction: Essays in Honor of C. Vann Woodward*, ed. J. Morgan Kousser and James M. McPherson (New York: Oxford University Press, 1982), p. 146.
168. Waters, "Ethnic and Racial Identities of Second Generation Black Immigrants in New York City."
169. Personal communication between authors and Yanick St. Jean, September 1994; Waters, "Ethnic and Racial Identities of Second Generation Black Immigrants in New York City."
170. Personal communication between authors and Yanick St. Jean, September 1994.
171. Paul Farmer, *AIDS and Accusation* (Berkeley: University of California Press, 1992), pp. 215–226.
172. Milton Gordon, *Assimilation in American Life* (New York: Oxford University Press, 1964), p. 78.
173. Talcott Parsons, "Full Citizenship for the Negro American? A Sociological Problem," in *The Negro American*, ed. Talcott Parsons and Kenneth B. Clark (Boston: Houghton Mifflin, 1965), p. 740; see also pp. 714–715.
174. Nathan Glazer, *Affirmative Discrimination* (New York: Basic Books, 1975), pp. 40–76; Daniel P. Moynihan, *The Negro Family* (Washington, DC: U.S. Government Printing Office, 1965); Frazier, *The Negro Church in America*; Myrdal, *An American Dilemma.*
175. Robert Blauner, *Racial Oppression in America* (New York: Harper & Row, 1972), pp. 51–110.
176. Wade, *Slavery in the Cities*, pp. 273–275; Herman D. Bloch, *The Circle of Discrimination* (New York: New York University Press, 1969), pp. ix–xiii.
177. Wilhelm, *Who Needs the Negro?*; Robert L. Allen, *Black Awakening in Capitalist America* (Garden City, NY: Doubleday/Anchor Books, 1970), pp. 4–6; *Report of the National Advisory Commission on Civil Disorders* (New York: Bantam, 1968), pp. 278–279.
178. Marimba Ani, *Yurugu: An African-Centered Critique of European Cultural Thought and Behavior* (Trenton, NJ: Africa World Press, 1994), pp. 567–569.
179. Feagin and Sikes, *Living with Racism*, p. vii; on the health costs of racial discrimination, see David R. Williams, Harold W. Neighbors, and James S. Jackson, "Racial/Ethnic Discrimination and Health: Findings from Community Studies," *American Journal of Public Health* 93 (February 2003): 200–208.

Chapter 8

1. Juan Gonzalez, *Harvest of Empire: A History of Latinos in America* (New York: Penguin Books, 2000), p. xii; Ruben Navarrette, "Calm Down, It's Not an Assault on America," Realclearpolitics Blog, May 03, 2006, www.realclearpolitics.com/articles/2006/05/calm_down_its_not_an_assault_o.html (retrieved October 26, 2006).
2. U.S. Census Bureau, "The Hispanic Population," Census 2000 Brief, May 2001, pp. 1–2, www.census.gov/prod/cen2000.
3. Edward Múrguía, "On Latino/Hispanic Ethnic Identity," *Latino Studies Journal* 2, no. 3 (September 1991): 8–18.
4. "Hispanics: A People in Motion," research report, Pew Hispanic Center, Washington, DC, January 2005, p. 3.

5. Teresa L. Amott and Julie A. Matthaei, *Race, Gender, and Work* (Boston: South End Press, 1991), pp. 64–67.
6. Américo Paredes, *With His Pistol in His Hand* (Austin: University of Texas Press, 1958), pp. 3–14; Rodolfo Acuña, *Occupied America* (San Francisco: Canfield Press, 1972), pp. 10–12.
7. Acuña, *Occupied America*, p. 15; S. Dale McLemore, "The Origin of Mexican American Subordination in Texas," *Social Science Quarterly* 53 (March 1973): 665–667; Rodolfo Alvarez, "The Psycho-Historical and Socioeconomic Development of the Chicano Community in the United States," *Social Science Quarterly* 53 (March 1973): 925; David Montejano, *Anglos and Mexicans in the Making of Texas, 1836–1986* (Austin: University of Texas Press, 1987).
8. William Lord, "Myths and Realities of the Alamo," *American West* 5 (May 1968): 20–25.
9. Carl N. Degler, *Out of Our Past* (New York: Harper, 1959), pp. 109–110; Acuña, *Occupied America*, pp. 23–29.
10. Joan Moore and Harry Pachon, *Hispanics in the United States* (Englewood Cliffs, NJ: Prentice Hall, 1985), pp. 18, 22–23; Leo Grebler, Joan W. Moore, and Ralph G. Guzmán, *The Mexican-American People* (New York: The Free Press, 1970), pp. 43–44; Acuña, *Occupied America*, p. 105; Joan W. Moore, "Colonialism: The Case of the Mexican Americans," *Social Problems* 17 (Spring 1970): 468–469.
11. Moore and Pachon, *Hispanics in the United States*, p. 21; Ellwyn R. Stoddard, *Mexican Americans* (New York: Random House, 1973), pp. 9–13; Carey McWilliams, *North from Mexico* (New York: Greenwood Press, 1968), pp. 70–76; Acuña, *Occupied America*, pp. 60–62; Grebler, Moore, and Guzmán, *The Mexican American People*, pp. 43–44; Nancie L. Gonzales, *The Spanish-Americans of New Mexico* (Albuquerque: University of New Mexico Press, 1967), pp. 204–210.
12. Alvarez, "Psycho-Historical and Socioeconomic Development," p. 925.
13. Oscar J. Martinez, "On the Size of the Chicano Population: New Estimates: 1850–1900," *Aztlán* 6 (Spring 1975): 55–56; U.S. Department of Justice, Immigration and Naturalization Service, *Annual Report* (Washington, DC, 1975), pp. 62–64; Julian Samora, *Los Mojados: The Wetback Story* (Notre Dame, IN: University of Notre Dame Press, 1971), pp. 7–8.
14. Leo Grebler, *Mexican Immigration to the United States: The Record and Its Implications* (Los Angeles: UCLA Mexican-American Study Project, 1965), pp. 20–21.
15. Mark Reisler, *By the Sweat of Their Brow: Mexican Immigrant Labor in the United States, 1900–1940* (Westport, CT: Greenwood Press, 1976); Grebler, *Mexican Immigration to the United States*, pp. 23–24; Manuel Gamio, *Mexican Immigration to the United States* (New York: Dover, 1971), pp. 171–174; Ronald Takaki, *A Different Mirror* (Boston: Little, Brown, 1993), pp. 326–334.
16. Samora, *Los Mojados*, pp. 48–52.
17. Gilberto Cardenas, "United States Immigration Policy Toward Mexico," *Chicano Law Review* 2 (Summer 1975): 73–75; Grebler, *Mexican Immigration to the United States*, p. 26.
18. Samora, *Los Mojados*, pp. 18–19, 24–25, 44–46, 57; Joan Moore, *Mexican Americans*, 2nd ed. (Englewood Cliffs, NJ: Prentice Hall, 1976), pp. 49–51; Strategy Research Corporation, *1991 U.S. Hispanic Market* (Miami: Strategy Research Corporation, 1991), pp. 39, 51.
19. Cardenas, "United States Immigration Policy Toward Mexico," pp. 84–85; Cheryl Anderson, "Immigration Bill Under Attack on Several Fronts," *Austin American-Statesman*, December 12, 1982, p. C1.
20. Luis Alberto Urrea, *By the Lake of Sleeping Children: The Secret Life of the Mexican Border* (New York: Anchor Books), 1996, p. 18; see also Ann V. Millard and Jorge Chapa, *Apple Pie and Enchiladas: Latino Newcomers in the Rural Midwest* (Austin: University of Texas Press, 2004).
21. See Ilan Stavans, *The Hispanic Condition: Reflections on Culture and Identity in America* (New York: HarperCollins, 1995).
22. Ibid., p. 22.
23. See Gonzalez, *Harvest of Empire*, pp. 234–236.
24. Michael Fix and Jeffrey S. Passel, *Immigration and Immigrants: Setting the Record Straight* (Washington, DC: Urban Institute, 1994), p. 24.
25. Jeffrey S. Passel, "Estimates of the Size and Characteristics of the Undocumented Population," research report, Pew Hispanic Center, Washington, DC, March 2005, p. 1; Leo R. Chávez, *Shadowed Lives: Undocumented Immigrants in American Society* (Orlando, FL: Harcourt Brace Jovanovich, 1992), pp. 19–151.
26. Douglas S. Massey, "Five Myths About Immigration," *Immigration Policy in Focus* 4 (August 2005), p. 1; Fix and Passel, *Immigration and Immigrants*, pp. 24–25, 51, 60, 62, 71, 81.
27. Stephen Koepp, "Rotten Shame: Who Will Pick the Crops?" *Time*, June 22, 1987, p. 49.
28. Jacqueline Maria Hagan and Susan González Baker, "Implementing the U.S. Legalization Program," *International Migration Review* 27 (Fall 1993): 514; Susan González Baker and Frank Bean, "The Legalization Programs of the 1986 Immigration Reform and Control Act," in *In Defense of the Alien*, ed. Lydio F. Tomasi (New York: Center for Migration Studies, 1990), pp. 3–11; Susan González Baker, *The Cautious Welcome: The Legalization Programs of the Immigration Reform and Control Act* (Washington, DC: Urban Institute, 1990); data provided by Demographics Statistics Branch, Immigration and Naturalization Service, January 1995.

29. Jose A. Pagan and Alberto Davila, "On-the-Job Training, Immigration Reform, and the True Wages of Native Male Workers," *Industrial Relations* 35 (January 1996): 45–58.
30. Lisa Lollock, *The Foreign Born Population in the United States: March 2000*, Current Population Reports, P20-534, (Washington, DC: U.S. Census Bureau, 2001); Karen A. Woodrow and Jeffrey S. Passel, "Post-IRCA Undocumented Immigration to the United States," in *Undocumented Migration to the United States*, ed. Frank Bean, Barry Edmonston, and Jeffrey Passel (Santa Monica, CA: Rand Corporation, 1990), p. 42.
31. Quoted from *The Los Angeles Times* in Donaldo Macedo, "Foreword," in Enrique T. Trueba, *Latinos Unidos: From Cultural Diversity to the Politics of Solidarity* (Lanham, MD: Rowman & Littlefield, 1999), pp. xviii–xix.
32. Lynda Gorov, "Poor Immigrants Face New Hurdles," *Boston Globe*, November 30, 1997, p. A1.
33. "Major Provisions of 'The Secure Fence Act of 2006,'" Justice for Immigrants, Press Release, www.justiceforimmigrants.org/HR6061.html (retrieved October 22, 2006); "Fencing in Immigration Reform," American Friends Service Committee, Press Release, www.afsc.org/news/2006/fencing-in-immigration-reform.htm (retrieved October 22, 2006).
34. Rakesh Kochhar, "Latino Labor Report," research report, Pew Hispanic Center, Washington, DC, September 27, 2006, p. 7; see also Gonzalez, *Harvest of Empire*, p. 197.
35. Quotations are from Arnoldo De León, "Initial Contacts: Niggers, Redskins, and Greasers," in *The Latino/a Condition: A Critical Reader*, ed. Richard Delgado and Jean Stefancic (New York: New York University Press, 1998), p. 161.
36. Quoted in Philip D. Ortego, "The Chicano Renaissance," in *Introduction to Chicano Studies*, ed. Livie I. Duran and H. Russell Bernard (New York: Macmillan, 1973), p. 337.
37. Ricardo Romo, *East Lost Angeles: History of a Barrio* (Austin: University of Texas Press, 1983), pp. 89–111.
38. Cardenas, "United States Immigration Policy Toward Mexico," pp. 70–71.
39. Quoted in Ralph Guzmán, "The Function of Anglo-American Racism in the Political Development of Chicanos," in *La Causa Politica*, ed. F. Chris Garcia (South Bend, IN: University of Notre Dame Press, 1974), p. 22.
40. McWilliams, *North from Mexico*, p. 213.
41. William Sheldon, "Educational Research and Statistics: The Intelligence of Mexican-American Children," in *In Their Place*, ed. Lewis H. Carlson and George A. Colburn (New York: John Wiley, 1972), pp. 149–151.
42. Quoted in Guillermo V. Flores, "Race and Culture in the Internal Colony: Keeping the Chicano in His Place," in "Structures of Dependency," ed. Frank Bonilla and Robert Girling. Manuscript, research seminar, Stanford, CA, 1973, p. 194.
43. Quoted in George A. Martinez, "Mexican Americans and Whiteness," in *The Latino/a Condition*, p. 178.
44. Quoted in Otto Santa Ana, "'Like an Animal I Was Treated': Anti-Immigrant Metaphor in U.S. Public Discourse," *Discourse & Society* 10 (1994): 220.
45. Octavio Ignacio Romano, "The Anthropology and Sociology of the Mexican-Americans," *El Grito* 2 (Fall 1968): 13–19; Oscar Lewis, *Five Families* (New York: John Wiley, 1962); William Madsen, *Mexican Americans of South Texas* (New York: Holt, Rinehart & Winston, 1964).
46. G. Marin, "Stereotyping Hispanics," *International Journal of Intercultural Relations* 8 (1984): 17–27.
47. On the issues in these paragraphs see, generally, Américo Paredes, *With His Pistol in His Hand*; Romano, "The Anthropology and Sociology of the Mexican Americans"; Stoddard, *Mexican Americans*, pp. 42–44; Lea Ybarra, "Empirical and Theoretical Developments in the Study of the Chicano Family," in *The State of Chicano Research on Family, Labor, and Migration*, ed. Armando Valdez, Albert Camarillo, and Tomás Almaguer (Stanford, CA: Stanford Center for Chicano Research, 1983), p. 96.
48. Linda A. Jackson, "Stereotypes, Emotions, Behavior, and Overall Attitudes Toward Hispanics by Anglos," Research Report 10, Julian Samora Research Institute, Michigan State University, East Lansing, MI, January 1995, www.jsri.msu/RandS/research/irr/rr10.htm (retrieved June 9, 2001).
49. National Conference of Christians and Jews, *Taking America's Pulse: The National Conference Survey on Inter-Group Relations* (New York: National Conference, 1994).
50. Charles N. Weaver, "Work Attitudes of Mexican Americans," *Hispanic Journal of Behavioral Sciences* 22 (August 2000): 275–295.
51. "America's Immigration Quandary: No Consensus on Immigration Problem or Proposed Fixes," research report, Pew Hispanic Center, Washington, DC, March 30, 2006, pp. 1–4.
52. James H. Johnson, Jr., Karen D. Johnson-Webb, and Walter C. Farrell, Jr., "A Profile of Hispanic Newcomers to North Carolina," *Popular Government* 65 (Fall 1999): 2–12.
53. "Blood on the Border," *Intelligence Report* (Southern Poverty Law Center), Spring 2001, pp. 8–11; Navarrette, "Calm Down, It's Not an Assault on America."

54. Samuel P. Huntington, "The Erosion of American National Interests," Foreign Affairs (September/October 1997), p. 28ff.
55. Joe Kelly and Stacy L. Smith, "Generally Movies Give Boys a D: Portraying Males as Dominant, Disconnected and Dangerous," research report, Duluth, Minnesota, Dadsanddaughters.org, 2006, p. 4; National Council of La Raza, "Distorted Reality: Hispanic Characters in TV Entertainment," September 1994. See also Gregory Freeman, *Crisis*, October 1994, p. 5; Travis L. Dixon and Daniel Linz, "Overrepresentation and Underrepresentation of African Americans and Latinos as Lawbreakers on Television News," *Journal of Communication* 50 (2000): 131–135; Children Now and National Hispanic Foundation for the Arts, "Latinos on Prime Time: 2001-02 Prime Time Television Season," 2002, http://72.14.209.104/search?q=cache:x880r4C_busJ:www.hispanicarts.org/Media/LatinosonPrimeTimeIII.pdf+%22latinos+on+prime+time%22+2001-2002&hl=en&gl=us&ct=clnk&cd=1 (retrieved November 13, 2006).
56. Ansel Martinez, "Study Shows Television Shows Stereotype Hispanics," *All Things Considered* (Washington, DC: National Public Radio), September 10, 1994.
57. Marco Portales, *Crowding Out Latinos: Mexican Americans in the Public Consciousness* (Philadelphia: Temple University Press, 2000), p. 101.
58. Ibid., p. 31.
59. Santa Ana, "'Like an Animal I Was Treated'", pp. 194–220; see also Otto Santa Ana, *Brown Tide Rising: Metaphors of Latinos in Contemporary American Public Discourse* (Austin: University of Texas Press, 2002). We draw on a foreword for this volume.
60. Jane H. Hill, "Mock Spanish: A Site for the Indexical Reproduction of Racism in American English," unpublished research paper, University of Arizona, Tucson, 1995.
61. Rosina Lippi-Green, *English with an Accent* (New York: Routledge, 1997), pp. 238–239.
62. David E. López and Ricardo D. Stanton-Salazar, "Mexican Americans: A Second Generation at Risk," in *Ethnicities: Children of Immigrants in America*, ed. Rubén Rumbaut and Alejandro Portes (Berkeley: University of California Press, 2001), pp. 57-90.
63. Joe R. Feagin and Danielle Dirks, "'Who Is White?': College Students' Assessments of Key U.S. Racial and Ethnic Groups," unpublished research manuscript, Texas A&M University, College Station, TX, 2006; "Reaction to Lou Dobbs Town Hall on Broken Borders," MyDD, www.mydd.com/story/2006/10/27/112734/61 (retrieved October 27, 2006).
64. Ariela J. Gross, "Texas Mexicans and the Politics of Whiteness," *Law and History Review* 21 (Spring 2003), www.historycooperative.org/journals/lhr/21.1/comment_gross.html (Retrieved October 30, 2006); the survey is in Tatcho Mindiola, Néstor Rodríguez, and Yolanda Flores Niemann, "Intergroup Relations Between African Americans and Hispanics in Harris County," unpublished research report, Center for Mexican American Studies, University of Houston, 1996; Pew Hispanic Center/Kaiser Family Foundation, "2002 National Survey of Latinos," research report, Washington, DC, December 2002, pp. 32–33.
65. U.S. Census Bureau, "Overview of Race and Hispanic Origin," Census 2000 Brief, March 2001, pp. 2–5, www.census.gov/prod/cen2000.
66. E. J. Hobsbawm, *Primitive Rebels* (New York: W. W. Norton, 1959), pp. 15–16; Paredes, *With His Pistol in His Hand*, pp. 27–32; McWilliams, *North from Mexico*, p. 127; Moore, "Colonialism," p. 466; Stoddard, *Mexican Americans*, p. 181.
67. Ralph H. Turner and Lewis M. Killian, *Collective Behavior* (Englewood Cliffs, NJ: Prentice Hall, 1957), pp. 125–128; McWilliams, *North from Mexico*, pp. 229–238.
68. Navarrette, "Calm Down, It's Not an Assault on America."
69. Armondo Morales, *Ando Sangrando* (Fair Lawn, NJ: R. E. Burdick, 1972), pp. 100–108.
70. U.S. Commission on Civil Rights, *Mexican Americans and the Administration of Justice in the Southwest* (Washington, DC, 1970), pp. 6–10; Robert Lee Maril, *Poorest of Americans* (South Bend, IN: University of Notre Dame Press, 1989), p. 52; Andrea Ford and Sheryl Stolberg, "Latinos Tell Panel of Anger at Police Conduct," *The Los Angeles Times*, May 21, 1991, p. A1.
71. Patrick J. McDonnell, "Latinos Recover Optimism Lost in '90s," *The Los Angeles Times*, March 11, 2001.
72. Raymond Smith, "The Chase and Beating Incident," *Press-Enterprise* (Riverside, CA), March 30, 1997, p. B1.
73. Antonio H. Rodríguez and Carlos A. Chávez, "Latinos Unite in Self-Defense on Proposition 187," *The Los Angeles Times*, October 21, 1994, p. B7; Beth Shuster and Chip Johnson, "Hundreds of Students Stage Walkouts to Protest Proposition 187," *The Los Angeles Times*, October 21, 1994, p. B3; Frank Trejo, "Thousands of Hispanics March in Washington; Texas Residents Join Call for End to Discrimination, Rights Abuses," *Dallas Morning News*, October 13, 1996, p. 1.
74. Andrew Gumbel, "A Million Turn out for Proimmigration March in Los Angeles," *The Independent*, March 27, 2006, www.findarticles.com/p/articles/mi_qn4158/is_20060327/ai_n16175884 (retrieved October 17, 2006); Robert Suro and Gabriel Escobar, "2006 National Survey of Latinos: The Immigration Debate," research report, Pew Hispanic Center,

Washington, DC, July 2006, pp. 8—9; and William I. Robinson, "'Aqui estamos y no nos vamos!' Global Capital and Immigrant Rights," *Race & Class* 48 (2006): 77–91.

75. Abel G. Rubio, *Stolen Heritage* (Austin, TX: Eakin Press, 1986); Clark Knowlton, "Recommendations for the Solution of Land Tenure Problems Among the Spanish Americans," in *Chicano: The Evolution of a People*, ed. Renato Rosaldo, Robert A. Calvert, and Gustav L. Seligmann (San Francisco: Rinehart Press, 1973), pp. 334–335; George I. Sánchez, *Forgotten People* (Albuquerque: University of New Mexico Press, 1940), p. 61; Arnoldo Deleón, *The Tejano Community, 1836–1900* (Albuquerque: University of New Mexico Press, 1982), pp. 63–91.
76. Tomas Almaguer, "Historical Notes on Chicano Oppression: The Dialectics of Racial and Class Domination in North America," *Atzlán* 5 (Spring–Fall 1974): 38–39; Richard del Castillo, "Myth and Reality: Chicano Economic Mobility in Los Angeles, 1850–1880," *Atzlán* 6 (Summer 1975): 153–154; Charles Wollenberg, "Huelga, 1928 Style: The Imperial Valley Canteloupe Workers' Strike," in *Chicano*, ed. Rosaldo, Calvert, and Seligmann, pp. 185–188; Amott and Matthaei, *Race, Gender, and Work*, pp. 76–77.
77. Samora, *Los Mojados*, p. 130; Grebler, Moore, and Guzmán, *The Mexican-American People*, p. 91.
78. Ruth H. Tuck, *Not with the Fist* (New York: Harcourt, Brace & World, 1946), pp. 173–183; Anne Brunton, "The Chicano Migrants," in *Introduction to Chicano Studies*, ed. Duran and Bernard, pp. 489–492; McWilliams, *North from Mexico*, pp. 217–218.
79. Roberto Suro, "Border Boom's Dirty Residue Imperils U.S.–Mexico Trade," *The New York Times*, March 31, 1991, p. 1; Patrick McDonnell, "Foreign-Owned Companies Add to Mexico's Pollution," *The Los Angeles Times*, November 18, 1991, p. A1; Richard W. Stevenson, "Economic Scene: The Hidden Costs of Mexico Plants," *The New York Times*, July 19, 1991, p. D2; Judy Pasternak, "Firms Find a Haven from U.S. Environmental Rules," *The Los Angeles Times*, November 19, 1991, p. A1; Patrick McDonnell, "Mexico: Progress and Promise," *The Los Angeles Times*, October 22, 1991, p. 11.
80. Chávez, *Shadowed Lives*, pp. 19, 139–155.
81. Teresa Puente, "When Hope Turns into Slavery," *Chicago Tribune*, August 10, 1997, p. 1C; Pierrette Hondagneu-Sotelo, *Domestica: Immigrant Workers Cleaning and Caring in the Shadows of Affluence* (Berkeley: University of California Press, 2001), p. 210.
82. "A Time for Courage," *Newsday*, April 6, 2001, p. A48.
83. Devah Pager and Bruce Western "Discrimination in Low-Wage Labor Markets: Evidence from an Experimental Audit Study in New York City," research paper, Princeton University, http://72.14.209.104/search?q=cache:hltEuw40fgkJ:paa2005.princeton.edu/download.aspx%3FsubmissionId%3D50874+discrimination+job+Hispanic+testers+matched+cities+research&hl=en&gl=us&ct=clnk&cd=1H (retrieved October 24, 2006).
84. Philip Moss and Chris Tilly, *Stories Employers Tell: Race, Skill, and Hiring in America* (New York: Russell Sage, 2001), pp. 130–150.
85. Millard and Chapa, *Apple Pie and Enchiladas*, p. 5.
86. López and Stanton-Salazar, "Mexican Americans: A Second Generation at Risk," in *Ethnicities*, p. 76.
87. Lawrence D. Bobo and Susah A. Suh, "Surveying Racial Discrimination: Analyses from a Multiethnic Labor Market," in *Prismatic Metropolis: Inequality in Los Angeles*, ed. Lawrence D. Bobo, Melvin L. Oliver, James H. Johnson, Jr., and Abel Valenzuela, Jr. (New York: Russell Sage, 2000) p. 528; John Zogby, John Bruce, and Rebecca Wittman, "Hispanic Perspectives," Zogby International report, June 2004, p. 16; "2006 National Survey of Latinos, pp. 4–5.
88. Jim Doyle, "Court Curbs 'English-Only' Company Rules," *San Francisco Chronicle*, October 5, 1991, p. A12; Juan Perea, "English-Only Rules and the Right to Speak One's Primary Language in the Workplace," *University of Michigan Journal of Law Reform* 23, no. 2 (Winter 1990): 265–318.
89. *Garcia* v. *Gloor* 618 F.2d 264 (5th Cir. 1980), *cert. denied*, 449 U.S. 1113 (1981).
90. *Gutierrez* v. *Municipal Court*, 838 F.2d at 1039, quotations from Perea, "English-Only Rules," pp. 271–272; *Gutierrez* v. *Municipal Court*, *vacated as moot*, 109 S. Ct. 1736 (1989).
91. *Garcia* v. *Spun Steak Co.*, DC NCalif, No. C91-1949 RHS, October 14, 1991; Doyle, "Court Curbs 'English-Only' Company Rules."
92. *Sandoval* v. *Hagan*, 197 F3d 484 (11thCir. 1999); *Alexander* v. *Sandoval*, Case No. 991908, decided April 24, 2001; Lawrence Siegel, The Argument for a Constitutional Right to Communication and Language," *Journal of Deaf Studies and Deaf Education* 7 (2002): 258–266; and Associated Press, "School Settles Bias Suit; Texas University to Pay $2 Million," April 21, 2001.
93. Gilda Laura Ochoa, "Mexican Americans' Attitudes toward and Interactions with Mexican Immigrants: A Qualitative Analysis of Conflict and Cooperation," *Social Science Quarterly* 81 (March 2000): 84–105.
94. U.S. Bureau of the Census, "2005 American Community Survey, American Fact Finder: Selected

Population Profile in the United States," http://factfinder.census.gov (retrieved June 15, 2007); see also U.S. Department of Labor, Bureau of Labor Statistics, "Annual Average Data, Table 6: "Employment Status of the Hispanic or Latino Population by Sex, Age, and Detailed Ethnic Group January 2006," ftp://ftp.bls.gov/pub/special.requests/lf/aat6.txt (retrieved October 17, 2006); U.S. Bureau of the Census, "Historical Income Data—Families, Table F-5. Race and Hispanic Origin of Householder—Families by Median and Mean Income: 1947 to 2004," published December 20, 2005, www.census.gov/hhes/www/income/histinc/f05.html. The data in Table 8.1 are from Office of Personnel Management, www.opm, September 30, 2004.

95. U.S. Bureau of the Census, "2005 American Community Survey, American Fact Finder: Selected Population Profile in the United States," http://factfinder.census.gov (retrieved June 15, 2007); see also U.S. Bureau of the Census, "The Hispanic Population in the United States: 2004," published December 14, 2005, www.census.gov/population/www/socdemo/hispanic/cps2004.html

96. U.S. Bureau of the Census, Asset Ownership of Households, Table 4, Characteristics: 2000, published January 28, 2005, www.census.gov/hhes/www/wealth/1998_2000/wlth00-4.html; Rakesh Kochhar, "The Wealth of Hispanic Households: 1996 to 2002," research report, Pew Hispanic Center, Washington, DC, October 18, 2004, p. 3.

97. López and Stanton-Salazar, "Mexican Americans: A Second Generation at Risk"; Zulema Valdez, "Segmented Assimilation Among Mexicans in the Southwest," *Sociological Quarterly* 47 (2006): 397; Zulema Valdez, "Review of 'Italians Then, Mexicans Now: Immigrant Origins and Second Generation Progress, 1890 to 2000,'" *Contemporary Sociology* 35 (2006), pp. 595—596.

98. Joan Moore and Raquel Pinderhughes, *In the Barrios: Latinos and the Underclass Debate* (New York: Russell Sage, 1993).

99. Avelardo Valdez, "Persistent Poverty, Crime, and Drugs: U.S.–Mexican Border Region," in *In the Barrios: Latinos and the Underclass Debate*, ed. Joan Moore and Raquel Pinderhughes (New York: Sage, 1993), pp. 184–194.

100. Nestor Rodríguez, "Economic Restructuring and Latino Growth in Houston," in *In the Barrios: Latinos and the Underclass Debate*, ed. Moore and Pinderhughes, pp. 101–126; see Edward Telles, "Mexican Americans and the American Nation: A Response to Professor Huntington," *Aztlán* 31 (Fall 2006): 7–23.

101. National Fair Housing Advocate, "Farmworkers Represented by CRLA and the County of Riverside Settle Major Fair Housing Case," www.fairhousing.com/news_archive/releases/crla5-23-00.html (retrieved March 1, 2001).

102. Dan Rozek, "Elgin Denies Housing Bias Against Hispanics," *Chicago Sun-Times*, October 3, 2000, p. 32; "Center Calls for the Rejection of Anti-Immigrant Ordinances," Southern Poverty Law Center Report, September 2006, p. 3.

103. Fair Housing Council of Fresno County, "Audit Uncovers Blatant Discrimination Against Hispanics, African Americans and Families with Children in Fresno County," press release, Fresno, CA, October 6, 1997; San Antonio Fair Housing Council, "San Antonio Metropolitan Area Rental Audit 1997," San Antonio, TX, 1997; Daryl Strickland, "O. C. Business Plus; Yoder-Shrader Settles Housing Bias Suit," *The Los Angeles Times*, August 1, 2000, p. C3.

104. "Hispanics: A People in Motion," p. 7.

105. Moore, *Mexican Americans*, p. 33.

106. *Garza* v. *County of Los Angeles*, 918 F.2d 763; 1990 U.S. App.; *Williams* v. *City of Dallas*, 734 F. Supp. 1317; 1990 U.S. Dist.

107. U.S. Hispanic Leadership Institute, "Latino Vote," www.ushli.org/about_us.html (retrieved October 26, 2006).

108. "Hispanics and the 2006 Election," research report, Pew Hispanic Center, Washington, DC, October 2006, pp. 1–3.

109. Zogby, Bruce, and Wittman, "Hispanic Perspectives," p. 7. Data on officials in these paragraphs are from Juan Gómez-Quiñones, *Chicano Politics: Reality and Promise, 1940–1990* (Albuquerque: University of New Mexico Press, 1990), pp. 167–169, 173; *National Association of Latino Elected and Appointed Officials, National Report* 11, no. 1 (Fourth Quarter 1991): 1, 3; and personal communications with Rodolfo de la Garza and Robert Brischetto. Hector Tobar and Richard Simon, "Molina's First Goal Expand County Board," *The Los Angeles Times*, February 21, 1991, p. A1; Carla Rivera, "Heated Meeting Marks Burke's Debut as Leader," *The Los Angeles Times*, December 8, 1993, p. B3.

110. The National Association of Latino Elected and Appointed Officials Educational Fund, press release, May 9, 2001.

111. Juan Gonzalez, *Harvest of Empire*, p. 169.

112. See Gregory Rodriguez, "Mayoral Election; A Novel Latino Strategy," *The Los Angeles Times*, June 3, 2001, p. M1.

113. Compiled from data on National Association of Latino Elected and Appointed Officials Educational Fund, www.naleo.org.

114. Ibid.; and from U.S. House website.

115. Rodolfo O. de la Garza, Nestor Rodríguez, and Harry Pachon, "The Domestic and Foreign Policy

Consequences of Mexican and Central American Immigration: Mexican-American Perspectives," in *Immigration and International Relations*, ed. Georges Vernes (Santa Monica, CA: Rand Corporation, 1990), pp. 135–147; Kenneth J. Meier and Laurence J. O'Toole, Jr., "Political Control Versus Bureaucratic Values: Reframing the Debate," *Public Administration Review* (March/April 2006): 177–188.

116. Ray Suarez, "Latinos Politics," National Public Radio, *Talk of the Nation*, August 5, 1997; Telles, "Mexican Americans and the American Nation," p. 17.

117. Marjorie Connelly, "The 1994 Elections," *The New York Times*, November 13, 1994, p. 24; Bob Wing, "White Power in Election," *ColorLines*, Spring 2001, www.arc.org/C_Lines/CLArchive (retrieved June 19, 2001); "How Did Latinos Really Vote in 2004?" National Council of La Raza, memorandum, January 15, 2005; "Hispanic Voters Reassessing Ties to Republicans," *Hispanic News*, October 24, 2006, www.hispanic.cc/hispanic_voters_reassessing_ties_to_republicans.htm (retrieved October 27, 2006).

118. *Hernandez* v. *Texas*, 347 U.S. 482 (1954). Cited in Ricardo Romo, "Mexican Americans in the New West," in *The Twentieth-Century West*, ed. Gerald D. Nash and Richard W. Etulian (Albuquerque: University of New Mexico Press, 1989), p. 135.

119. U.S. Commission on Civil Rights, *Mexican Americans and the Administration of Justice in the Southwest*, pp. 79–86; U.S. Bureau of Labor Statistics, Current Population Survey, Table 11, Household Data, www.bls.gov/cps/cpsaat11.pdf (retrieved November 9, 2006).

120. Ibid., pp. 66–69; Robert Walters and Mark Curriden, "A Jury of One's Peers? Investigating Underrepresentation in Jury Venires," *Judge's Journal* 43 (Fall 2004): 17–21; *Hernandez* v. *New York*, 1991, 111 S. Ct. 1859; Juan Perea, "*Hernandez* v. *New York*: Courts, Prosecutors, and the Fear of Spanish," *Hofstra Law Review* 21 (Fall 1992): 1–61.

121. David B. Rottman and Randall M. Hansen, "How Recent Court Users View the State Courts: Perceptions of Whites, African-Americans, and Latinos," http://72.14.209.104/search?q=cache:reUHK336gmIJ:www.flcourts.org/gen_public/family/diversity/bin/perceptions2.pdf+How+Recent+Court+Users+View+the+State+Courts:&hl=en&gl=us&ct=clnk&cd=1 (retrieved October 27, 2006); Police Assessment Resource Center, "Racial Profiling," March 2002, research report, pp. 7–8; Police Assessment Resource Center and Vera Institute of Justice, "Assessing Police-Community Relations in Pasadena, California," Los Angeles, CA, research report, August 2006, p. 70.

122. Romo, "Mexican Americans in the New West," pp. 136–139; Michael V. Miller and James D. Preston, "Vertical Ties and the Redistribution of Power in Crystal City," *Social Science Quarterly* 53 (March 1973): 772–782; John S. Shockley, *Chicano Revolt in a Texas Town* (Notre Dame, IN: University of Notre Dame Press, 1974), pp. 28–148, 162–177; Maril, *Poorest of Americans*, p. 52; Armando Gutiérrez and Herbert Hirsch, "The Militant Challenge to the American Ethos: 'Chicanos' and the 'Mexican Americans,'" *Social Science Quarterly* 53 (March 1973): 844–845; Carlos Muñoz, Jr., *Youth, Identity, Power: The Chicano Movement* (New York: Verso, 1989); Ignacio M. Garcia, *United We Win* (Tucson: University of Arizona Press, 1989), pp. 228–231.

123. Marta Cotera, "Feminism, the Chicana and Anglo Versions," in *Twice a Minority*, ed. Margarita B. Melville (St. Louis: C. V. Mosby, 1980), p. 231; see also Amott and Matthaei, *Race, Gender, and Work*, pp. 83–84; Cotera, *Feminism*, pp. 213–233.

124. McWilliams, *North from Mexico*, pp. 191–193; Grebler, Moore, and Guz1án, *The Mexican-American People*, pp. 91–92; Stoddard, *Mexican Americans*, p. 180; Gamio, *Mexican Immigration to the United States*, pp. 135–138.

125. Grebler, Moore, and Guzmán, *The Mexican-American People*, pp. 543–545; Stoddard, *Mexican Americans*, p. 188; Moore, *Mexican Americans*, p. 152; U.S. Commission on Civil Rights, *Mexican Americans and the Administration of Justice in the Southwest*, pp. 15–17; Rees Lloyd and Peter Montague, "Ford and La Raza: 'They Stole Our Land and Gave Us Powdered Milk,'" in *Introduction to Chicano Studies*, ed. Duran and Bernard, pp. 376–378; Frances L. Swadesh, "The Alianza Movement: Catalyst for Social Change in New Mexico," in *Chicano*, ed. Rosaldo, Calvert, and Seligmann, pp. 270–274.

126. Robert Pear, "U.S. Sues Houston to Block Election," *The New York Times*, October 22, 1991, p. A16; William Grady and Thomas Hardy, "Court Orders New Remap," *Chicago Tribune*, December 14, 1991, p. 1; Kenneth Weiss, "Latinos to Challenge Court Plan," *The Los Angeles Times*, December 17, 1991, p. B1.

127. Mark Bixler, "Latino Advocacy Groups Plan Offices Here for Anti-Bias Efforts," *Atlanta Journal and Constitution*, May 30, 2001, p. 3B.

128. Mary Pardo, "Mexican American Women Grassroots Community Activists: 'Mothers of East Los Angeles,'" *Frontiers* XI, no. 1 (1990): 4.

129. Jacques E. Levy, *César Chávez* (New York: W. W. Norton, 1975), pp. 182–201; Peter Matthiessen, *Sal Si Puedes* (New York: Delta Books, 1969), pp. 59–216; John G. Dunne, *Delano* (New York: Farrar, Straus & Giroux, 1967), pp. 110–167.

130. Levy, *César Chávez*, pp. 495, 522–535.

131. J. Craig Jenkins, *The Politics of Insurgency* (New York: Columbia University Press, 1985), pp. x–xi; Robert Reinhold, "Environmental Agency Moves to End Most Uses of Deadly Agricultural Pesticide," *The New York Times*, September 6, 1991, p. A17; "Cubans in the United States," research report, Pew Hispanic Center, Washington, DC, August 2006, p. 6.
132. Ann Bancroft, "10,000 at Rally for Farm Workers," *San Francisco Chronicle*, April 25, 1994, p. A1; "UFW Chronology," www.ufw.org/_page.php?menu=research&inc=_page.php?menu=research&inc=history/01.html (retrieved October 17, 2006).
133. Mark Arax, "UFW Pledges New Activism as March Ends," *The Los Angeles Times*, April 25, 1994, p. A3; Letisia Marquez, "Farm workers union has work cut out for it," *Ventura County Star*, March 29, 2001, http://web.insidevc.com/news/372065.shtml (retrieved July 2, 2001).
134. Hector L. Delgado, *New Immigrants, Old Unions: Undocumented Workers in Los Angeles* (Philadelphia: Temple University Press, 1993).
135. Margaret M. Zamudio, "Organizing Labor Among Difference: The Impact of Race/Ethnicity, Citizenship, and Gender on Working-Class Solidarity," in *Places and Politics in the Age of Global Capitalism*, ed. Arif Dirlik (Lanham, MD: Rowman & Littlefield, 2001), p. 116; Antonio Olivo, "Hotel Workers, Riot Police Clash During Protest," *The Los Angeles Times*, August 4, 2000, p. B1.
136. Glenn Bracey II, "Black and Latino Coalitions and Interest Convergence Theory: A Case Study of the Justice for Janitors Campaign in Houston, Texas," master's thesis, Texas A&M University, College Station, TX, forthcoming, 2007; we also draw on Peter Costantini, "A New Internationalism Rising," Inter Press Service International Association, January 9, 2006, www.ipsnews.net/news.asp?idnews=31695 (retrieved October 30, 2006).
137. Frank D. Bean and Stephanie Bell-Rose, "Immigration and Its Relation to Race and Ethnicity in the United States," in *Immigration and Opportunity: Race, Ethnicity, and Employment in the United States*, ed. Frank D. Bean and Stephanie Bell-Rose (New York: Russell Sage, 1999), pp. 13–14; a more optimistic view is Rakesh Kochhar, "Growth in the Foreign-Born Workforce and Employment of the Native Born," research report, Pew Hispanic Center, Washington, DC, August 2006, pp. 1–4.
138. Martin Kasindorf and Maria Puente, "Hispanics, Blacks Find Futures Entangled," *USA Today*, September 10, 1999, p. 4.
139. Ibid.
140. Chandler Davidson and Charles M. Gaitz, "Ethnic Attitudes as a Basis for Minority Cooperation in a Southwestern Metropolis," *Social Science Quarterly* 53 (March 1973): 747–748; Néstor Rodríguez, "U.S. Immigration and Intergroup Relations in the Late 20th Century: African Americans and Latinos," *Social Justice* 23 (1996): 111–124;. Bracey, "Black and Latino Coalitions and Interest Convergence Theory."
141. Thomas P. Carter, *Mexican Americans in School* (New York: College Entrance Examination Board, 1970), pp. 204–205.; George I. Sánchez, "History, Culture, and Education," in *La Raza*, ed. Julian Samora (Notre Dame, IN: University of Notre Dame Press, 1966), pp. 1–26; Paul Taylor, *An American-Mexican Frontier* (Chapel Hill: University of North Carolina Press, 1934), pp. 196–204; Guadalupe San Miguel, Jr., *Let All of Them Take Heed: Mexican Americans and the Campaign for Educational Equality in Texas, 1910–1981* (Austin: University of Texas Press, 1987), pp. 1–58.
142. Charles Wollenberg, *All Deliberate Speed: Segregation and Exclusion in California Schools, 1855–1975* (Berkeley: University of California Press, 1976), pp. 125–135.
143. Carter, *Mexican Americans in School*, pp. 97–102; Thomas P. Carter, "The Negative Self-Concept of Mexican-American Students," *School and Society* 96 (March 30, 1968): 217–220; George I. Sánchez, "Bilingualism and Mental Measures, a Word of Caution," *Journal of Applied Psychology*, December 1934, pp. 767–769. See also Wollenberg, *All Deliberate Speed*, pp. 118–119; Jane Mercer, *Labelling the Mentally Retarded* (Berkeley: University of California Press, 1973), pp. 96–189.
144. Gary Orfield and Chugmei Lee, *Racial Transformation and the Changing Nature of Segregation* (Cambridge, MA: Harvard Civil Rights Project, 2006), pp. 11–12.
145. Quoted in Gail Russell Chaddock, "U.S. Schools Slip Back Toward Segregation," *The Christian Science Monitor*, July 18, 2001, www.csmonitor.com.
146. Juan F. Perea, "Demography and Distrust: An Essay on American Languages, Cultural Pluralism, and Official English," *Minnesota Law Review* 77 (1992): 269.
147. See Kenji Hakuta and Eugene E. Garcia, "Bilingualism and Education," *American Psychologist* 44 (February 1989): 374–379; Dick Kirschten, "Speaking English," *National Review*, June 17, 1989, pp. 1556–1561; Manuel Ramirez and Alfredo Castaneda, *Cultural Democracy, Bicognitive Development, and Education* (New York: Academic Press, 1974); San Miguel, Jr., *Let All of Them Take Heed*.
148. James Crawford, "Language Politics in the U.S.A.: The Paradox of Bilingual Education," *Social Justice* 25 (Fall 1998), http://ourworld.compuserve.com/homepages/JWCRAWFORD/paradox.htm (retrieved November 13, 2006).

149. Susan Baker and Kenji Hakuta, "Bilingual Education and Latino Civil Rights," www.law.harvard.edu/groups/civilrights/papers/bilingual/bilingual.html (retrieved July 2, 2001).
150. U.S. Bureau of the Census, *1950 Census of Population*, P-E no. 3C, Table 3; U.S. Census Bureau, "Hispanic Population, Table 7.1: Educational Attainment of the Population 25 Years and Over by Sex, Hispanic Origin, and Race: March 2000," published March 6, 2001, www.census.gov/population/www/socdemo/hispanic.html; U.S. Bureau of the Census, "2005 American Community Survey, American Fact Finder: Selected Population Profile in the United States," http://factfinder.census.gov (retrieved June 15, 2007).
151. "Educational System Fails Chicano Students at Every Level, Says Report," *Staff and News Wire Report*, March 24, 2006, www.diverseeducation.com/artman/publish/article_5664.shtml (October 17, 2006); U.S. Census Bureau, "The Foreign-Born Population, Table 4.1: Latin American Foreign-Born Population by Sex, Age, and Region of Birth: March 2000," published January 03, 2001, www.census.gov/population/www/socdemo/foreign.html.
152. Quoted in Beth Barrett, "College Disparity Costly: Mexican-Americans' Wage Gap Up, Study Says," *Daily News of Los Angeles*, May 27, 1997, p. N1.
153. U.S. Census Bureau, Current Population Survey, October 1999, p. 4; Barbara Kantrowitz with Lourdes Rosado, "Falling Further Behind," *Newsweek*, August 19, 1991, p. 60; "Cubans in the United States," pp. 5–7.
154. The research in this and the following paragraph is reported in Harriett Romo and Toni Falbo, *Defying the Odds: Keeping Latino Youth in School* (Austin: University of Texas Press, 1995).
155. Ibid.
156. Zogby, Bruce, and Wittman, "Hispanic Perspectives," pp. 11–12.
157. Concha Delgado-Gaitan and Henry Trueba, *Crossing Cultural Borders: Education for Immigrant Families in America* (Philadelphia: The Falmer Press, 1991); Richard Fry, "The High Schools Hispanics Attend," research report, Pew Hispanic Center, Washington, DC, November 2005, pp. i–ii.
158. Catherine Walsh, *Pedagogy and the Struggle for Voice* (New York: Bergin and Garvey, 1991), pp. 95–113, quotation on p. 112.
159. José A. Cobas and Joe R. Feagin, "Language Oppression and Resistance: The Case of Latinos in the United States," *Ethnic and Racial Studies*, forthcoming, 2008.
160. Paul Vanderwood, "Religion: Official, Popular, and Otherwise," *Mexican Studies* 16 (Summer 2000): 418.
161. Moore, *Mexican Americans*, pp. 88–91; Stoddard, *Mexican Americans*, p. 93; Grebler, Moore, and Guzmán, *The Mexican-American People*, pp. 459–460; Gómez-Quiñones, *Chicano Politics*, p. 179; "Latinos Shift Loyalties," *Christian Century*, April 6, 1994, p. 344.
162. David A. Badillo, "Mexicanos and Suburban Parish Communities," *Journal of Urban History* 31 (November 2004): 23–42; see also Grebler, Moore, and Guzmán, *The Mexican-American People*, pp. 436–439, 473–477.
163. Telles, "Mexican Americans and the American Nation," p. 16.
164. Jill Leovy, "More Hispanics Hear Call of Witnesses," *Seattle Times*, March 25, 1991, p. E1; Vanderwood, "Religion," pp. 476–477.
165. "The Mixture as Never Before," *The Economist*, March 11, 2000.
166. Edward Múrguía, *Assimilation, Colonialism, and the Mexican American People* (Austin: University of Texas Press, 1975), pp. 4–5.; Rodolfo Alvarez, "The Unique Psycho-Historical Experience of the Mexican-American People," *Social Science Quarterly* 52 (June 1971): 15–29; Stoddard, *Mexican Americans*, p. 103; Benjamin S. Bradshaw and Frank Bean, "Trends in the Fertility of Mexican Americans, 1950–1970," *Social Science Quarterly* 53 (March 1973): 696–697.
167. Strategy Research Corporation, *1991 U.S. Hispanic Market*, pp. 107–108.
168. Zogby, Bruce, and Wittman, "Hispanic Perspectives," pp 15; "Hispanic Attitudes Toward Learning English," research report, Pew Hispanic Center, Washington, DC, June 2006, p. 1; and Rubén Rumbaut, Douglas S. Massey, and Frank D. Bean, "Linguistic Life Expectancies," *Population and Development Review* (September 2006): 1–2; Telles, "Mexican Americans and the American Nation," p. 13.
169. "Newcomers Eager to Learn English Face Waiting Lines Across the Nation," National Association of Latino Elected and Appointed Officials, October 6, 2006, www.naleo.org/pr100606.html (retrieved October 17, 2006).
170. Frank Bean, Susan Brown, and Rubén Rumbaut, "Mexican Immigrant Political and Economic Incorporation," *Perspectives on Politics* 4 (June 2006): 312; Robert Suro, "A Developing Identity: Hispanics in the United States," *Carnegie Reporter*, Spring 2006, pp. 24–25.
171. Edward Múrguía and Edward E. Telles, "Phenotype and Schooling Among Mexican Americans," *Sociology of Education* 69 (October 1996): 276–289.
172. López and Stanton-Salazar, "Mexican Americans: A Second Generation at Risk," in *Ethnicities*, pp. 57–90; Cobas and Joe R. Feagin, "Language Oppression and Resistance," forthcoming.

173. Strategy Research Corporation, *1991 U.S. Hispanic Market*, pp. 111–115; Edward Múrguía, *Chicano Intermarriage: A Theoretical and Empirical Study* (San Antonio, TX: Trinity University Press, 1982), pp. 45–51; Amitai Etzioni, "The Monochrome Society," *Heritage Foundation Policy Review*, February 2001, p. 53.
174. Telles, "Mexican Americans and the American Nation," p. 15; p. 56; Marta I. Cruz-Janzen, "Lives on the Crossfire," *Race, Gender & Class* 9 (2002): 55–57.
175. Walter Connor, "Who Are the Mexican Americans? A Note on Comparability," in *Mexican-Americans in Comparative Perspective*, ed. Connor, pp. 4–28; López and Stanton-Salazar, "Mexican Americans: A Second Generation at Risk," in *Ethnicities*, pp. 57–90
176. Cheskin Company, *Hispanic Trends* (Redwood Shores, CA: Cheskin, 2002), p. 5.
177. Peter Skerry, "Not Much Cooking," *Brookings Review*, June 22, 1993, p. 42.
178. Montejano, *Anglos and Mexicans in the Making of Texas, 1836–1986;* Múrguía, *Assimilation, Colonialism, and the Mexican American People*, p. 112; Edward Múrguía and Misael Obregon, "From Colorlism to Presentation in the Case of Mexican Americans and African Americans," unpublished research paper, Texas A&M University College Station, TX, 2006.
179. Mireya Navarro, "Complaint to Spanish TV: Not Enough Americans; Few U.S. Plots for Growing U.S. Audience," *The New York Times*, August 21, 2000, p. B1; *Hispanic Trends*, p. 15.
180. See Achy Obejas, "A Changing Nation: Shades of Future Seen in Census Report on Hispanics," *Chicago Tribune*, March 31, 1996, p. 1; Cheskin Company, *Hispanic Trends*, p. 15.
181. Acuña, *Occupied America*, p. 3.
182. Alvarez, "Psycho-Historical and Socioeconomic Development," pp. 928–930.
183. Múrguía, *Assimilation, Colonialism, and the Mexican American People*, pp. 8–9.
184. John U. Ogbu, *Minority Education and Caste* (New York: Academic Press, 1987), pp. 236–237; and John Obgu, "Variability in Minority Responses to Schooling: Nonimmigrants vs. Immigrants," in *Interpretive Ethnography of Education*, ed. George Spindler and Louise Spinder (Hillsdale, NJ: Lawrence Erlbaum, 1987), pp. 255–275.
185. Barrera, *Race and Class in the Southwest*, p. 213.
186. Geoffrey Fox, *Hispanic Nation: Culture, Politics, and the Constructing of Identity* (Tucson: University of Arizona Press, 1996), pp. 240–241.
187. Nathan Glazer, "The Political Distinctiveness of the Mexican Americans," in *Mexican-Americans in Comparative Perspective*, ed. Walter Connor (Washington, DC: Urban Institute, 1985), pp. 212–216.
188. Rodolfo Acuña, *Anything but Mexican: Chicanos in Contemporary Los Angeles* (London: Verso, 1996), p. 8; the historical data are from Gross, "Texas Mexicans and the Politics of Whiteness."
189. Nestor Rodriguez, personal communication, March 1996.
190. Yolanda Flores-Niemann, Tatcho Mindiola, and Nestor Rodriguez, "U.S.-Born and Foreign-Born Latinas' Perceptions of Black/Brown Relations: Implications for Future Inter-Group Relations," unpublished research paper, University of Houston, 1997, pp. 12–13.
191. Gilda L. Ochoa, *Becoming Neighbors in a Mexican American Community: Power, Conflict and Solidarity* (Austin: University of Texas Press, 2004), p. 128.
192. Fox, *Hispanic Nation*, p. 241.
193. Felix M. Padilla, *Latino Ethnic Consciousness: The Case of Mexican Americans and Puerto Ricans in Chicago* (Notre Dame, IN: University of Notre Dame Press, 1985), pp. 7. See also pp. 138–139; and Andrés Torres, "Latinos in New England: An Introduction," in *Latinos in New England*, ed. Andrés Torres (Philadelphia: Temple University Press, 2006), p. 17.
194. Múrguía, "On Latino/Hispanic Ethnic Identity."
195. Massey, "Five Myths About Immigration," pp. 1–13.

Chapter 9

1. Daniel Adams, "Puerto Ricans Vote on Independence from U.S.," *The Independent*, December 9, 1991, p. 14.
2. U.S. Census Bureau, *2005 American Community Survey*, "General Demographic Characteristics: 2005," http://factfinder.census.gov (retrieved November 05, 2006).
3. Ibid.; Enrique Fernandez, "Puerto Rican Independence: Is It a Dream?" *Newsday*, February 27, 1992, p. 94.
4. See Eric Williams, *From Columbus to Castro: The History of the Caribbean 1492–1969* (London: André Deutsch: 1970), pp. 109, 291.
5. Manuel Maldonado-Denis, *Puerto Rico, A Socio-Historic Interpretation*, trans. Elena Vialo (New York: Random House/Vintage Books, 1972), pp. 13–19; Luis Antonio Cardona, *A History of the Puerto Ricans in the U.S.A.* (Rockville, MD: Carreta Press, 1990), pp. 8–9; Williams, *From Columbus to Castro*, pp. 109, 291.
6. U.S. Commission on Civil Rights, *Puerto Ricans in the Continental United States: An Uncertain Future* (Washington, DC, 1976), pp. 11–12; Jorge Heine, "A

People Apart," *Wilson Quarterly* 4, no. 2 (Spring 1980): 119–123.

7. Maldonado-Denis, *Puerto Rico*, p. 77.
8. U.S. Commission on Civil Rights, *Puerto Ricans in the Continental United States*, p. 12.
9. Maldonado-Denis, *Puerto Rico*, pp. 305–306; Heine, "A People Apart," p. 123.
10. U.S. Bureau of the Census, *Statistical Abstract of the United States 1994*, Table 1342 (Washington, DC, 1994), p. 835.
11. Kristin S. Krause, "Post-incentive Puerto Rico; Island's Future as Manufacturing Center in Doubt as Congress Phases out Income Tax Break," *Traffic World*, October 27, 1997, p. 20; César F. Rosado Marzán, "Facing Financial Crisis, Puerto Rican Government Lays off 100,000," *Labor Notes*, http://labornotes.org/node/232 (retrieved November 10, 2006).
12. Adalberto Lopez, "The Puerto Rican Diaspora: A Survey," in *Puerto Rico and Puerto Ricans: Studies in History and Society*, ed. Adalberto Lopez and James Petras (New York: John Wiley, 1974), p. 318; Clara E. Rodríguez, *Puerto Ricans: Born in the U.S.A.* (Boston: Unwin Hyman, 1989), pp. 1–10.
13. Jack Agueros, "Halfway to Dick and Jane," in *The Immigrant Experience: The Anguish of Becoming American*, ed. Thomas C. Wheeler (New York: Dial Press, 1971), p. 93.
14. Cardona, *A History of the Puerto Ricans in the U.S.A.*, pp. 95–96.
15. U.S. Commission on Civil Rights, *Puerto Ricans in the Continental United States*, p. 25; Rodríguez, *Puerto Ricans*, pp. 4–13; Cardona, *A History of the Puerto Ricans in the U.S.A.*, pp. 95–112; Felix M. Padilla, *Puerto Rican Chicago* (Notre Dame, IN: University of Notre Dame Press, 1987), pp. 66–72.
16. Pedro A. Rivera, "Angel and Aurea," *Wilson Quarterly* 4, no. 2 (Spring 1980): 146–152; Rodríguez, *Puerto Ricans*, pp. 4–8, 28; Gina M. Pérez, *The Near Northwest Side Story: Migration, Displacement, and Puerto Rican Families* (Berkeley: University of California Press, 2004), pp. 196–198; the "emotional bridges" quote is from Elizabeth M. Aranda, *Emotional Bridges to Puerto Rico: Migration, Return Migration, and the Struggles of Incorporation* (Lanham, MD: Rowman & Littlefield, 2007), pp. 172–176.
17. U.S. Bureau of the Census, *American Community Survey*, "General Demographic Characteristics: 2005," http://factfinder.census.gov/servlet/ADPTable?_bm=y&-context=adp&-qr_name=ACS_2005_EST_G00_DP1&-ds_name=ACS_2005_EST_G00_&-tree_id=305&-redoLog=false&-_caller=geoselect&-geo_id=04000US36&-format=&-_lang=en (retrieved November 5, 2006); Elizabeth Aranda, personal communication, November 15, 2006.
18. Candice Choi, "Fewer Puerto Ricans in NYC, but More Mexicans, Asian Indians," DiversityInc.com, www.diversityinc.com (retrieved July 8, 2001).
19. Bart Jones, "Census 2000: Island's Little El Salvador," *Newsday*, May 23, 2001, p. A2.
20. Ibid.; Kern Resource Center, "Spanish for Health Care Workers," Bakersfield, CA, http://72.14.209.104/search?q=cache:brQ2ex8Gy7sJ:www.health-careers.org/resources/Spanish%2520Handbook%2520Revised.pdf+%22million+Salvadorans%22+%222000+census%22+2005&hl=en&gl=us&ct=clnk&cd=1 (retrieved November 13, 2006).
21. Quoted in Frank Bonilla, "Beyond Survival: Porque Sequiremos Siendo Puertoriquenos," in *Puerto Rico and Puerto Ricans*, ed. Lopez and Petras, p. 439.
22. Alfredo Lopez, *The Puerto Rican Papers* (Indianapolis, IN: Bobbs-Merrill, 1973), p. 120.
23. Quoted in ibid., p. 211.
24. Danice K. Eaton et. al., "Youth Risk Behavior Surveillance—United States, 2005," *Morbidity and Mortality Weekly Report* 55(SS05) (June 9, 2006): 1–108.
25. Kristal Brent Zook, "Esai Morales, Good Cop; 'NYPD Blue' Casts New Recruit Against Type," *Washington Post*, May 21, 2001, p. C1.
26. Quoted in Juan Gonzalez, *Harvest of Empire: A History of Latinos in America* (New York: Penguin, 2000), p. 253.
27. Nathan Glazer and Daniel P. Moynihan, *Beyond the Melting Pot* (Cambridge: M.I.T. Press and Harvard University Press, 1963), pp. 88–90.
28. Oscar Lewis, *La Vida* (New York: Random House, 1965).
29. Mirta Ojito, "A Movement Is Born; New Britain Puerto Ricans React to Report Revealing Bias," *The New York Times*, June 28, 1997, p. 23.
30. Associated Press, "Congressman Criticized for Vieques 'Welfare' Slam," June 20, 2001, http://salon.com/politics/wire/2001/06/20/welfare/index.html; Dexter Filkins, "Racial Slurs and Intrigue on City Island," *The New York Times*, February 16, 2001, p. B3.
31. Marta I. Cruz-Janzen, "Latinegras," *Frontiers* 22 (2001): 18; Rodríguez, *Puerto Ricans*, pp. 51–56.
32. Ramón Grosfoguel and Chloe S. Georas, "'Coloniality of Power" and Racial Dynamics: Notes Toward a Reinterpretation of Latino Caribbeans in New York City," *Identities: Global Studies in Culture and Power* 7 (2000): 85–125.
33. Piri Thomas, *Down These Mean Streets* (New York: Knopf, 1967), pp. 85–86.
34. Rodríguez, *Puerto Ricans*, pp. 56–59, 79.
35. Ibid., pp. 60–61; Angel R. Martínez, "The Effects of Acculturation and Racial Identity on Self-Esteem and Psychological Well-Being Among Young Puerto

Ricans," Ph.D. thesis, City University of New York, 1988; Joe R. Feagin and Danielle Dirks, "Who Is White?": College Students' Assessments of Key US Racial and Ethnic Groups," unpublished manuscript, Texas A&M University, 2004.

36. Rodríguez, *Puerto Ricans*, pp. 61–68; Pew Hispanic Center/Kaiser Family Foundation, "2002 National Survey of Latinos," research report, Washington, DC, December 2002, pp. 32–33.
37. Jesús Colon, "The Early Days," in *The Puerto Ricans: A Documentary History*, ed. Kal Wagenheim (Garden City, NY: Doubleday/Anchor Books, 1973), p. 286.
38. Thomas, *Down These Mean Streets*, pp. 102–104.
39. Rodríguez, *Puerto Ricans*, p. 2; U.S. Commission on Civil Rights, *Puerto Ricans in the Continental United States*, p. 54; Frank Bonilla and Ricardo Campos, "A Wealth of Poor: Puerto Ricans in the New Economic Order," *Daedalus* 110 (Spring 1981): 158.
40. U.S. Bureau of the Census, "2005 American Community Survey, American Fact Finder: Selected Population Profile in the United States," http://factfinder.census.gov (retrieved June 16, 2007); see also U.S. Bureau of the Census, "The Hispanic Population in the United States: 2004, Detailed Tables, Table 10.2: Occupation of the Employed Civilian Population 16 Years and over by Sex and Hispanic Origin Type: 2004," published December 14, 2005, www.census.gov/population/www/socdemo/hispanic/cps2004.html.
41. Juan Gonzalez, "Puerto Ricans on the Mainland," *Perspectives* 13 (Winter 1982): 16; U.S. Commission on Civil Rights, *Puerto Ricans in the Continental United States*, p. 52; Bonilla and Campos, "A Wealth of Poor," p. 160.
42. U.S. Department of Labor, Bureau of Labor Statistics, "Annual Average Data, Table 6: "Employment Status of the Hispanic or Latino population by Sex, Age, and Detailed Ethnic Group," ftp://ftp.bls.gov/pub/special.requests/lf/aat6.txt (retrieved November 6, 2006).
43. Gonzalez, *Harvest of Empire*, p. 95.
44. "Latinos and Hospital," *Gotham Gazette*, www.gothamgazette.com/resource/housing/report/10 (retrieved November 14, 2006); see also U.S. Commission on Civil Rights, *Puerto Ricans in the Continental United States*, pp. 59–62.
45. Western Regional Office, U.S. Commission on Civil Rights, *Puerto Ricans in California* (Washington, DC, 1980), p. 17.
46. Devah Pager and Bruce Western "Discrimination in Low-Wage Labor Markets: Evidence from an Experimental Audit Study in New York City," research paper, Princeton University, http://72.14.209.104/search?q=cache:hltEuw40fgkJ:paa2005.princeton.edu/download.aspx%3FsubmissionId%3D50874+discrimination+job+Hispanic+testers+matched+cities+research&hl=en&gl=us&ct=clnk&cd=1H (retrieved October 24, 2006); Aranda, *Emotional Bridges to Puerto Rico*, p. 174; Rodríguez, Puerto Ricans, pp. 92–93.
47. U.S. Commission on Civil Rights, *Puerto Ricans in the Continental United States*, p. 60; Vilma Ortiz, "Latinos and Industrial Change in New York and Los Angeles," unpublished research paper, 1990; Clara E. Rodríguez, "Economic Factors Affecting Puerto Ricans in New York," in *Labor Migration Under Capitalism: The Puerto Rican Experience*, ed. History Task Force (New York: Center for Puerto Rican Studies, 1979), pp. 208–210; Rodríguez, *Puerto Ricans*, pp. 85–91.
48. Mercer L. Sullivan, "Puerto Ricans in Sunset Park, Brooklyn: Poverty Amidst Ethnic and Economic Diversity," in *In the Barrios*, ed. Joan Moore and Raquel Pinderhughes (New York: Russell Sage, 1993), pp. 1–25.
49. U.S. Bureau of the Census, "2005 American Community Survey, American Fact Finder: Selected Population Profile in the United States," http://factfinder.census.gov (retrieved June 15, 2007); see also U.S. Bureau of the Census, "Hispanic Population in the United States, Table 11.2: Earnings of Full-Time, Year-Round Workers 15 Years and Over in 2003 by Sex and Hispanic Origin Type: 2004," published December 14, 2005, www.census.gov/population/socdemo/hispanic/ASEC2004/2004CPS_tab11.2a.html.
50. Francisco Rivera-Batiz, "The Socioeconomic Status of Hispanic New Yorkers," research report, Pew Hispanic Center, Washington, DC, 2002, p. 26.
51. Agueros, "Halfway to Dick and Jane," pp. 96–102; Rivera, "Angel and Aurea," p. 148.
52. See Padilla, *Puerto Rican Chicago*, pp. 117–123; U.S. Bureau of the Census, *The Hispanic Population in the United States: March 1993*, Current Population Reports P20–475 (Washington, DC, 1994), pp. 16–17; Rodríguez, *Puerto Ricans*, pp. 106–116.
53. Jordan Green, "City Life; Gentrification Puts Whites on the Hook," *Newsday*, June 21, 2001, p. A45; Arlene Dávila, *Barrio Dreams: Puerto Ricans, Latinos, and the Neoliberal City* (Berkeley: University of California Press, 2004).
54. Joseph Mallia, "Matter of Rights in Freeport," *Newsday*, February 11, 2001, p. G17; Joseph Mallia, "Complaints Against Inspectors," *Newsday*, January 25, 2001, p. A8.
55. Randal Archibold, "Mount Kisco Agrees to Extend Ban on Bias Against Hispanics," *The New York Times*, February 8, 2001, p. B7; "Federal Court Finds That

Brookhaven Discriminated Against Latinos in Evicting Day Laborers and Day Laborers," Puerto Rican Legal Defense and Education Fund, press release, December 16, 2005.

56. Lance Freeman, "A Note on the Influence of African Heritage on Segregation: The Case of Dominicans," *Urban Affairs Review* 35 (September 1999): 137–146; Grosfoguel and Georas, "'Coloniality of Power and Racial Dynamics," p. 110.
57. Pew Hispanic Center/Kaiser Family Foundation, "2002 National Survey of Latinos," research report, Washington, D.C., December 2002, pp. 72–76; see also Clay F. Richards, "Jobs Top Latinos' List of Concerns," *Newsday*, October 13, 1991, p. 27.
58. U.S. Bureau of the Census, "2005 American Community Survey, American Fact Finder: Selected Population Profile in the United States," http://factfinder.census.gov (retrieved June 15, 2007).
59. Rodríguez, *Puerto Ricans*, pp. 122–123, 127; see George Borjas and Marta Tienda, eds. *Hispanics in the U.S. Economy* (New York: Academic Press, 1985); Lucy Hood, "High School Students at Risk: The Challenge of Dropouts and Pushouts," *Challenge Papers*, Carnegie Corporation, New York, 2004, pp. 1–16.
60. Milga Morales-Nadal, "Puerto Rican/Latino(a) Vistas on Culture and Education," unpublished research paper, 1991, n.p.
61. Rodríguez, *Puerto Ricans*, pp. 139–140.
62. Ibid.; Hood, "High School Students at Risk"; Gary Orfield and Chugmei Lee, *Racial Transformation and the Changing Nature of Segregation* (Cambridge, MA: Harvard Civil Rights Project, 2006), p. 11.
63. Quoted in U.S. Commission on Civil Rights, *Puerto Ricans in the Continental United States*, p. 99; Rodríguez, *Puerto Ricans*, pp. 126.
64. Quoted in U.S. Commission on Civil Rights, *Puerto Ricans in the Continental United States*, p. 103.
65. Pérez, *The Near Northwest Side Story*, pp. 157–191; Rodríguez, *Puerto Ricans*, pp. 139–148; Edna Acosta-Belén and Carlos Santiago, *Puerto Ricans in the United States: A Contemporary Portrait* (Boulder, CO: Lynne Rienner, 2006), p. 159.
66. Catherine Walsh, *Pedagogy and the Struggle for Voice* (New York: Bergin and Garvey, 1991), pp. 101, 127.
67. Ibid., p. ix.
68. Ibid., pp. vii–xi, 1–27, 65–68, quotations from p. vii.
69. Migration Division, Department of Labor and Human Resources, Commonwealth of Puerto Rico, *Puerto Rican Voter Registration in New York City* (New York: Commonwealth of Puerto Rico, 1988), pp. 5–6.
70. General information was provided by the Midwest–Northeast Voter Registration Education Project; Pew Hispanic Center/Kaiser Family Foundation, "2002 National Survey of Latinos," pp. 64–65.
71. In this and the following section we draw on comments provided by Maria Merrill-Ramirez and information provided by the Midwest–Northeast Voter Registration Education Project (now the U.S. Hispanic Leadership Institute).
72. Some information here provided by the Midwest–Northeast Voter Registration Education Project (now the U.S. Hispanic Leadership Institute); "About NHCSL," www.nhcsl.org/about.html (retrieved November 22, 2006).
73. Lopez, "The Puerto Rican Diaspora," p. 329; Western Regional Office, U.S. Commission on Civil Rights, *Puerto Ricans in California*, p. 16.
74. *Building a Road Towards Tomorrow*, Midwest–Northeast Voter Registration Education Project Newsbulletin (Chicago, 1991); David E. Pitt, "Puerto Rico Expands New York Voter Drive," *The New York Times*, October 14, 1987, p. A18; "Puerto Rico Governor to Announce Nation's Largest Nonpartisan Hispanic Voter Registration Campaign Succeeded in Registering over 300,000 Hispanic Voters," Hispanic Prwire, www.hispanicprwire.com/news.php?l=in&id=2865&cha=10 (retrieved November 22, 2006).
75. Shannah Kurland, "Brown Power vs. Black Power," *ColorLines*, Spring 2001, www.ard.org/C_Lines/CLArchive.htm; Lori Robinson, Paul Cuadros, Alysia Tate, and Raul Yzaguirre, "In the Pursuit of Opportunities and Justice, Should the Black and Latino Communities Join Forces or Go It Alone?" *The Crisis*, January/February 2004, www.findarticles.com/p/articles/mi_qa4081/is_200401/ai_n9382156/pg_1 (retrieved November 26, 2006).
76. Lopez, *The Puerto Rican Papers*, pp., 55–58.
77. Bonilla and Campos, "A Wealth of Poor," pp. 166–167; Larry Rohter, "Puerto Rico Votes to Retain Status as Commonwealth," *The New York Times*, November 15, 1993, p. A1; Gonzalez, *Harvest of Empire*, pp. 263–266.
78. Rubén Berríos Martínez, "Puerto Rico's Decolonization," *Foreign Affairs*, November/December 1997; "Puerto Rico Crosscurrents Likely to Wash over Florida," *Broward Daily Business Review*, March 21, 1997, p. A5.
79. Georgie Anne Geyer, "Puerto Rico Should Teach the Language That Binds," *Tulsa World*, September 5, 1997, p. A21; "Regional Congress Rejects Puerto Rico Colonial Regime," Prensa Latina, November 22, 2006, www.independencia.net/noticias/pl_ingl_congr_rejects_colol_status22n06.html (retrieved November 26, 2006).

80. Associated Press, "Congressman Criticized for Vieques 'Welfare' Slam," June 20, 2001, http://salon.com/politics/wire (retrieved July 3, 2001).
81. Joseph Fitzpatrick, "Puerto Ricans," in *Harvard Encyclopedia of Ethnic Groups*, ed. Stephen Thernstrom (Cambridge, MA: Harvard University Press, 1981), p. 866; Padilla, *Puerto Rican Chicago*, pp. 54, 99–143.
82. John Adam Moreau, "My Parents, They Cry for Joy," in *The Puerto Ricans*, ed. Wagenheim, pp. 327–330.
83. Lopez, "The Puerto Rican Diaspora," p. 331.
84. Ibid., pp. 331–332.
85. Acosta-Belén and Santiago, *Puerto Ricans in the United States*, pp. 157–165.
86. Pérez, *The Near Northwest Side Story*, pp. 152-154; Gonzalez, "Puerto Ricans on the Mainland," p. 17; Padilla, *Puerto Rican Chicago*, pp. 117–125; Steven A. Holmes, "Puerto Ricans' Alienation Is Cited in Miami Rampage," *The New York Times*, December 5, 1990, p. A24.
87. Jennifer Weil, Joe Williams, and Alice McQuillan, "Violence Follows Parade: 42 Arrested as Cops and Angry Crowd Clash in Bronx," (New York) *Daily News*, June 12, 2001, p. 7; Pérez, *The Near Northwest Side Story*, p. 169.
88. Lopez, "The Puerto Rican Diaspora," p. 332; Acosta-Belén and Santiago, *Puerto Ricans in the United States*, pp. 160–167.
89. Quoted in Gigi Anders, "Talking the Talk," *American Journalism Review*, November 2000, p. 30.
90. Joseph Torres, "Racism Mars Puerto Rican Parade," New America News Service, September 10, 1997; "National Puerto Rican Day Parade 2005," www.nationalpuertoricandayparade.org/parade.html (retrieved November 26, 2006).
91. Fitzpatrick, "Puerto Ricans," p. 865; Susan E. Eichenberger, "Where Two or More Are Gathered: The Inclusion of Puerto Ricans in Multiethnic Latino Parishes in Southeastern United States," Ph.D. dissertation, University of Florida, Gainesville, 2004.
92. Andrew Greeley, "Defection Among Hispanics (Updated)," *America* 177 (September 27, 1997): 12–13; Acosta-Belén and Santiago, *Puerto Ricans in the United States*, pp. 185.
93. Joseph P. Fitzpatrick, *Puerto Rican Americans: The Meaning of Migration to the Mainland* (Englewood Cliffs, NJ: Prentice Hall, 1971), pp. 22–43.
94. Elena Padilla, *Up from Puerto Rico* (New York: Columbia University Press, 1958). See also Walsh, *Pedagogy and the Struggle for Voice*, pp. 101–102; Milton Gordon, *Assimilation in American Life* (New York: Oxford University Press, 1964), pp. 75–77.
95. Maldonado-Denis, *Puerto Rico*, p. 319.
96. Lloyd H. Rogler and Rosemary Santana Cooney, *Puerto Rican Families in New York City: Intergenerational Processes* (Maplewood, NJ: Waterfront Press, 1984), pp. 76–79; Strategy Research Corporation, *1991 U.S. Hispanic Market* (Miami, 1991), p. 78; Rubén Rumbaut, Douglas S. Massey, and Frank D. Bean, "Linguistic Life Expectancies," *Population and Development Review* (September 2006): 1–2; Telles, "Mexican Americans and the American Nation," p. 11.
97. Fitzpatrick, *Puerto Rican Americans*, p. 43.
98. Aranda, *Emotional Bridges to Puerto Rico*, p. 175.
99. Dávila, *Barrio Dreams*, p. 18; see also chap. 8.
100. Aranda, *Emotional Bridges to Puerto Rico*, pp. 60–120; Greta A. Gilbertson, Joseph P. Fitzpatrick, and Lijun Yang, "Hispanic Intermarriage in New York City," *International Migration Review* 30 (Summer 1996): 445–459; Sharon Lee and Barry Edmonston, "New Marriages, New Families: U.S. Racial and Hispanic Intermarriage," *Population Bulletin*, June 2005, pp. 13–15.
101. Rogler and Cooney, *Puerto Rican Families in New York City*, pp. 76–79; Acosta-Belén and Santiago, *Puerto Ricans in the United States*, pp. 226–228.
102. Nancy Rivera Brooks, "Barbie's Online Critics See Guise in Dolls; Toys: Puerto Rican Incarnation Is at Center of Latest Mattel Brouhaha. First, the Hair . . . ," *The Los Angeles Times*, November 21, 1997, p. D1; see also Acosta-Belén and Santiago, *Puerto Ricans in the United States*, pp. 15–17.
103. Gonzalez, *Harvest of Empire*, p. 95.
104. See Lopez, "The Puerto Rican Diaspora," p. 343.
105. Bonilla and Campos, "A Wealth of Poor," p. 172.
106. Felix Robert Masud-Piloto, *With Open Arms: Cuban Migration to the U.S.* (Totowa, NJ: Rowman & Littlefield, 1988), pp. 7–11.
107. Ibid., pp. 13–20.
108. Ibid., p. 11.
109. Ibid., pp. 20–35.
110. Ibid., pp. 1, 32–35, 39–41; "U.S. Hispanics: Who They Are, Whence They Came, and Why," in *The Hispanic Almanac* (Washington, DC: Hispanic Policy Development Project, 1984), pp. 17–18; Antonio Jorge and Raul Moncarz, *The Political Economy of Cubans in South Florida* (Miami: Institute of Interamerican Studies, 1987), pp. 4, 18; Hugh Thomas, *Cuba: The Pursuit of Freedom* (New York: Harper & Row, 1971), p. 117; Silvia Pedraza-Bailey, "Cuba's Exiles: Portrait of a Refugee Migration," *International Migration Review* 19, no. 1 (Spring 1985): 9–11, 23; Silvia Pedraza, "Cubans in Exile (1959–1989): The State of the Research," *Scholarship on the Cuban Experience: A Dialogue Among Cubanists*, ed. Damian Fernandez (Gainesville: University of Florida, 1992).
111. Masud-Piloto, *With Open Arms*, pp. 1–5, 83–87.
112. Pedraza-Bailey, "Cuba's Exiles," pp. 15–17; Michael G. Wenk, "Adjustment and Assimilation: The Cuban

Refugee Experience," *International Migration Review* 3, no. 1 (Fall 1968): 44, 48.

113. Pedraza-Bailey, "Cuba's Exiles," pp. 22–26; Masud-Piloto, *With Open Arms*, pp. 92–108.
114. Masud-Piloto, *With Open Arms*, pp. 83–87; Zulema E. Suarez, "Cuban Americans in Exile: Myths and Reality," in *Family Ethnicity: Strength in Diversity*, ed. Harriette P. McAdoo (Thousand Oaks, CA: Sage, 1999), pp. 135–152.
115. Tim Golden, "U.S.-Cuban Accord Sets off a Surge of New Refugees," *The New York Times*, September 11, 1994, p. 1; "Prepared Statement of the Honorable Phylis E. Oakley, Assistant Secretary of State, Bureau of Population, Refugees and Migration, Before the Senate Committee on the Judiciary, Subcommittee on Immigration," Federal News Service, July 31, 1997; Andrew I. Schoenholtz and Thomas F. Muther, Jr., "Immigration and Nationality," *The International Lawyer* 33 (Summer 1999): 517.
116. U.S. Census Bureau, *The Hispanic Population*, Census 2000 Brief, May 2001, pp. 1, 7, 8.
117. Lisandro Perez, "Immigrant Economic Adjustment and Family Organization: The Cuban Success Story Reexamined," *International Migration Review* 20, no. 1 (Spring 1986): 13.
118. "Trouble in Paradise," *Time*, November 23, 1981, pp. 24–32; Max J. Castro and Guillermo J. Grenier, "Black–Latino Relations Under Conditions of Latino Empowerment: The Miami Case," unpublished research proposal, Miami, 1991, pp. 3–4; Jeffrey Schmalz, "Miami Tensions Simmering 3 Months After Violence," *The New York Times*, April 10, 1989, p. A8; Holmes, "Puerto Ricans' Alienation Is Cited in Miami Rampage," p. A24.
119. Mike Clary, "Black, Cuban Racial Chasm Splits Miami," *The Los Angeles Times*, March 23, 1997, p. A1.
120. "757 Haitians Cleared to Seek Refuge in U.S.," *The New York Times*, December 10, 1991, p. A8.
121. Mirta Ojito "Best of Friends, Worlds Apart," *The New York Times*, June 5, 2000, p. 1A.
122. Ibid.
123. Myriam Marquez, "'Ugly Cuban-American' a Malicious Stereotype," *Houston Chronicle*, April 20, 2000, p. A29.
124. Susan Eckstein, "Cuban Émigrés and the American Dream," *Perspectives on Politics* 4 (June 2006): 305.
125. U.S. Census Bureau, "Hispanic Population in the United States, Table 14.1: Poverty Status of the Population in 1999 by Sex, Age, Hispanic Origin, and Race: March 2000," published March 6, 2001, www.census.gov/population/www/socdemo/hispanic.html; U.S. Bureau of the Census, "2005 American Community Survey, American Fact Finder: Selected Population Profile in the United States," http://factfinder.census.gov/servlet/IPTable?_bm=y&-context=ip&-reg=ACS_2005_EST_G00_S0201:403;ACS_2005_EST_G00_S0201PR:403;ACS_2005_EST_G00_S0201T:403;ACS_2005_EST_G00_S0201TPR:403&-qr_name=ACS_2005_EST_G00_S0201&-qr_name=ACS_2005_EST_G00_S0201PR&-qr_name=ACS_2005_EST_G00_S0201T&-qr_name=ACS_2005_EST_G00_S0201TPR&-ds_name=ACS_2005_EST_G00_&-tree_id=305&-redoLog=false&-geo_id=01000US&-search_results=01000US&-format=&-_lang-en (retrieved December 6, 2006).
126. Matt Spetalnick, "Florida Declares English Official Language," *Reuter Library Report*, November 9, 1988, n.p.
127. Neil A. Lewis, "Committee Rejects Bush Nominee to Key Appellate Court in South," *The New York Times*, April 12, 1991, pp. A1, A11.
128. Philip Shenon, "FBI Suspends Veteran Agent," *The New York Times*, March 5, 1990, p. A1.
129. David Kidwell, "Miami Agent Lashes out at DEA," *Miami Herald*, February 22, 2001, p. 1B.
130. Jorge and Moncarz, *The Political Economy of Cubans in South Florida*, pp. 16–19.
131. Ibid., p. 9.
132. Perez, "Immigrant Economic Adjustment and Family Organization," pp. 4–7; Silvia Pedraza-Bailey, "Cubans and Mexicans in the United States: The Functions of Political and Economic Migration," *Cuban Studies* 11, no. 2/12, no. 1 (July 1981–January 1982); Alejandro Portes and Robert L. Bach, *Latin American Journey* (Berkeley: University of California Press, 1985), pp. 200–220.
133. Grosfoguel and Georas, "'Coloniality of Power and Racial Dynamics," p. 113; other data here are from David E. Hayes-Bautista and Robert M. Stein, "Los Angeles; A Choice of Two Destinies: Will It Be Miami or San Antonio?" *The Los Angeles Times*, March 11, 2001 p. 1M.
134. Perez, "Immigrant Economic Adjustment and Family Organization," pp. 4–20.
135. Ibid., quotation on p. 18.
136. U.S. Census Bureau, "Hispanic Population, Table 1: Selected Summary Measures of Age and Income by Hispanic Origin and Race: March 2000," published March 6, 2001, www.census.gov/population/www/socdemo/hispanic.html; U.S. Census Bureau, "Hispanic Population, Table 13.1: Total Money Income in 1999 of Families by Type, and by Hispanic Origin and Race of Householder; published March 6, 2001, www.census.gov/population/www/socdemo/hispanic.html; U.S. Census Bureau, "Hispanic Population, Table 14.1: Poverty Status of the Population in 1999 by Sex, Age, Hispanic Origin, and Race," published March 6, 2001, www.census.gov/population/www/

socdemo/hispanic.html; U.S. Census Bureau, "Hispanic Population, Table 15.1: Poverty Status of Families in 1999 by Family Type, and by Hispanic Origin and Race of Householder," published March 6, 2001, www.census.gov/population/www/socdemo/hispanic.html; U.S. Census Bureau, "Hispanic Population, Table 7.1: Educational Attainment of the Population 25 Years and Over by Sex, Hispanic Origin, and Race: March 2000," published March 6, 2001, www.census.gov/population/www/socdemo/hispanic.html; U.S. Bureau of the Census, "The Hispanic Population in the United States: 2004 Detailed Tables: Table 14.2: Poverty Status of the Population in 2003 by Sex, Age, and Hispanic Origin Type: 2004," published December 14, 2005, www.census.gov/population/www/socdemo/hispanic/cps2004.html; U.S. Bureau of the Census, "2005 American Community Survey, American Fact Finder: Selected Population Profile in the United States."

137. See also U.S. Census Bureau, "Hispanic Population, Table 14.1: Poverty Status of the Population in 1999 by Sex, Age, Hispanic Origin, and Race"; U.S. Census Bureau, "Hispanic Population, Table 15.1: Poverty Status of Families in 1999 by Family Type, and by Hispanic Origin and Race of Householder."
138. Quoted in "Widespread Political Efforts Open New Era for Hispanics," *Congressional Quarterly*, October 23, 1982, p. 2,709.
139. Jorge and Moncarz, *The Political Economy of Cubans in South Florida*, p. 30; Masud-Piloto, *With Open Arms*, p. 16; "Cubans in the United States," research report, Pew Hispanic Center, Washington, DC, August 25, 2006, pp. 6–7.
140. Some information was provided by the Midwest–Northeast Voter Registration Education Project; Clary, "Black, Cuban Racial Chasm Splits Miami"; "Survey of Cuban and Cuban American Resident Adults in Miami-Dade and Broward," Bendixen & Associates, September 2006, www.miami.com/multimedia/miami/news/Cuban%20Exile%20Poll.pdf (retrieved December 7, 2006).
141. Andrew Gumbel, "U.S. Presidential Election: Mayor Denies 'Betrayal' of Democrats," *The Independent* (London), December 4, 2000, p. 12.
142. See Samuel P. Huntington, "The Erosion of American National Interests," *Foreign Affairs*, September/October 1997, p. 28.
143. Jorge Mas Santos, "Make a Difference. Have a Purpose. Shine a Light," February 7, 2001, www.canfnet.org (retrieved July 12, 2001); Ana Menendez, "The 'Transition' has Begun—In Cuba and U.S.," MiamiHerald.Com, December 6, 2006, www.miami.com/mld/miamiherald/16173093.htm (retrieved December 7, 2006).
144. "Survey of Cuban and Cuban American Resident Adults in Miami-Dade and Broward"; Eckstein, "Cuban Émigrés and the American Dream," pp. 301–303.
145. Richard Boudreaus, "Cuba Strikes Democracy Movement," *The Los Angeles Times*, January 19, 1992, p. A1; Deborah Sharp, "Execution in Cuba," *USA Today*, January 22, 1992, p. 3A.; "Summary of Results for Individual Questions of Political Attitudes Survey of Cuban Americans, 2004,"Florida International University, http://72.14.209.104/search?q=cache:RBN7YmdR9SIJ:www.engagingamerica.org/ajc/pdffiles/ethnic/cugs1.doc+%22survey+of+Cuban+Americans%22&hl=en&gl=us&ct=clnk&cd=4 (retrieved December 7, 2006); Peter Kornbluh and Jon Elliston, "Will Congress Kill TV Marti?" *The Nation*, August 22/29, 1994, pp. 194–196; "Radio and TV. Marti," Council on Hemispheric Affairs, March 29, 2006, www.coha.org/2006/03/29/radio-and-tv-marti-washington-guns-after-castro-at-any-cost (retrieved December 7, 2006).
146. Kirk Nielsen, "Sail Away and Stay and Stay," Miami New Times Online, May 10, 2001, www.miaminewtimes.com (retrieved July 12, 2001); "Bush Urges Cubans to Push Democracy," CNN.COM, www.cnn.com/2006/POLITICS/08/03/us.cuba/index.html (retrieved August 3, 2006).
147. Cathay Smith, "Santería: The Way of the Saints," http://home.wlu.edu/~lubint/Touchstone/Santeria-Smith.htm (retrieved November 19, 2006); "Cubans in the United States," p. 7;. Eichenberger, "Where Two or More Are Gathered."
148. Jon Nordheimer, "Where Old Havana Plays," *The New York Times*, April 3, 1991, p. C1; Eckstein, "Cuban Émigrés and the American Dream," pp. 297—299.
149. Deborah Sontag, "The Lasting Exile of Cuban Spirits," *The New York Times*, September 11, 1994, sec. 4, p. 1; the survey is cited in "Cubans in the United States," p. 7; "Survey of Cuban and Cuban American Resident Adults in Miami-Dade and Broward."
150. Kelly M. Barlow, Donald M. Taylor, and Wallace E. Lambert, "Ethnicity in America and Feeling 'American,'" *Journal of Psychology* 134 (November 2000): 581–600.
151. Portes and Bach, *Latin American Journey*, pp. 91–93, 193–199.
152. Hayes-Bautista and Stein, "Los Angeles: A Choice of Two Destinies."
153. Amie Parnes, "First Communions Turn Lavish in South Florida; Cuban-Americans Among Big Spenders," *Boston Globe*, June 27, 2001, p. A2.
154. Portes and Bach, *Latin American Journey*, pp. 246–247.

155. "Trouble in Paradise," pp. 30–31.
156. Data in this and the following paragraph are from Strategy Research Corporation, *1991 U.S. Hispanic Market*, pp. 78–130; Eckstein, "Cuban Émigrés and the American Dream," p. 299.
157. Matea Gold, "Cultural Celebration Sways to a Cuban Beat; Heritage: About 20,000 Attend L.A.'s Third Annual Cuban American Festival of Art, Music, and Food in Echo Park," *The Los Angeles Times*, May 19, 1997, p. B1; "2002 National Survey of Latinos," pp. 32–33.
158. Andrew Meadows, "Catering to Latin Tastes; Tapping the Hispanic Market," *Tampa (Fla.) Tribune*, April 20, 2001, p. 1, Business & Finance.
159. Private communication with Maria Merril-Ramirez, July 1982.
160. Robert Suro and Gabriel Escobar, "2006 National Survey of Latinos: The Immigration Debate," research report, Pew Hispanic Center, Washington, DC, July 2006, p. 16.
161. Stephanie Armour, "Welcome Mat Rolls out for Hispanic Workers: Corporate America Cultivates Talent as Ethnic Population Booms," *USA Today*, April 12, 2001, p. 1B.

Chapter 10

1. Mitsuye Yamada, "Invisibility Is an Unnatural Disaster: Reflections of an Asian American Woman," in *Feminist Theory Reader: Local and Global Perspectives*, eds. Carole K. McCann and Seung-Kyung Kim (New York: Routledge, 2003), p. 174.
2. U.S. Bureau of the Census, *U.S. Census of Population, 1980: Asian and Pacific Islander Population in the United States*, PC80-2-1E (Washington, DC, 1988), p. 1; U.S. Bureau of the Census, *1990 Census of Population: Social and Economic Characteristics: United States*, CP-2-1 (Washington, DC, 1993), pp. 105–106; U.S. Bureau of the Census, "American Fact Finder: Census 2000 Demographic Profile Highlights: Selected Population Group," http://factfinder.census.gov/home/saff/main.html?_lang=en; (retrieved December 1, 2006); U.S. Bureau of the Census, "2005 American Community Survey, American Fact Finder: Selected Population Profile in the United States," http://factfinder.census.gov/servlet/IPTable?_bm=y&-context=ip&-reg=ACS_2005_EST_G00_S0201:022;ACS_2005_EST_G00_S0201PR:022;ACS_2005_EST_G00_S0201T:022;ACS_2005_EST_G00_S0201TPR:022&-qr_name=ACS_2005_EST_G00_S0201&-qr_name=ACS_2005_EST_G00_S0201PR&-qr_name=ACS_2005_EST_G00_S0201T&-qr_name=ACS_2005_EST_G00_S0201TPR&-ds_name=ACS_2005_EST_G00_&-tree_id=305&-redoLog=false&-geo_id=01000US&-search_results=01000US&-format=&-_lang=en (retrieved December 5, 2006).
3. U.S. Commission on Civil Rights, *Civil Rights Issues Facing Asian Americans in the 1990s* (Washington, DC: U.S. Government Printing Office, 1992), p. 15; Robert Daniels, *Coming to America* (New York: HarperCollins, 1990), p. 350.
4. Kathryn Tolbert, "Pacific Grim," *Boston Globe Sunday Magazine*, March 29, 1992, p. 14.
5. Ronald Takaki, *Strangers from a Different Shore: A History of Asian Americans* (New York: Penguin, 1989), p. 7.
6. Alan T. Moriyama, *Imingaisha: Japanese Immigration Companies and Hawaii, 1894–1908* (Honolulu: University of Hawaii Press, 1985); Wayne Patterson, *The Korean Frontier in America: Immigration to Hawaii, 1896–1910* (Honolulu: University of Hawaii Press, 1988).
7. Roger Daniels, *The Politics of Prejudice* (New York: Atheneum, 1969), pp. 3–6; Hilary Conroy, *The Japanese Frontier in Hawaii, 1868–1898* (Berkeley: University of California Press, 1953), passim; Moriyama, *Imingaisha*, pp. xvi–xix.
8. Takaki, *Strangers from a Different Shore*, p. 179.
9. U.S. Immigration and Naturalization Service, *1975 Annual Report* (Washington, DC, 1975), pp. 62–66.
10. Arinori Mori, *The Japanese in America* (Japan Advertiser Press, 1926), pp. 19–21; Kaizo Naka, *Social and Economic Conditions Among Japanese Farmers in California* (San Francisco: R & E Research Associates, 1974), p. 6; John Modell, "On Being an Issei: Orientations Toward America," Unpublished research paper presented to the American Anthropological Association, San Diego, November 1970, p. 4.
11. Sucheng Chan, *Asian Americans: An Interpretive History* (Boston: Twayne, 1991), pp. 103–117; Roger Daniels, *Asian America: Chinese and Japanese in the United States Since 1850* (Seattle: University of Washington Press, 1988), pp. 100–154.
12. Jacobus tenBroek, Edward N. Barnhart, and Floyd W. Matson, *Prejudice, War, and the Constitution* (Berkeley: University of California Press, 1968), pp. 42–43; *Takao Ozawa* v. *United States*, 260 U.S. 178 (1922); Takaki, *Strangers from a Distant Shore*, pp. 14–15.
13. Hillary Conroy and T. Scott Miyakawa, "Foreword," in *East Across the Pacific*, ed. Hillary Conroy and T. Scott Miyakawa (Santa Barbara, CA: ABC-CLIO, 1972), pp. xiv–xv.
14. The statistics are from U.S. Census Bureau publications.
15. Takaki, *Strangers from a Different Shore*, pp. 479–481.

16. Robert G. Lee, *Orientals: Asian Americans in Popular Culture* (Philadelphia: Temple University Press, 1999), p. 8.
17. E. Manchester-Boddy, *Japanese in America* (San Francisco: R & E Research Associates, 1970), pp. 25–30.
18. V. S. McClatchy, *Japanese Immigration and Colonization*, reprint ed. (San Francisco: R & E Research Associates, 1970), p. 42.
19. Quoted in Edward K. Strong, Jr., *The Second-Generation Japanese Problem* (Stanford, CA: Stanford University Press, 1934), p. 133.
20. tenBroek, Barnhart, and Matson, *Prejudice, War, and the Constitution*, p. 31.
21. Dennis M. Ogawa, *From Japs to Japanese* (Berkeley, CA: McCutchan, 1971), p. 12; Carey McWilliams, *Brothers Under the Skin*, rev. ed. (Boston: Little, Brown, 1964), pp. 148–149; Stanley Sue and Harry H. L. Kitano, "Stereotypes as a Measure of Success," *Journal of Social Issues* 29 (1973): 83–98.
22. tenBroek, Barnhart, and Matson, *Prejudice, War, and the Constitution*, pp. 66–70.
23. Quoted in Ogawa, *From Japs to Japanese*, p. 11.
24. U.S. Department of the Interior, War Relocation Authority, *Myths and Facts About the Japanese American* (Washington, DC, 1945), pp. 7–8; Ogawa, *From Japs to Japanese*, pp. 35–54. Survey data document attitude changes in the period 1942–1961. See also Roger Daniels, "Why It Happened Here," in *The Social Reality of Ethnic America*, ed. R. Gomez et al. (Lexington, MA: D. C. Heath, 1971), p. 236.
25. Council on Interracial Books for Children, *Stereotypes, Distortions and Omissions in U.S. History Textbooks* (New York: Racism and Sexism Resource Center for Educators, 1977), pp. 42–46; Funie Hsu, "Textbook Companies Dictating Whitewashed History," *AsianWeek*, September 2, 2005, http://news.asianweek.com/news (retrieved December 17, 2006); Sam Chu Lin, "Extended Life for 'Chinese Experience' Series," *AsianWeek*, February 20, 2004, http://news.asianweek.com/news (retrieved December 17, 2006); "Latest Headline News," Media Action Network for Asian Americans, http://www.manaa.org (retrieved December 18, 2006).
26. Letta Tayler, "Dateline: Washington," States News Service, May 8, 1987, n.p.; Takaki, *Strangers from a Different Shore*, p. 6.
27. Mia Tuan, *Forever Foreigners or Honorary Whites?: The Asian American Experience Today* (New Brunswick, NJ: Rutgers University Press, 1998), p. 1.
28. Karl Taro Greenfield, "Return of the Yellow Peril," *Nation*, May 11, 1992, p. 636; Michael Crichton, *Rising Sun* (New York: Knopf, 1991).
29. Helen Zia, *Asian American Dreams: The Emergence of an American People* (New York: Farrar, Straus & Giroux, 2000), p. 134.
30. Erika Hayasaki, "'Pearl Harbor' Making Its Marks," *The Los Angeles Times*, May 29, 2001, p. 6–1.
31. Steven A. Chin, "KFRC Deejay Draws Suspension for On-Air Derogatory Remarks," *San Francisco Examiner*, December 6, 1994, p. A2; "Current Affairs," *JACL News*, www.jacl.org/index.php (retrieved December 19, 2006); Media Action Network for Asian Americans, "Latest Headline News," www.manaa.org (retrieved December 18, 2006).
32. Herbert B. Johnson, *Discrimination Against the Japanese in California* (Berkeley, CA: Courier, 1907), pp. 73–74; Daniels, *The Politics of Prejudice*, pp. 33–34; Howard H. Sugimoto, "The Vancouver Riots of 1907: A Canadian Episode," in *East Across the Pacific*, ed. Conroy and Miyakawa, pp. 92–110.
33. Jean Pajus, *The Real Japanese California* (San Francisco: R & E Research Associates, 1971), pp. 164–166; Daniels, *The Politics of Prejudice*, p. 87; tenBroek, Barnhart, and Matson, *Prejudice, War, and the Constitution*, p. 73.
34. Lemuel F. Ignacio, *Asian Americans and Pacific Islanders* (San Jose, CA: Pilipino Development Associates, 1976), pp. 95–96; tenBroek, Barnhart, and Matson, *Prejudice, War, and the Constitution*, passim; Raymond Y. Okamura, "The American Concentration camps: A Cover-up Through Euphemistic Terminology," in *Understanding Prejudice and Discrimination*, ed. Scott Plous (New York: McGraw-Hill, 2003), pp. 149–164.
35. Dorothy Swaine Thomas and Richard S. Nishimoto, *The Spoilage* (Berkeley: University of California Press, 1946), pp. 8–16; tenBroek, Barnhart, and Matson, *Prejudice, War, and the Constitution*, pp. 118–120.
36. tenBroek, Barnhart, and Matson, *Prejudice, War, and the Constitution*, pp. 120, 126–129, 130; Thomas and Nishimoto, *The Spoilage*, pp. 10–20; Edward H. Spicer et al., *Impounded People* (Tucson: University of Arizona Press, 1969), pp. 141–241.
37. Richard Drinnon, *Keeper of Concentration Camps* (Berkeley: University of California Press, 1987), pp. 47, 153; quotation from Valerie Matsumoto, "Japanese American Women During World War II," in *Unequal Sisters*, ed. Ellen C. DuBois and Vicki L. Ruiz (New York: Routledge, 1990), p. 373.
38. Thomas and Nishimoto, *The Spoilage*, pp. 54–71; tenBroek, Barnhart, and Matson, *Prejudice, War, and the Constitution*, pp. 126–132, 149–155; Spicer et al., *Impounded People*, pp. 252–280.
39. Leonard Bloom and Ruth Riemer, *Removal and Return* (Berkeley: University of California Press, 1949),

pp. 124–157, 198–204; tenBroek, Barnhart, and Matson, *Prejudice, War, and the Constitution*, pp. 155–177, 180–181.

40. Bradford Smith, *Americans from Japan* (New York; Lippincott, 1948), pp. 10–12, 202–276; Carey McWilliams, *Prejudice* (Boston: Little, Brown, 1944), p. 4; tenBroek, Barnhart, and Matson, *Prejudice, War, and the Constitution*, pp. 211–223; Harry H. L. Kitano, *Japanese Americans*, 2nd ed. (Englewood Cliffs, NJ: Prentice Hall, 1976), pp. 82–88; S. Frank Miyamoto, "The Forced Evacuation of the Japanese Minority During World War II," *Journal of Social Issues* 29 (1973): 11–29.
41. Drinnon, *Keeper of Concentration Camps*, pp. 255–256. See also Christopher Thorne, *Allies of a Kind* (New York: Oxford University Press, 1978).
42. Kitano, *Japanese Americans*, p. 73.
43. Gary Y. Okihiro, "Japanese Resistance in America's Concentration Camps: A Re-evaluation," *Amerasia Journal* 2 (Fall 1973): 20–34; Arthur A. Hansen and David A. Hacker, "The Manzanar Riot: An Ethnic Perspective," *Amerasia Journal* 3 (Fall 1974): 112–142. See also Roger Daniels, *Concentration Camps, U.S.A.* (New York: Holt, Rinehart & Winston, 1971).
44. See the Southern Poverty Law Center's Intelligence Report, March 1994, pp. 17–29; C. N. Le, "Anti-Asian Racism and Violence," *Asian-Nation*, www.asian-nation.org/racism.shtml (retrieved December 21, 2006). The Watada story is in Mike Honda, "Watada Chose to Stop Fighting," *San Francisco Chronicle*, January 30, 2007, www. thankyoult. org/content/view/107/23 (retrieved February 2, 2007); and "Ehren Watada," http://en.wikipedia.org/wiki/Ehren_Watada (retrieved February 2, 2007).
45. Ivan H. Light, *Ethnic Enterprise in America* (Berkeley: University of California Press, 1972), pp. 174–179; Bill Hosokawa, *The Nisei* (New York: Morrow, 1969), pp. 199–200; Kitano, *Japanese Americans*, pp. 55–58.
46. Hosokawa, *The Nisei*, pp. 439–446; Kitano, *Japanese Americans*, pp. 89–90.
47. Nathaniel C. Nash, "House Votes Payments to Japanese Americans," *The New York Times*, September 18, 1987, p. A15.
48. Ken Miller, "U.S. Pays Japanese Internees $20,000—and Apologies," Gannett News Service, October 9, 1990, n.p.
49. Santiago O'Donnell and Psyche Pascual, "Kato Slaying Raises Fears of Hate Crime," *The Los Angeles Times*, March 1, 1992, p. B1.
50. Benjamin Forgey, "Imagery Says It All at New Monument; Artistry, Apology Merge at Japanese American Memorial," *The Washington Post*, June 30, 2001, p. C1.
51. Rodolfo Acuña, *Occupied America* (San Francisco: Canfield Press, 1972), pp. 212–213.
52. Quoted in Harry H. L. Kitano and Roger Daniels, *Asian Americans: Emerging Minorities*, 3rd ed. (Englewood Cliffs, NJ: Prentice Hall, 2001), p. 47.
53. Kitano, *Japanese Americans*, pp. 174–186; Daniel Inouye and Lawrence Elliot, *Journey to Washington* (Englewood Cliffs, NJ: Prentice Hall, 1967), pp. 248–250; Hosokawa, *The Nisei*, pp. 460–469.
54. Hosokawa, *The Nisei*, pp. 486–487.
55. Stanley Karnow, "Apathetic Asian Americans?" *The Washington Post*, November 29, 1992, p. C1; Jeffrey Passel, "The Latino and Asian Vote," www.urban.org/publications/900723.html (retrieved December 19, 2006).
56. "Slur Stirs Party In-fighting," *Commercial Appeal*, May 4, 1994, p. 5A.
57. U.S. Commission on Civil Rights, *Recent Activities Against Citizens and Residents of Asian Descent* (Washington, DC, 1986), pp. 3–6.
58. Kenneth Walsh, Gloria Borger, Susan Dentzer, and Carla A. Robbins, "The 'America First' Fallacies," *U.S. News & World Report*, February 3, 1992, p. 22.
59. O'Donnell and Pascual, "Kato Slaying Raises Fears of Hate Crime," p. B1.
60. Kitano and Daniels, *Asian Americans*, 3rd ed., p. 83.
61. Yuji Ichioka, "A Buried Past," *Amerasia Journal* 1 (July 1971): 1–25; Karl Yoneda, "100 Years of Japanese Labor History in the U.S.A.," in *Roots*, ed. Amy Tachiki et al. (Los Angeles: UCLA Asian American Studies Center, 1971), pp. 150–157; Takaki, *Strangers from a Different Shore*, p. 200.
62. See *Roots*, ed. Tachiki et al.
63. Russell Endo and William Wei, "On the Development of Asian American Studies Programs," in *Reflections on Shattered Windows*, ed. Gary Y. Okihiro et al. (Pullman: Washington State University Press, 1988), pp. 6–12.
64. "Prepared Testimony of Karen Narasaki, Executive Director, National Asian Pacific American Legal Consortium, Before the House Judiciary Committee," Subcommittee on the Constitution, Subcommittee Hearing on H.R. 1909: The Civil Rights Act of 1997, Federal News Service, June 26, 1997; Randal C. Archibold, "UC Irvine Expected to Offer Asian Studies Major; Education: On a Campus Where More Than Half the Students Are of Asian Background, Absence of Such a Program Has Been a Concern and a Topic of Protests," *The Los Angeles Times*, May 13, 1997, p. A3.
65. Wired News Report, "E-mail Hate Scribe Sentenced," *Wired News*, www.wired.com/news/print/0,1294,12090,00.html (retrieved August 12, 2001).

66. Cited in Sidney L. Gulick, *The American Japanese Problem* (New York: Scribner's, 1914), p. 11; Japanese Association of the Pacific Northwest, *Japanese Immigration* (San Francisco: R & E Research Associates, 1972), pp. 22–25; Daniels, *The Politics of Prejudice*, pp. 7, 10–12.
67. Edna Bonacich and John Modell, *The Economic Basis of Ethnic Solidarity* (Berkeley: University of California Press, 1980), pp. 38–47.
68. Kitano, *Japanese Americans*, pp. 19–21; Light, *Ethnic Enterprise in America*, pp. 27–29; S. Frank Miyamoto, "An Immigrant Community in America," in *East Across the Pacific*, ed. Conroy and Miyakawa, pp. 223–225.
69. Gulick, *The American Japanese Problem*, pp. 11, 32–33; Light, *Ethnic Enterprise in America*, p. 71.
70. See also Roger Daniels, "Japanese Immigrants on the Western Frontier: The Issei in California, 1890–1940," in *East Across the Pacific*, ed. Conroy and Miyakawa, p. 85.
71. Pajus, *The Real Japanese California*, pp. 147–151; Light, *Ethnic Enterprise in America*, p. 76.
72. Bloom and Riemer, *Removal and Return*, pp. 115–117; Strong, *The Second-Generation Japanese Problem*, pp. 209–211.
73. Bloom and Riemer, *Removal and Return*, pp. 17–20.
74. Evelyn Nakano Glenn, "The Dialectics of Wage Work: Japanese American Women and Domestic Service, 1905–1940," in *Unequal Sisters*, ed. DuBois and Ruiz, p. 345.
75. Ibid., p. 369.
76. Bloom and Riemer, *Removal and Return*, pp. 44, 144.
77. Bonacich and Modell, *The Economic Basis of Ethnic Solidarity*, pp. 256–259.
78. U.S. Bureau of the Census, "American Fact Finder: 2005 American Community Survey," http://factfinder.census.gov (retrieved June 13, 2007).
79. Ibid.
80. Kitano and Daniels, *Asian Americans,* 3rd ed., p. 81; "Asian Representation Increasing on TV, Slowly," *Goldsea Intelligence,* http://goldsea.com/Asiagate/612/08tv.html (retrieved December 13, 2006).
81. U.S. Commission on Civil Rights, *Success of Asian Americans: Fact or Fiction?* (Washington, DC, 1980), pp. 14–15.
82. Harry H. L. Kitano and Roger Daniels, *Asian Americans: Emerging Minorities* (Englewood Cliffs, NJ: Prentice Hall, 1988), p. 171; S. B. Woo, "How to Vote in 2004 to Win 'The Big Interests,'" *80-20Initiative,* www.80-20initiative.net/empower.html (retrieved December 20, 2006).
83. Winfred Yu, "Asian Americans Charge Prejudice Slows Climb to Management Ranks," *The Wall Street Journal*, September 11, 1985, n.p., quoted in Takaki, *Strangers from a Different Shore*, p. 476.
84. Takaki, *Strangers from a Different Shore*, pp. 475–477; Woo, "How to Vote in 2004 to Win 'The Big Interests.'"
85. Art Pine, "Marines Pin Bars on Man They Dismissed," *The Los Angeles Times*, March 19, 1994, p. A4; Judy Tachibana, "Triumph over Racism in the Marines," *Sacramento Bee*, April 20, 1994, p. B3.
86. K. K. Kawakami, *The Japanese Question* (New York: Macmillan, 1921), pp. 143–145; John Modell, "Tradition and Opportunity: The Japanese Immigrant in America," *Pacific Historical Review* 40 (May 1971): 163–182.
87. Johnson, *Discrimination Against the Japanese in California*, pp. 3–20, 40–47; Franklin Hichborn, *The Story of the Session of the California Legislature of 1909* (San Francisco: James H. Barry Press, 1909), p. 207; Pajus, *The Real Japanese California*, pp. 170–178; Kawakami, *The Japanese Question*, pp. 168–169.
88. William Petersen, *Japanese Americans* (New York: Random House, 1971), p. 183; Strong, *The Second-Generation Japanese Problem*, pp. 201–204; Kawakami, *The Japanese Question*, pp. 146–151; Pajus, *The Real Japanese California*, p. 181.
89. Pajus, *The Real Japanese California*, p. 183; Strong, *The Second-Generation Japanese Problem*, pp. 185–188.
90. U.S. Bureau of the Census, "American Fact Finder: 2005 American Community Survey," http://factfinder.census.gov (retrieved June 13, 2007).
91. U.S. Commission on Civil Rights, *Social Indicators of Equality for Minorities and Women* (Washington, DC, 1978), pp. 24–26; U.S. Bureau of the Census, *1990 Census of Population: Social and Economic Characteristics: California*, pp. 181, 246.
92. Manchester-Boddy, *Japanese in America*, p. 118.
93. Petersen, *Japanese Americans*, p. 177; Manchester-Boddy, *Japanese in America*, pp. 114–118.
94. Andrew W. Lind, *Hawaii's Japanese* (Princeton, NJ: Princeton University Press, 1946), pp. 212–257; Petersen, *Japanese Americans*, pp. 177–178, 185.
95. Hosokawa, *The Nisei*, p. 131; Kitano, *Japanese Americans*, p. 115; Christie Kiefer, *Changing Cultures, Changing Lives* (San Francisco: Jossey-Bass, 1974), pp. 34–38; Petersen, *Japanese Americans*, p. 187.
96. John Dart, "Military Opens Chaplain Ranks to Buddhists," *The Los Angeles Times*, October 27, 1987, p. 1.
97. John Modell, "The Japanese American Family: A Perspective for Future Investigations," *Pacific Historical Review* 37 (February 1968): 79; Joe R. Feagin and Nancy Fujitaki, "On the Assimilation of Japanese Americans," *Amerasia Journal* 1 (February 1972): 15–17.
98. Tuan, *Forever Foreigners*, p. 155.
99. Peter Y. Hong, "Japanese American Newspaper's Layoffs Anger Community," *The Los Angeles Times*, November 15, 1997, p. B1. See newspaper at http://www.rafu.com.

100. Petersen, *Japanese Americans*, pp. 6–7; Light, *Ethnic Enterprise in America*, passim; William Caudill, "Japanese American Personality and Acculturation," *Genetic Psychology Monographs* 45 (1952): 3–102; Kitano and Daniels, *Asian Americans*, p. 179.
101. Paul Spickard, *Mixed Blood* (Madison: University of Wisconsin Press, 1988), p. 347.
102. David J. O'Brien and Stephen S. Fugita, "Generational Differences in Japanese Americans' Perceptions and Feelings About Social Relationships Between Themselves and Caucasian Americans," in *Culture, Ethnicity, and Identity*, ed. William McCready (New York: Academic Press, 1983), pp. 235–236; Rosalind S. Chou, "Malady of the Model Minority: White Racism's Assault on Asian Americans," Master's thesis, (Texas A&M University, College Station, TX, 2007).
103. Darrel Montero, *Japanese Americans: Changing Patterns of Ethnic Affiliation over Three Generations* (Boulder, CO: Westview Press, 1980), p. 80; Petersen, *Japanese Americans*, pp. 220–224; Modell, "The Japanese American Family," pp. 76–79; Kitano, *Japanese Americans*, pp. 189, 196; George Kagiwada, "Assimilation of Nisei in Los Angeles," in *East Across the Pacific*, ed. Conroy and Miyakawa, p. 273.
104. Feagin and Fujitaki, "On the Assimilation of Japanese Americans," p. 23.
105. Akemi Kikumura and Harry H. L. Kitano, "Interracial Marriage: A Picture of Japanese Americans," *Journal of Social Issues* 29 (1973): 67–81; John N. Tinker, "Intermarriage and Ethnic Boundaries: The Japanese American Case," *Journal of Social Issues* 29 (1973): 55; John W. Connor, *Tradition and Change in Three Generations of Japanese Americans* (Chicago: Nelson-Hall, 1977), p. 308; Gene N. Levine and Colbert Rhodes, *The Japanese American Community* (New York: Praeger, 1981), p. 145.
106. Larry H. Shinagawa and Gin Yong Pang, "Asian American Panethnicity and Intermarriage," in *Asian Americans: Experiences and Perspectives*, ed. Timothy P. Fong and Larry H. Shinagawa (Upper Saddle River, NJ: Prentice Hall, 2000), pp. 334–343; C. N. Le, "Interracial Dating and Marriage," *Asian-Nation*, www.asian-nation.org/interracial.shtml (retrieved December 21, 2006).
107. O'Brien and Fugita, "Generational Differences," pp. 231–235.
108. Kitano and Daniels, *Asian Americans*, p. 80; Annie Nakao, "Homing in on Japan," *San Francisco Chronicle*, September 10, 2000, www.sfgate.com/cgi-bin/article.cgi?file=/examiner/archive/2000/09/10/NEWS12211.dtl (retrieved December 21, 2006).
109. Kitano and Daniels, *Asian Americans*, p. 81.
110. Ibid., pp. 191–192.
111. Petersen, *Japanese Americans*, pp. 214–221.
112. Greg Mayeda, "Japanese Americans Don't Lose Identity," *The New York Times*, December 28, 1995, p. A20; Nakao, "Homing in on Japan."
113. Edna Bonacich, "United States Capitalist Development: A Background to Asian Immigration," in *Labor Immigration Under Capitalism*, ed. Lucie Cheng and Edna Bonacich (Berkeley: University of California Press, 1984), p. 82.
114. *U.S.* v. *Bhagat Singh Thind*, 261 U.S. 215 (1923).
115. Shinagawa and Pang, "Asian American Panethnicity and Intermarriage," in Fong and Shinagawa, *Asian Americans*, pp. 343–344.
116. Takaki, *Strangers from a Different Shore*, p. 474.
117. Robert Blauner, *Racial Oppression in America* (New York: Harper & Row, 1972), pp. 54–55; Paul Takagi, "The Myth of 'Assimilation in American Life,'" *Amerasia Journal* 2 (Fall 1973): 149–158; Peter Uhlenberg, "Demographic Correlates of Group Achievement: Contrasting Patterns of Mexican-Americans and Japanese-Americans," *Demography* 9 (February 1972): 119–128.
118. B. Suzuki, "Education and the Socialization of Asian Americans," in *Asian Americans: Social and Psychological Perspectives*, ed. R. Endo, S. Sue, and N. Wagner (Palo Alto, CA: Science & Behavior Books, 1980), 2:155–178; William Petersen, "Success Story, Japanese-American Style," *The New York Times*, January 9, 1966, p. 21; "Success Story of One Minority Group in the U.S.," *U.S. News & World Report*, December 26, 1966, pp. 73–76; Thomas Sowell, *Ethnic America* (New York: Basic Books, 1981).
119. Amado Cabezas and Gary Kawaguchi, "Empirical Evidence for Continuing Asian American Inequality: The Human Capital Model and Labor Market Segmentation," in *Reflections on Shattered Windows*, pp. 144–164.
120. Studies cited in Amado Cabezas, "Testimony to U.S. Commission on Civil Rights," in *Civil Rights Issues of Asian and Pacific Americans* (Washington, DC: U.S. Government Printing Office, 1980), pp. 389–393. See also Takaki, *Strangers from a Different Shore*, p. 475.
121. Takagi, "The Myth of 'Assimilation in American Life,'" pp. 149–158; Ogawa, *From Jap to Japanese*, pp. 43ff.
122. "When You're Smiling: The Deadly Legacy of Internment," a documentary produced and directed by Janice D. Tanaka, Visual Communications, 1999.
123. Brad Knickerbocker, "U.S. Japanese Retain Cultural Ties," *The Christian Science Monitor*, July 27, 1993, p. 11.
124. Miranda Ewell, "Japanese American Still Trying to Find a Way to Belong in U.S.; Asians Have Achieved

Measurable Success but Continue to Face a Complex Racial and Ethnic Landscape," *Orange County (CA) Register*, August 19, 1996, p. A10.

125. JACL, "Causes of Anti-Asian Sentiment," www.jacl.org/antihate/index.html (retrieved December 21, 2006).
126. David Mura, "Whites: How to Face the Angry Racial Tribes," *Utne Reader*, July/August 1992, p. 80. See also David Mura, *Turning Japanese: Memoirs of a Sansei* (New York: Atlantic Monthly Press, 1991).
127. Charles Burress, "Looking to Hawaii for Harmony: Japanese American Panel Wants a Model for the New California," *San Francisco Chronicle*, October 21, 1997, p. A17.

Chapter 11

1. Elaine H. Kim, "They Armed in Self-Defense," *Newsweek*, May 18, 1992, p. 10.
2. Vickie Nam, "Introduction," in *YELL-Oh Girls*, ed. Vickie Nam (New York: Quill, 2001), pp. 111–116; Michael Kim, "Out and About: Coming of Age in a Straight White World," in *Asian American X: An Intersection of 21st Century Asian American Voices*, eds. Arar Han and John Hsu (Ann Arbor, MI: University of Michigan Press, 2004), p. 141.
3. U.S. Department of Homeland Security, "Yearbook of Immigration Statistics: 2005, Table 2: Legal Permanent Resident Flow by Region and Country of Last Residence: Fiscal Years 1820 to 2005," published December 18, 2006, www.dhs.gov/ximgtn/statistics/publications/LPR05.shtm.
4. Ronald Takaki, *A Different Mirror* (Boston: Little, Brown, 1993), pp. 211–214; Roger Daniels, *Asian America: Chinese and Japanese in the United States Since 1850* (Seattle: University of Washington Press, 1988), pp. 16–17, 44; Bill Ong Hing, *Making and Remaking Asian America Through Immigration Policy: 1850–1990* (Stanford, CA: Stanford University Press, 1993), p. 23, 48–49, 80.
5. U.S. Commission on Civil Rights, *Recent Activities Against Citizens and Residents of Asian Descent* (Washington, DC, 1986), p. 7.
6. Immigration and Naturalization Service, *1985 Statistical Yearbook*, pp. 2–5; Ronald Takaki, *Strangers from a Different Shore: A History of Asian Americans* (Boston: Little, Brown, 1989), pp. 111–112.
7. U.S. Commission on Civil Rights, *Recent Activities Against Citizens and Residents of Asian Descent*, p. 8.
8. U.S. Commission on Civil Rights, *The Tarnished Golden Door: Civil Rights Issues in Immigration* (Washington, DC, 1980), p. 10.
9. Immigration and Naturalization Service, *1985 Statistical Yearbook*, pp. 2–5; U.S. Census Bureau, "Table DP-1: Profile of General Demographic Characteristics for the United States: 2000," www.census.gov (retrieved August 29, 2001); U.S. Census Bureau, http://factfinder.census.gov/basicfacts.html (retrieved August 29, 2001); U.S. Bureau of the Census, "American Fact Finder: Census 2000 Demographic Profile Highlights: Selected Population Group," http://factfinder.census.gov/home/saff/main.html?_lang=en (retrieved December 16, 2006); U.S. Bureau of the Census, "2005 American Community Survey, American Fact Finder: Selected Population Profile in the United States," http://factfinder.census.gov/servlet/IPTable?_bm=y&-context=ip &-reg=ACS_2005_EST_G00_S0201:022;ACS_2005_EST_G00_S0201PR:022;ACS_2005_EST_G00_S0201T:022;ACS_2005_EST_G00_S0201TPR:022&-qr_name=ACS_2005_EST_G00_S0201&-qr_name=ACS_2005_EST_G00_S0201PR&-qr_name=ACS_2005_EST_G00_S0201T&-qr_name=ACS_2005_EST_G00_S0201TPR&-ds_name=ACS_2005_EST_G00_&-tree_id=305&-redoLog=false&-geo_id=01000US&-search_results=01000US&-format=&-_lang=en (retrieved December 16, 2006).
10. Stephan Thernstrom, ed., *Harvard Encyclopedia of American Ethnic Groups* (Cambridge, MA: Harvard University Press, 1981), pp. 357–359.
11. U.S. Commission on Civil Rights, *Recent Activities Against Citizens and Residents of Asian Descent*, p. 9.
12. Vanessa Ho, "Filipinos' American Dream Comes True," *Seattle Times*, April 29, 1992, p. B1.
13. David Pierson, "Plight of Filipino Vets Studied," *The Los Angeles Times*, August 1, 2001, Part 2, p. 8
14. U.S. Census Bureau, "Table DP-1: Profile of General Demographic Characteristics for the United States: 2000"; U.S. Census Bureau, http://factfinder.census.gov/basicfacts.html; U.S. Bureau of the Census, "American Fact Finder: Census 2000 Demographic Profile Highlights: Selected Population Group"; U.S. Bureau of the Census, "2005 American Community Survey, American Fact Finder: Selected Population Profile in the United States."
15. Wayne Patterson, *The Korean Frontier in America: Immigration to Hawaii, 1896–1910* (Honolulu: University of Hawaii Press, 1988), p. 177; Takaki, *Strangers from a Different Shore*, pp. 270–271; U.S. Commission on Civil Rights, *Recent Activities Against Citizens and Residents of Asian Descent*, p. 9.
16. Warren Y. Kim, *Koreans in America* (Seoul: Po Chin Chai Printing Co., 1971), pp. 22–25.
17. David M. Reimers, *Still the Golden Door: The Third World Comes to America* (New York: Columbia

University Press, 1985), pp. 110–111; U.S. Department of Homeland Security, "Yearbook of Immigration Statistics: 2005, Table 2: Legal Permanent Resident Flow by Region and Country of Last Residence: Fiscal Years 1820 to 2005," published December 18, 2006,www.dhs.gov/ximgtn/statistics/publications/LPR05.shtm.

18. U.S. Census Bureau, "Table DP-1: Profile of General Demographic Characteristics for the United States: 2000"; U.S. Census Bureau, http://factfinder.census.gov/basicfacts.html; U.S. Bureau of the Census, "American Fact Finder: Census 2000 Demographic Profile Highlights: Selected Population Group"; U.S. Bureau of the Census, "2005 American Community Survey, American Fact Finder: Selected Population Profile in the United States."
19. Darrel Montero, *Vietnamese Americans: Patterns of Resettlement and Socioeconomic Adaptation in the United States* (Boulder, CO: Westview Press, 1979), pp. 1–3.
20. Morrison G. Wong and Charles Hirschman, "The New Asian Immigrants," in *Culture, Ethnicity, and Identity*, ed. William C. McCready (New York: Academic Press, 1983), p. 381.
21. U.S. Bureau of the Census, *1990 Census of Population: United States Summary*, CP-2-1 (Washington, DC, 1993), p. 4; U.S. Census Bureau, "Table DP-1: Profile of General Demographic Characteristics for the United States: 2000"; U.S. Census Bureau, http://factfinder.census.gov/basicfacts.html.
22. Ibid.
23. This paragraph draws on research of Arun Jain, as cited in Marcia Mogelonsky, "Asian-Indian Americans," *American Demographics*, August 1995, p. 36.
24. U.S. Bureau of the Census, "American Fact Finder: Census 2000 Demographic Profile Highlights: Selected Population Group"; U.S. Bureau of the Census, "2005 American Community Survey, American Fact Finder: Selected Population Profile in the United States."
25. Min Zhou and James V. Gatewood, "Introduction: Revisiting Contemporary Asian America," in *Contemporary Asian America: A Multidisciplinary Reader*, ed. Min Zhou and James V. Gatewood (New York: New York University Press, 2000), p. 35.
26. Ibid., p. 10.
27. Harry H. L. Kitano and Roger Daniels, *Asian Americans: Emerging Minorities* (Englewood Cliffs, NJ: Prentice Hall, 1988), p. 176.
28. Quoted in K. Connie Kang, "Building Bridges to Equality," *The Los Angeles Times*, January 7, 1995, p. A1.
29. See "Prepared Testimony of Karen Narasaki, Executive Director, National Asian Pacific American Legal Consortium Before the House Judiciary Committee, Subcommittee on the Constitution," Subcommittee Hearing on H.R. 1909: The Civil Rights Act of 1997, Federal News Service, June 26, 1997; Nazli Kibria, "College and Notions of 'Asian Americans,'" in *The Second Generation: Ethnic Identity Among Asian Americans*, ed. Pyong Gap Min (Lanham, MD: Rowman & Littlefield, 2002), p. 204; Leland T. Saito, "The Politics of Adaptation and the 'Good Immigrant': Japanese Americans and the New Chinese Immigrants," in *Asian and Latino Immigrants in a Restructuring Economy: The Metamorphosis of Southern California*, eds. Marta Lopez-Garza and David R. Diaz (Palo Alto, CA: Stanford University Press, 2001), pp. 332–349.
30. Claire Jean Kim, "The Racial Triangulation of Asian Americans," *Politics and Society* 27 (March 1999): 105–138.
31. *Plessy* v. *Ferguson* 163 U.S. 537, 561 (1896).
32. Quoted in Takaki, *Strangers from a Different Shore*, p. 370.
33. Miriam Sharma, "Labor Migration and Class Formation Among the Filipinos in Hawaii, 1940–1946," in *Labor Immigration Under Capitalism*, ed. Lucie Cheng and Edna Bonacich (Berkeley: University of California Press, 1984), pp. 583, 593.
34. Montero, *Vietnamese Americans*, pp. 3–4.
35. Paul Sweeney, "Tolerance in a Texas Town," *Texas Observer*, September 17, 1982, pp. 7–9; K. Connie Kang, "U.S. Asians Seen as 'Alien,' Study Finds," *The Los Angeles Times*, March 2, 2000, p. A3; Steve Emmons and David Reyes, "Gangs, Crime Top Fears of Vietnamese in Orange County," *The Los Angeles Times*, February 5, 1989, p. 3; Anti-Defamation League, "American Attitudes Towards Chinese Americans and Asian Americans," Press Release, April 25, 2001, www.adl.org/misc/american_attitudes_towards_chinese.asp (retrieved December 20, 2006).
36. As quoted in C. N. Le, "Sex and the Asian Man," *Asian-Nation*, www.asian-nation.org/asian-man.shtml (retrieved December 28, 2006). The text was originally written by David Pierson for the *Los Angeles Times*.
37. C. N. Le, "Cosmetic and Plastic Surgery," *Asian-Nation*, www.asian-nation.org/cosmetic-surgery.shtml (retrieved December 21, 2006); Olivia Chung, "Finding My Eye-Identity," in *YELL-Oh Girls*, p. 139; on white male sexism, see Meggy Wang, "For Those Who Love Yellow Girls," in *YELL-Oh Girls*, pp. 129–132, and other essays in this book.
38. C. N. Le, "Martial Arts Movies Kick @#!" *Asian-Nation*, www.asian-nation.org/martial-arts.shtml (retrieved December 28, 2006).

39. Helen Zia, *Asian American Dreams: The Emergence of an American People* (New York: Farrar, Straus, and Co., 2000), p. 199.
40. Sonni Efron, "'Saigon' Is Under Fire Once More," *The Los Angeles Times*, September 7, 1990, p. F1; Holly Hee Won Coughlin, "My Breakup with Miss Saigon," *Minnesota Women's Press*, July 7, 1999, www.modelminority.com (retrieved December 31, 2006); Center for Integration and Improvement of Journalism, *News Watch: A Critical Look at Coverage of People of Color* (San Francisco: San Francisco State University, 1994), pp. 40–43.
41. Ling-chi Wang, "Foreign Money Is No Friend of Ours," in *Asian Americans: Experiences and Perspectives*, ed. Timothy P. Fong and Larry H. Shinagawa (Upper Saddle River, NJ: Prentice Hall, 2000), p. 402.
42. Mia Tuan, *Forever Foreigners or Honorary Whites?: The Asian American Experience Today* (New Brunswick, NJ: Rutgers University Press, 1998), p. 154; Steven Rosenfeld, Liane Hansen, "Asian Americans," *NPR Weekend Sunday*, November 23, 1997; Andrea Stone and Robert Silvers, "Asian Americans See Rising Racism," *USA Today*, July 15, 1997, p. 8A.
43. "Daphne Kwok, Organization of Chinese Americans, and John O'Sullivan, *National Review*, Discuss Recent Cover Story for That Magazine That Asian Americans Are Saying Is Offensive and Racist," NBC News Transcripts, March 21, 1997; Mae M. Cheng, "Magazine Cover Ripped; Coalition Calls *National Review* Illustration Racist," *Newsday*, April 11, 1997, p. A4.
44. Doris Lin, "The Death of (http://Icebox.com's) Mr. Wong," USAsians.net, http://us_asians.tripod.com/articles-mrwong.html (retrieved December 14, 2006).
45. Jennifer Fang, "Team America: Racism, Idiocy, and Two Men's Pursuit to Piss Off as Many People as Possible," *Asian Media Watch*, October 28, 2004, www.asianmediawatch.net/teamamerica/review.html (retrieved December 17, 2006).
46. Zia, *Asian American Dreams*, p. 109; *YELL-Oh Girls*, pp. 111–200; *Asian American X*, passim.
47. Sharmila Rudrappa, "Disciplining Desire in Making the Home: Engendering Ethnicity in Indian Immigrant Families," in *The Second Generation*, p. 85.
48. U.S. Commission on Civil Rights, *Civil Rights Issues Facing Asian Americans in the 1990s* (Washington, DC: U.S. Government Printing Office, 1992), pp. 5–6; U.S. Commission on Civil Rights, *Recent Activities Against Citizens and Residents of Asian Descent*, pp. 3–6; Jocelyn Y. Stewart, "Lest Hate Victim Be Forgotten," *The Los Angeles Times*, January 25, 2001, p. A1.
49. U.S. Department of Justice, "Criminal Justice Information Services Uniform Crime Reports," press release for June 1994; Lena H. Sun, "Anti-Asian American Incidents Rising, Civil Rights Group Says; Organization Executives to Meet with Reno Today," *The Washington Post*, September 9, 1997, p. A2; "Prepared Testimony of Karen Narasaki," Federal News Service, June 26, 1997.
50. U.S. Commission on Civil Rights, *Civil Rights Issues Facing Asian Americans in the 1990s*, pp. 22–48; "Hate Crimes Rise in Orange County," *The Race Relations Reporter*, May 15, 1999, p. 1; Orange County Human Relations Commission, "Hate Crimes and Incidents in Orange County," http://64.233.161.104/ search?q=cache:2B69Ym6YOgAJ:www.ochumanrelations.org/pdf/Hate_Crime_report.pdf+%22orange+county%22+reported+%22hate+crimes%22+2005&hl=en&gl=us&ct=clnk&cd=3 (retrieved January 1, 2007).
51. David Reyes, "Coalition Urges More Prosecutions of Hate Crimes," *The Los Angeles Times*, September 9, 1994, p. B1; Mara Rose Williams, "Asian Americans Say Police Are Biased," *Atlanta Journal and Constitution*, September 9, 1994, p. C5; Maryland Advisory Committee, U.S. Commission on Civil Rights, "City Services and the Justice System: Do Korean American Storeowners in Baltimore, Maryland Get Equal Treatment?" July 2004, http:// 64.233.161.104/search?q=cache:3QEAKAn9wJ:www.usccr.gov/pubs/sac/md0704.pdf+%22adequate+police+protection%22+%22asian+americans%22&hl=en&gl=us&ct=clnk&cd=1 (retrieved January 1, 2007).
52. U.S. Commission on Civil Rights, *Civil Rights Issues Facing Asian Americans in the 1990s*, pp. 49–69, quotation from p. 52.
53. Mimi Ko, "Forum to Examine Police Harassment," *The Los Angeles Times*, June 11, 1994, p. B2; see also Utah Task Force on Racial and Ethnic Fairness in the Legal System, "Perceptions of Racial and Ethnic Fairness in the Criminal Justice System: Listening to Utahns," Client Committee Report on Public Hearings," 1999, http://64.233.161.104/search?q=cache:2i_I1Gbt5K0J:www.utcourts.gov/specproj/retaskforce/clrpt24.pdf+photographing+youths+%22gang%22+%22racial+profiling%22+%22asian+american%22&hl=en&gl=us&ct=clnk&cd=4 (retrieved January 1, 2007).
54. U.S. Commission on Civil Rights, *Civil Rights Issues Facing Asian Americans in the 1990s*, pp. 5–6; U.S. Commission on Civil Rights, *Recent Activities Against Citizens and Residents of Asian Descent*, pp. 3–6.
55. Ann Bancroft, "Jury Gets Racist Firebombings Case in Sacramento," *San Francisco Chronicle*, August 25, 1994, p. A20.
56. U.S. Commission on Civil Rights, *Recent Activities Against Citizens and Residents of Asian Descent*, pp. 43–44; U.S. Commission on Civil Rights, *Civil Rights*

Issues Facing Asian Americans in the 1990s, pp. 25–26; quotation from p. 28.

57. U.S. Commission on Civil Rights, *Civil Rights Issues Facing Asian Americans in the 1990s*, pp. 25–26.
58. Ibid., pp. 26–28; "Hate Crime in Queens," *AsianWeek*, August 25, 2006, http://news.asianweek.com (retrieved December 18, 2006).
59. Julie Chao, "Berkeley Students Claim Bias in D.C.; Asian Americans Offended by Guards," *San Francisco Examiner*, September 30, 1997, p. A1.
60. Harry H. L. Kitano and Roger Daniels, *Asian Americans: Emerging Minorities*, 3rd ed. (Englewood Cliffs, NJ: Prentice Hall, 2001), pp. 54–55; "Rights Commission Schedules Briefing on Scapegoating of Asian-Americans," ACLU press release, October 23, 1997.
61. Howard A. DeWitt, *Anti-Filipino Movements in California: A History, Bibliography and Study Guide* (San Francisco: R & E Research Associates, 1976), pp. 27–66.
62. Ibid.
63. David Ibata, "Asians Seek Spot in America's Melting Pot," *Chicago Tribune*, April 26, 1992, p. 1.
64. Stewart, "Lest Hate Victim Be Forgotten," p. A1; 2/9/06; "Death Climbs to 8 in Postal Rampage," *Asianweek.com*, February 9, 2006, www.asianam.org/hate.htm (retrieved January 2, 2007).
65. Gus Mercado, "Lessons Learned from the Texas 10 Trials," National Federation of Filipino American Associations, www.naffaa.org/2005naffaa/files/texas10lessons.pdf (retrieved January 3, 2007).
66. Andrea Ford, "Slain Girl Was Not Stealing Juice, Police Say," *The Los Angeles Times*, March 19, 1991, p. B1; Itabari Njeri, "Perspectives on Race Relations," *The Los Angeles Times*, November 29, 1991, p. B5; Mike Davis, "In L.A., Burning All Illusions," Nation 254, no. 21 (June 1, 1992): 743–746, quotation on p. 745.
67. Kim, "They Armed in Self-Defense," p. 10.
68. Hsia-Chuan Hsia, "Imported Racism and Indigenous Biases: The Impacts of the U.S. Media on Taiwanese Images of African Americans," research paper presented at the Annual Meeting of the American Sociological Association, Los Angeles, August 5–9, 1994.
69. See Joe R. Feagin, *Racist America: Roots, Current Realities, and Future Reparations* (New York: Routledge, 2000), chap. 7.
70. Claire Jean Kim, *Bitter Fruit: The Politics of Black—Korean Conflict in New York City* (New Haven, CT: Yale University Press, 2000), p. 11.
71. Moon H. Jo, "Korean Merchants in the Black Community: Prejudice Among the Victims of Prejudice," *Ethnic and Racial Studies* 15 (1992): 395–411; Robert L. Bach, *Changing Relations: Newcomers and Established Residents in U.S. Communities* (New York: Ford Foundation, 1993).
72. Nancy Abelmann and John Lie, *Blue Dreams: Korean Americans and the Los Angeles Riots* (Cambridge, MA: Harvard University Press, 1995), pp. 140–141.
73. Quoted in Njeri, "Perspectives on Race Relations," p. B5.
74. Ku-Sup Chin, "New Immigrants, Industrial Flexibility, and Ethnic Conflicts: Korean and Hispanic Immigrants in the Los Angeles Garment Industry," paper presented at the Annual Meeting of the American Sociological Association, Los Angeles, August 5–9, 1994.
75. U.S. Commission on Civil Rights, *Recent Activities Against Citizens and Residents of Asian Descent*, pp. 50–52; Sweeney, "Tolerance in a Texas Town," pp. 7–10.
76. Michael McCabe, "U.S. Leaders Urged to Fight Hate Crimes," *San Francisco Chronicle*, February 29, 1992, p. A1; Zia, *Asian American Dreams*, p. 91.
77. Eric K. Yamamoto, "Healing Our Own," Boston College, www.bc.edu/bc_org/avp/law/lwsch/journals/bctwj/20_1/08_TXT.htm (retrieved January 2, 2007).
78. Jonathan Schuppe and Aditi Kinkhabwala, "Education a Family Affair; Asian Indians Work Hard for Success in Classroom," *Asbury Park Press* (Neptune, NJ), August 17, 1997, p. 27A; "Documented Incidents of Xenophobia and Intolerance in Political Discourse," South Asian Leaders of Tomorrow (SAALT), press release, August 30, 2006.
79. Zia, *Asian American Dreams*, pp. 219–221.
80. Arlene Newman, "Festival Reflects Indians' Growth," *The New York Times*, August 18, 1991, sec. 12NJ, p. 1; Joel Kotkin, "Asian Indians in California Spotlight After Years in Shadows," *The Washington Post*, May 6, 1990, p. H2; Asian American Legal Defense and Education Fund, "Public Statement from Concerned Organizations Regarding the Recent Incidents in Edison, NJ Involving the South Asian Community," www.aaldef.org/article.php? article_id=144 (retrieved December 13, 2006).
81. "Asian Americans Called the New "Sleeping Giant' of California Politics," *AsianConnections.com*, September 7, 2006, http://asianconnections.com (retrieved December 18, 2006); U.S. House of Representatives, "Daily Press Gallery: Demographics," published November 13, 2006, www.house.gov/daily/hpg.htm.
82. K. Connie Kang, "Group Seeks to Boost Profile of Asian American Voters," *The Los Angeles Times*, August 22, 2000, p. B1; telephone interview with New York City Council office, January 18, 2002; "The Immigrant Vote in New York City Is Topic of Panel Discussion," *Barnard Campus News*, Wednesday, May 2, 2001, p. 1; "Asians in State Legislatures and Voting Age Population," *Vietnamese American Demographics*,

www.ncvaonline.org/demographics.shtml (retrieved January 2, 2007).

83. Paul Ong and Don Nakanishi, "Becoming Citizens, Becoming Voters," in *Asian Americans*, ed. Fong and Shinagawa, pp. 380–383; "The Immigrant Vote in New York City Is Topic of Panel Discussion," *Barnard Campus News*, Wednesday, May 2, 2001; U.S. Commission on Civil Rights, *Civil Rights Issues Facing Asian Americans in the 1990s*, pp. 157–163.
84. Asian American Legal Defense and Education Fund, "The Asian American Vote 2004: A Report on the Multilingual Exit Poll in the 2004 Presidential Election," *Outlook*, Fall 2006, www.aaldef.org/article.php?article_id=67 (retrieved December 13, 2006).
85. Daniels, *Asian America*, p. 113; Zhou and Gatewood, "Introduction: Revisiting Contemporary Asian America," p. 27.
86. Yen Le Espiritu, *Asian American Panethnicity* (Philadelphia: Temple University Press, 1992), pp. 19–49; see also Edward W. Said, *Orientalism* (New York: Vintage Books, 1979).
87. Lisa Lowe, "Heterogeneity, Hybridity, Multiplicity: Marking Asian American Differences," *Diaspora* 1 (1991): 31; Espiritu, *Asian American Panethnicity*, pp. 47–49.
88. Espiritu, *Asian American Panethnicity*, pp. 50–51; Paul Sweeney, "Asian Americans Gain Clout," *American Demographics* 8 (February 1986): 18–19; Kang, "Building Bridges to Equality."
89. Frank Wu, "Asian Americans Finally Organize the NCAPA," New America News Service, November 27, 1997.
90. Carla Rivera, "Orange County Focus," *The Los Angeles Times*, April 28, 1992, p. B3; K. Connie Kang, "Korean Groups Back Union Fight for Jobs," *The Los Angeles Times*, November 17, 1994, p. B1.
91. Peter Kwong, *Chinatown, N.Y.: Labor and Politics, 1930–1950* (New York: Monthly Review Press, 1979), pp. 45–67; Judy Yung, "The Social Awakening of Chinese American Women," in *Unequal Sisters*, ed. Ellen Carol DuBois and Vicki L. Ruiz (New York: Routledge, 1990), p. 196.
92. Martin F. Nolan, "California Confronts the Politics of Growth," *Boston Globe*, October 23, 1991, p. 1.
93. Kitano and Daniels, *Asian Americans*, p. 49.
94. K. Connie Kang, "Activist for a New Era of Civil Rights; Berkeley Professor Has Fought Many Battles for the Asian American Community in the Past Three Decades," *The Los Angeles Times*, July 6, 2001, part 2, p. 1.
95. For earlier issues, see Nicholas Lemann, "Growing Pains," *Atlantic Monthly*, January 1988, pp. 57–62.
96. Pei-te Lien, M. Margaret Conway, and Janelle Wong, *The Politics of Asian Americans: Diversity and Community* (New York: Routledge, 2004), p. vii.
97. Frank Wu, "What Do Chinese Americans Think of China?" New America News Service, October 30, 1997; see "Issues," Committee of 100, www.committee100.org/aboutus/aboutus_issues.htm (retrieved January 3, 2007); K. Connie Kang, "The 2008 Summer Games; Chinese Americans Feel Joy, Concern at Choice," *The Los Angeles Times*, July 14, 2001, p. A10.
98. John Gregory Dunne, *Delano: The Story of the California Grape Strike* (New York: Farrar, Straus & Giroux, 1967), p. 77; Lemuel F. Ignacio, *Asian Americans and Pacific Islanders* (San Jose, CA: Pilipino Development Associates, 1976), pp. 11–56; Kitano and Daniels, *Asian Americans*, p. 86.
99. Michelle Mizal, "Filipino Americans Hope to Build Unity; Group Also Hopes to Build Political Clout at D.C. Event," *Virginian-Pilot* (Norfolk, VA), August 21, 1997, p. B1.
100. Kitano and Daniels, *Asian Americans*, 3rd ed., p. 117.
101. "D.C. Groups Congratulate David Wu and Stress the Importance of the APA Vote," Asian Pacific American Institute for Congressional Studies, press release, November 9, 1998.
102. James T. Madore, "Long-Quiet Asian Group Starts to Mobilize," *The Christian Science Monitor*, May 20, 1988, p. 7; "Filipino Americans Protest S.F. Memorial," United Press International, March 31, 1997.
103. Bong-youn Choy, *Koreans in America* (Chicago: Nelson-Hall, 1979), pp. 141–189; "Programs," Korean American Coalition, www.kacdc.org/programs/index.html (retrieved January 3, 2007).
104. Quoted in Greg La Motte, "Asian Americans: A Diverse Voting Block," Cable News Network, June 1, 1992, transcript no. 76-5.
105. Julie Ha, "Korean American Political Power," New America News Service, March 18, 1997.
106. Zia, *Asian American Dreams*, p. 184; Wendy Koch, "Asians Are Becoming More Vocal in the Debate," *USA Today*, May 2, 2006, p. 7A.
107. "Korean Americans Send 100,000 Dollars in Aid to North Korea," Agence France Presse, April 3, 1997; Barbara Slavin, "Korean-Americans Want Families on Agenda," *USA Today*, May 9, 2001, p. 13A; "Korean Americans Fear Ramifications of Nuclear Test," *The Online News Hour*, October 31, 2006, http://64.233.161.104/search?q=cache:RURtiM2z30gJ:www.pbs.org/newshour/bb/politics/july-dec06/koreanams_1031.html+%22korean+americans% 22+2006+family+%22north+korea%22+government+policy&hl=en&gl=us&ct=clnk&cd=1 (retrieved January 3, 2007).

108. Steve Emmons and David Reyes, "The Orange County Poll," *The Los Angeles Times,* February 5, 1989, p. 1; "Vietnamese Americans," *Wikipedia,* http://en.wikipedia.org/wiki/Vietnamese_America n (retrieved January 3, 2007).
109. Ibid.
110. Quyen Do, "Little Saigon Readies for Community Balloting; Vietnamese Americans Will Elect Their Unofficial Leaders," *Orange County (CA) Register,* January 13, 1996, p. B1; Bert Eljera, "Big Plans for Little Saigon," www.asianweek.com/ 051796/Little Saigon.html (retrieved August 15, 2001); Leland Saito, personal communication, April 18, 2001; "Vietnamese Americans," *Wikipedia.*
111. Carolyn Leung, "Redefining Advocacy for the Southeast Asian American Community," *Journal of Asian American Studies* 3 (2000): 237–241.
112. Kotkin, "Asian Indians in California Spotlight After Years in Shadows," p. H2; Newman, "Festival Reflects Indians' Growth," sec. 12NJ, p. 1; Vindu P. Goel, "The Rise of Asian Indians," (Cleveland) *Plain Dealer,* July 28, 1996, p. 8.
113. Zia, *Asian American Dreams,* pp. 198–202; Tianlong Yu, "Challenging the Politics of the 'Model Minority' Stereotype," *Equity & Excellence in Education* 39 (2006): 328; "The Continuing Impact of September 11th and the South Asian Community," *South Asian American Leaders of Tomorrow,* http://64.233.161.104/search?q=cache:p_ e8QXcjwUEJ:www.saalt.org/pdfs/PhillyImpact9-11.pdf+%22south+asian+coalition%22+indian+-india+-villages+-servitude&hl=en&gl=us&ct=clnk&cd=2 (retrieved January 3, 2007).
114. U.S. Commission on Civil Rights, *Civil Rights Issues Facing Asian Americans in the 1990s,* pp. 131–136, 145–148.
115. Ibid; Edward Iwata, "Boards Seat Few Asian-Pacific Americans," April 14, 2004, *USA Today,* www.usatoday.com/money/companies/management/2004-04-14-asian-americans_x.htm; E. J. Park, "Asian Americans in Silicon Valley: Race and Ethnicity in the Postindustrial Economy," unpublished doctoral dissertation, University of California, Berkeley, Department of Ethnic Studies, 1992; Cliff Cheng, "Are Asian American Employees a Model Minority or Just a Minority?" *Journal of Applied Behavioral Science* 33, no. 3 (September 1997): 277–290.
116. U.S. Commission on Civil Rights, *Civil Rights Issues Facing Asian Americans in the 1990s,* pp. 131–136, 153–156; Johanna Shih, "Circumventing Discrimination: Gender and Ethnic Strategies in Silicon Valley," *Gender & Society* 20 (April 2006): 177–206; National Asian Pacific American Women's Forum, Press Release, www.napawf.org/file/issues/issues-wage_gap.pdf (retrieved January 4, 2007).
117. "Got the Look? Abercrombie & Fitch's Hiring Policy: Hot or Not?" *Current Events* 103 (2003), p. 3.
118. U.S. Commission on Civil Rights, *Civil Rights Issues Facing Asian Americans in the 1990s*, pp. 136–148.
119. *Harvard Encyclopedia of American Ethnic Groups*, ed. Thernstrom, pp. 218–220; Takaki, *Strangers from a Different Shore*, pp. 374–375.
120. Reimers, *Still the Golden Door*, p. 107.
121. Zhou and Gatewood, "Introduction: Revisiting Contemporary Asian America," in *Contemporary Asian America: A Multidisciplinary Reader*, ed. Zhou and Gatewood, p. 10.
122. Bettina Boxall, "Asian Indians Remake Silicon Valley; Immigrants: As Their Numbers Surge, High-Tech Skills Ease the Transition for Many," *The Los Angeles Times*, July 6, 2001 p. A1; "Demand for Asian Exec a Sign of the Times," *Nwasianweekly.Com*, July 30, 2005, www.nwasianweekly.com/20052431/editorial20052431.htm (retrieved December 20, 2006).
123. U.S. Bureau of the Census, "2005 American Community Survey, American Fact Finder: Selected Population Profile," http://factfinder.census.gov/servlet/IPCharIterationServlet?_ts=184605613460; retrieved December 18, 2006; U.S. Bureau of the Census, "American Fact Finder: Selected Population Profile in the United States," http://factfinder. census.gov/servlet/IPTable?_bm=y&-geo_id=01000US&-qr_name=ACS_2005_EST_G00_S0201&-qr_name=ACS_2005_EST_G00_S0201PR&-qr_name=ACS_2005_EST_G00_S0201T&-qr_name=ACS_2005_EST_G00_S0201TPR&-reg=ACS_2005_EST_G00_S0201:016;ACS_2005_EST_G00_S0201PR:016;ACS_2005_EST_G00_S0201T:016;ACS_2005_EST_G00_S0201TPR:016&-ds_name=ACS_2005_EST_G00_&-_lang=en&-format= (retrieved December 29, 2006).
124. U.S. Bureau of the Census, *1990 Census of Population: Social and Economic Characteristics: United States Summary*, pp. 44, 111–112.
125. Roger Daniels, *Coming to America* (New York: HarperCollins, 1990), p. 355; C. N. Le, "Writers, Artists and Entertainers," *Asian-Nation*, www.asian-nation.org/artists.shtml (retrieved December 28, 2006).
126. U.S. Bureau of the Census, "2005 American Community Survey, American Fact Finder: Select Population Profile," http://factfinder.census.gov/servlet/IPCharIterationServlet?_ts=184605613460 (retrieved December 18, 2006).
127. U.S. Bureau of the Census, *1990 Census of Population: Asians and Pacific Islanders in the United States*, pp. 76, 111, 146.

128. Jan Lin, *Reconstructing Chinatown: Ethnic Enclave, Global Change* (Minneapolis: University of Minnesota Press, 1998). p. ix.
129. Leland Saito, personal communication, Fall 1998; and Leland Saito, *Race and Politics: Asian Americans, Latinos, and Whites in a Los Angeles Suburb* (Urbana: University of Illinois Press, 1998), pp. 39–54.
130. Takaki, *Strangers from a Different Shore*, pp. 322–323, quotation from p. 323.
131. Steve Lohr, "Filipinos Flocking to the U.S. as Manila's Troubles Grow," *The New York Times*, June 6, 1985, p. A14.
132. U.S. Bureau of the Census, "American Fact Finder, Selected Population Profile in the United States," http://factfinder.census.gov/servlet/IPTable?_bm=y&-geo_id=01000US&-qr_name=ACS_2005_EST_G00_S0201&-qr_name=ACS_2005_EST_G00_S0201PR&-qr_name=ACS_2005_EST_G00_S0201T&-qr_name=ACS_2005_EST_G00_S0201TPR&-reg=ACS_2005_EST_G00_S0201:019;ACS_2005_EST_G00_S0201PR:019;ACS_2005_EST_G00_S0201T:019;ACS_2005_EST_G00_S0201TPR:019&-ds_name=ACS_2005_EST_G00_&-_lang=en&-redoLog=false&-format= (retrieved December 29, 2006).
133. United Press International, press release, March 30, 1988.
134. Irene Chang, "Ruling on Foreign Language Ban Criticized," *The Los Angeles Times*, October 26, 1991, p. B3; Kari Gibson, "English Only Court Cases Involving the U.S. Workplace: The Myths of Language Use and the Homogenization of Bilingual Workers' Identities," *Second Language Studies* 22 (Spring 2004): 1–6.
135. Choy, *Koreans in America*, pp. 123–133.
136. U.S. Bureau of the Census, *1990 Census of Population: Social and Economic Characteristics: United States Summary*, pp. 47, 113; U.S. Bureau of the Census, *1990 Census of the Population: Social and Economic Characteristics: Urbanized Areas*, CP-2-1C (Washington, DC, 1993), p. 4759; Takaki, *Strangers from a Different Shore*, pp. 441–444; Reimers, *Still the Golden Door*, pp. 111–112; Ivan Light, "Immigrant Entrepreneurs in America: Koreans in Los Angeles," in *Clamor at the Gates*, ed. Nathan Glazer (San Francisco: ICS Press, 1985), p. 162.
137. "Korean Americans Adjust to Life in Korea," New America News Service, February 3, 1997.
138. Pyong Gap Min, *Changes and Conflicts: Korean Immigrant Families in New York* (Boston: Allyn & Bacon, 1998), p. 120.
139. Survey by Eui-Young Yu, cited in Emily MacFarquhar, "Fighting over the Dream," *U.S. News & World Report*, May 18, 1991, p. 34; Ivan Light and Edna Bonacich, *Immigrant Entrepreneurs* (Berkeley: University of California Press, 1988); Keeley Webster, "Brokers, Investors Banking on Koreatown's Growing Attraction," *California Real Estate Journal*, June 12, 2006, http://209.85.165.104/search?q=cache:FVGTS8TQWqUJ:themercuryla.com/the-extras/banking-on-koreatown.php+%22moving+ back+to+koreatown%22+%22los+angeles%22&hl=en&gl=us&ct=clnk&cd=1 (retrieved January 5, 2007).
140. U.S. Bureau of the Census, 1990 *Census of Population: Social and Economic Characteristics: United States Summary*, pp. 44, 48, 111, 117, 119; Asian American Legal Defense and Education Fund, "Aaldef Releases Groundbreaking Report on Low-Wage Korean Workers," " *Outlook*, Fall 2006, www.aaldef.org/article.php?article_id=206 (retrieved December 13, 2006); Aruna Lee, "Korean Americans: Crackdown Could Hurt Linked Communities," *New America Media*, March 30, 2006, http://news.newamericamedia.org/news/view_article.html? article_id=c43694580a1dbba141a6e50e37d93577.
141. Montero, *Vietnamese Americans*, p. 39.
142. "Prepared Testimony of Karen Narasaki," Federal News Service, June 26, 1997; Linh Ngo, "The Lawsuit," in *YELL-Oh Girls*, pp. 150–153.
143. Dennis McLellan, "Writer Urges the U.S. to See 'A Hidden Treasure of Talents,'" *The Los Angeles Times*, February 7, 1992, p. E3; Sonni Efron, "Few Viet Exiles Find U.S. Riches," *The Los Angeles Times*, April 29, 1990, p. A1;. U.S. Bureau of the Census, "American Fact Finder, Selected Population Profile in the United States," http://factfinder.census.gov/servlet/IPTable?_bm=y&-geo_id=01000US&-qr_name=ACS_2005_EST_G00_S0201&-qr_name=ACS_2005_EST_G00_S0201PR&-qr_name=ACS_2005_EST_G00_S0201T&-qr_name=ACS_2005_EST_G00_S0201TPR&-reg=ACS_2005_EST_G00_S0201:019;ACS_2005_EST_G00_S0201PR:019;ACS_2005_EST_G00_S0201T:019;ACS_2005_EST_G00_S0201TPR:019&-ds_name=ACS_2005_EST_G00_&-_lang=en&-redoLog=false&-format= (retrieved December 29, 2006).
144. See "Asian, Indian Firms Growing," *Omaha World Herald*, August 5, 1996, p. 13.
145. The study is cited in Boxall, "Asian Indians Remake Silicon Valley"; "The Market: Potential and Opportunity," http://mediakit.indusbusinessjournal.com/03_ibj_mediakit07_market_potential.pdf (retrieved January 5, 2007).
146. U.S. Bureau of the Census, "American Fact Finder, Selected Population Profile in the United States," http://factfinder.census.gov/servlet/IPTable?_bm=y&-geo_id=01000US&qr_name=ACS_2005_EST_G00_S0201&-qr_name=ACS_2005_EST_G00_S020 1PR&-qr_name=ACS_2005_EST_G00_S0201T&-qr_ name=ACS_2005_EST_G00_S0201TPR&-reg=ACS_2005_EST_G00_S0201:019;ACS_2005_EST_

G00_S0201PR:019;ACS_2005_EST_G00_S0201T:019;ACS_2005_EST_G00_S0201TPR:019&-ds_name=ACS_2005_EST_G00_&-_lang=en&-redoLog=false&-format= (retrieved December 29, 2006); "The Market: Potential and Opportunity."

147. Boxall, "Asian Indians Remake Silicon Valley."
148. "Prepared Testimony of Karen Narasaki," Federal News Service, June 26, 1997.
149. Leland Saito, personal communication, Fall 1998.
150. Angela Kim and Christine Yeh, "Stereotypes of Asian American Students," *ERIC Digest*, February 2002, http://searcheric.org/digests/ed462510.html (retrieved December 21, 2006).
151. U.S. Commission on Civil Rights, *Civil Rights Issues Facing Asian Americans in the 1990s*, pp. 68–99.
152. Somini Sengupta, "Not All Asian Americans Prospering, Study Reports; Students' Academic Success Obscuring Needs," *Dallas Morning News*, November 14, 1997, p. 44A; Sonia M. Pérez, Ka Ying Yang, Marian Wright Edelman, and James M. Jones, "Growing Up American," *Children of Immigrant Families* 14 (Summer 2004): 119–138.
153. Kim and Yeh, "Stereotypes of Asian American Students."
154. Michelle Ott, "The Incidence of Anti-Asian Violence in High Schools," Bates College, 1994, cited in Peter Nien-Chu Kiang, "We Could Shape It: Organizing for Asian Pacific American Student Empowerment," in Asian Americans, ed. Fong and Shinagawa, p. 126; Asian American Legal Defense and Education Fund, "Educational Equity," www.aaldef.org/education.php (retrieved December 13, 2006).
155. Long Le, "The Dark Side of the Asian American 'Model Student,'" August 2, 2006, http://news.newamericamedia.org/news (retrieved January 5, 2007); Donna Leinwand, "Racist Threats Set Penn State on Edge," USA Today, May 3, 2001, p. 3A.
156. U.S. Bureau of the Census, *Statistical Abstract of the United States 1994* (Washington, DC, 1994), pp. 49, 157.
157. U.S. Bureau of the Census, "2005 American Community Survey, American Fact Finder: Select Population Profile," http://factfinder.census.gov/servlet/IPCharIterationServlet?_ts=184605613460 (retrieved December 18, 2006).
158. Schuppe and Kinkhabwala, "Education a Family Affair"; Melita Marie Garza, "Asians Feel Bias Built on Perceptions," *Chicago Tribune*, August 7, 1994, p. C1.
159. Eloise Salholz et al., "Do Colleges Set Asian Quotas?" *Newsweek*, February 9, 1987, p. 60.
160. U.S. Commission on Civil Rights, *Civil Rights Issues Facing Asian Americans in the 1990s*, pp. 109–112.
161. Madore, "Long-Quiet Asian Group Starts to Mobilize," p. 7.
162. Ronald Takaki, "Is Race Surmountable? Thomas Sowell's Celebration of Japanese-American 'Success,'" in *Ethnicity and the Work Force*, ed. Winston A. Van Horne (Madison: University of Wisconsin Press, 1985), pp. 218–220.
163. Senate Judiciary Committee, "Capitol Hill Hearings," September 20, 1991; "Prepared Testimony of Karen Narasaki," Federal News Service, June 26, 1997; for late 2000s positions, see www.napaba.org.
164. Mogelonsky, "Asian-Indian Americans," pp. 32–38; Takaki, *Strangers from a Different Shore*, p. 473.
165. Tuan, *Forever Foreigners*, p. 155.
166. Kitano and Daniels, *Asian Americans*, pp. 190–192; Takaki, *Strangers from a Different Shore*, p. 473.
167. Saito, *Race and Politics*, p. 61.
168. Emmons and Reyes, "Gangs, Crime Top Fears of Vietnamese in Orange County," p. 3; Emmons and Reyes, "The Orange County Poll," p. 1.
169. Scott Gold, "A Generation Removed: Lessons and Legacies 25 Years After Vietnam," *The Los Angeles Times*, April 28, 2000, p. M3.
170. Daniels, *Coming to America*, p. 367; Reimers, *Still the Golden Door*, p. 111.
171. Karen Pyke, "'The Normal American Family' as an Interpretive Structure of Family Life Among Adult Children of Korean and Vietnamese Immigrants," unpublished paper, University of Florida, Gainesville, 1997; see also Pyong Gap Min and Joann Hong, "Ethnic Attachment Among Second-Generation Korean Americans, in *The Second Generation*, pp. 113–126; Christine Yeh, "Age, Acculturation, Cultural Adjustment, and Mental Health Symptoms of Chinese, Korean, and Japanese Immigrant Youths," *Cultural Diversity and Ethnic Minority Psychology* 9 (2003); 34–48.
172. Durriya Z. Khairullah and Zahid Y. Khairullah, "Behavioural Acculturation and Demographic Characteristics of Asian Indian Immigrants in the United States of America," *International Journal of Sociology* 19 (1999): 57–80; Boxall, "Asian Indians Remake Silicon Valley."
173. John Dillin, "More Blacks Enter Middle Class," *The Christian Science Monitor*, August 9, 1991, p. 7; Shinagawa and Pang, "Asian American Panethnicity and Intermarriage," in *Asian Americans*, ed. Fong and Shinagawa, p. 341.
174. Shinagawa and Pang, "Asian American Panethnicity and Intermarriage," pp. 334–343; C. N. Le, "Interracial Dating and Marriage," Asian-Nation, www.asian-nation.org/interracial.shtml (retrieved December 21, 2006).

175. Shinagawa and Pang, "Asian American Panethnicity and Intermarriage," pp. 334–343.
176. Kumiko Nemoto, "Intimacy, Desire, and the Construction of Self in Relationships Between Asian American Women and White American Men," *Journal of Asian American Studies* 9 (2006), p. 51.
177. Nazli Kibria, "The Construction of 'Asian American': Reflections on Intermarriage and Ethnic Identity Among Second-Generation Chinese and Korean Americans," *Ethnic and Racial Studies*, 20 (July 1997): 523–544; Nazli Kibria, *Becoming Asian American: Second Generation Chinese and Korean American Identities* (Baltimore, MD: Johns Hopkins University Press, 2002), pp. 175–199.
178. Shinagawa and Pang, "Asian American Panethnicity and Intermarriage," p. 343.
179. B. Suzuki, "Education and the Socialization of Asian Americans," in *Asian Americans: Social and Psychological Perspectives*, ed. R. Endo, S. Sue, and N. Wagner (Palo Alto, CA: Science & Behavior Books, 1980), 2:155–178.
180. Robert G. Lee, *Orientals: Asian Americans in Popular Culture* (Philadelphia: Temple University Press, 1999), pp. 188, 189.
181. Ishmael Reed, "America's Color Bind: The Modeling of Minorities," *San Francisco Examiner*, November 19, 1987, p. A20; "Success Story of One Minority Group in the U.S.," *U.S. News & World Report*, December 26, 1966, pp. 73–76.
182. We draw here on Feagin, *Racist America*, chap. 7.
183. See, for example, Dinesh D'Souza, *The End of Racism: Principles for a Multiracial Society* (New York: The Free Press, 1995).
184. Frank Wu, "Neither Black nor White: Asian Americans and Affirmative Action," *Boston College Third World Law Journal* 15 (1995): 249–250.
185. Gary Y. Okihiro, "Is Yellow Black or White?" in *Asian Americans: Experiences and Perspectives*, ed. Fong and Shinagawa, p. 75.
186. Richard L. Zweigenhaft and William Domhoff, *Diversity in the Power Elite: Have Women and Minorities Reached the Top?* (New Haven, CT: Yale University Press, 1998).
187. Min Zhou, "Growing Up American: The Challenge Confronting Immigrant Children and Children of Immigrants," *Annual Review of Sociology* 23 (1997): 63–95.
188. Gloria Luz R. Martinez and Wayne J. Villemez, "Assimilation in the United States: Occupational Attainment of Asian Americans, 1980," paper presented at the American Sociological Association meetings, Chicago, 1987, pp. 31–32; U.S. Commission on Civil Rights, *Civil Rights Issues Facing Asian Americans in the 1990s*, pp. 103–136.
189. Yen Le Espiritu, "Multiple Identities of Second-Generation Filipinos," in *The Second Generation*, p. 45; Hung Cam Thai, "Formation of Ethnic Identity Among Second-Generation Vietnamese Americans," in *The Second Generation*, p. 76; Tuan, *Forever Foreigners*, p. 159.
190. Wendy Lin, "Asians, Latinos Rip Voting Plan," *Newsday*, May 29, 1992, p. 4.
191. See Kwang Chung Kim and Won Moo Hurh, "Korean Americans and the 'Success' Image: A Critique," *Amerasia* 10 (Fall/Winter 1983): 15.
192. Daniels, *Coming to America*, pp. 388–389.

Chapter 12

1. "Easy Targets: Arab Americans Fight Bias," tolerance.org, October 7, 2005, www.tolerance.org/news/article_tol.jsp?id=1305.
2. Nadine Naber, "Muslim First, Arab Second: A Strategic Politics of Race and Gender," *The Muslim World* 95 (October 2005): 479–481; we draw here on comments from Karyn Mc-Kinney Marvasti. We are indebted to her and to Gary David, Amir Marvasti, and Pinar Batur for comments on this chapter.
3. See Amir Marvasti and Karyn D. McKinney, *Middle Eastern Lives In America* (Lanham, MD: Rowman & Littlefield, 2004).
4. Joseph R. Haiek, *Arab American Almanac*, 3rd ed. (Glendale, CA: News Circle Publishing, 1984), pp. 20–32.
5. Ibid., p. 33; Gary Orfalea, *The Arab Americans: A History* (Northampton, MA: Olive Branch Press, 2006), pp. 44–46; Haiek, *Arab American Almanac*, pp. 33–42.
6. Gary David, *The Mosaic of Middle Eastern Communities in Metropolitan Detroit* (Detroit: United Way Community Services, 1999), pp. 7–9.
7. Nadine Naber, "Ambiguous Insiders: An Investigation of Arab-American Invisibility," *Ethnic and Racial Studies* 23 (January 2000): 41.
8. U.S. Bureau of the Census: "We the People of Arab Ancestry in the United States: Table 1: Population with Arab Ancestry by Detailed Group," published March 2005, www.census.gov/prod/2005pubs/censr-21.pdf.
9. Randa A. Kayyali, *The Arab Americans* (Westport, CT: Greenwood Press, 2006), pp. 58–62.
10. Naber, "Ambiguous Insiders," pp. 37–61; and John Zogby, "Arab America Today," 1990, www.arabaai.org (retrieved January 26, 2001).
11. Alixa Naff, *Becoming American: The Early Arab Immigrant Experience* (Carbondale, IL: Southern Illinois

University Press, 1985), pp. 3–4; Zogby, "Arab America Today"; Kayyali, *The Arab Americans*, pp. 24–36.
12. Kayyali, *The Arab Americans*, pp. 24–26.
13. David, *The Mosaic of Middle Eastern Communities in Metropolitan Detroit*, p. 17.
14. Naff, *Becoming American*, p. 16.
15. David, *The Mosaic of Middle Eastern Communities in Metropolitan Detroit*, pp. 17–19.
16. Michael W. Suleiman, "Introduction: The Arab Immigrant Experience," in *Arabs in America: Building a New Future*, ed. Michael W. Suleiman (Philadelphia: Temple University Press, 1999), p. 7; Haney Lopez, *White by Law: The Legal Construction of Race* (New York: New York University Press, 1996), pp. 204–208.
17. Naber, "Ambiguous Insiders," p. 39.
18. Evelyn Shakir, *Bint Arab: Arab and Arab American Women in the United States* (Westport, CT: Praeger, 1997), p. 81; Kayyali, *The Arab Americans*, p. 53.
19. Edward W. Said, *Orientalism* (New York: Vintage Books, 1979), p. 287.
20. Ibid.; Shelly Shade, "The Image of the Arab in America: Analysis of a Poll on American Attitudes," *Middle East Journal* 35 (Spring 1981): 143–162.
21. Lydia Saad, "Anti-Muslim Feelings Fairly Common in U.S.: Nearly 40% of Americans Admit Feeling Prejudice," Gallup Poll, http://news.aol.com/gallup/story (retrieved January 13, 2007).
22. Terrel Bell, *The Thirteenth Man: A Reagan Cabinet Memoir* (New York: The Free Press, 1988), pp. 103–105.
23. Said, *Orientalism*, p. 286; Therese Saliba, "Resisting Invisibility: Arab Americans in Academia and Activism," in *Arabs in America*, p. 310.
24. Shakir, *Bint Arab*, p. 1.
25. Karyn McKinney Marvasti, personal communication, December 2006.
26. See Said, *Orientalism*; we draw here on comments from Karyn McKinney Marvasti (December 2006).
27. Quoted in Said, *Orientalism*, p. 79.
28. David, *The Mosaic of Middle Eastern Communities in Metropolitan Detroit*, p. 39.
29. Shakir, *Bint Arab*, pp. 2, 5.
30. Kayyali, *The Arab Americans*, p. 80; we also draw here on comments from Karyn McKinney Marvasti (December 2006); and "Women in National Parliaments," Interracial-Parliamentary Union, www.ipu.org/wmn-e/classif.htm (retrieved January 13, 2007).
31. Shakir, *Bint Arab*, p. 10.
32. Kristine Ajrouch, "Family and Ethnic Identity in an Arab-American Community," in *Arabs in America*, p. 129.
33. Shakir, *Bint Arab*, p. 112.
34. Ibid., p. 81.
35. Joe R. Feagin and Danielle Dirks, "'Who Is White?': College Students' Assessments of Key US Racial and Ethnic Groups," unpublished research manuscript, Texas A&M University, College Station, TX, 2006.
36. Alana Semuels, "Workplace Bias Against Muslims, Arabs on Rise," *The Los Angeles Times*, October 3, 2006, www.adc.org/index.php?id=2973 (retrieved January 17, 2007).
37. Shakir, *Bint Arab*, p. 116; Marvasti and McKinney, *Middle Eastern Lives in America*, pp. 129–132; Fatima Agha Al-Hayani, "Arabs and the American Legal System: Cultural and Political Ramifications," in *Arabs in America*, p. 80.
38. Said, *Orientalism*, p. 321; on U.S. ethnocentrism with regard to Iraq and other Middle Eastern countries, see Antony J. Blinken, "Winning the War of Ideas," *Washington Quarterly* 25 (Spring 2002): 101–114.
39. Zogby, "Arab America Today."
40. Mowahid Shah, "The FBI and the Civil Rights of Arab-Americans," *ADC Issues*, number 5, Washington DC, 1986.
41. Gary David, e-mail communication, March 2001.
42. Shakir, *Bint Arab*, p. 86; Kathleen M. Moore, "A Closer Look at Anti-Terrorism Law," in *Arabs in America*, p. 80.
43. "Islam in the United States, a Tentative Ascent, a Conversation with Yvonne Haddad," http://usinfo.state.gov/usa/islam/hadad.htm (retrieved June 4, 2001); Kathryn A. Ruff, "Scared to Donate," *New York University Journal of Legislation and Public Policy* 9 (2006): 448–449; "Poll Shows Declining Arab American Support for Bush," *Arabic Newspaper Online*, www.arabmedia.com/page1.html (retrieved January 17, 2007); "Hamilton College Muslim America Poll," www.hamilton.edu/news/more_news/display.cfm?ID=4607 (retrieved January 17, 2007).
44. Naber, "Ambiguous Insiders," p. 49; Leadership Conference on Civil Rights, "Faces of Hate Crimes," www.civilrights.org/programs/hate_crimes/faces/index.html#3 (retrieved January 24, 2002).
45. American-Arab Anti-Discrimination Committee (ADC), "ADC Fact Sheet: The Condition of Arab Americans Post 9/11," www.adc.org/terror_attack/9-11aftermath.pdf, p. 1 (retrieved January 24, 2002); Peter Finn, "Hijackers Depicted as Elite Group," *The Washington Post*, November 5, 2001, p. Al.
46. American-Arab Anti-Discrimination Committee (ADC), "ADC Fact Sheet: The Condition of Arab Americans Post 9/11," p. 2; we draw here on comments from Karyn McKinney Marvasti (January 2007).
47. Marvasti and McKinney, *Middle Eastern Lives in America*, p. 49.

48. Mark Fitzgerald, "Arab Americans Boycott '*Chicago Sun-Times*'" *Jerusalem Post*, November 1, 2000, p. 1; quote is from Naber, "Ambiguous Insiders," p. 46.
49. " Muslim-American Activism: Discussion of Legal Issues Facing Muslim Communities in the United States," *Washington Report of Middle Eastern Affairs*, June 2000, pp. 88–89; see also Marvasti and McKinney, *Middle Eastern Lives in America*, pp. 129–132.
50. Nikki Tait, "Immigrants Earn Their Rewards: Arab-American Community," *Financial Times*, February 28, 2000, p. 6. See also Gary David, *Intercultural Relationships Across the Counter: An Interactional Analysis of In-Situ Service Encounters*, unpublished dissertation, Wayne State University, Detroit, MI, 1999; Kayyali, *The Arab Americans*, pp. 142–144.
51. Abdon M. Pallasch, "Arab, Jewish Law Groups Convene; Attorneys Here Seeking Common Ground," *Chicago Sun-Times*, November 10, 2000, p. 12; for more recent efforts, see the discussion at the Arab-American Bar Association of Illinois website, http://72.14.209.104/search?q=cache:k3A1of3teO8J:www.arabbar.org/art-govrept.asp+Arab-American+Bar+Association+and+the+Decalogue+Society+of+-Jewish+lawyers&hl=en&gl=us&ct=clnk&cd=7 (retrieved January 16, 2007); Albor Ruiz, "Group Fights Spread of Mideast Hate Here," New York Daily News, November 6, 2000, p. 6.
52. Leo Standora et al., "Violence Shaking up Arabs, Jews in City," *New York Daily News*, October 13, 2000, p. 37.
53. "2006 Arab American Candidates," Arab American Institute, www.aaiusa.org/get-involved/382/2006-arab-american-candidates (retrieved January 17, 2007); Teresa Watanabe, "American Muslims Look for Ways to Harness Political Power," *The Los Angeles Times*, October 1, 2000, p. B3; Friday Watch-Fire Prayer Alert, *Intercessors for America*, www.ifapray.org/FridayWatch-FireAlert/FWF-6_23_2006.html (retrieved January 17, 2007).
54. Andrea Stone, "Arab Vote Is Critical in Michigan," *USA Today*, November 1, 2000, p. 12A; Kayyali, *The Arab Americans*, pp. 136–137; Zev Chafets, "Arab Enclave on Pols' Map," *New York Daily News*, November 3, 2000, p. 6; Casey Kasem, "Famous Arab Americans," Arab American Institute Foundation, www.aaiusa.org/arab-americans/23/famous-arab-americans (retrieved January 8, 2007).
55. Shakir, *Bint Arab*, p. 88.
56. Quoted in E. R. Shipp, "Anti-Muslim Bigotry Is Bad Political Strategy," *New York Daily News*, November 5, 2000, p. 45.
57. Bonnie Squires, "Americans Warming to Arab Cause?" *Philadelphia Daily News*, as reprinted on http://www.arab-aai.org (retrieved January 26, 2001); Orfalea, The Arab Americans, pp. 327–328; Martin Sieff, "Analysis: Poll Adds to Pressure on Israel," UPI Press Release, December 14, 2006.
58. Janine Zacharia, "Arab Americans Send Record Number of Delegates to Democratic Convention," *Jerusalem Post*, August 17, 2000, p. 2; David, *The Mosaic of Middle Eastern Communities in Metropolitan Detroit*, p. 23.
59. David, *The Mosaic of Middle Eastern Communities in Metropolitan Detroit*, p. 51.
60. Watanabe, "American Muslims Look for Ways to Harness Political Power," p. B3.
61. Naber, "Ambiguous Insiders," pp. 37–61; and Zogby, "Arab America Today."
62. U.S. Bureau of the Census: "We the People of Arab Ancestry in the United States: Figure 11: Occupation 2000," published March 2005, www.census.gov/prod/2005pubs/censr-21.pdf.
63. U.S. Bureau of the Census: "We the People of Arab Ancestry in the United States: Figure 13: Median Family Income: 1999; Figure 14: Poverty Rate by Broad Age Group: 1999," published March 2005, www.census.gov/prod/2005pubs/censr-21.pdf.
64. Zogby, "Arab America Today"; David, *The Mosaic of Middle Eastern Communities in Metropolitan Detroit*, pp. 9–49; Tait, "Immigrants Earn Their Rewards: Arab-American Community," p. 6.
65. Chafets, "Arab Enclave on Pols' Map," p. 6.
66. Suleiman, "Introduction," p. 16; U.S. Bureau of the Census: "We the People of Arab Ancestry in the United States: Figure 9: Educational Attainment: 2000," published March 2005, www.census.gov/prod/2005pubs/censr-21.pdf.
67. David, *The Mosaic of Middle Eastern Communities in Metropolitan Detroit*, p. 40.
68. Jane Adas, "Museum of the City of New York Examines Local Arab Americans," *Washington Report of Middle Eastern Affairs*, April 2000, pp. 51–52, 83.
69. Wendy Schwartz, "Arab American Students in Public Schools," http://eric-web.tc.columbia.edu/digests/dig142.htm (retrieved June 4, 2001).
70. Kayyali, *The Arab Americans*, p. 100.
71. "Islam in the United States, a Tentative Ascent, a Conversation with Yvonne Haddad"; U.S. Diplomatic Mission to Germany, "Religions of America," http://usa.usembassy.de/society-religion.htm (retrieved January 18, 2007).
72. Shakir, *Bint Arab*, pp. 115–116.
73. Abdul Malik, "Muslims in America: Profile 2001," www.soundvision.com/yearinreview/2001/profile.shtml (retrieved June 4, 2001).
74. "Islam in the United States, a Tentative Ascent, a Conversation with Yvonne Haddad."

75. Ibid.
76. Suad Joseph, "Against the Grain of the Nation—The Arab," in *Arabs in America: Building a New Future*, ed. Suleiman, p. 261.
77. Suleiman, "Introduction," p. 15.
78. Naber, "Ambiguous Insiders," p. 40.
79. Naff, *Becoming American*, p. 15.
80. David, *The Mosaic of Middle Eastern Communities in Metropolitan Detroit*, pp. 32–34.
81. Zogby, "Arab America Today"; Kayyali, *The Arab Americans*, pp. 83–84.
82. Denise Al-Johar, "Muslim Marriages in America: Reflecting New Identities," *The Muslim World* 95 (October 2005): 558–572; Shakir, *Bint Arab*, p. 116.
83. Zogby, "Arab America Today"; Kayyali, *The Arab Americans*, pp. 109–110.
84. Gary David and Kenneth Kahtan Ayouby, "Being Arab and Becoming Americanized," unpublished research paper, Bentley College, Waltham, MA, 2001, p. 34.
85. Mariam Sami, "As Cap Replaces Kaffiyeh, Arab Parents Look for Help," *The New York Times*, November 2, 1997, Sec. 14, p. 10.
86. Richard A. Chapman, "Arab-American Teenagers Share Their Culture in Video," *Chicago Sun-Times*, November 28, 1996, p. 22; and David, *The Mosaic of Middle Eastern Communities in Metropolitan Detroit*, p. 39.
87. Naber, "Muslim First, Arab Second," p. 494.
88. Quoted in David, *The Mosaic of Middle Eastern Communities in Metropolitan Detroit*, p. 37.
89. David and Ayouby, p. 35. See also pp. 4, 37.
90. Ibid., p. 15.
91. Shakir, *Bint Arab*, p. 112.
92. Naber, "Ambiguous Insiders," pp. 50–51.

Chapter 13

1. Nat Hentoff, "Free Expression Comes to Boston Latin," *The Washington Post*, February 8, 1992, p. A21.
2. Quoted in Ilan Stavans, *The Hispanic Condition: Reflections on Culture and Identity in America* (New York: HarperCollins, 1995), p. 166.
3. Stavans, *The Hispanic Condition: Reflections on Culture and Identity in America*, p. 167.
4. S. H. Murdock, *An America Challenged: Population Change and the Future of the United States* (Boulder, CO: Westview Press, 1995), pp. 33–47.
5. Buchanan is quoted in Clarence Page, "U.S. Media Should Stop Abetting Intolerance," *Toronto Star*, December 27, 1991, p. A27; Pat Buchanan, *State of Emergency, The Third World Invasion and Conquest of America* (New York: Thomas Dunne Books, 2006).
6. Samuel P. Huntington, "The Erosion of American National Interests," *Foreign Affairs* (September/October 1997): 28.
7. Arthur Schlesinger, *The Disuniting of America: Reflections on a Multicultural Society* (New York: W. W. Norton, 1991), pp. 13, 124–125.
8. U.S. Department of Homeland Security, "2005 Yearbook of Immigration Statistics: Office of Immigration Statistics," published November 2006, www.dhs.gov/xlibrary/assets/statistics/yearbook/2005/OIS_2005_Yearbook.pdf; see also Immigration and Naturalization Service, *Fiscal Year 1998 Statistical Yearbook* (Washington, DC: U.S. Government Printing Office, 1999), Table 2, www.ins.gov/graphics/aboutins/statistics/98immtbl.pdf (retrieved August 31, 2001). Note that the data are incomplete for certain time periods and that the definition of some countries has sometimes changed at different points in time.
9. Andrew Piatt, "The Crux of the Immigration Question," *North American Review* 199 (June 1914): 866, quoted in Rita J. Simon and Susan H. Alexander, *The Ambivalent Welcome: Print Media, Public Opinion, and Immigration* (Westport, CT: Praeger, 1993), p. 59.
10. U.S. Census Bureau, Table DP-1: Profile of General Demographic Characteristics for the United States: 2000, www.census.gov (retrieved August 29, 2001).
11. Wendy Lin, "Stakes are High in Lottery for U.S. Green Cards," *Newsday*, October 13, 1991, p. 19.
12. Pew Research Center, "America's Immigration Quandary: No Consensus on Immigration Problem or Proposed Fixes," http://people-press.org/reports/display.php3?PageID=1045 (retrieved January 19, 2007); "Canadians View Immigration as Having Positive Economic Effect, Reports Recent Canada–U.S. Public Opinion Poll," Canada NewsWire, www.newswire.ca/releases/May2000/06/c2434.html (retrieved August 27, 2001).
13. Cited in Shawn Foster, "Immigrants: Blessing or Curse for Utah?" *Salt Lake Tribune*, November 10, 1994, p. A1; the National Academy report is quoted in Center for Continuing Study of the California Economy, "The Impact of Immigration on the California Economy," California, September 2005, p. 40. This report has other recent data showing a very small effect on native workers' jobs and incomes.
14. Immigration and Naturalization Service, *Fiscal Year 1998 Statistical Yearbook* (Washington, DC: U.S. Government Printing Office, 1999), Tables 1–3, www.ins.gov/graphics/aboutins/statistics/98immtbl.pdf (retrieved August 31, 2001).

15. Ibid.
16. Quoted in Keith Henderson, "Immigration as an Economic Engine," *The Christian Science Monitor*, March 27, 1992, p. 9. See also Ben Wattenberg, *The First Universal Nation* (New York: The Free Press, 1990).
17. Hector Tobar and Robin Fields, "21st-Century Cities: What Is Happening in Urban America?" *Milwaukee Journal Sentinel*, May 11, 2001, p. 19A.
18. Juan Gonzalez, *Harvest of Empire: A History of Latinos in America* (New York: Penguin Books, 2000), pp. xii–xix.
19. Israel Zangwill, *The Melting Pot* (New York: Macmillan, 1925), p. 33.
20. Milton M. Gordon, *Assimilation in American Life* (New York: Oxford University Press, 1964), pp. 72–73.
21. Mitchell Chang, "Measuring the Impact of a Diversity Requirement on Students' Level of Racial Prejudice," University of California, Los Angeles, 1999, http://209.85.165.104/search?q=cache:M0zg0lQn2NUJ:www.diversityweb.org/digest/W00/research2.html+Universities+have+a+diversity+requirement%22&hl=en&gl=us&ct=clnk&cd=1 (retrieved January 19, 2007); Terry Lefton, "Building Bridges in the Big Apple," *Teaching Tolerance* 1, no. 1 (Spring 1992): 8–13; Ralph Blumenthal, "Black Youth Is Killed by Whites; Brooklyn Attack Is Called Racial," *The New York Times*, August 25, 1989, p. A1; for late 2000s data on colleges and universities, see www.diversityweb.org.
22. Quoted in Itabari Njeri, "Beyond the Melting Pot; in America, Blending in Was Once the Ideal," *The Los Angeles Times*, January 13, 1991, p. E1.
23. Arthur Schlesinger, Jr., "Speaking Up: A Look at Noteworthy Addresses in the Southland," *The Los Angeles Times*, February 7, 1992, p. B2.
24. Andrés Torres, *Between Melting Pot and Mosaic: African Americans and Puerto Ricans in the New York Political Economy* (Philadelphia: Temple University Press, 1995), pp. 2–6.
25. Ibid., p. 4.
26. Amitai Etzioni, "Community of Communities," *Washington Quarterly*, 19 (Summer 1996): 127–138.
27. Cited in Bobbie Harville, "History: Knowledge Is Lacking; Americans' Understanding of the Country's History Is Thin, a New Survey Reveals," *Dayton Daily News*, July 14, 1996, p. 15A.
28. James W. Loewen, *Lies My Teacher Told Me: Everything Your American History Textbook Got Wrong* (New York: The New Press, 1995), p. 163.
29. Quoted in Njeri, "Beyond the Melting Pot," p. E1.
30. Ted Gordon and Wahneema Lubiano, "The Statement of the Black Faculty Caucus," in *Debating P.C.*, ed. Paul Berman (New York: Dell, 1992), p. 251.
31. Ibid., pp. 251–253.
32. Joe R. Feagin and Melvin P. Sikes, *Living with Racism* (Boston: Beacon, 1994), p. 222.
33. William H. Frey, "Diversity Spreads Out," *Living Cities Census Series*, Brookings Institution, March 2006, pp. 19–21; see also William H. Frey, "Immigration, Domestic Migration, and Demographic Balkanization in America: New Evidence from the 1990s," *Population and Development Review* 22 (December 1996): 741–763; Frey, "Immigration, Domestic Migration, and Demographic Balkanization in America," p. 758; see also William H. Frey, "The New White Flight," *American Demographics* (April 1994): 1–6.
34. Frey, "Diversity Spreads Out," pp. 18-19.
35. See Joe R. Feagin, "The Future of U.S. Society in an Era of Racism, Group Segregation, and Demographic Revolution," in *Sociology for the Twenty-First Century: Continuities and Cutting Edges*, ed. J. L. Abu-Lughod (Chicago: University of Chicago Press, 1999), pp. 199–212.

Part III

1. W. E. B. DuBois, *The World and Africa* (New York: International Publishers, 1965 [1946]), p. 23.

Chapter 14

1. Peter Turnley et al., "Graceland," *Newsweek*, May 9, 1994, pp. 30–33.
2. Paul Taylor, "In New South Africa, Pace of Change Has Race Tensions Simmering," *The Washington Post*, July 21, 1994, p. A20.
3. Patrick Bond, "From Racial to Class Apartheid: South Africa's Frustrating Decade of Freedom," *Monthly Review*, March 2004, p. 49.
4. Marion Lloyd, "In Brazil, a New Debate over Color," *The Chronicle of Higher Education*, February 13, 2004, p. 6.
5. F. Scott Fitzgerald, *The Great Gatsby* (New York: Penguin Books, 1983), p. 19.
6. For a fuller discussion of certain issues raised here, see Pinar Batur, "Centering on Global Racism and Anti-Racism: From Everyday Life to Global Complexity," *Sociological Spectrum* 19 (1999): 467–484.
7. Pinar Batur, "Racial and Ethnic Inequality and Struggle from the Colonial Era to the Present: Drawing the Global Color Line," in *The Global Color Line: Racial and Ethnic Inequality and Struggle from a Global*

Perspective, ed. Pinar Batur and Joe Feagin (Stamford, CT: JAI Press, 1999), pp. 3–21.

8. Zia Sardar, Ashis Nandy, and Merryl Wyn Davies, *Barbaric Others: A Manifesto on Western Racism* (London: Pluto Press, 1993), pp. 8–9.
9. Oliver C. Cox, *Caste, Class and Race: A Study in Social Dynamics* (Garden City, NY: Doubleday, 1948), pp. 331–332.
10. Ibid., p. 334.
11. Albert Memmi, *The Colonizer and the Colonized* (New York: Orion Press, 1965).
12. Ronald Takaki, *Iron Cages* (New York: Oxford University Press, 1990), p. 12.
13. Joseph Arthur de Gobineau, *Selected Political Writings*, ed. M. D. Biddiss (New York: Harper & Row, 1970), p. 136.
14. Pinar Batur, "Racial and Ethnic Inequality."
15. Frantz Fanon, "The Pitfalls of National Consciousness," and "On National Culture," in *The Wretched of the Earth*, trans. Constance Farrington (New York: Grove Press, 1963); Anthony Brewer, *Marxist Theories of Imperialism* (New York: Routledge, 1986).
16. Albert Memmi, *The Pillar of Salt* (Boston: Beacon Press, 1992), p. 331.
17. Pinar Batur, "Centering on Global Racism."
18. Leonard Thompson, *A History of South Africa* (New Haven, CT: Yale University Press, 1990); Nigel Worden, *The Making of Modern South Africa: Conquest, Segregation and Apartheid* (Oxford: Blackwell, 1994); Basil Davidson, *Africa in History* (New York: Collier Books, 1991); Roland Oliver and Anthony Atmore, *Africa Since 1800*, 3rd ed. (Cambridge: Cambridge University Press, 1989); Joseph Harris, *Africans and Their History* (New York: Mentor, 1987).
19. Leonard Thompson, *Political Mythology of Apartheid* (New Haven, CT: Yale University Press, 1985), p. 71.
20. Ibid., pp. 72–73.
21. Worden, *Making of Modern South Africa*, pp. 11–12.
22. Thompson, *Political Mythology of Apartheid*, p. 75.
23. Ibid., p. 76.
24. Ibid., p. 70.
25. Davidson, *Africa in History*, p. 269.
26. Thompson, *History of South Africa*, pp. 111–112.
27. Allister Sparks, *The Mind of South Africa* (New York: Knopf, 1990), pp. 148–149.
28. The quote is from Thompson, *History of South Africa*, p. 184; see also Sparks, *Mind of South Africa*, p. 153.
29. Merle Lipton, *Capitalism and Apartheid: South Africa, 1910–1984* (Totowa, NJ: Rowman & Allenheld, 1985), pp. 14–15.
30. Thompson, *History of South Africa*; Oliver and Atmore, *Africa Since 1800*, p. 295.
31. Thompson, *History of South Africa*, p. 206; Lipton, *Capitalism and Apartheid*.
32. Francis Meli, *South Africa Belongs to Us: A History of the ANC* (Bloomington: Indiana University Press, 1988).
33. Nozipho Diseko, "The Origins and Development of the South African Student's Movement (SASM): 1968–1976," *Journal of South African Studies* 18 (March 1991): 40–62.
34. Howard Barrell, "The Turn to the Masses: The African National Congress' Strategic Review of 1978–1979," *Journal of South African Studies* 18 (March 1991): 64–92.
35. Bill Keller, "In South Africa, a White 'Third Force' of Violence Is Confirmed," *The New York Times*, March 20, 1994, sec. 4, p. 5.
36. Thompson, *History of South Africa*.
37. Bill Keller, "Rival Visions of a Post-Apartheid Future Divide South Africa's Zulus," *The New York Times*, April 4, 1994, p. A1; Tom Masland and Joseph Conteras, "Ballots or Bullets," *Newsweek*, April 11, 1994, pp. 34–37.
38. Bond, "From Racial to Class Apartheid."
39. Linda Vergnani, "South African President's Views on AIDS Cloud International Gathering of Scientists," *The Chronicle of Higher Education*, July 7, 2000, p. A43.
40. Clare Kapp, "South African's Hope for a New Era in HIV/AIDS Policies," *Lancet*, November 18, 2006, p. 1759.
41. Janis van der Westhuizen, "Alarms over AIDS in South Africa," *Alternatives* 30 (2005): 276.
42. "Race About Race: South Africa's Racial Election," *The Economist*, December 9, 2000, p. 5.
43. Frantz Fanon, *Black Skin, White Masks*, transl. Charles Markmann (New York: Grove Weidenfeld, 1967), p. 87.
44. "The Colours of Brazil," *The Economist*, May 10, 1986, p. 42.
45. Lloyd, "In Brazil, a New Debate over Color," p.6
46. Charles Whitaker, "Blacks in Brazil: The Myth and the Reality," *Ebony*, February 1991, pp. 41, 60–64.
47. Lloyd, "In Brazil, a New Debate over Color," p. 6.
48. Daniela Hart, "Racial Bias Entrenched," *Chronicle of Higher Education*, July 20, 1988, p. A31–A32.
49. E. Bradford Burns, *A History of Brazil*, 3rd ed. (New York: Cornell Press, 1993), pp. 23–27.
50. Thomas Skidmore and Peter Smith, *Modern Latin America*, 2nd ed. (Oxford: Oxford University Press, 1994), p. 140; Burns, *History of Brazil*, pp. 216–217.
51. Michael Hanchard, *Orpheus and Power: The* Movimento Negro *of Rio de Janeiro and São Paulo, Brazil,*

1945–1988 (Princeton, NJ: Princeton University Press, 1994). pp. 43–45.

52. Thomas Skidmore, *Black into White: Race and Nationality in Brazilian Thought* (Oxford: Oxford University Press, 1974), pp. 48–69; Dain Borges, "Puffy, Ugly, Slothful and Inert: Degeneration in Brazilian Social Thought, 1880–1940," *Journal of Latin American Studies* 25 (1993): 235–256.
53. Thomas Sanders, "Racial Discrimination and Black Consciousness in Brazil," *American Universities Field Staff Reports* 42 (1981); Hanchard, *Orpheus and Power*.
54. Sanders, "Racial Discrimination and Black Consciousness in Brazil," p. 2.
55. George Andrews, "Racial Inequality in Brazil and the United States: A Statistical Comparison," *Journal of Social History* 26 (1992): 234; see also Peggy Webster and Jeffrey Dwyer, "The Cost of Being Nonwhite in Brazil," *Sociology and Social Research* 72 (1988): 136–142.
56. Andrews, "Racial Inequality in Brazil and the United States," pp. 256–257.
57. Mala Htun, "Racial Quotas for a Racial Democracy," *NACLA Report on the Americas*, January–February 2005, pp. 21–22.
58. Howard Winant, "Rethinking Race in Brazil," *Journal of Latin American Studies* 24 (1992): 173–192.
59. Anthony Faiola, "Yet Another Fresh Start for Brazil," *Washington Post National Weekly Edition*, October 20, 1997, p. 19.
60. David Kennedy, "Who Are Brazil's *Indigenas*: Contributions of Census Data Analysis to Anthropological Demography on Indigenous Populations," *Human Organization* 59 (2000): 311; "Threat to Brazil's Indians," *Geographical* 73 (June 2001): 12.
61. "Brazil's Unfinished Battle for Racial Democracy," *The Economist*, April 22, 2000, p. 31.
62. Francisco Oliviera, "A Bible and an Automatic," *Index on Censorship* 28 (January 1999): 115.
63. Quoted in Whitaker, "Racial Bias Entrenched."
64. Nicole Roberge, "Brazil Experiences the Growing Pains of Affirmative Action," *Diverse Education*, June 1, 2006, p. 16.
65. Ibid.
66. Lloyd, "In Brazil, a New Debate over Color."
67. Fanon, *Wretched of the Earth*, p. 41.
68. Pierre Birnbaum, *Anti-Semitism in France: A Political History from Leon Blum to the Present*, transl. Miriam Kochan (Oxford: Blackwell, 1992), p. 1.
69. Stephen Wilson, *Ideology and Experience: Antisemitism in France at the Time of the Dreyfus Affair* (Rutherford, NJ: Fairleigh Dickinson University Press, 1982).
70. Alan Riding, "Mitterand's Mistakes: Vichy Past Is Unveiled," *The New York Times*, September 9, 1994, p. A4.
71. Maxim Silverman, *Deconstructing the Nation: Immigration, Racism and Citizenship in Modern France* (London: Routledge, 1992), p. 10.
72. Douglas Johnson, "The Making of the French Nation," in *The National Question in Europe in Historical Context*, ed. Mikulas Teich and Roy Porter (Cambridge: Cambridge University Press, 1993), p. 59.
73. Silverman, *Deconstructing the Nation*, pp. 3–4.
74. R. D. Grillo, *Ideologies and Institutions in Urban France* (Cambridge: Cambridge University Press, 1985), p. 65.
75. Silverman, *Deconstructing the Nation*, p. 3.
76. Julia Kristeva, *Nations Without Nationalism* (New York: Columbia University Press, 1993), pp. 97–98.
77. Catherine Wihtol De Wenden, "North African Immigration and the French Political Imaginary," in *Race, Discourse and Power in France*, ed. Maxim Silverman (Brookfield, VT: Gower, 1991), p. 108.
78. Daniel Singer, "Liberte, Egalite, Racisme?, *Nation*, October 21, 1996, p. 19.
79. Kristeva, *Nations Without Nationalism*, pp. 13–14.
80. Chris Woodall, "Arabicide in France: An Interview with Fausto Giudice," *Race and Class* 35 (1993): 21–33.
81. Ibid.
82. Youssef Ibrahim, "France Bans Muslim Scarf in Its Schools," *The New York Times*, September 11, 1994, p. 4.
83. Letitia Creamean, "Membership of Foreigners: Algerians in France," *Arab Studies Quarterly* 16 (1996): 49–67.
84. Alice Chasan, "Border Skirmishes: European Integration vs. Ugly Atavisms," *World Press Review*, January 2000, p. 2.
85. "French TV Executive, Former TV Host Fined for Racist Song Performed on Air About Blacks," *Jet*, April 1, 1996, p. 65.
86. Robert Aldrich, "Colonial Past, Post-Colonial Present," *History Australia* 3 (2006): 14.1–14.10.
87. Frank Johnson, "The Rioters Want "liberte, egalite, fraternite"; What They Don't Want Is an Islamic State," *The Spectator*, November 19, 2005, p. 32.
88. Ibid.
89. Stephanie Giry, "France and Its Muslims (Terrorism)," *Foreign Affairs* 85 (September–October 2006): 87.
90. Pinar Batur, "The Discourse of Counterattack: Ethnic Movements and the Formation of Ethnic Identity," Ph.D. dissertation, University of Texas, Austin, 1992.

91. Samuel Totten and W. S. Parson, *The Century of Genocide* (New York: Routledge, 2004), p. xxviii.
92. Ibid., p. xxxix.
93. Scott Straus, "Darfur and the Genocide Debate," *Foreign Affairs* 84 (2004): 123–133.
94. Asafa Jalata, "State Terrorism and Globalization: The Cases of Ethiopia and Sudan," *International Journal of Comparative Sociology* 46 (2005): 79–102.
95. Paul Salopek, "Shattered Sudan," *National Geographic*, February 2003, p. 2; Karen Lange, " The Nuba: Still Standing," *National Geographic*, February 2003, p. 4.
96. Straus, "Darfur and the Genocide Debate."
97. Cynthia E. Smith and Tony Pipa, "The Politics of Genocide: U.S. Rhetoric vs. Inaction in Darfur, 7 April–26 September 2004," *Kennedy School Review* 6 (2004): 131–141.
98. Nouraee Andisheh, ""Don't Panic!" *Weekly Planet* 18/40 (2006): 16.

Photo Credits

Preface and Chapter 1: p. xvii, Arthur Tilley/Taxi/Getty Images; p. 3, Esbin Anderson, The Image Works; p. 8, AP Wide World Photos; p. 11, Jonathan Nourok, PhotoEdit Inc.; p. 19, Bob Daemmrich, Stock Boston.

Chapter 2: p. 25, Kunio Awaki, Corbis/Stock Market; p. 30, Corbis/Bettmann; p. 36, A. Ramey, PhotoEdit Inc.; p. 40, Merritt Vincent, PhotoEdit Inc.

Chapter 3: p. 63, The Granger Collection, New York; p. 65, Corbis/Bettmann; p. 71, Steven Rubin, The Image Works; p. 82, Rudi Von Brief, PhotoEdit Inc.

Chapter 4: p. 84, Courtesy of the Library of Congress; p. 90, ALBERT EINSTEIN and related rights TM/© of The Hebrew University of Jerusalem, used under license. Represented exclusively by Corbis Corporation; p. 102, Judy Gelles, Stock Boston; p. 104, Lewis W. Hine, Getty Images Inc.—Hulton Archive Photos.

Chapter 5: p. 112, David Karp, AP Wide World Photos; p. 117, AP Wide World Photos; p. 121, Tannen Maury, The Image Works; p. 126, Corbis/Bettmann.

Chapter 6: p. 135, Charles Coffey; p. 139, Corbis/Bettmann; p. 156, David Lassman, The Image Works; p. 158, Charles Coffey; p. 161, © VisionsofAmerica/Joe Sohm/Getty Images.

Chapter 7: p. 165, Jim West, Alamy Images; p. 176, AP Wide World Photos; p. 191, UPI, Corbis/Bettmann; p. 193, Maria Mulas; p. 199, Scott Applewhite, AP Wide World Photos.

Chapter 8: p. 205, © A. Ramey/PhotoEdit—All rights reserved; p. 211, Robert Holmes, Robert Holmes Photography; p. 227, Getty Images, Inc.—Agence France Presse; p. 230, AP Wide World Photos; p. 237, Bob Daemmrich, Stock Boston.

Chapter 9: p. 244, Alan Diaz, AP Wide World Photos; p. 258, Agence France Presse/Getty Images; p. 262, Hazel Hankin, Stock Boston; p. 266, Joe Marquette, AP/Wide World Photos; p. 272, Sylwia Kapuscinski, Getty Images, Inc.

Chapter 10: p. 279, Damian Dovarganes, AP Wide World Photos; p. 287, AP Wide World Photos; p. 289, Time Boyle, Getty Images, Inc.; p. 295, Christian Simonpietri, Corbis/Sygma.

Chapter 11: p. 303, Copyright Lia Chang Gallery; p. 317, AP Wide World Photos; p. 320, AP Wide World Photos; p. 322, Stock Boston; p. 329, The New York Times; p. 332, Bob Deammrich, The Image Works.

Chapter 12: p. 341, Bizuayehu Tesfaye, AP Wide World Photos; p. 351, Bill Mokdad; p. 352, Justin Sullivan, Getty Images, Inc.; p. 356, Bill Mokdad; p. 357, AP Wide World Photos.

Chapter 13: p. 362, Corbis/Bettmann; p. 365, AP Wide World Photos; p. 369, Lara Jo Regan, Getty Images, Inc.; p. 372, AP Wide World Photos.

Chapter 14: p. 380, Jean-Jaques Gonzalez, The Image Works; p. 386, AP Wide World Photos; p. 388, Eraldo Peres, AP Wide World Photos; p. 393 AP Wide World Photos.

Index